BLACK PANTHER

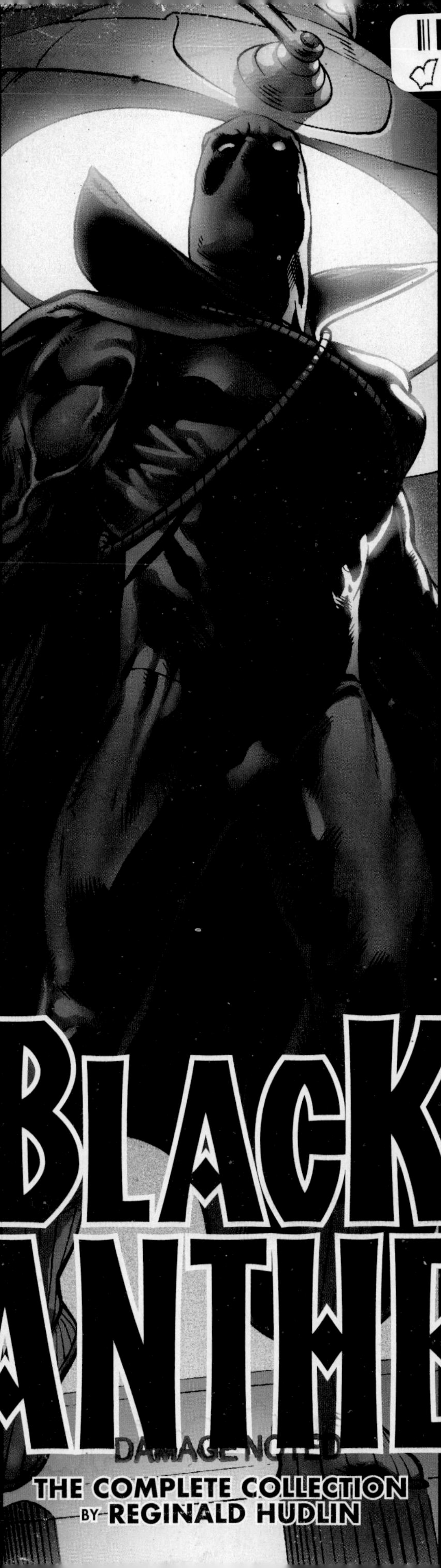

DAMAGE NOTED

THE COMPLETE COLLECTION
BY REGINALD HUDLIN

—— BLACK PANTHER CREATED BY **STAN LEE** & **JACK KIRBY** ——

COLLECTION EDITOR **MARK D. BEAZLEY**
ASSISTANT EDITOR **CAITLIN O'CONNELL**
ASSOCIATE MANAGING EDITOR **KATERI WOODY**
ASSOCIATE MANAGER, DIGITAL ASSETS **JOE HOCHSTEIN**
SENIOR EDITOR, SPECIAL PROJECTS **JENNIFER GRÜNWALD**
VP PRODUCTION & SPECIAL PROJECTS **JEFF YOUNGQUIST**
RESEARCH & LAYOUT **JEPH YORK**
PRODUCTION **SALENA MAHINA**
BOOK DESIGNER **ADAM DEL RE**
SVP PRINT, SALES & MARKETING **DAVID GABRIEL**

EDITOR IN CHIEF **C.B. CEBULSKI**
CHIEF CREATIVE OFFICER **JOE QUESADA**
PRESIDENT **DAN BUCKLEY**
EXECUTIVE PRODUCER **ALAN FINE**

BLACK PANTHER BY REGINALD HUDLIN: THE COMPLETE COLLECTION VOL. 2. Contains material originally published in magazine form as BLACK PANTHER #19-34 and ANNUAL #1. First printing 2017. ISBN# 978-1-302-90947-5. Published by MARVEL WORLDWIDE, INC., a subsidiary of MARVEL ENTERTAINMENT, LLC. OFFICE OF PUBLICATION: 135 West 50th Street, New York, NY 10020. Copyright © 2017 MARVEL. No similarity between any of the names, characters, persons, and/or institutions in this magazine with those of any living or dead person or institution is intended, and any such similarity which may exist is purely coincidental. **Printed in the U.S.A.** DAN BUCKLEY, President, Marvel Entertainment; JOE QUESADA, Chief Creative Officer; TOM BREVOORT, SVP of Publishing; DAVID BOGART, SVP of Business Affairs & Operations, Publishing & Partnership; C.B. CEBULSKI, VP of Brand Management & Development, Asia; DAVID GABRIEL, SVP of Sales & Marketing, Publishing; JEFF YOUNGQUIST, VP of Production & Special Projects; DAN CARR, Executive Director of Publishing Technology; ALEX MORALES, Director of Publishing Operations; SUSAN CRESPI, Production Manager; STAN LEE, Chairman Emeritus. For information regarding advertising in Marvel Comics or on Marvel.com, please contact Jonathan Parkhideh, VP of Digital Media & Marketing Solutions, at jparkhideh@marvel.com. For Marvel subscription inquiries, please call 888-511-5480. **Manufactured between 11/10/2017 and 12/12/2017 by LSG COMMUNICATIONS INC., KENDALLVILLE, IN, USA.**

10 9 8 7 6 5 4 3 2 1

BLACK PANTHER

WRITTEN BY

REGINALD HUDLIN

BLACK PANTHER #19-22
"WORLD TOUR"

PENCILS BY
SCOT EATON (#19) & **MANUEL GARCIA** (#20-22)

INKS BY
ANDREW HENNESSY (#19) **MARK MORALES** & **SANDU FLOREA** (#20) AND **JAY LEISTEN** (#21-22) WITH **SEAN PARSONS** (#22)

COLORS BY
DEAN WHITE (#19) & **MATT MILLA** (#20-22)

SPECIAL THANKS TO
IRENE LEE

BLACK PANTHER #23-25
"WAR CRIMES"

PENCILS BY
KOI TURNBULL (#23-24) & **MARCUS TO** (#24-25)

INKS BY
DON HO & **JEFF de LOS SANTOS** WITH **SAL REGLA** (#23-24) & **NICK NIX** (#24)

COLORS BY
J.D. SMITH

SPECIAL THANKS TO
JASON GORDER

BLACK PANTHER #26-27   BLACK PANTHER #28-30
"TWO PLUS TWO"   "FOUR THE HARD WAY"

PENCILS BY
FRANCIS PORTELA

INKS BY
VICTOR OLAZABA (#26-27) & **FRANCIS PORTELA** (#28-30)

COLORS BY
VAL STAPLES

BLACK PANTHER #31-34
"LITTLE GREEN MEN"

PENCILS BY
FRANCIS PORTELA (#31-32) **ANDREA DI VITO** (#32-33) & **CAFU** (#34)

INKS BY
FRANCIS PORTELA (#31-32) **ANDREA DI VITO** (#32-33) & **BIT** (#34)

COLORS BY
VAL STAPLES

BLACK PANTHER ANNUAL #1
"BLACK TO THE FUTURE"

PENCILS BY
LARRY STROMAN & KEN LASHLEY

INKS BY
ROLAND PARIS CARLOS CUEVAS & **JON SIBAL**

COLORS BY
MATT MILLA & **VAL STAPLES**

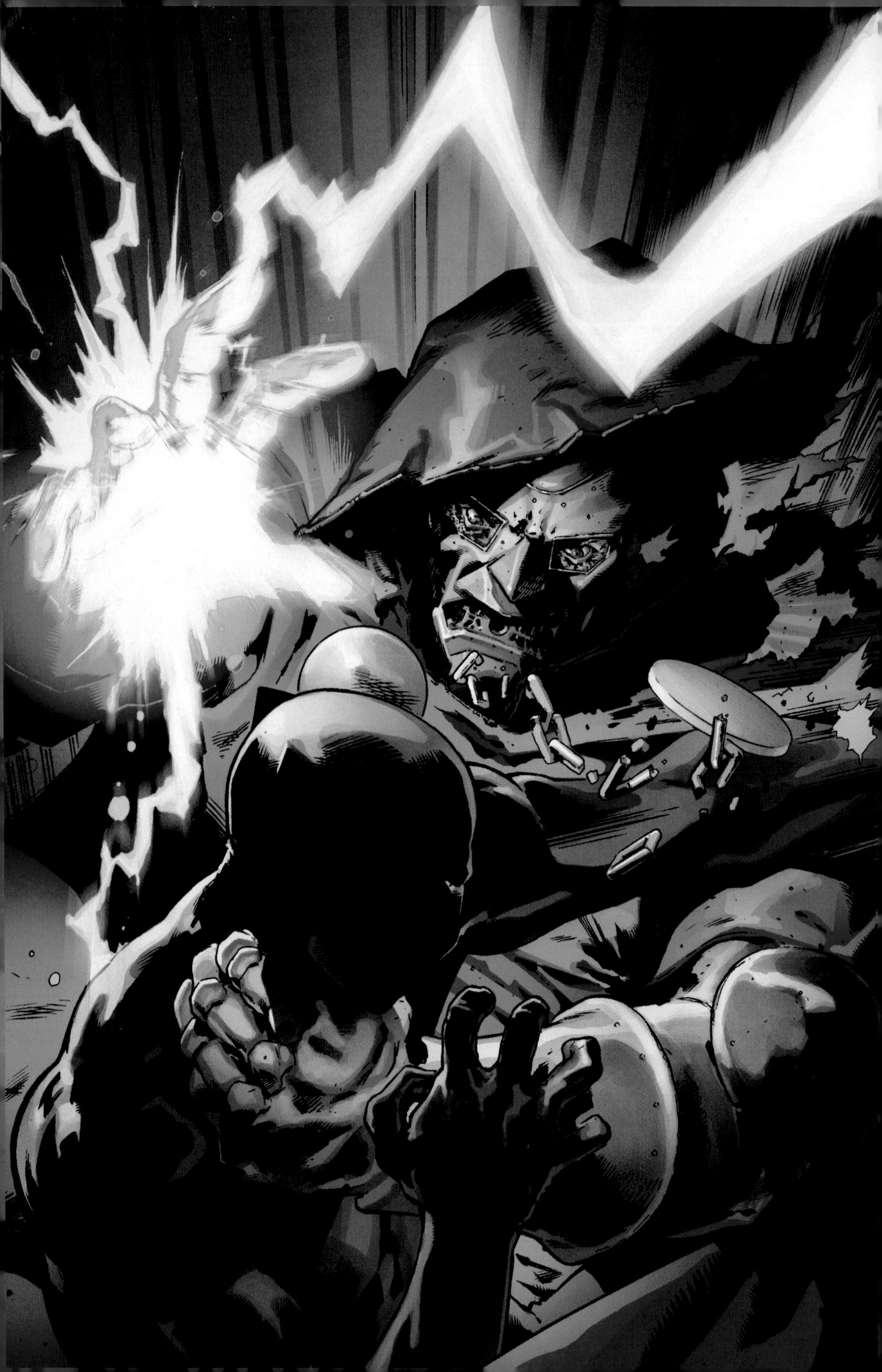

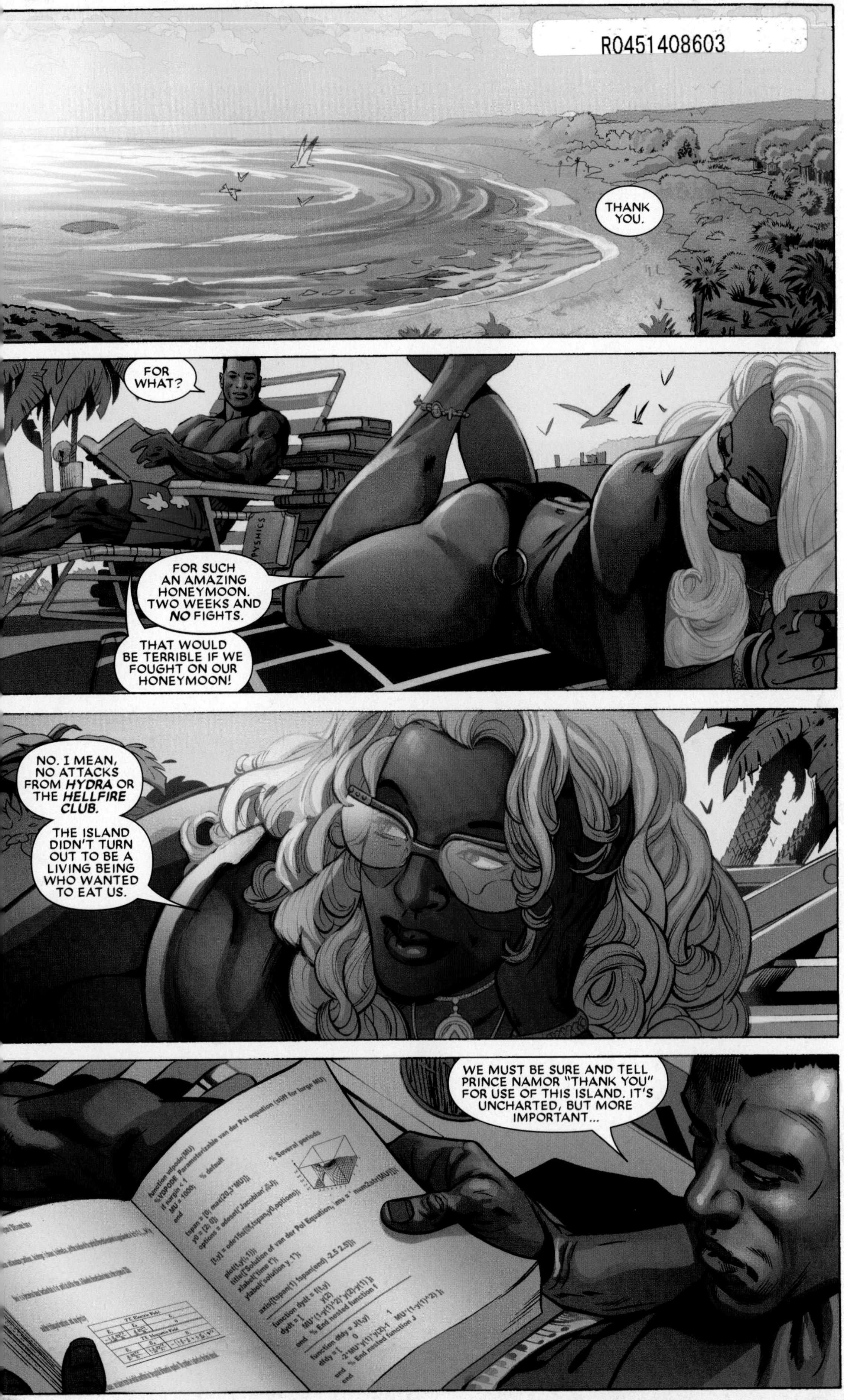
THANK YOU.
FOR WHAT?
PYSHICS
FOR SUCH AN AMAZING HONEYMOON. TWO WEEKS AND NO FIGHTS.
THAT WOULD BE TERRIBLE IF WE FOUGHT ON OUR HONEYMOON!
NO. I MEAN, NO ATTACKS FROM HYDRA OR THE HELLFIRE CLUB.
THE ISLAND DIDN'T TURN OUT TO BE A LIVING BEING WHO WANTED TO EAT US.
WE MUST BE SURE AND TELL PRINCE NAMOR "THANK YOU" FOR USE OF THIS ISLAND. IT'S UNCHARTED, BUT MORE IMPORTANT...

"...HE'S GOT THE MOST DANGEROUS SEA CREATURES ON EARTH PATROLLING THE WATERS AROUND THE ISLAND FOR MILES."

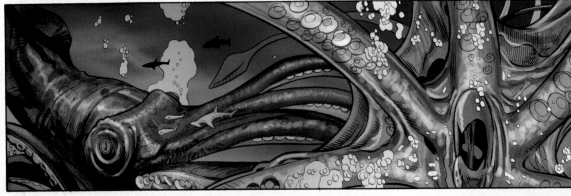

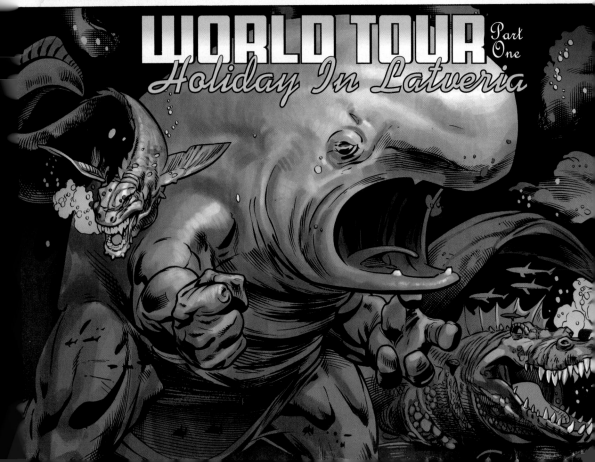

WORLD TOUR Part One
Holiday In Latveria

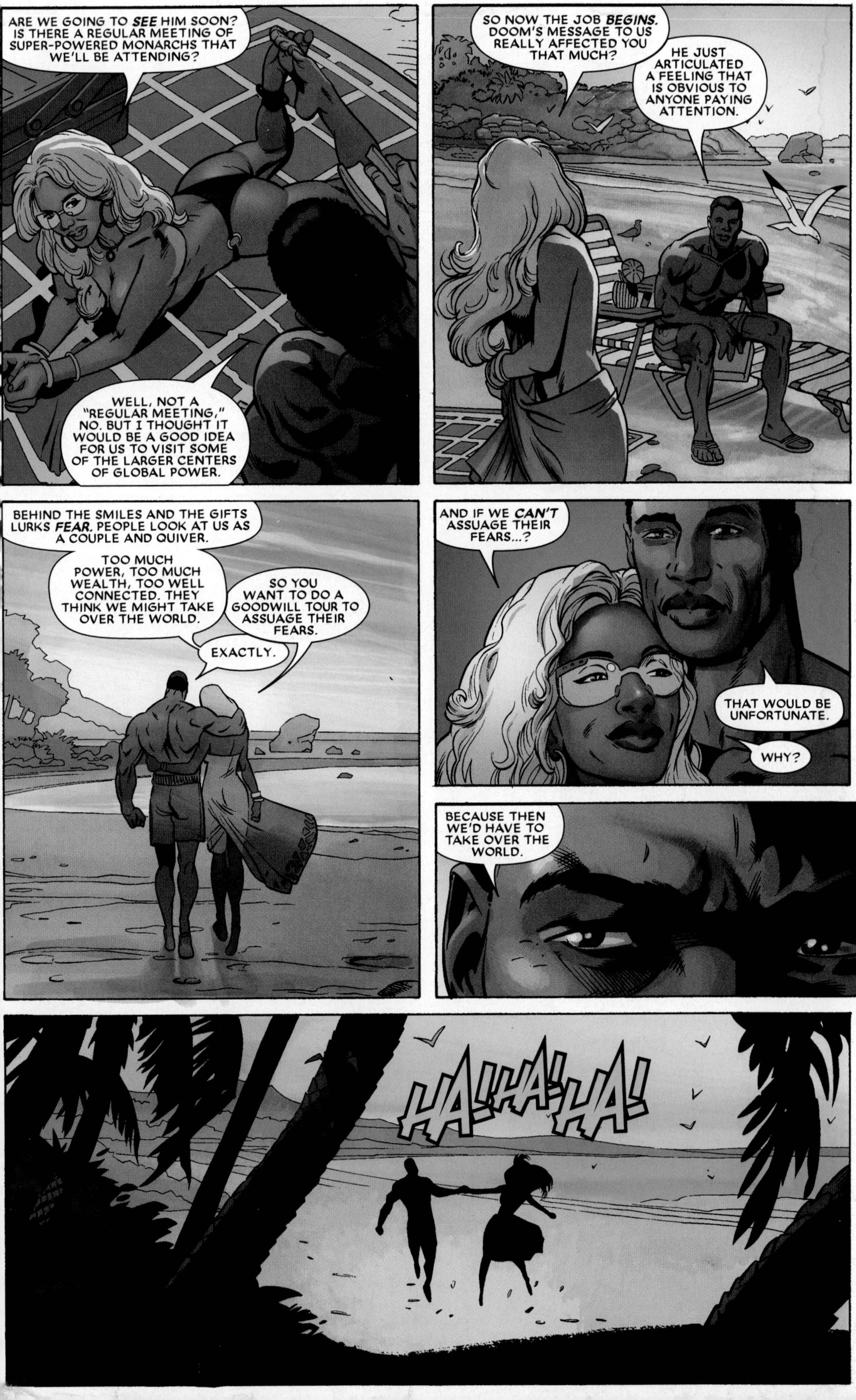
ARE WE GOING TO SEE HIM SOON? IS THERE A REGULAR MEETING OF SUPER-POWERED MONARCHS THAT WE'LL BE ATTENDING?
WELL, NOT A "REGULAR MEETING," NO. BUT I THOUGHT IT WOULD BE A GOOD IDEA FOR US TO VISIT SOME OF THE LARGER CENTERS OF GLOBAL POWER.
SO NOW THE JOB BEGINS. DOOM'S MESSAGE TO US REALLY AFFECTED YOU THAT MUCH?
HE JUST ARTICULATED A FEELING THAT IS OBVIOUS TO ANYONE PAYING ATTENTION.
BEHIND THE SMILES AND THE GIFTS LURKS FEAR. PEOPLE LOOK AT US AS A COUPLE AND QUIVER.
TOO MUCH POWER, TOO MUCH WEALTH, TOO WELL CONNECTED. THEY THINK WE MIGHT TAKE OVER THE WORLD.
SO YOU WANT TO DO A GOODWILL TOUR TO ASSUAGE THEIR FEARS.
EXACTLY.
AND IF WE CAN'T ASSUAGE THEIR FEARS...?
THAT WOULD BE UNFORTUNATE.
WHY?
BECAUSE THEN WE'D HAVE TO TAKE OVER THE WORLD.
HA! HA! HA!

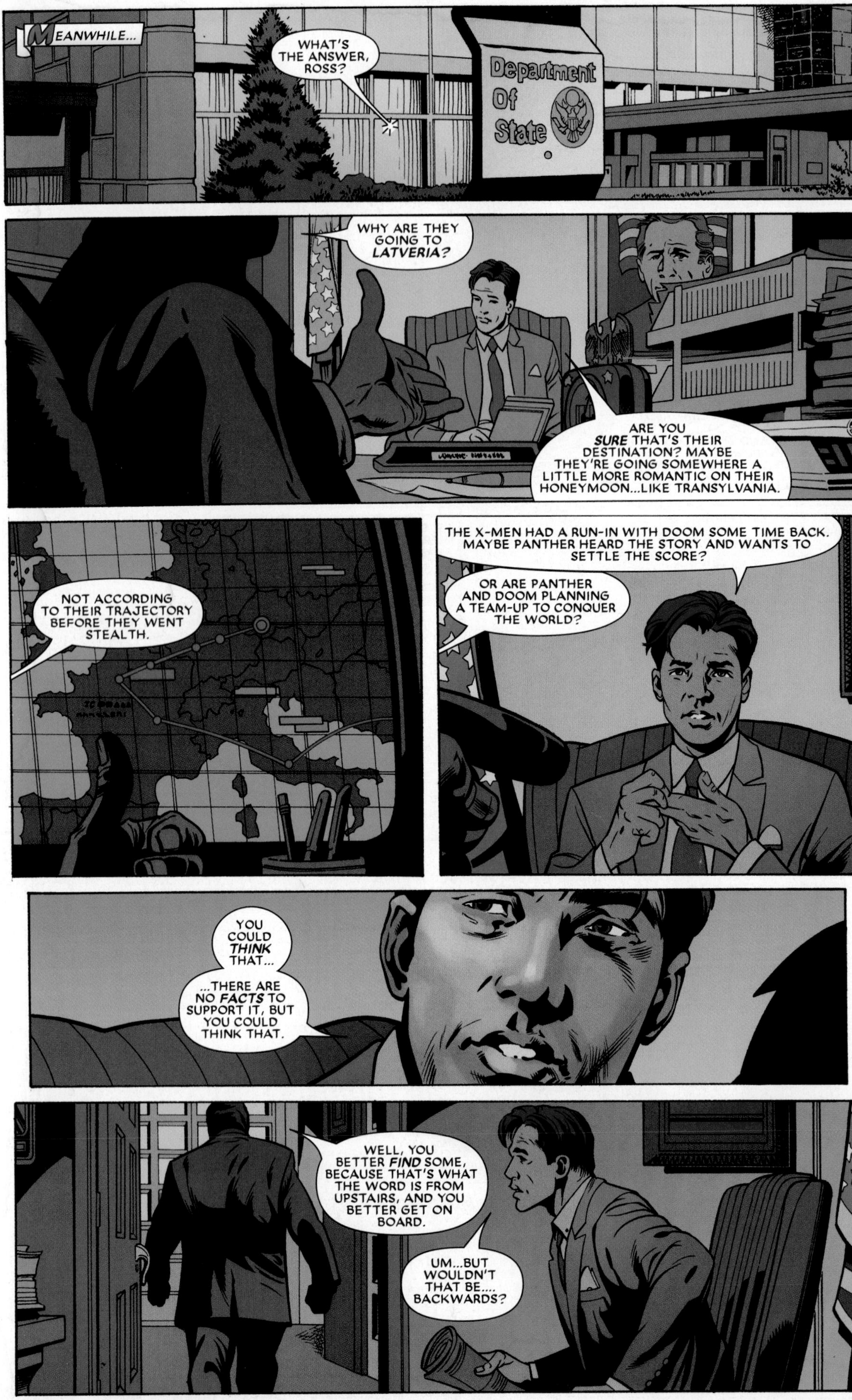
MEANWHILE...
WHAT'S THE ANSWER, ROSS?
Department Of State
WHY ARE THEY GOING TO LATVERIA?
ARE YOU SURE THAT'S THEIR DESTINATION? MAYBE THEY'RE GOING SOMEWHERE A LITTLE MORE ROMANTIC ON THEIR HONEYMOON...LIKE TRANSYLVANIA.
NOT ACCORDING TO THEIR TRAJECTORY BEFORE THEY WENT STEALTH.
THE X-MEN HAD A RUN-IN WITH DOOM SOME TIME BACK. MAYBE PANTHER HEARD THE STORY AND WANTS TO SETTLE THE SCORE?
OR ARE PANTHER AND DOOM PLANNING A TEAM-UP TO CONQUER THE WORLD?
YOU COULD THINK THAT...
...THERE ARE NO FACTS TO SUPPORT IT, BUT YOU COULD THINK THAT.
WELL, YOU BETTER FIND SOME, BECAUSE THAT'S WHAT THE WORD IS FROM UPSTAIRS, AND YOU BETTER GET ON BOARD.
UM...BUT WOULDN'T THAT BE.... BACKWARDS?

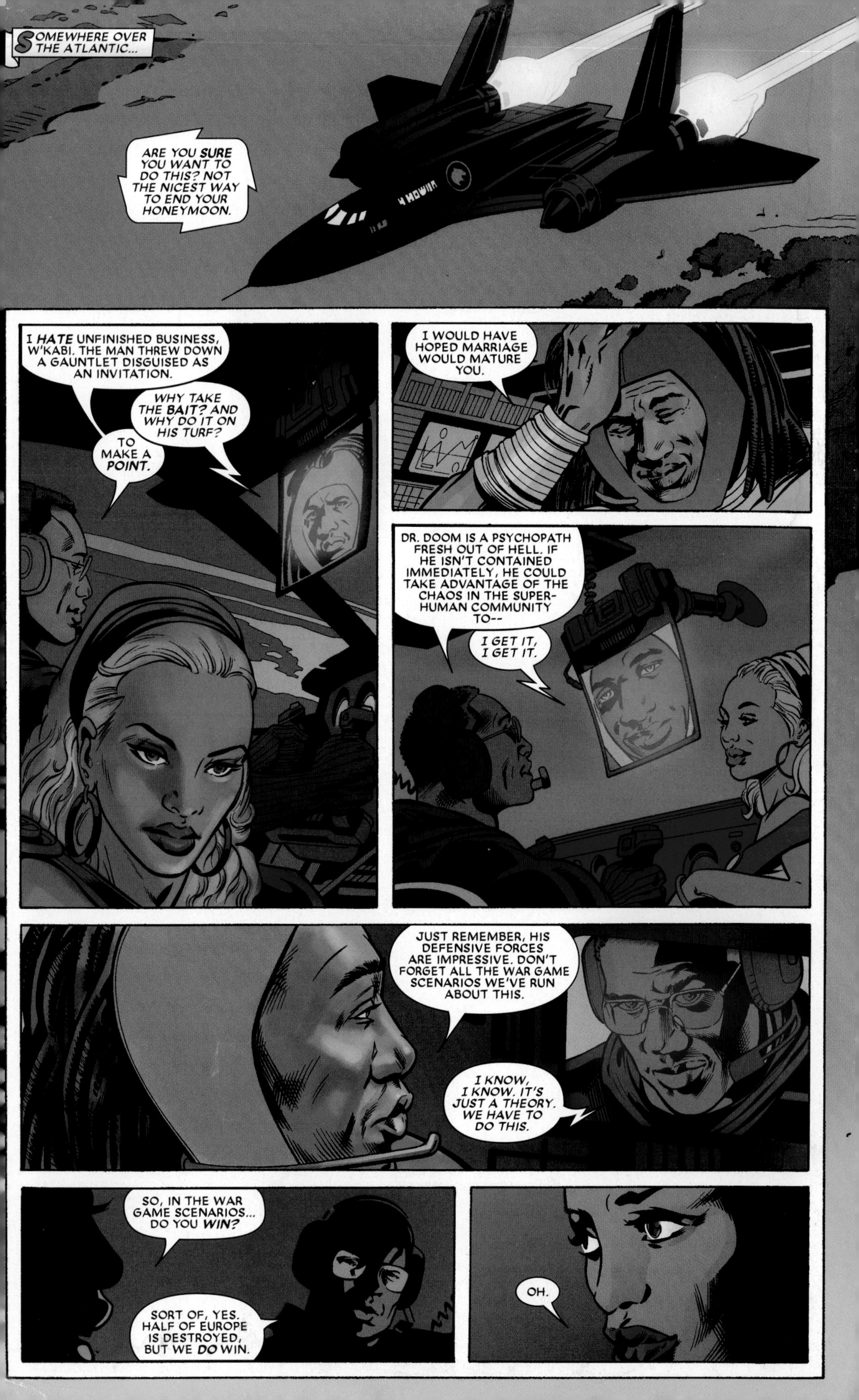
SOMEWHERE OVER THE ATLANTIC...
ARE YOU SURE YOU WANT TO DO THIS? NOT THE NICEST WAY TO END YOUR HONEYMOON.
I HATE UNFINISHED BUSINESS, W'KABI. THE MAN THREW DOWN A GAUNTLET DISGUISED AS AN INVITATION.
WHY TAKE THE BAIT? AND WHY DO IT ON HIS TURF?
TO MAKE A POINT.
I WOULD HAVE HOPED MARRIAGE WOULD MATURE YOU.
DR. DOOM IS A PSYCHOPATH FRESH OUT OF HELL. IF HE ISN'T CONTAINED IMMEDIATELY, HE COULD TAKE ADVANTAGE OF THE CHAOS IN THE SUPER-HUMAN COMMUNITY TO--
I GET IT, I GET IT.
JUST REMEMBER, HIS DEFENSIVE FORCES ARE IMPRESSIVE. DON'T FORGET ALL THE WAR GAME SCENARIOS WE'VE RUN ABOUT THIS.
I KNOW, I KNOW. IT'S JUST A THEORY. WE HAVE TO DO THIS.
SO, IN THE WAR GAME SCENARIOS... DO YOU WIN?
SORT OF, YES. HALF OF EUROPE IS DESTROYED, BUT WE DO WIN.
OH.

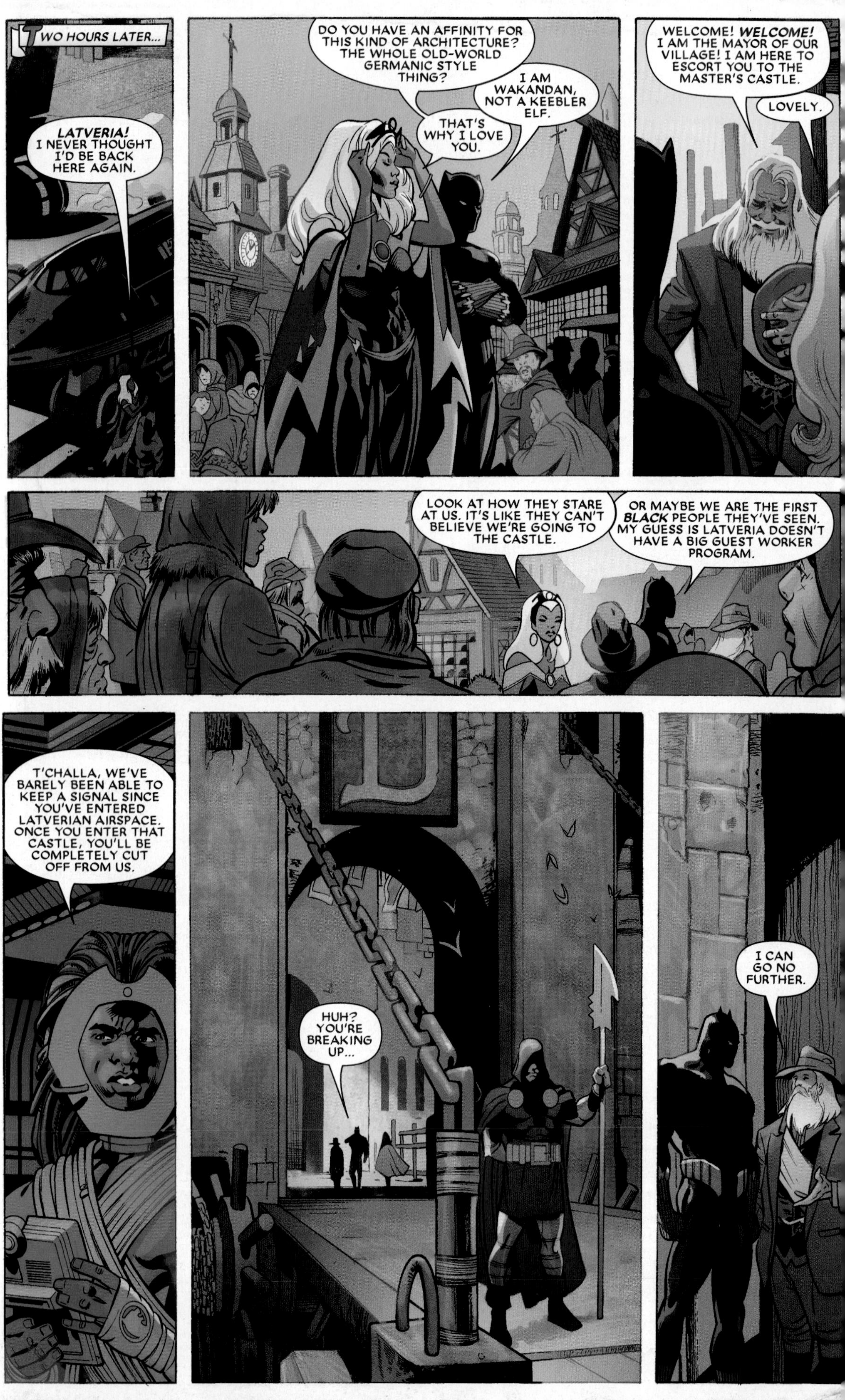
TWO HOURS LATER...
LATVERIA! I NEVER THOUGHT I'D BE BACK HERE AGAIN.
DO YOU HAVE AN AFFINITY FOR THIS KIND OF ARCHITECTURE? THE WHOLE OLD-WORLD GERMANIC STYLE THING?
I AM WAKANDAN, NOT A KEEBLER ELF.
THAT'S WHY I LOVE YOU.
WELCOME! WELCOME! I AM THE MAYOR OF OUR VILLAGE! I AM HERE TO ESCORT YOU TO THE MASTER'S CASTLE.
LOVELY.
LOOK AT HOW THEY STARE AT US. IT'S LIKE THEY CAN'T BELIEVE WE'RE GOING TO THE CASTLE.
OR MAYBE WE ARE THE FIRST BLACK PEOPLE THEY'VE SEEN. MY GUESS IS LATVERIA DOESN'T HAVE A BIG GUEST WORKER PROGRAM.
T'CHALLA, WE'VE BARELY BEEN ABLE TO KEEP A SIGNAL SINCE YOU'VE ENTERED LATVERIAN AIRSPACE. ONCE YOU ENTER THAT CASTLE, YOU'LL BE COMPLETELY CUT OFF FROM US.
HUH? YOU'RE BREAKING UP...
I CAN GO NO FURTHER.

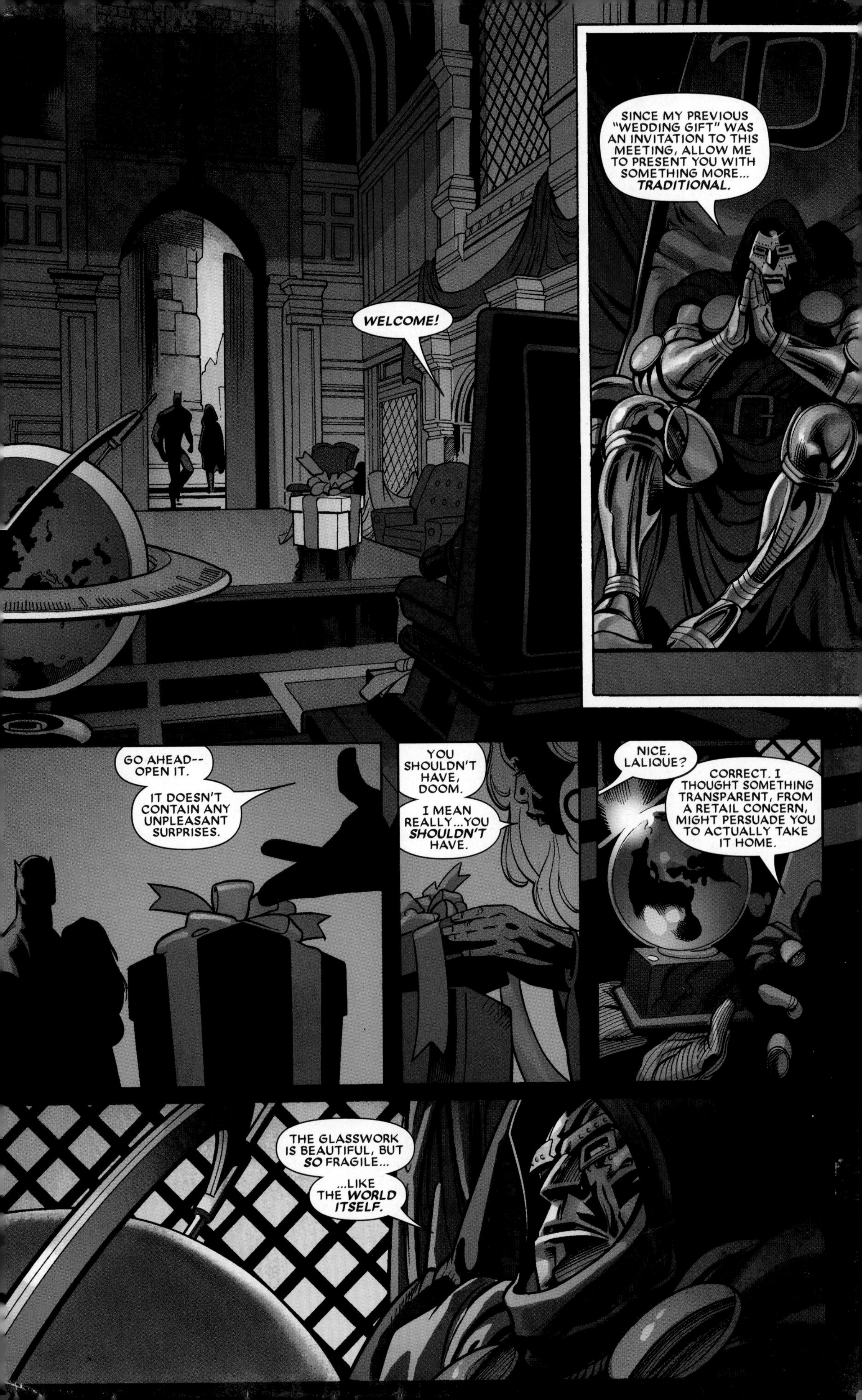
WELCOME!
SINCE MY PREVIOUS "WEDDING GIFT" WAS AN INVITATION TO THIS MEETING, ALLOW ME TO PRESENT YOU WITH SOMETHING MORE... *TRADITIONAL.*
GO AHEAD-- OPEN IT.
IT DOESN'T CONTAIN ANY UNPLEASANT SURPRISES.
YOU SHOULDN'T HAVE, DOOM.
I MEAN REALLY...YOU *SHOULDN'T* HAVE.
NICE. LALIQUE?
CORRECT. I THOUGHT SOMETHING TRANSPARENT, FROM A RETAIL CONCERN, MIGHT PERSUADE YOU TO ACTUALLY TAKE IT HOME.
THE GLASSWORK IS BEAUTIFUL, BUT *SO* FRAGILE...
...LIKE THE *WORLD ITSELF.*

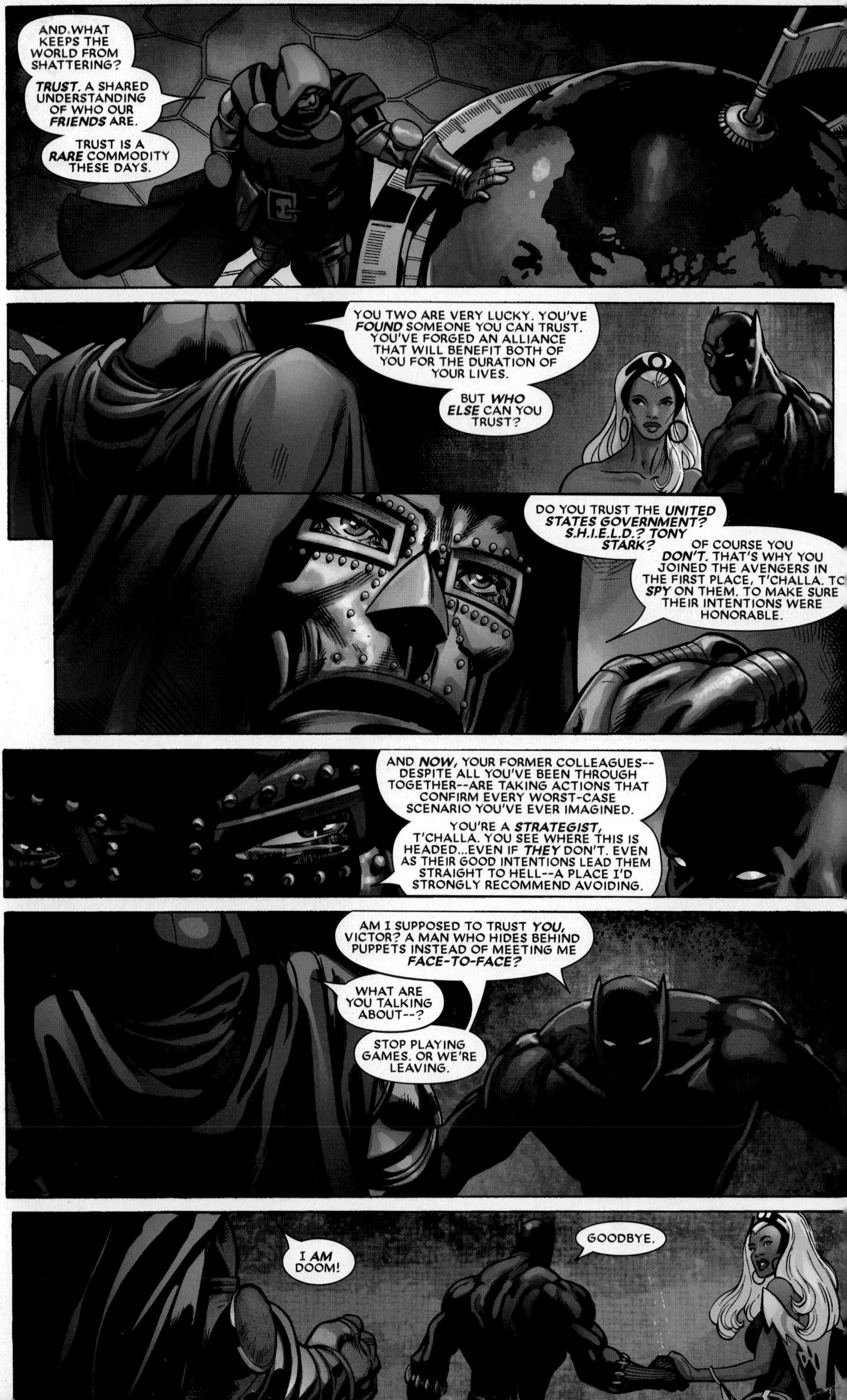
AND WHAT KEEPS THE WORLD FROM SHATTERING?
TRUST. A SHARED UNDERSTANDING OF WHO OUR FRIENDS ARE.
TRUST IS A RARE COMMODITY THESE DAYS.
YOU TWO ARE VERY LUCKY. YOU'VE FOUND SOMEONE YOU CAN TRUST. YOU'VE FORGED AN ALLIANCE THAT WILL BENEFIT BOTH OF YOU FOR THE DURATION OF YOUR LIVES.
BUT WHO ELSE CAN YOU TRUST?
DO YOU TRUST THE UNITED STATES GOVERNMENT? S.H.I.E.L.D.? TONY STARK?
OF COURSE YOU DON'T. THAT'S WHY YOU JOINED THE AVENGERS IN THE FIRST PLACE, T'CHALLA. TO SPY ON THEM. TO MAKE SURE THEIR INTENTIONS WERE HONORABLE.
AND NOW, YOUR FORMER COLLEAGUES--DESPITE ALL YOU'VE BEEN THROUGH TOGETHER--ARE TAKING ACTIONS THAT CONFIRM EVERY WORST-CASE SCENARIO YOU'VE EVER IMAGINED.
YOU'RE A STRATEGIST, T'CHALLA. YOU SEE WHERE THIS IS HEADED...EVEN IF THEY DON'T. EVEN AS THEIR GOOD INTENTIONS LEAD THEM STRAIGHT TO HELL--A PLACE I'D STRONGLY RECOMMEND AVOIDING.
AM I SUPPOSED TO TRUST YOU, VICTOR? A MAN WHO HIDES BEHIND PUPPETS INSTEAD OF MEETING ME FACE-TO-FACE?
WHAT ARE YOU TALKING ABOUT--?
STOP PLAYING GAMES. OR WE'RE LEAVING.
I AM DOOM!
GOODBYE.

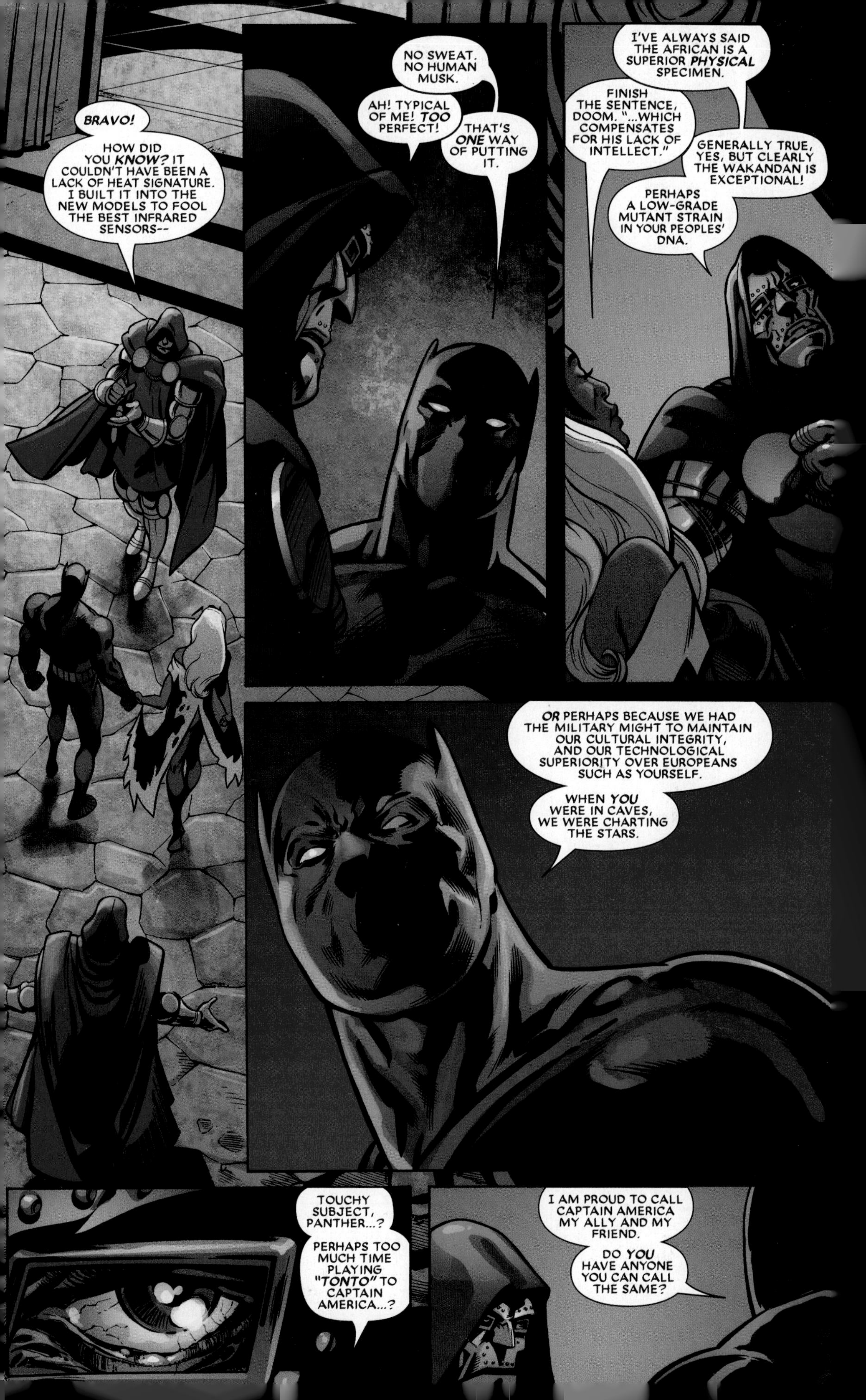

BRAVO!
HOW DID YOU KNOW? IT COULDN'T HAVE BEEN A LACK OF HEAT SIGNATURE. I BUILT IT INTO THE NEW MODELS TO FOOL THE BEST INFRARED SENSORS--
NO SWEAT. NO HUMAN MUSK.
AH! TYPICAL OF ME! TOO PERFECT!
THAT'S ONE WAY OF PUTTING IT.
I'VE ALWAYS SAID THE AFRICAN IS A SUPERIOR PHYSICAL SPECIMEN.
FINISH THE SENTENCE, DOOM. "...WHICH COMPENSATES FOR HIS LACK OF INTELLECT."
GENERALLY TRUE, YES, BUT CLEARLY THE WAKANDAN IS EXCEPTIONAL!
PERHAPS A LOW-GRADE MUTANT STRAIN IN YOUR PEOPLES' DNA.
OR PERHAPS BECAUSE WE HAD THE MILITARY MIGHT TO MAINTAIN OUR CULTURAL INTEGRITY, AND OUR TECHNOLOGICAL SUPERIORITY OVER EUROPEANS SUCH AS YOURSELF.
WHEN YOU WERE IN CAVES, WE WERE CHARTING THE STARS.
TOUCHY SUBJECT, PANTHER...?
PERHAPS TOO MUCH TIME PLAYING "TONTO" TO CAPTAIN AMERICA...?
I AM PROUD TO CALL CAPTAIN AMERICA MY ALLY AND MY FRIEND.
DO YOU HAVE ANYONE YOU CAN CALL THE SAME?

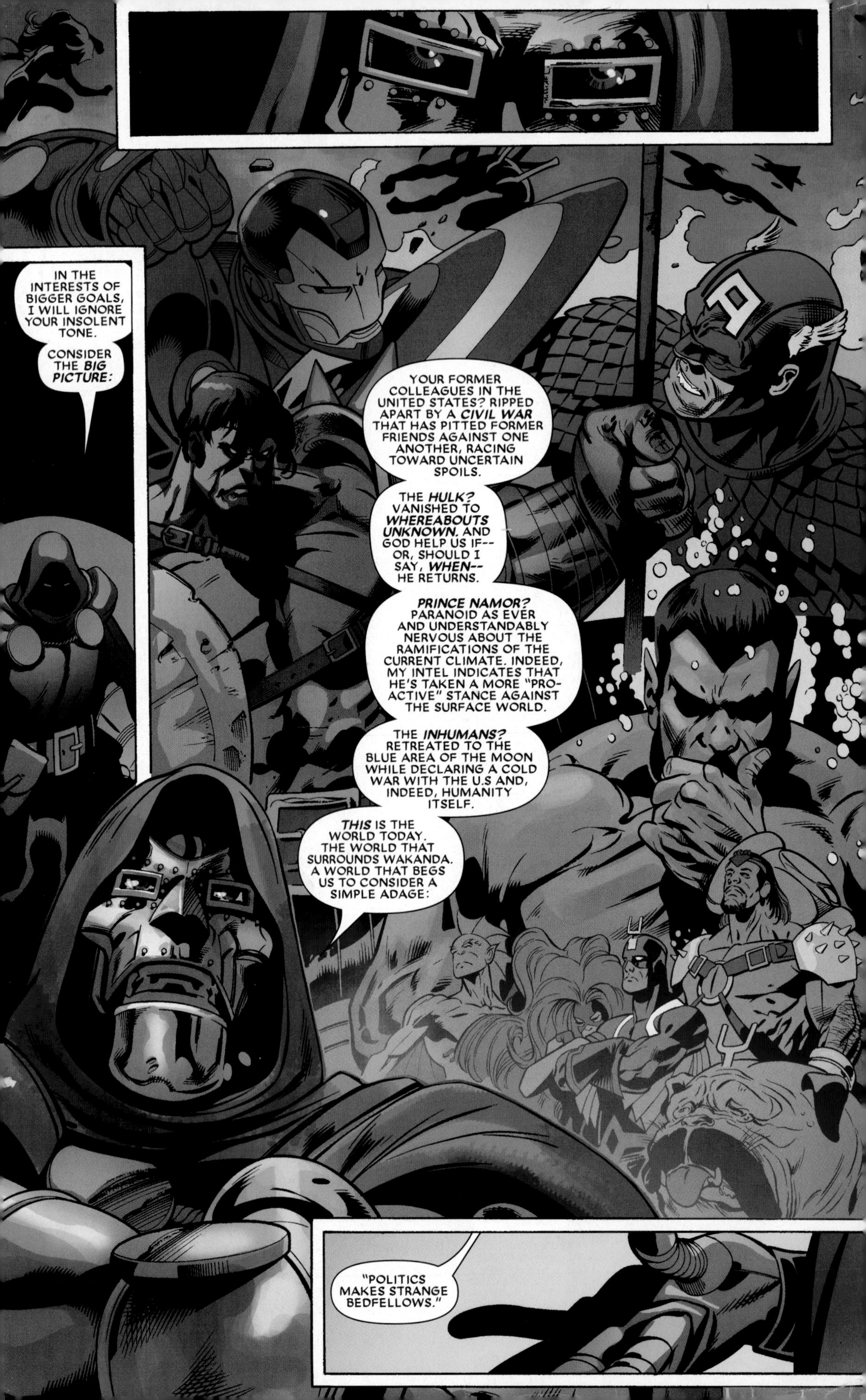

IN THE INTERESTS OF BIGGER GOALS, I WILL IGNORE YOUR INSOLENT TONE.
CONSIDER THE *BIG PICTURE:*
YOUR FORMER COLLEAGUES IN THE UNITED STATES? RIPPED APART BY A *CIVIL WAR* THAT HAS PITTED FORMER FRIENDS AGAINST ONE ANOTHER, RACING TOWARD UNCERTAIN SPOILS.
THE *HULK?* VANISHED TO *WHEREABOUTS UNKNOWN.* AND GOD HELP US IF-- OR, SHOULD I SAY, *WHEN--* HE RETURNS.
PRINCE NAMOR? PARANOID AS EVER AND UNDERSTANDABLY NERVOUS ABOUT THE RAMIFICATIONS OF THE CURRENT CLIMATE. INDEED, MY INTEL INDICATES THAT HE'S TAKEN A MORE "PRO-ACTIVE" STANCE AGAINST THE SURFACE WORLD.
THE *INHUMANS?* RETREATED TO THE BLUE AREA OF THE MOON WHILE DECLARING A COLD WAR WITH THE U.S AND, INDEED, HUMANITY ITSELF.
THIS IS THE WORLD TODAY. THE WORLD THAT SURROUNDS WAKANDA. A WORLD THAT BEGS US TO CONSIDER A SIMPLE ADAGE:
"POLITICS MAKES STRANGE BEDFELLOWS."

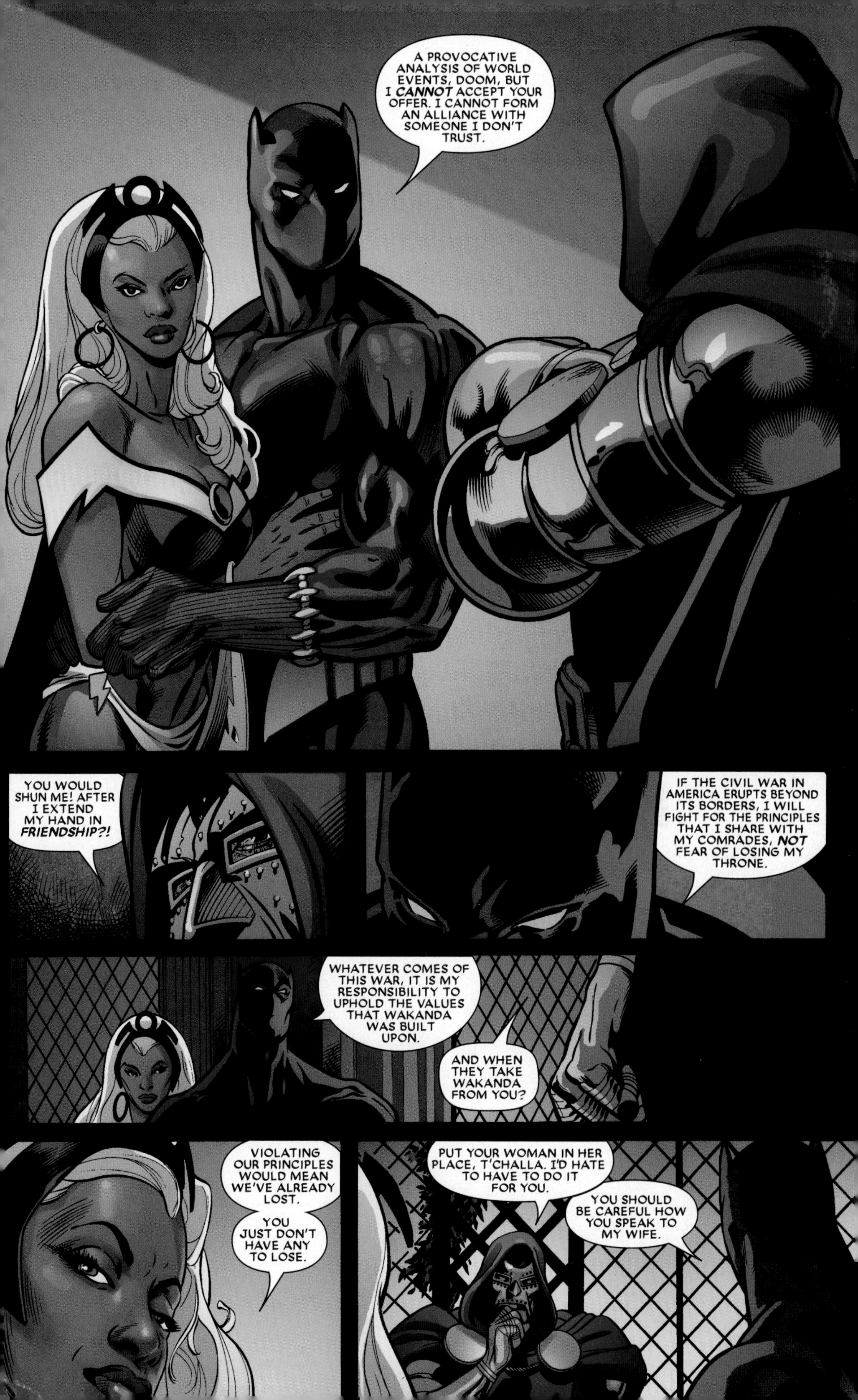
A PROVOCATIVE ANALYSIS OF WORLD EVENTS, DOOM, BUT I CANNOT ACCEPT YOUR OFFER. I CANNOT FORM AN ALLIANCE WITH SOMEONE I DON'T TRUST.
YOU WOULD SHUN ME! AFTER I EXTEND MY HAND IN FRIENDSHIP?!
IF THE CIVIL WAR IN AMERICA ERUPTS BEYOND ITS BORDERS, I WILL FIGHT FOR THE PRINCIPLES THAT I SHARE WITH MY COMRADES, NOT FEAR OF LOSING MY THRONE.
WHATEVER COMES OF THIS WAR, IT IS MY RESPONSIBILITY TO UPHOLD THE VALUES THAT WAKANDA WAS BUILT UPON.
AND WHEN THEY TAKE WAKANDA FROM YOU?
VIOLATING OUR PRINCIPLES WOULD MEAN WE'VE ALREADY LOST.
YOU JUST DON'T HAVE ANY TO LOSE.
PUT YOUR WOMAN IN HER PLACE, T'CHALLA. I'D HATE TO HAVE TO DO IT FOR YOU.
YOU SHOULD BE CAREFUL HOW YOU SPEAK TO MY WIFE.

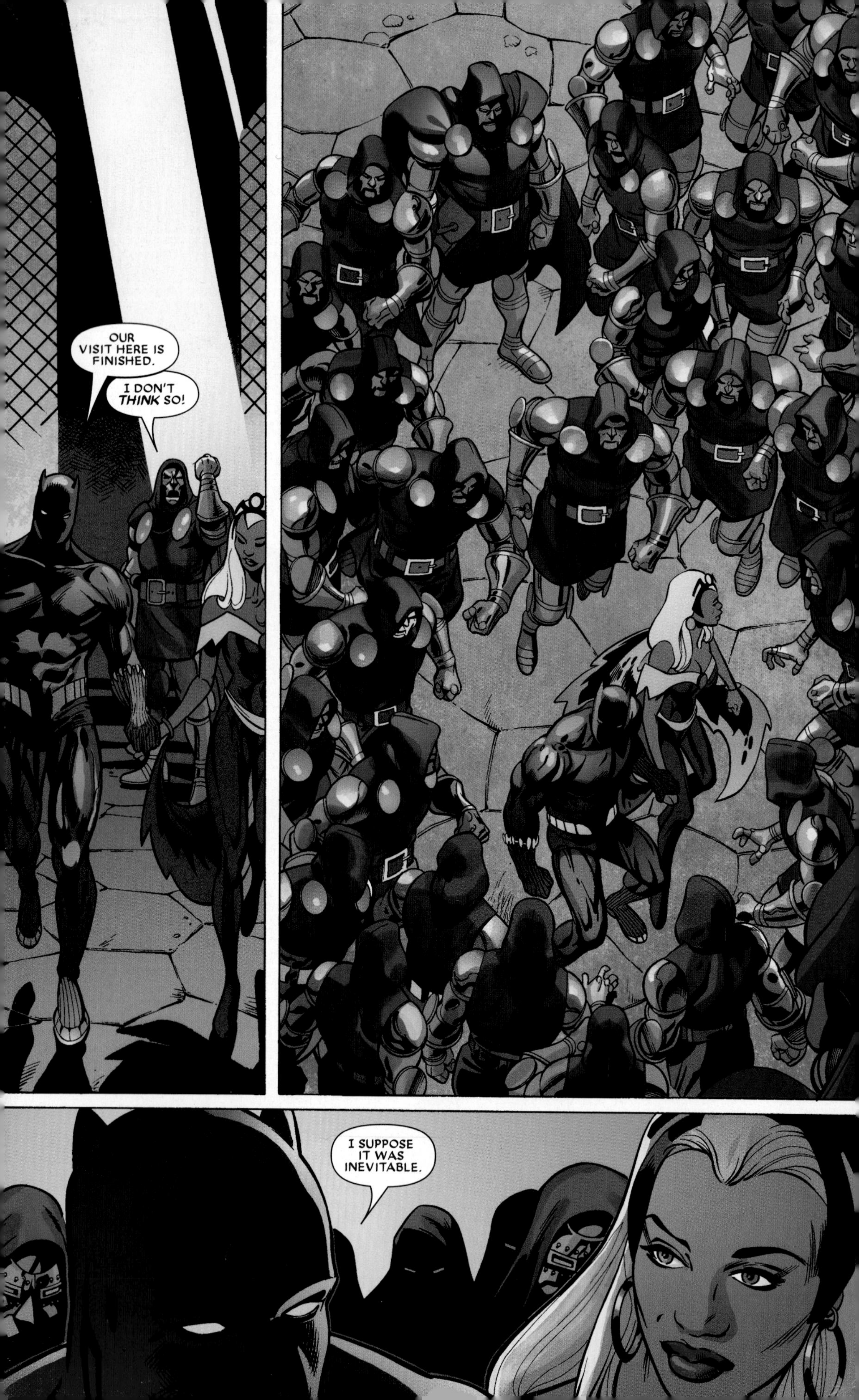

OUR VISIT HERE IS FINISHED.
I DON'T THINK SO!
I SUPPOSE IT WAS INEVITABLE.

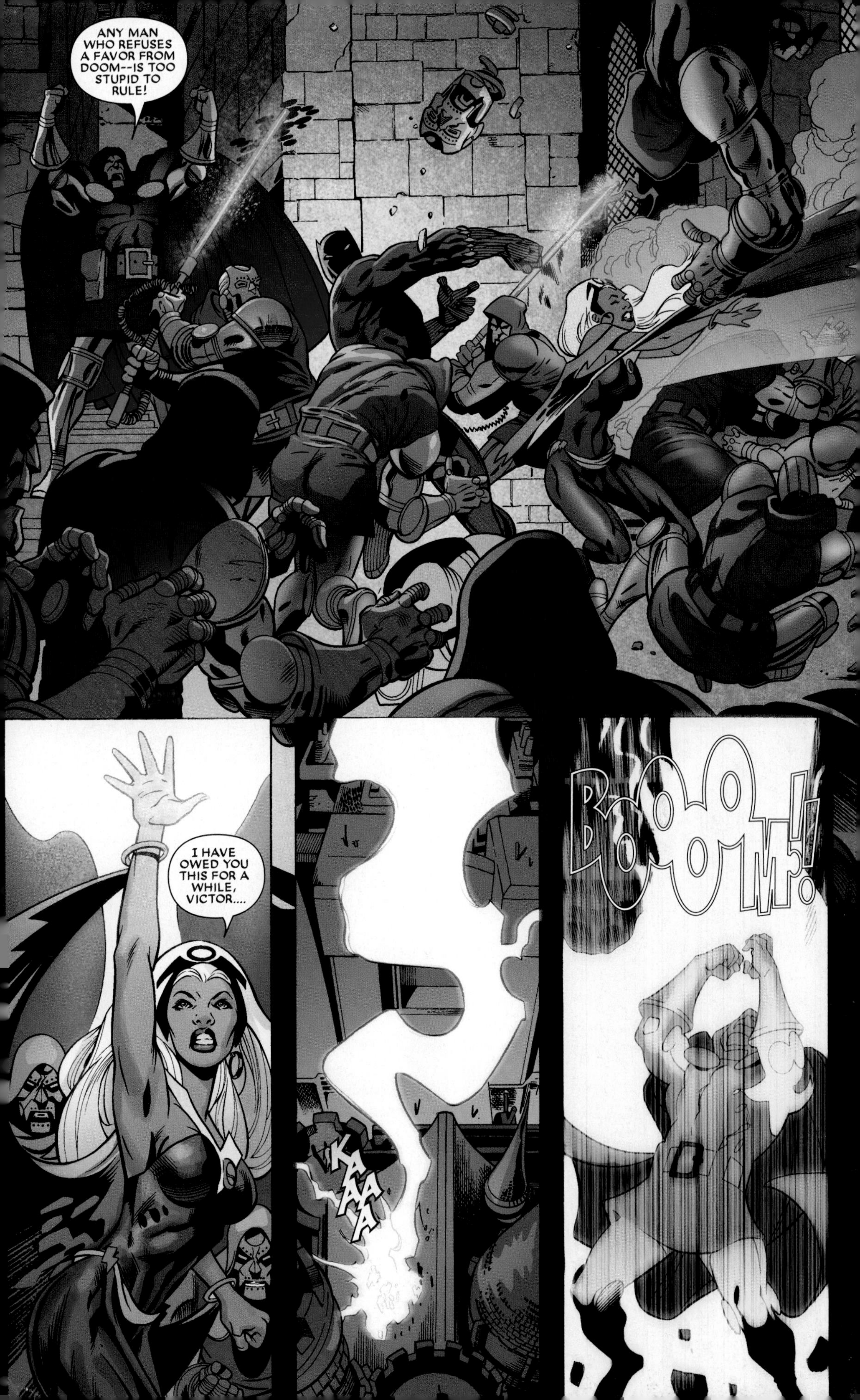
ANY MAN WHO REFUSES A FAVOR FROM DOOM--IS TOO STUPID TO RULE!
I HAVE OWED YOU THIS FOR A WHILE, VICTOR....
KAAAA
BOOOOOM!!

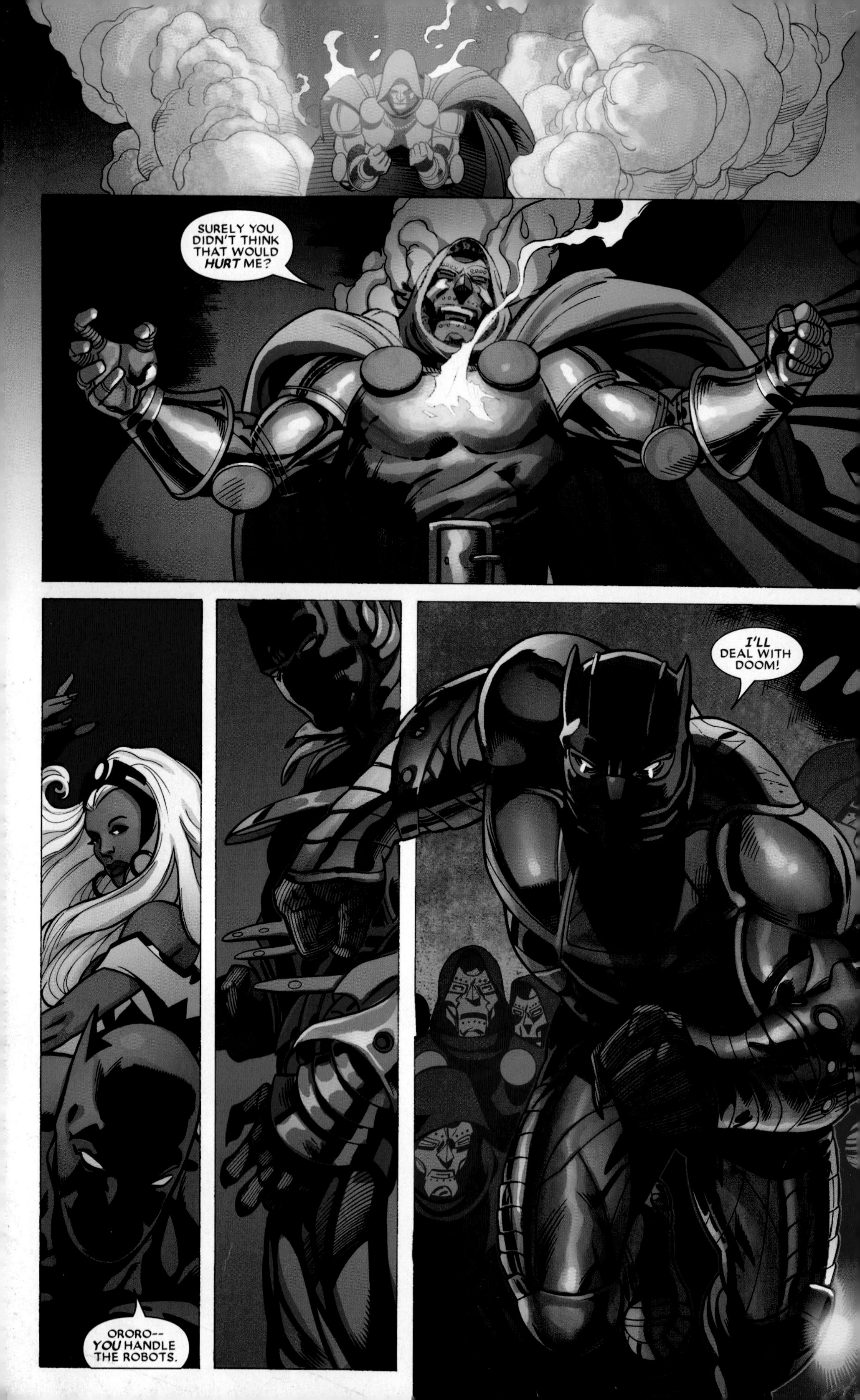
SURELY YOU DIDN'T THINK THAT WOULD *HURT* ME?
ORORO-- *YOU* HANDLE THE ROBOTS.
I'LL DEAL WITH DOOM!

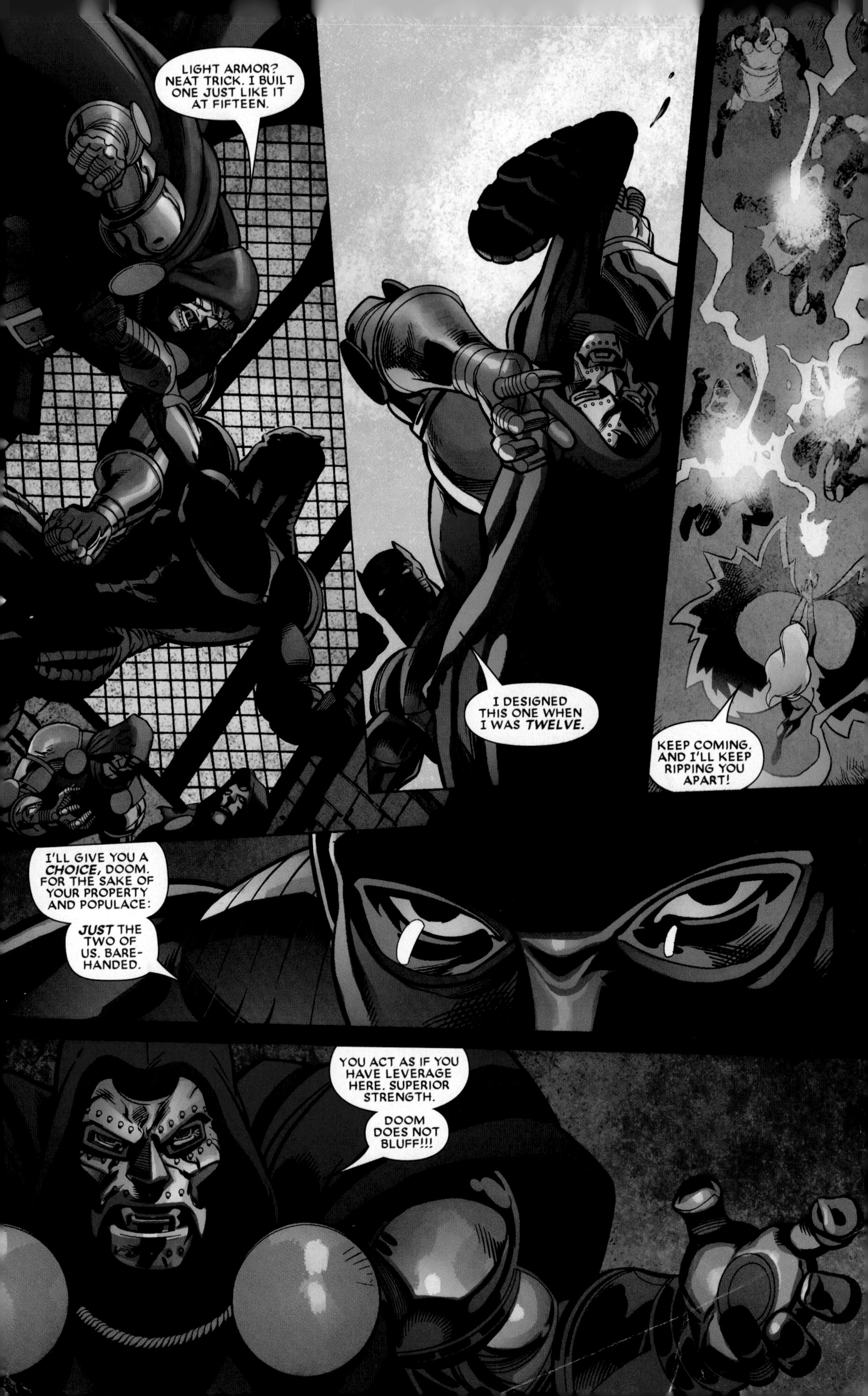
LIGHT ARMOR? NEAT TRICK. I BUILT ONE JUST LIKE IT AT FIFTEEN.
I DESIGNED THIS ONE WHEN I WAS *TWELVE.*
KEEP COMING. AND I'LL KEEP RIPPING YOU APART!
I'LL GIVE YOU A *CHOICE,* DOOM. FOR THE SAKE OF YOUR PROPERTY AND POPULACE:
JUST THE TWO OF US. BARE-HANDED.
YOU ACT AS IF YOU HAVE LEVERAGE HERE. SUPERIOR STRENGTH.
DOOM DOES NOT BLUFF!!!

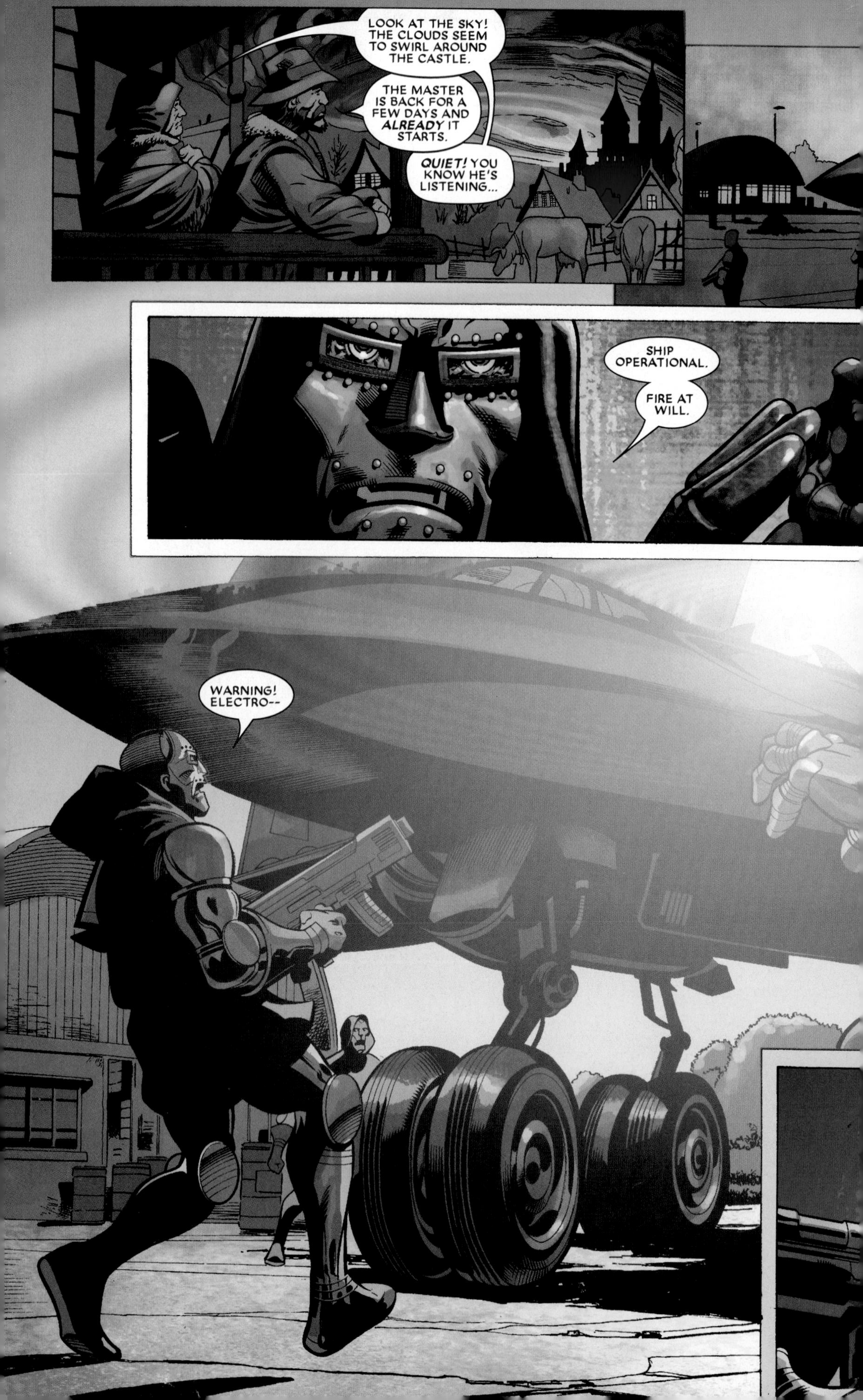
LOOK AT THE SKY! THE CLOUDS SEEM TO SWIRL AROUND THE CASTLE.
THE MASTER IS BACK FOR A FEW DAYS AND ALREADY IT STARTS.
QUIET! YOU KNOW HE'S LISTENING...
SHIP OPERATIONAL.
FIRE AT WILL.
WARNING! ELECTRO--

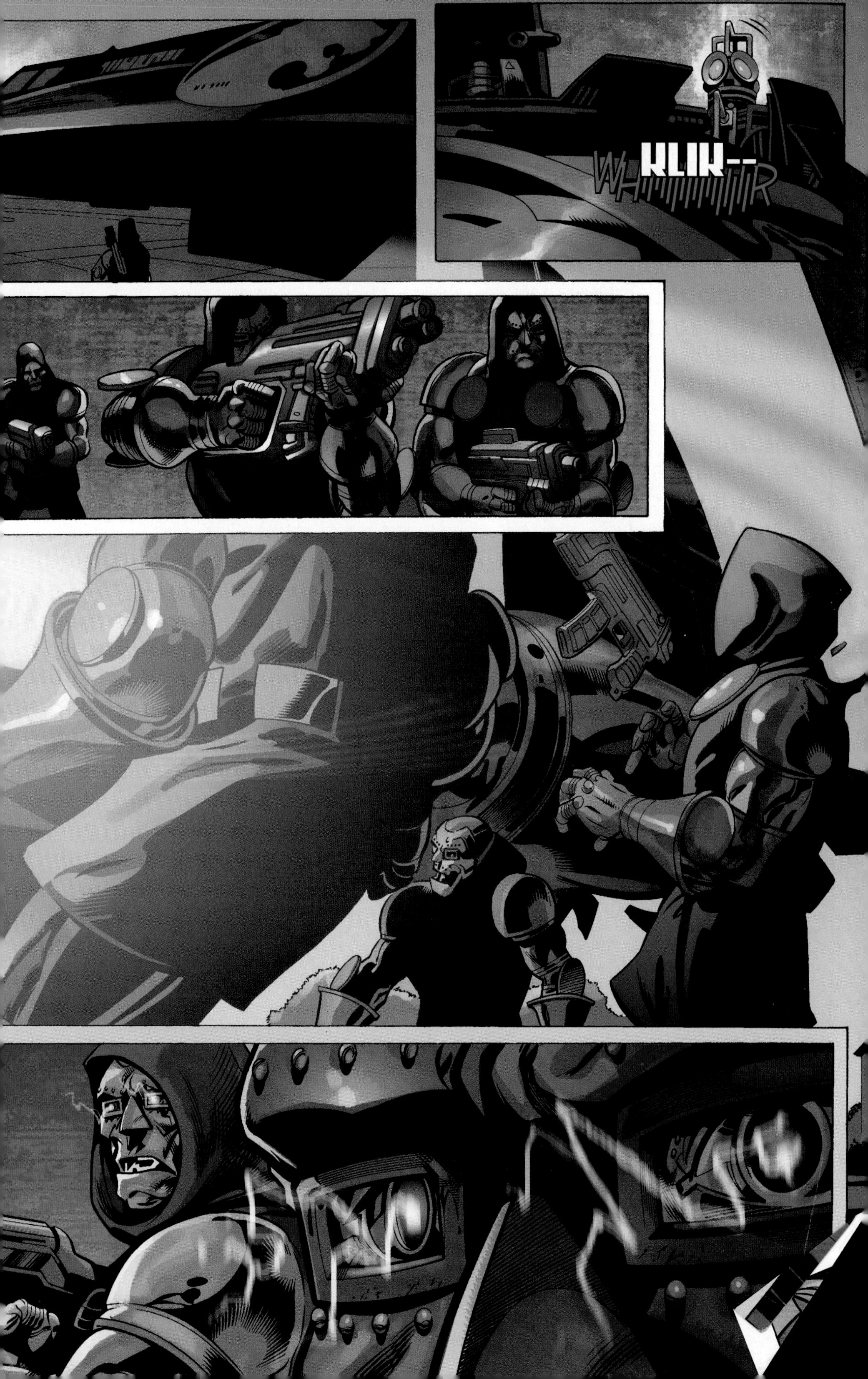
KLIK--

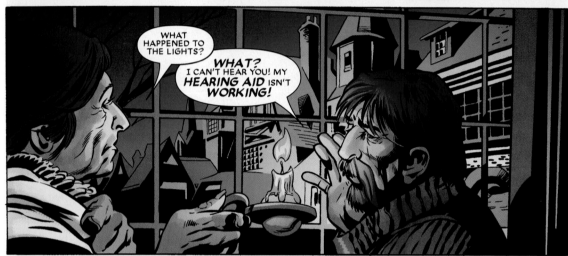

WHAT HAPPENED TO THE LIGHTS?

WHAT? I CAN'T HEAR YOU! MY HEARING AID ISN'T WORKING!

LOOKS LIKE SOMEONE CUT YOUR PUPPETS' STRINGS, DOOM.

AN ELECTROMAGNETIC PULSE? YOU FOOL!

DO YOU KNOW WHAT YOU'VE DONE?

WELL, I BUILT IT, SO YES, I DO.

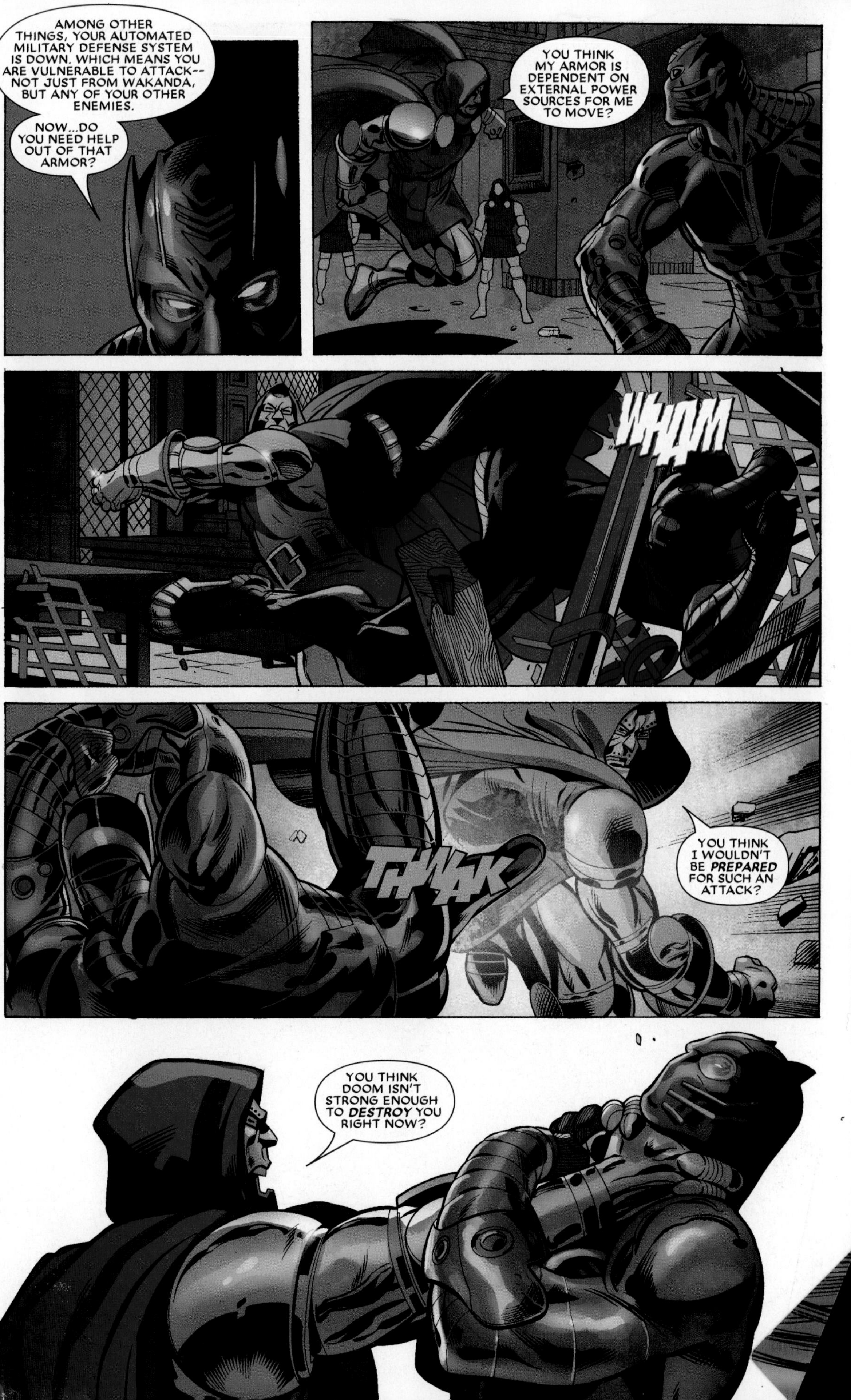
AMONG OTHER THINGS, YOUR AUTOMATED MILITARY DEFENSE SYSTEM IS DOWN. WHICH MEANS YOU ARE VULNERABLE TO ATTACK-- NOT JUST FROM WAKANDA, BUT ANY OF YOUR OTHER ENEMIES.
NOW...DO YOU NEED HELP OUT OF THAT ARMOR?
YOU THINK MY ARMOR IS DEPENDENT ON EXTERNAL POWER SOURCES FOR ME TO MOVE?
WHAM
THWAK
YOU THINK I WOULDN'T BE PREPARED FOR SUCH AN ATTACK?
YOU THINK DOOM ISN'T STRONG ENOUGH TO DESTROY YOU RIGHT NOW?

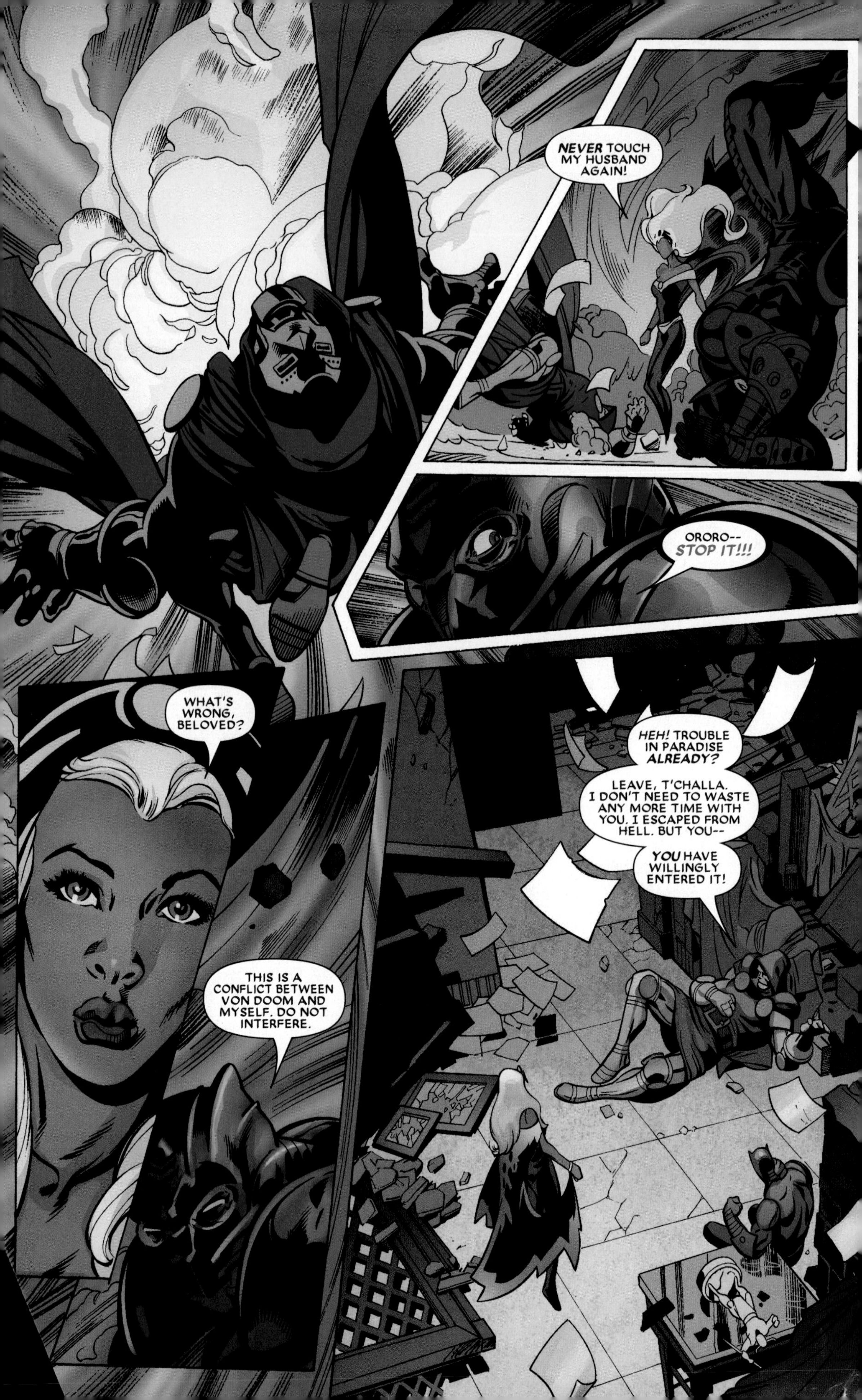

NEVER TOUCH MY HUSBAND AGAIN!
ORORO-- STOP IT!!!
WHAT'S WRONG, BELOVED?
THIS IS A CONFLICT BETWEEN VON DOOM AND MYSELF. DO NOT INTERFERE.
HEH! TROUBLE IN PARADISE ALREADY?
LEAVE, T'CHALLA. I DON'T NEED TO WASTE ANY MORE TIME WITH YOU. I ESCAPED FROM HELL. BUT YOU--
YOU HAVE WILLINGLY ENTERED IT!

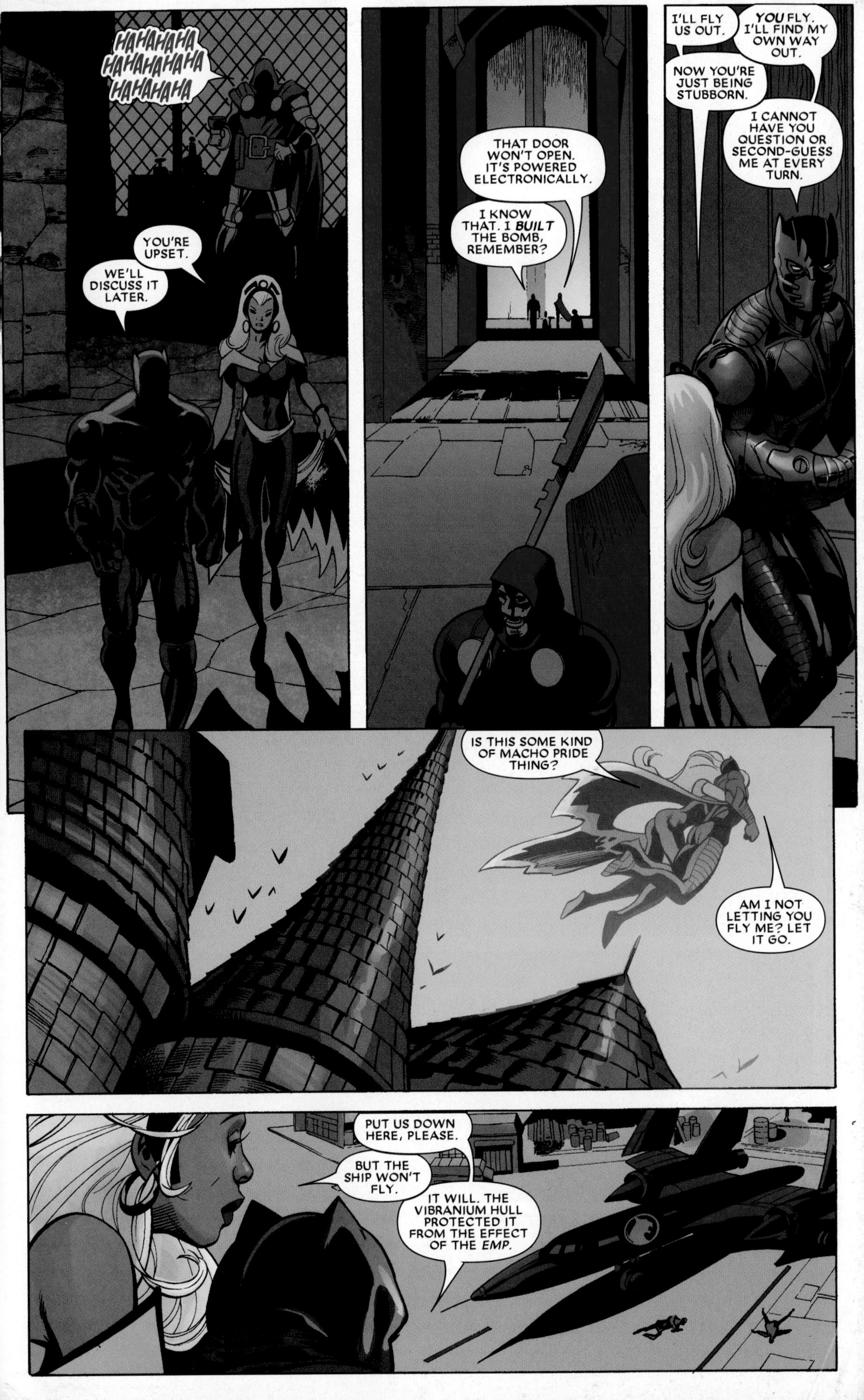
HAHAHAHA
HAHAHAHAHA
HAHAHAHA
YOU'RE UPSET.
WE'LL DISCUSS IT LATER.
THAT DOOR WON'T OPEN. IT'S POWERED ELECTRONICALLY.
I KNOW THAT. I *BUILT* THE BOMB, REMEMBER?
I'LL FLY US OUT.
YOU FLY. I'LL FIND MY OWN WAY OUT.
NOW YOU'RE JUST BEING STUBBORN.
I CANNOT HAVE YOU QUESTION OR SECOND-GUESS ME AT EVERY TURN.
IS THIS SOME KIND OF MACHO PRIDE THING?
AM I NOT LETTING YOU FLY ME? LET IT GO.
PUT US DOWN HERE, PLEASE.
BUT THE SHIP WON'T FLY.
IT WILL. THE VIBRANIUM HULL PROTECTED IT FROM THE EFFECT OF THE *EMP*.

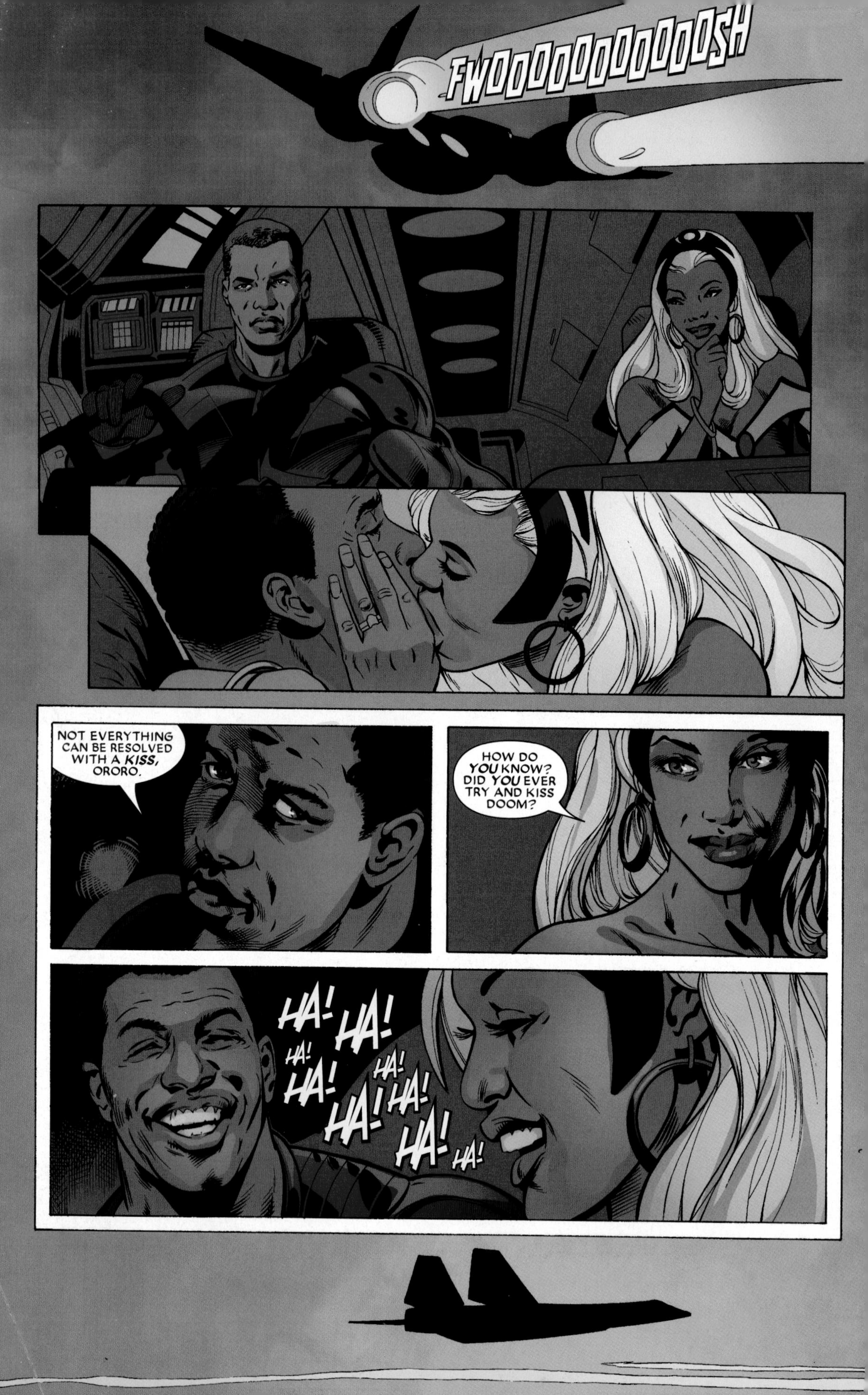
FWOOOOOOOOOOOSH
NOT EVERYTHING CAN BE RESOLVED WITH A KISS, ORORO.
HOW DO YOU KNOW? DID YOU EVER TRY AND KISS DOOM?
HA! HA! HA! HA! HA! HA! HA! HA! HA!

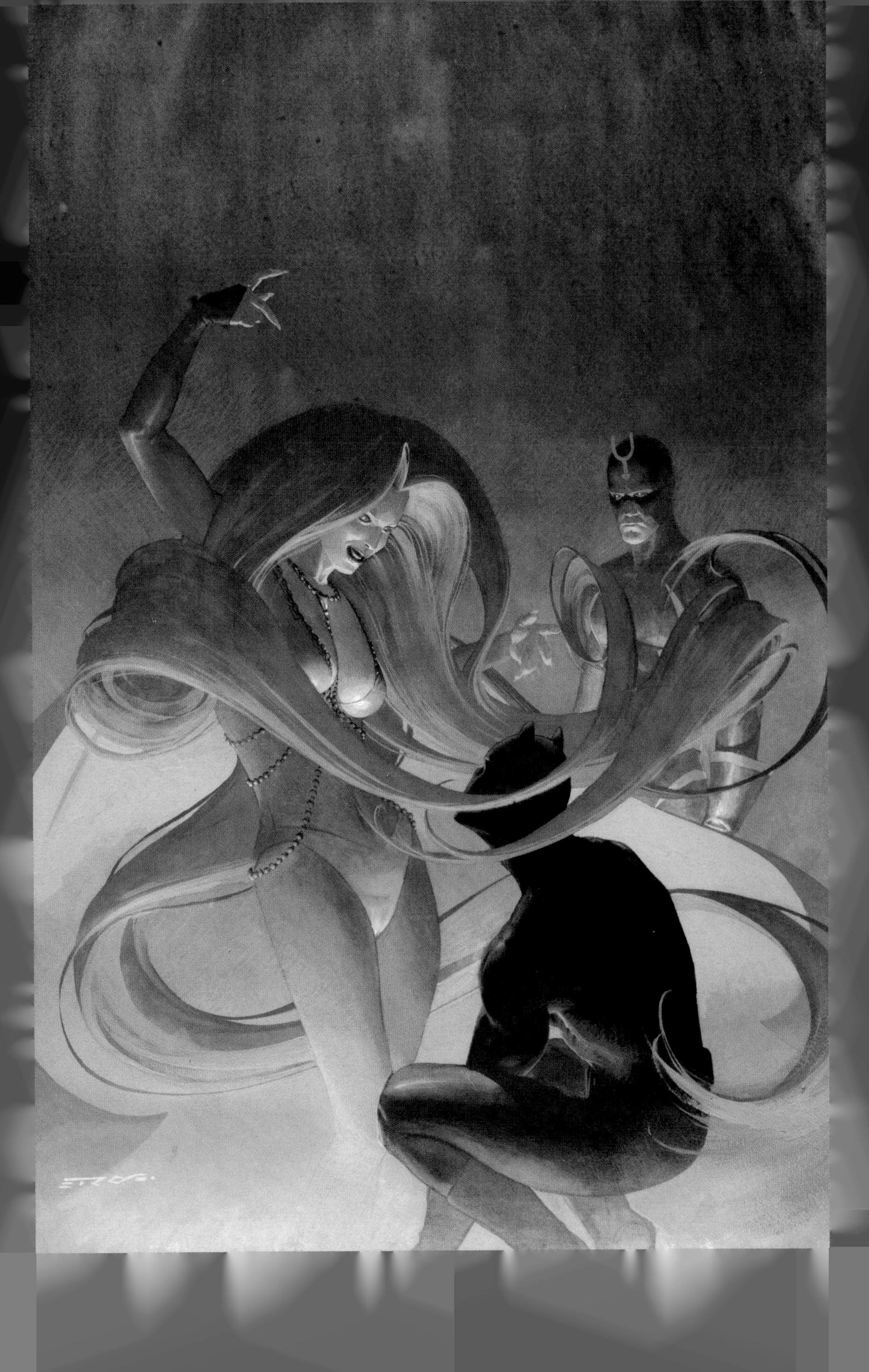

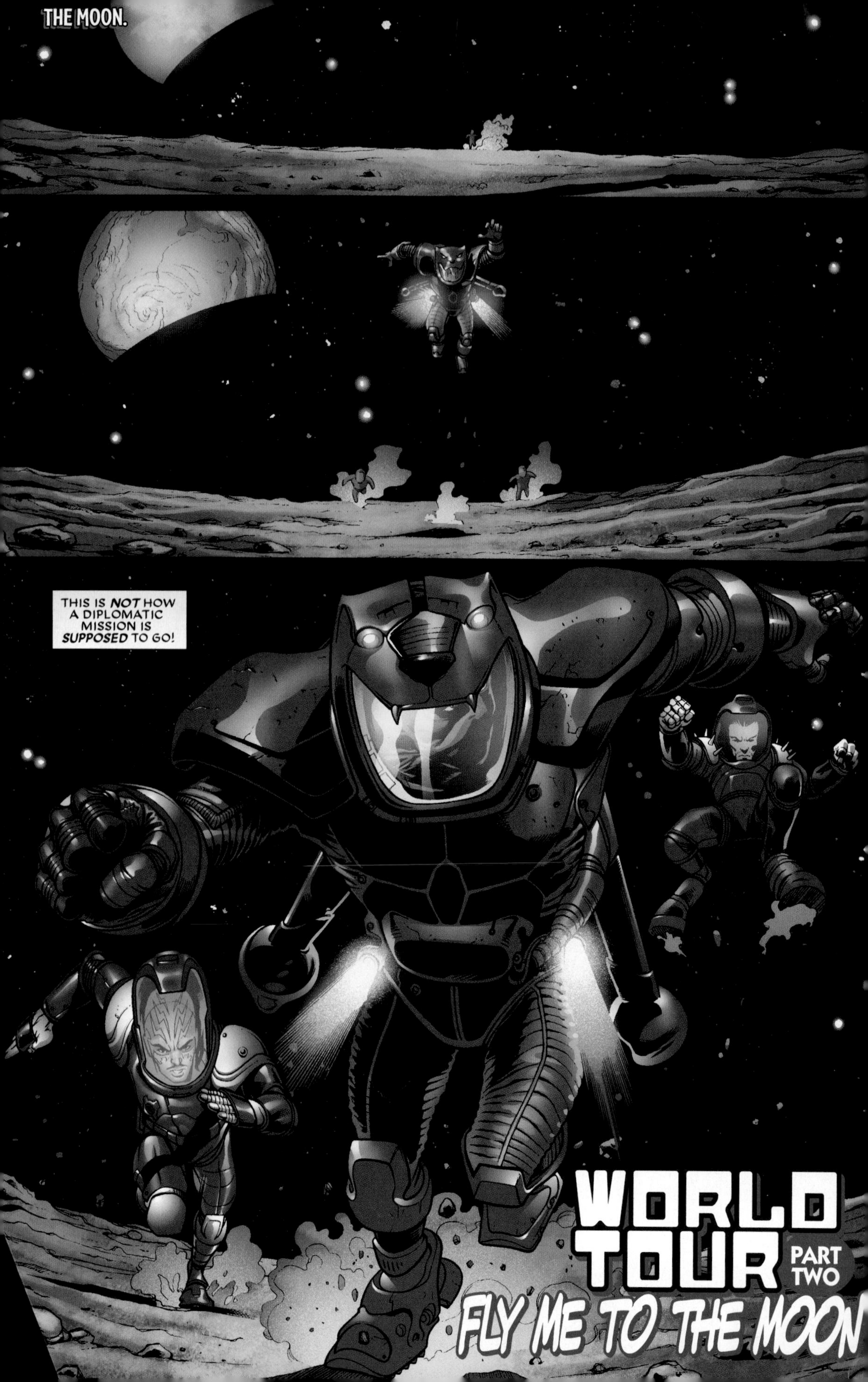
THE MOON.
THIS IS NOT HOW A DIPLOMATIC MISSION IS SUPPOSED TO GO!
WORLD TOUR PART TWO
FLY ME TO THE MOON

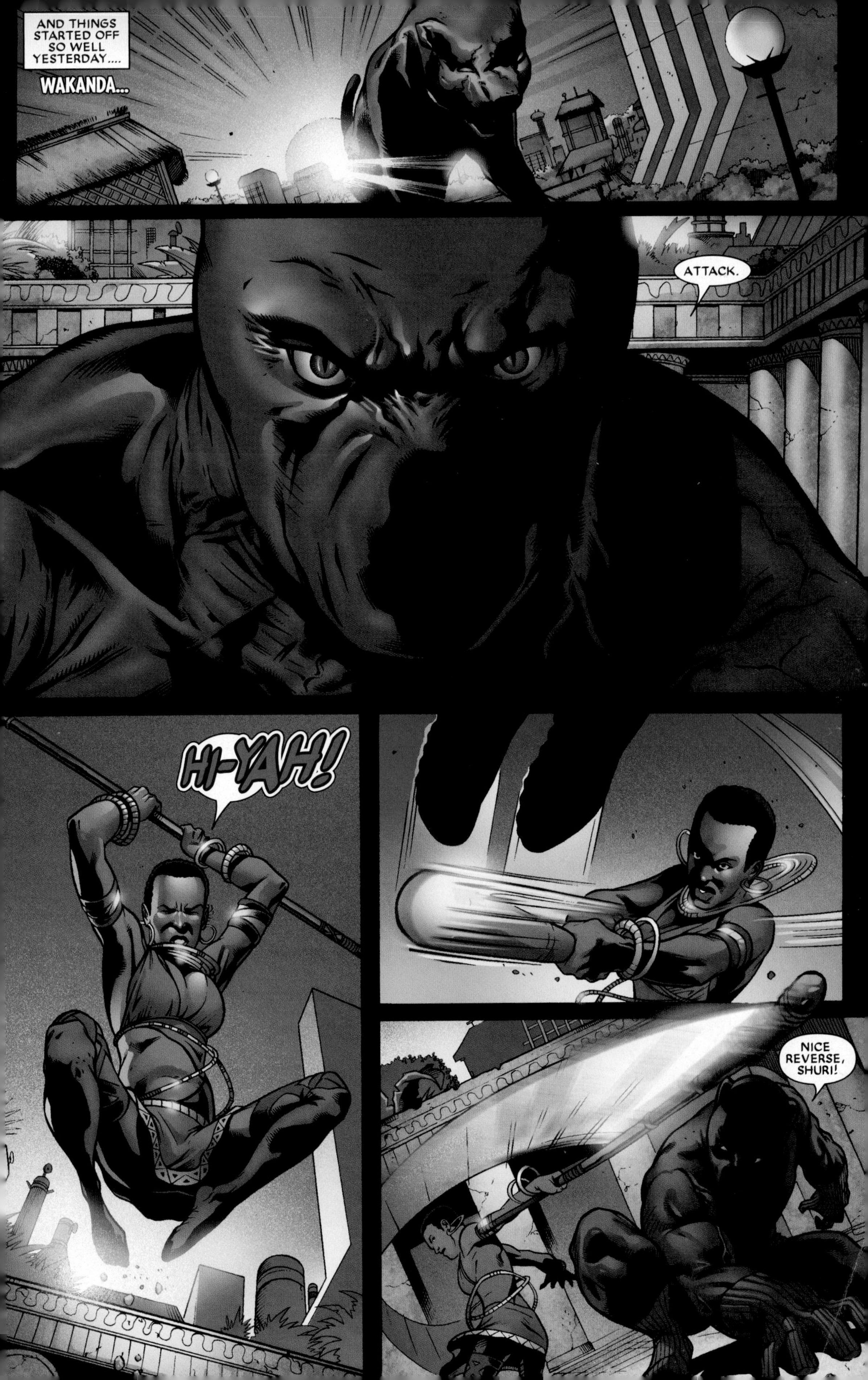
AND THINGS STARTED OFF SO WELL YESTERDAY....
WAKANDA...
ATTACK.
HI-YAH!
NICE REVERSE, SHURI!

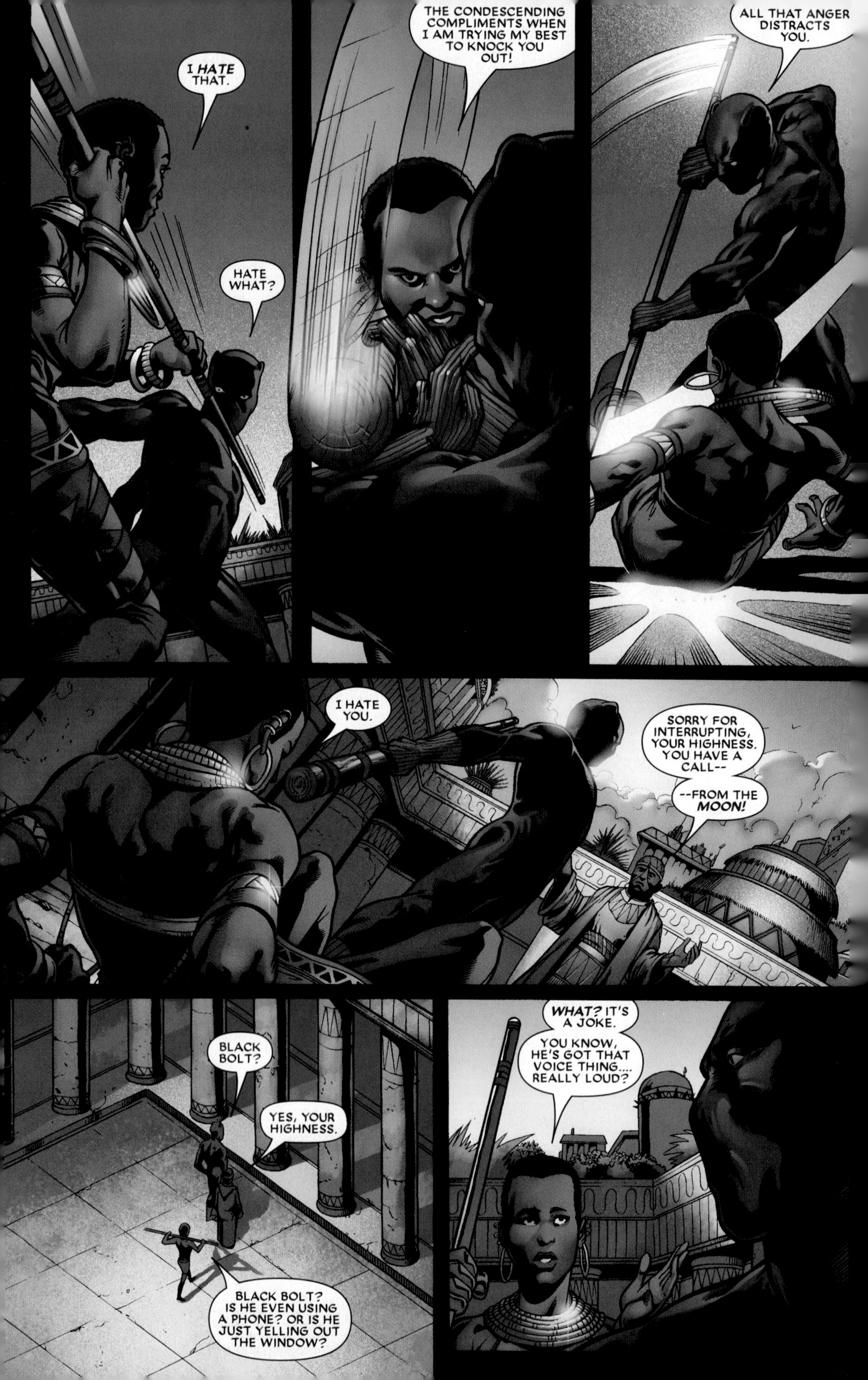
I HATE THAT.
HATE WHAT?
THE CONDESCENDING COMPLIMENTS WHEN I AM TRYING MY BEST TO KNOCK YOU OUT!
ALL THAT ANGER DISTRACTS YOU.
I HATE YOU.
SORRY FOR INTERRUPTING, YOUR HIGHNESS. YOU HAVE A CALL--
--FROM THE MOON!
BLACK BOLT?
YES, YOUR HIGHNESS.
BLACK BOLT? IS HE EVEN USING A PHONE? OR IS HE JUST YELLING OUT THE WINDOW?
WHAT? IT'S A JOKE.
YOU KNOW, HE'S GOT THAT VOICE THING.... REALLY LOUD?

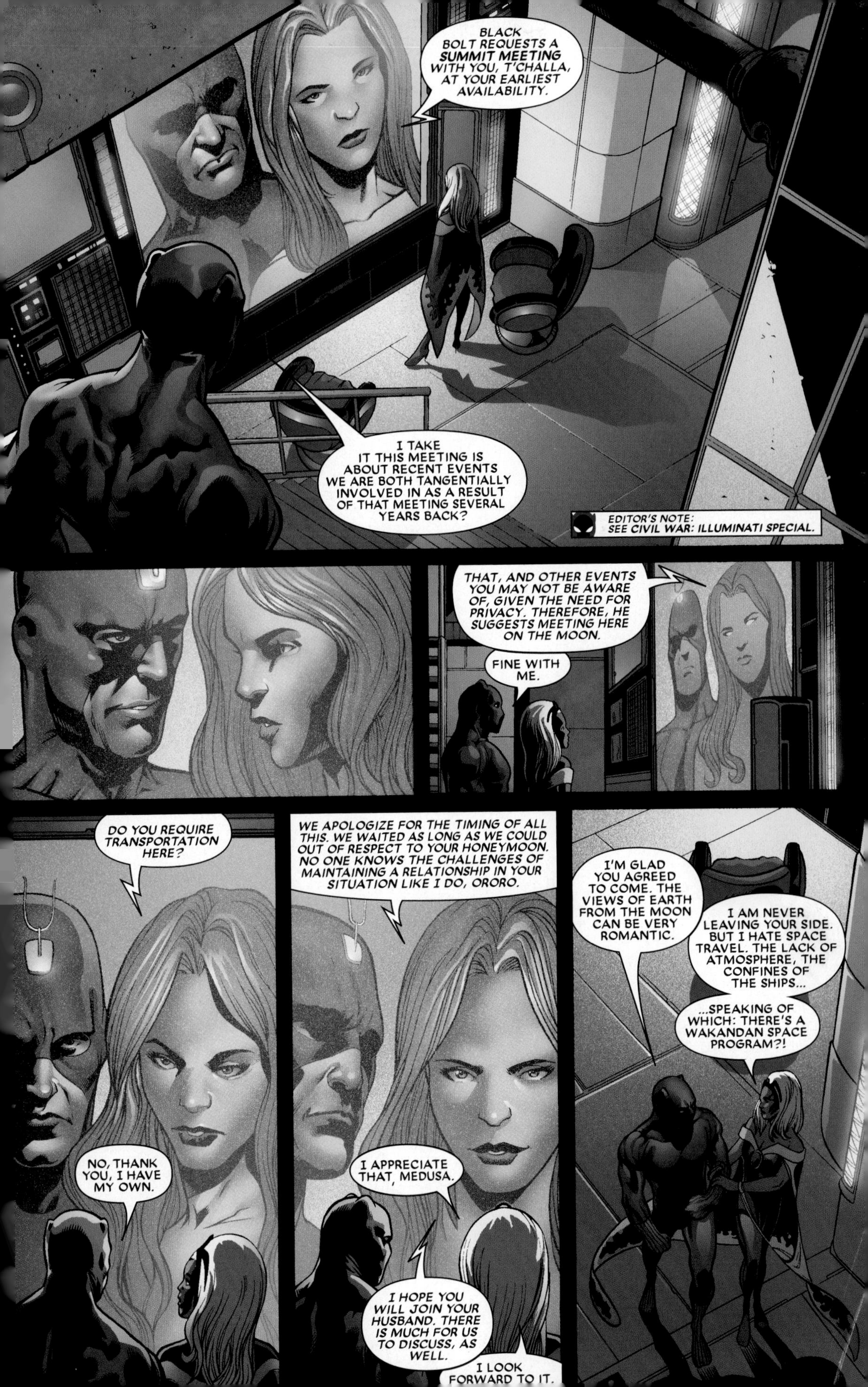
BLACK BOLT REQUESTS A SUMMIT MEETING WITH YOU, T'CHALLA, AT YOUR EARLIEST AVAILABILITY.
I TAKE IT THIS MEETING IS ABOUT RECENT EVENTS WE ARE BOTH TANGENTIALLY INVOLVED IN AS A RESULT OF THAT MEETING SEVERAL YEARS BACK?
EDITOR'S NOTE: SEE CIVIL WAR: ILLUMINATI SPECIAL.
THAT, AND OTHER EVENTS YOU MAY NOT BE AWARE OF, GIVEN THE NEED FOR PRIVACY. THEREFORE, HE SUGGESTS MEETING HERE ON THE MOON.
FINE WITH ME.
DO YOU REQUIRE TRANSPORTATION HERE?
NO, THANK YOU, I HAVE MY OWN.
WE APOLOGIZE FOR THE TIMING OF ALL THIS. WE WAITED AS LONG AS WE COULD OUT OF RESPECT TO YOUR HONEYMOON. NO ONE KNOWS THE CHALLENGES OF MAINTAINING A RELATIONSHIP IN YOUR SITUATION LIKE I DO, ORORO.
I APPRECIATE THAT, MEDUSA.
I HOPE YOU WILL JOIN YOUR HUSBAND. THERE IS MUCH FOR US TO DISCUSS, AS WELL.
I LOOK FORWARD TO IT.
I'M GLAD YOU AGREED TO COME. THE VIEWS OF EARTH FROM THE MOON CAN BE VERY ROMANTIC.
I AM NEVER LEAVING YOUR SIDE. BUT I HATE SPACE TRAVEL. THE LACK OF ATMOSPHERE, THE CONFINES OF THE SHIPS...
...SPEAKING OF WHICH: THERE'S A WAKANDAN SPACE PROGRAM?!

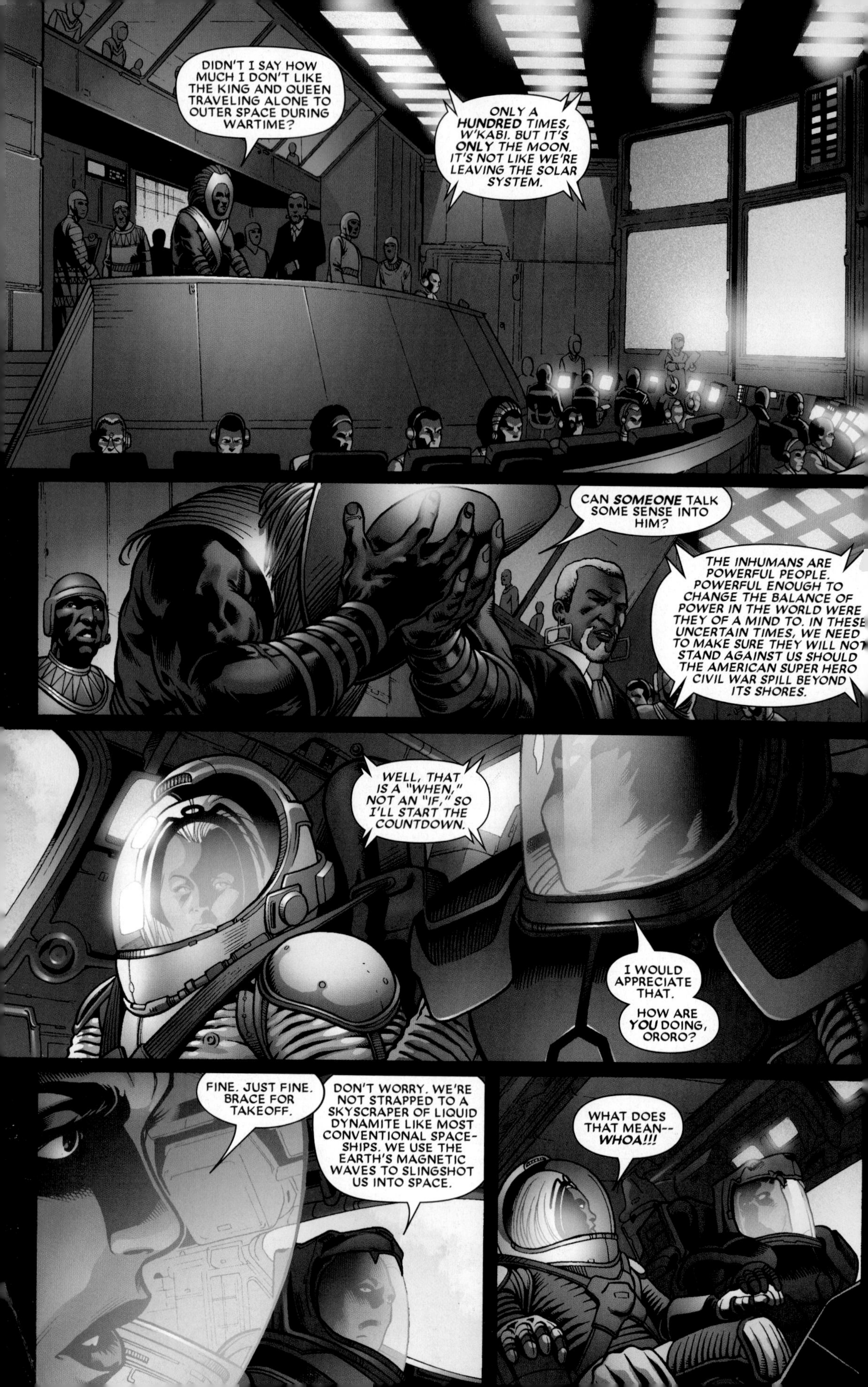
DIDN'T I SAY HOW MUCH I DON'T LIKE THE KING AND QUEEN TRAVELING ALONE TO OUTER SPACE DURING WARTIME?
ONLY A HUNDRED TIMES, W'KABI. BUT IT'S ONLY THE MOON. IT'S NOT LIKE WE'RE LEAVING THE SOLAR SYSTEM.
CAN SOMEONE TALK SOME SENSE INTO HIM?
THE INHUMANS ARE POWERFUL PEOPLE. POWERFUL ENOUGH TO CHANGE THE BALANCE OF POWER IN THE WORLD WERE THEY OF A MIND TO. IN THESE UNCERTAIN TIMES, WE NEED TO MAKE SURE THEY WILL NOT STAND AGAINST US SHOULD THE AMERICAN SUPER HERO CIVIL WAR SPILL BEYOND ITS SHORES.
WELL, THAT IS A "WHEN," NOT AN "IF," SO I'LL START THE COUNTDOWN.
I WOULD APPRECIATE THAT.
HOW ARE YOU DOING, ORORO?
FINE. JUST FINE. BRACE FOR TAKEOFF.
DON'T WORRY. WE'RE NOT STRAPPED TO A SKYSCRAPER OF LIQUID DYNAMITE LIKE MOST CONVENTIONAL SPACE-SHIPS. WE USE THE EARTH'S MAGNETIC WAVES TO SLINGSHOT US INTO SPACE.
WHAT DOES THAT MEAN-- WHOA!!!

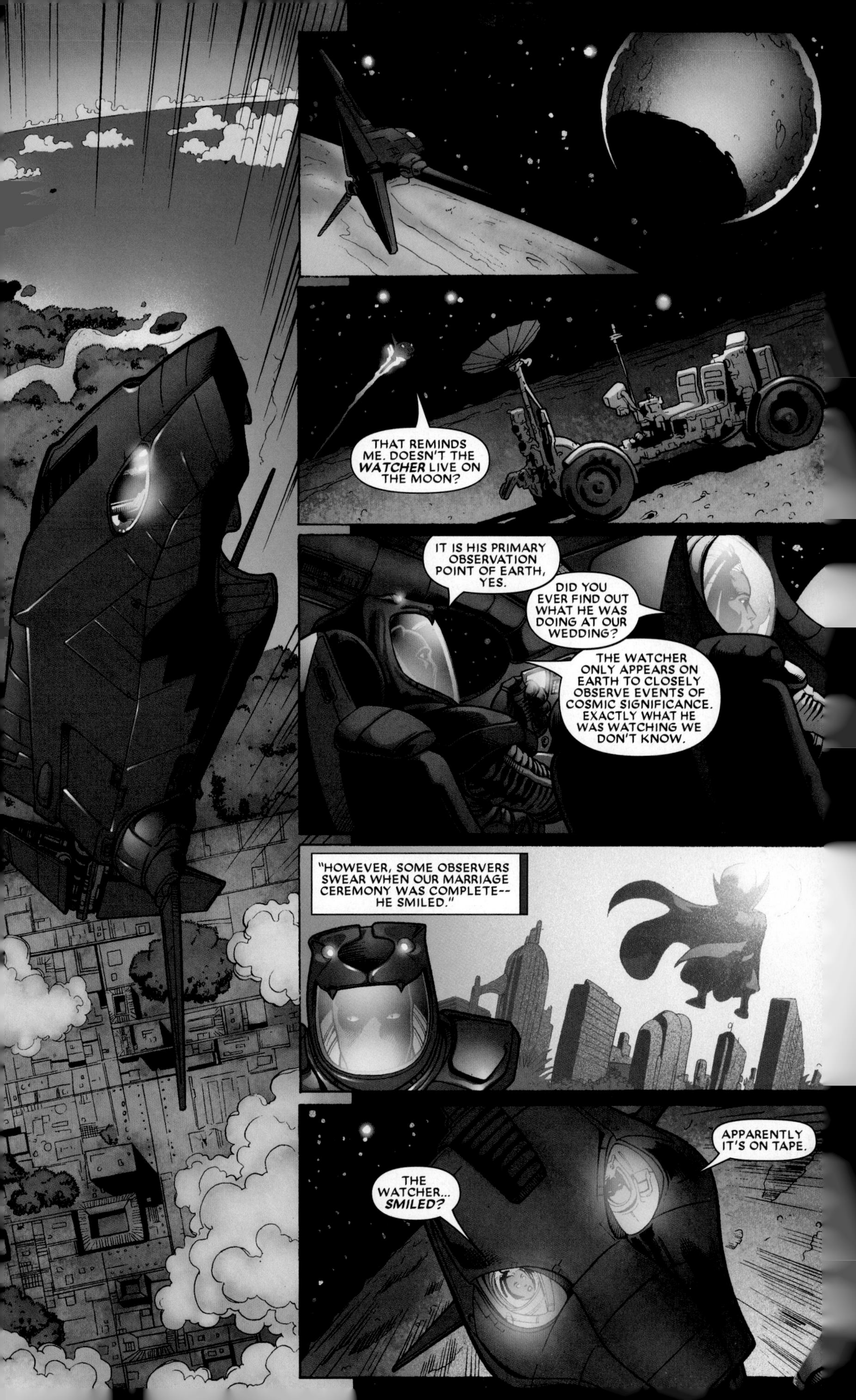
THAT REMINDS ME. DOESN'T THE *WATCHER* LIVE ON THE MOON?
IT IS HIS PRIMARY OBSERVATION POINT OF EARTH, YES.
DID YOU EVER FIND OUT WHAT HE WAS DOING AT OUR WEDDING?
THE WATCHER ONLY APPEARS ON EARTH TO CLOSELY OBSERVE EVENTS OF COSMIC SIGNIFICANCE. EXACTLY WHAT HE WAS WATCHING WE DON'T KNOW.
"HOWEVER, SOME OBSERVERS SWEAR WHEN OUR MARRIAGE CEREMONY WAS COMPLETE-- HE SMILED."
APPARENTLY IT'S ON TAPE.
THE WATCHER... *SMILED?*

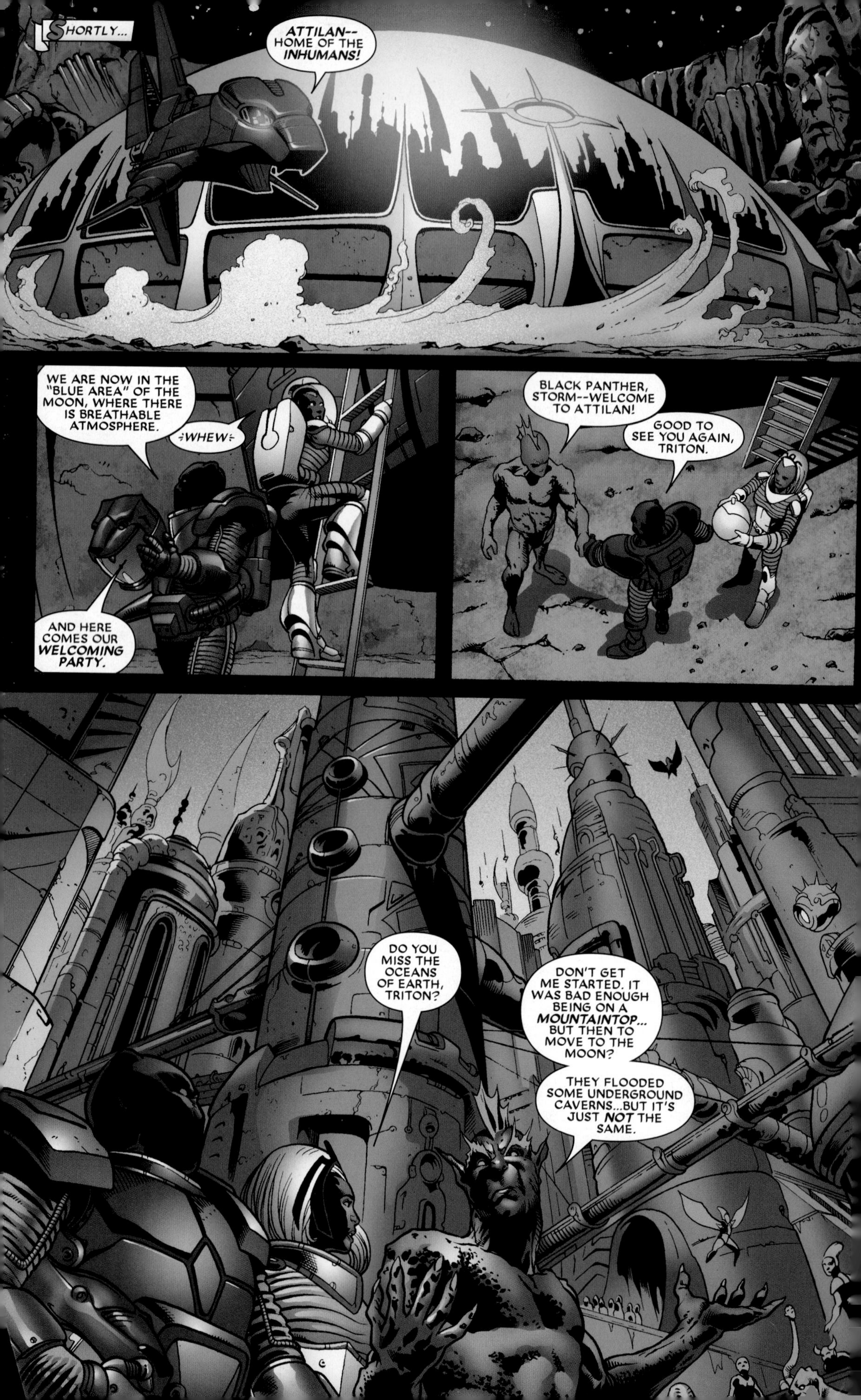
SHORTLY...
ATTILAN-- HOME OF THE INHUMANS!
WE ARE NOW IN THE "BLUE AREA" OF THE MOON, WHERE THERE IS BREATHABLE ATMOSPHERE.
=WHEW=
AND HERE COMES OUR WELCOMING PARTY.
BLACK PANTHER, STORM--WELCOME TO ATTILAN!
GOOD TO SEE YOU AGAIN, TRITON.
DO YOU MISS THE OCEANS OF EARTH, TRITON?
DON'T GET ME STARTED. IT WAS BAD ENOUGH BEING ON A MOUNTAINTOP... BUT THEN TO MOVE TO THE MOON?
THEY FLOODED SOME UNDERGROUND CAVERNS...BUT IT'S JUST NOT THE SAME.

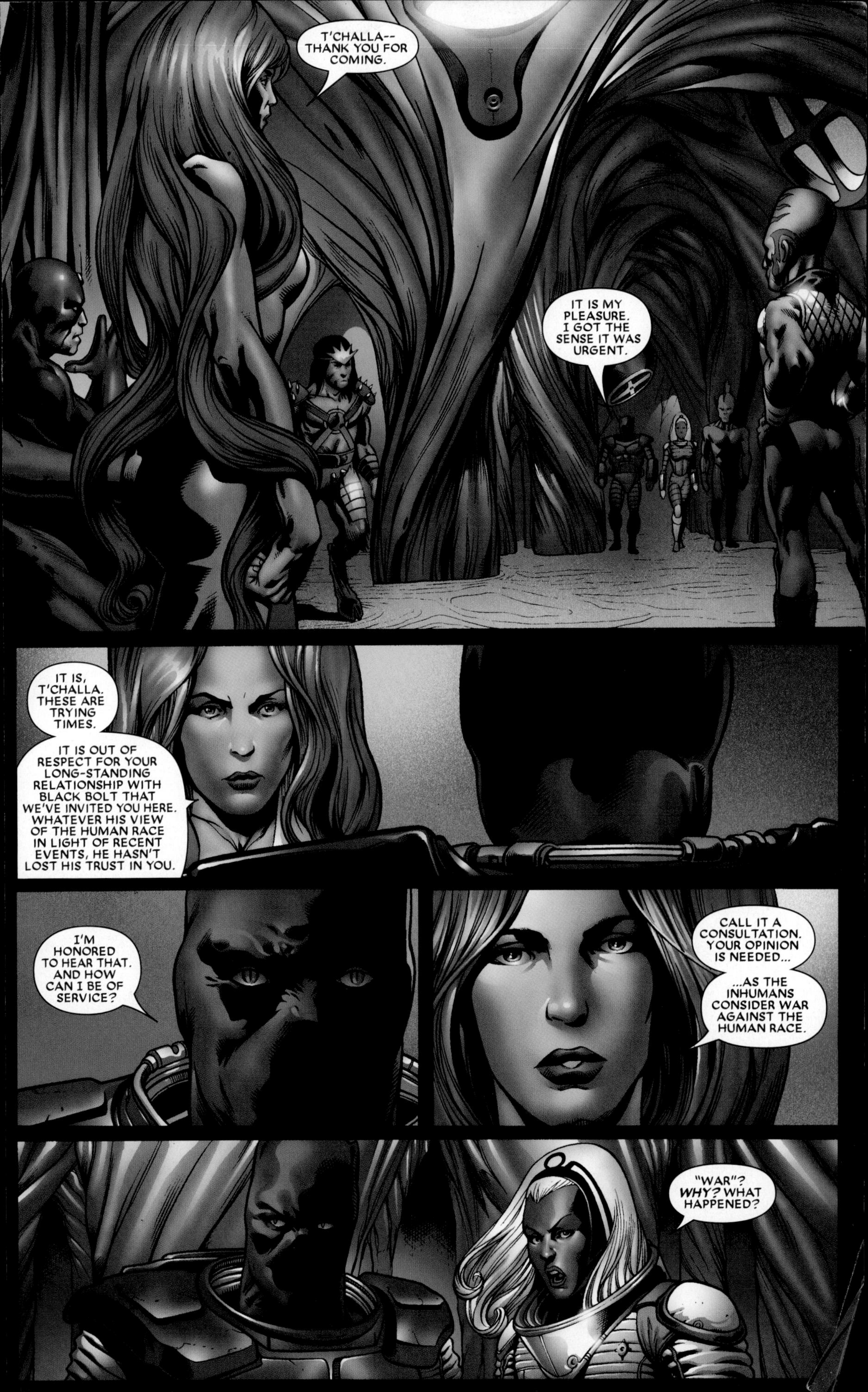
T'CHALLA-- THANK YOU FOR COMING.
IT IS MY PLEASURE. I GOT THE SENSE IT WAS URGENT.
IT IS, T'CHALLA. THESE ARE TRYING TIMES.
IT IS OUT OF RESPECT FOR YOUR LONG-STANDING RELATIONSHIP WITH BLACK BOLT THAT WE'VE INVITED YOU HERE. WHATEVER HIS VIEW OF THE HUMAN RACE IN LIGHT OF RECENT EVENTS, HE HASN'T LOST HIS TRUST IN YOU.
I'M HONORED TO HEAR THAT. AND HOW CAN I BE OF SERVICE?
CALL IT A CONSULTATION. YOUR OPINION IS NEEDED...
...AS THE INHUMANS CONSIDER WAR AGAINST THE HUMAN RACE.
"WAR"? *WHY?* WHAT HAPPENED?

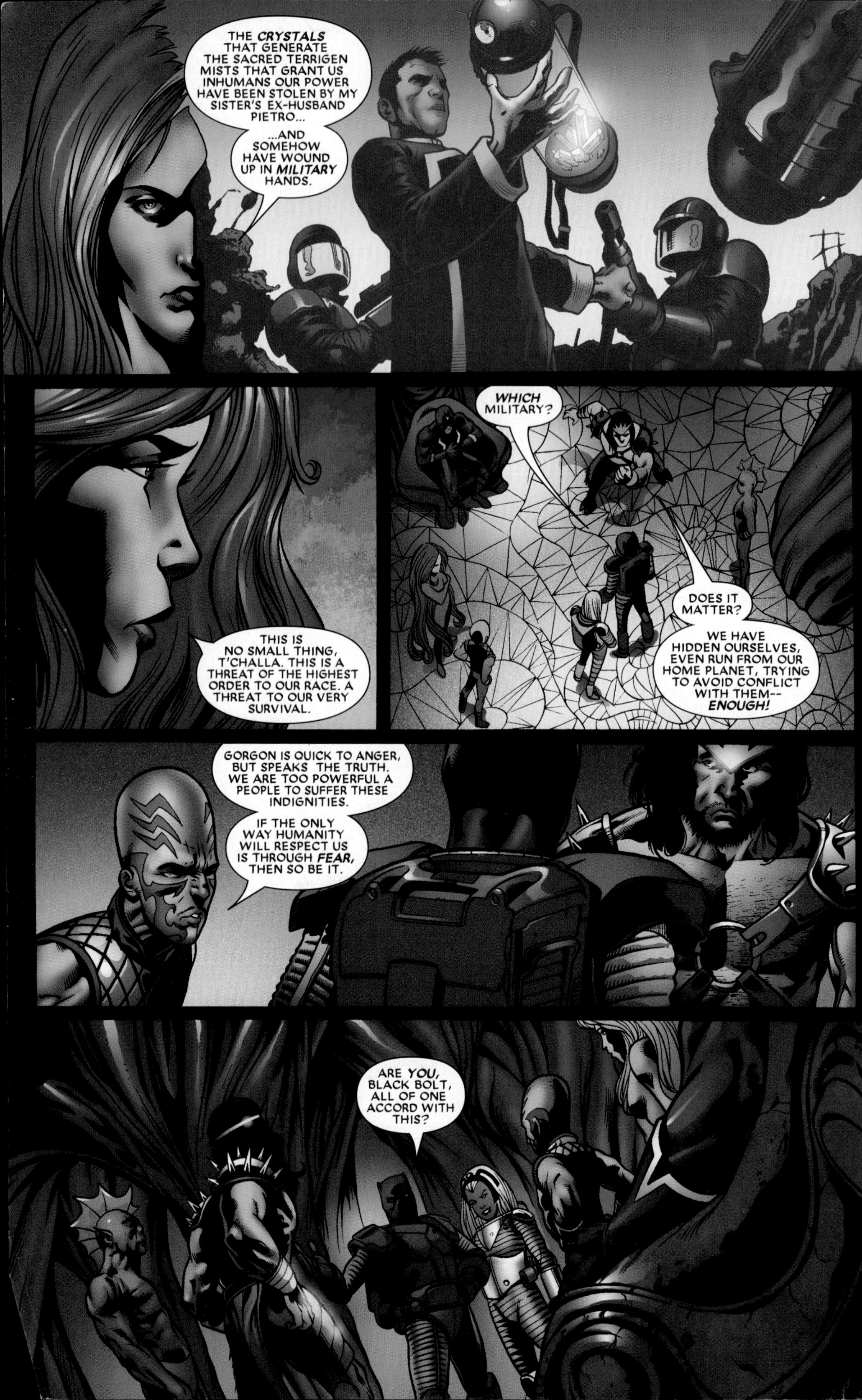
THE *CRYSTALS* THAT GENERATE THE SACRED TERRIGEN MISTS THAT GRANT US INHUMANS OUR POWER HAVE BEEN STOLEN BY MY SISTER'S EX-HUSBAND PIETRO...
...AND SOMEHOW HAVE WOUND UP IN *MILITARY* HANDS.
THIS IS NO SMALL THING, T'CHALLA. THIS IS A THREAT OF THE HIGHEST ORDER TO OUR RACE. A THREAT TO OUR VERY SURVIVAL.
WHICH MILITARY?
DOES IT MATTER?
WE HAVE HIDDEN OURSELVES, EVEN RUN FROM OUR HOME PLANET, TRYING TO AVOID CONFLICT WITH THEM-- *ENOUGH!*
GORGON IS QUICK TO ANGER, BUT SPEAKS THE TRUTH. WE ARE TOO POWERFUL A PEOPLE TO SUFFER THESE INDIGNITIES.
IF THE ONLY WAY HUMANITY WILL RESPECT US IS THROUGH *FEAR,* THEN SO BE IT.
ARE *YOU,* BLACK BOLT, ALL OF ONE ACCORD WITH THIS?

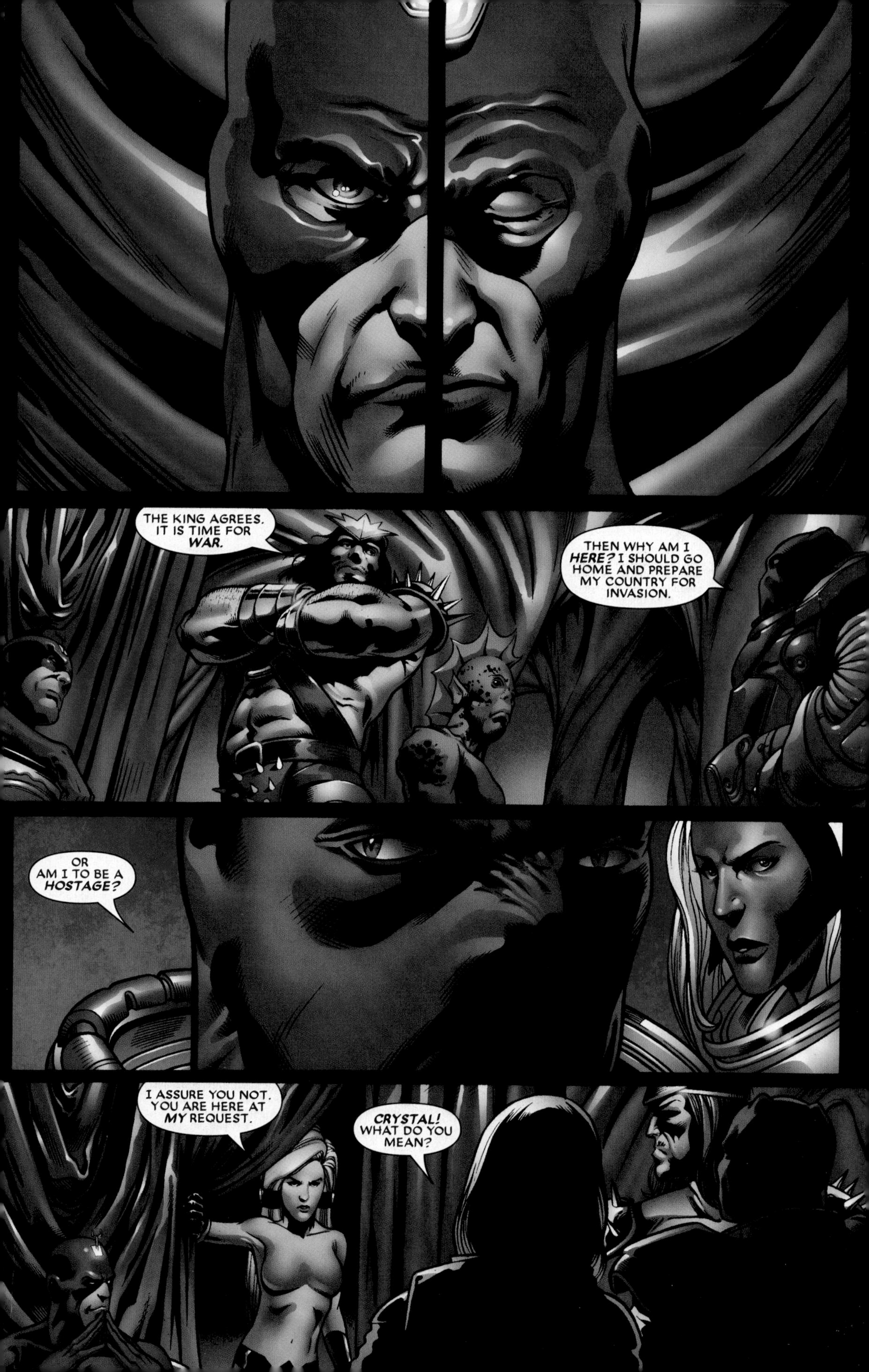
THE KING AGREES. IT IS TIME FOR WAR.
THEN WHY AM I HERE? I SHOULD GO HOME AND PREPARE MY COUNTRY FOR INVASION.
OR AM I TO BE A HOSTAGE?
I ASSURE YOU NOT. YOU ARE HERE AT MY REQUEST.
CRYSTAL! WHAT DO YOU MEAN?

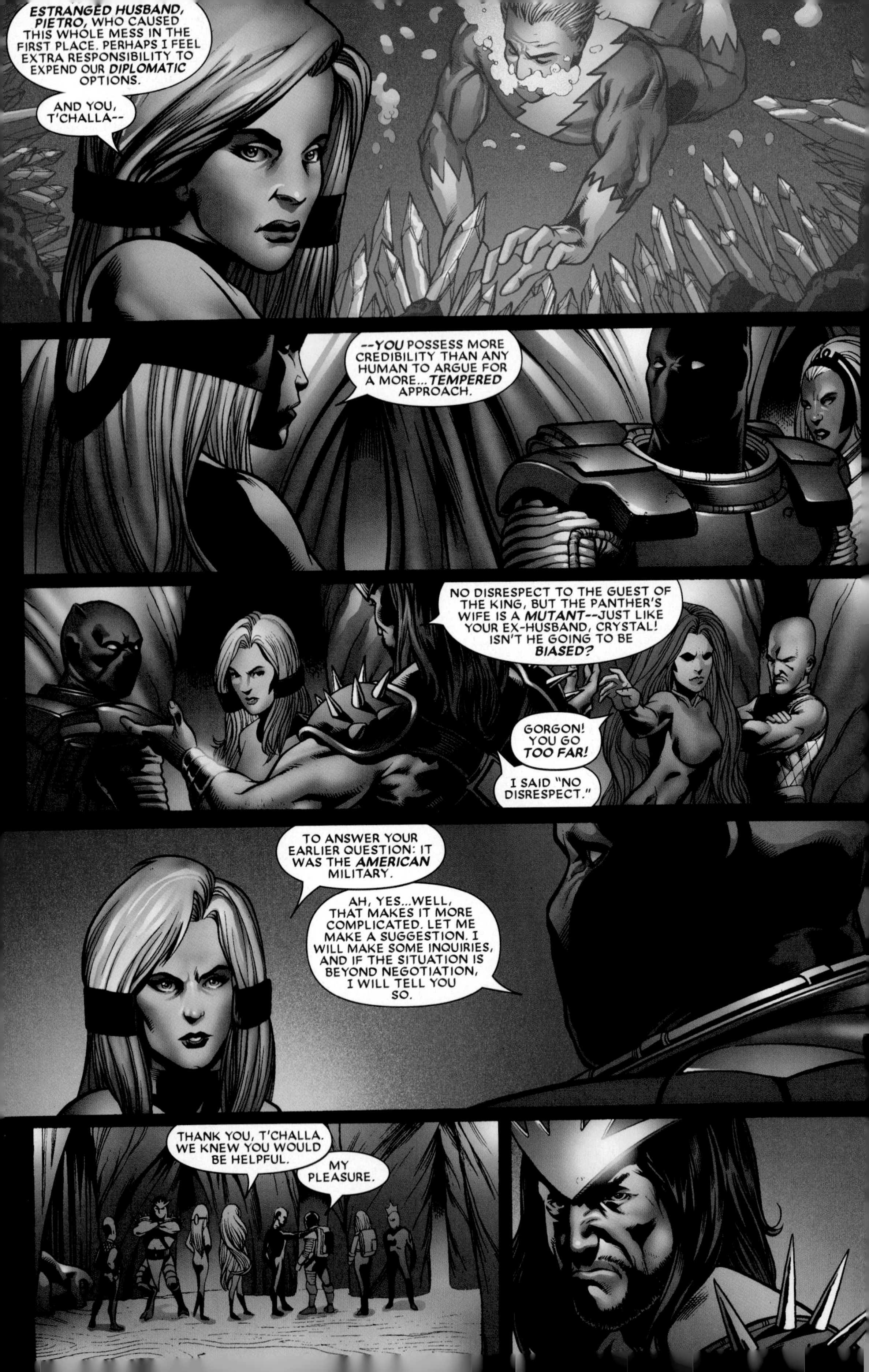
ESTRANGED HUSBAND, PIETRO, WHO CAUSED THIS WHOLE MESS IN THE FIRST PLACE. PERHAPS I FEEL EXTRA RESPONSIBILITY TO EXPEND OUR DIPLOMATIC OPTIONS.
AND YOU, T'CHALLA--
--YOU POSSESS MORE CREDIBILITY THAN ANY HUMAN TO ARGUE FOR A MORE... TEMPERED APPROACH.
NO DISRESPECT TO THE GUEST OF THE KING, BUT THE PANTHER'S WIFE IS A MUTANT--JUST LIKE YOUR EX-HUSBAND, CRYSTAL! ISN'T HE GOING TO BE BIASED?
GORGON! YOU GO TOO FAR!
I SAID "NO DISRESPECT."
TO ANSWER YOUR EARLIER QUESTION: IT WAS THE AMERICAN MILITARY.
AH, YES... WELL, THAT MAKES IT MORE COMPLICATED. LET ME MAKE A SUGGESTION. I WILL MAKE SOME INQUIRIES, AND IF THE SITUATION IS BEYOND NEGOTIATION, I WILL TELL YOU SO.
THANK YOU, T'CHALLA. WE KNEW YOU WOULD BE HELPFUL.
MY PLEASURE.

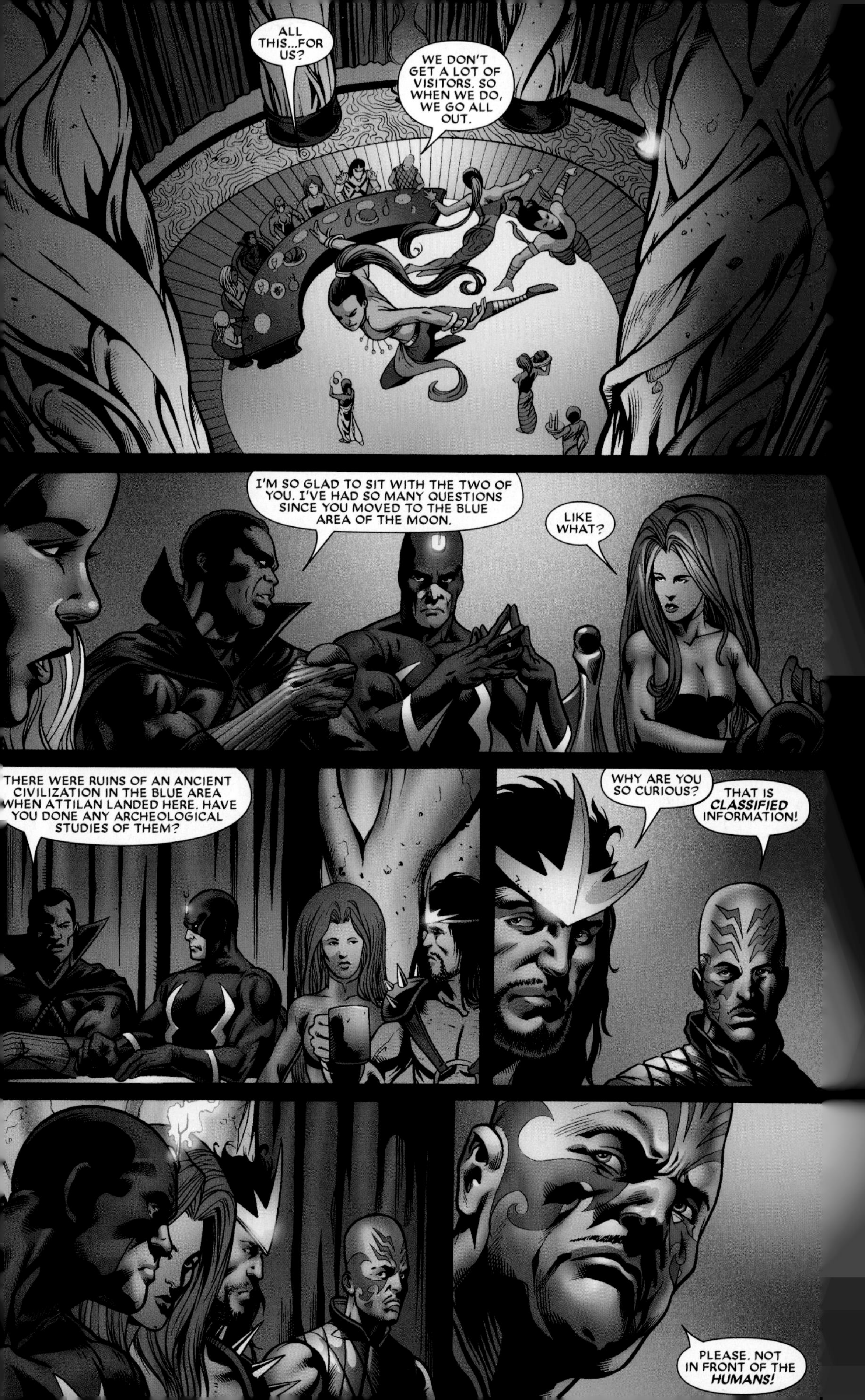

ALL THIS...FOR US?
WE DON'T GET A LOT OF VISITORS. SO WHEN WE DO, WE GO ALL OUT.
I'M SO GLAD TO SIT WITH THE TWO OF YOU. I'VE HAD SO MANY QUESTIONS SINCE YOU MOVED TO THE BLUE AREA OF THE MOON.
LIKE WHAT?
THERE WERE RUINS OF AN ANCIENT CIVILIZATION IN THE BLUE AREA WHEN ATTILAN LANDED HERE. HAVE YOU DONE ANY ARCHEOLOGICAL STUDIES OF THEM?
WHY ARE YOU SO CURIOUS?
THAT IS *CLASSIFIED* INFORMATION!
PLEASE. NOT IN FRONT OF THE *HUMANS!*

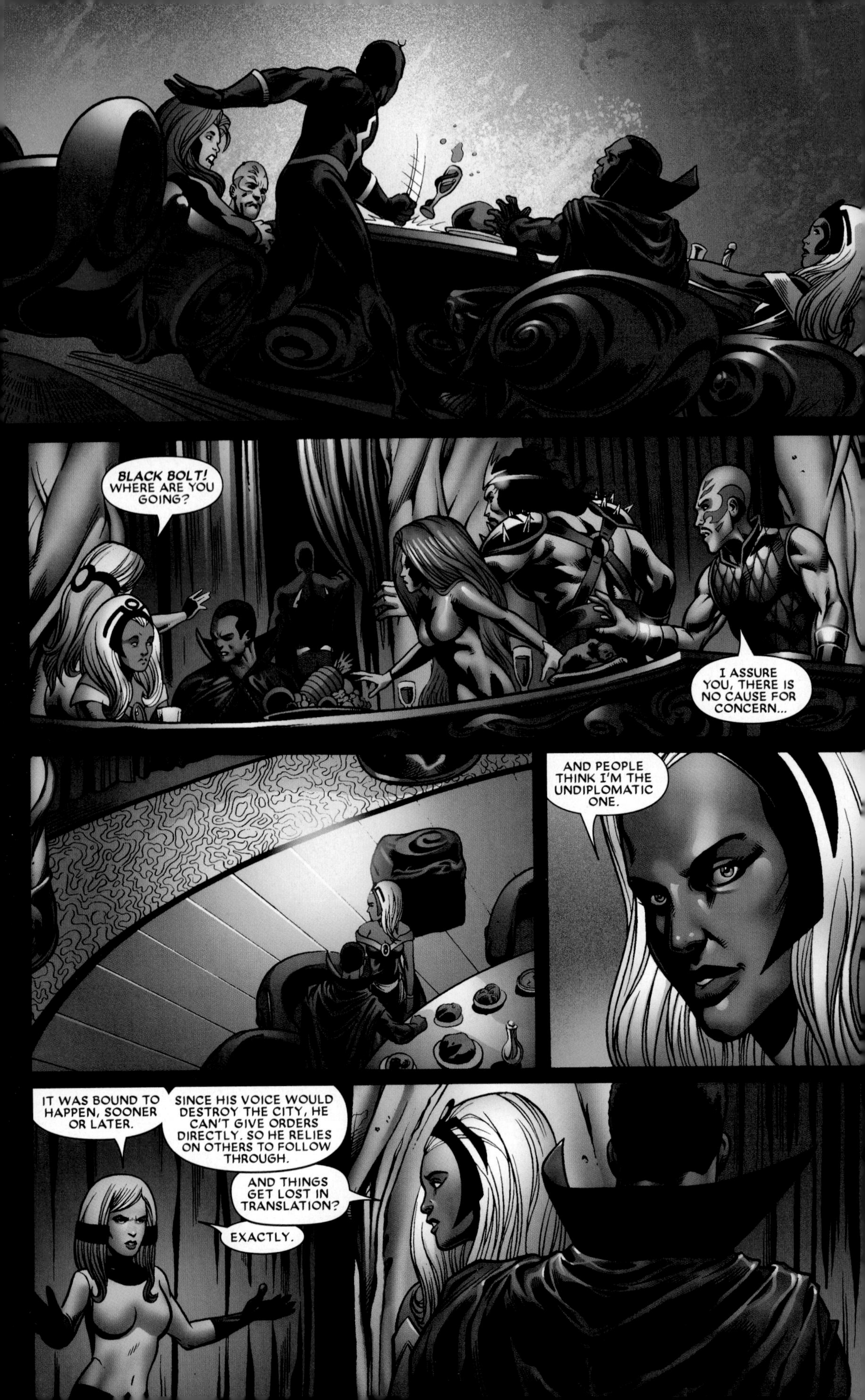
BLACK BOLT! WHERE ARE YOU GOING?
I ASSURE YOU, THERE IS NO CAUSE FOR CONCERN...
AND PEOPLE THINK I'M THE UNDIPLOMATIC ONE.
IT WAS BOUND TO HAPPEN, SOONER OR LATER.
SINCE HIS VOICE WOULD DESTROY THE CITY, HE CAN'T GIVE ORDERS DIRECTLY. SO HE RELIES ON OTHERS TO FOLLOW THROUGH.
AND THINGS GET LOST IN TRANSLATION?
EXACTLY.

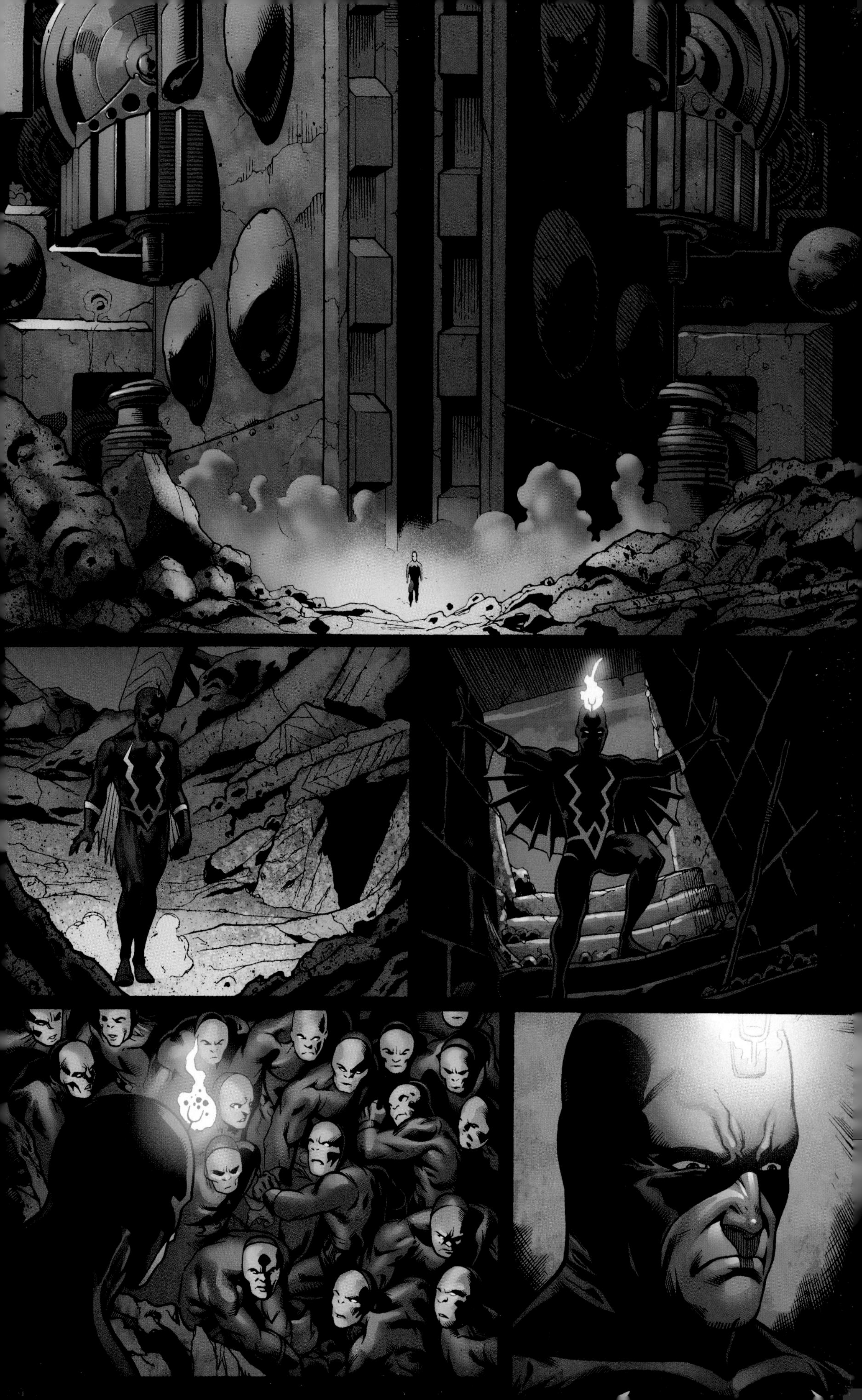

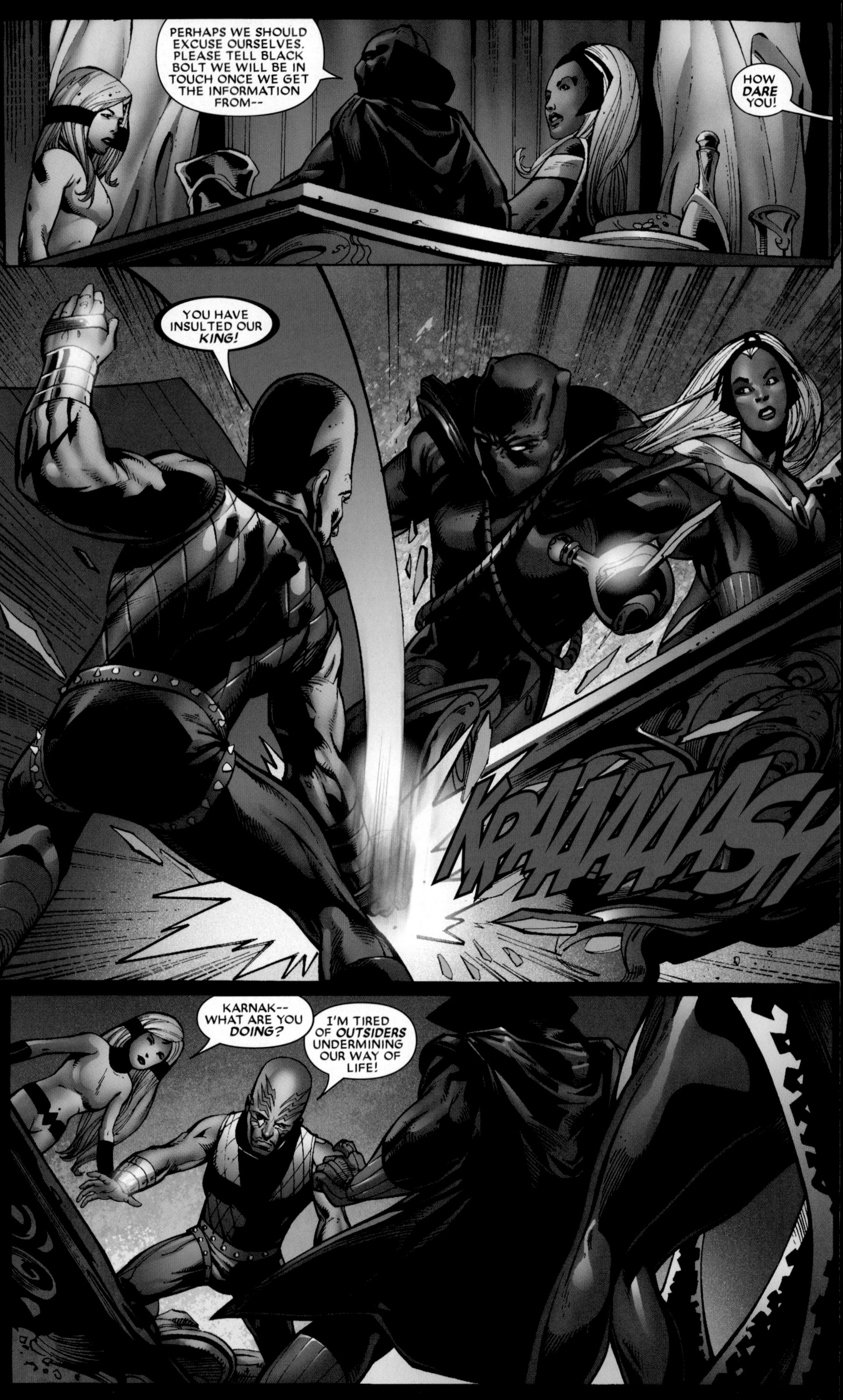
PERHAPS WE SHOULD EXCUSE OURSELVES. PLEASE TELL BLACK BOLT WE WILL BE IN TOUCH ONCE WE GET THE INFORMATION FROM--
HOW DARE YOU!
YOU HAVE INSULTED OUR KING!
KRAAAAASH
KARNAK-- WHAT ARE YOU DOING?
I'M TIRED OF OUTSIDERS UNDERMINING OUR WAY OF LIFE!

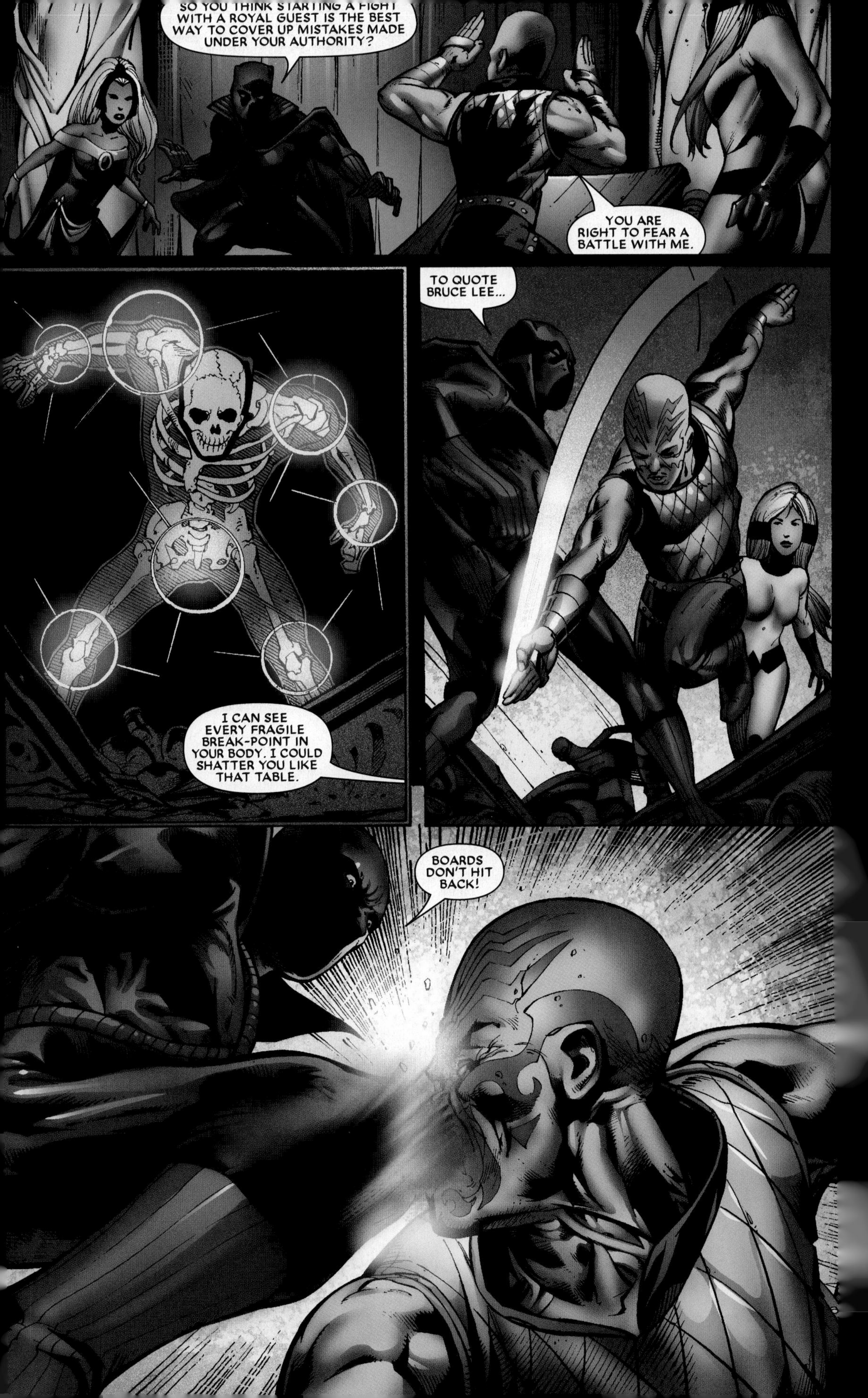
SO YOU THINK STARTING A FIGHT WITH A ROYAL GUEST IS THE BEST WAY TO COVER UP MISTAKES MADE UNDER YOUR AUTHORITY?
YOU ARE RIGHT TO FEAR A BATTLE WITH ME.
I CAN SEE EVERY FRAGILE BREAK-POINT IN YOUR BODY. I COULD SHATTER YOU LIKE THAT TABLE.
TO QUOTE BRUCE LEE...
BOARDS DON'T HIT BACK!

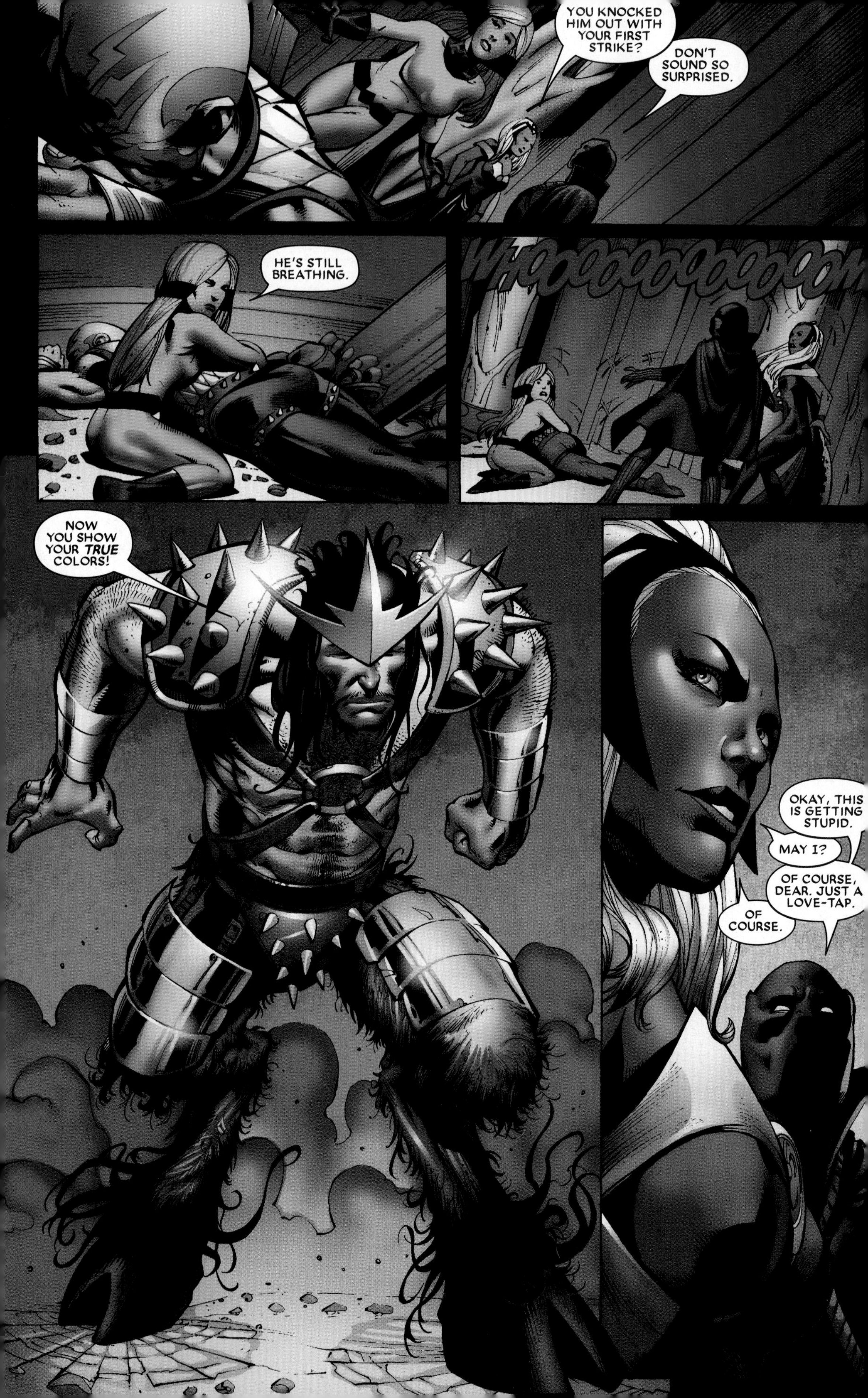
YOU KNOCKED HIM OUT WITH YOUR FIRST STRIKE?
DON'T SOUND SO SURPRISED.
HE'S STILL BREATHING.
WHOOOOOOOOOOOOOM
NOW YOU SHOW YOUR TRUE COLORS!
OKAY, THIS IS GETTING STUPID.
MAY I?
OF COURSE, DEAR. JUST A LOVE-TAP.
OF COURSE.

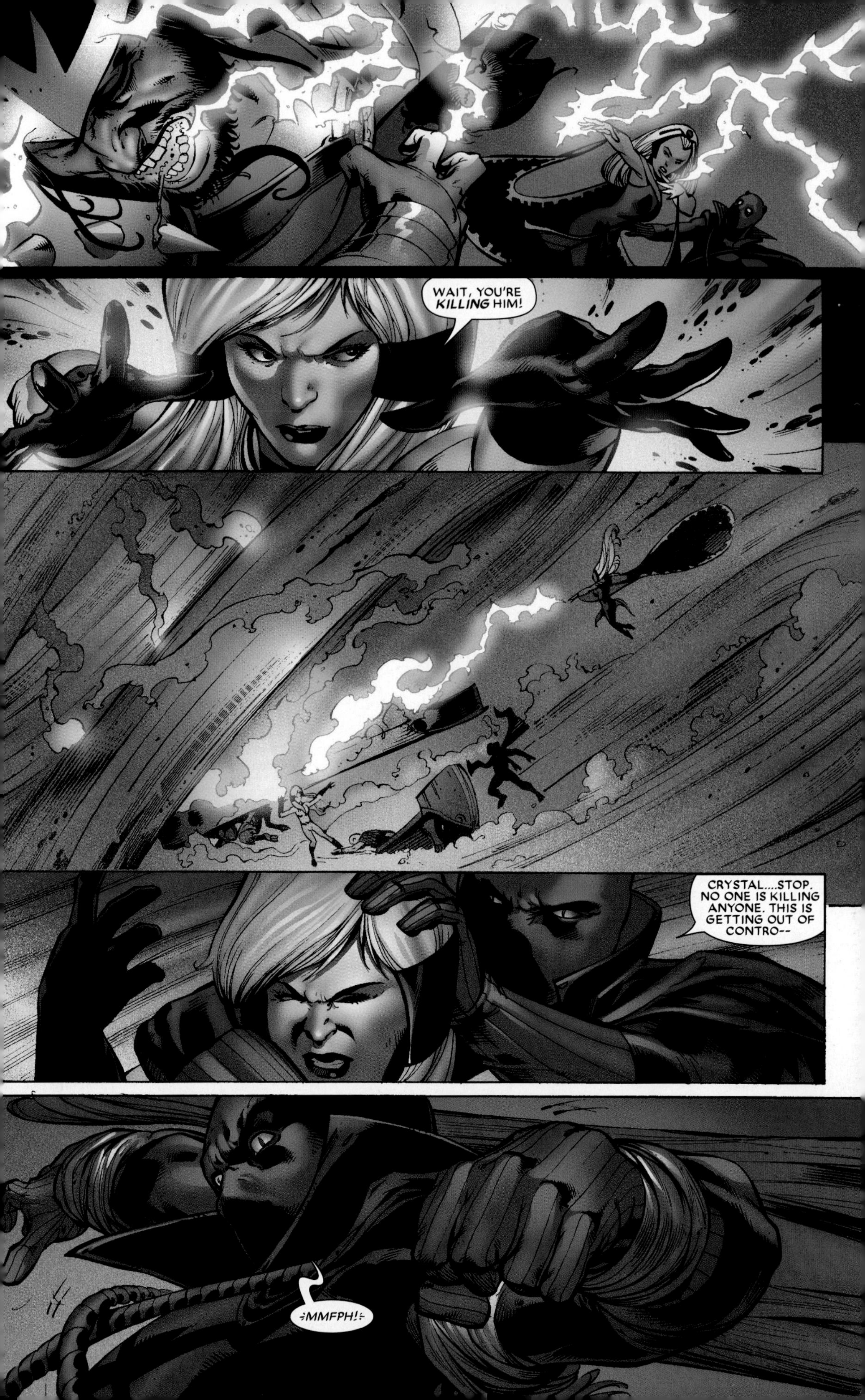
WAIT, YOU'RE *KILLING* HIM!
CRYSTAL....STOP. NO ONE IS KILLING ANYONE. THIS IS GETTING OUT OF CONTRO--
MMFPH!

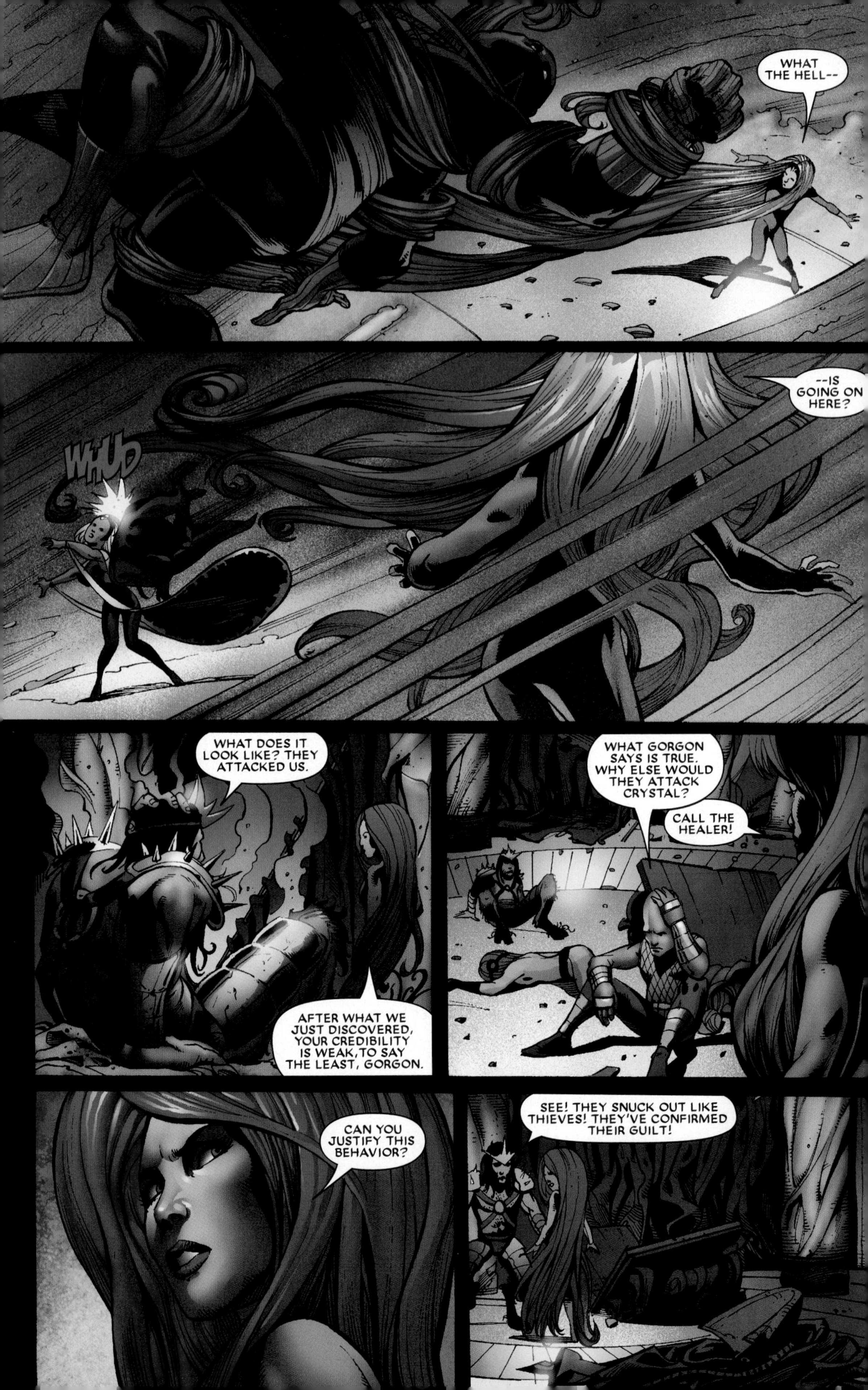
WHAT THE HELL--
--IS GOING ON HERE?
WHUD
WHAT DOES IT LOOK LIKE? THEY ATTACKED US.
AFTER WHAT WE JUST DISCOVERED, YOUR CREDIBILITY IS WEAK, TO SAY THE LEAST, GORGON.
WHAT GORGON SAYS IS TRUE. WHY ELSE WOULD THEY ATTACK CRYSTAL?
CALL THE HEALER!
CAN YOU JUSTIFY THIS BEHAVIOR?
SEE! THEY SNUCK OUT LIKE THIEVES! THEY'VE CONFIRMED THEIR GUILT!

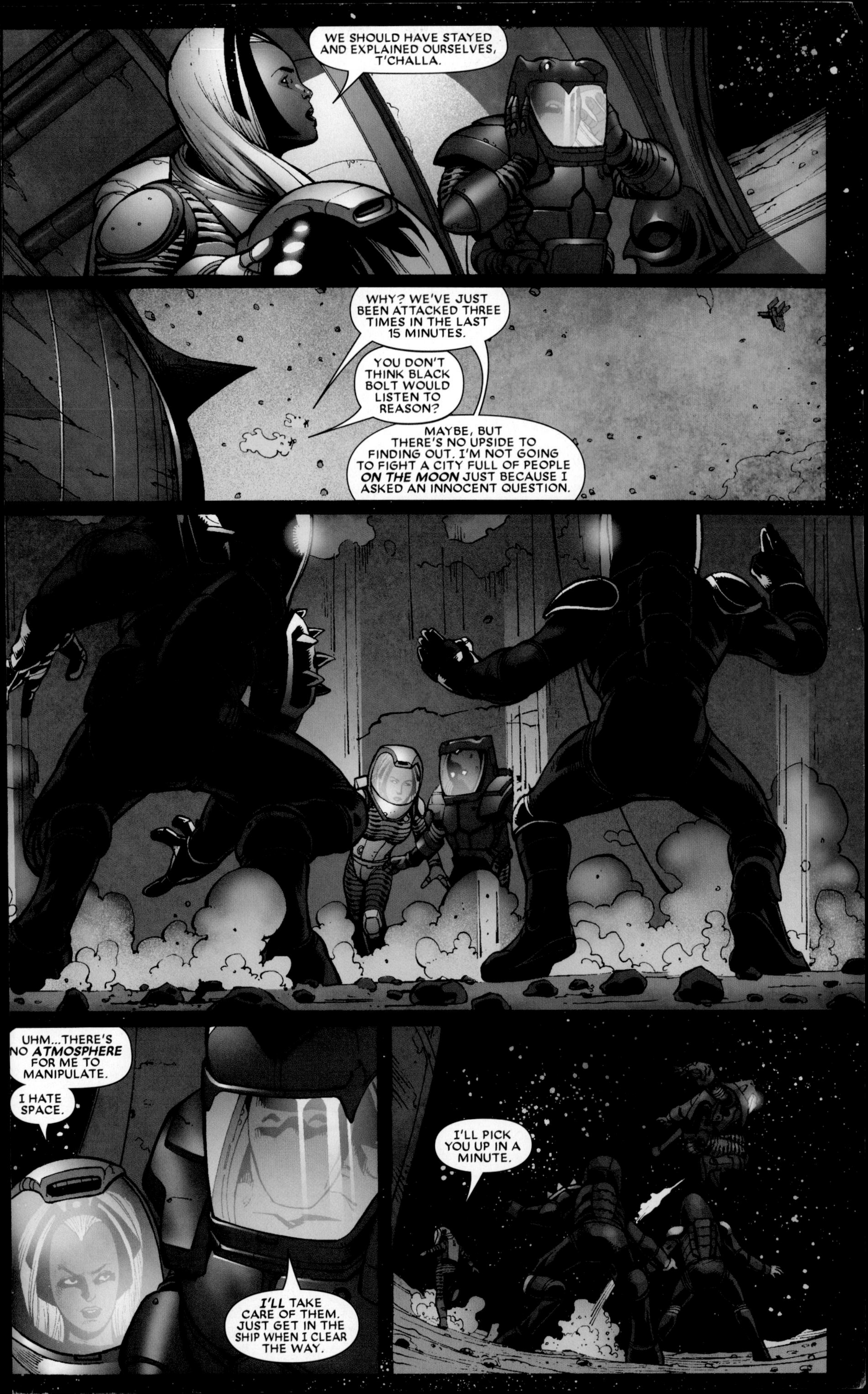
WE SHOULD HAVE STAYED AND EXPLAINED OURSELVES, T'CHALLA.
WHY? WE'VE JUST BEEN ATTACKED THREE TIMES IN THE LAST 15 MINUTES.
YOU DON'T THINK BLACK BOLT WOULD LISTEN TO REASON?
MAYBE, BUT THERE'S NO UPSIDE TO FINDING OUT. I'M NOT GOING TO FIGHT A CITY FULL OF PEOPLE *ON THE MOON* JUST BECAUSE I ASKED AN INNOCENT QUESTION.
UHM...THERE'S NO *ATMOSPHERE* FOR ME TO MANIPULATE.
I HATE SPACE.
I'LL TAKE CARE OF THEM. JUST GET IN THE SHIP WHEN I CLEAR THE WAY.
I'LL PICK YOU UP IN A MINUTE.

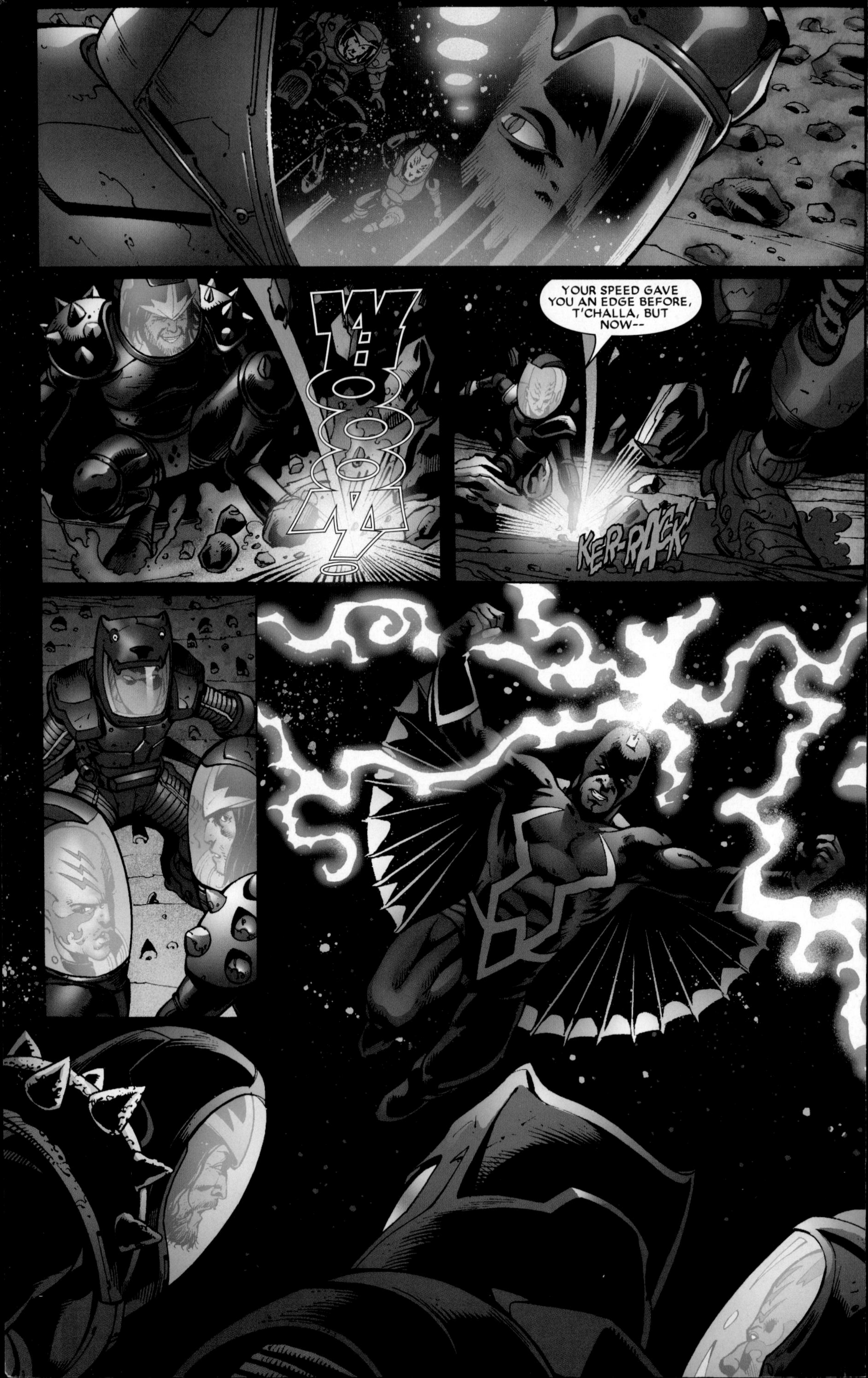
WHOOOOM
YOUR SPEED GAVE YOU AN EDGE BEFORE, T'CHALLA, BUT NOW--
KER-RACK!

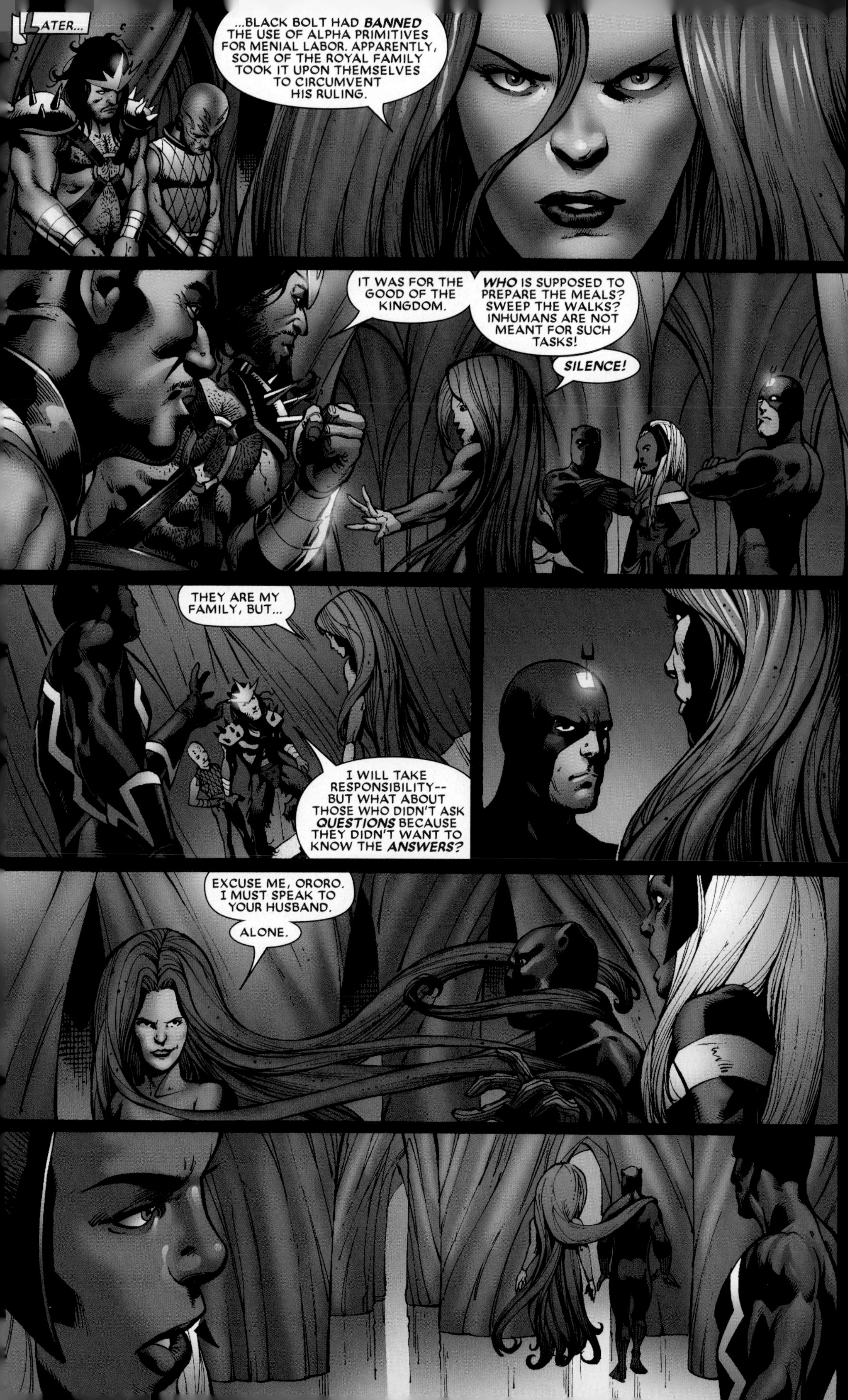
LATER...
...BLACK BOLT HAD BANNED THE USE OF ALPHA PRIMITIVES FOR MENIAL LABOR. APPARENTLY, SOME OF THE ROYAL FAMILY TOOK IT UPON THEMSELVES TO CIRCUMVENT HIS RULING.
IT WAS FOR THE GOOD OF THE KINGDOM.
WHO IS SUPPOSED TO PREPARE THE MEALS? SWEEP THE WALKS? INHUMANS ARE NOT MEANT FOR SUCH TASKS!
SILENCE!
THEY ARE MY FAMILY, BUT...
I WILL TAKE RESPONSIBILITY-- BUT WHAT ABOUT THOSE WHO DIDN'T ASK QUESTIONS BECAUSE THEY DIDN'T WANT TO KNOW THE ANSWERS?
EXCUSE ME, ORORO. I MUST SPEAK TO YOUR HUSBAND.
ALONE.

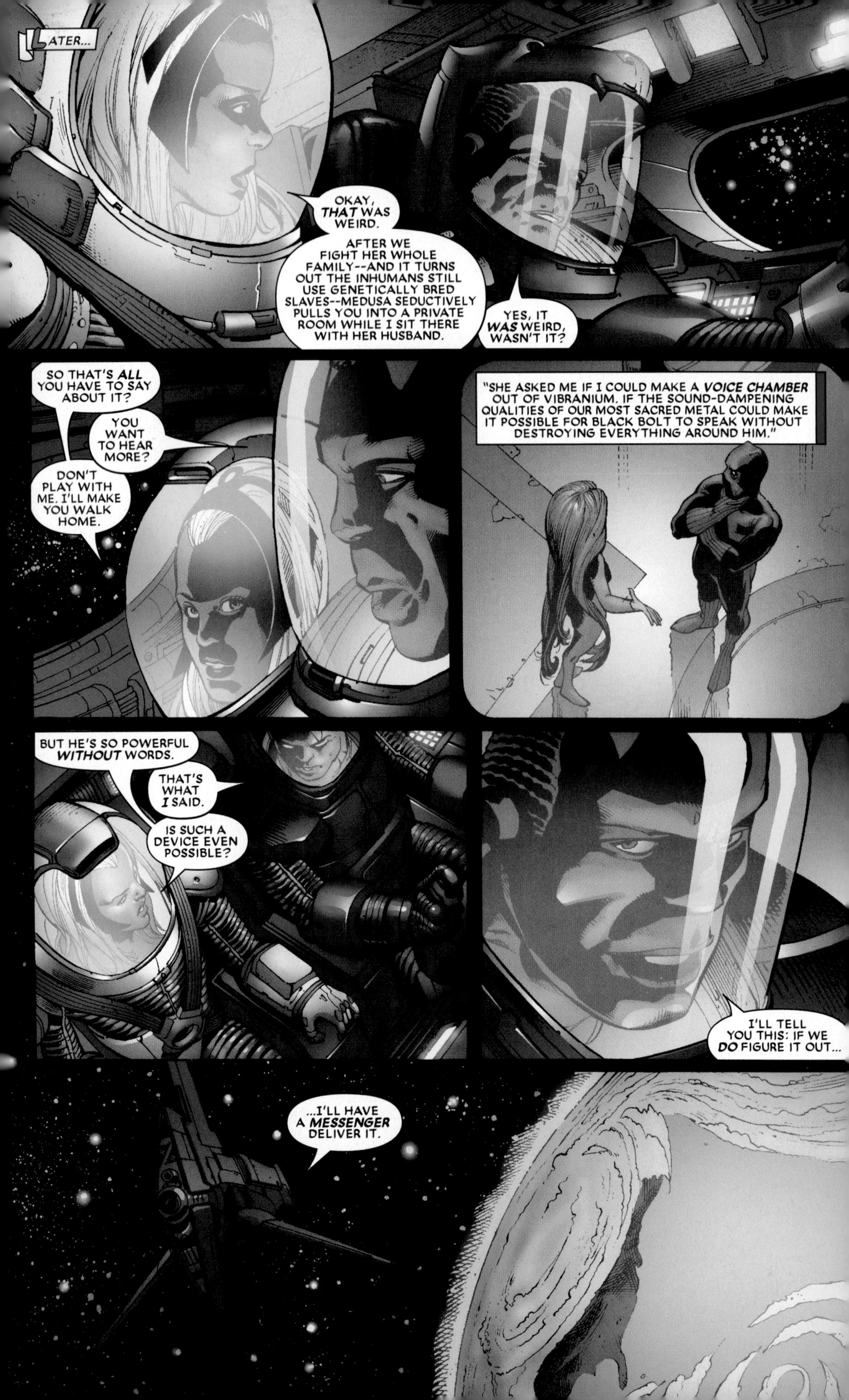
LATER...
OKAY, THAT WAS WEIRD.
AFTER WE FIGHT HER WHOLE FAMILY--AND IT TURNS OUT THE INHUMANS STILL USE GENETICALLY BRED SLAVES--MEDUSA SEDUCTIVELY PULLS YOU INTO A PRIVATE ROOM WHILE I SIT THERE WITH HER HUSBAND.
YES, IT WAS WEIRD, WASN'T IT?
SO THAT'S ALL YOU HAVE TO SAY ABOUT IT?
YOU WANT TO HEAR MORE?
DON'T PLAY WITH ME. I'LL MAKE YOU WALK HOME.
"SHE ASKED ME IF I COULD MAKE A VOICE CHAMBER OUT OF VIBRANIUM. IF THE SOUND-DAMPENING QUALITIES OF OUR MOST SACRED METAL COULD MAKE IT POSSIBLE FOR BLACK BOLT TO SPEAK WITHOUT DESTROYING EVERYTHING AROUND HIM."
BUT HE'S SO POWERFUL WITHOUT WORDS.
THAT'S WHAT I SAID.
IS SUCH A DEVICE EVEN POSSIBLE?
I'LL TELL YOU THIS: IF WE DO FIGURE IT OUT...
...I'LL HAVE A MESSENGER DELIVER IT.

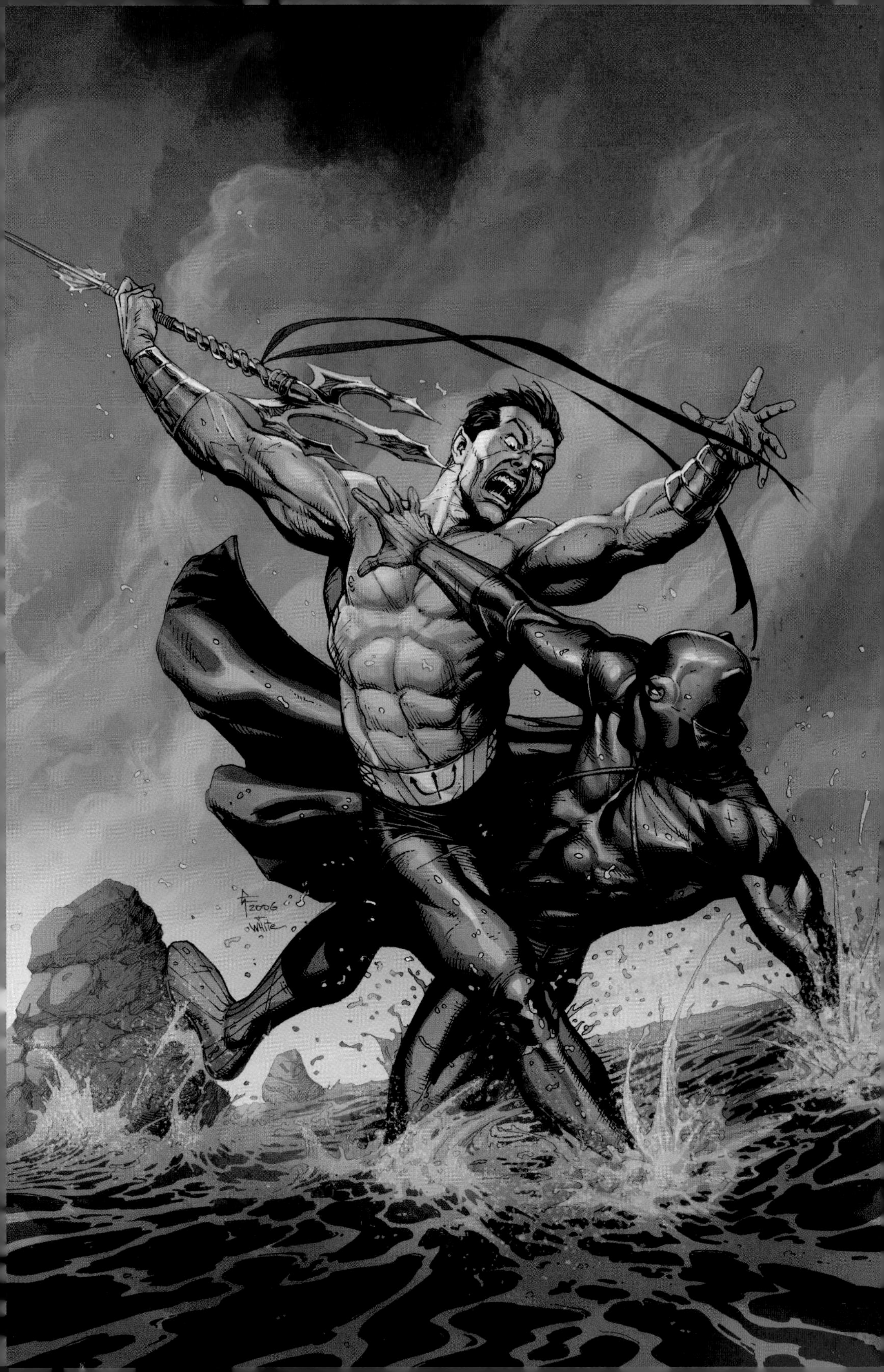
2006
WHITE

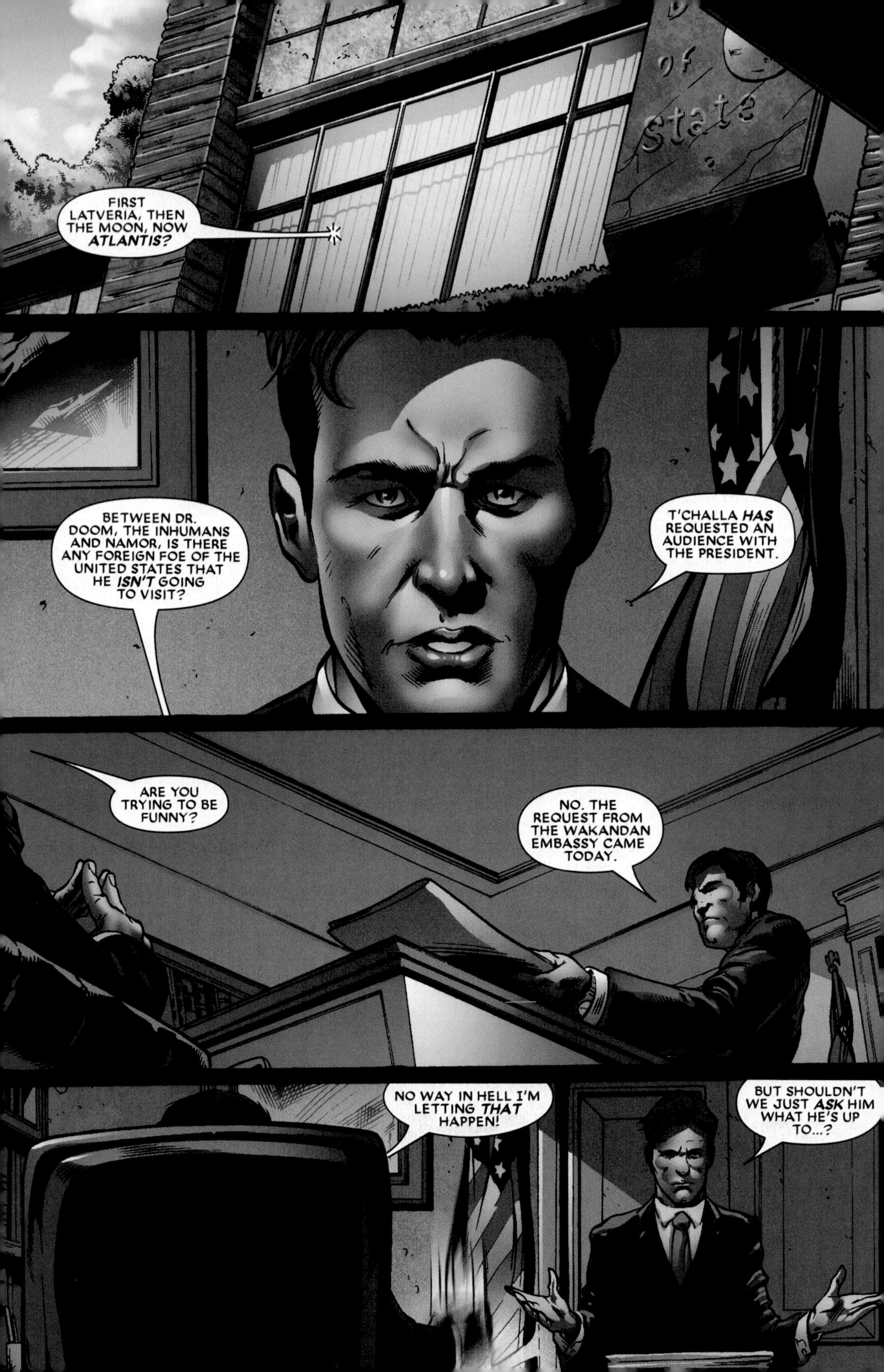
of
state
FIRST LATVERIA, THEN THE MOON, NOW ATLANTIS?
BETWEEN DR. DOOM, THE INHUMANS AND NAMOR, IS THERE ANY FOREIGN FOE OF THE UNITED STATES THAT HE ISN'T GOING TO VISIT?
T'CHALLA HAS REQUESTED AN AUDIENCE WITH THE PRESIDENT.
ARE YOU TRYING TO BE FUNNY?
NO. THE REQUEST FROM THE WAKANDAN EMBASSY CAME TODAY.
NO WAY IN HELL I'M LETTING THAT HAPPEN!
BUT SHOULDN'T WE JUST ASK HIM WHAT HE'S UP TO...?

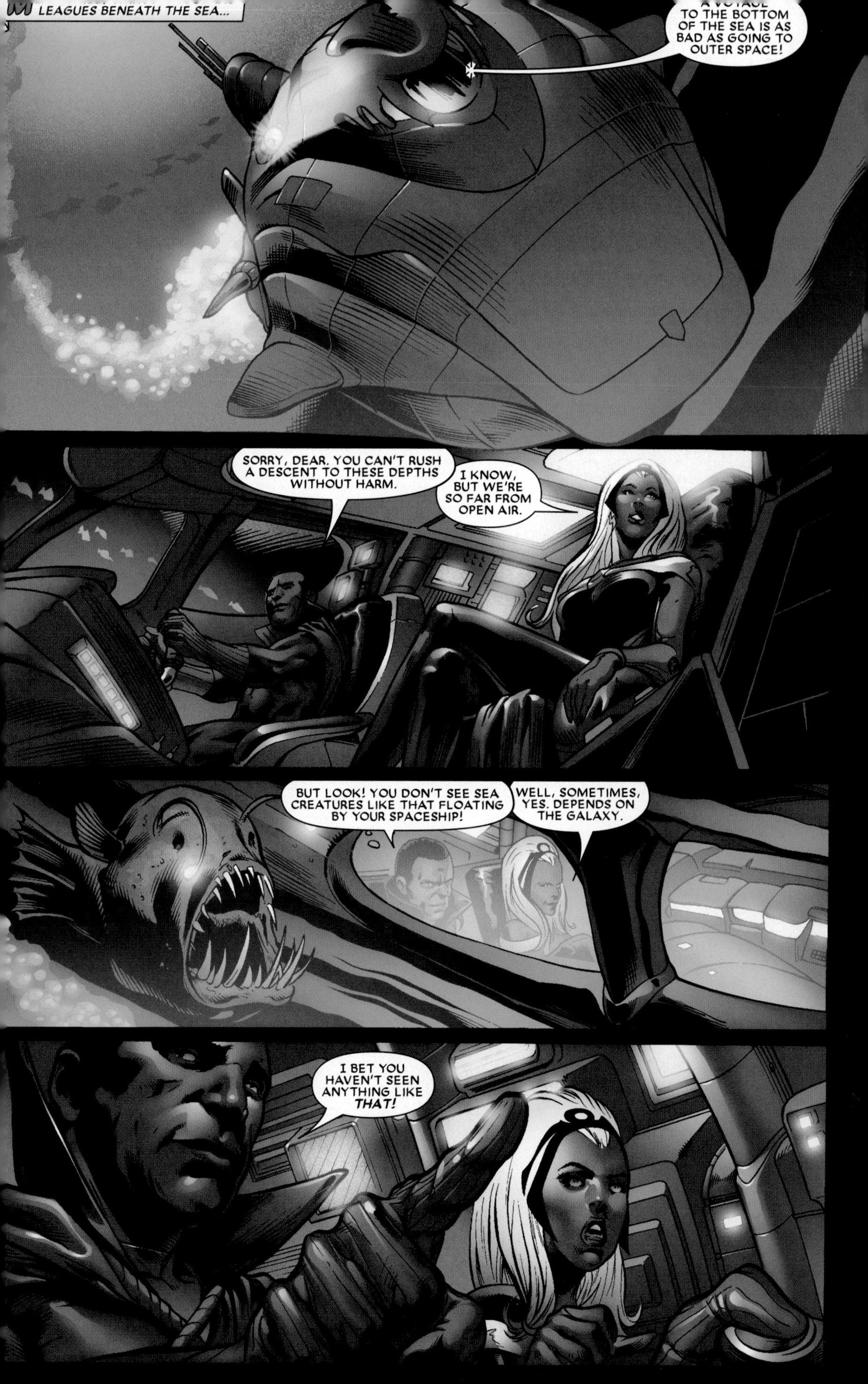
LEAGUES BENEATH THE SEA...
TO THE BOTTOM OF THE SEA IS AS BAD AS GOING TO OUTER SPACE!
SORRY, DEAR. YOU CAN'T RUSH A DESCENT TO THESE DEPTHS WITHOUT HARM.
I KNOW, BUT WE'RE SO FAR FROM OPEN AIR.
BUT LOOK! YOU DON'T SEE SEA CREATURES LIKE THAT FLOATING BY YOUR SPACESHIP!
WELL, SOMETIMES, YES. DEPENDS ON THE GALAXY.
I BET YOU HAVEN'T SEEN ANYTHING LIKE *THAT!*

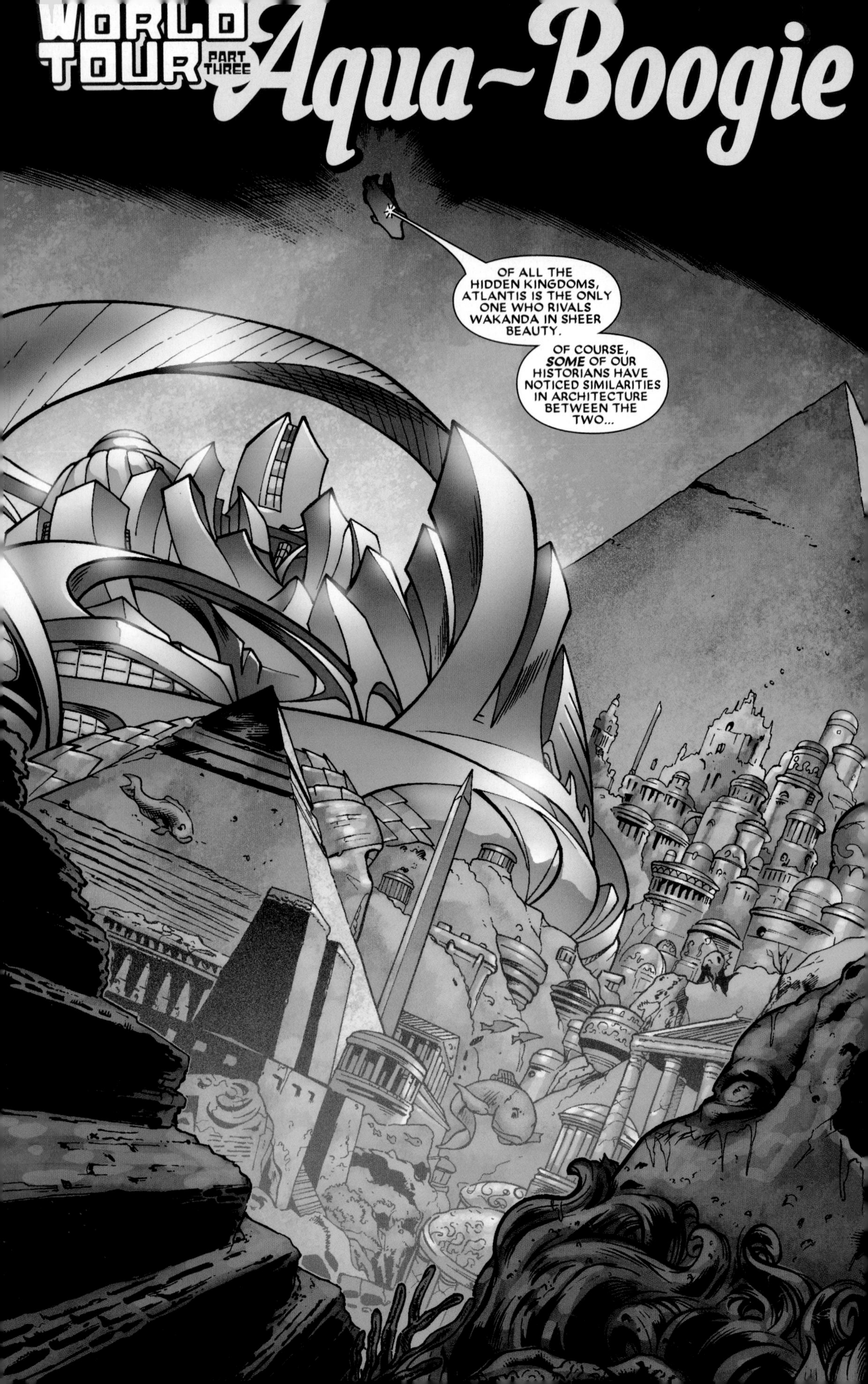
WORLD TOUR PART THREE
Aqua~Boogie
OF ALL THE HIDDEN KINGDOMS, ATLANTIS IS THE ONLY ONE WHO RIVALS WAKANDA IN SHEER BEAUTY.
OF COURSE, SOME OF OUR HISTORIANS HAVE NOTICED SIMILARITIES IN ARCHITECTURE BETWEEN THE TWO...

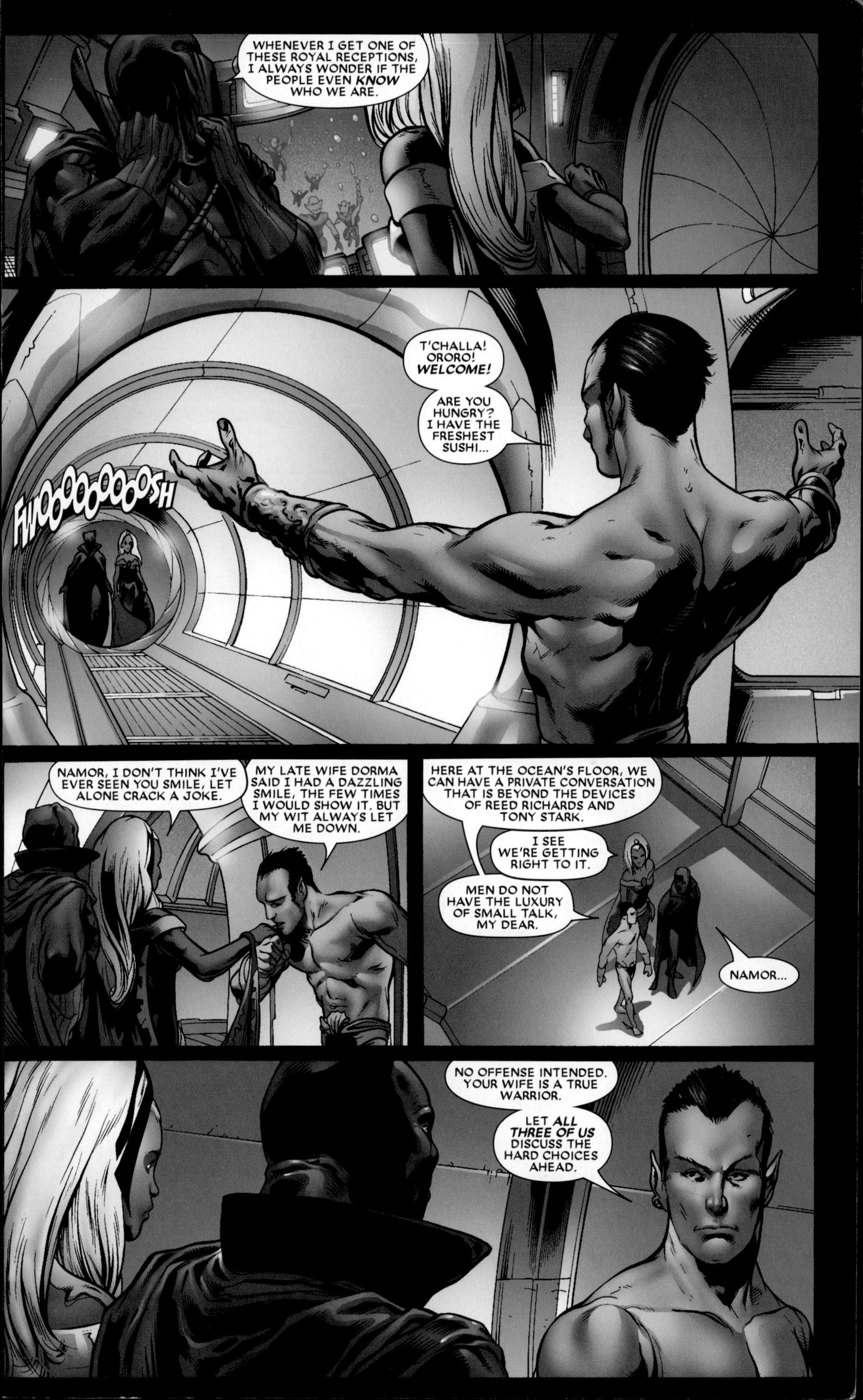
WHENEVER I GET ONE OF THESE ROYAL RECEPTIONS, I ALWAYS WONDER IF THE PEOPLE EVEN *KNOW* WHO WE ARE.
T'CHALLA! ORORO! ***WELCOME!***
ARE YOU HUNGRY? I HAVE THE FRESHEST SUSHI...
FWOOOOOOOOOOSH
NAMOR, I DON'T THINK I'VE EVER SEEN YOU SMILE, LET ALONE CRACK A JOKE.
MY LATE WIFE DORMA SAID I HAD A DAZZLING SMILE, THE FEW TIMES I WOULD SHOW IT. BUT MY WIT ALWAYS LET ME DOWN.
HERE AT THE OCEAN'S FLOOR, WE CAN HAVE A PRIVATE CONVERSATION THAT IS BEYOND THE DEVICES OF REED RICHARDS AND TONY STARK.
I SEE WE'RE GETTING RIGHT TO IT.
MEN DO NOT HAVE THE LUXURY OF SMALL TALK, MY DEAR.
NAMOR...
NO OFFENSE INTENDED. YOUR WIFE IS A TRUE WARRIOR.
LET ***ALL THREE OF US*** DISCUSS THE HARD CHOICES AHEAD.

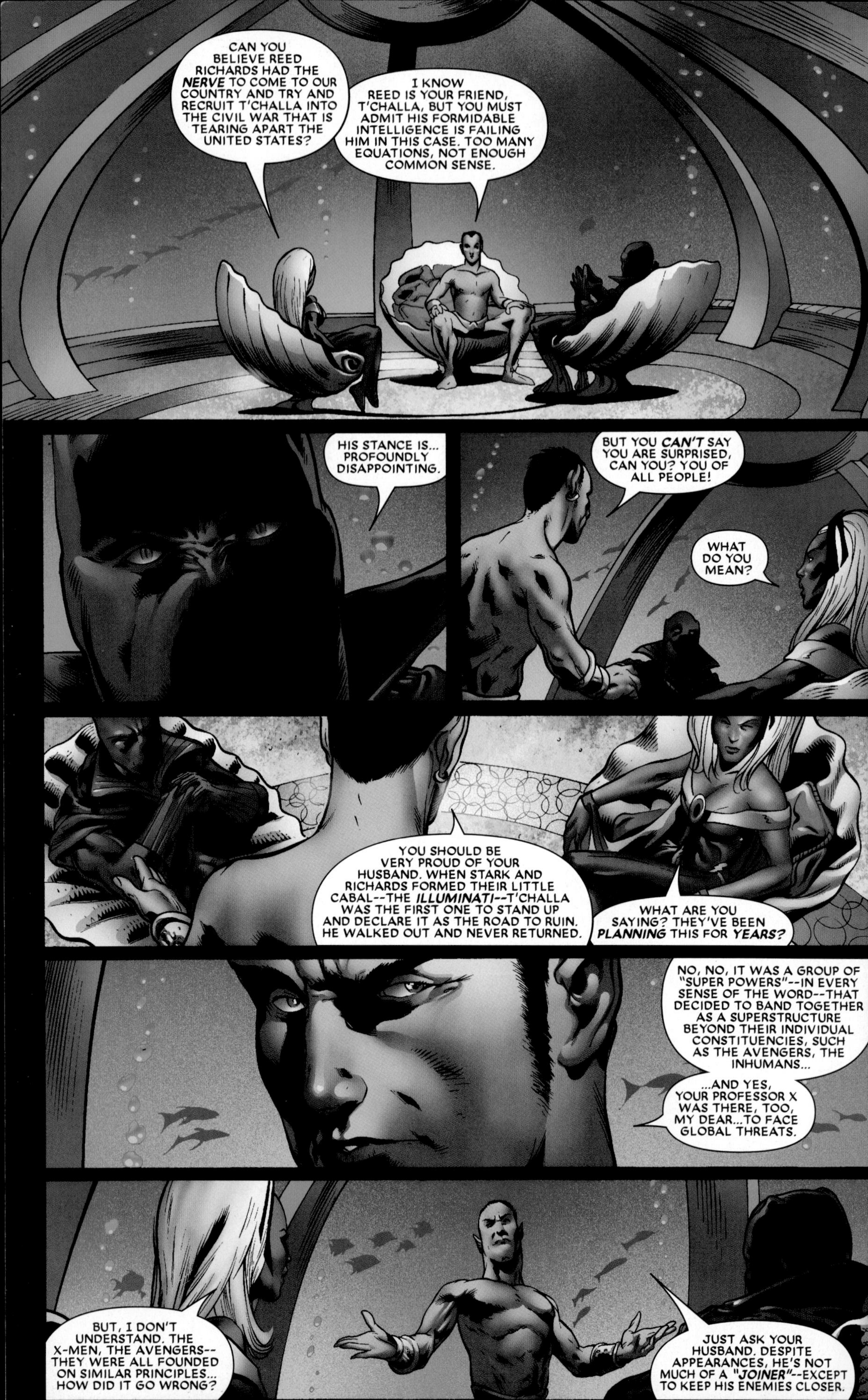
CAN YOU BELIEVE REED RICHARDS HAD THE NERVE TO COME TO OUR COUNTRY AND TRY AND RECRUIT T'CHALLA INTO THE CIVIL WAR THAT IS TEARING APART THE UNITED STATES?
I KNOW REED IS YOUR FRIEND, T'CHALLA, BUT YOU MUST ADMIT HIS FORMIDABLE INTELLIGENCE IS FAILING HIM IN THIS CASE. TOO MANY EQUATIONS, NOT ENOUGH COMMON SENSE.
HIS STANCE IS... PROFOUNDLY DISAPPOINTING.
BUT YOU CAN'T SAY YOU ARE SURPRISED, CAN YOU? YOU OF ALL PEOPLE!
WHAT DO YOU MEAN?
YOU SHOULD BE VERY PROUD OF YOUR HUSBAND. WHEN STARK AND RICHARDS FORMED THEIR LITTLE CABAL--THE ILLUMINATI--T'CHALLA WAS THE FIRST ONE TO STAND UP AND DECLARE IT AS THE ROAD TO RUIN. HE WALKED OUT AND NEVER RETURNED.
WHAT ARE YOU SAYING? THEY'VE BEEN PLANNING THIS FOR YEARS?
NO, NO, IT WAS A GROUP OF "SUPER POWERS"--IN EVERY SENSE OF THE WORD--THAT DECIDED TO BAND TOGETHER AS A SUPERSTRUCTURE BEYOND THEIR INDIVIDUAL CONSTITUENCIES, SUCH AS THE AVENGERS, THE INHUMANS...
...AND YES, YOUR PROFESSOR X WAS THERE, TOO, MY DEAR...TO FACE GLOBAL THREATS.
BUT, I DON'T UNDERSTAND. THE X-MEN, THE AVENGERS--THEY WERE ALL FOUNDED ON SIMILAR PRINCIPLES... HOW DID IT GO WRONG?
JUST ASK YOUR HUSBAND. DESPITE APPEARANCES, HE'S NOT MUCH OF A "JOINER"--EXCEPT TO KEEP HIS ENEMIES CLOSER.

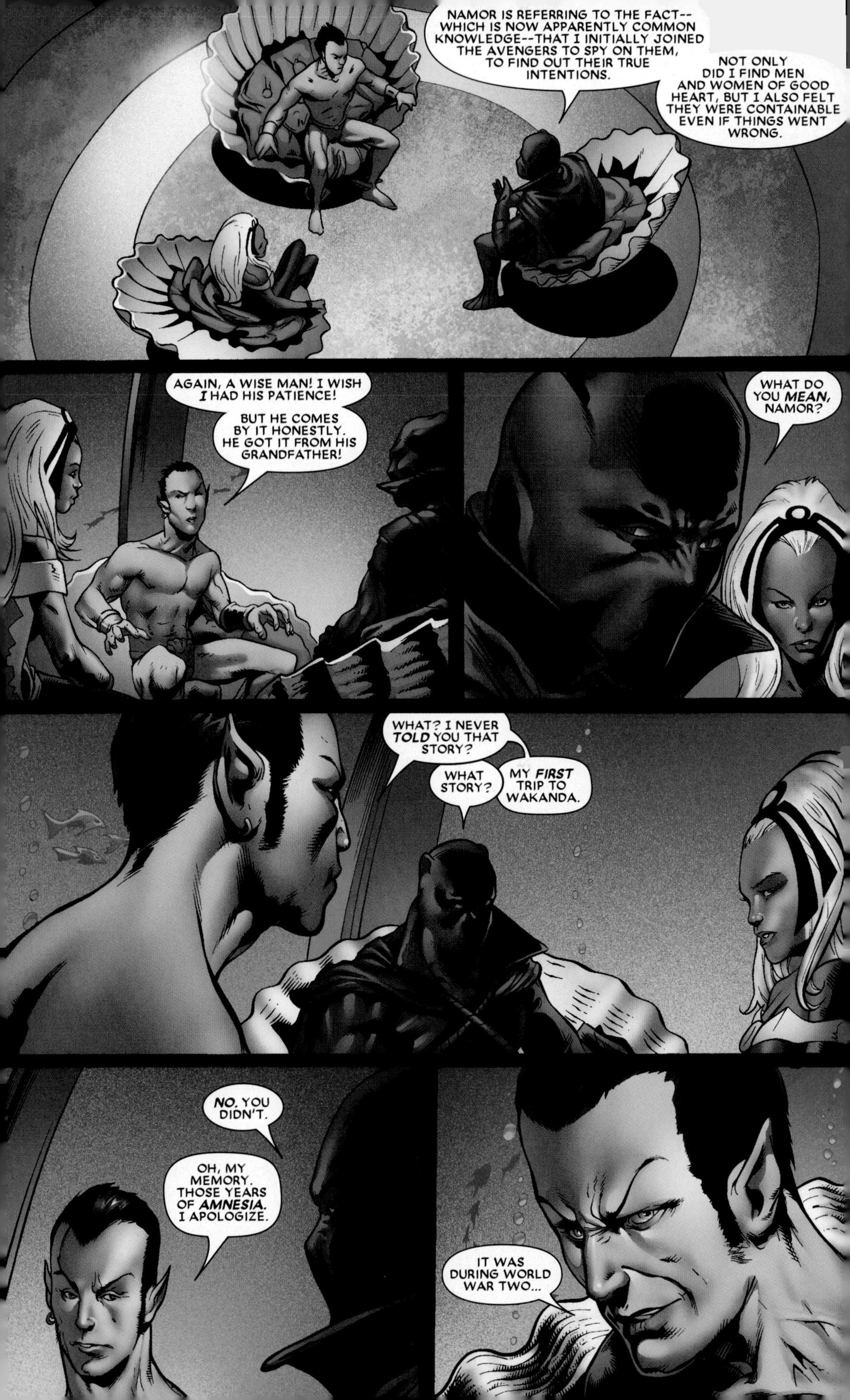

NAMOR IS REFERRING TO THE FACT--WHICH IS NOW APPARENTLY COMMON KNOWLEDGE--THAT I INITIALLY JOINED THE AVENGERS TO SPY ON THEM, TO FIND OUT THEIR TRUE INTENTIONS.
NOT ONLY DID I FIND MEN AND WOMEN OF GOOD HEART, BUT I ALSO FELT THEY WERE CONTAINABLE EVEN IF THINGS WENT WRONG.
AGAIN, A WISE MAN! I WISH *I* HAD HIS PATIENCE!
BUT HE COMES BY IT HONESTLY. HE GOT IT FROM HIS GRANDFATHER!
WHAT DO YOU *MEAN*, NAMOR?
WHAT? I NEVER *TOLD* YOU THAT STORY?
WHAT STORY?
MY *FIRST* TRIP TO WAKANDA.
NO. YOU DIDN'T.
OH, MY MEMORY. THOSE YEARS OF *AMNESIA.* I APOLOGIZE.
IT WAS DURING WORLD WAR TWO...

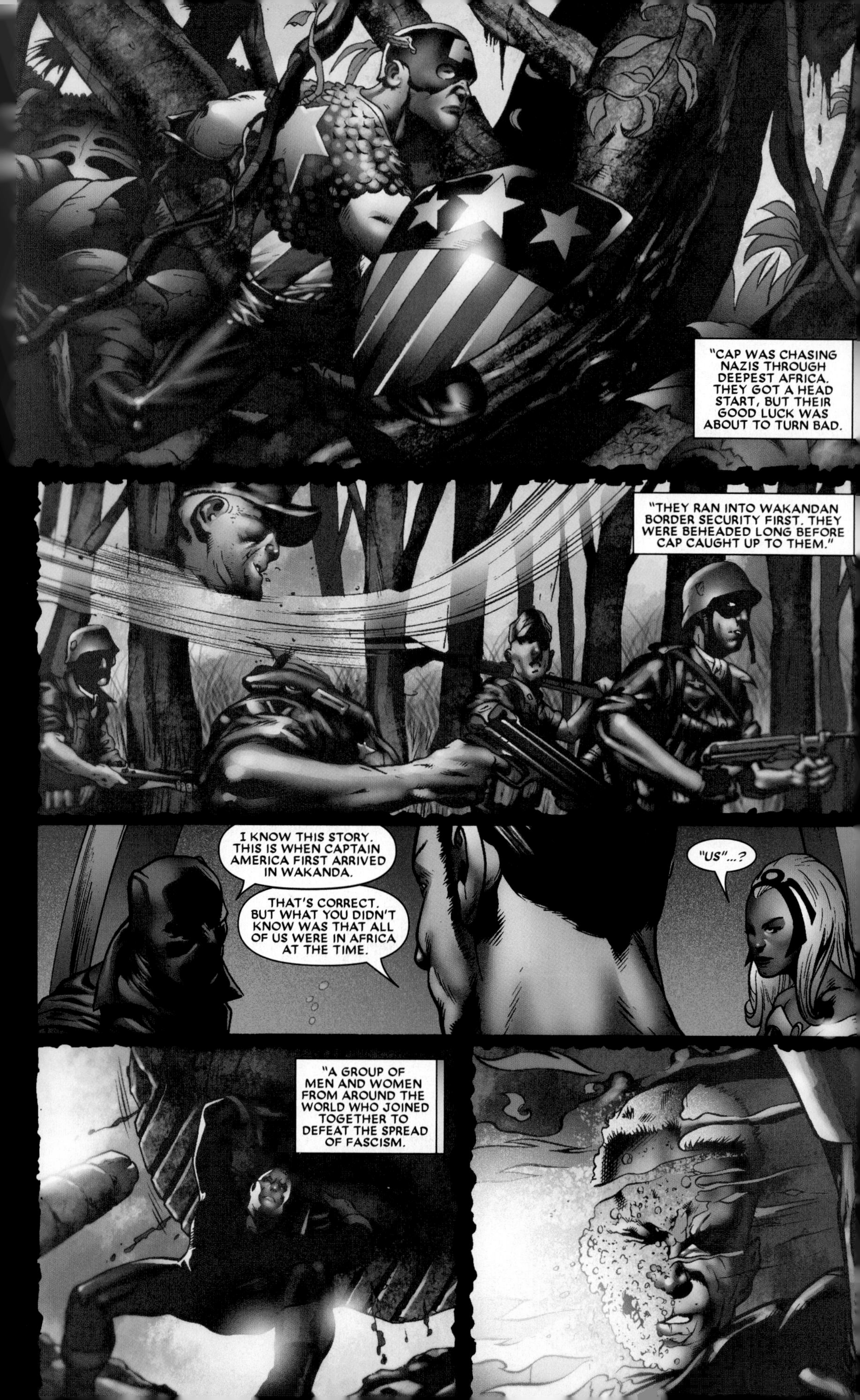
"CAP WAS CHASING NAZIS THROUGH DEEPEST AFRICA. THEY GOT A HEAD START, BUT THEIR GOOD LUCK WAS ABOUT TO TURN BAD.
"THEY RAN INTO WAKANDAN BORDER SECURITY FIRST. THEY WERE BEHEADED LONG BEFORE CAP CAUGHT UP TO THEM."
I KNOW THIS STORY. THIS IS WHEN CAPTAIN AMERICA FIRST ARRIVED IN WAKANDA.
THAT'S CORRECT. BUT WHAT YOU DIDN'T KNOW WAS THAT ALL OF US WERE IN AFRICA AT THE TIME.
"US"...?
"A GROUP OF MEN AND WOMEN FROM AROUND THE WORLD WHO JOINED TOGETHER TO DEFEAT THE SPREAD OF FASCISM.

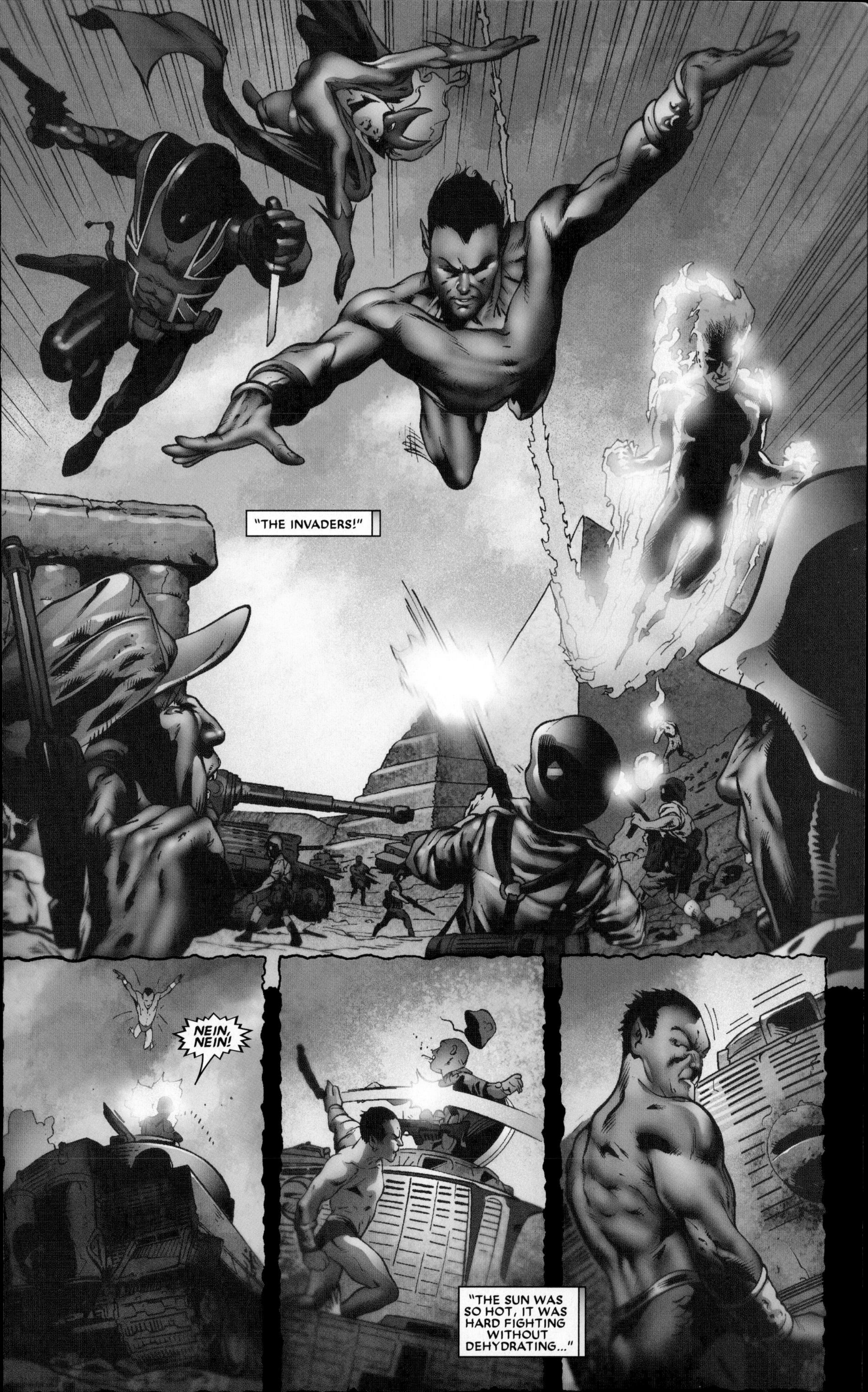
"THE INVADERS!"
NEIN, NEIN!
"THE SUN WAS SO HOT, IT WAS HARD FIGHTING WITHOUT DEHYDRATING..."

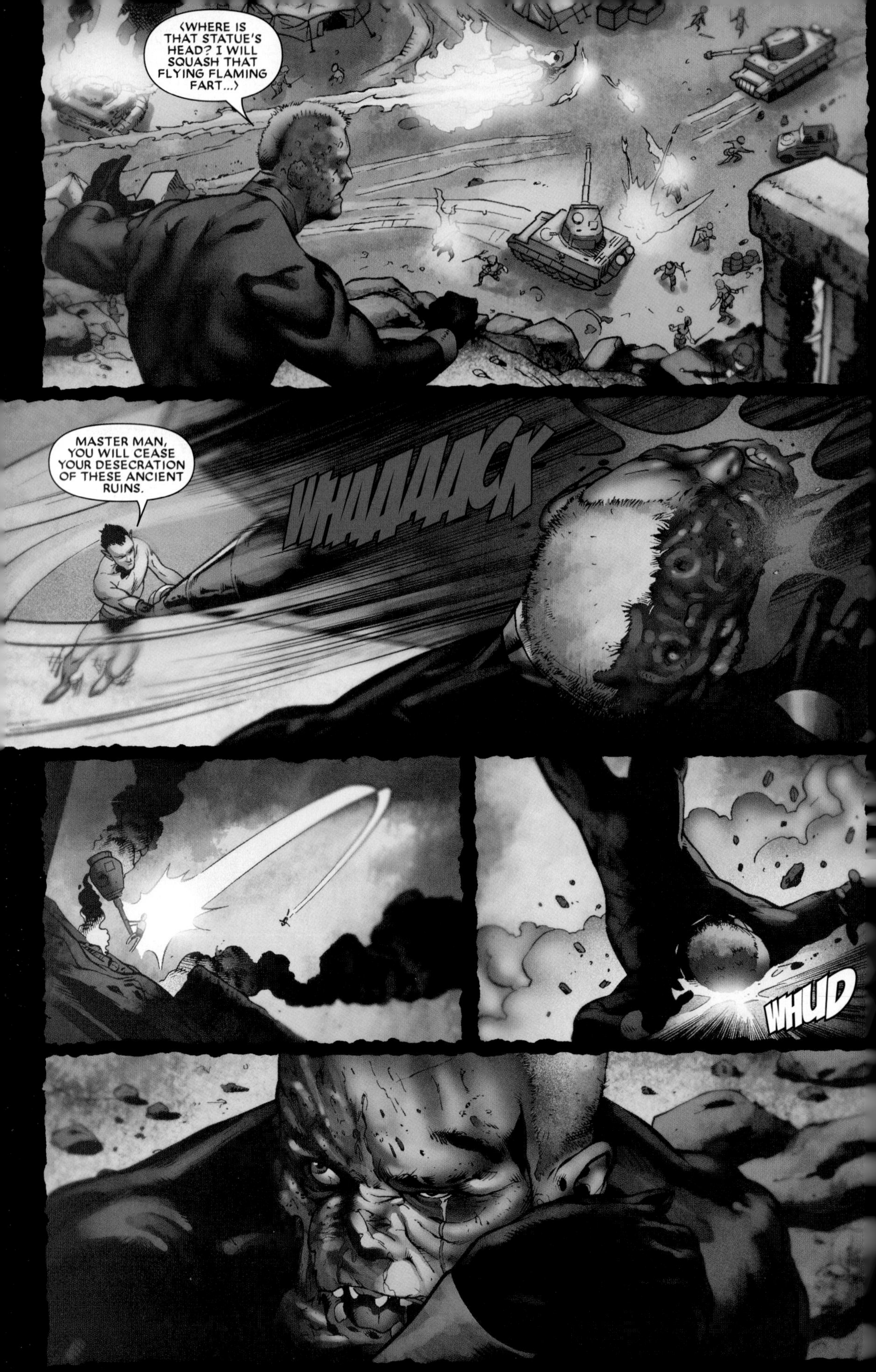
‹WHERE IS THAT STATUE'S HEAD? I WILL SQUASH THAT FLYING FLAMING FART...›
MASTER MAN, YOU WILL CEASE YOUR DESECRATION OF THESE ANCIENT RUINS.
WHAAAAACK
WHUD

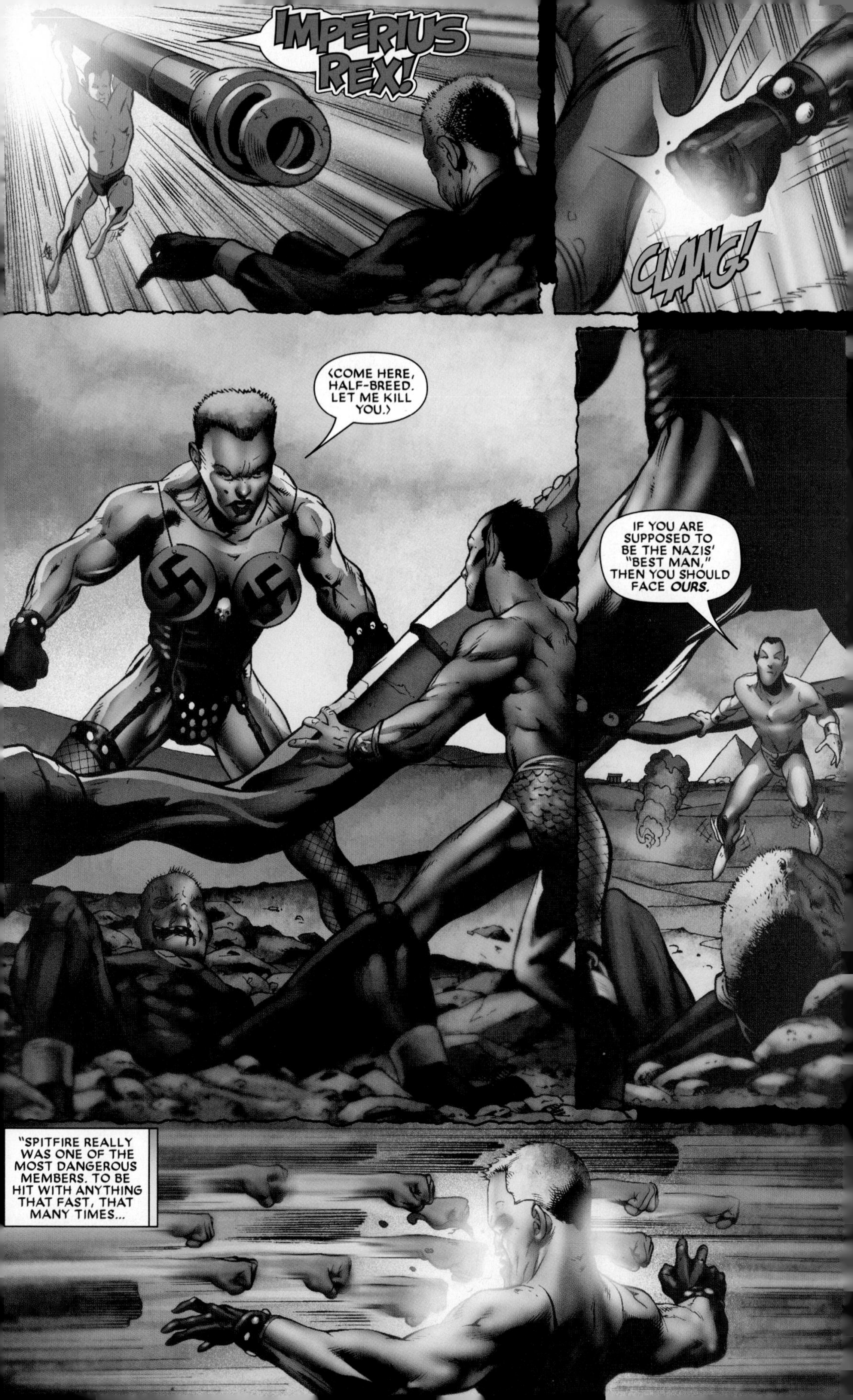
IMPERIUS REX!
CLANG!
‹COME HERE, HALF-BREED. LET ME KILL YOU.›
IF YOU ARE SUPPOSED TO BE THE NAZIS' "BEST MAN," THEN YOU SHOULD FACE *OURS.*
"SPITFIRE REALLY WAS ONE OF THE MOST DANGEROUS MEMBERS. TO BE HIT WITH ANYTHING THAT FAST, THAT MANY TIMES...

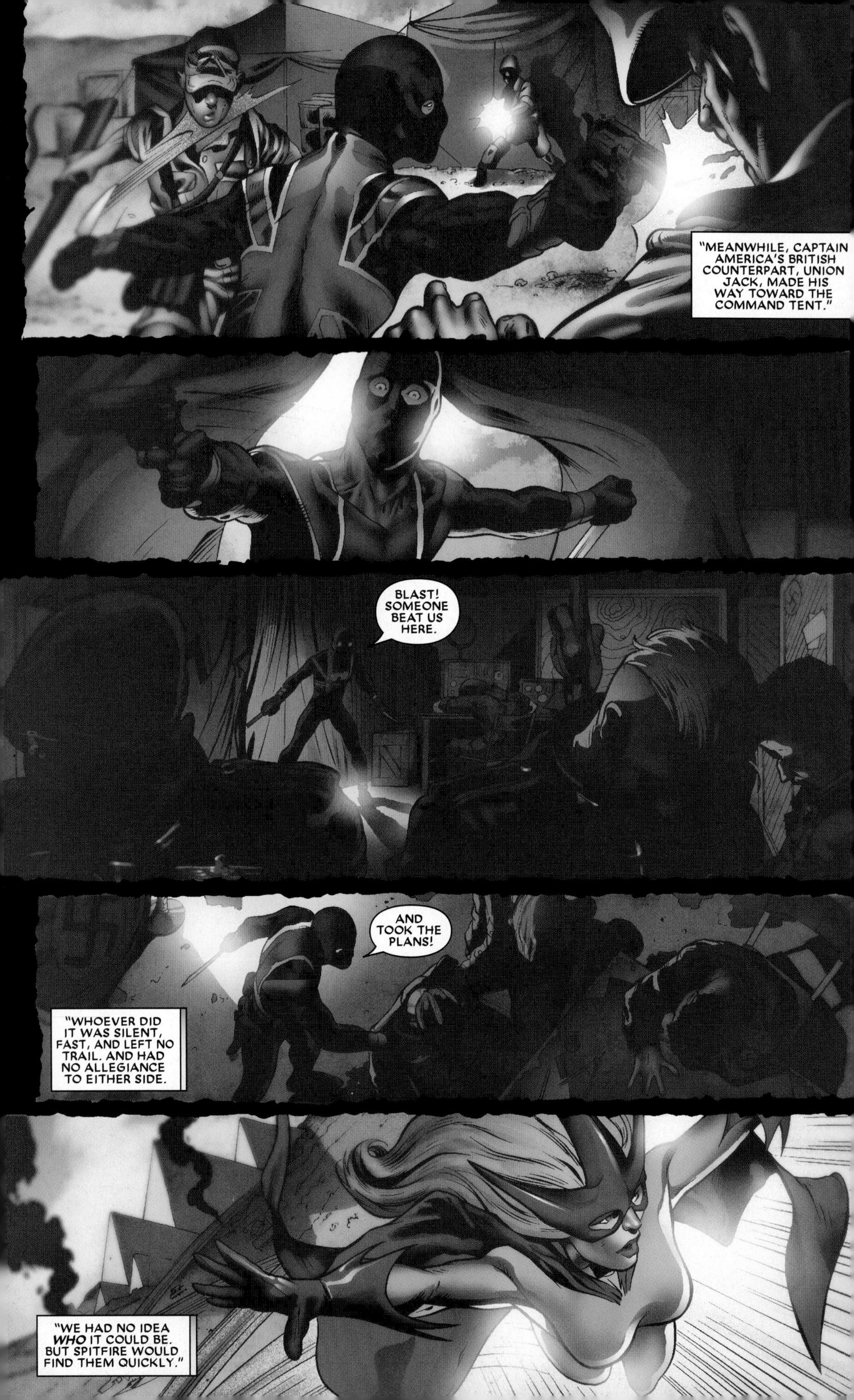
"MEANWHILE, CAPTAIN AMERICA'S BRITISH COUNTERPART, UNION JACK, MADE HIS WAY TOWARD THE COMMAND TENT."
BLAST! SOMEONE BEAT US HERE.
AND TOOK THE PLANS!
"WHOEVER DID IT WAS SILENT, FAST, AND LEFT NO TRAIL. AND HAD NO ALLEGIANCE TO EITHER SIDE.
"WE HAD NO IDEA *WHO* IT COULD BE. BUT SPITFIRE WOULD FIND THEM QUICKLY."

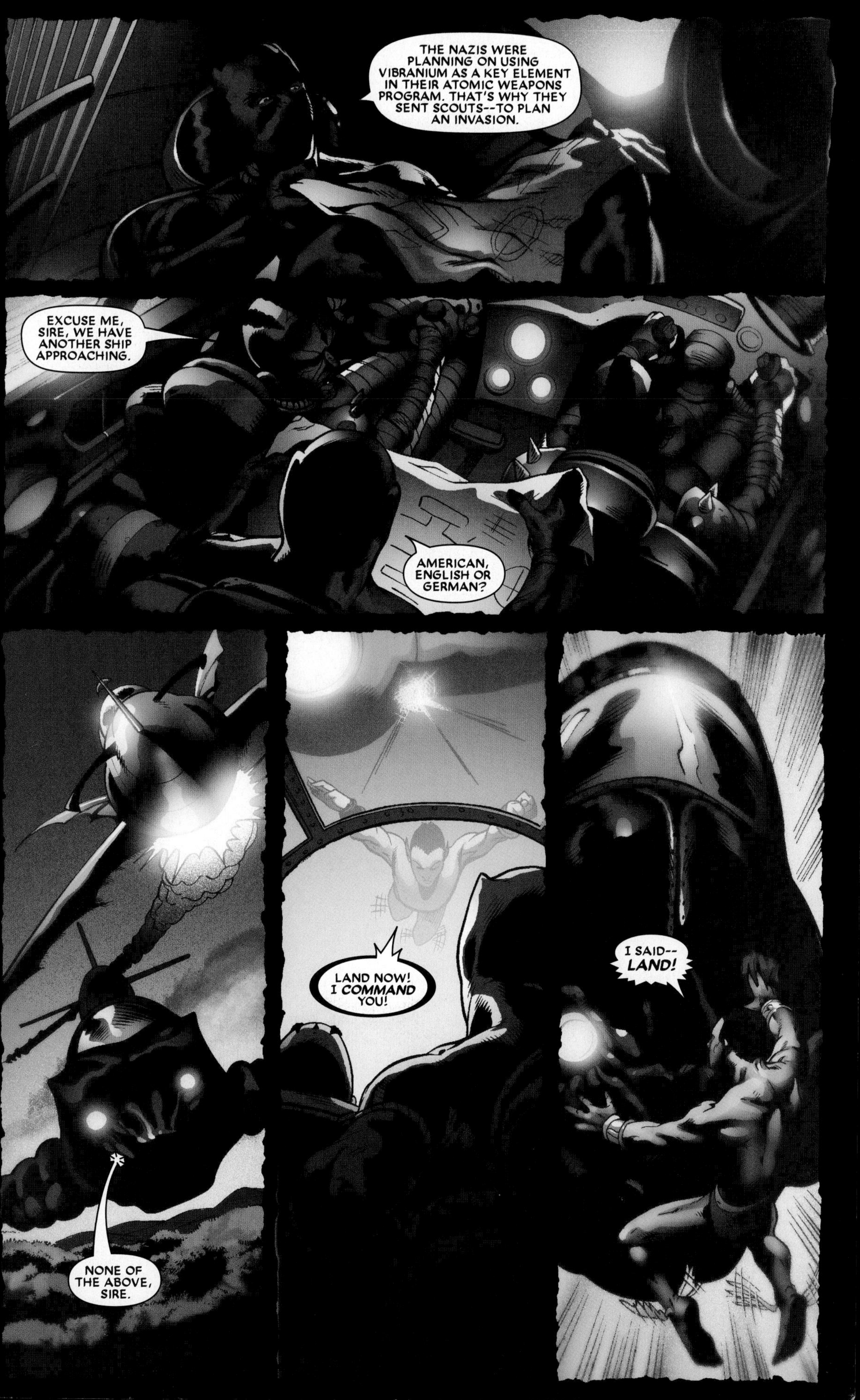
THE NAZIS WERE PLANNING ON USING VIBRANIUM AS A KEY ELEMENT IN THEIR ATOMIC WEAPONS PROGRAM. THAT'S WHY THEY SENT SCOUTS--TO PLAN AN INVASION.
EXCUSE ME, SIRE, WE HAVE ANOTHER SHIP APPROACHING.
AMERICAN, ENGLISH OR GERMAN?
NONE OF THE ABOVE, SIRE.
LAND NOW! I *COMMAND* YOU!
I SAID-- *LAND!*

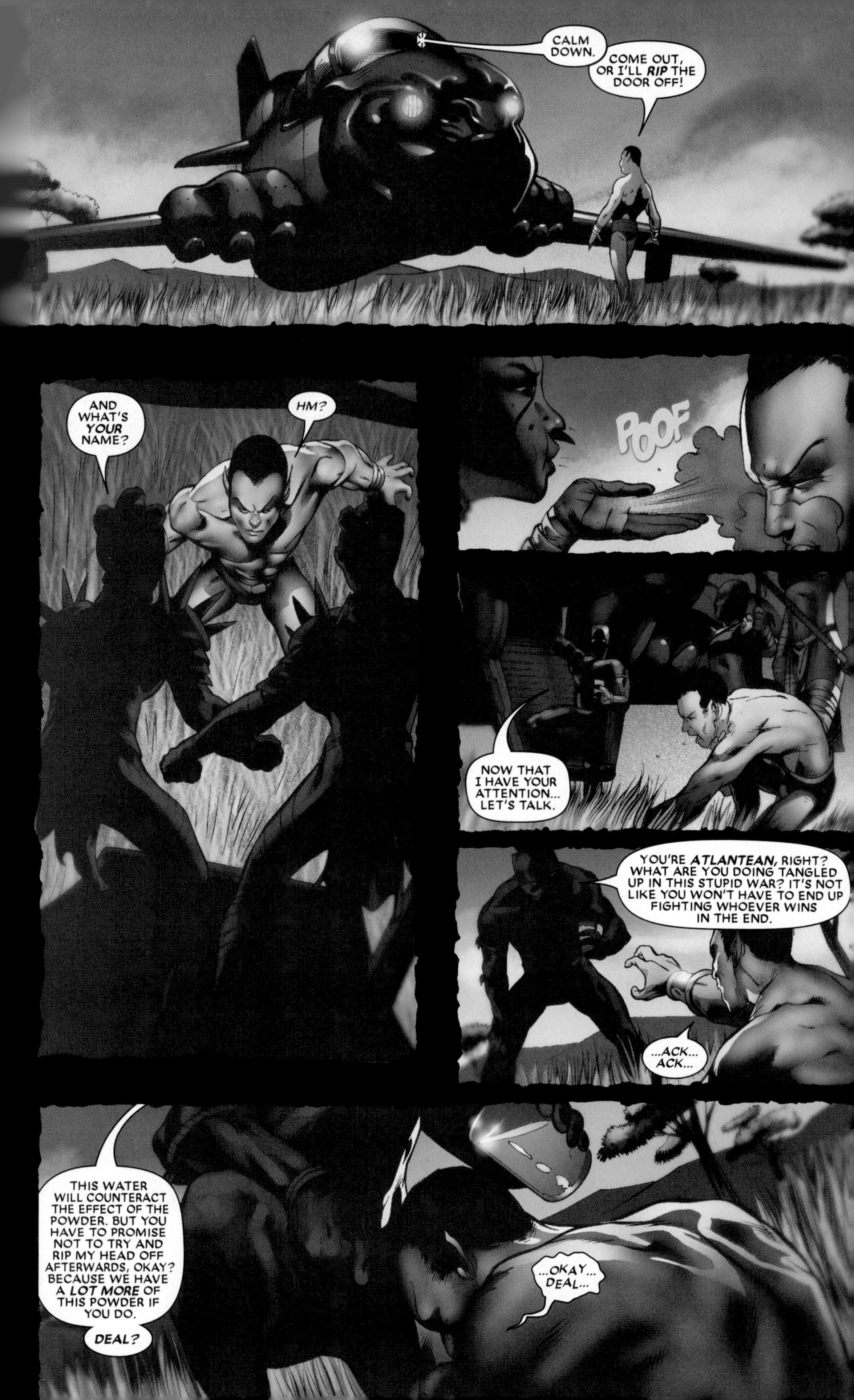
CALM DOWN.
COME OUT, OR I'LL RIP THE DOOR OFF!
AND WHAT'S YOUR NAME?
HM?
POOF
NOW THAT I HAVE YOUR ATTENTION... LET'S TALK.
YOU'RE ATLANTEAN, RIGHT? WHAT ARE YOU DOING TANGLED UP IN THIS STUPID WAR? IT'S NOT LIKE YOU WON'T HAVE TO END UP FIGHTING WHOEVER WINS IN THE END.
...ACK... ACK...
THIS WATER WILL COUNTERACT THE EFFECT OF THE POWDER. BUT YOU HAVE TO PROMISE NOT TO TRY AND RIP MY HEAD OFF AFTERWARDS, OKAY? BECAUSE WE HAVE A LOT MORE OF THIS POWDER IF YOU DO.
DEAL?
...OKAY... DEAL...

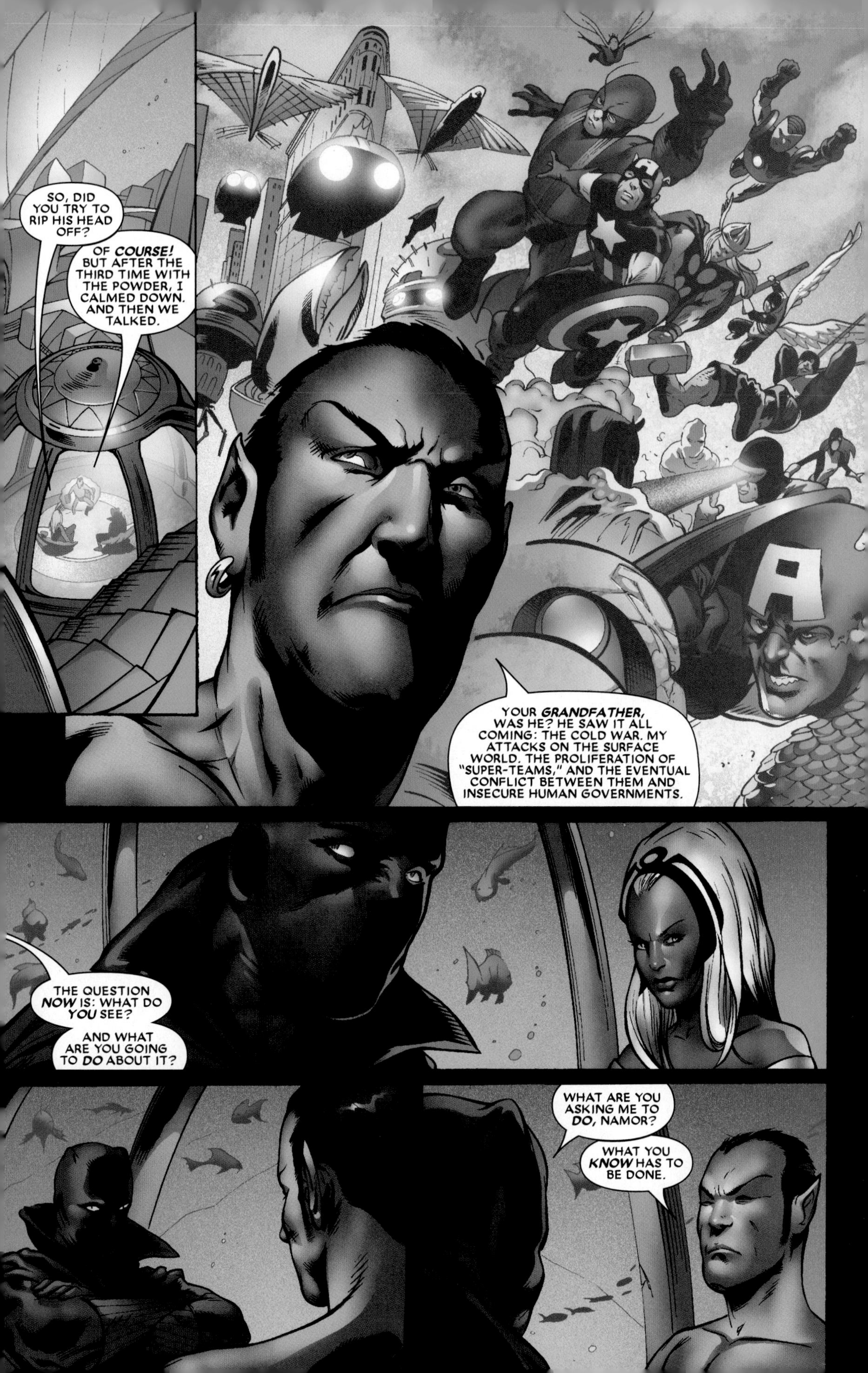
SO, DID YOU TRY TO RIP HIS HEAD OFF?
OF COURSE! BUT AFTER THE THIRD TIME WITH THE POWDER, I CALMED DOWN. AND THEN WE TALKED.
YOUR GRANDFATHER, WAS HE? HE SAW IT ALL COMING: THE COLD WAR. MY ATTACKS ON THE SURFACE WORLD. THE PROLIFERATION OF "SUPER-TEAMS," AND THE EVENTUAL CONFLICT BETWEEN THEM AND INSECURE HUMAN GOVERNMENTS.
THE QUESTION NOW IS: WHAT DO YOU SEE?
AND WHAT ARE YOU GOING TO DO ABOUT IT?
WHAT ARE YOU ASKING ME TO DO, NAMOR?
WHAT YOU KNOW HAS TO BE DONE.

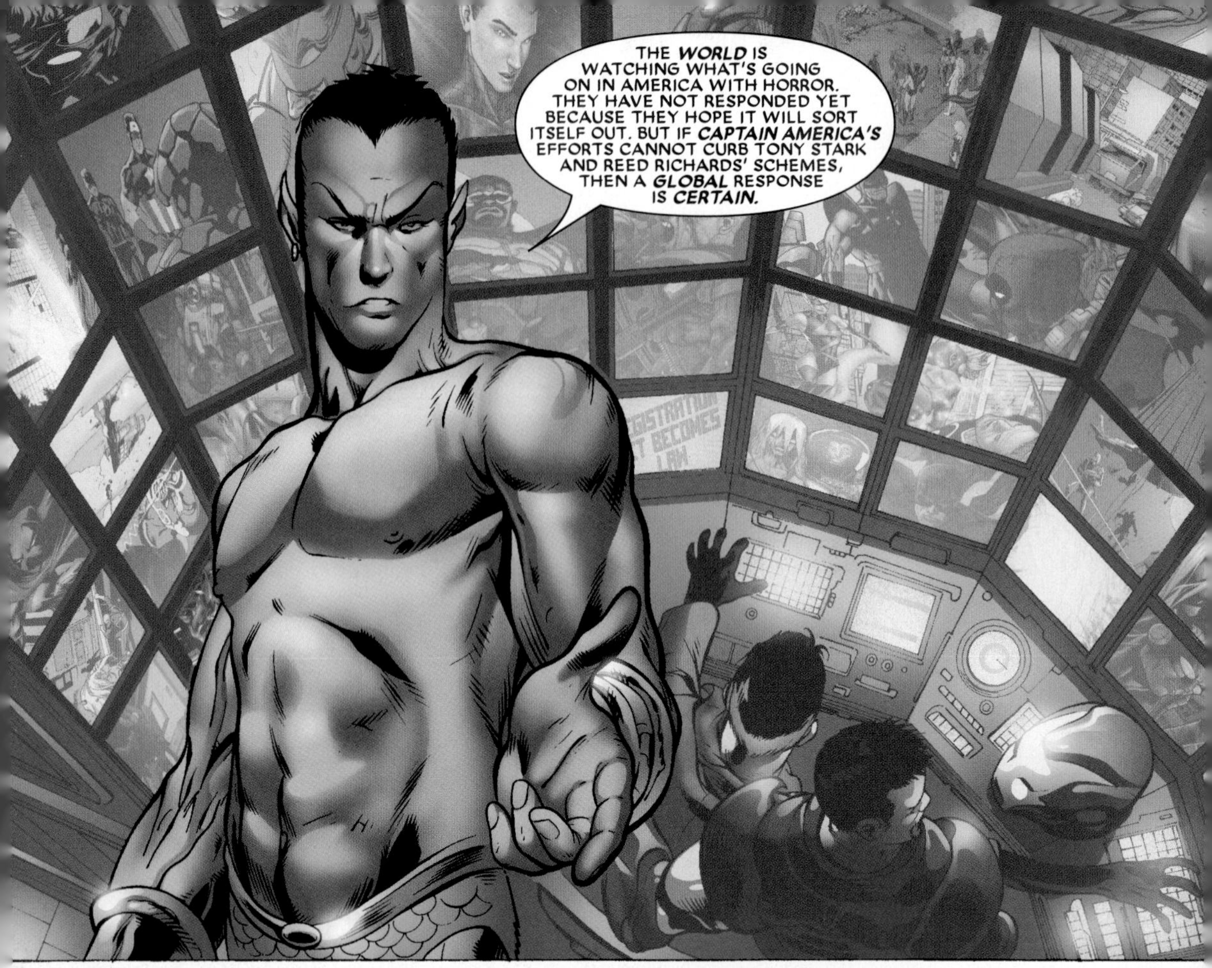
THE WORLD IS WATCHING WHAT'S GOING ON IN AMERICA WITH HORROR. THEY HAVE NOT RESPONDED YET BECAUSE THEY HOPE IT WILL SORT ITSELF OUT. BUT IF CAPTAIN AMERICA'S EFFORTS CANNOT CURB TONY STARK AND REED RICHARDS' SCHEMES, THEN A GLOBAL RESPONSE IS CERTAIN.

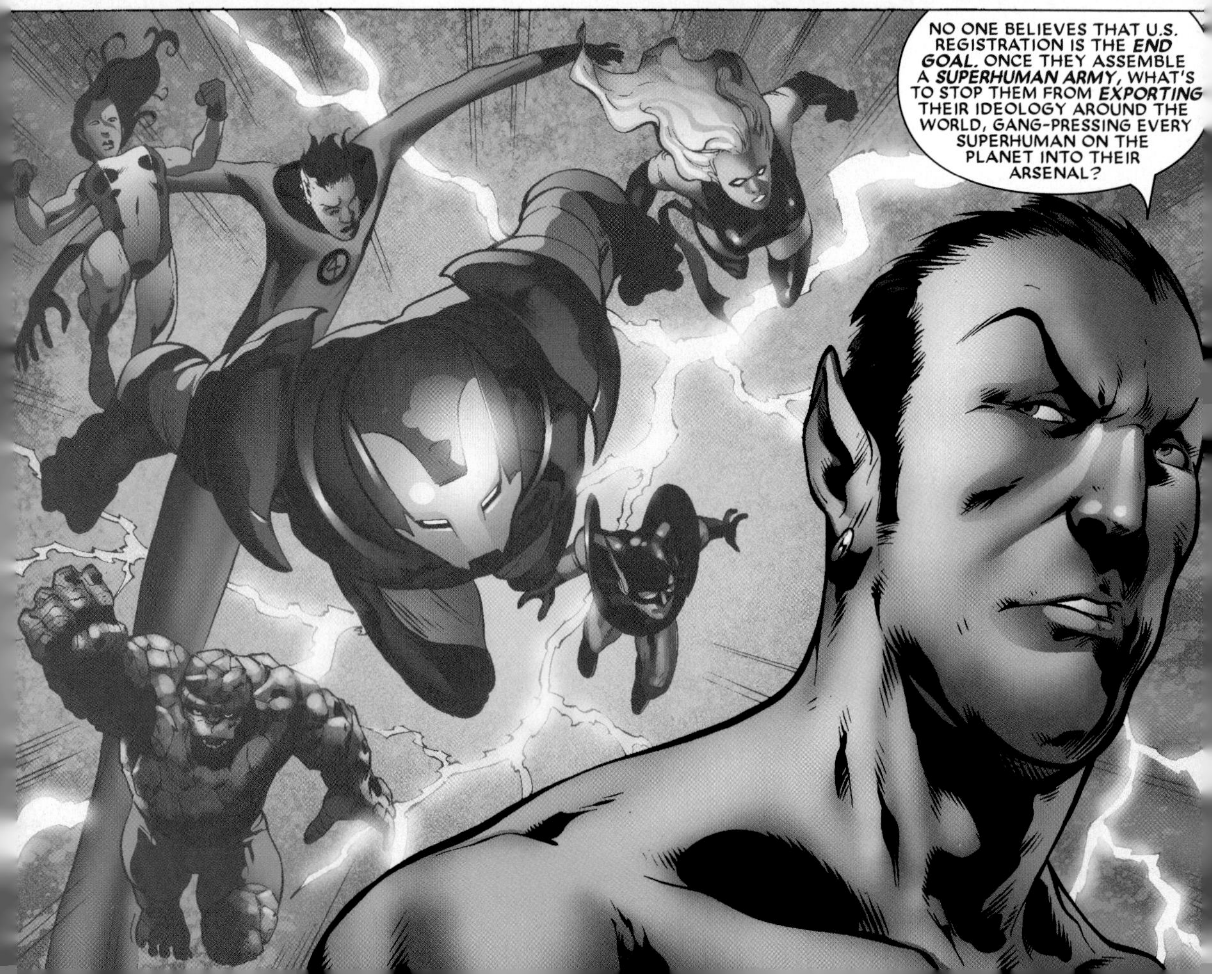
NO ONE BELIEVES THAT U.S. REGISTRATION IS THE END GOAL. ONCE THEY ASSEMBLE A SUPERHUMAN ARMY, WHAT'S TO STOP THEM FROM EXPORTING THEIR IDEOLOGY AROUND THE WORLD, GANG-PRESSING EVERY SUPERHUMAN ON THE PLANET INTO THEIR ARSENAL?

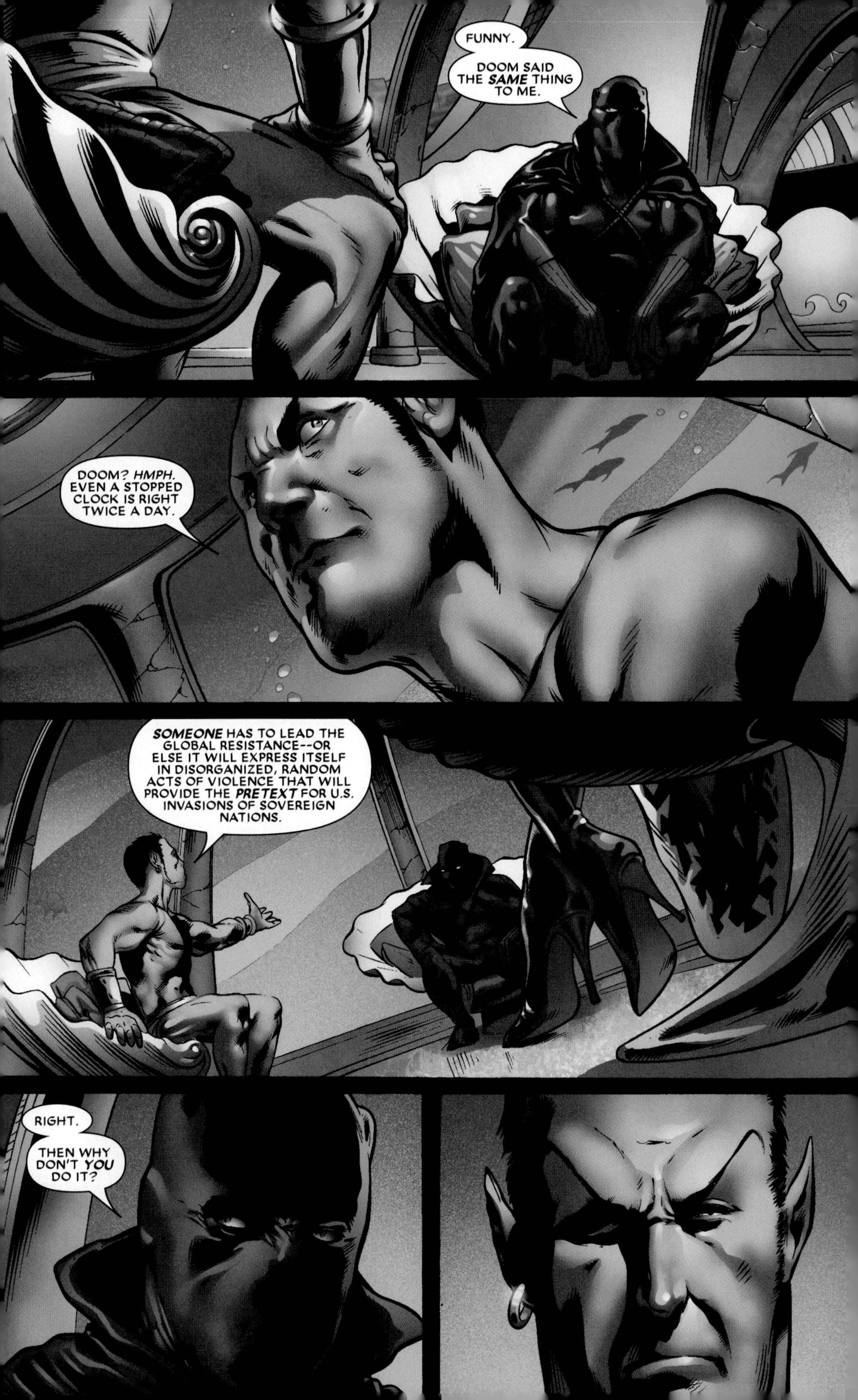
FUNNY.
DOOM SAID THE SAME THING TO ME.
DOOM? HMPH. EVEN A STOPPED CLOCK IS RIGHT TWICE A DAY.
SOMEONE HAS TO LEAD THE GLOBAL RESISTANCE--OR ELSE IT WILL EXPRESS ITSELF IN DISORGANIZED, RANDOM ACTS OF VIOLENCE THAT WILL PROVIDE THE PRETEXT FOR U.S. INVASIONS OF SOVEREIGN NATIONS.
RIGHT.
THEN WHY DON'T YOU DO IT?

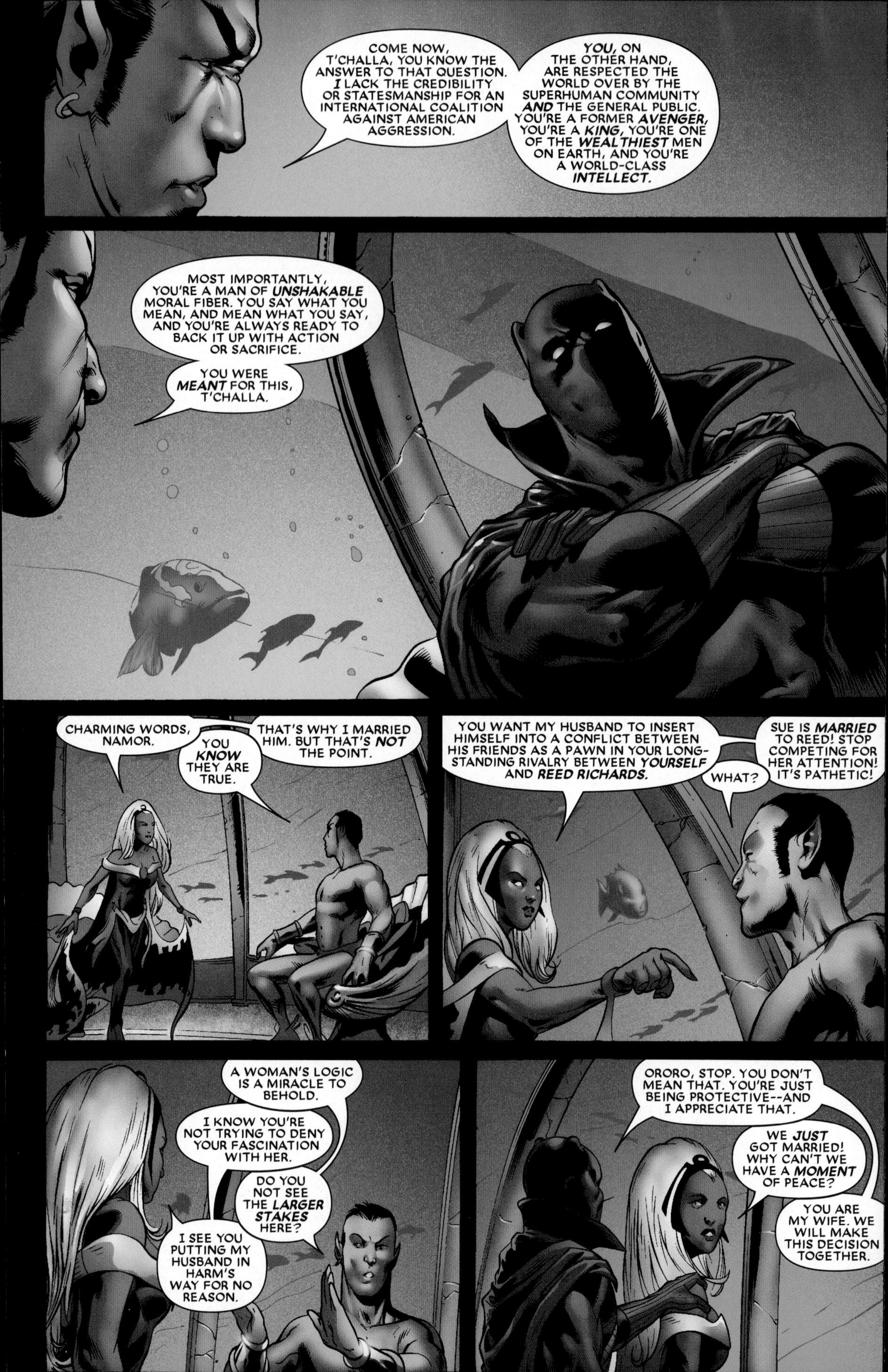
COME NOW, T'CHALLA, YOU KNOW THE ANSWER TO THAT QUESTION. I LACK THE CREDIBILITY OR STATESMANSHIP FOR AN INTERNATIONAL COALITION AGAINST AMERICAN AGGRESSION.
YOU, ON THE OTHER HAND, ARE RESPECTED THE WORLD OVER BY THE SUPERHUMAN COMMUNITY AND THE GENERAL PUBLIC. YOU'RE A FORMER AVENGER, YOU'RE A KING, YOU'RE ONE OF THE WEALTHIEST MEN ON EARTH, AND YOU'RE A WORLD-CLASS INTELLECT.
MOST IMPORTANTLY, YOU'RE A MAN OF UNSHAKABLE MORAL FIBER. YOU SAY WHAT YOU MEAN, AND MEAN WHAT YOU SAY, AND YOU'RE ALWAYS READY TO BACK IT UP WITH ACTION OR SACRIFICE.
YOU WERE MEANT FOR THIS, T'CHALLA.
CHARMING WORDS, NAMOR.
YOU KNOW THEY ARE TRUE.
THAT'S WHY I MARRIED HIM. BUT THAT'S NOT THE POINT.
YOU WANT MY HUSBAND TO INSERT HIMSELF INTO A CONFLICT BETWEEN HIS FRIENDS AS A PAWN IN YOUR LONG-STANDING RIVALRY BETWEEN YOURSELF AND REED RICHARDS.
WHAT?
SUE IS MARRIED TO REED! STOP COMPETING FOR HER ATTENTION! IT'S PATHETIC!
A WOMAN'S LOGIC IS A MIRACLE TO BEHOLD.
I KNOW YOU'RE NOT TRYING TO DENY YOUR FASCINATION WITH HER.
DO YOU NOT SEE THE LARGER STAKES HERE?
I SEE YOU PUTTING MY HUSBAND IN HARM'S WAY FOR NO REASON.
ORORO, STOP. YOU DON'T MEAN THAT. YOU'RE JUST BEING PROTECTIVE--AND I APPRECIATE THAT.
WE JUST GOT MARRIED! WHY CAN'T WE HAVE A MOMENT OF PEACE?
YOU ARE MY WIFE. WE WILL MAKE THIS DECISION TOGETHER.

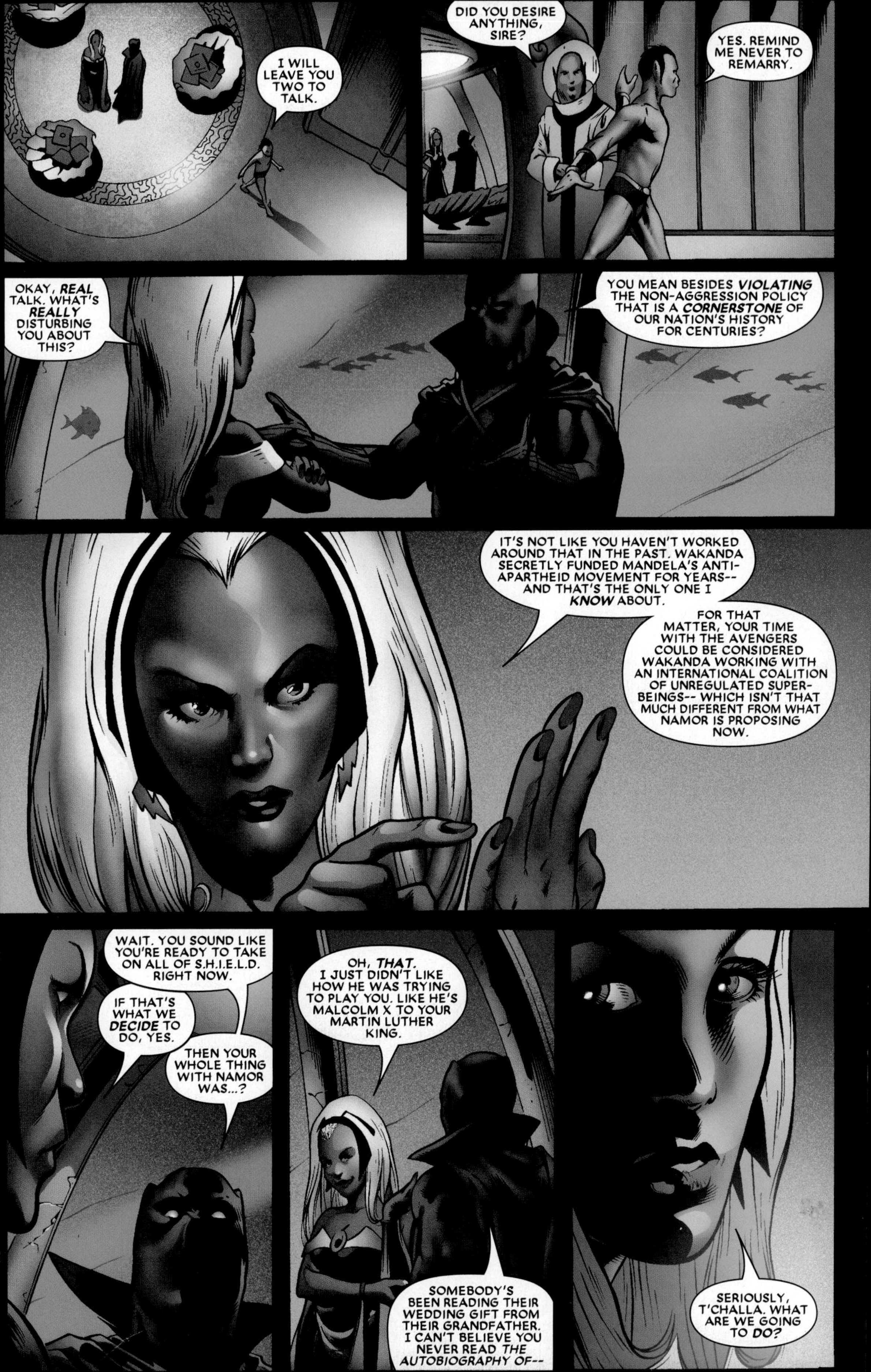
I WILL LEAVE YOU TWO TO TALK.
DID YOU DESIRE ANYTHING, SIRE?
YES. REMIND ME NEVER TO REMARRY.
OKAY, *REAL* TALK. WHAT'S *REALLY* DISTURBING YOU ABOUT THIS?
YOU MEAN BESIDES *VIOLATING* THE NON-AGGRESSION POLICY THAT IS A *CORNERSTONE* OF OUR NATION'S HISTORY FOR CENTURIES?
IT'S NOT LIKE YOU HAVEN'T WORKED AROUND THAT IN THE PAST. WAKANDA SECRETLY FUNDED MANDELA'S ANTI-APARTHEID MOVEMENT FOR YEARS-- AND THAT'S THE ONLY ONE I *KNOW* ABOUT.
FOR THAT MATTER, YOUR TIME WITH THE AVENGERS COULD BE CONSIDERED WAKANDA WORKING WITH AN INTERNATIONAL COALITION OF UNREGULATED SUPER-BEINGS-- WHICH ISN'T THAT MUCH DIFFERENT FROM WHAT NAMOR IS PROPOSING NOW.
WAIT. YOU SOUND LIKE YOU'RE READY TO TAKE ON ALL OF S.H.I.E.L.D. RIGHT NOW.
IF THAT'S WHAT WE *DECIDE* TO DO, YES.
THEN YOUR WHOLE THING WITH NAMOR WAS...?
OH, *THAT.* I JUST DIDN'T LIKE HOW HE WAS TRYING TO PLAY YOU. LIKE HE'S MALCOLM X TO YOUR MARTIN LUTHER KING.
SOMEBODY'S BEEN READING THEIR WEDDING GIFT FROM THEIR GRANDFATHER. I CAN'T BELIEVE YOU NEVER READ *THE AUTOBIOGRAPHY OF--*
SERIOUSLY, T'CHALLA. WHAT ARE WE GOING TO *DO?*

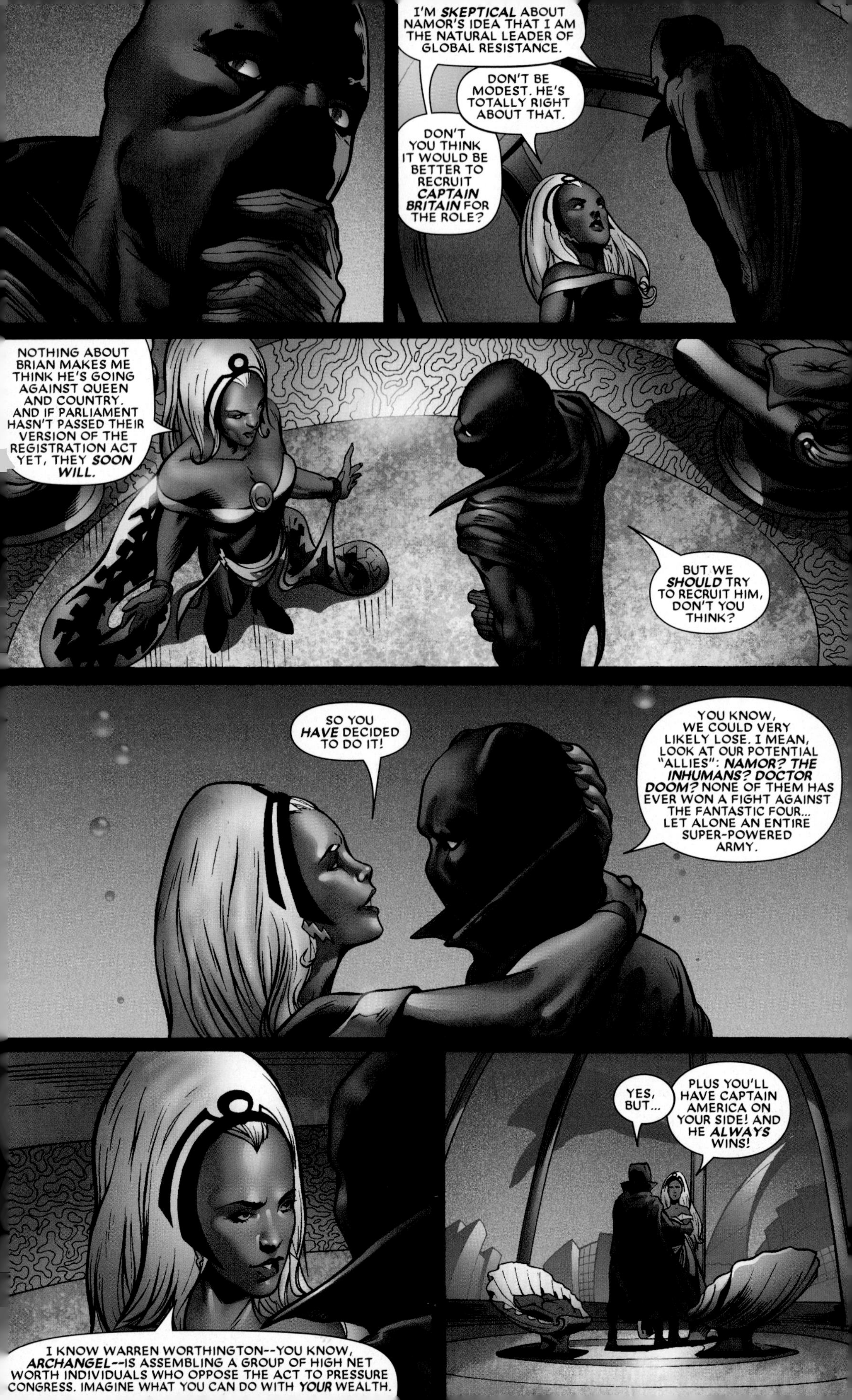

I'M SKEPTICAL ABOUT NAMOR'S IDEA THAT I AM THE NATURAL LEADER OF GLOBAL RESISTANCE.
DON'T YOU THINK IT WOULD BE BETTER TO RECRUIT CAPTAIN BRITAIN FOR THE ROLE?
DON'T BE MODEST. HE'S TOTALLY RIGHT ABOUT THAT.
NOTHING ABOUT BRIAN MAKES ME THINK HE'S GOING AGAINST QUEEN AND COUNTRY. AND IF PARLIAMENT HASN'T PASSED THEIR VERSION OF THE REGISTRATION ACT YET, THEY SOON WILL.
BUT WE SHOULD TRY TO RECRUIT HIM, DON'T YOU THINK?
SO YOU HAVE DECIDED TO DO IT!
YOU KNOW, WE COULD VERY LIKELY LOSE. I MEAN, LOOK AT OUR POTENTIAL "ALLIES": NAMOR? THE INHUMANS? DOCTOR DOOM? NONE OF THEM HAS EVER WON A FIGHT AGAINST THE FANTASTIC FOUR... LET ALONE AN ENTIRE SUPER-POWERED ARMY.
I KNOW WARREN WORTHINGTON--YOU KNOW, ARCHANGEL--IS ASSEMBLING A GROUP OF HIGH NET WORTH INDIVIDUALS WHO OPPOSE THE ACT TO PRESSURE CONGRESS. IMAGINE WHAT YOU CAN DO WITH YOUR WEALTH.
YES, BUT...
PLUS YOU'LL HAVE CAPTAIN AMERICA ON YOUR SIDE! AND HE ALWAYS WINS!

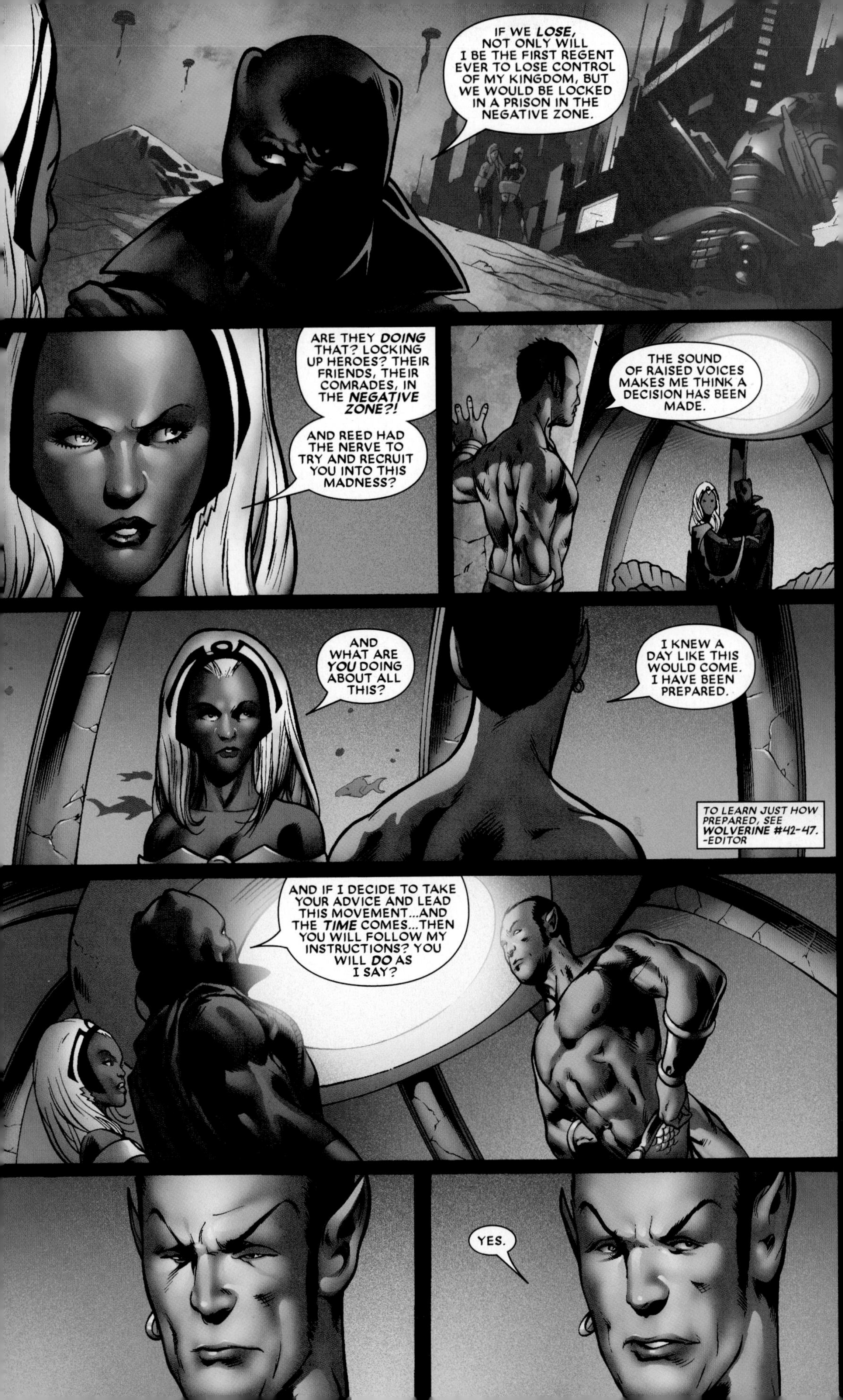
IF WE LOSE, NOT ONLY WILL I BE THE FIRST REGENT EVER TO LOSE CONTROL OF MY KINGDOM, BUT WE WOULD BE LOCKED IN A PRISON IN THE NEGATIVE ZONE.
ARE THEY DOING THAT? LOCKING UP HEROES? THEIR FRIENDS, THEIR COMRADES, IN THE NEGATIVE ZONE?!
AND REED HAD THE NERVE TO TRY AND RECRUIT YOU INTO THIS MADNESS?
THE SOUND OF RAISED VOICES MAKES ME THINK A DECISION HAS BEEN MADE.
AND WHAT ARE YOU DOING ABOUT ALL THIS?
I KNEW A DAY LIKE THIS WOULD COME. I HAVE BEEN PREPARED.
TO LEARN JUST HOW PREPARED, SEE WOLVERINE #42-47. -EDITOR
AND IF I DECIDE TO TAKE YOUR ADVICE AND LEAD THIS MOVEMENT...AND THE TIME COMES...THEN YOU WILL FOLLOW MY INSTRUCTIONS? YOU WILL DO AS I SAY?
YES.

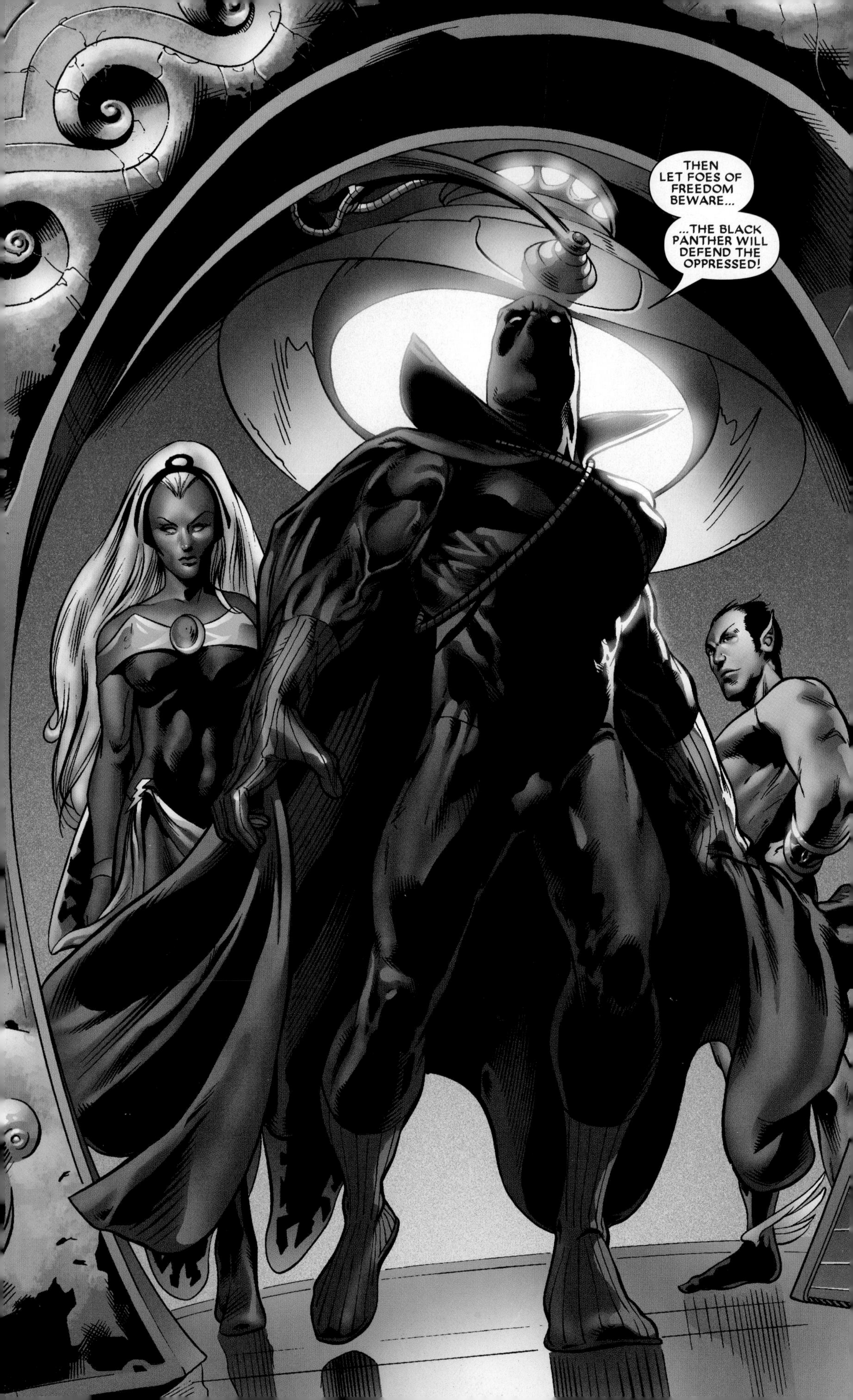
THEN LET FOES OF FREEDOM BEWARE...
...THE BLACK PANTHER WILL DEFEND THE OPPRESSED!

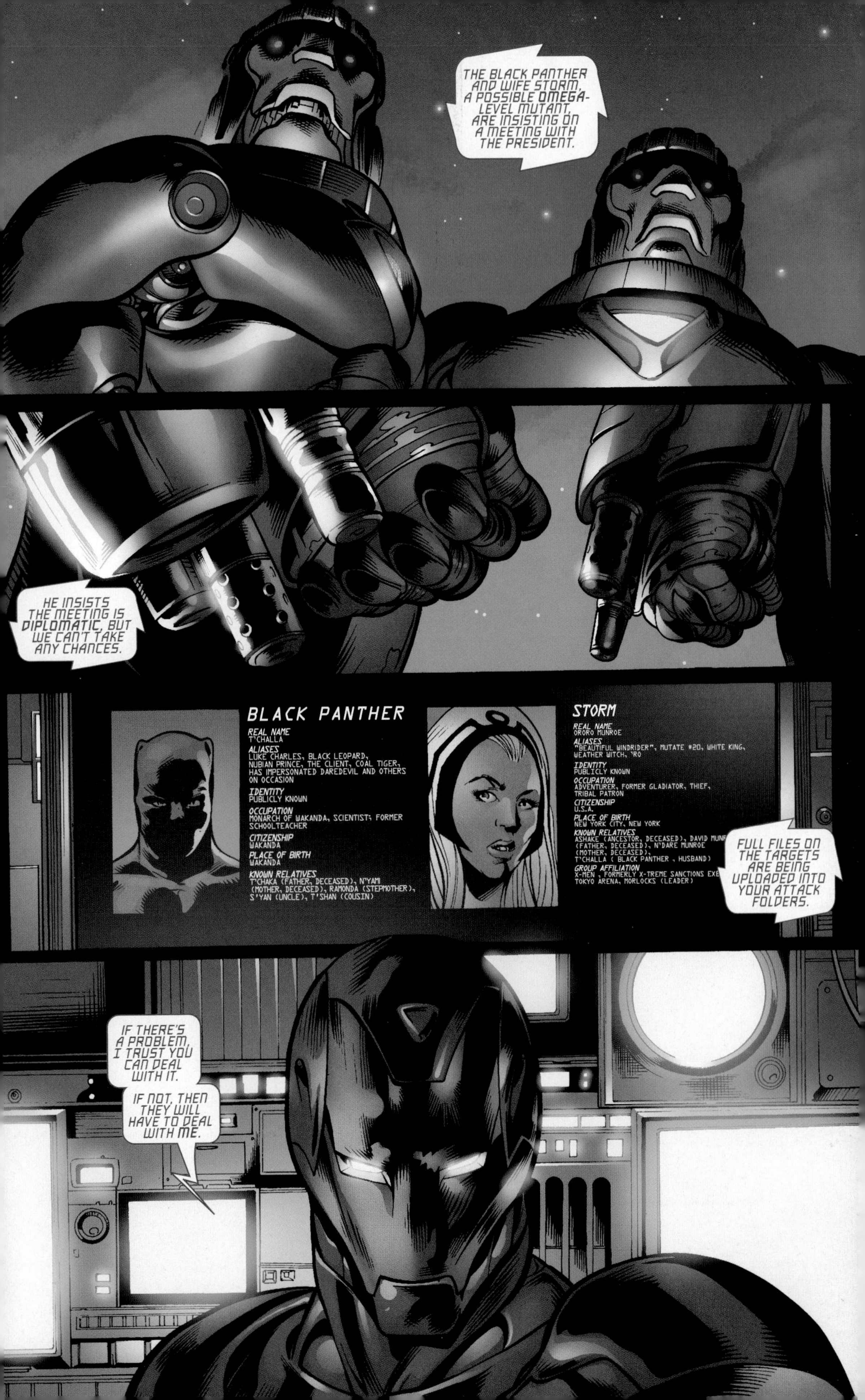
THE BLACK PANTHER AND WIFE STORM, A POSSIBLE OMEGA-LEVEL MUTANT, ARE INSISTING ON A MEETING WITH THE PRESIDENT.
HE INSISTS THE MEETING IS DIPLOMATIC, BUT WE CAN'T TAKE ANY CHANCES.
BLACK PANTHER
REAL NAME
T'CHALLA
ALIASES
LUKE CHARLES, BLACK LEOPARD, NUBIAN PRINCE, THE CLIENT, COAL TIGER, HAS IMPERSONATED DAREDEVIL AND OTHERS ON OCCASION
IDENTITY
PUBLICLY KNOWN
OCCUPATION
MONARCH OF WAKANDA, SCIENTIST; FORMER SCHOOLTEACHER
CITIZENSHIP
WAKANDA
PLACE OF BIRTH
WAKANDA
KNOWN RELATIVES
T'CHAKA (FATHER, DECEASED), N'YAMI (MOTHER, DECEASED), RAMONDA (STEPMOTHER), S'YAN (UNCLE), T'SHAN (COUSIN)
STORM
REAL NAME
ORORO MUNROE
ALIASES
"BEAUTIFUL WINDRIDER", MUTATE #20, WHITE KING, WEATHER WITCH, 'RO
IDENTITY
PUBLICLY KNOWN
OCCUPATION
ADVENTURER, FORMER GLADIATOR, THIEF, TRIBAL PATRON
CITIZENSHIP
U.S.A.
PLACE OF BIRTH
NEW YORK CITY, NEW YORK
KNOWN RELATIVES
ASHAKE (ANCESTOR, DECEASED), DAVID MUNR (FATHER, DECEASED), N'DARE MUNROE (MOTHER, DECEASED), T'CHALLA (BLACK PANTHER , HUSBAND)
GROUP AFFILIATION
X-MEN , FORMERLY X-TREME SANCTIONS EXE TOKYO ARENA, MORLOCKS (LEADER)
FULL FILES ON THE TARGETS ARE BEING UPLOADED INTO YOUR ATTACK FOLDERS.
IF THERE'S A PROBLEM, I TRUST YOU CAN DEAL WITH IT.
IF NOT, THEN THEY WILL HAVE TO DEAL WITH ME.

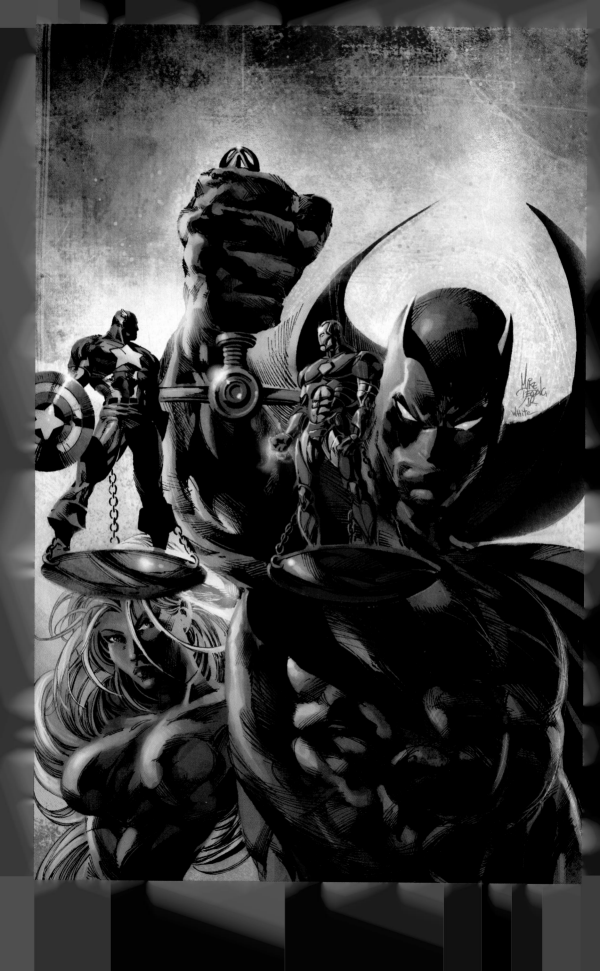

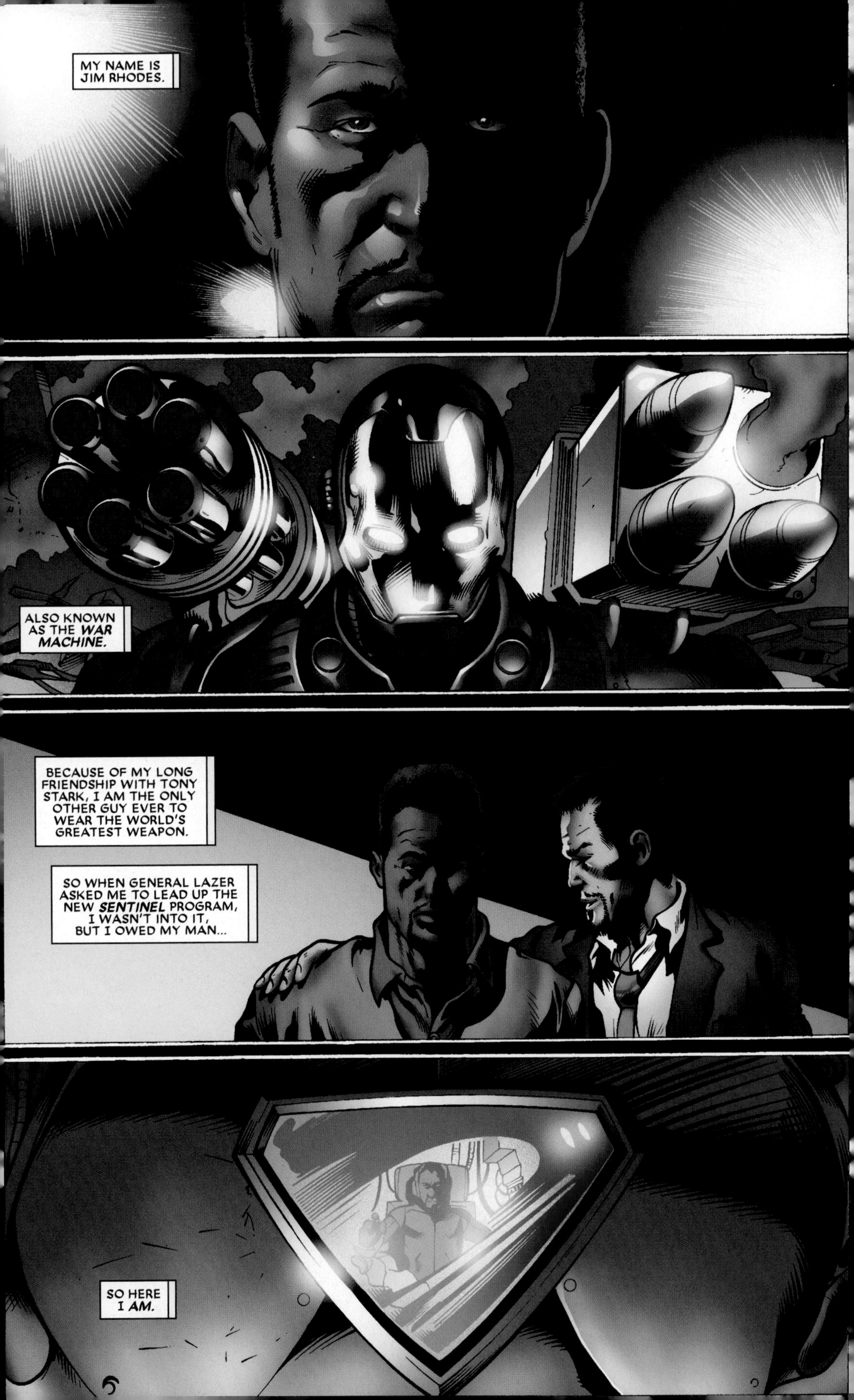
MY NAME IS JIM RHODES.
ALSO KNOWN AS THE *WAR MACHINE.*
BECAUSE OF MY LONG FRIENDSHIP WITH TONY STARK, I AM THE ONLY OTHER GUY EVER TO WEAR THE WORLD'S GREATEST WEAPON.
SO WHEN GENERAL LAZER ASKED ME TO LEAD UP THE NEW *SENTINEL* PROGRAM, I WASN'T INTO IT, BUT I OWED MY MAN...
SO HERE I *AM.*

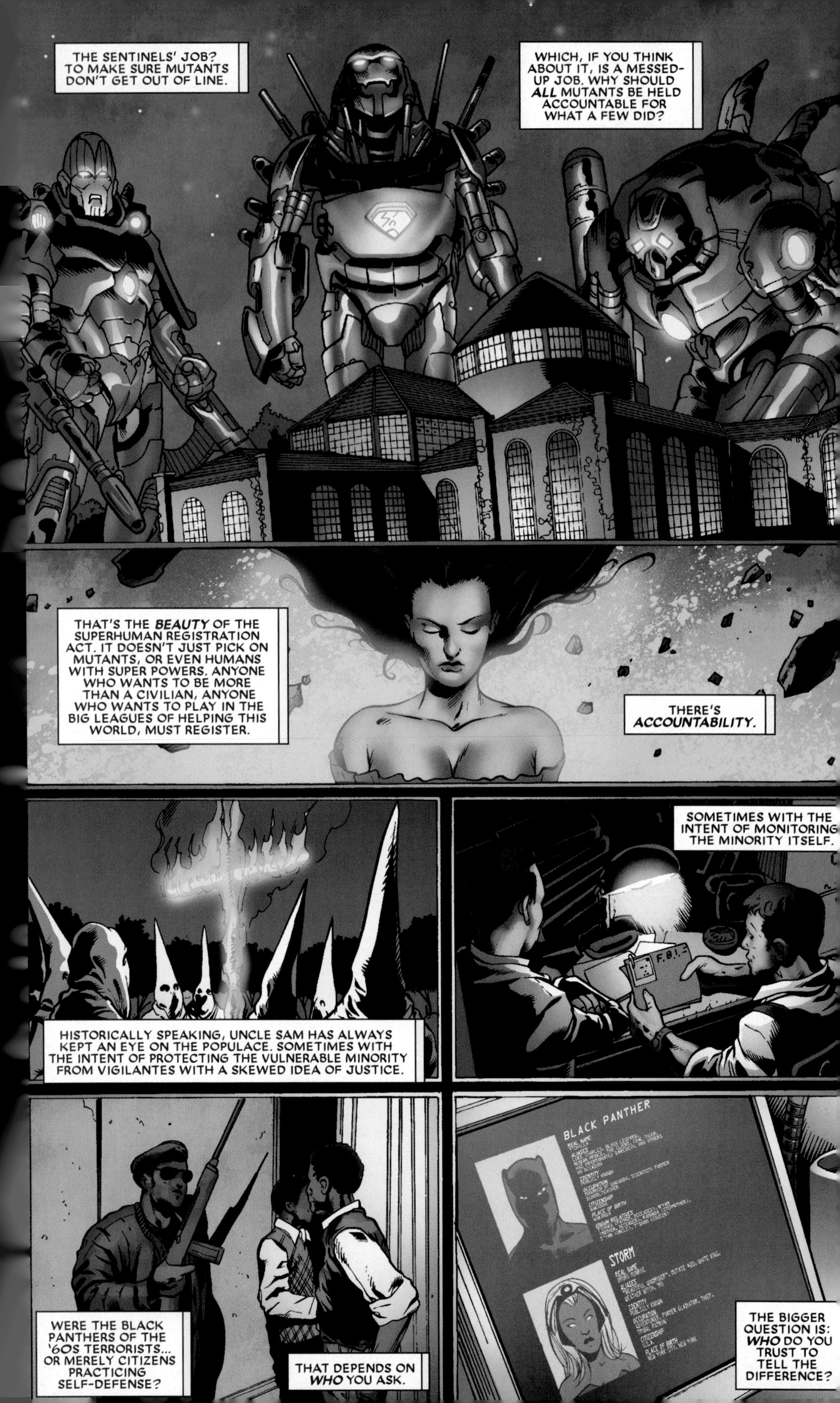
THE SENTINELS' JOB? TO MAKE SURE MUTANTS DON'T GET OUT OF LINE.
WHICH, IF YOU THINK ABOUT IT, IS A MESSED-UP JOB. WHY SHOULD *ALL* MUTANTS BE HELD ACCOUNTABLE FOR WHAT A FEW DID?
THAT'S THE *BEAUTY* OF THE SUPERHUMAN REGISTRATION ACT. IT DOESN'T JUST PICK ON MUTANTS, OR EVEN HUMANS WITH SUPER POWERS. ANYONE WHO WANTS TO BE MORE THAN A CIVILIAN, ANYONE WHO WANTS TO PLAY IN THE BIG LEAGUES OF HELPING THIS WORLD, MUST REGISTER.
THERE'S *ACCOUNTABILITY.*
HISTORICALLY SPEAKING, UNCLE SAM HAS ALWAYS KEPT AN EYE ON THE POPULACE. SOMETIMES WITH THE INTENT OF PROTECTING THE VULNERABLE MINORITY FROM VIGILANTES WITH A SKEWED IDEA OF JUSTICE.
SOMETIMES WITH THE INTENT OF MONITORING THE MINORITY ITSELF.
F.B.I.
WERE THE BLACK PANTHERS OF THE '60S TERRORISTS... OR MERELY CITIZENS PRACTICING SELF-DEFENSE?
THAT DEPENDS ON *WHO* YOU ASK.
BLACK PANTHER
STORM
THE BIGGER QUESTION IS: *WHO* DO YOU TRUST TO TELL THE DIFFERENCE?

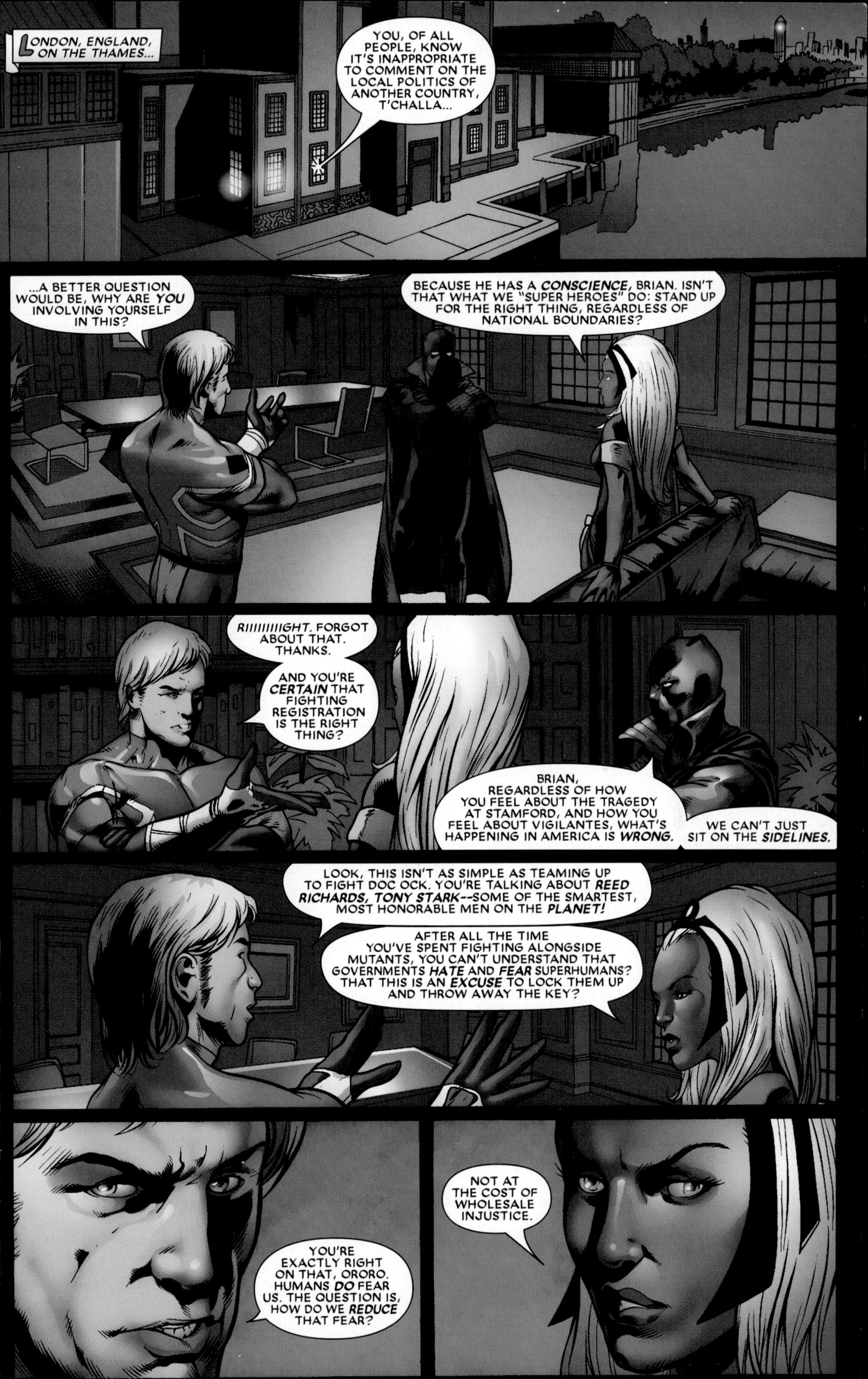
LONDON, ENGLAND, ON THE THAMES...
YOU, OF ALL PEOPLE, KNOW IT'S INAPPROPRIATE TO COMMENT ON THE LOCAL POLITICS OF ANOTHER COUNTRY, T'CHALLA...
...A BETTER QUESTION WOULD BE, WHY ARE YOU INVOLVING YOURSELF IN THIS?
BECAUSE HE HAS A CONSCIENCE, BRIAN. ISN'T THAT WHAT WE "SUPER HEROES" DO: STAND UP FOR THE RIGHT THING, REGARDLESS OF NATIONAL BOUNDARIES?
RIIIIIIIIGHT. FORGOT ABOUT THAT. THANKS.
AND YOU'RE CERTAIN THAT FIGHTING REGISTRATION IS THE RIGHT THING?
BRIAN, REGARDLESS OF HOW YOU FEEL ABOUT THE TRAGEDY AT STAMFORD, AND HOW YOU FEEL ABOUT VIGILANTES, WHAT'S HAPPENING IN AMERICA IS WRONG.
WE CAN'T JUST SIT ON THE SIDELINES.
LOOK, THIS ISN'T AS SIMPLE AS TEAMING UP TO FIGHT DOC OCK. YOU'RE TALKING ABOUT REED RICHARDS, TONY STARK--SOME OF THE SMARTEST, MOST HONORABLE MEN ON THE PLANET!
AFTER ALL THE TIME YOU'VE SPENT FIGHTING ALONGSIDE MUTANTS, YOU CAN'T UNDERSTAND THAT GOVERNMENTS HATE AND FEAR SUPERHUMANS? THAT THIS IS AN EXCUSE TO LOCK THEM UP AND THROW AWAY THE KEY?
YOU'RE EXACTLY RIGHT ON THAT, ORORO. HUMANS DO FEAR US. THE QUESTION IS, HOW DO WE REDUCE THAT FEAR?
NOT AT THE COST OF WHOLESALE INJUSTICE.

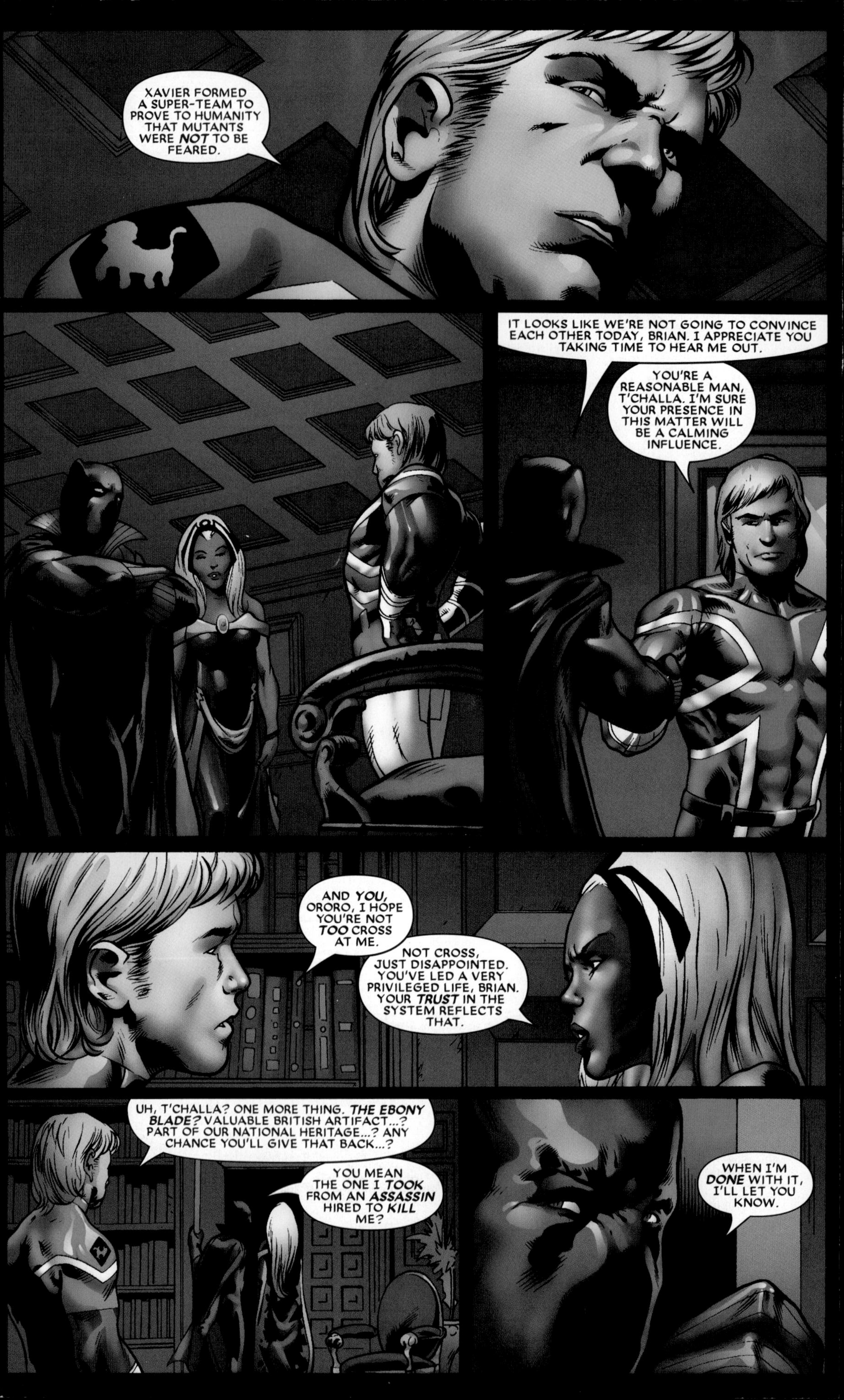
XAVIER FORMED A SUPER-TEAM TO PROVE TO HUMANITY THAT MUTANTS WERE *NOT* TO BE FEARED.
IT LOOKS LIKE WE'RE NOT GOING TO CONVINCE EACH OTHER TODAY, BRIAN. I APPRECIATE YOU TAKING TIME TO HEAR ME OUT.
YOU'RE A REASONABLE MAN, T'CHALLA. I'M SURE YOUR PRESENCE IN THIS MATTER WILL BE A CALMING INFLUENCE.
AND *YOU*, ORORO, I HOPE YOU'RE NOT *TOO* CROSS AT ME.
NOT CROSS, JUST DISAPPOINTED. YOU'VE LED A VERY PRIVILEGED LIFE, BRIAN. YOUR *TRUST* IN THE SYSTEM REFLECTS THAT.
UH, T'CHALLA? ONE MORE THING. *THE EBONY BLADE?* VALUABLE BRITISH ARTIFACT...? PART OF OUR NATIONAL HERITAGE...? ANY CHANCE YOU'LL GIVE THAT BACK...?
YOU MEAN THE ONE I *TOOK* FROM AN *ASSASSIN* HIRED TO *KILL* ME?
WHEN I'M *DONE* WITH IT, I'LL LET YOU KNOW.

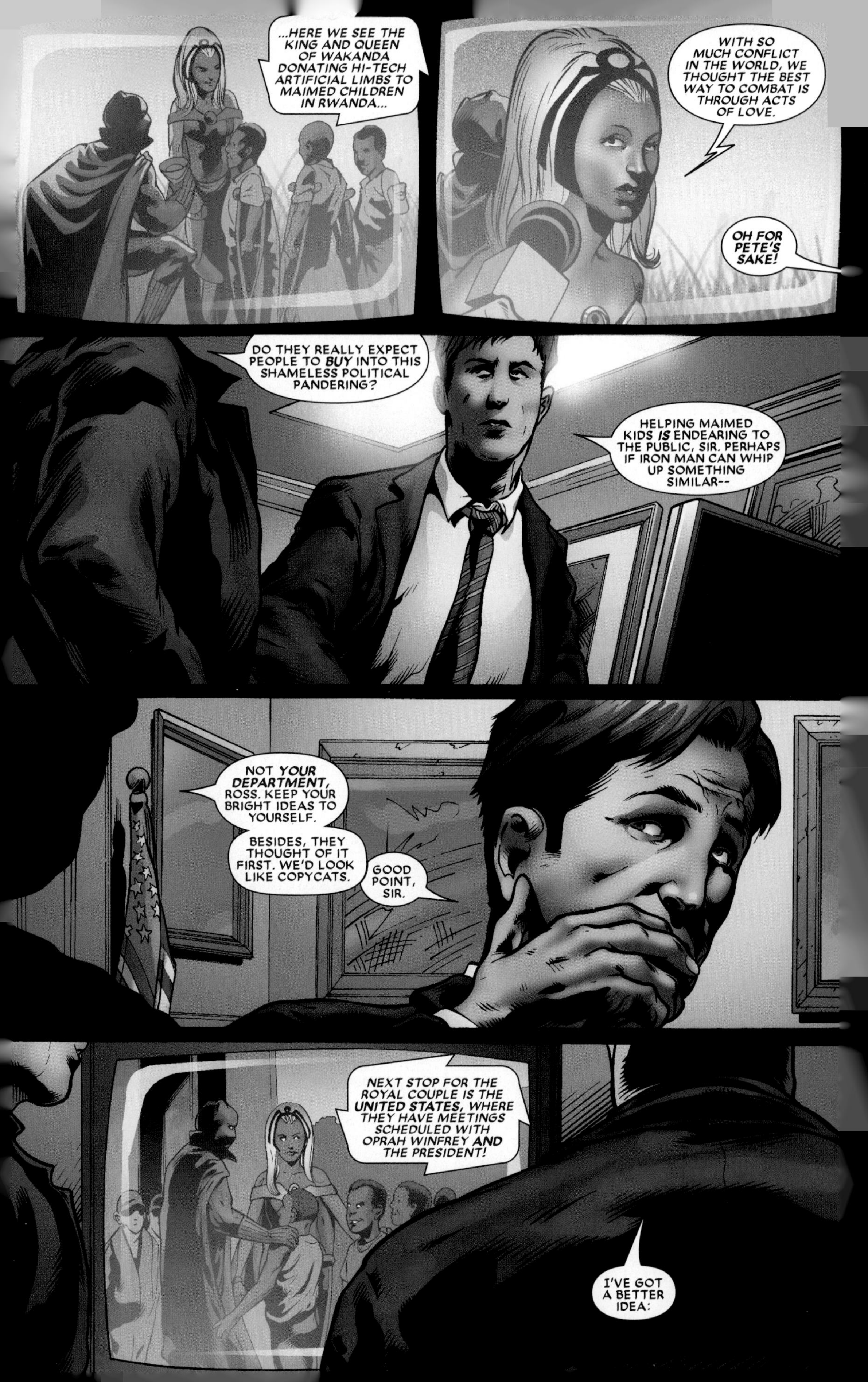
...HERE WE SEE THE KING AND QUEEN OF WAKANDA DONATING HI-TECH ARTIFICIAL LIMBS TO MAIMED CHILDREN IN RWANDA...
WITH SO MUCH CONFLICT IN THE WORLD, WE THOUGHT THE BEST WAY TO COMBAT IS THROUGH ACTS OF LOVE.
OH FOR PETE'S SAKE!
DO THEY REALLY EXPECT PEOPLE TO BUY INTO THIS SHAMELESS POLITICAL PANDERING?
HELPING MAIMED KIDS IS ENDEARING TO THE PUBLIC, SIR. PERHAPS IF IRON MAN CAN WHIP UP SOMETHING SIMILAR--
NOT YOUR DEPARTMENT, ROSS. KEEP YOUR BRIGHT IDEAS TO YOURSELF.
BESIDES, THEY THOUGHT OF IT FIRST. WE'D LOOK LIKE COPYCATS.
GOOD POINT, SIR.
NEXT STOP FOR THE ROYAL COUPLE IS THE UNITED STATES, WHERE THEY HAVE MEETINGS SCHEDULED WITH OPRAH WINFREY AND THE PRESIDENT!
I'VE GOT A BETTER IDEA:

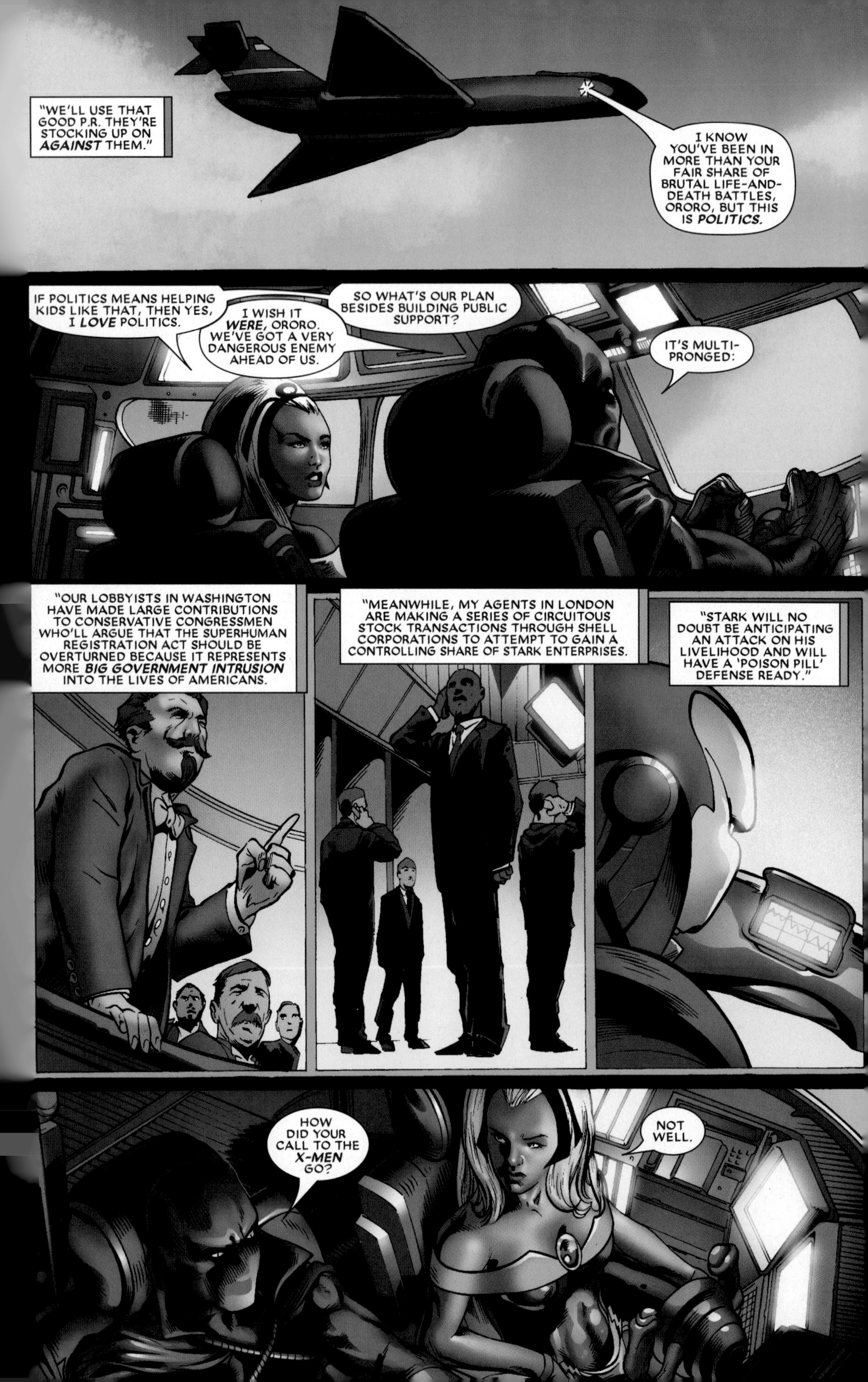
"WE'LL USE THAT GOOD P.R. THEY'RE STOCKING UP ON AGAINST THEM."
I KNOW YOU'VE BEEN IN MORE THAN YOUR FAIR SHARE OF BRUTAL LIFE-AND-DEATH BATTLES, ORORO, BUT THIS IS POLITICS.
IF POLITICS MEANS HELPING KIDS LIKE THAT, THEN YES, I LOVE POLITICS.
I WISH IT WERE, ORORO. WE'VE GOT A VERY DANGEROUS ENEMY AHEAD OF US.
SO WHAT'S OUR PLAN BESIDES BUILDING PUBLIC SUPPORT?
IT'S MULTI-PRONGED:
"OUR LOBBYISTS IN WASHINGTON HAVE MADE LARGE CONTRIBUTIONS TO CONSERVATIVE CONGRESSMEN WHO'LL ARGUE THAT THE SUPERHUMAN REGISTRATION ACT SHOULD BE OVERTURNED BECAUSE IT REPRESENTS MORE BIG GOVERNMENT INTRUSION INTO THE LIVES OF AMERICANS.
"MEANWHILE, MY AGENTS IN LONDON ARE MAKING A SERIES OF CIRCUITOUS STOCK TRANSACTIONS THROUGH SHELL CORPORATIONS TO ATTEMPT TO GAIN A CONTROLLING SHARE OF STARK ENTERPRISES.
"STARK WILL NO DOUBT BE ANTICIPATING AN ATTACK ON HIS LIVELIHOOD AND WILL HAVE A 'POISON PILL' DEFENSE READY."
HOW DID YOUR CALL TO THE X-MEN GO?
NOT WELL.

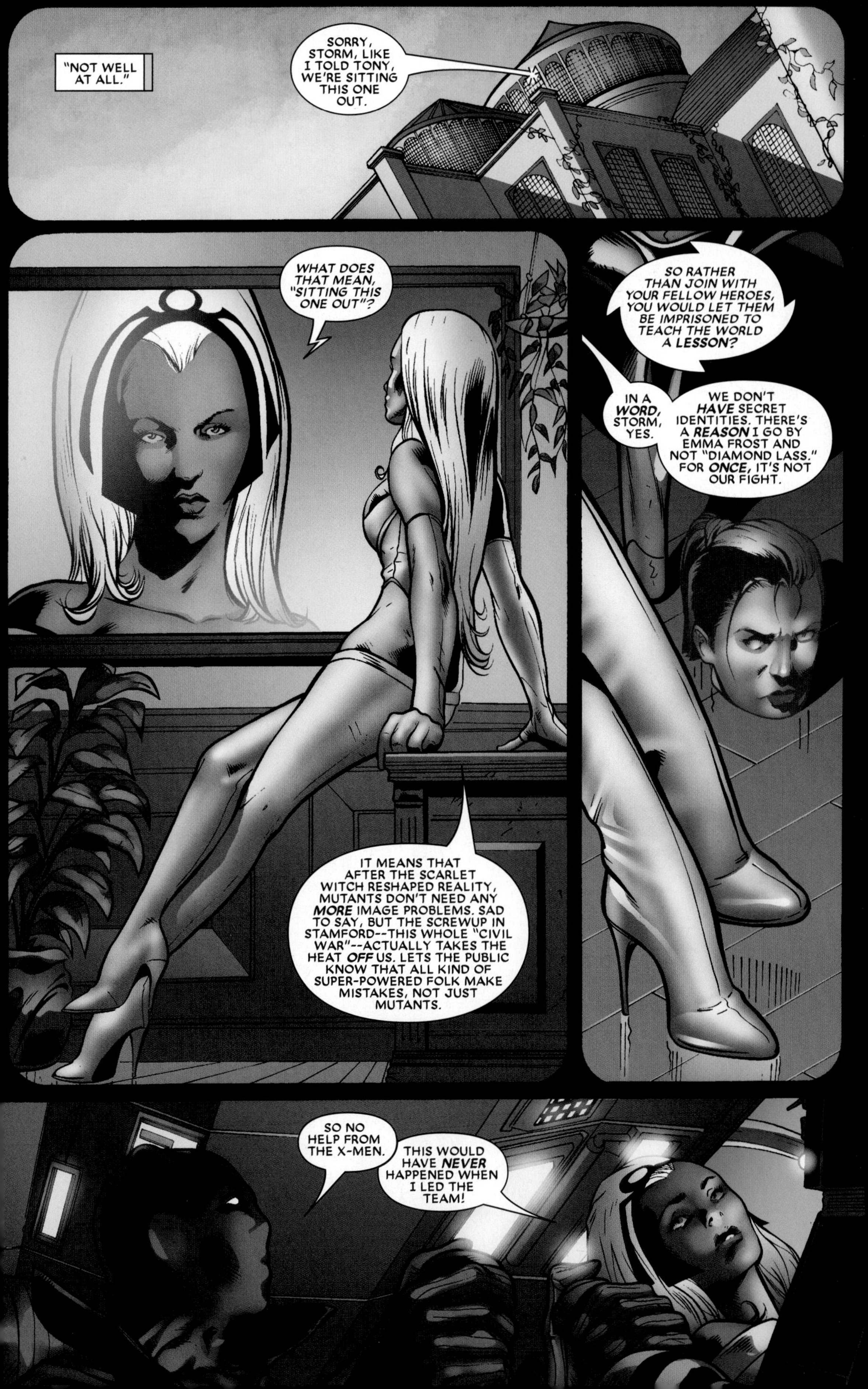
"NOT WELL AT ALL."
SORRY, STORM, LIKE I TOLD TONY, WE'RE SITTING THIS ONE OUT.
WHAT DOES THAT MEAN, "SITTING THIS ONE OUT"?
IT MEANS THAT AFTER THE SCARLET WITCH RESHAPED REALITY, MUTANTS DON'T NEED ANY MORE IMAGE PROBLEMS. SAD TO SAY, BUT THE SCREWUP IN STAMFORD--THIS WHOLE "CIVIL WAR"--ACTUALLY TAKES THE HEAT OFF US. LETS THE PUBLIC KNOW THAT ALL KIND OF SUPER-POWERED FOLK MAKE MISTAKES, NOT JUST MUTANTS.
SO RATHER THAN JOIN WITH YOUR FELLOW HEROES, YOU WOULD LET THEM BE IMPRISONED TO TEACH THE WORLD A LESSON?
IN A WORD, STORM, YES.
WE DON'T HAVE SECRET IDENTITIES. THERE'S A REASON I GO BY EMMA FROST AND NOT "DIAMOND LASS." FOR ONCE, IT'S NOT OUR FIGHT.
SO NO HELP FROM THE X-MEN.
THIS WOULD HAVE NEVER HAPPENED WHEN I LED THE TEAM!

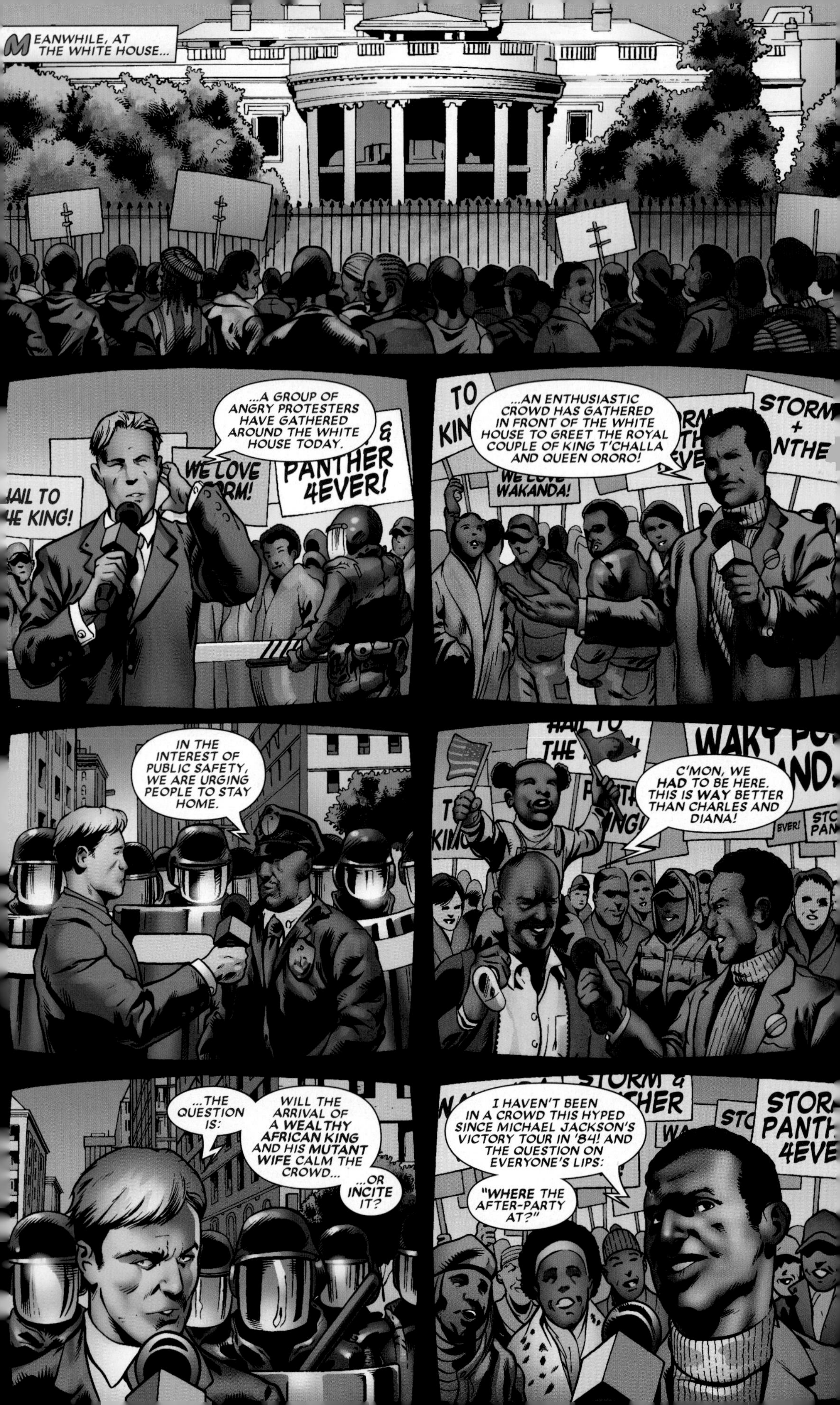
MEANWHILE, AT THE WHITE HOUSE...
...A GROUP OF ANGRY PROTESTERS HAVE GATHERED AROUND THE WHITE HOUSE TODAY.
PANTHER 4EVER!
...AN ENTHUSIASTIC CROWD HAS GATHERED IN FRONT OF THE WHITE HOUSE TO GREET THE ROYAL COUPLE OF KING T'CHALLA AND QUEEN ORORO!
WAKANDA!
IN THE INTEREST OF PUBLIC SAFETY, WE ARE URGING PEOPLE TO STAY HOME.
C'MON, WE HAD TO BE HERE. THIS IS WAY BETTER THAN CHARLES AND DIANA!
...THE QUESTION IS:
WILL THE ARRIVAL OF A WEALTHY AFRICAN KING AND HIS MUTANT WIFE CALM THE CROWD...
...OR INCITE IT?
I HAVEN'T BEEN IN A CROWD THIS HYPED SINCE MICHAEL JACKSON'S VICTORY TOUR IN '84! AND THE QUESTION ON EVERYONE'S LIPS:
"WHERE THE AFTER-PARTY AT?"

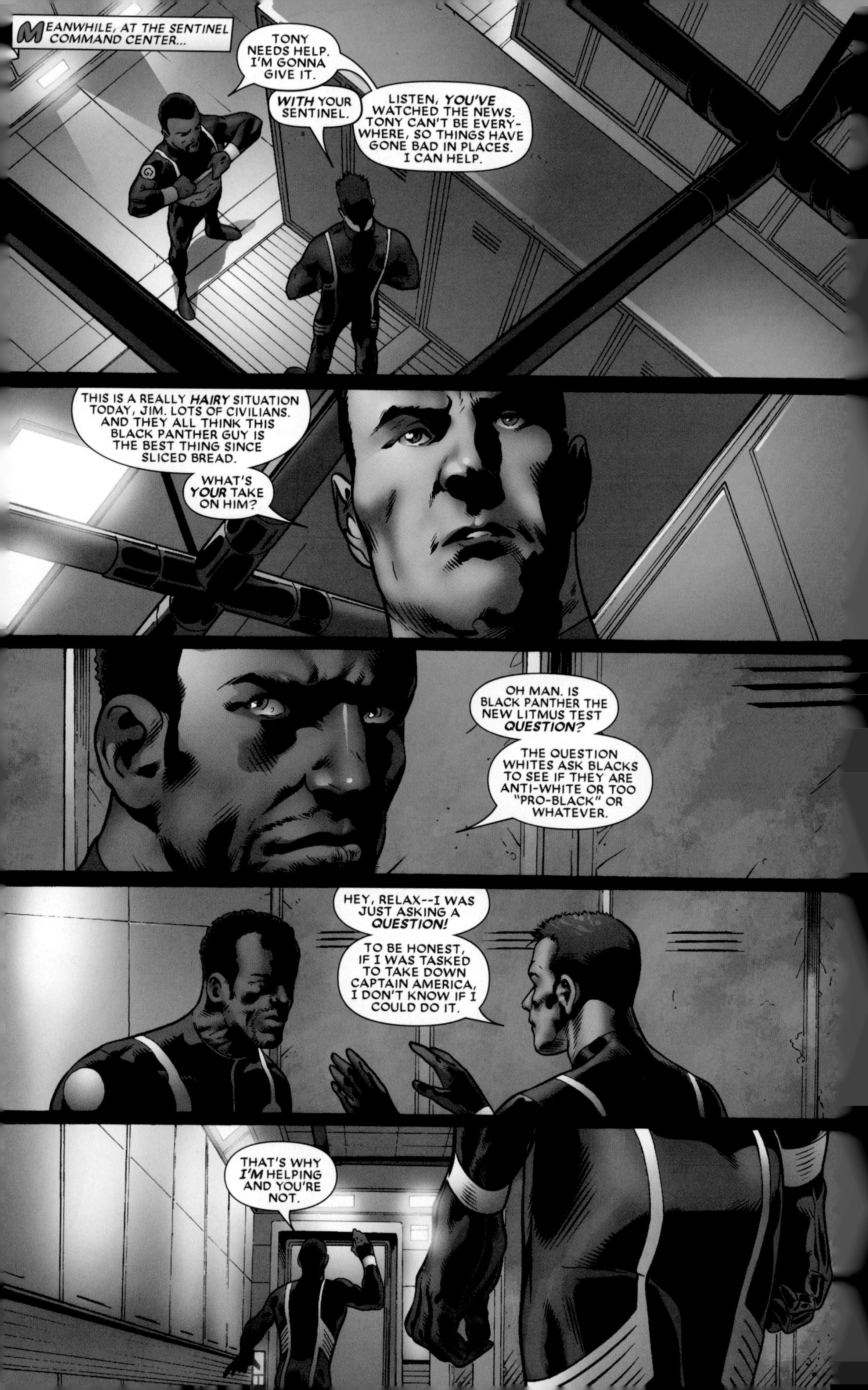
MEANWHILE, AT THE SENTINEL COMMAND CENTER...
TONY NEEDS HELP. I'M GONNA GIVE IT.
WITH YOUR SENTINEL.
LISTEN, YOU'VE WATCHED THE NEWS. TONY CAN'T BE EVERYWHERE, SO THINGS HAVE GONE BAD IN PLACES. I CAN HELP.
THIS IS A REALLY HAIRY SITUATION TODAY, JIM. LOTS OF CIVILIANS. AND THEY ALL THINK THIS BLACK PANTHER GUY IS THE BEST THING SINCE SLICED BREAD.
WHAT'S YOUR TAKE ON HIM?
OH MAN. IS BLACK PANTHER THE NEW LITMUS TEST QUESTION?
THE QUESTION WHITES ASK BLACKS TO SEE IF THEY ARE ANTI-WHITE OR TOO "PRO-BLACK" OR WHATEVER.
HEY, RELAX--I WAS JUST ASKING A QUESTION!
TO BE HONEST, IF I WAS TASKED TO TAKE DOWN CAPTAIN AMERICA, I DON'T KNOW IF I COULD DO IT.
THAT'S WHY I'M HELPING AND YOU'RE NOT.

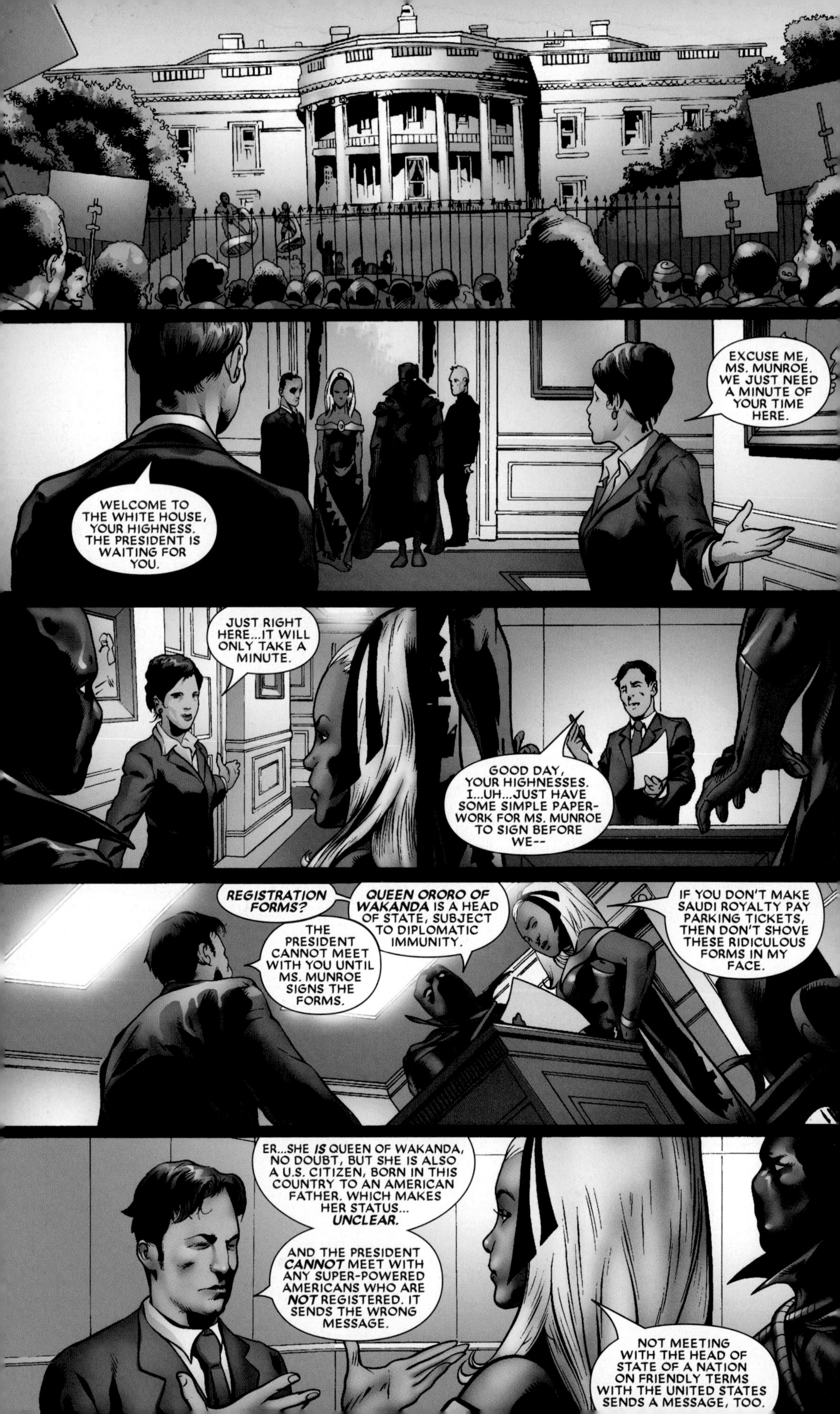
EXCUSE ME, MS. MUNROE. WE JUST NEED A MINUTE OF YOUR TIME HERE.
WELCOME TO THE WHITE HOUSE, YOUR HIGHNESS. THE PRESIDENT IS WAITING FOR YOU.
JUST RIGHT HERE...IT WILL ONLY TAKE A MINUTE.
GOOD DAY, YOUR HIGHNESSES. I...UH...JUST HAVE SOME SIMPLE PAPER-WORK FOR MS. MUNROE TO SIGN BEFORE WE--
REGISTRATION FORMS?
THE PRESIDENT CANNOT MEET WITH YOU UNTIL MS. MUNROE SIGNS THE FORMS.
QUEEN ORORO OF WAKANDA IS A HEAD OF STATE, SUBJECT TO DIPLOMATIC IMMUNITY.
IF YOU DON'T MAKE SAUDI ROYALTY PAY PARKING TICKETS, THEN DON'T SHOVE THESE RIDICULOUS FORMS IN MY FACE.
ER...SHE IS QUEEN OF WAKANDA, NO DOUBT, BUT SHE IS ALSO A U.S. CITIZEN, BORN IN THIS COUNTRY TO AN AMERICAN FATHER. WHICH MAKES HER STATUS... UNCLEAR.
AND THE PRESIDENT CANNOT MEET WITH ANY SUPER-POWERED AMERICANS WHO ARE NOT REGISTERED. IT SENDS THE WRONG MESSAGE.
NOT MEETING WITH THE HEAD OF STATE OF A NATION ON FRIENDLY TERMS WITH THE UNITED STATES SENDS A MESSAGE, TOO.

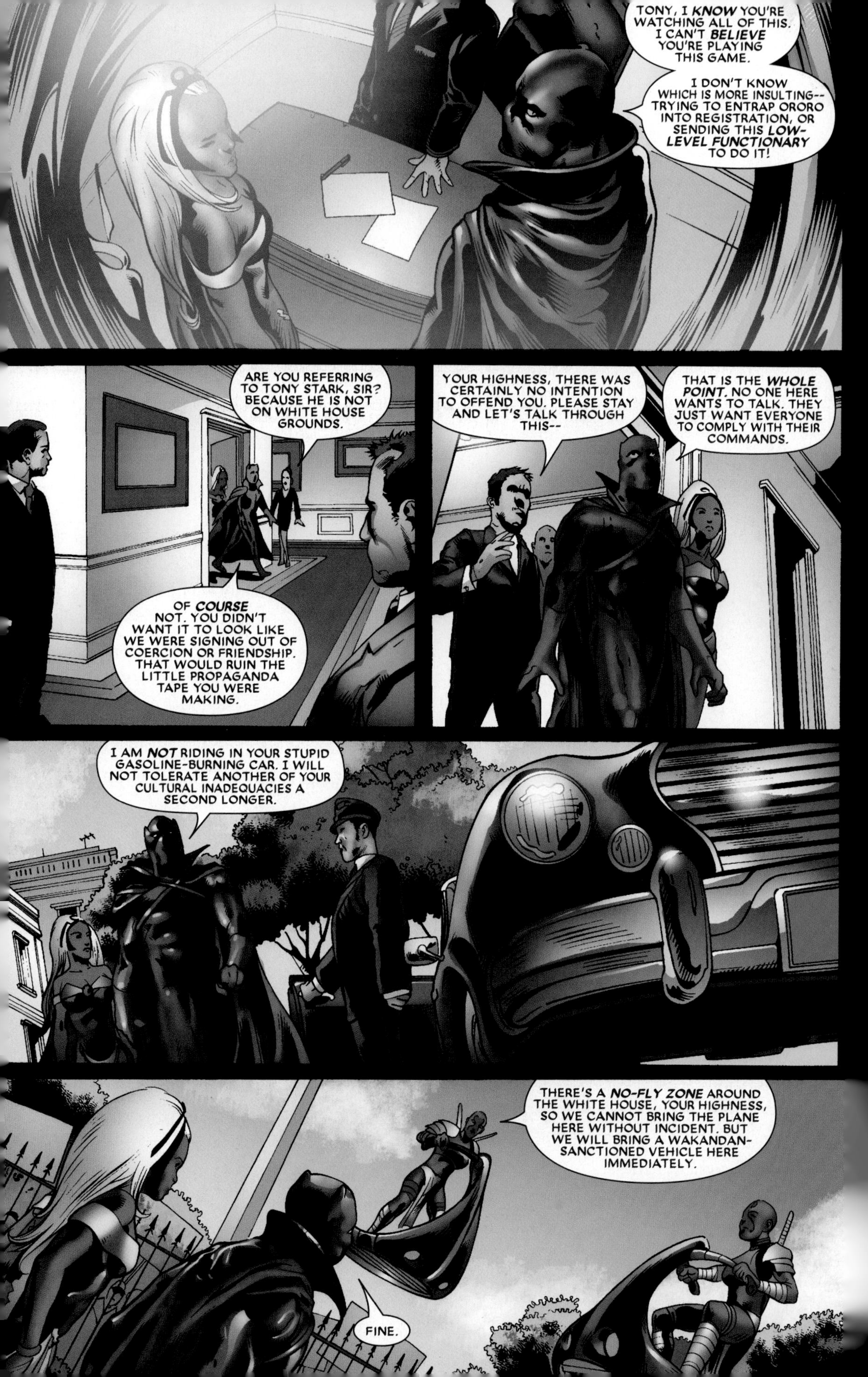
TONY, I KNOW YOU'RE WATCHING ALL OF THIS. I CAN'T BELIEVE YOU'RE PLAYING THIS GAME.
I DON'T KNOW WHICH IS MORE INSULTING-- TRYING TO ENTRAP ORORO INTO REGISTRATION, OR SENDING THIS LOW-LEVEL FUNCTIONARY TO DO IT!
ARE YOU REFERRING TO TONY STARK, SIR? BECAUSE HE IS NOT ON WHITE HOUSE GROUNDS.
OF COURSE NOT. YOU DIDN'T WANT IT TO LOOK LIKE WE WERE SIGNING OUT OF COERCION OR FRIENDSHIP. THAT WOULD RUIN THE LITTLE PROPAGANDA TAPE YOU WERE MAKING.
YOUR HIGHNESS, THERE WAS CERTAINLY NO INTENTION TO OFFEND YOU. PLEASE STAY AND LET'S TALK THROUGH THIS--
THAT IS THE WHOLE POINT. NO ONE HERE WANTS TO TALK. THEY JUST WANT EVERYONE TO COMPLY WITH THEIR COMMANDS.
I AM NOT RIDING IN YOUR STUPID GASOLINE-BURNING CAR. I WILL NOT TOLERATE ANOTHER OF YOUR CULTURAL INADEQUACIES A SECOND LONGER.
THERE'S A NO-FLY ZONE AROUND THE WHITE HOUSE, YOUR HIGHNESS, SO WE CANNOT BRING THE PLANE HERE WITHOUT INCIDENT. BUT WE WILL BRING A WAKANDAN-SANCTIONED VEHICLE HERE IMMEDIATELY.
FINE.

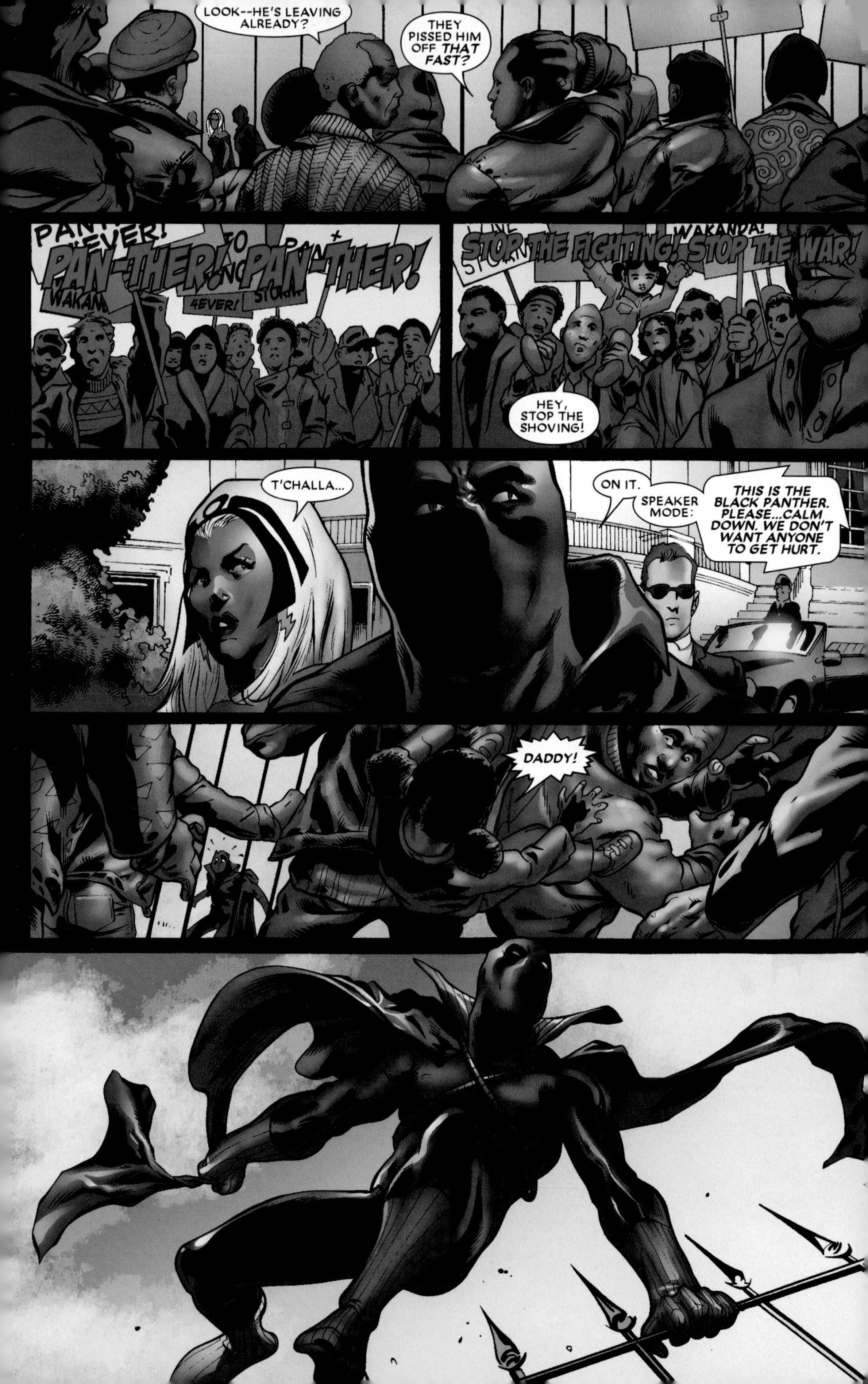

LOOK--HE'S LEAVING ALREADY?
THEY PISSED HIM OFF THAT FAST?
PAN-THER! PAN-THER!
4EVER!
STOP THE FIGHTING! STOP THE WAR!
WAKANDA!
HEY, STOP THE SHOVING!
T'CHALLA...
ON IT.
SPEAKER MODE:
THIS IS THE BLACK PANTHER. PLEASE...CALM DOWN. WE DON'T WANT ANYONE TO GET HURT.
DADDY!

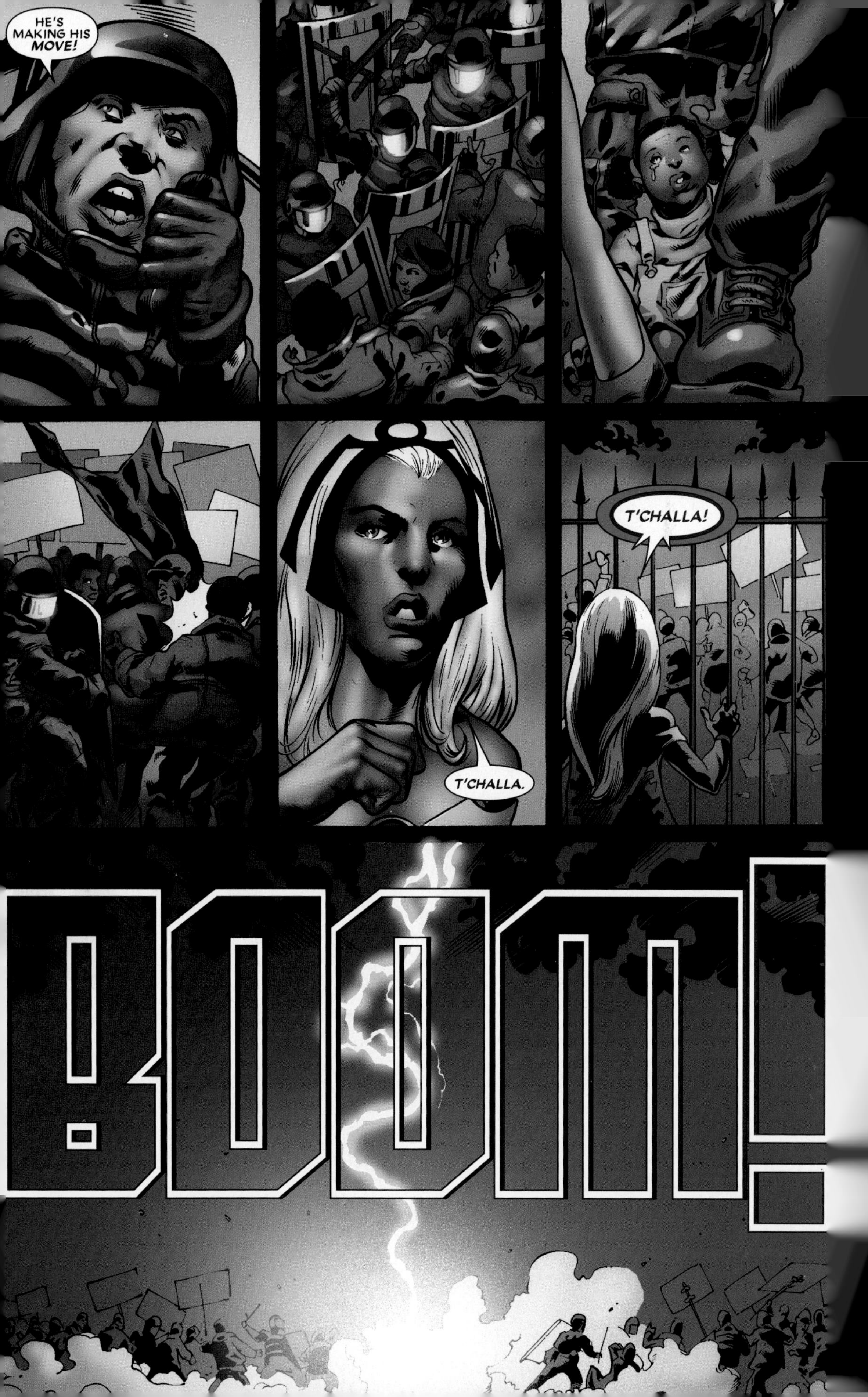
HE'S MAKING HIS MOVE!
T'CHALLA.
T'CHALLA!
BOOM!

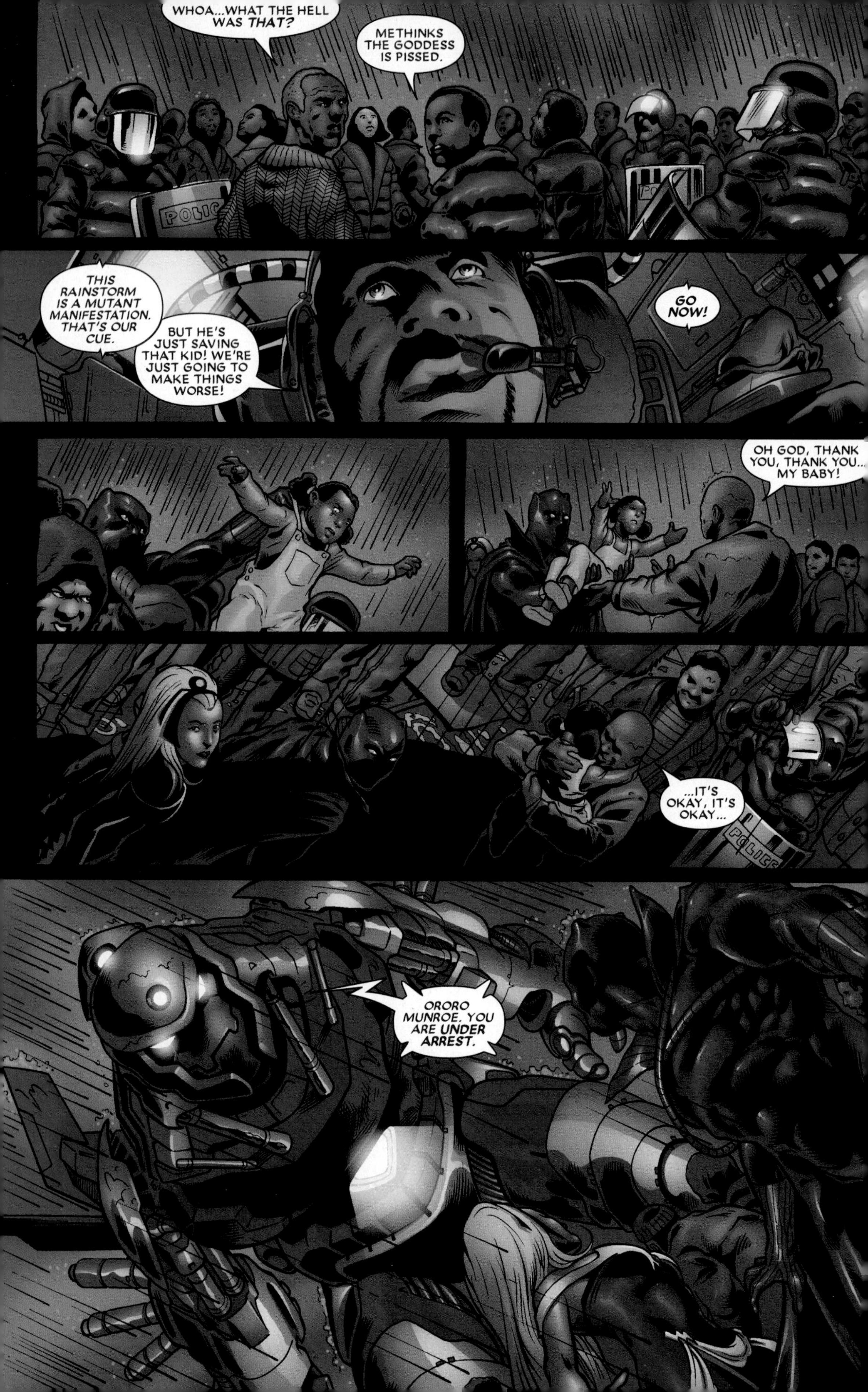
WHOA...WHAT THE HELL WAS THAT?
METHINKS THE GODDESS IS PISSED.
THIS RAINSTORM IS A MUTANT MANIFESTATION. THAT'S OUR CUE.
BUT HE'S JUST SAVING THAT KID! WE'RE JUST GOING TO MAKE THINGS WORSE!
GO NOW!
OH GOD, THANK YOU, THANK YOU... MY BABY!
...IT'S OKAY, IT'S OKAY...
ORORO MUNROE. YOU ARE UNDER ARREST.

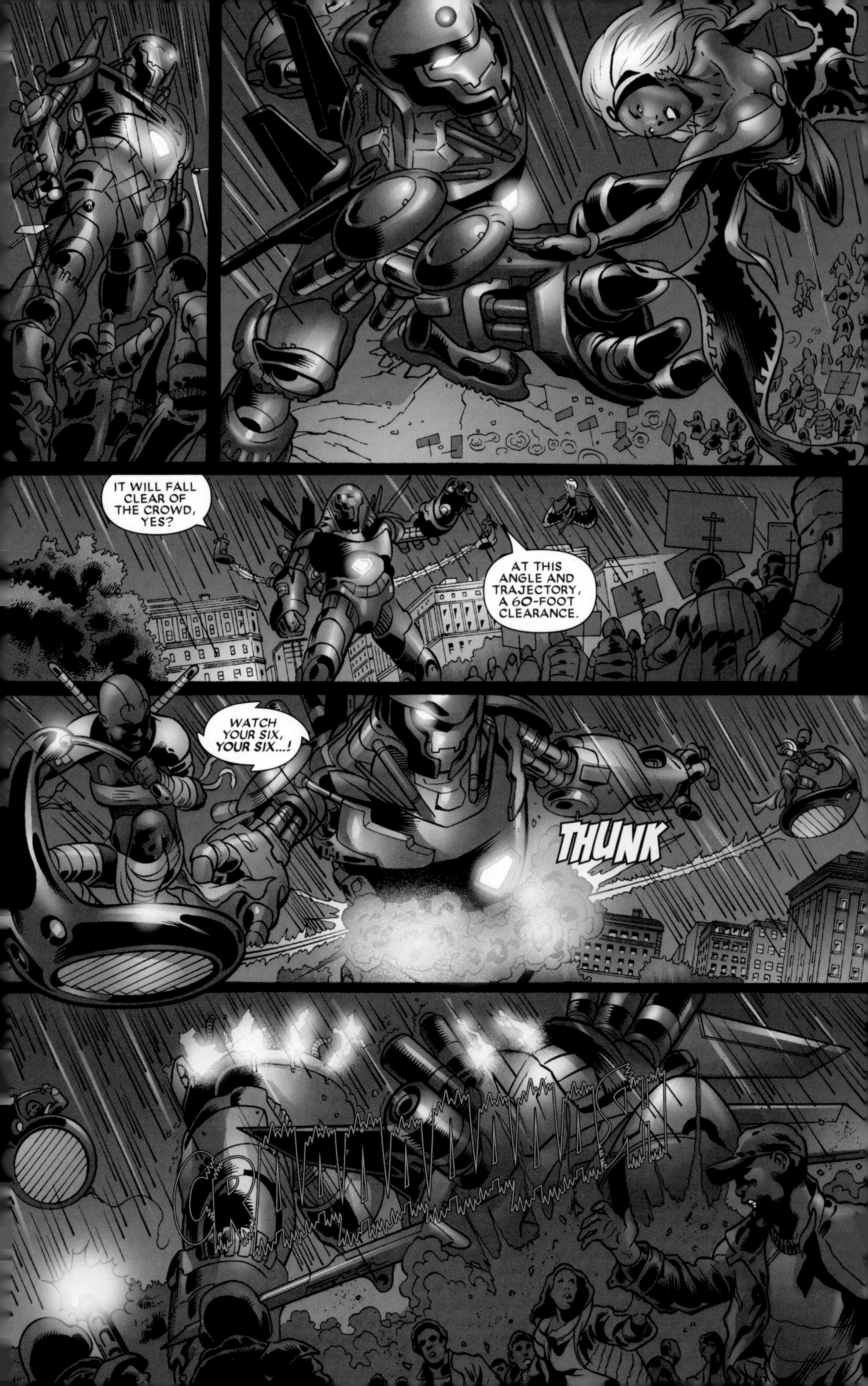
IT WILL FALL CLEAR OF THE CROWD, YES?
AT THIS ANGLE AND TRAJECTORY, A 60-FOOT CLEARANCE.
WATCH YOUR SIX, YOUR SIX...!
THUNK

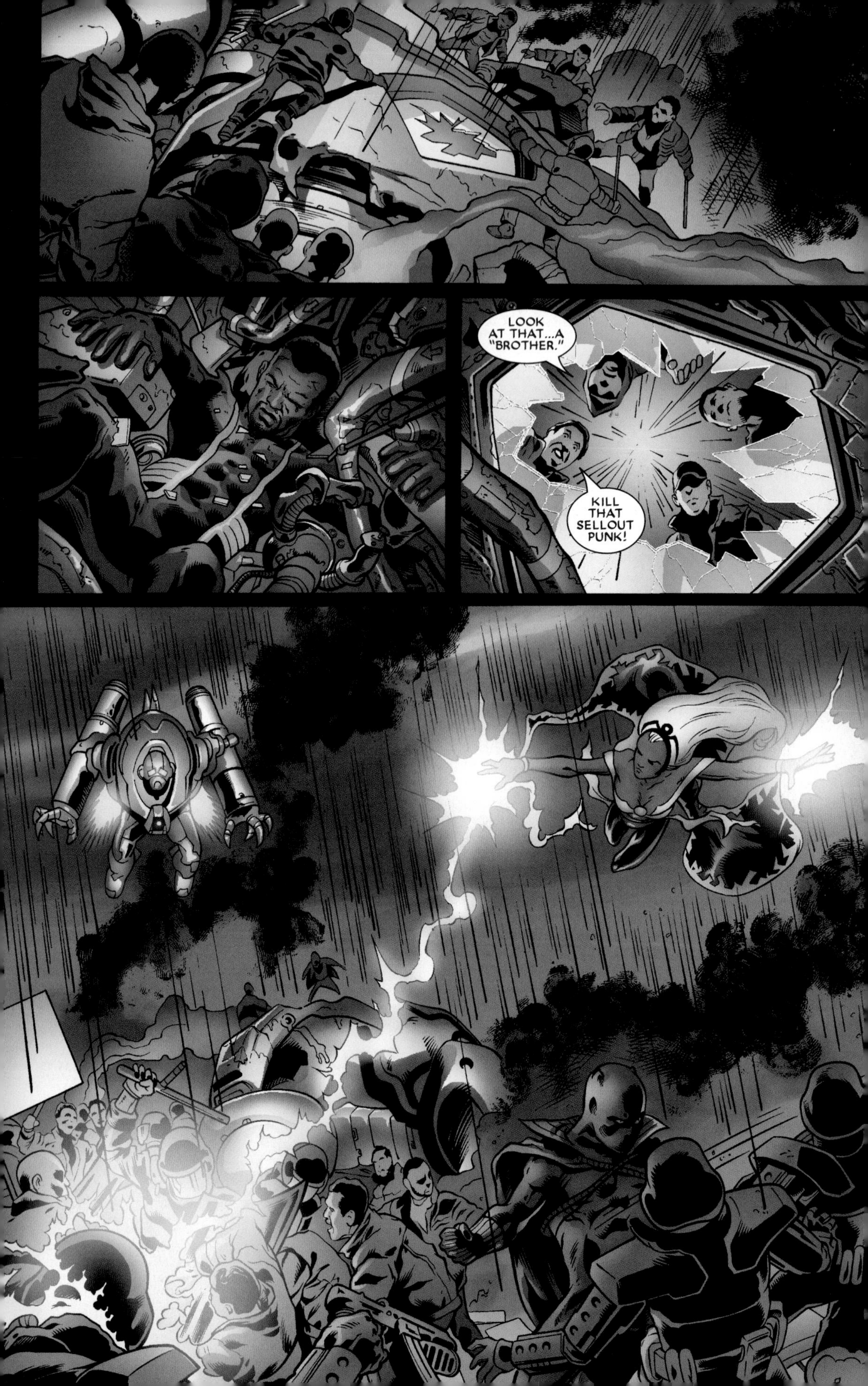
LOOK AT THAT...A "BROTHER."
KILL THAT SELLOUT PUNK!

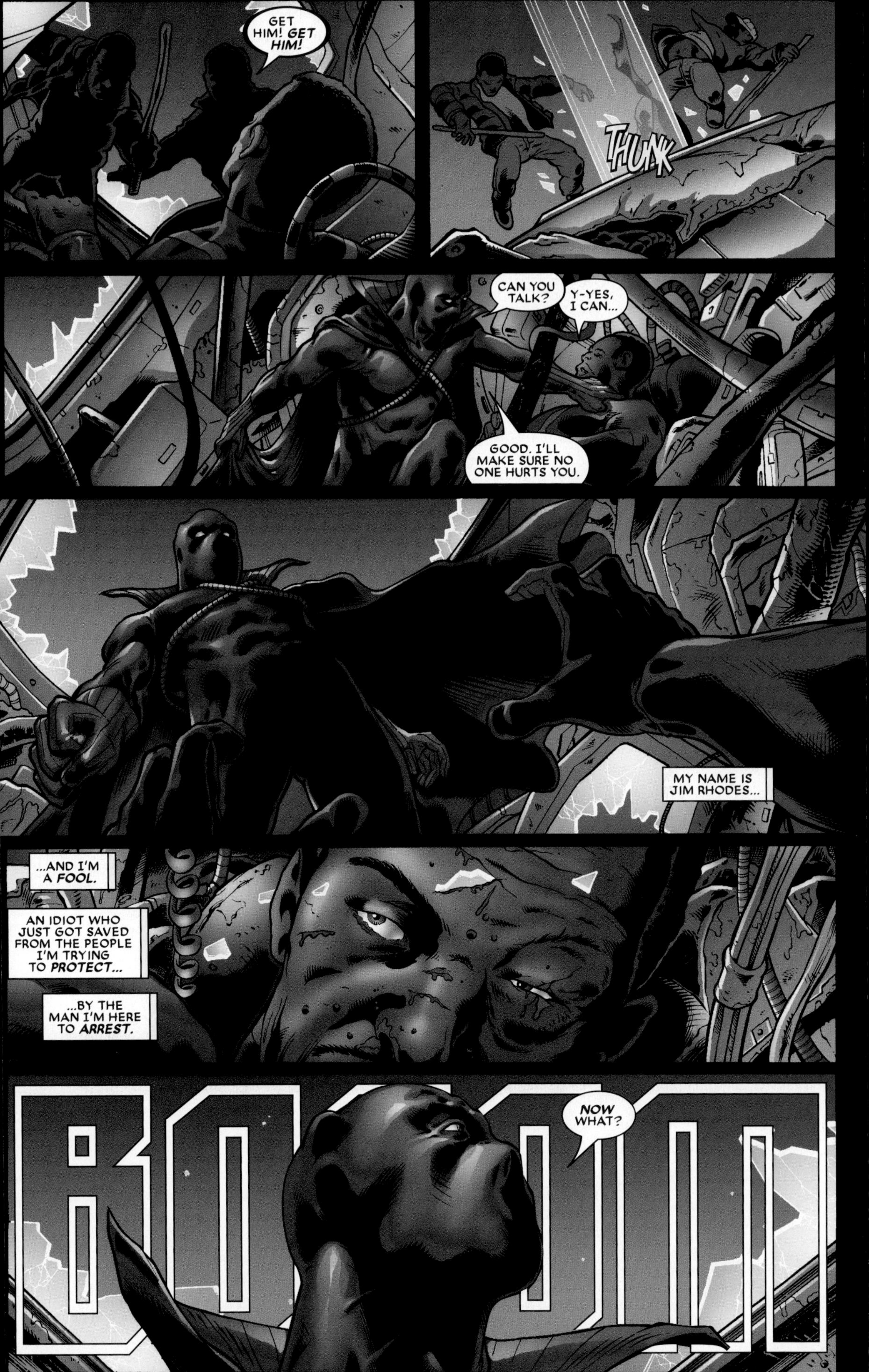
GET HIM! GET HIM!
THUNK
CAN YOU TALK?
Y-YES, I CAN...
GOOD. I'LL MAKE SURE NO ONE HURTS YOU.
MY NAME IS JIM RHODES...
...AND I'M A FOOL.
AN IDIOT WHO JUST GOT SAVED FROM THE PEOPLE I'M TRYING TO PROTECT...
...BY THE MAN I'M HERE TO ARREST.
NOW WHAT?

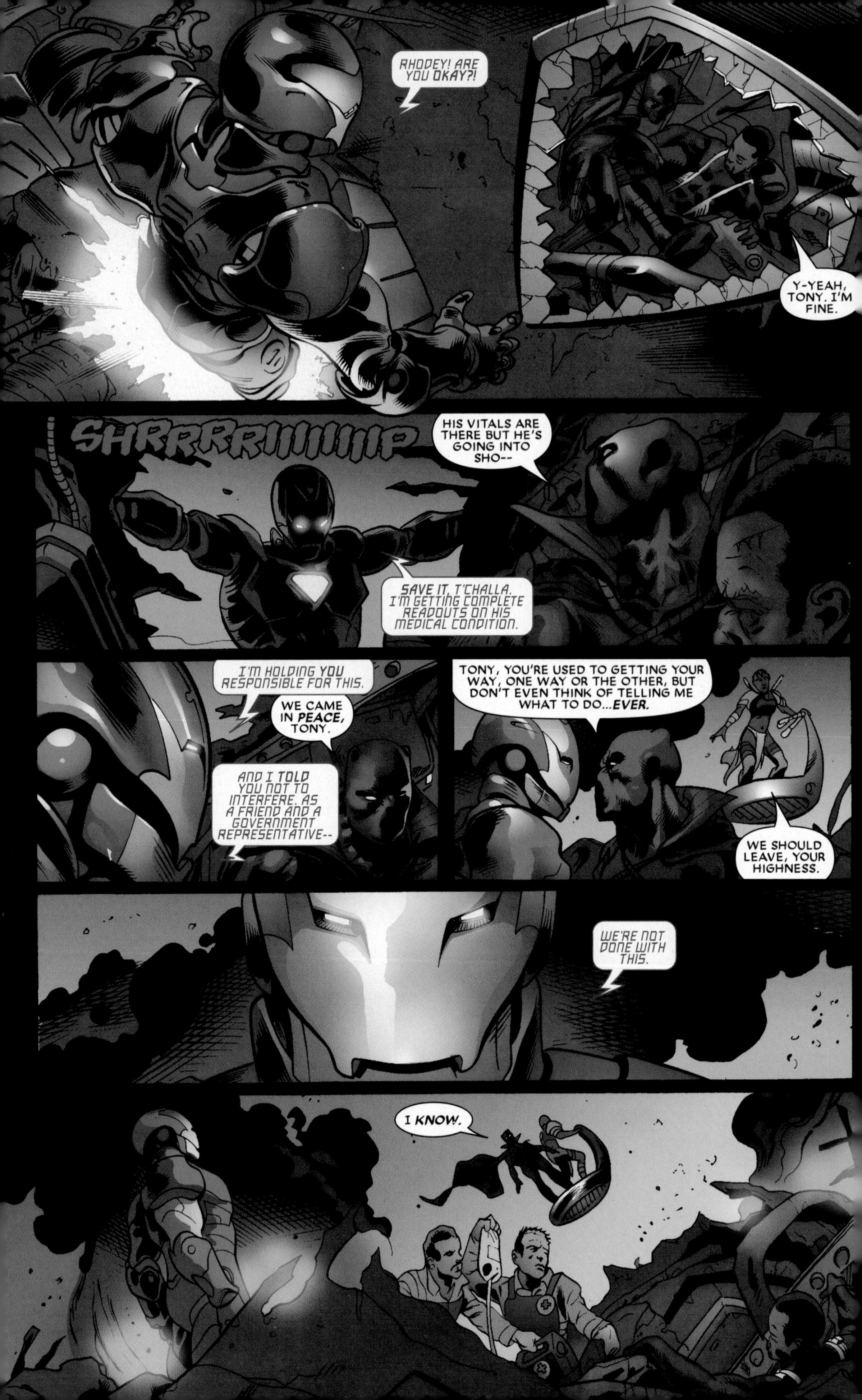

RHODEY! ARE YOU OKAY?!
Y-YEAH, TONY. I'M FINE.
SHRRRRIIIIIIIP
HIS VITALS ARE THERE BUT HE'S GOING INTO SHO--
SAVE IT, T'CHALLA. I'M GETTING COMPLETE READOUTS ON HIS MEDICAL CONDITION.
I'M HOLDING YOU RESPONSIBLE FOR THIS.
WE CAME IN PEACE, TONY.
AND I TOLD YOU NOT TO INTERFERE. AS A FRIEND AND A GOVERNMENT REPRESENTATIVE--
TONY, YOU'RE USED TO GETTING YOUR WAY, ONE WAY OR THE OTHER, BUT DON'T EVEN THINK OF TELLING ME WHAT TO DO...EVER.
WE SHOULD LEAVE, YOUR HIGHNESS.
WE'RE NOT DONE WITH THIS.
I KNOW.

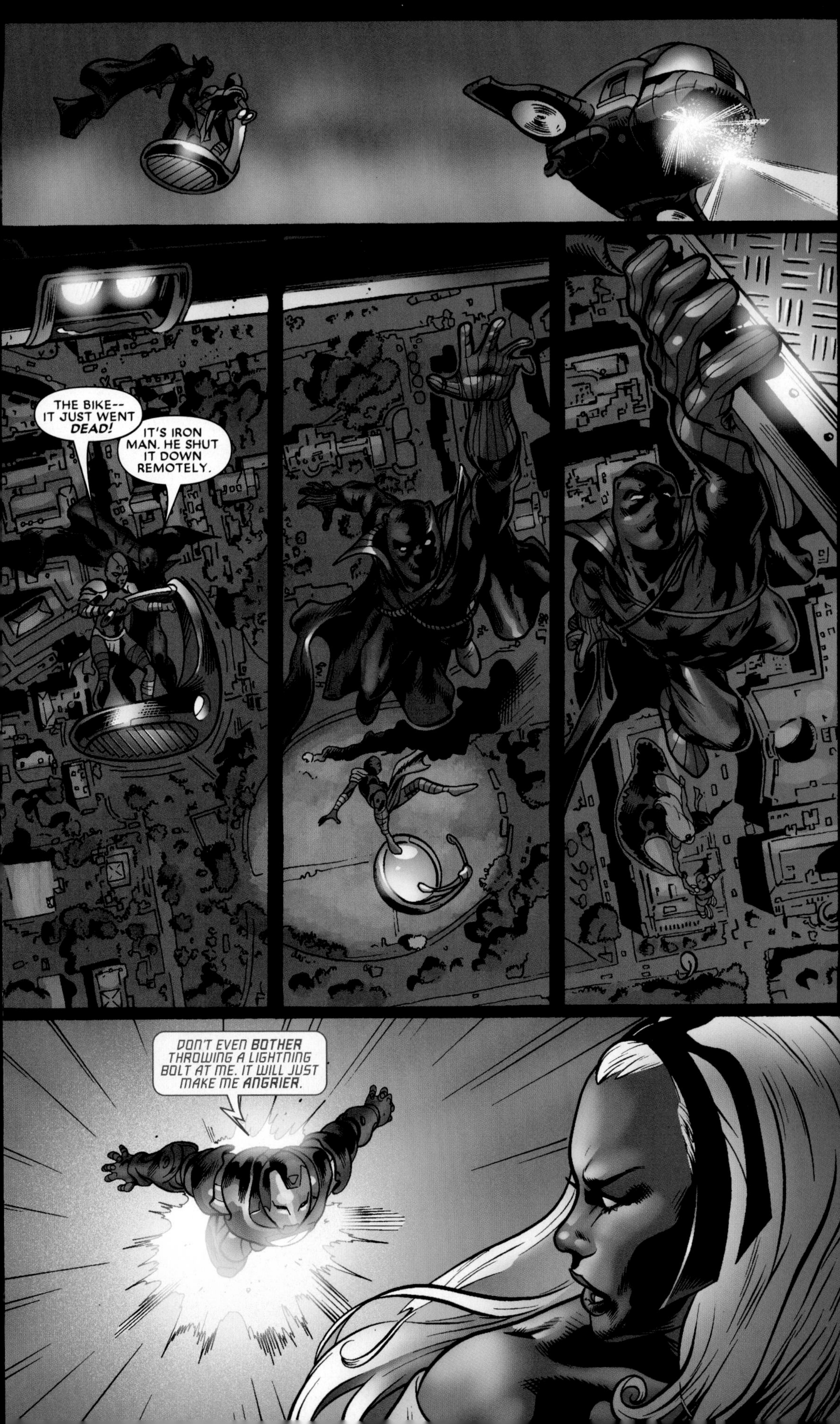
THE BIKE-- IT JUST WENT DEAD!
IT'S IRON MAN. HE SHUT IT DOWN REMOTELY.
DON'T EVEN BOTHER THROWING A LIGHTNING BOLT AT ME. IT WILL JUST MAKE ME ANGRIER.

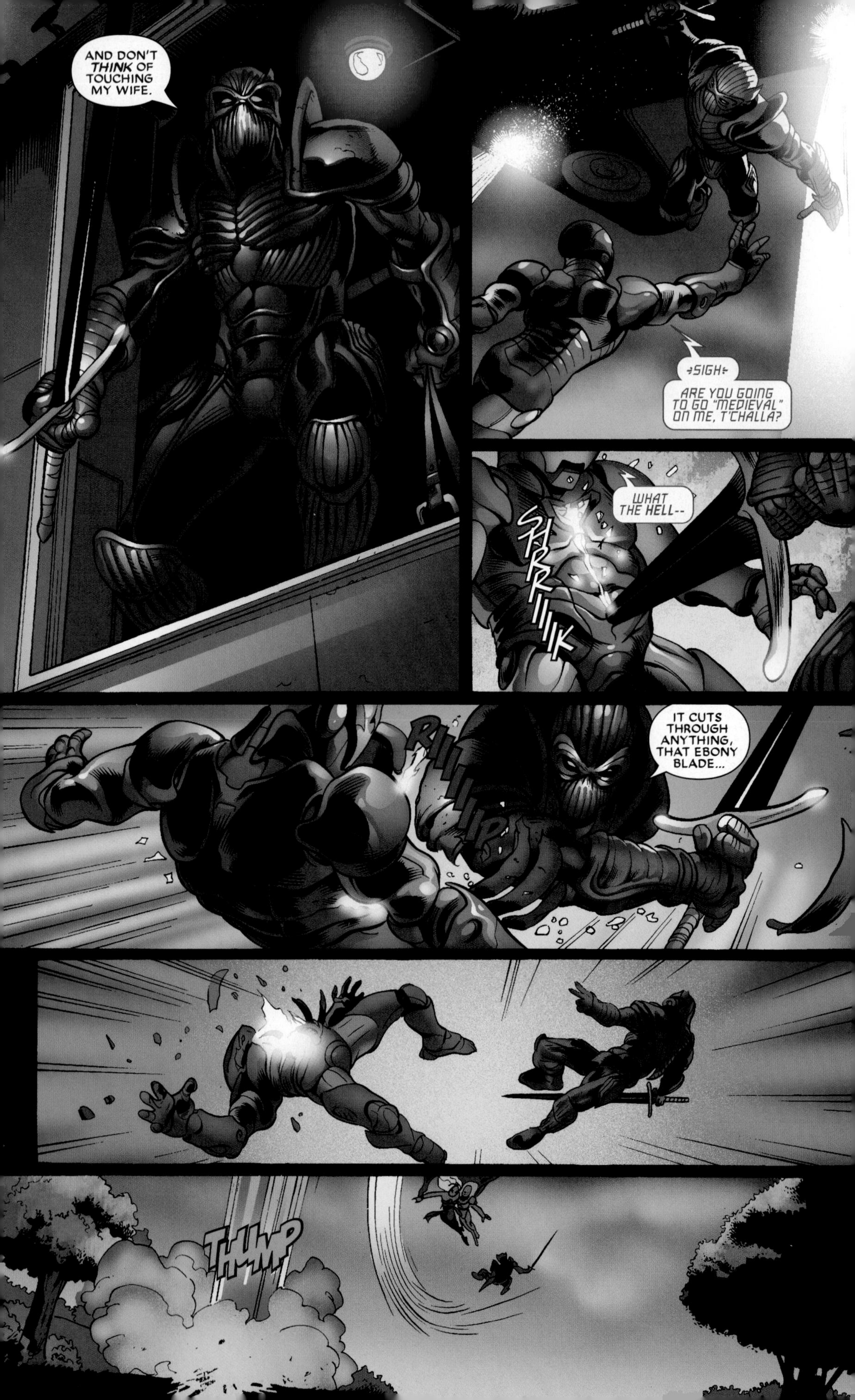
AND DON'T THINK OF TOUCHING MY WIFE.
SIGH
ARE YOU GOING TO GO "MEDIEVAL" ON ME, T'CHALLA?
WHAT THE HELL--
SHRRIIIIK
RIIIIIIP
IT CUTS THROUGH ANYTHING, THAT EBONY BLADE...
THUMP

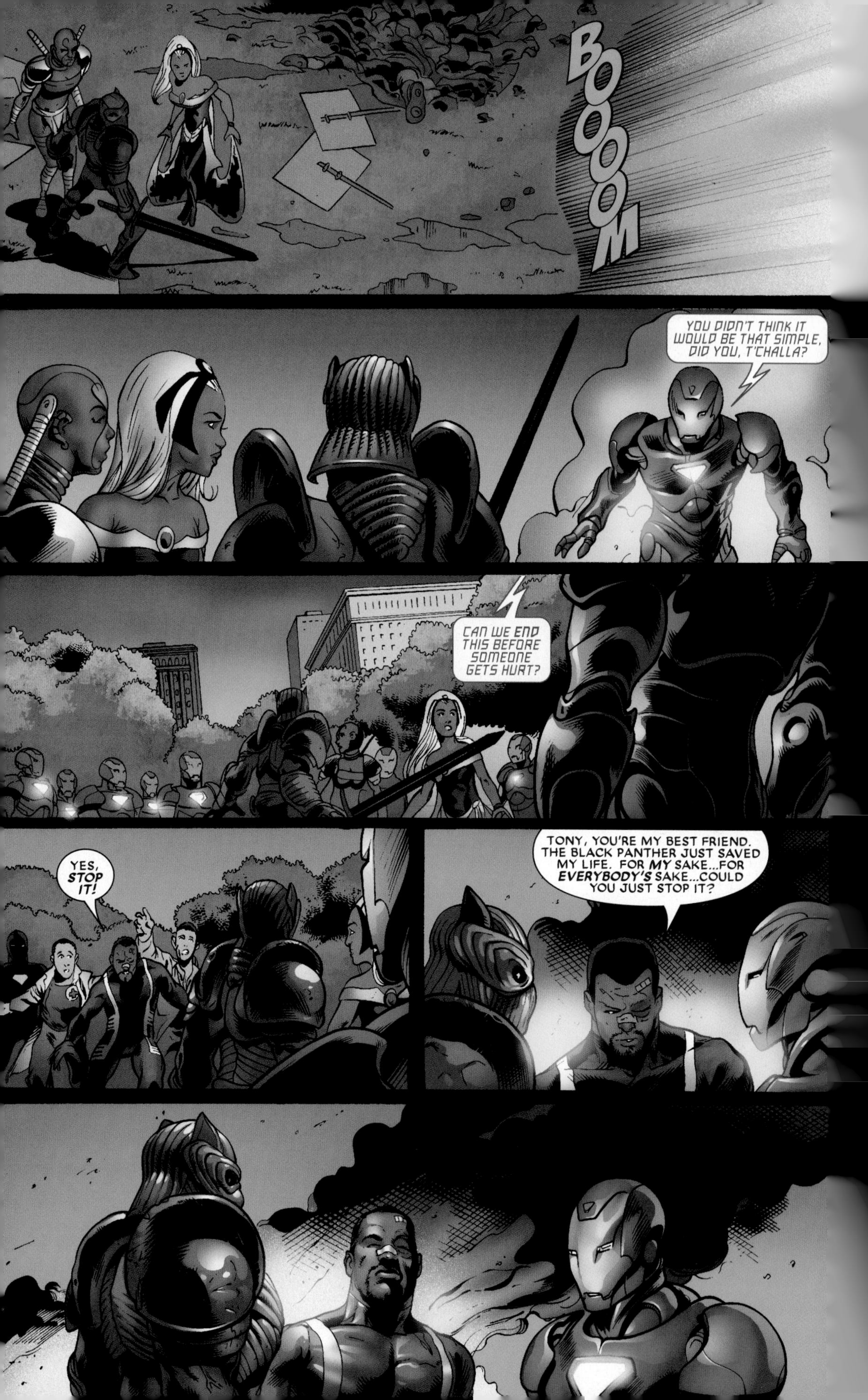
BOOOOM
YOU DIDN'T THINK IT WOULD BE THAT SIMPLE, DID YOU, T'CHALLA?
CAN WE END THIS BEFORE SOMEONE GETS HURT?
YES, STOP IT!
TONY, YOU'RE MY BEST FRIEND. THE BLACK PANTHER JUST SAVED MY LIFE. FOR MY SAKE...FOR EVERYBODY'S SAKE...COULD YOU JUST STOP IT?

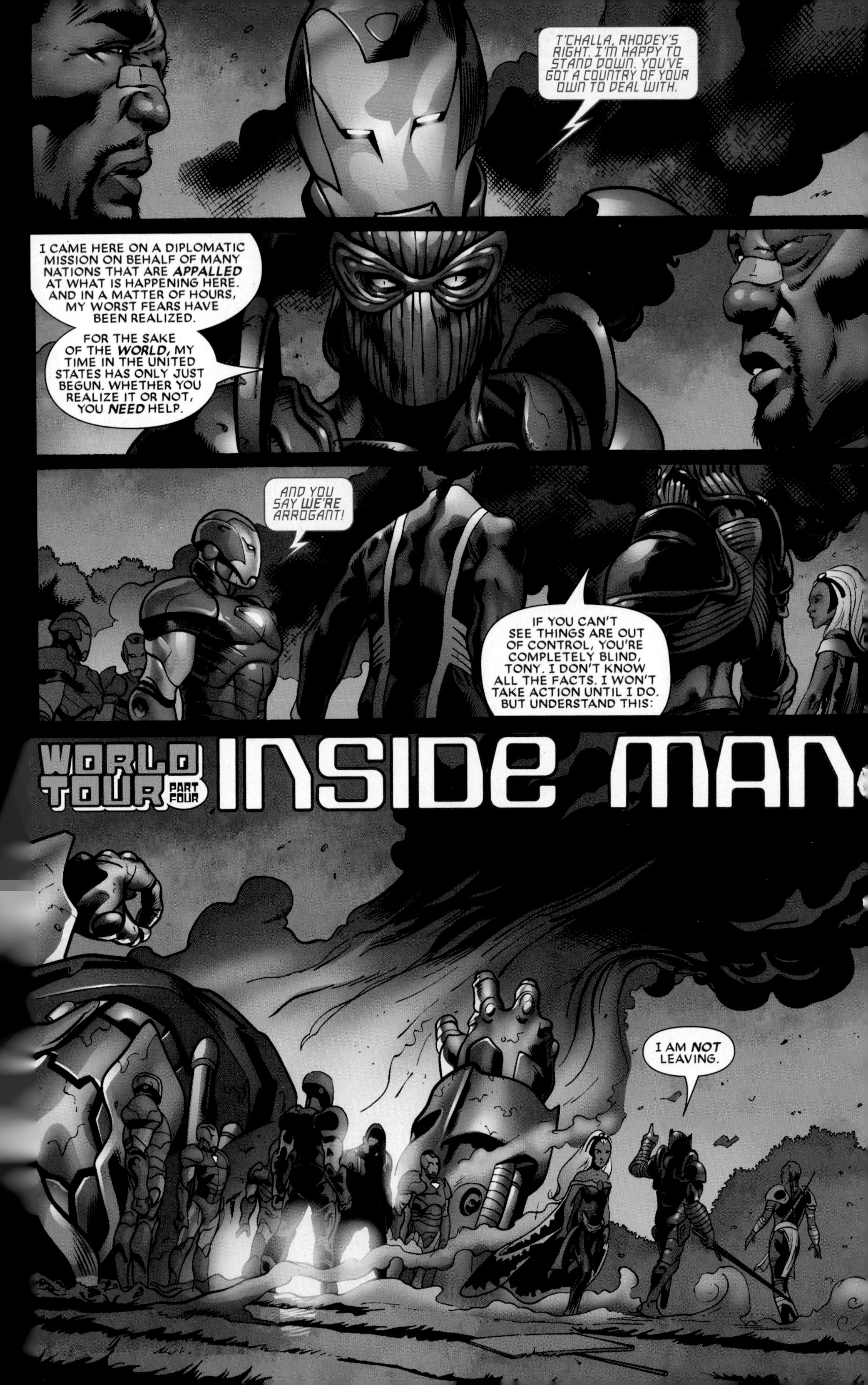
T'CHALLA, RHODEY'S RIGHT. I'M HAPPY TO STAND DOWN. YOU'VE GOT A COUNTRY OF YOUR OWN TO DEAL WITH.
I CAME HERE ON A DIPLOMATIC MISSION ON BEHALF OF MANY NATIONS THAT ARE APPALLED AT WHAT IS HAPPENING HERE. AND IN A MATTER OF HOURS, MY WORST FEARS HAVE BEEN REALIZED.
FOR THE SAKE OF THE WORLD, MY TIME IN THE UNITED STATES HAS ONLY JUST BEGUN. WHETHER YOU REALIZE IT OR NOT, YOU NEED HELP.
AND YOU SAY WE'RE ARROGANT!
IF YOU CAN'T SEE THINGS ARE OUT OF CONTROL, YOU'RE COMPLETELY BLIND, TONY. I DON'T KNOW ALL THE FACTS. I WON'T TAKE ACTION UNTIL I DO. BUT UNDERSTAND THIS:
WORLD TOUR PART FOUR
INSIDE MAN
I AM NOT LEAVING.

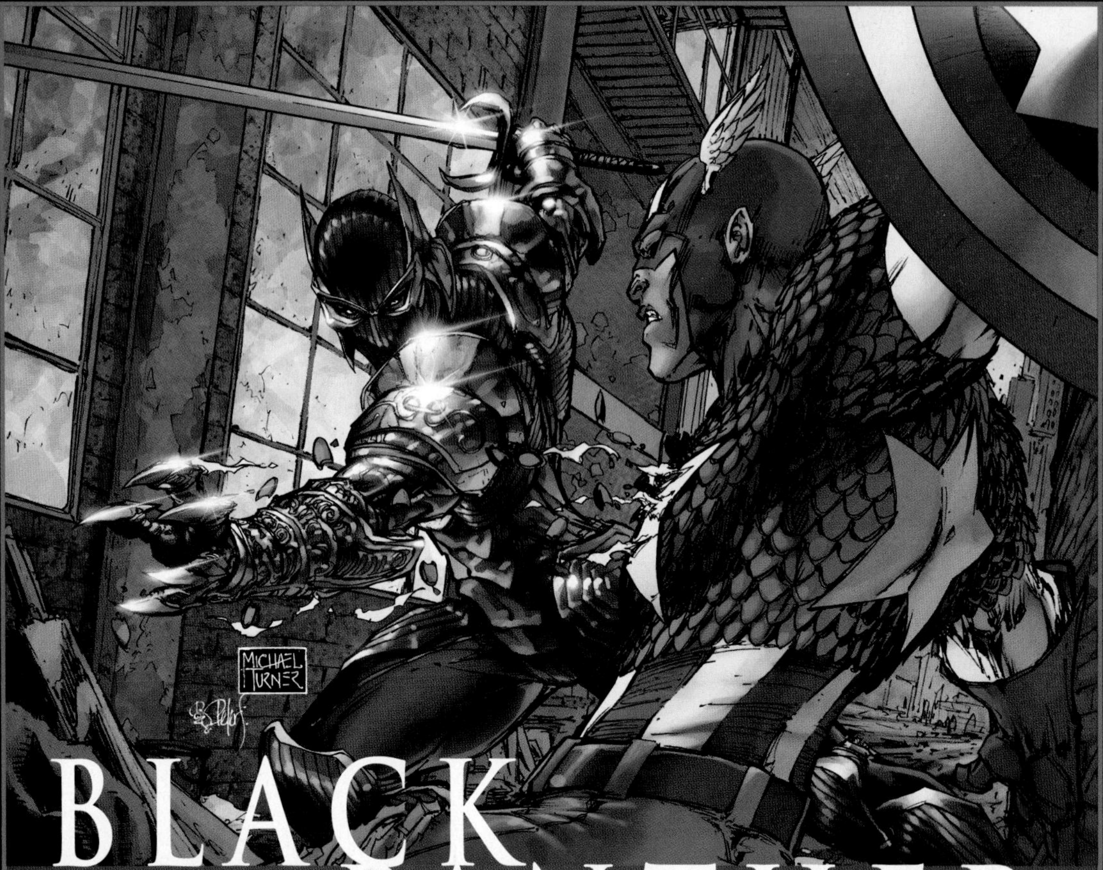
MICHAEL TURNER

BLACK PANTHER

A MARVEL COMICS EVENT

CIVIL WAR

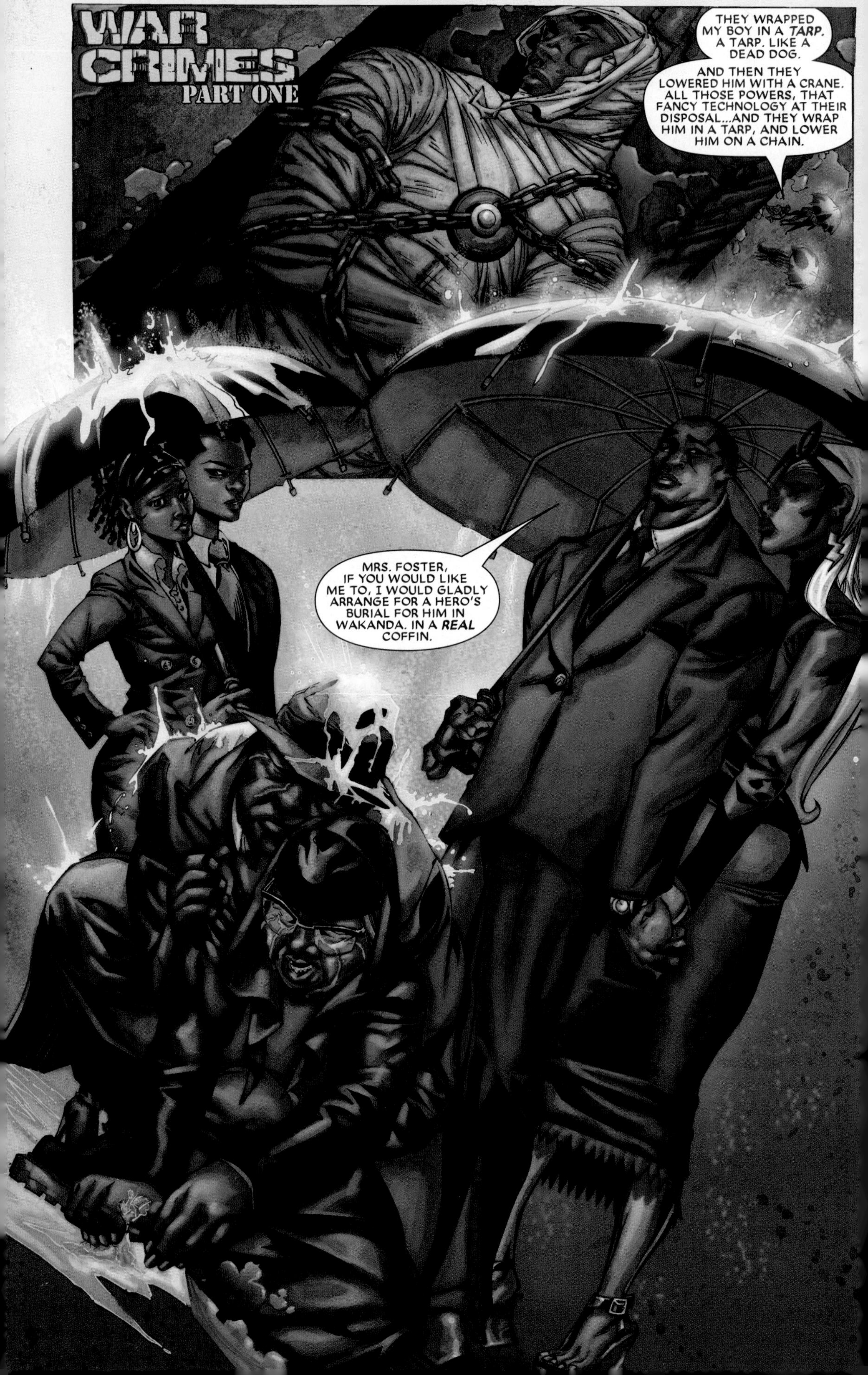
WAR CRIMES
PART ONE
THEY WRAPPED MY BOY IN A TARP. A TARP. LIKE A DEAD DOG.
AND THEN THEY LOWERED HIM WITH A CRANE. ALL THOSE POWERS, THAT FANCY TECHNOLOGY AT THEIR DISPOSAL...AND THEY WRAP HIM IN A TARP, AND LOWER HIM ON A CHAIN.
MRS. FOSTER, IF YOU WOULD LIKE ME TO, I WOULD GLADLY ARRANGE FOR A HERO'S BURIAL FOR HIM IN WAKANDA. IN A REAL COFFIN.

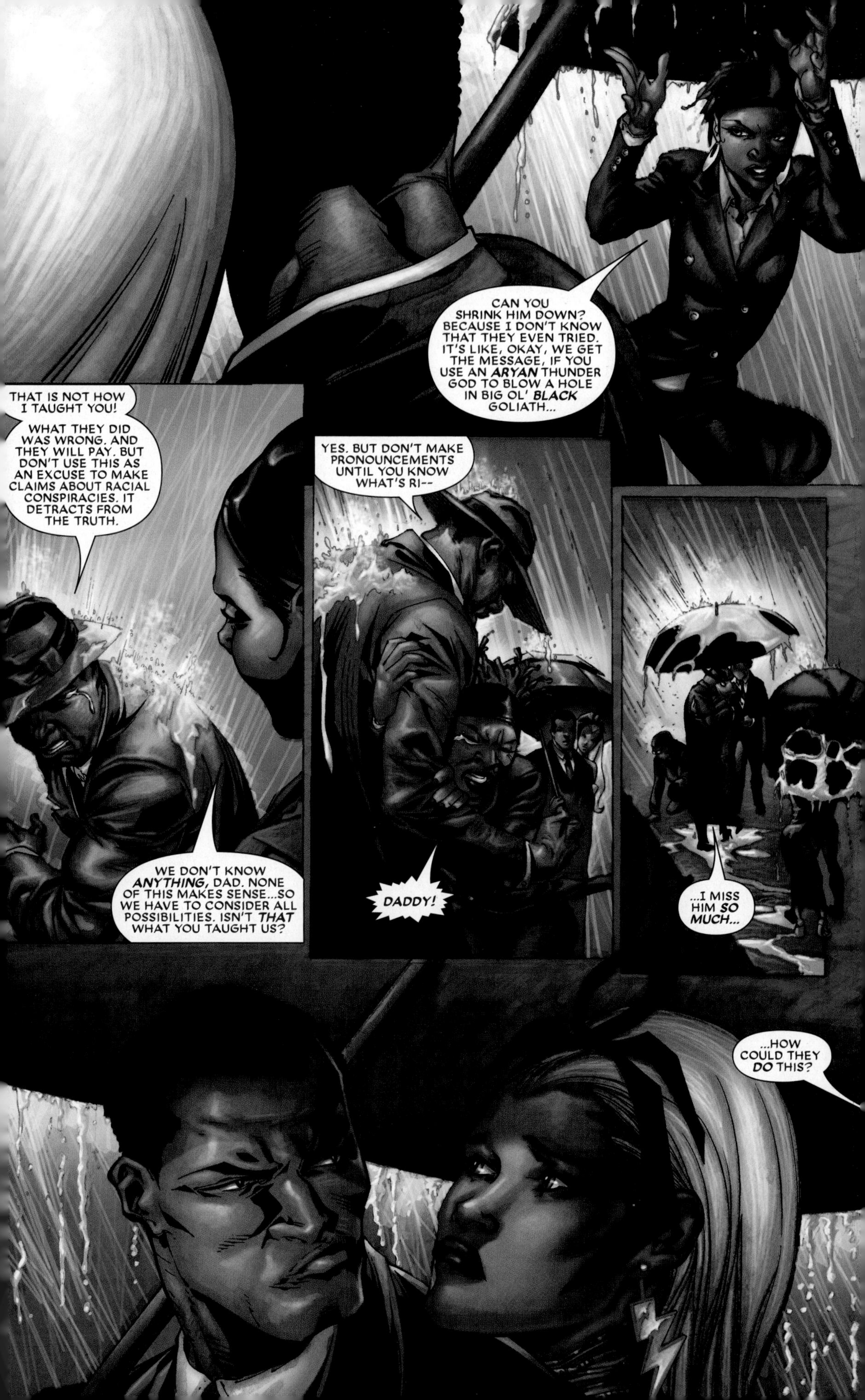
CAN YOU SHRINK HIM DOWN? BECAUSE I DON'T KNOW THAT THEY EVEN TRIED. IT'S LIKE, OKAY, WE GET THE MESSAGE, IF YOU USE AN ARYAN THUNDER GOD TO BLOW A HOLE IN BIG OL' BLACK GOLIATH...
THAT IS NOT HOW I TAUGHT YOU!
WHAT THEY DID WAS WRONG. AND THEY WILL PAY. BUT DON'T USE THIS AS AN EXCUSE TO MAKE CLAIMS ABOUT RACIAL CONSPIRACIES. IT DETRACTS FROM THE TRUTH.
WE DON'T KNOW ANYTHING, DAD. NONE OF THIS MAKES SENSE...SO WE HAVE TO CONSIDER ALL POSSIBILITIES. ISN'T THAT WHAT YOU TAUGHT US?
YES. BUT DON'T MAKE PRONOUNCEMENTS UNTIL YOU KNOW WHAT'S RI--
DADDY!
...I MISS HIM SO MUCH...
...HOW COULD THEY DO THIS?

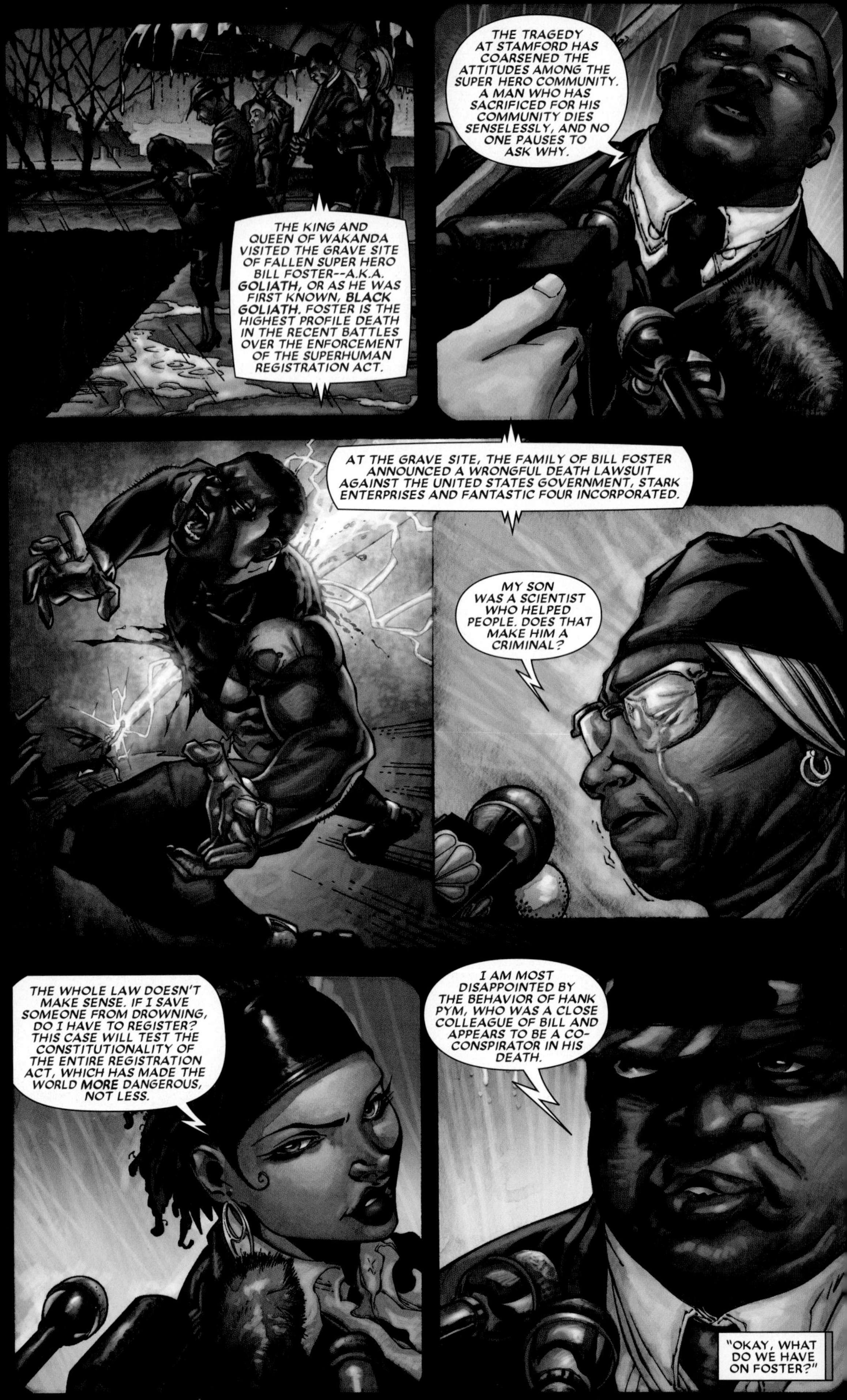
THE KING AND QUEEN OF WAKANDA VISITED THE GRAVE SITE OF FALLEN SUPER HERO BILL FOSTER--A.K.A. GOLIATH, OR AS HE WAS FIRST KNOWN, BLACK GOLIATH. FOSTER IS THE HIGHEST PROFILE DEATH IN THE RECENT BATTLES OVER THE ENFORCEMENT OF THE SUPERHUMAN REGISTRATION ACT.
THE TRAGEDY AT STAMFORD HAS COARSENED THE ATTITUDES AMONG THE SUPER HERO COMMUNITY. A MAN WHO HAS SACRIFICED FOR HIS COMMUNITY DIES SENSELESSLY, AND NO ONE PAUSES TO ASK WHY.
AT THE GRAVE SITE, THE FAMILY OF BILL FOSTER ANNOUNCED A WRONGFUL DEATH LAWSUIT AGAINST THE UNITED STATES GOVERNMENT, STARK ENTERPRISES AND FANTASTIC FOUR INCORPORATED.
MY SON WAS A SCIENTIST WHO HELPED PEOPLE. DOES THAT MAKE HIM A CRIMINAL?
THE WHOLE LAW DOESN'T MAKE SENSE. IF I SAVE SOMEONE FROM DROWNING, DO I HAVE TO REGISTER? THIS CASE WILL TEST THE CONSTITUTIONALITY OF THE ENTIRE REGISTRATION ACT, WHICH HAS MADE THE WORLD MORE DANGEROUS, NOT LESS.
I AM MOST DISAPPOINTED BY THE BEHAVIOR OF HANK PYM, WHO WAS A CLOSE COLLEAGUE OF BILL AND APPEARS TO BE A CO-CONSPIRATOR IN HIS DEATH.
"OKAY, WHAT DO WE HAVE ON FOSTER?"

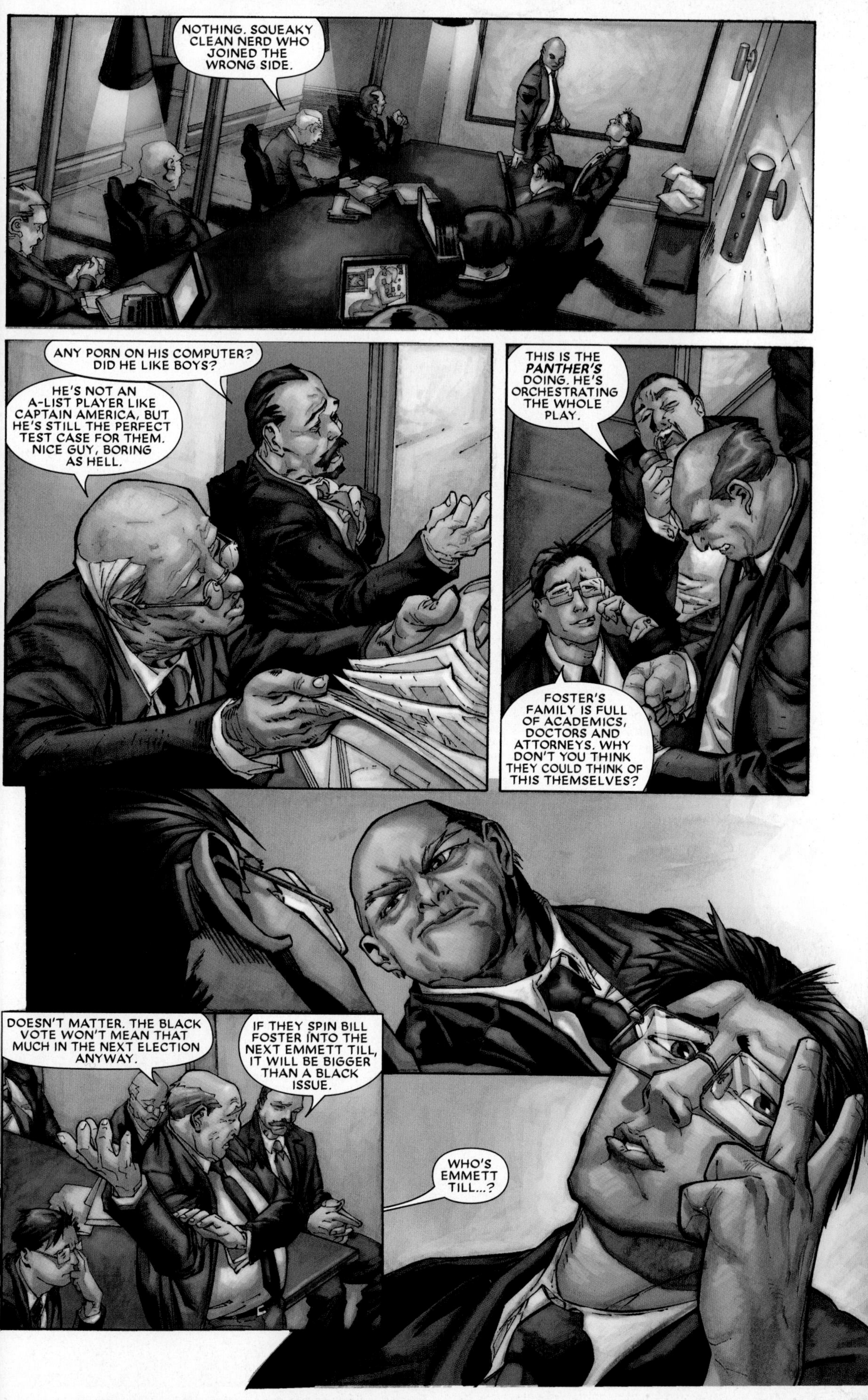
NOTHING. SQUEAKY CLEAN NERD WHO JOINED THE WRONG SIDE.
ANY PORN ON HIS COMPUTER? DID HE LIKE BOYS?
HE'S NOT AN A-LIST PLAYER LIKE CAPTAIN AMERICA, BUT HE'S STILL THE PERFECT TEST CASE FOR THEM. NICE GUY, BORING AS HELL.
THIS IS THE PANTHER'S DOING. HE'S ORCHESTRATING THE WHOLE PLAY.
FOSTER'S FAMILY IS FULL OF ACADEMICS, DOCTORS AND ATTORNEYS. WHY DON'T YOU THINK THEY COULD THINK OF THIS THEMSELVES?
DOESN'T MATTER. THE BLACK VOTE WON'T MEAN THAT MUCH IN THE NEXT ELECTION ANYWAY.
IF THEY SPIN BILL FOSTER INTO THE NEXT EMMETT TILL, IT WILL BE BIGGER THAN A BLACK ISSUE.
WHO'S EMMETT TILL...?

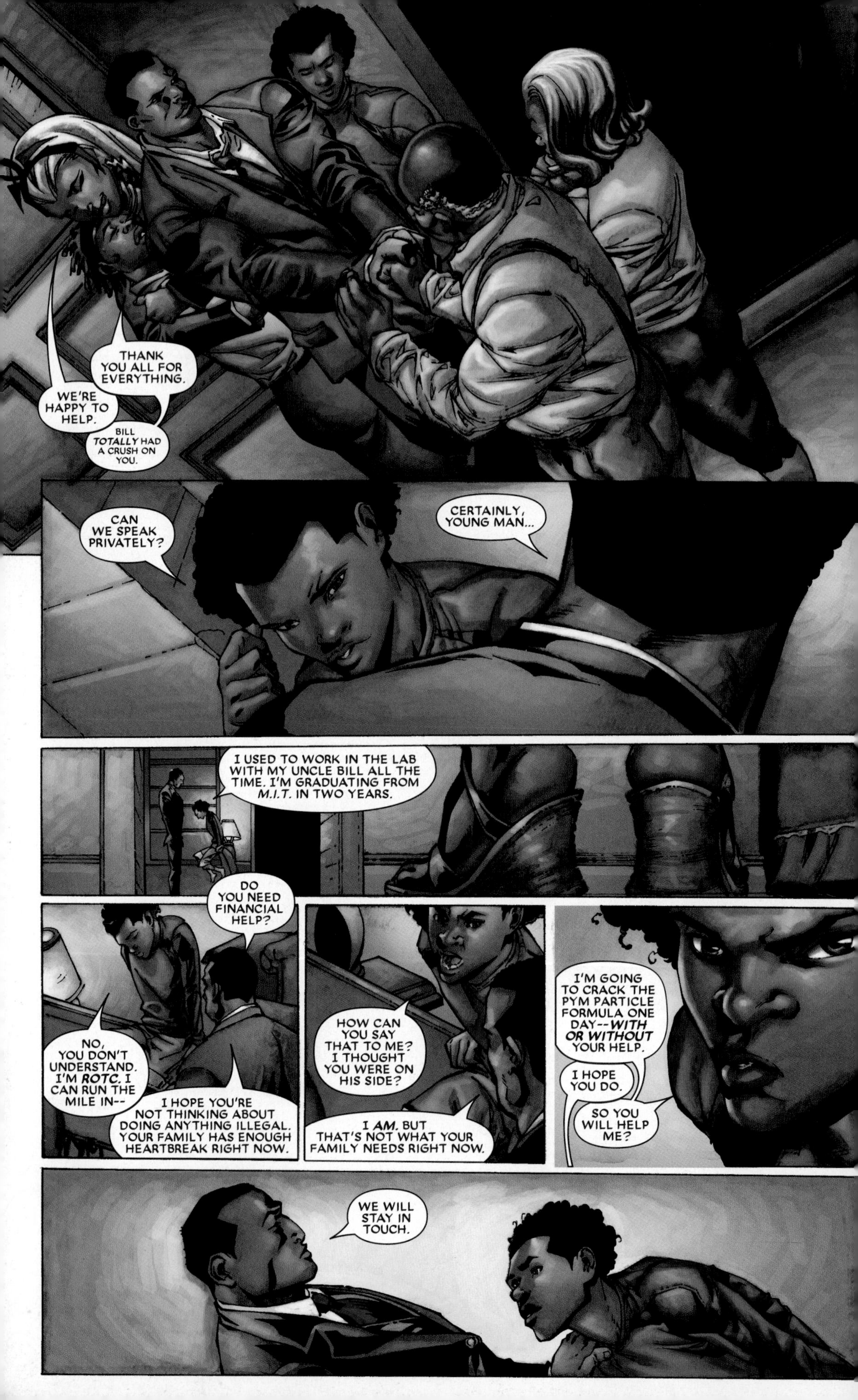
THANK YOU ALL FOR EVERYTHING.
WE'RE HAPPY TO HELP.
BILL TOTALLY HAD A CRUSH ON YOU.
CAN WE SPEAK PRIVATELY?
CERTAINLY, YOUNG MAN...
I USED TO WORK IN THE LAB WITH MY UNCLE BILL ALL THE TIME. I'M GRADUATING FROM M.I.T. IN TWO YEARS.
DO YOU NEED FINANCIAL HELP?
NO, YOU DON'T UNDERSTAND. I'M ROTC. I CAN RUN THE MILE IN--
I HOPE YOU'RE NOT THINKING ABOUT DOING ANYTHING ILLEGAL. YOUR FAMILY HAS ENOUGH HEARTBREAK RIGHT NOW.
HOW CAN YOU SAY THAT TO ME? I THOUGHT YOU WERE ON HIS SIDE?
I AM. BUT THAT'S NOT WHAT YOUR FAMILY NEEDS RIGHT NOW.
I'M GOING TO CRACK THE PYM PARTICLE FORMULA ONE DAY--WITH OR WITHOUT YOUR HELP.
I HOPE YOU DO.
SO YOU WILL HELP ME?
WE WILL STAY IN TOUCH.

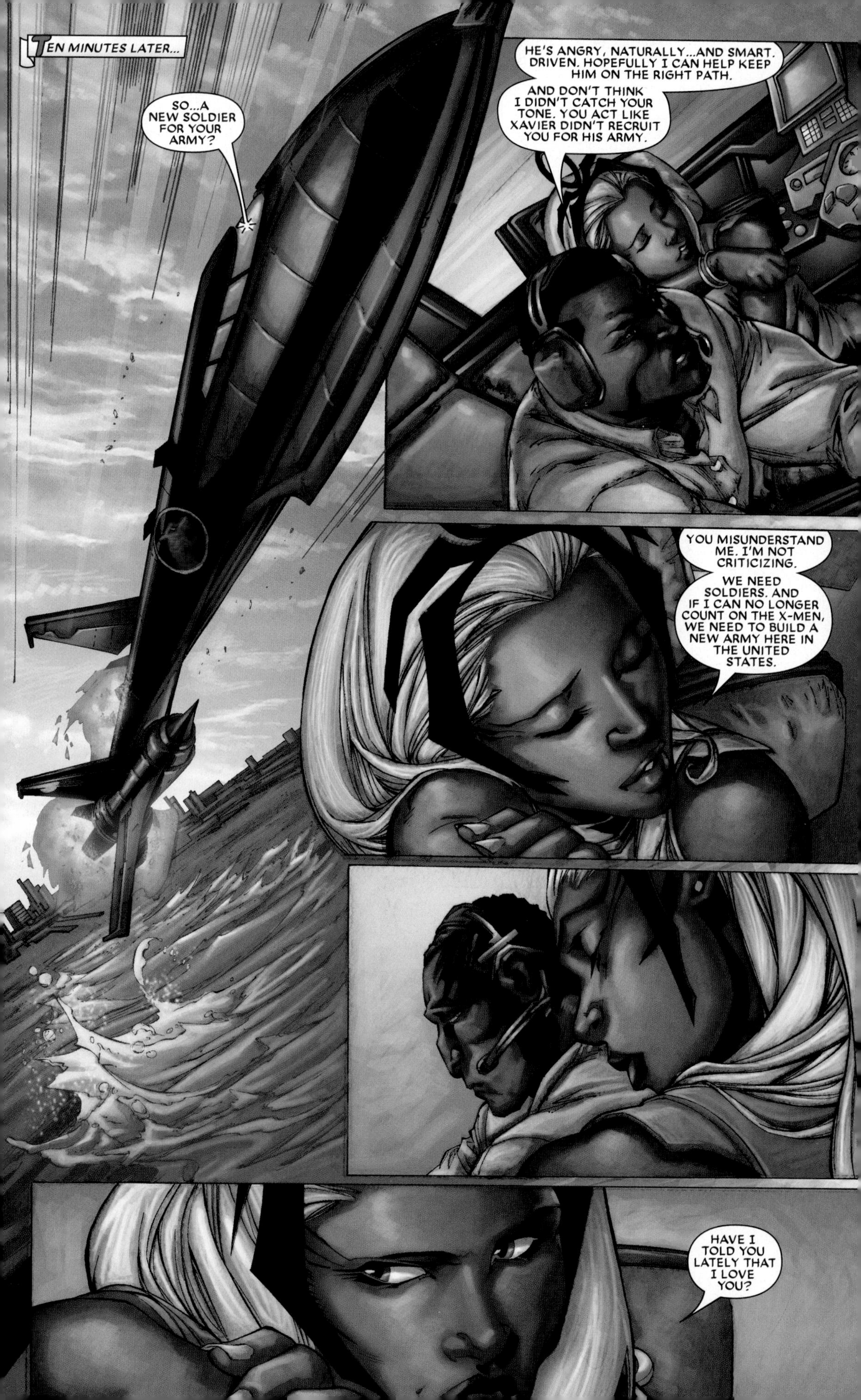
TEN MINUTES LATER...
SO...A NEW SOLDIER FOR YOUR ARMY?
HE'S ANGRY, NATURALLY...AND SMART. DRIVEN. HOPEFULLY I CAN HELP KEEP HIM ON THE RIGHT PATH.
AND DON'T THINK I DIDN'T CATCH YOUR TONE. YOU ACT LIKE XAVIER DIDN'T RECRUIT YOU FOR HIS ARMY.
YOU MISUNDERSTAND ME. I'M NOT CRITICIZING.
WE NEED SOLDIERS. AND IF I CAN NO LONGER COUNT ON THE X-MEN, WE NEED TO BUILD A NEW ARMY HERE IN THE UNITED STATES.
HAVE I TOLD YOU LATELY THAT I LOVE YOU?

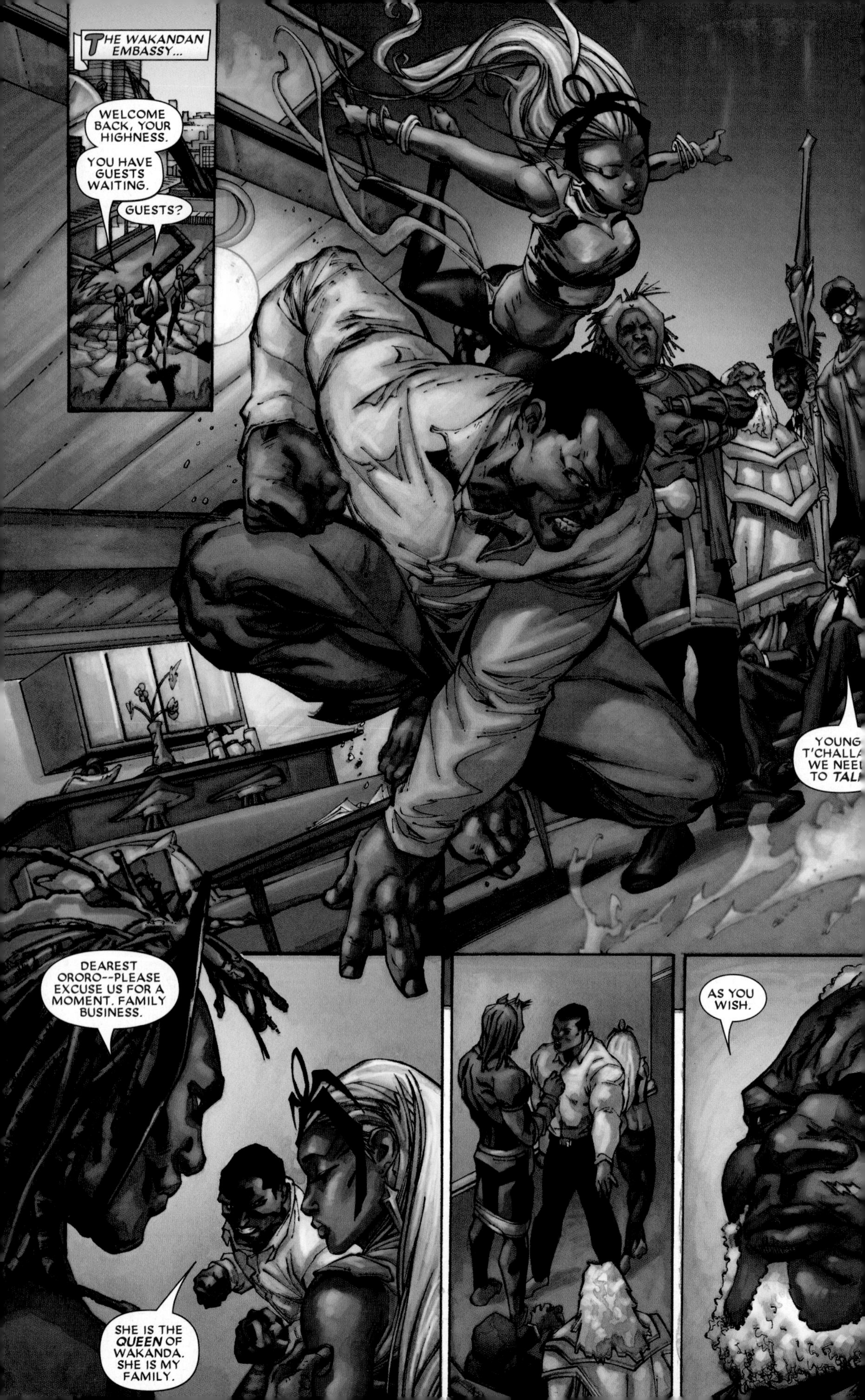

THE WAKANDAN EMBASSY...
WELCOME BACK, YOUR HIGHNESS.
YOU HAVE GUESTS WAITING.
GUESTS?
YOUNG T'CHALLA WE NEE TO TAL
DEAREST ORORO--PLEASE EXCUSE US FOR A MOMENT. FAMILY BUSINESS.
SHE IS THE QUEEN OF WAKANDA. SHE IS MY FAMILY.
AS YOU WISH.

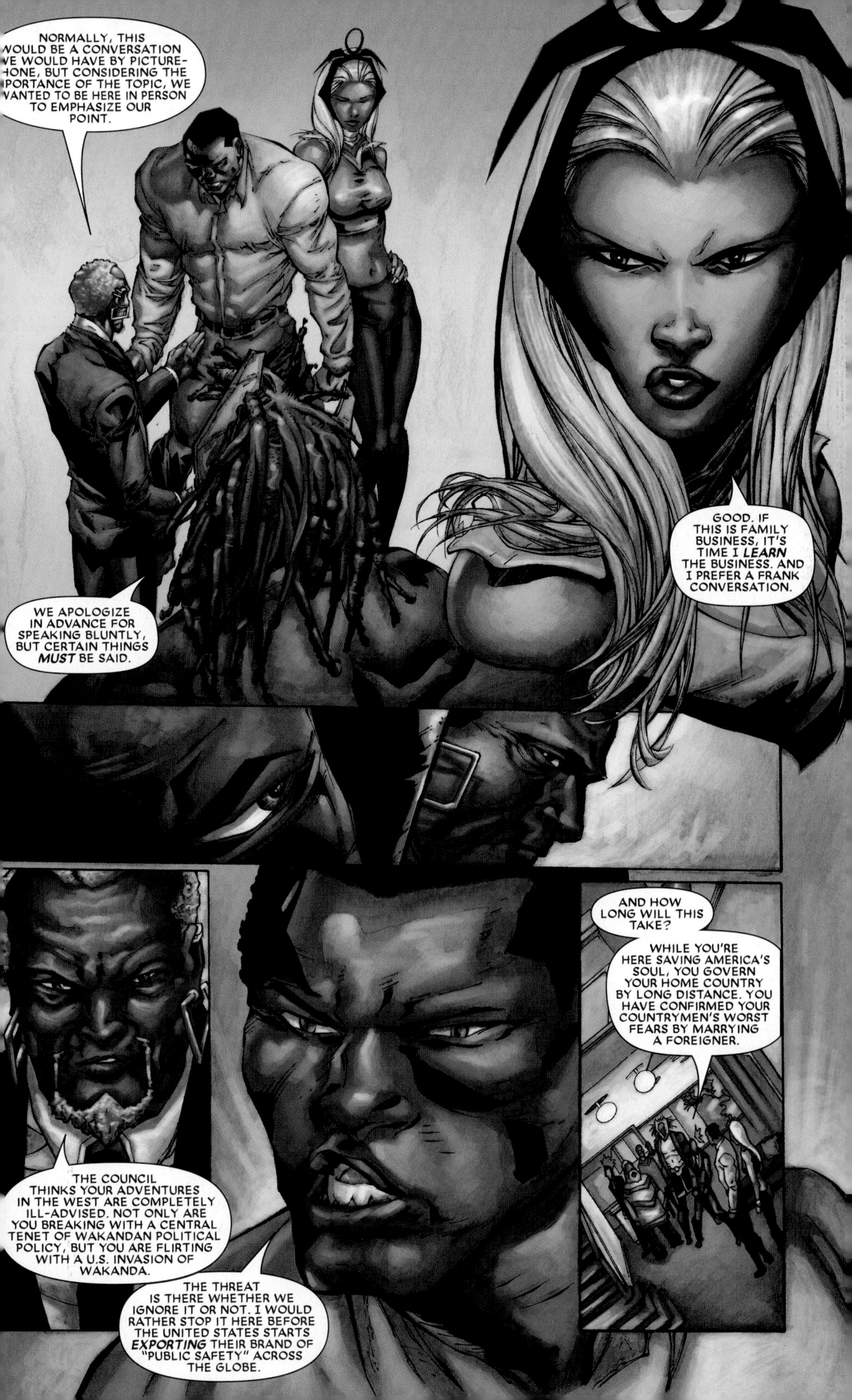
NORMALLY, THIS WOULD BE A CONVERSATION WE WOULD HAVE BY PICTURE-PHONE, BUT CONSIDERING THE IMPORTANCE OF THE TOPIC, WE WANTED TO BE HERE IN PERSON TO EMPHASIZE OUR POINT.
GOOD. IF THIS IS FAMILY BUSINESS, IT'S TIME I *LEARN* THE BUSINESS. AND I PREFER A FRANK CONVERSATION.
WE APOLOGIZE IN ADVANCE FOR SPEAKING BLUNTLY, BUT CERTAIN THINGS *MUST* BE SAID.
AND HOW LONG WILL THIS TAKE?
WHILE YOU'RE HERE SAVING AMERICA'S SOUL, YOU GOVERN YOUR HOME COUNTRY BY LONG DISTANCE. YOU HAVE CONFIRMED YOUR COUNTRYMEN'S WORST FEARS BY MARRYING A FOREIGNER.
THE COUNCIL THINKS YOUR ADVENTURES IN THE WEST ARE COMPLETELY ILL-ADVISED. NOT ONLY ARE YOU BREAKING WITH A CENTRAL TENET OF WAKANDAN POLITICAL POLICY, BUT YOU ARE FLIRTING WITH A U.S. INVASION OF WAKANDA.
THE THREAT IS THERE WHETHER WE IGNORE IT OR NOT. I WOULD RATHER STOP IT HERE BEFORE THE UNITED STATES STARTS *EXPORTING* THEIR BRAND OF "PUBLIC SAFETY" ACROSS THE GLOBE.

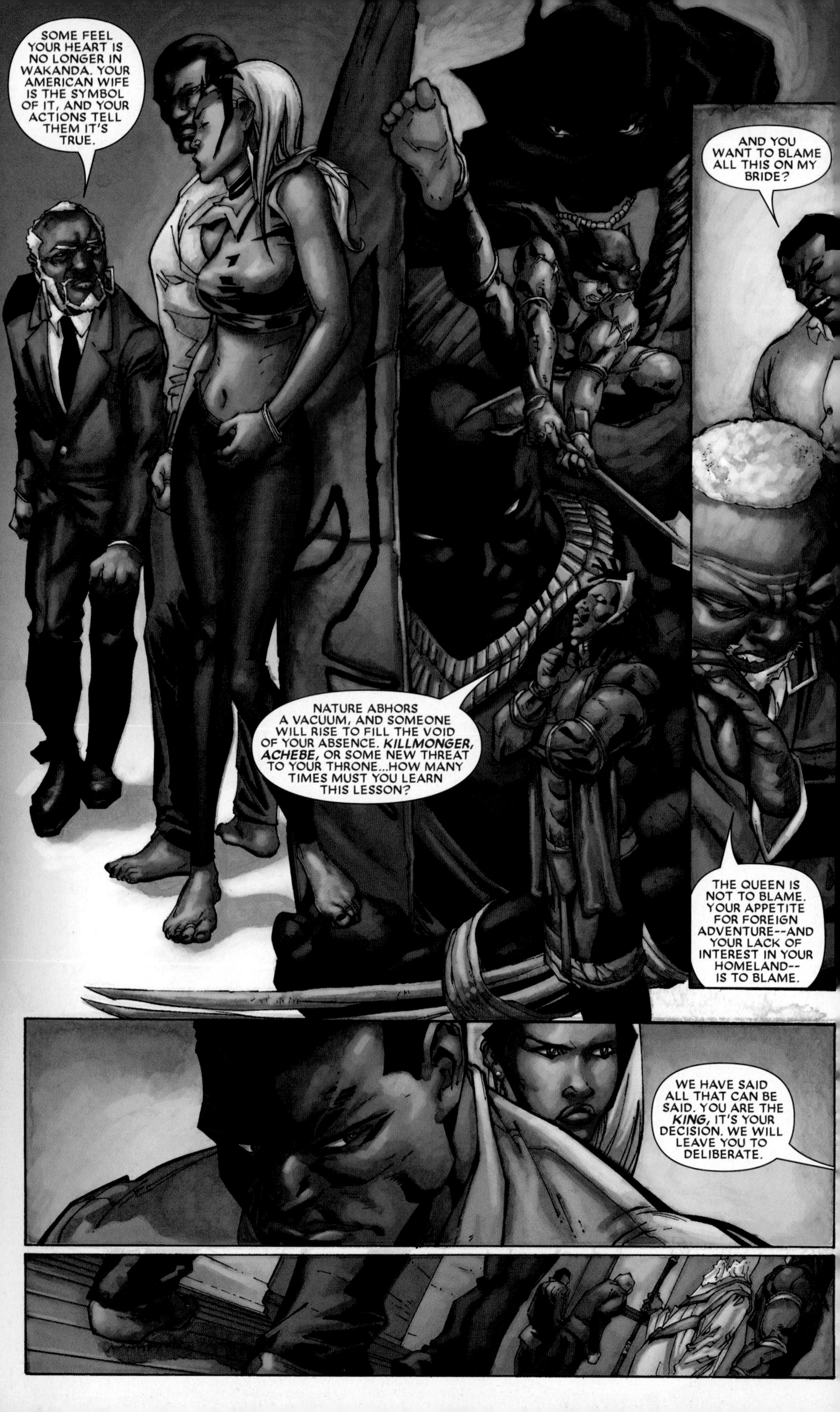
SOME FEEL YOUR HEART IS NO LONGER IN WAKANDA. YOUR AMERICAN WIFE IS THE SYMBOL OF IT, AND YOUR ACTIONS TELL THEM IT'S TRUE.
AND YOU WANT TO BLAME ALL THIS ON MY BRIDE?
NATURE ABHORS A VACUUM, AND SOMEONE WILL RISE TO FILL THE VOID OF YOUR ABSENCE. KILLMONGER, ACHEBE, OR SOME NEW THREAT TO YOUR THRONE...HOW MANY TIMES MUST YOU LEARN THIS LESSON?
THE QUEEN IS NOT TO BLAME. YOUR APPETITE FOR FOREIGN ADVENTURE--AND YOUR LACK OF INTEREST IN YOUR HOMELAND--IS TO BLAME.
WE HAVE SAID ALL THAT CAN BE SAID. YOU ARE THE KING, IT'S YOUR DECISION. WE WILL LEAVE YOU TO DELIBERATE.

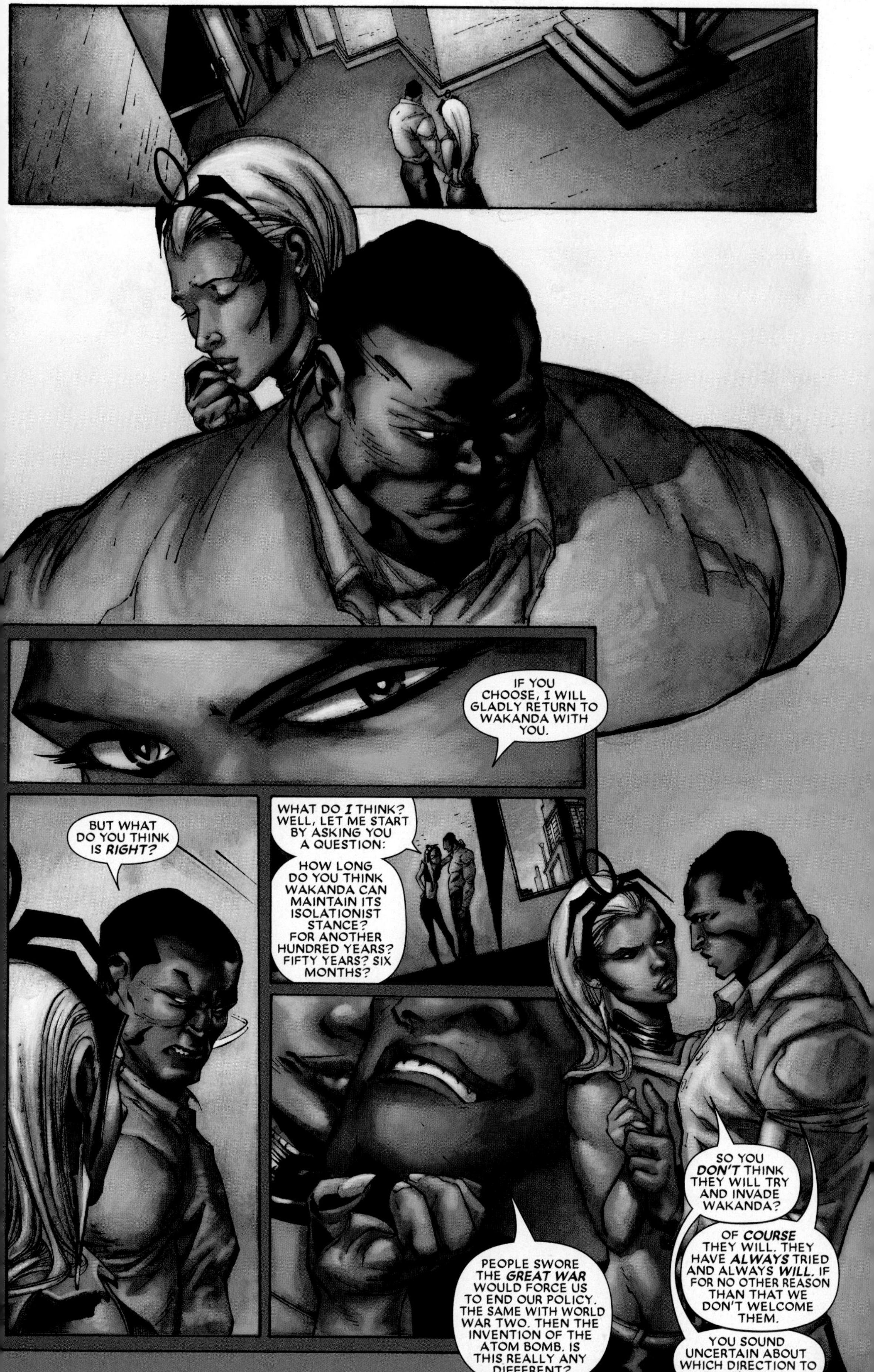
IF YOU CHOOSE, I WILL GLADLY RETURN TO WAKANDA WITH YOU.
BUT WHAT DO YOU THINK IS *RIGHT?*
WHAT DO *I* THINK? WELL, LET ME START BY ASKING YOU A QUESTION:
HOW LONG DO YOU THINK WAKANDA CAN MAINTAIN ITS ISOLATIONIST STANCE? FOR ANOTHER HUNDRED YEARS? FIFTY YEARS? SIX MONTHS?
PEOPLE SWORE THE *GREAT WAR* WOULD FORCE US TO END OUR POLICY. THE SAME WITH WORLD WAR TWO. THEN THE INVENTION OF THE ATOM BOMB. IS THIS REALLY ANY DIFFERENT?
SO YOU *DON'T* THINK THEY WILL TRY AND INVADE WAKANDA?
OF *COURSE* THEY WILL. THEY HAVE *ALWAYS* TRIED AND ALWAYS *WILL.* IF FOR NO OTHER REASON THAN THAT WE DON'T WELCOME THEM.
YOU SOUND UNCERTAIN ABOUT WHICH DIRECTION TO GO, T'CHALLA.

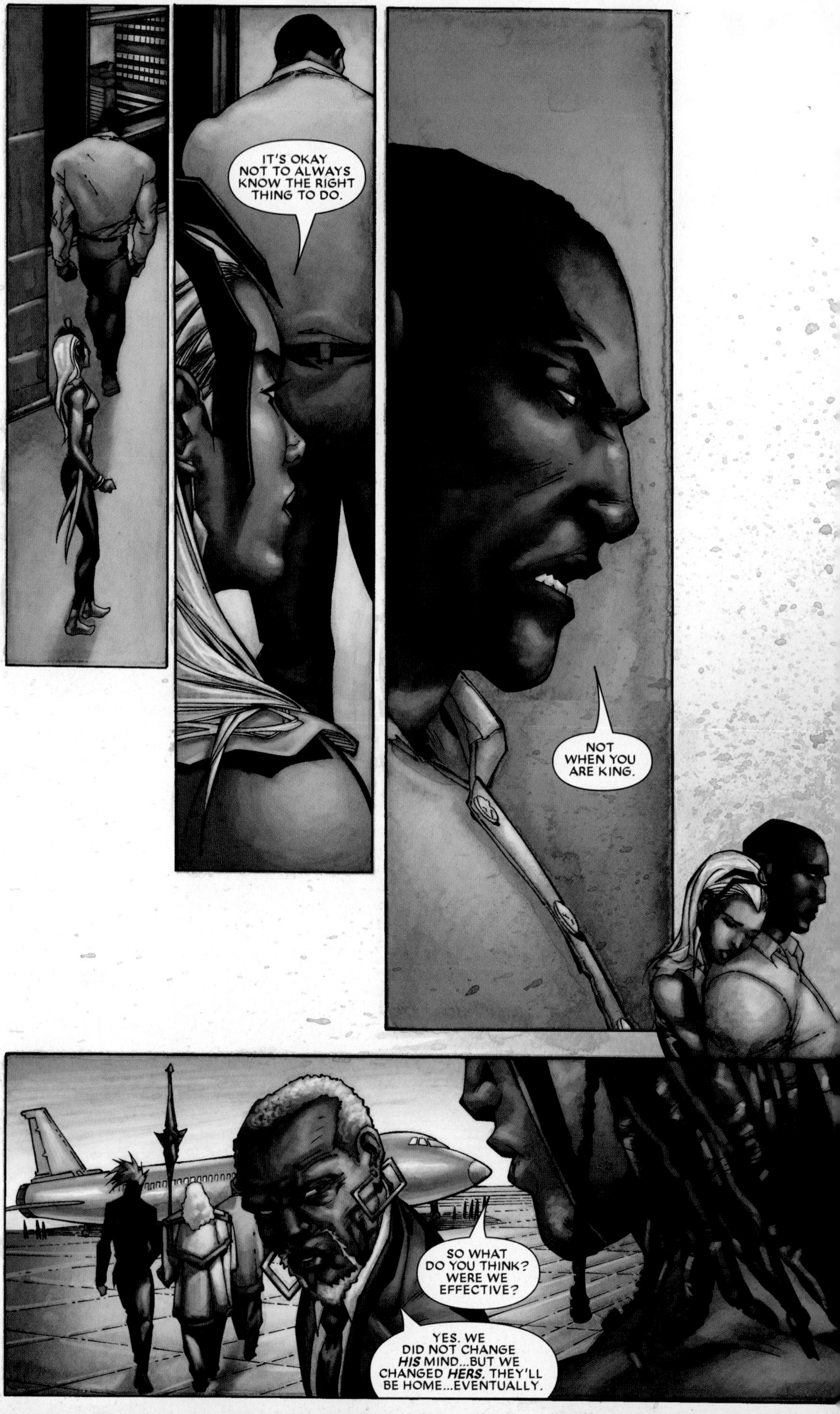
IT'S OKAY NOT TO ALWAYS KNOW THE RIGHT THING TO DO.
NOT WHEN YOU ARE KING.
SO WHAT DO YOU THINK? WERE WE EFFECTIVE?
YES. WE DID NOT CHANGE *HIS* MIND...BUT WE CHANGED *HERS.* THEY'LL BE HOME...EVENTUALLY.

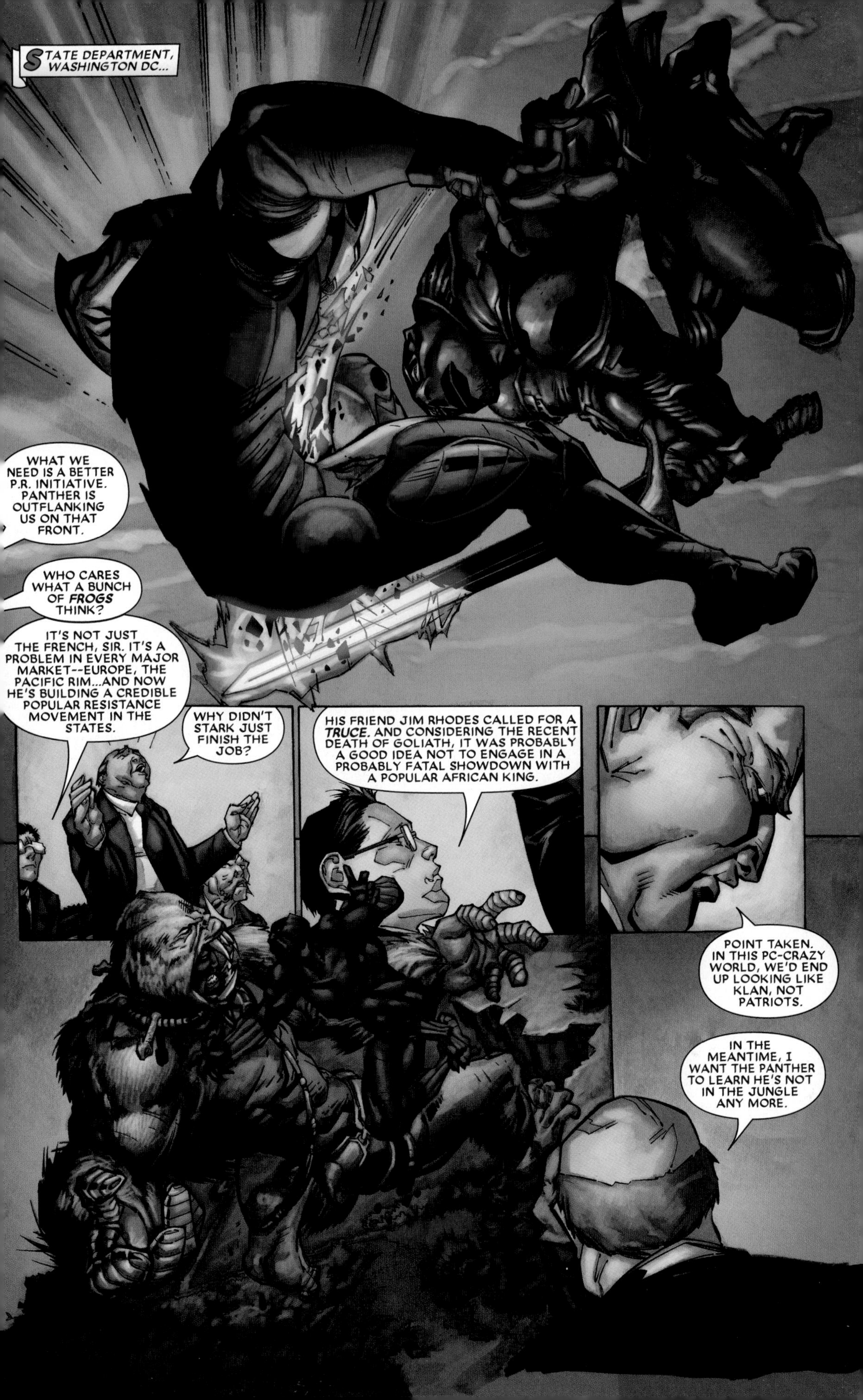
STATE DEPARTMENT, WASHINGTON DC...
WHAT WE NEED IS A BETTER P.R. INITIATIVE. PANTHER IS OUTFLANKING US ON THAT FRONT.
WHO CARES WHAT A BUNCH OF FROGS THINK?
IT'S NOT JUST THE FRENCH, SIR. IT'S A PROBLEM IN EVERY MAJOR MARKET--EUROPE, THE PACIFIC RIM...AND NOW HE'S BUILDING A CREDIBLE POPULAR RESISTANCE MOVEMENT IN THE STATES.
WHY DIDN'T STARK JUST FINISH THE JOB?
HIS FRIEND JIM RHODES CALLED FOR A TRUCE. AND CONSIDERING THE RECENT DEATH OF GOLIATH, IT WAS PROBABLY A GOOD IDEA NOT TO ENGAGE IN A PROBABLY FATAL SHOWDOWN WITH A POPULAR AFRICAN KING.
POINT TAKEN. IN THIS PC-CRAZY WORLD, WE'D END UP LOOKING LIKE KLAN, NOT PATRIOTS.
IN THE MEANTIME, I WANT THE PANTHER TO LEARN HE'S NOT IN THE JUNGLE ANY MORE.

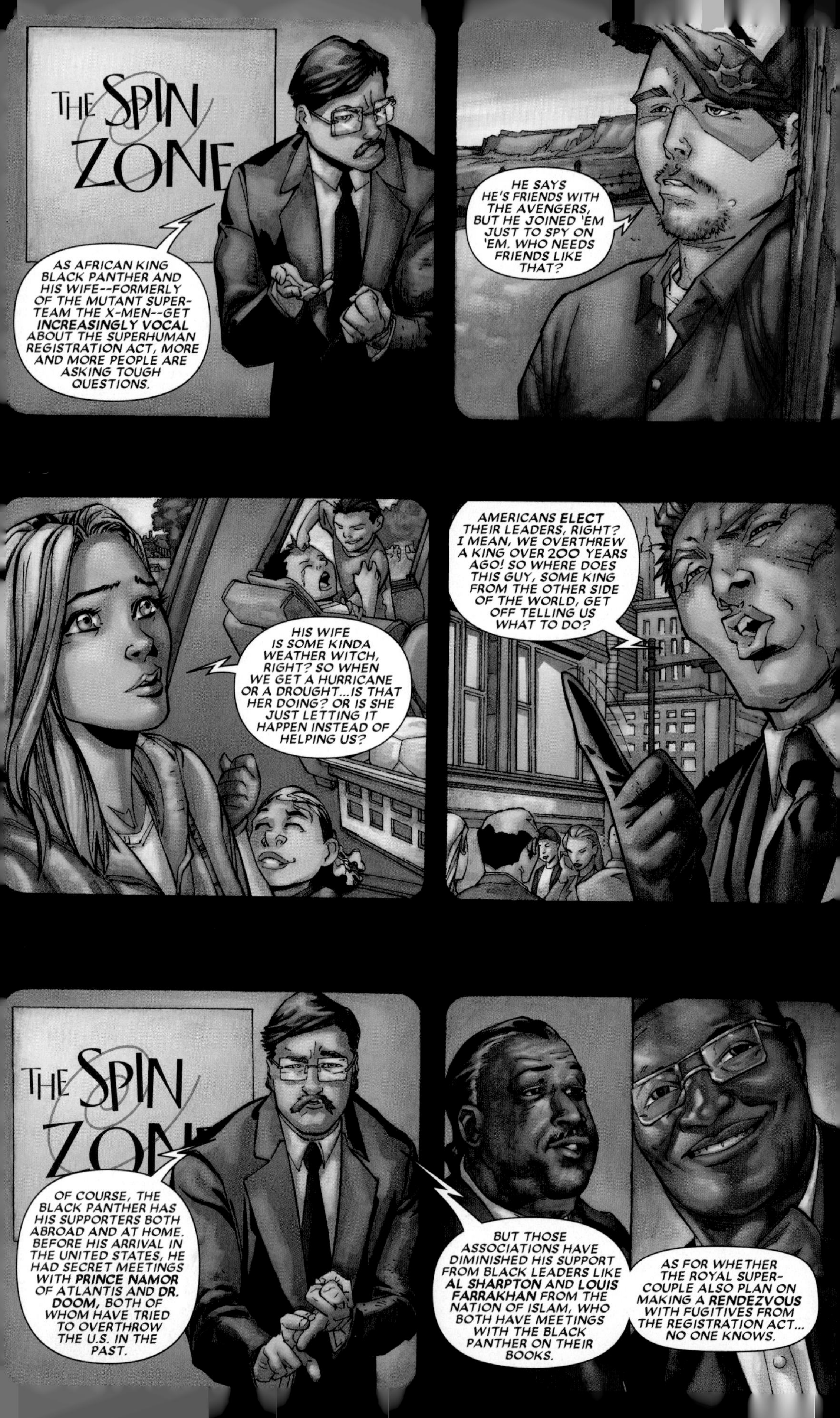
THE SPIN ZONE
AS AFRICAN KING BLACK PANTHER AND HIS WIFE--FORMERLY OF THE MUTANT SUPER-TEAM THE X-MEN--GET INCREASINGLY VOCAL ABOUT THE SUPERHUMAN REGISTRATION ACT, MORE AND MORE PEOPLE ARE ASKING TOUGH QUESTIONS.
HE SAYS HE'S FRIENDS WITH THE AVENGERS, BUT HE JOINED 'EM JUST TO SPY ON 'EM. WHO NEEDS FRIENDS LIKE THAT?
HIS WIFE IS SOME KINDA WEATHER WITCH, RIGHT? SO WHEN WE GET A HURRICANE OR A DROUGHT...IS THAT HER DOING? OR IS SHE JUST LETTING IT HAPPEN INSTEAD OF HELPING US?
AMERICANS ELECT THEIR LEADERS, RIGHT? I MEAN, WE OVERTHREW A KING OVER 200 YEARS AGO! SO WHERE DOES THIS GUY, SOME KING FROM THE OTHER SIDE OF THE WORLD, GET OFF TELLING US WHAT TO DO?
THE SPIN ZONE
OF COURSE, THE BLACK PANTHER HAS HIS SUPPORTERS BOTH ABROAD AND AT HOME. BEFORE HIS ARRIVAL IN THE UNITED STATES, HE HAD SECRET MEETINGS WITH PRINCE NAMOR OF ATLANTIS AND DR. DOOM, BOTH OF WHOM HAVE TRIED TO OVERTHROW THE U.S. IN THE PAST.
BUT THOSE ASSOCIATIONS HAVE DIMINISHED HIS SUPPORT FROM BLACK LEADERS LIKE AL SHARPTON AND LOUIS FARRAKHAN FROM THE NATION OF ISLAM, WHO BOTH HAVE MEETINGS WITH THE BLACK PANTHER ON THEIR BOOKS.
AS FOR WHETHER THE ROYAL SUPER-COUPLE ALSO PLAN ON MAKING A RENDEZVOUS WITH FUGITIVES FROM THE REGISTRATION ACT... NO ONE KNOWS.

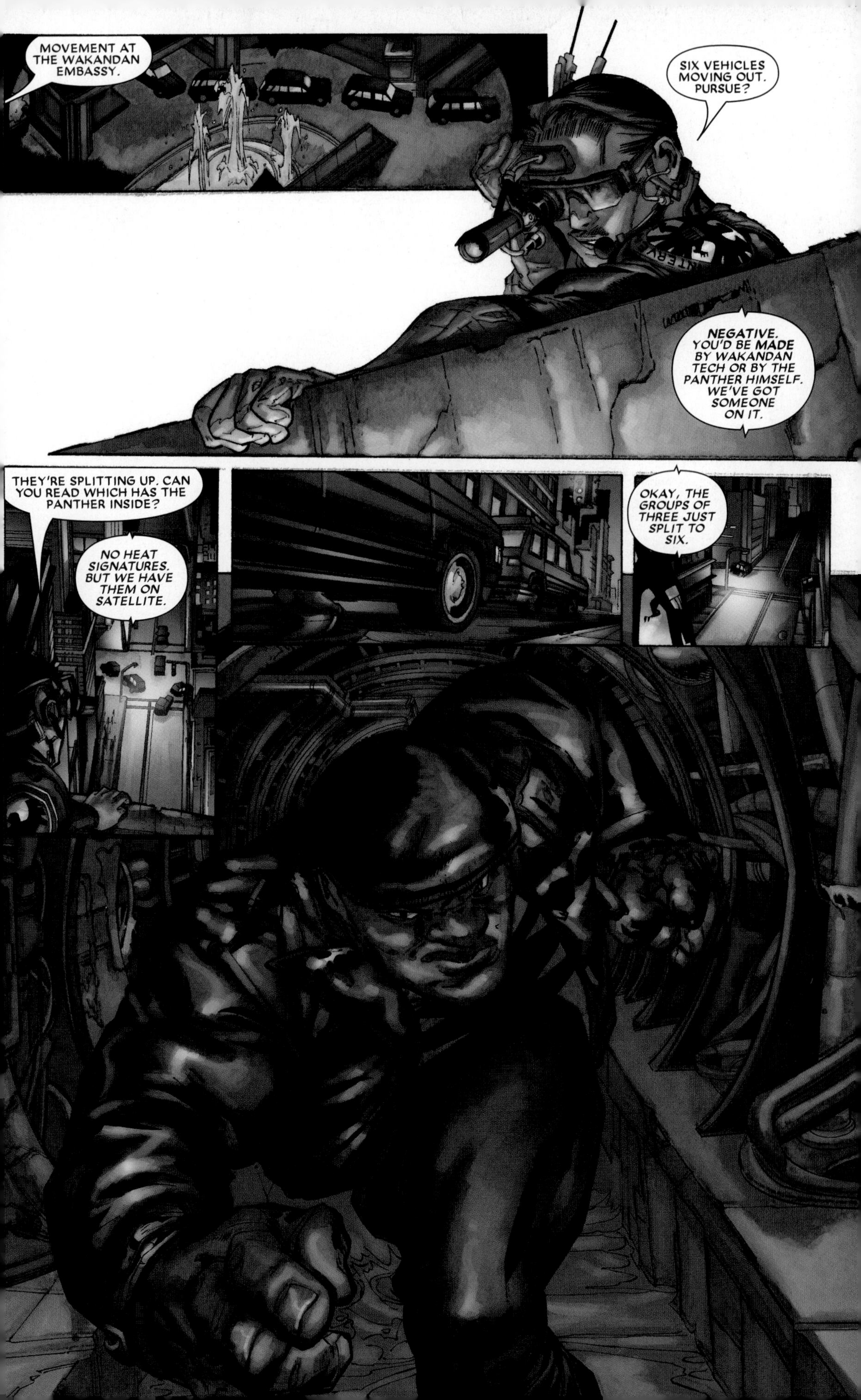

MOVEMENT AT THE WAKANDAN EMBASSY.
SIX VEHICLES MOVING OUT. PURSUE?
NEGATIVE. YOU'D BE MADE BY WAKANDAN TECH OR BY THE PANTHER HIMSELF. WE'VE GOT SOMEONE ON IT.
THEY'RE SPLITTING UP. CAN YOU READ WHICH HAS THE PANTHER INSIDE?
NO HEAT SIGNATURES. BUT WE HAVE THEM ON SATELLITE.
OKAY, THE GROUPS OF THREE JUST SPLIT TO SIX.

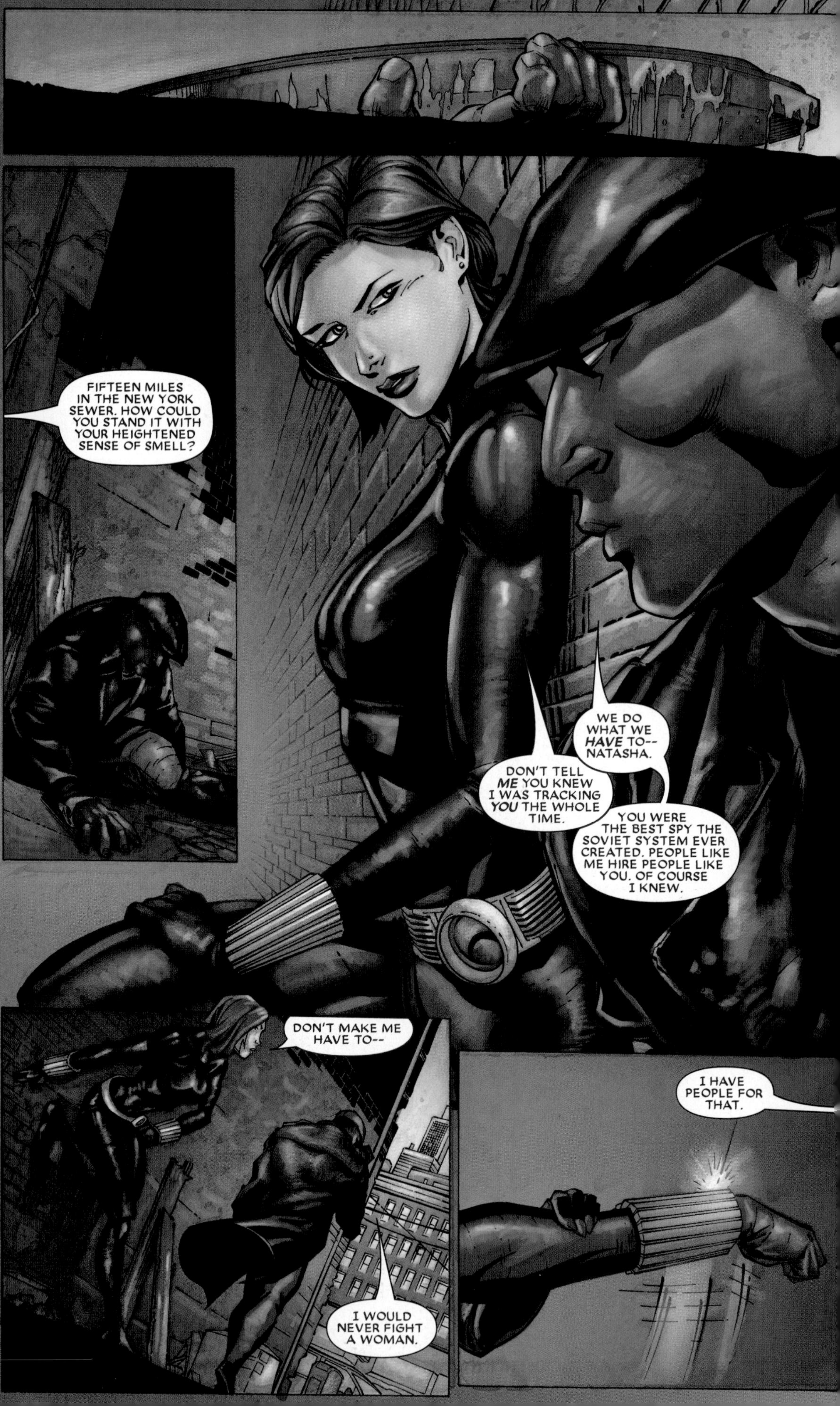
FIFTEEN MILES IN THE NEW YORK SEWER. HOW COULD YOU STAND IT WITH YOUR HEIGHTENED SENSE OF SMELL?
WE DO WHAT WE HAVE TO-- NATASHA.
DON'T TELL ME YOU KNEW I WAS TRACKING YOU THE WHOLE TIME.
YOU WERE THE BEST SPY THE SOVIET SYSTEM EVER CREATED. PEOPLE LIKE ME HIRE PEOPLE LIKE YOU. OF COURSE I KNEW.
DON'T MAKE ME HAVE TO--
I WOULD NEVER FIGHT A WOMAN.
I HAVE PEOPLE FOR THAT.

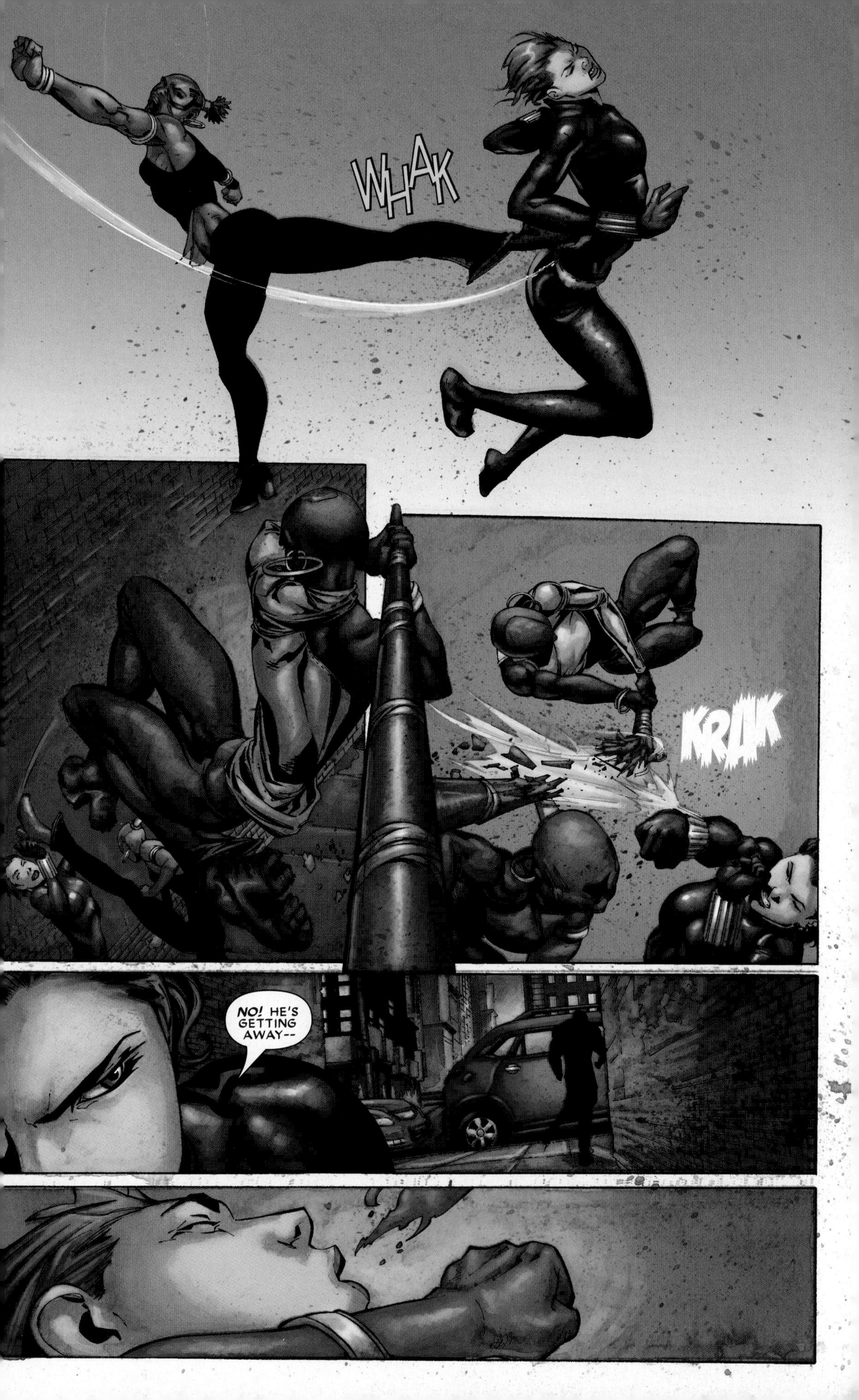

WHAK
KRAK
NO! HE'S GETTING AWAY--

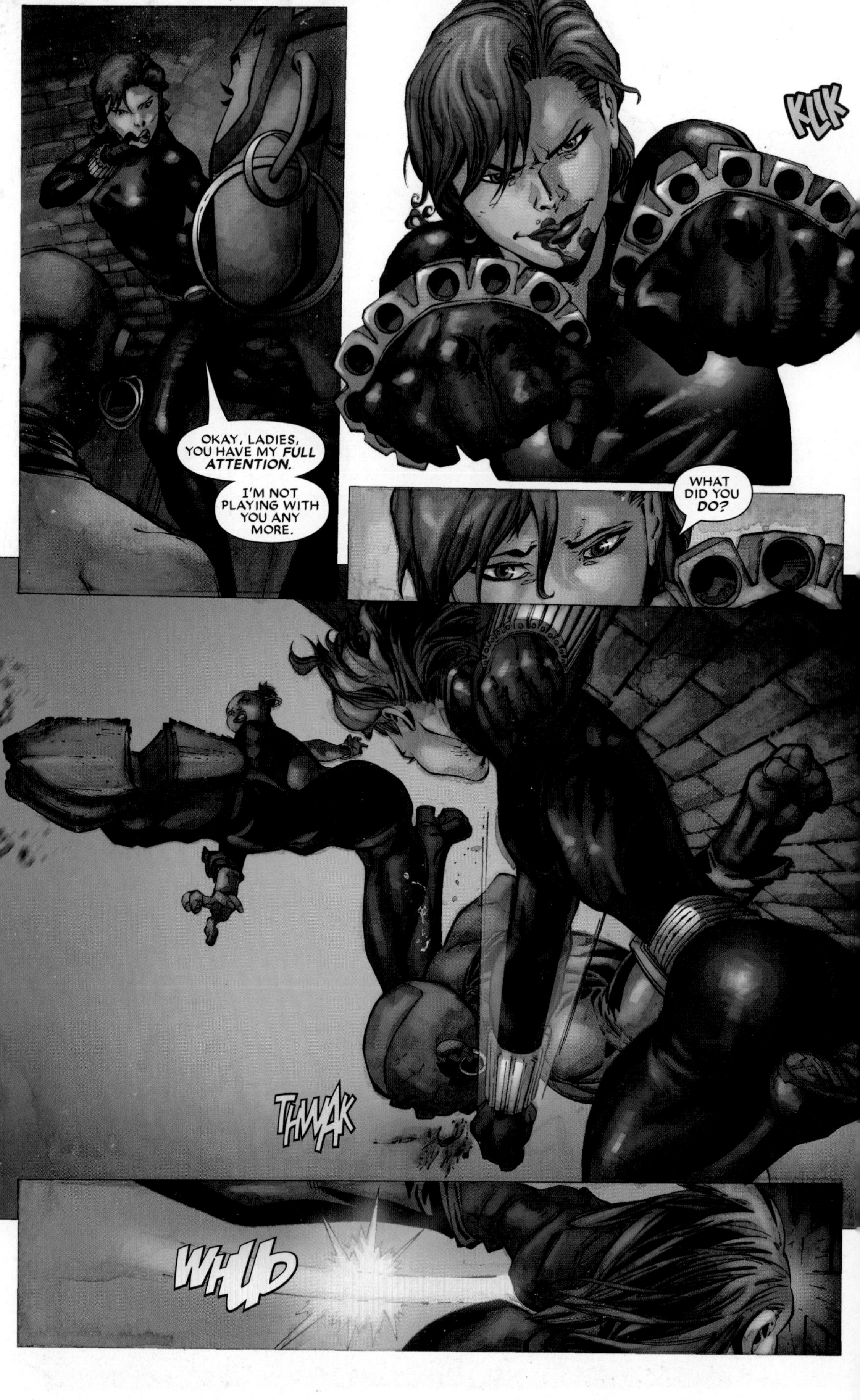
OKAY, LADIES, YOU HAVE MY FULL ATTENTION.
I'M NOT PLAYING WITH YOU ANY MORE.
KLIK
WHAT DID YOU DO?
THWAK
WHUD

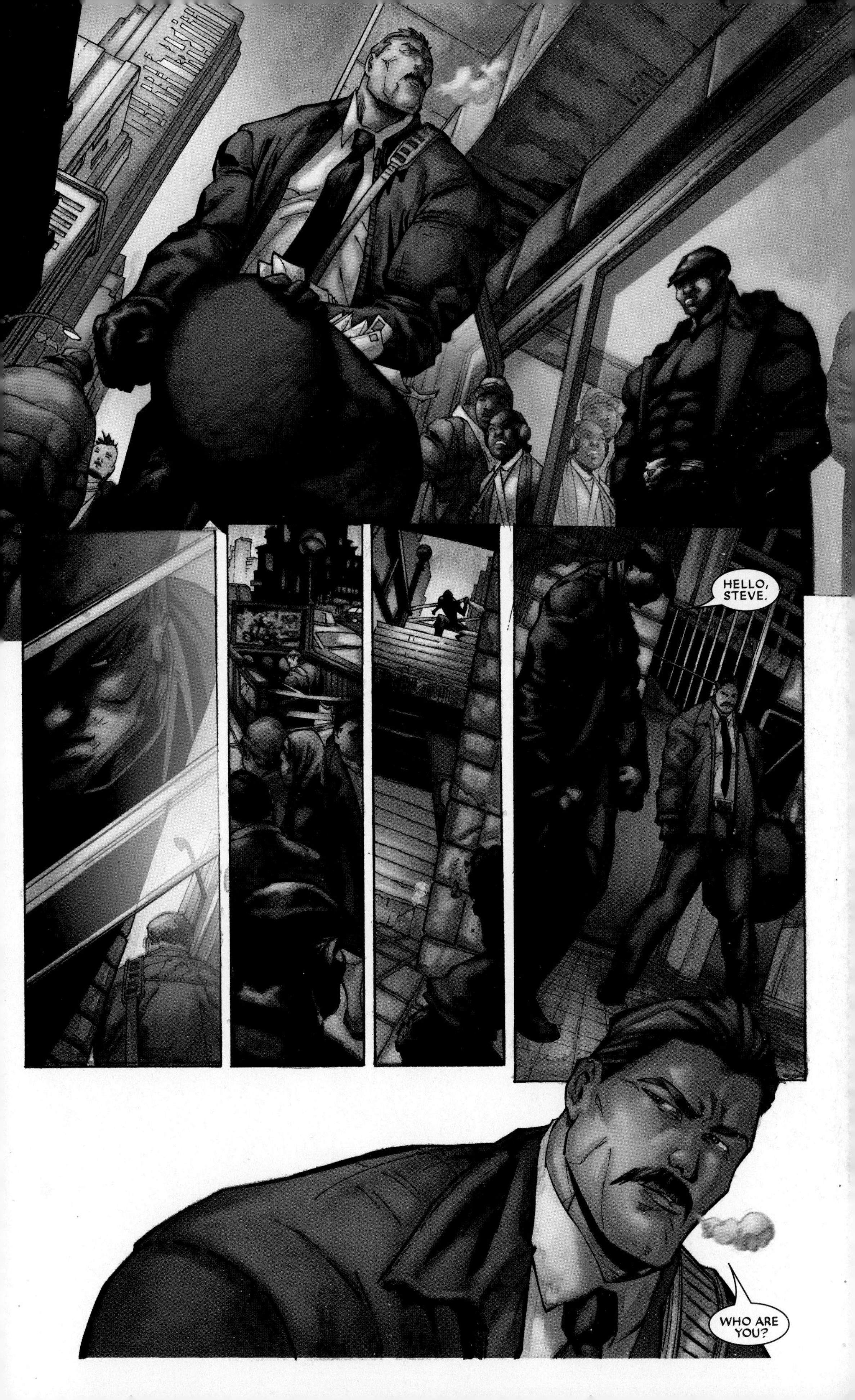
HELLO, STEVE.
WHO ARE YOU?

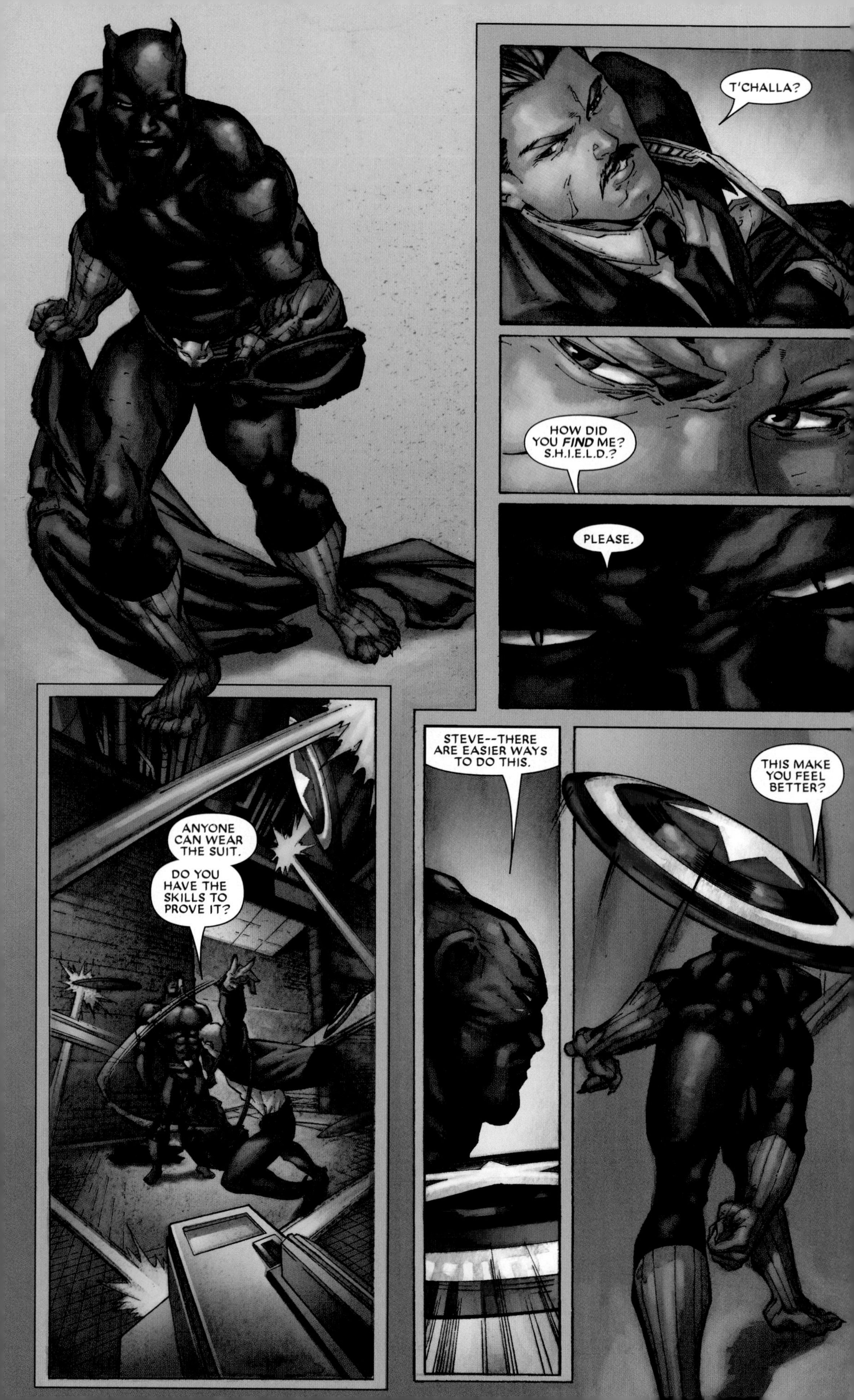
T'CHALLA?
HOW DID YOU FIND ME? S.H.I.E.L.D.?
PLEASE.
ANYONE CAN WEAR THE SUIT.
DO YOU HAVE THE SKILLS TO PROVE IT?
STEVE--THERE ARE EASIER WAYS TO DO THIS.
THIS MAKE YOU FEEL BETTER?

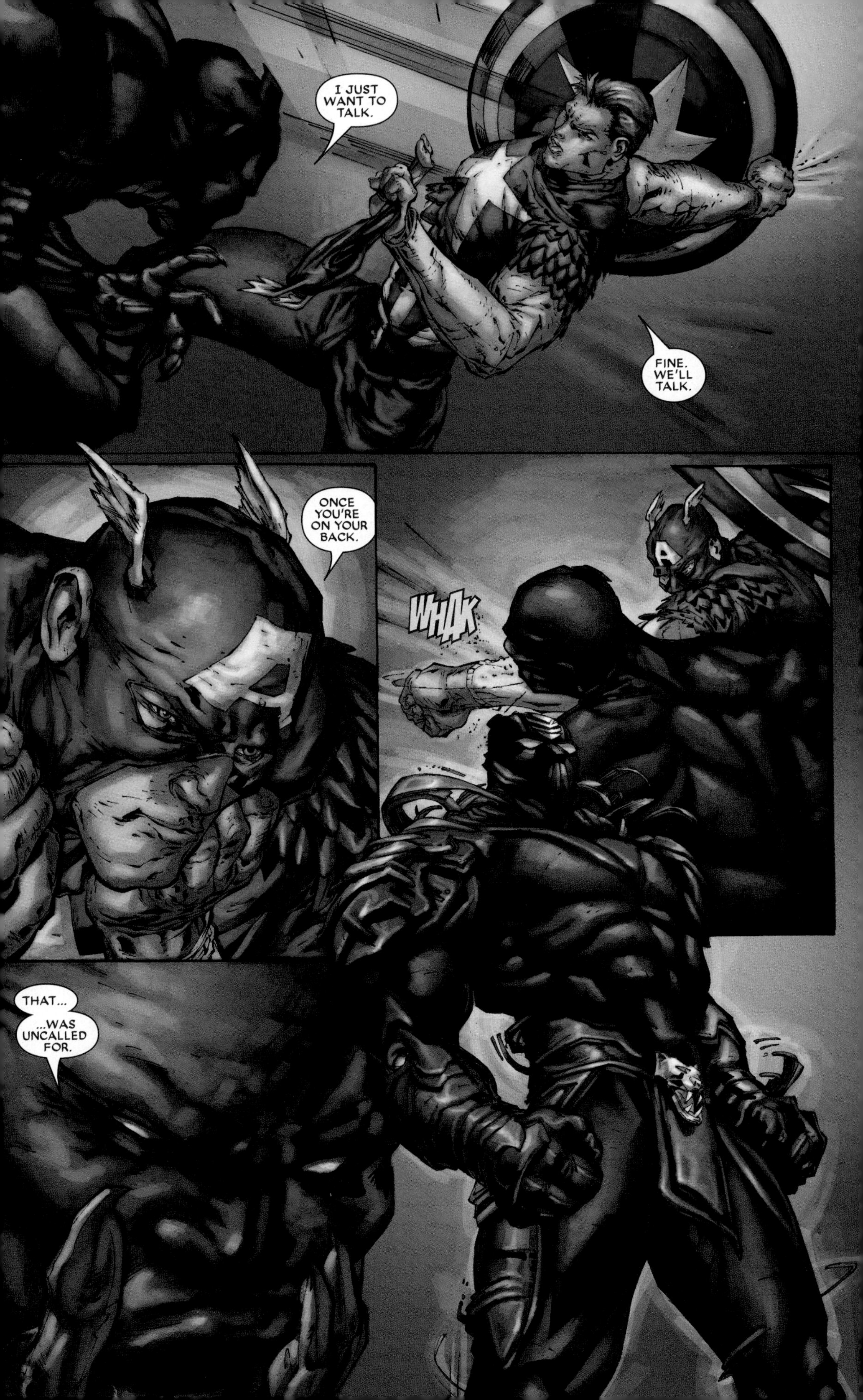
I JUST WANT TO TALK.
FINE. WE'LL TALK.
ONCE YOU'RE ON YOUR BACK.
WHAK
THAT...
...WAS UNCALLED FOR.

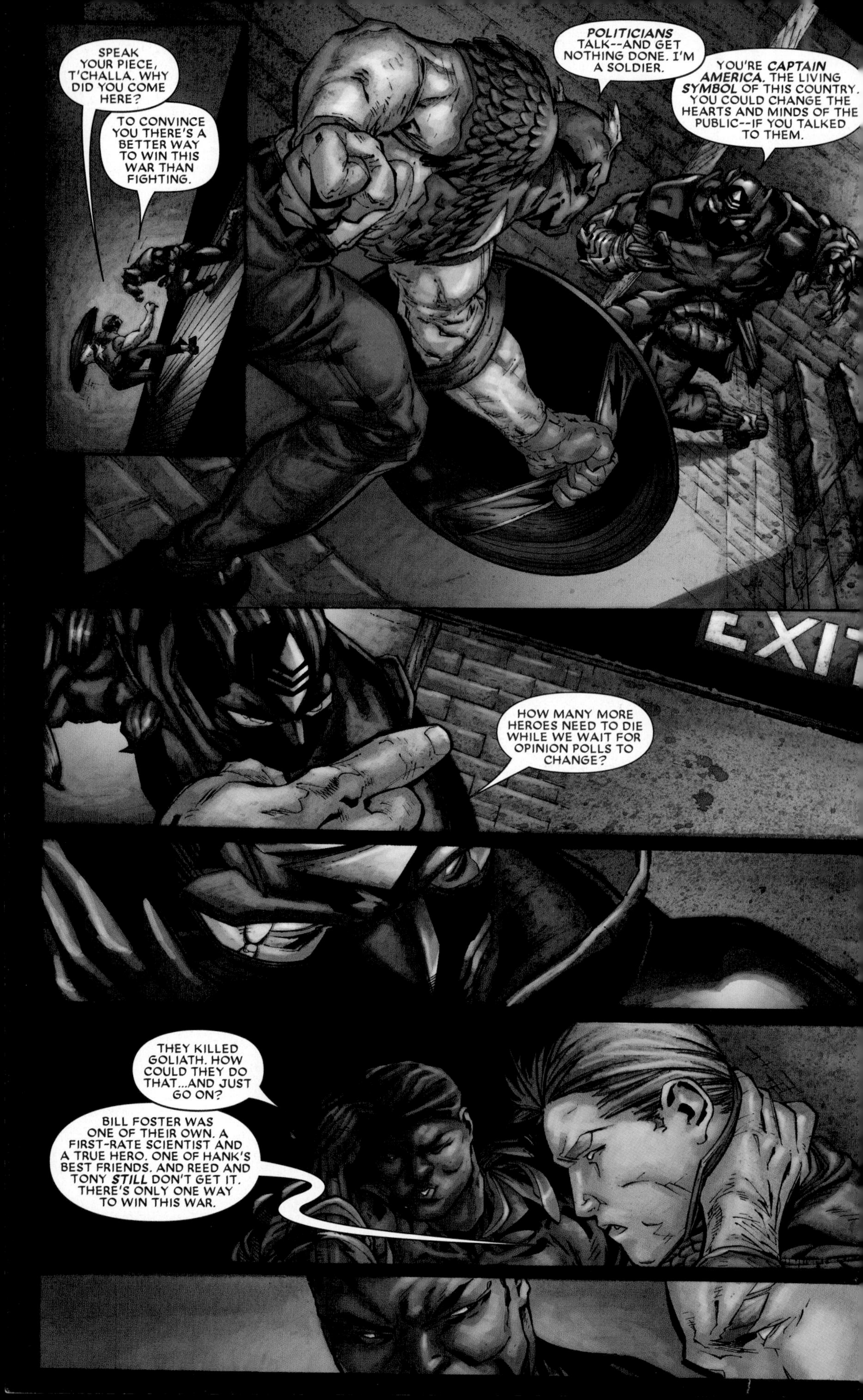
SPEAK YOUR PIECE, T'CHALLA. WHY DID YOU COME HERE?
TO CONVINCE YOU THERE'S A BETTER WAY TO WIN THIS WAR THAN FIGHTING.
POLITICIANS TALK--AND GET NOTHING DONE. I'M A SOLDIER.
YOU'RE CAPTAIN AMERICA. THE LIVING SYMBOL OF THIS COUNTRY. YOU COULD CHANGE THE HEARTS AND MINDS OF THE PUBLIC--IF YOU TALKED TO THEM.
EXIT
HOW MANY MORE HEROES NEED TO DIE WHILE WE WAIT FOR OPINION POLLS TO CHANGE?
THEY KILLED GOLIATH. HOW COULD THEY DO THAT...AND JUST GO ON?
BILL FOSTER WAS ONE OF THEIR OWN. A FIRST-RATE SCIENTIST AND A TRUE HERO. ONE OF HANK'S BEST FRIENDS. AND REED AND TONY STILL DON'T GET IT. THERE'S ONLY ONE WAY TO WIN THIS WAR.

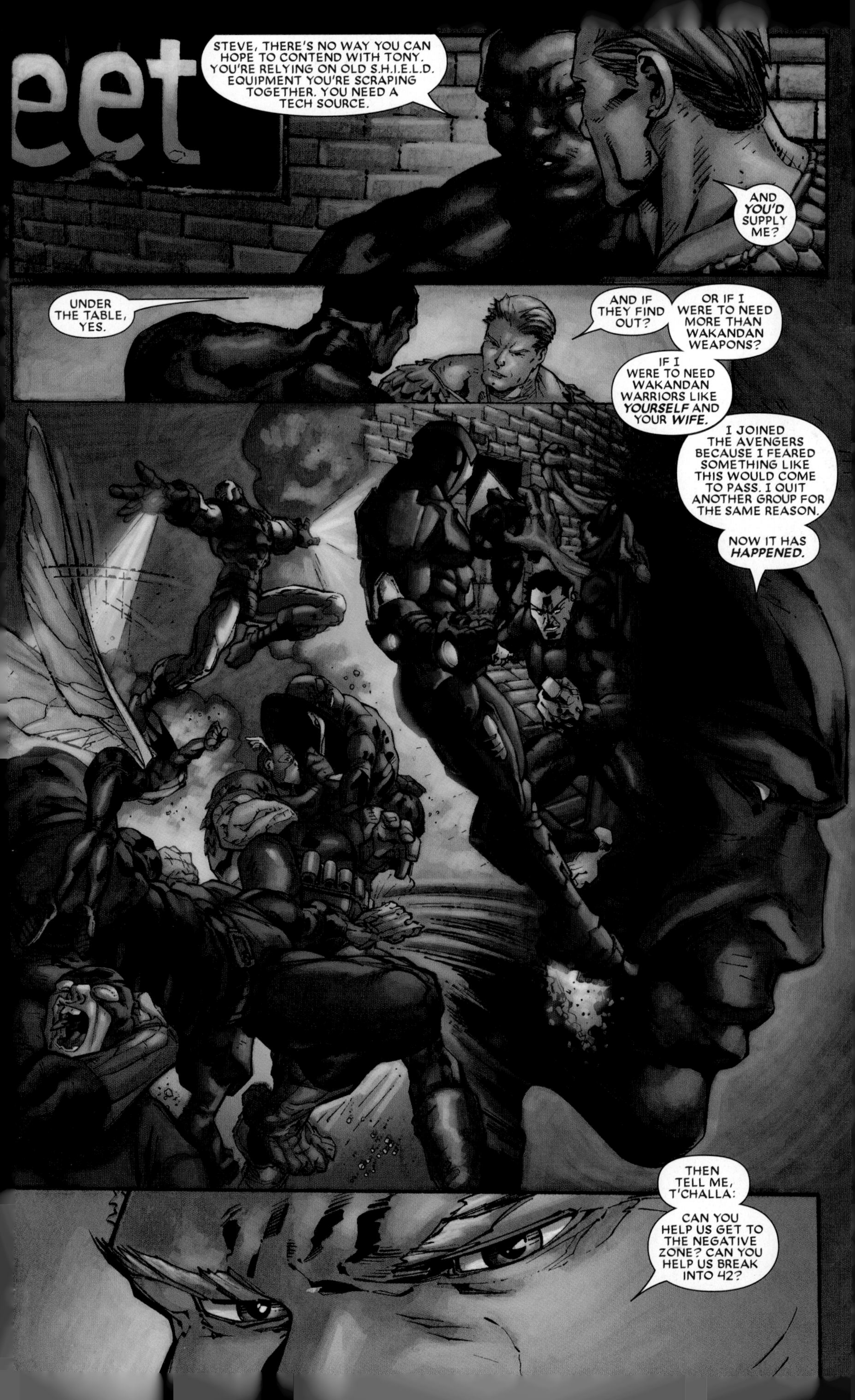
eet
STEVE, THERE'S NO WAY YOU CAN HOPE TO CONTEND WITH TONY. YOU'RE RELYING ON OLD S.H.I.E.L.D. EQUIPMENT YOU'RE SCRAPING TOGETHER. YOU NEED A TECH SOURCE.
AND *YOU'D* SUPPLY ME?
UNDER THE TABLE, YES.
AND IF THEY FIND OUT?
OR IF I WERE TO NEED MORE THAN WAKANDAN WEAPONS?
IF I WERE TO NEED WAKANDAN WARRIORS LIKE ***YOURSELF*** AND YOUR ***WIFE.***
I JOINED THE AVENGERS BECAUSE I FEARED SOMETHING LIKE THIS WOULD COME TO PASS. I QUIT ANOTHER GROUP FOR THE SAME REASON.
NOW IT HAS ***HAPPENED.***
THEN TELL ME, T'CHALLA:
CAN YOU HELP US GET TO THE NEGATIVE ZONE? CAN YOU HELP US BREAK INTO 42?

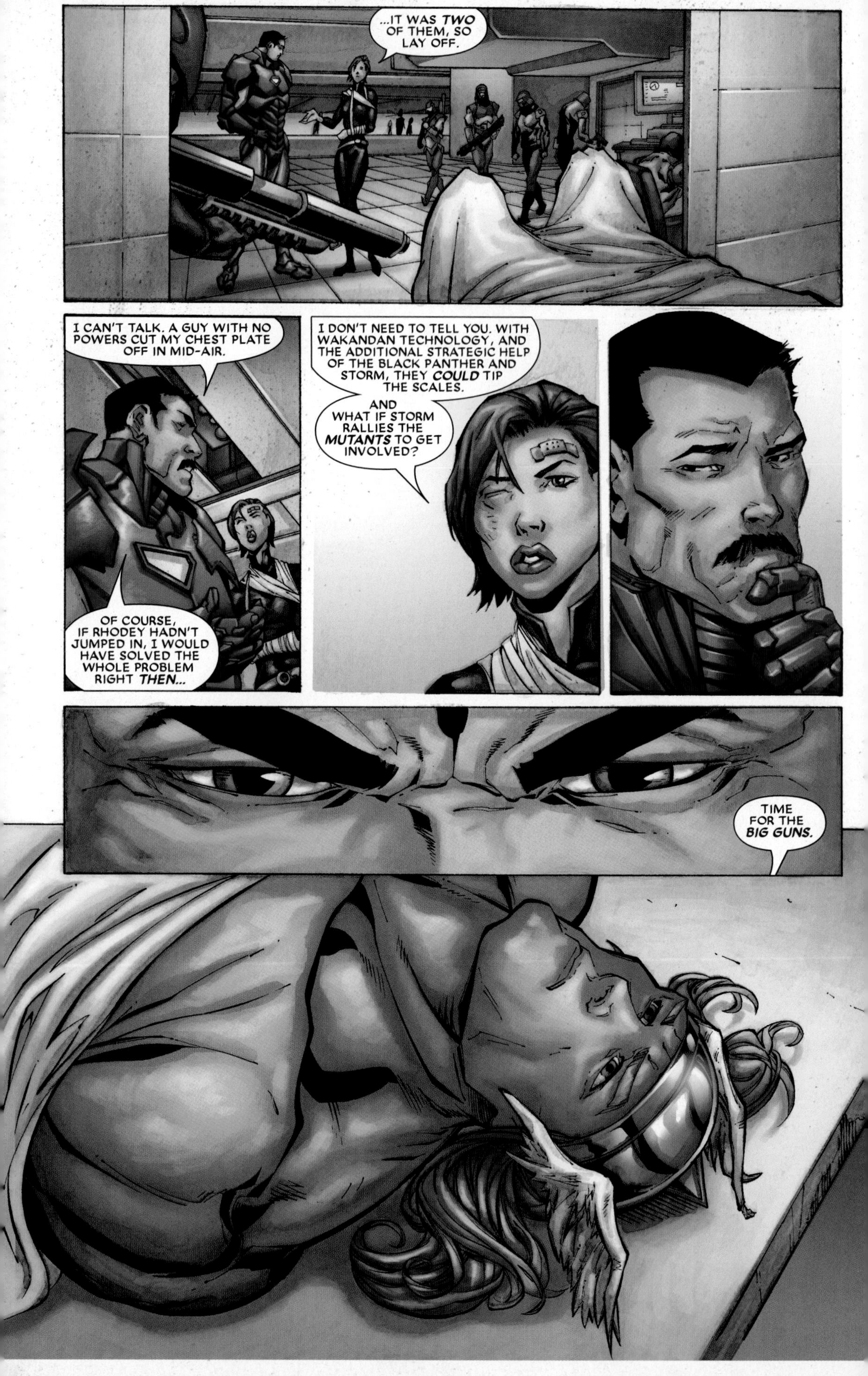
...IT WAS TWO OF THEM, SO LAY OFF.
I CAN'T TALK. A GUY WITH NO POWERS CUT MY CHEST PLATE OFF IN MID-AIR.
OF COURSE, IF RHODEY HADN'T JUMPED IN, I WOULD HAVE SOLVED THE WHOLE PROBLEM RIGHT THEN...
I DON'T NEED TO TELL YOU. WITH WAKANDAN TECHNOLOGY, AND THE ADDITIONAL STRATEGIC HELP OF THE BLACK PANTHER AND STORM, THEY COULD TIP THE SCALES.
AND WHAT IF STORM RALLIES THE MUTANTS TO GET INVOLVED?
TIME FOR THE BIG GUNS.

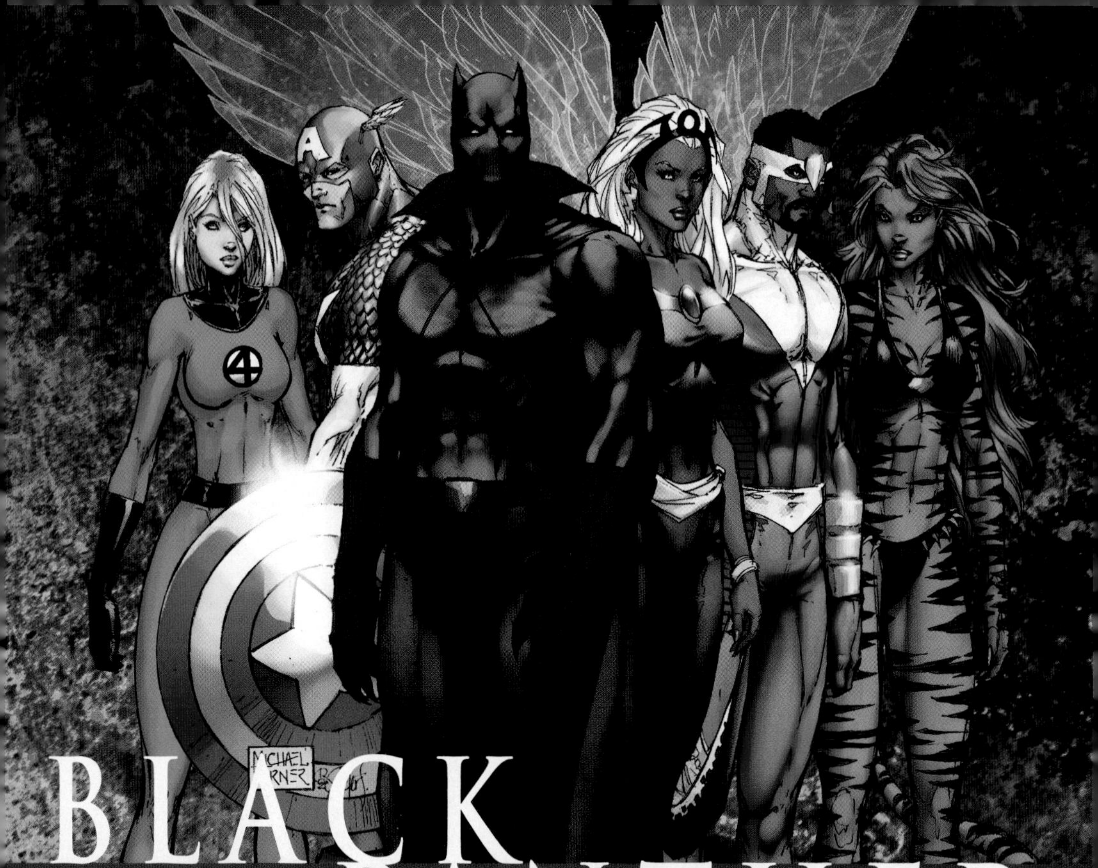

BLACK PANTHER

A MARVEL COMICS EVENT

CIVIL WAR

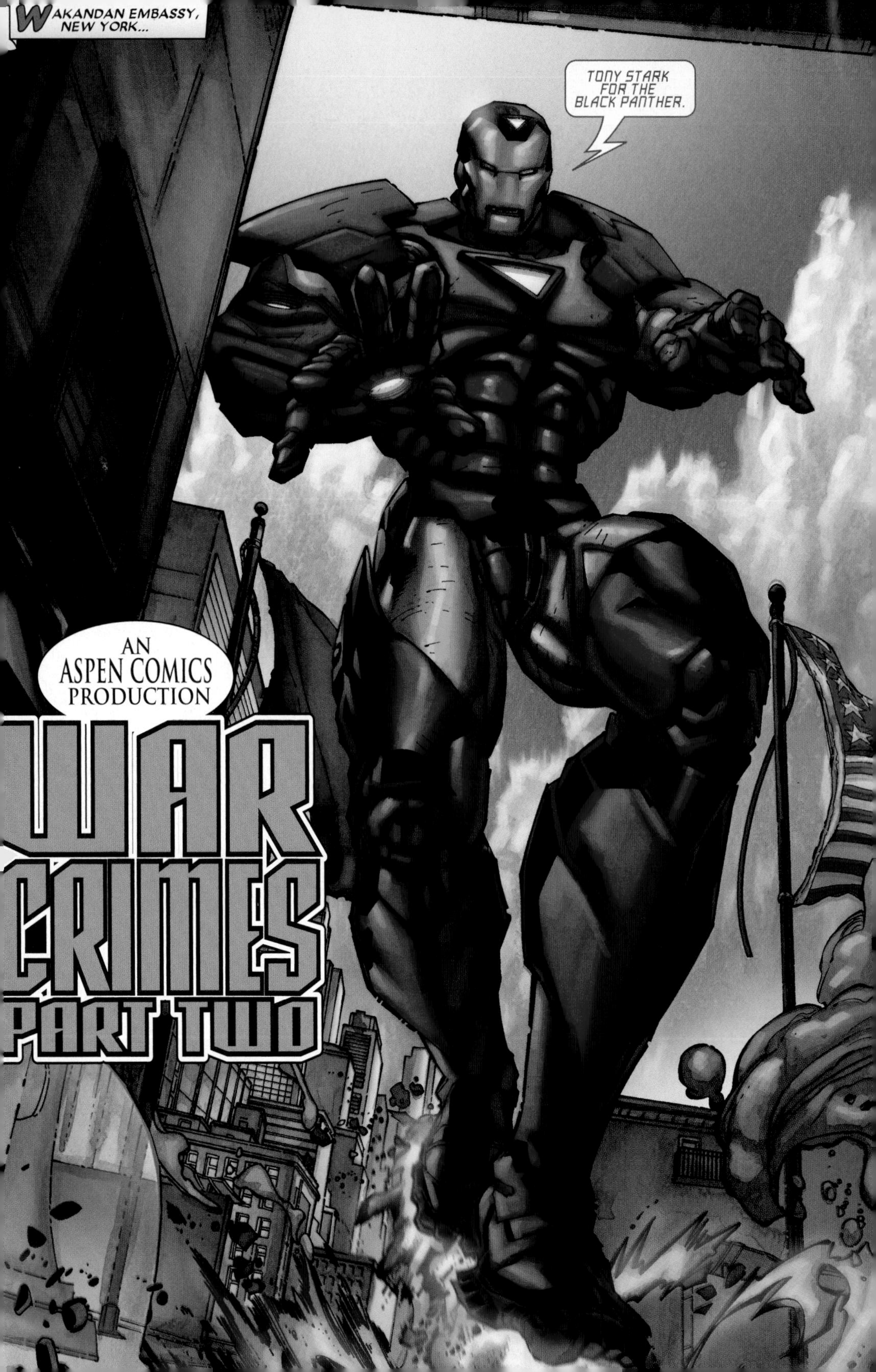
WAKANDAN EMBASSY, NEW YORK...
TONY STARK FOR THE BLACK PANTHER.
AN ASPEN COMICS PRODUCTION
WAR CRIMES PART TWO

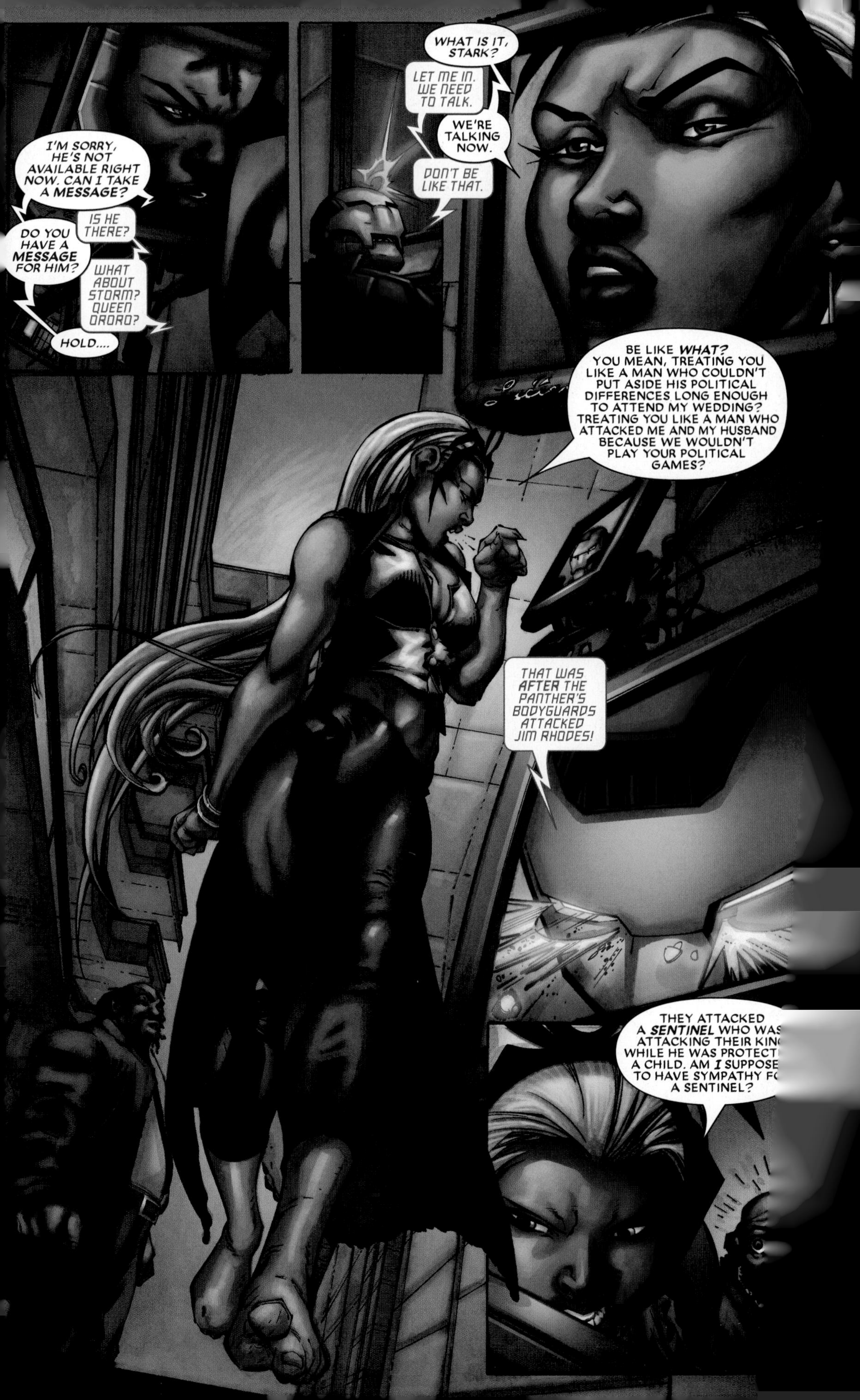
I'M SORRY, HE'S NOT AVAILABLE RIGHT NOW. CAN I TAKE A MESSAGE?
IS HE THERE?
DO YOU HAVE A MESSAGE FOR HIM?
WHAT ABOUT STORM? QUEEN ORORO?
HOLD....
WHAT IS IT, STARK?
LET ME IN. WE NEED TO TALK.
WE'RE TALKING NOW.
DON'T BE LIKE THAT.
BE LIKE WHAT? YOU MEAN, TREATING YOU LIKE A MAN WHO COULDN'T PUT ASIDE HIS POLITICAL DIFFERENCES LONG ENOUGH TO ATTEND MY WEDDING? TREATING YOU LIKE A MAN WHO ATTACKED ME AND MY HUSBAND BECAUSE WE WOULDN'T PLAY YOUR POLITICAL GAMES?
THAT WAS AFTER THE PANTHER'S BODYGUARDS ATTACKED JIM RHODES!
THEY ATTACKED A SENTINEL WHO WAS ATTACKING THEIR KING WHILE HE WAS PROTECT A CHILD. AM I SUPPOSE TO HAVE SYMPATHY FO A SENTINEL?

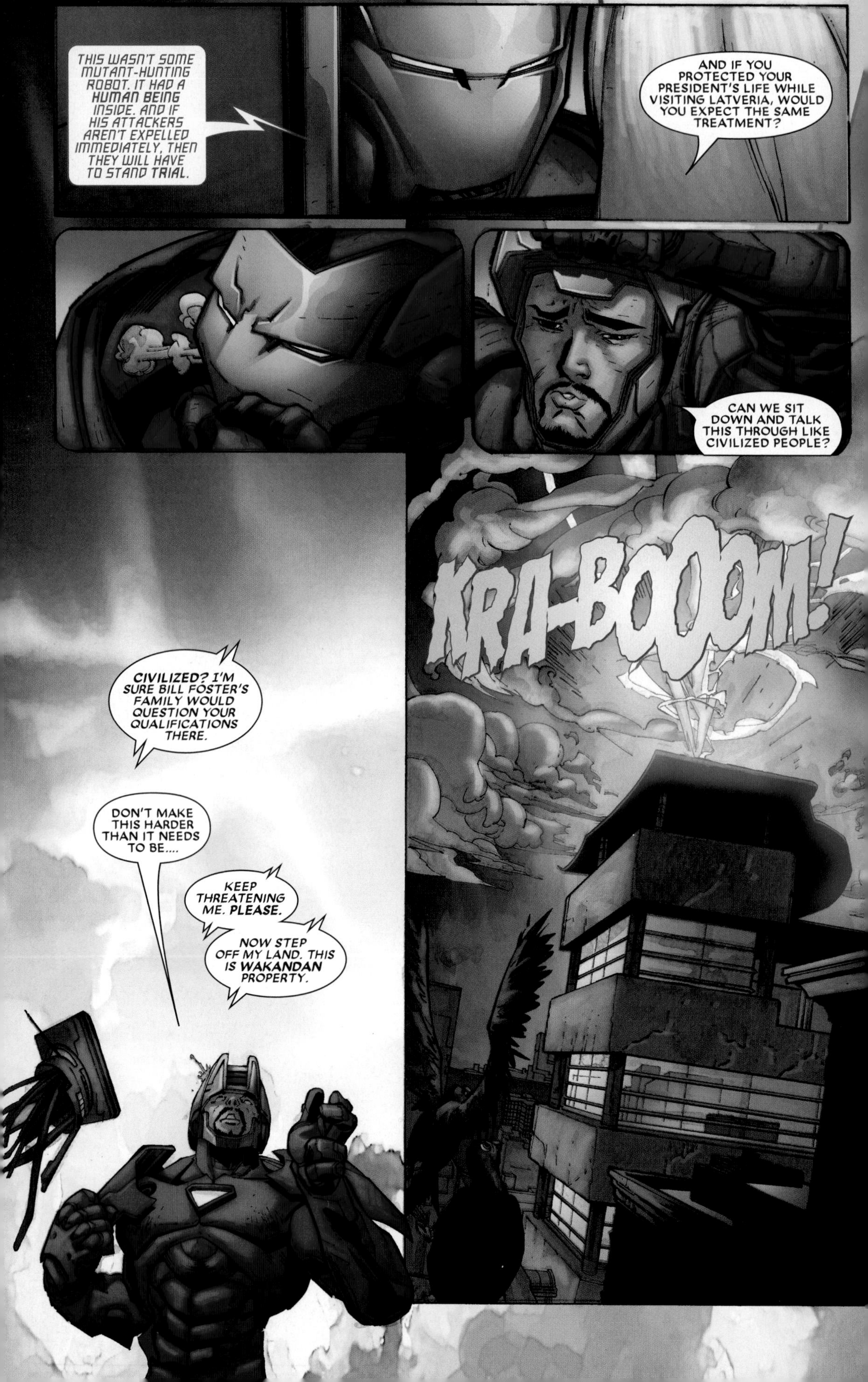
THIS WASN'T SOME MUTANT-HUNTING ROBOT. IT HAD A HUMAN BEING INSIDE. AND IF HIS ATTACKERS AREN'T EXPELLED IMMEDIATELY, THEN THEY WILL HAVE TO STAND TRIAL.
AND IF YOU PROTECTED YOUR PRESIDENT'S LIFE WHILE VISITING LATVERIA, WOULD YOU EXPECT THE SAME TREATMENT?
CAN WE SIT DOWN AND TALK THIS THROUGH LIKE CIVILIZED PEOPLE?
KRA-BOOOM!
CIVILIZED? I'M SURE BILL FOSTER'S FAMILY WOULD QUESTION YOUR QUALIFICATIONS THERE.
DON'T MAKE THIS HARDER THAN IT NEEDS TO BE....
KEEP THREATENING ME. PLEASE.
NOW STEP OFF MY LAND. THIS IS WAKANDAN PROPERTY.

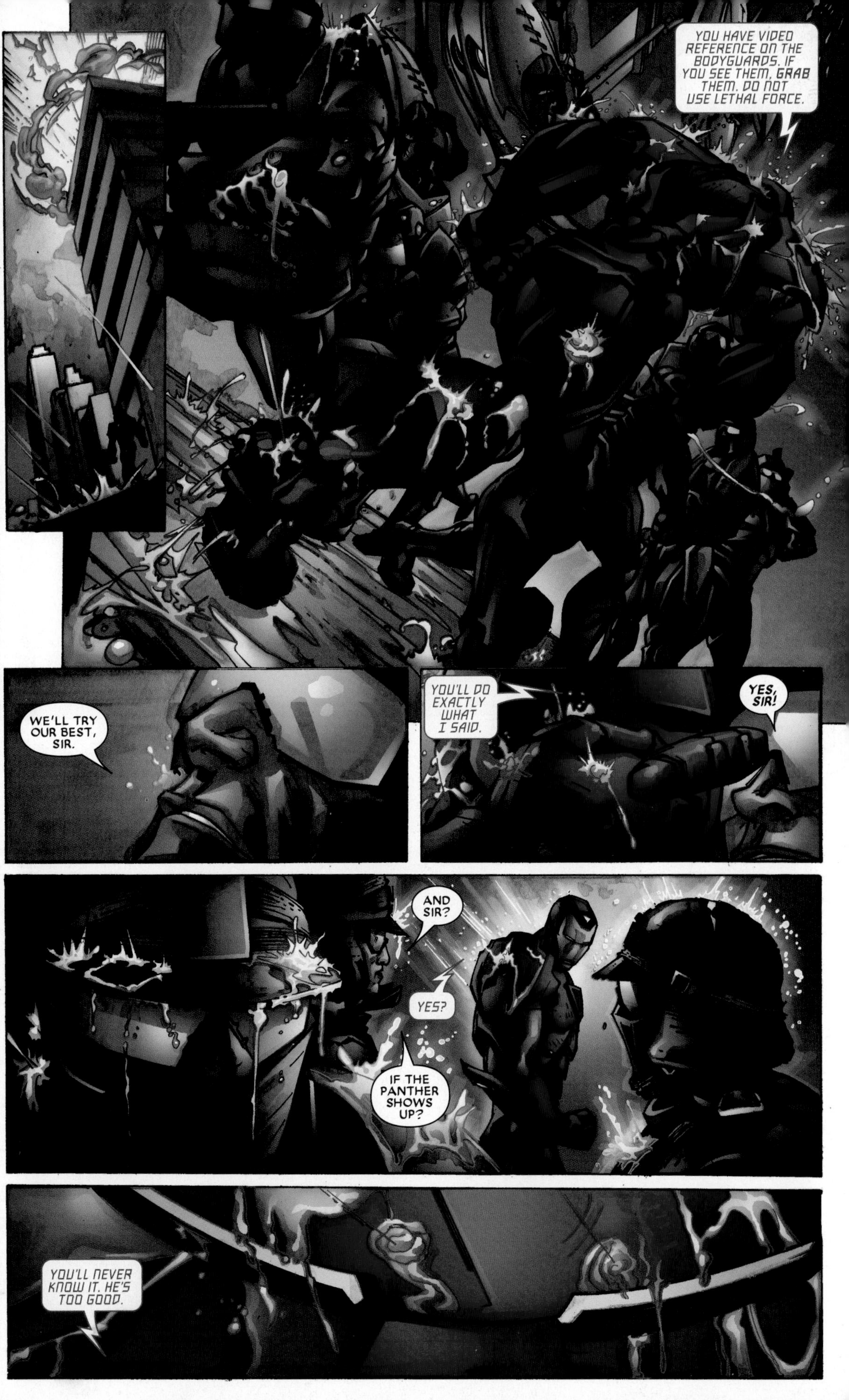
YOU HAVE VIDEO REFERENCE ON THE BODYGUARDS. IF YOU SEE THEM, GRAB THEM. DO NOT USE LETHAL FORCE.
WE'LL TRY OUR BEST, SIR.
YOU'LL DO EXACTLY WHAT I SAID.
YES, SIR!
AND SIR?
YES?
IF THE PANTHER SHOWS UP?
YOU'LL NEVER KNOW IT. HE'S TOO GOOD.

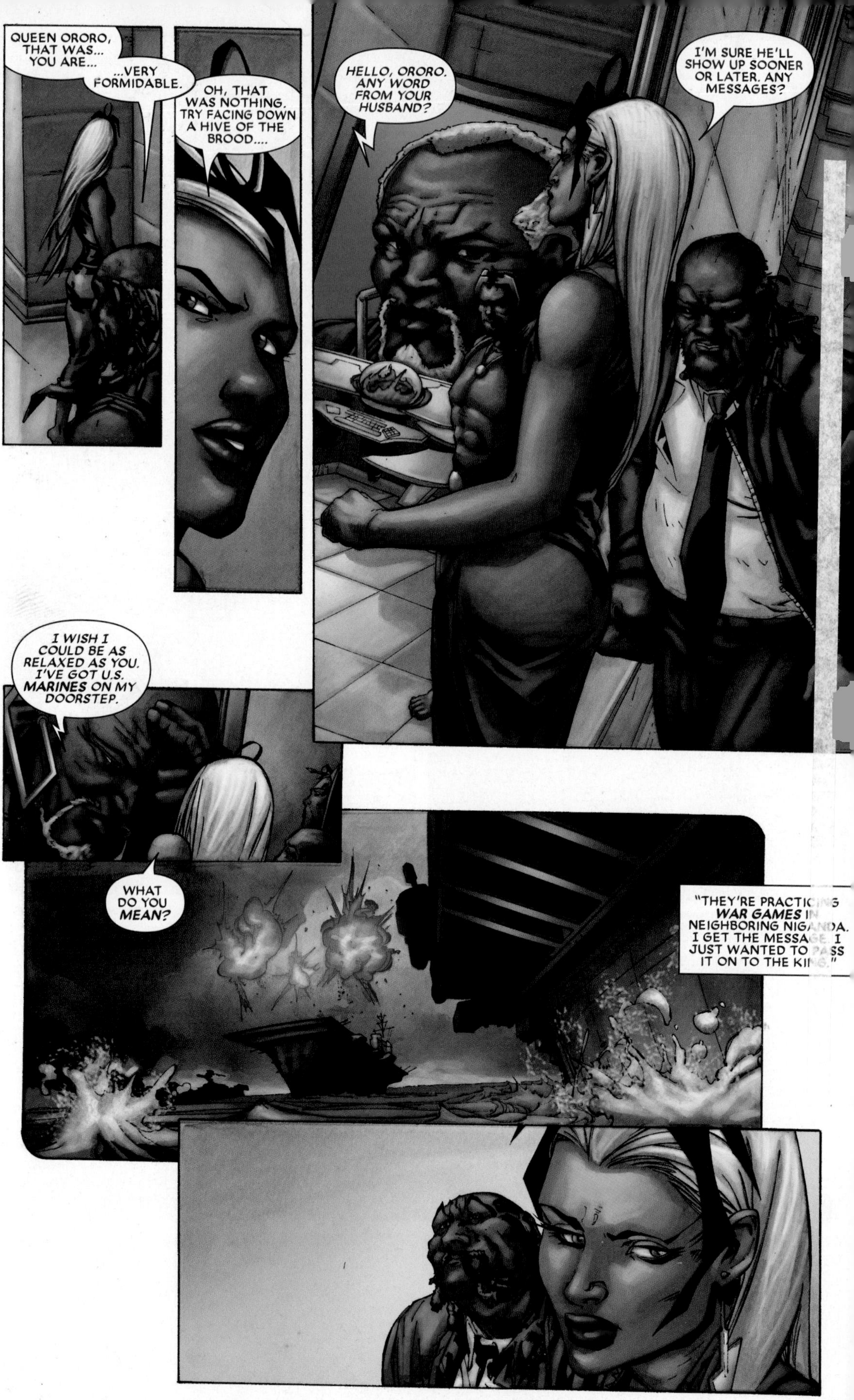
QUEEN ORORO, THAT WAS... YOU ARE...
...VERY FORMIDABLE.
OH, THAT WAS NOTHING. TRY FACING DOWN A HIVE OF THE BROOD....
HELLO, ORORO. ANY WORD FROM YOUR HUSBAND?
I'M SURE HE'LL SHOW UP SOONER OR LATER. ANY MESSAGES?
I WISH I COULD BE AS RELAXED AS YOU. I'VE GOT U.S. MARINES ON MY DOORSTEP.
WHAT DO YOU MEAN?
"THEY'RE PRACTICING WAR GAMES IN NEIGHBORING NIGANDA. I GET THE MESSAGE. I JUST WANTED TO PASS IT ON TO THE KING."

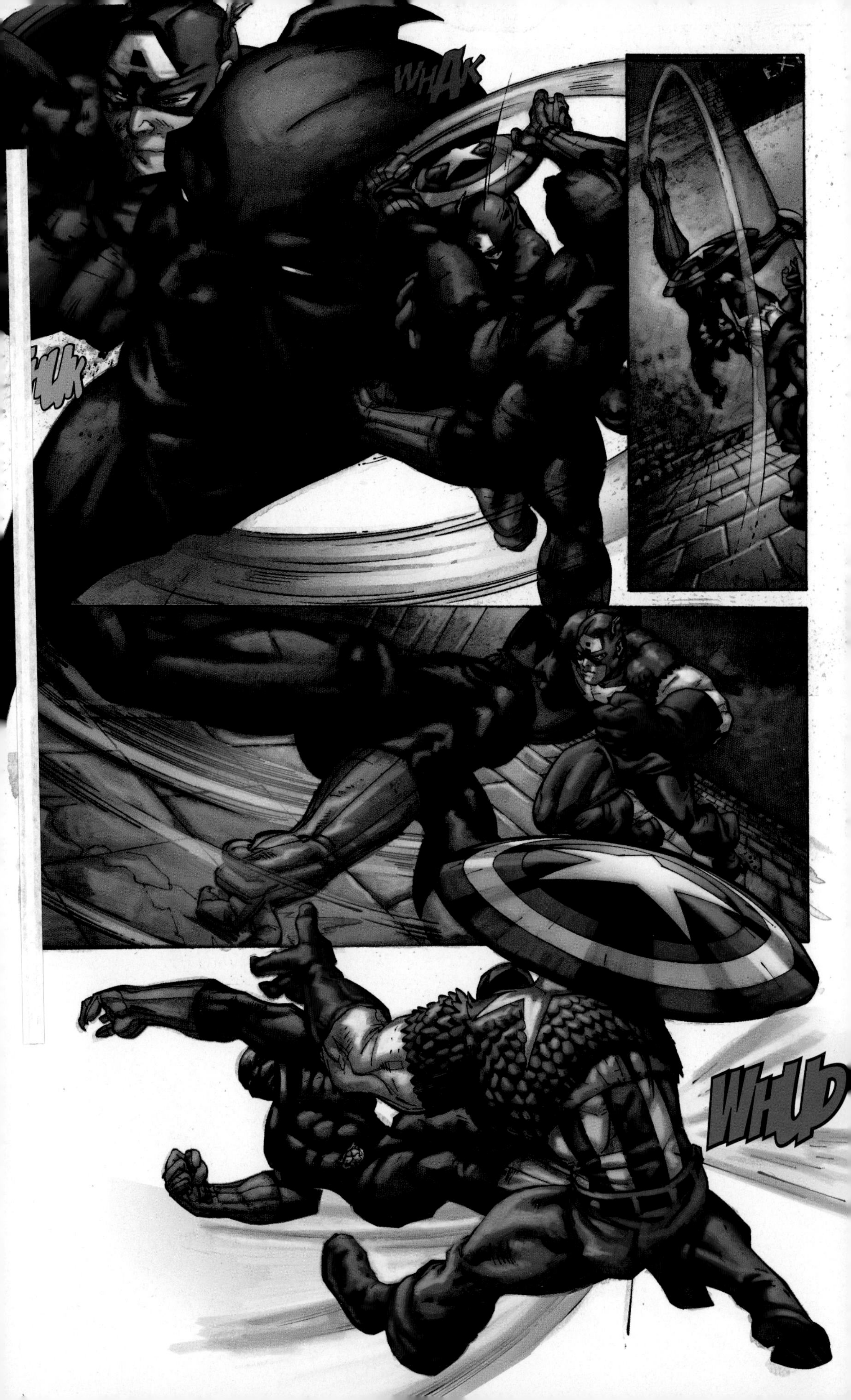
WHAK
WHUP

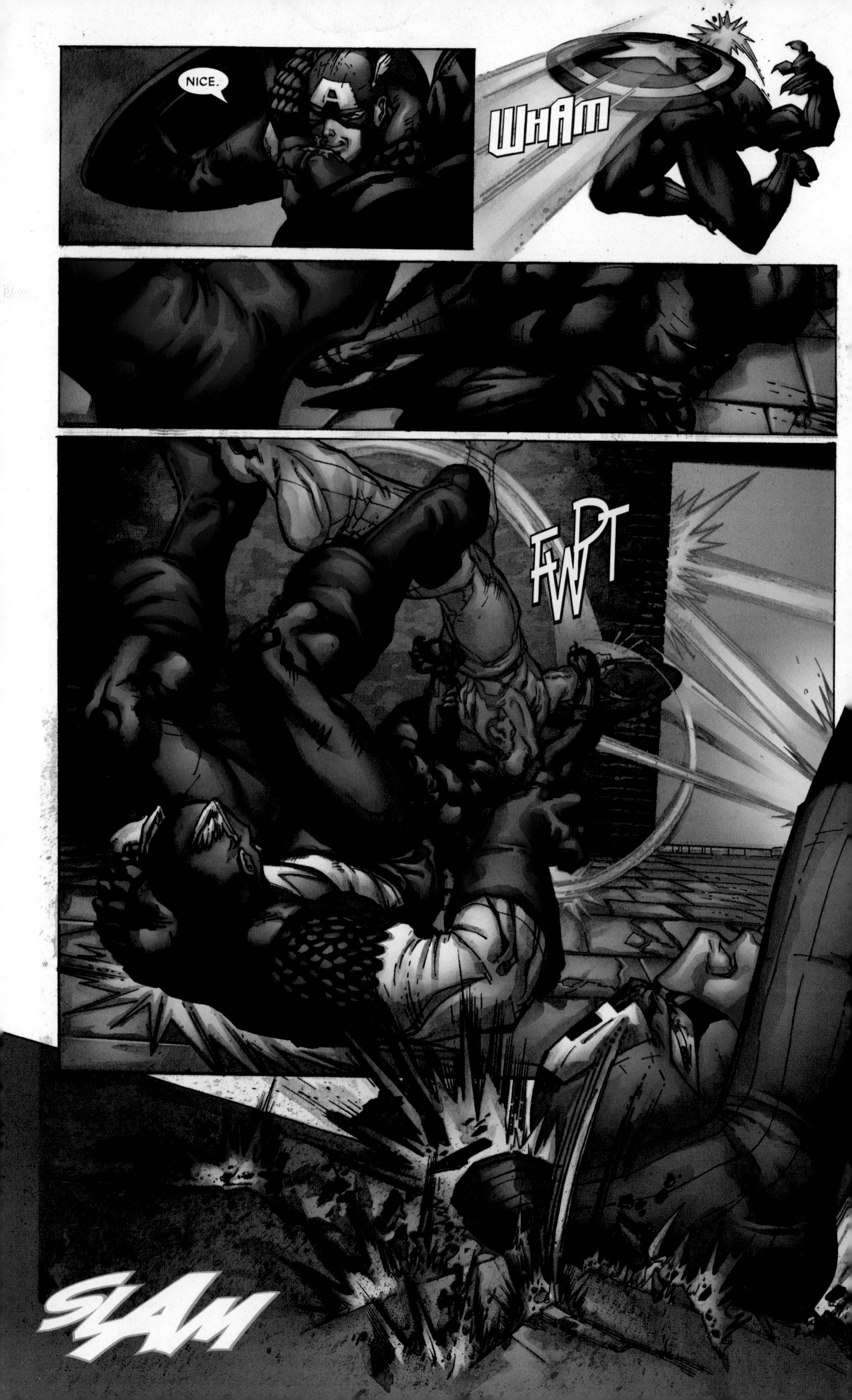
NICE.
WHAM
FWPT
SLAM

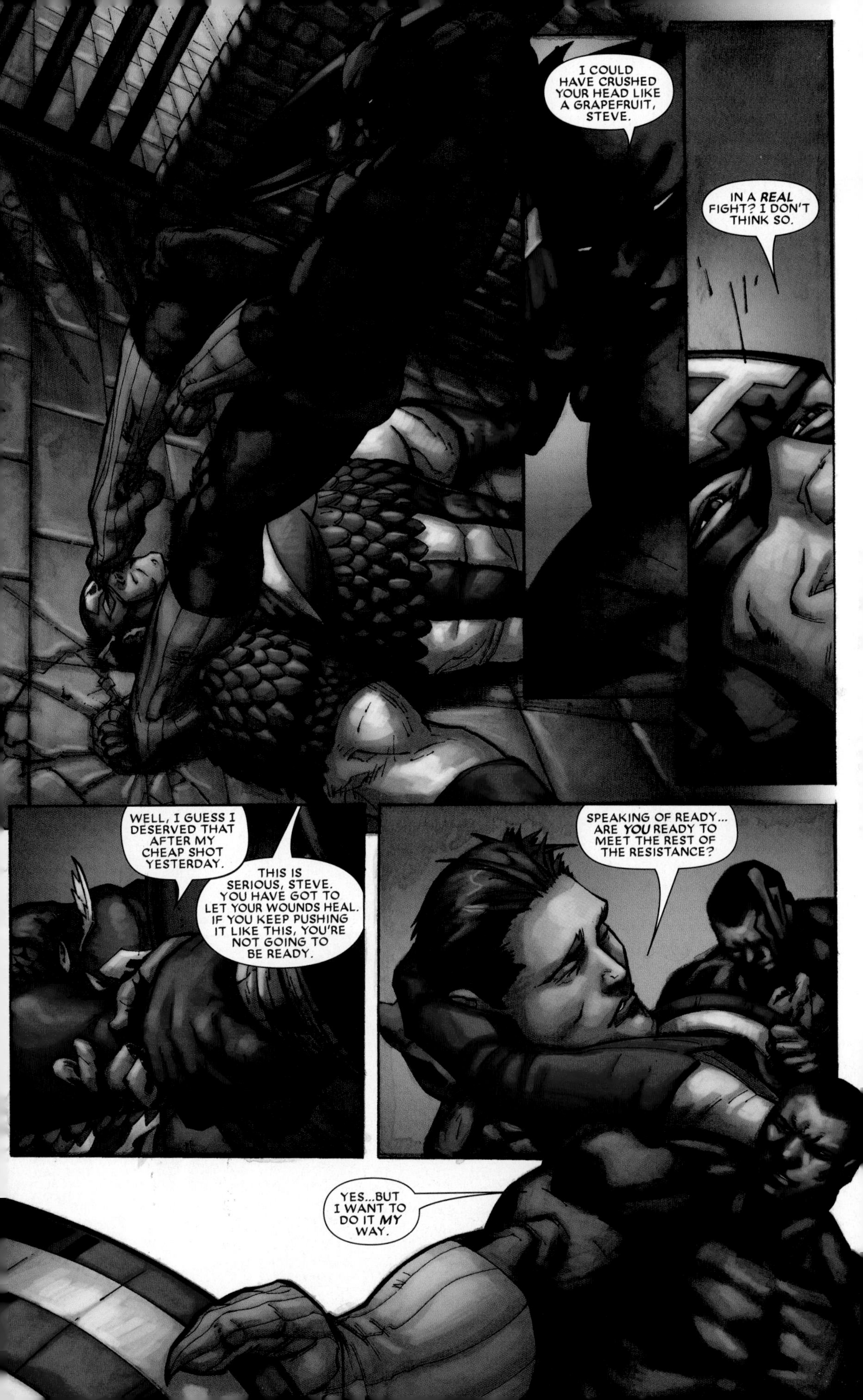
I COULD HAVE CRUSHED YOUR HEAD LIKE A GRAPEFRUIT, STEVE.
IN A REAL FIGHT? I DON'T THINK SO.
WELL, I GUESS I DESERVED THAT AFTER MY CHEAP SHOT YESTERDAY.
THIS IS SERIOUS, STEVE. YOU HAVE GOT TO LET YOUR WOUNDS HEAL. IF YOU KEEP PUSHING IT LIKE THIS, YOU'RE NOT GOING TO BE READY.
SPEAKING OF READY... ARE YOU READY TO MEET THE REST OF THE RESISTANCE?
YES...BUT I WANT TO DO IT MY WAY.

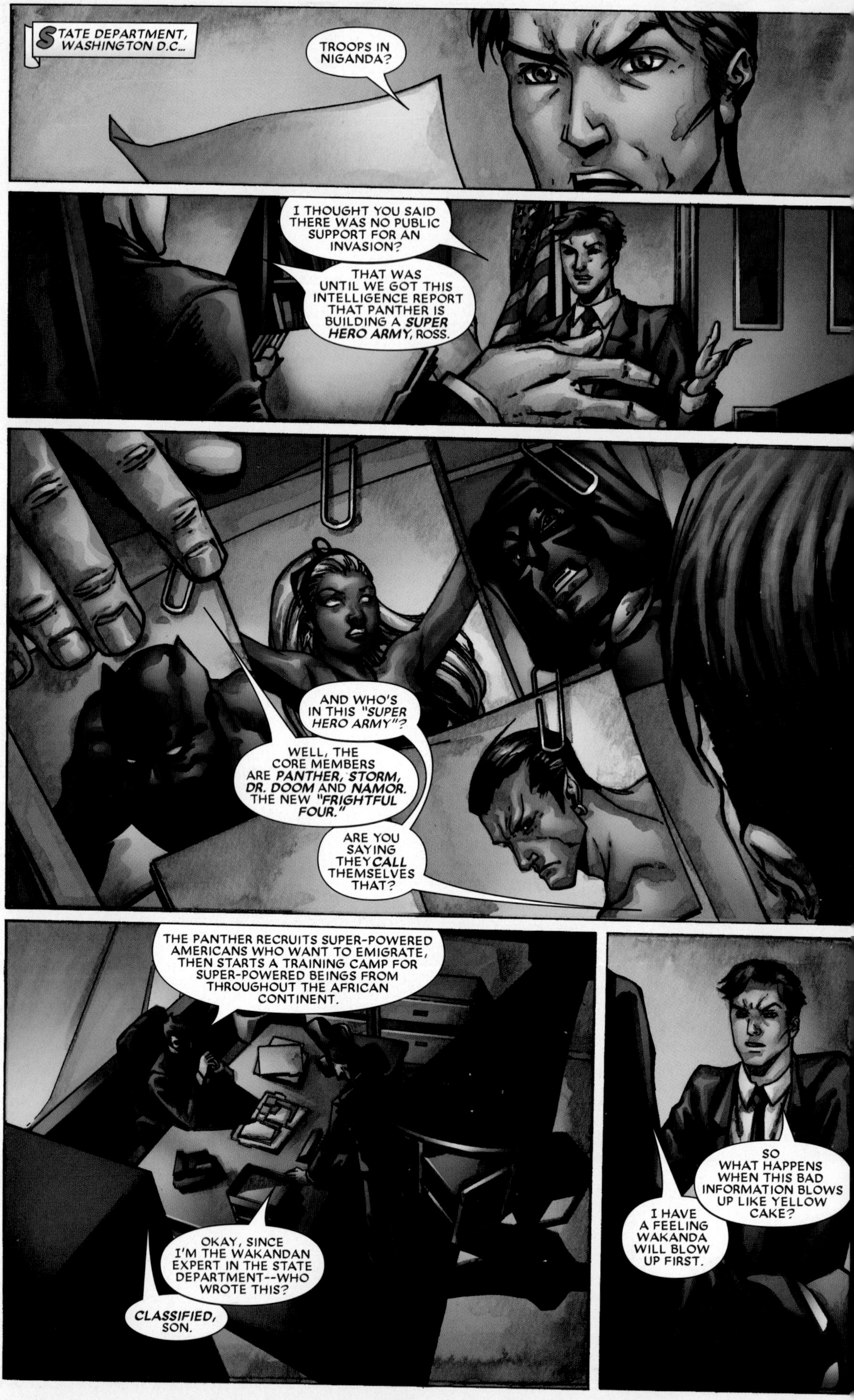
STATE DEPARTMENT, WASHINGTON D.C...
TROOPS IN NIGANDA?
I THOUGHT YOU SAID THERE WAS NO PUBLIC SUPPORT FOR AN INVASION?
THAT WAS UNTIL WE GOT THIS INTELLIGENCE REPORT THAT PANTHER IS BUILDING A SUPER HERO ARMY, ROSS.
AND WHO'S IN THIS "SUPER HERO ARMY"?
WELL, THE CORE MEMBERS ARE PANTHER, STORM, DR. DOOM AND NAMOR. THE NEW "FRIGHTFUL FOUR."
ARE YOU SAYING THEY CALL THEMSELVES THAT?
THE PANTHER RECRUITS SUPER-POWERED AMERICANS WHO WANT TO EMIGRATE, THEN STARTS A TRAINING CAMP FOR SUPER-POWERED BEINGS FROM THROUGHOUT THE AFRICAN CONTINENT.
OKAY, SINCE I'M THE WAKANDAN EXPERT IN THE STATE DEPARTMENT--WHO WROTE THIS?
CLASSIFIED, SON.
SO WHAT HAPPENS WHEN THIS BAD INFORMATION BLOWS UP LIKE YELLOW CAKE?
I HAVE A FEELING WAKANDA WILL BLOW UP FIRST.

WAKANDA...

BROTHER VOODOO! HOW GOES IT?

WELL, THANK YOU. WAKANDAN HOSPITALITY IS EXTRAORDINARY.

DO YOU THINK MORE OF YOUR COUNTRYMEN WILL TAKE UP T'CHALLA'S OFFER?

WELL, I HOPE A SPEEDY RESOLUTION OF THE REGISTRATION CRISIS IN THE UNITED STATES WILL MAKE IT A NONISSUE.

BUT IN THE MEANTIME, I HAVE BEEN WORKING WITH YOUR PRIESTS HERE. THERE'S BEEN A FASCINATING EXCHANGE OF IDEAS. I HAD NO IDEA HOW CLOSELY THE SPIRITUAL AND THE SCIENTIFIC WERE IN WAKANDA.

IT'S ALL A CONTINUUM TO US.

I'M STILL SEARCHING FOR THE WHEREABOUTS OF THAT SHAPE-SHIFTER OR BODY STEALER WHO WAS AT THE WEDDING.

STILL NO PERCEPTION OF HIM? OR HER?

NOT YET. THEY KNOW THEY ARE BEING HUNTED. BUT EVENTUALLY THEY WILL MAKE A PLAY FOR A POWERFUL HOST. AND THAT'S WHEN THEY WILL BE CAUGHT.

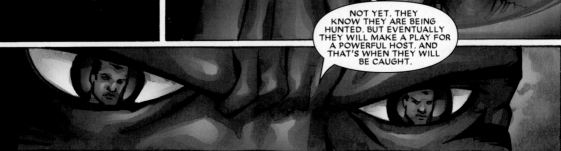

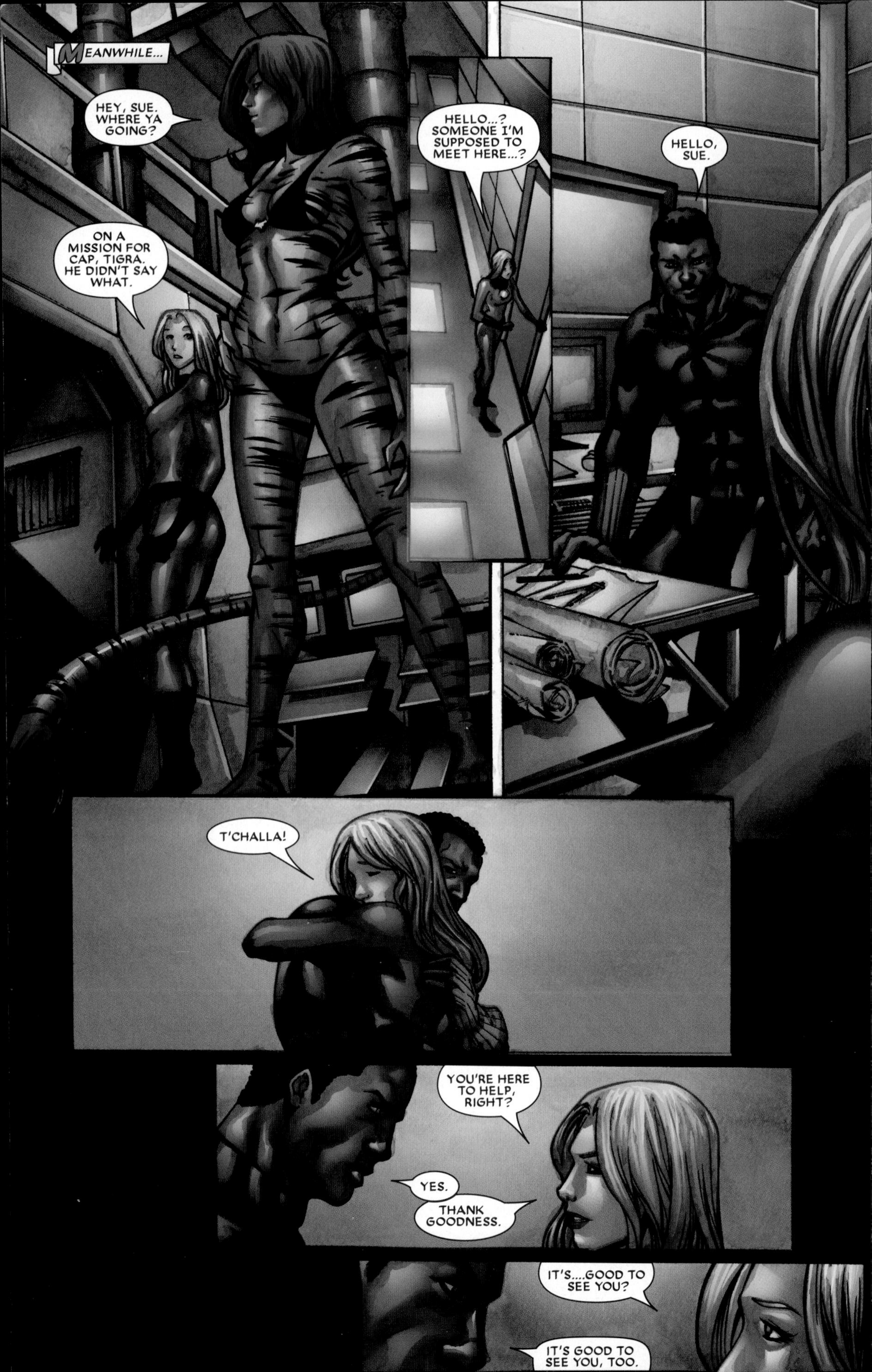
MEANWHILE...
HEY, SUE. WHERE YA GOING?
ON A MISSION FOR CAP, TIGRA. HE DIDN'T SAY WHAT.
HELLO...? SOMEONE I'M SUPPOSED TO MEET HERE...?
HELLO, SUE.
T'CHALLA!
YOU'RE HERE TO HELP, RIGHT?
YES.
THANK GOODNESS.
IT'S....GOOD TO SEE YOU?
IT'S GOOD TO SEE YOU, TOO.

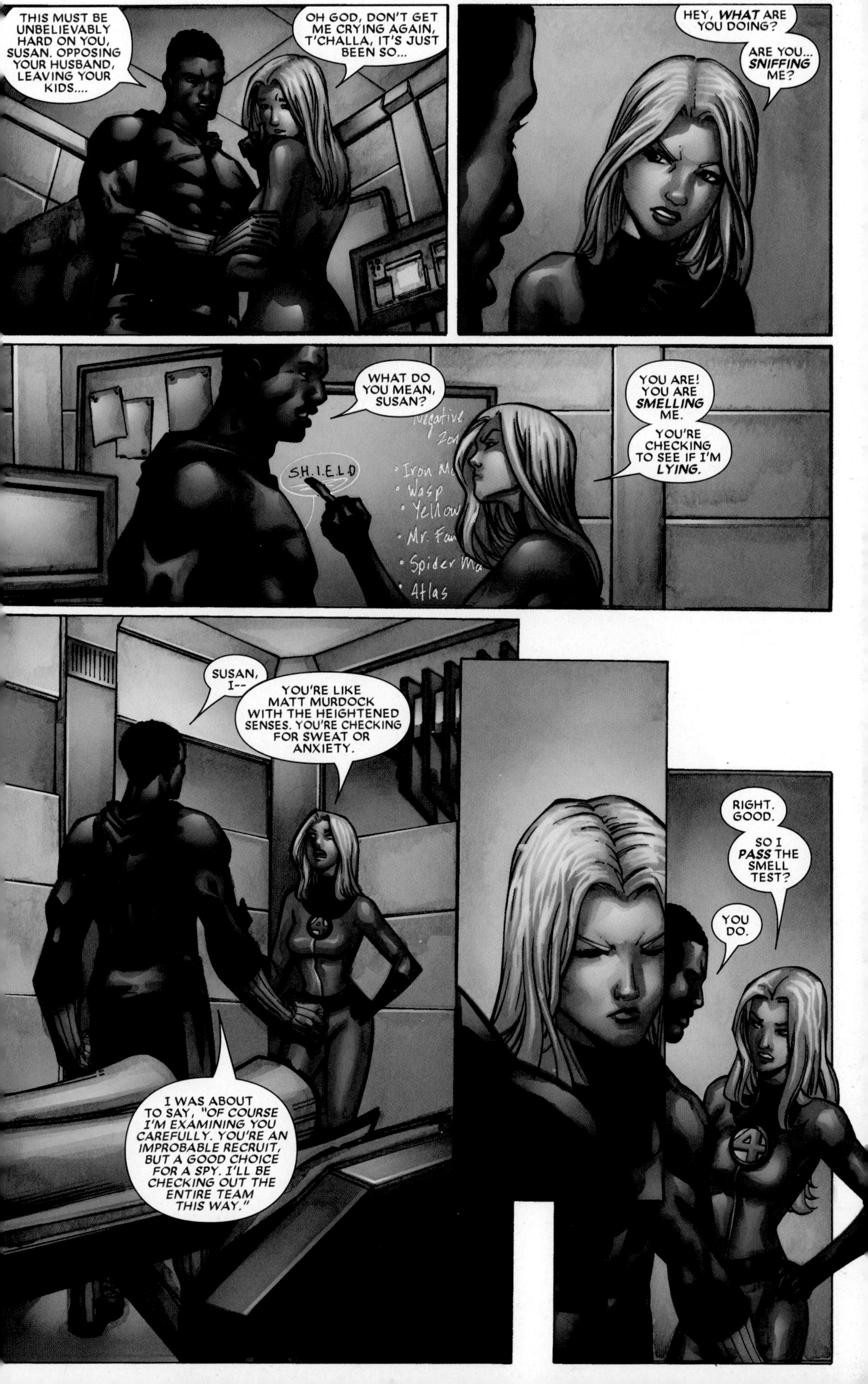

THIS MUST BE UNBELIEVABLY HARD ON YOU, SUSAN. OPPOSING YOUR HUSBAND, LEAVING YOUR KIDS....
OH GOD, DON'T GET ME CRYING AGAIN, T'CHALLA, IT'S JUST BEEN SO...
HEY, WHAT ARE YOU DOING?
ARE YOU... SNIFFING ME?
WHAT DO YOU MEAN, SUSAN?
Negative Zon
S.H.I.E.L.D
Iron M
Wasp
Yellow
Mr. Fa
Spider Ma
Atlas
YOU ARE! YOU ARE SMELLING ME.
YOU'RE CHECKING TO SEE IF I'M LYING.
SUSAN, I--
YOU'RE LIKE MATT MURDOCK WITH THE HEIGHTENED SENSES. YOU'RE CHECKING FOR SWEAT OR ANXIETY.
I WAS ABOUT TO SAY, "OF COURSE I'M EXAMINING YOU CAREFULLY. YOU'RE AN IMPROBABLE RECRUIT, BUT A GOOD CHOICE FOR A SPY. I'LL BE CHECKING OUT THE ENTIRE TEAM THIS WAY."
RIGHT. GOOD.
SO I PASS THE SMELL TEST?
YOU DO.

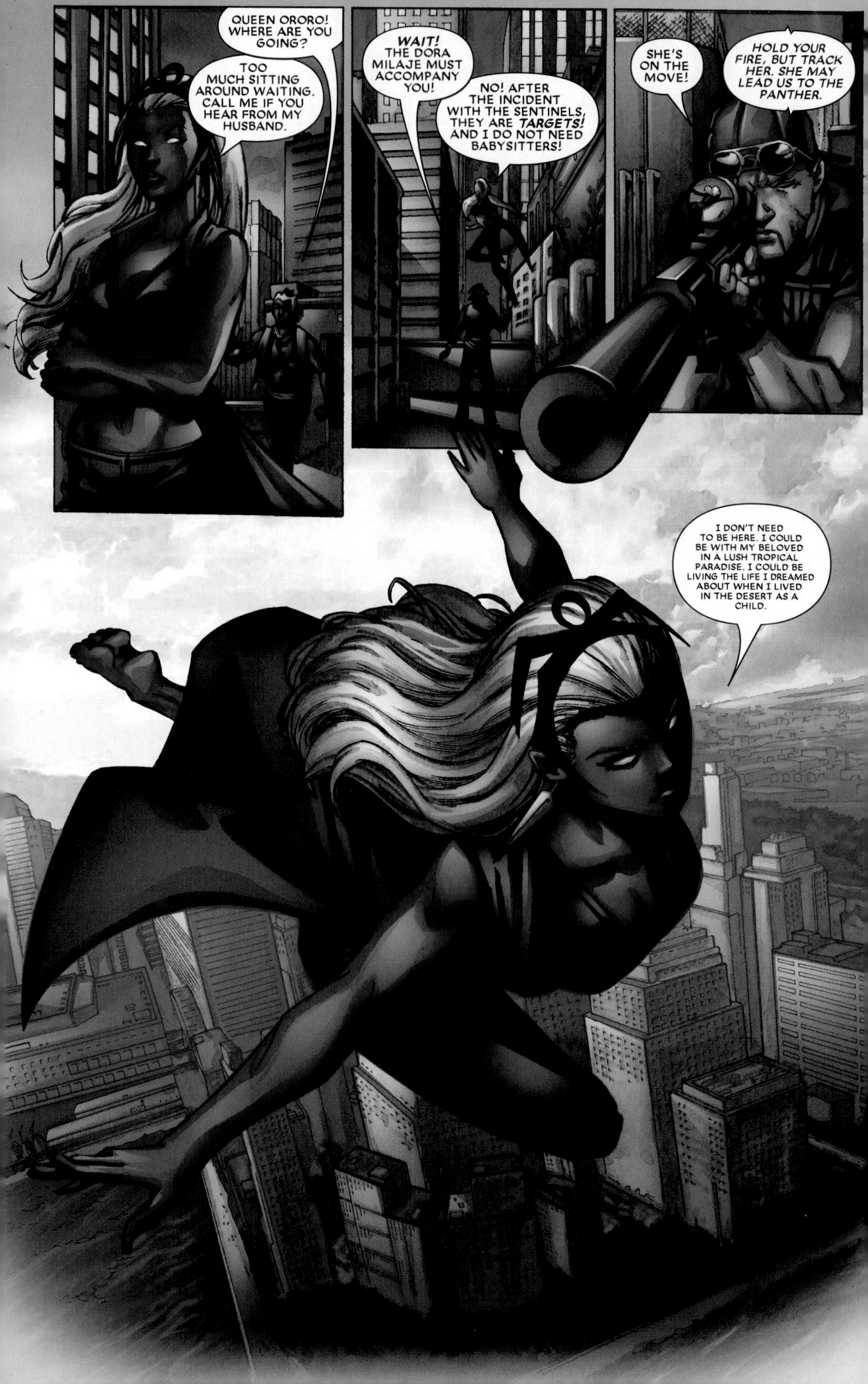
QUEEN ORORO! WHERE ARE YOU GOING?
TOO MUCH SITTING AROUND WAITING. CALL ME IF YOU HEAR FROM MY HUSBAND.
WAIT! THE DORA MILAJE MUST ACCOMPANY YOU!
NO! AFTER THE INCIDENT WITH THE SENTINELS, THEY ARE TARGETS! AND I DO NOT NEED BABYSITTERS!
SHE'S ON THE MOVE!
HOLD YOUR FIRE, BUT TRACK HER. SHE MAY LEAD US TO THE PANTHER.
I DON'T NEED TO BE HERE. I COULD BE WITH MY BELOVED IN A LUSH TROPICAL PARADISE. I COULD BE LIVING THE LIFE I DREAMED ABOUT WHEN I LIVED IN THE DESERT AS A CHILD.

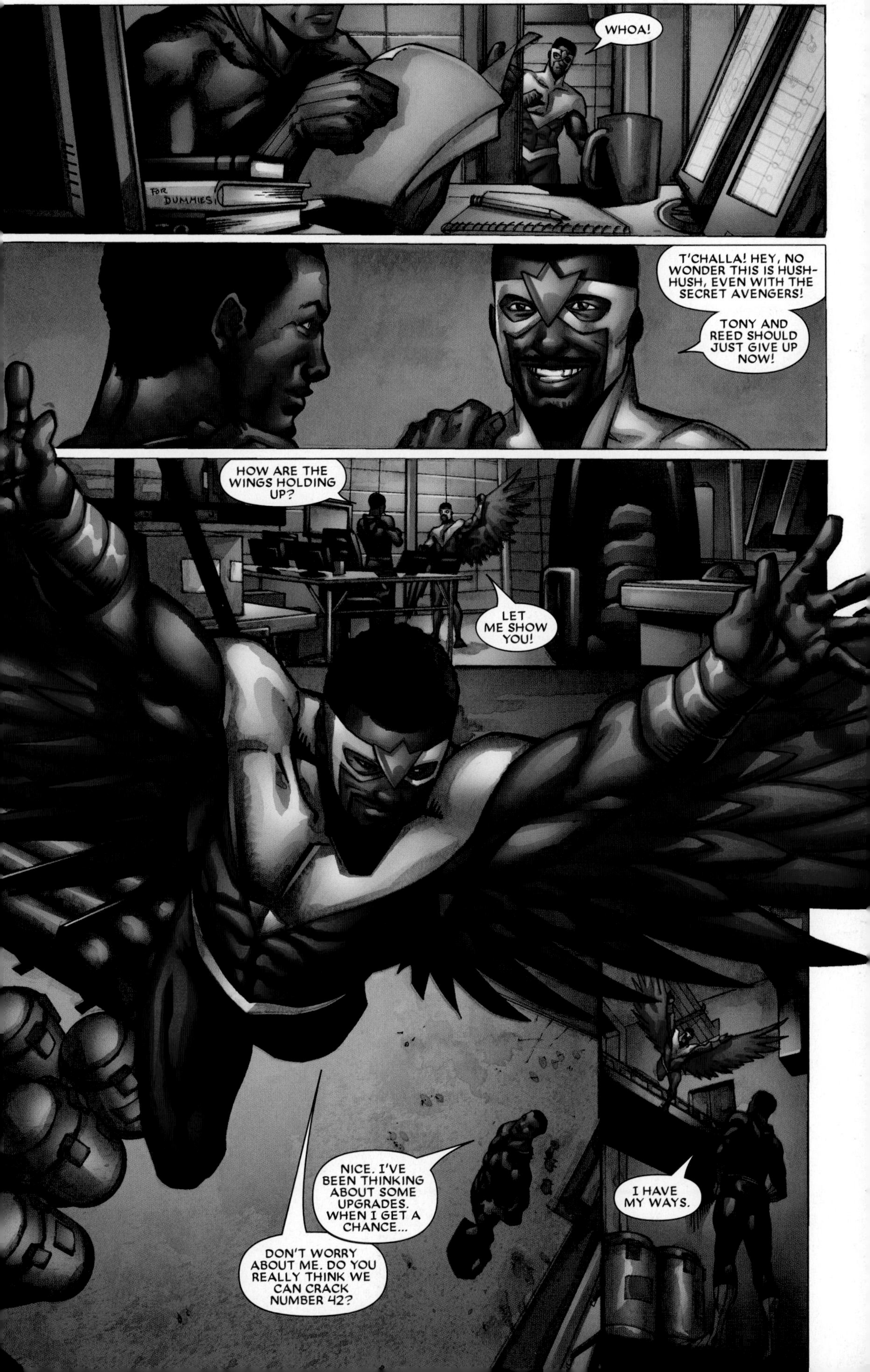
WHOA!
FOR DUMMIES
T'CHALLA! HEY, NO WONDER THIS IS HUSH-HUSH, EVEN WITH THE SECRET AVENGERS!
TONY AND REED SHOULD JUST GIVE UP NOW!
HOW ARE THE WINGS HOLDING UP?
LET ME SHOW YOU!
NICE. I'VE BEEN THINKING ABOUT SOME UPGRADES. WHEN I GET A CHANCE...
DON'T WORRY ABOUT ME. DO YOU REALLY THINK WE CAN CRACK NUMBER 42?
I HAVE MY WAYS.

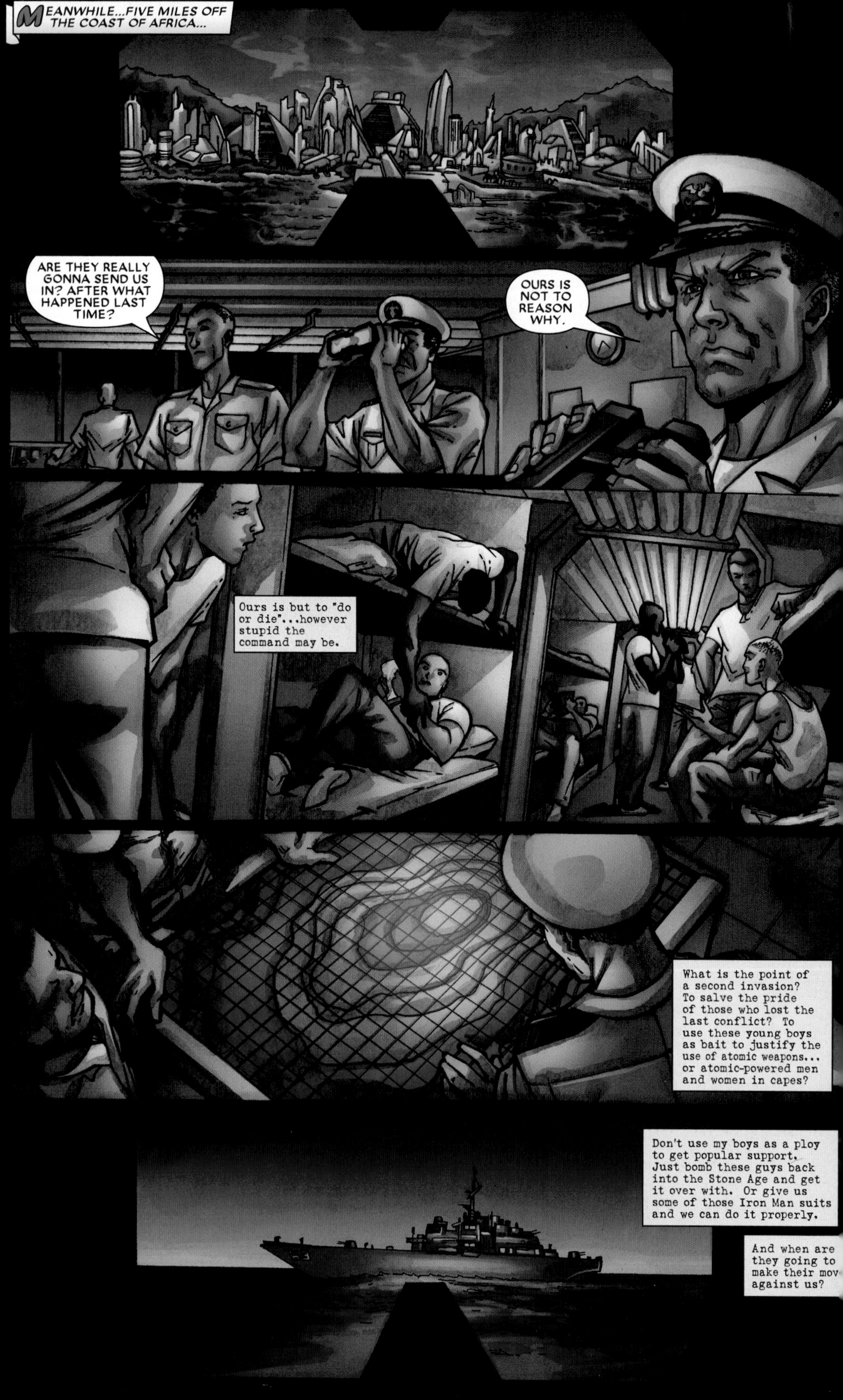
MEANWHILE...FIVE MILES OFF THE COAST OF AFRICA...
ARE THEY REALLY GONNA SEND US IN? AFTER WHAT HAPPENED LAST TIME?
OURS IS NOT TO REASON WHY.
Ours is but to "do or die"...however stupid the command may be.
What is the point of a second invasion? To salve the pride of those who lost the last conflict? To use these young boys as bait to justify the use of atomic weapons... or atomic-powered men and women in capes?
Don't use my boys as a ploy to get popular support. Just bomb these guys back into the Stone Age and get it over with. Or give us some of those Iron Man suits and we can do it properly.
And when are they going to make their mov against us?

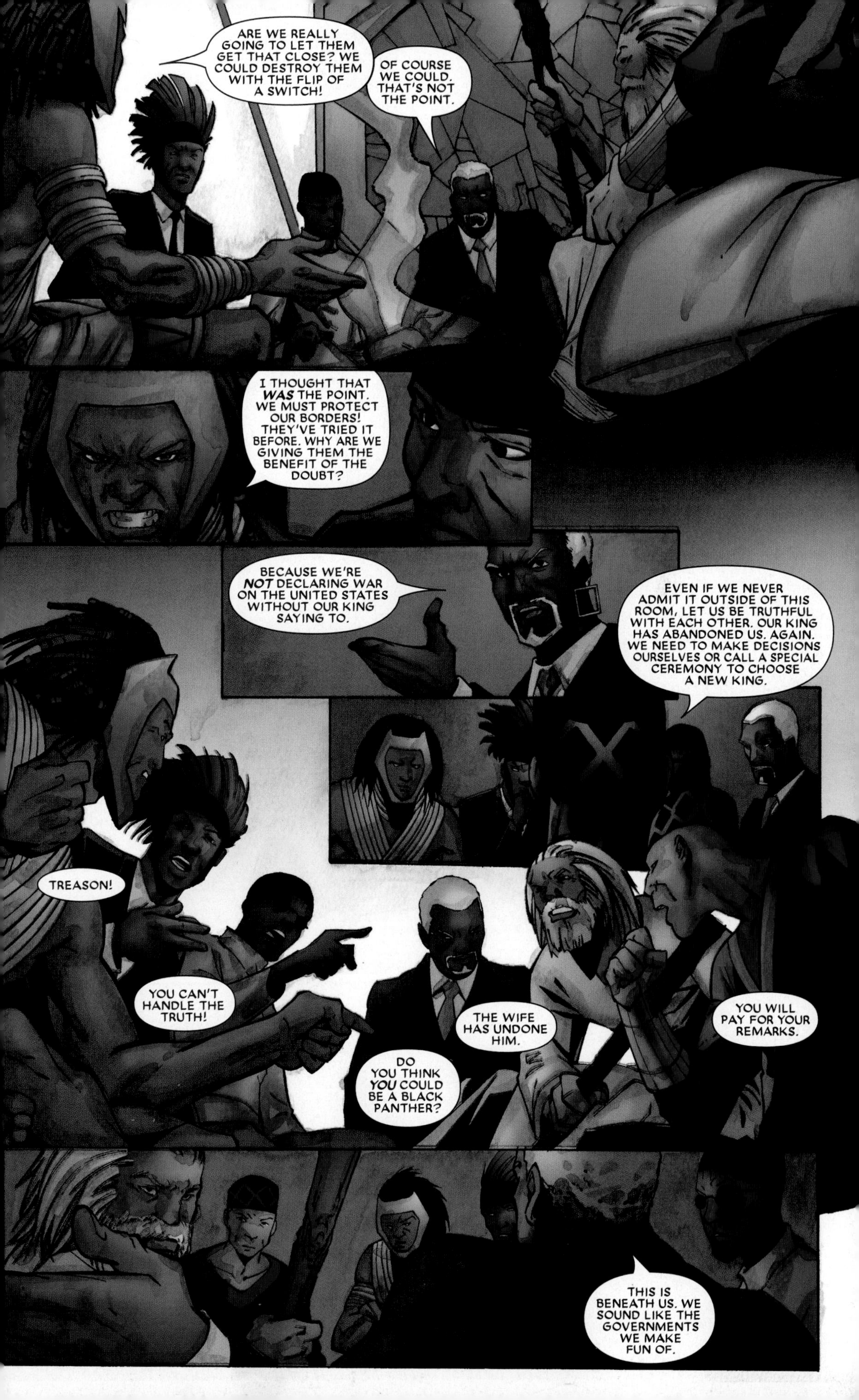
ARE WE REALLY GOING TO LET THEM GET THAT CLOSE? WE COULD DESTROY THEM WITH THE FLIP OF A SWITCH!
OF COURSE WE COULD. THAT'S NOT THE POINT.
I THOUGHT THAT WAS THE POINT. WE MUST PROTECT OUR BORDERS! THEY'VE TRIED IT BEFORE. WHY ARE WE GIVING THEM THE BENEFIT OF THE DOUBT?
BECAUSE WE'RE NOT DECLARING WAR ON THE UNITED STATES WITHOUT OUR KING SAYING TO.
EVEN IF WE NEVER ADMIT IT OUTSIDE OF THIS ROOM, LET US BE TRUTHFUL WITH EACH OTHER. OUR KING HAS ABANDONED US. AGAIN. WE NEED TO MAKE DECISIONS OURSELVES OR CALL A SPECIAL CEREMONY TO CHOOSE A NEW KING.
TREASON!
YOU CAN'T HANDLE THE TRUTH!
THE WIFE HAS UNDONE HIM.
DO YOU THINK YOU COULD BE A BLACK PANTHER?
YOU WILL PAY FOR YOUR REMARKS.
THIS IS BENEATH US. WE SOUND LIKE THE GOVERNMENTS WE MAKE FUN OF.

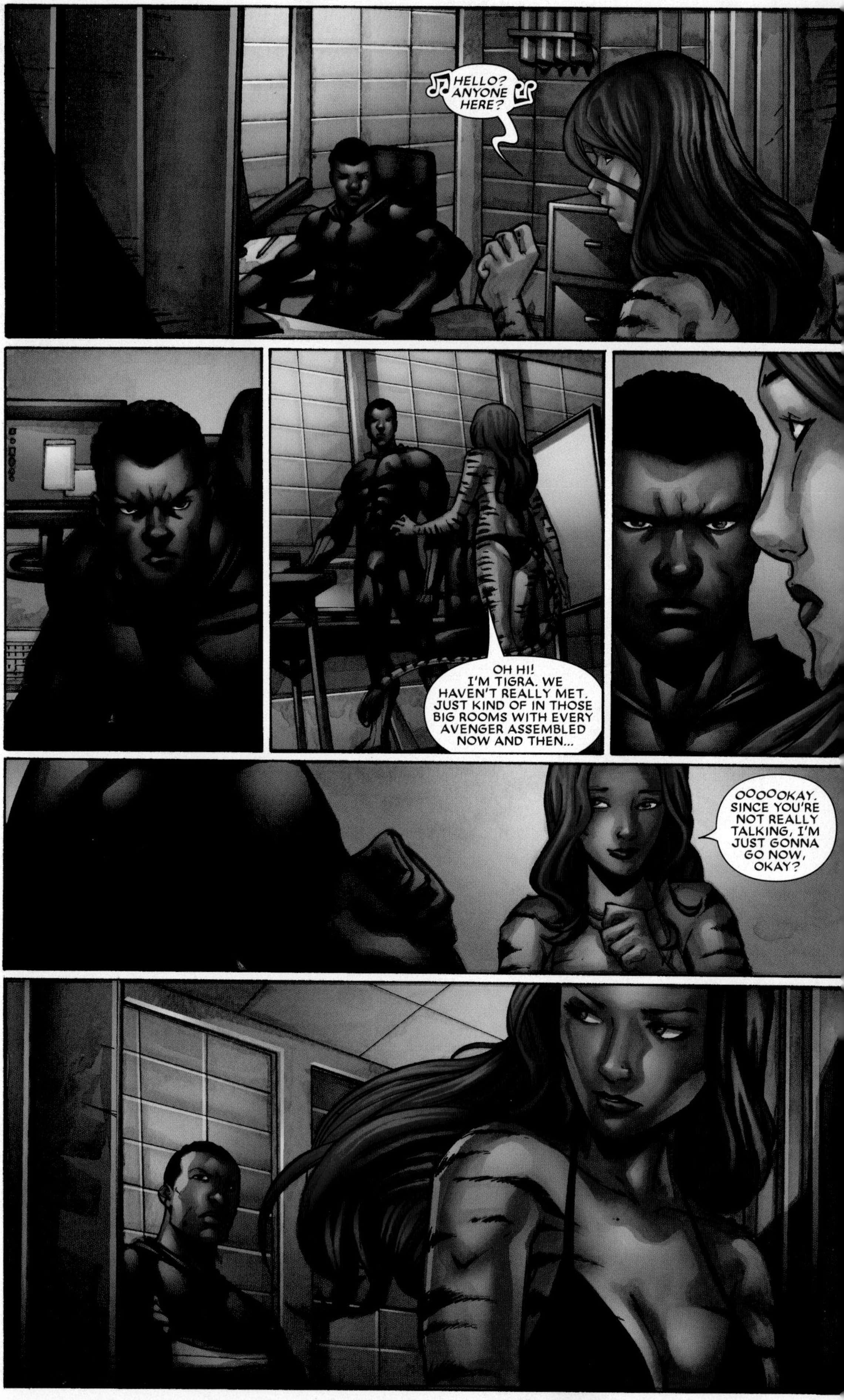
HELLO? ANYONE HERE?
OH HI! I'M TIGRA. WE HAVEN'T REALLY MET. JUST KIND OF IN THOSE BIG ROOMS WITH EVERY AVENGER ASSEMBLED NOW AND THEN...
OOOOOKAY. SINCE YOU'RE NOT REALLY TALKING, I'M JUST GONNA GO NOW, OKAY?

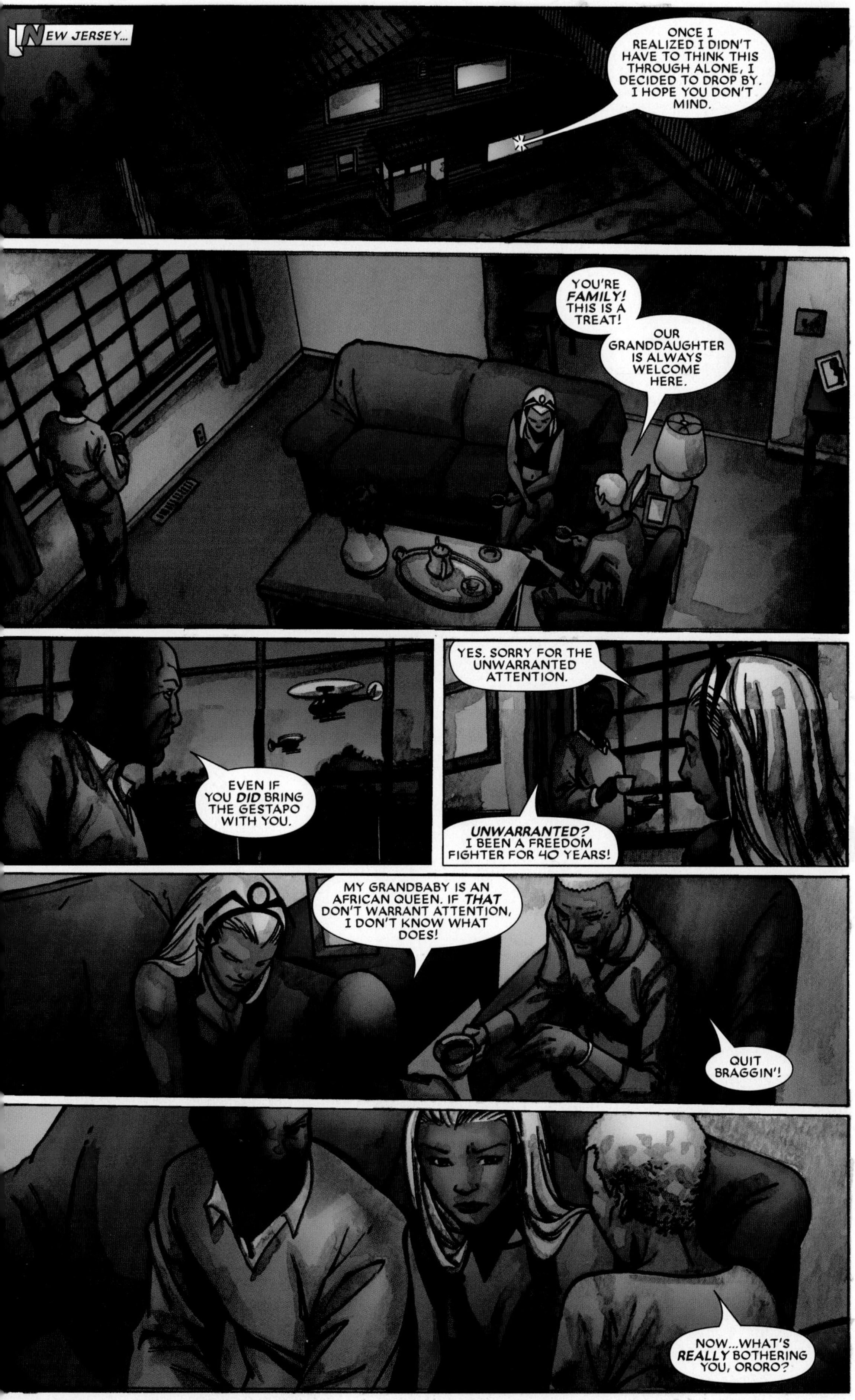
NEW JERSEY...
ONCE I REALIZED I DIDN'T HAVE TO THINK THIS THROUGH ALONE, I DECIDED TO DROP BY. I HOPE YOU DON'T MIND.
YOU'RE FAMILY! THIS IS A TREAT!
OUR GRANDDAUGHTER IS ALWAYS WELCOME HERE.
EVEN IF YOU DID BRING THE GESTAPO WITH YOU.
YES. SORRY FOR THE UNWARRANTED ATTENTION.
UNWARRANTED? I BEEN A FREEDOM FIGHTER FOR 40 YEARS!
MY GRANDBABY IS AN AFRICAN QUEEN. IF THAT DON'T WARRANT ATTENTION, I DON'T KNOW WHAT DOES!
QUIT BRAGGIN'!
NOW...WHAT'S REALLY BOTHERING YOU, ORORO?

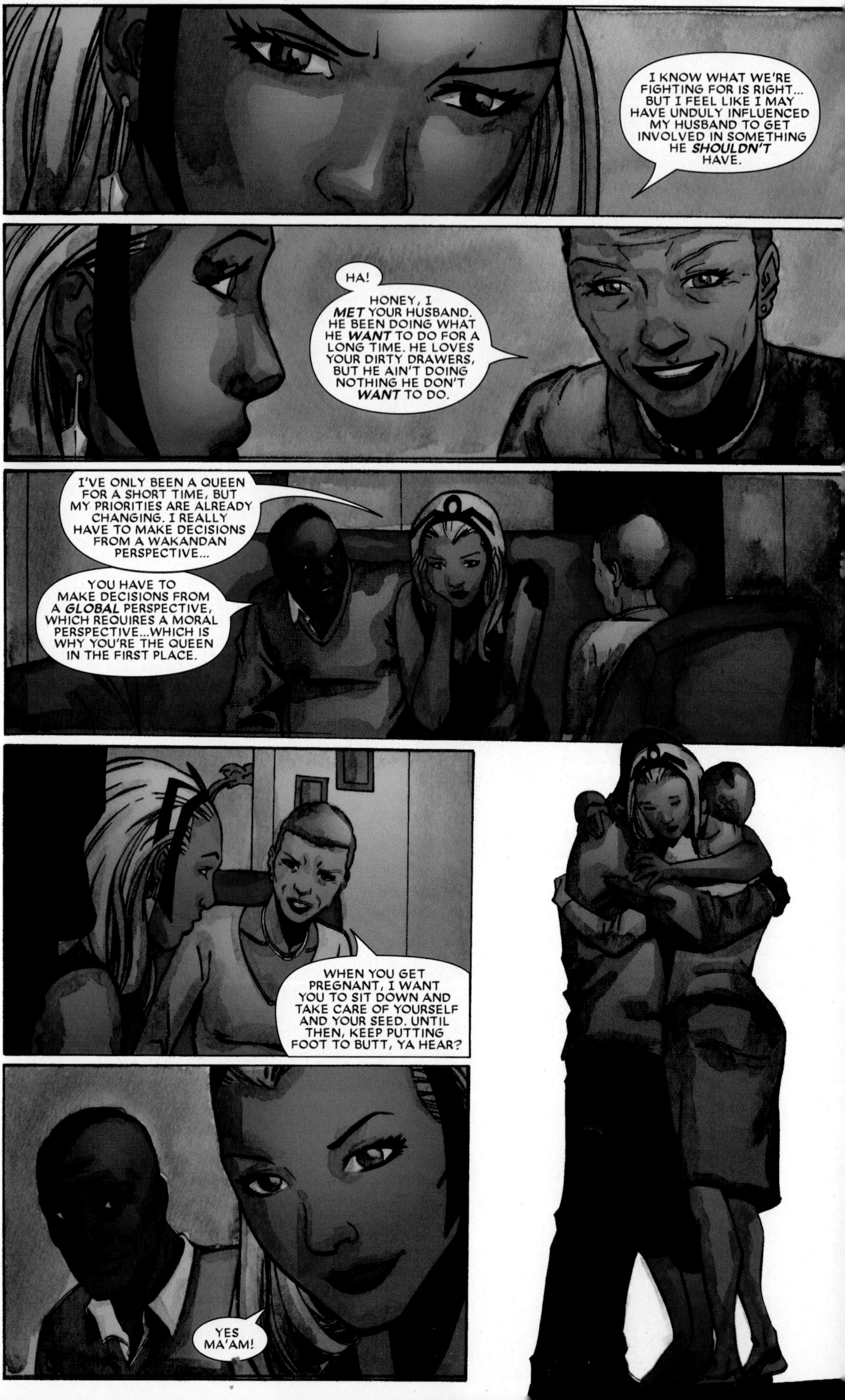
I KNOW WHAT WE'RE FIGHTING FOR IS RIGHT... BUT I FEEL LIKE I MAY HAVE UNDULY INFLUENCED MY HUSBAND TO GET INVOLVED IN SOMETHING HE SHOULDN'T HAVE.
HA!
HONEY, I MET YOUR HUSBAND. HE BEEN DOING WHAT HE WANT TO DO FOR A LONG TIME. HE LOVES YOUR DIRTY DRAWERS, BUT HE AIN'T DOING NOTHING HE DON'T WANT TO DO.
I'VE ONLY BEEN A QUEEN FOR A SHORT TIME, BUT MY PRIORITIES ARE ALREADY CHANGING. I REALLY HAVE TO MAKE DECISIONS FROM A WAKANDAN PERSPECTIVE...
YOU HAVE TO MAKE DECISIONS FROM A GLOBAL PERSPECTIVE, WHICH REQUIRES A MORAL PERSPECTIVE...WHICH IS WHY YOU'RE THE QUEEN IN THE FIRST PLACE.
WHEN YOU GET PREGNANT, I WANT YOU TO SIT DOWN AND TAKE CARE OF YOURSELF AND YOUR SEED. UNTIL THEN, KEEP PUTTING FOOT TO BUTT, YA HEAR?
YES MA'AM!

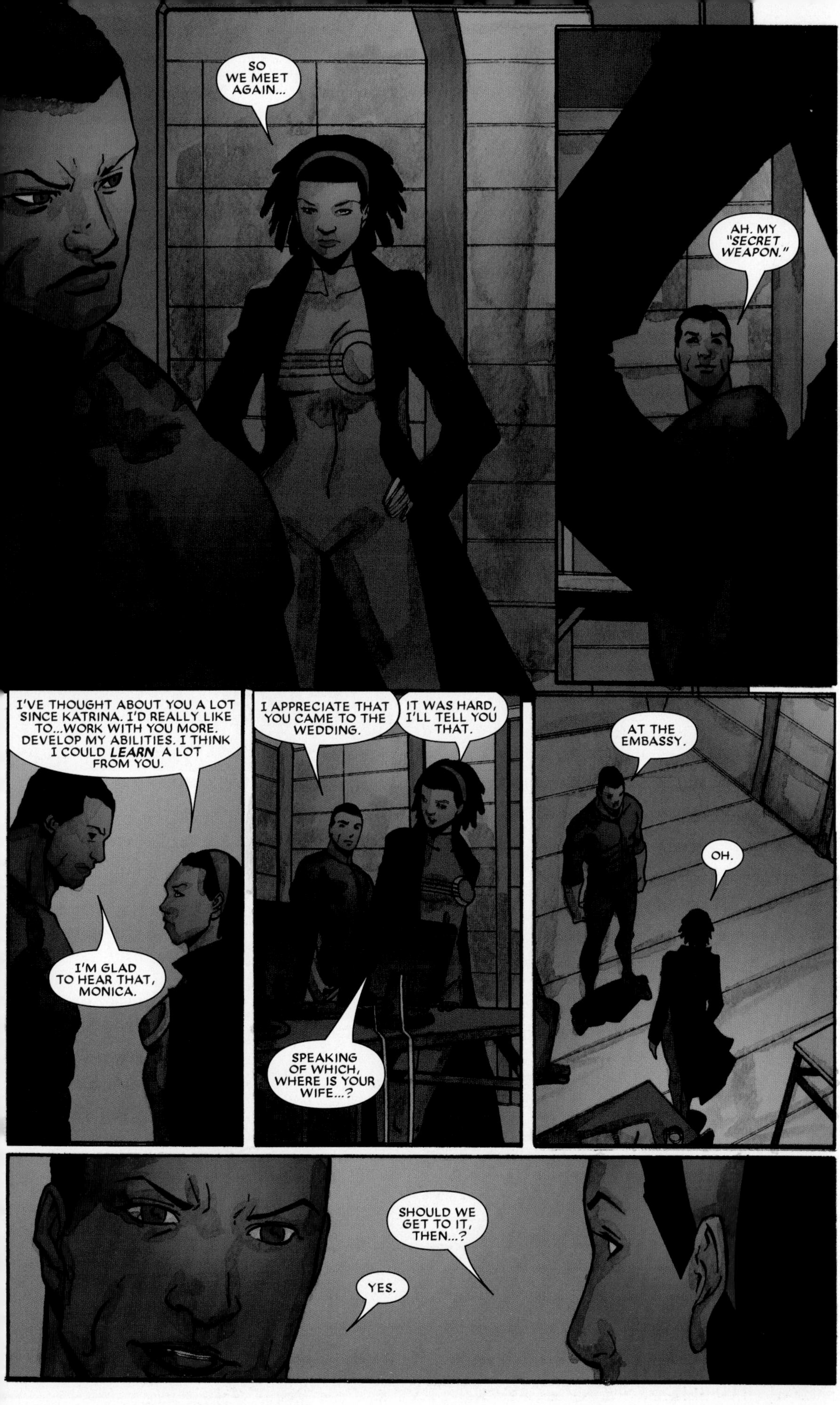
SO WE MEET AGAIN...
AH. MY "SECRET WEAPON."
I'VE THOUGHT ABOUT YOU A LOT SINCE KATRINA. I'D REALLY LIKE TO...WORK WITH YOU MORE. DEVELOP MY ABILITIES. I THINK I COULD LEARN A LOT FROM YOU.
I'M GLAD TO HEAR THAT, MONICA.
I APPRECIATE THAT YOU CAME TO THE WEDDING.
IT WAS HARD, I'LL TELL YOU THAT.
SPEAKING OF WHICH, WHERE IS YOUR WIFE...?
AT THE EMBASSY.
OH.
SHOULD WE GET TO IT, THEN...?
YES.

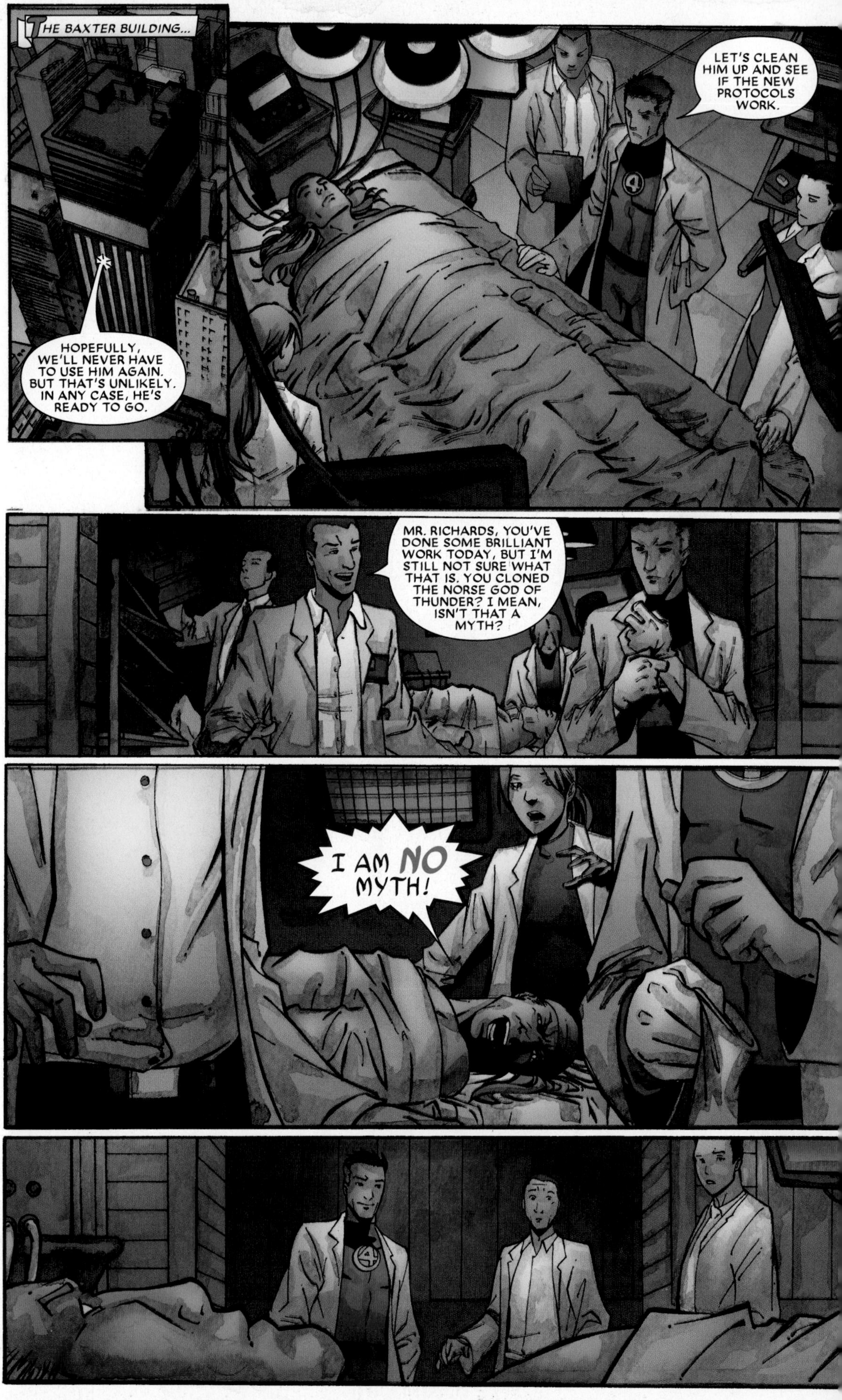
THE BAXTER BUILDING...
HOPEFULLY, WE'LL NEVER HAVE TO USE HIM AGAIN. BUT THAT'S UNLIKELY. IN ANY CASE, HE'S READY TO GO.
LET'S CLEAN HIM UP AND SEE IF THE NEW PROTOCOLS WORK.
MR. RICHARDS, YOU'VE DONE SOME BRILLIANT WORK TODAY, BUT I'M STILL NOT SURE WHAT THAT IS. YOU CLONED THE NORSE GOD OF THUNDER? I MEAN, ISN'T THAT A MYTH?
I AM NO MYTH!

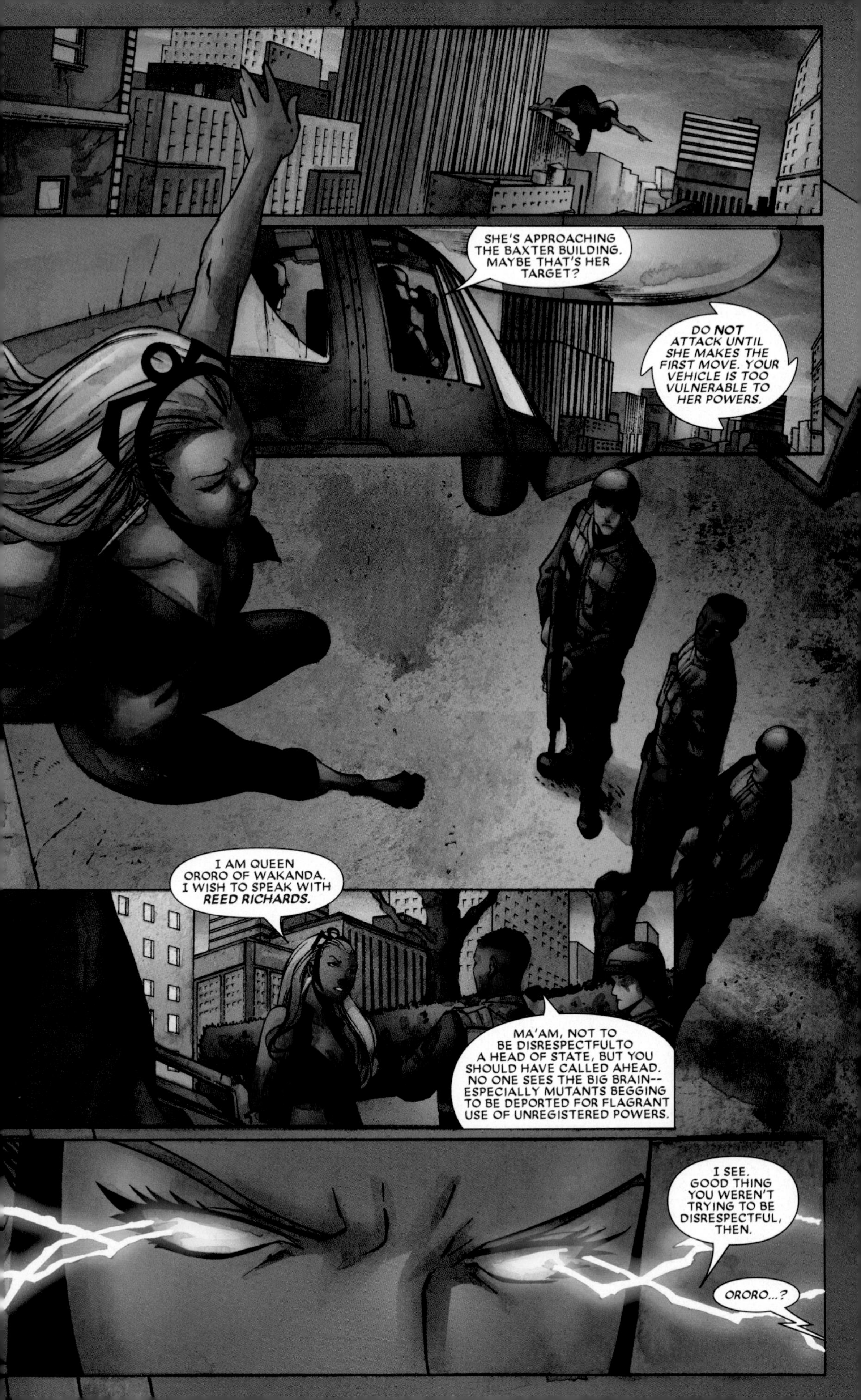

SHE'S APPROACHING THE BAXTER BUILDING. MAYBE THAT'S HER TARGET?
DO NOT ATTACK UNTIL SHE MAKES THE FIRST MOVE. YOUR VEHICLE IS TOO VULNERABLE TO HER POWERS.
I AM QUEEN ORORO OF WAKANDA. I WISH TO SPEAK WITH REED RICHARDS.
MA'AM, NOT TO BE DISRESPECTFULTO A HEAD OF STATE, BUT YOU SHOULD HAVE CALLED AHEAD. NO ONE SEES THE BIG BRAIN-- ESPECIALLY MUTANTS BEGGING TO BE DEPORTED FOR FLAGRANT USE OF UNREGISTERED POWERS.
I SEE. GOOD THING YOU WEREN'T TRYING TO BE DISRESPECTFUL, THEN.
ORORO...?

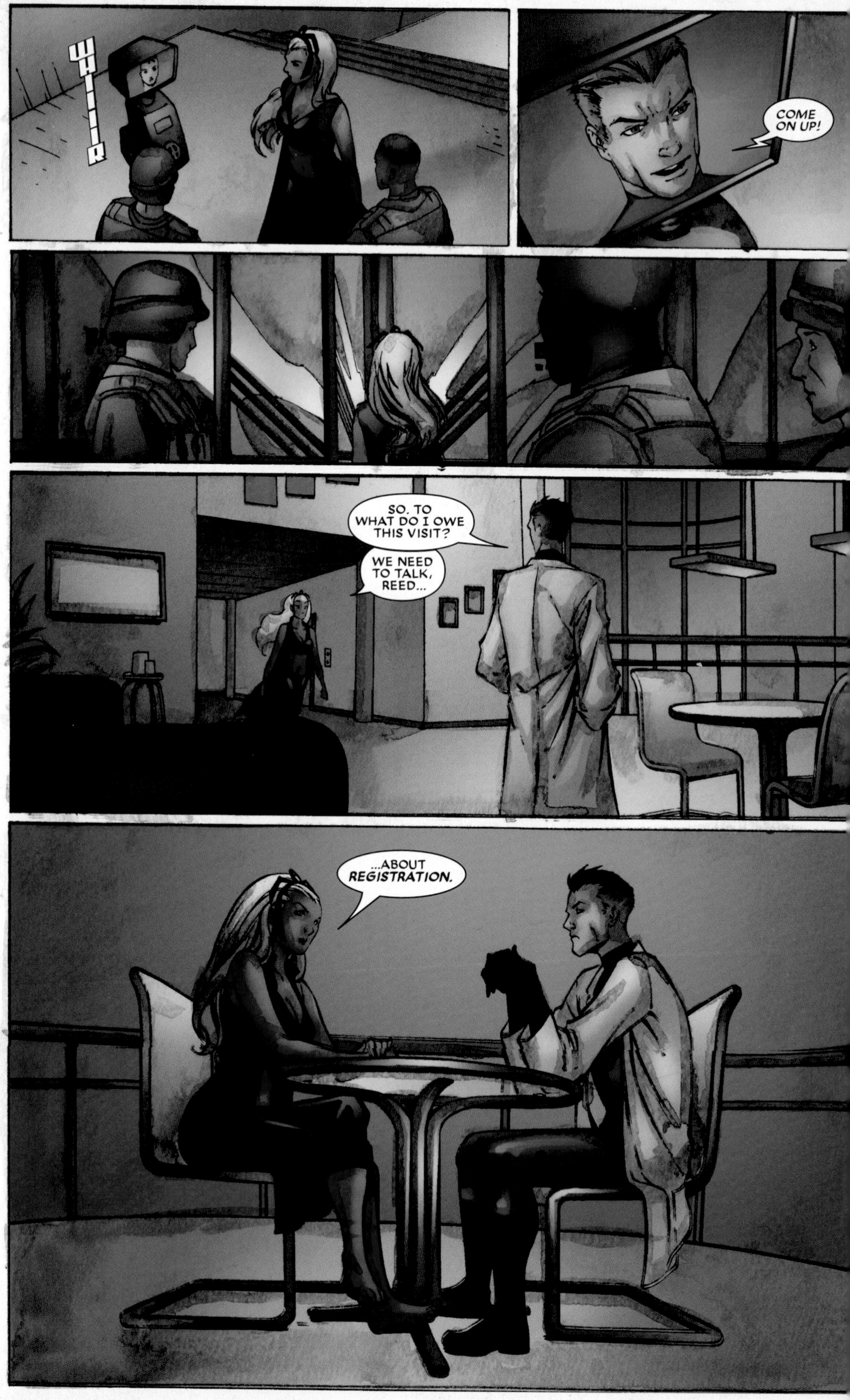
WHIIIR
COME ON UP!
SO. TO WHAT DO I OWE THIS VISIT?
WE NEED TO TALK, REED...
...ABOUT REGISTRATION.

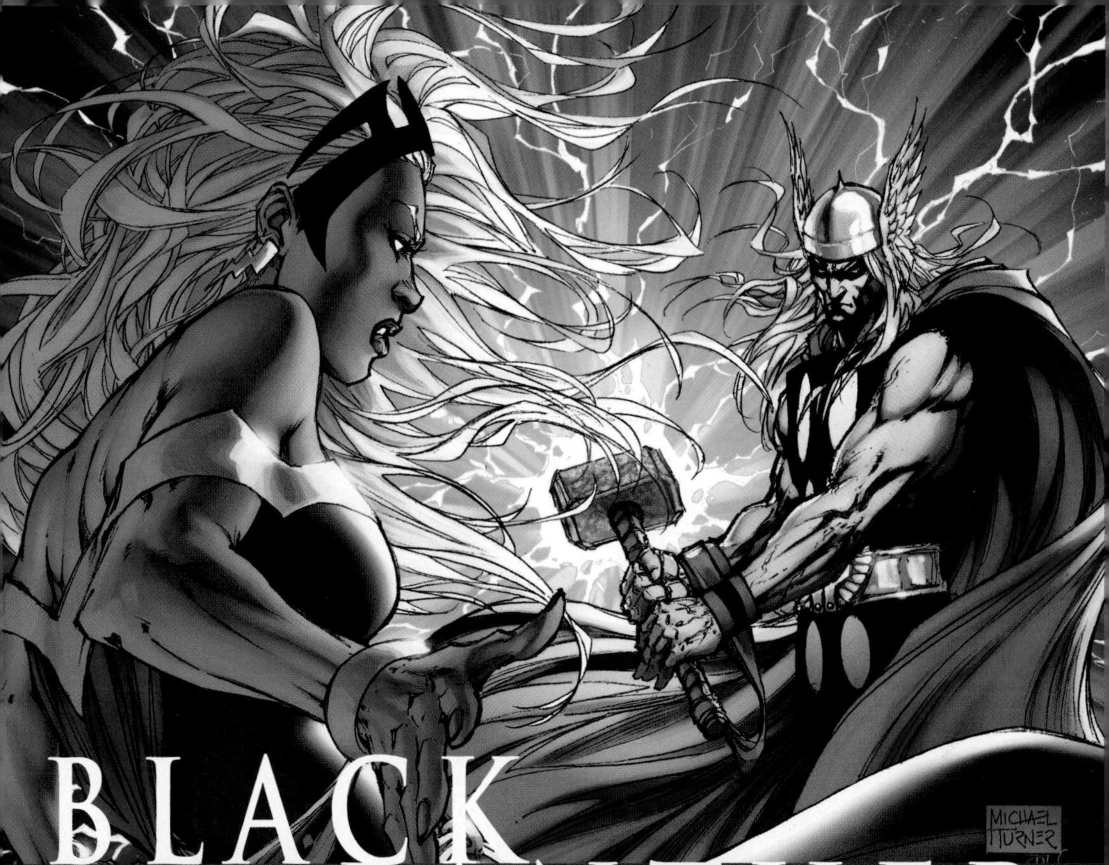
MICHAEL TURNER

BLACK PANTHER

A MARVEL COMICS EVENT

CIVIL WAR

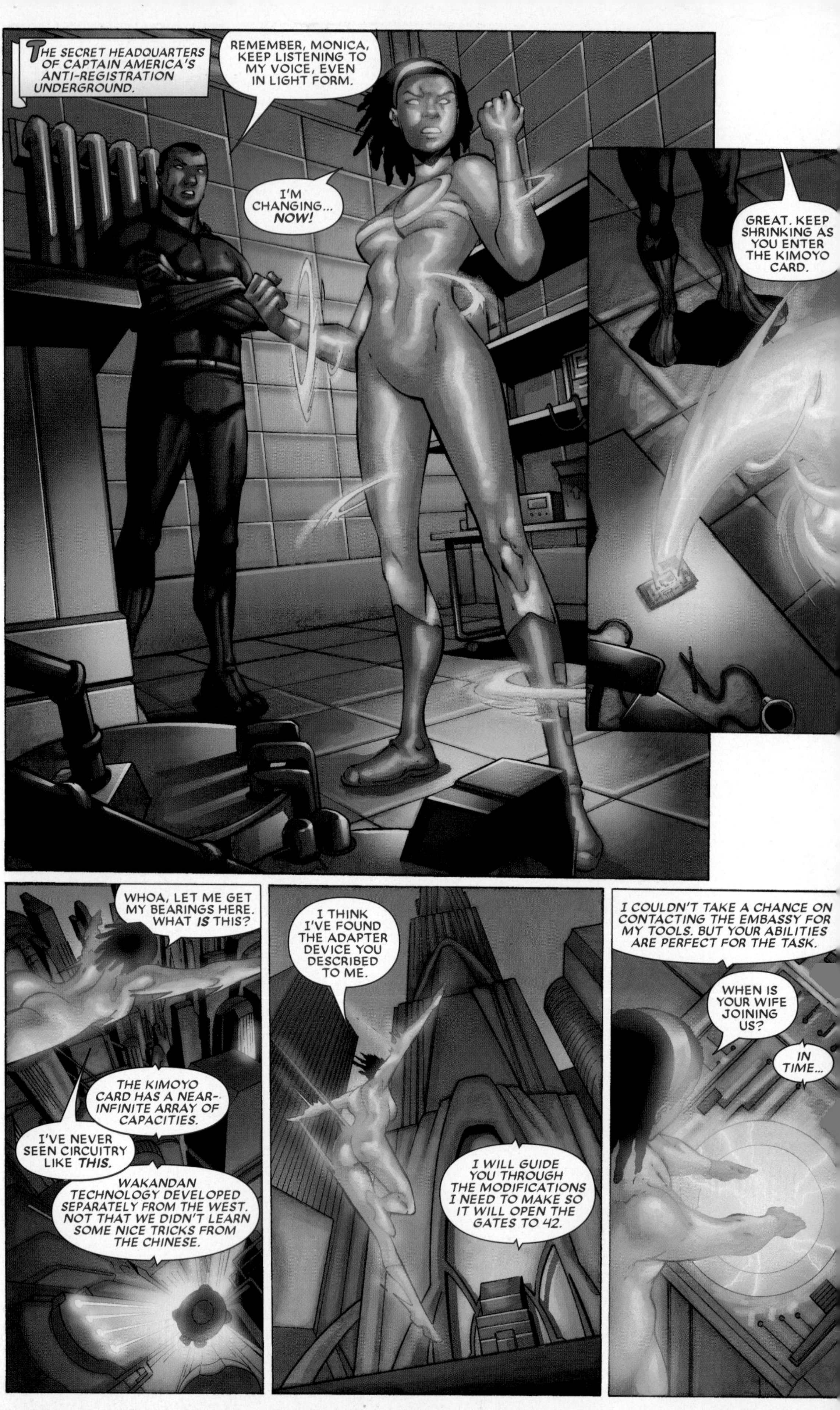
THE SECRET HEADQUARTERS OF CAPTAIN AMERICA'S ANTI-REGISTRATION UNDERGROUND.
REMEMBER, MONICA, KEEP LISTENING TO MY VOICE, EVEN IN LIGHT FORM.
I'M CHANGING... NOW!
GREAT. KEEP SHRINKING AS YOU ENTER THE KIMOYO CARD.
WHOA, LET ME GET MY BEARINGS HERE. WHAT IS THIS?
THE KIMOYO CARD HAS A NEAR-INFINITE ARRAY OF CAPACITIES.
I'VE NEVER SEEN CIRCUITRY LIKE THIS.
WAKANDAN TECHNOLOGY DEVELOPED SEPARATELY FROM THE WEST. NOT THAT WE DIDN'T LEARN SOME NICE TRICKS FROM THE CHINESE.
I THINK I'VE FOUND THE ADAPTER DEVICE YOU DESCRIBED TO ME.
I WILL GUIDE YOU THROUGH THE MODIFICATIONS I NEED TO MAKE SO IT WILL OPEN THE GATES TO 42.
I COULDN'T TAKE A CHANCE ON CONTACTING THE EMBASSY FOR MY TOOLS. BUT YOUR ABILITIES ARE PERFECT FOR THE TASK.
WHEN IS YOUR WIFE JOINING US?
IN TIME...

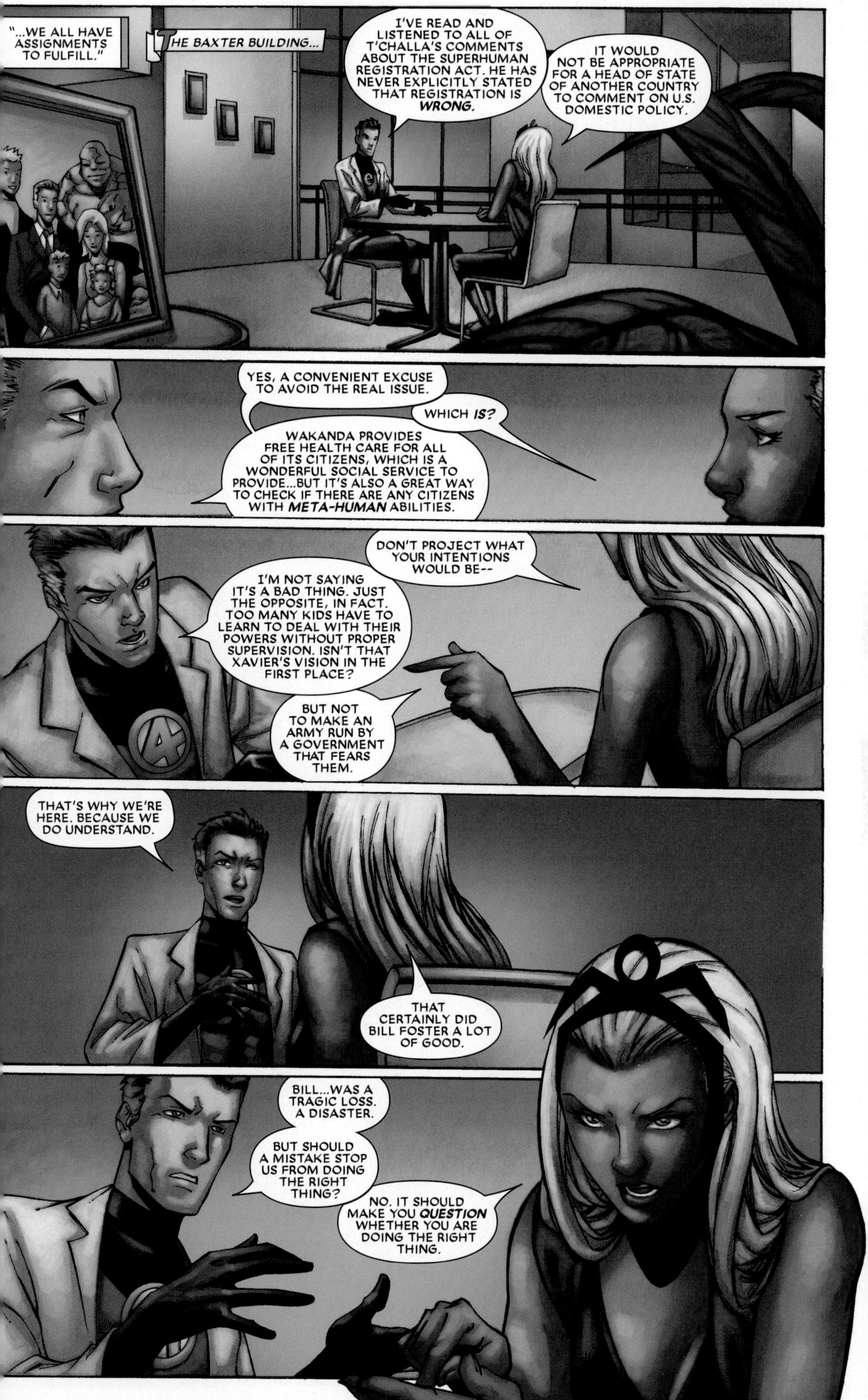
"...WE ALL HAVE ASSIGNMENTS TO FULFILL."
THE BAXTER BUILDING...
I'VE READ AND LISTENED TO ALL OF T'CHALLA'S COMMENTS ABOUT THE SUPERHUMAN REGISTRATION ACT. HE HAS NEVER EXPLICITLY STATED THAT REGISTRATION IS *WRONG.*
IT WOULD NOT BE APPROPRIATE FOR A HEAD OF STATE OF ANOTHER COUNTRY TO COMMENT ON U.S. DOMESTIC POLICY.
YES, A CONVENIENT EXCUSE TO AVOID THE REAL ISSUE.
WHICH *IS?*
WAKANDA PROVIDES FREE HEALTH CARE FOR ALL OF ITS CITIZENS, WHICH IS A WONDERFUL SOCIAL SERVICE TO PROVIDE...BUT IT'S ALSO A GREAT WAY TO CHECK IF THERE ARE ANY CITIZENS WITH *META-HUMAN* ABILITIES.
DON'T PROJECT WHAT YOUR INTENTIONS WOULD BE--
I'M NOT SAYING IT'S A BAD THING. JUST THE OPPOSITE, IN FACT. TOO MANY KIDS HAVE TO LEARN TO DEAL WITH THEIR POWERS WITHOUT PROPER SUPERVISION. ISN'T THAT XAVIER'S VISION IN THE FIRST PLACE?
BUT NOT TO MAKE AN ARMY RUN BY A GOVERNMENT THAT FEARS THEM.
THAT'S WHY WE'RE HERE. BECAUSE WE DO UNDERSTAND.
THAT CERTAINLY DID BILL FOSTER A LOT OF GOOD.
BILL...WAS A TRAGIC LOSS. A DISASTER.
BUT SHOULD A MISTAKE STOP US FROM DOING THE RIGHT THING?
NO. IT SHOULD MAKE YOU *QUESTION* WHETHER YOU ARE DOING THE RIGHT THING.

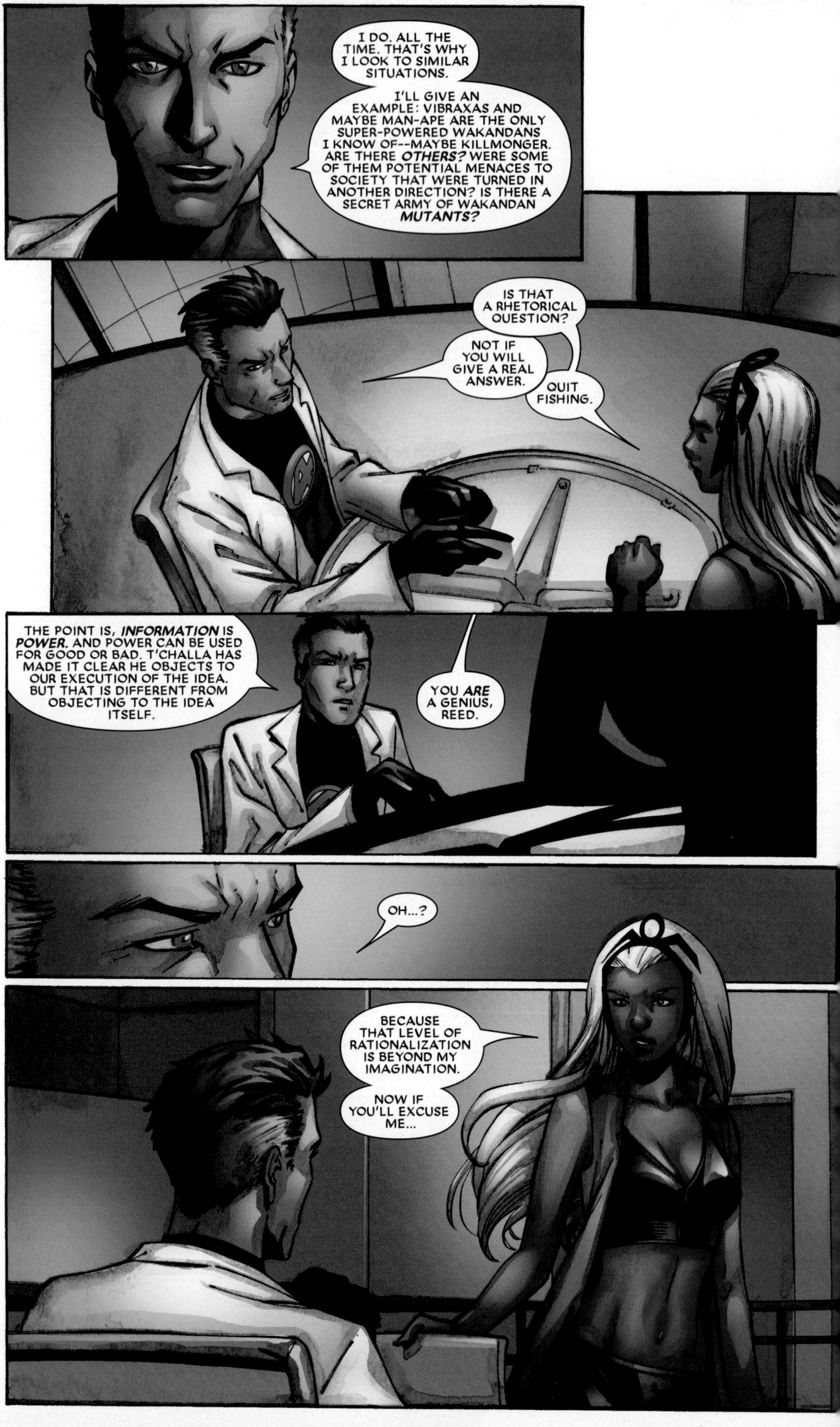

I DO. ALL THE TIME. THAT'S WHY I LOOK TO SIMILAR SITUATIONS.
I'LL GIVE AN EXAMPLE: VIBRAXAS AND MAYBE MAN-APE ARE THE ONLY SUPER-POWERED WAKANDANS I KNOW OF--MAYBE KILLMONGER. ARE THERE *OTHERS?* WERE SOME OF THEM POTENTIAL MENACES TO SOCIETY THAT WERE TURNED IN ANOTHER DIRECTION? IS THERE A SECRET ARMY OF WAKANDAN *MUTANTS?*
IS THAT A RHETORICAL QUESTION?
NOT IF YOU WILL GIVE A REAL ANSWER.
QUIT FISHING.
THE POINT IS, *INFORMATION* IS *POWER.* AND POWER CAN BE USED FOR GOOD OR BAD. T'CHALLA HAS MADE IT CLEAR HE OBJECTS TO OUR EXECUTION OF THE IDEA. BUT THAT IS DIFFERENT FROM OBJECTING TO THE IDEA ITSELF.
YOU *ARE* A GENIUS, REED.
OH...?
BECAUSE THAT LEVEL OF RATIONALIZATION IS BEYOND MY IMAGINATION.
NOW IF YOU'LL EXCUSE ME...

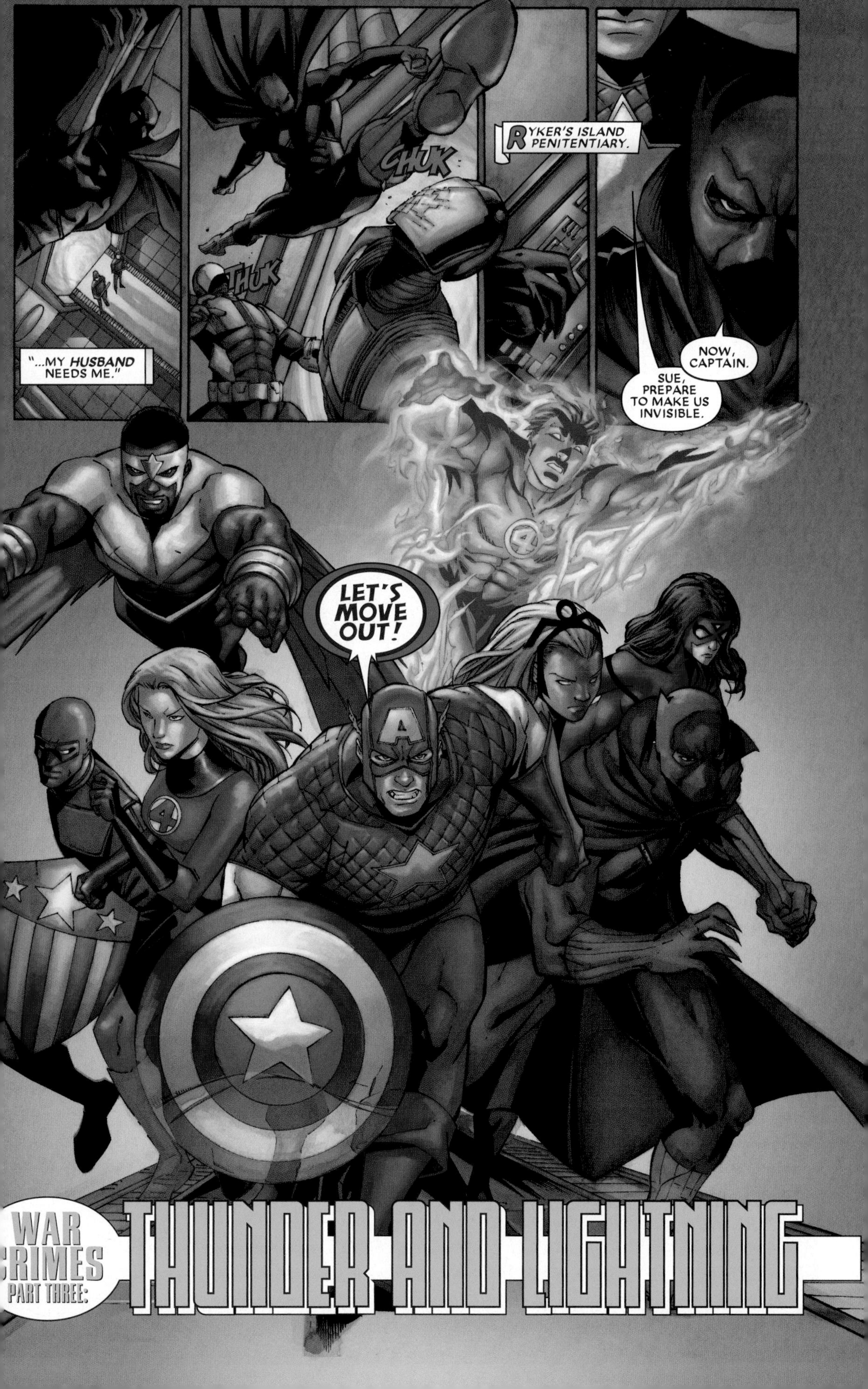
"...MY HUSBAND NEEDS ME."
CHUK
THUK
RYKER'S ISLAND PENITENTIARY.
NOW, CAPTAIN.
SUE, PREPARE TO MAKE US INVISIBLE.
LET'S MOVE OUT!
WAR CRIMES PART THREE:
THUNDER AND LIGHTNING

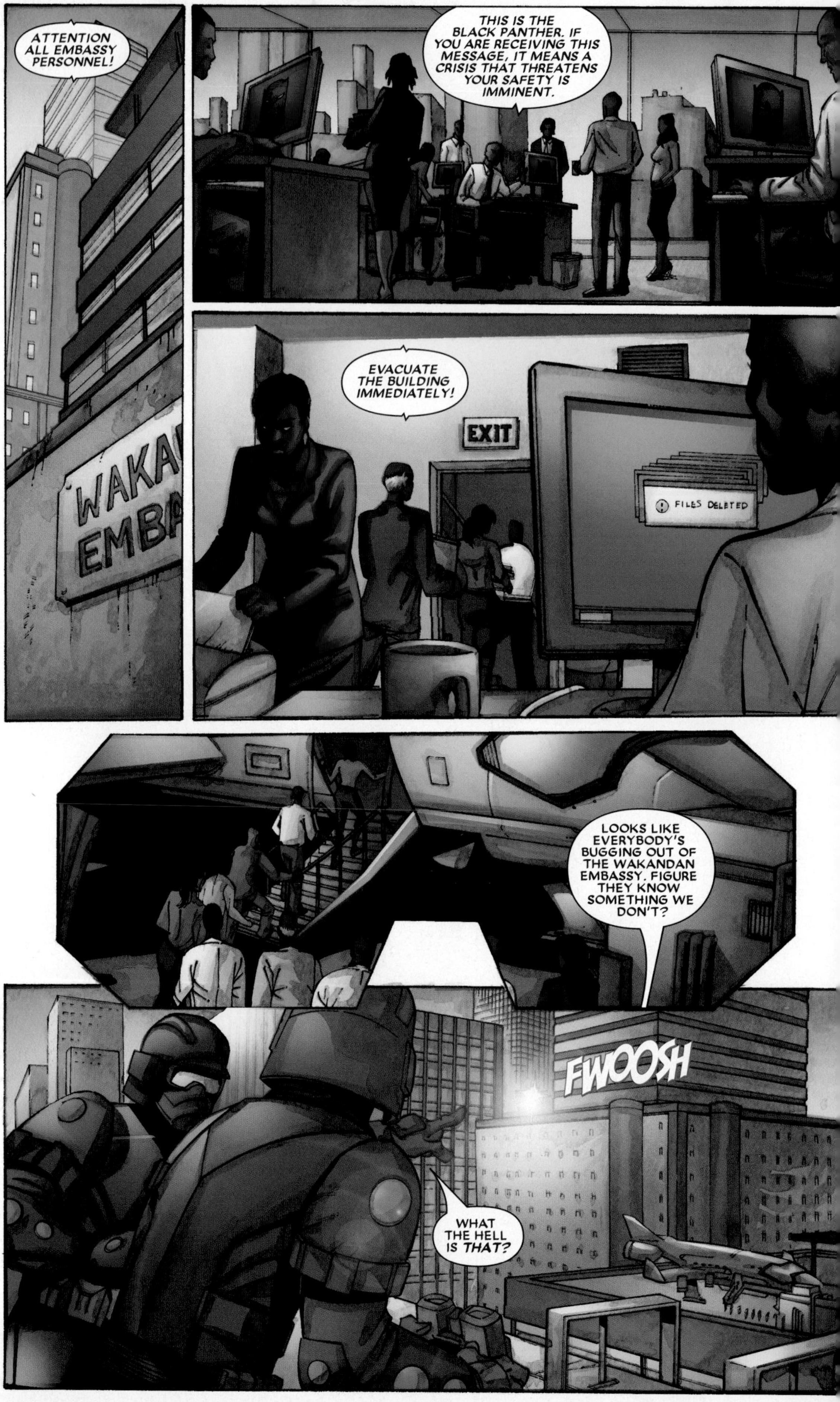
ATTENTION ALL EMBASSY PERSONNEL!
WAKA
EMB
THIS IS THE BLACK PANTHER. IF YOU ARE RECEIVING THIS MESSAGE, IT MEANS A CRISIS THAT THREATENS YOUR SAFETY IS IMMINENT.
EVACUATE THE BUILDING IMMEDIATELY!
EXIT
FILES DELETED
LOOKS LIKE EVERYBODY'S BUGGING OUT OF THE WAKANDAN EMBASSY. FIGURE THEY KNOW SOMETHING WE DON'T?
FWOOSH
WHAT THE HELL IS *THAT?*

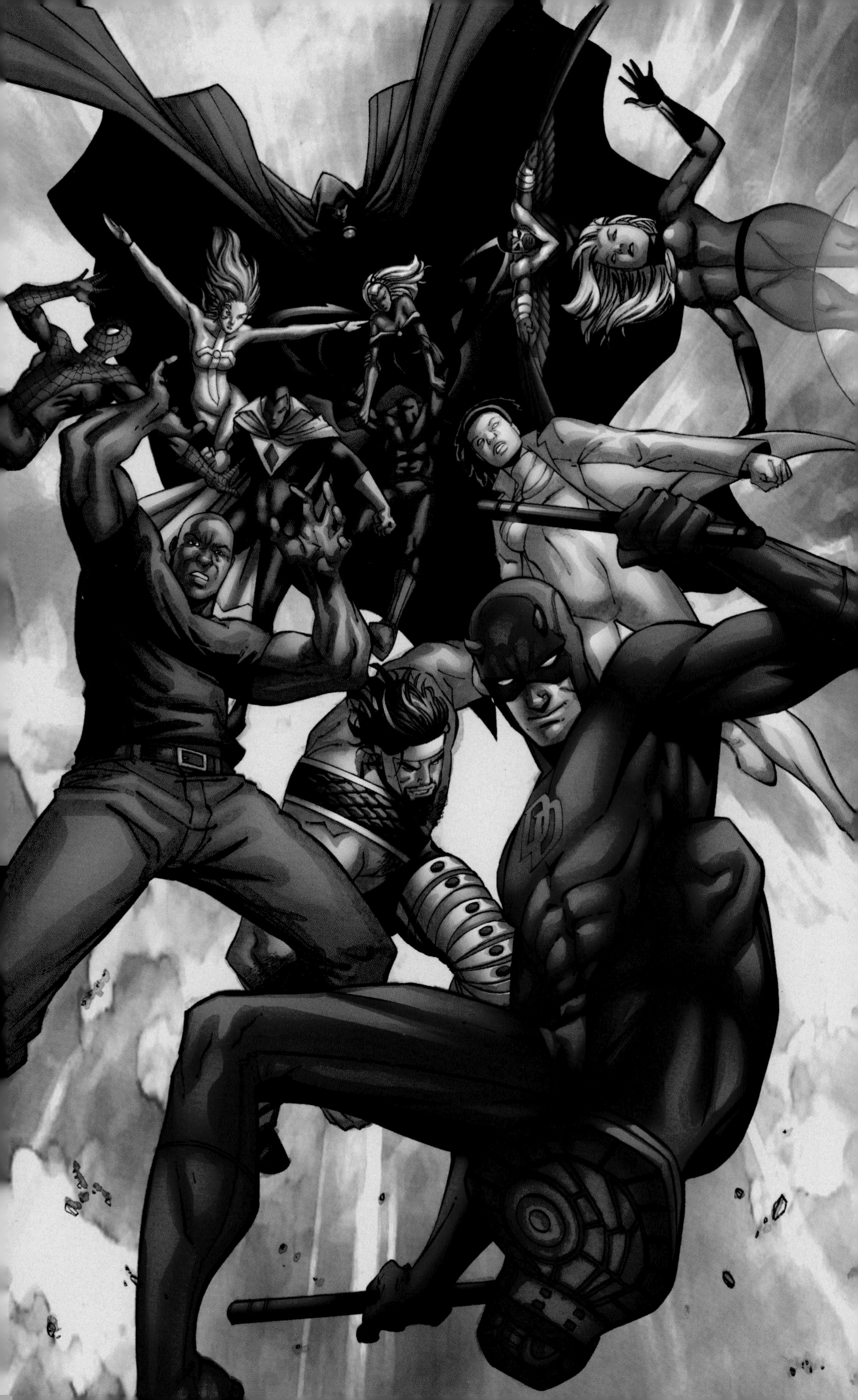

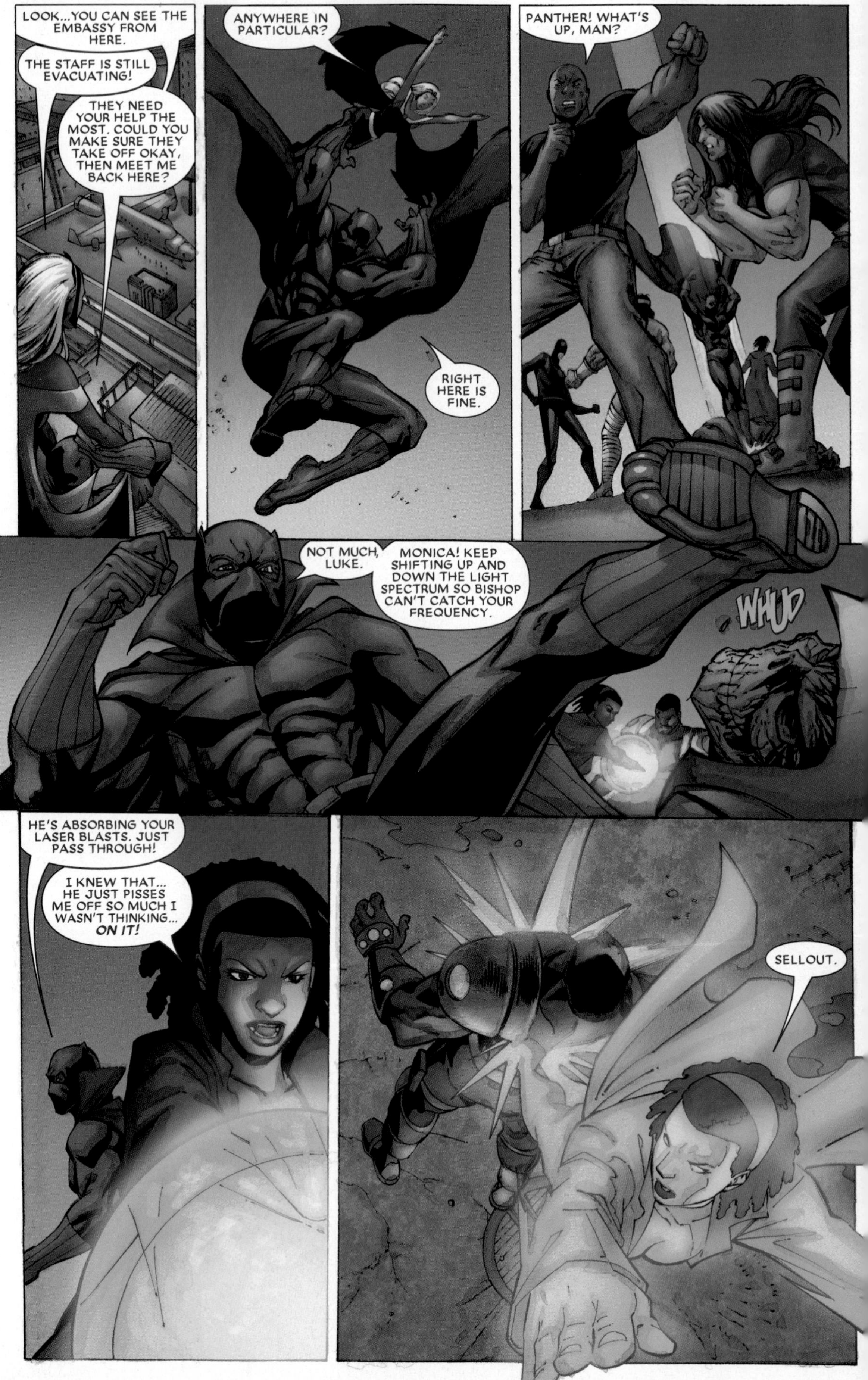
LOOK...YOU CAN SEE THE EMBASSY FROM HERE.
THE STAFF IS STILL EVACUATING!
THEY NEED YOUR HELP THE MOST. COULD YOU MAKE SURE THEY TAKE OFF OKAY, THEN MEET ME BACK HERE?
ANYWHERE IN PARTICULAR?
RIGHT HERE IS FINE.
PANTHER! WHAT'S UP, MAN?
NOT MUCH, LUKE.
MONICA! KEEP SHIFTING UP AND DOWN THE LIGHT SPECTRUM SO BISHOP CAN'T CATCH YOUR FREQUENCY.
WHUD
HE'S ABSORBING YOUR LASER BLASTS. JUST PASS THROUGH!
I KNEW THAT... HE JUST PISSES ME OFF SO MUCH I WASN'T THINKING... ON IT!
SELLOUT.

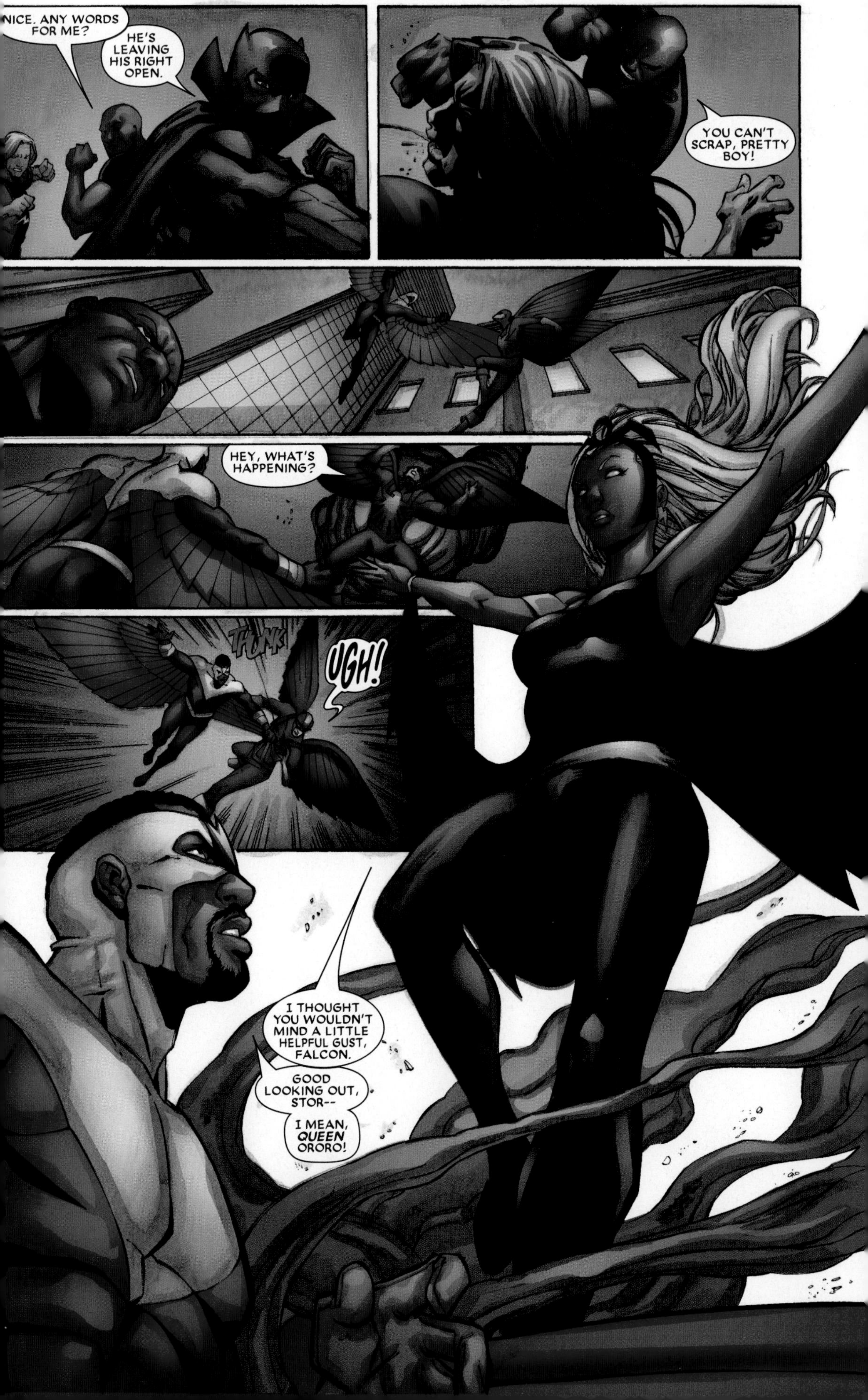
NICE. ANY WORDS FOR ME?
HE'S LEAVING HIS RIGHT OPEN.
YOU CAN'T SCRAP, PRETTY BOY!
HEY, WHAT'S HAPPENING?
THUNK
UGH!
I THOUGHT YOU WOULDN'T MIND A LITTLE HELPFUL GUST, FALCON.
GOOD LOOKING OUT, STOR--
I MEAN, *QUEEN* ORORO!

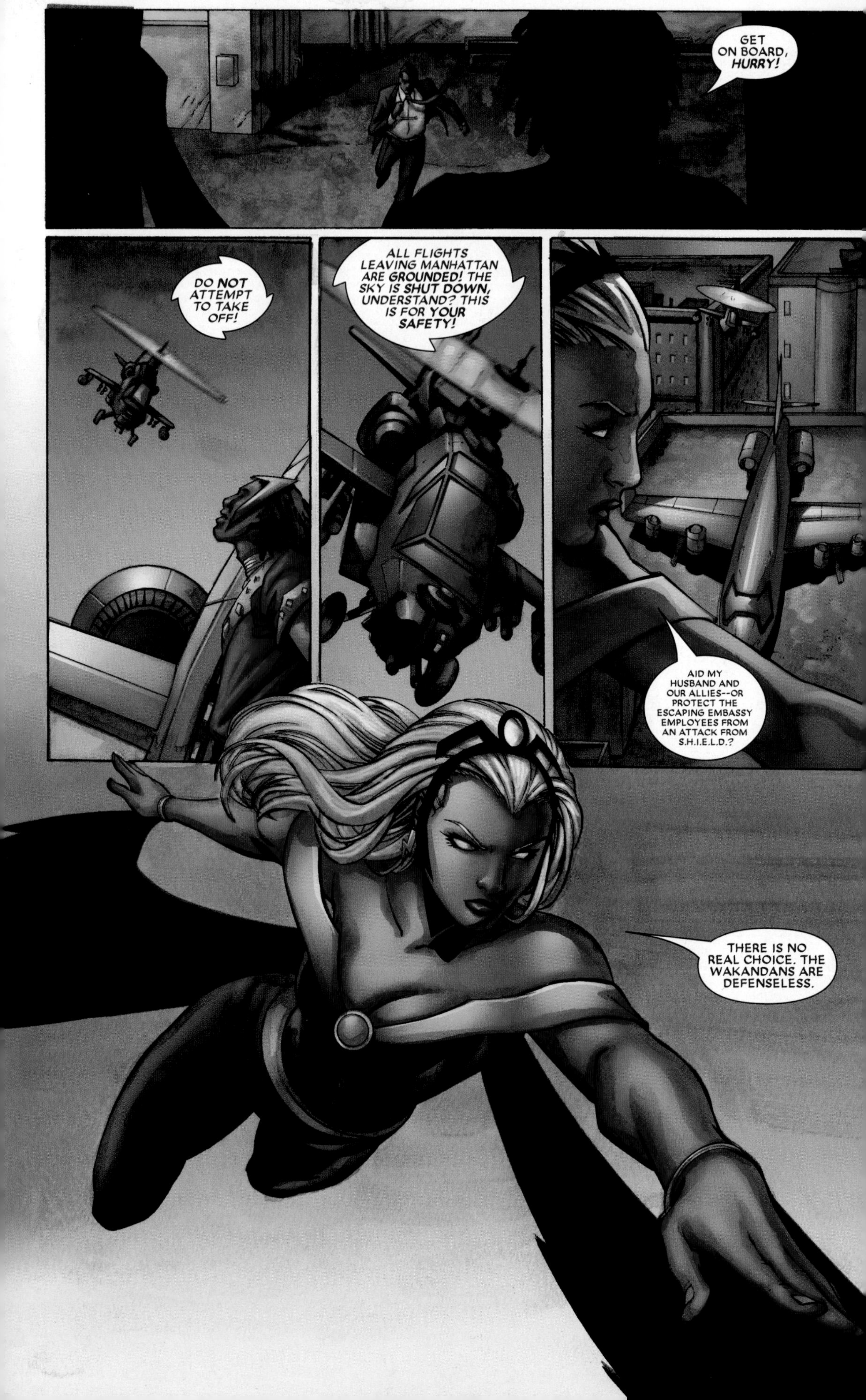
GET ON BOARD, HURRY!
DO NOT ATTEMPT TO TAKE OFF!
ALL FLIGHTS LEAVING MANHATTAN ARE GROUNDED! THE SKY IS SHUT DOWN, UNDERSTAND? THIS IS FOR YOUR SAFETY!
AID MY HUSBAND AND OUR ALLIES--OR PROTECT THE ESCAPING EMBASSY EMPLOYEES FROM AN ATTACK FROM S.H.I.E.L.D.?
THERE IS NO REAL CHOICE. THE WAKANDANS ARE DEFENSELESS.

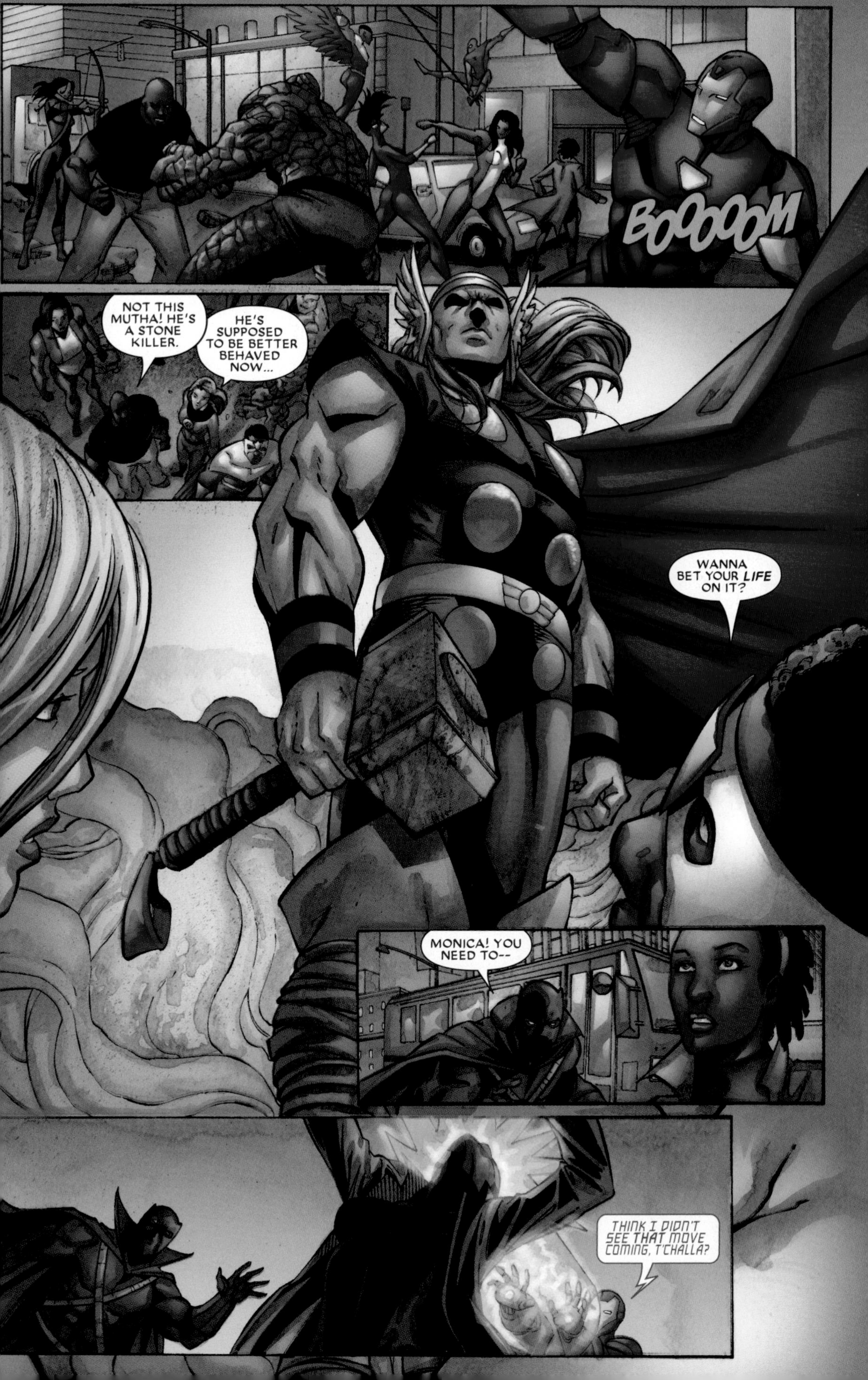
BOOOOOM
NOT THIS MUTHA! HE'S A STONE KILLER.
HE'S SUPPOSED TO BE BETTER BEHAVED NOW...
WANNA BET YOUR LIFE ON IT?
MONICA! YOU NEED TO--
THINK I DIDN'T SEE THAT MOVE COMING, T'CHALLA?

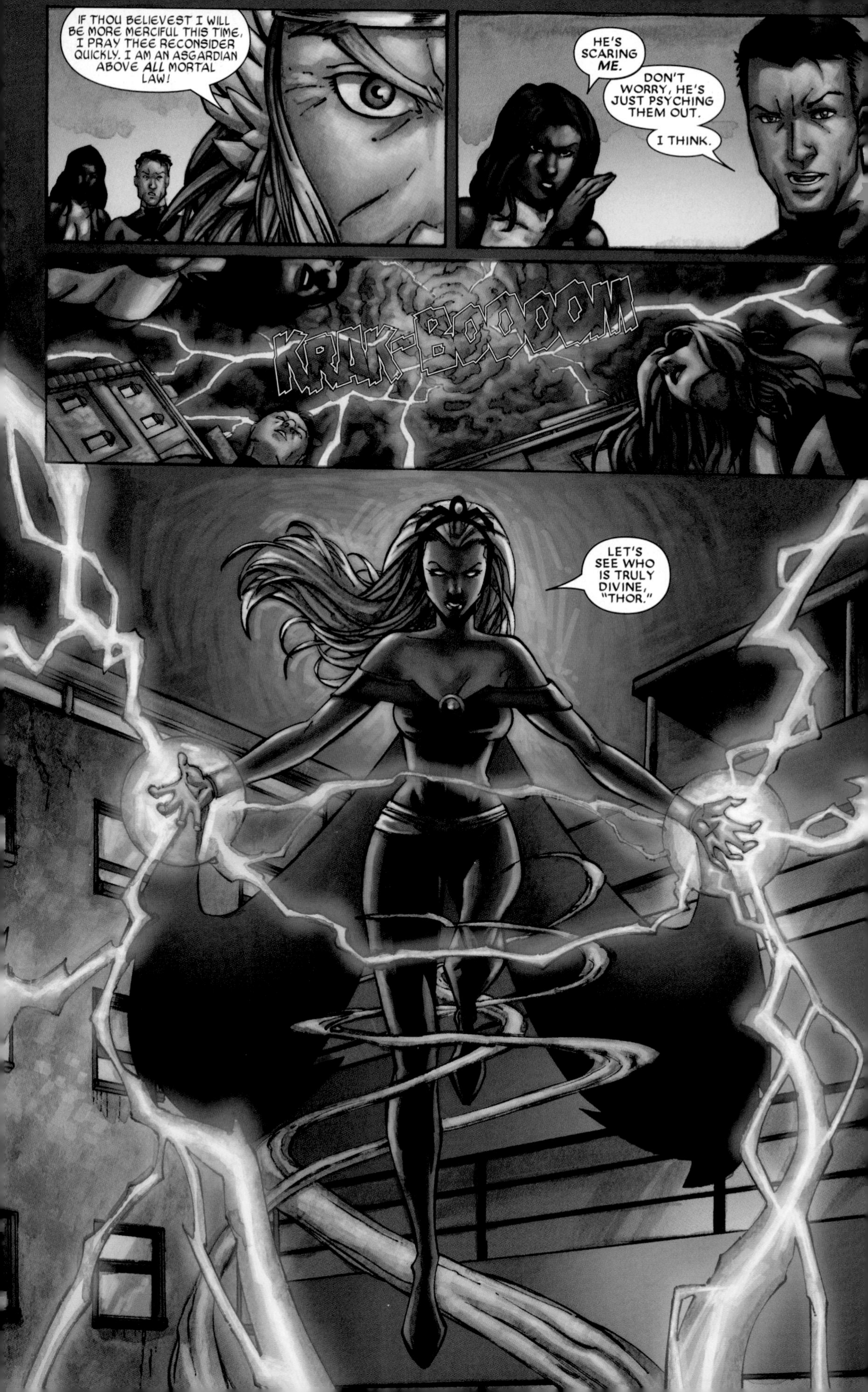
IF THOU BELIEVEST I WILL BE MORE MERCIFUL THIS TIME, I PRAY THEE RECONSIDER QUICKLY. I AM AN ASGARDIAN ABOVE ALL MORTAL LAW!
HE'S SCARING ME.
DON'T WORRY, HE'S JUST PSYCHING THEM OUT.
I THINK.
KRAK-BOOOOM
LET'S SEE WHO IS TRULY DIVINE, "THOR."

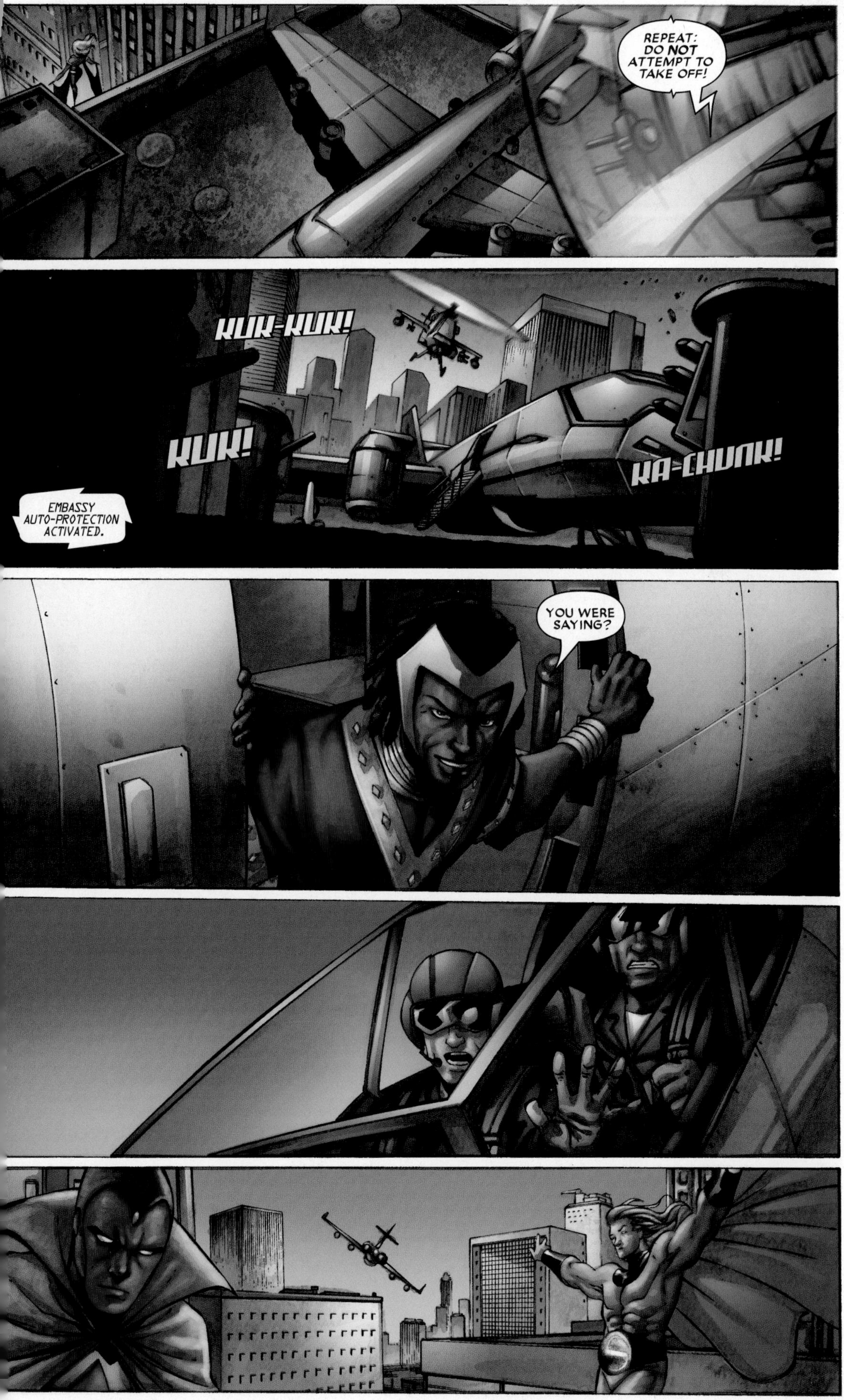
REPEAT: DO NOT ATTEMPT TO TAKE OFF!
KUK-KUK!
KUK!
KA-CHUNK!
EMBASSY AUTO-PROTECTION ACTIVATED.
YOU WERE SAYING?

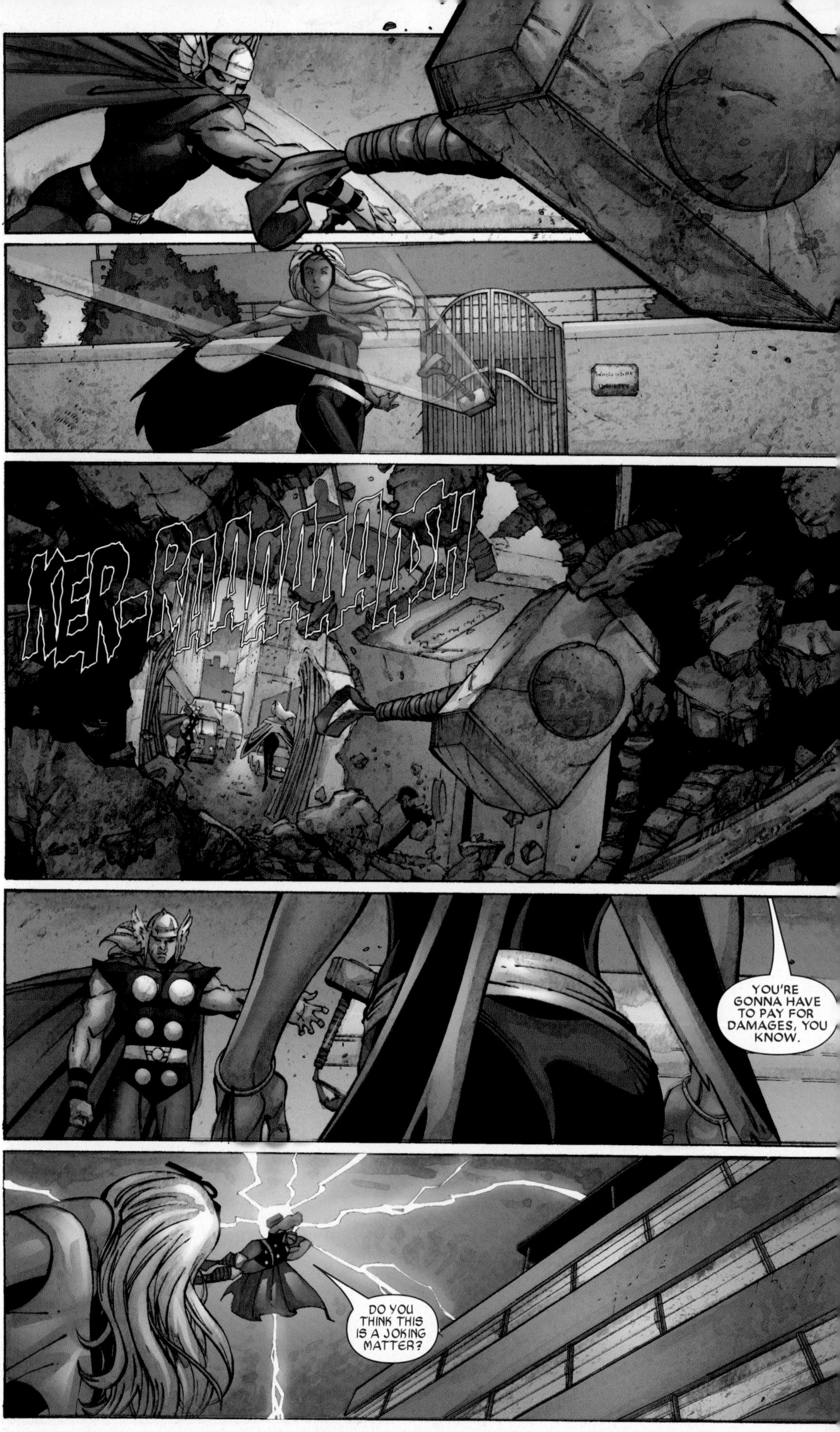
KER-RAAAAAAASH
YOU'RE GONNA HAVE TO PAY FOR DAMAGES, YOU KNOW.
DO YOU THINK THIS IS A JOKING MATTER?

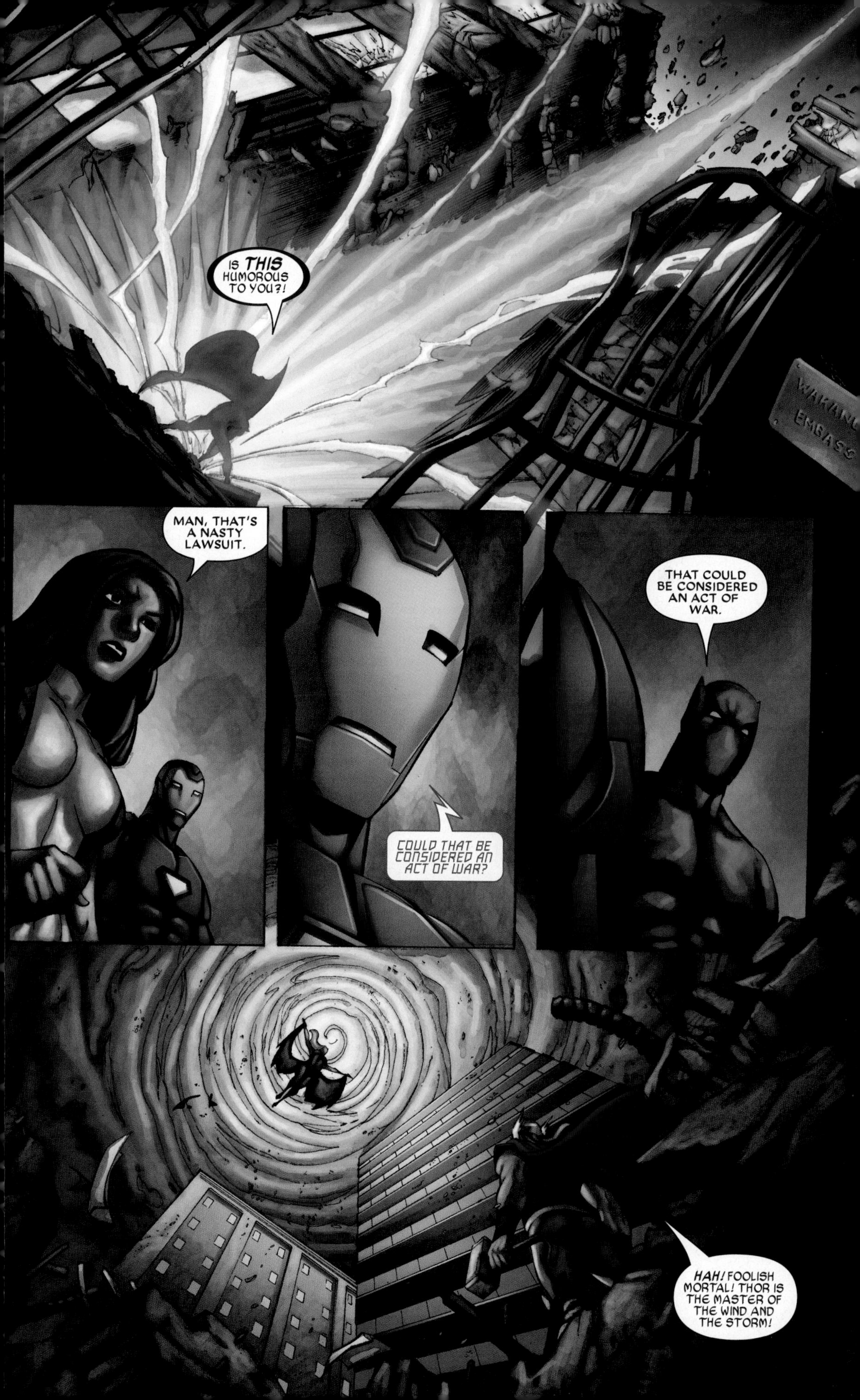
IS THIS HUMOROUS TO YOU?!
MAN, THAT'S A NASTY LAWSUIT.
COULD THAT BE CONSIDERED AN ACT OF WAR?
THAT COULD BE CONSIDERED AN ACT OF WAR.
HAH! FOOLISH MORTAL! THOR IS THE MASTER OF THE WIND AND THE STORM!

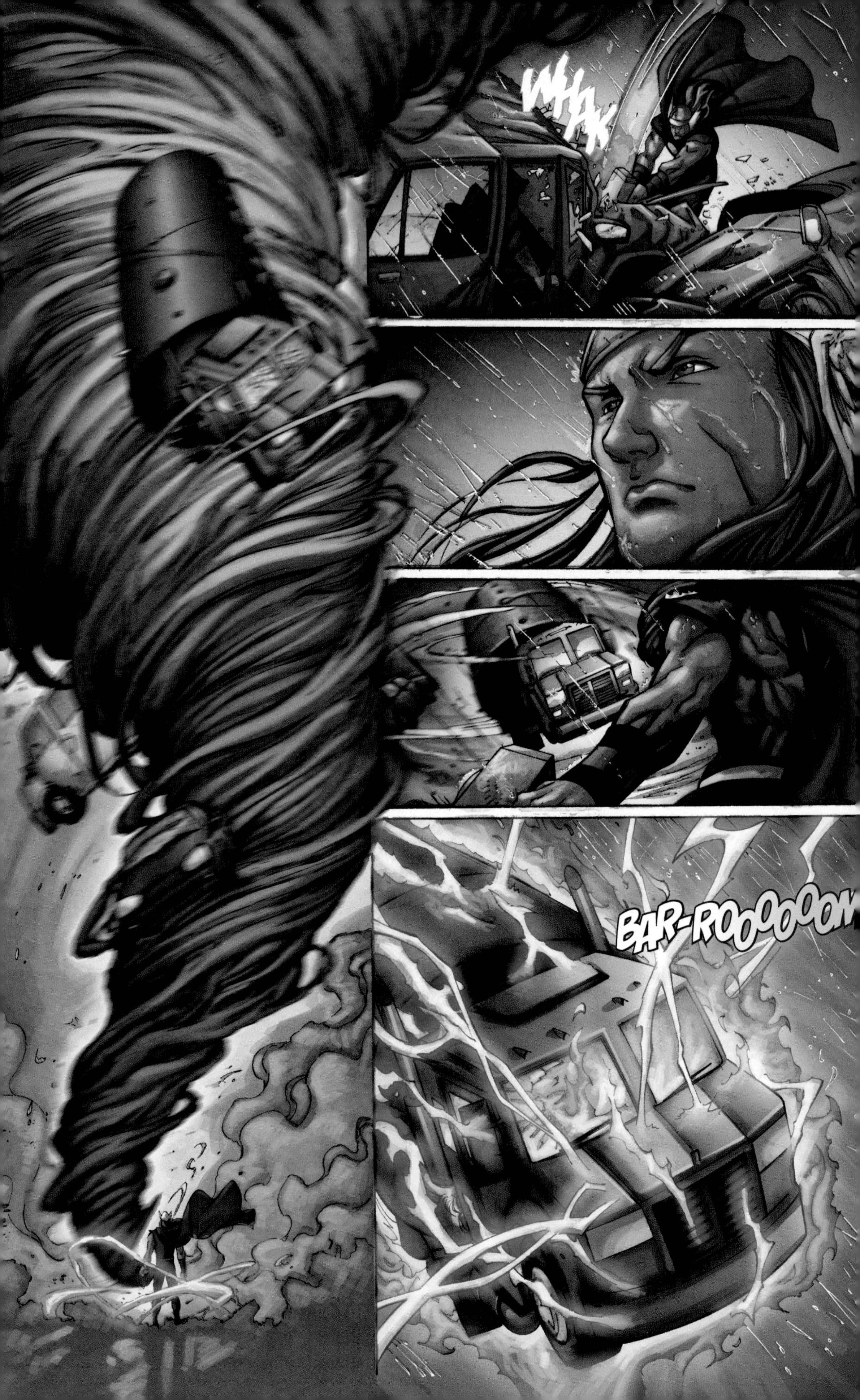
WHAK
BAR-ROOOOOOOM

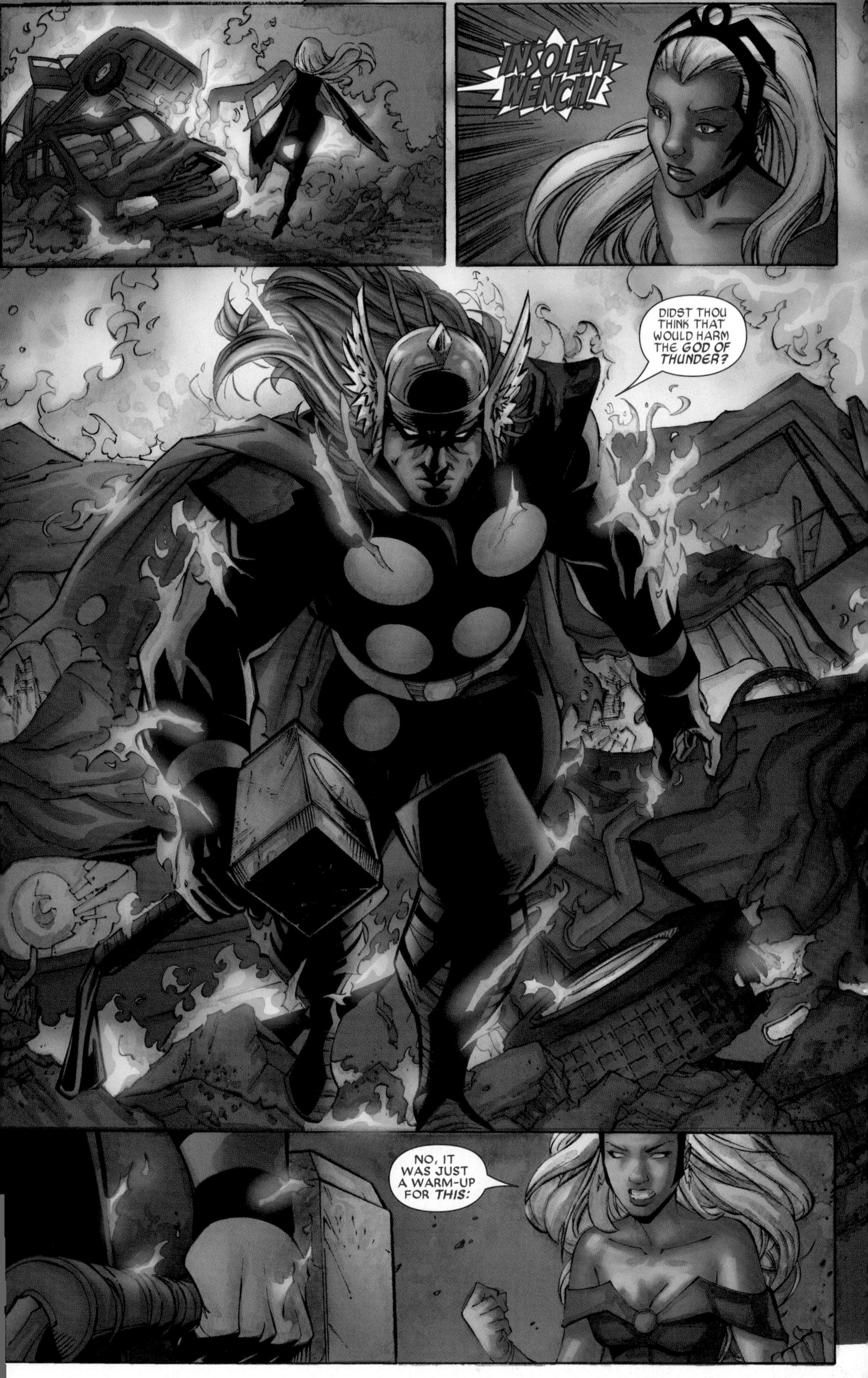
INSOLENT WENCH!
DIDST THOU THINK THAT WOULD HARM THE GOD OF THUNDER?
NO, IT WAS JUST A WARM-UP FOR THIS:

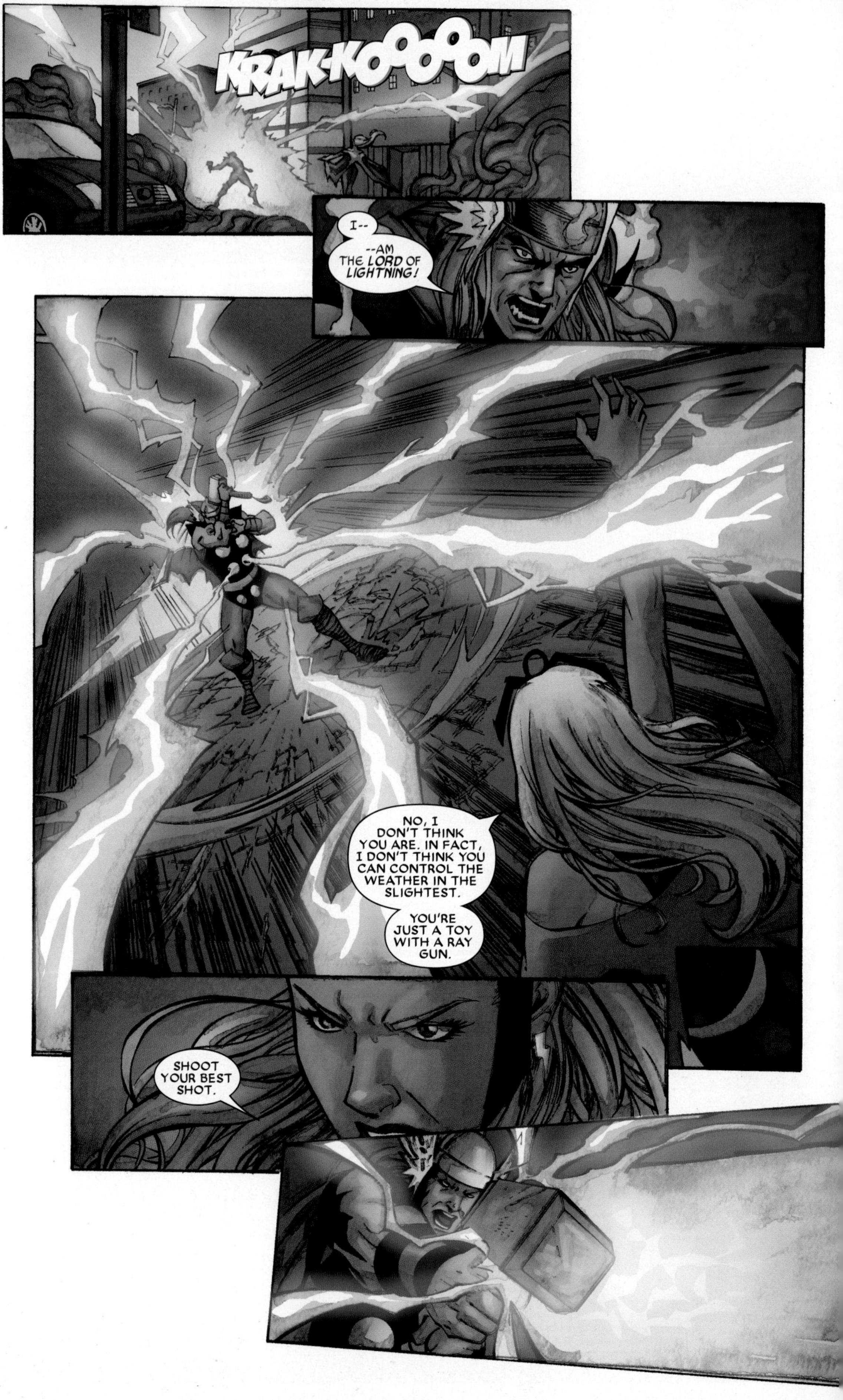
KRAK-KOOOOOM
I--
--AM THE LORD OF LIGHTNING!
NO, I DON'T THINK YOU ARE. IN FACT, I DON'T THINK YOU CAN CONTROL THE WEATHER IN THE SLIGHTEST.
YOU'RE JUST A TOY WITH A RAY GUN.
SHOOT YOUR BEST SHOT.

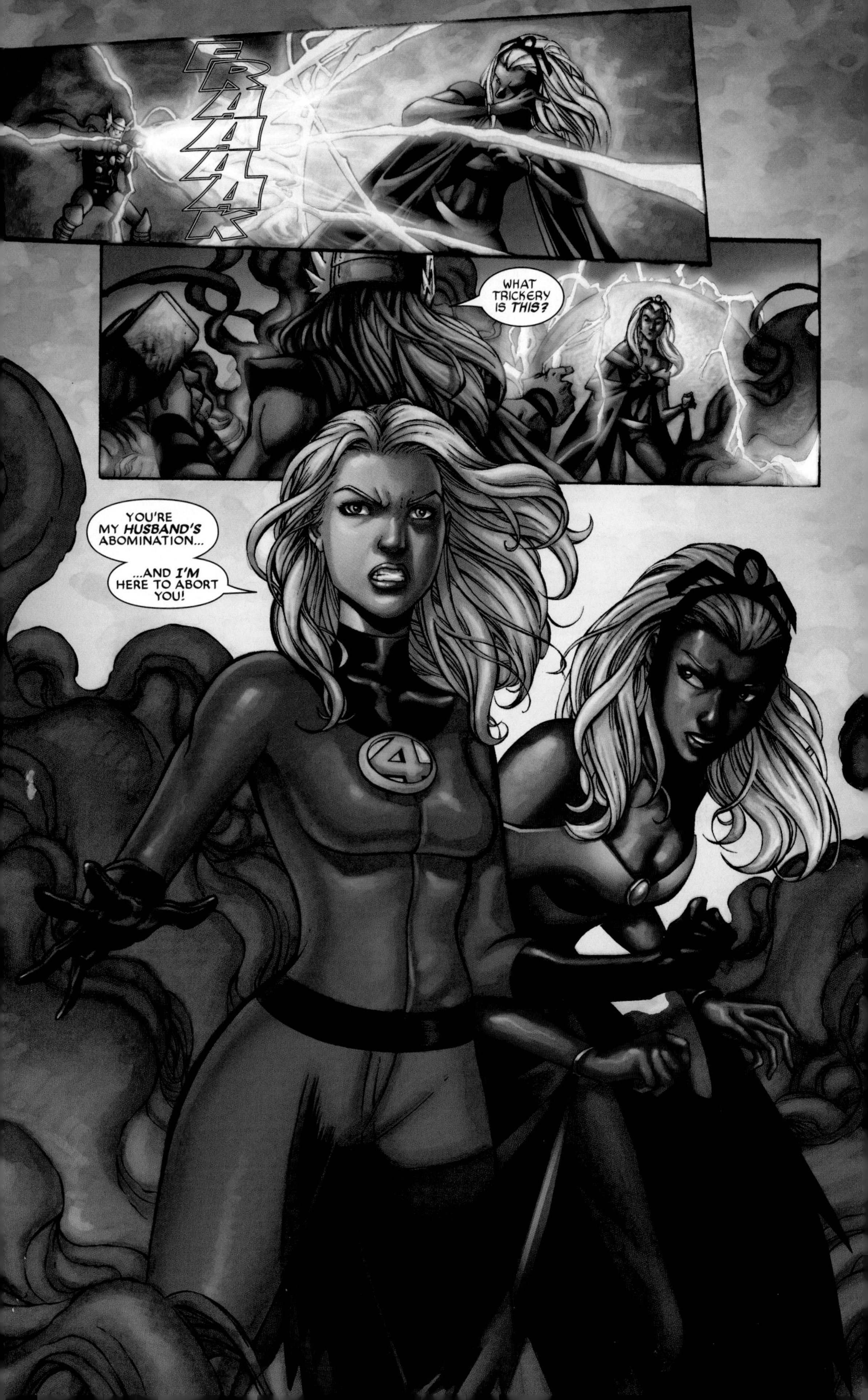
FRAAAAK
WHAT TRICKERY IS THIS?
YOU'RE MY HUSBAND'S ABOMINATION...
...AND I'M HERE TO ABORT YOU!

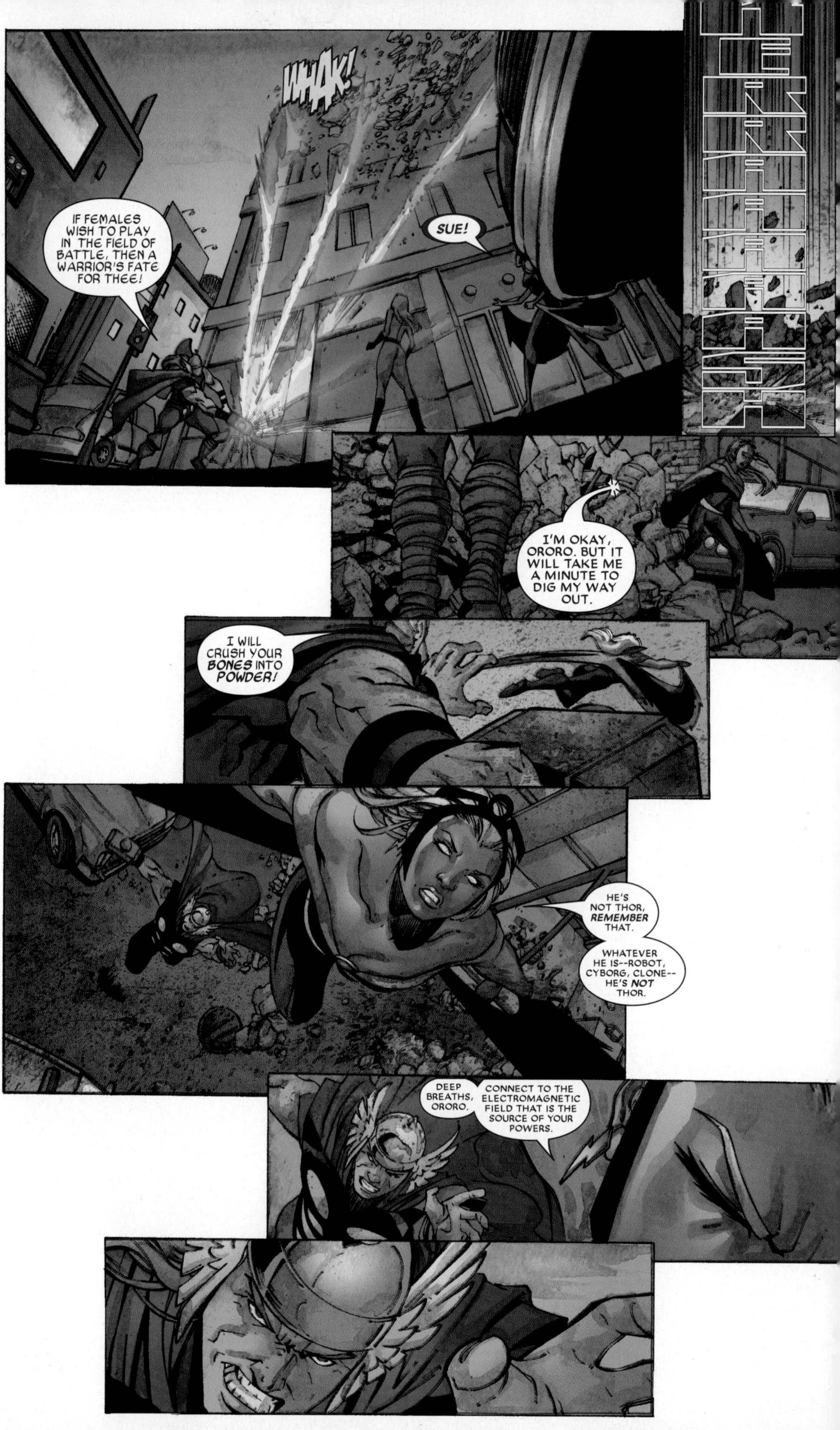
WHAK!
IF FEMALES WISH TO PLAY IN THE FIELD OF BATTLE, THEN A WARRIOR'S FATE FOR THEE!
SUE!
I'M OKAY, ORORO. BUT IT WILL TAKE ME A MINUTE TO DIG MY WAY OUT.
I WILL CRUSH YOUR BONES INTO POWDER!
HE'S NOT THOR, REMEMBER THAT.
WHATEVER HE IS--ROBOT, CYBORG, CLONE-- HE'S NOT THOR.
DEEP BREATHS, ORORO.
CONNECT TO THE ELECTROMAGNETIC FIELD THAT IS THE SOURCE OF YOUR POWERS.

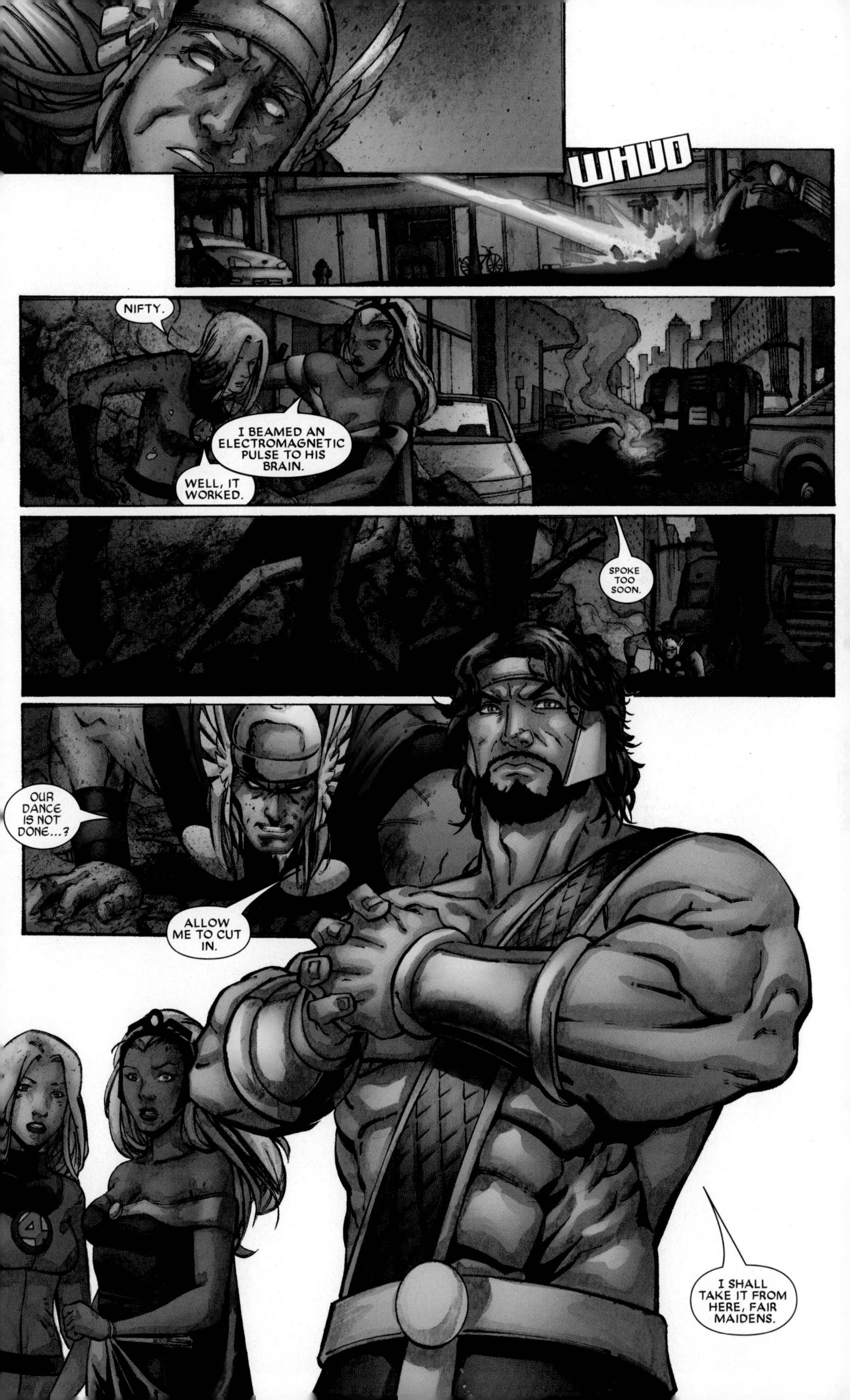
WHUD
NIFTY.
I BEAMED AN ELECTROMAGNETIC PULSE TO HIS BRAIN.
WELL, IT WORKED.
SPOKE TOO SOON.
OUR DANCE IS NOT DONE...?
ALLOW ME TO CUT IN.
I SHALL TAKE IT FROM HERE, FAIR MAIDENS.

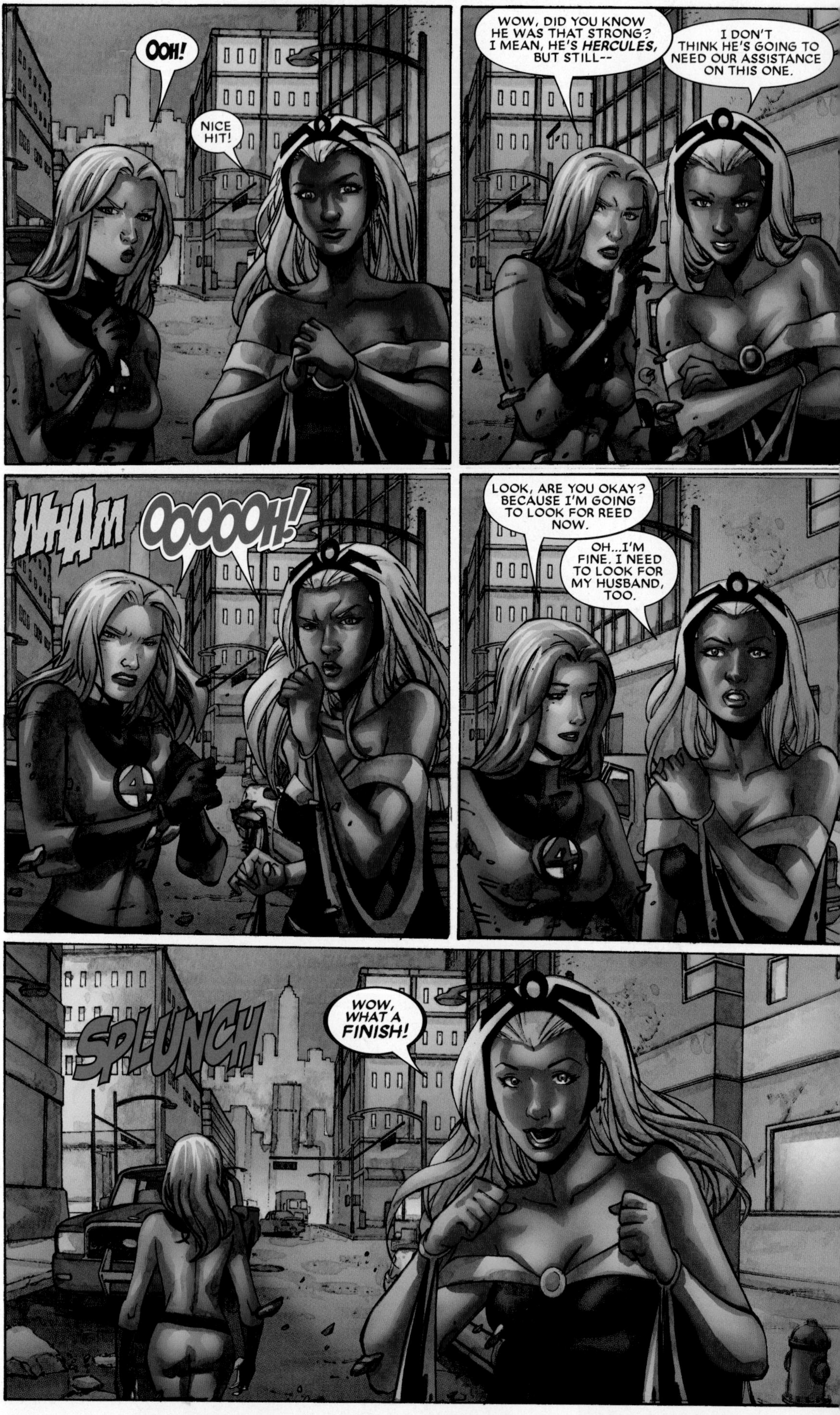
OOH!
NICE HIT!
WOW, DID YOU KNOW HE WAS THAT STRONG? I MEAN, HE'S HERCULES, BUT STILL--
I DON'T THINK HE'S GOING TO NEED OUR ASSISTANCE ON THIS ONE.
WHAM
OOOOOH!
LOOK, ARE YOU OKAY? BECAUSE I'M GOING TO LOOK FOR REED NOW.
OH...I'M FINE. I NEED TO LOOK FOR MY HUSBAND, TOO.
SPLUNCH
WOW, WHAT A FINISH!

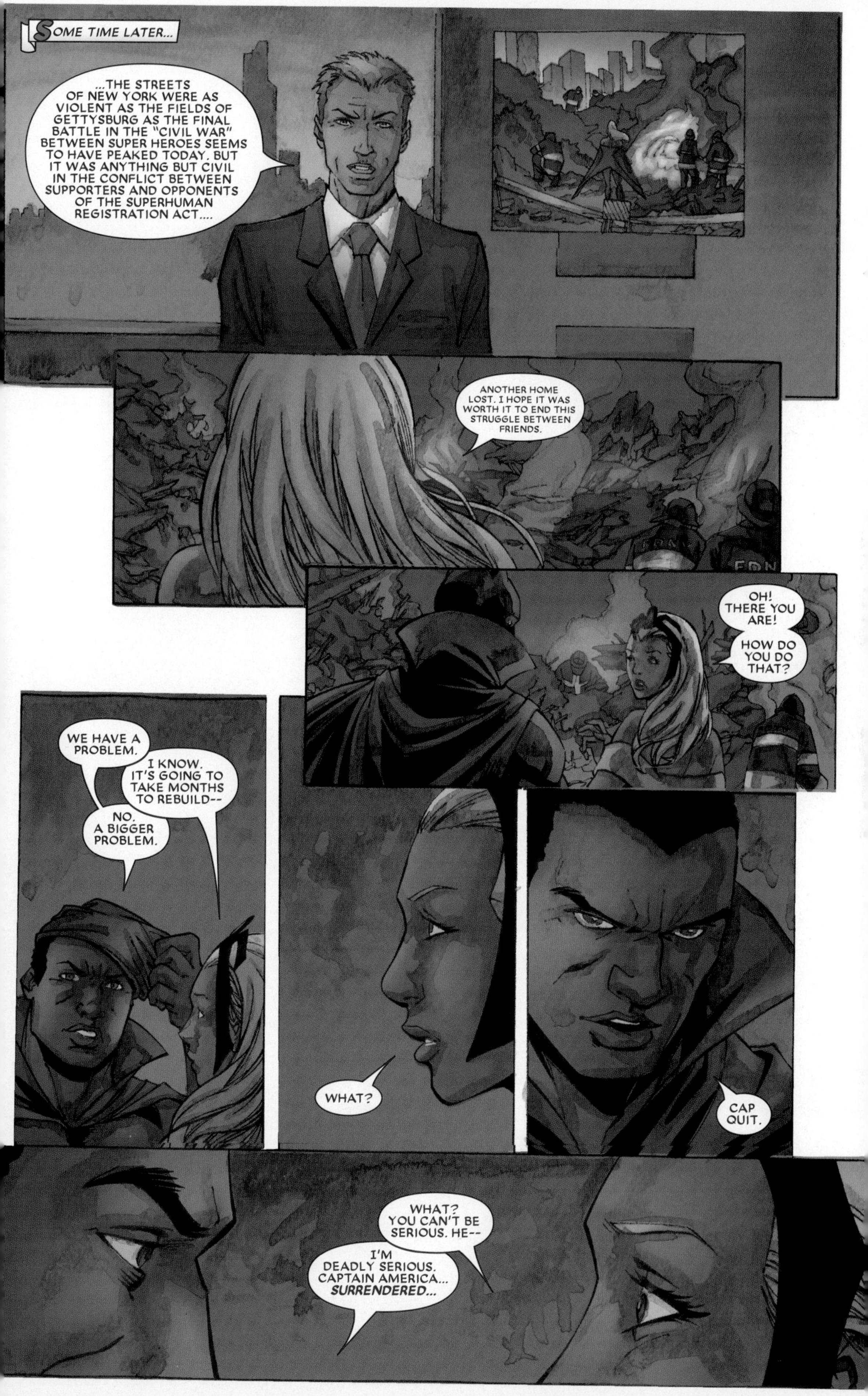
SOME TIME LATER...
...THE STREETS OF NEW YORK WERE AS VIOLENT AS THE FIELDS OF GETTYSBURG AS THE FINAL BATTLE IN THE "CIVIL WAR" BETWEEN SUPER HEROES SEEMS TO HAVE PEAKED TODAY. BUT IT WAS ANYTHING BUT CIVIL IN THE CONFLICT BETWEEN SUPPORTERS AND OPPONENTS OF THE SUPERHUMAN REGISTRATION ACT....
ANOTHER HOME LOST. I HOPE IT WAS WORTH IT TO END THIS STRUGGLE BETWEEN FRIENDS.
OH! THERE YOU ARE!
HOW DO YOU DO THAT?
WE HAVE A PROBLEM.
I KNOW. IT'S GOING TO TAKE MONTHS TO REBUILD--
NO. A BIGGER PROBLEM.
WHAT?
CAP QUIT.
WHAT? YOU CAN'T BE SERIOUS. HE--
I'M DEADLY SERIOUS. CAPTAIN AMERICA... SURRENDERED...

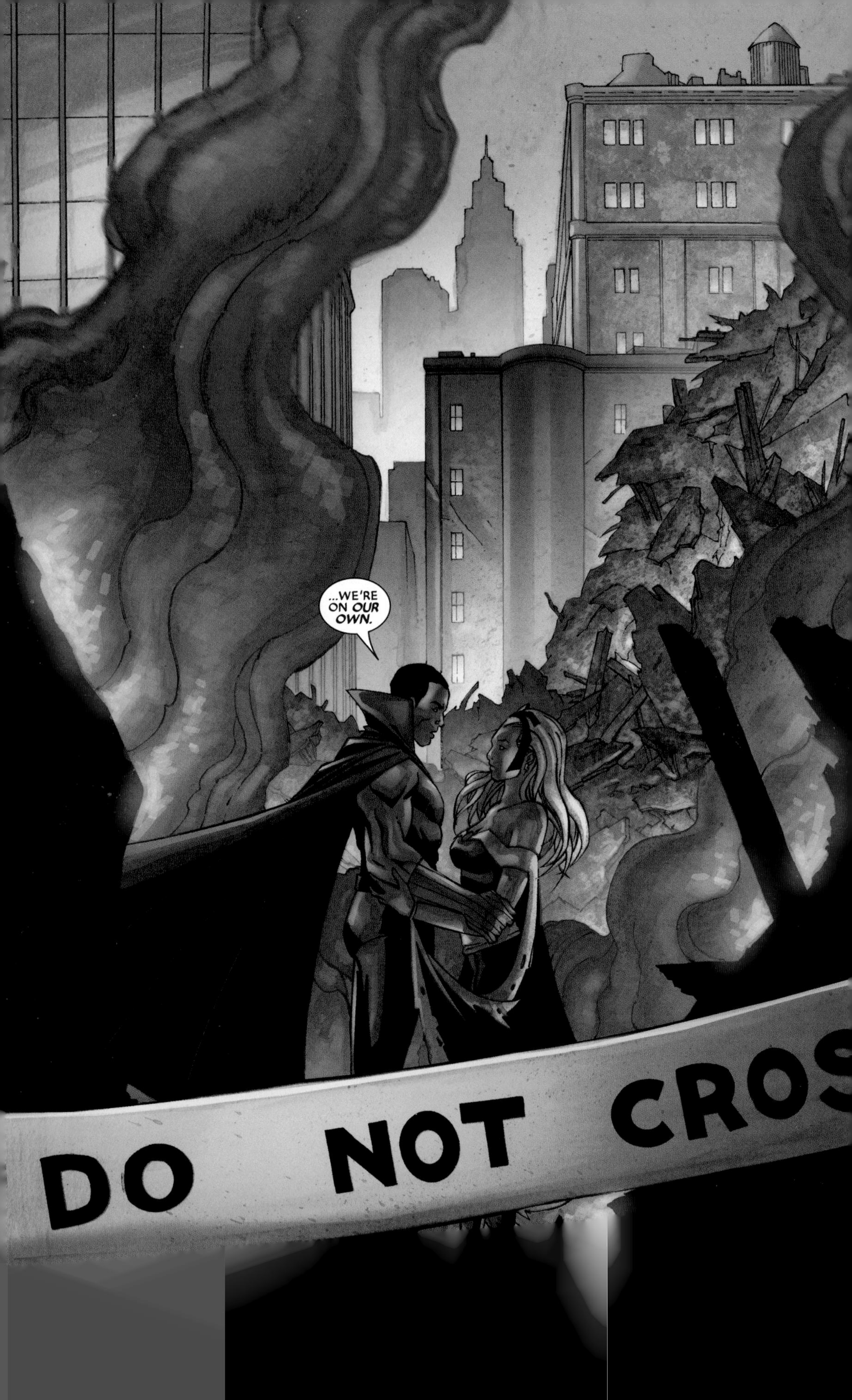
...WE'RE ON OUR OWN.
DO NOT CROS

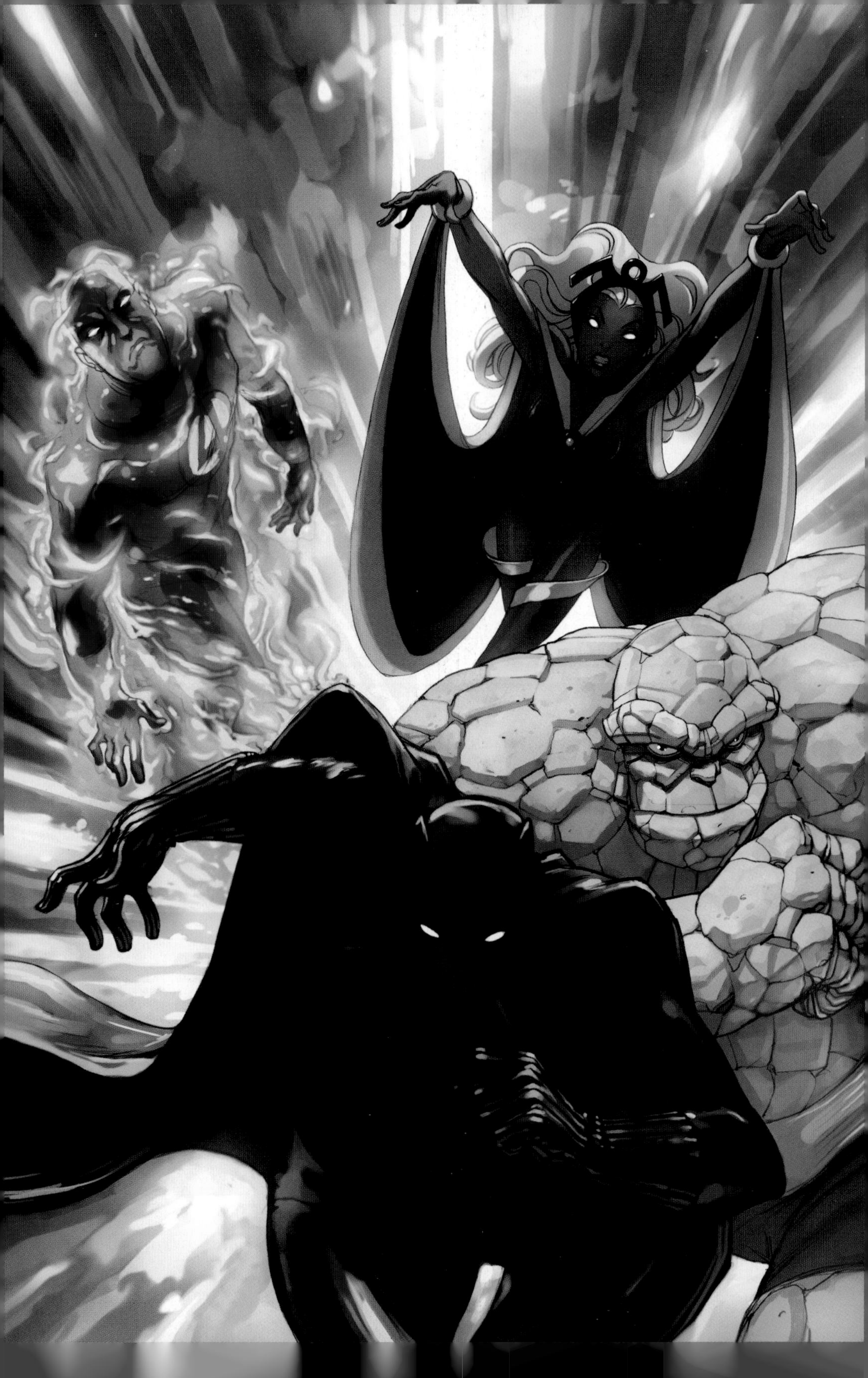

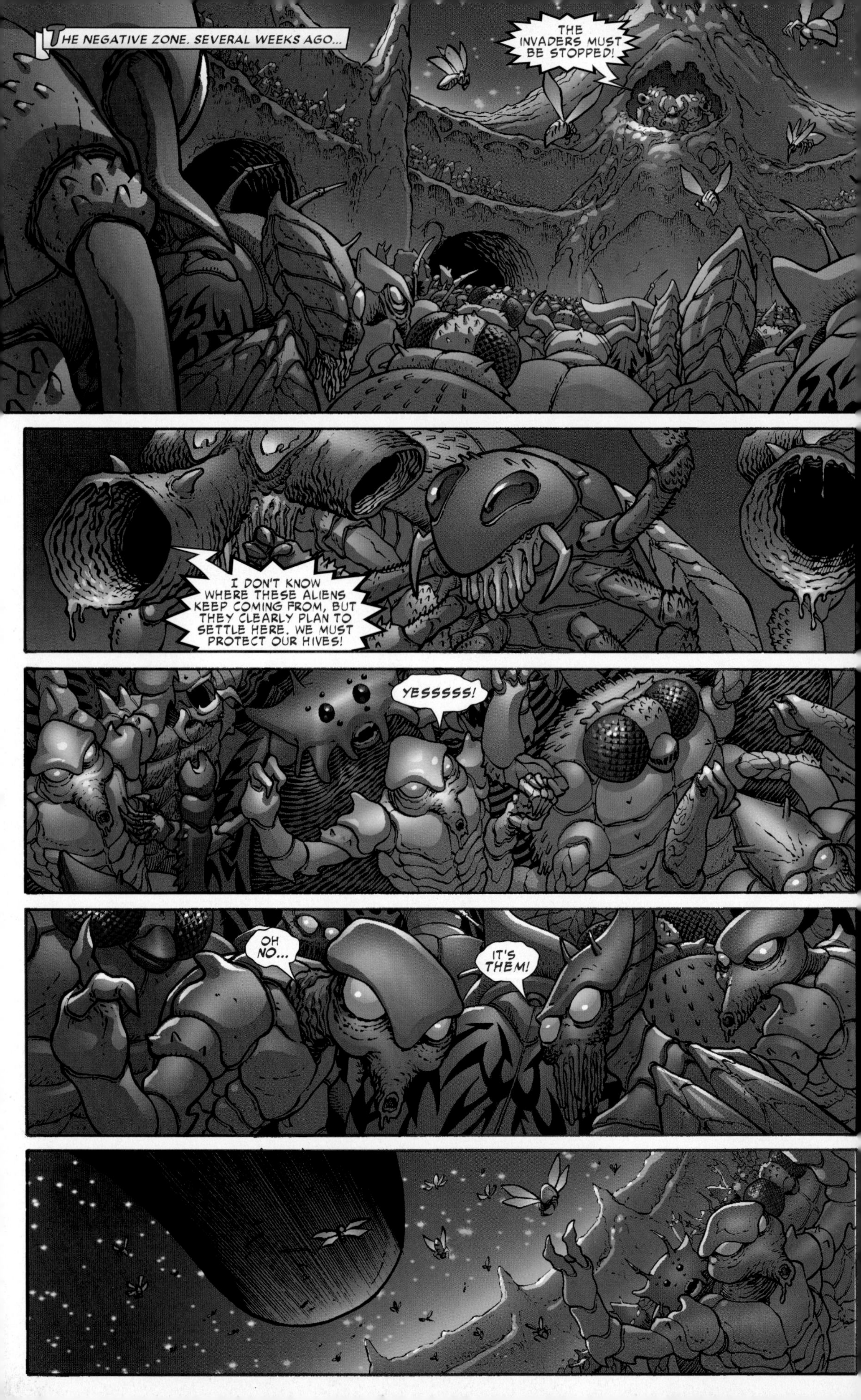
THE NEGATIVE ZONE. SEVERAL WEEKS AGO...
THE INVADERS MUST BE STOPPED!
I DON'T KNOW WHERE THESE ALIENS KEEP COMING FROM, BUT THEY CLEARLY PLAN TO SETTLE HERE. WE MUST PROTECT OUR HIVES!
YESSSSS!
OH NO...
IT'S THEM!

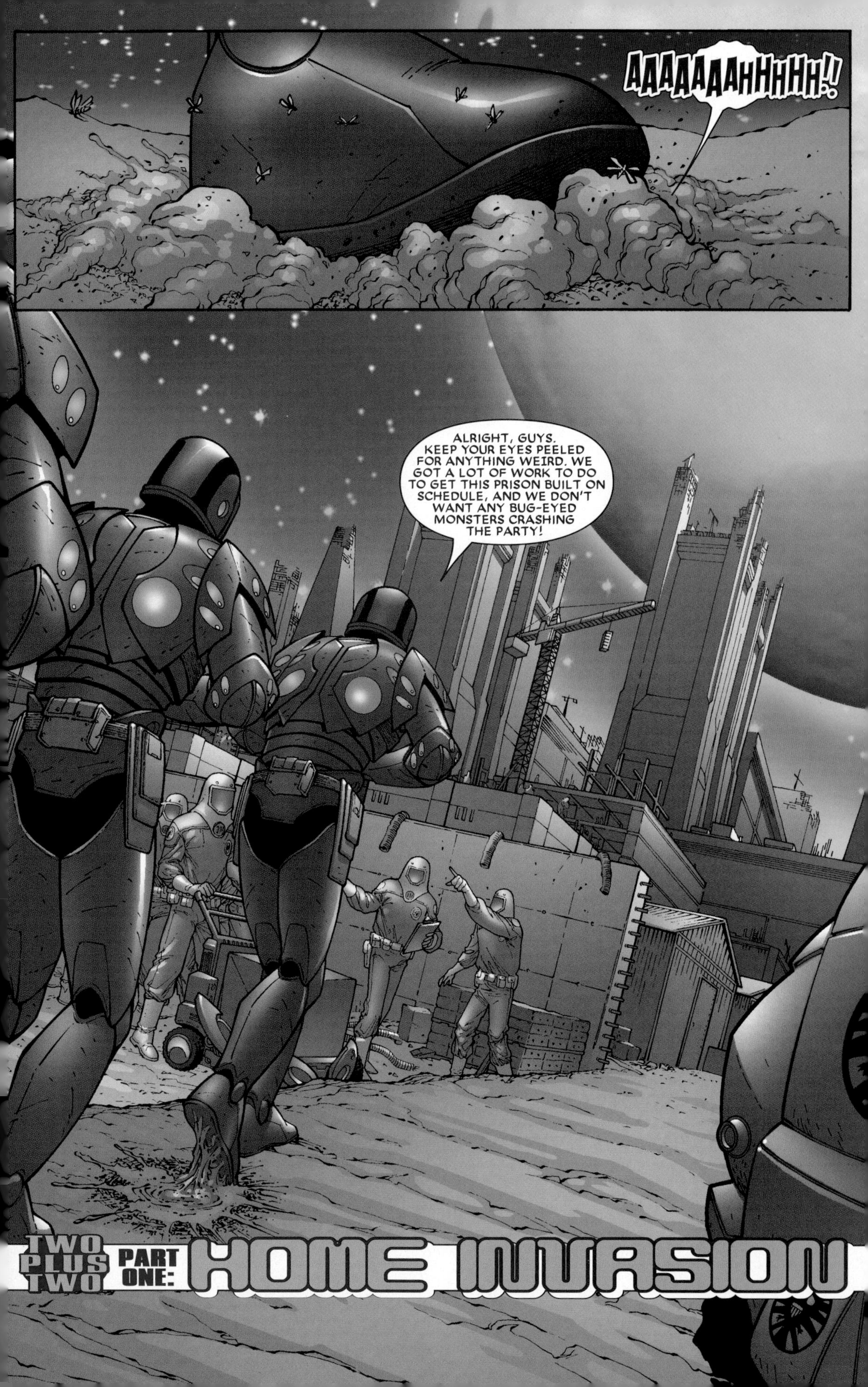
AAAAAAAHHHHH!!
ALRIGHT, GUYS. KEEP YOUR EYES PEELED FOR ANYTHING WEIRD. WE GOT A LOT OF WORK TO DO TO GET THIS PRISON BUILT ON SCHEDULE, AND WE DON'T WANT ANY BUG-EYED MONSTERS CRASHING THE PARTY!
TWO PLUS TWO PART ONE: HOME INVASION

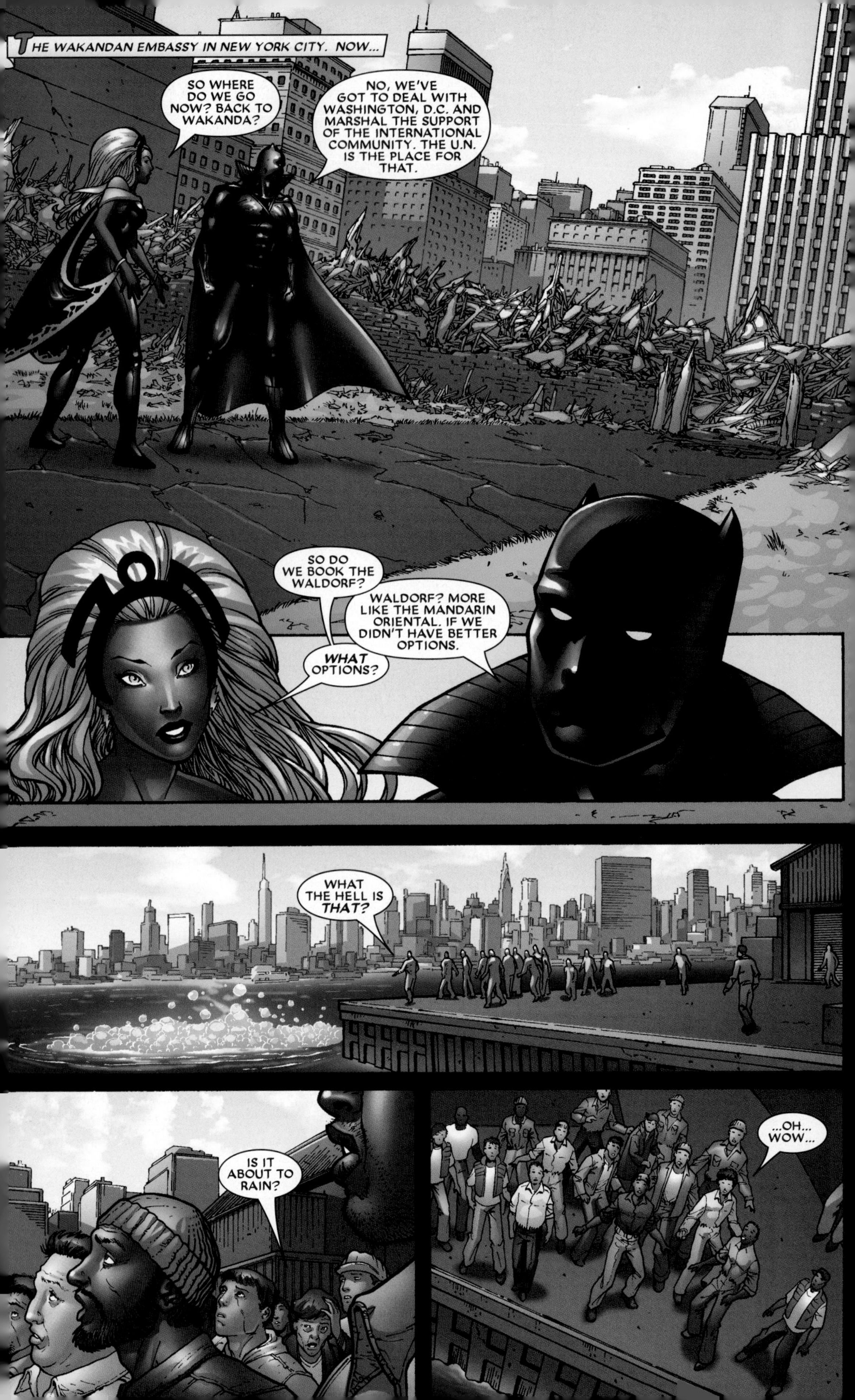
THE WAKANDAN EMBASSY IN NEW YORK CITY. NOW...
SO WHERE DO WE GO NOW? BACK TO WAKANDA?
NO, WE'VE GOT TO DEAL WITH WASHINGTON, D.C. AND MARSHAL THE SUPPORT OF THE INTERNATIONAL COMMUNITY. THE U.N. IS THE PLACE FOR THAT.
SO DO WE BOOK THE WALDORF?
WALDORF? MORE LIKE THE MANDARIN ORIENTAL. IF WE DIDN'T HAVE BETTER OPTIONS.
WHAT OPTIONS?
WHAT THE HELL IS THAT?
IS IT ABOUT TO RAIN?
...OH... WOW...

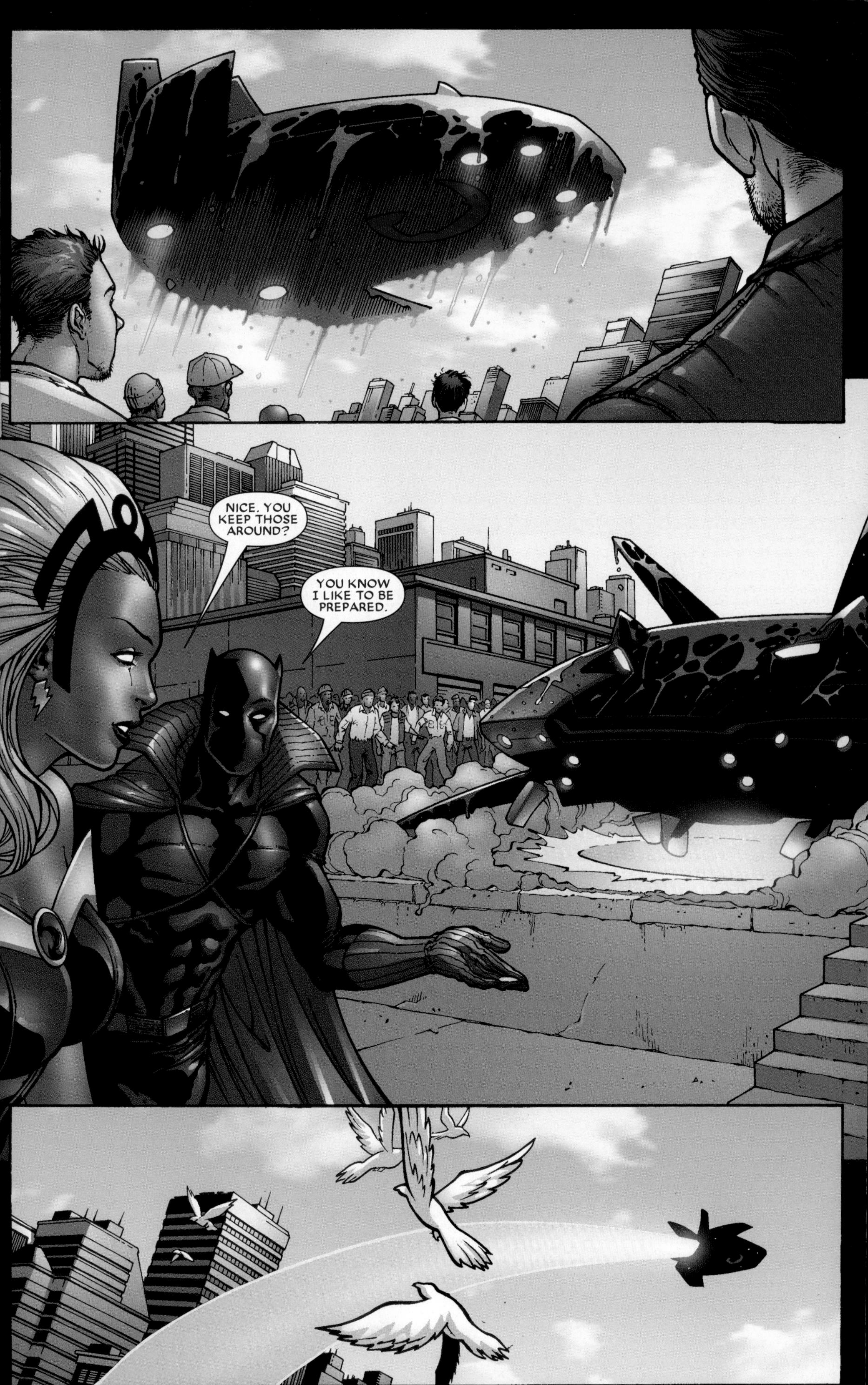
NICE. YOU KEEP THOSE AROUND?
YOU KNOW I LIKE TO BE PREPARED.

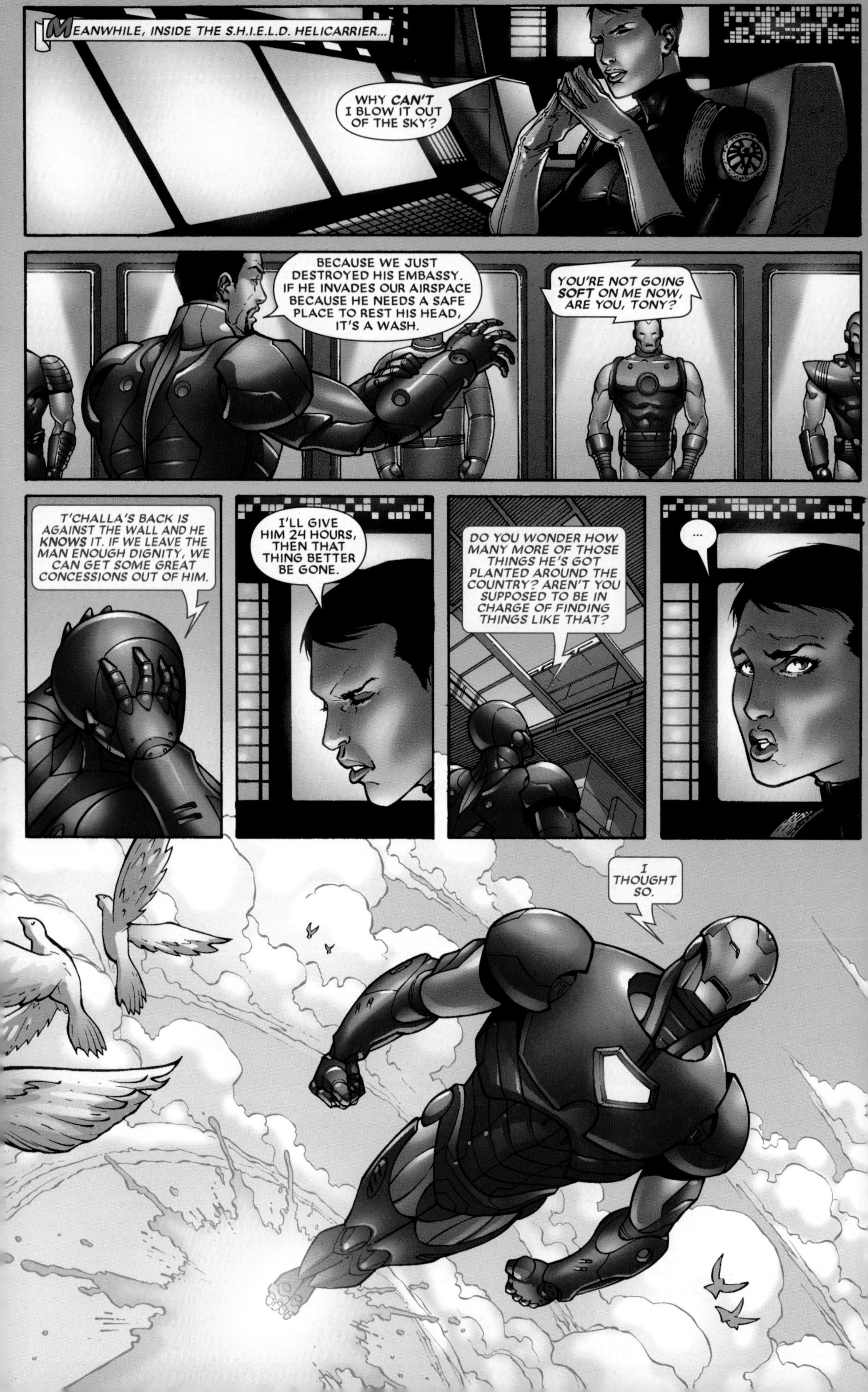
MEANWHILE, INSIDE THE S.H.I.E.L.D. HELICARRIER...
WHY CAN'T I BLOW IT OUT OF THE SKY?
BECAUSE WE JUST DESTROYED HIS EMBASSY. IF HE INVADES OUR AIRSPACE BECAUSE HE NEEDS A SAFE PLACE TO REST HIS HEAD, IT'S A WASH.
YOU'RE NOT GOING SOFT ON ME NOW, ARE YOU, TONY?
T'CHALLA'S BACK IS AGAINST THE WALL AND HE KNOWS IT. IF WE LEAVE THE MAN ENOUGH DIGNITY, WE CAN GET SOME GREAT CONCESSIONS OUT OF HIM.
I'LL GIVE HIM 24 HOURS, THEN THAT THING BETTER BE GONE.
DO YOU WONDER HOW MANY MORE OF THOSE THINGS HE'S GOT PLANTED AROUND THE COUNTRY? AREN'T YOU SUPPOSED TO BE IN CHARGE OF FINDING THINGS LIKE THAT?
...
I THOUGHT SO.

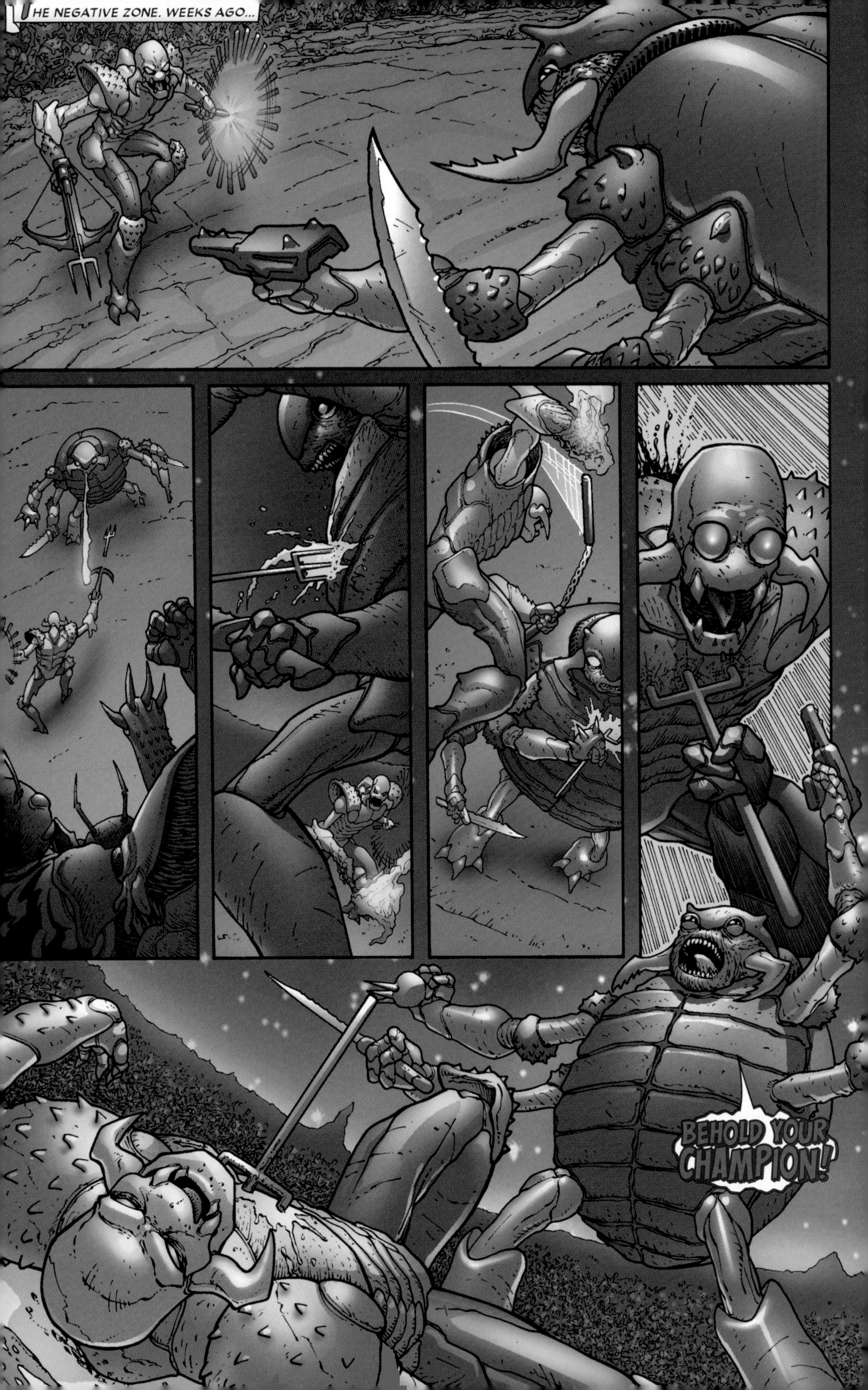
THE NEGATIVE ZONE. WEEKS AGO...
BEHOLD YOUR CHAMPION!

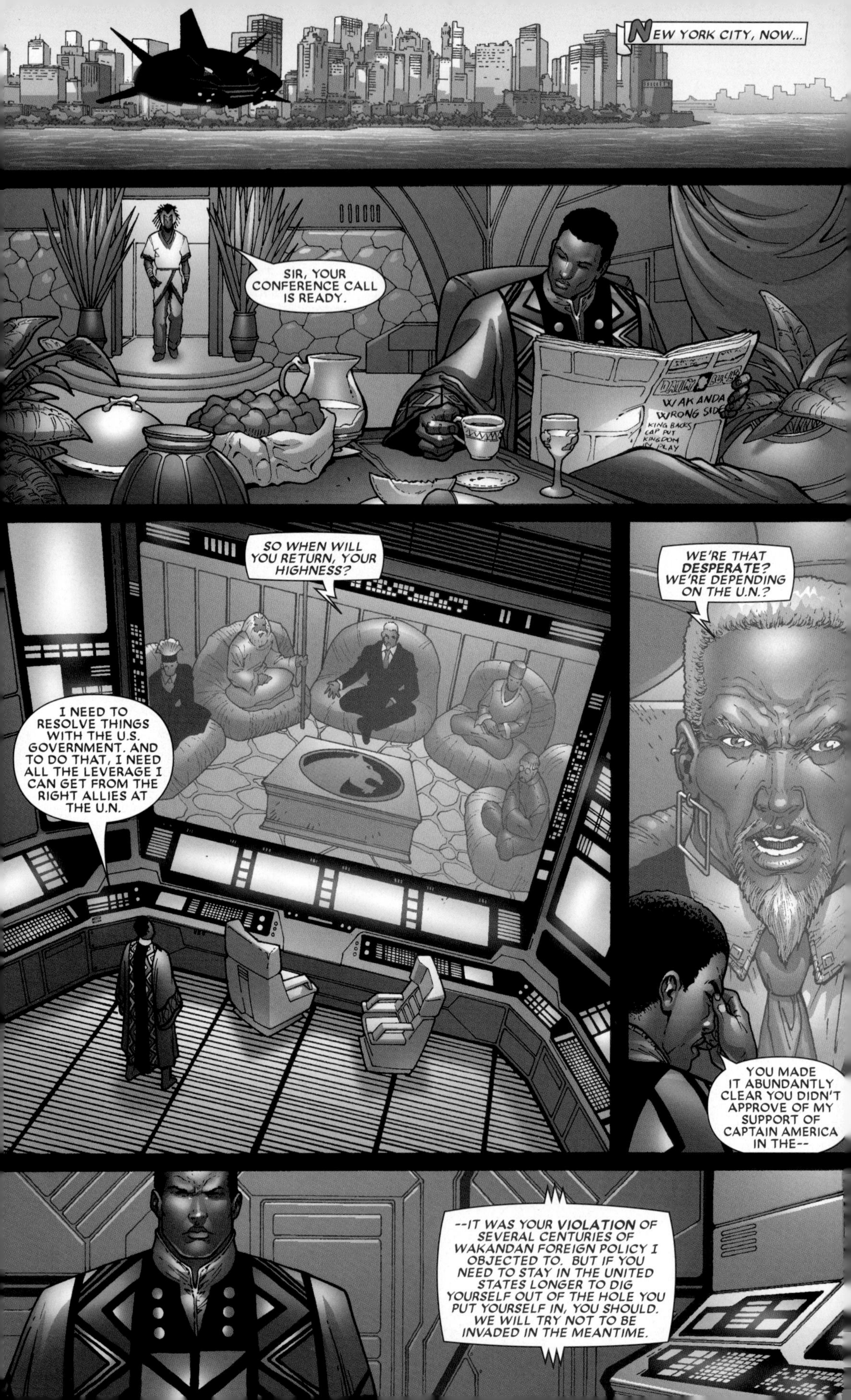
NEW YORK CITY, NOW...
SIR, YOUR CONFERENCE CALL IS READY.
WAKANDA WRONG SIDE
KING BACKS CAP PUT KINGDOM IN PLAY
SO WHEN WILL YOU RETURN, YOUR HIGHNESS?
I NEED TO RESOLVE THINGS WITH THE U.S. GOVERNMENT. AND TO DO THAT, I NEED ALL THE LEVERAGE I CAN GET FROM THE RIGHT ALLIES AT THE U.N.
WE'RE THAT DESPERATE? WE'RE DEPENDING ON THE U.N.?
YOU MADE IT ABUNDANTLY CLEAR YOU DIDN'T APPROVE OF MY SUPPORT OF CAPTAIN AMERICA IN THE--
--IT WAS YOUR VIOLATION OF SEVERAL CENTURIES OF WAKANDAN FOREIGN POLICY I OBJECTED TO. BUT IF YOU NEED TO STAY IN THE UNITED STATES LONGER TO DIG YOURSELF OUT OF THE HOLE YOU PUT YOURSELF IN, YOU SHOULD. WE WILL TRY NOT TO BE INVADED IN THE MEANTIME.

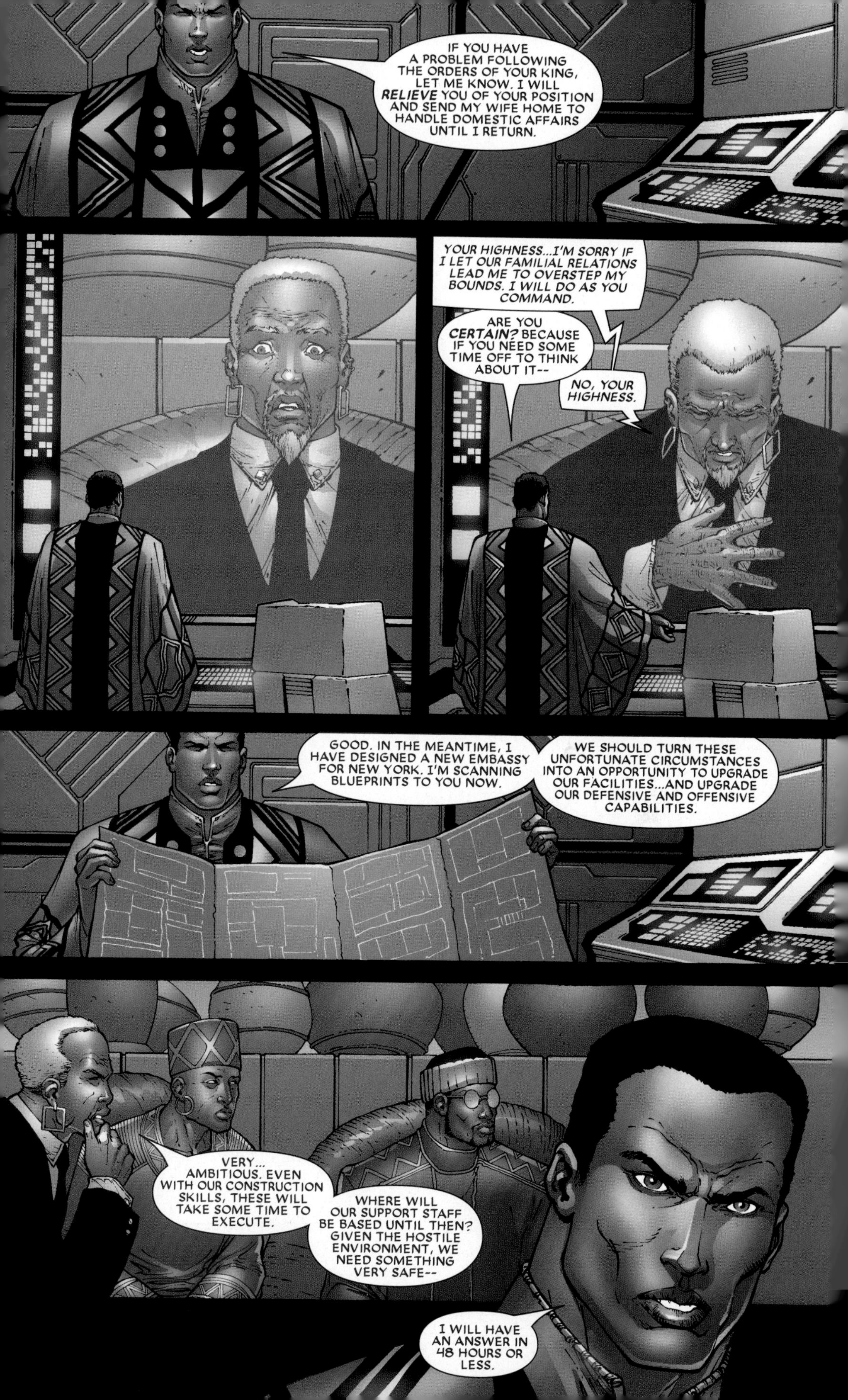
IF YOU HAVE A PROBLEM FOLLOWING THE ORDERS OF YOUR KING, LET ME KNOW. I WILL RELIEVE YOU OF YOUR POSITION AND SEND MY WIFE HOME TO HANDLE DOMESTIC AFFAIRS UNTIL I RETURN.
YOUR HIGHNESS...I'M SORRY IF I LET OUR FAMILIAL RELATIONS LEAD ME TO OVERSTEP MY BOUNDS. I WILL DO AS YOU COMMAND.
ARE YOU CERTAIN? BECAUSE IF YOU NEED SOME TIME OFF TO THINK ABOUT IT--
NO, YOUR HIGHNESS.
GOOD. IN THE MEANTIME, I HAVE DESIGNED A NEW EMBASSY FOR NEW YORK. I'M SCANNING BLUEPRINTS TO YOU NOW.
WE SHOULD TURN THESE UNFORTUNATE CIRCUMSTANCES INTO AN OPPORTUNITY TO UPGRADE OUR FACILITIES...AND UPGRADE OUR DEFENSIVE AND OFFENSIVE CAPABILITIES.
VERY... AMBITIOUS. EVEN WITH OUR CONSTRUCTION SKILLS, THESE WILL TAKE SOME TIME TO EXECUTE.
WHERE WILL OUR SUPPORT STAFF BE BASED UNTIL THEN? GIVEN THE HOSTILE ENVIRONMENT, WE NEED SOMETHING VERY SAFE--
I WILL HAVE AN ANSWER IN 48 HOURS OR LESS.

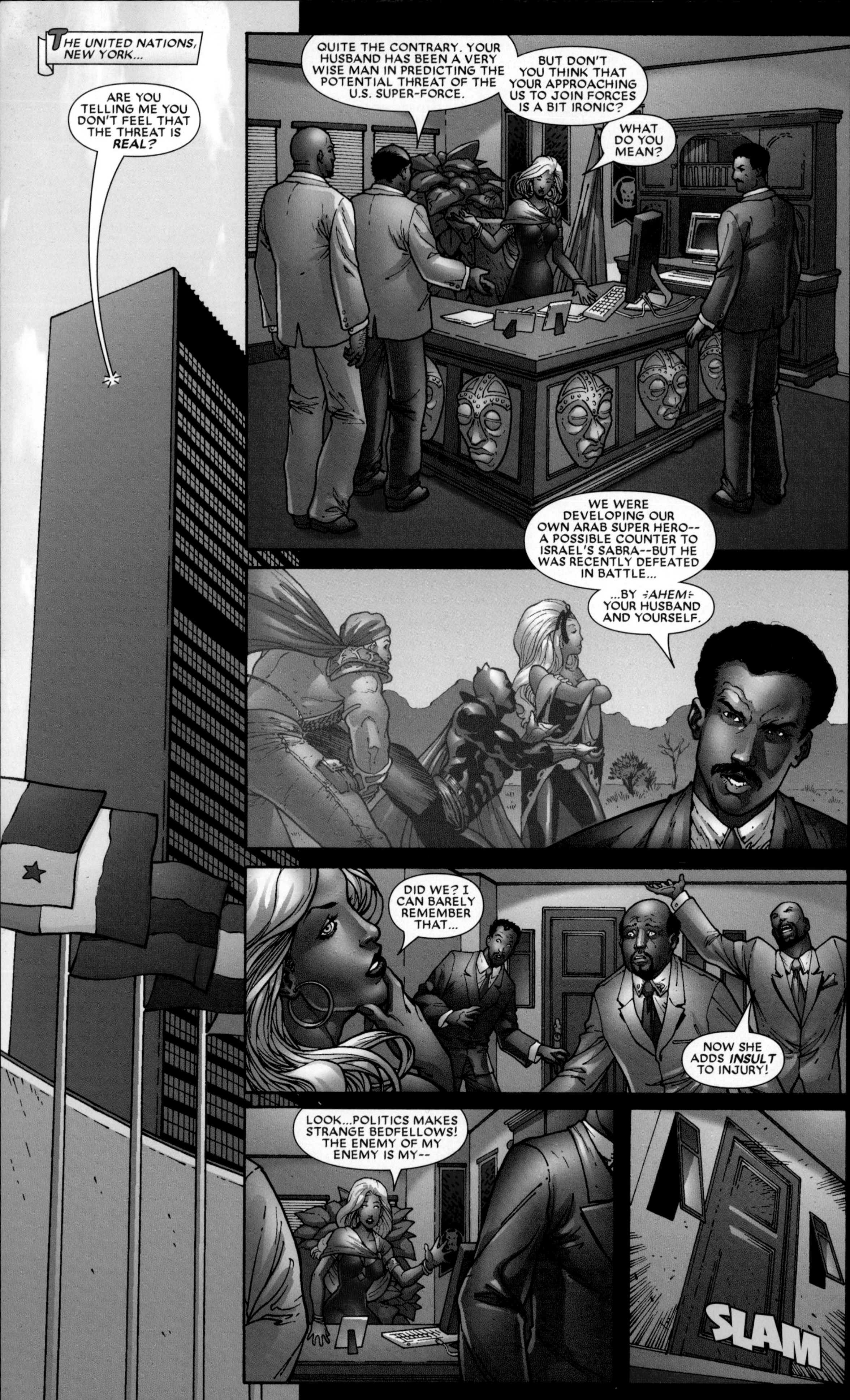
THE UNITED NATIONS, NEW YORK...
ARE YOU TELLING ME YOU DON'T FEEL THAT THE THREAT IS REAL?
QUITE THE CONTRARY. YOUR HUSBAND HAS BEEN A VERY WISE MAN IN PREDICTING THE POTENTIAL THREAT OF THE U.S. SUPER-FORCE.
BUT DON'T YOU THINK THAT YOUR APPROACHING US TO JOIN FORCES IS A BIT IRONIC?
WHAT DO YOU MEAN?
WE WERE DEVELOPING OUR OWN ARAB SUPER HERO-- A POSSIBLE COUNTER TO ISRAEL'S SABRA--BUT HE WAS RECENTLY DEFEATED IN BATTLE...
...BY -AHEM- YOUR HUSBAND AND YOURSELF.
DID WE? I CAN BARELY REMEMBER THAT...
NOW SHE ADDS INSULT TO INJURY!
LOOK...POLITICS MAKES STRANGE BEDFELLOWS! THE ENEMY OF MY ENEMY IS MY--
SLAM

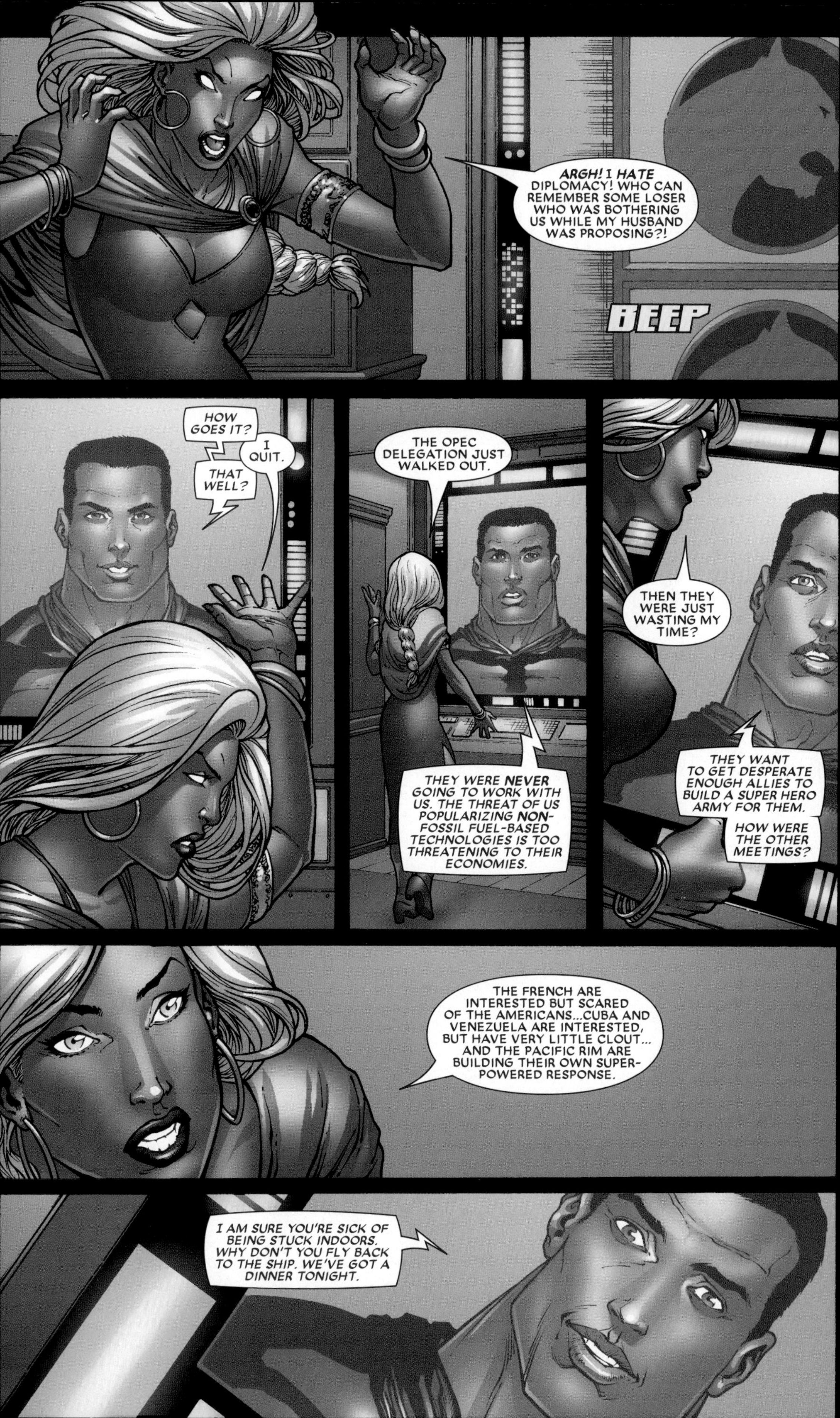
ARGH! I HATE DIPLOMACY! WHO CAN REMEMBER SOME LOSER WHO WAS BOTHERING US WHILE MY HUSBAND WAS PROPOSING?!
BEEP
HOW GOES IT?
I QUIT.
THAT WELL?
THE OPEC DELEGATION JUST WALKED OUT.
THEY WERE NEVER GOING TO WORK WITH US. THE THREAT OF US POPULARIZING NON-FOSSIL FUEL-BASED TECHNOLOGIES IS TOO THREATENING TO THEIR ECONOMIES.
THEN THEY WERE JUST WASTING MY TIME?
THEY WANT TO GET DESPERATE ENOUGH ALLIES TO BUILD A SUPER HERO ARMY FOR THEM.
HOW WERE THE OTHER MEETINGS?
THE FRENCH ARE INTERESTED BUT SCARED OF THE AMERICANS...CUBA AND VENEZUELA ARE INTERESTED, BUT HAVE VERY LITTLE CLOUT... AND THE PACIFIC RIM ARE BUILDING THEIR OWN SUPER-POWERED RESPONSE.
I AM SURE YOU'RE SICK OF BEING STUCK INDOORS. WHY DON'T YOU FLY BACK TO THE SHIP. WE'VE GOT A DINNER TONIGHT.

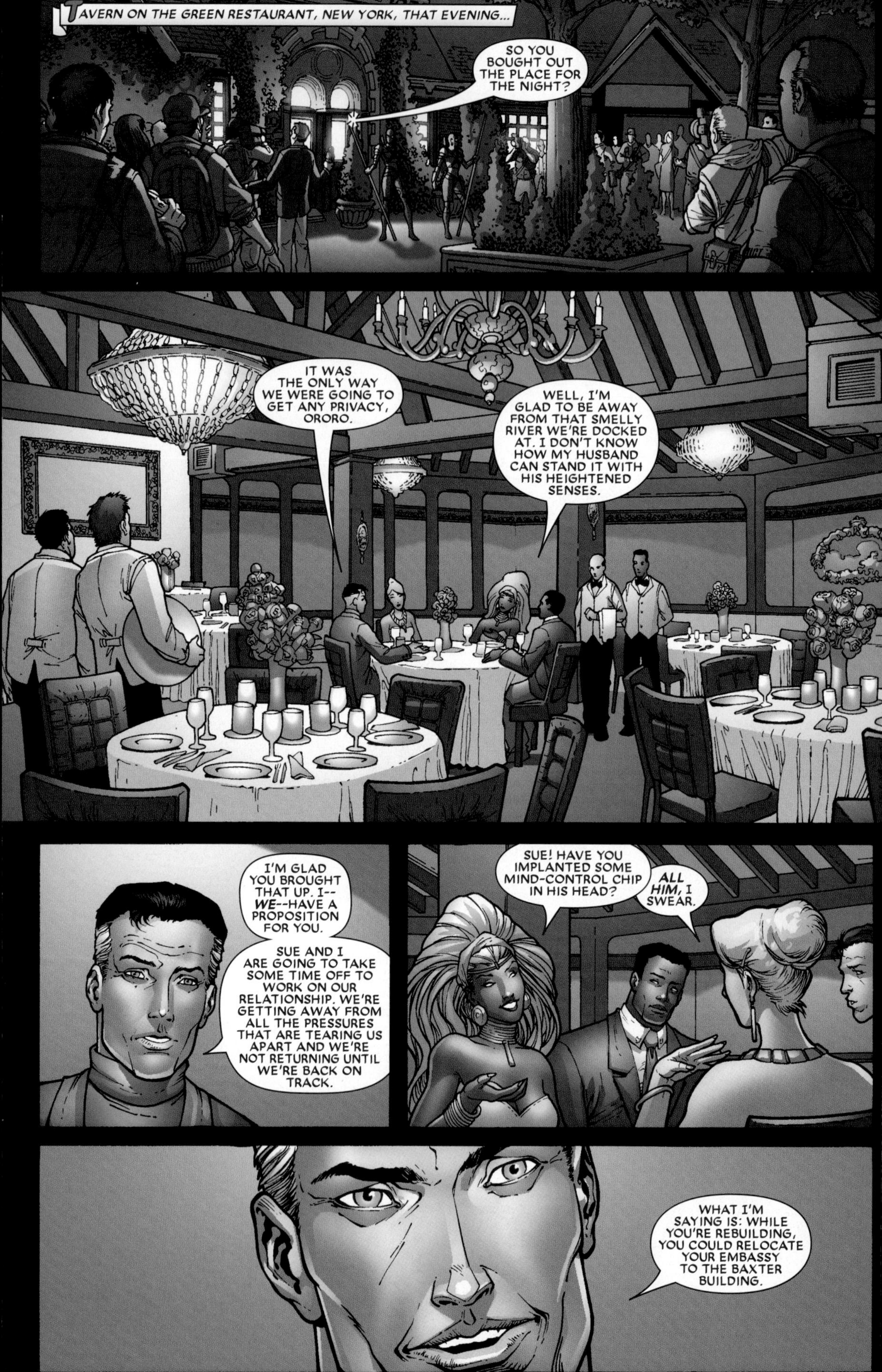
TAVERN ON THE GREEN RESTAURANT, NEW YORK, THAT EVENING...
SO YOU BOUGHT OUT THE PLACE FOR THE NIGHT?
IT WAS THE ONLY WAY WE WERE GOING TO GET ANY PRIVACY, ORORO.
WELL, I'M GLAD TO BE AWAY FROM THAT SMELLY RIVER WE'RE DOCKED AT. I DON'T KNOW HOW MY HUSBAND CAN STAND IT WITH HIS HEIGHTENED SENSES.
I'M GLAD YOU BROUGHT THAT UP. I-- *WE*--HAVE A PROPOSITION FOR YOU.
SUE AND I ARE GOING TO TAKE SOME TIME OFF TO WORK ON OUR RELATIONSHIP. WE'RE GETTING AWAY FROM ALL THE PRESSURES THAT ARE TEARING US APART AND WE'RE NOT RETURNING UNTIL WE'RE BACK ON TRACK.
SUE! HAVE YOU IMPLANTED SOME MIND-CONTROL CHIP IN HIS HEAD?
ALL HIM, I SWEAR.
WHAT I'M SAYING IS: WHILE YOU'RE REBUILDING, YOU COULD RELOCATE YOUR EMBASSY TO THE BAXTER BUILDING.

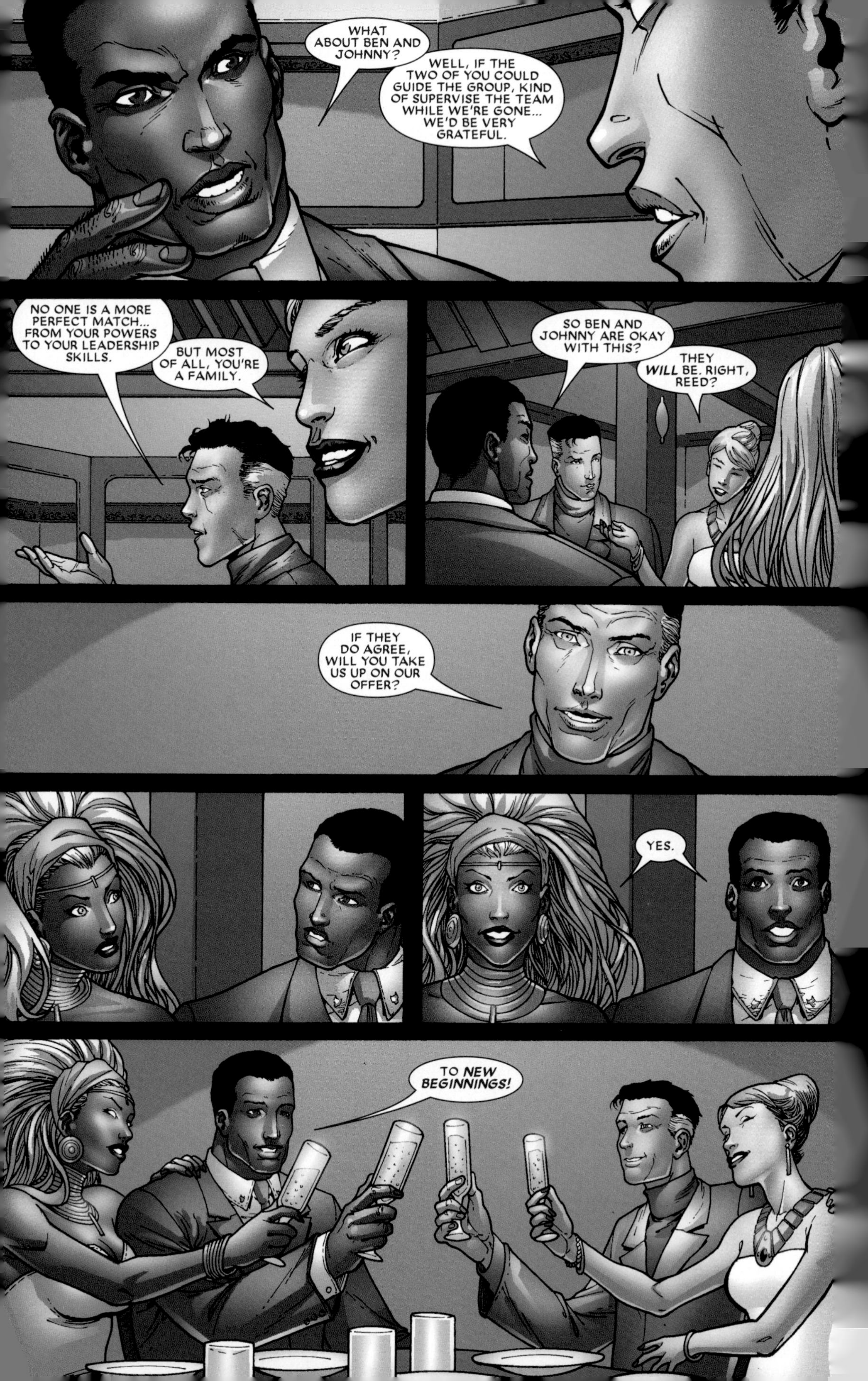
WHAT ABOUT BEN AND JOHNNY?
WELL, IF THE TWO OF YOU COULD GUIDE THE GROUP, KIND OF SUPERVISE THE TEAM WHILE WE'RE GONE... WE'D BE VERY GRATEFUL.
NO ONE IS A MORE PERFECT MATCH... FROM YOUR POWERS TO YOUR LEADERSHIP SKILLS.
BUT MOST OF ALL, YOU'RE A FAMILY.
SO BEN AND JOHNNY ARE OKAY WITH THIS?
THEY *WILL* BE. RIGHT, REED?
IF THEY DO AGREE, WILL YOU TAKE US UP ON OUR OFFER?
YES.
TO *NEW BEGINNINGS!*

THE BAXTER BUILDING, LATER...

SECOND HONEYMOON? NIIICE!

I DIDN'T KNOW YOU HAD IT IN YOU, REED.

WHAT DO YOU MEAN, *SECOND HONEYMOON?* WE NEVER DID A FIRST!

DON'T WORRY, STRETCHO, WE'LL KEEP AN EYE ON EVERYTHING WHILE YOU'RE GONE.

÷GAAAK÷

SORRY ABOUT THAT, PAL.

ACTUALLY, WE WANTED TO TALK TO YOU ABOUT THAT. WE'VE FOUND REPLACEMENTS FOR OURSELVES.

"REPLACEMENTS"? WHAT DOES THAT MEAN?

WE'RE BIG BOYS. WE CAN TAKE CARE OF OURSELVES.

YEP. BEN'S ALMOST HOUSEBROKEN!

SHUT IT, YOU--

THANKS FOR MAKING THE POINT, CHILDREN.

OKAY, MAYBE YOU GOT A POINT. AS LONG AS THEY KNOW HOW TO USE ONE OF YOUR FLIBBERDEGIBIT IN CASE THERE'S TROUBLE THAT JOHNN CAN'T BURN AND I CAN'T PUNCH.

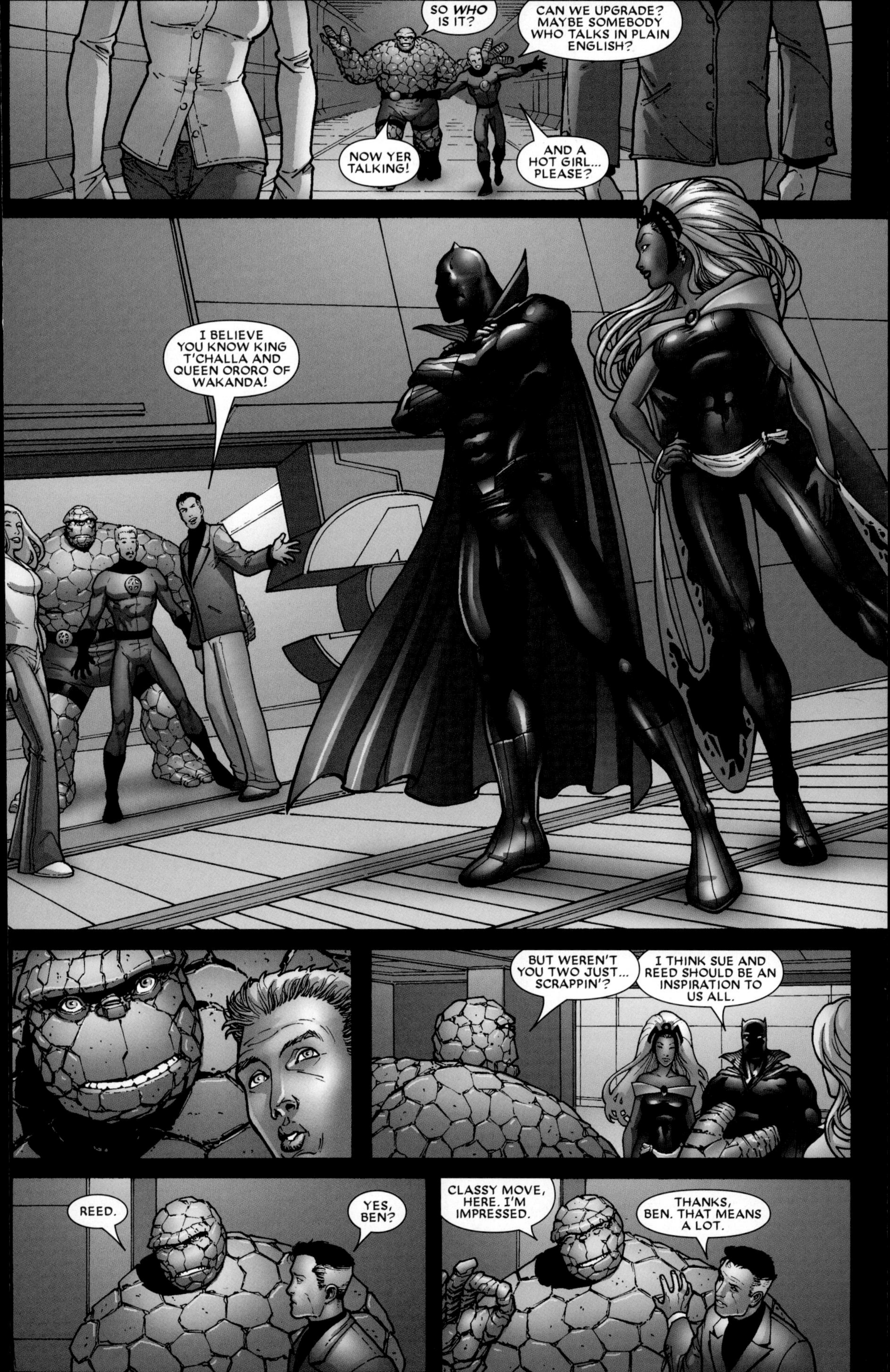
SO WHO IS IT?
CAN WE UPGRADE? MAYBE SOMEBODY WHO TALKS IN PLAIN ENGLISH?
NOW YER TALKING!
AND A HOT GIRL... PLEASE?
I BELIEVE YOU KNOW KING T'CHALLA AND QUEEN ORORO OF WAKANDA!
BUT WEREN'T YOU TWO JUST... SCRAPPIN'?
I THINK SUE AND REED SHOULD BE AN INSPIRATION TO US ALL.
REED.
YES, BEN?
CLASSY MOVE, HERE. I'M IMPRESSED.
THANKS, BEN. THAT MEANS A LOT.

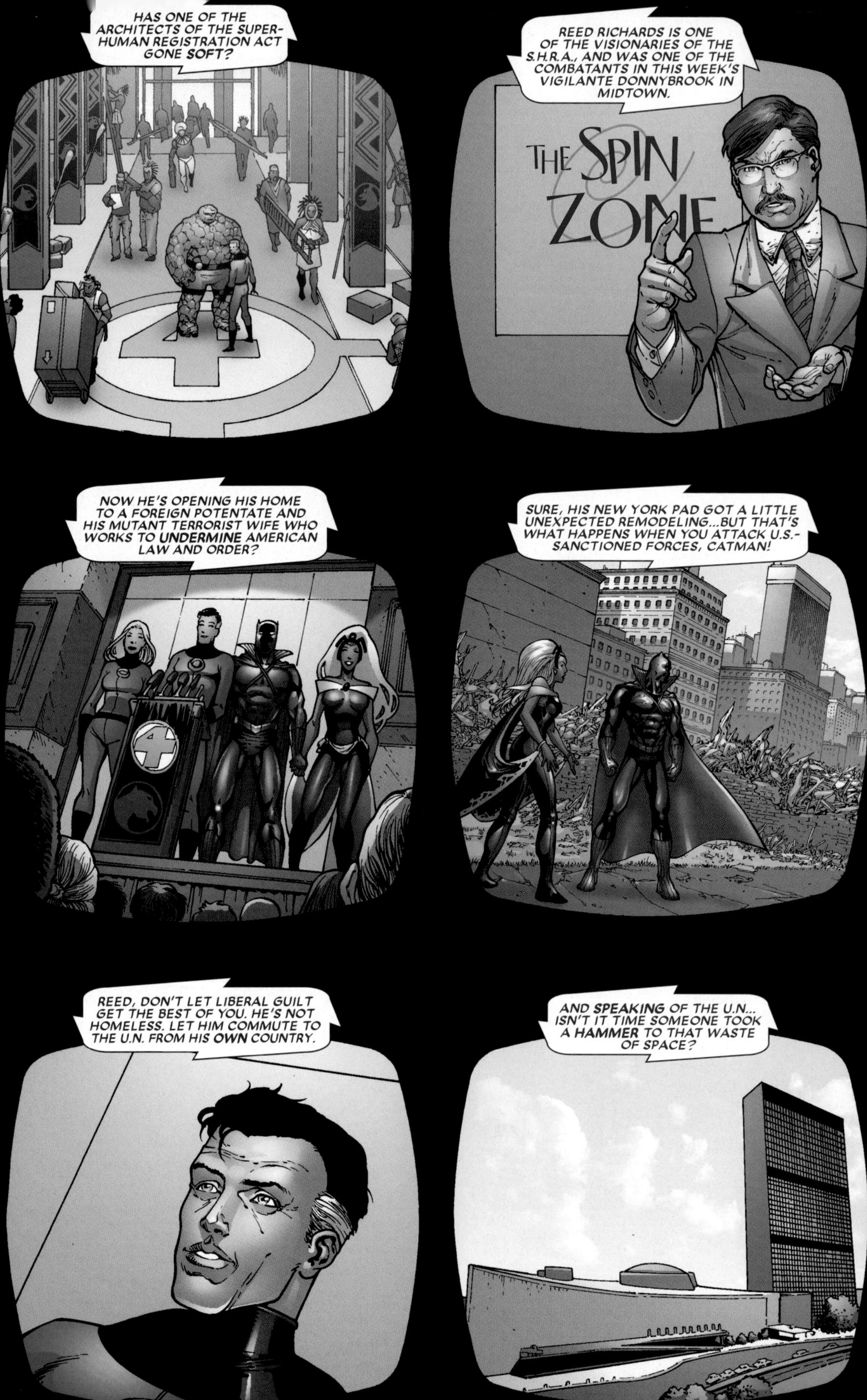
HAS ONE OF THE ARCHITECTS OF THE SUPER-HUMAN REGISTRATION ACT GONE SOFT?
REED RICHARDS IS ONE OF THE VISIONARIES OF THE S.H.R.A., AND WAS ONE OF THE COMBATANTS IN THIS WEEK'S VIGILANTE DONNYBROOK IN MIDTOWN.
THE SPIN ZONE
NOW HE'S OPENING HIS HOME TO A FOREIGN POTENTATE AND HIS MUTANT TERRORIST WIFE WHO WORKS TO UNDERMINE AMERICAN LAW AND ORDER?
SURE, HIS NEW YORK PAD GOT A LITTLE UNEXPECTED REMODELING...BUT THAT'S WHAT HAPPENS WHEN YOU ATTACK U.S.-SANCTIONED FORCES, CATMAN!
REED, DON'T LET LIBERAL GUILT GET THE BEST OF YOU. HE'S NOT HOMELESS. LET HIM COMMUTE TO THE U.N. FROM HIS OWN COUNTRY.
AND SPEAKING OF THE U.N... ISN'T IT TIME SOMEONE TOOK A HAMMER TO THAT WASTE OF SPACE?

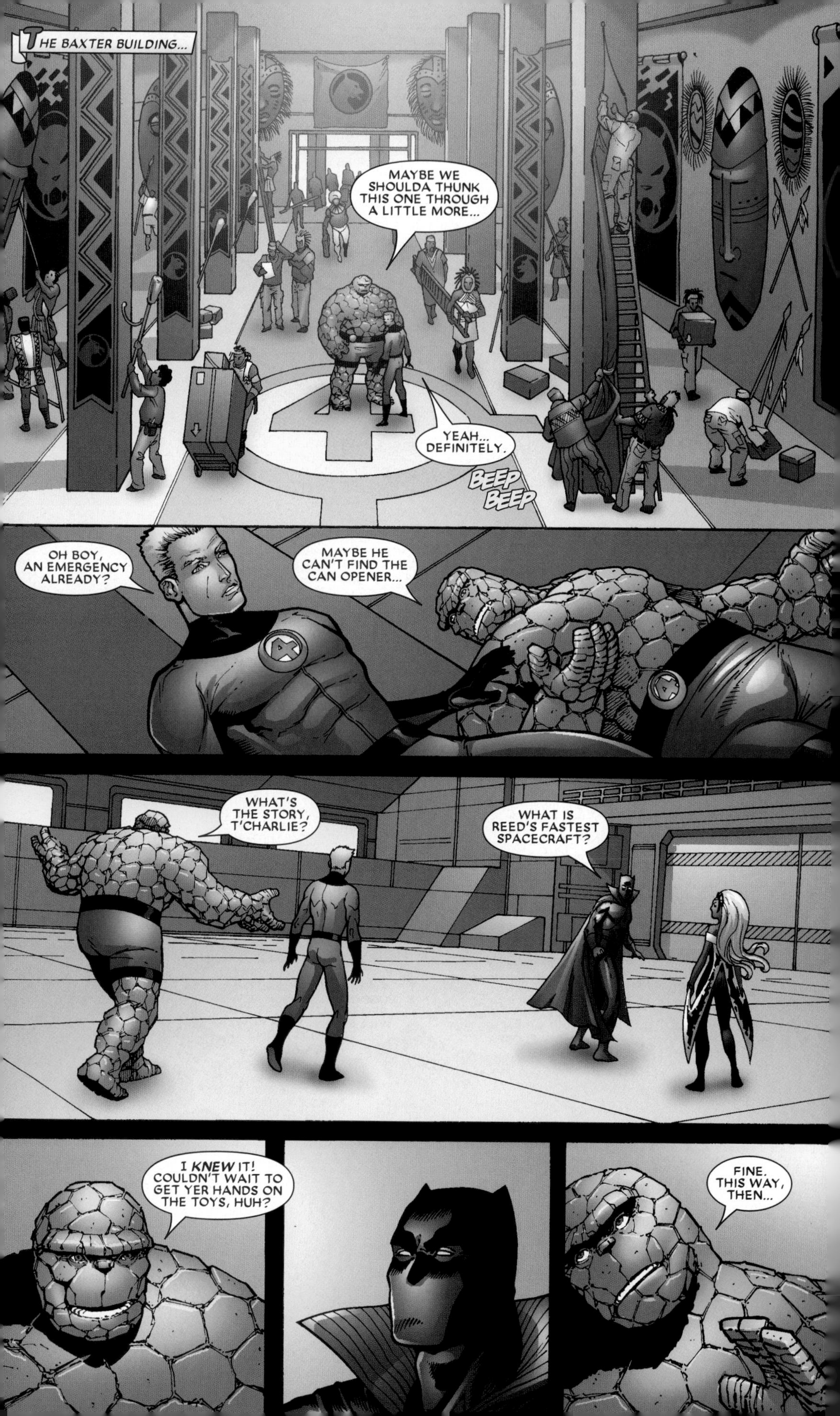
THE BAXTER BUILDING...
MAYBE WE SHOULDA THUNK THIS ONE THROUGH A LITTLE MORE...
YEAH... DEFINITELY.
BEEP BEEP
OH BOY, AN EMERGENCY ALREADY?
MAYBE HE CAN'T FIND THE CAN OPENER...
WHAT'S THE STORY, T'CHARLIE?
WHAT IS REED'S FASTEST SPACECRAFT?
I *KNEW* IT! COULDN'T WAIT TO GET YER HANDS ON THE TOYS, HUH?
FINE. THIS WAY, THEN...

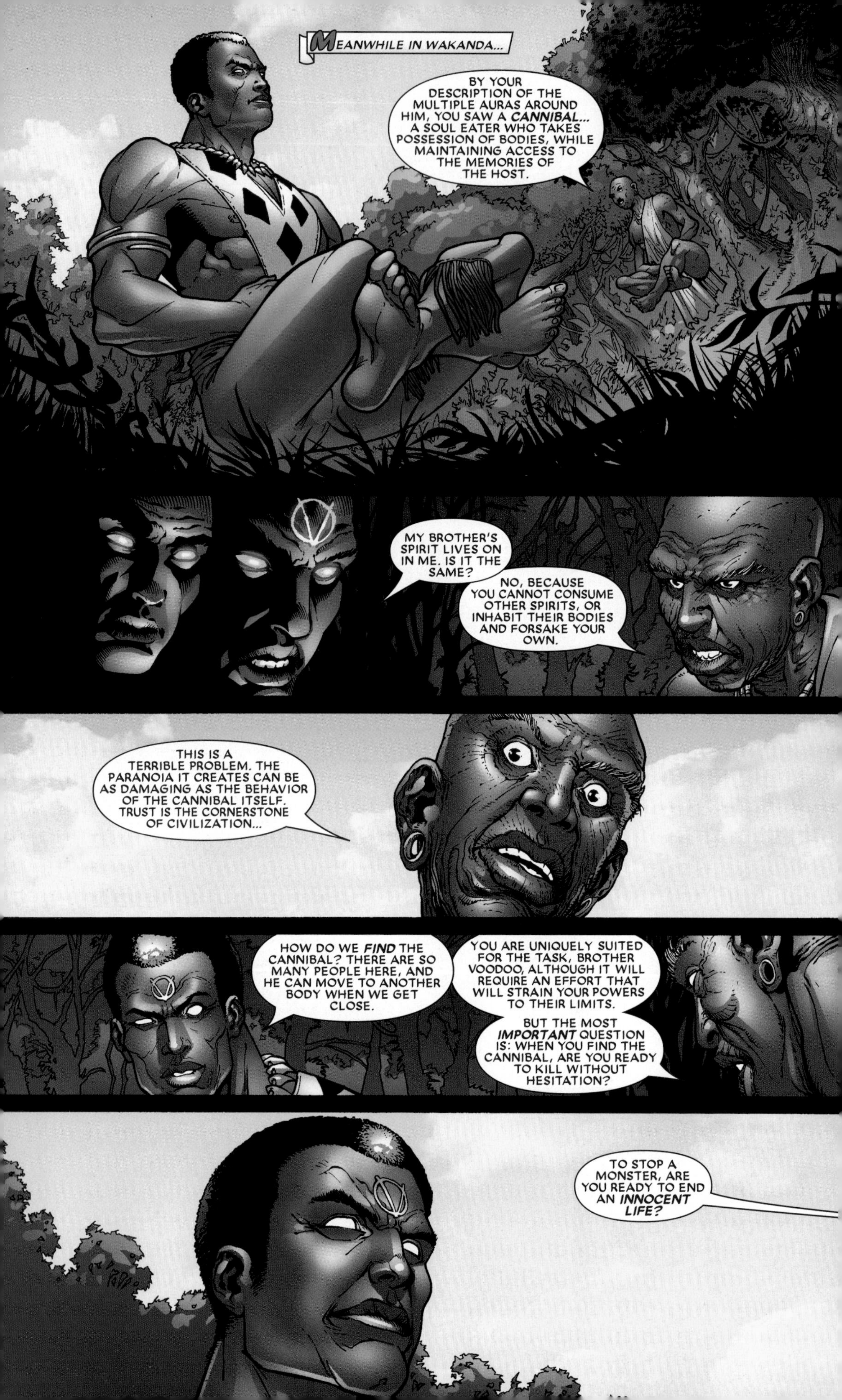
MEANWHILE IN WAKANDA...
BY YOUR DESCRIPTION OF THE MULTIPLE AURAS AROUND HIM, YOU SAW A CANNIBAL... A SOUL EATER WHO TAKES POSSESSION OF BODIES, WHILE MAINTAINING ACCESS TO THE MEMORIES OF THE HOST.
MY BROTHER'S SPIRIT LIVES ON IN ME. IS IT THE SAME?
NO, BECAUSE YOU CANNOT CONSUME OTHER SPIRITS, OR INHABIT THEIR BODIES AND FORSAKE YOUR OWN.
THIS IS A TERRIBLE PROBLEM. THE PARANOIA IT CREATES CAN BE AS DAMAGING AS THE BEHAVIOR OF THE CANNIBAL ITSELF. TRUST IS THE CORNERSTONE OF CIVILIZATION...
HOW DO WE FIND THE CANNIBAL? THERE ARE SO MANY PEOPLE HERE, AND HE CAN MOVE TO ANOTHER BODY WHEN WE GET CLOSE.
YOU ARE UNIQUELY SUITED FOR THE TASK, BROTHER VOODOO, ALTHOUGH IT WILL REQUIRE AN EFFORT THAT WILL STRAIN YOUR POWERS TO THEIR LIMITS.
BUT THE MOST IMPORTANT QUESTION IS: WHEN YOU FIND THE CANNIBAL, ARE YOU READY TO KILL WITHOUT HESITATION?
TO STOP A MONSTER, ARE YOU READY TO END AN INNOCENT LIFE?

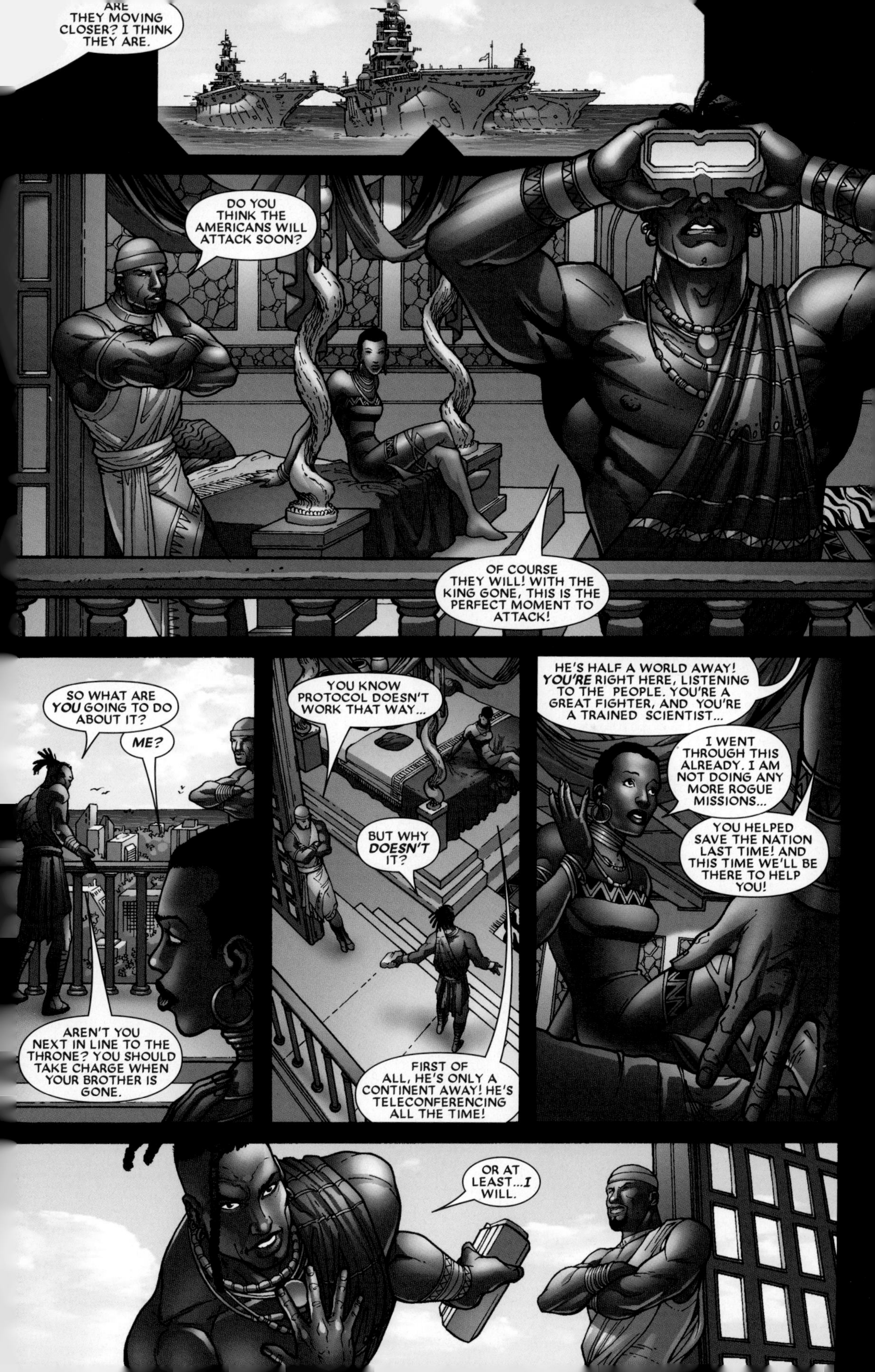

ARE THEY MOVING CLOSER? I THINK THEY ARE.
DO YOU THINK THE AMERICANS WILL ATTACK SOON?
OF COURSE THEY WILL! WITH THE KING GONE, THIS IS THE PERFECT MOMENT TO ATTACK!
SO WHAT ARE YOU GOING TO DO ABOUT IT?
ME?
AREN'T YOU NEXT IN LINE TO THE THRONE? YOU SHOULD TAKE CHARGE WHEN YOUR BROTHER IS GONE.
YOU KNOW PROTOCOL DOESN'T WORK THAT WAY...
BUT WHY DOESN'T IT?
FIRST OF ALL, HE'S ONLY A CONTINENT AWAY! HE'S TELECONFERENCING ALL THE TIME!
HE'S HALF A WORLD AWAY! YOU'RE RIGHT HERE, LISTENING TO THE PEOPLE. YOU'RE A GREAT FIGHTER, AND YOU'RE A TRAINED SCIENTIST...
I WENT THROUGH THIS ALREADY. I AM NOT DOING ANY MORE ROGUE MISSIONS...
YOU HELPED SAVE THE NATION LAST TIME! AND THIS TIME WE'LL BE THERE TO HELP YOU!
OR AT LEAST...I WILL.

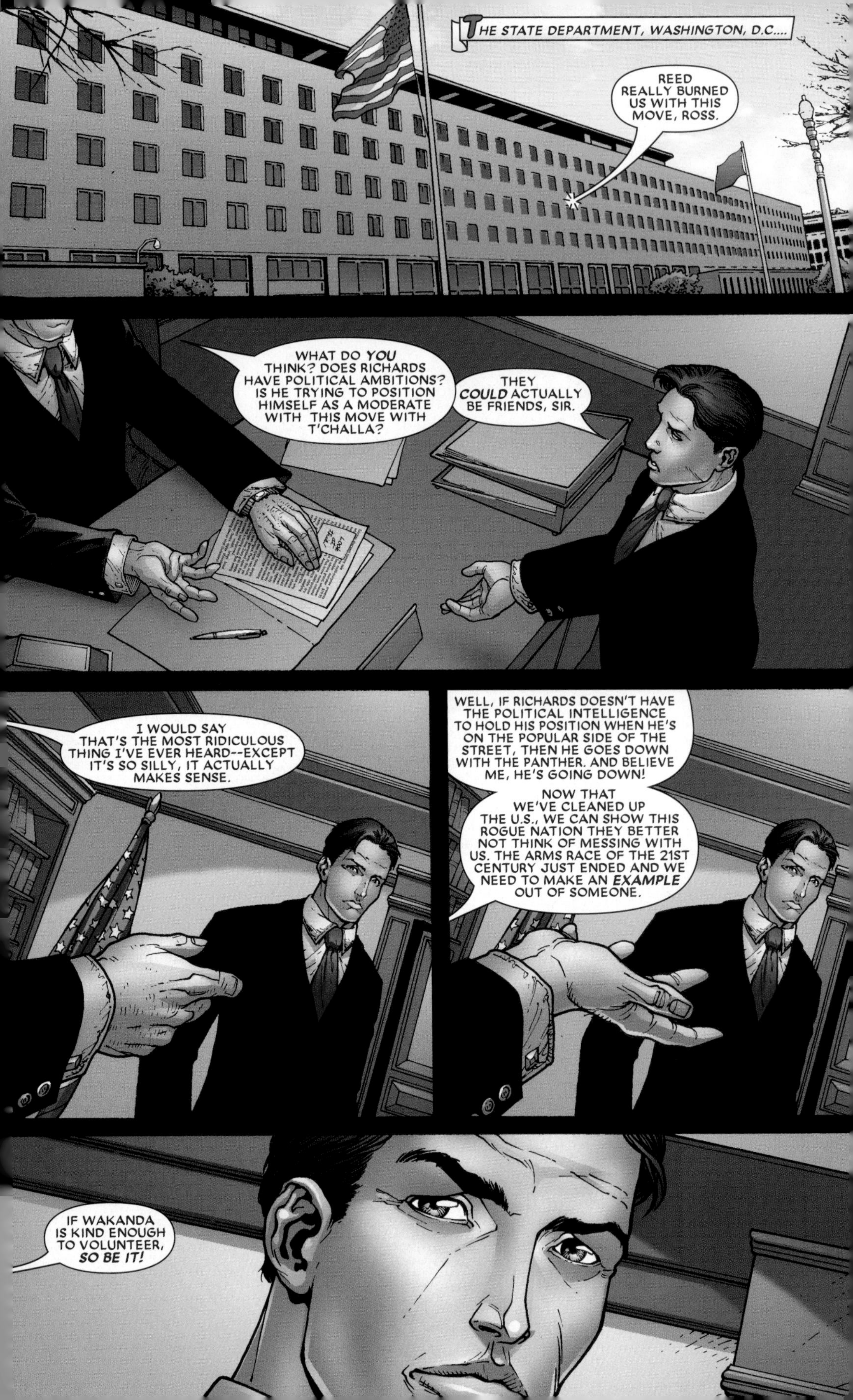
THE STATE DEPARTMENT, WASHINGTON, D.C....
REED REALLY BURNED US WITH THIS MOVE, ROSS.
WHAT DO YOU THINK? DOES RICHARDS HAVE POLITICAL AMBITIONS? IS HE TRYING TO POSITION HIMSELF AS A MODERATE WITH THIS MOVE WITH T'CHALLA?
THEY COULD ACTUALLY BE FRIENDS, SIR.
I WOULD SAY THAT'S THE MOST RIDICULOUS THING I'VE EVER HEARD--EXCEPT IT'S SO SILLY, IT ACTUALLY MAKES SENSE.
WELL, IF RICHARDS DOESN'T HAVE THE POLITICAL INTELLIGENCE TO HOLD HIS POSITION WHEN HE'S ON THE POPULAR SIDE OF THE STREET, THEN HE GOES DOWN WITH THE PANTHER. AND BELIEVE ME, HE'S GOING DOWN!
NOW THAT WE'VE CLEANED UP THE U.S., WE CAN SHOW THIS ROGUE NATION THEY BETTER NOT THINK OF MESSING WITH US. THE ARMS RACE OF THE 21ST CENTURY JUST ENDED AND WE NEED TO MAKE AN EXAMPLE OUT OF SOMEONE.
IF WAKANDA IS KIND ENOUGH TO VOLUNTEER, SO BE IT!

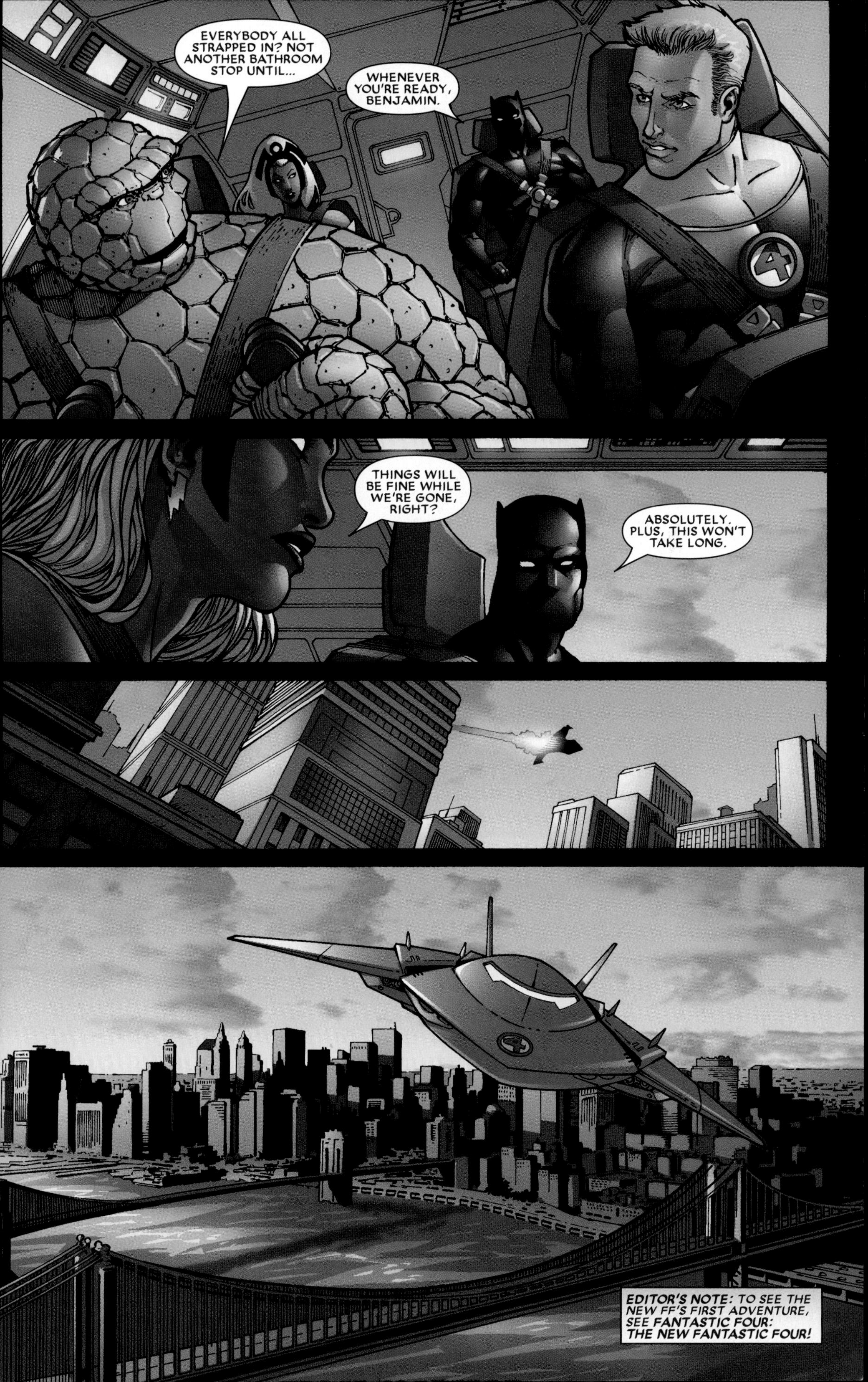
EVERYBODY ALL STRAPPED IN? NOT ANOTHER BATHROOM STOP UNTIL...
WHENEVER YOU'RE READY, BENJAMIN.
THINGS WILL BE FINE WHILE WE'RE GONE, RIGHT?
ABSOLUTELY. PLUS, THIS WON'T TAKE LONG.
EDITOR'S NOTE: TO SEE THE NEW FF'S FIRST ADVENTURE, SEE FANTASTIC FOUR: THE NEW FANTASTIC FOUR!

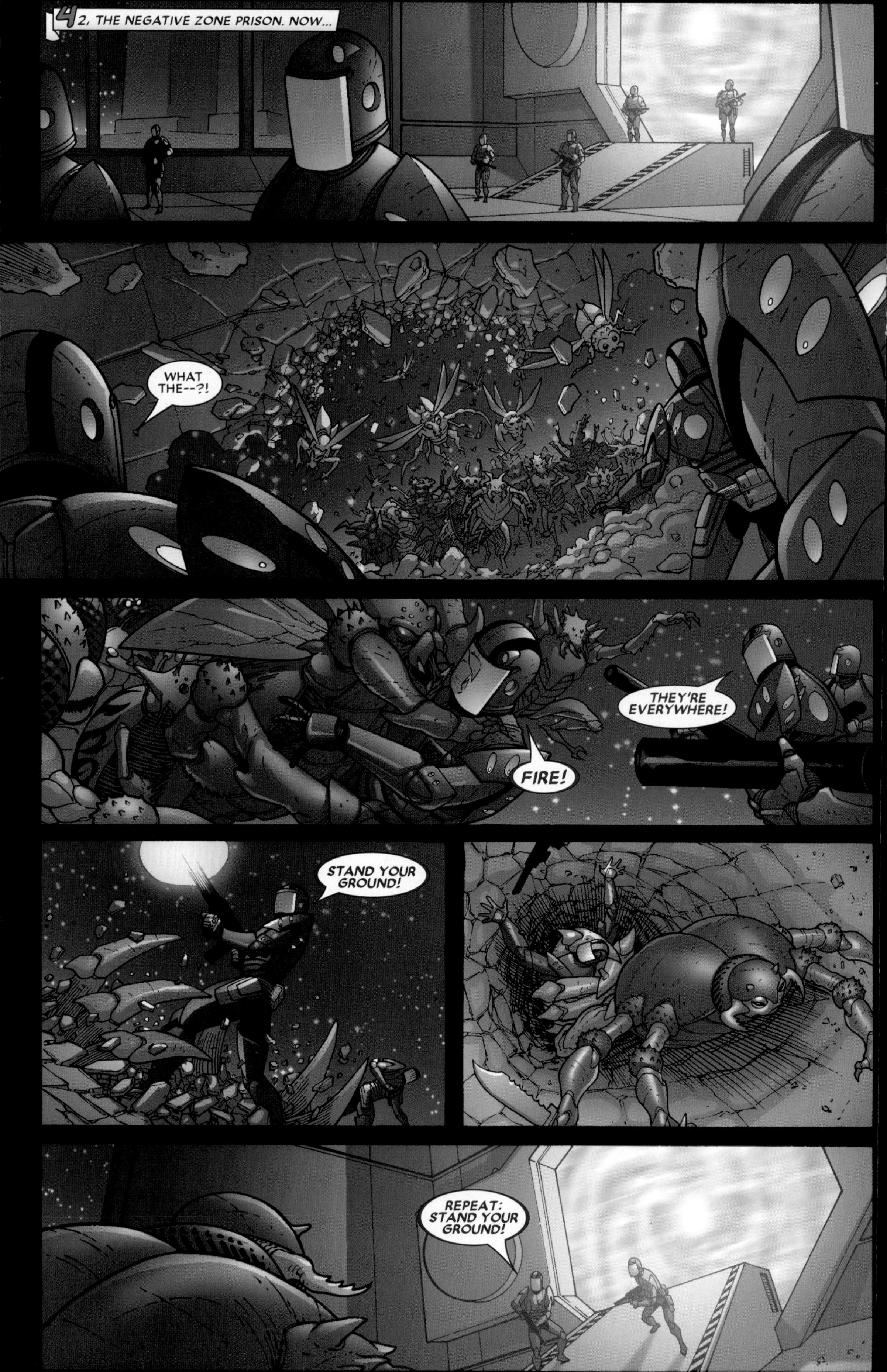
42, THE NEGATIVE ZONE PRISON. NOW...
WHAT THE--?!
THEY'RE EVERYWHERE!
FIRE!
STAND YOUR GROUND!
REPEAT: STAND YOUR GROUND!

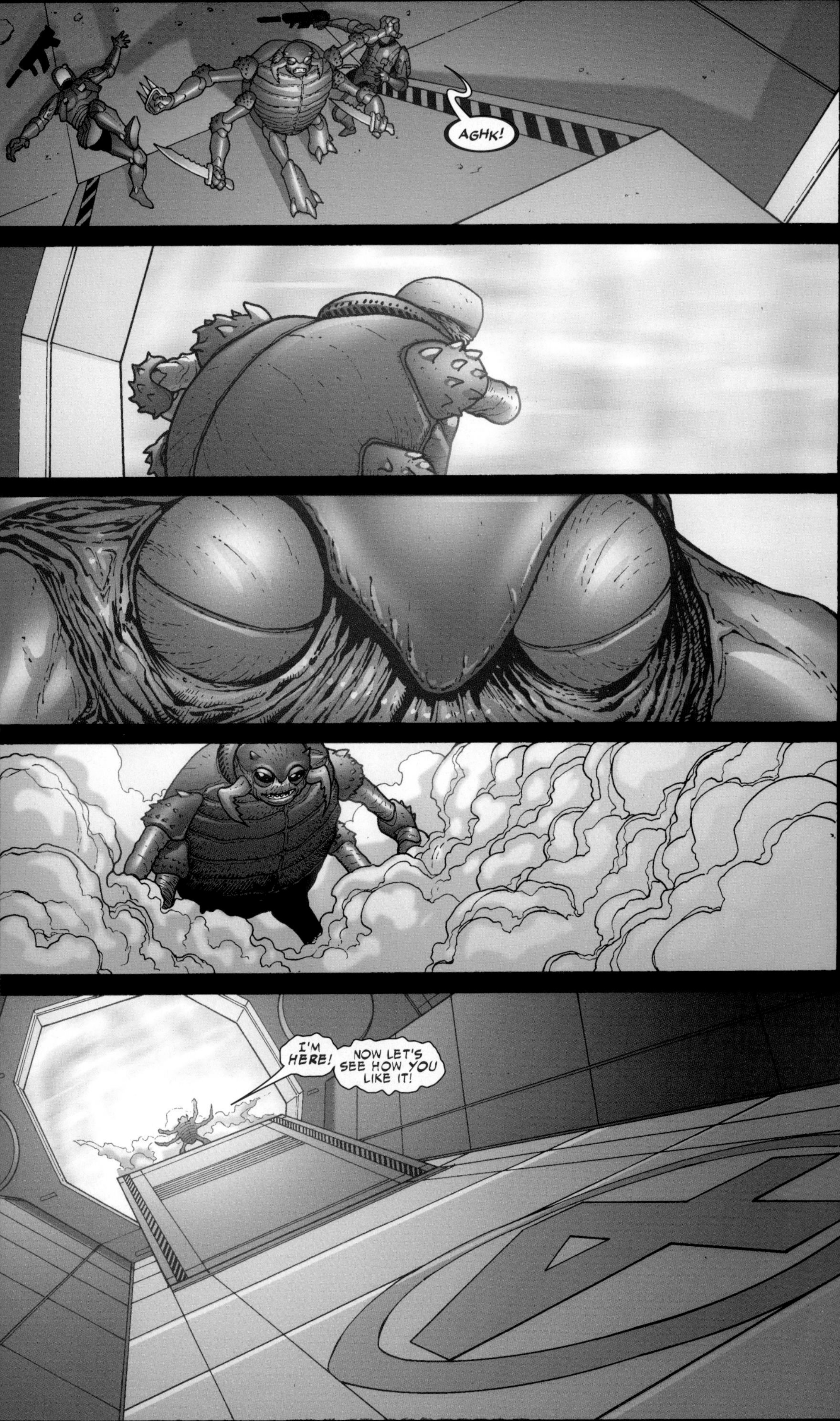
AGHK!
I'M HERE!
NOW LET'S SEE HOW YOU LIKE IT!

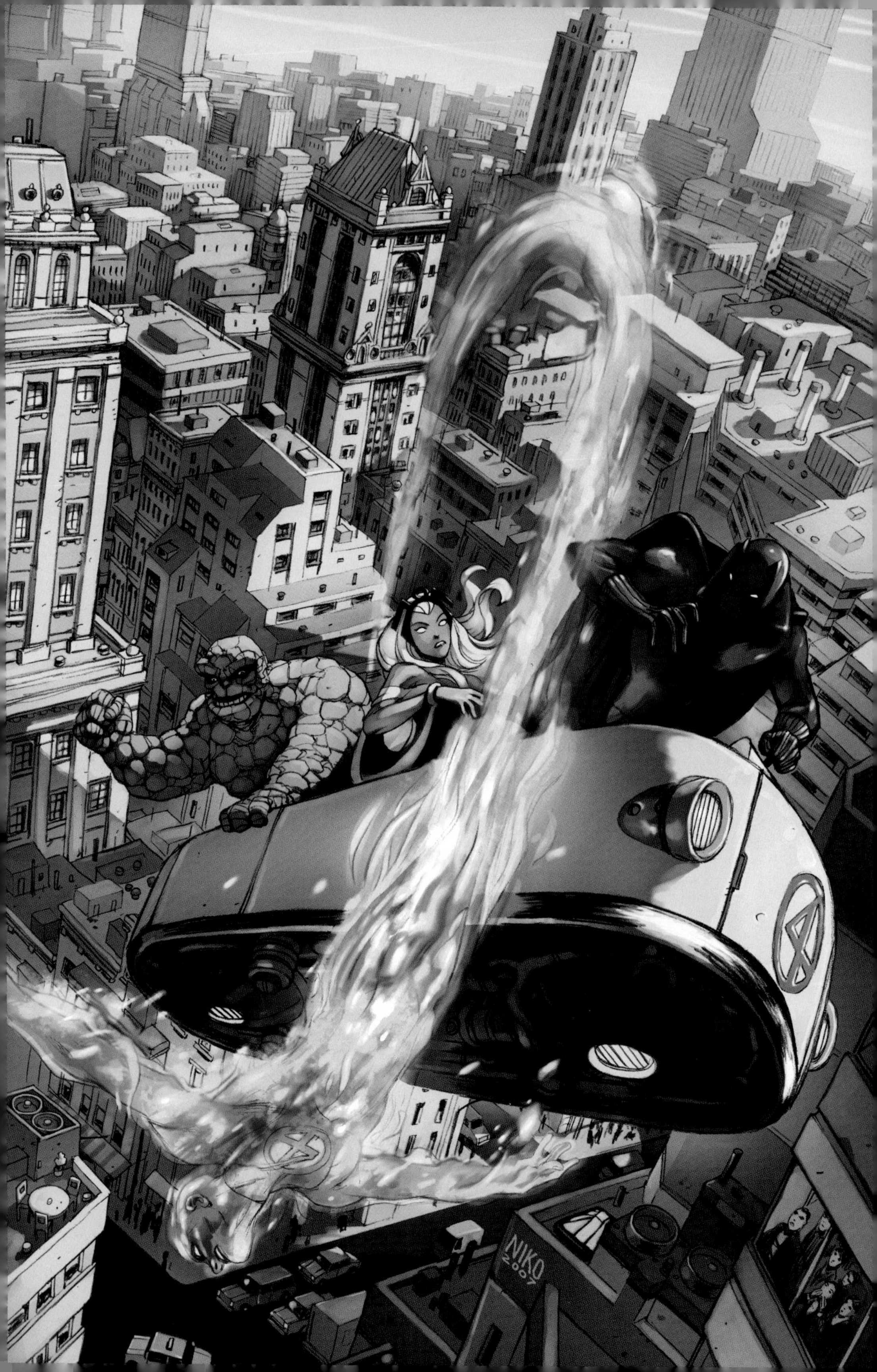
NIKO
2007

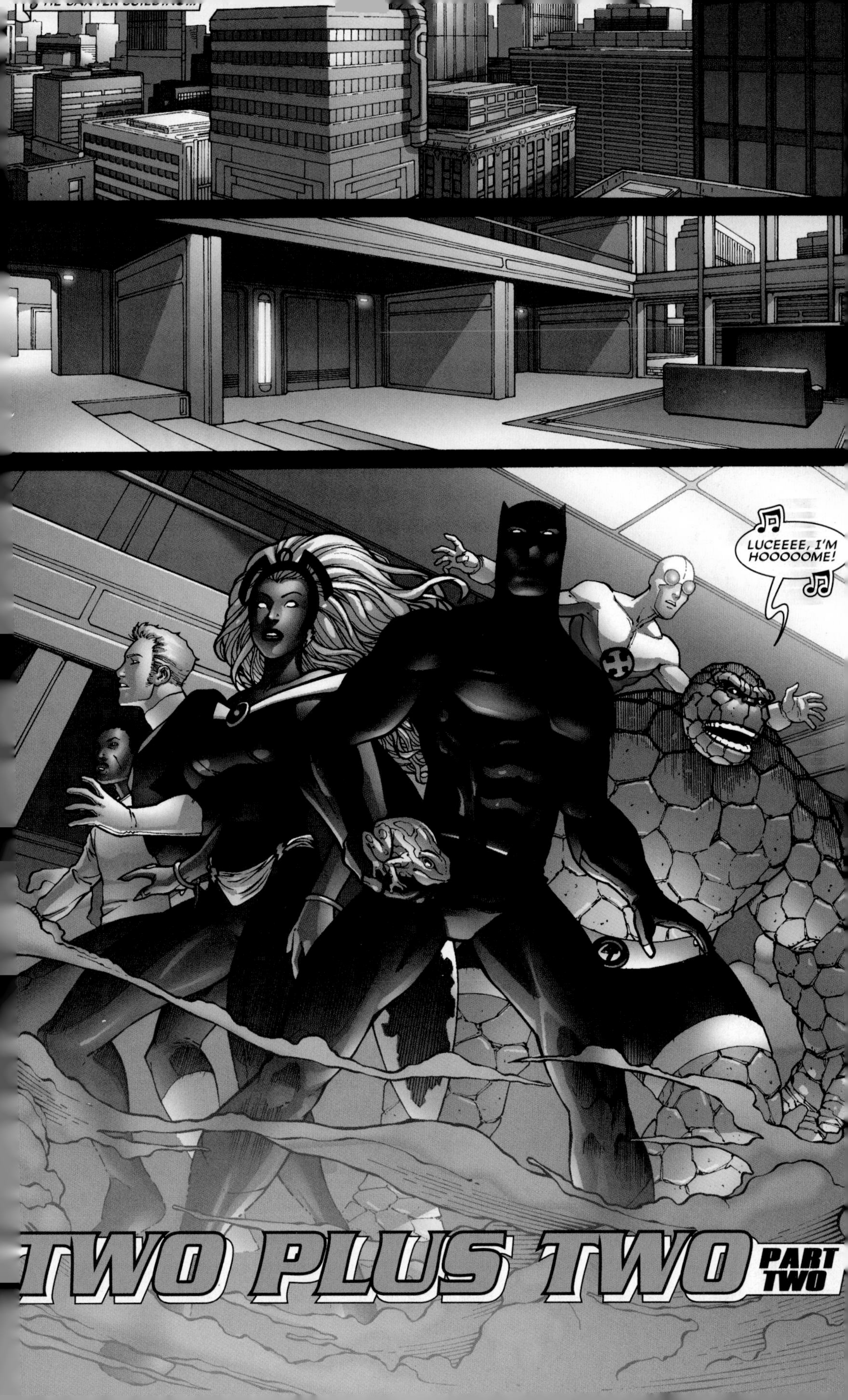
LUCEEEE, I'M HOOOOOME!
TWO PLUS TWO PART TWO

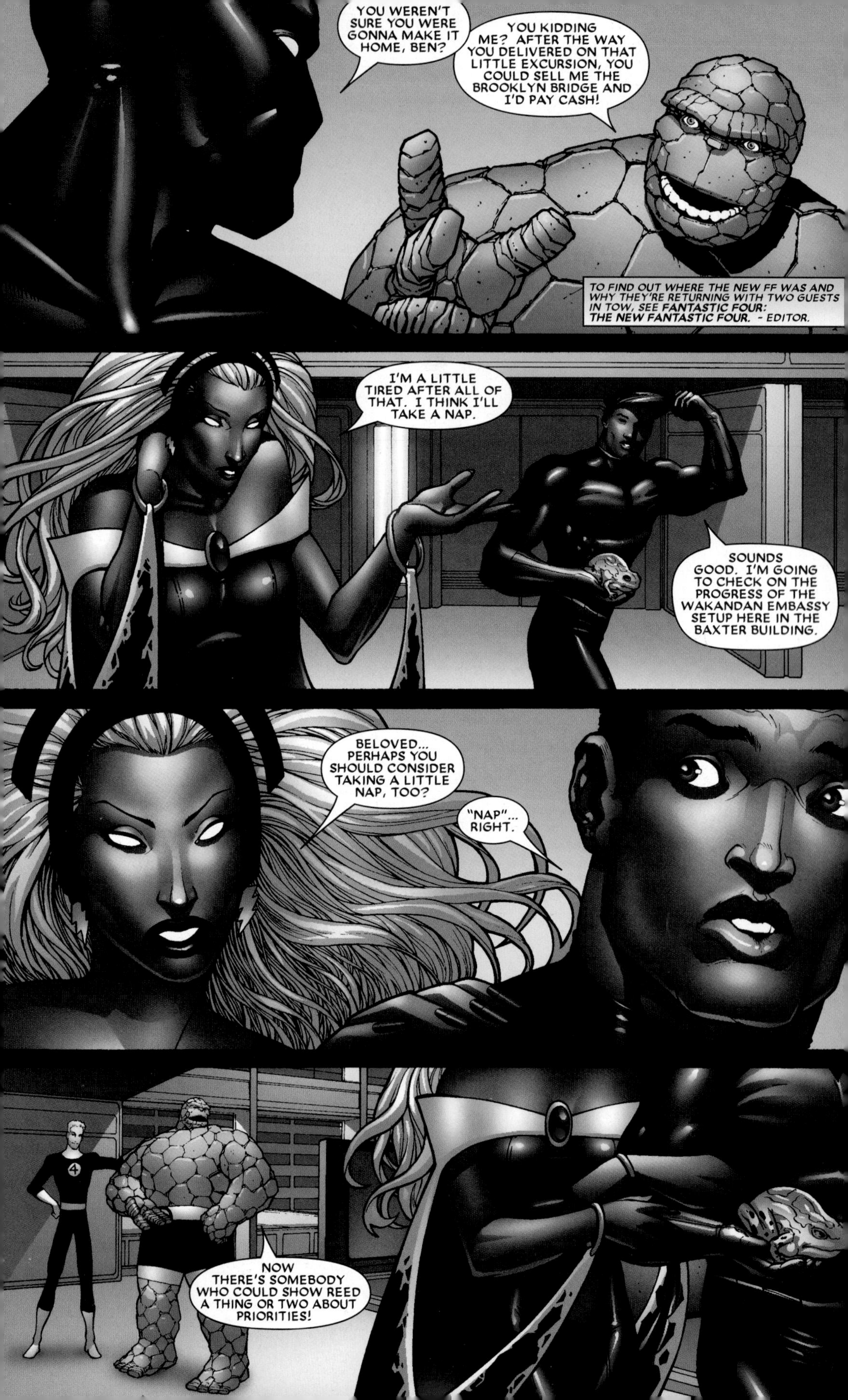
YOU WEREN'T SURE YOU WERE GONNA MAKE IT HOME, BEN?
YOU KIDDING ME? AFTER THE WAY YOU DELIVERED ON THAT LITTLE EXCURSION, YOU COULD SELL ME THE BROOKLYN BRIDGE AND I'D PAY CASH!
TO FIND OUT WHERE THE NEW FF WAS AND WHY THEY'RE RETURNING WITH TWO GUESTS IN TOW, SEE FANTASTIC FOUR: THE NEW FANTASTIC FOUR. - EDITOR.
I'M A LITTLE TIRED AFTER ALL OF THAT. I THINK I'LL TAKE A NAP.
SOUNDS GOOD. I'M GOING TO CHECK ON THE PROGRESS OF THE WAKANDAN EMBASSY SETUP HERE IN THE BAXTER BUILDING.
BELOVED... PERHAPS YOU SHOULD CONSIDER TAKING A LITTLE NAP, TOO?
"NAP"... RIGHT.
NOW THERE'S SOMEBODY WHO COULD SHOW REED A THING OR TWO ABOUT PRIORITIES!

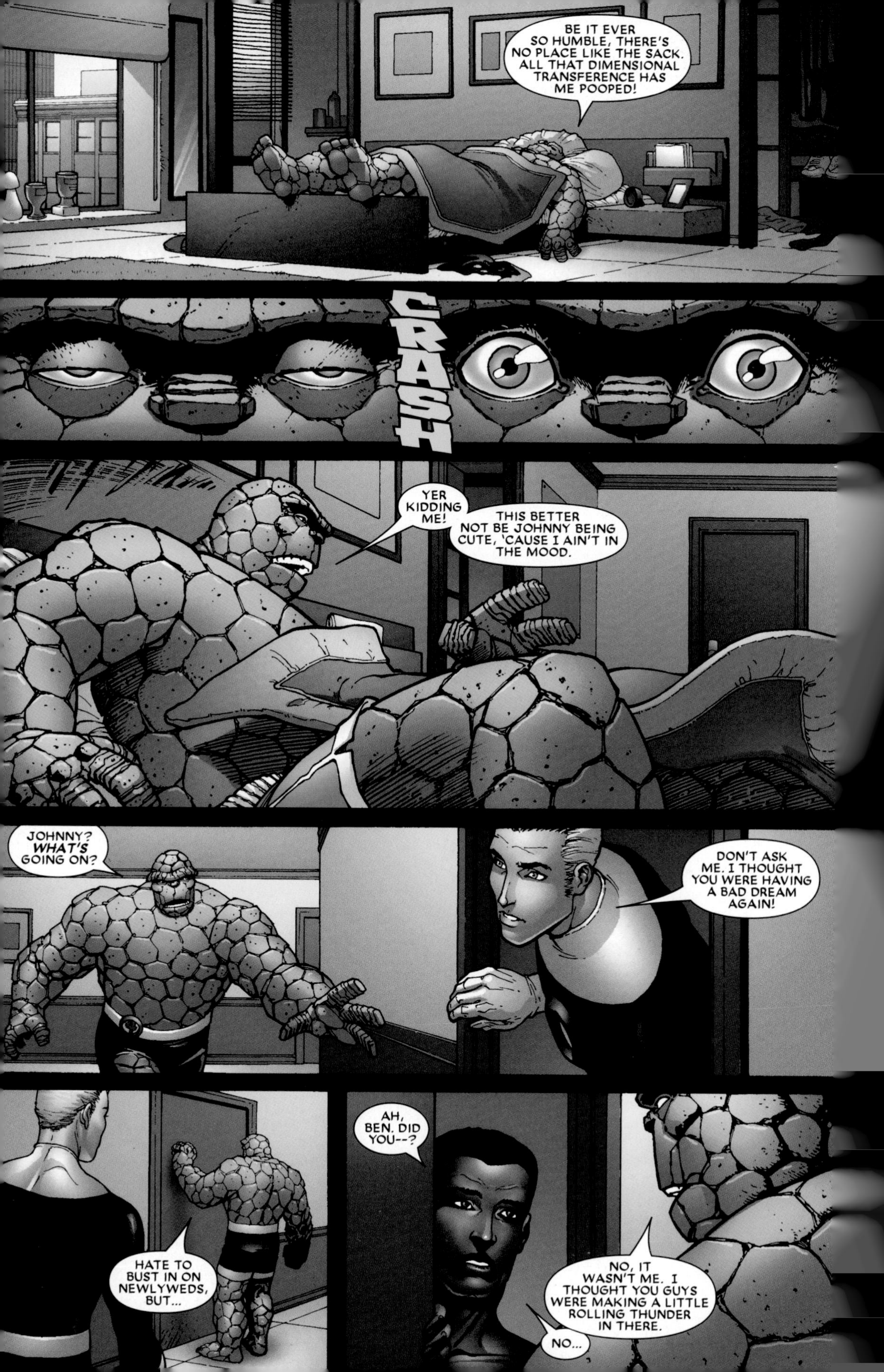
BE IT EVER SO HUMBLE, THERE'S NO PLACE LIKE THE SACK. ALL THAT DIMENSIONAL TRANSFERENCE HAS ME POOPED!
CRASH
YER KIDDING ME!
THIS BETTER NOT BE JOHNNY BEING CUTE, 'CAUSE I AIN'T IN THE MOOD.
JOHNNY? WHAT'S GOING ON?
DON'T ASK ME. I THOUGHT YOU WERE HAVING A BAD DREAM AGAIN!
HATE TO BUST IN ON NEWLYWEDS, BUT...
AH, BEN. DID YOU--?
NO, IT WASN'T ME. I THOUGHT YOU GUYS WERE MAKING A LITTLE ROLLING THUNDER IN THERE.
NO...

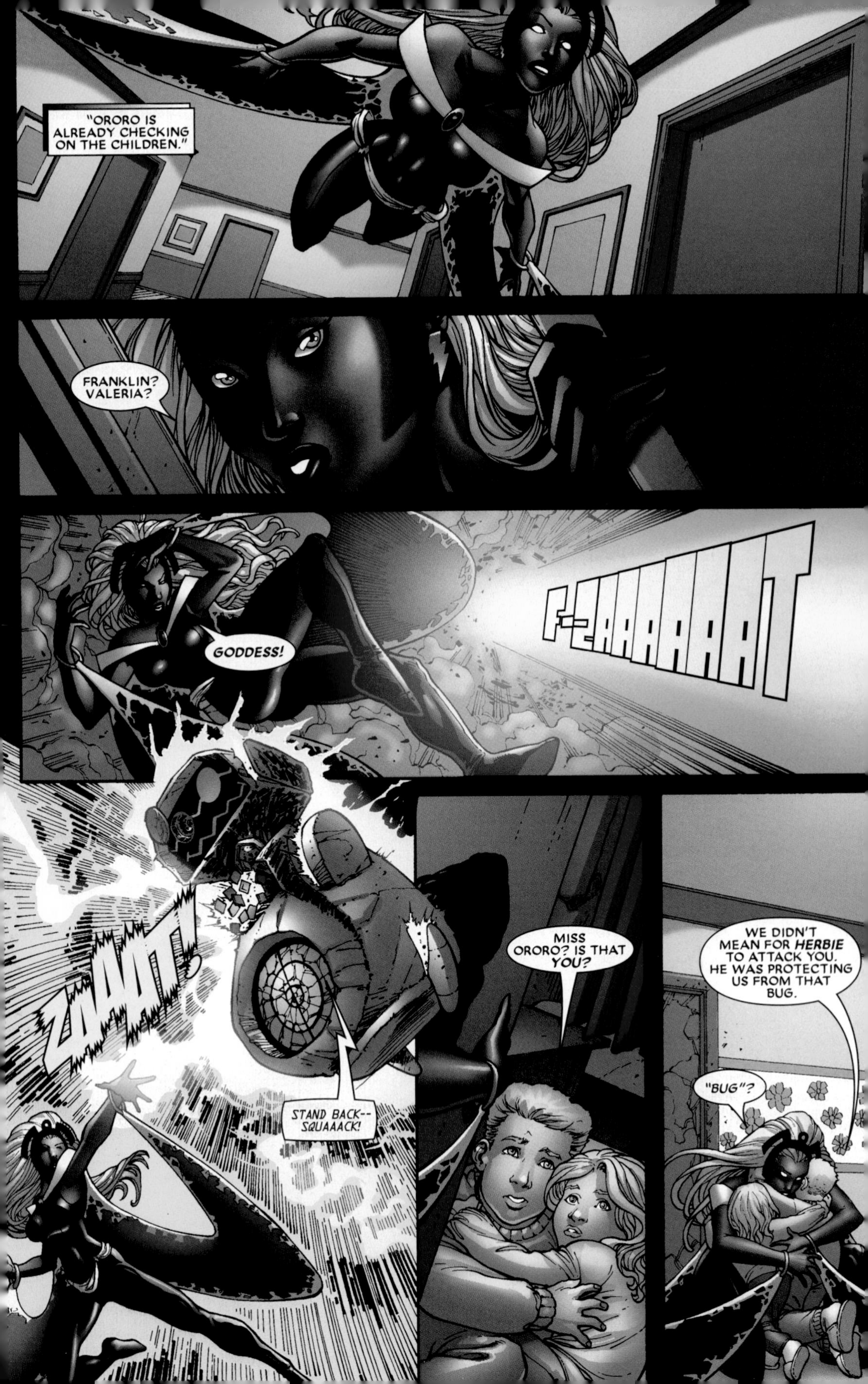
"ORORO IS ALREADY CHECKING ON THE CHILDREN."
FRANKLIN? VALERIA?
GODDESS!
F-ZAAAAAAAT
ZAAAT!
STAND BACK-- SQUAAACK!
MISS ORORO? IS THAT YOU?
WE DIDN'T MEAN FOR HERBIE TO ATTACK YOU. HE WAS PROTECTING US FROM THAT BUG.
"BUG"?

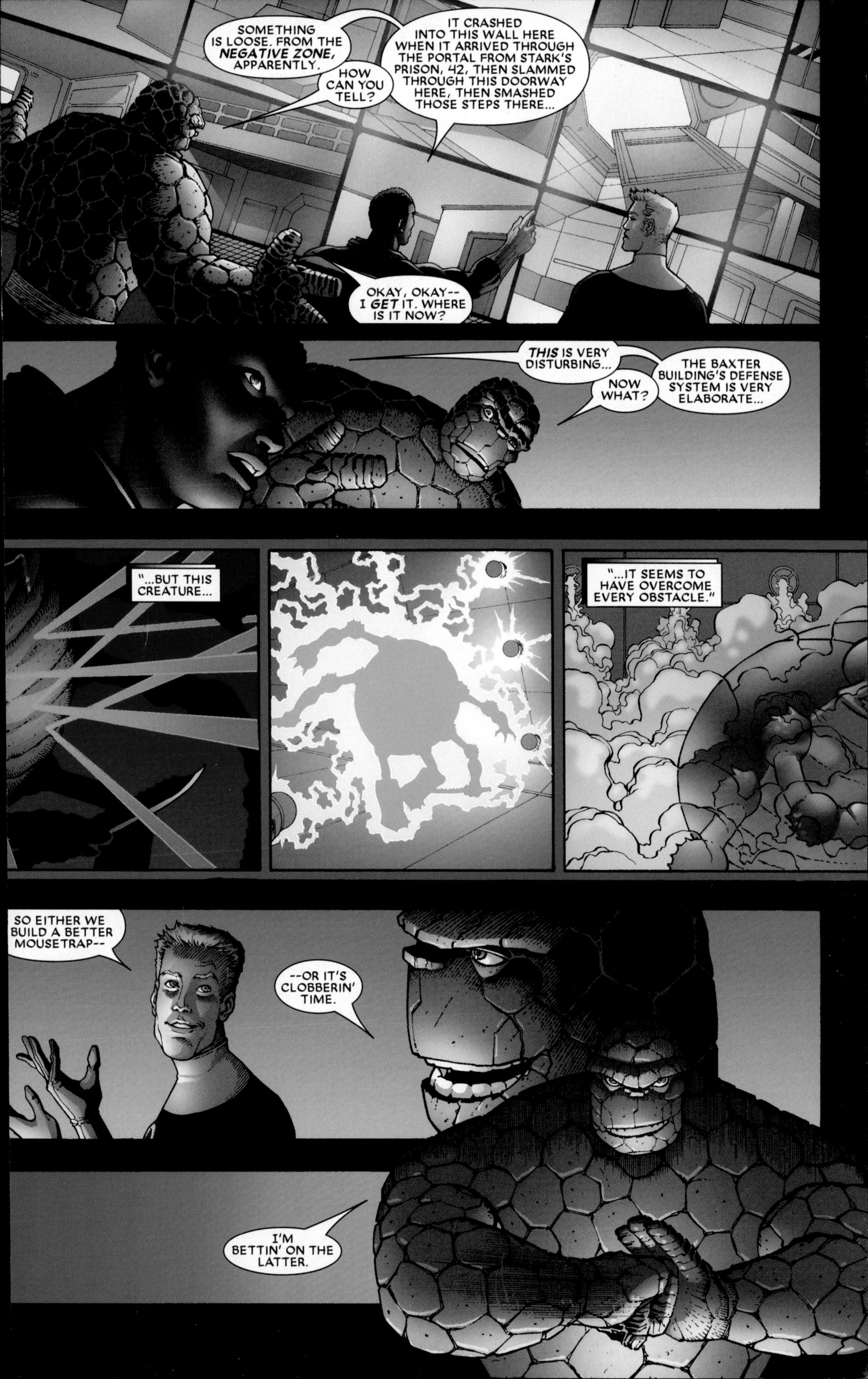

SOMETHING IS LOOSE. FROM THE *NEGATIVE ZONE,* APPARENTLY.
HOW CAN YOU TELL?
IT CRASHED INTO THIS WALL HERE WHEN IT ARRIVED THROUGH THE PORTAL FROM STARK'S PRISON, 42, THEN SLAMMED THROUGH THIS DOORWAY HERE, THEN SMASHED THOSE STEPS THERE...
OKAY, OKAY-- I *GET* IT. WHERE IS IT NOW?
THIS IS VERY DISTURBING...
NOW WHAT?
THE BAXTER BUILDING'S DEFENSE SYSTEM IS VERY ELABORATE...
"...BUT THIS CREATURE...
"...IT SEEMS TO HAVE OVERCOME EVERY OBSTACLE."
SO EITHER WE BUILD A BETTER MOUSETRAP--
--OR IT'S CLOBBERIN' TIME.
I'M BETTIN' ON THE LATTER.

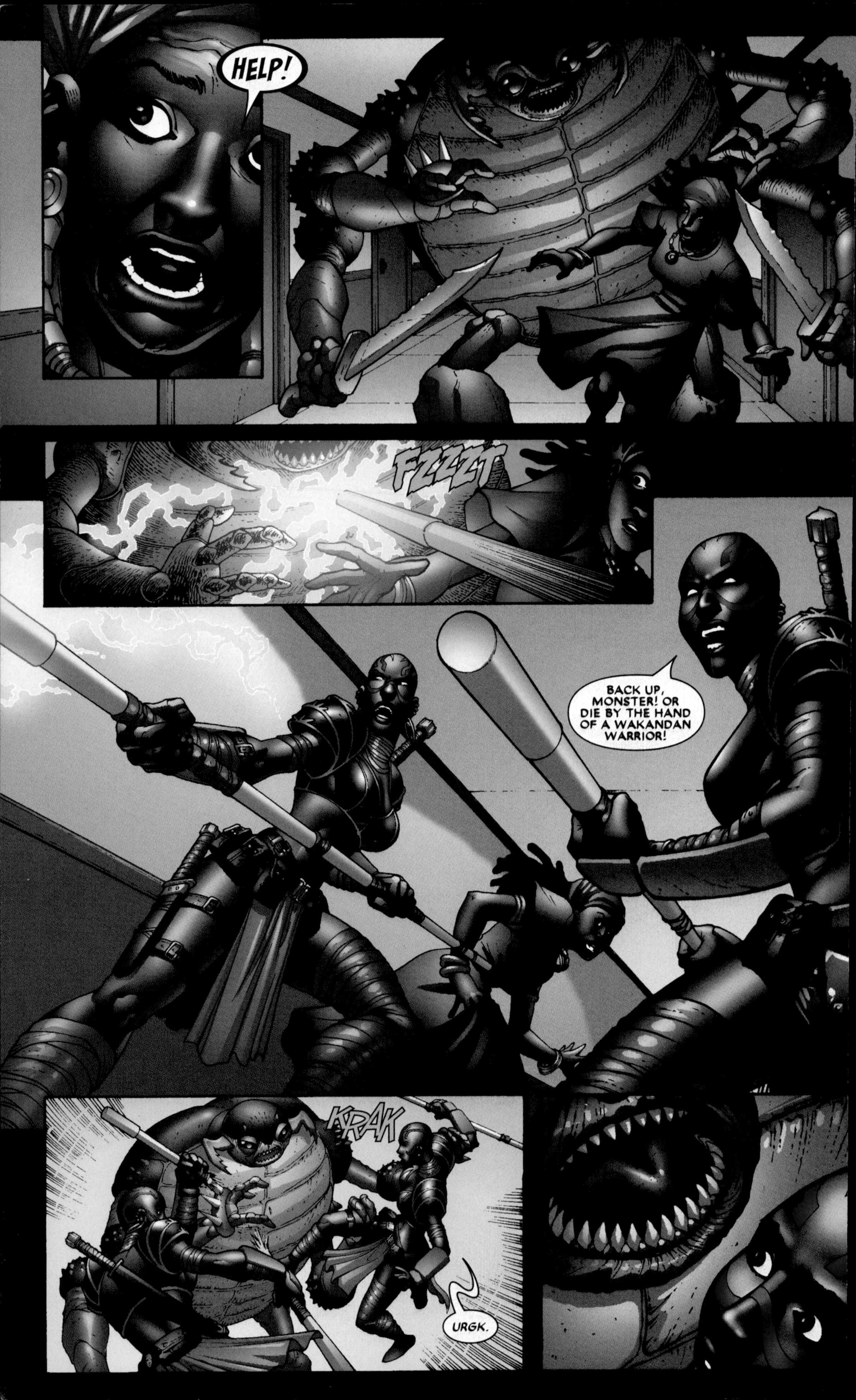
HELP!
FZZZT
BACK UP, MONSTER! OR DIE BY THE HAND OF A WAKANDAN WARRIOR!
KRAK
URGK.

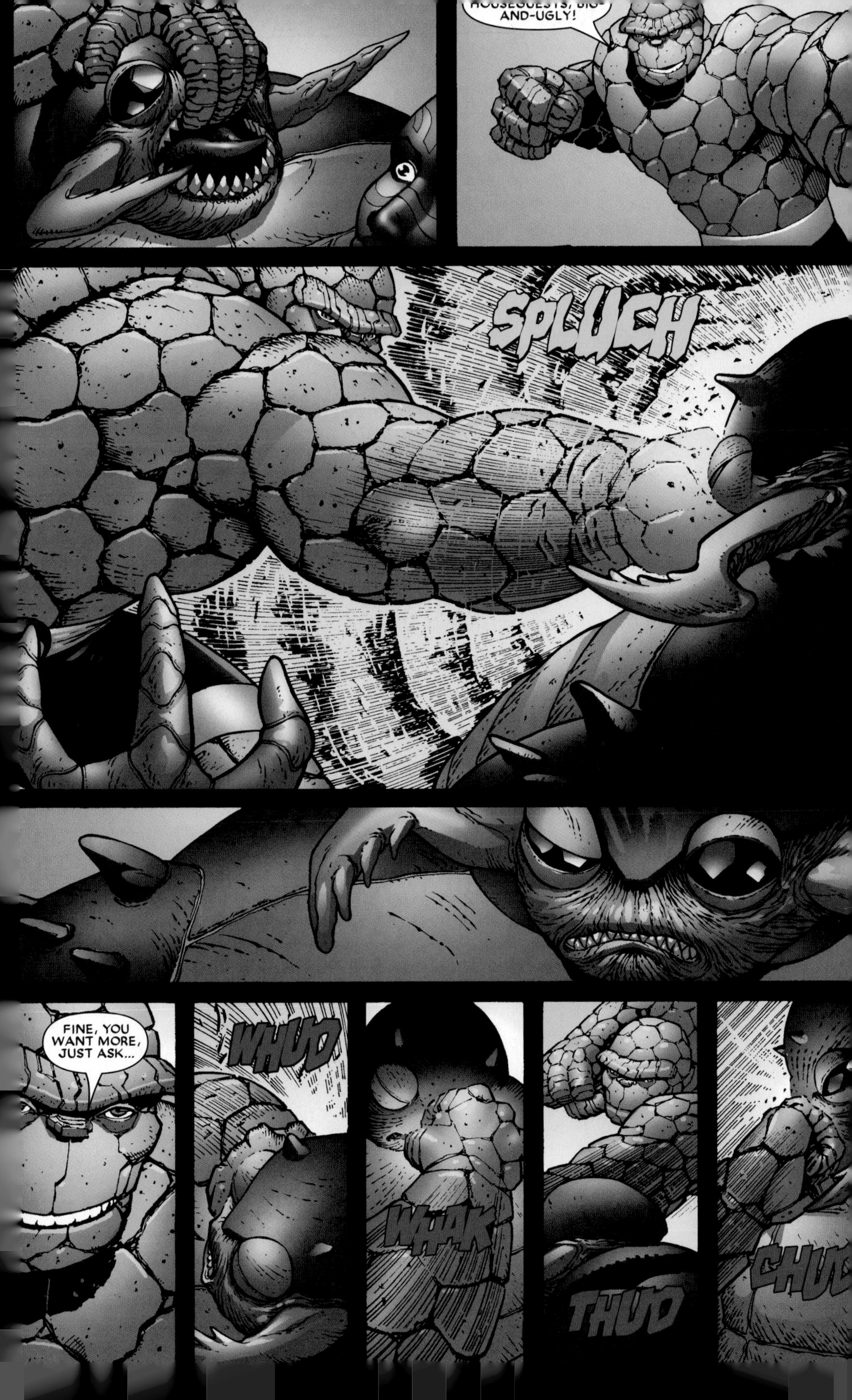
AND-UGLY!
SPLUCH
FINE, YOU WANT MORE, JUST ASK...
WHUD
WHAK
THUD
CHUD

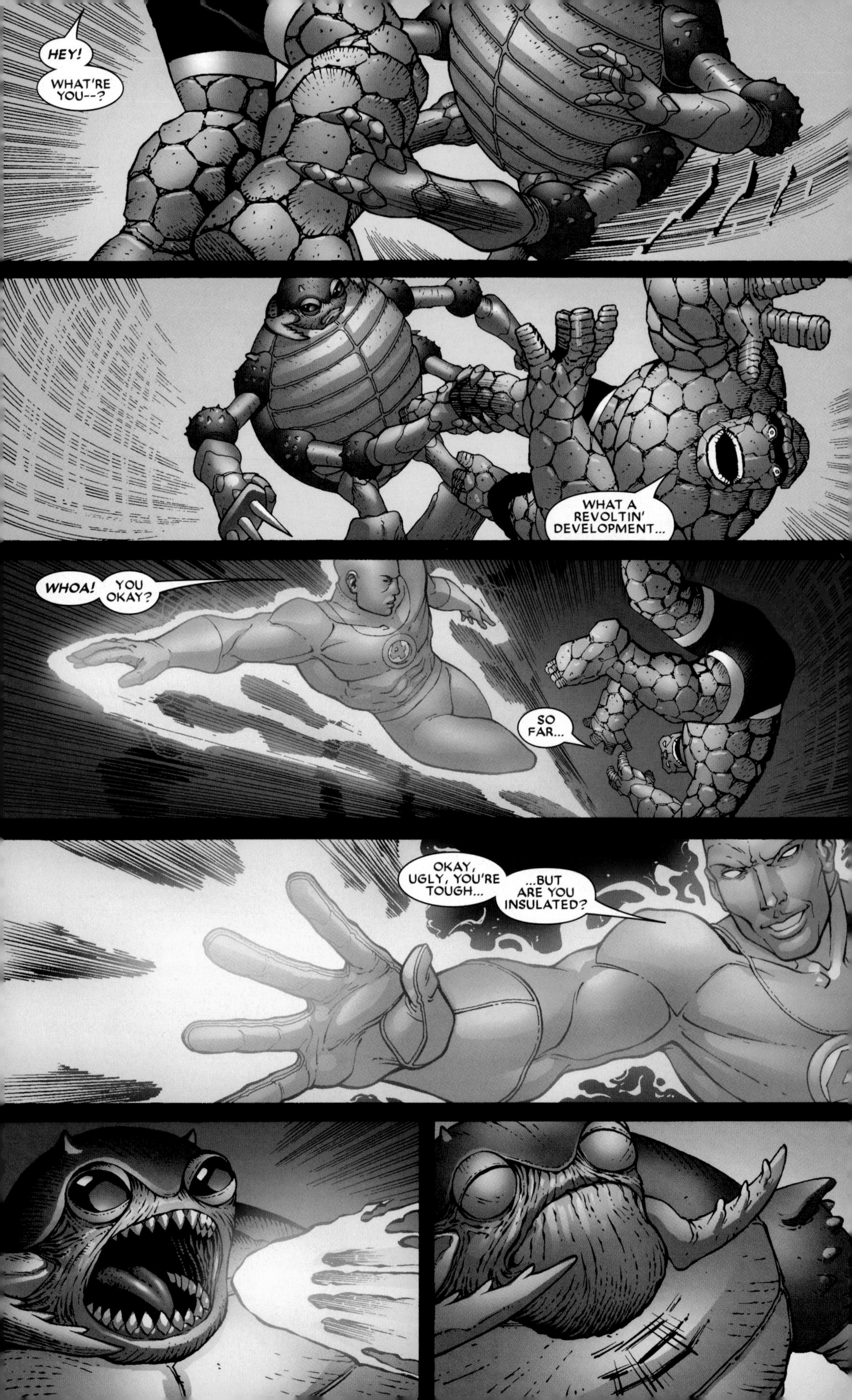
HEY!
WHAT'RE YOU--?
WHAT A REVOLTIN' DEVELOPMENT...
WHOA! YOU OKAY?
SO FAR...
OKAY, UGLY, YOU'RE TOUGH...
...BUT ARE YOU INSULATED?

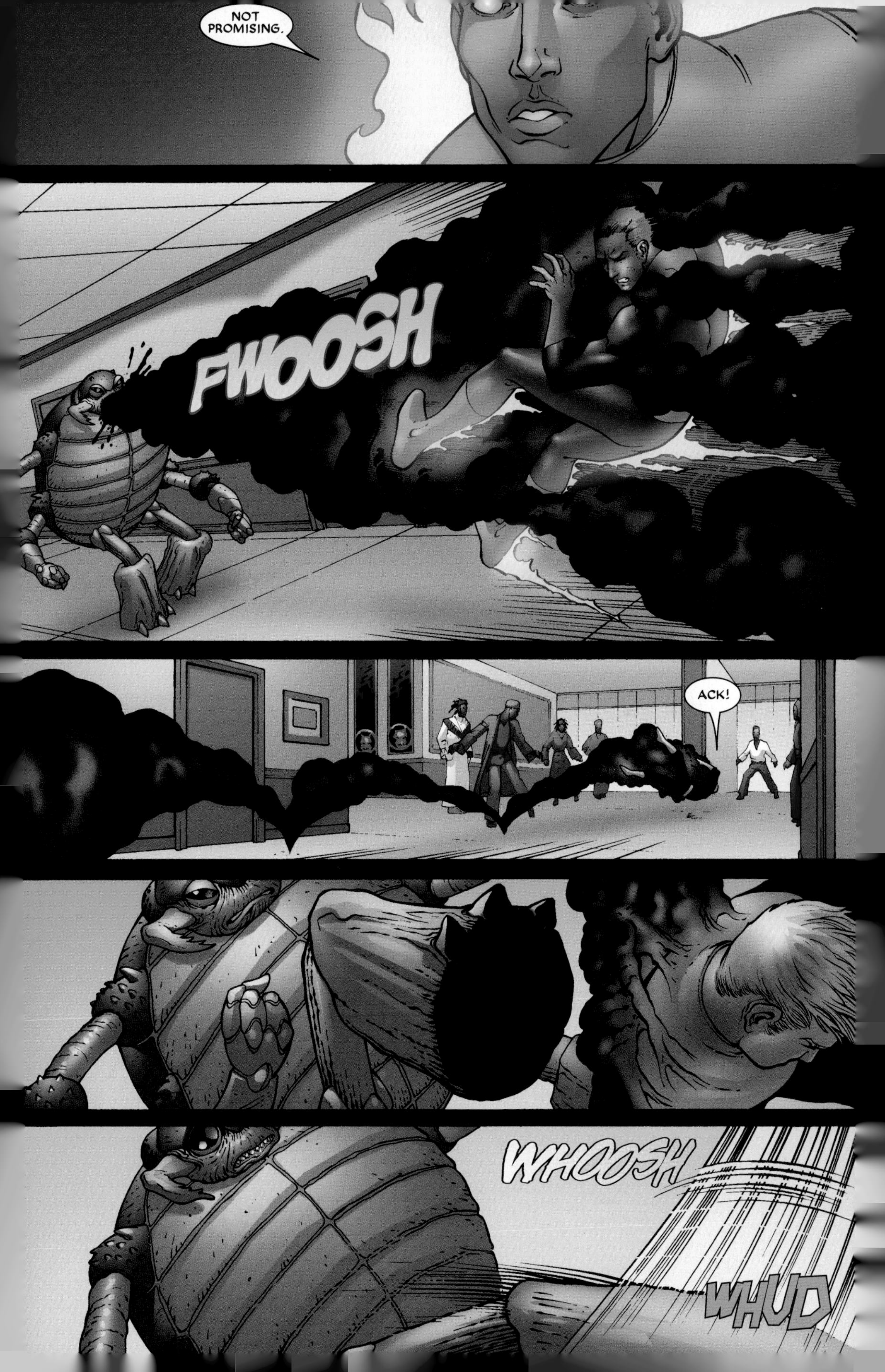

NOT PROMISING.
FWOOSH
ACK!
WHOOSH
WHUD

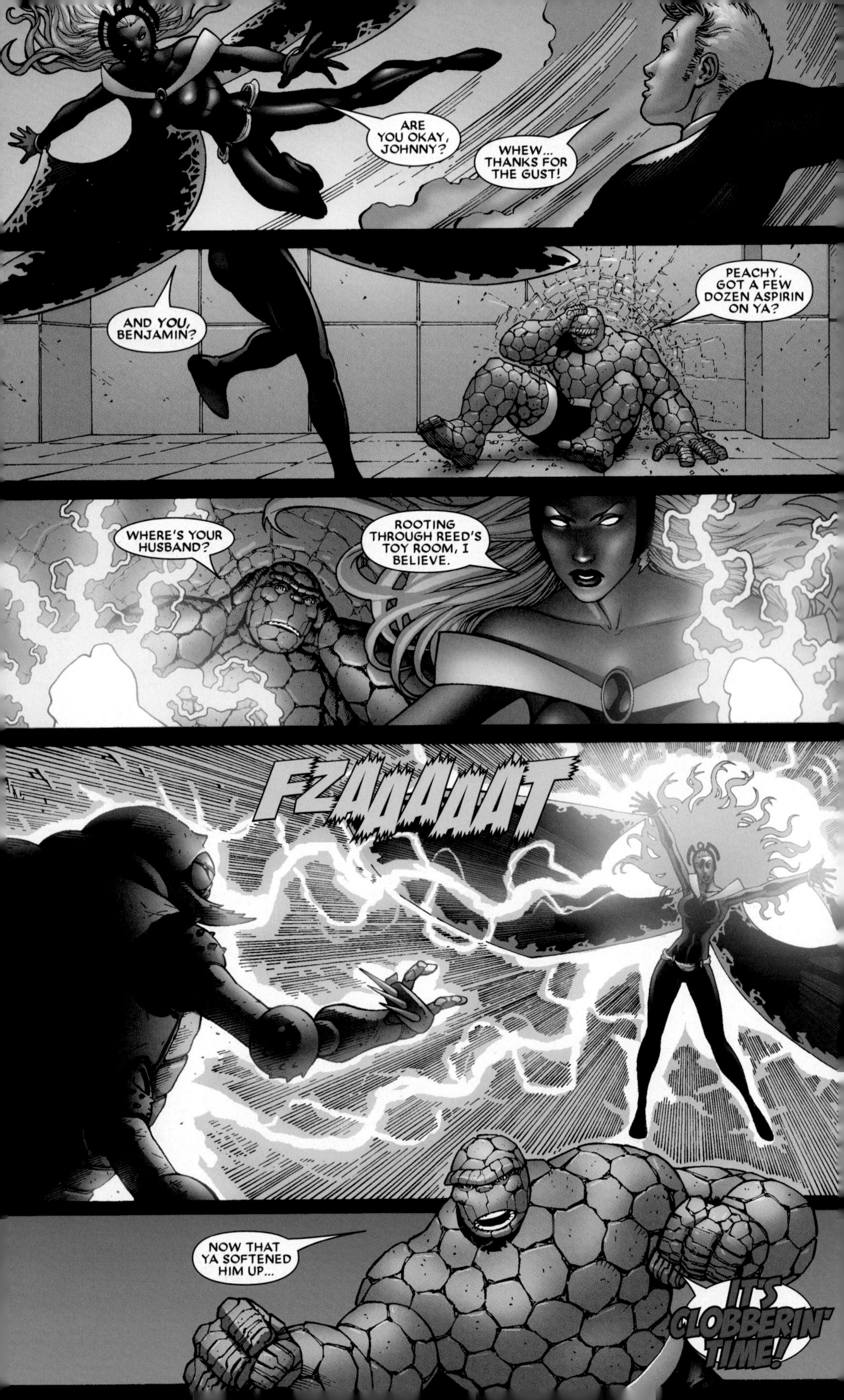
ARE YOU OKAY, JOHNNY?
WHEW... THANKS FOR THE GUST!
AND YOU, BENJAMIN?
PEACHY. GOT A FEW DOZEN ASPIRIN ON YA?
WHERE'S YOUR HUSBAND?
ROOTING THROUGH REED'S TOY ROOM, I BELIEVE.
FZAAAAAAT
NOW THAT YA SOFTENED HIM UP...
IT'S CLOBBERIN' TIME!

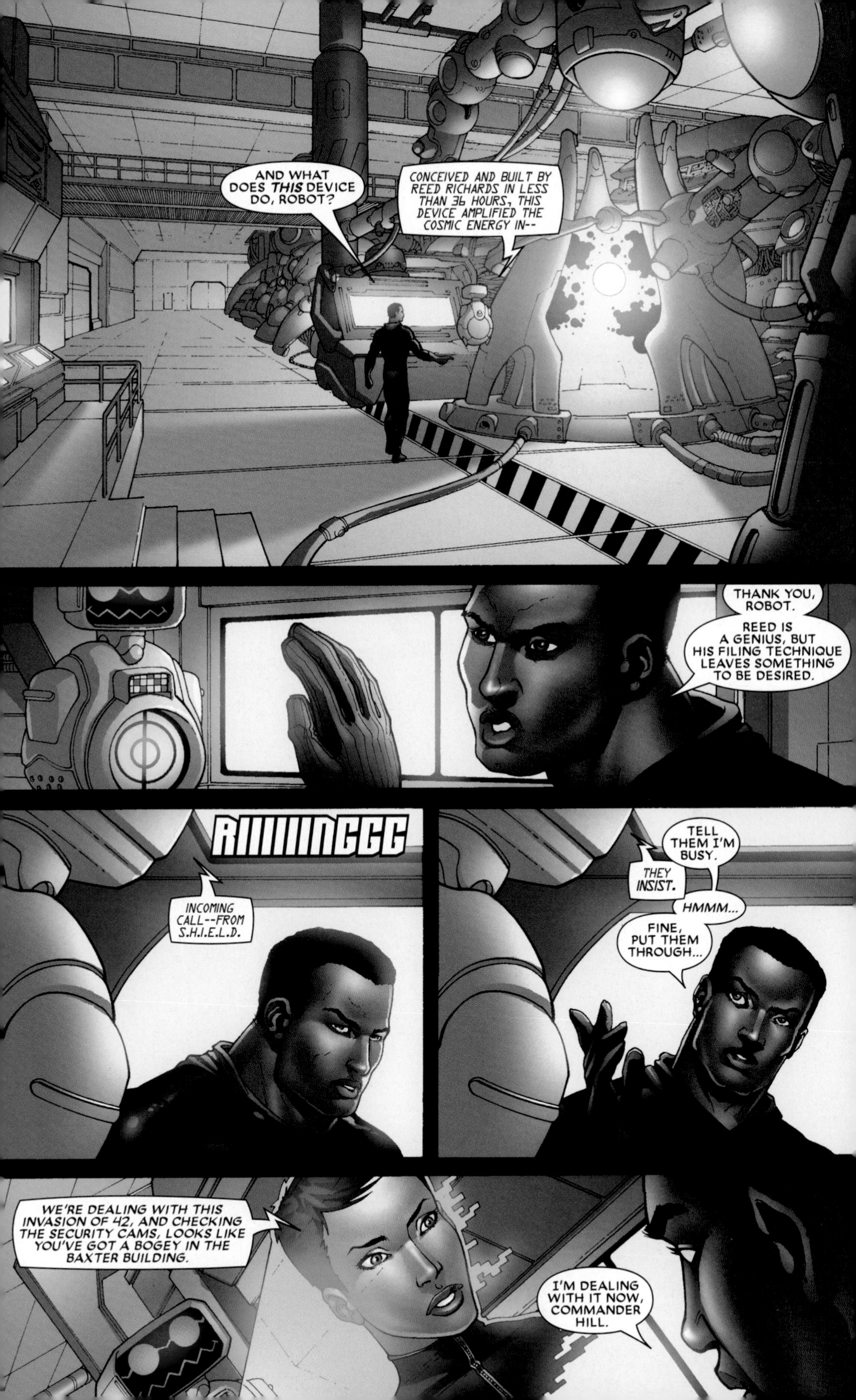
AND WHAT DOES *THIS* DEVICE DO, ROBOT?
CONCEIVED AND BUILT BY REED RICHARDS IN LESS THAN 36 HOURS, THIS DEVICE AMPLIFIED THE COSMIC ENERGY IN--
THANK YOU, ROBOT.
REED IS A GENIUS, BUT HIS FILING TECHNIQUE LEAVES SOMETHING TO BE DESIRED.
RIIIIINGGG
INCOMING CALL--FROM S.H.I.E.L.D.
TELL THEM I'M BUSY.
THEY *INSIST.*
HMMM...
FINE, PUT THEM THROUGH...
WE'RE DEALING WITH THIS INVASION OF 42, AND CHECKING THE SECURITY CAMS, LOOKS LIKE YOU'VE GOT A BOGEY IN THE BAXTER BUILDING.
I'M DEALING WITH IT NOW, COMMANDER HILL.

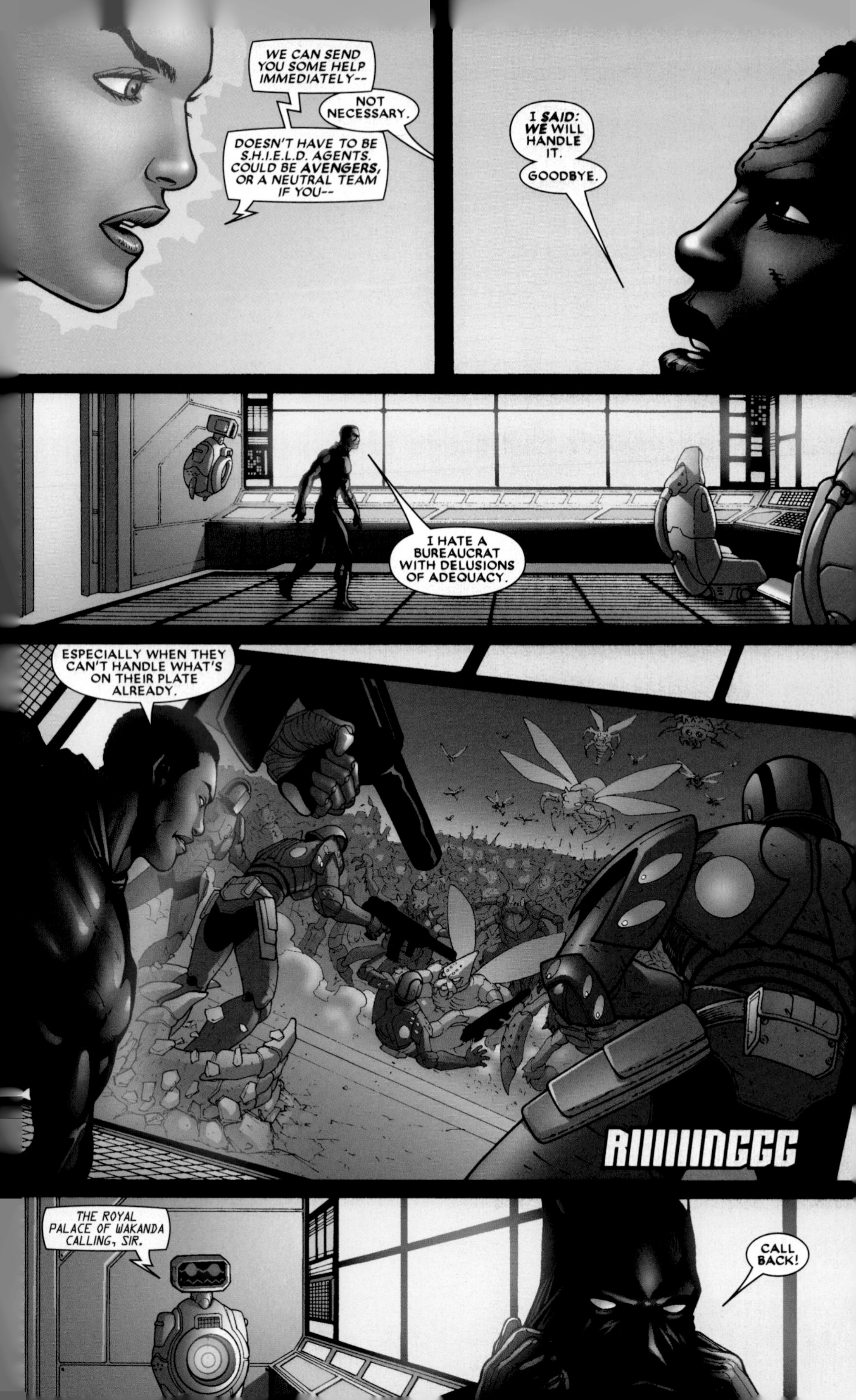
WE CAN SEND YOU SOME HELP IMMEDIATELY--
NOT NECESSARY.
DOESN'T HAVE TO BE S.H.I.E.L.D. AGENTS. COULD BE AVENGERS, OR A NEUTRAL TEAM IF YOU--
I SAID: WE WILL HANDLE IT.
GOODBYE.
I HATE A BUREAUCRAT WITH DELUSIONS OF ADEQUACY.
ESPECIALLY WHEN THEY CAN'T HANDLE WHAT'S ON THEIR PLATE ALREADY.
RIIIIINGGG
THE ROYAL PALACE OF WAKANDA CALLING, SIR.
CALL BACK!

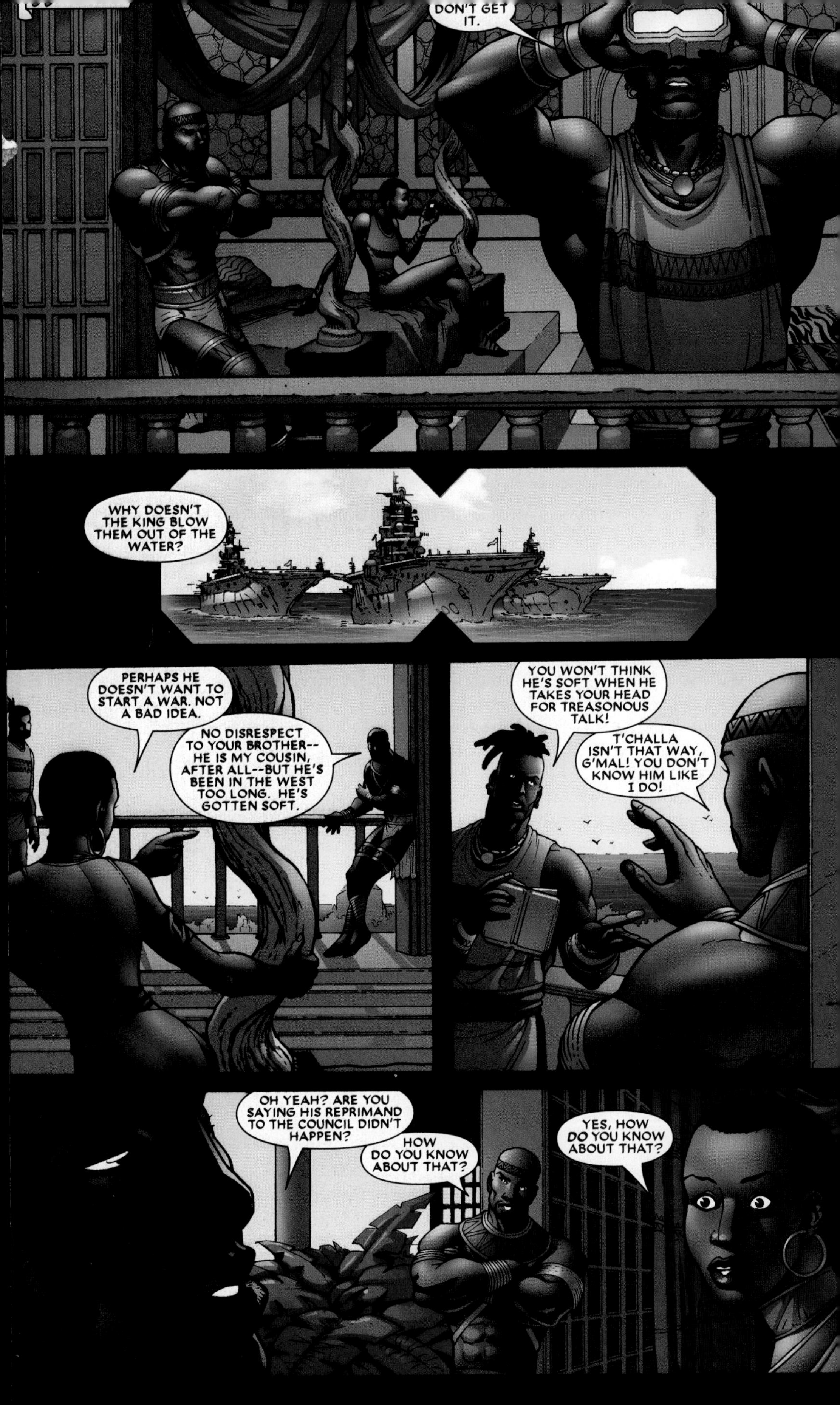
DON'T GET IT.
WHY DOESN'T THE KING BLOW THEM OUT OF THE WATER?
PERHAPS HE DOESN'T WANT TO START A WAR. NOT A BAD IDEA.
NO DISRESPECT TO YOUR BROTHER-- HE IS MY COUSIN, AFTER ALL--BUT HE'S BEEN IN THE WEST TOO LONG. HE'S GOTTEN SOFT.
YOU WON'T THINK HE'S SOFT WHEN HE TAKES YOUR HEAD FOR TREASONOUS TALK!
T'CHALLA ISN'T THAT WAY, G'MAL! YOU DON'T KNOW HIM LIKE I DO!
OH YEAH? ARE YOU SAYING HIS REPRIMAND TO THE COUNCIL DIDN'T HAPPEN?
HOW DO YOU KNOW ABOUT THAT?
YES, HOW DO YOU KNOW ABOUT THAT?

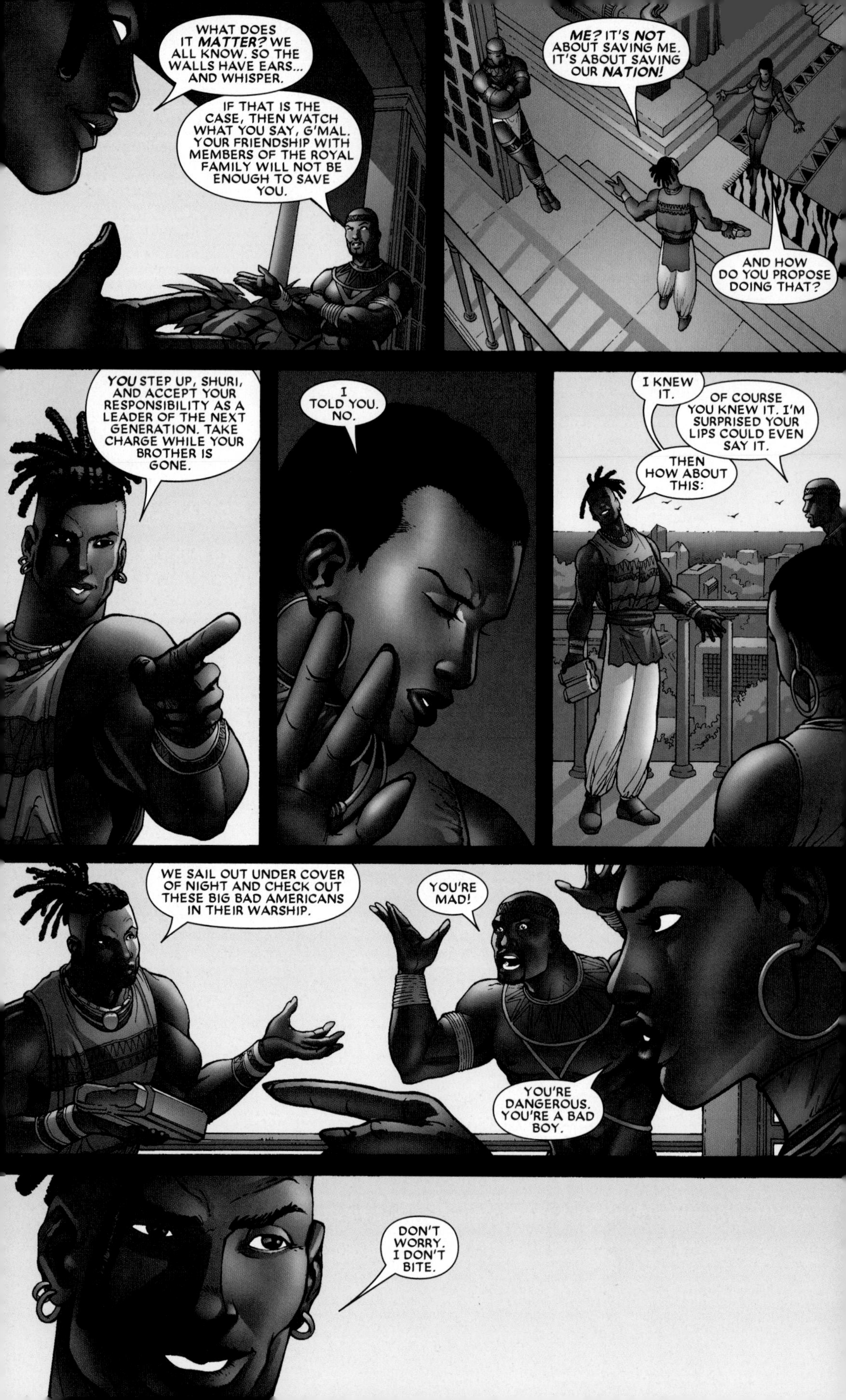
WHAT DOES IT MATTER? WE ALL KNOW. SO THE WALLS HAVE EARS... AND WHISPER.
IF THAT IS THE CASE, THEN WATCH WHAT YOU SAY, G'MAL. YOUR FRIENDSHIP WITH MEMBERS OF THE ROYAL FAMILY WILL NOT BE ENOUGH TO SAVE YOU.
ME? IT'S NOT ABOUT SAVING ME. IT'S ABOUT SAVING OUR NATION!
AND HOW DO YOU PROPOSE DOING THAT?
YOU STEP UP, SHURI, AND ACCEPT YOUR RESPONSIBILITY AS A LEADER OF THE NEXT GENERATION. TAKE CHARGE WHILE YOUR BROTHER IS GONE.
I TOLD YOU. NO.
I KNEW IT.
OF COURSE YOU KNEW IT. I'M SURPRISED YOUR LIPS COULD EVEN SAY IT.
THEN HOW ABOUT THIS:
WE SAIL OUT UNDER COVER OF NIGHT AND CHECK OUT THESE BIG BAD AMERICANS IN THEIR WARSHIP.
YOU'RE MAD!
YOU'RE DANGEROUS. YOU'RE A BAD BOY.
DON'T WORRY. I DON'T BITE.

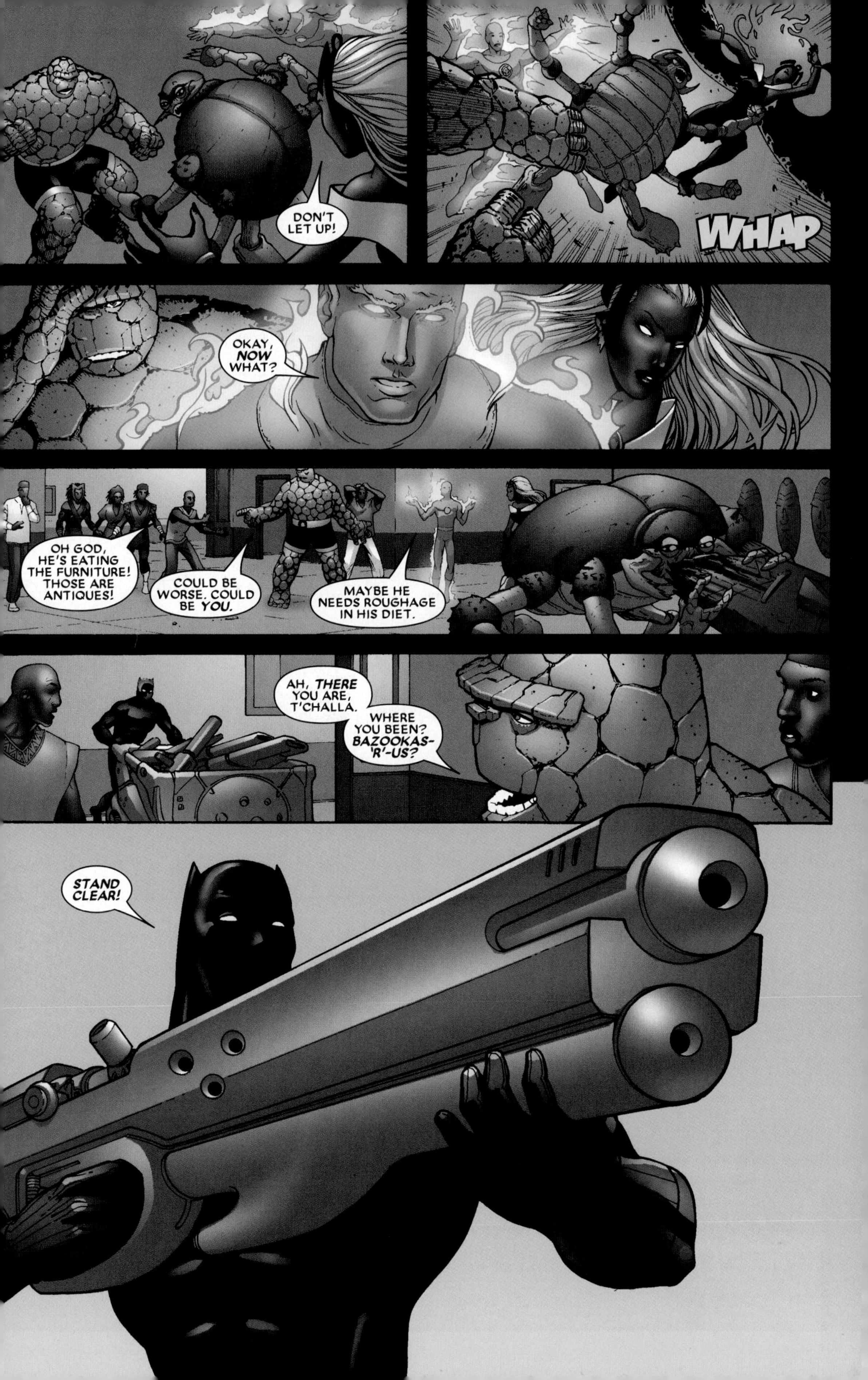
DON'T LET UP!
WHAP
OKAY, NOW WHAT?
OH GOD, HE'S EATING THE FURNITURE! THOSE ARE ANTIQUES!
COULD BE WORSE. COULD BE YOU.
MAYBE HE NEEDS ROUGHAGE IN HIS DIET.
AH, THERE YOU ARE, T'CHALLA.
WHERE YOU BEEN? BAZOOKAS-'R'-US?
STAND CLEAR!

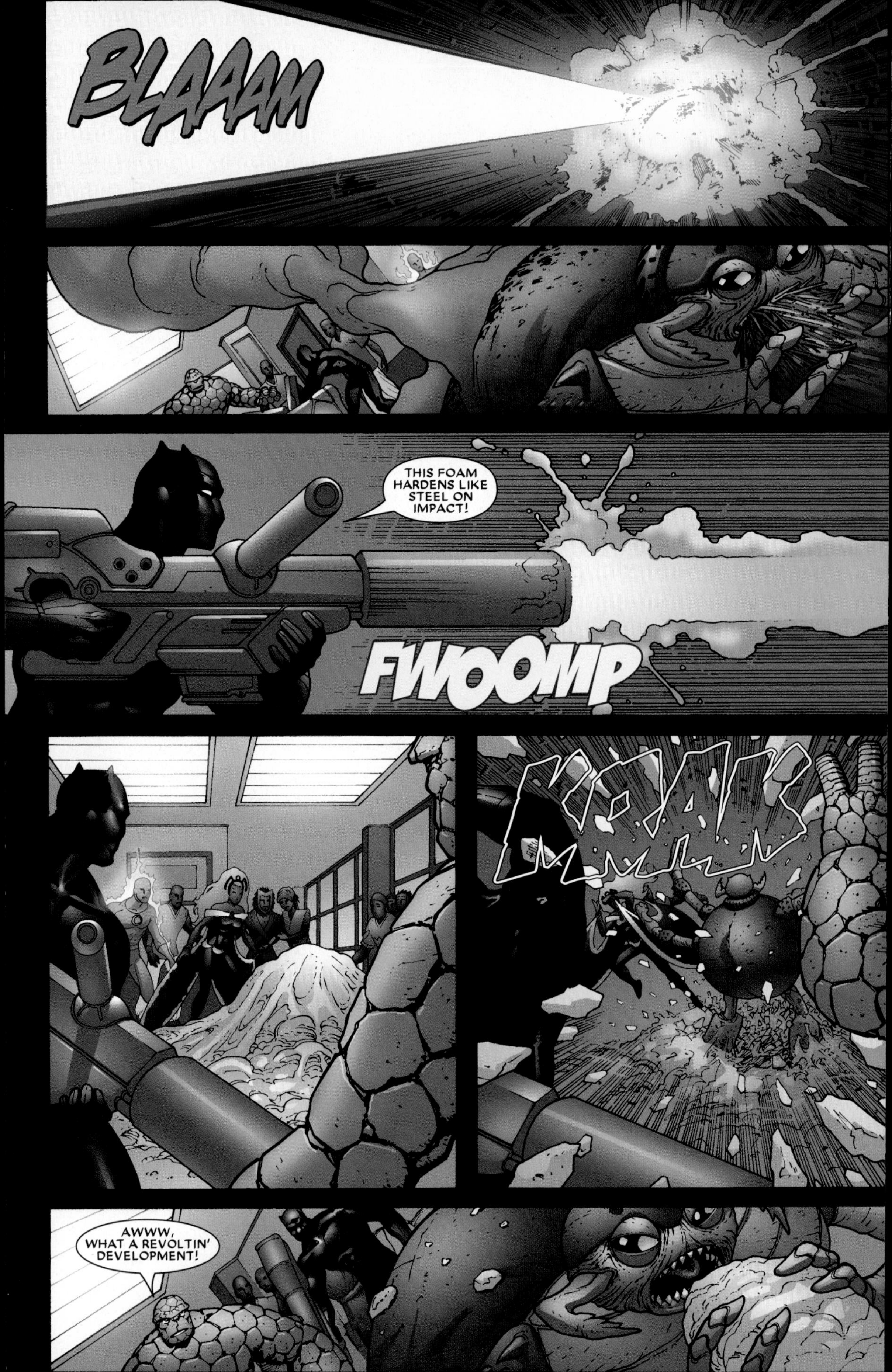
BLAAAM
THIS FOAM HARDENS LIKE STEEL ON IMPACT!
FWOOMP
AWWW, WHAT A REVOLTIN' DEVELOPMENT!

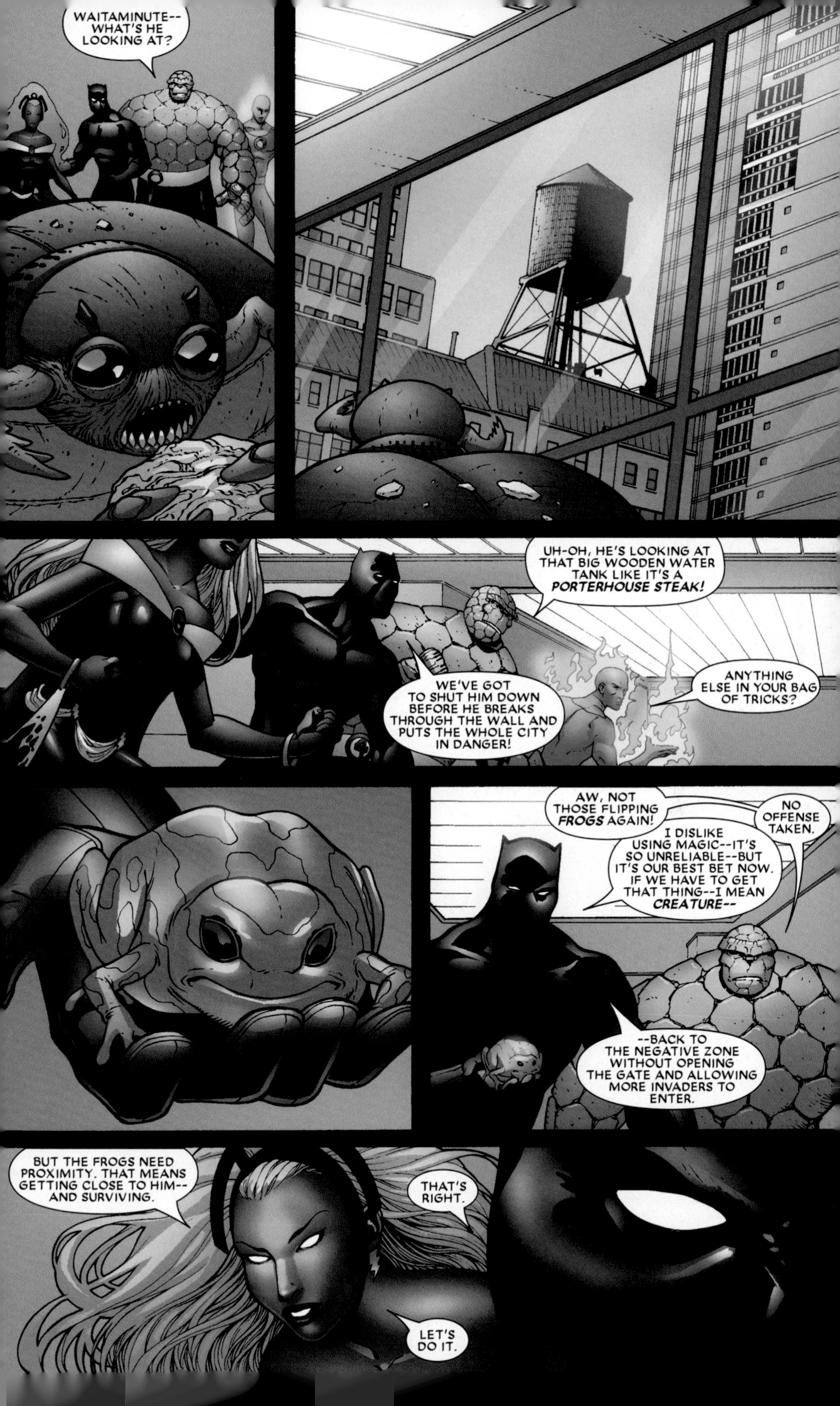
WAITAMINUTE-- WHAT'S HE LOOKING AT?
UH-OH, HE'S LOOKING AT THAT BIG WOODEN WATER TANK LIKE IT'S A PORTERHOUSE STEAK!
WE'VE GOT TO SHUT HIM DOWN BEFORE HE BREAKS THROUGH THE WALL AND PUTS THE WHOLE CITY IN DANGER!
ANYTHING ELSE IN YOUR BAG OF TRICKS?
AW, NOT THOSE FLIPPING FROGS AGAIN!
NO OFFENSE TAKEN.
I DISLIKE USING MAGIC--IT'S SO UNRELIABLE--BUT IT'S OUR BEST BET NOW. IF WE HAVE TO GET THAT THING--I MEAN CREATURE--
--BACK TO THE NEGATIVE ZONE WITHOUT OPENING THE GATE AND ALLOWING MORE INVADERS TO ENTER.
BUT THE FROGS NEED PROXIMITY. THAT MEANS GETTING CLOSE TO HIM--AND SURVIVING.
THAT'S RIGHT.
LET'S DO IT.

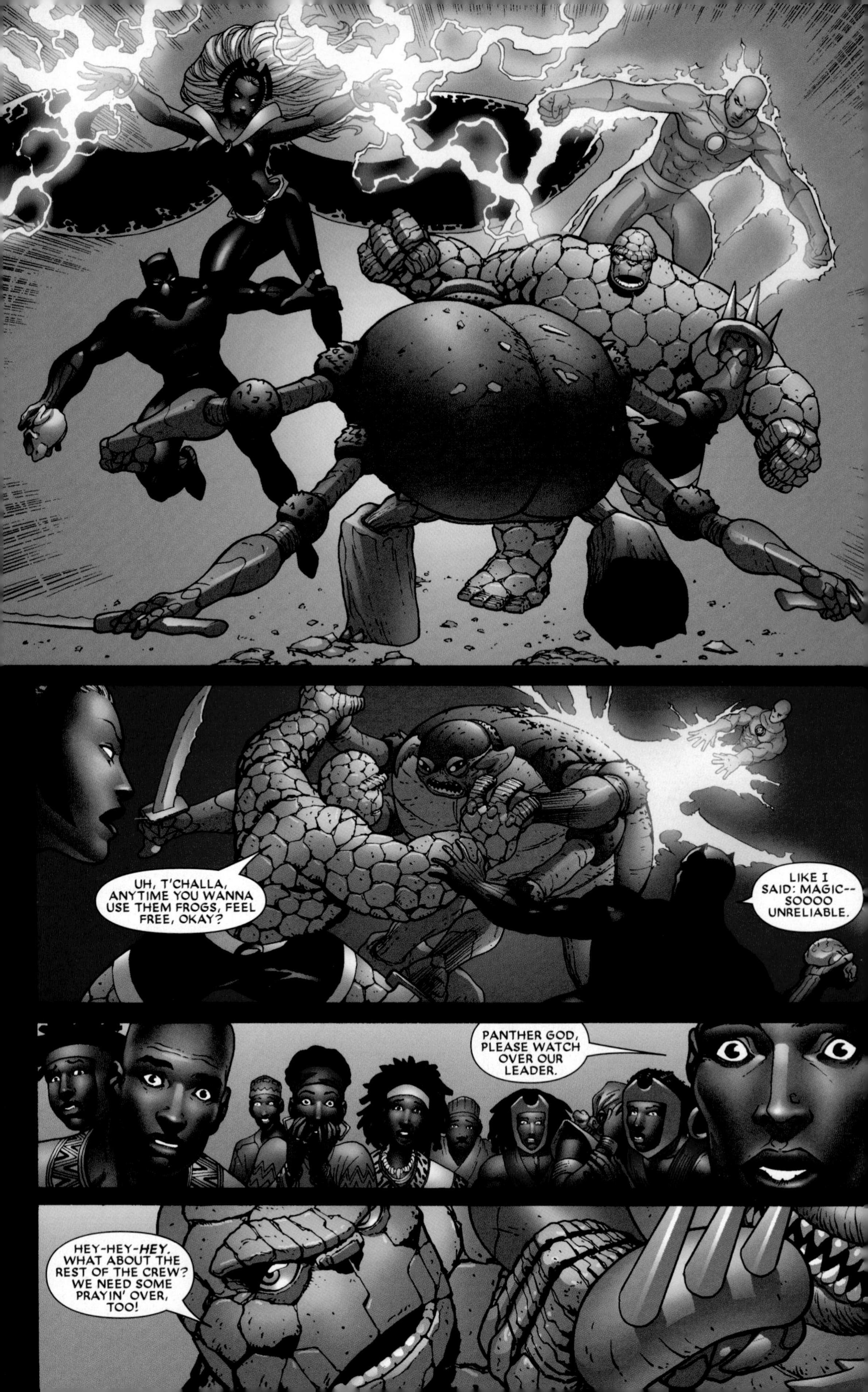
UH, T'CHALLA, ANYTIME YOU WANNA USE THEM FROGS, FEEL FREE, OKAY?
LIKE I SAID: MAGIC-- SOOOO UNRELIABLE.
PANTHER GOD, PLEASE WATCH OVER OUR LEADER.
HEY-HEY-*HEY*. WHAT ABOUT THE REST OF THE CREW? WE NEED SOME PRAYIN' OVER, TOO!

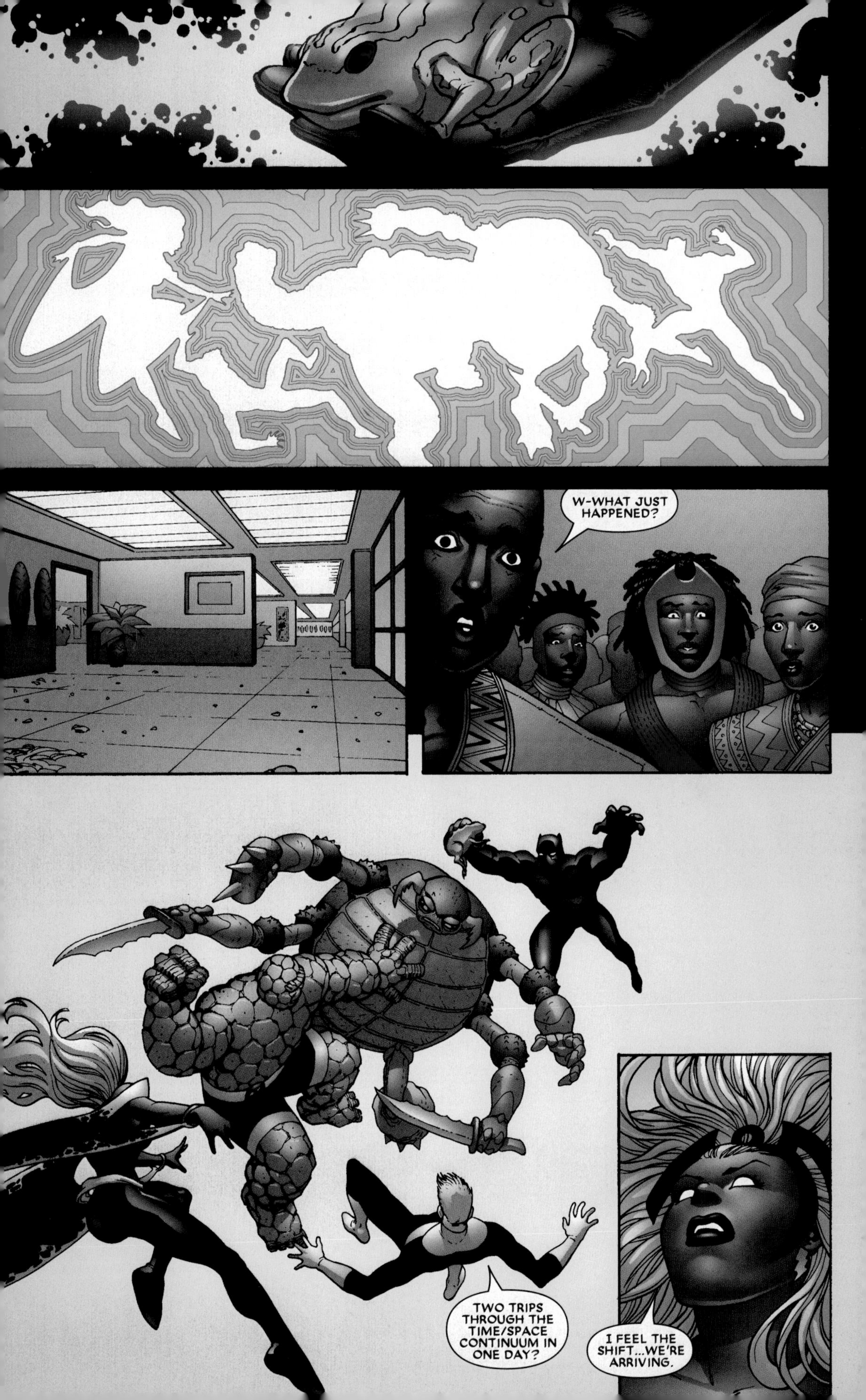
W-WHAT JUST HAPPENED?
TWO TRIPS THROUGH THE TIME/SPACE CONTINUUM IN ONE DAY?
I FEEL THE SHIFT...WE'RE ARRIVING.

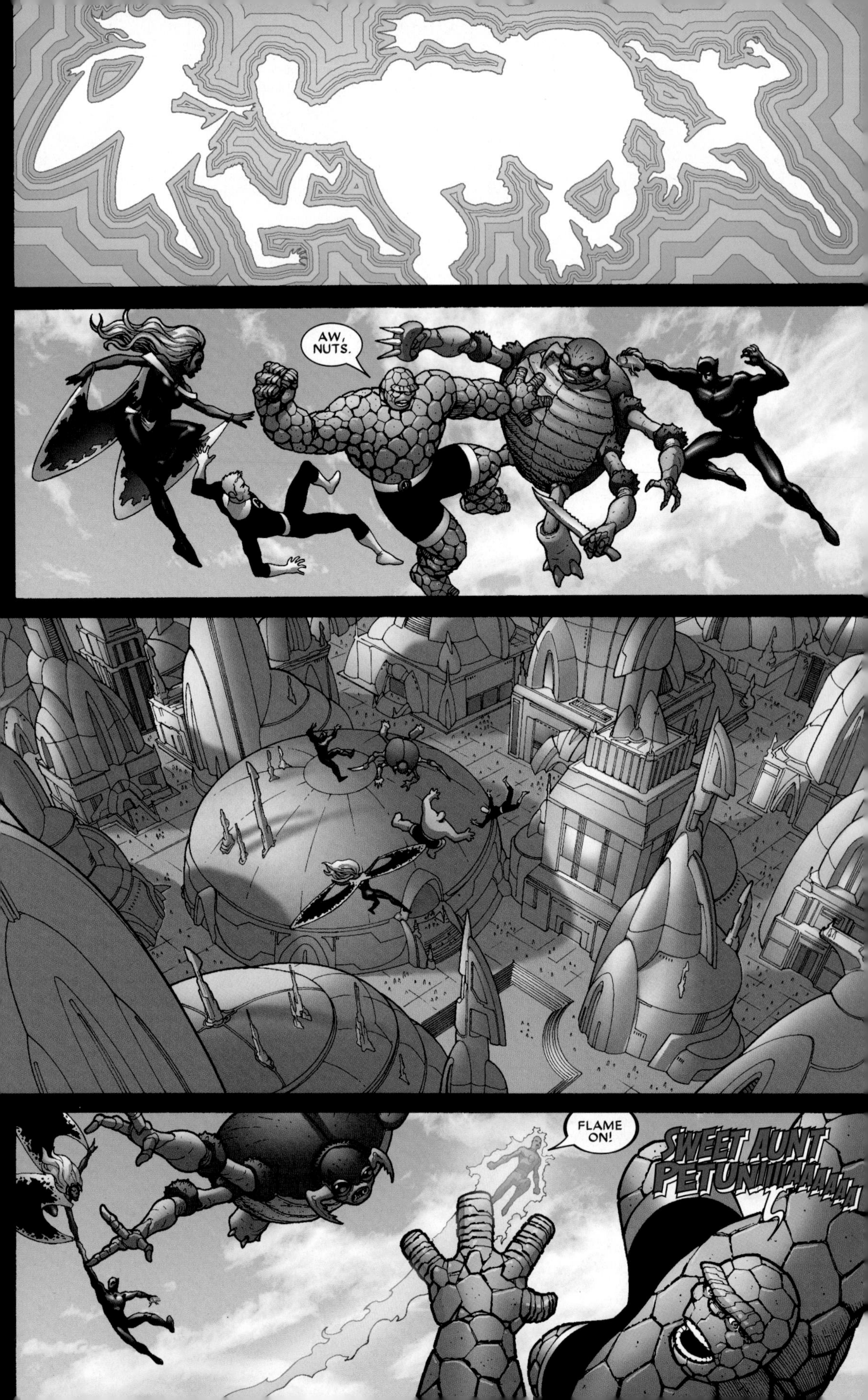
AW, NUTS.
FLAME ON!
SWEET AUNT PETUNIIIIAAAAAA!

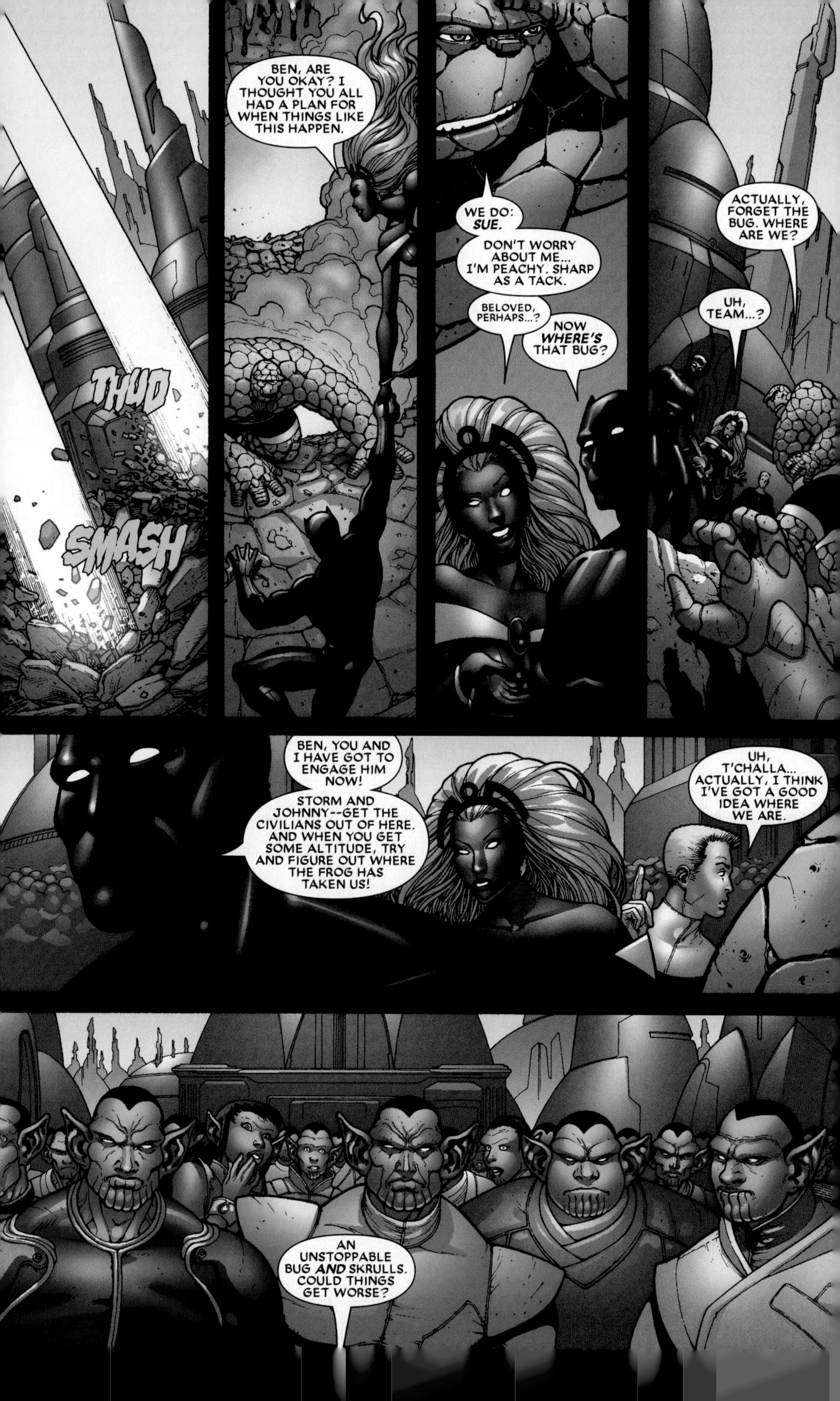
THUD
SMASH
BEN, ARE YOU OKAY? I THOUGHT YOU ALL HAD A PLAN FOR WHEN THINGS LIKE THIS HAPPEN.
WE DO: SUE.
DON'T WORRY ABOUT ME... I'M PEACHY. SHARP AS A TACK.
BELOVED, PERHAPS...?
NOW WHERE'S THAT BUG?
ACTUALLY, FORGET THE BUG. WHERE ARE WE?
UH, TEAM...?
BEN, YOU AND I HAVE GOT TO ENGAGE HIM NOW!
STORM AND JOHNNY--GET THE CIVILIANS OUT OF HERE. AND WHEN YOU GET SOME ALTITUDE, TRY AND FIGURE OUT WHERE THE FROG HAS TAKEN US!
UH, T'CHALLA... ACTUALLY, I THINK I'VE GOT A GOOD IDEA WHERE WE ARE.
AN UNSTOPPABLE BUG AND SKRULLS. COULD THINGS GET WORSE?

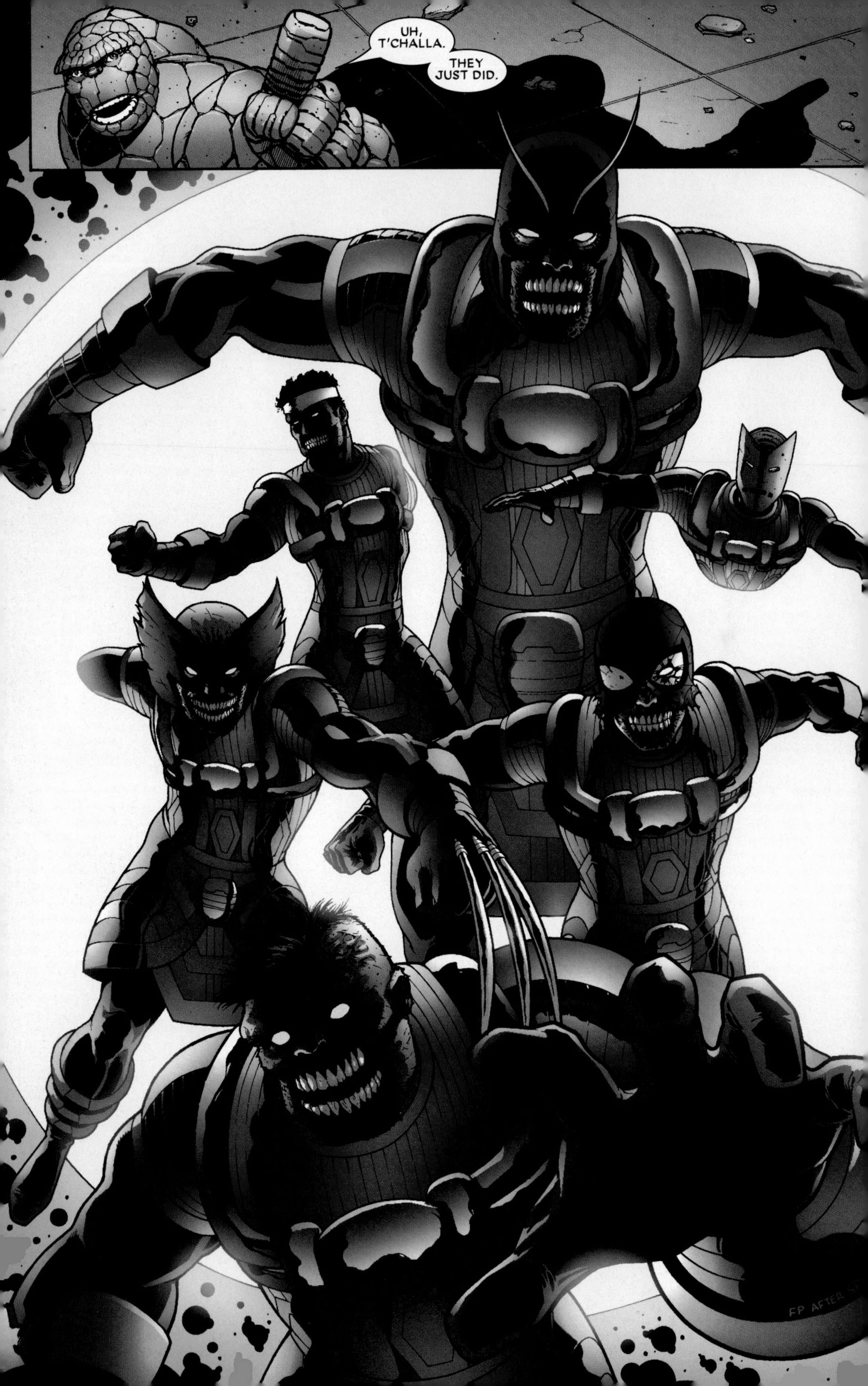
UH, T'CHALLA.
THEY JUST DID.

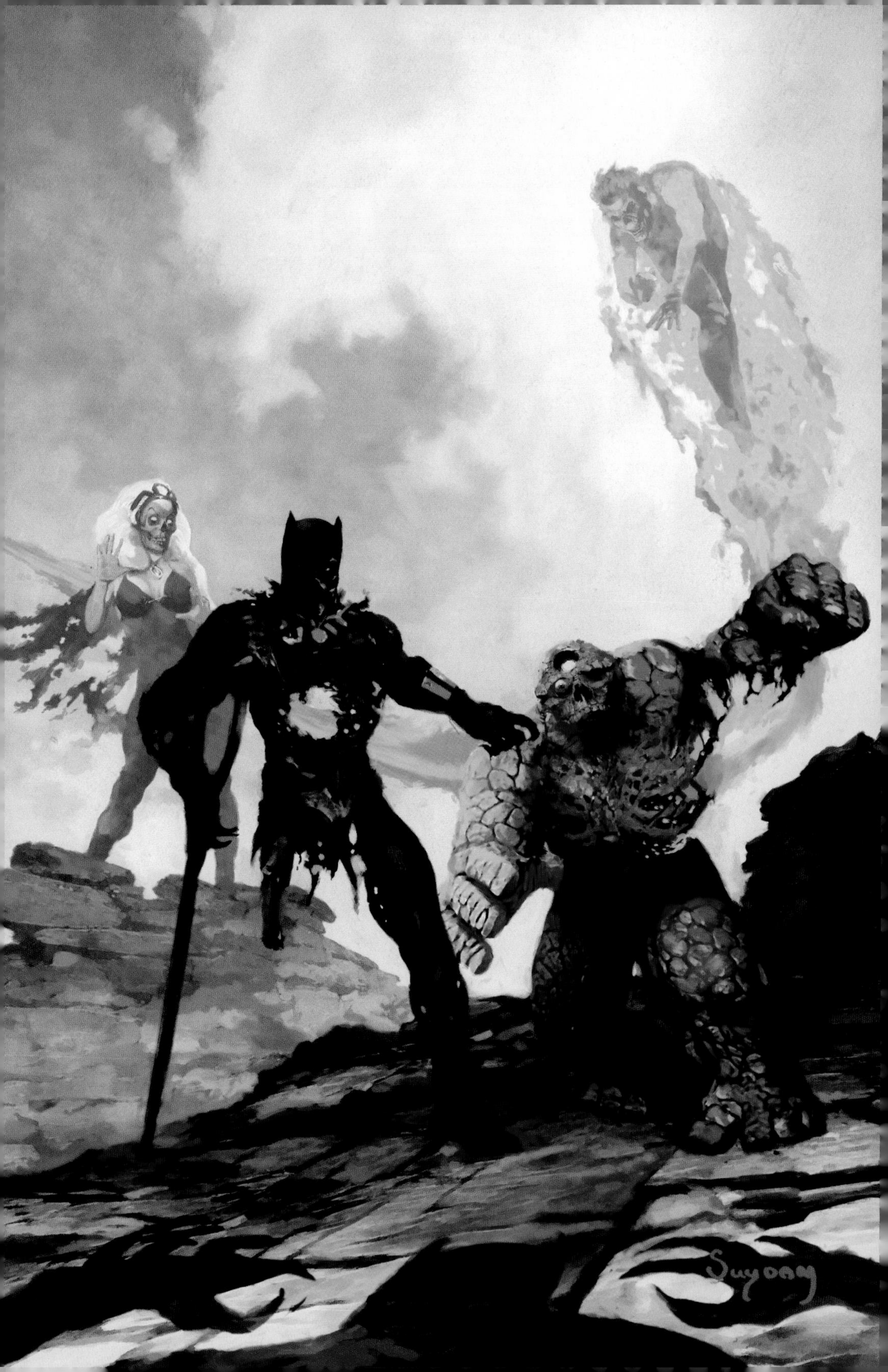
Suydam

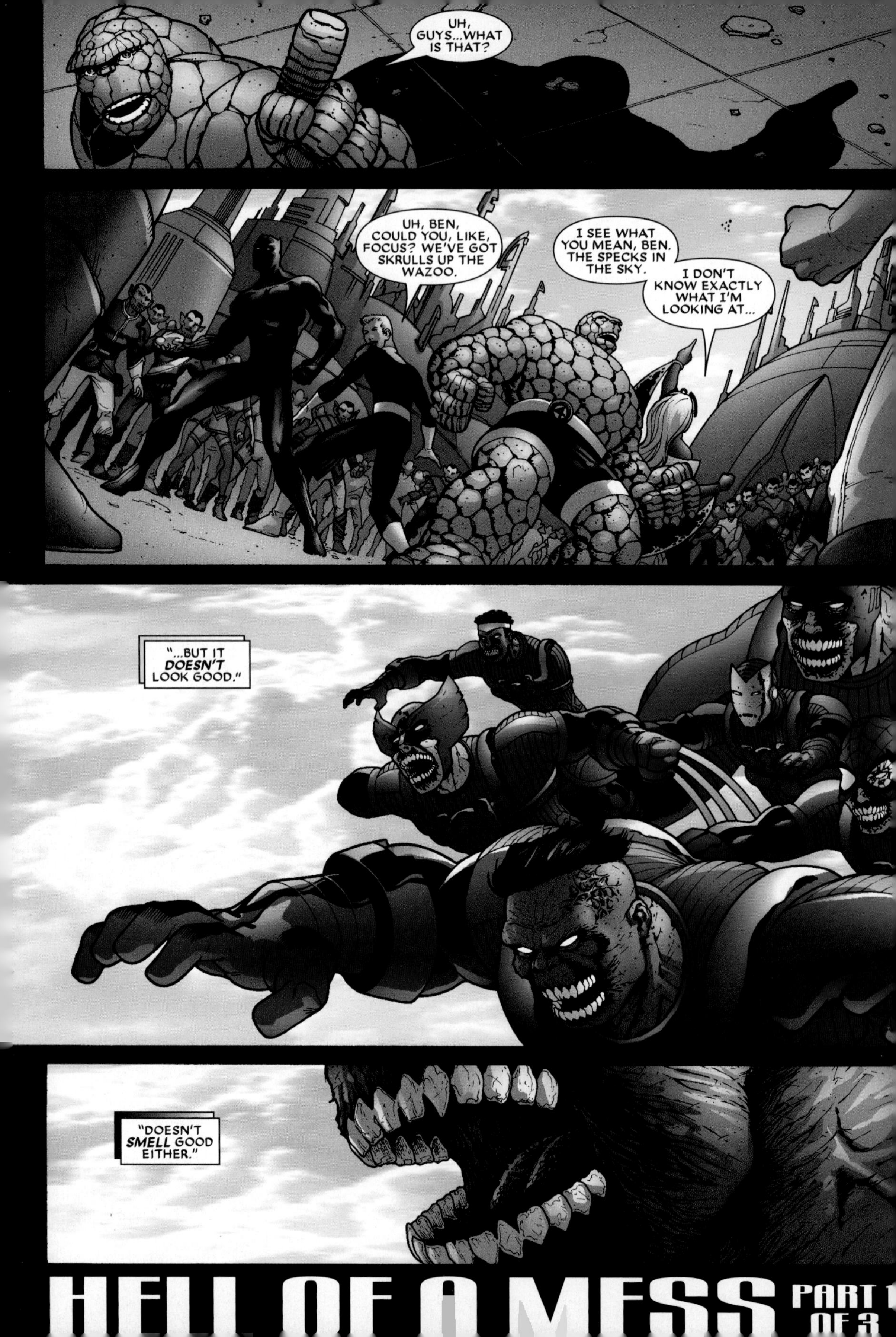
UH, GUYS...WHAT IS THAT?
UH, BEN, COULD YOU, LIKE, FOCUS? WE'VE GOT SKRULLS UP THE WAZOO.
I SEE WHAT YOU MEAN, BEN. THE SPECKS IN THE SKY.
I DON'T KNOW EXACTLY WHAT I'M LOOKING AT...
"...BUT IT DOESN'T LOOK GOOD."
"DOESN'T SMELL GOOD EITHER."
HELL OF A MESS PART 1 OF 3

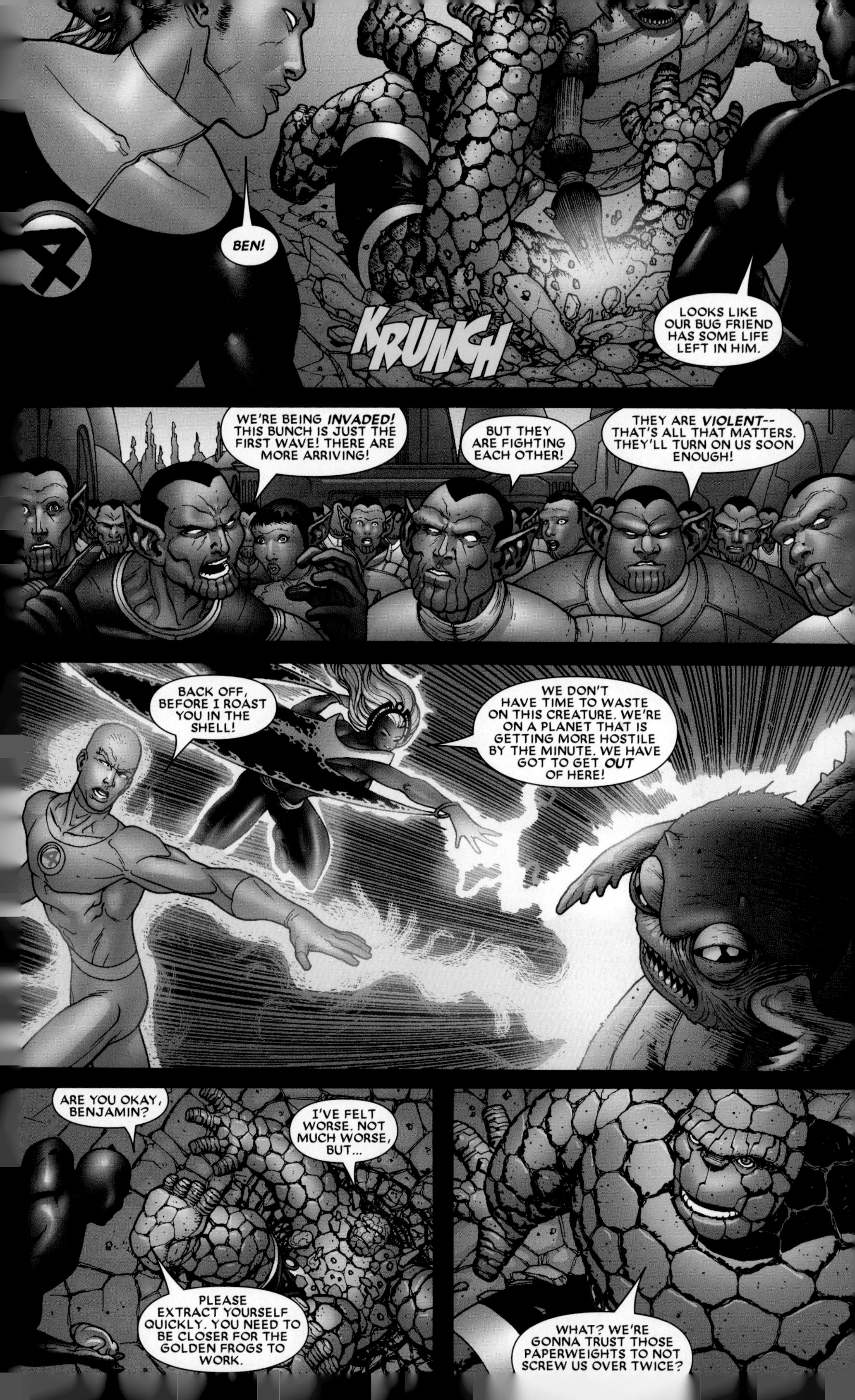
BEN!
KRUNCH
LOOKS LIKE OUR BUG FRIEND HAS SOME LIFE LEFT IN HIM.
WE'RE BEING *INVADED!* THIS BUNCH IS JUST THE FIRST WAVE! THERE ARE MORE ARRIVING!
BUT THEY ARE FIGHTING EACH OTHER!
THEY ARE *VIOLENT*-- THAT'S ALL THAT MATTERS. THEY'LL TURN ON US SOON ENOUGH!
BACK OFF, BEFORE I ROAST YOU IN THE SHELL!
WE DON'T HAVE TIME TO WASTE ON THIS CREATURE. WE'RE ON A PLANET THAT IS GETTING MORE HOSTILE BY THE MINUTE. WE HAVE GOT TO GET *OUT* OF HERE!
ARE YOU OKAY, BENJAMIN?
I'VE FELT WORSE. NOT MUCH WORSE, BUT...
PLEASE EXTRACT YOURSELF QUICKLY. YOU NEED TO BE CLOSER FOR THE GOLDEN FROGS TO WORK.
WHAT? WE'RE GONNA TRUST THOSE PAPERWEIGHTS TO NOT SCREW US OVER TWICE?

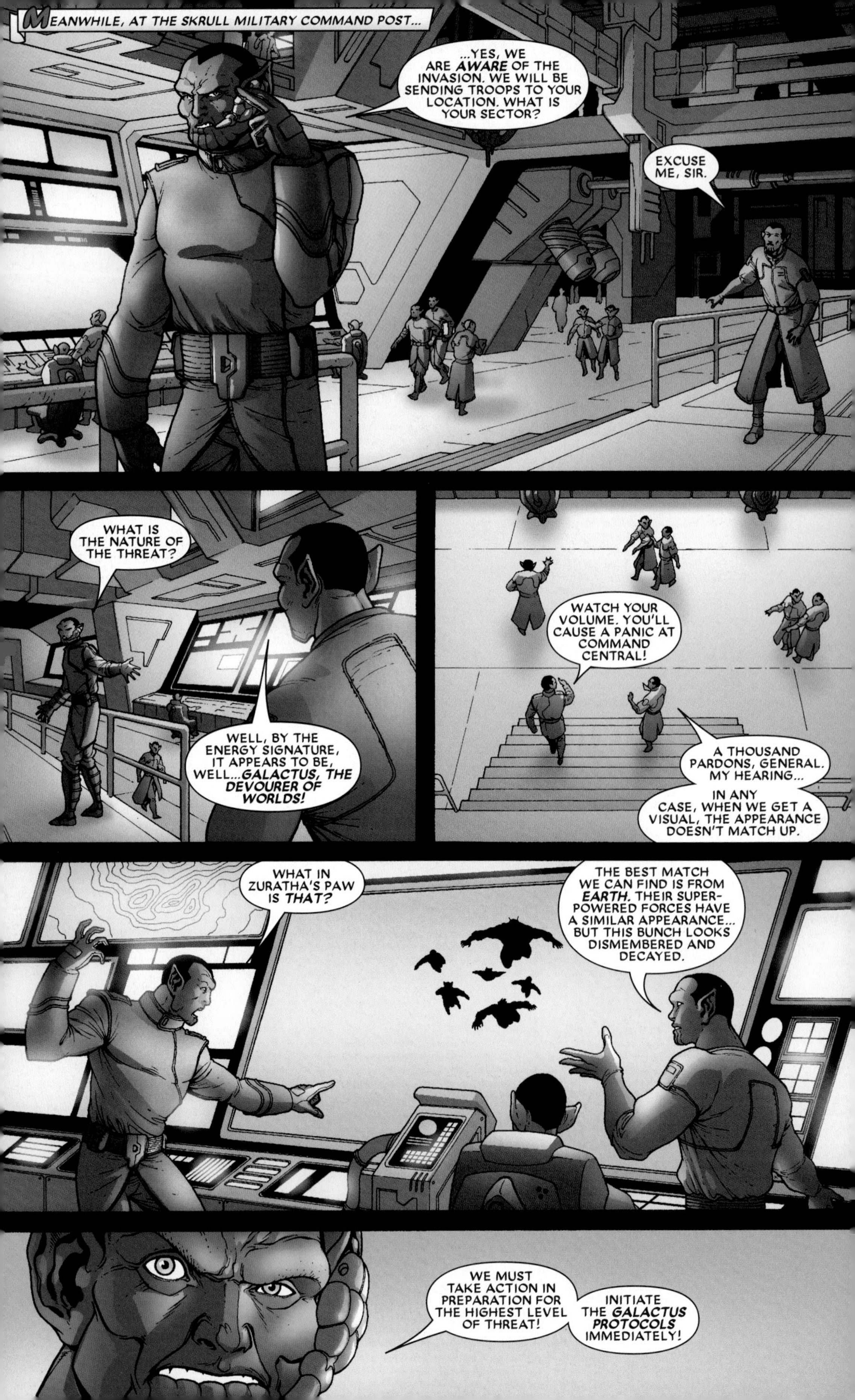
MEANWHILE, AT THE SKRULL MILITARY COMMAND POST...
...YES, WE ARE AWARE OF THE INVASION. WE WILL BE SENDING TROOPS TO YOUR LOCATION. WHAT IS YOUR SECTOR?
EXCUSE ME, SIR.
WHAT IS THE NATURE OF THE THREAT?
WELL, BY THE ENERGY SIGNATURE, IT APPEARS TO BE, WELL...GALACTUS, THE DEVOURER OF WORLDS!
WATCH YOUR VOLUME. YOU'LL CAUSE A PANIC AT COMMAND CENTRAL!
A THOUSAND PARDONS, GENERAL. MY HEARING...
IN ANY CASE, WHEN WE GET A VISUAL, THE APPEARANCE DOESN'T MATCH UP.
WHAT IN ZURATHA'S PAW IS THAT?
THE BEST MATCH WE CAN FIND IS FROM EARTH. THEIR SUPER-POWERED FORCES HAVE A SIMILAR APPEARANCE... BUT THIS BUNCH LOOKS DISMEMBERED AND DECAYED.
WE MUST TAKE ACTION IN PREPARATION FOR THE HIGHEST LEVEL OF THREAT!
INITIATE THE GALACTUS PROTOCOLS IMMEDIATELY!

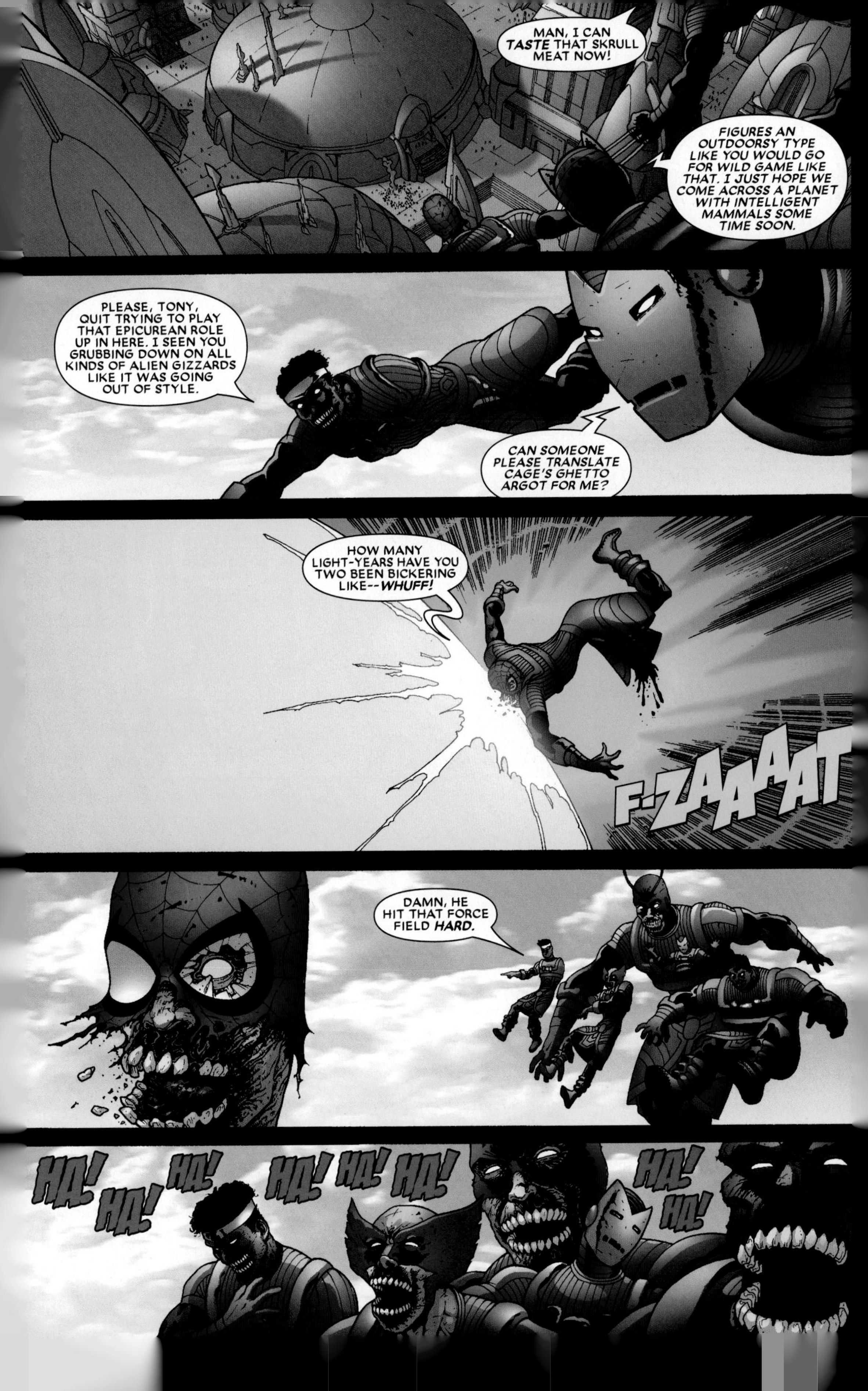
MAN, I CAN TASTE THAT SKRULL MEAT NOW!
FIGURES AN OUTDOORSY TYPE LIKE YOU WOULD GO FOR WILD GAME LIKE THAT. I JUST HOPE WE COME ACROSS A PLANET WITH INTELLIGENT MAMMALS SOME TIME SOON.
PLEASE, TONY, QUIT TRYING TO PLAY THAT EPICUREAN ROLE UP IN HERE. I SEEN YOU GRUBBING DOWN ON ALL KINDS OF ALIEN GIZZARDS LIKE IT WAS GOING OUT OF STYLE.
CAN SOMEONE PLEASE TRANSLATE CAGE'S GHETTO ARGOT FOR ME?
HOW MANY LIGHT-YEARS HAVE YOU TWO BEEN BICKERING LIKE--WHUFF!
F-ZAAAAT
DAMN, HE HIT THAT FORCE FIELD HARD.
HA! HA! HA! HA! HA! HA! HA! HA!

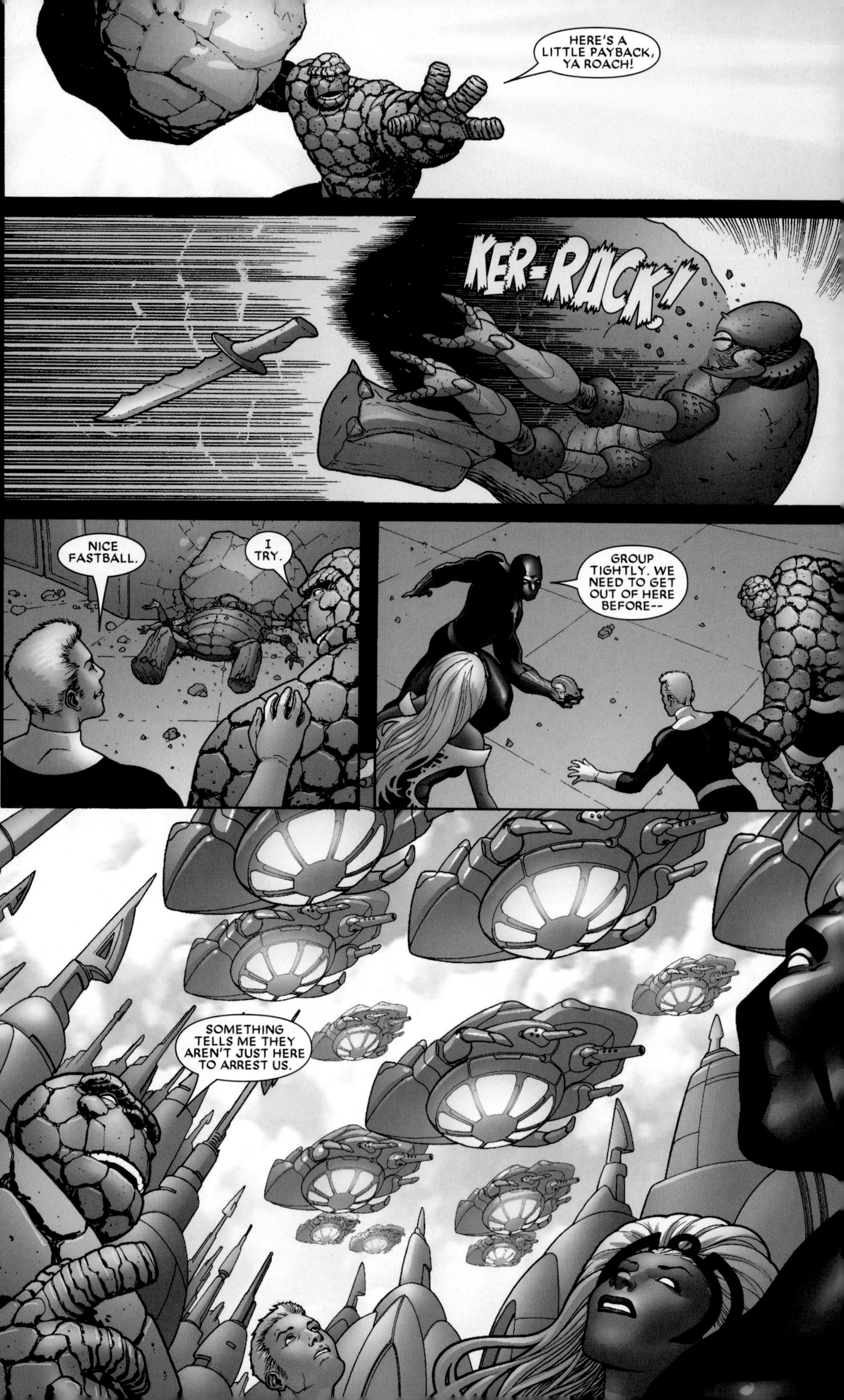
HERE'S A LITTLE PAYBACK, YA ROACH!
KER-RACK!
NICE FASTBALL.
I TRY.
GROUP TIGHTLY. WE NEED TO GET OUT OF HERE BEFORE--
SOMETHING TELLS ME THEY AREN'T JUST HERE TO ARREST US.

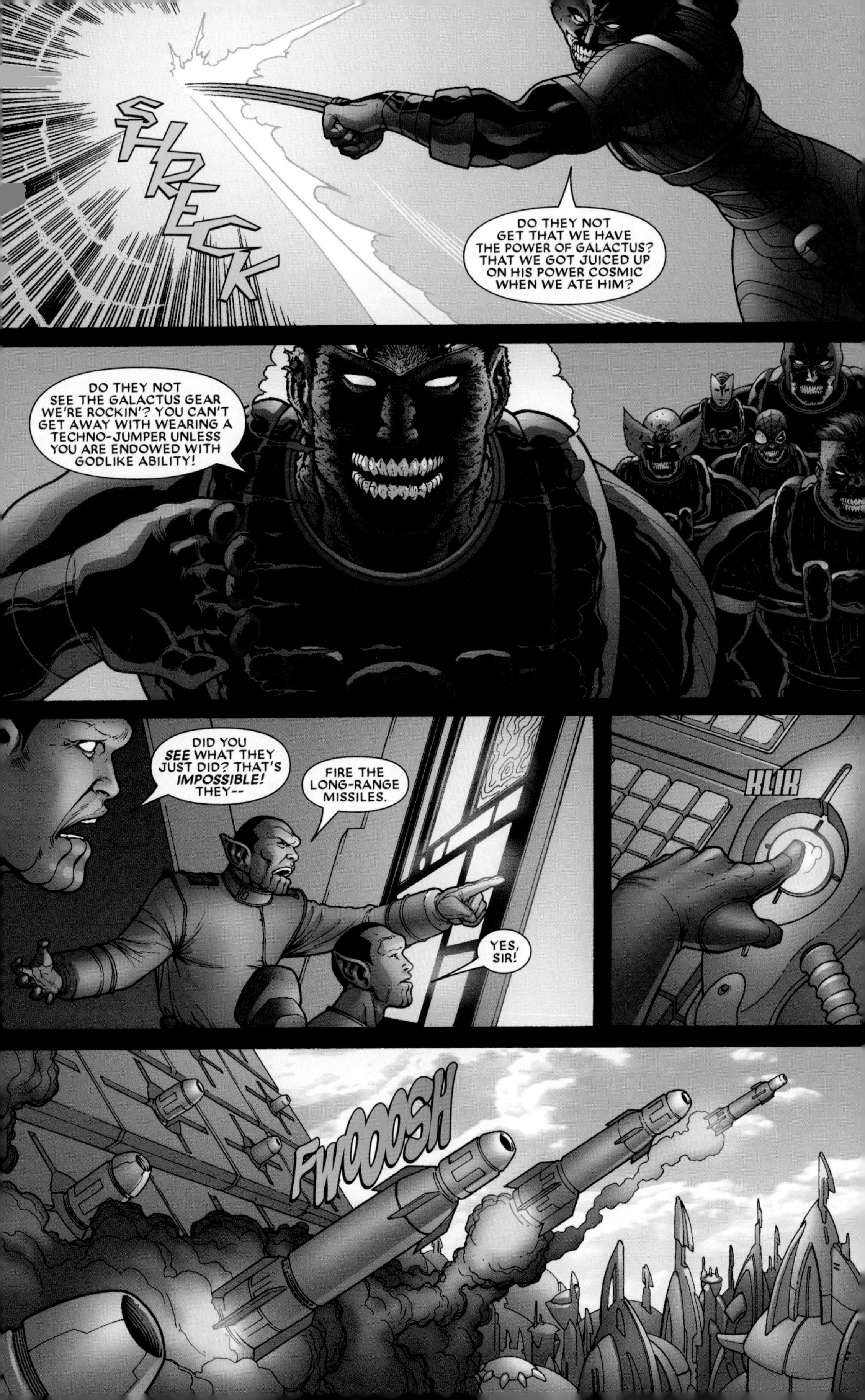
SHRECK
DO THEY NOT GET THAT WE HAVE THE POWER OF GALACTUS? THAT WE GOT JUICED UP ON HIS POWER COSMIC WHEN WE ATE HIM?
DO THEY NOT SEE THE GALACTUS GEAR WE'RE ROCKIN'? YOU CAN'T GET AWAY WITH WEARING A TECHNO-JUMPER UNLESS YOU ARE ENDOWED WITH GODLIKE ABILITY!
DID YOU *SEE* WHAT THEY JUST DID? THAT'S *IMPOSSIBLE!* THEY--
FIRE THE LONG-RANGE MISSILES.
YES, SIR!
KLIK
FWOOOSH

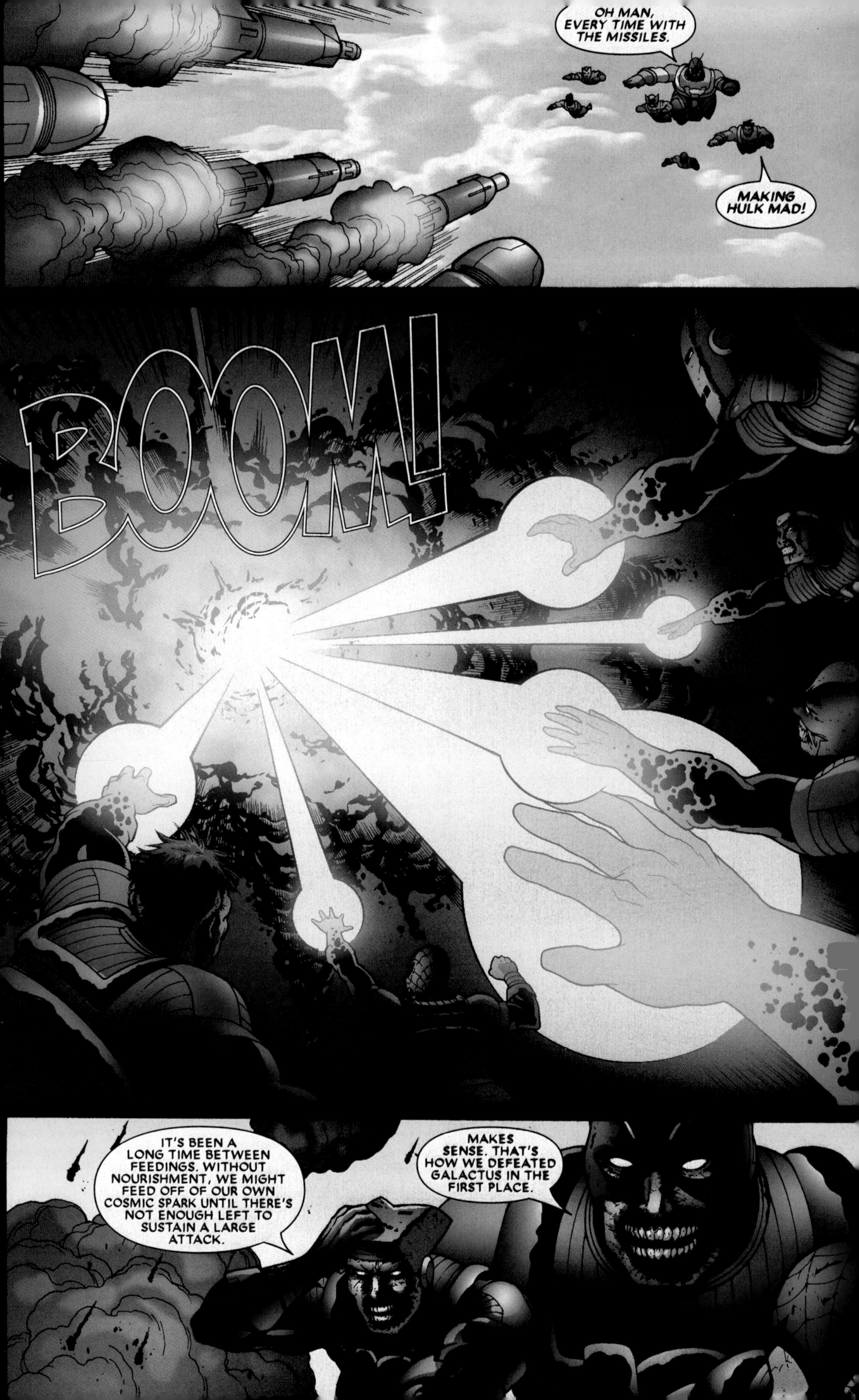
OH MAN, EVERY TIME WITH THE MISSILES.
MAKING HULK MAD!
BOOM!
IT'S BEEN A LONG TIME BETWEEN FEEDINGS. WITHOUT NOURISHMENT, WE MIGHT FEED OFF OF OUR OWN COSMIC SPARK UNTIL THERE'S NOT ENOUGH LEFT TO SUSTAIN A LARGE ATTACK.
MAKES SENSE. THAT'S HOW WE DEFEATED GALACTUS IN THE FIRST PLACE.

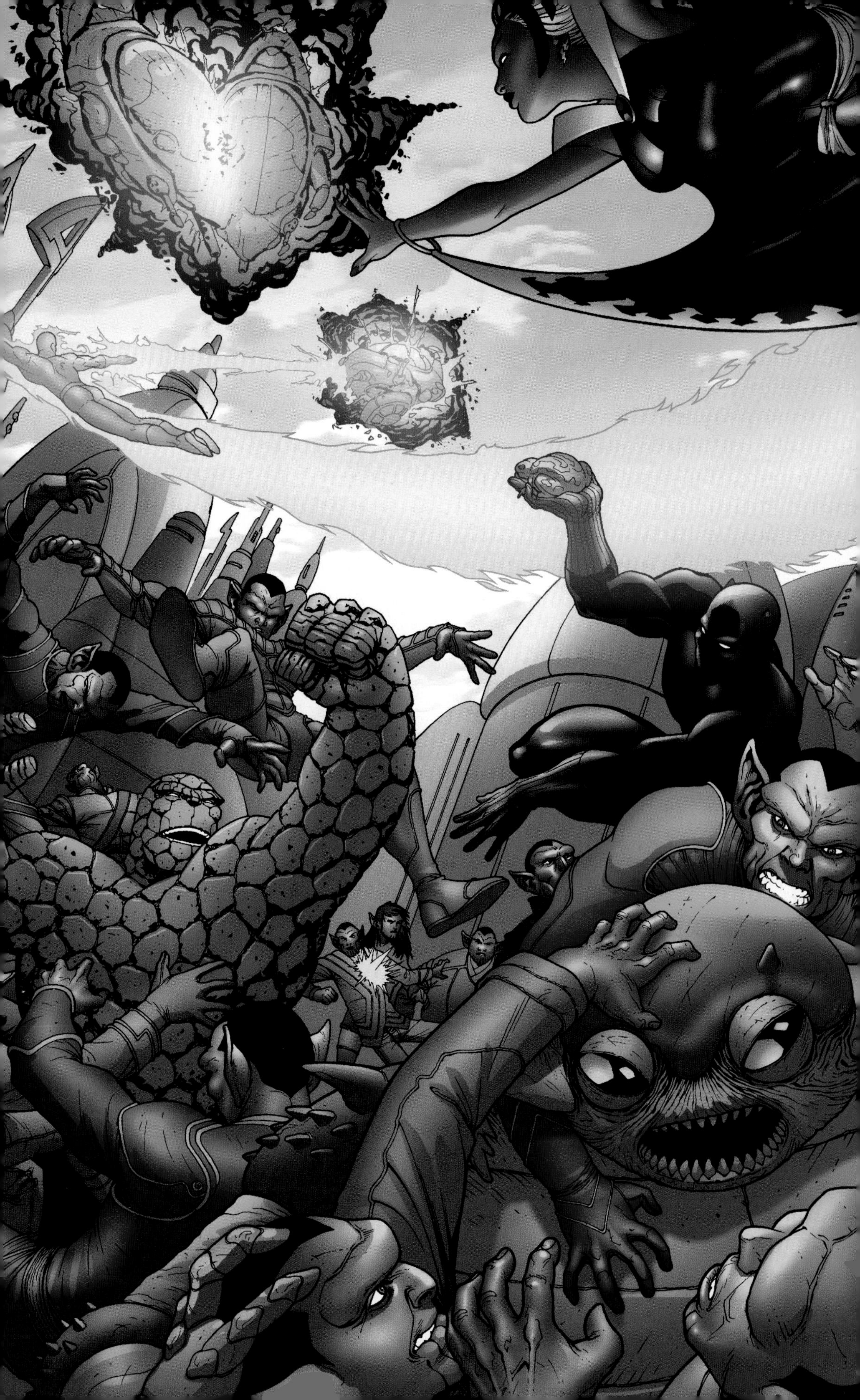

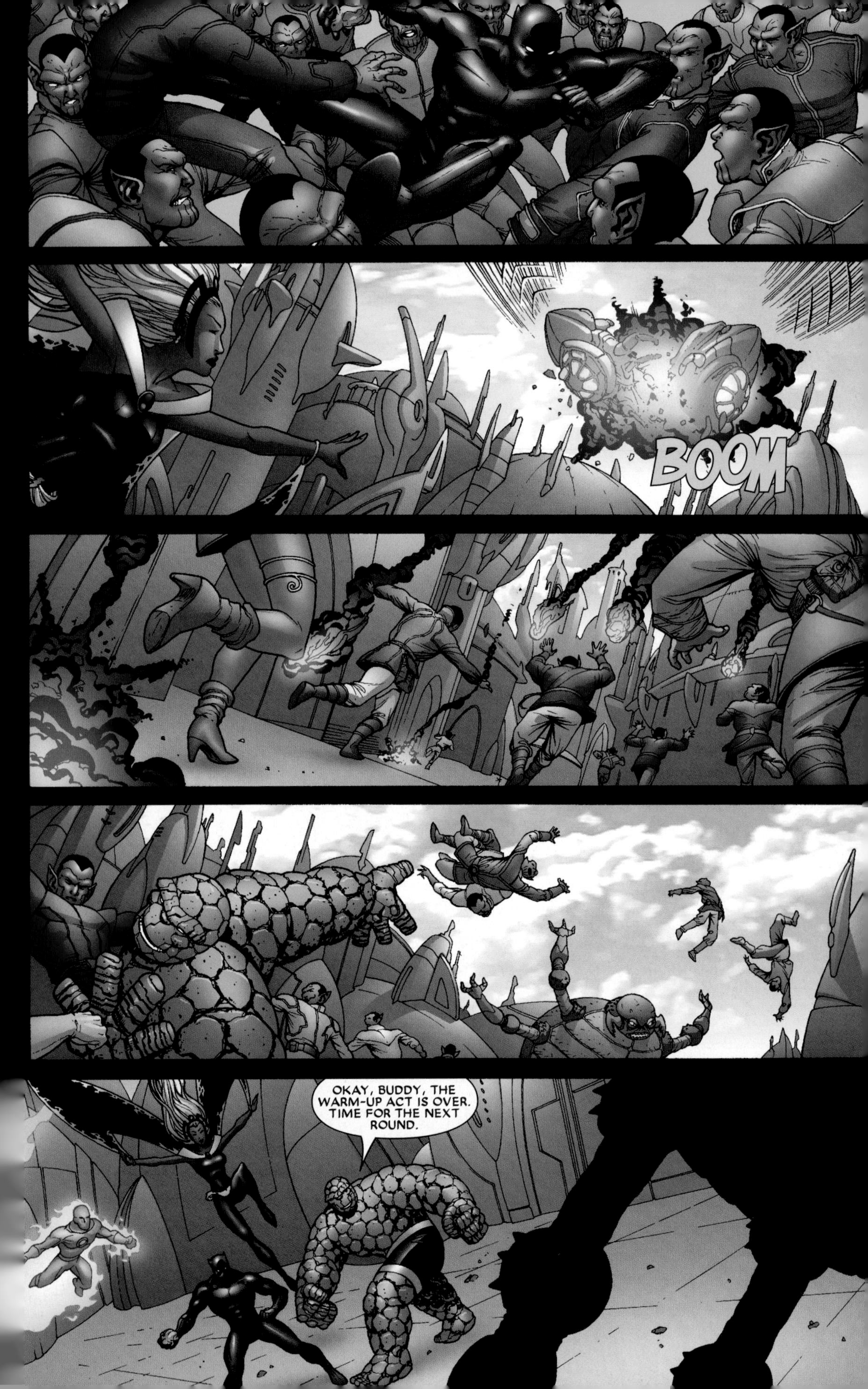
BOOM
OKAY, BUDDY, THE WARM-UP ACT IS OVER. TIME FOR THE NEXT ROUND.

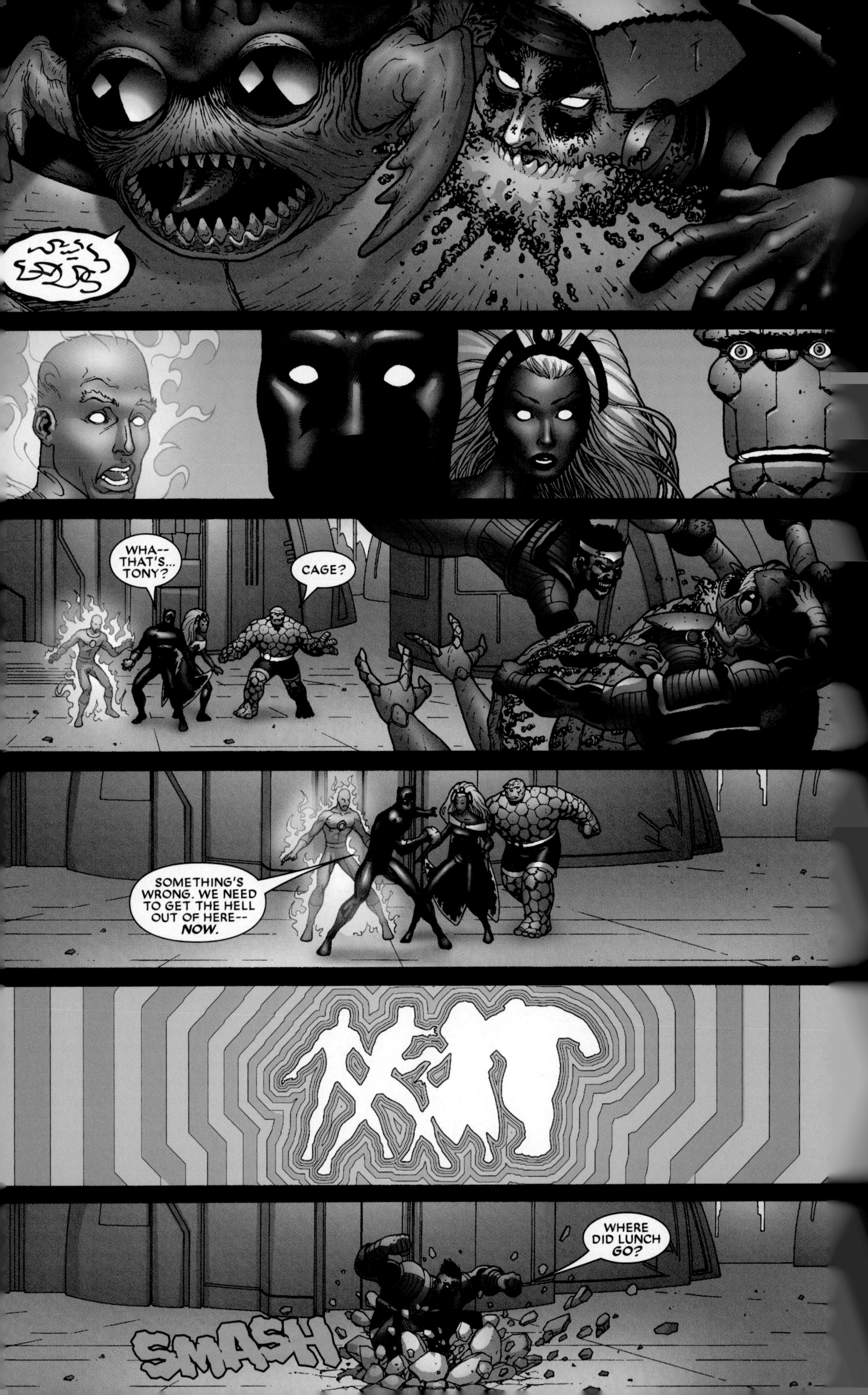
WHA-- THAT'S... TONY?
CAGE?
SOMETHING'S WRONG. WE NEED TO GET THE HELL OUT OF HERE-- NOW.
WHERE DID LUNCH GO?
SMASH

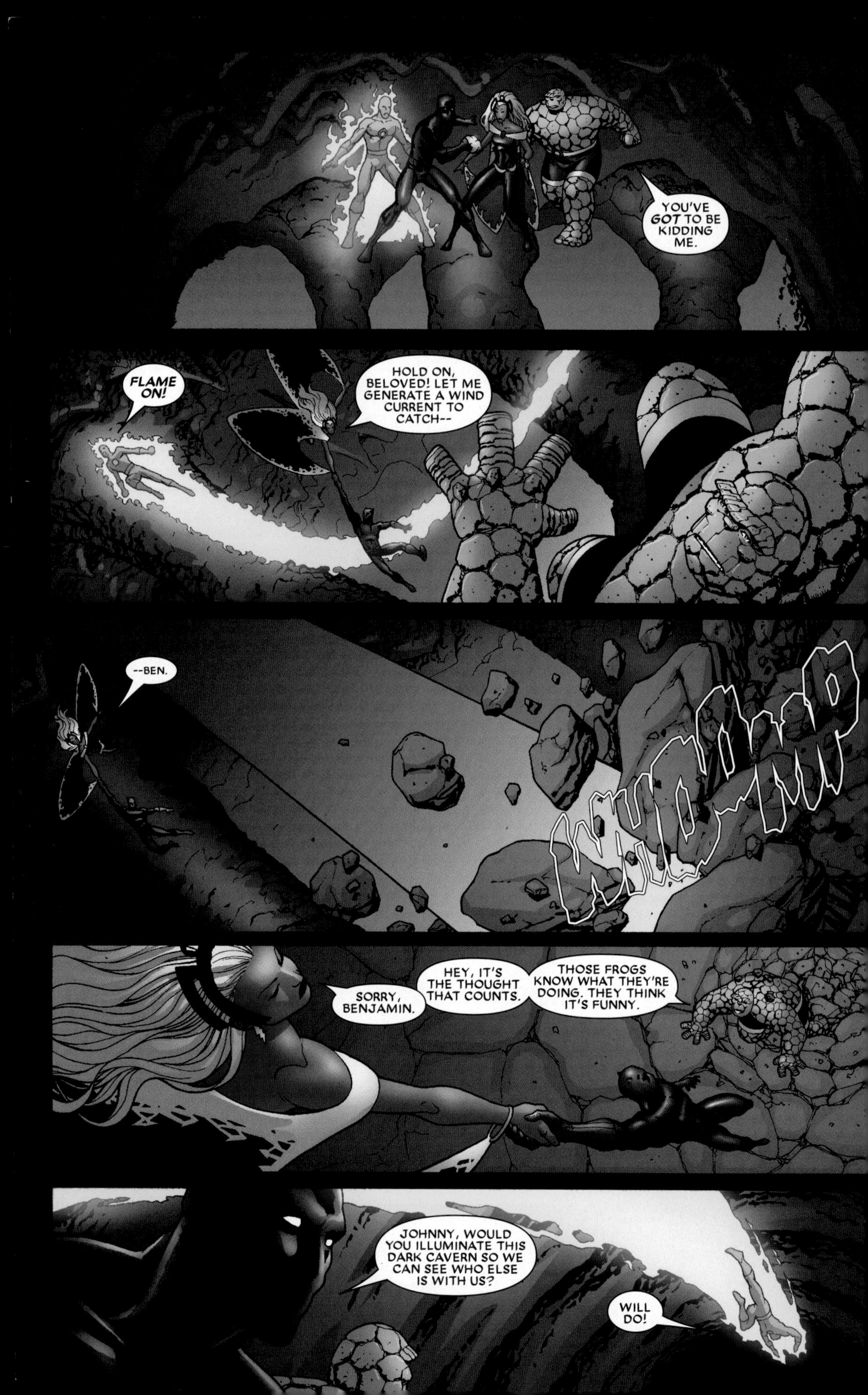
YOU'VE *GOT* TO BE KIDDING ME.
FLAME ON!
HOLD ON, BELOVED! LET ME GENERATE A WIND CURRENT TO CATCH--
--BEN.
WHOOMP
SORRY, BENJAMIN.
HEY, IT'S THE THOUGHT THAT COUNTS.
THOSE FROGS KNOW WHAT THEY'RE DOING. THEY THINK IT'S FUNNY.
JOHNNY, WOULD YOU ILLUMINATE THIS DARK CAVERN SO WE CAN SEE WHO ELSE IS WITH US?
WILL DO!

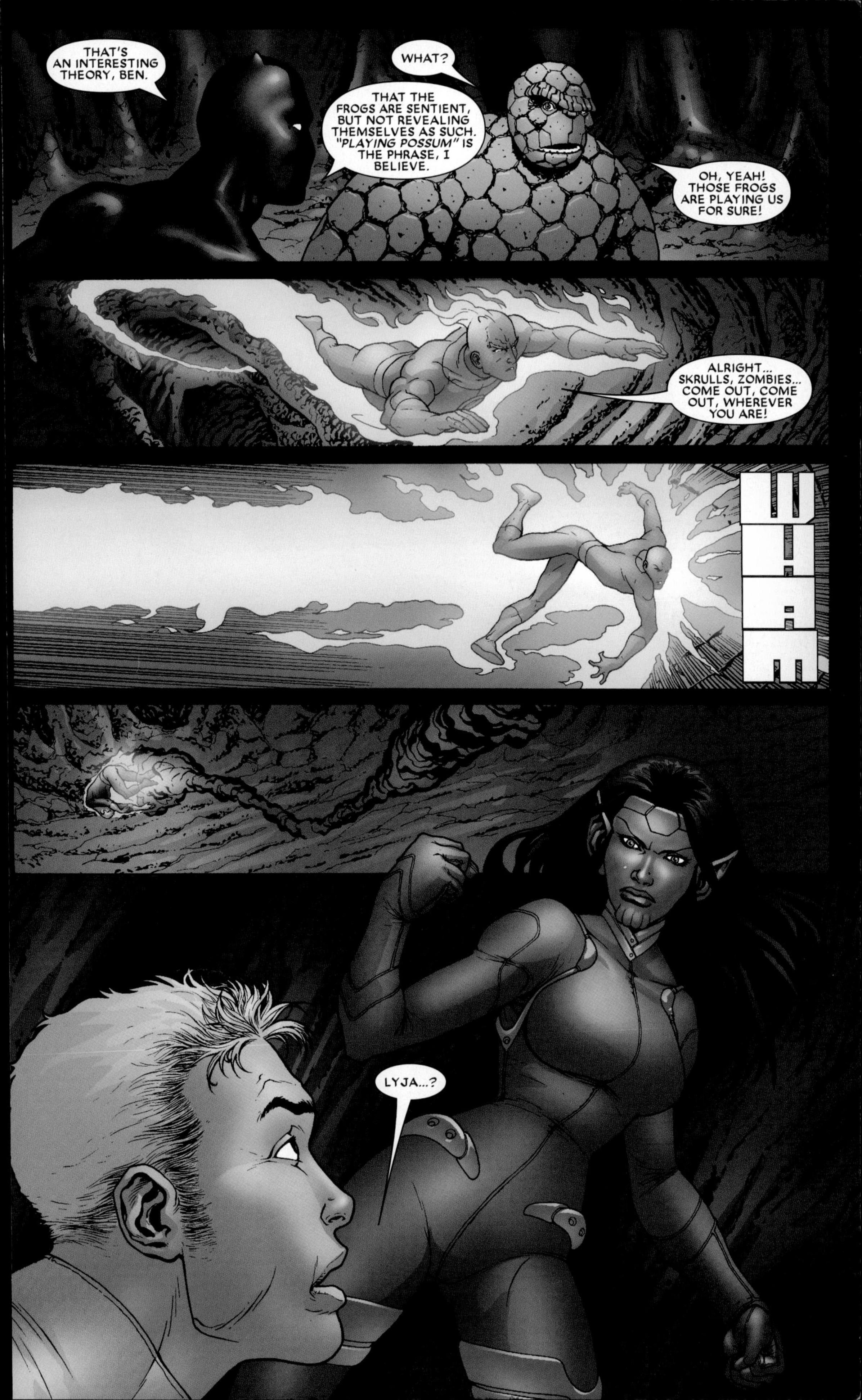
THAT'S AN INTERESTING THEORY, BEN.
WHAT?
THAT THE FROGS ARE SENTIENT, BUT NOT REVEALING THEMSELVES AS SUCH. "PLAYING POSSUM" IS THE PHRASE, I BELIEVE.
OH, YEAH! THOSE FROGS ARE PLAYING US FOR SURE!
ALRIGHT... SKRULLS, ZOMBIES... COME OUT, COME OUT, WHEREVER YOU ARE!
WHAM
LYJA...?

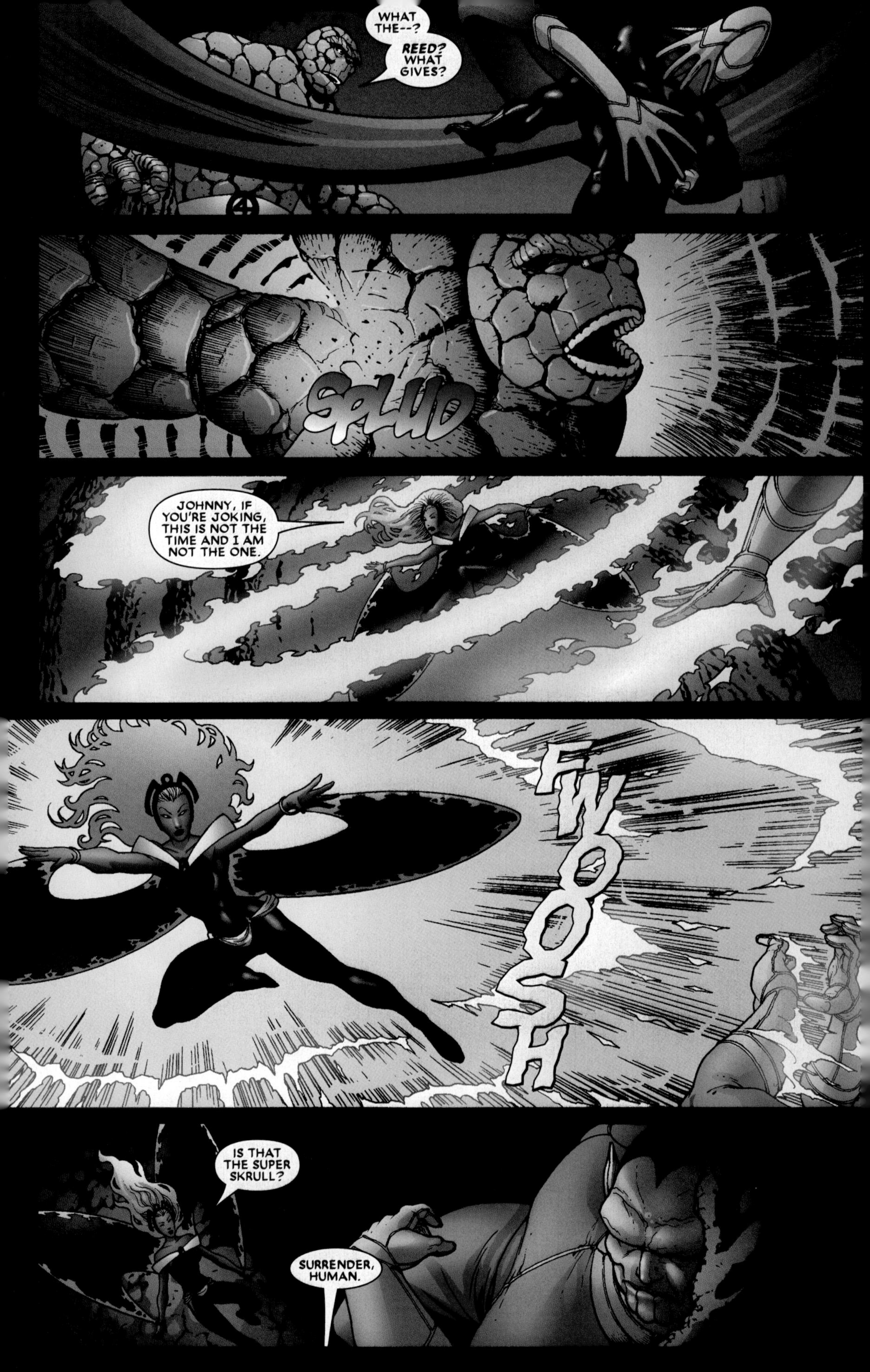

WHAT THE--? REED? WHAT GIVES?
SPLUD
JOHNNY, IF YOU'RE JOKING, THIS IS NOT THE TIME AND I AM NOT THE ONE.
FWOOSH
IS THAT THE SUPER SKRULL?
SURRENDER, HUMAN.

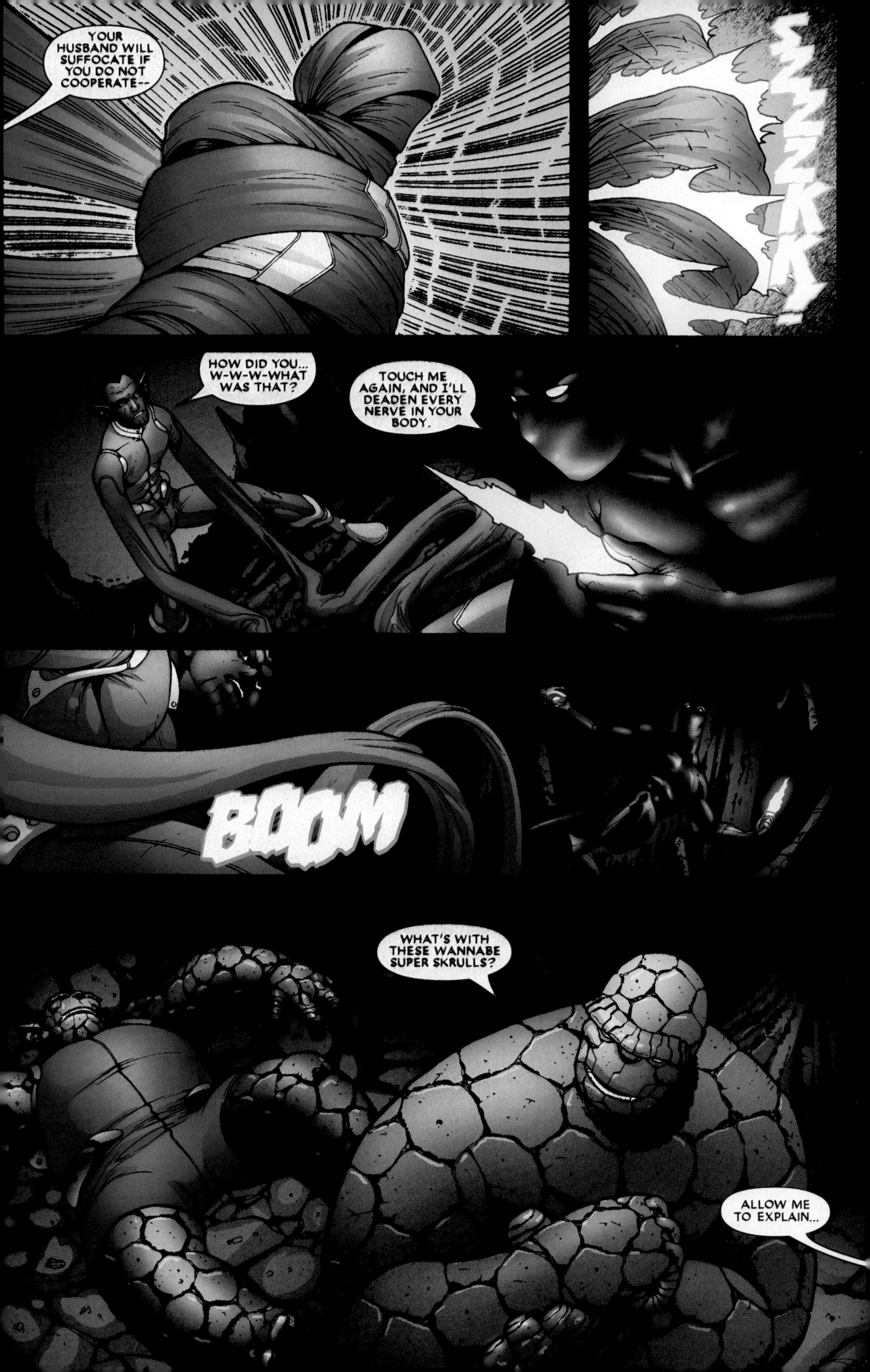
YOUR HUSBAND WILL SUFFOCATE IF YOU DO NOT COOPERATE--
SSSZZKK!
HOW DID YOU.. W-W-W-WHAT WAS THAT?
TOUCH ME AGAIN, AND I'LL DEADEN EVERY NERVE IN YOUR BODY.
BOOM
WHAT'S WITH THESE WANNABE SUPER SKRULLS?
ALLOW ME TO EXPLAIN...

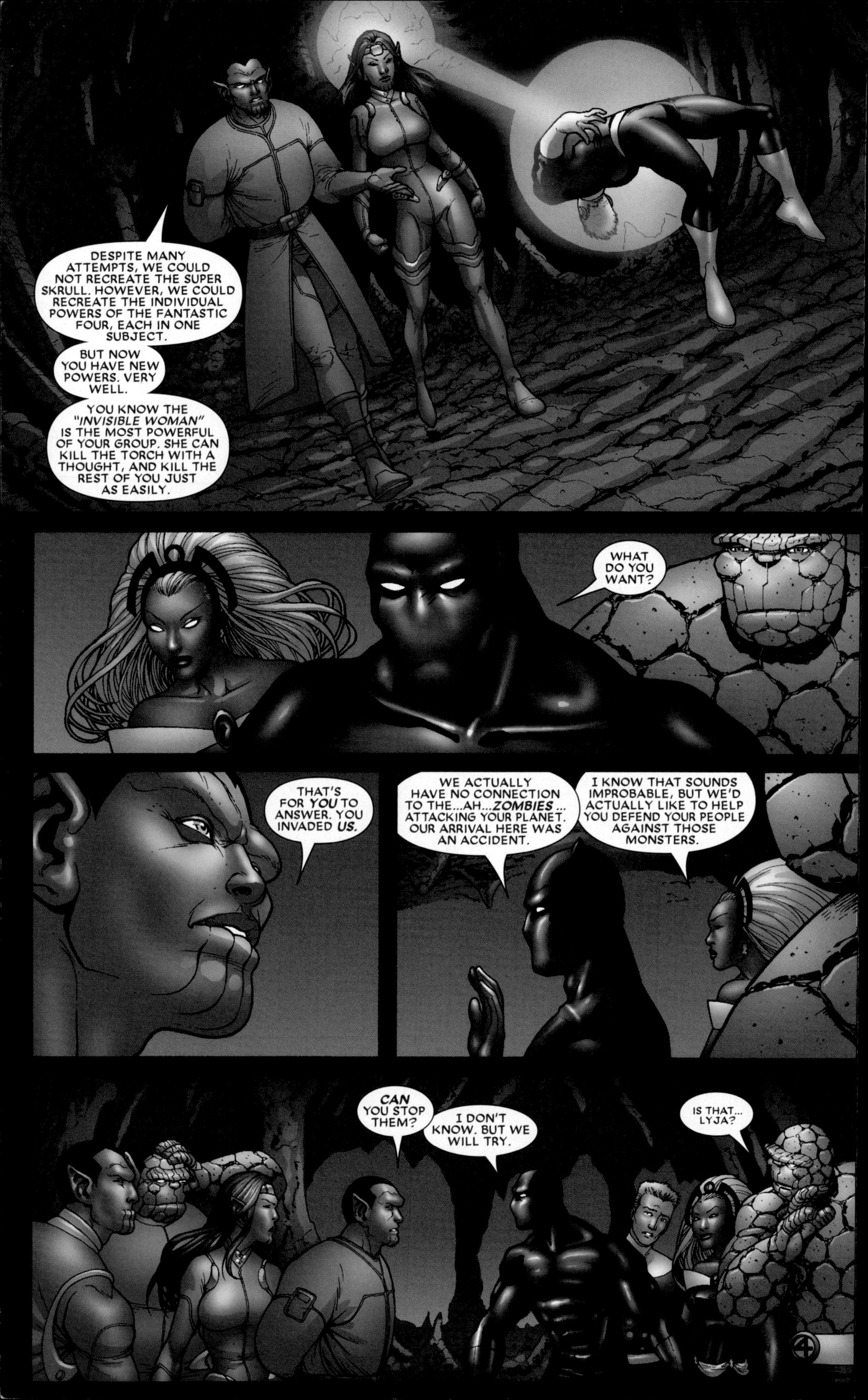
DESPITE MANY ATTEMPTS, WE COULD NOT RECREATE THE SUPER SKRULL. HOWEVER, WE COULD RECREATE THE INDIVIDUAL POWERS OF THE FANTASTIC FOUR, EACH IN ONE SUBJECT.
BUT NOW YOU HAVE NEW POWERS. VERY WELL.
YOU KNOW THE "INVISIBLE WOMAN" IS THE MOST POWERFUL OF YOUR GROUP. SHE CAN KILL THE TORCH WITH A THOUGHT, AND KILL THE REST OF YOU JUST AS EASILY.
WHAT DO YOU WANT?
THAT'S FOR YOU TO ANSWER. YOU INVADED US.
WE ACTUALLY HAVE NO CONNECTION TO THE...AH...ZOMBIES... ATTACKING YOUR PLANET. OUR ARRIVAL HERE WAS AN ACCIDENT.
I KNOW THAT SOUNDS IMPROBABLE, BUT WE'D ACTUALLY LIKE TO HELP YOU DEFEND YOUR PEOPLE AGAINST THOSE MONSTERS.
CAN YOU STOP THEM?
I DON'T KNOW. BUT WE WILL TRY.
IS THAT... LYJA?

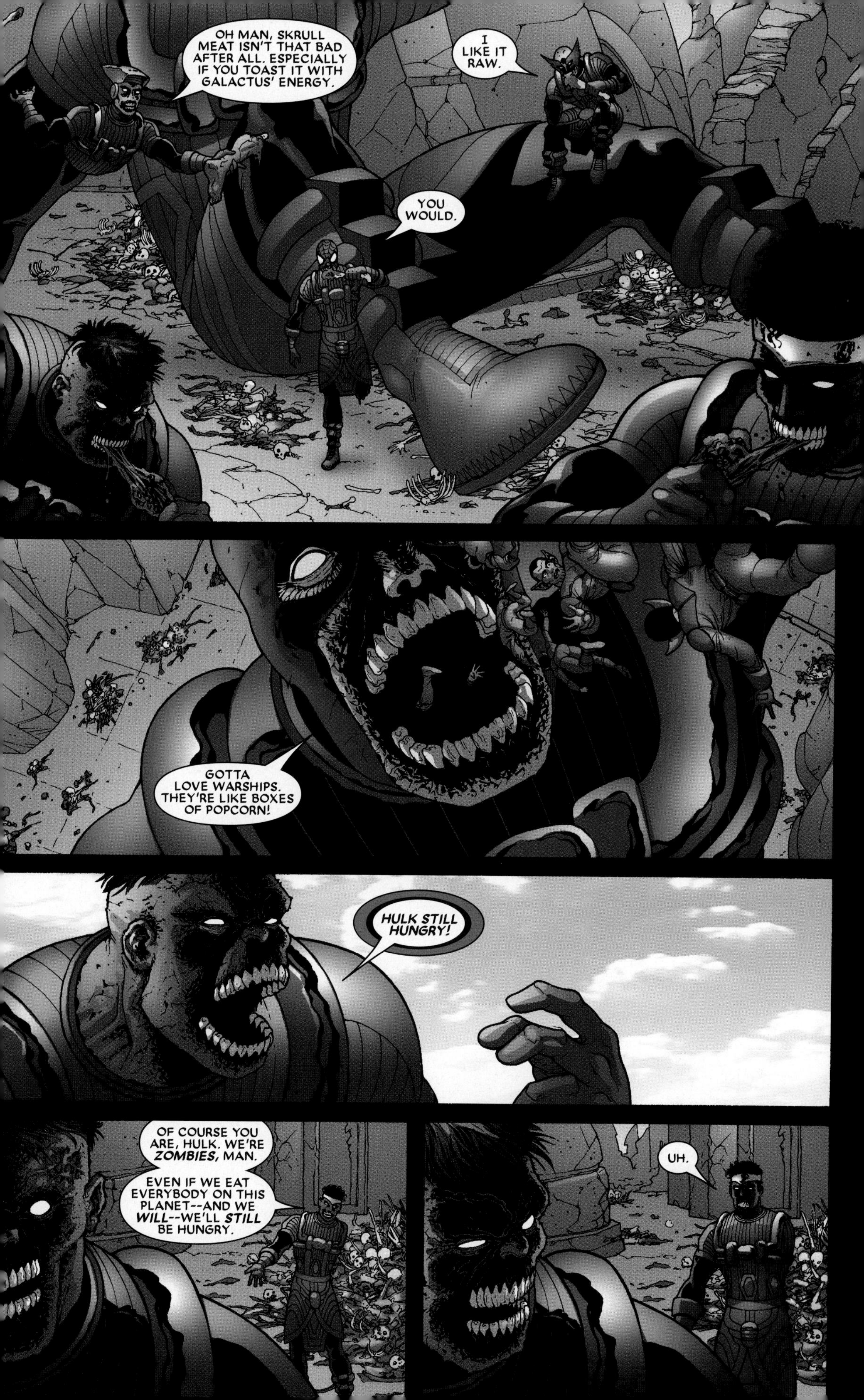
OH MAN, SKRULL MEAT ISN'T THAT BAD AFTER ALL. ESPECIALLY IF YOU TOAST IT WITH GALACTUS' ENERGY.
I LIKE IT RAW.
YOU WOULD.
GOTTA LOVE WARSHIPS. THEY'RE LIKE BOXES OF POPCORN!
HULK STILL HUNGRY!
OF COURSE YOU ARE, HULK. WE'RE ZOMBIES, MAN.
EVEN IF WE EAT EVERYBODY ON THIS PLANET--AND WE WILL--WE'LL STILL BE HUNGRY.
UH.

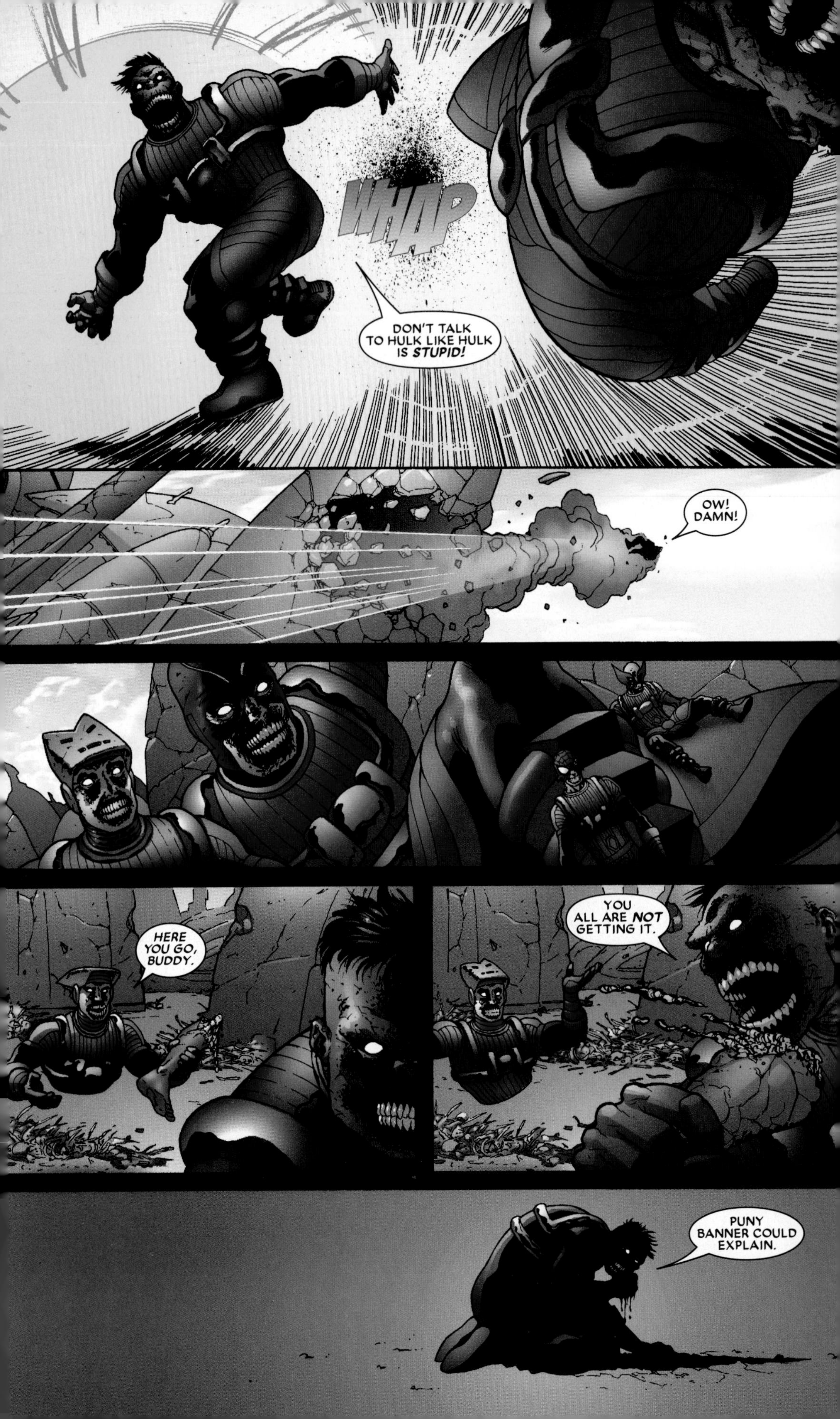
WHAP
DON'T TALK TO HULK LIKE HULK IS *STUPID!*
OW! DAMN!
HERE YOU GO, BUDDY.
YOU ALL ARE *NOT* GETTING IT.
PUNY BANNER COULD EXPLAIN.

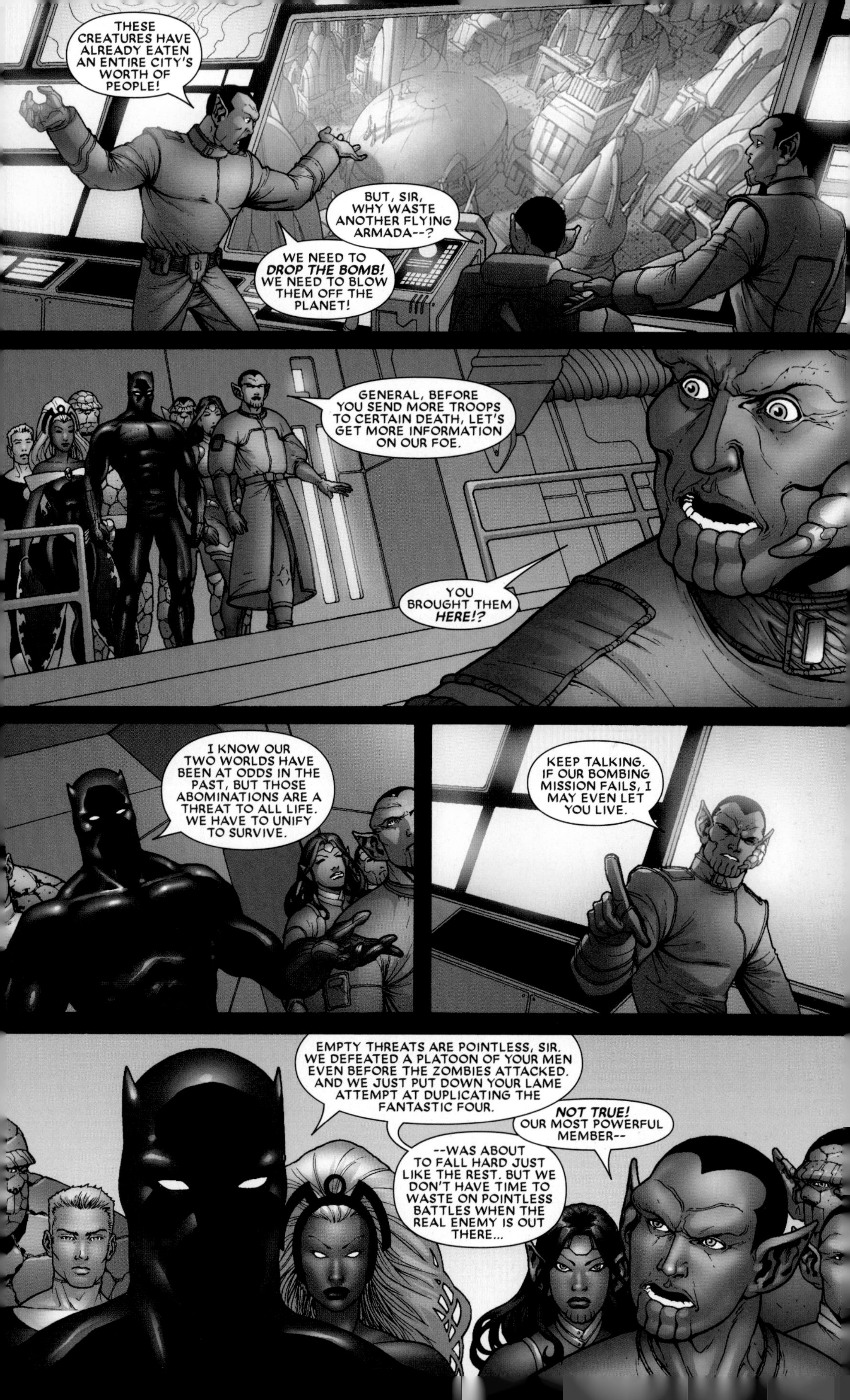
THESE CREATURES HAVE ALREADY EATEN AN ENTIRE CITY'S WORTH OF PEOPLE!
BUT, SIR, WHY WASTE ANOTHER FLYING ARMADA--?
WE NEED TO DROP THE BOMB! WE NEED TO BLOW THEM OFF THE PLANET!
GENERAL, BEFORE YOU SEND MORE TROOPS TO CERTAIN DEATH, LET'S GET MORE INFORMATION ON OUR FOE.
YOU BROUGHT THEM HERE!?
I KNOW OUR TWO WORLDS HAVE BEEN AT ODDS IN THE PAST, BUT THOSE ABOMINATIONS ARE A THREAT TO ALL LIFE. WE HAVE TO UNIFY TO SURVIVE.
KEEP TALKING. IF OUR BOMBING MISSION FAILS, I MAY EVEN LET YOU LIVE.
EMPTY THREATS ARE POINTLESS, SIR. WE DEFEATED A PLATOON OF YOUR MEN EVEN BEFORE THE ZOMBIES ATTACKED. AND WE JUST PUT DOWN YOUR LAME ATTEMPT AT DUPLICATING THE FANTASTIC FOUR.
NOT TRUE! OUR MOST POWERFUL MEMBER--
--WAS ABOUT TO FALL HARD JUST LIKE THE REST. BUT WE DON'T HAVE TIME TO WASTE ON POINTLESS BATTLES WHEN THE REAL ENEMY IS OUT THERE...

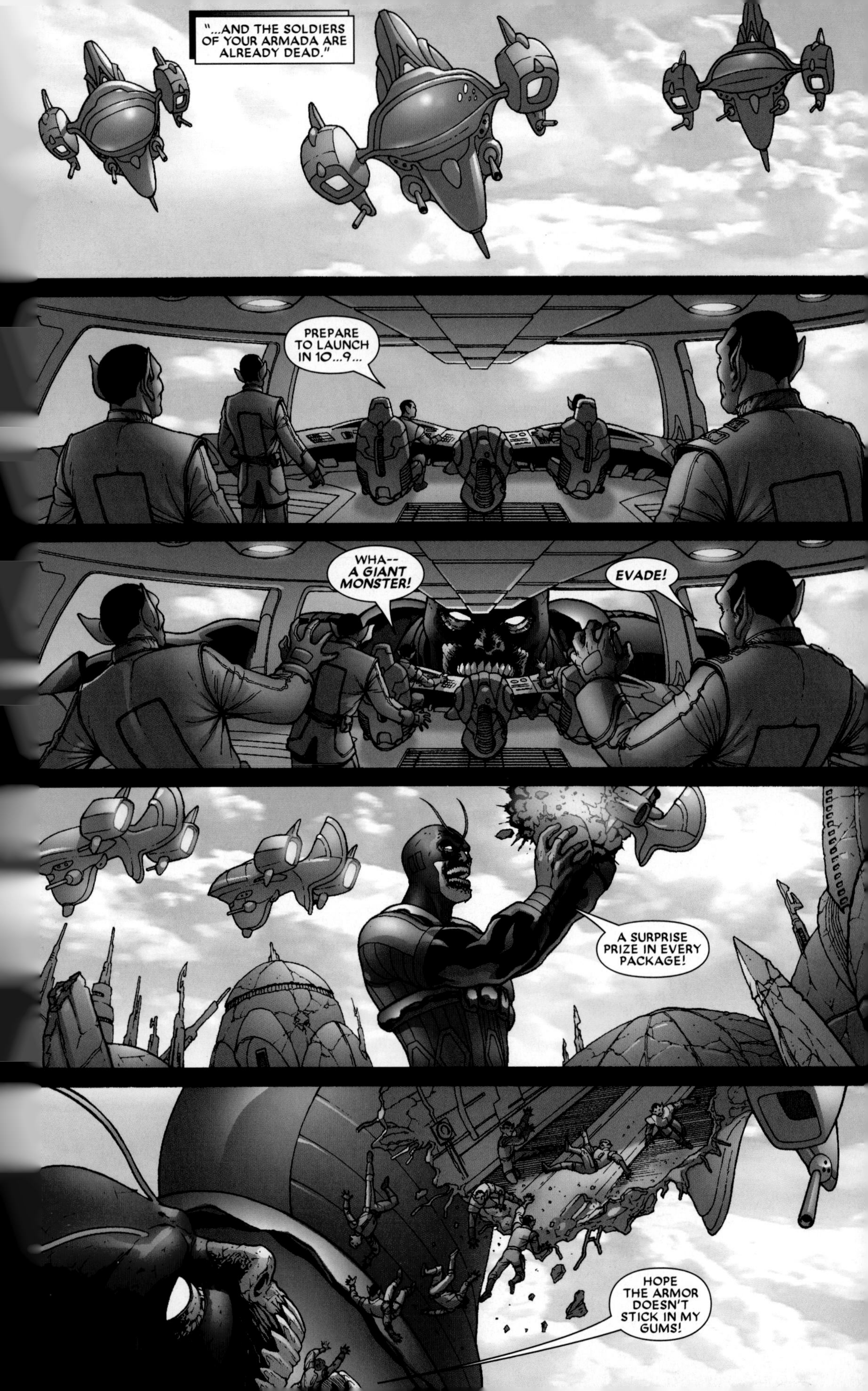
"...AND THE SOLDIERS OF YOUR ARMADA ARE ALREADY DEAD."
PREPARE TO LAUNCH IN 10...9...
WHA-- A GIANT MONSTER!
EVADE!
A SURPRISE PRIZE IN EVERY PACKAGE!
HOPE THE ARMOR DOESN'T STICK IN MY GUMS!

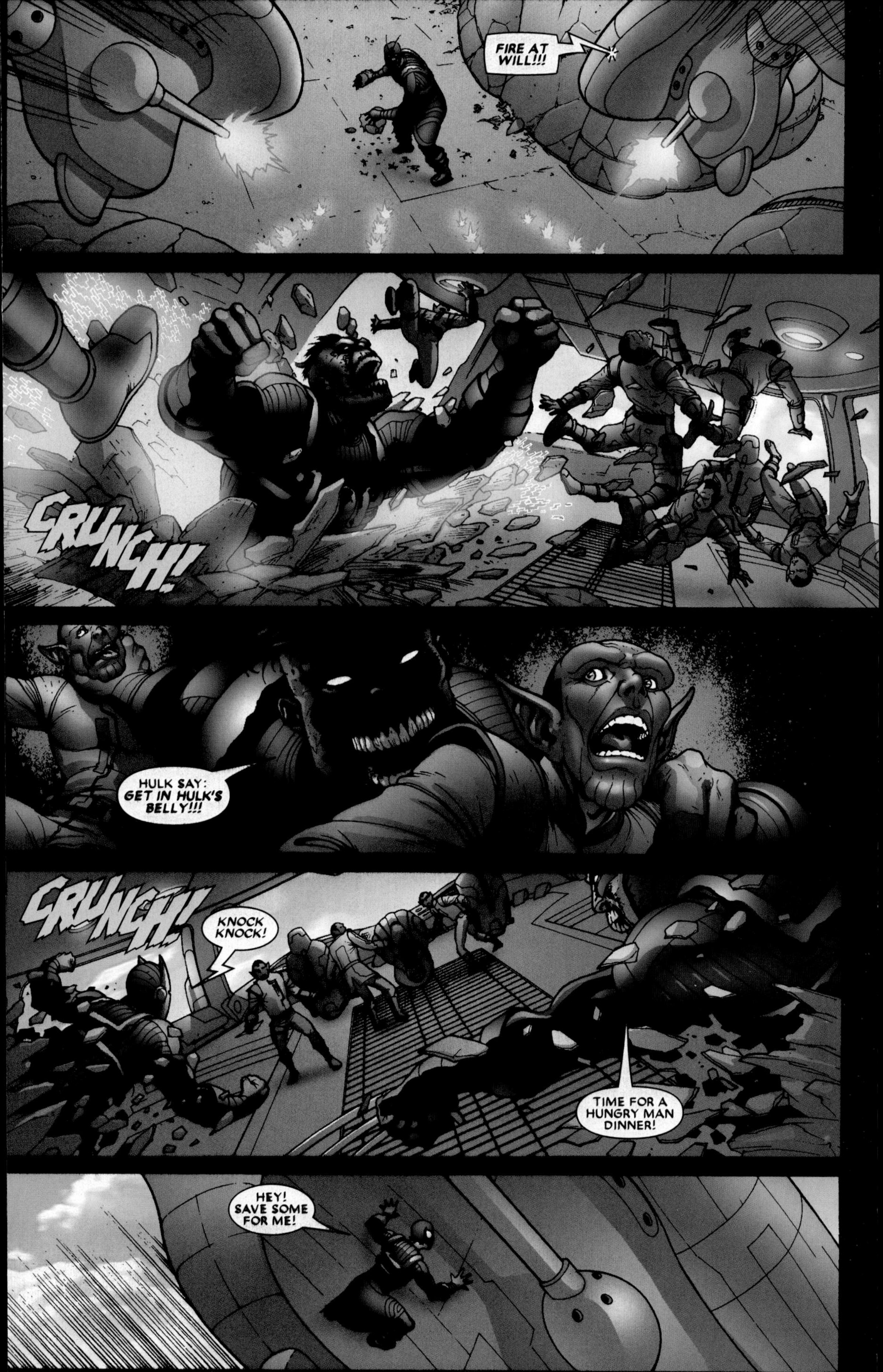
FIRE AT WILL!!!
CRUNCH!
HULK SAY: GET IN HULK'S BELLY!!!
CRUNCH!
KNOCK KNOCK!
TIME FOR A HUNGRY MAN DINNER!
HEY! SAVE SOME FOR ME!

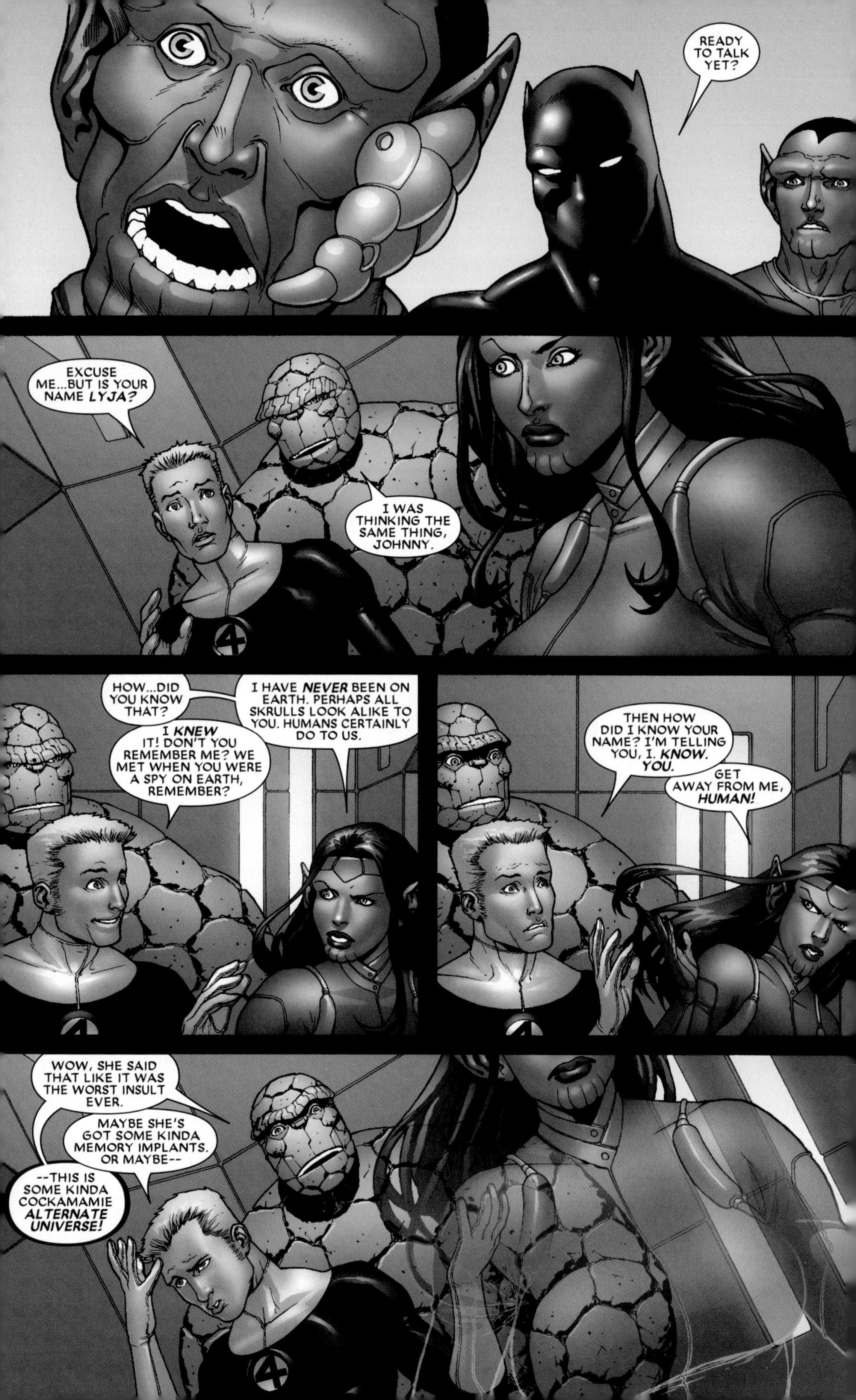
READY TO TALK YET?
EXCUSE ME...BUT IS YOUR NAME LYJA?
I WAS THINKING THE SAME THING, JOHNNY.
HOW...DID YOU KNOW THAT?
I KNEW IT! DON'T YOU REMEMBER ME? WE MET WHEN YOU WERE A SPY ON EARTH, REMEMBER?
I HAVE NEVER BEEN ON EARTH. PERHAPS ALL SKRULLS LOOK ALIKE TO YOU. HUMANS CERTAINLY DO TO US.
THEN HOW DID I KNOW YOUR NAME? I'M TELLING YOU, I. KNOW. YOU.
GET AWAY FROM ME, HUMAN!
WOW, SHE SAID THAT LIKE IT WAS THE WORST INSULT EVER.
MAYBE SHE'S GOT SOME KINDA MEMORY IMPLANTS. OR MAYBE--
--THIS IS SOME KINDA COCKAMAMIE ALTERNATE UNIVERSE!

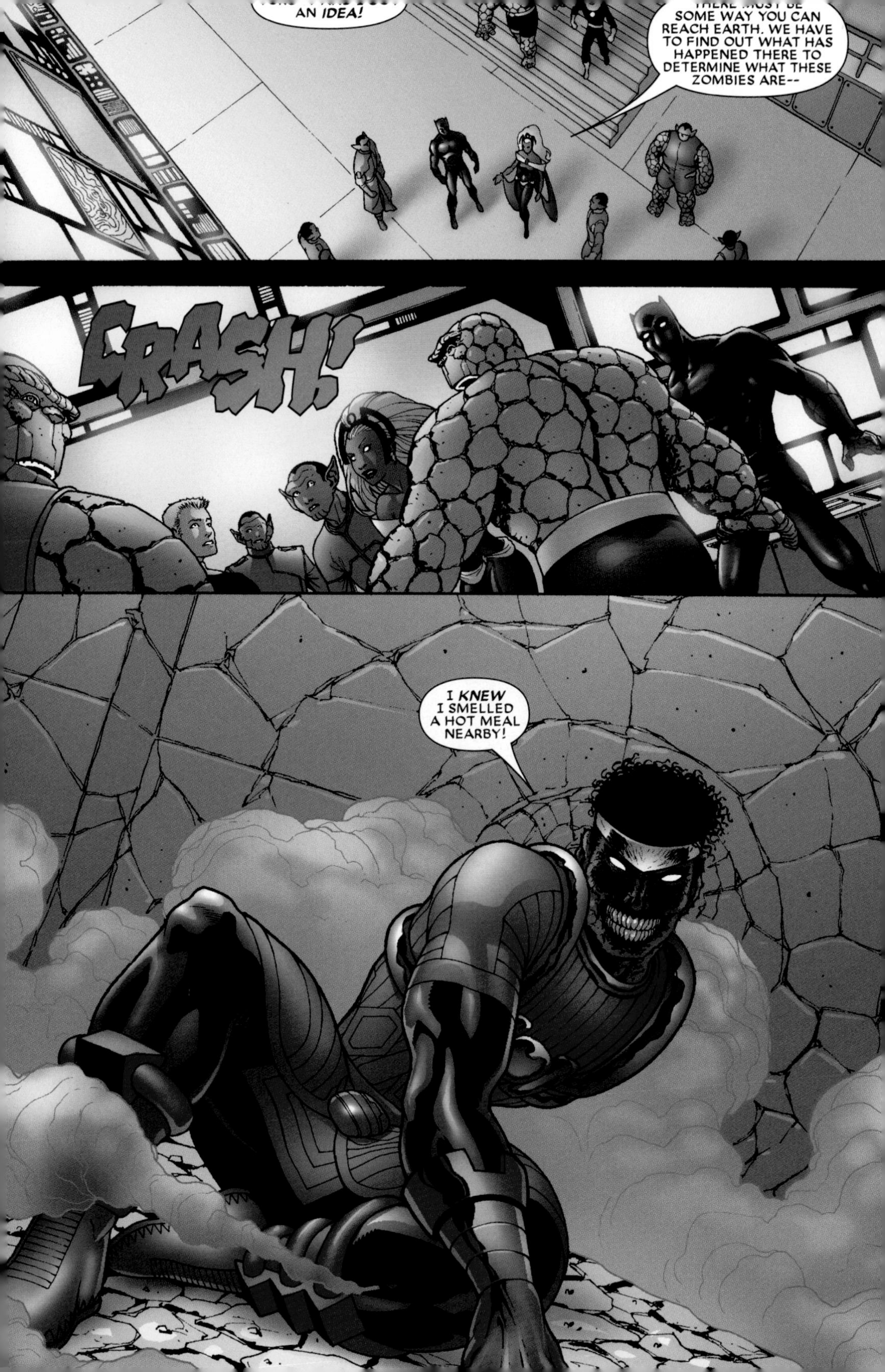
AN IDEA!
SOME WAY YOU CAN REACH EARTH. WE HAVE TO FIND OUT WHAT HAS HAPPENED THERE TO DETERMINE WHAT THESE ZOMBIES ARE--
CRASH!
I KNEW I SMELLED A HOT MEAL NEARBY!

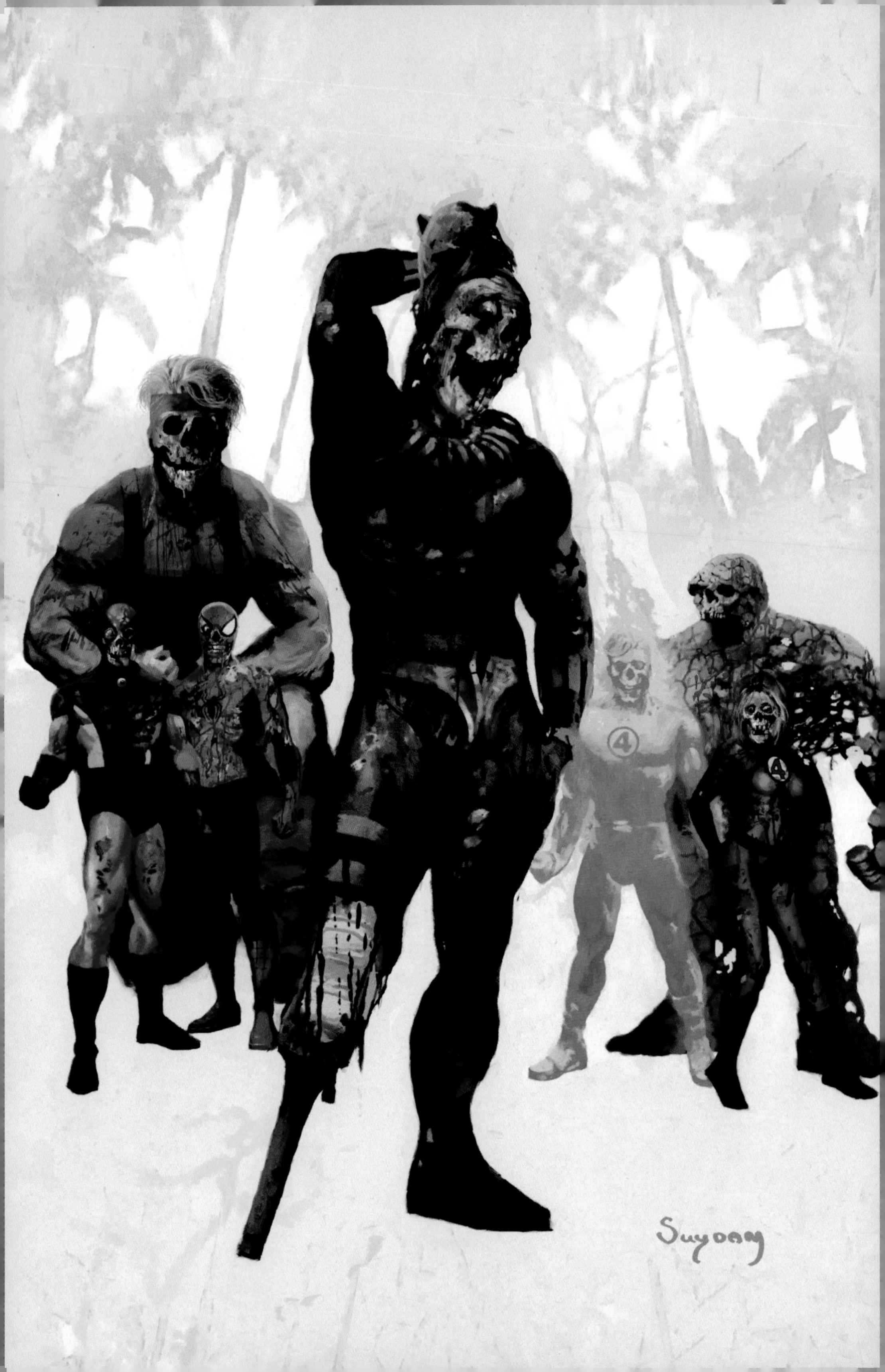
Suydam

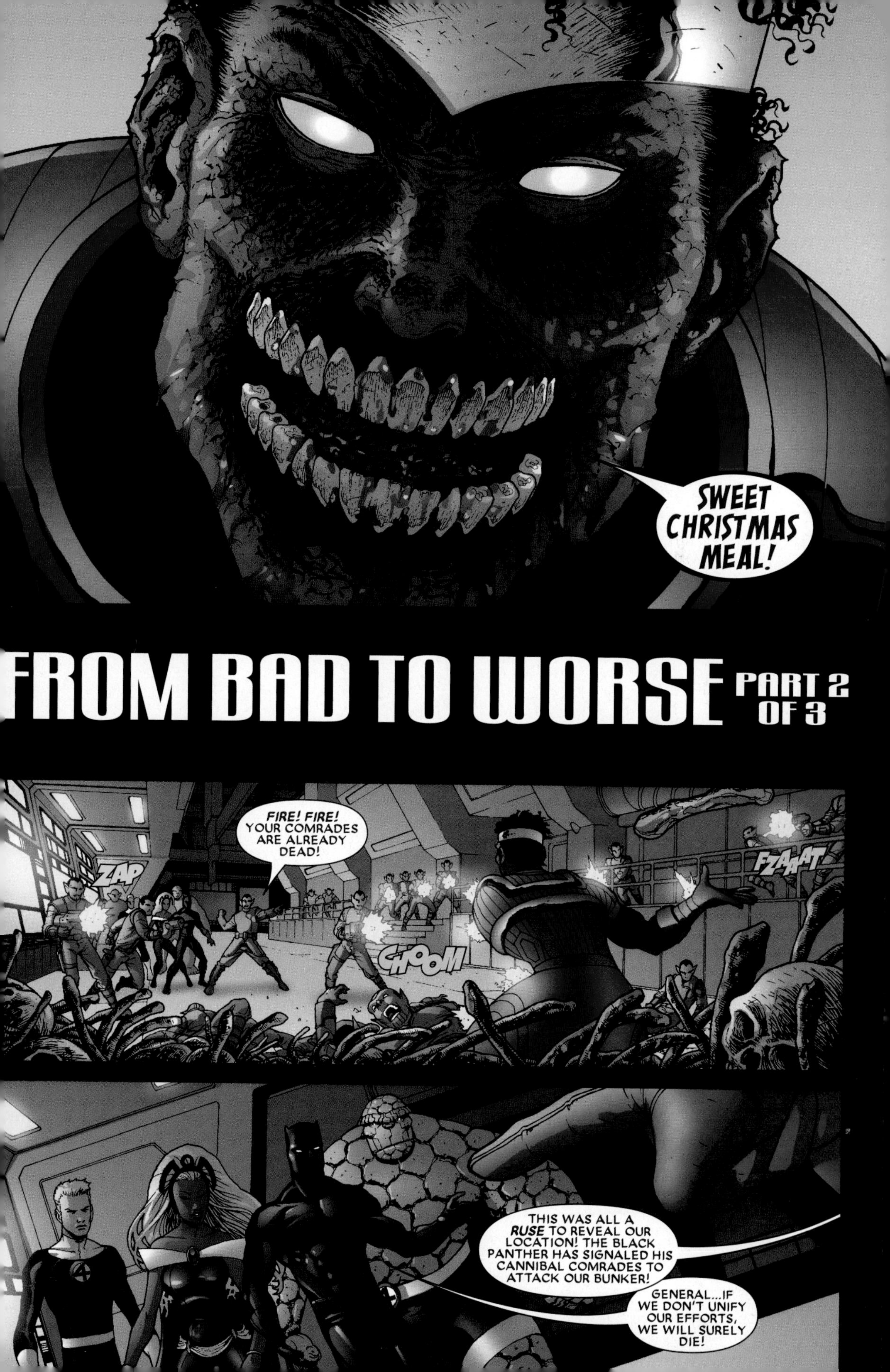
SWEET CHRISTMAS MEAL!
FROM BAD TO WORSE PART 2 OF 3
FIRE! FIRE! YOUR COMRADES ARE ALREADY DEAD!
ZAP
FZAAAT
CHOOM
THIS WAS ALL A RUSE TO REVEAL OUR LOCATION! THE BLACK PANTHER HAS SIGNALED HIS CANNIBAL COMRADES TO ATTACK OUR BUNKER!
GENERAL...IF WE DON'T UNIFY OUR EFFORTS, WE WILL SURELY DIE!

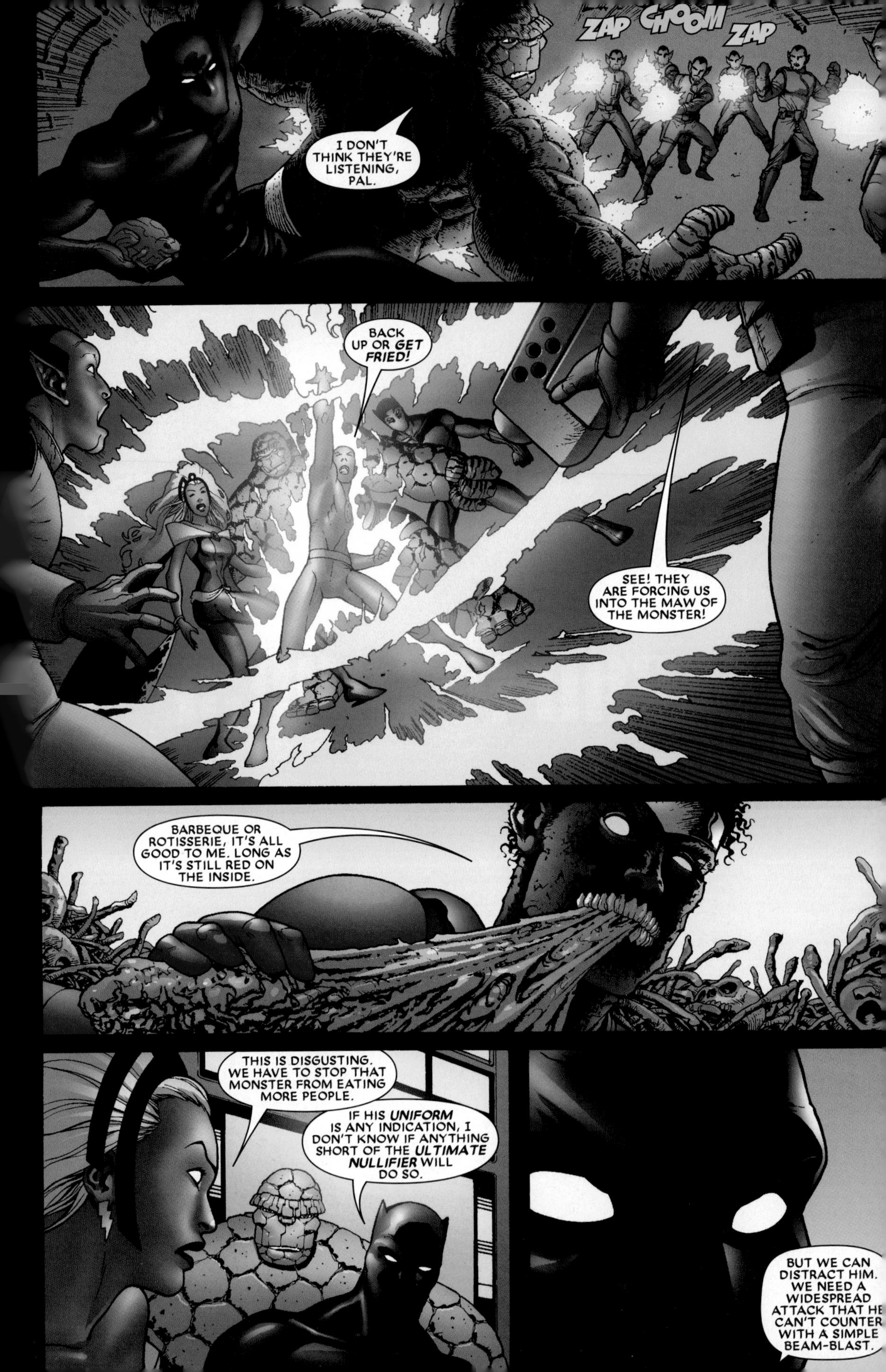
ZAP CHOOM ZAP
I DON'T THINK THEY'RE LISTENING, PAL.
BACK UP OR GET FRIED!
SEE! THEY ARE FORCING US INTO THE MAW OF THE MONSTER!
BARBEQUE OR ROTISSERIE, IT'S ALL GOOD TO ME. LONG AS IT'S STILL RED ON THE INSIDE.
THIS IS DISGUSTING. WE HAVE TO STOP THAT MONSTER FROM EATING MORE PEOPLE.
IF HIS UNIFORM IS ANY INDICATION, I DON'T KNOW IF ANYTHING SHORT OF THE ULTIMATE NULLIFIER WILL DO SO.
BUT WE CAN DISTRACT HIM. WE NEED A WIDESPREAD ATTACK THAT HE CAN'T COUNTER WITH A SIMPLE BEAM-BLAST.

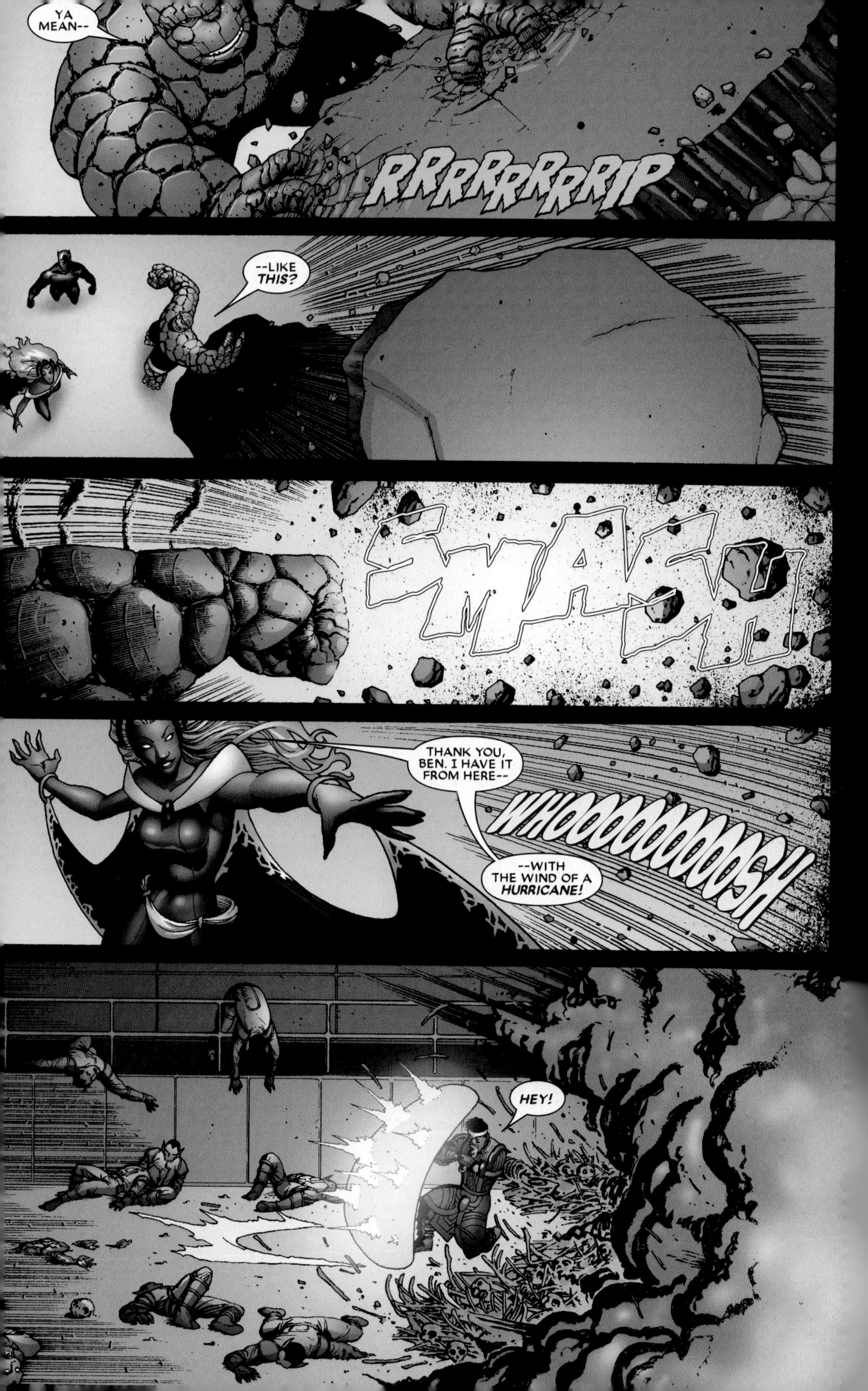
YA MEAN--
RRRRRRRRRIP
--LIKE THIS?
SMACK
THANK YOU, BEN. I HAVE IT FROM HERE--
WHOOOOOOOOOSH
--WITH THE WIND OF A HURRICANE!
HEY!

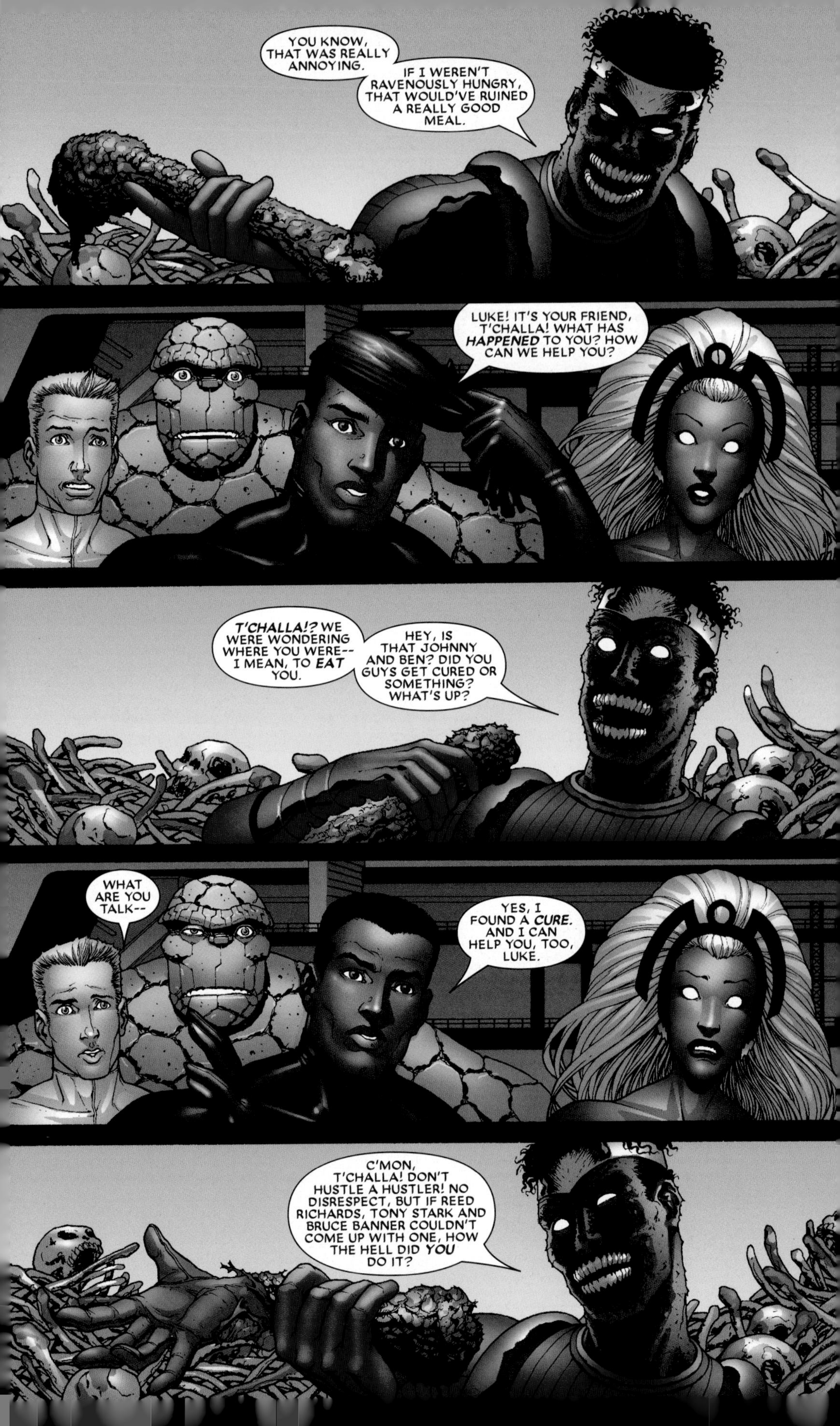
YOU KNOW, THAT WAS REALLY ANNOYING.
IF I WEREN'T RAVENOUSLY HUNGRY, THAT WOULD'VE RUINED A REALLY GOOD MEAL.
LUKE! IT'S YOUR FRIEND, T'CHALLA! WHAT HAS *HAPPENED* TO YOU? HOW CAN WE HELP YOU?
T'CHALLA!? WE WERE WONDERING WHERE YOU WERE-- I MEAN, TO *EAT* YOU.
HEY, IS THAT JOHNNY AND BEN? DID YOU GUYS GET CURED OR SOMETHING? WHAT'S UP?
WHAT ARE YOU TALK--
YES, I FOUND A *CURE.* AND I CAN HELP YOU, TOO, LUKE.
C'MON, T'CHALLA! DON'T HUSTLE A HUSTLER! NO DISRESPECT, BUT IF REED RICHARDS, TONY STARK AND BRUCE BANNER COULDN'T COME UP WITH ONE, HOW THE HELL DID *YOU* DO IT?

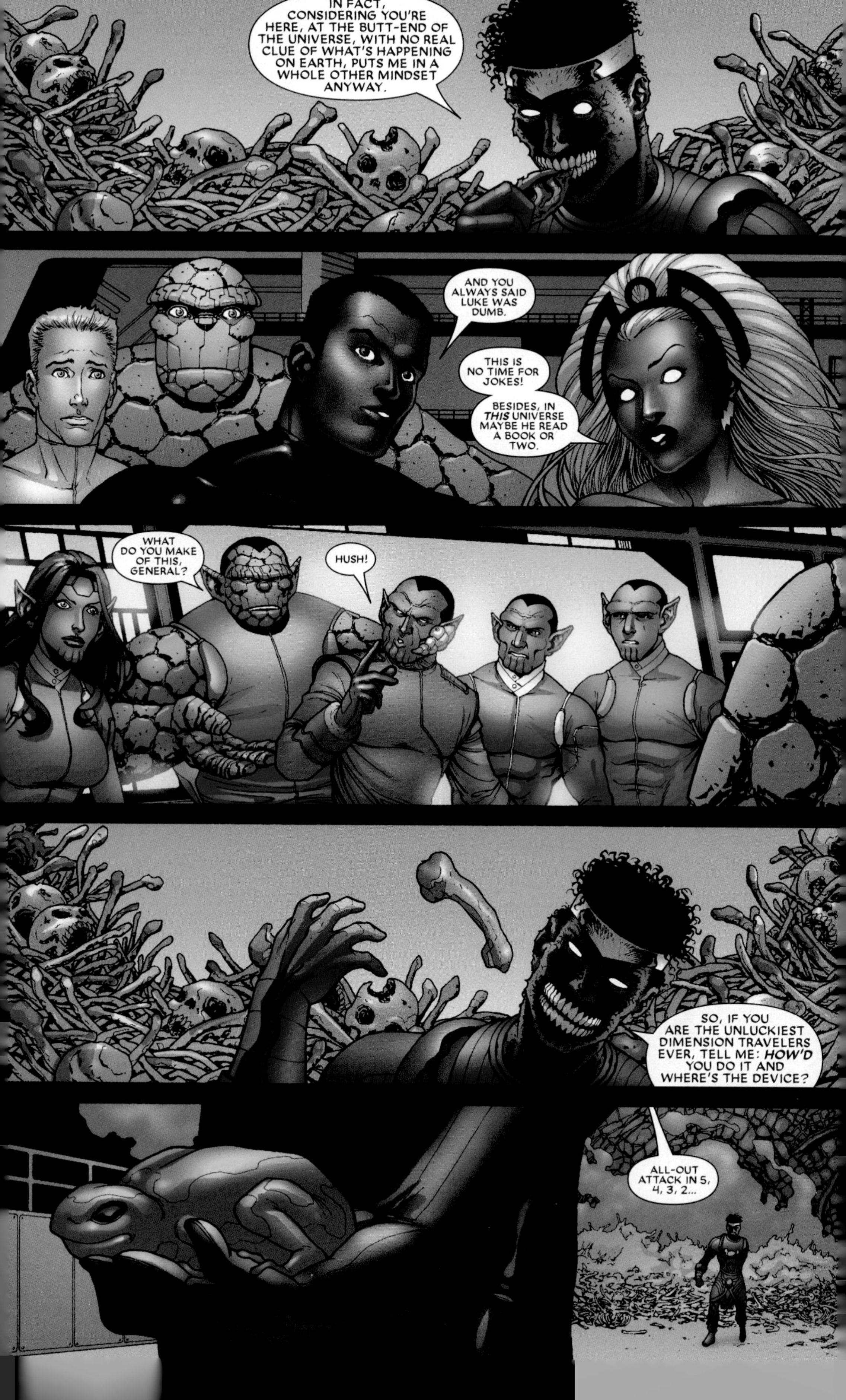
IN FACT, CONSIDERING YOU'RE HERE, AT THE BUTT-END OF THE UNIVERSE, WITH NO REAL CLUE OF WHAT'S HAPPENING ON EARTH, PUTS ME IN A WHOLE OTHER MINDSET ANYWAY.
AND YOU ALWAYS SAID LUKE WAS DUMB.
THIS IS NO TIME FOR JOKES!
BESIDES, IN *THIS* UNIVERSE MAYBE HE READ A BOOK OR TWO.
WHAT DO YOU MAKE OF THIS, GENERAL?
HUSH!
SO, IF YOU ARE THE UNLUCKIEST DIMENSION TRAVELERS EVER, TELL ME: *HOW'D* YOU DO IT AND WHERE'S THE DEVICE?
ALL-OUT ATTACK IN 5, 4, 3, 2...

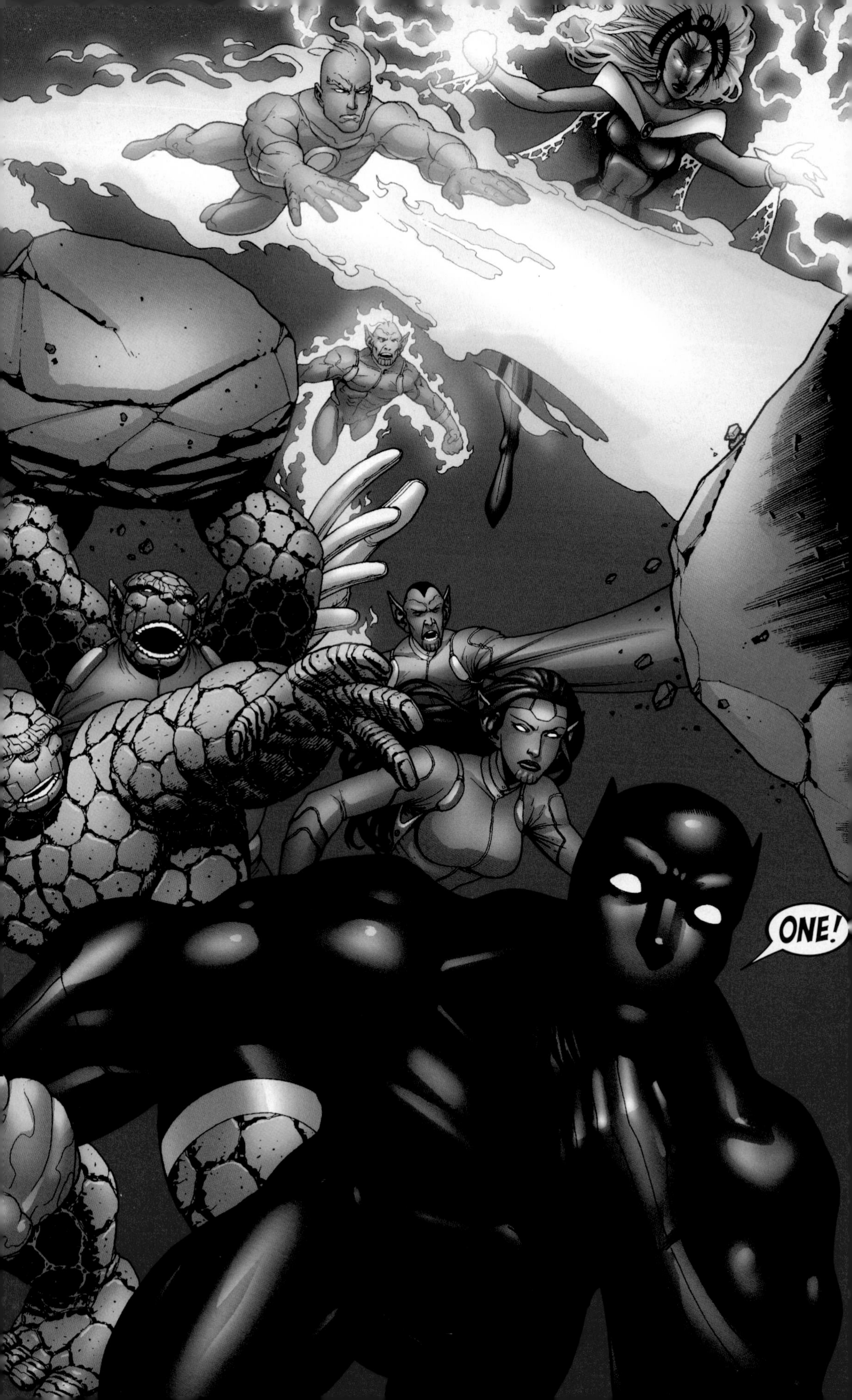
ONE!

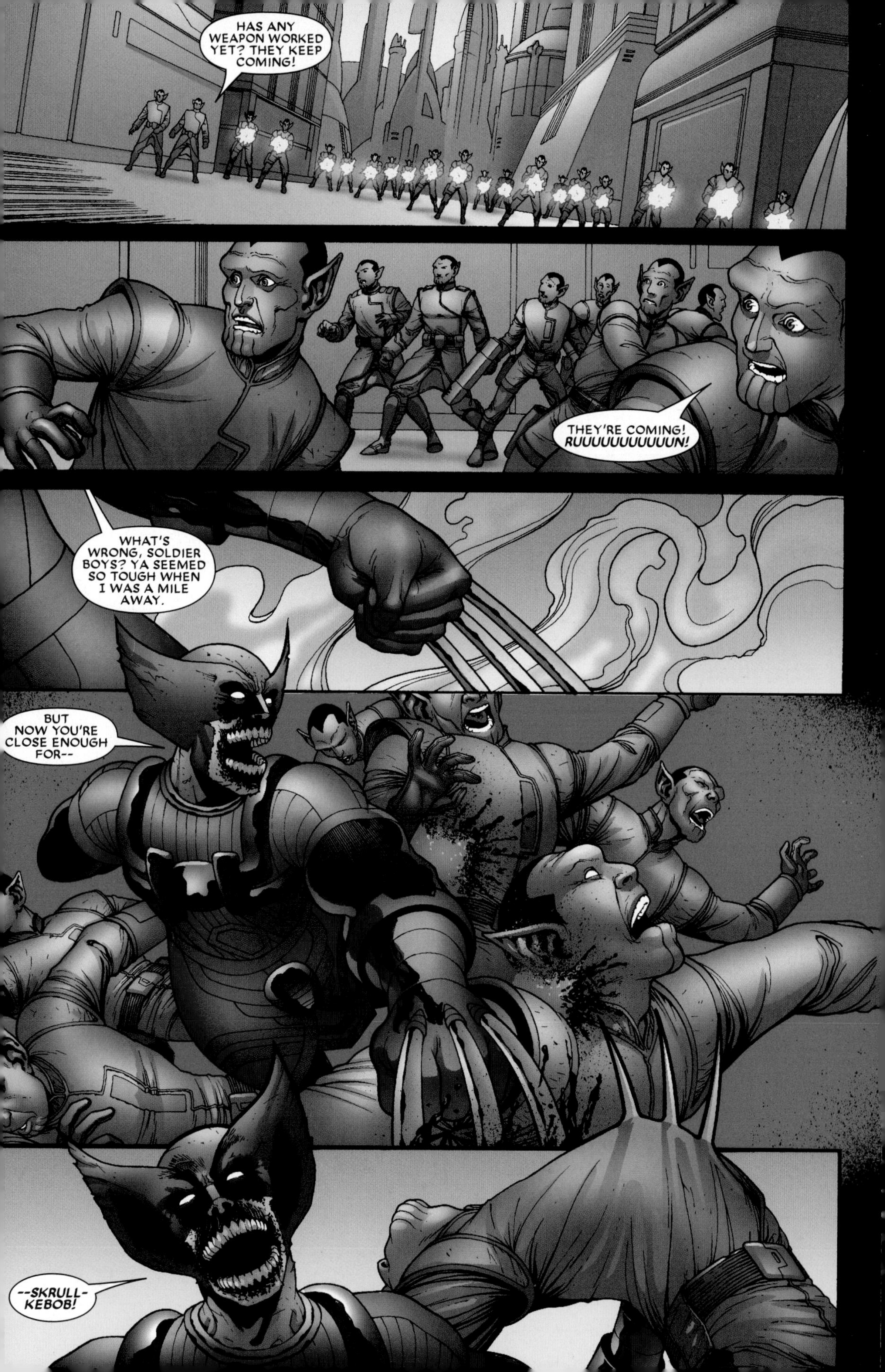
HAS ANY WEAPON WORKED YET? THEY KEEP COMING!
THEY'RE COMING! RUUUUUUUUUUUN!
WHAT'S WRONG, SOLDIER BOYS? YA SEEMED SO TOUGH WHEN I WAS A MILE AWAY.
BUT NOW YOU'RE CLOSE ENOUGH FOR--
--SKRULL-KEBOB!

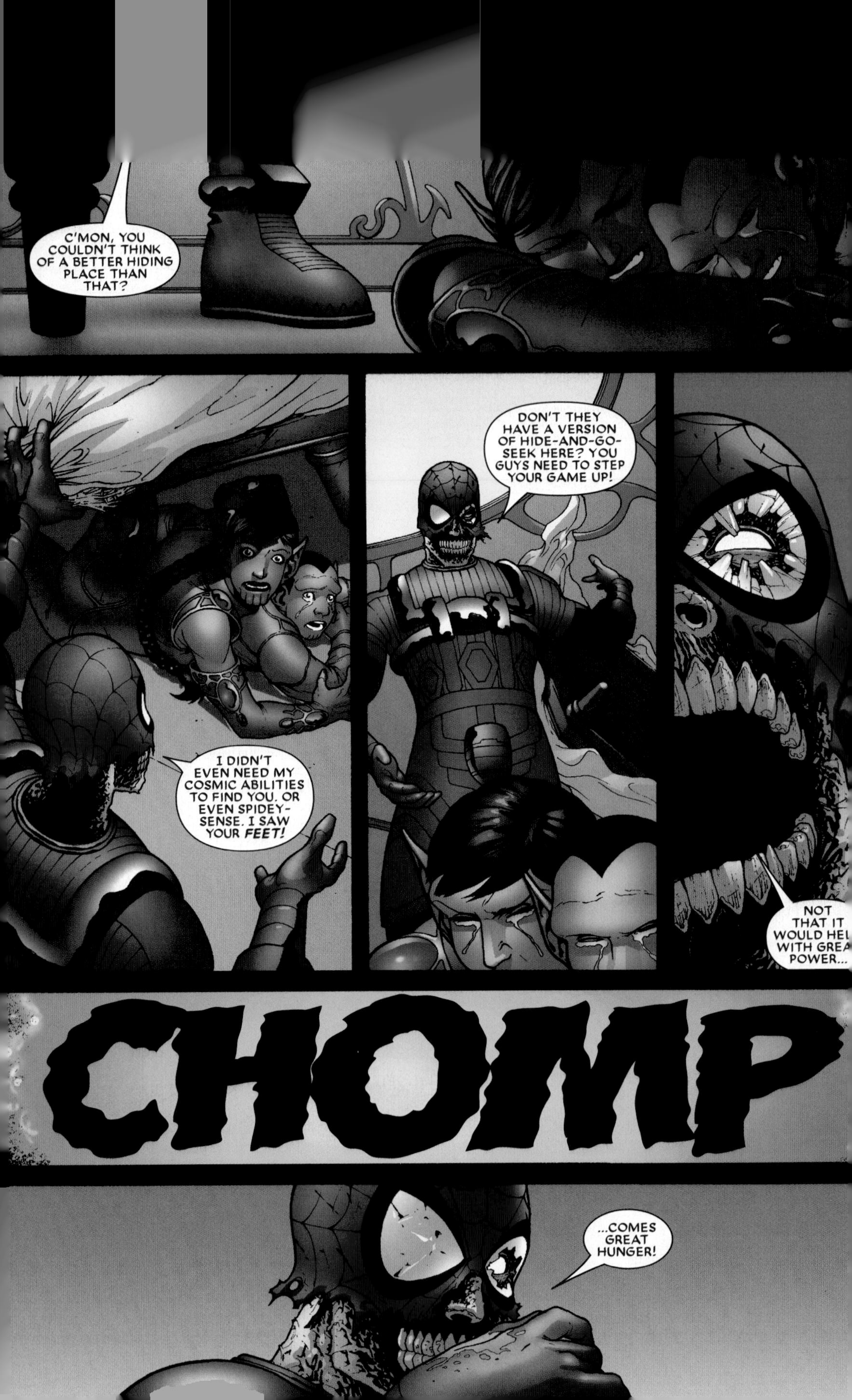
C'MON, YOU COULDN'T THINK OF A BETTER HIDING PLACE THAN THAT?
I DIDN'T EVEN NEED MY COSMIC ABILITIES TO FIND YOU. OR EVEN SPIDEY-SENSE. I SAW YOUR FEET!
DON'T THEY HAVE A VERSION OF HIDE-AND-GO-SEEK HERE? YOU GUYS NEED TO STEP YOUR GAME UP!
NOT THAT IT WOULD HEL WITH GREA POWER...
CHOMP
...COMES GREAT HUNGER!

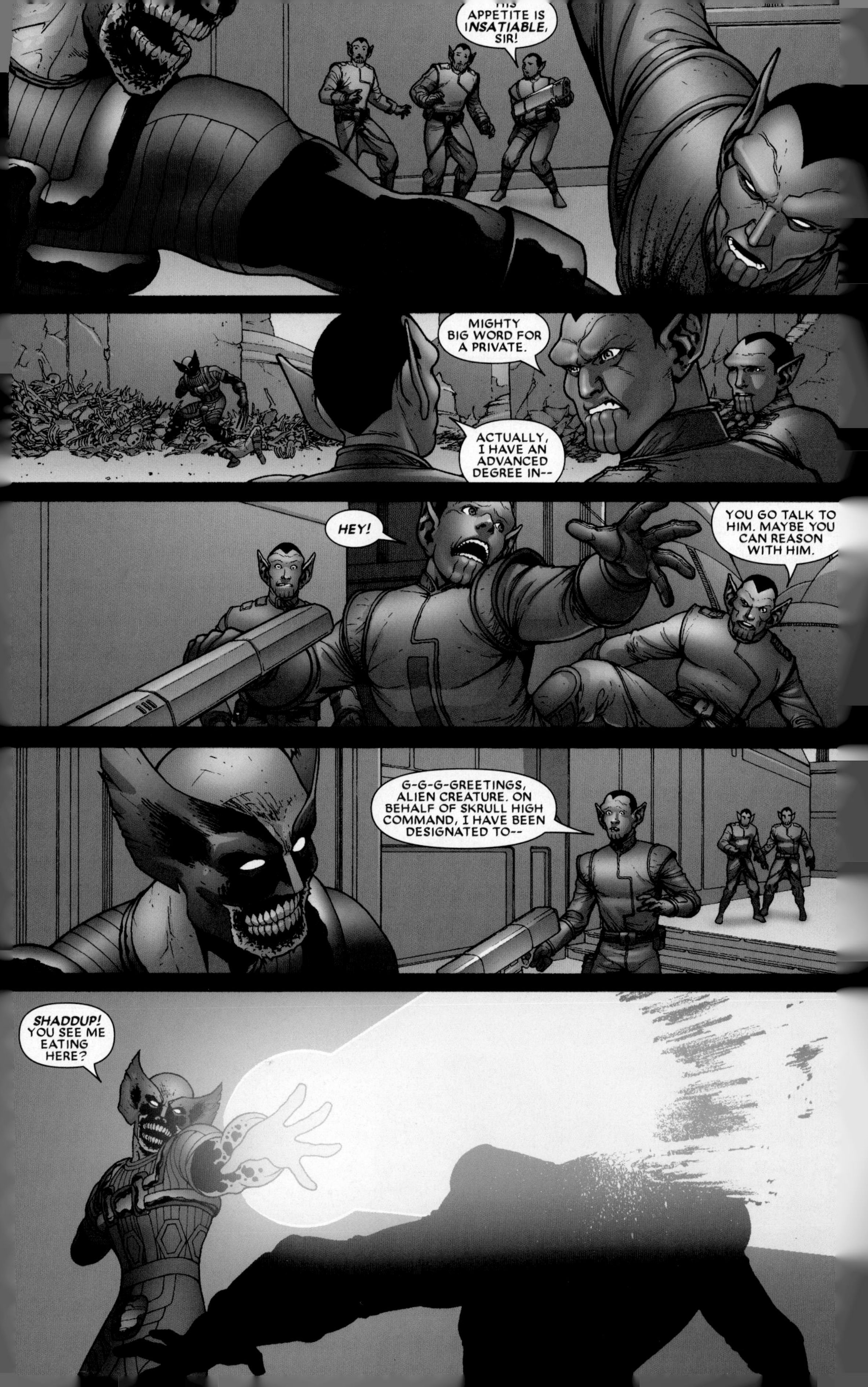
APPETITE IS INSATIABLE, SIR!
MIGHTY BIG WORD FOR A PRIVATE.
ACTUALLY, I HAVE AN ADVANCED DEGREE IN--
HEY!
YOU GO TALK TO HIM. MAYBE YOU CAN REASON WITH HIM.
G-G-G-GREETINGS, ALIEN CREATURE. ON BEHALF OF SKRULL HIGH COMMAND, I HAVE BEEN DESIGNATED TO--
SHADDUP! YOU SEE ME EATING HERE?

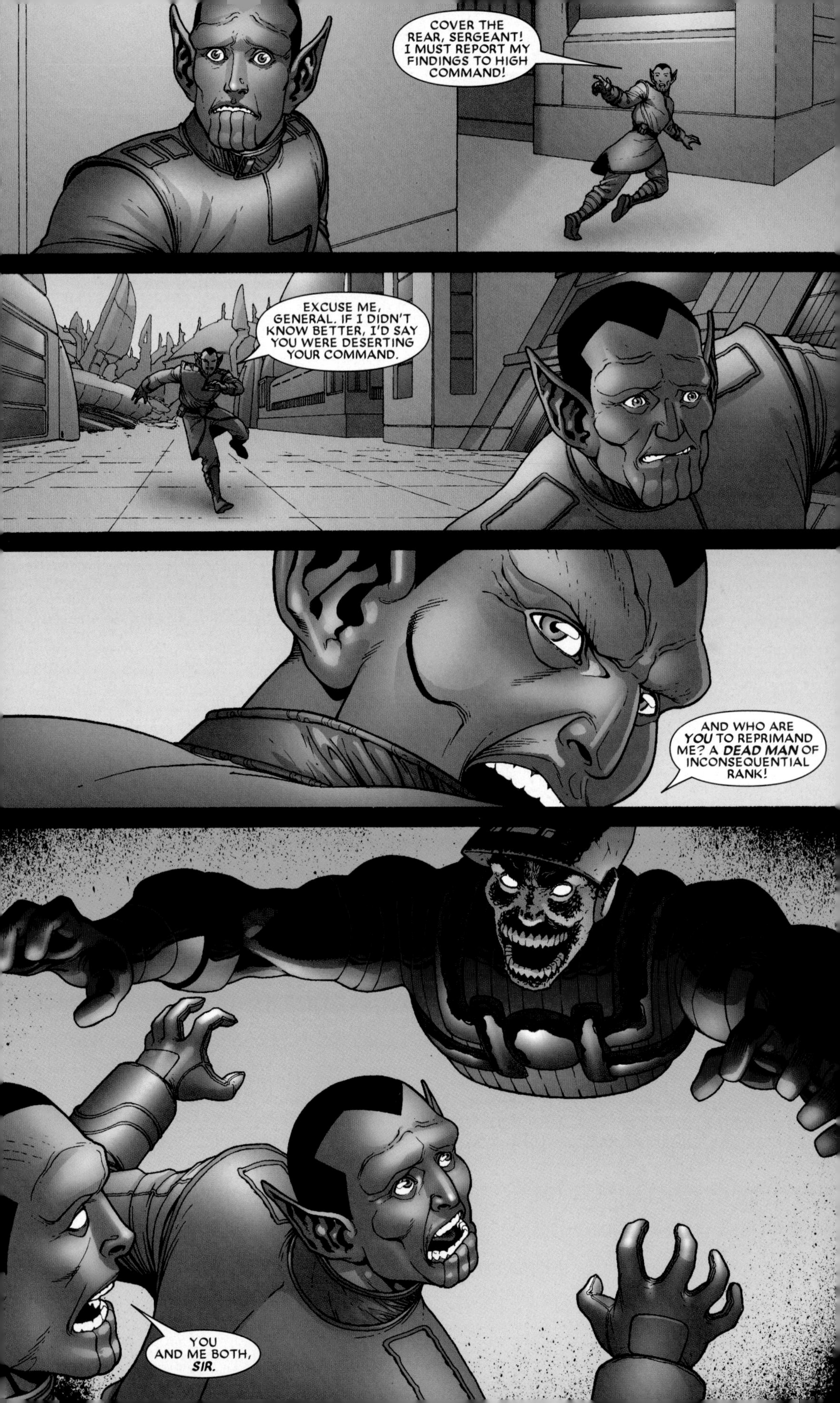
COVER THE REAR, SERGEANT! I MUST REPORT MY FINDINGS TO HIGH COMMAND!
EXCUSE ME, GENERAL. IF I DIDN'T KNOW BETTER, I'D SAY YOU WERE DESERTING YOUR COMMAND.
AND WHO ARE YOU TO REPRIMAND ME? A DEAD MAN OF INCONSEQUENTIAL RANK!
YOU AND ME BOTH, SIR.

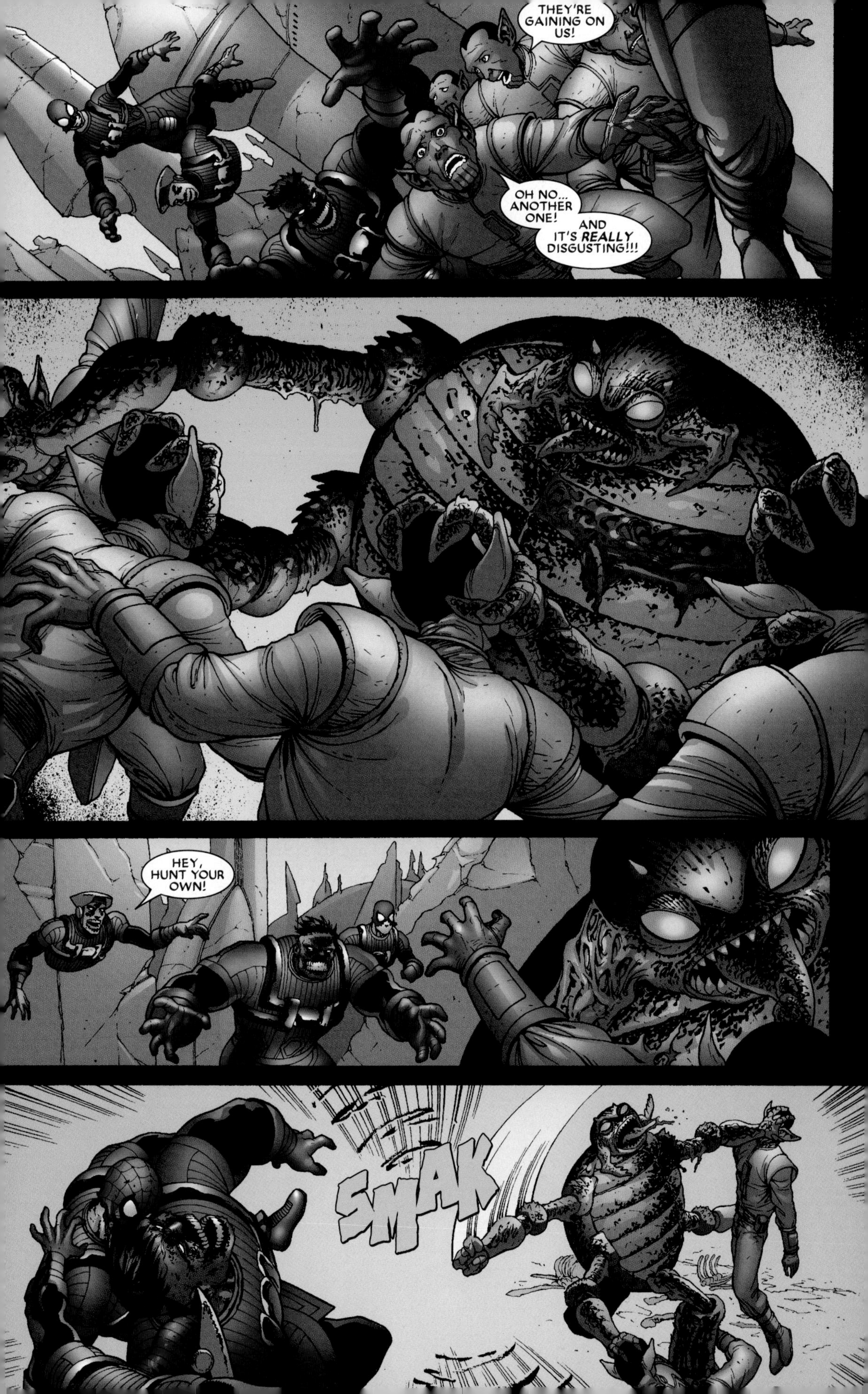
THEY'RE GAINING ON US!
OH NO... ANOTHER ONE!
AND IT'S REALLY DISGUSTING!!!
HEY, HUNT YOUR OWN!
SMAK

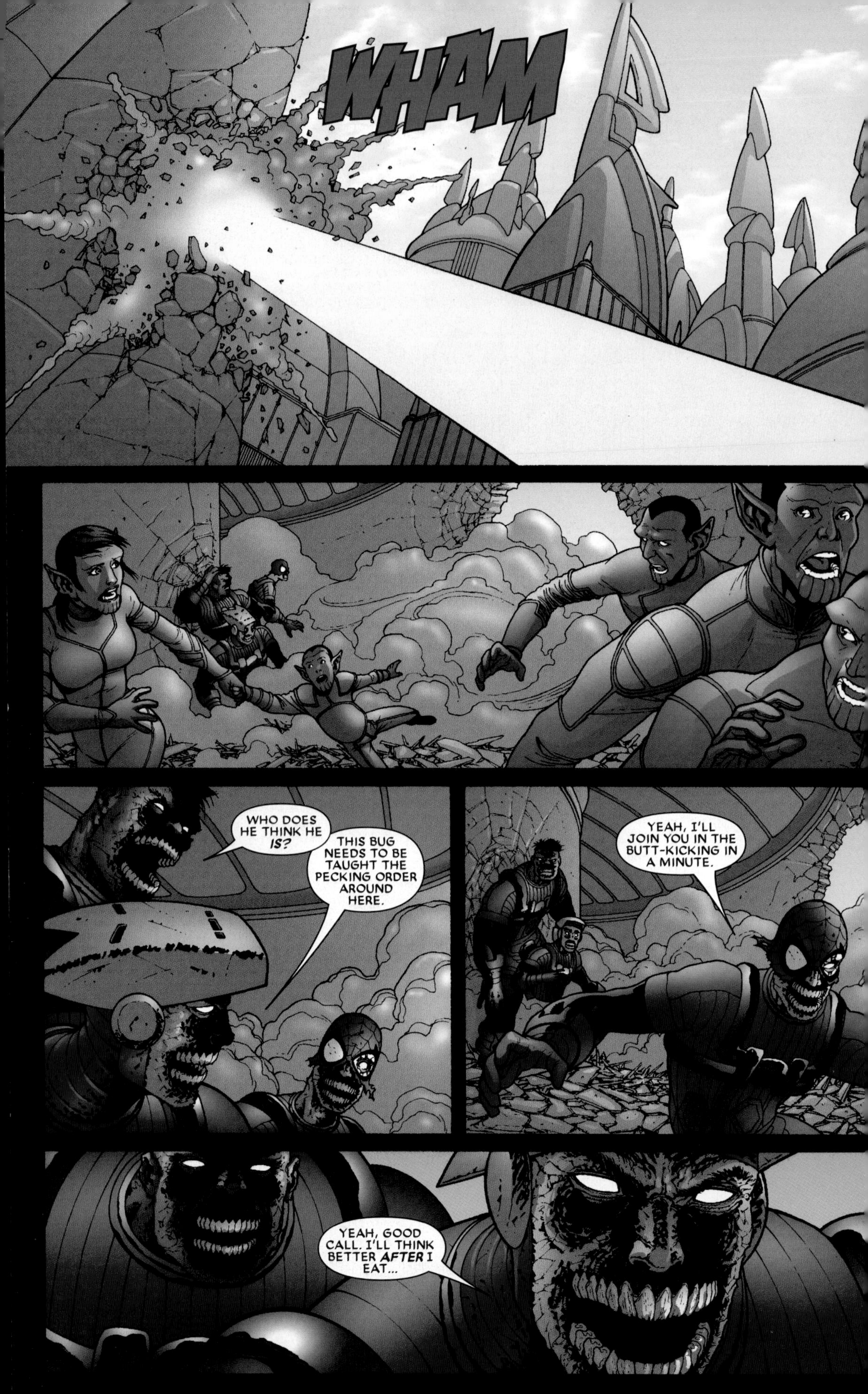
WHAM
WHO DOES HE THINK HE IS?
THIS BUG NEEDS TO BE TAUGHT THE PECKING ORDER AROUND HERE.
YEAH, I'LL JOIN YOU IN THE BUTT-KICKING IN A MINUTE.
YEAH, GOOD CALL. I'LL THINK BETTER AFTER I EAT...

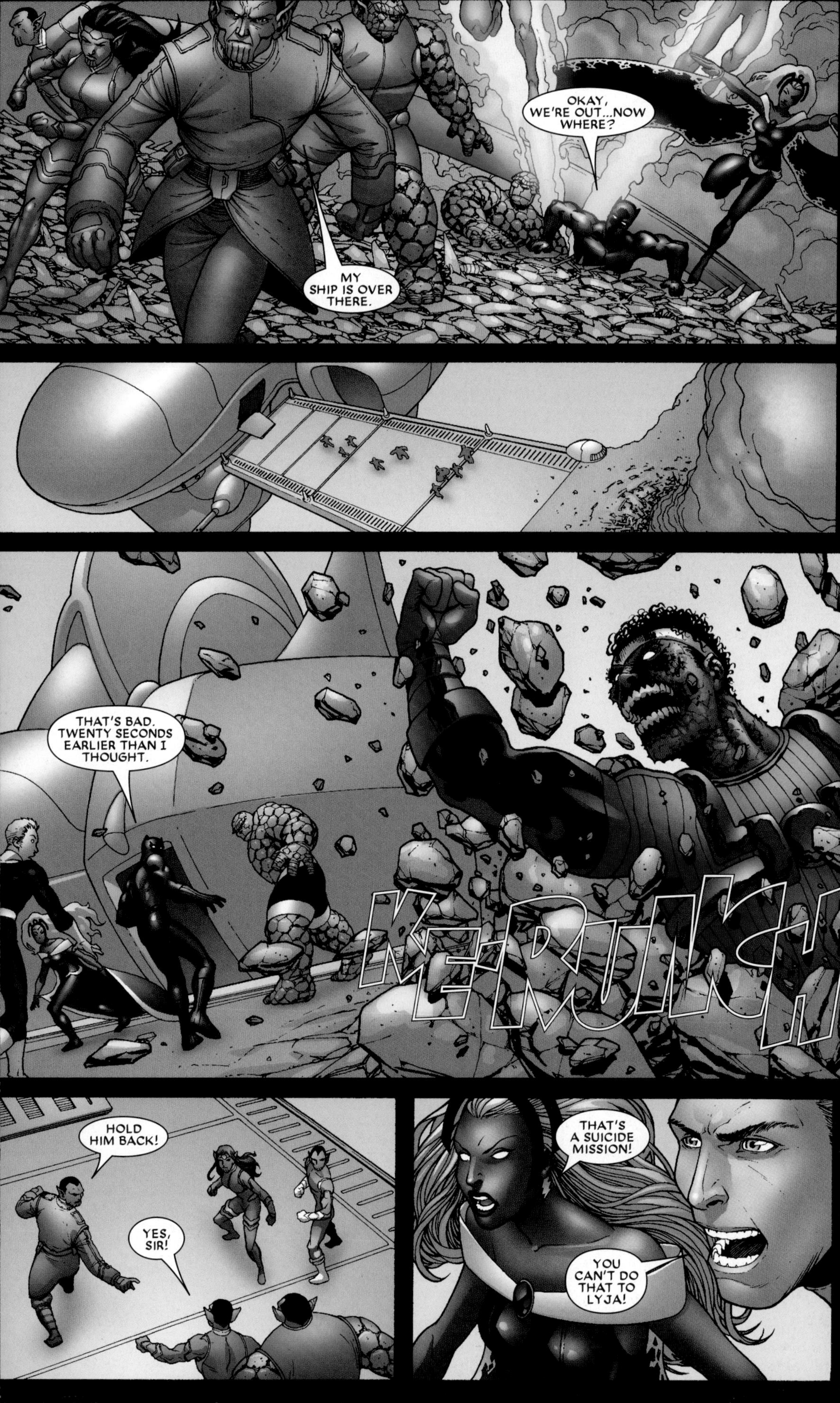
OKAY, WE'RE OUT...NOW WHERE?
MY SHIP IS OVER THERE.
THAT'S BAD. TWENTY SECONDS EARLIER THAN I THOUGHT.
KE-RUNCH
HOLD HIM BACK!
YES, SIR!
THAT'S A SUICIDE MISSION!
YOU CAN'T DO THAT TO LYJA!

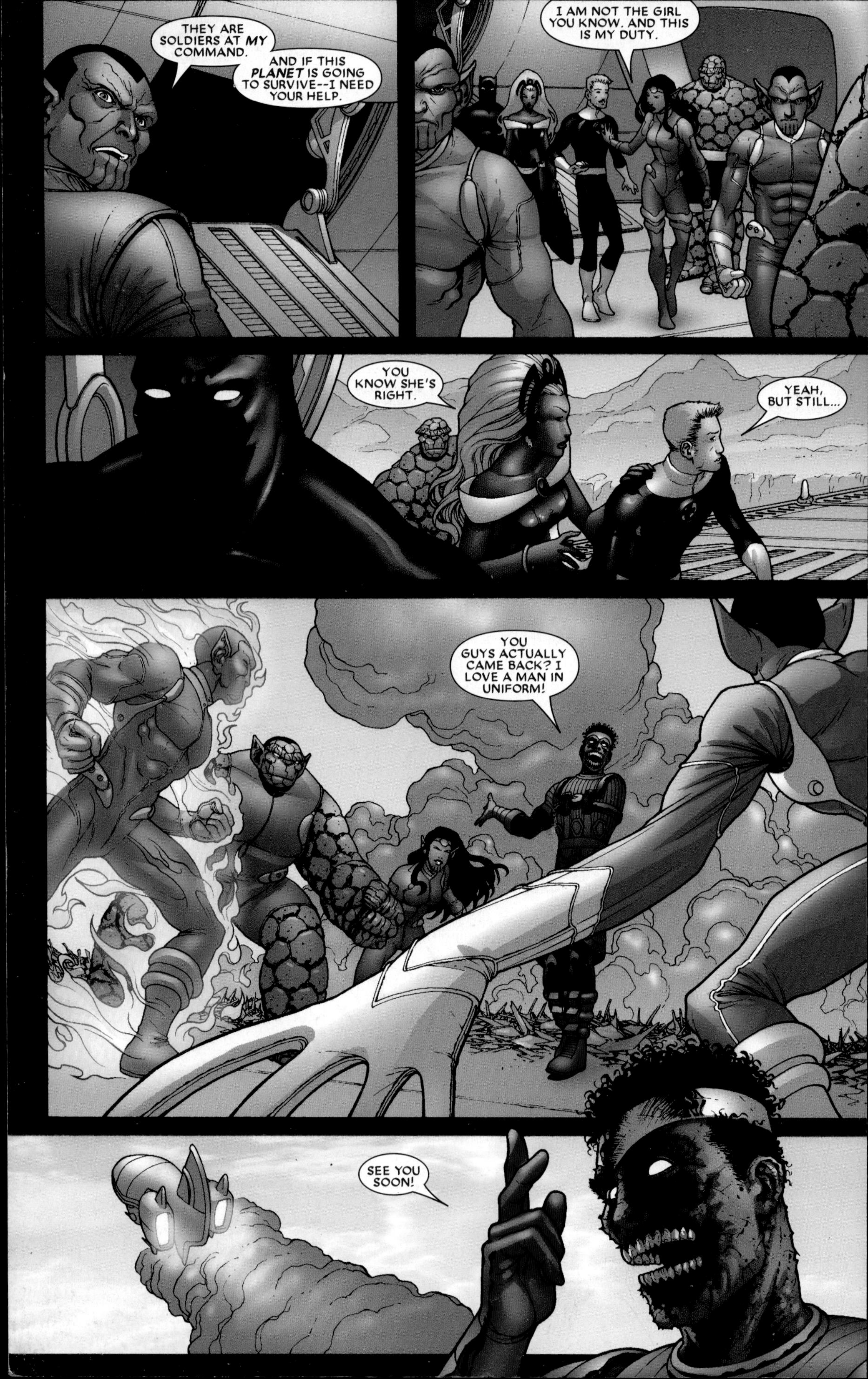
THEY ARE SOLDIERS AT MY COMMAND.
AND IF THIS PLANET IS GOING TO SURVIVE--I NEED YOUR HELP.
I AM NOT THE GIRL YOU KNOW. AND THIS IS MY DUTY.
YOU KNOW SHE'S RIGHT.
YEAH, BUT STILL...
YOU GUYS ACTUALLY CAME BACK? I LOVE A MAN IN UNIFORM!
SEE YOU SOON!

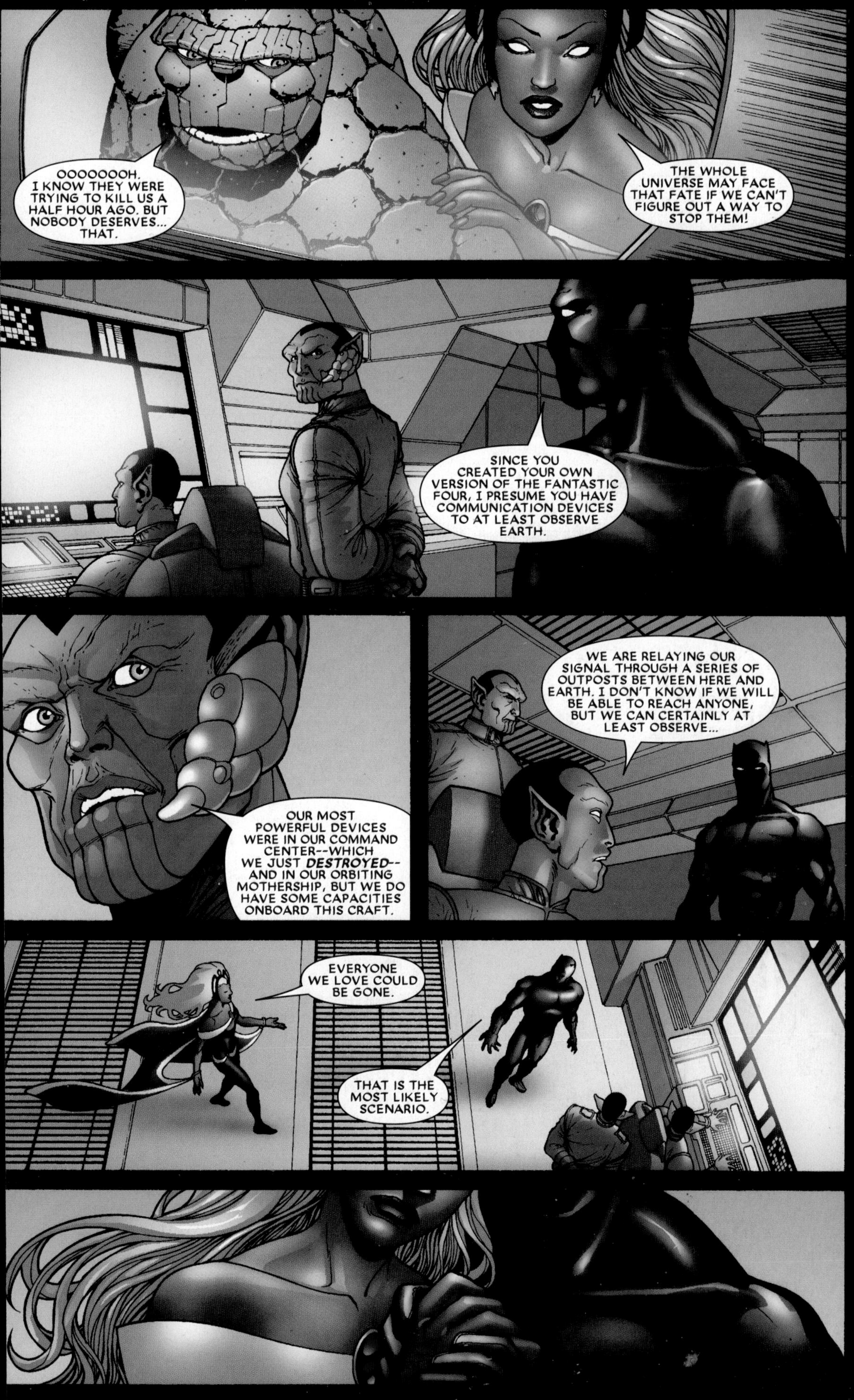

OOOOOOOH. I KNOW THEY WERE TRYING TO KILL US A HALF HOUR AGO. BUT NOBODY DESERVES... THAT.
THE WHOLE UNIVERSE MAY FACE THAT FATE IF WE CAN'T FIGURE OUT A WAY TO STOP THEM!
SINCE YOU CREATED YOUR OWN VERSION OF THE FANTASTIC FOUR, I PRESUME YOU HAVE COMMUNICATION DEVICES TO AT LEAST OBSERVE EARTH.
OUR MOST POWERFUL DEVICES WERE IN OUR COMMAND CENTER--WHICH WE JUST *DESTROYED*--AND IN OUR ORBITING MOTHERSHIP, BUT WE DO HAVE SOME CAPACITIES ONBOARD THIS CRAFT.
WE ARE RELAYING OUR SIGNAL THROUGH A SERIES OF OUTPOSTS BETWEEN HERE AND EARTH. I DON'T KNOW IF WE WILL BE ABLE TO REACH ANYONE, BUT WE CAN CERTAINLY AT LEAST OBSERVE...
EVERYONE WE LOVE COULD BE GONE.
THAT IS THE MOST LIKELY SCENARIO.

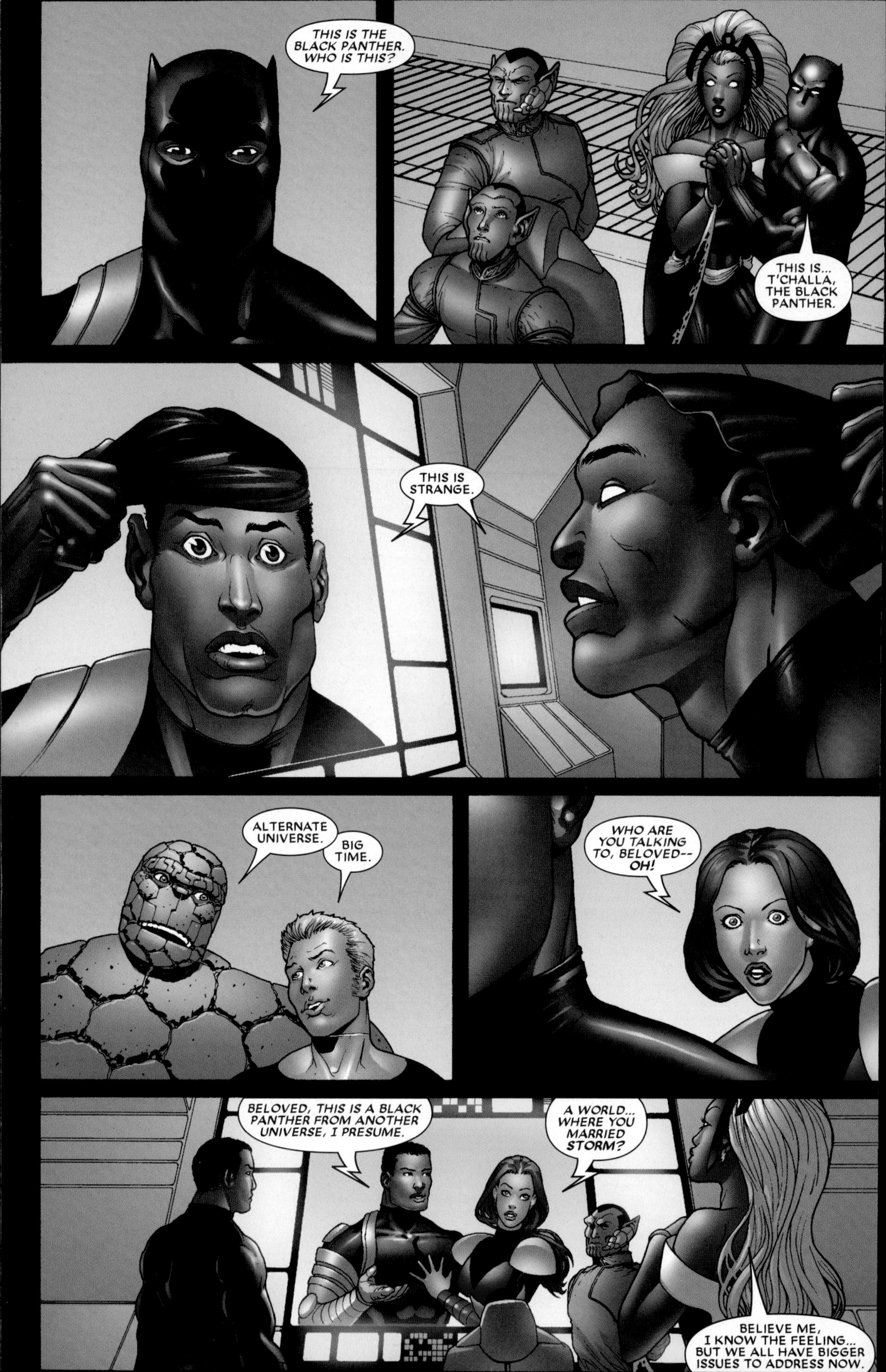

THIS IS THE BLACK PANTHER. WHO IS THIS?
THIS IS... T'CHALLA, THE BLACK PANTHER.
THIS IS STRANGE.
ALTERNATE UNIVERSE.
BIG TIME.
WHO ARE YOU TALKING TO, BELOVED-- OH!
BELOVED, THIS IS A BLACK PANTHER FROM ANOTHER UNIVERSE, I PRESUME.
A WORLD... WHERE YOU MARRIED STORM?
BELIEVE ME, I KNOW THE FEELING... BUT WE ALL HAVE BIGGER ISSUES TO ADDRESS NOW.

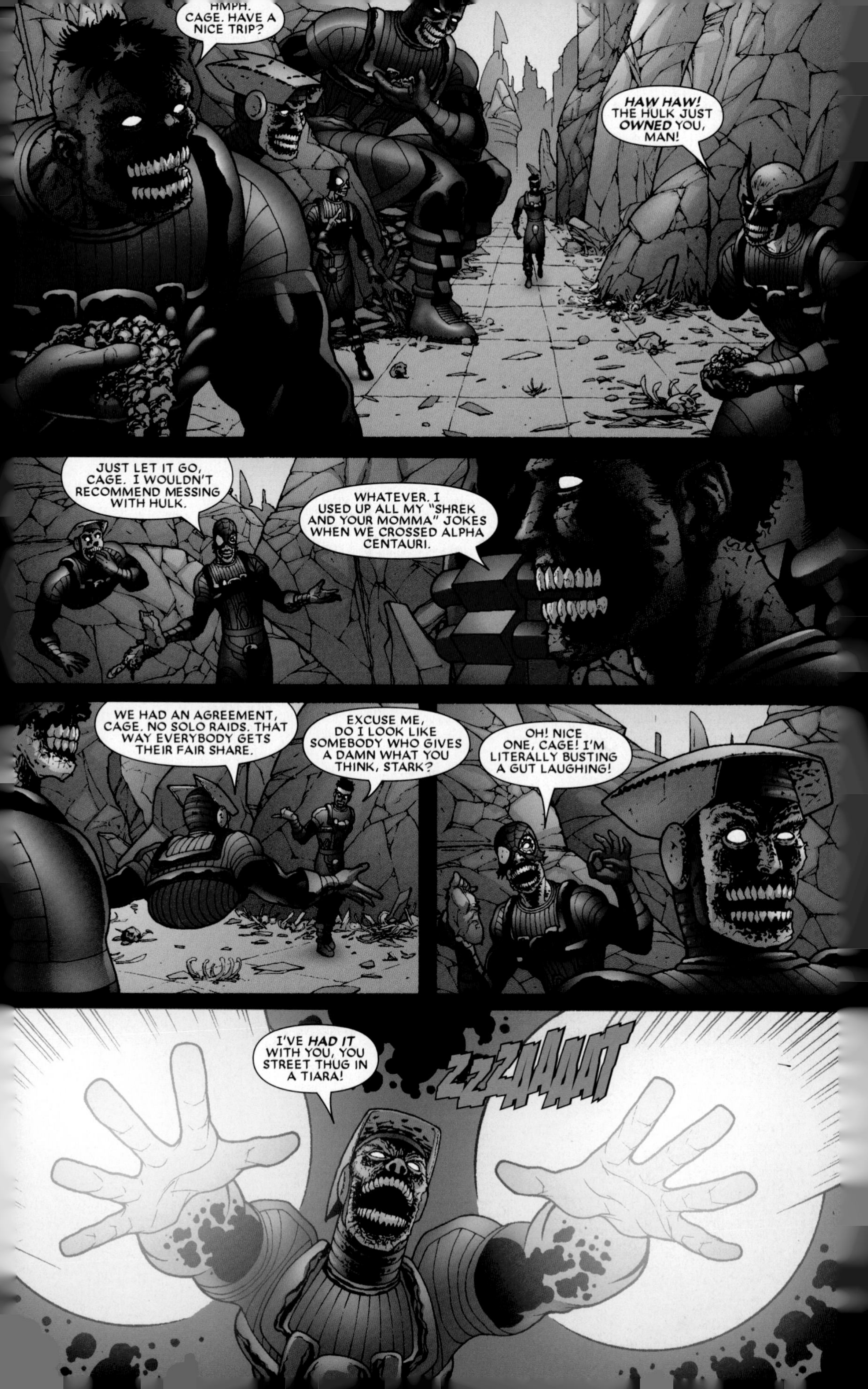
HMPH. CAGE. HAVE A NICE TRIP?
HAW HAW! THE HULK JUST OWNED YOU, MAN!
JUST LET IT GO, CAGE. I WOULDN'T RECOMMEND MESSING WITH HULK.
WHATEVER. I USED UP ALL MY "SHREK AND YOUR MOMMA" JOKES WHEN WE CROSSED ALPHA CENTAURI.
WE HAD AN AGREEMENT, CAGE. NO SOLO RAIDS. THAT WAY EVERYBODY GETS THEIR FAIR SHARE.
EXCUSE ME, DO I LOOK LIKE SOMEBODY WHO GIVES A DAMN WHAT YOU THINK, STARK?
OH! NICE ONE, CAGE! I'M LITERALLY BUSTING A GUT LAUGHING!
I'VE HAD IT WITH YOU, YOU STREET THUG IN A TIARA!
ZZZAAAAAT

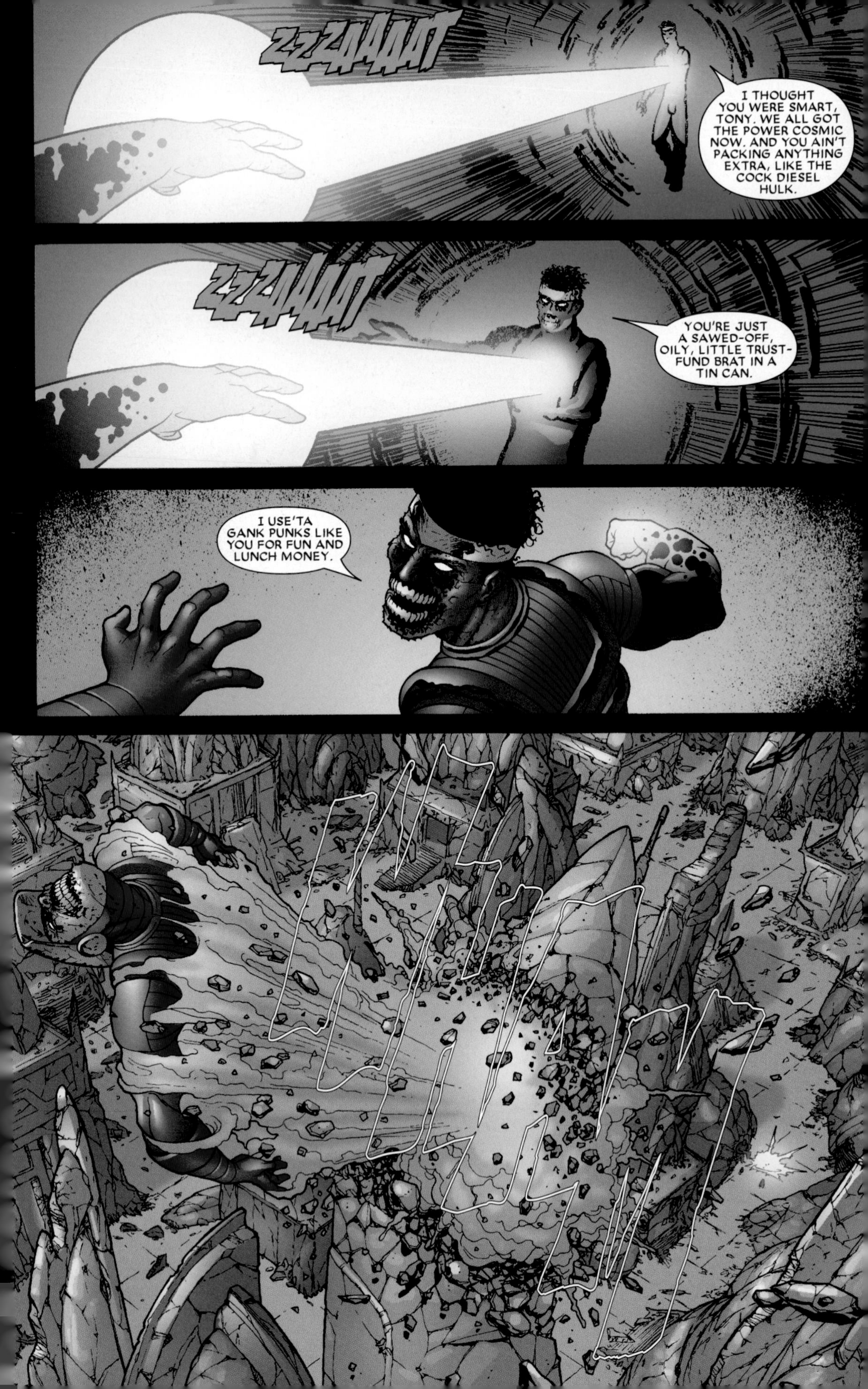
ZZZAAAAAT
I THOUGHT YOU WERE SMART, TONY. WE ALL GOT THE POWER COSMIC NOW. AND YOU AIN'T PACKING ANYTHING EXTRA, LIKE THE COCK DIESEL HULK.
ZZZAAAAAT
YOU'RE JUST A SAWED-OFF, OILY, LITTLE TRUST-FUND BRAT IN A TIN CAN.
I USE'TA GANK PUNKS LIKE YOU FOR FUN AND LUNCH MONEY.

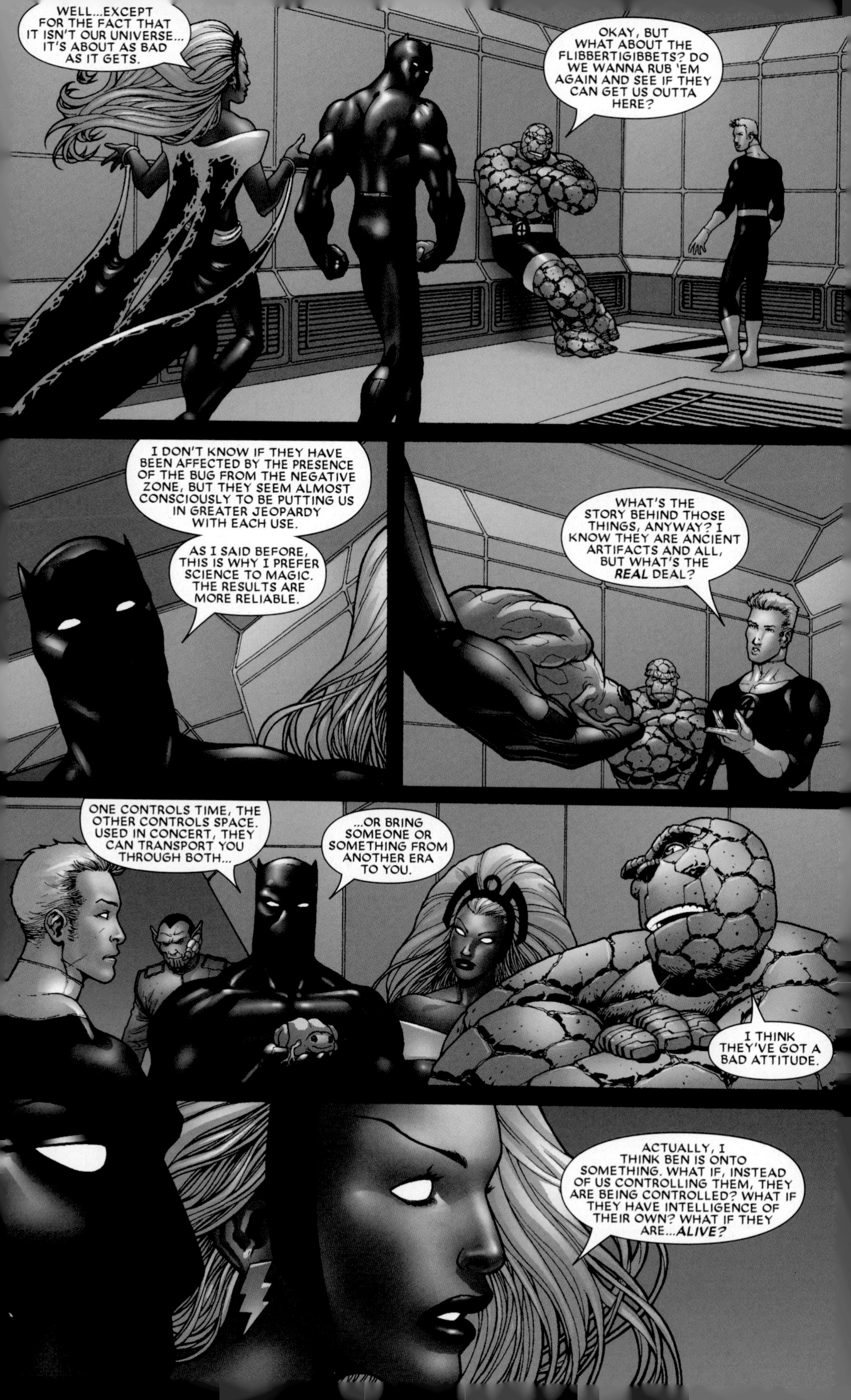
WELL...EXCEPT FOR THE FACT THAT IT ISN'T OUR UNIVERSE... IT'S ABOUT AS BAD AS IT GETS.
OKAY, BUT WHAT ABOUT THE FLIBBERTIGIBBETS? DO WE WANNA RUB 'EM AGAIN AND SEE IF THEY CAN GET US OUTTA HERE?
I DON'T KNOW IF THEY HAVE BEEN AFFECTED BY THE PRESENCE OF THE BUG FROM THE NEGATIVE ZONE, BUT THEY SEEM ALMOST CONSCIOUSLY TO BE PUTTING US IN GREATER JEOPARDY WITH EACH USE.
AS I SAID BEFORE, THIS IS WHY I PREFER SCIENCE TO MAGIC. THE RESULTS ARE MORE RELIABLE.
WHAT'S THE STORY BEHIND THOSE THINGS, ANYWAY? I KNOW THEY ARE ANCIENT ARTIFACTS AND ALL, BUT WHAT'S THE *REAL* DEAL?
ONE CONTROLS TIME, THE OTHER CONTROLS SPACE. USED IN CONCERT, THEY CAN TRANSPORT YOU THROUGH BOTH...
...OR BRING SOMEONE OR SOMETHING FROM ANOTHER ERA TO YOU.
I THINK THEY'VE GOT A BAD ATTITUDE.
ACTUALLY, I THINK BEN IS ONTO SOMETHING. WHAT IF, INSTEAD OF US CONTROLLING THEM, THEY ARE BEING CONTROLLED? WHAT IF THEY HAVE INTELLIGENCE OF THEIR OWN? WHAT IF THEY ARE...*ALIVE?*

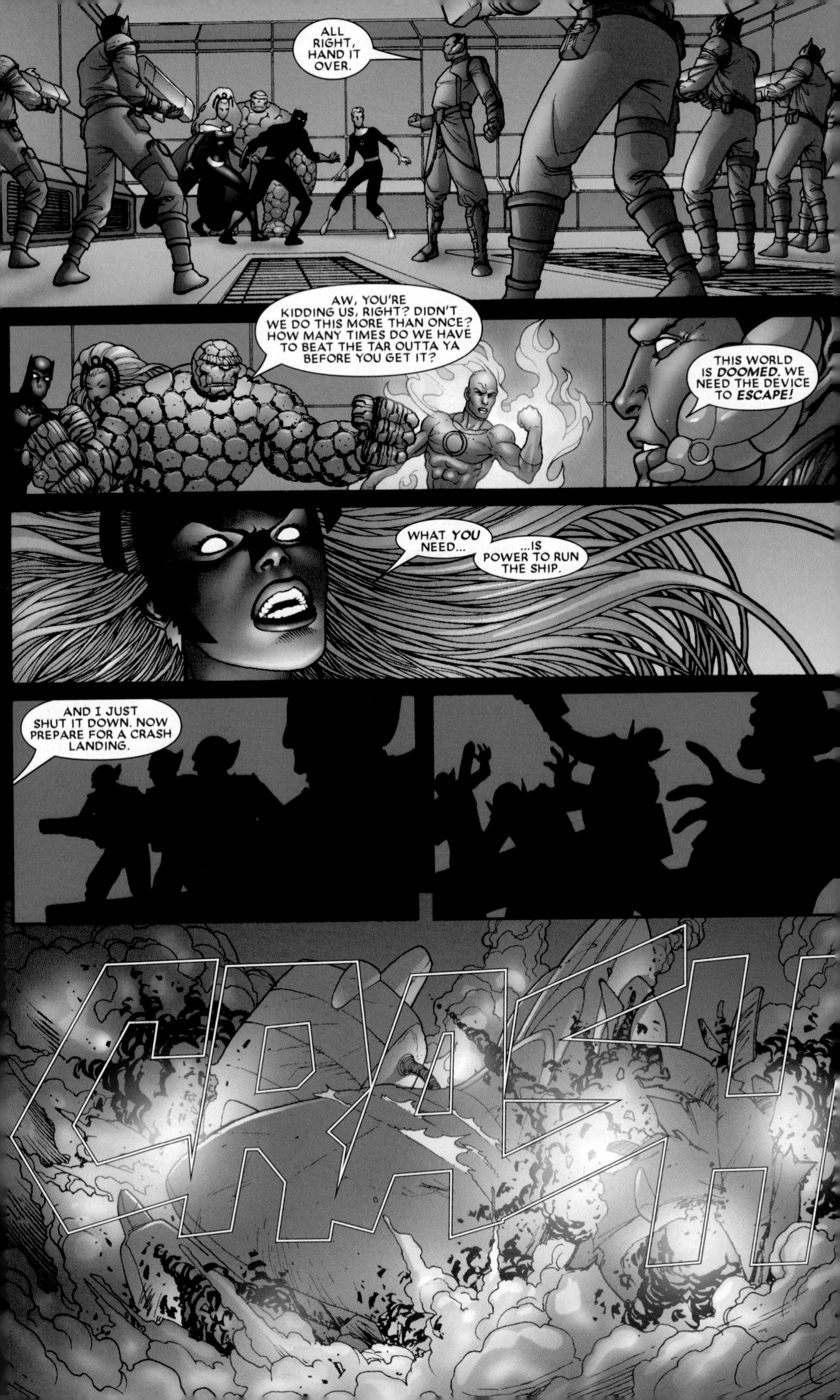
ALL RIGHT, HAND IT OVER.
AW, YOU'RE KIDDING US, RIGHT? DIDN'T WE DO THIS MORE THAN ONCE? HOW MANY TIMES DO WE HAVE TO BEAT THE TAR OUTTA YA BEFORE YOU GET IT?
THIS WORLD IS **DOOMED.** WE NEED THE DEVICE TO **ESCAPE!**
WHAT **YOU** NEED...
...IS POWER TO RUN THE SHIP.
AND I JUST SHUT IT DOWN. NOW PREPARE FOR A CRASH LANDING.
CRASH

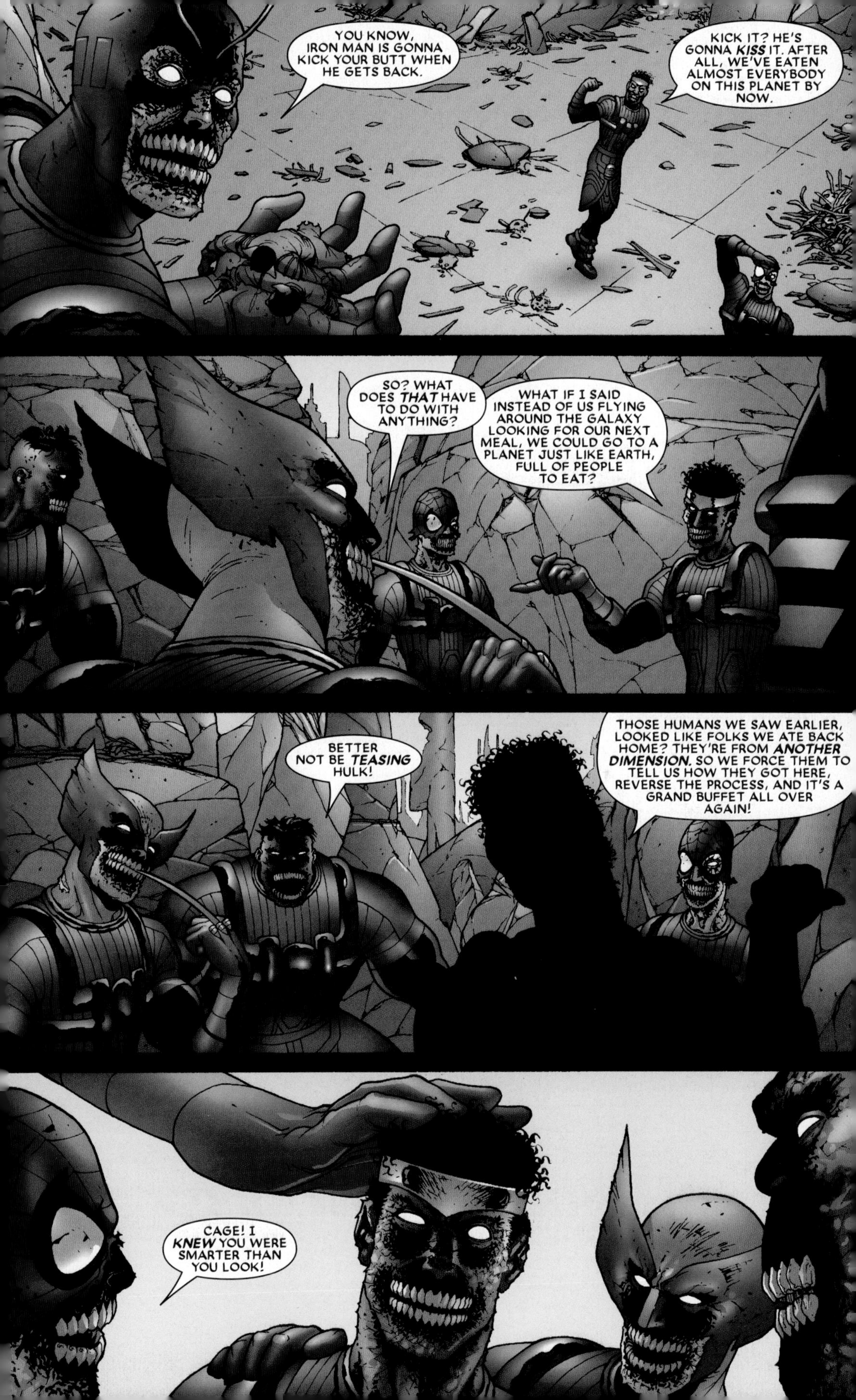
YOU KNOW, IRON MAN IS GONNA KICK YOUR BUTT WHEN HE GETS BACK.
KICK IT? HE'S GONNA KISS IT. AFTER ALL, WE'VE EATEN ALMOST EVERYBODY ON THIS PLANET BY NOW.
SO? WHAT DOES THAT HAVE TO DO WITH ANYTHING?
WHAT IF I SAID INSTEAD OF US FLYING AROUND THE GALAXY LOOKING FOR OUR NEXT MEAL, WE COULD GO TO A PLANET JUST LIKE EARTH, FULL OF PEOPLE TO EAT?
BETTER NOT BE TEASING HULK!
THOSE HUMANS WE SAW EARLIER, LOOKED LIKE FOLKS WE ATE BACK HOME? THEY'RE FROM ANOTHER DIMENSION. SO WE FORCE THEM TO TELL US HOW THEY GOT HERE, REVERSE THE PROCESS, AND IT'S A GRAND BUFFET ALL OVER AGAIN!
CAGE! I KNEW YOU WERE SMARTER THAN YOU LOOK!

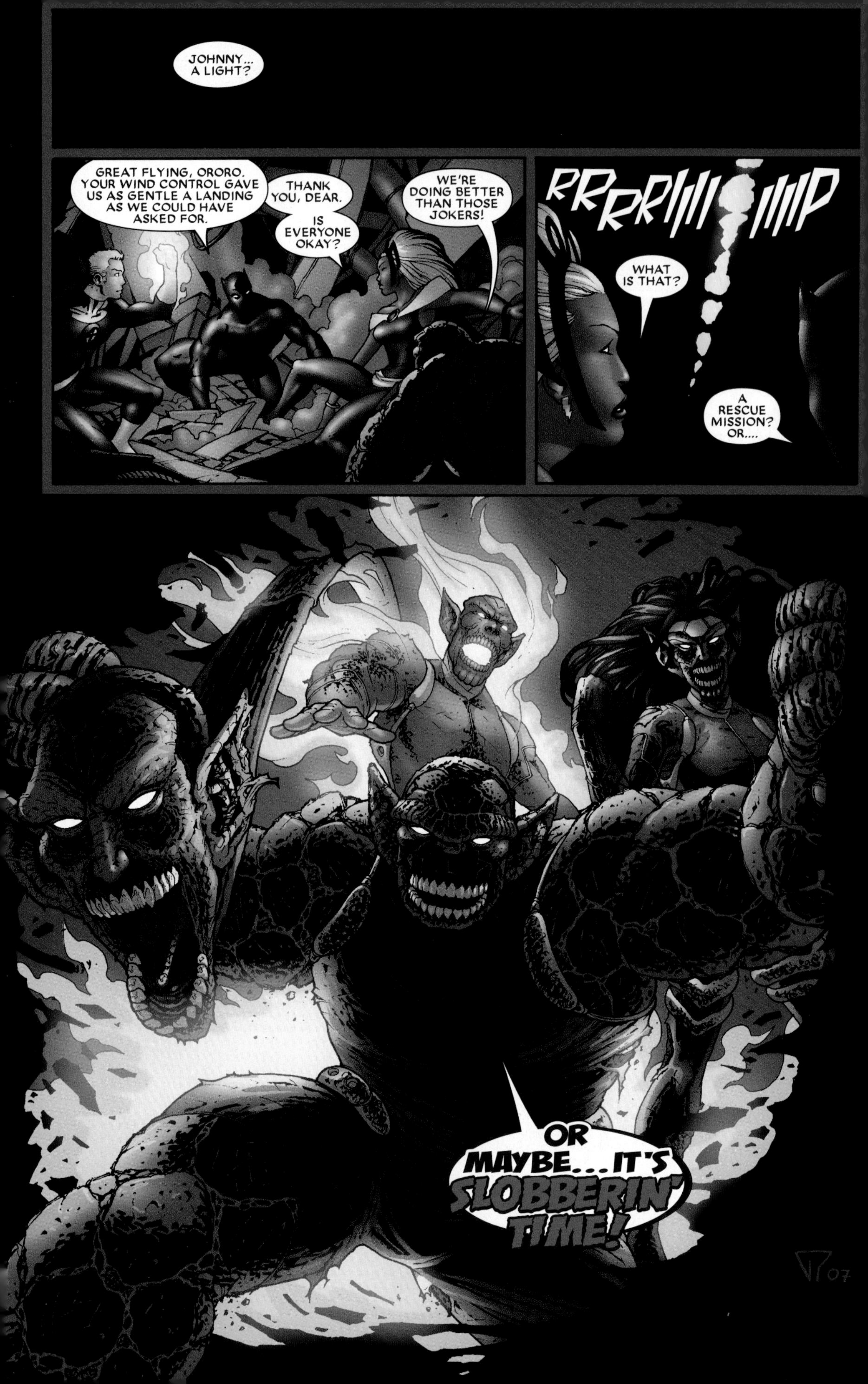
JOHNNY... A LIGHT?
GREAT FLYING, ORORO. YOUR WIND CONTROL GAVE US AS GENTLE A LANDING AS WE COULD HAVE ASKED FOR.
THANK YOU, DEAR.
IS EVERYONE OKAY?
WE'RE DOING BETTER THAN THOSE JOKERS!
RRRRRIIIIIIIIMP
WHAT IS THAT?
A RESCUE MISSION? OR....
OR MAYBE...IT'S SLOBBERIN' TIME!

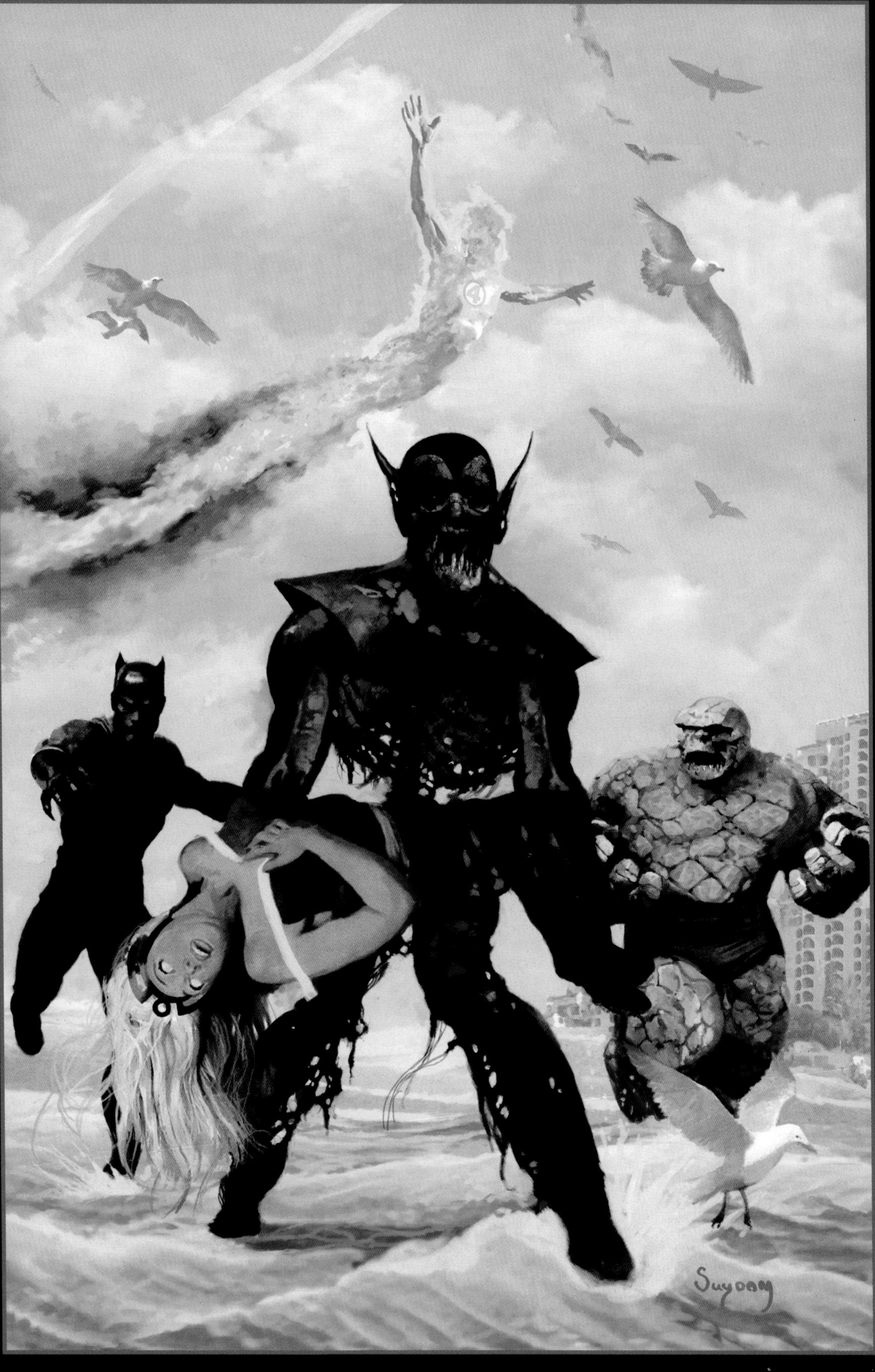
Suydam

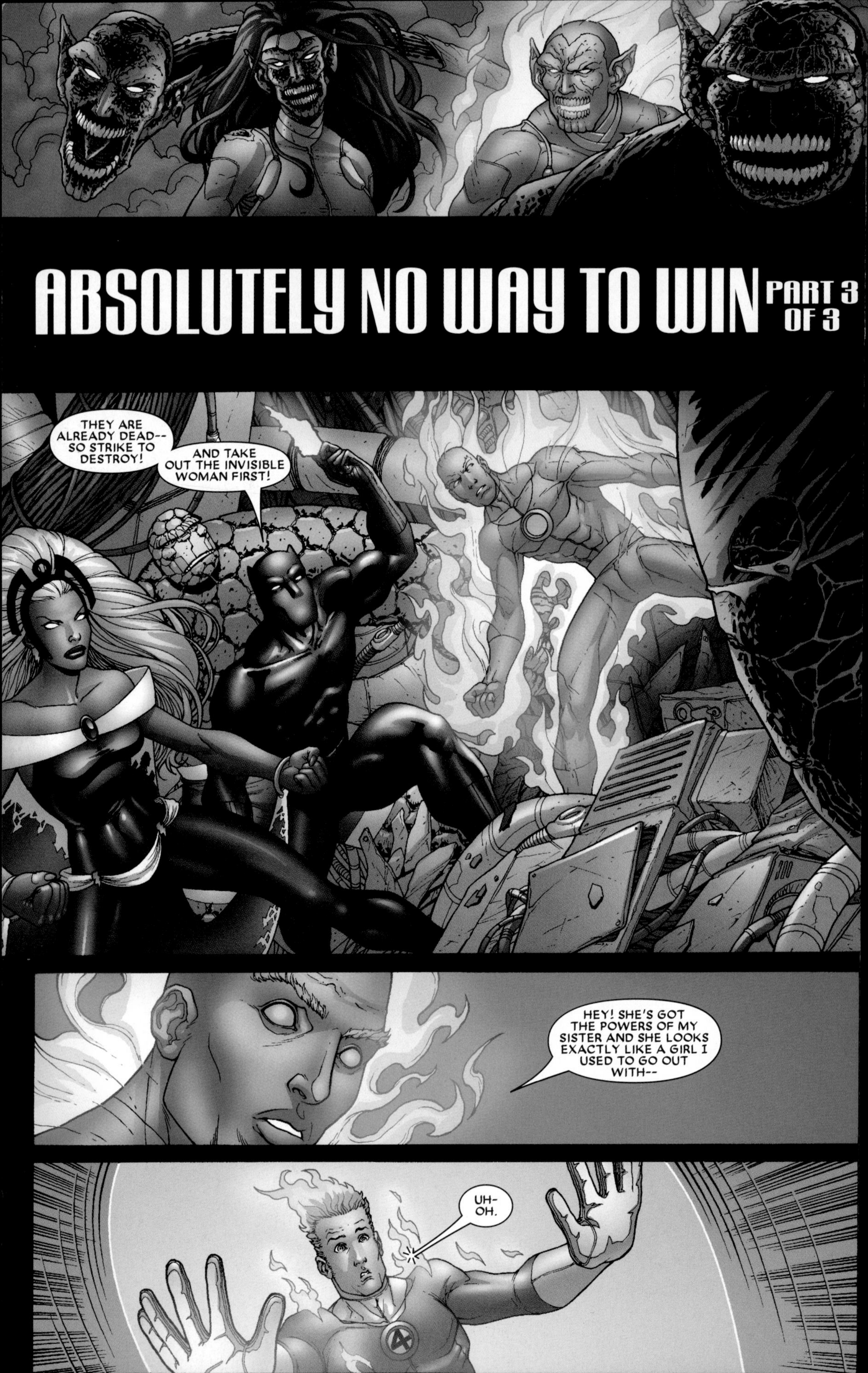
ABSOLUTELY NO WAY TO WIN PART 3 OF 3
THEY ARE ALREADY DEAD-- SO STRIKE TO DESTROY!
AND TAKE OUT THE INVISIBLE WOMAN FIRST!
HEY! SHE'S GOT THE POWERS OF MY SISTER AND SHE LOOKS EXACTLY LIKE A GIRL I USED TO GO OUT WITH--
UH-OH.

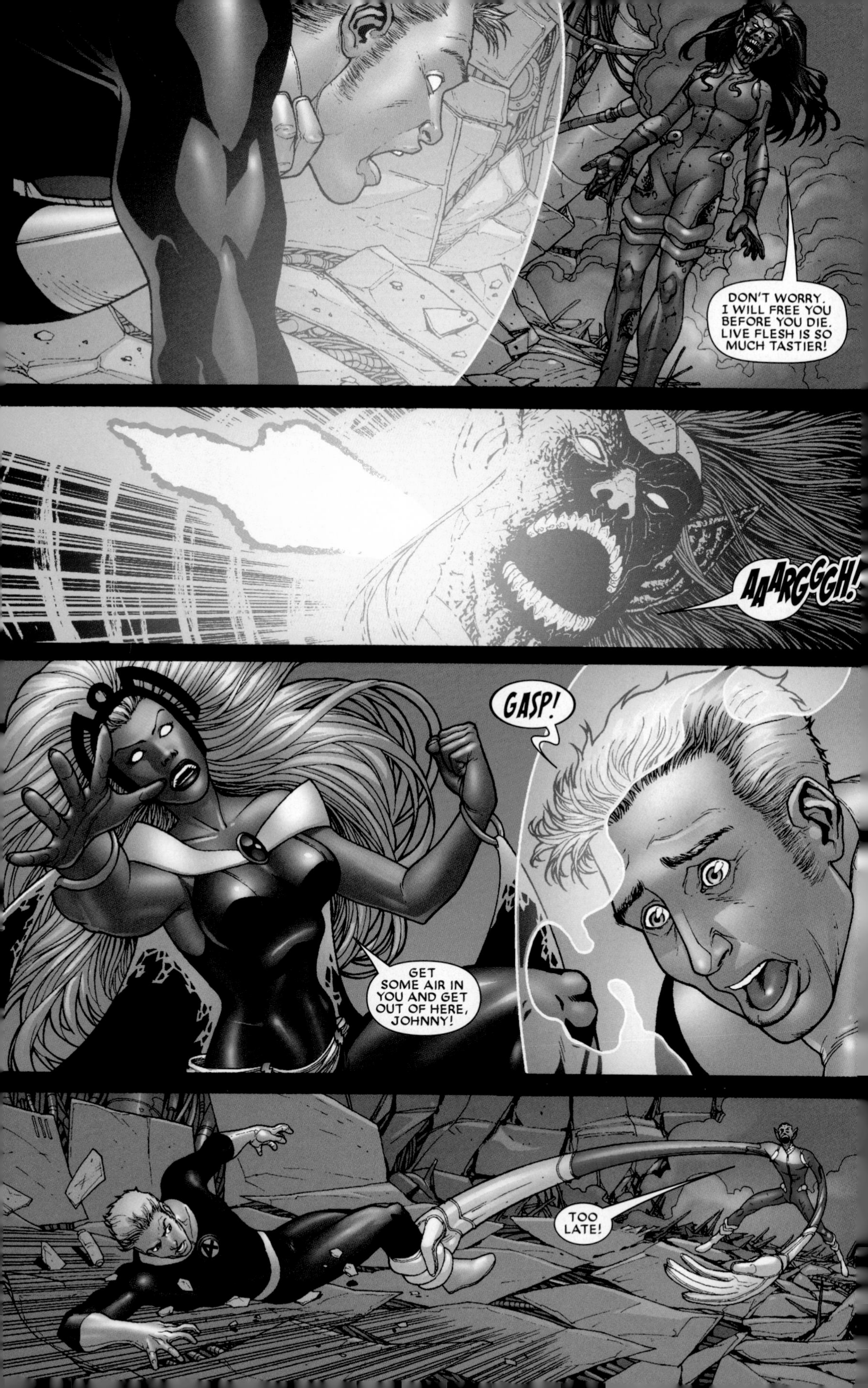
DON'T WORRY. I WILL FREE YOU BEFORE YOU DIE. LIVE FLESH IS SO MUCH TASTIER!
AAARGGGH!
GASP!
GET SOME AIR IN YOU AND GET OUT OF HERE, JOHNNY!
TOO LATE!

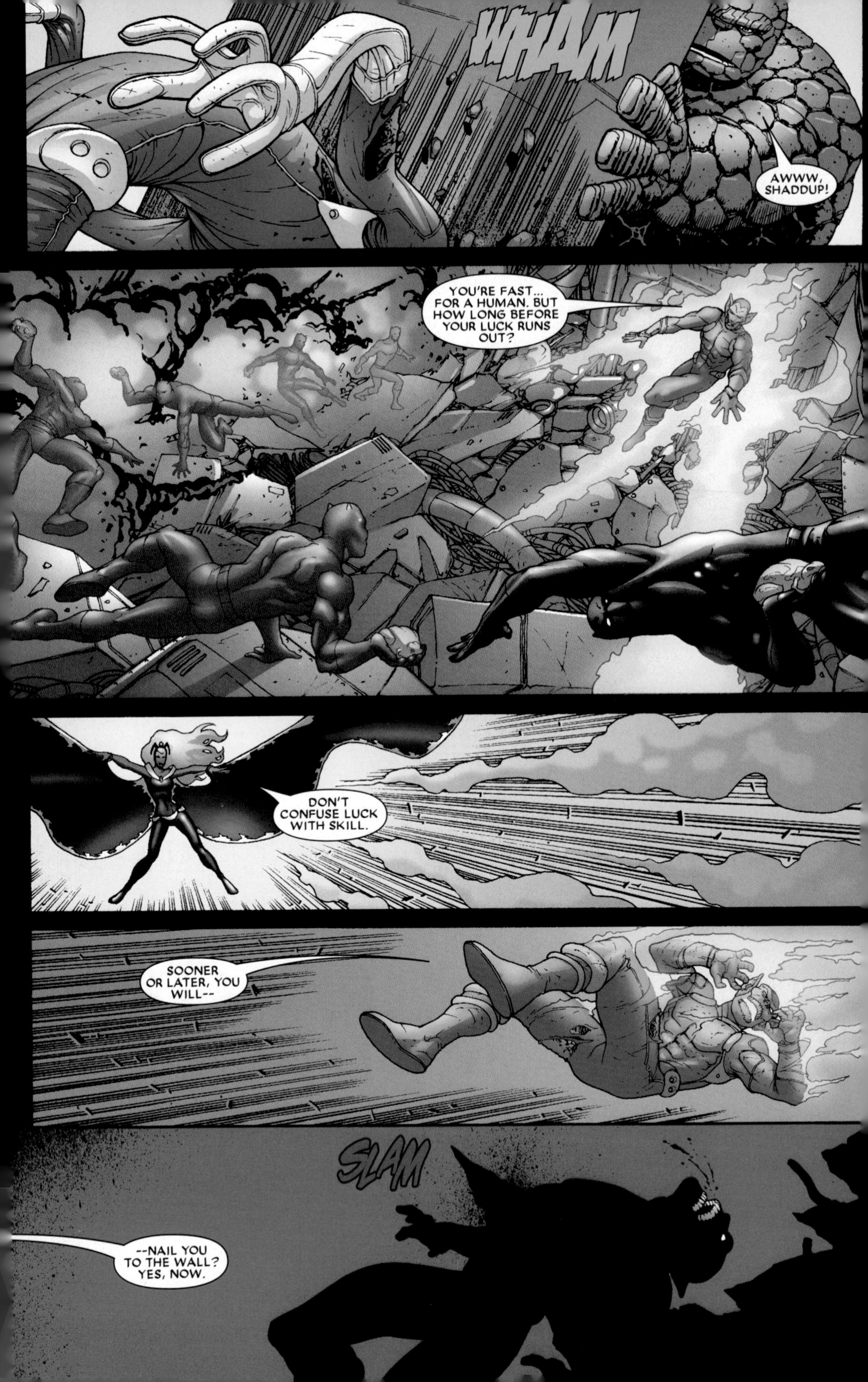
WHAM
AWWW, SHADDUP!
YOU'RE FAST... FOR A HUMAN. BUT HOW LONG BEFORE YOUR LUCK RUNS OUT?
DON'T CONFUSE LUCK WITH SKILL.
SOONER OR LATER, YOU WILL--
SLAM
--NAIL YOU TO THE WALL? YES, NOW.

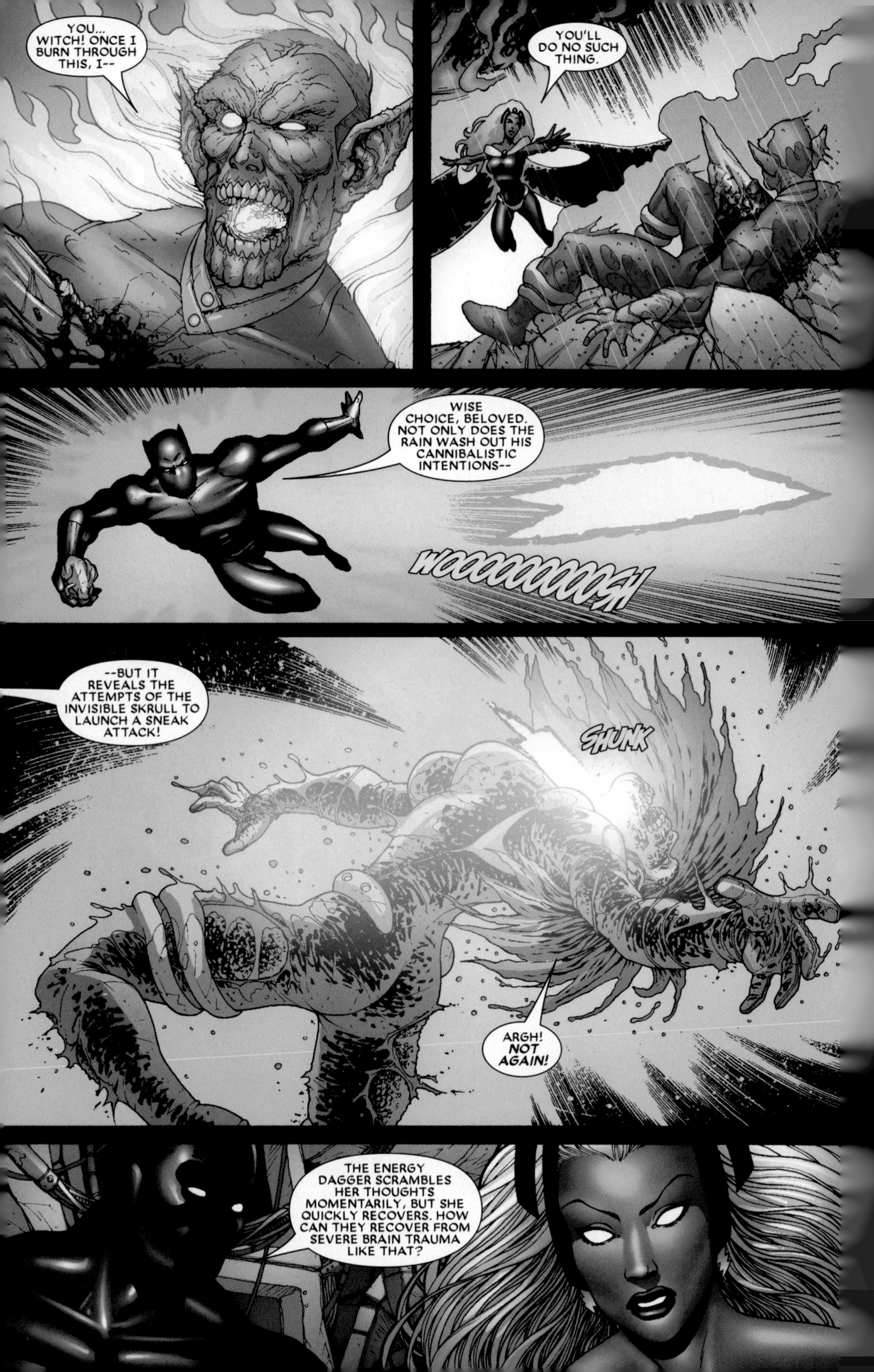
YOU... WITCH! ONCE I BURN THROUGH THIS, I--
YOU'LL DO NO SUCH THING.
WISE CHOICE, BELOVED. NOT ONLY DOES THE RAIN WASH OUT HIS CANNIBALISTIC INTENTIONS--
WOOOOOOOOOSH
--BUT IT REVEALS THE ATTEMPTS OF THE INVISIBLE SKRULL TO LAUNCH A SNEAK ATTACK!
SHUNK
ARGH! NOT AGAIN!
THE ENERGY DAGGER SCRAMBLES HER THOUGHTS MOMENTARILY, BUT SHE QUICKLY RECOVERS. HOW CAN THEY RECOVER FROM SEVERE BRAIN TRAUMA LIKE THAT?

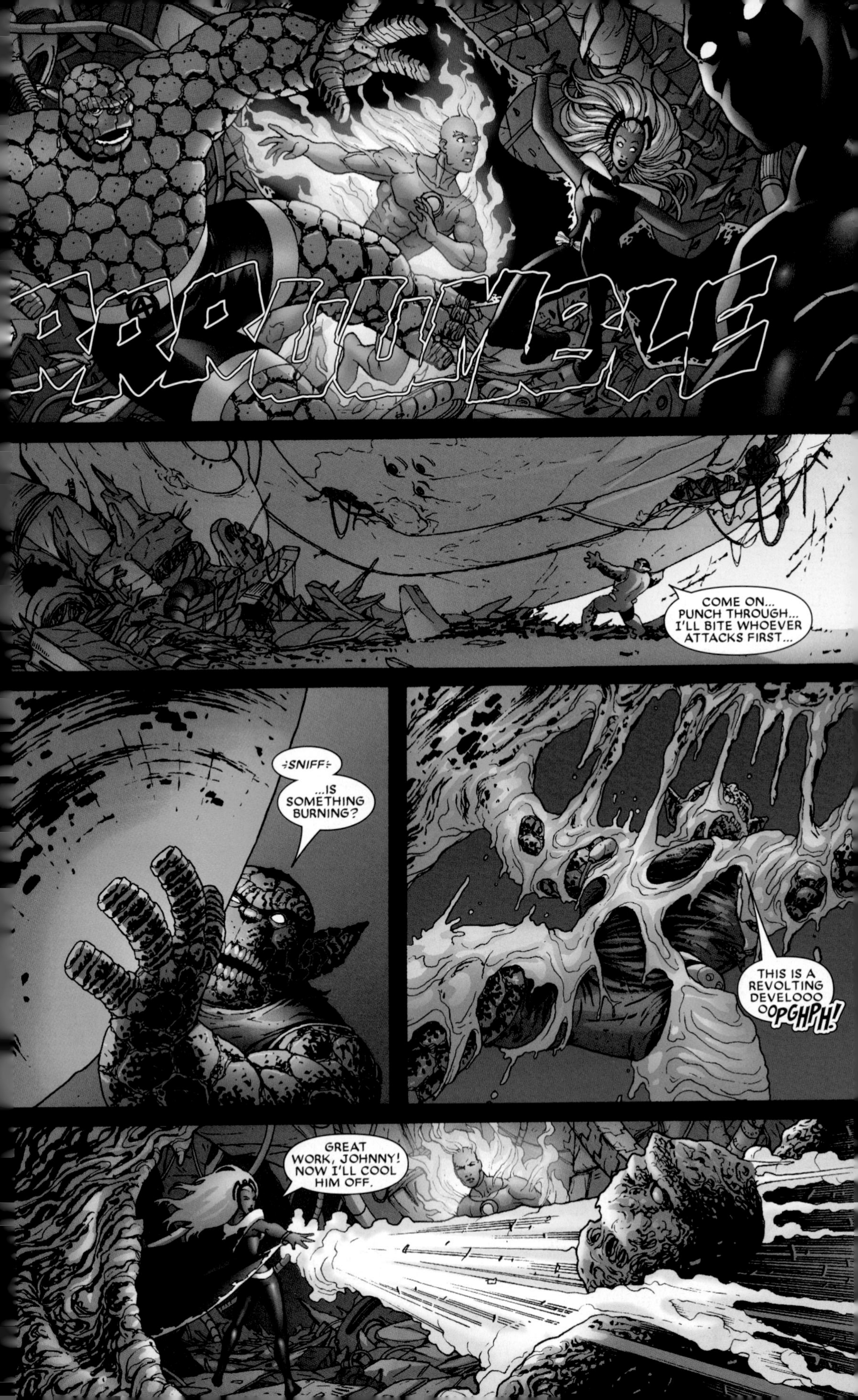
KRRUUMBLE
COME ON... PUNCH THROUGH... I'LL BITE WHOEVER ATTACKS FIRST...
-SNIFF-
...IS SOMETHING BURNING?
THIS IS A REVOLTING DEVELOOO OOPGHPH!
GREAT WORK, JOHNNY! NOW I'LL COOL HIM OFF.

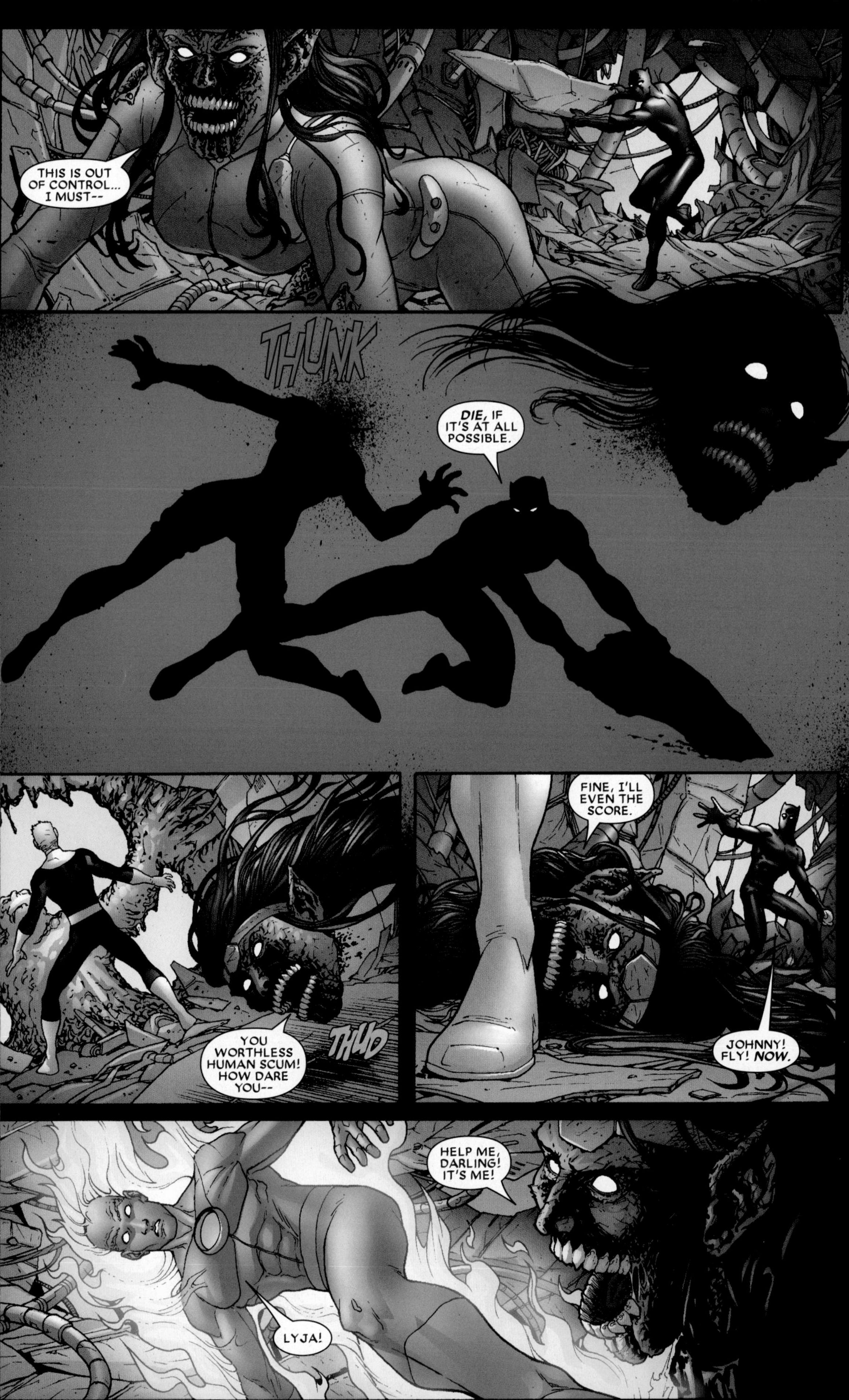
THIS IS OUT OF CONTROL... I MUST--
THUNK
DIE, IF IT'S AT ALL POSSIBLE.
YOU WORTHLESS HUMAN SCUM! HOW DARE YOU--
THUD
FINE, I'LL EVEN THE SCORE.
JOHNNY! FLY! *NOW*.
HELP ME, DARLING! IT'S ME!
LYJA!

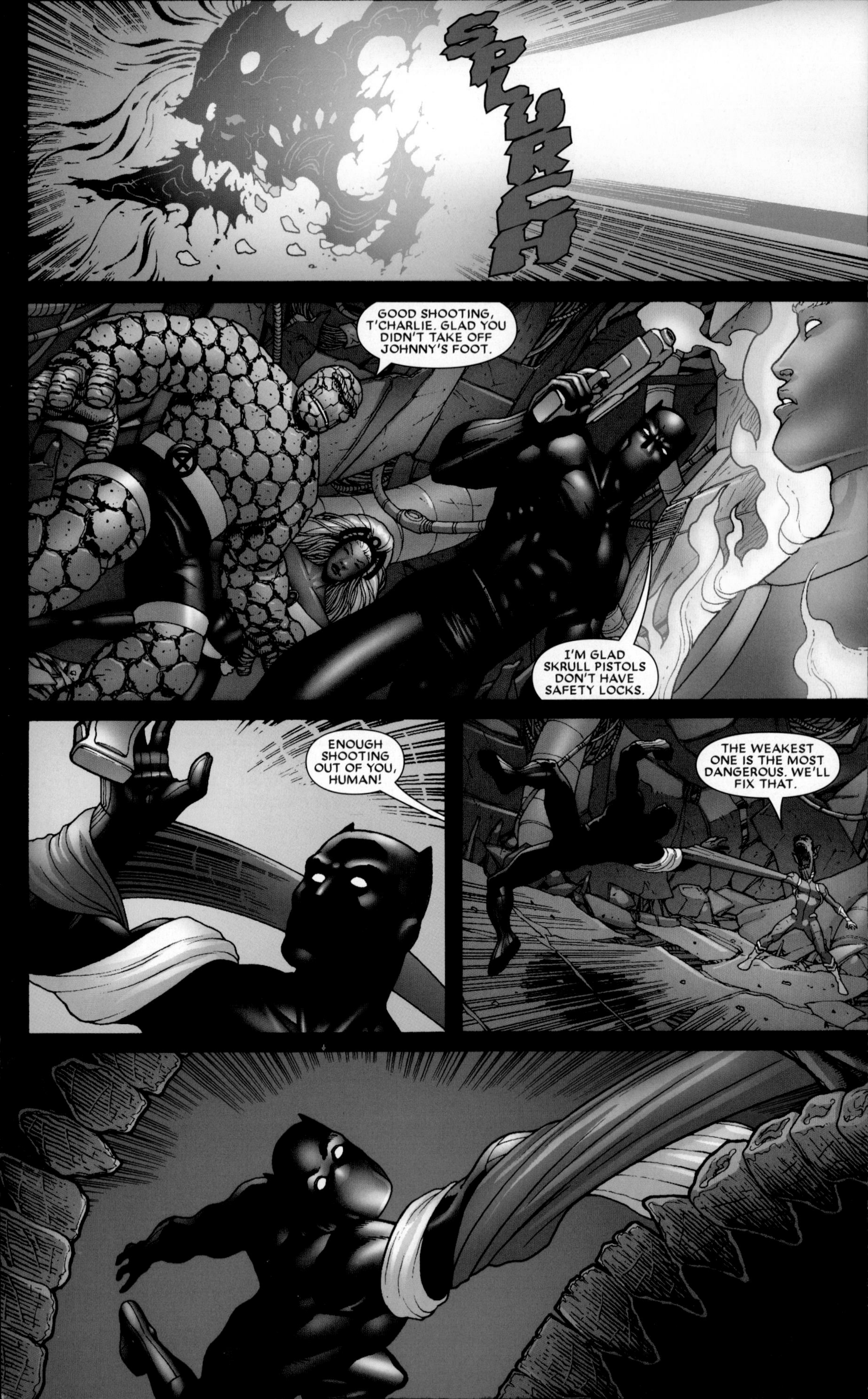
SPLURCH
GOOD SHOOTING, T'CHARLIE. GLAD YOU DIDN'T TAKE OFF JOHNNY'S FOOT.
I'M GLAD SKRULL PISTOLS DON'T HAVE SAFETY LOCKS.
ENOUGH SHOOTING OUT OF YOU, HUMAN!
THE WEAKEST ONE IS THE MOST DANGEROUS. WE'LL FIX THAT.

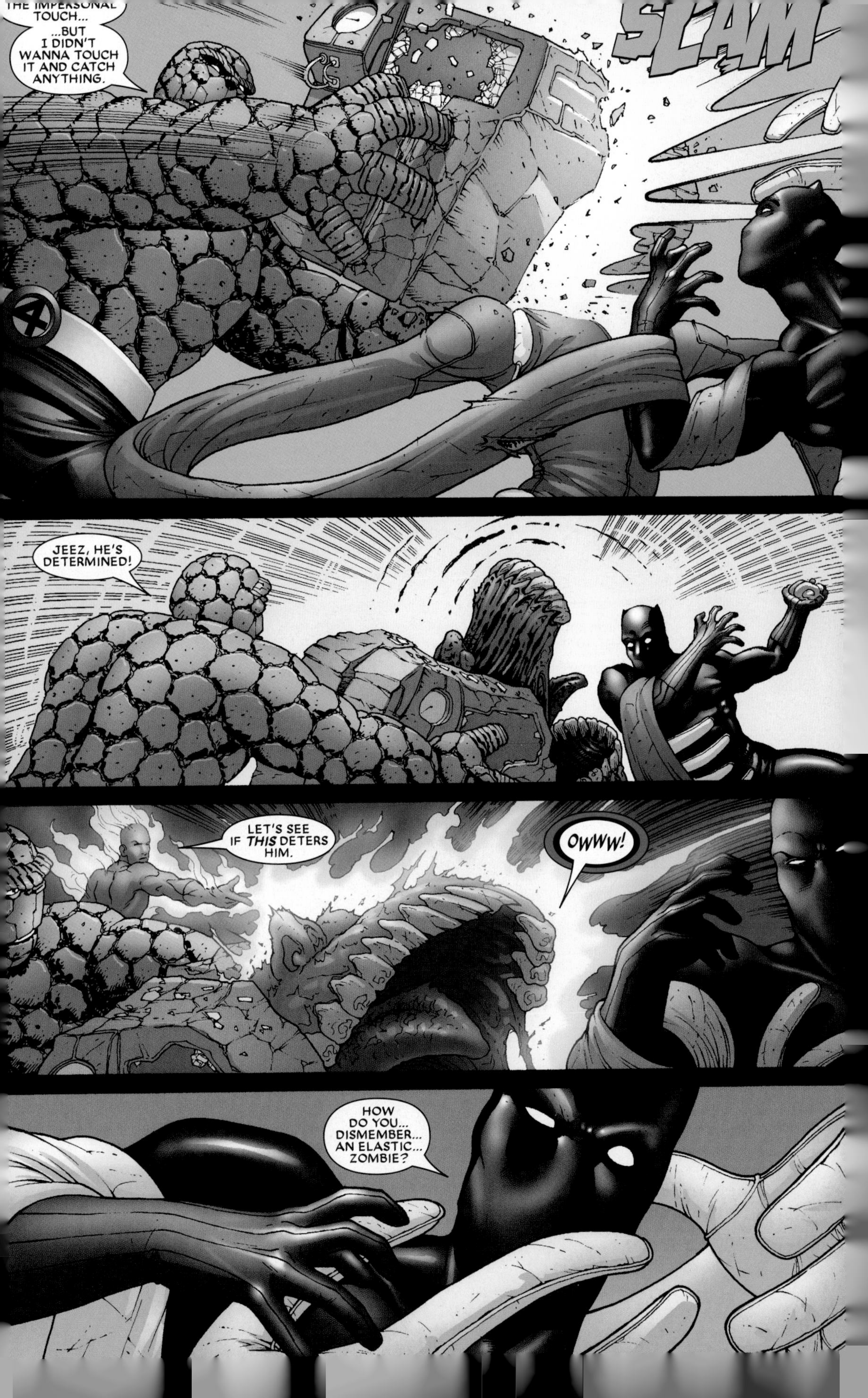
THE IMPERSONAL TOUCH... ...BUT I DIDN'T WANNA TOUCH IT AND CATCH ANYTHING.
SLAM
JEEZ, HE'S DETERMINED!
LET'S SEE IF THIS DETERS HIM.
OWWW!
HOW DO YOU... DISMEMBER... AN ELASTIC... ZOMBIE?

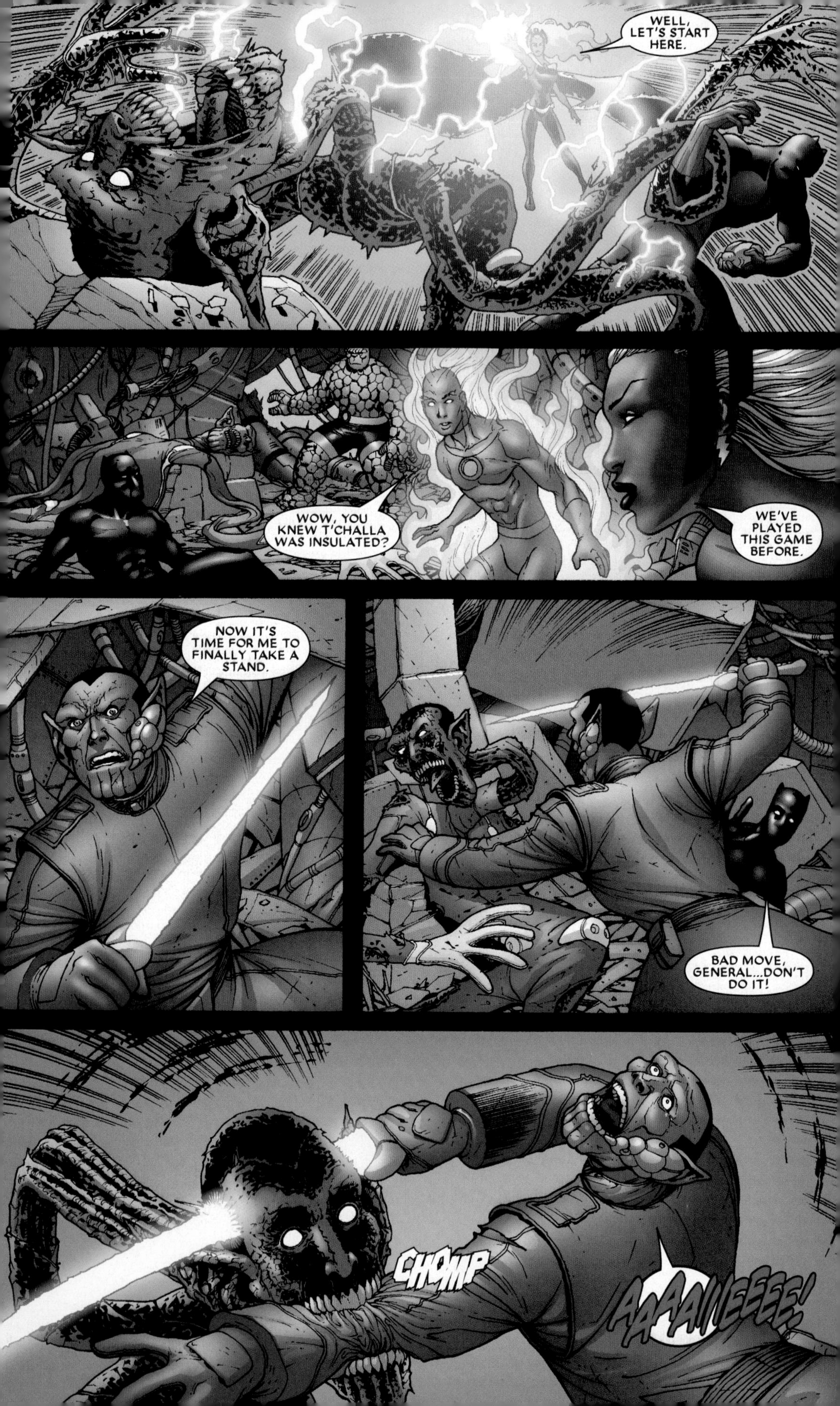
WELL, LET'S START HERE.
WOW, YOU KNEW T'CHALLA WAS INSULATED?
WE'VE PLAYED THIS GAME BEFORE.
NOW IT'S TIME FOR ME TO FINALLY TAKE A STAND.
BAD MOVE, GENERAL...DON'T DO IT!
CHOMP
AAAAIIEEEE!

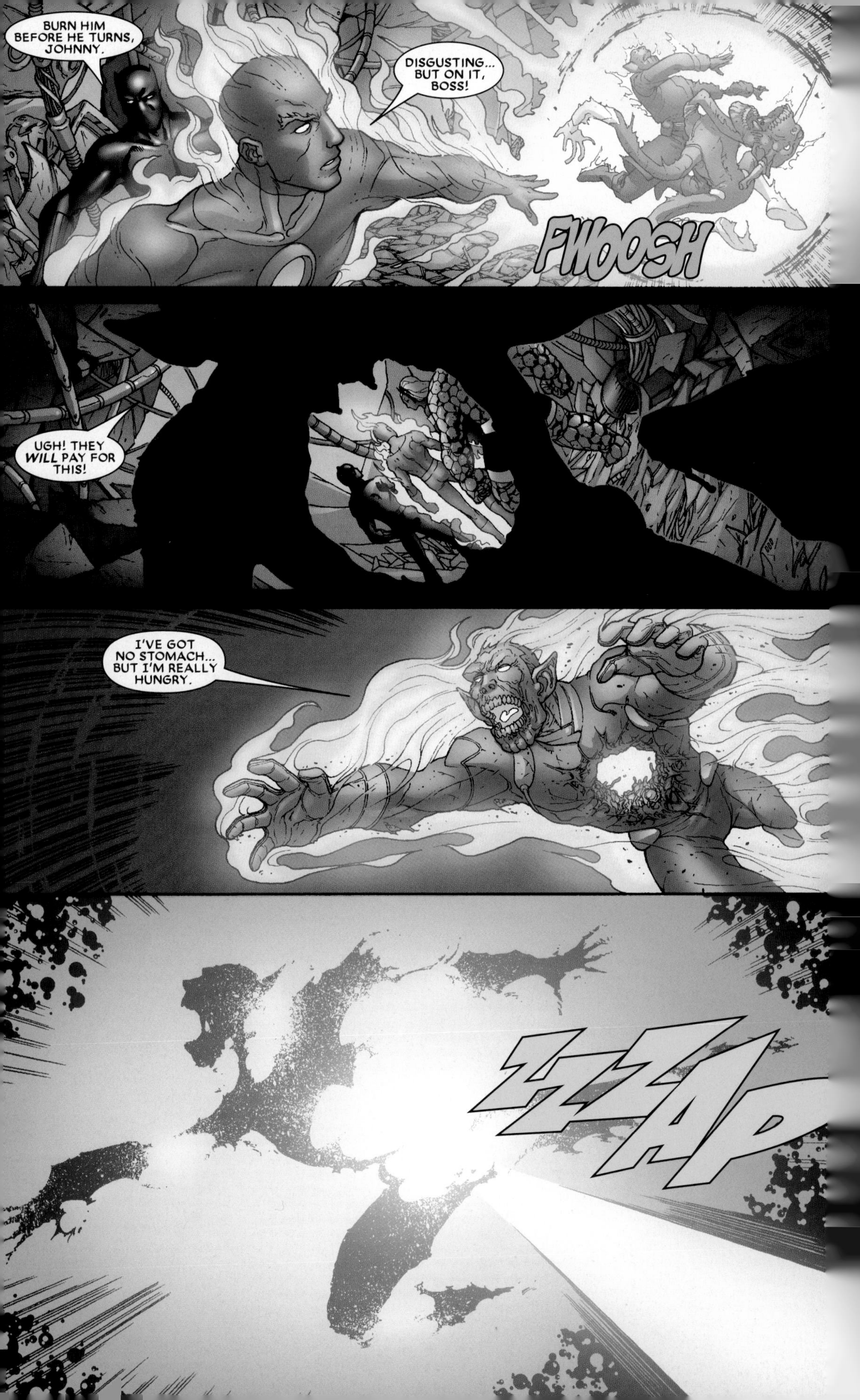
BURN HIM BEFORE HE TURNS, JOHNNY.
DISGUSTING... BUT ON IT, BOSS!
FWOOSH
UGH! THEY WILL PAY FOR THIS!
I'VE GOT NO STOMACH... BUT I'M REALLY HUNGRY.
ZZAP

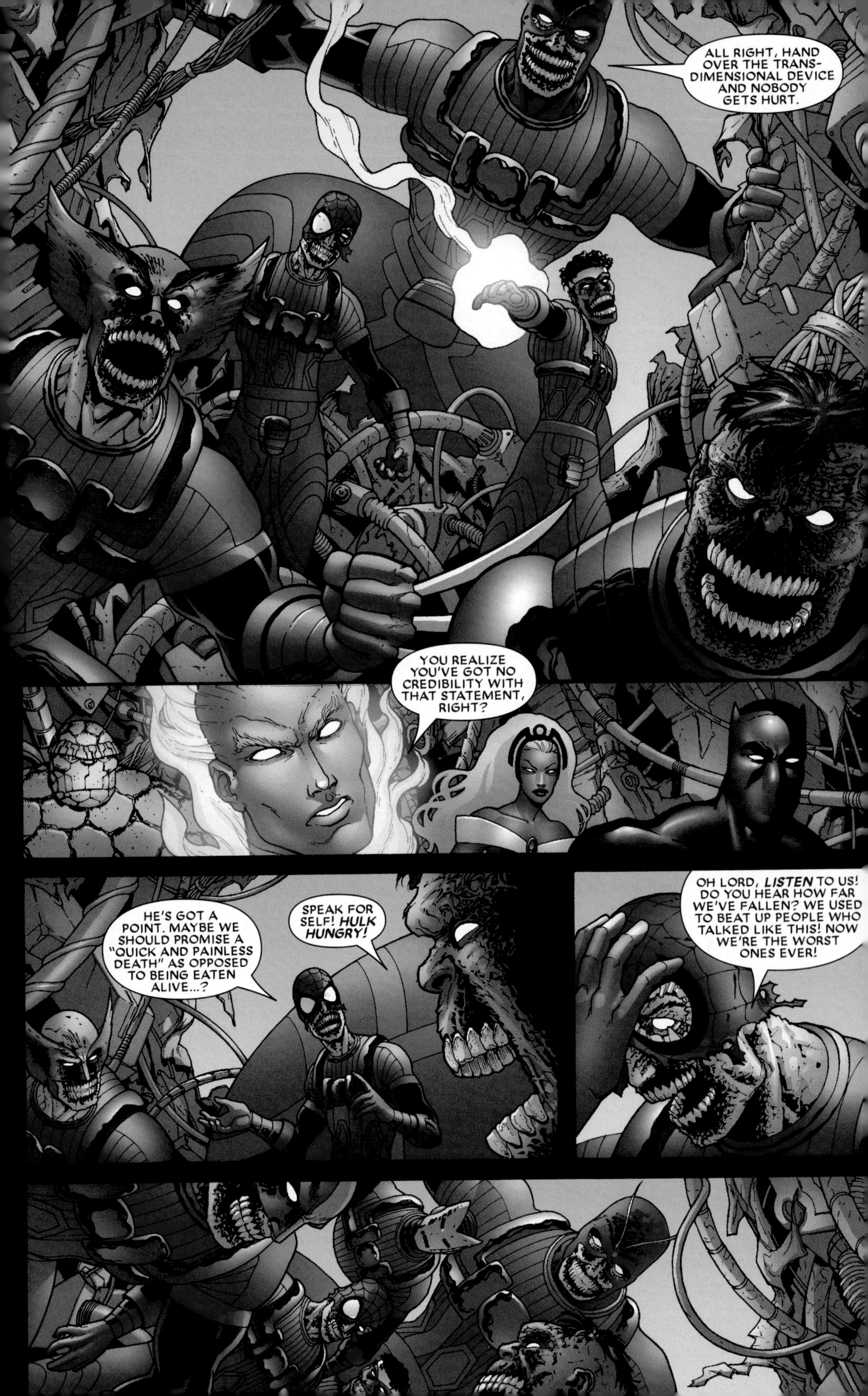
ALL RIGHT, HAND OVER THE TRANS-DIMENSIONAL DEVICE AND NOBODY GETS HURT.
YOU REALIZE YOU'VE GOT NO CREDIBILITY WITH THAT STATEMENT, RIGHT?
HE'S GOT A POINT. MAYBE WE SHOULD PROMISE A "QUICK AND PAINLESS DEATH" AS OPPOSED TO BEING EATEN ALIVE...?
SPEAK FOR SELF! HULK HUNGRY!
OH LORD, LISTEN TO US! DO YOU HEAR HOW FAR WE'VE FALLEN? WE USED TO BEAT UP PEOPLE WHO TALKED LIKE THIS! NOW WE'RE THE WORST ONES EVER!

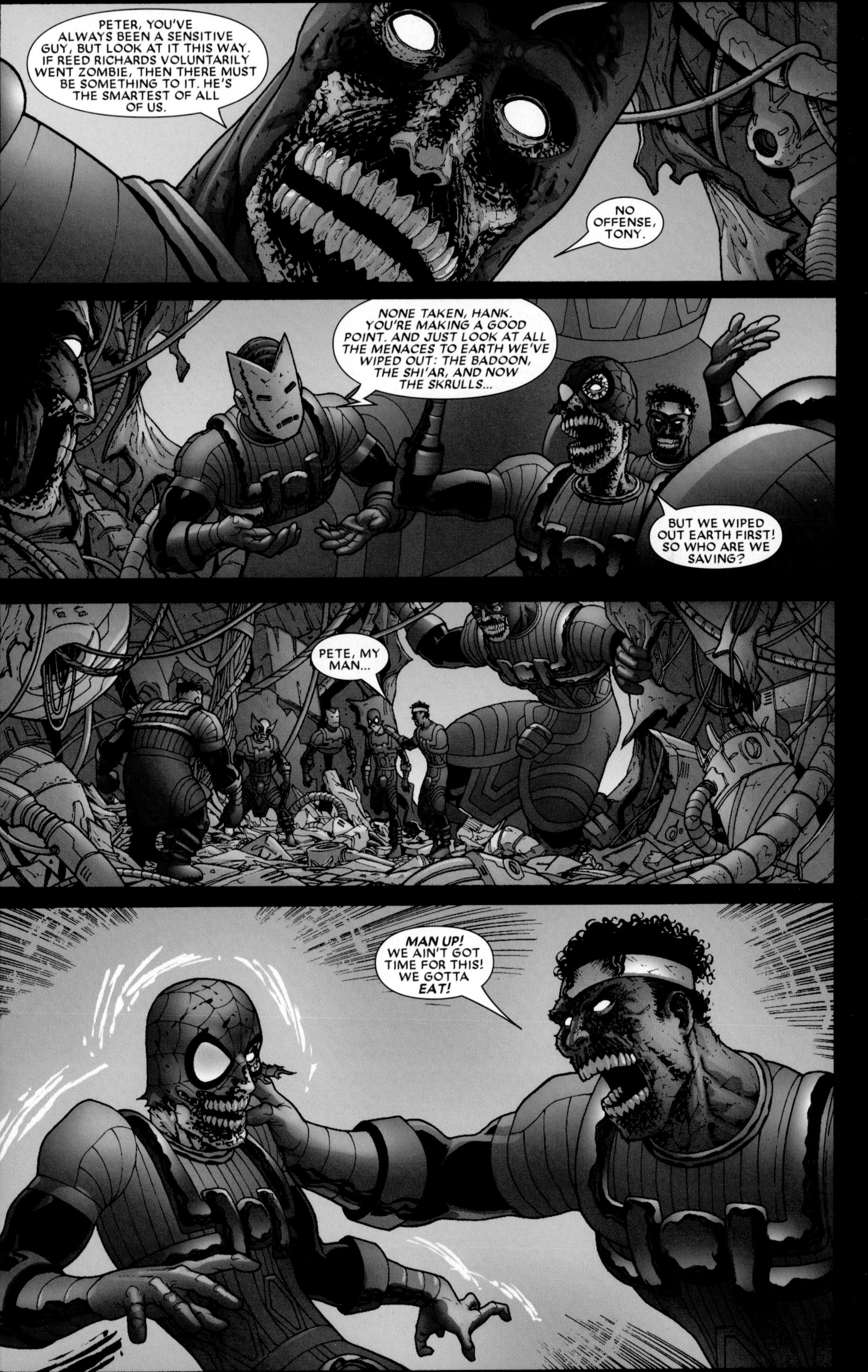
PETER, YOU'VE ALWAYS BEEN A SENSITIVE GUY, BUT LOOK AT IT THIS WAY. IF REED RICHARDS VOLUNTARILY WENT ZOMBIE, THEN THERE MUST BE SOMETHING TO IT. HE'S THE SMARTEST OF ALL OF US.
NO OFFENSE, TONY.
NONE TAKEN, HANK. YOU'RE MAKING A GOOD POINT. AND JUST LOOK AT ALL THE MENACES TO EARTH WE'VE WIPED OUT: THE BADOON, THE SHI'AR, AND NOW THE SKRULLS...
BUT WE WIPED OUT EARTH FIRST! SO WHO ARE WE SAVING?
PETE, MY MAN...
MAN UP! WE AIN'T GOT TIME FOR THIS! WE GOTTA EAT!

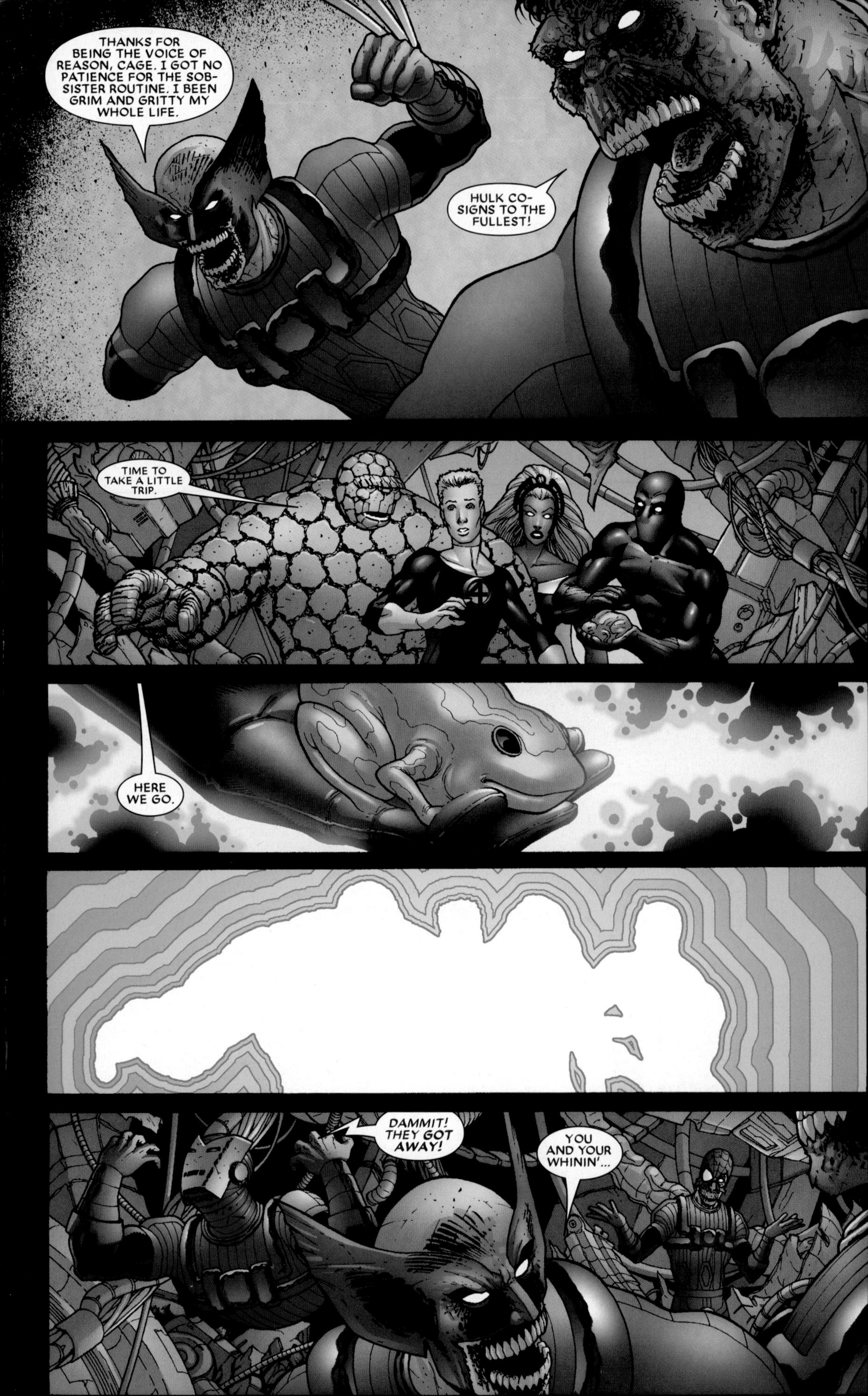
THANKS FOR BEING THE VOICE OF REASON, CAGE. I GOT NO PATIENCE FOR THE SOB-SISTER ROUTINE. I BEEN GRIM AND GRITTY MY WHOLE LIFE.
HULK CO-SIGNS TO THE FULLEST!
TIME TO TAKE A LITTLE TRIP.
HERE WE GO.
DAMMIT! THEY GOT AWAY!
YOU AND YOUR WHININ'...

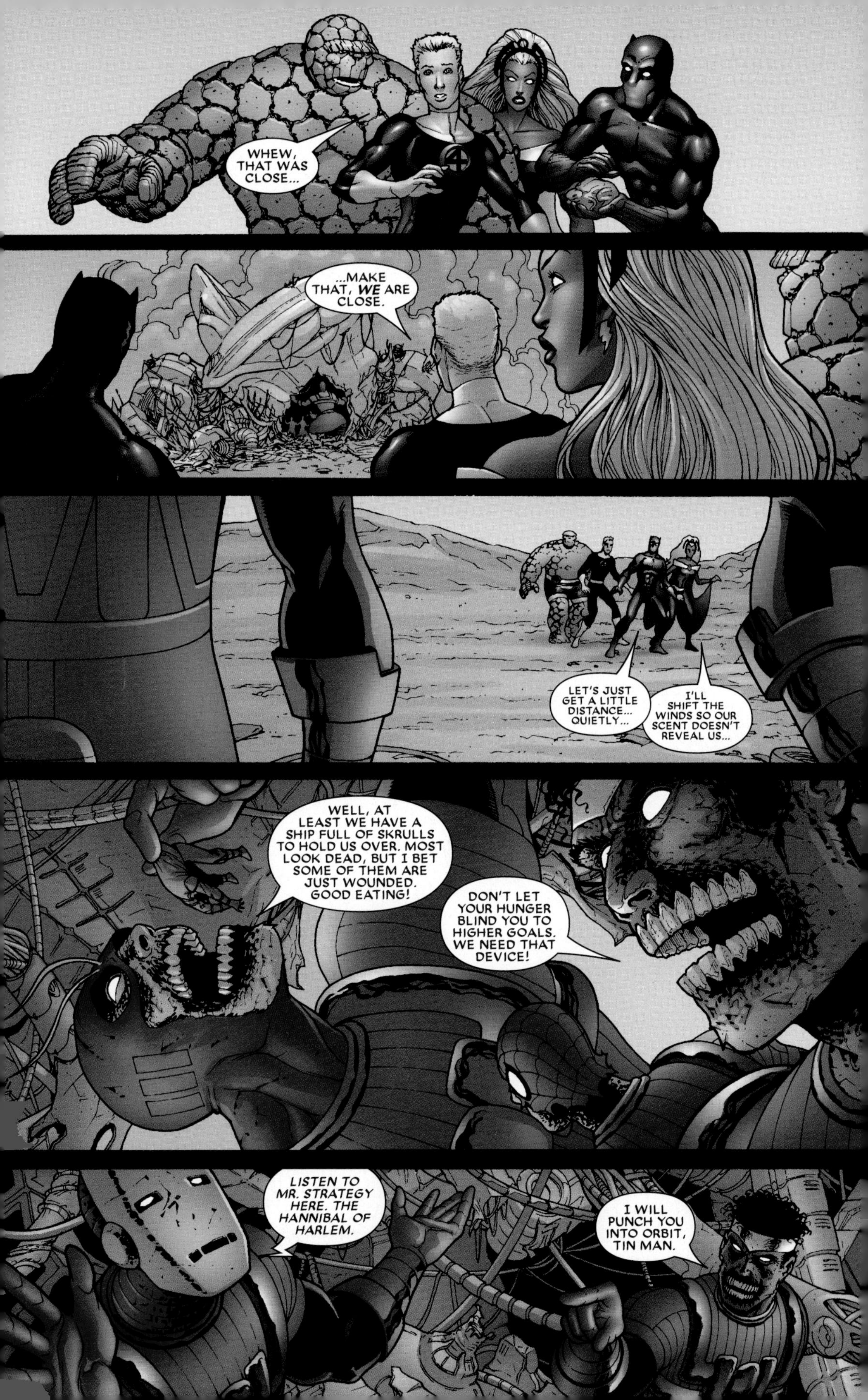
WHEW, THAT WAS CLOSE...
...MAKE THAT, WE ARE CLOSE.
LET'S JUST GET A LITTLE DISTANCE... QUIETLY...
I'LL SHIFT THE WINDS SO OUR SCENT DOESN'T REVEAL US...
WELL, AT LEAST WE HAVE A SHIP FULL OF SKRULLS TO HOLD US OVER. MOST LOOK DEAD, BUT I BET SOME OF THEM ARE JUST WOUNDED. GOOD EATING!
DON'T LET YOUR HUNGER BLIND YOU TO HIGHER GOALS. WE NEED THAT DEVICE!
LISTEN TO MR. STRATEGY HERE. THE HANNIBAL OF HARLEM.
I WILL PUNCH YOU INTO ORBIT, TIN MAN.

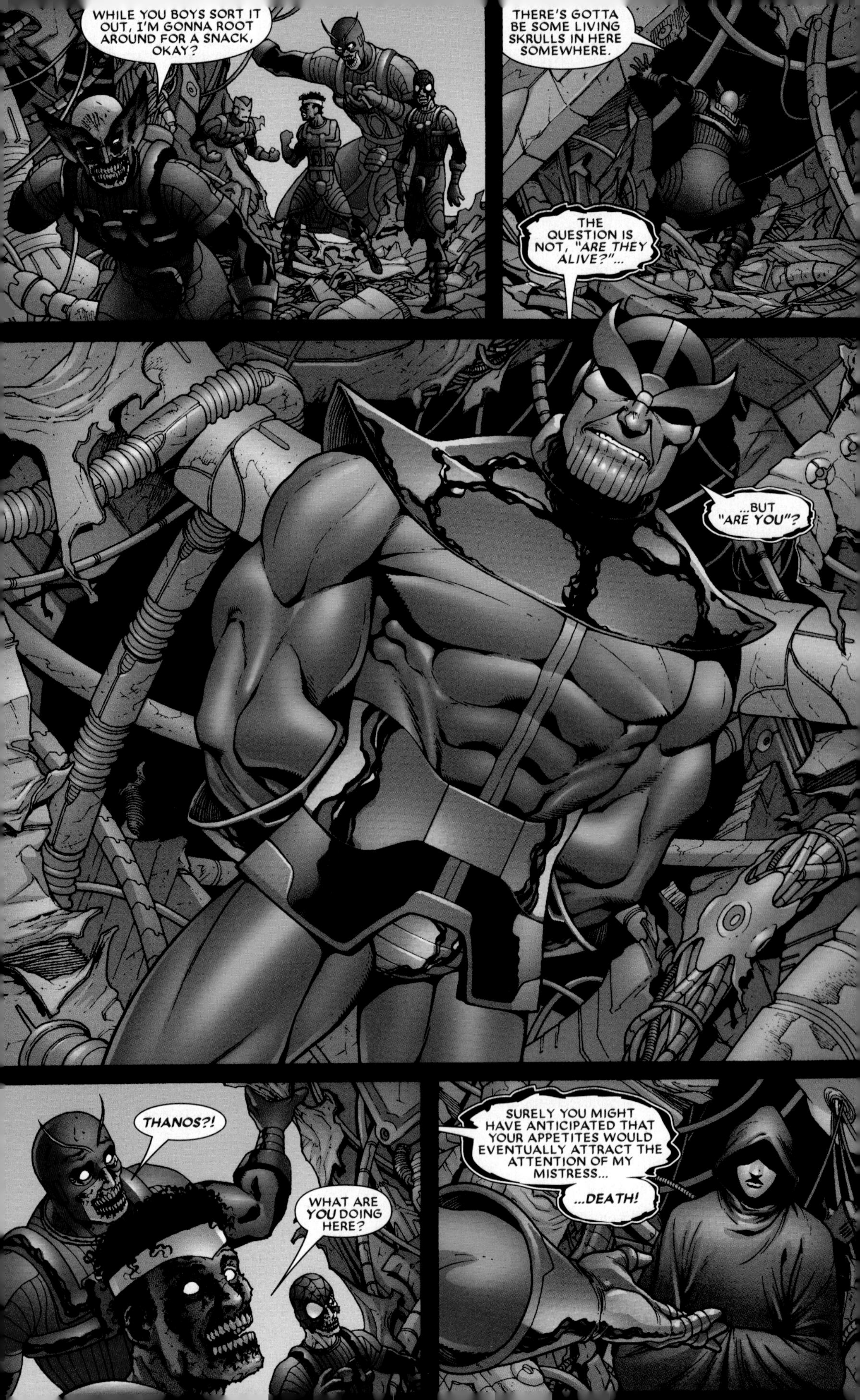
WHILE YOU BOYS SORT IT OUT, I'M GONNA ROOT AROUND FOR A SNACK, OKAY?
THERE'S GOTTA BE SOME LIVING SKRULLS IN HERE SOMEWHERE.
THE QUESTION IS NOT, "ARE THEY ALIVE?"...
...BUT "ARE YOU"?
THANOS?!
WHAT ARE YOU DOING HERE?
SURELY YOU MIGHT HAVE ANTICIPATED THAT YOUR APPETITES WOULD EVENTUALLY ATTRACT THE ATTENTION OF MY MISTRESS...
...DEATH!

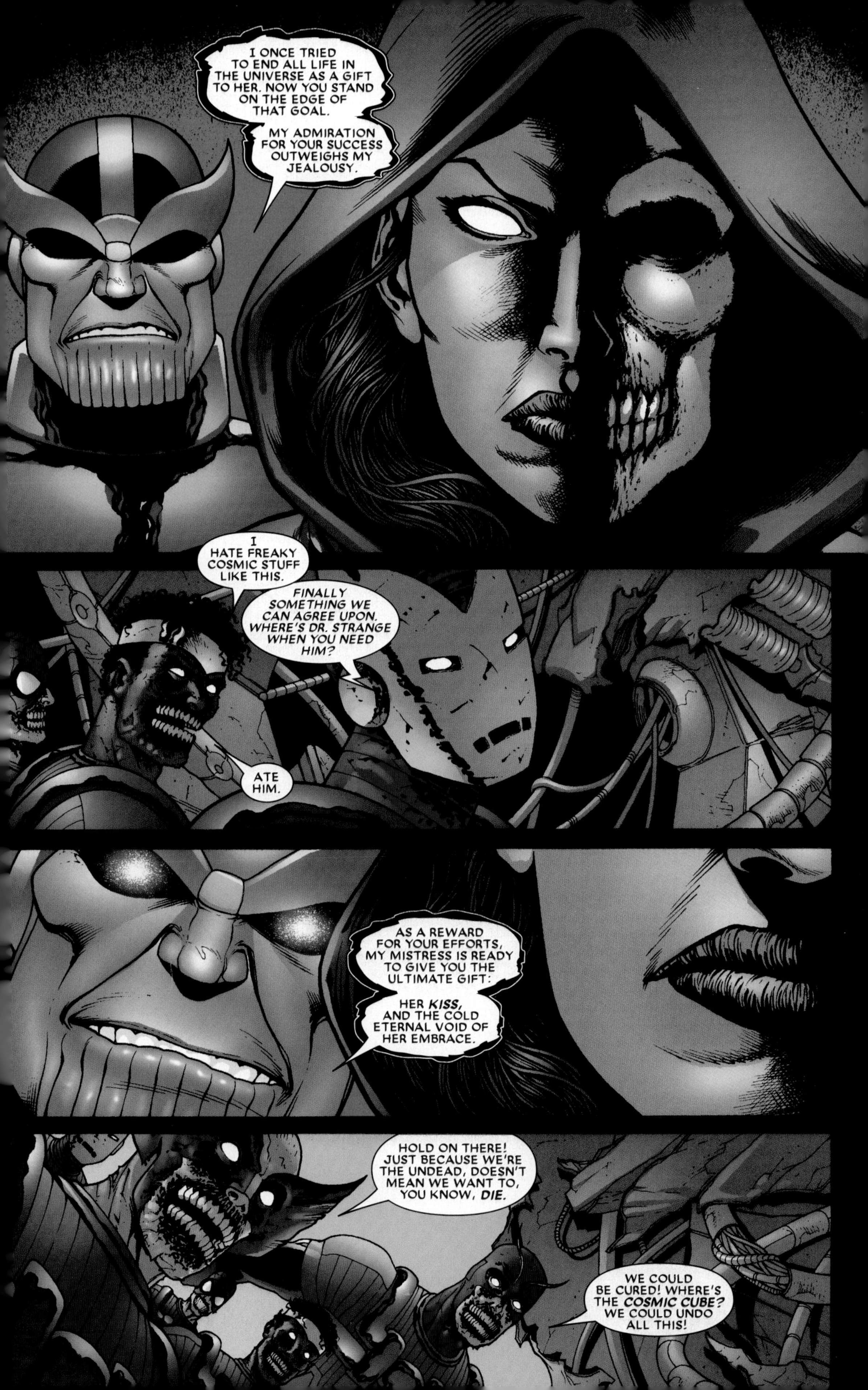
I ONCE TRIED TO END ALL LIFE IN THE UNIVERSE AS A GIFT TO HER. NOW YOU STAND ON THE EDGE OF THAT GOAL.
MY ADMIRATION FOR YOUR SUCCESS OUTWEIGHS MY JEALOUSY.
I HATE FREAKY COSMIC STUFF LIKE THIS.
FINALLY SOMETHING WE CAN AGREE UPON. WHERE'S DR. STRANGE WHEN YOU NEED HIM?
ATE HIM.
AS A REWARD FOR YOUR EFFORTS, MY MISTRESS IS READY TO GIVE YOU THE ULTIMATE GIFT:
HER ***KISS,*** AND THE COLD ETERNAL VOID OF HER EMBRACE.
HOLD ON THERE! JUST BECAUSE WE'RE THE UNDEAD, DOESN'T MEAN WE WANT TO, YOU KNOW, ***DIE.***
WE COULD BE CURED! WHERE'S THE ***COSMIC CUBE?*** WE COULD UNDO ALL THIS!

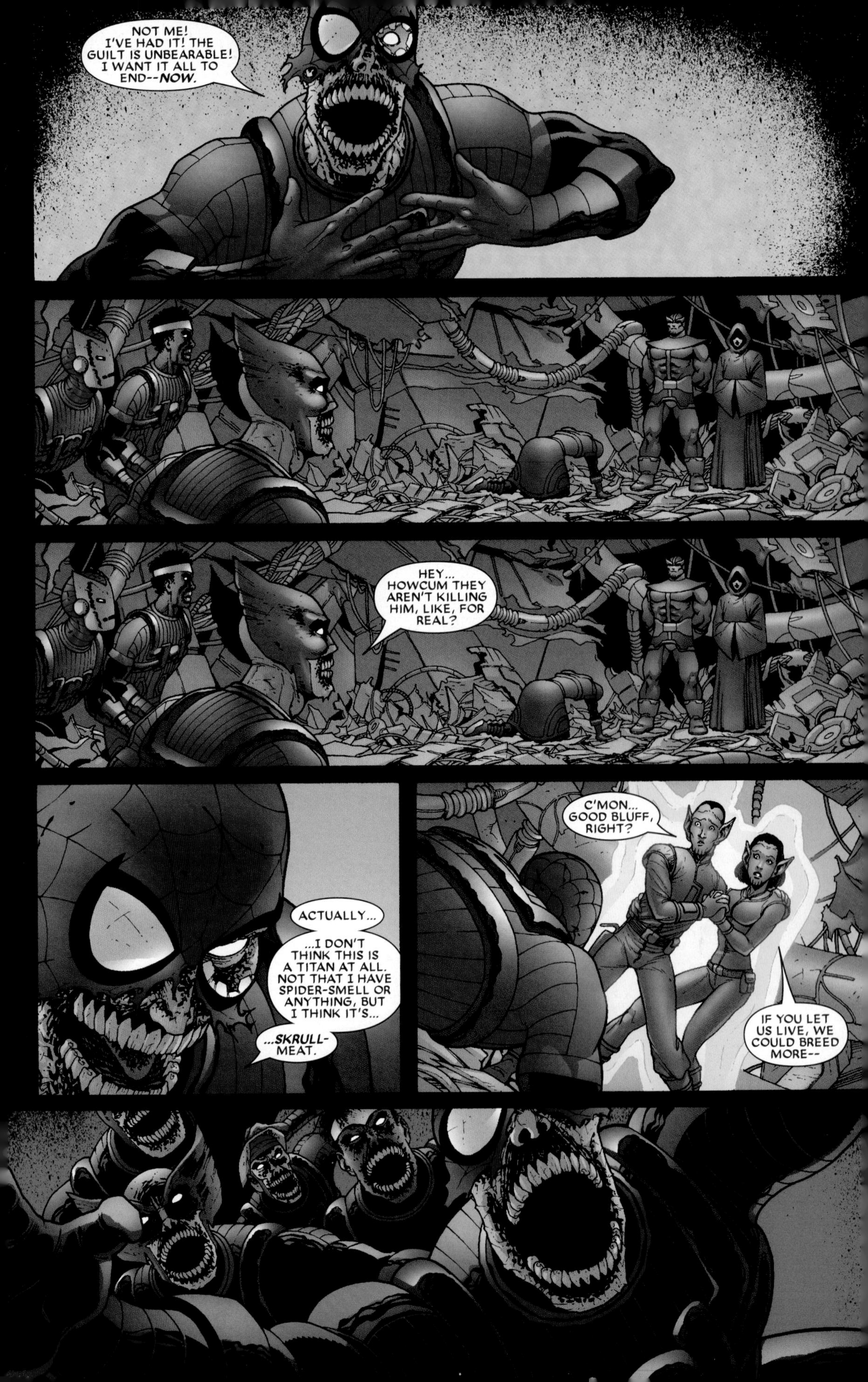

NOT ME! I'VE HAD IT! THE GUILT IS UNBEARABLE! I WANT IT ALL TO END--NOW.
HEY... HOWCUM THEY AREN'T KILLING HIM, LIKE, FOR REAL?
ACTUALLY...
...I DON'T THINK THIS IS A TITAN AT ALL. NOT THAT I HAVE SPIDER-SMELL OR ANYTHING, BUT I THINK IT'S...
...SKRULL-MEAT.
C'MON... GOOD BLUFF, RIGHT?
IF YOU LET US LIVE, WE COULD BREED MORE--

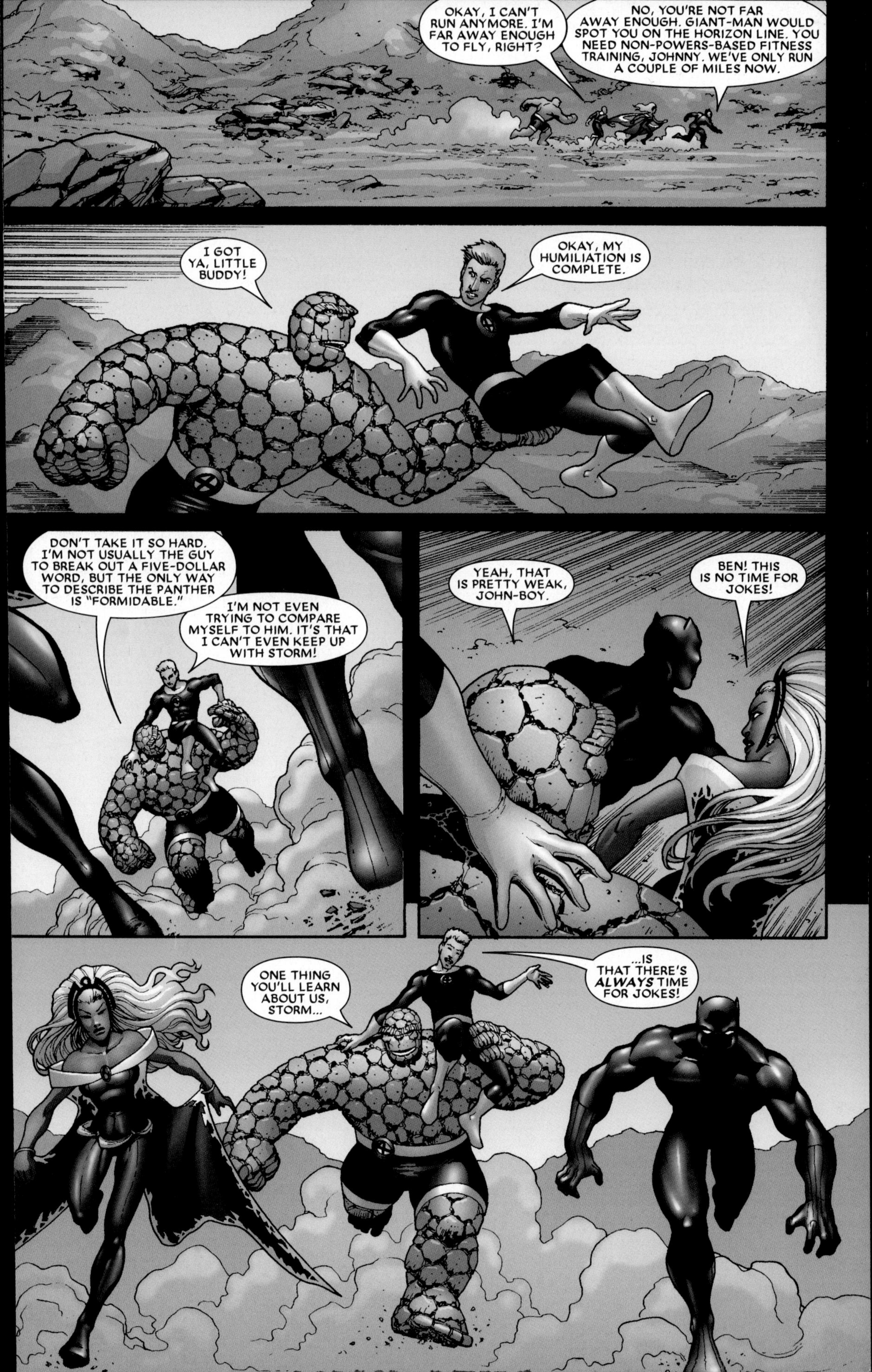
OKAY, I CAN'T RUN ANYMORE. I'M FAR AWAY ENOUGH TO FLY, RIGHT?
NO, YOU'RE NOT FAR AWAY ENOUGH. GIANT-MAN WOULD SPOT YOU ON THE HORIZON LINE. YOU NEED NON-POWERS-BASED FITNESS TRAINING, JOHNNY. WE'VE ONLY RUN A COUPLE OF MILES NOW.
I GOT YA, LITTLE BUDDY!
OKAY, MY HUMILIATION IS COMPLETE.
DON'T TAKE IT SO HARD. I'M NOT USUALLY THE GUY TO BREAK OUT A FIVE-DOLLAR WORD, BUT THE ONLY WAY TO DESCRIBE THE PANTHER IS "FORMIDABLE."
I'M NOT EVEN TRYING TO COMPARE MYSELF TO HIM. IT'S THAT I CAN'T EVEN KEEP UP WITH STORM!
YEAH, THAT IS PRETTY WEAK, JOHN-BOY.
BEN! THIS IS NO TIME FOR JOKES!
ONE THING YOU'LL LEARN ABOUT US, STORM...
...IS THAT THERE'S ALWAYS TIME FOR JOKES!

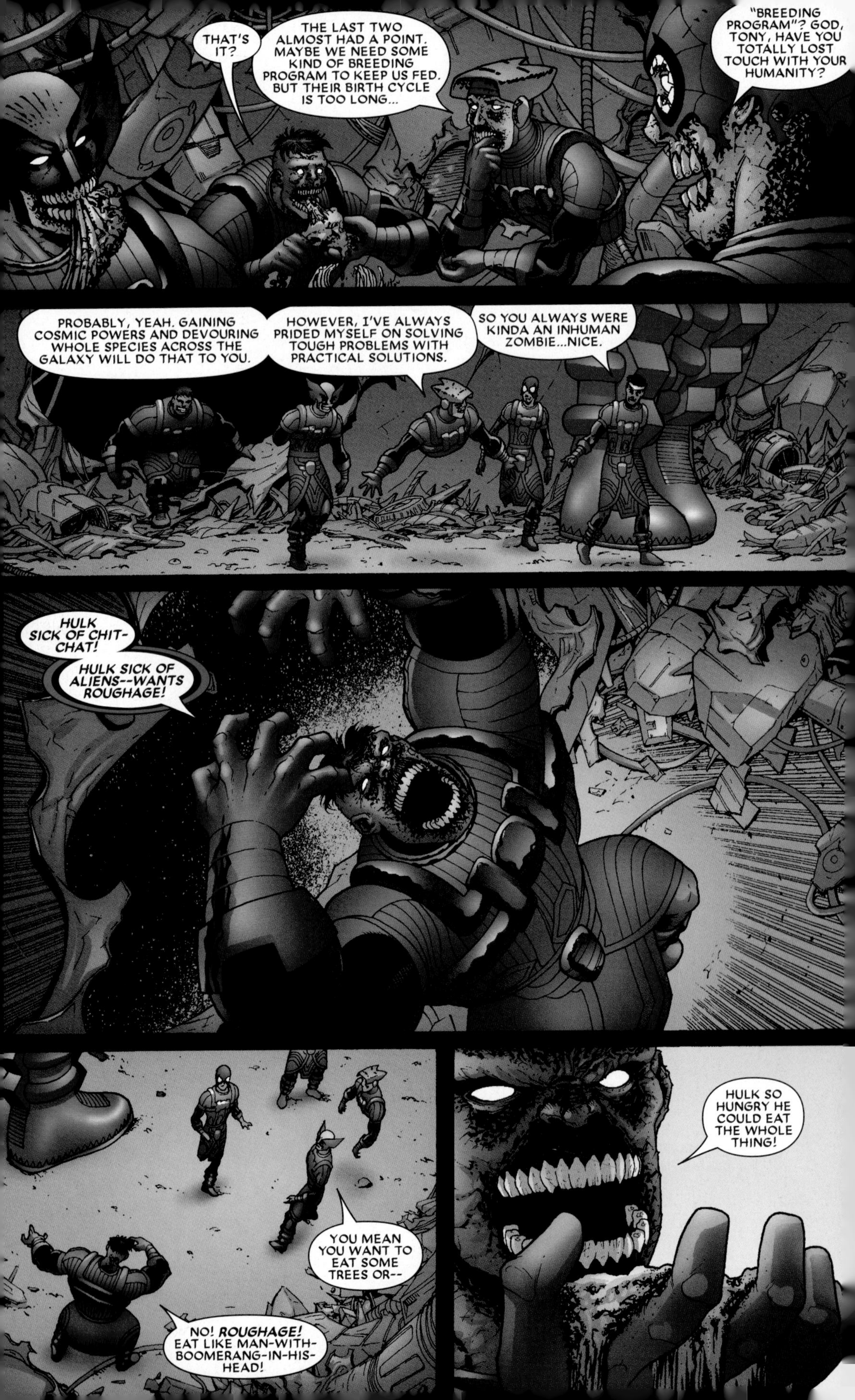
THAT'S IT?
THE LAST TWO ALMOST HAD A POINT. MAYBE WE NEED SOME KIND OF BREEDING PROGRAM TO KEEP US FED. BUT THEIR BIRTH CYCLE IS TOO LONG...
"BREEDING PROGRAM"? GOD, TONY, HAVE YOU TOTALLY LOST TOUCH WITH YOUR HUMANITY?
PROBABLY, YEAH. GAINING COSMIC POWERS AND DEVOURING WHOLE SPECIES ACROSS THE GALAXY WILL DO THAT TO YOU.
HOWEVER, I'VE ALWAYS PRIDED MYSELF ON SOLVING TOUGH PROBLEMS WITH PRACTICAL SOLUTIONS.
SO YOU ALWAYS WERE KINDA AN INHUMAN ZOMBIE...NICE.
HULK SICK OF CHIT-CHAT!
HULK SICK OF ALIENS--WANTS ROUGHAGE!
YOU MEAN YOU WANT TO EAT SOME TREES OR--
NO! *ROUGHAGE!* EAT LIKE MAN-WITH-BOOMERANG-IN-HIS-HEAD!
HULK SO HUNGRY HE COULD EAT THE WHOLE THING!

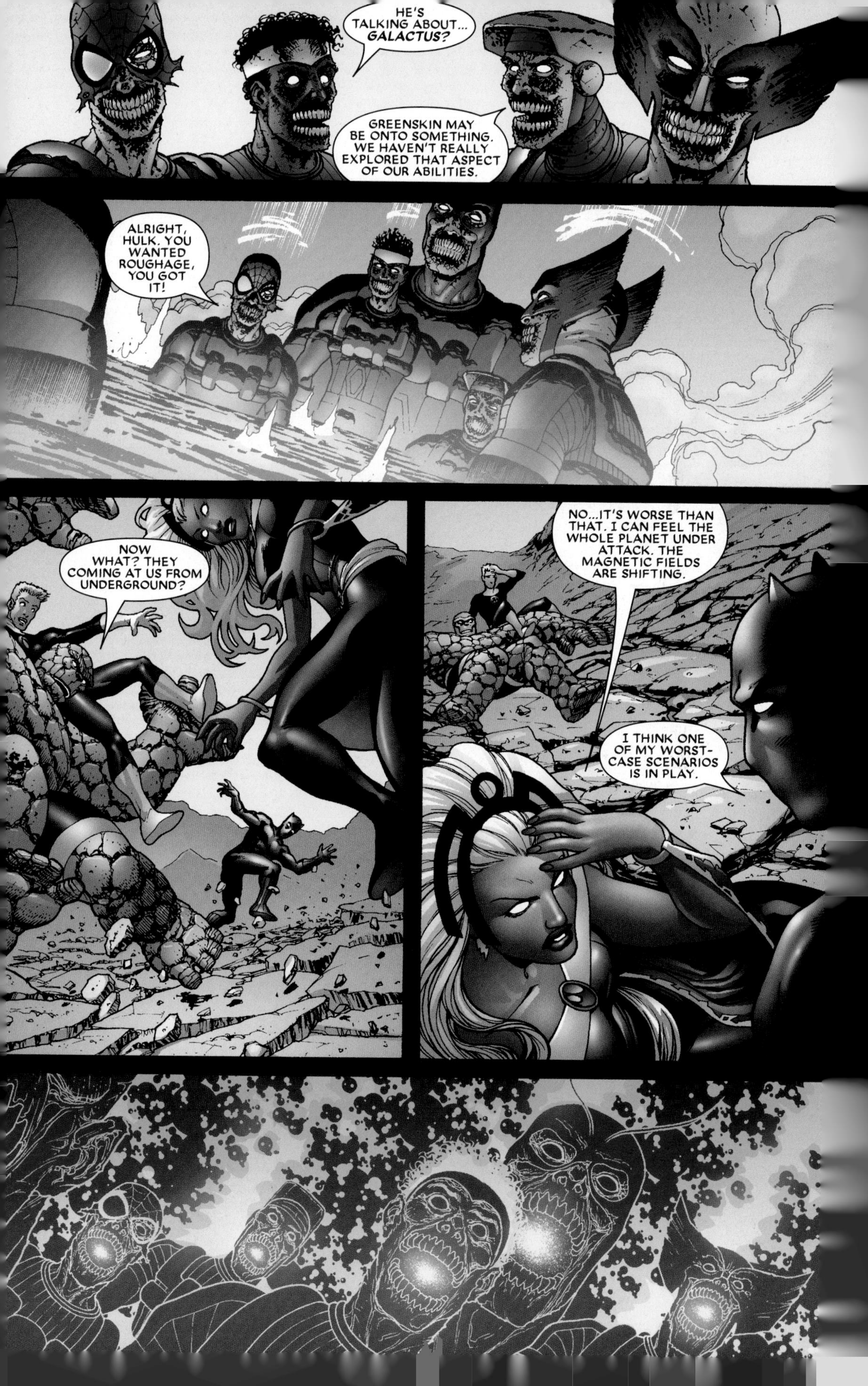
HE'S TALKING ABOUT... GALACTUS?
GREENSKIN MAY BE ONTO SOMETHING. WE HAVEN'T REALLY EXPLORED THAT ASPECT OF OUR ABILITIES.
ALRIGHT, HULK. YOU WANTED ROUGHAGE, YOU GOT IT!
NOW WHAT? THEY COMING AT US FROM UNDERGROUND?
NO...IT'S WORSE THAN THAT. I CAN FEEL THE WHOLE PLANET UNDER ATTACK. THE MAGNETIC FIELDS ARE SHIFTING.
I THINK ONE OF MY WORST-CASE SCENARIOS IS IN PLAY.

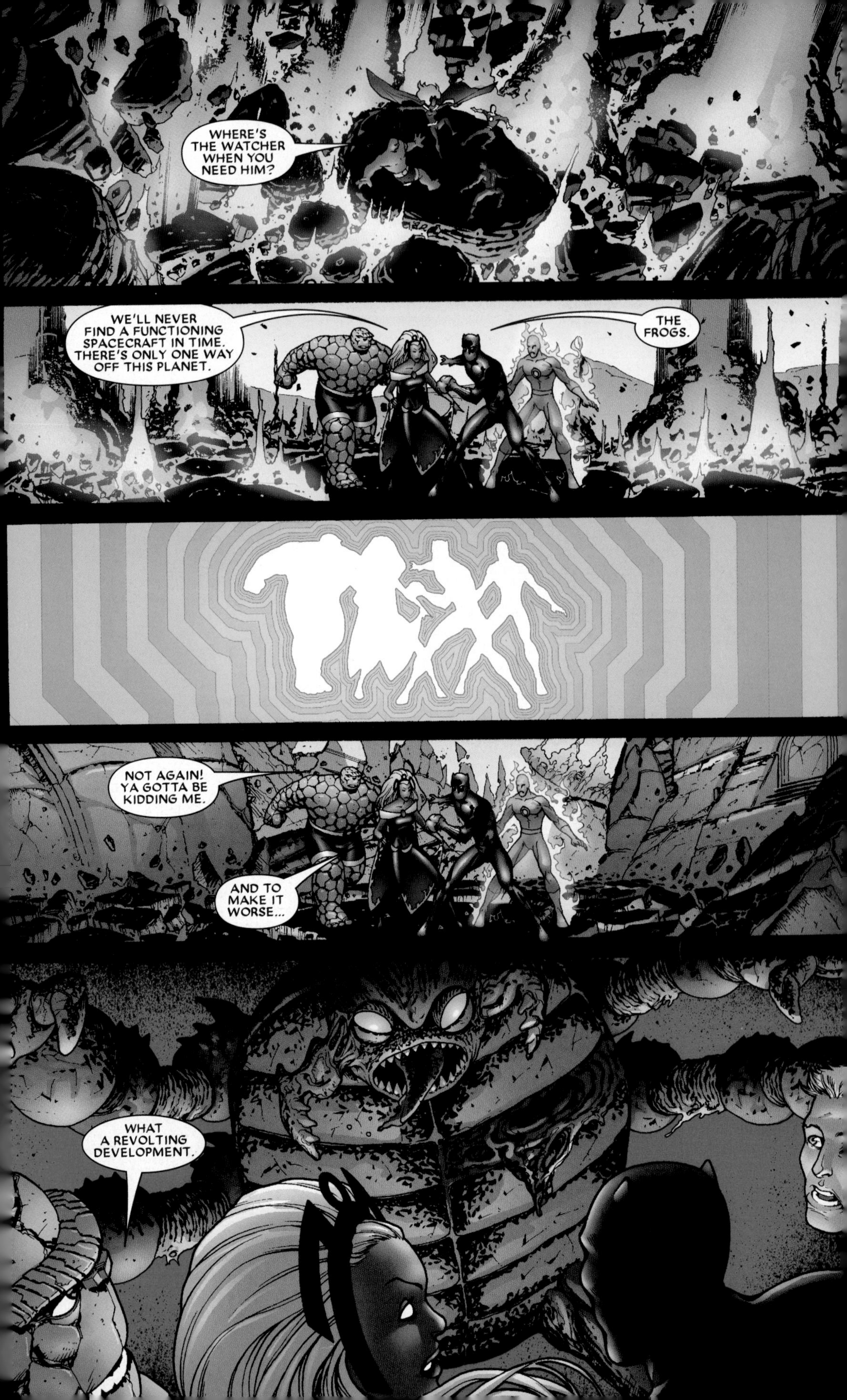
WHERE'S THE WATCHER WHEN YOU NEED HIM?
WE'LL NEVER FIND A FUNCTIONING SPACECRAFT IN TIME. THERE'S ONLY ONE WAY OFF THIS PLANET.
THE FROGS.
NOT AGAIN! YA GOTTA BE KIDDING ME.
AND TO MAKE IT WORSE...
WHAT A REVOLTING DEVELOPMENT.

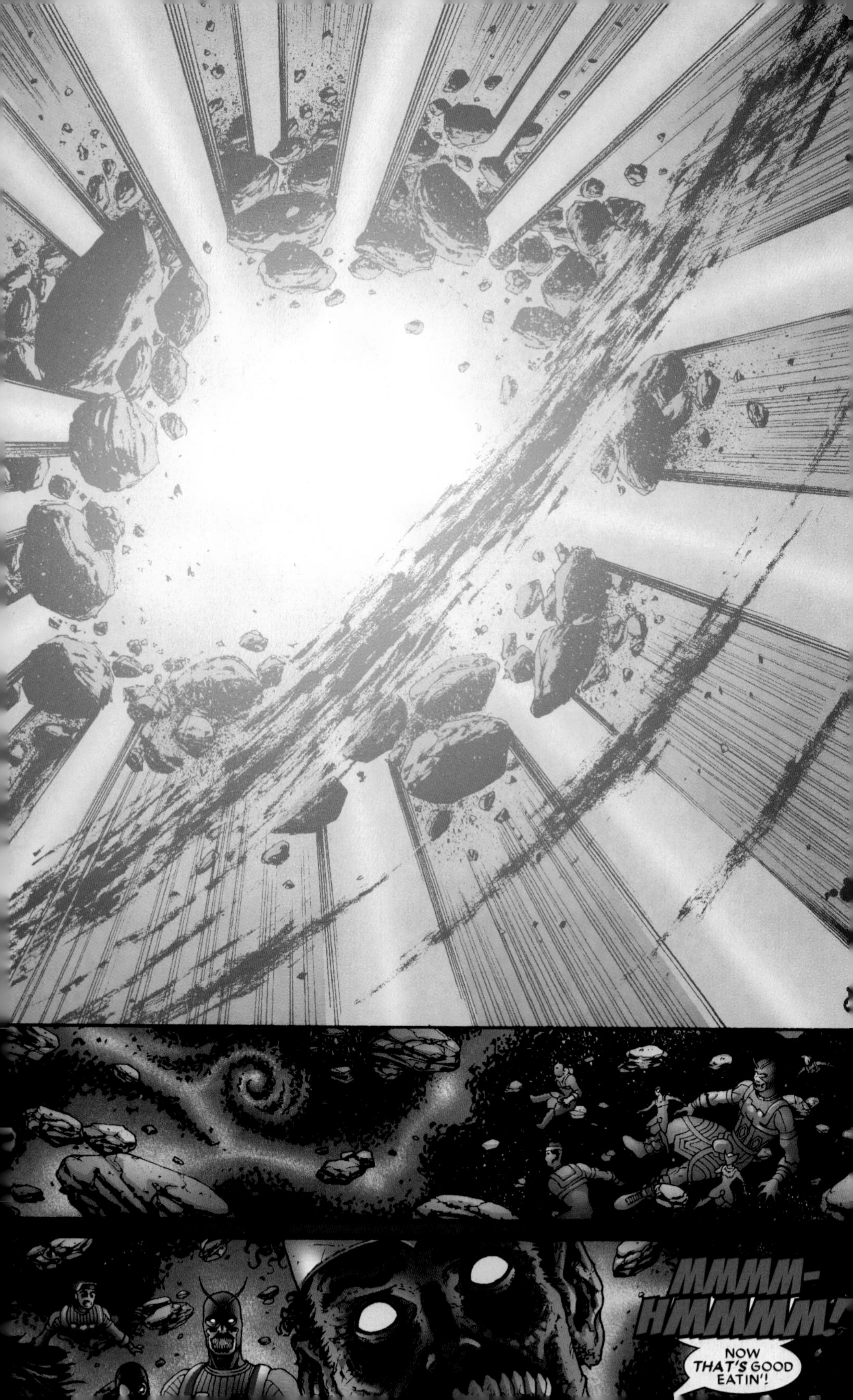
MMMM-HMMMM!
NOW THAT'S GOOD EATIN'!

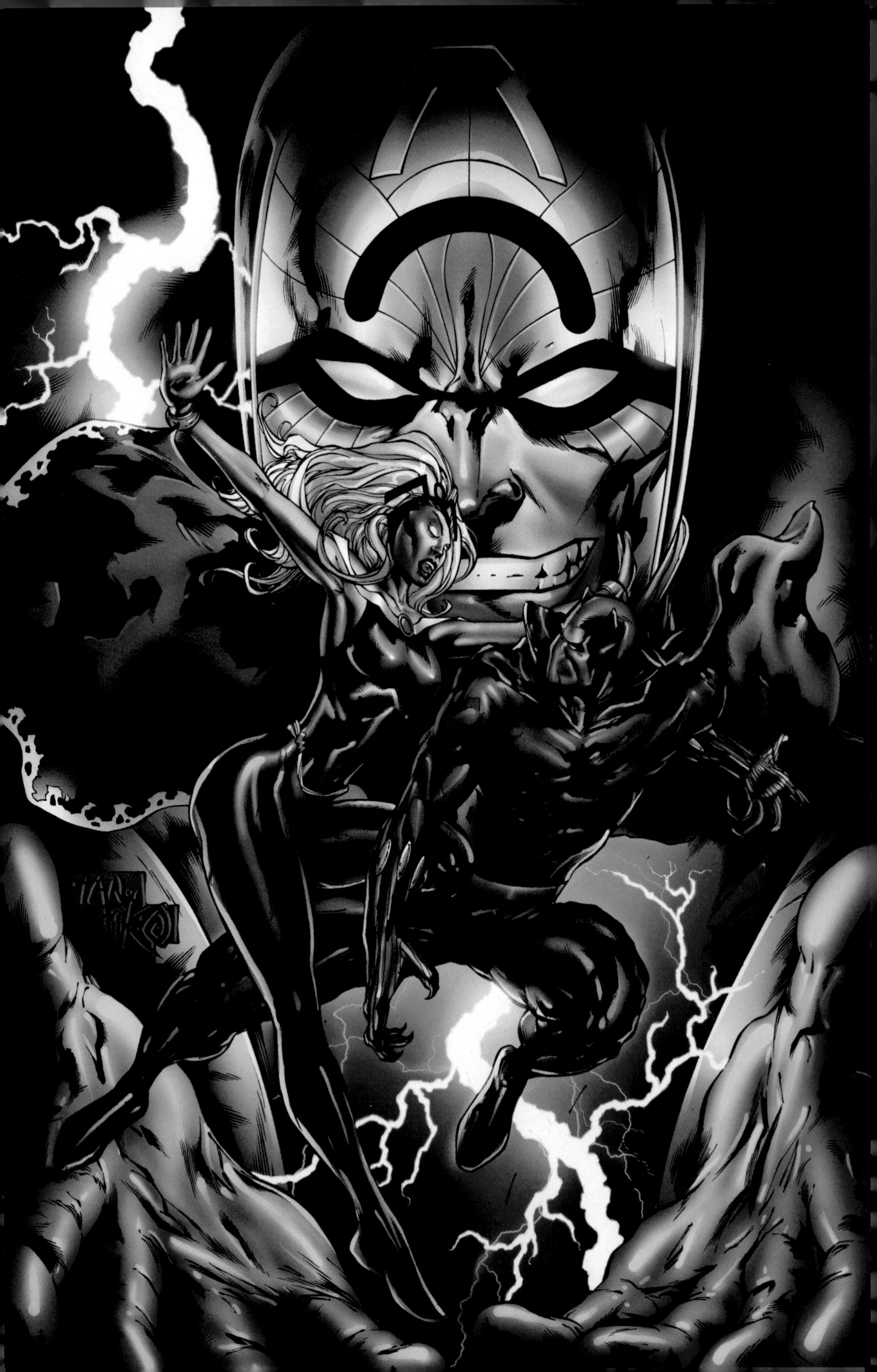

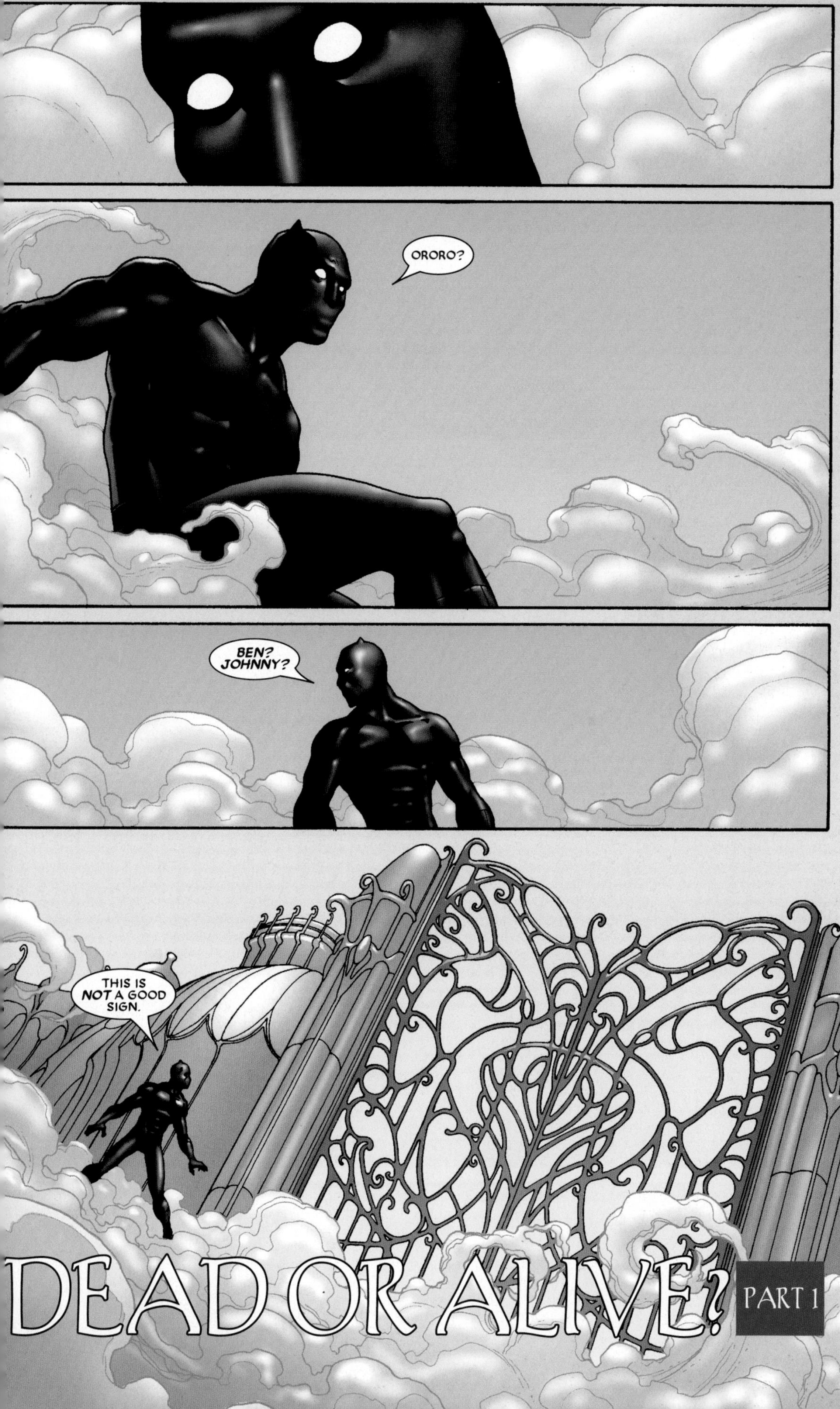
ORORO?
BEN? JOHNNY?
THIS IS NOT A GOOD SIGN.
DEAD OR ALIVE? PART 1

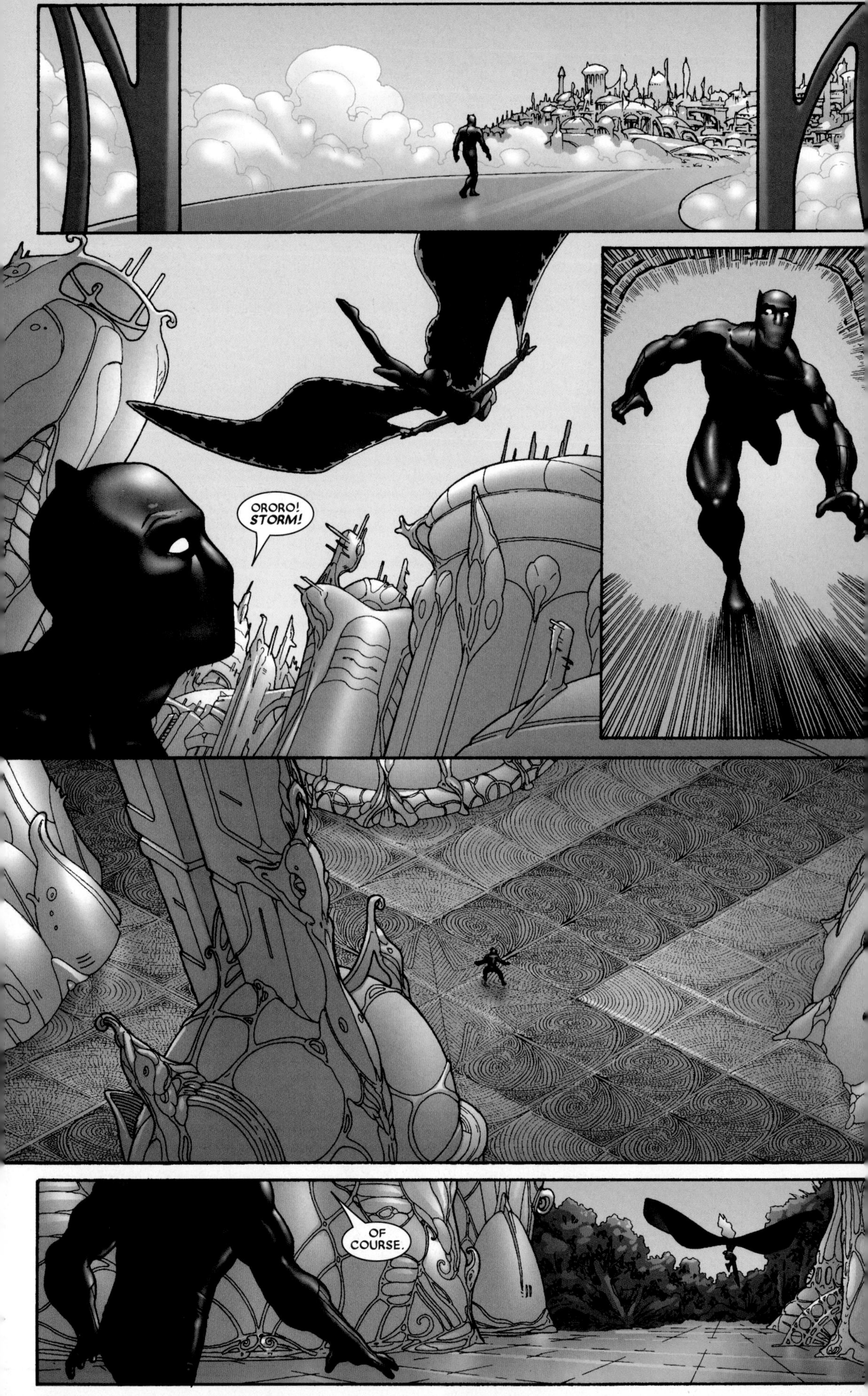
ORORO! STORM!
OF COURSE.

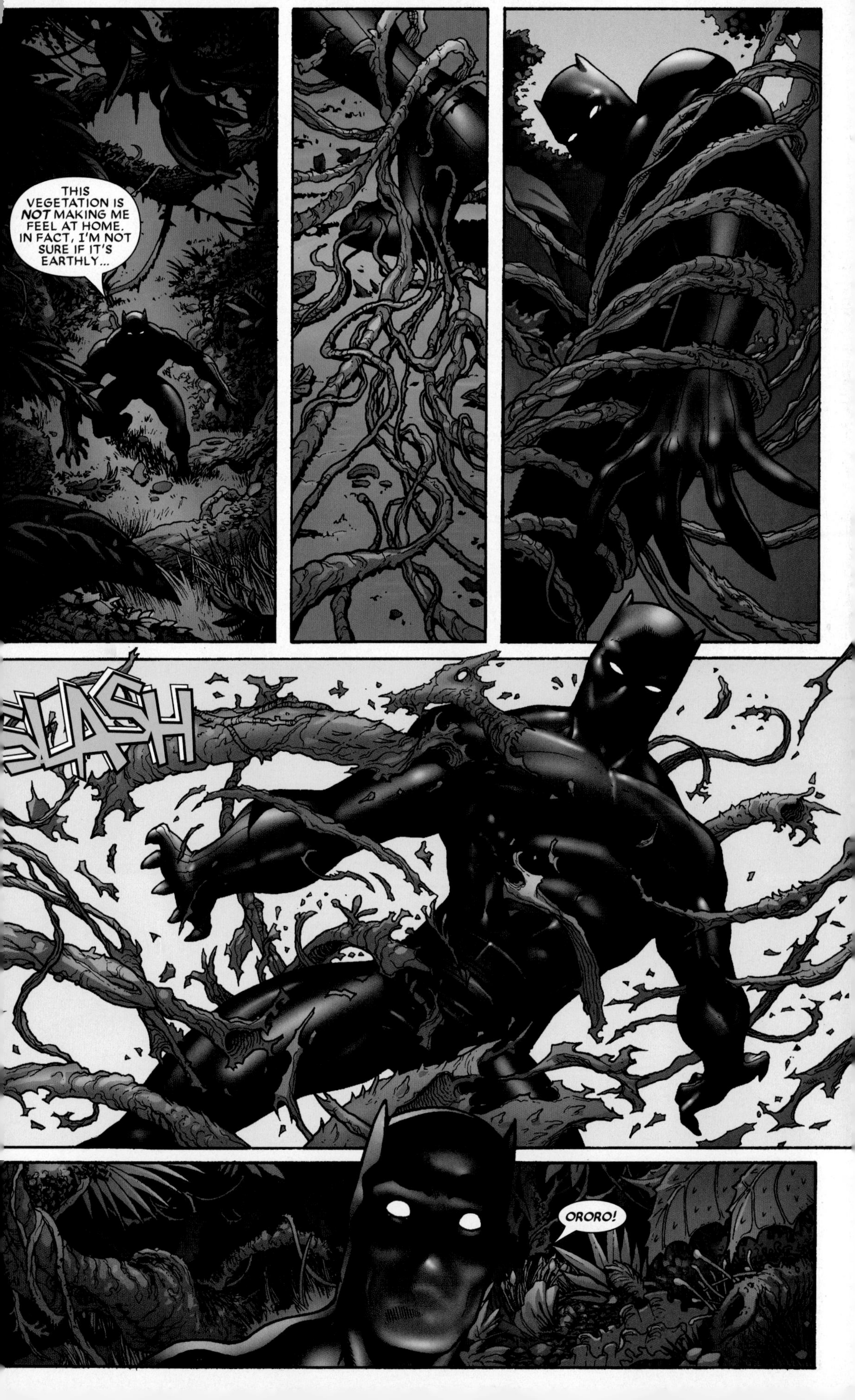
THIS VEGETATION IS NOT MAKING ME FEEL AT HOME. IN FACT, I'M NOT SURE IF IT'S EARTHLY...
SLASH
ORORO!

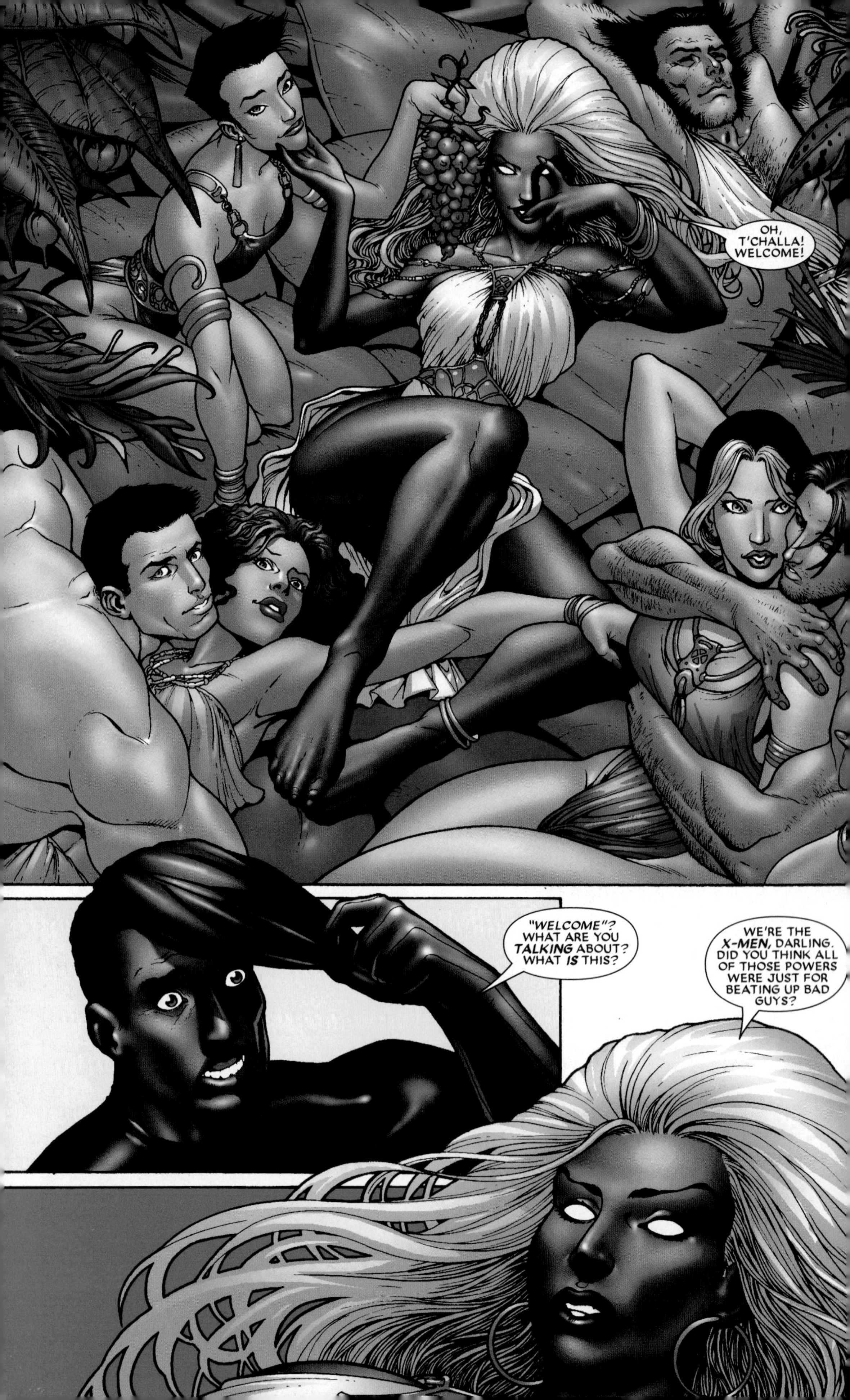

OH, T'CHALLA! WELCOME!
"WELCOME"? WHAT ARE YOU TALKING ABOUT? WHAT IS THIS?
WE'RE THE X-MEN, DARLING. DID YOU THINK ALL OF THOSE POWERS WERE JUST FOR BEATING UP BAD GUYS?

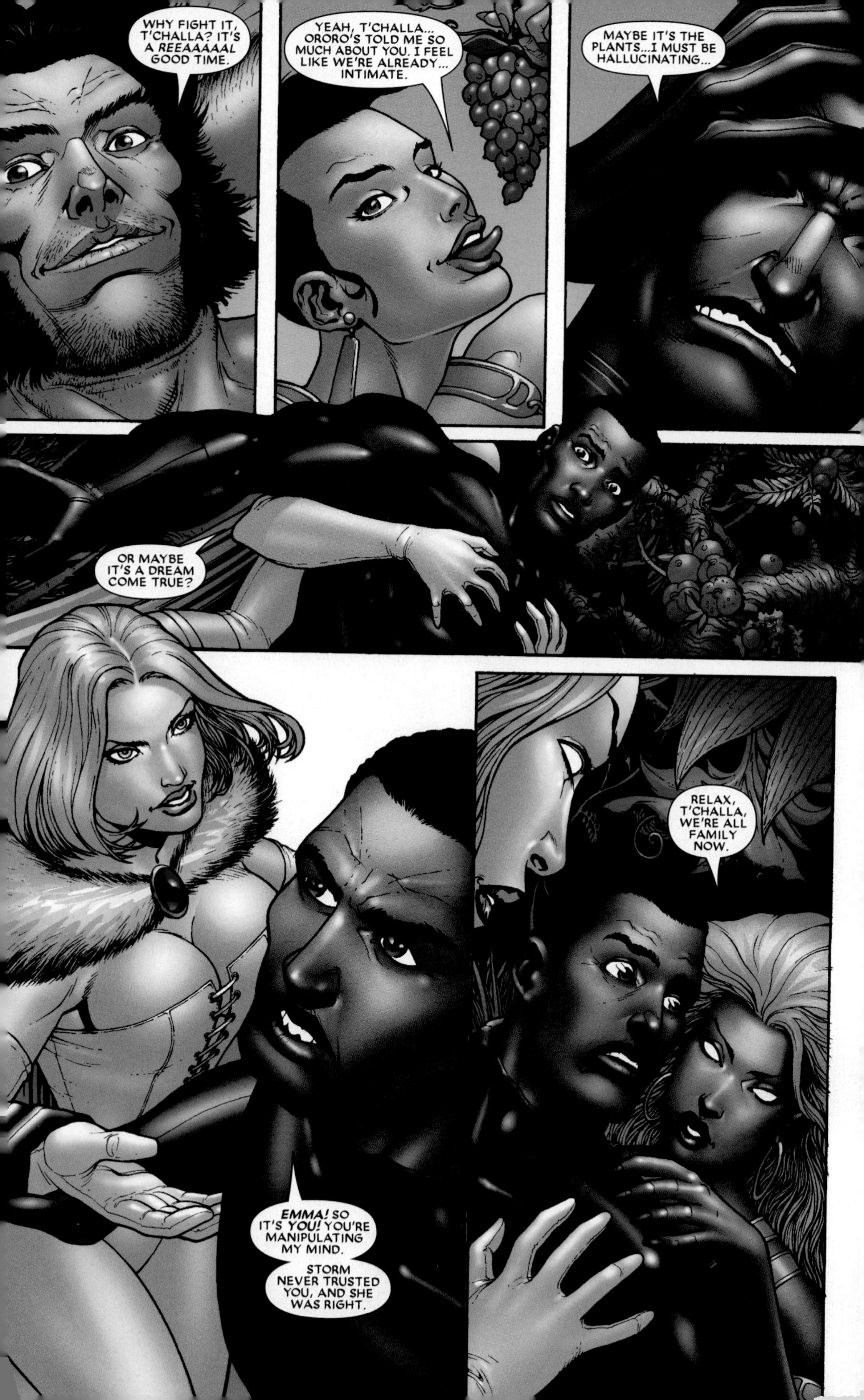

WHY FIGHT IT, T'CHALLA? IT'S A *REEAAAAAAL* GOOD TIME.
YEAH, T'CHALLA... ORORO'S TOLD ME SO MUCH ABOUT YOU. I FEEL LIKE WE'RE ALREADY... INTIMATE.
MAYBE IT'S THE PLANTS...I MUST BE HALLUCINATING...
OR MAYBE IT'S A DREAM COME TRUE?
EMMA! SO IT'S **YOU!** YOU'RE MANIPULATING MY MIND.
STORM NEVER TRUSTED YOU, AND SHE WAS RIGHT.
RELAX, T'CHALLA, WE'RE ALL FAMILY NOW.

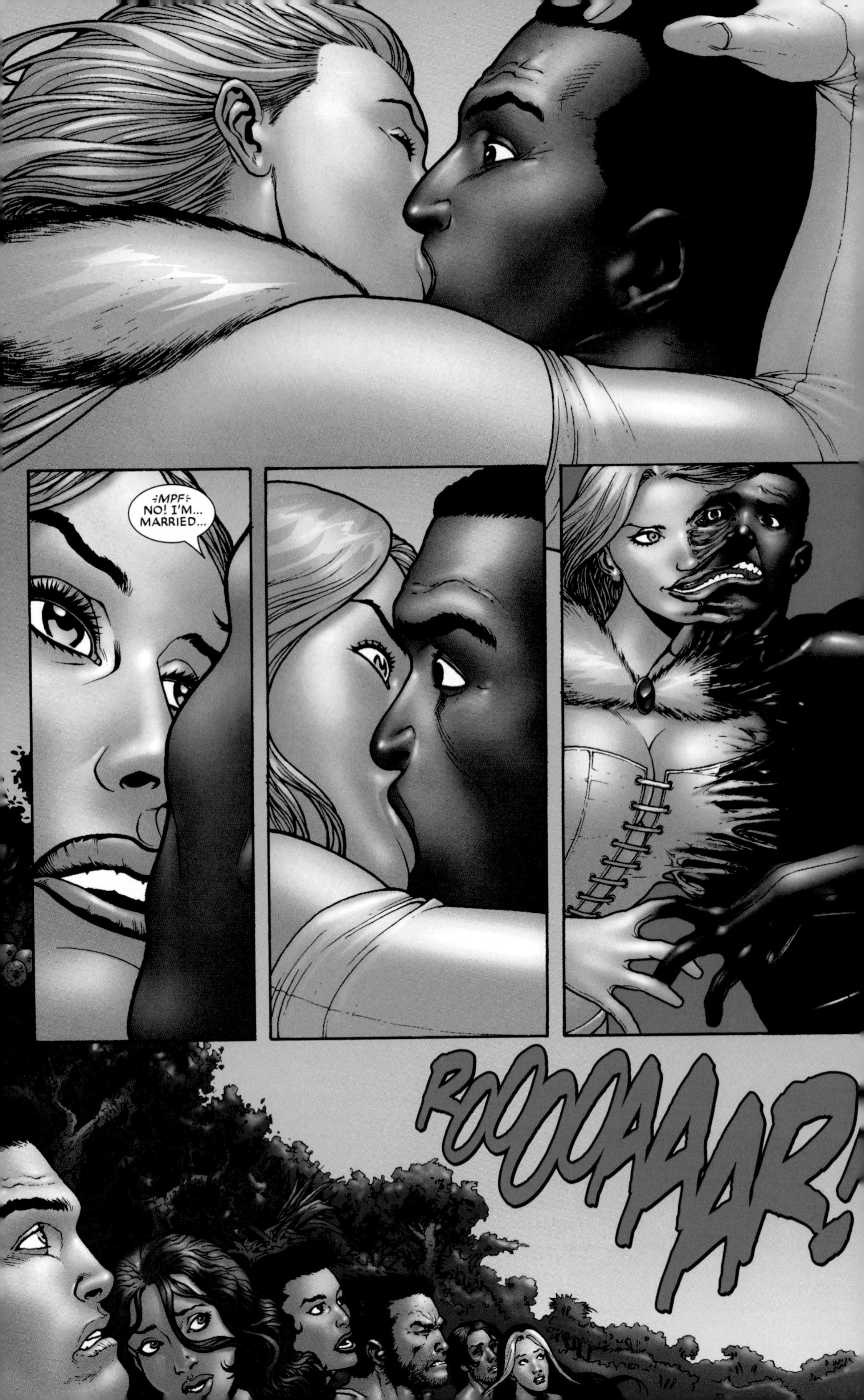

MPF
NO! I'M... MARRIED...
ROOOAAAR!

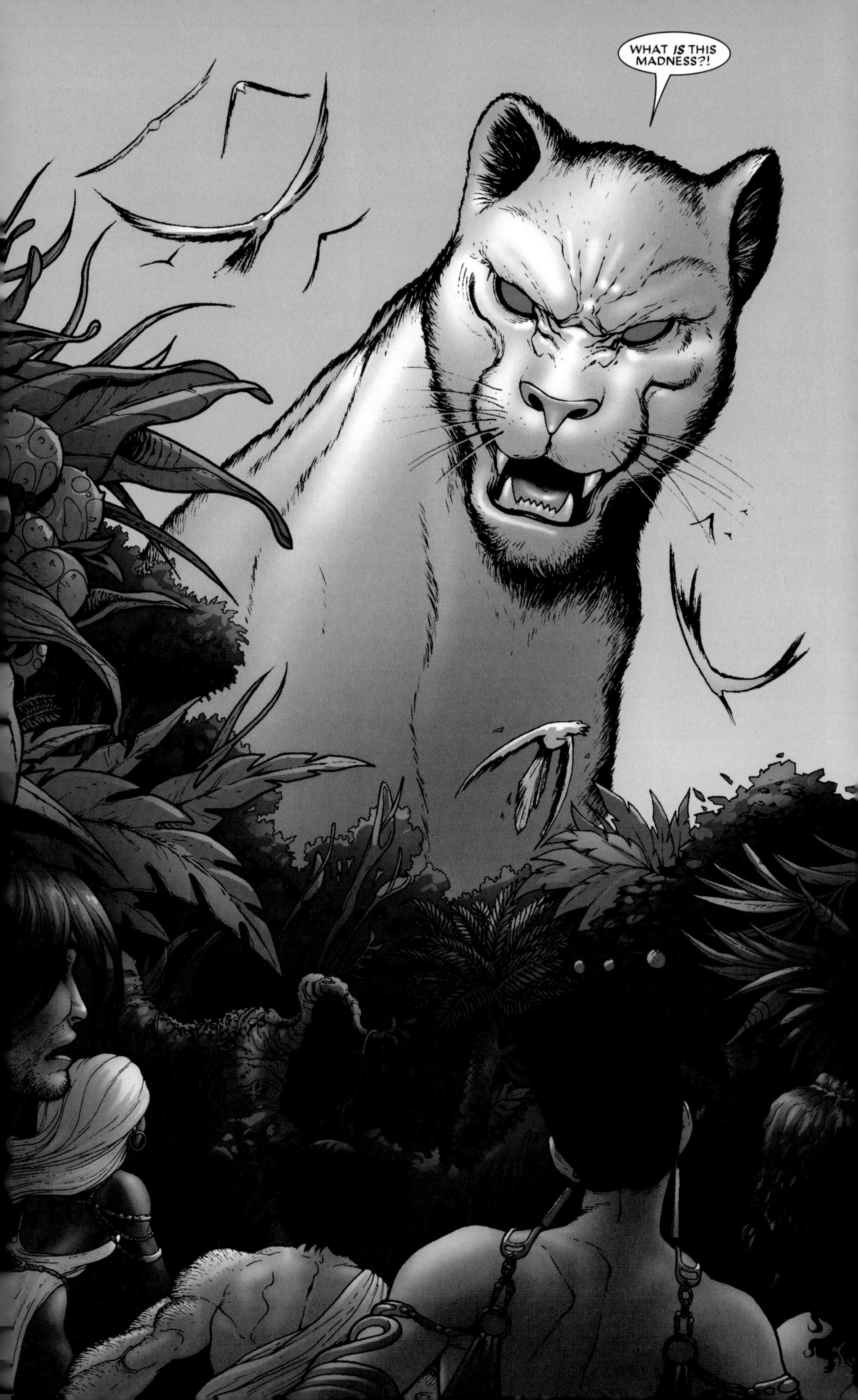
WHAT IS THIS MADNESS?!

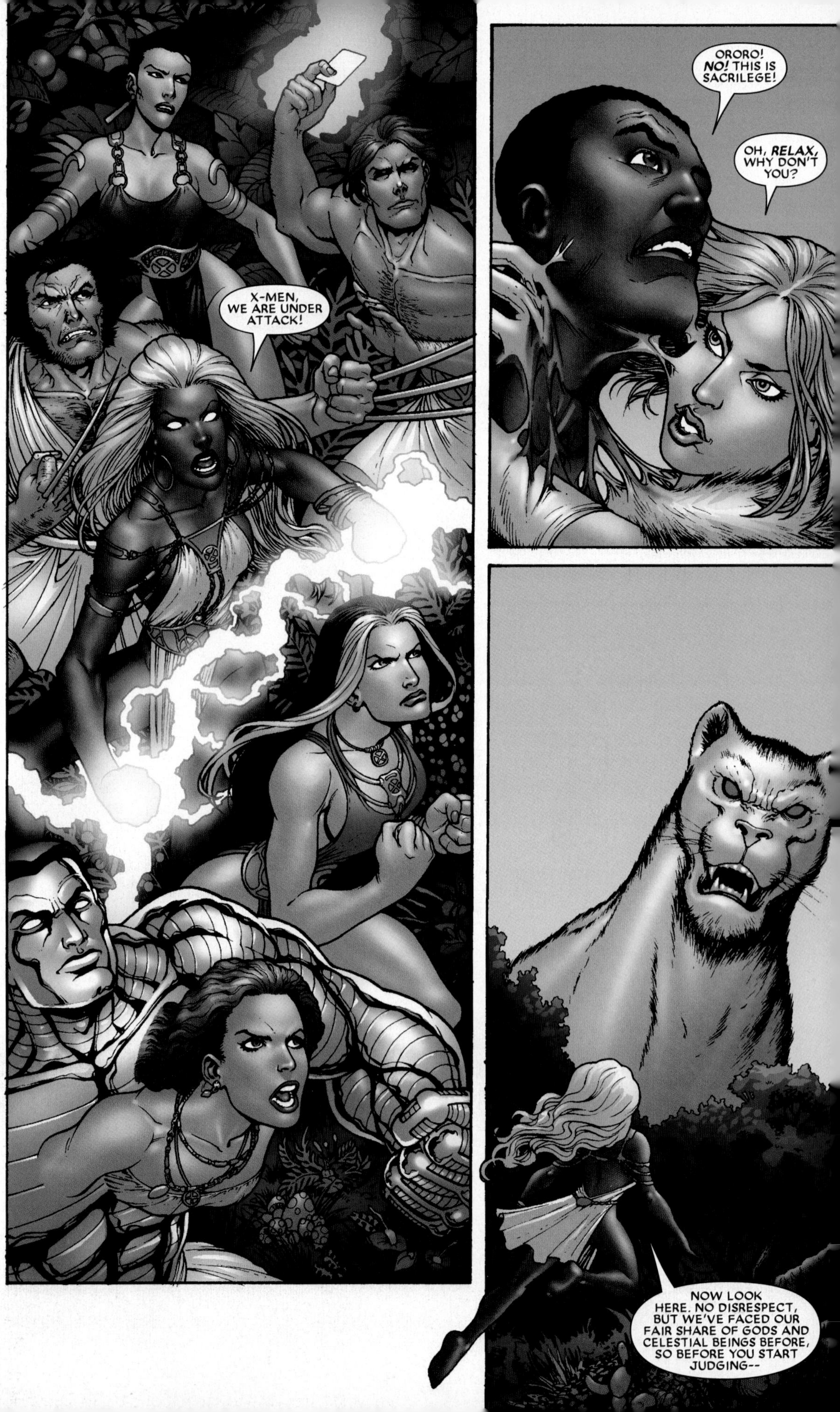
X-MEN, WE ARE UNDER ATTACK!
ORORO! NO! THIS IS SACRILEGE!
OH, RELAX, WHY DON'T YOU?
NOW LOOK HERE. NO DISRESPECT, BUT WE'VE FACED OUR FAIR SHARE OF GODS AND CELESTIAL BEINGS BEFORE, SO BEFORE YOU START JUDGING--

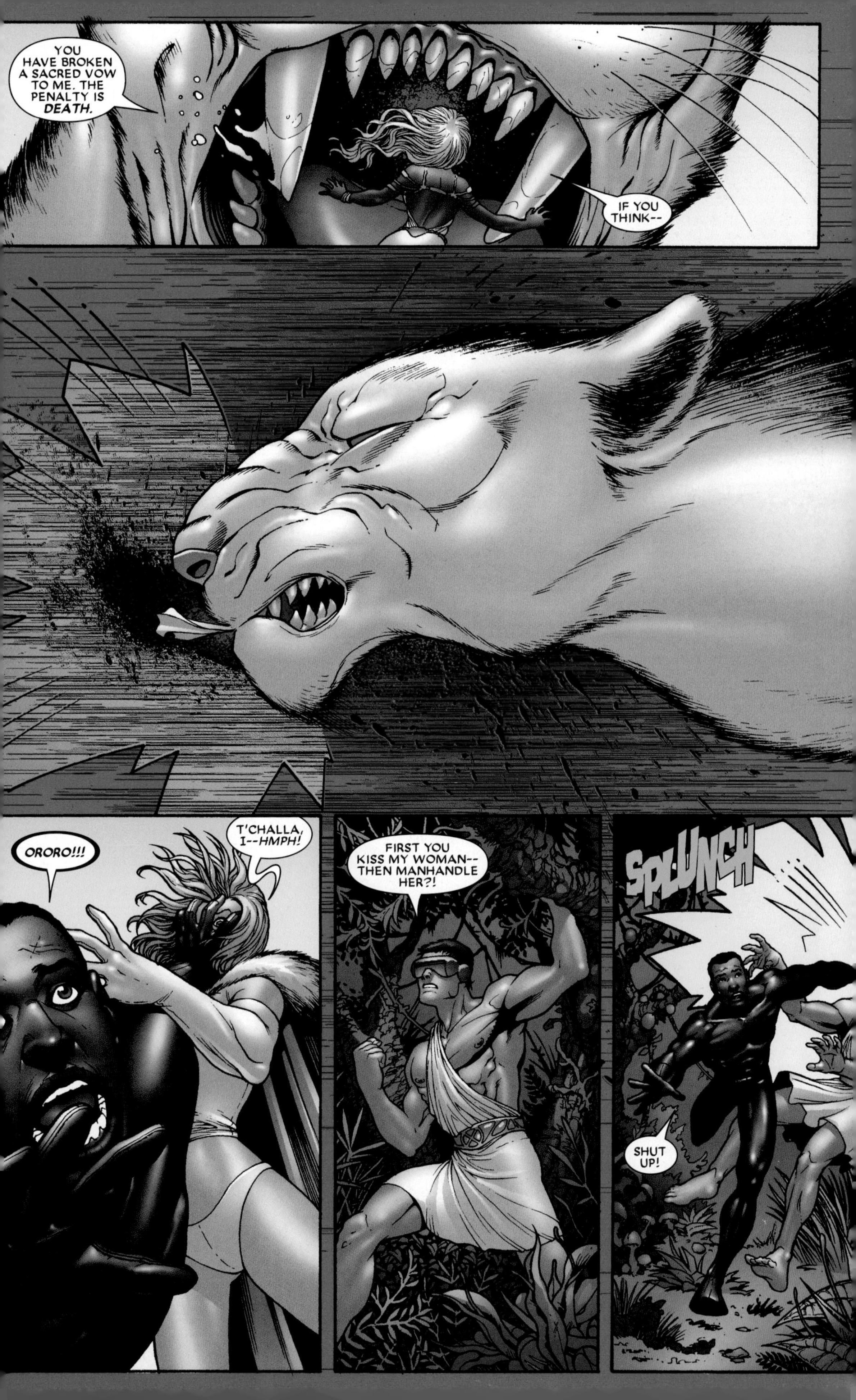
YOU HAVE BROKEN A SACRED VOW TO ME. THE PENALTY IS *DEATH.*
IF YOU THINK--
ORORO!!!
T'CHALLA, I--*HMPH!*
FIRST YOU KISS MY WOMAN--THEN MANHANDLE HER?!
SPLUNCH
SHUT UP!

NICE ONE. ALWAYS WANTED TO DO THAT.

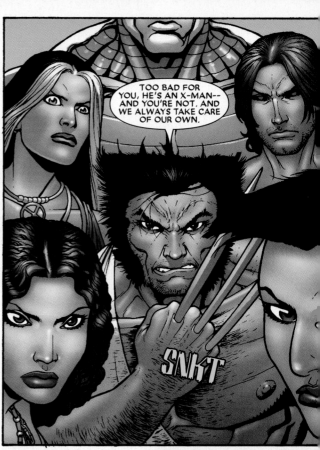

TOO BAD FOR YOU, HE'S AN X-MAN-- AND YOU'RE NOT. AND WE ALWAYS TAKE CARE OF OUR OWN.

SNKT

THIS--

--IS--

WHAK

--INSANE!

KRROOM

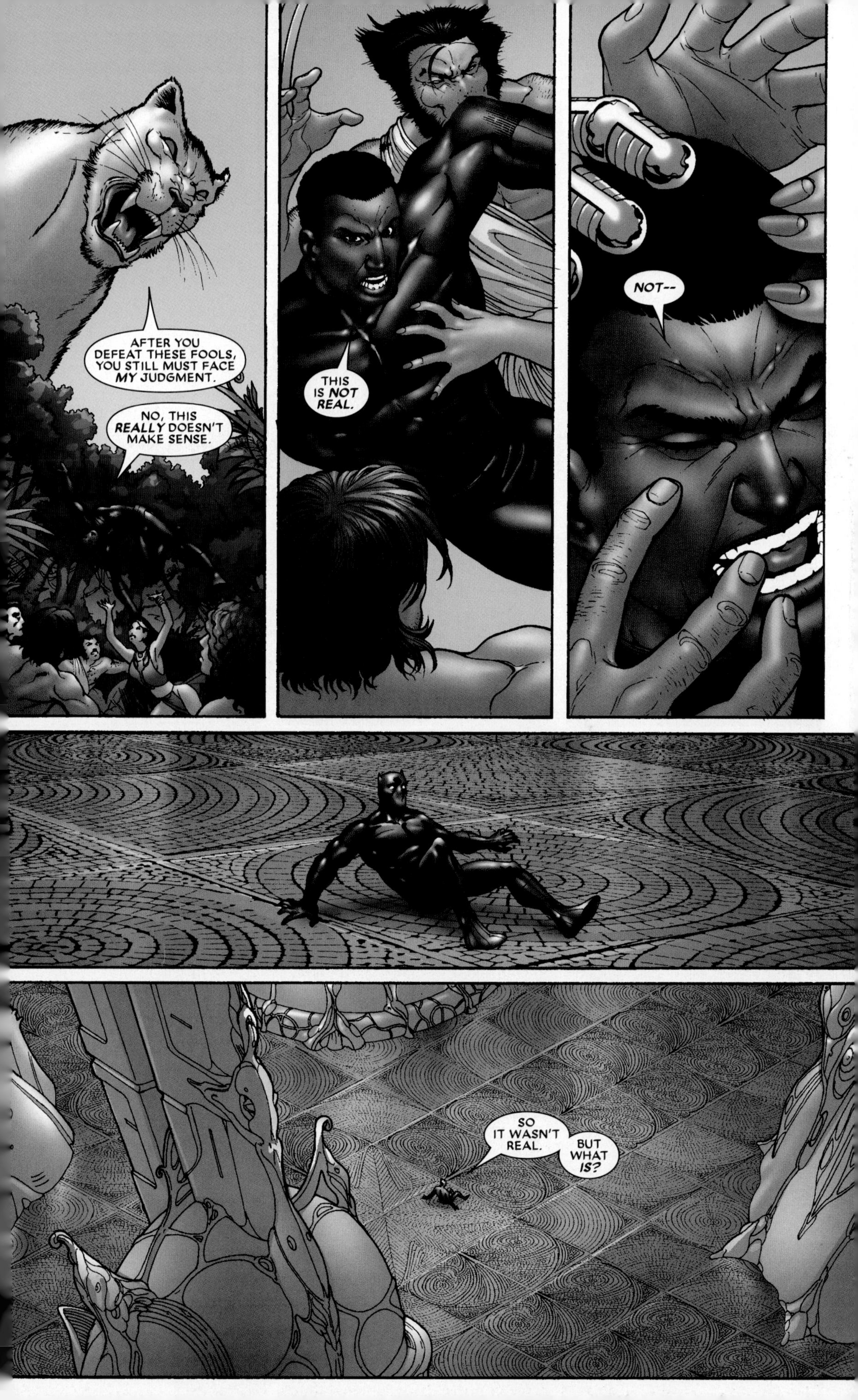
AFTER YOU DEFEAT THESE FOOLS, YOU STILL MUST FACE MY JUDGMENT.
NO, THIS REALLY DOESN'T MAKE SENSE.
THIS IS NOT REAL.
NOT--
SO IT WASN'T REAL.
BUT WHAT IS?

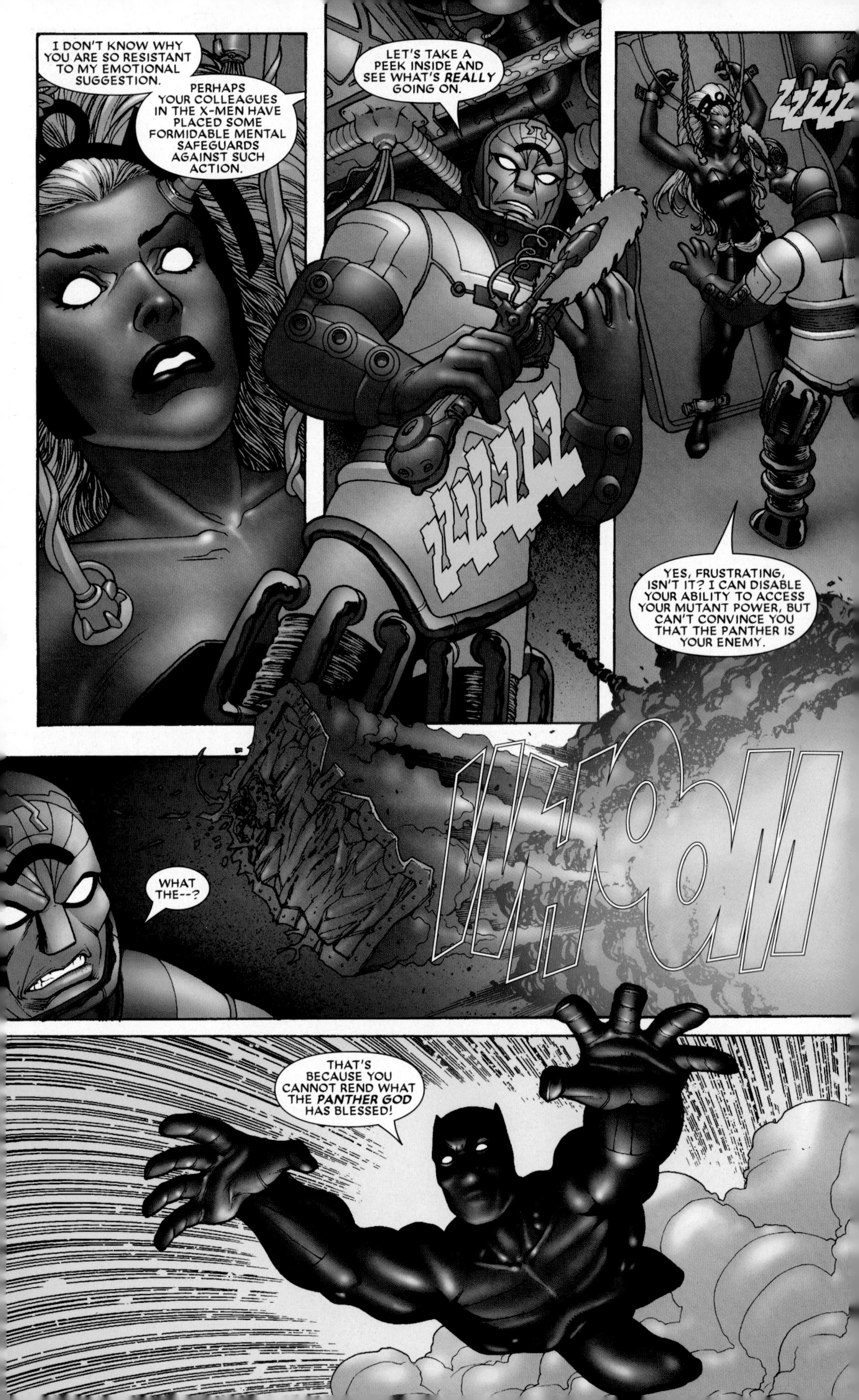
I DON'T KNOW WHY YOU ARE SO RESISTANT TO MY EMOTIONAL SUGGESTION.
PERHAPS YOUR COLLEAGUES IN THE X-MEN HAVE PLACED SOME FORMIDABLE MENTAL SAFEGUARDS AGAINST SUCH ACTION.
LET'S TAKE A PEEK INSIDE AND SEE WHAT'S *REALLY* GOING ON.
ZZZZZZ
ZZZZ
YES, FRUSTRATING, ISN'T IT? I CAN DISABLE YOUR ABILITY TO ACCESS YOUR MUTANT POWER, BUT CAN'T CONVINCE YOU THAT THE PANTHER IS YOUR ENEMY.
WHOOM
WHAT THE--?
THAT'S BECAUSE YOU CANNOT REND WHAT THE *PANTHER GOD* HAS BLESSED!

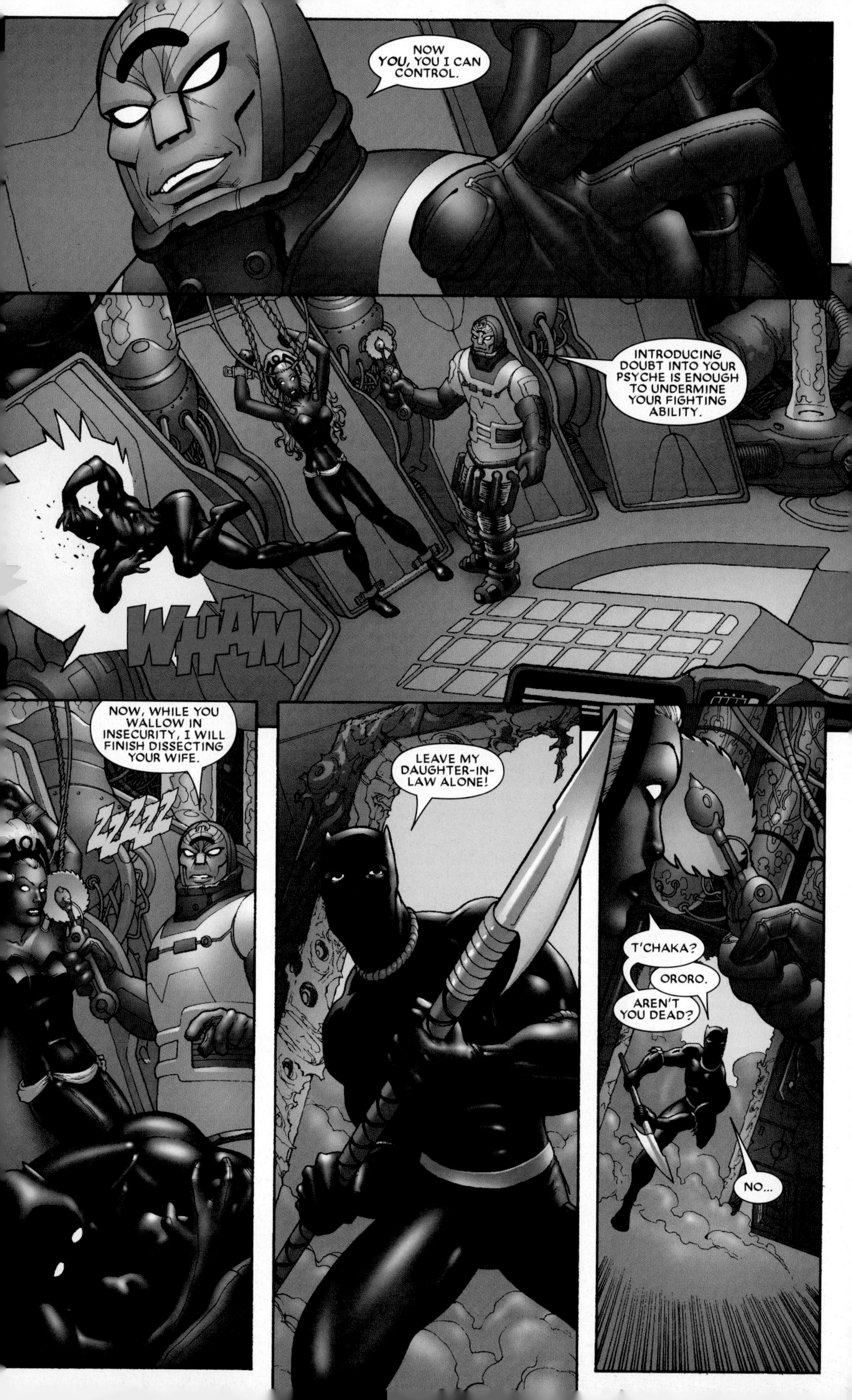
NOW YOU, YOU I CAN CONTROL.
INTRODUCING DOUBT INTO YOUR PSYCHE IS ENOUGH TO UNDERMINE YOUR FIGHTING ABILITY.
WHAM
NOW, WHILE YOU WALLOW IN INSECURITY, I WILL FINISH DISSECTING YOUR WIFE.
ZZZZZ
LEAVE MY DAUGHTER-IN-LAW ALONE!
T'CHAKA?
ORORO.
AREN'T YOU DEAD?
NO...

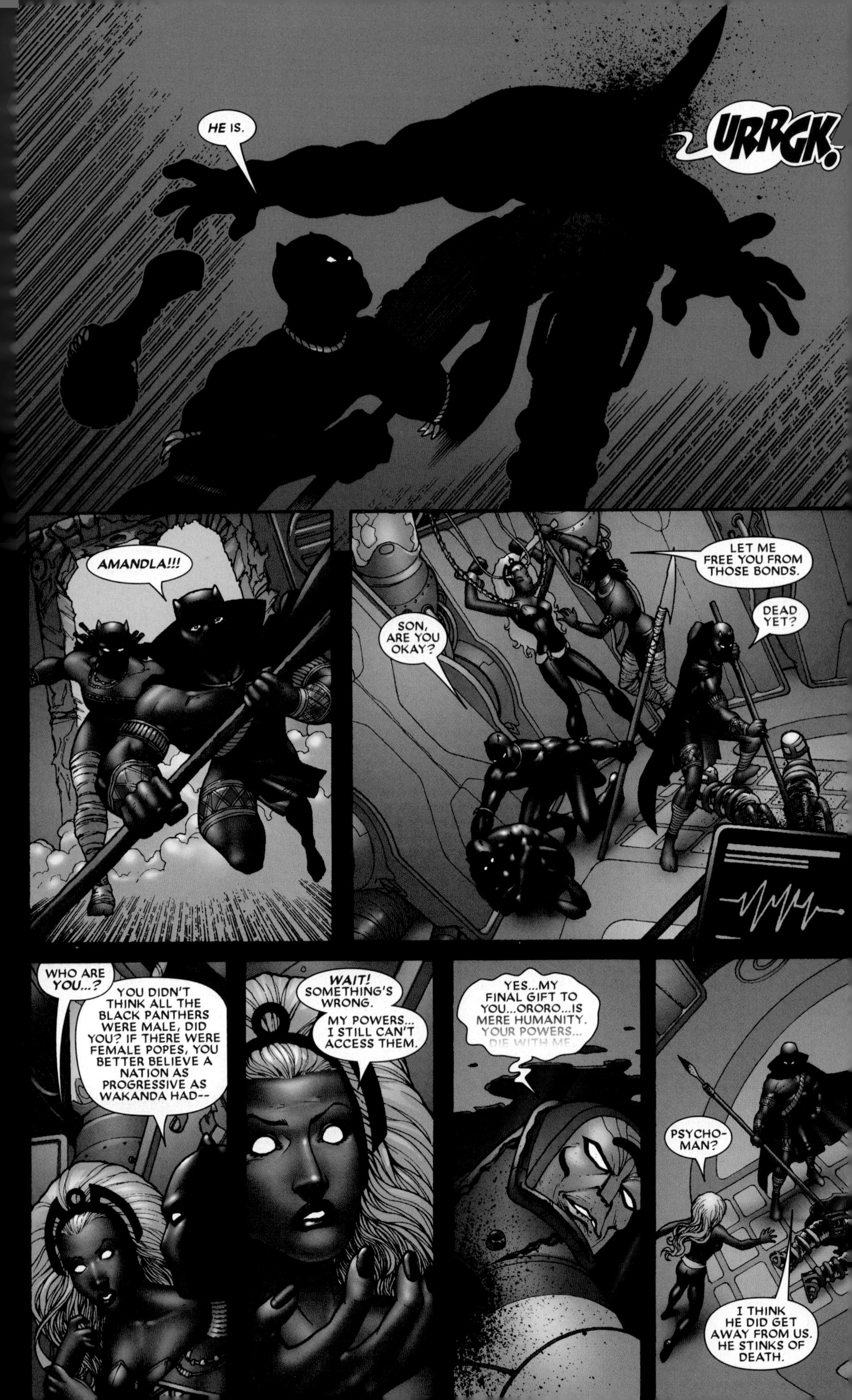

HE IS.
URRGK!
AMANDLA!!!
LET ME FREE YOU FROM THOSE BONDS.
SON, ARE YOU OKAY?
DEAD YET?
WHO ARE YOU...?
YOU DIDN'T THINK ALL THE BLACK PANTHERS WERE MALE, DID YOU? IF THERE WERE FEMALE POPES, YOU BETTER BELIEVE A NATION AS PROGRESSIVE AS WAKANDA HAD--
WAIT! SOMETHING'S WRONG.
MY POWERS... I STILL CAN'T ACCESS THEM.
YES...MY FINAL GIFT TO YOU...ORORO...IS MERE HUMANITY. YOUR POWERS... DIE WITH ME...
PSYCHO-MAN?
I THINK HE DID GET AWAY FROM US. HE STINKS OF DEATH.

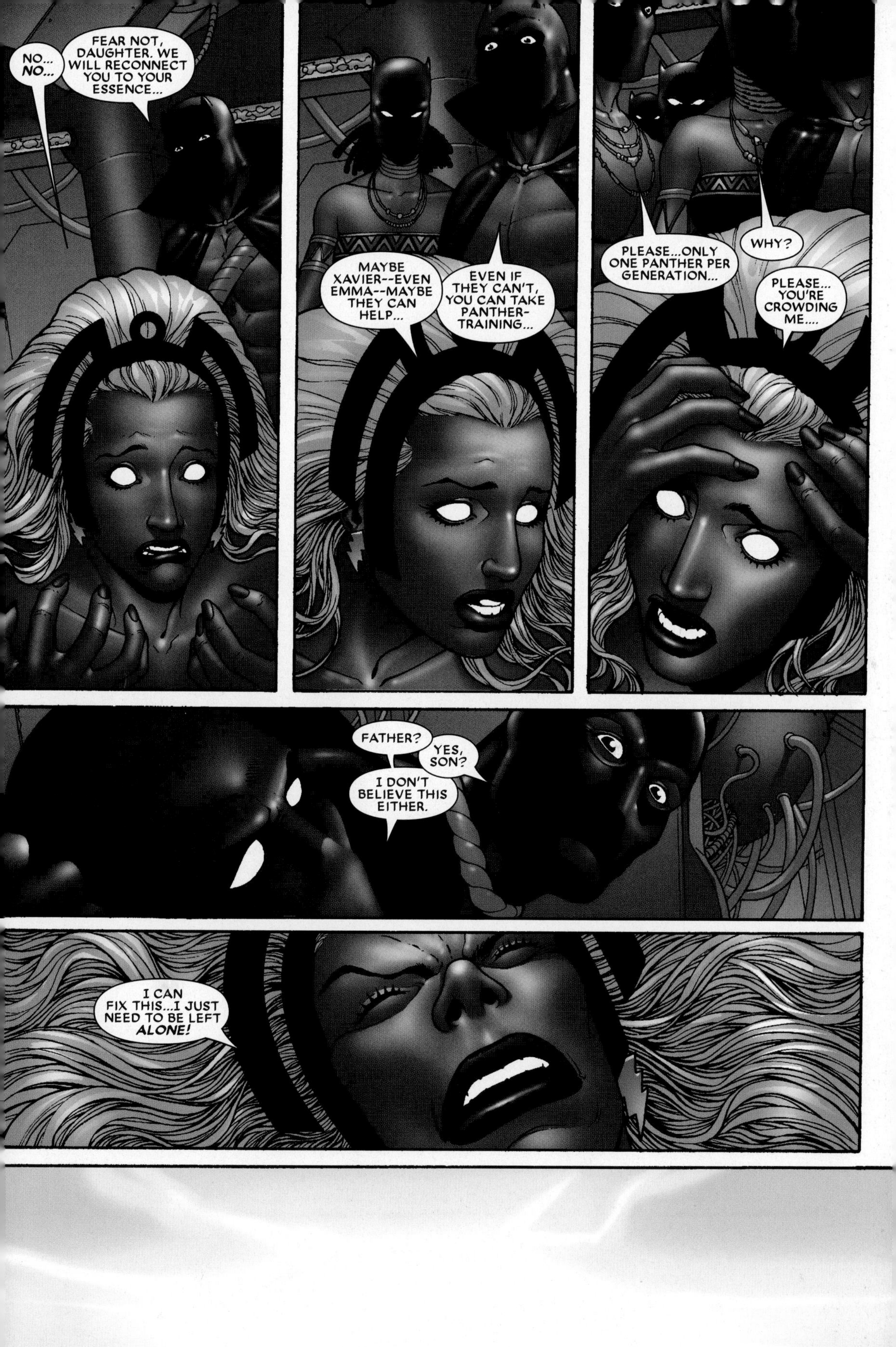
NO... NO...
FEAR NOT, DAUGHTER. WE WILL RECONNECT YOU TO YOUR ESSENCE...
MAYBE XAVIER--EVEN EMMA--MAYBE THEY CAN HELP...
EVEN IF THEY CAN'T, YOU CAN TAKE PANTHER-TRAINING...
PLEASE...ONLY ONE PANTHER PER GENERATION...
WHY?
PLEASE... YOU'RE CROWDING ME....
FATHER?
YES, SON?
I DON'T BELIEVE THIS EITHER.
I CAN FIX THIS...I JUST NEED TO BE LEFT ALONE!

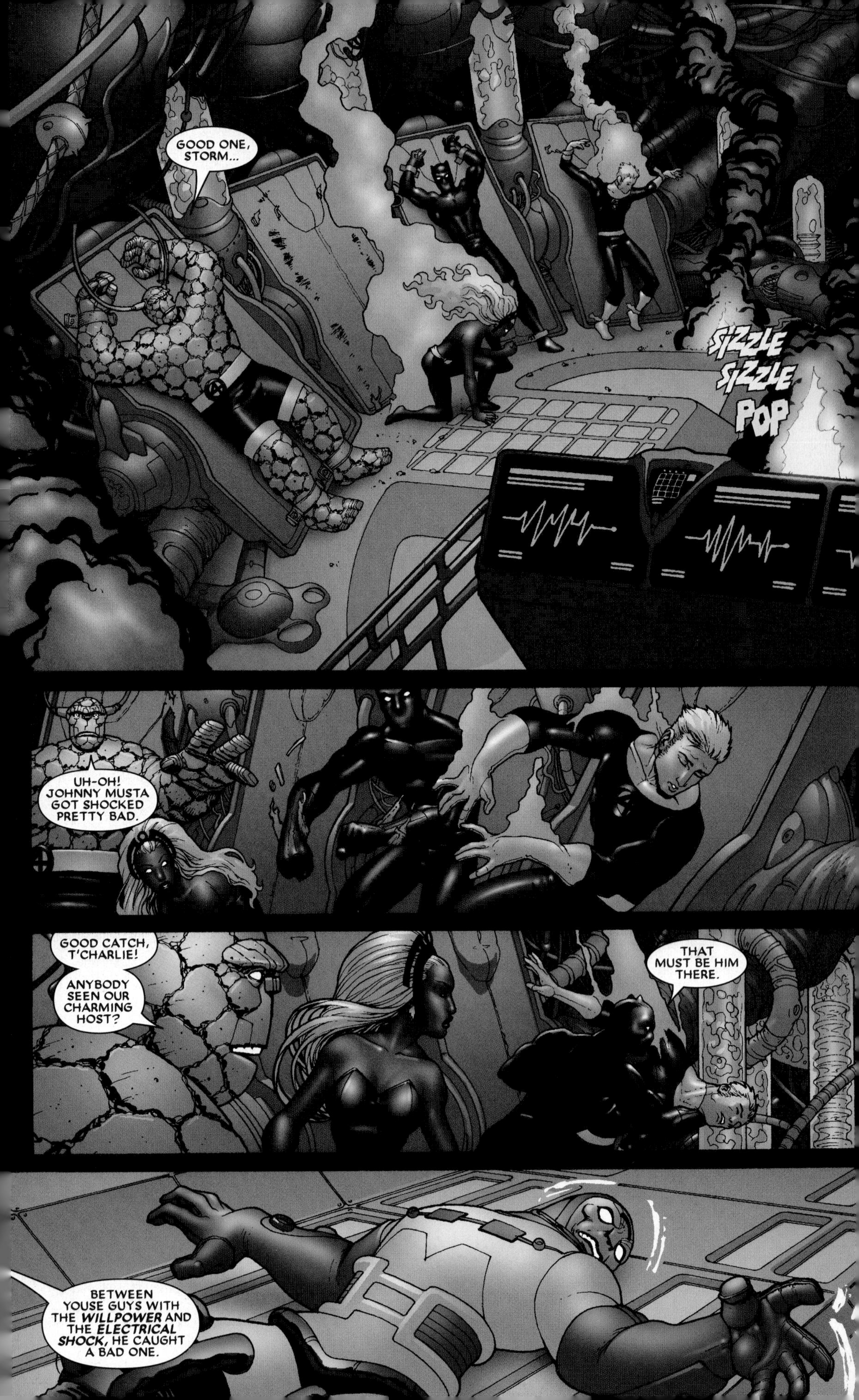
GOOD ONE, STORM...
SIZZLE SIZZLE POP
UH-OH! JOHNNY MUSTA GOT SHOCKED PRETTY BAD.
GOOD CATCH, T'CHARLIE!
ANYBODY SEEN OUR CHARMING HOST?
THAT MUST BE HIM THERE.
BETWEEN YOUSE GUYS WITH THE *WILLPOWER* AND THE *ELECTRICAL SHOCK,* HE CAUGHT A BAD ONE.

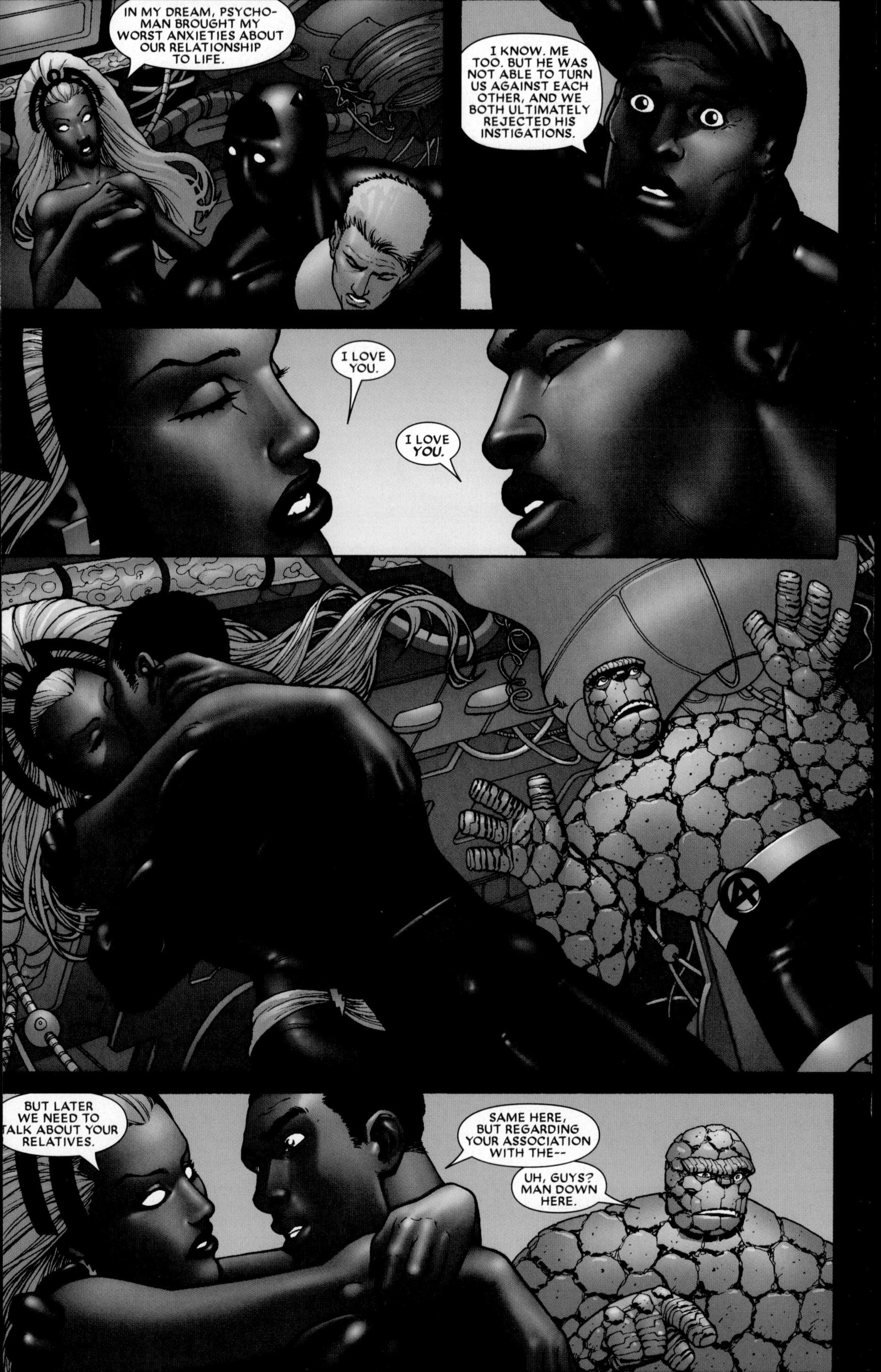
IN MY DREAM, PSYCHO-MAN BROUGHT MY WORST ANXIETIES ABOUT OUR RELATIONSHIP TO LIFE.
I KNOW. ME TOO. BUT HE WAS NOT ABLE TO TURN US AGAINST EACH OTHER, AND WE BOTH ULTIMATELY REJECTED HIS INSTIGATIONS.
I LOVE YOU.
I LOVE *YOU.*
BUT LATER WE NEED TO TALK ABOUT YOUR RELATIVES.
SAME HERE, BUT REGARDING YOUR ASSOCIATION WITH THE--
UH, GUYS? MAN DOWN HERE.

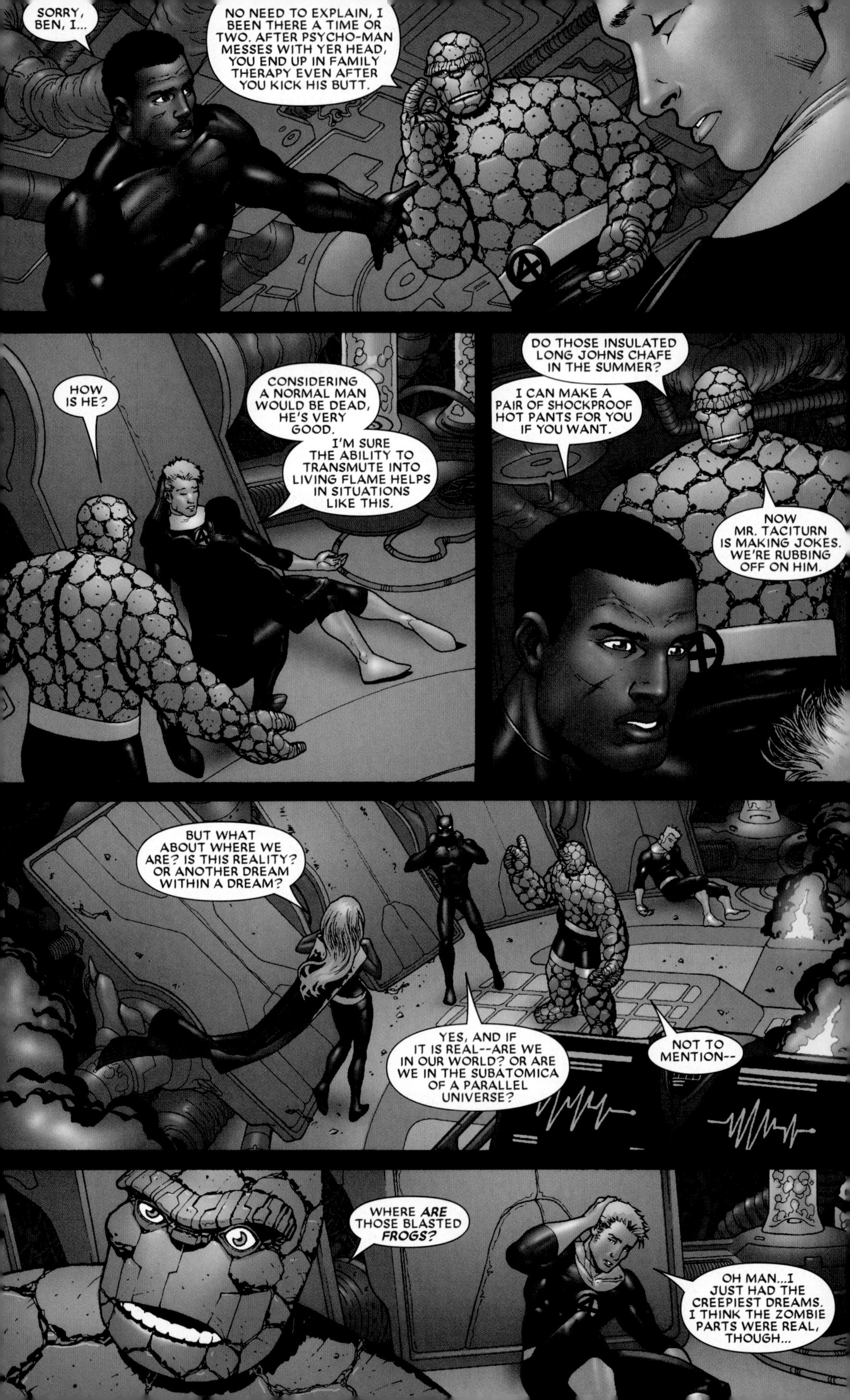
SORRY, BEN, I...
NO NEED TO EXPLAIN, I BEEN THERE A TIME OR TWO. AFTER PSYCHO-MAN MESSES WITH YER HEAD, YOU END UP IN FAMILY THERAPY EVEN AFTER YOU KICK HIS BUTT.
HOW IS HE?
CONSIDERING A NORMAL MAN WOULD BE DEAD, HE'S VERY GOOD.
I'M SURE THE ABILITY TO TRANSMUTE INTO LIVING FLAME HELPS IN SITUATIONS LIKE THIS.
DO THOSE INSULATED LONG JOHNS CHAFE IN THE SUMMER?
I CAN MAKE A PAIR OF SHOCKPROOF HOT PANTS FOR YOU IF YOU WANT.
NOW MR. TACITURN IS MAKING JOKES. WE'RE RUBBING OFF ON HIM.
BUT WHAT ABOUT WHERE WE ARE? IS THIS REALITY? OR ANOTHER DREAM WITHIN A DREAM?
YES, AND IF IT IS REAL--ARE WE IN OUR WORLD? OR ARE WE IN THE SUBATOMICA OF A PARALLEL UNIVERSE?
NOT TO MENTION--
WHERE *ARE* THOSE BLASTED *FROGS?*
OH MAN...I JUST HAD THE CREEPIEST DREAMS. I THINK THE ZOMBIE PARTS WERE REAL, THOUGH...

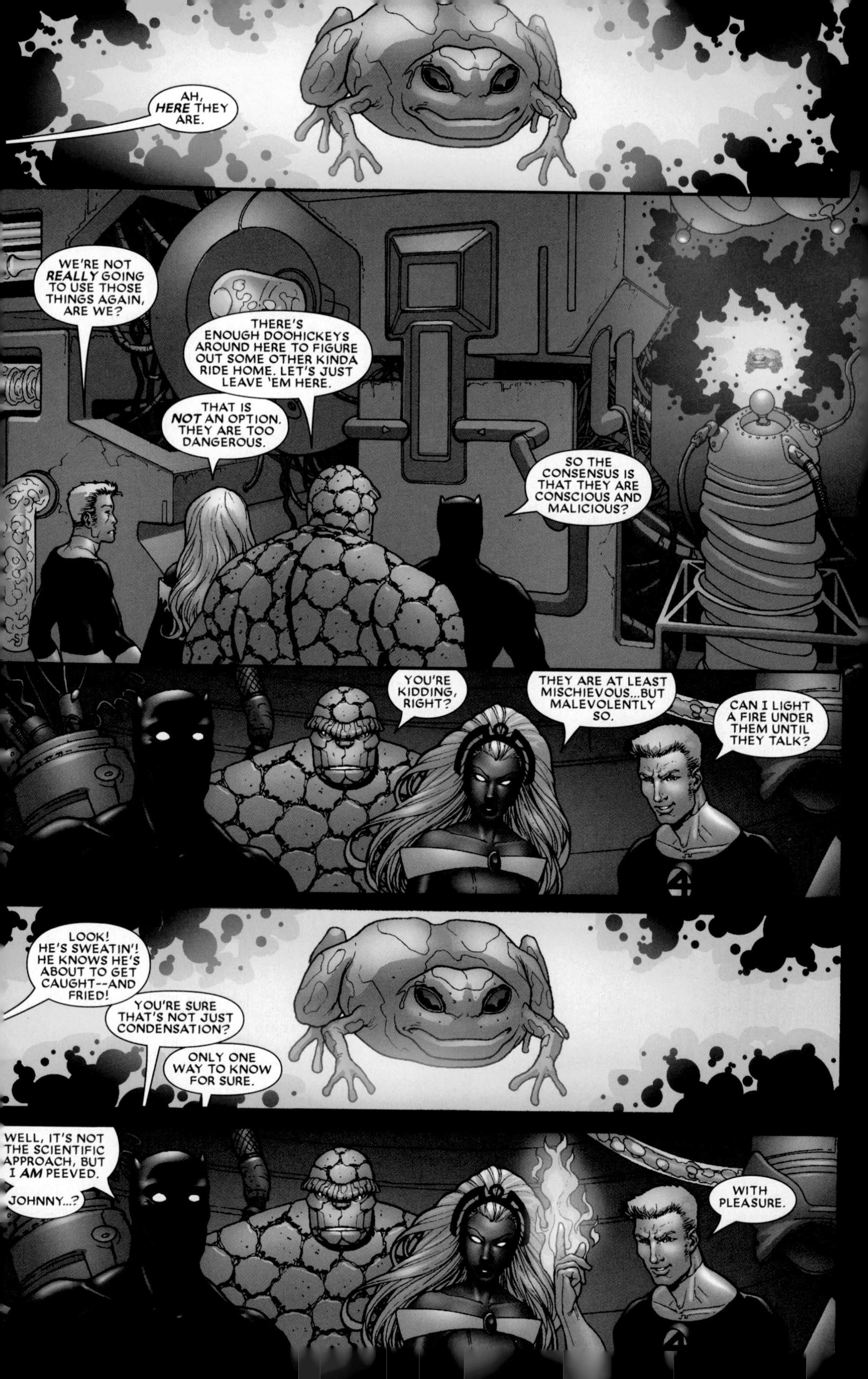
AH, HERE THEY ARE.
WE'RE NOT REALLY GOING TO USE THOSE THINGS AGAIN, ARE WE?
THERE'S ENOUGH DOOHICKEYS AROUND HERE TO FIGURE OUT SOME OTHER KINDA RIDE HOME. LET'S JUST LEAVE 'EM HERE.
THAT IS NOT AN OPTION. THEY ARE TOO DANGEROUS.
SO THE CONSENSUS IS THAT THEY ARE CONSCIOUS AND MALICIOUS?
YOU'RE KIDDING, RIGHT?
THEY ARE AT LEAST MISCHIEVOUS...BUT MALEVOLENTLY SO.
CAN I LIGHT A FIRE UNDER THEM UNTIL THEY TALK?
LOOK! HE'S SWEATIN'! HE KNOWS HE'S ABOUT TO GET CAUGHT--AND FRIED!
YOU'RE SURE THAT'S NOT JUST CONDENSATION?
ONLY ONE WAY TO KNOW FOR SURE.
WELL, IT'S NOT THE SCIENTIFIC APPROACH, BUT I AM PEEVED.
JOHNNY...?
WITH PLEASURE.

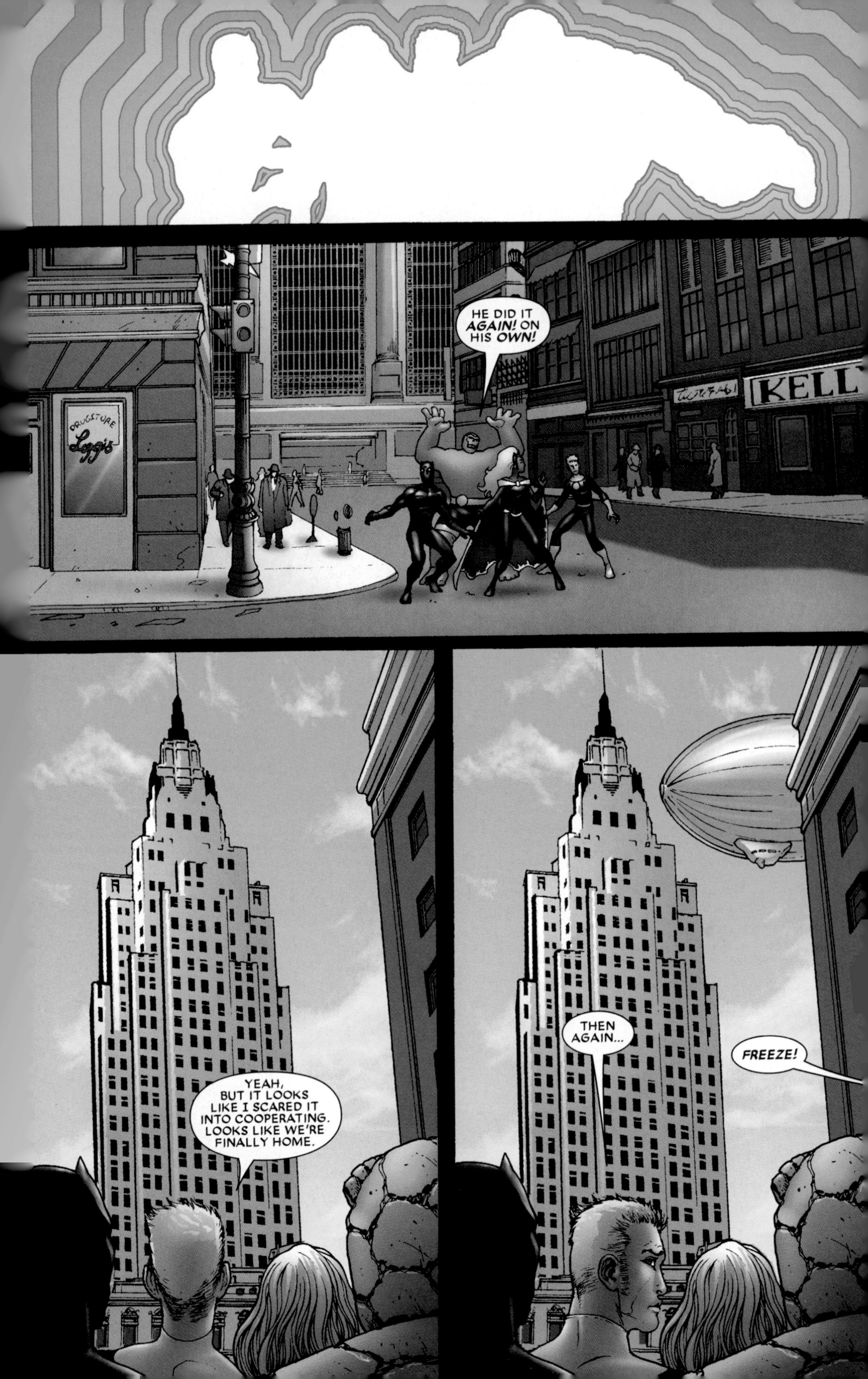
HE DID IT AGAIN! ON HIS OWN!
DRUGSTORE
Luigi's
KELL
YEAH, BUT IT LOOKS LIKE I SCARED IT INTO COOPERATING. LOOKS LIKE WE'RE FINALLY HOME.
THEN AGAIN...
FREEZE!

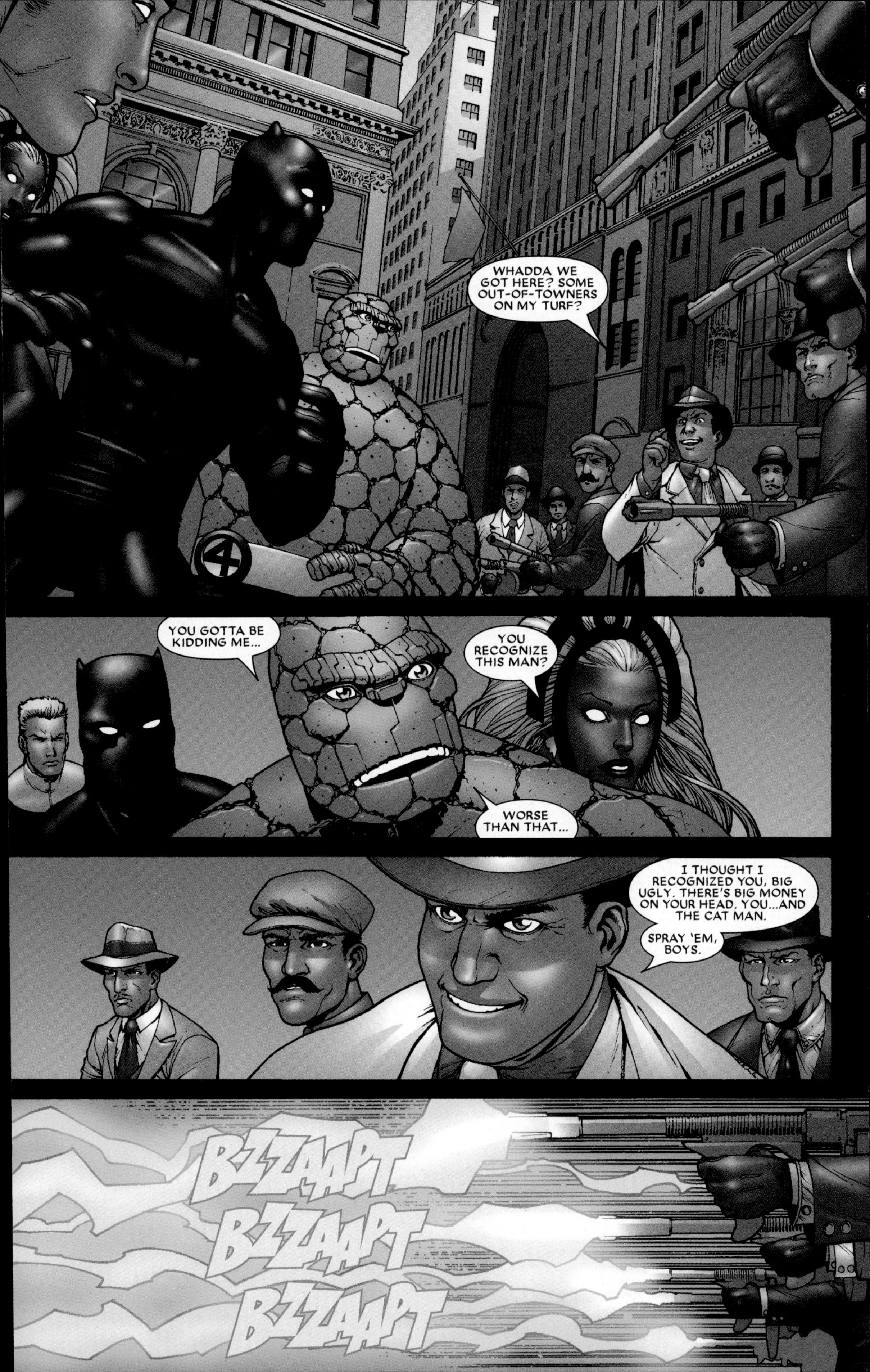
WHADDA WE GOT HERE? SOME OUT-OF-TOWNERS ON MY TURF?
YOU GOTTA BE KIDDING ME...
YOU RECOGNIZE THIS MAN?
WORSE THAN THAT...
I THOUGHT I RECOGNIZED YOU, BIG UGLY. THERE'S BIG MONEY ON YOUR HEAD. YOU...AND THE CAT MAN.
SPRAY 'EM, BOYS.
BZZAAPT
BZZAAPT
BZZAAPT

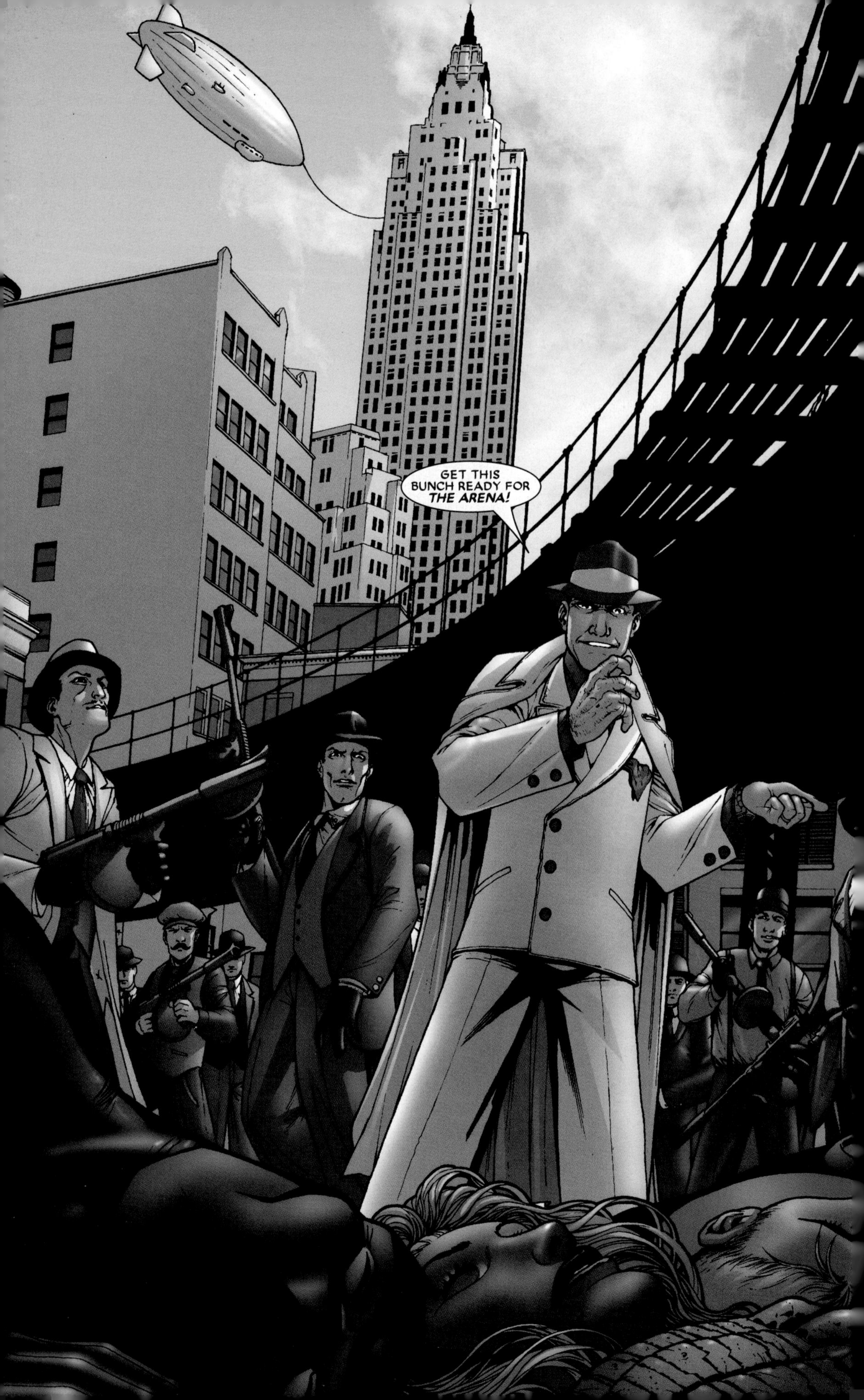
GET THIS BUNCH READY FOR THE ARENA!

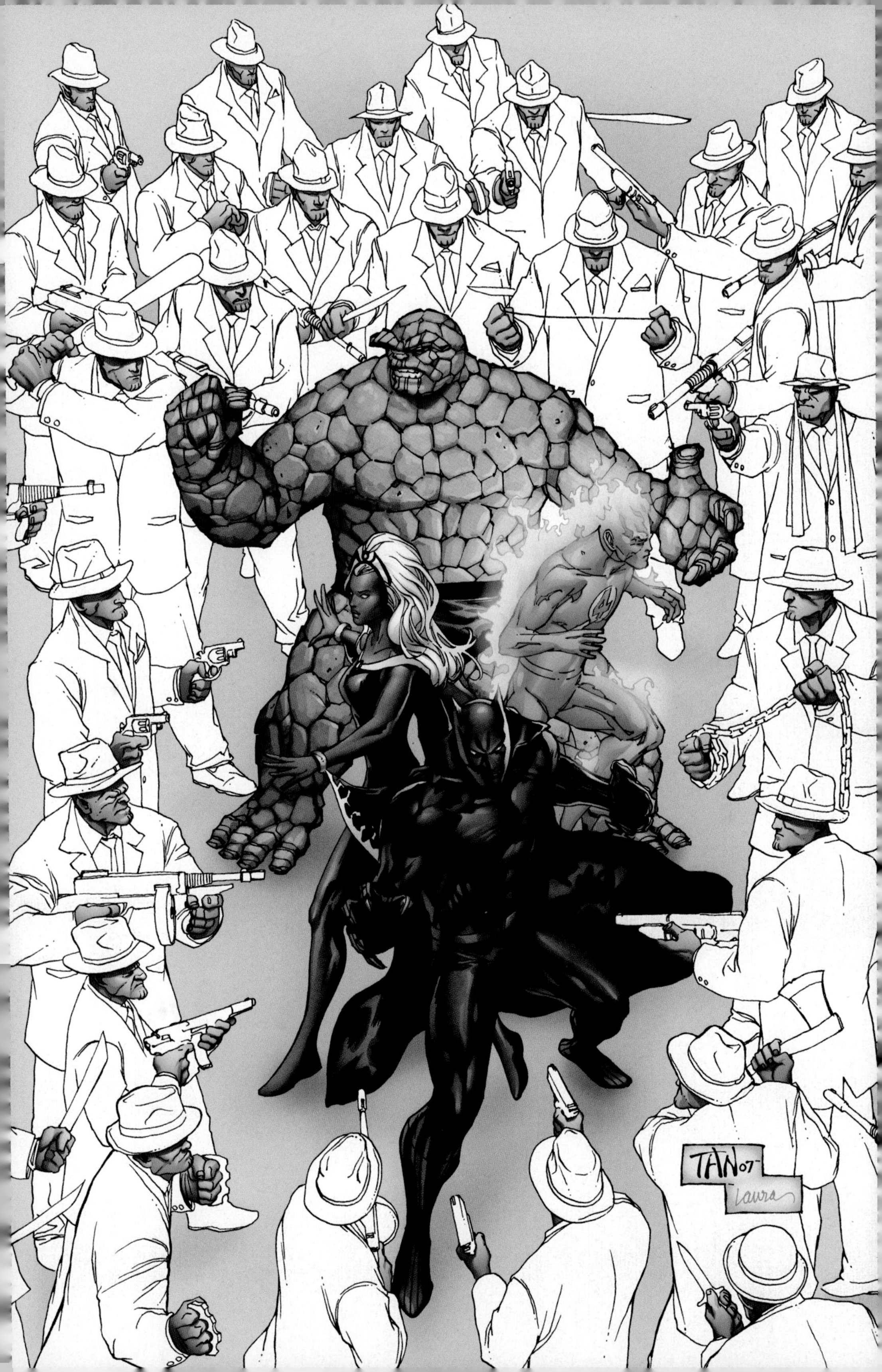
TAN 07
Laura

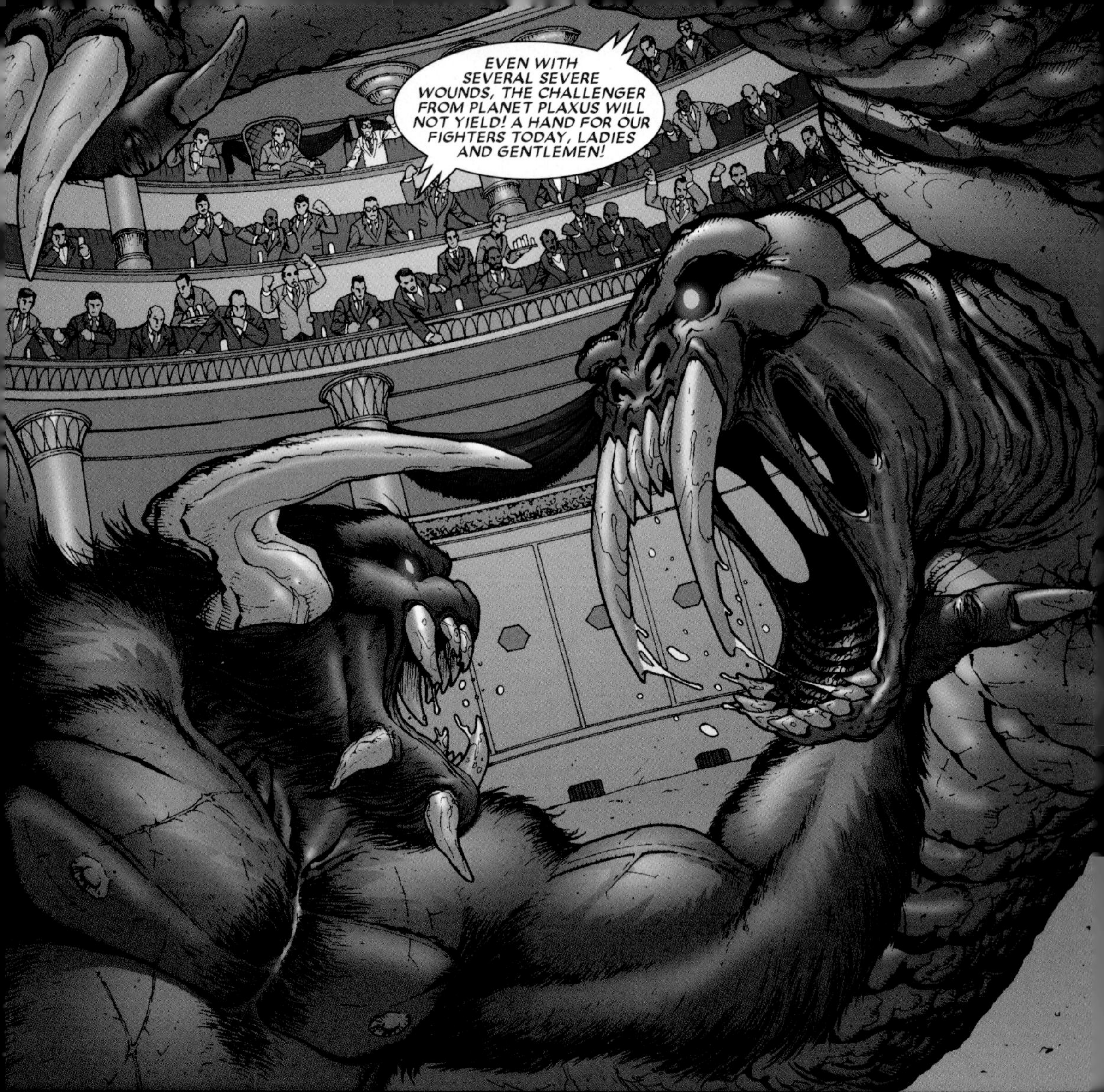
EVEN WITH SEVERAL SEVERE WOUNDS, THE CHALLENGER FROM PLANET PLAXUS WILL NOT YIELD! A HAND FOR OUR FIGHTERS TODAY, LADIES AND GENTLEMEN!

GANGSTA LEAN
PART 2

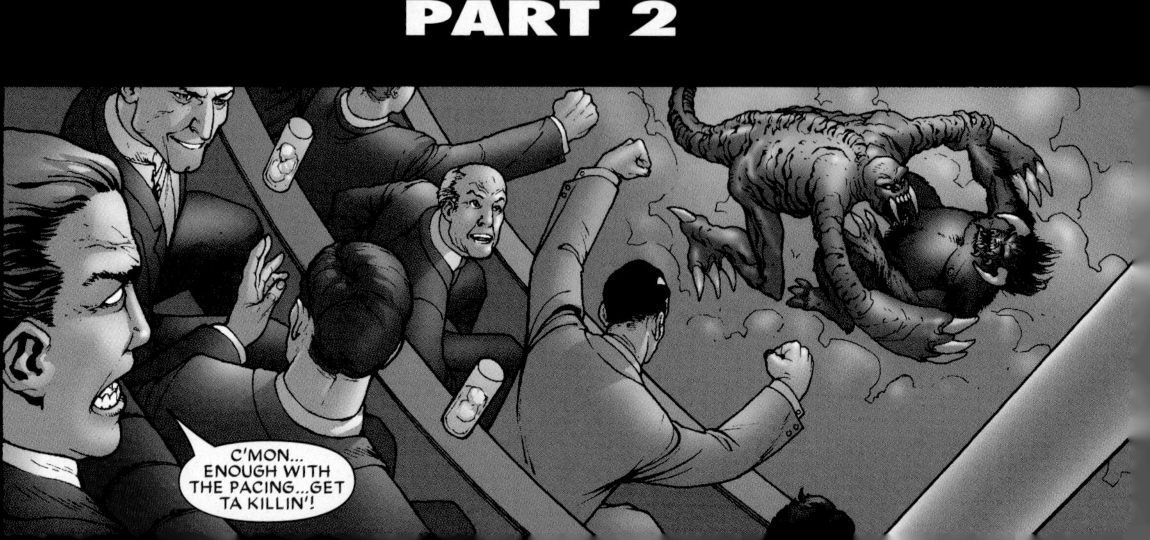
C'MON... ENOUGH WITH THE PACING...GET TA KILLIN'!

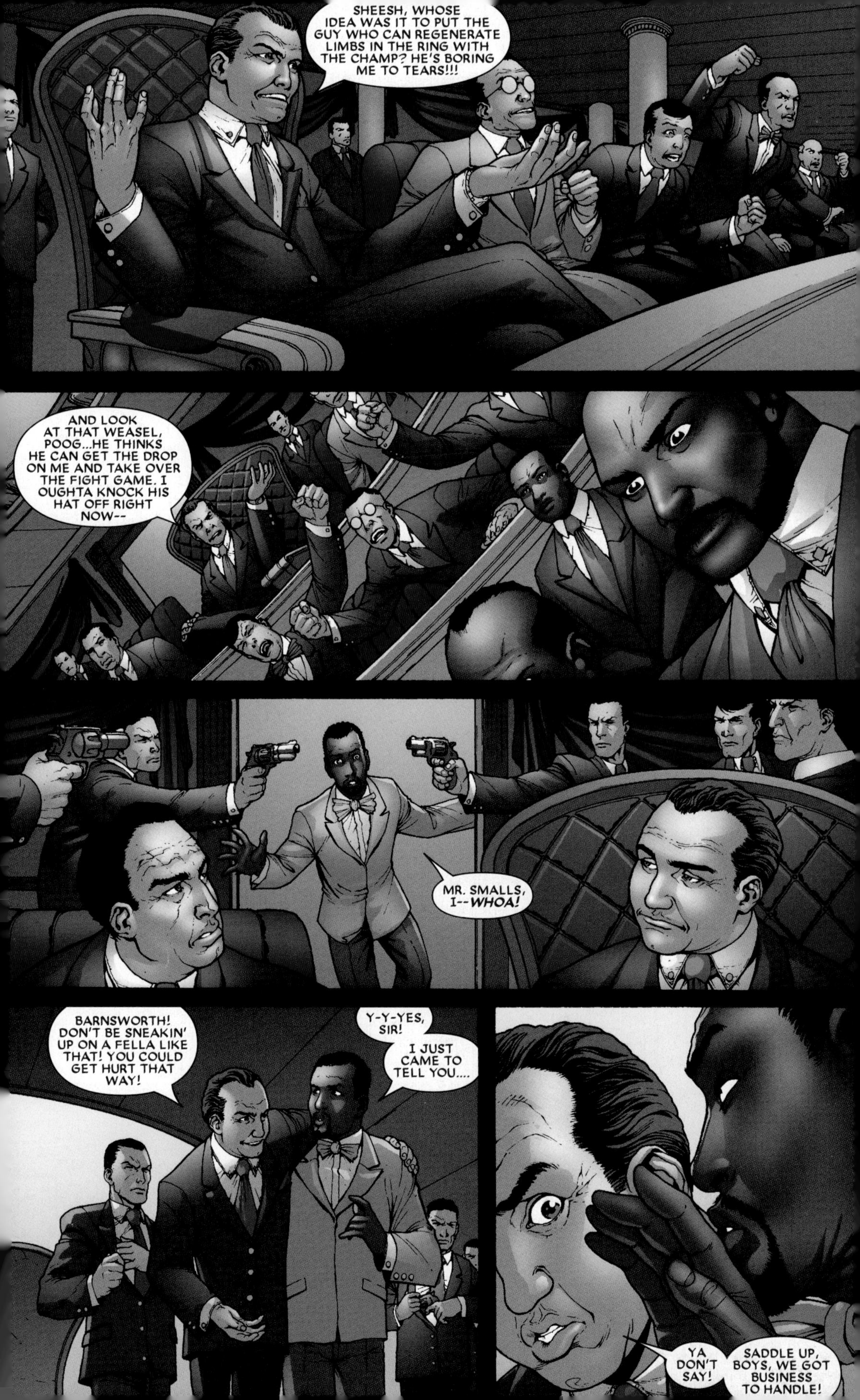
SHEESH, WHOSE IDEA WAS IT TO PUT THE GUY WHO CAN REGENERATE LIMBS IN THE RING WITH THE CHAMP? HE'S BORING ME TO TEARS!!!
AND LOOK AT THAT WEASEL, POOG...HE THINKS HE CAN GET THE DROP ON ME AND TAKE OVER THE FIGHT GAME. I OUGHTA KNOCK HIS HAT OFF RIGHT NOW--
MR. SMALLS, I--*WHOA!*
BARNSWORTH! DON'T BE SNEAKIN' UP ON A FELLA LIKE THAT! YOU COULD GET HURT THAT WAY!
Y-Y-YES, SIR!
I JUST CAME TO TELL YOU....
YA DON'T SAY!
SADDLE UP, BOYS, WE GOT BUSINESS TO HANDLE!

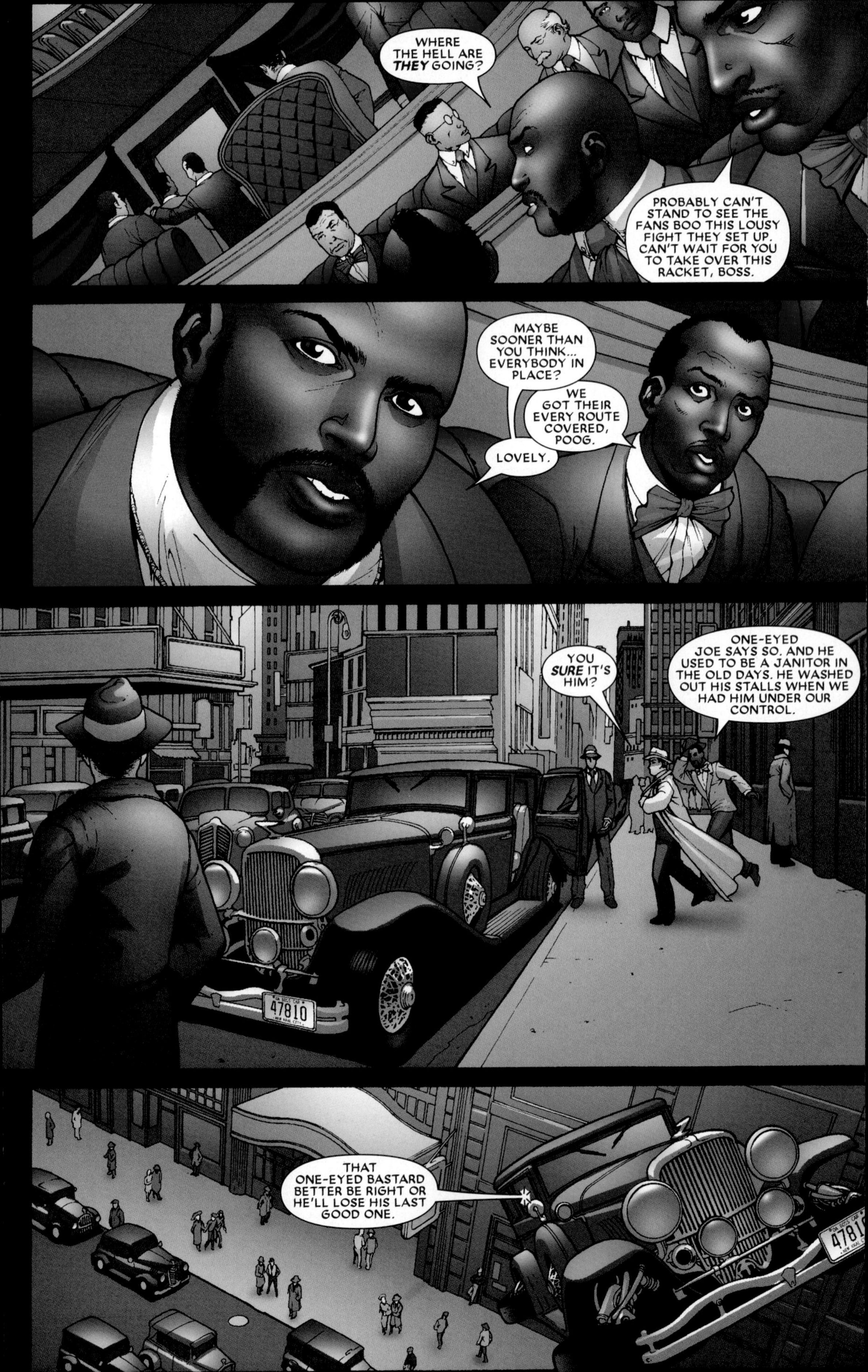
WHERE THE HELL ARE *THEY* GOING?
PROBABLY CAN'T STAND TO SEE THE FANS BOO THIS LOUSY FIGHT THEY SET UP. CAN'T WAIT FOR YOU TO TAKE OVER THIS RACKET, BOSS.
MAYBE SOONER THAN YOU THINK... EVERYBODY IN PLACE?
WE GOT THEIR EVERY ROUTE COVERED, POOG.
LOVELY.
YOU *SURE* IT'S HIM?
ONE-EYED JOE SAYS SO. AND HE USED TO BE A JANITOR IN THE OLD DAYS. HE WASHED OUT HIS STALLS WHEN WE HAD HIM UNDER OUR CONTROL.
47810
THAT ONE-EYED BASTARD BETTER BE RIGHT OR HE'LL LOSE HIS LAST GOOD ONE.

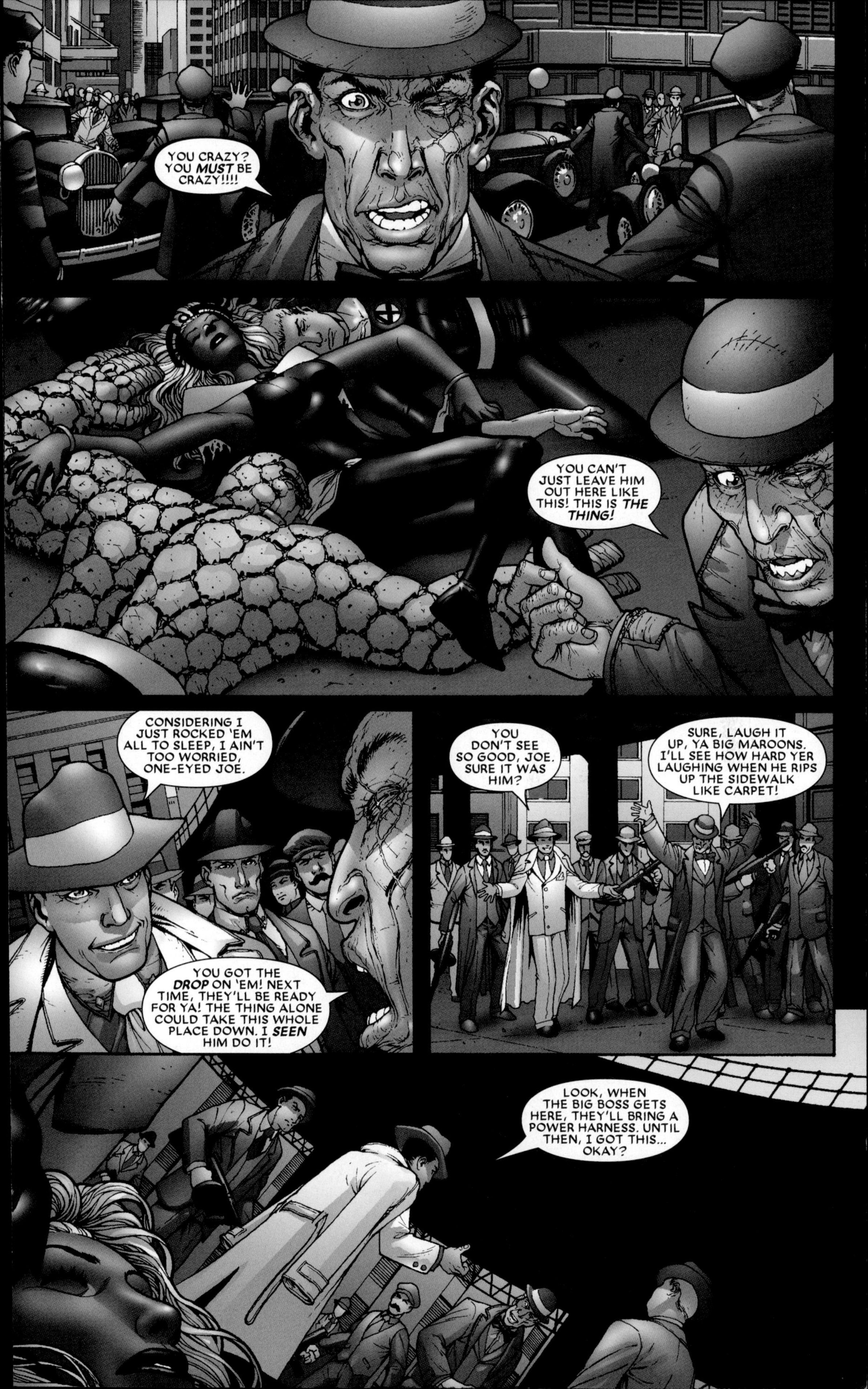
YOU CRAZY? YOU MUST BE CRAZY!!!!
YOU CAN'T JUST LEAVE HIM OUT HERE LIKE THIS! THIS IS THE THING!
CONSIDERING I JUST ROCKED 'EM ALL TO SLEEP, I AIN'T TOO WORRIED, ONE-EYED JOE.
YOU GOT THE DROP ON 'EM! NEXT TIME, THEY'LL BE READY FOR YA! THE THING ALONE COULD TAKE THIS WHOLE PLACE DOWN. I SEEN HIM DO IT!
YOU DON'T SEE SO GOOD, JOE. SURE IT WAS HIM?
SURE, LAUGH IT UP, YA BIG MAROONS. I'LL SEE HOW HARD YER LAUGHING WHEN HE RIPS UP THE SIDEWALK LIKE CARPET!
LOOK, WHEN THE BIG BOSS GETS HERE, THEY'LL BRING A POWER HARNESS. UNTIL THEN, I GOT THIS... OKAY?

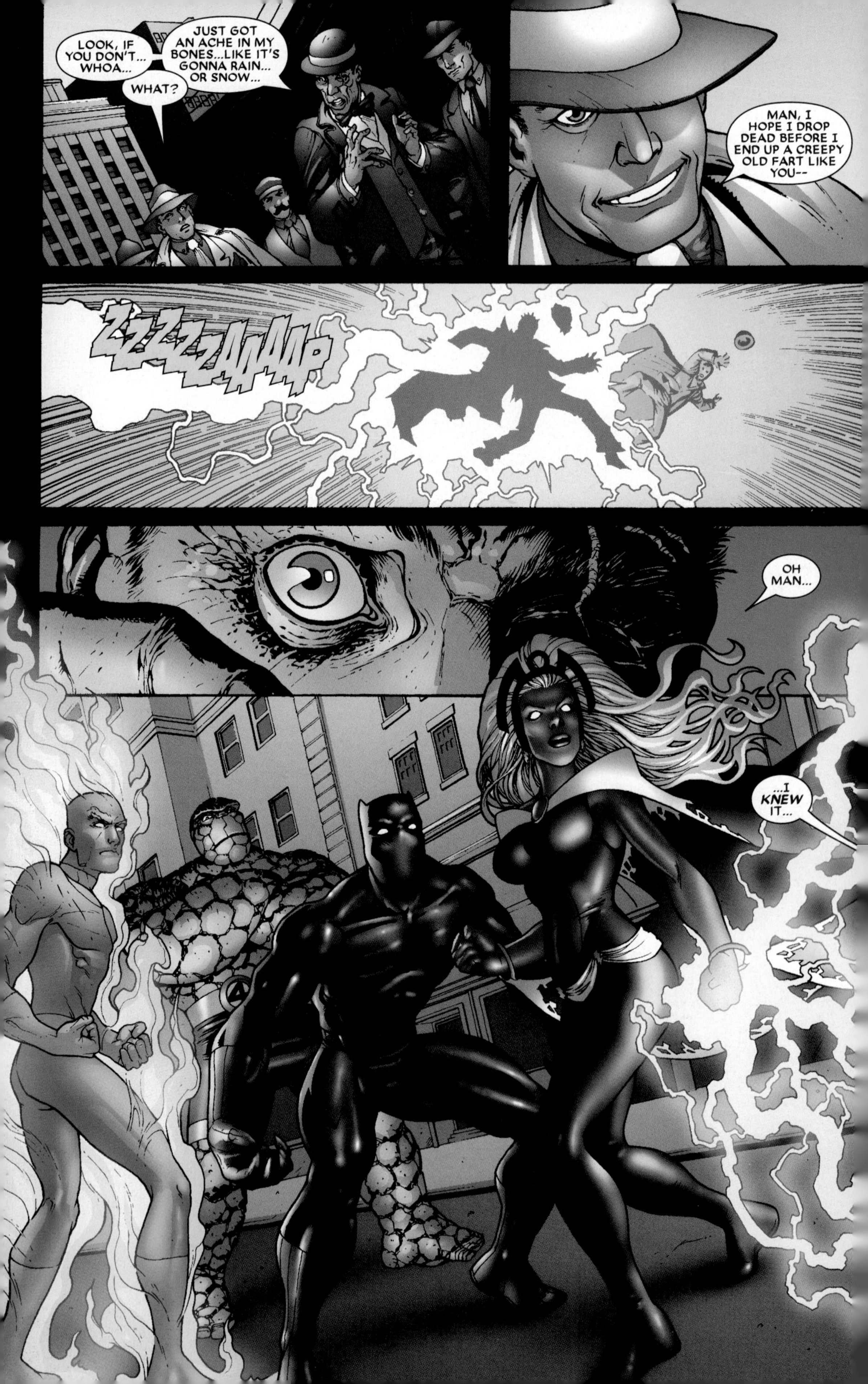

LOOK, IF YOU DON'T... WHOA...
JUST GOT AN ACHE IN MY BONES...LIKE IT'S GONNA RAIN... OR SNOW...
WHAT?
MAN, I HOPE I DROP DEAD BEFORE I END UP A CREEPY OLD FART LIKE YOU--
ZZZZZAAAAP
OH MAN...
...I KNEW IT...

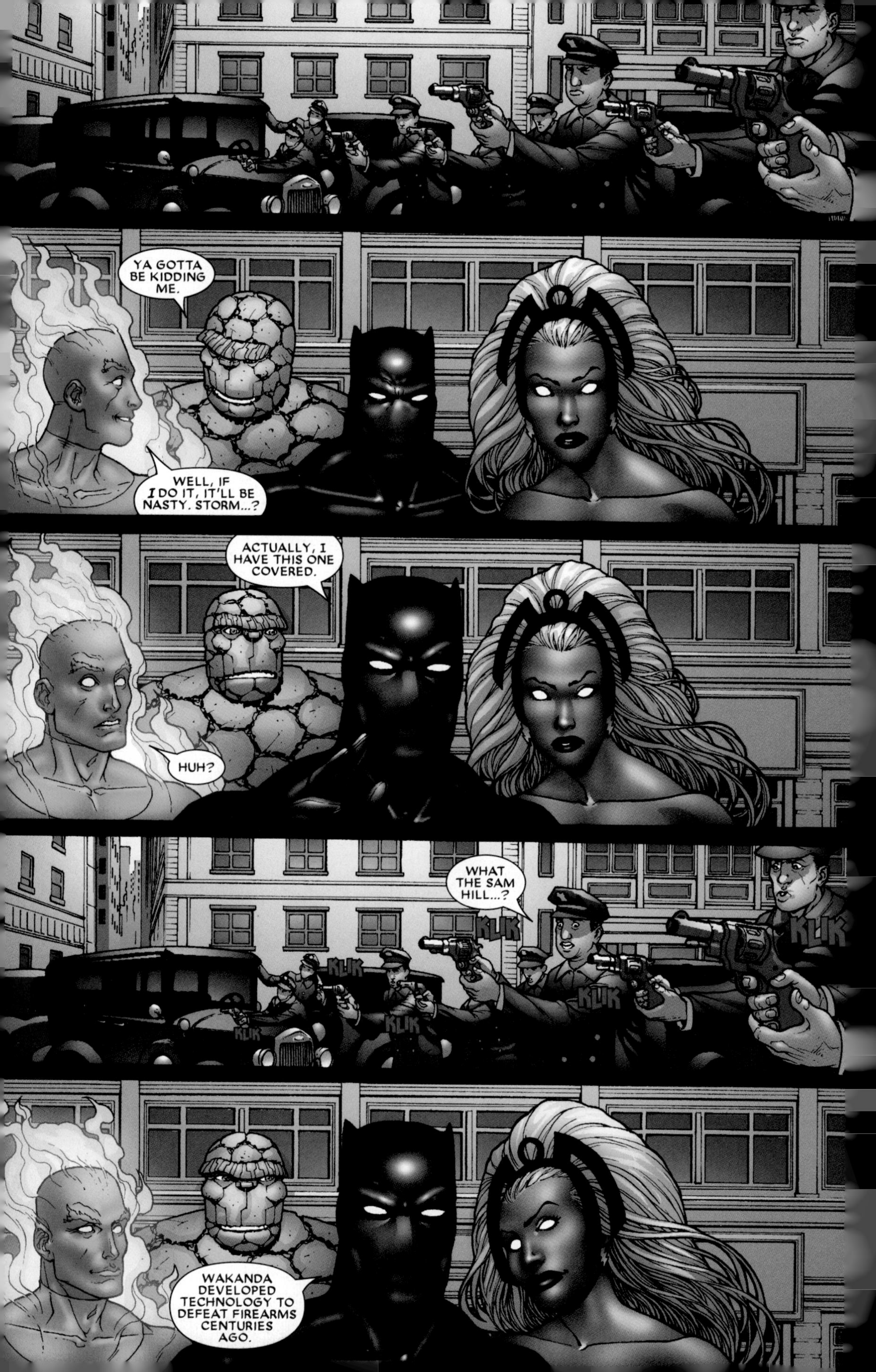
YA GOTTA BE KIDDING ME.
WELL, IF I DO IT, IT'LL BE NASTY. STORM...?
ACTUALLY, I HAVE THIS ONE COVERED.
HUH?
WHAT THE SAM HILL...?
KLIK
KLIK
KLIK
KLIK
KLIK
KLIK
WAKANDA DEVELOPED TECHNOLOGY TO DEFEAT FIREARMS CENTURIES AGO.

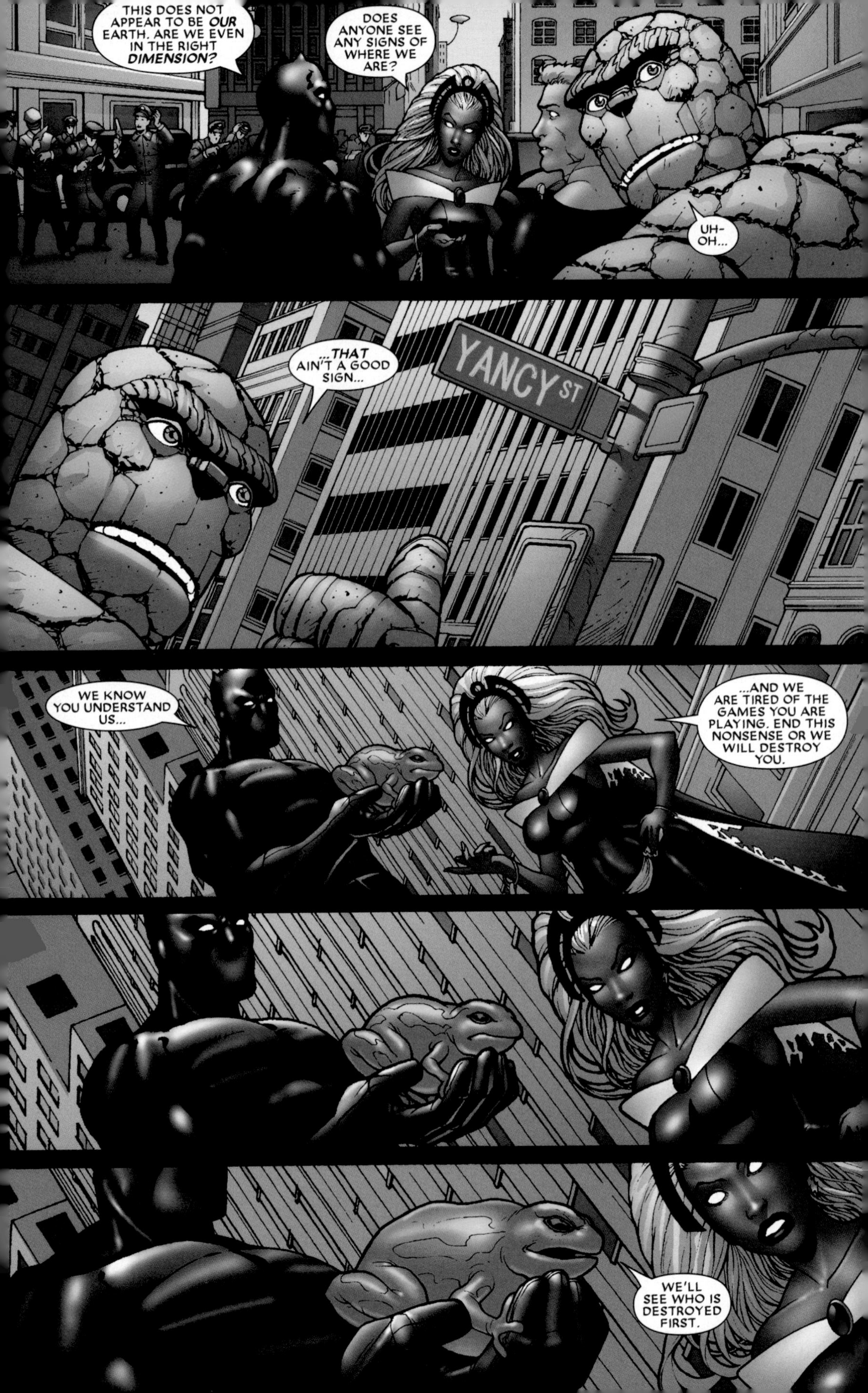
THIS DOES NOT APPEAR TO BE OUR EARTH. ARE WE EVEN IN THE RIGHT DIMENSION?
DOES ANYONE SEE ANY SIGNS OF WHERE WE ARE?
UH-OH...
...THAT AIN'T A GOOD SIGN...
YANCY ST
WE KNOW YOU UNDERSTAND US...
...AND WE ARE TIRED OF THE GAMES YOU ARE PLAYING. END THIS NONSENSE OR WE WILL DESTROY YOU.
WE'LL SEE WHO IS DESTROYED FIRST.

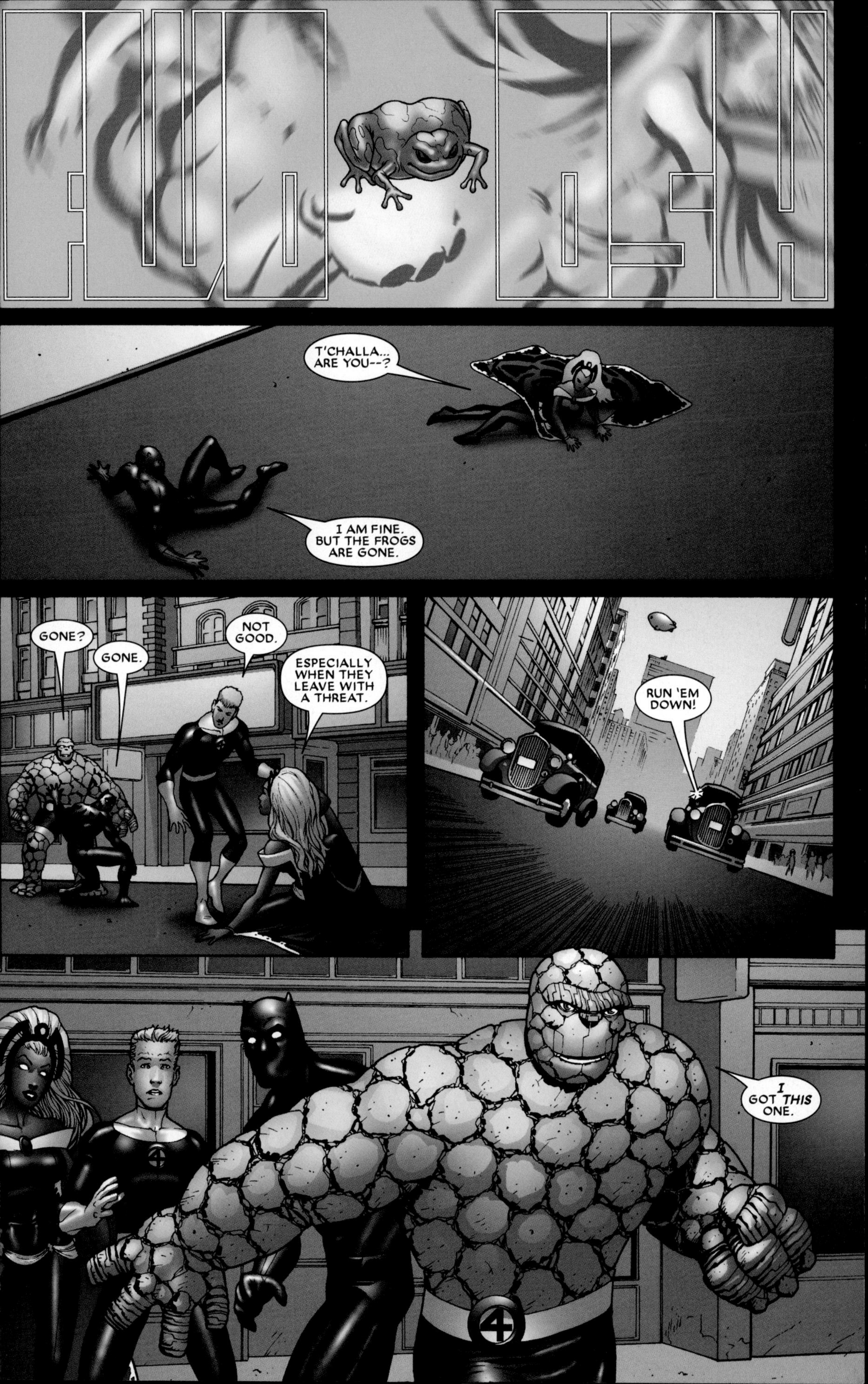
T'CHALLA... ARE YOU--?
I AM FINE. BUT THE FROGS ARE GONE.
GONE?
GONE.
NOT GOOD.
ESPECIALLY WHEN THEY LEAVE WITH A THREAT.
RUN 'EM DOWN!
I GOT THIS ONE.

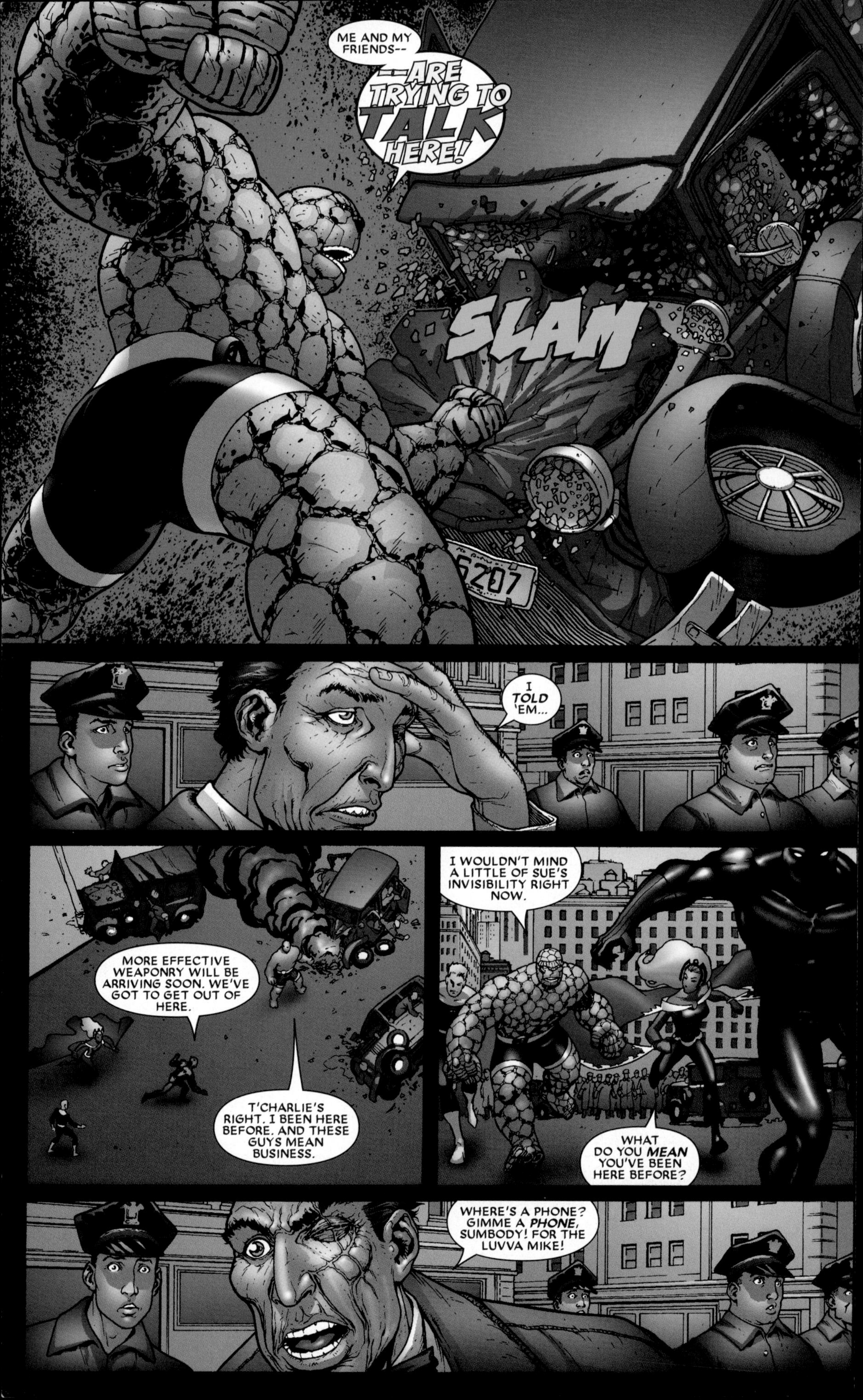
ME AND MY FRIENDS--
--ARE TRYING TO TALK HERE!
SLAM
6207
I TOLD 'EM...
MORE EFFECTIVE WEAPONRY WILL BE ARRIVING SOON. WE'VE GOT TO GET OUT OF HERE.
T'CHARLIE'S RIGHT. I BEEN HERE BEFORE. AND THESE GUYS MEAN BUSINESS.
I WOULDN'T MIND A LITTLE OF SUE'S INVISIBILITY RIGHT NOW.
WHAT DO YOU MEAN YOU'VE BEEN HERE BEFORE?
WHERE'S A PHONE? GIMME A PHONE, SUMBODY! FOR THE LUVVA MIKE!

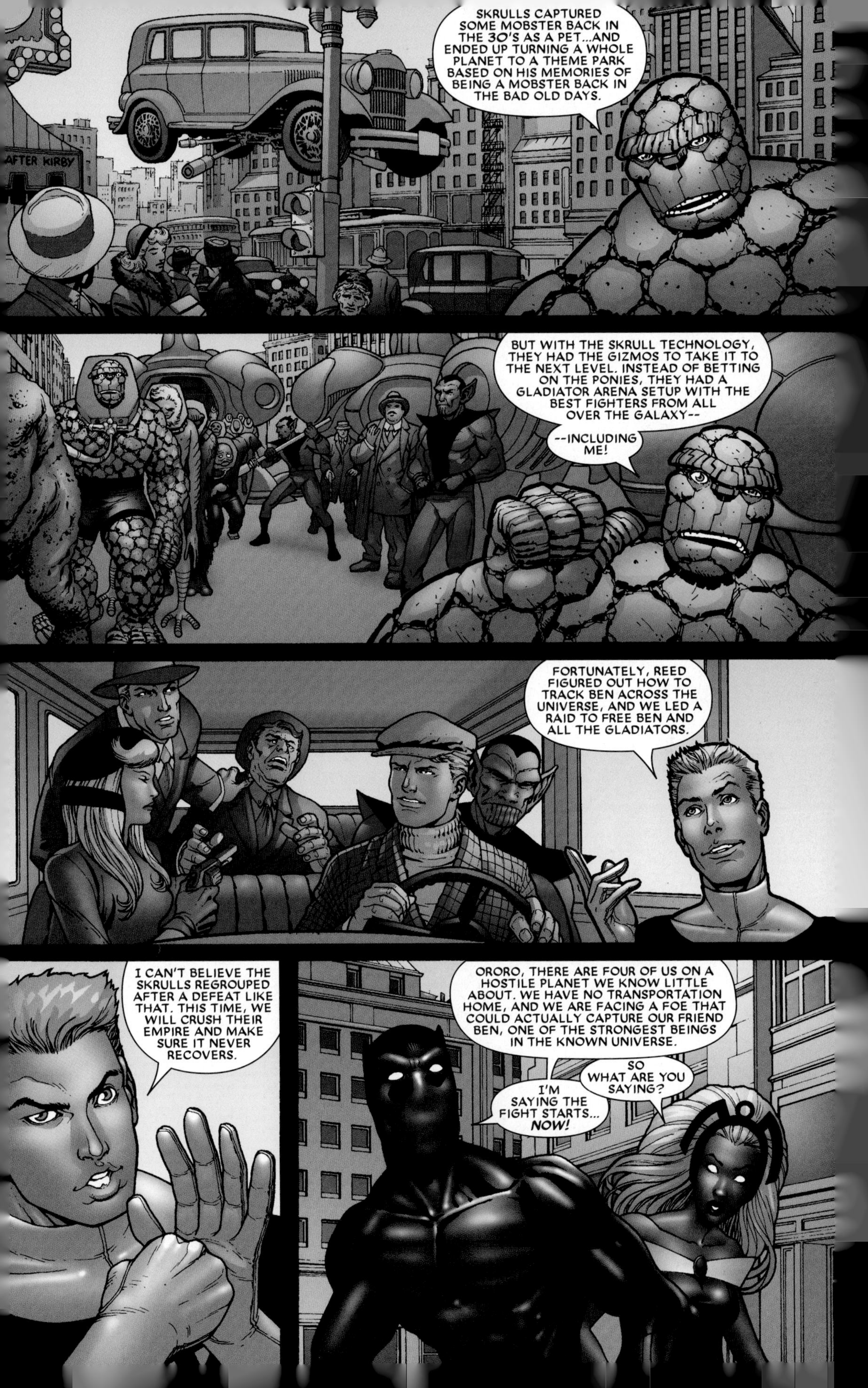
AFTER KIRBY
SKRULLS CAPTURED SOME MOBSTER BACK IN THE 30'S AS A PET...AND ENDED UP TURNING A WHOLE PLANET TO A THEME PARK BASED ON HIS MEMORIES OF BEING A MOBSTER BACK IN THE BAD OLD DAYS.
BUT WITH THE SKRULL TECHNOLOGY, THEY HAD THE GIZMOS TO TAKE IT TO THE NEXT LEVEL. INSTEAD OF BETTING ON THE PONIES, THEY HAD A GLADIATOR ARENA SETUP WITH THE BEST FIGHTERS FROM ALL OVER THE GALAXY--
--INCLUDING ME!
FORTUNATELY, REED FIGURED OUT HOW TO TRACK BEN ACROSS THE UNIVERSE, AND WE LED A RAID TO FREE BEN AND ALL THE GLADIATORS.
I CAN'T BELIEVE THE SKRULLS REGROUPED AFTER A DEFEAT LIKE THAT. THIS TIME, WE WILL CRUSH THEIR EMPIRE AND MAKE SURE IT NEVER RECOVERS.
ORORO, THERE ARE FOUR OF US ON A HOSTILE PLANET WE KNOW LITTLE ABOUT. WE HAVE NO TRANSPORTATION HOME, AND WE ARE FACING A FOE THAT COULD ACTUALLY CAPTURE OUR FRIEND BEN, ONE OF THE STRONGEST BEINGS IN THE KNOWN UNIVERSE.
SO WHAT ARE YOU SAYING?
I'M SAYING THE FIGHT STARTS... *NOW!*

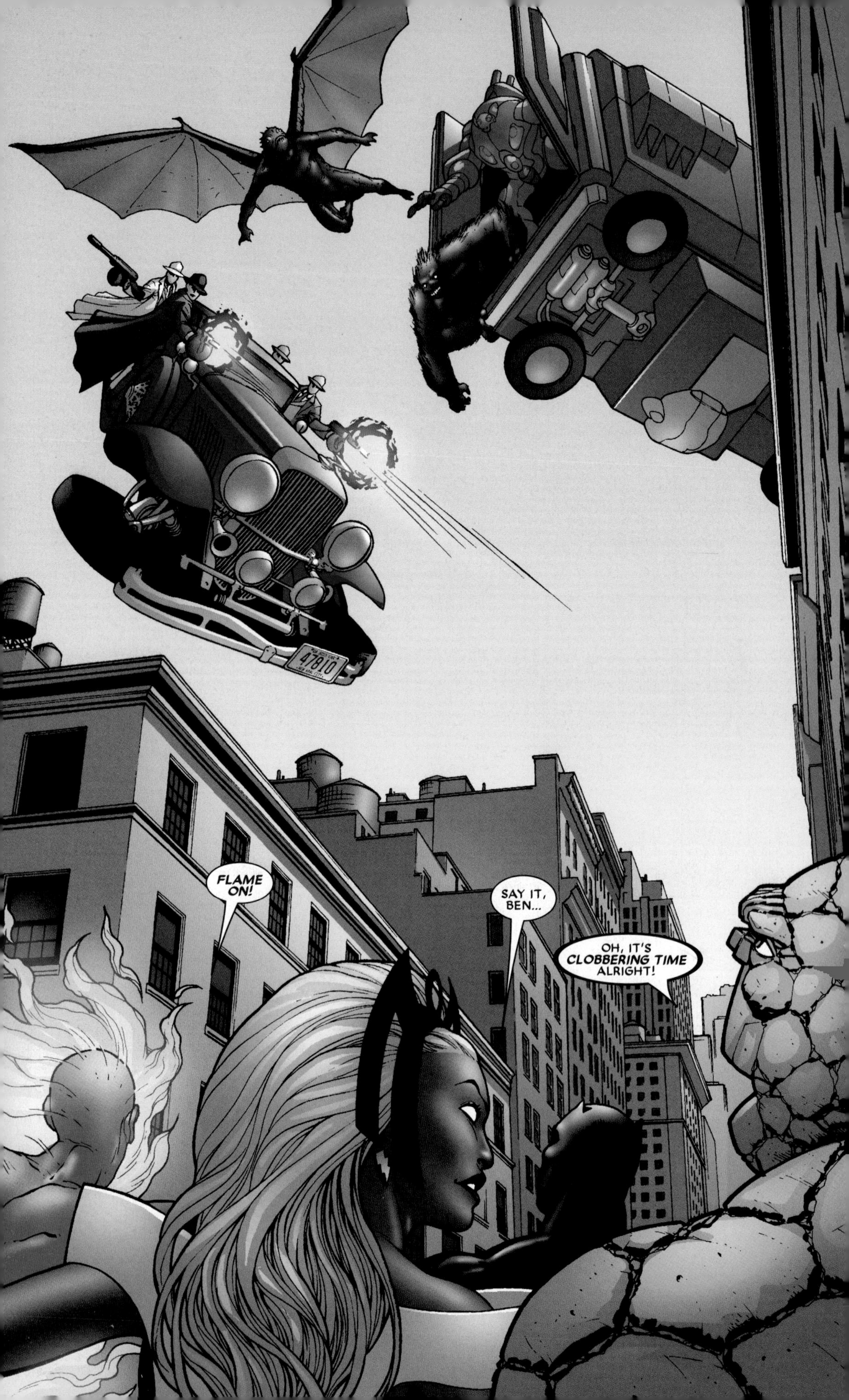
FLAME ON!
SAY IT, BEN...
OH, IT'S CLOBBERING TIME ALRIGHT!

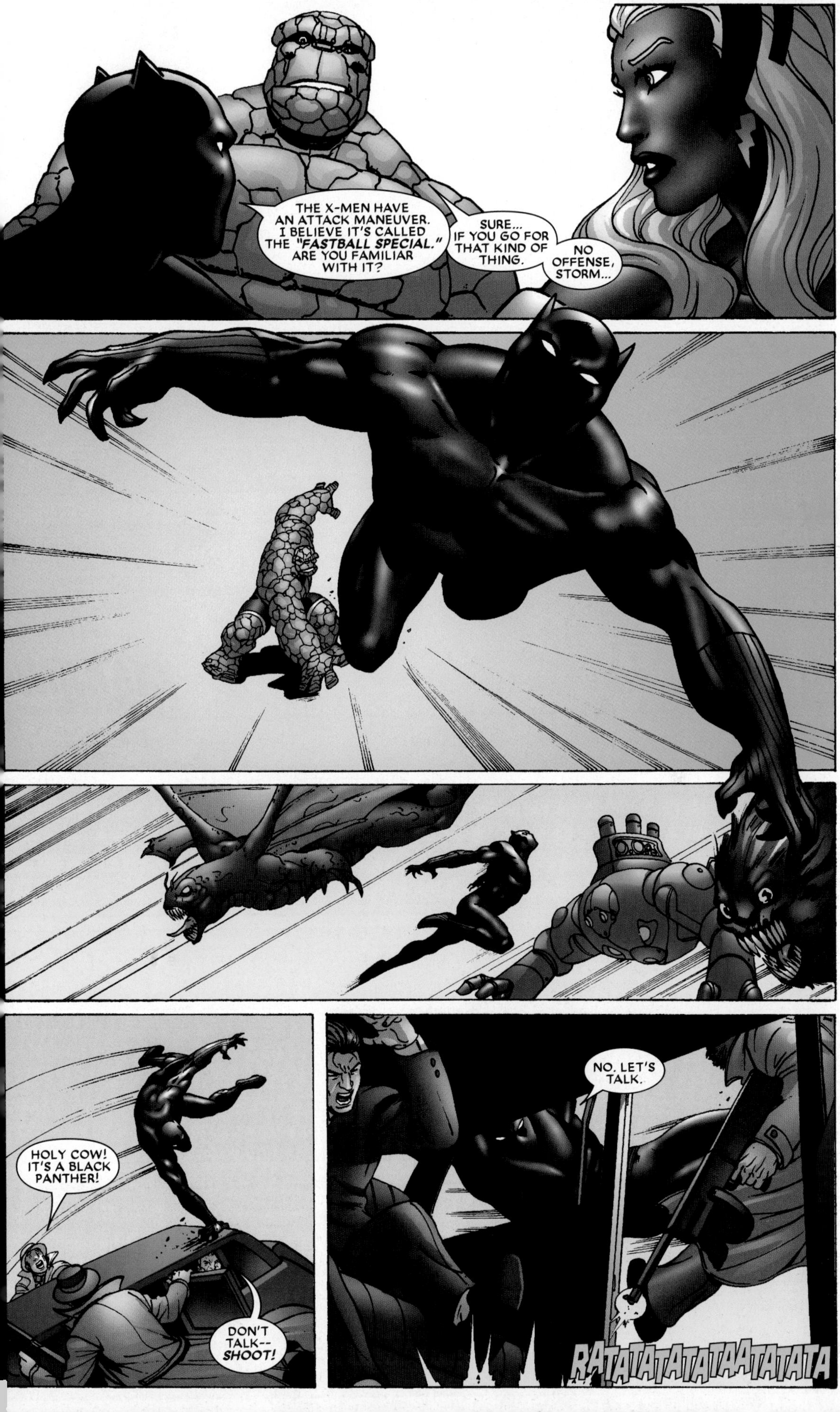
THE X-MEN HAVE AN ATTACK MANEUVER. I BELIEVE IT'S CALLED THE "FASTBALL SPECIAL." ARE YOU FAMILIAR WITH IT?
SURE... IF YOU GO FOR THAT KIND OF THING.
NO OFFENSE, STORM...
HOLY COW! IT'S A BLACK PANTHER!
DON'T TALK-- SHOOT!
NO. LET'S TALK.
RATATATATATATAATATATA

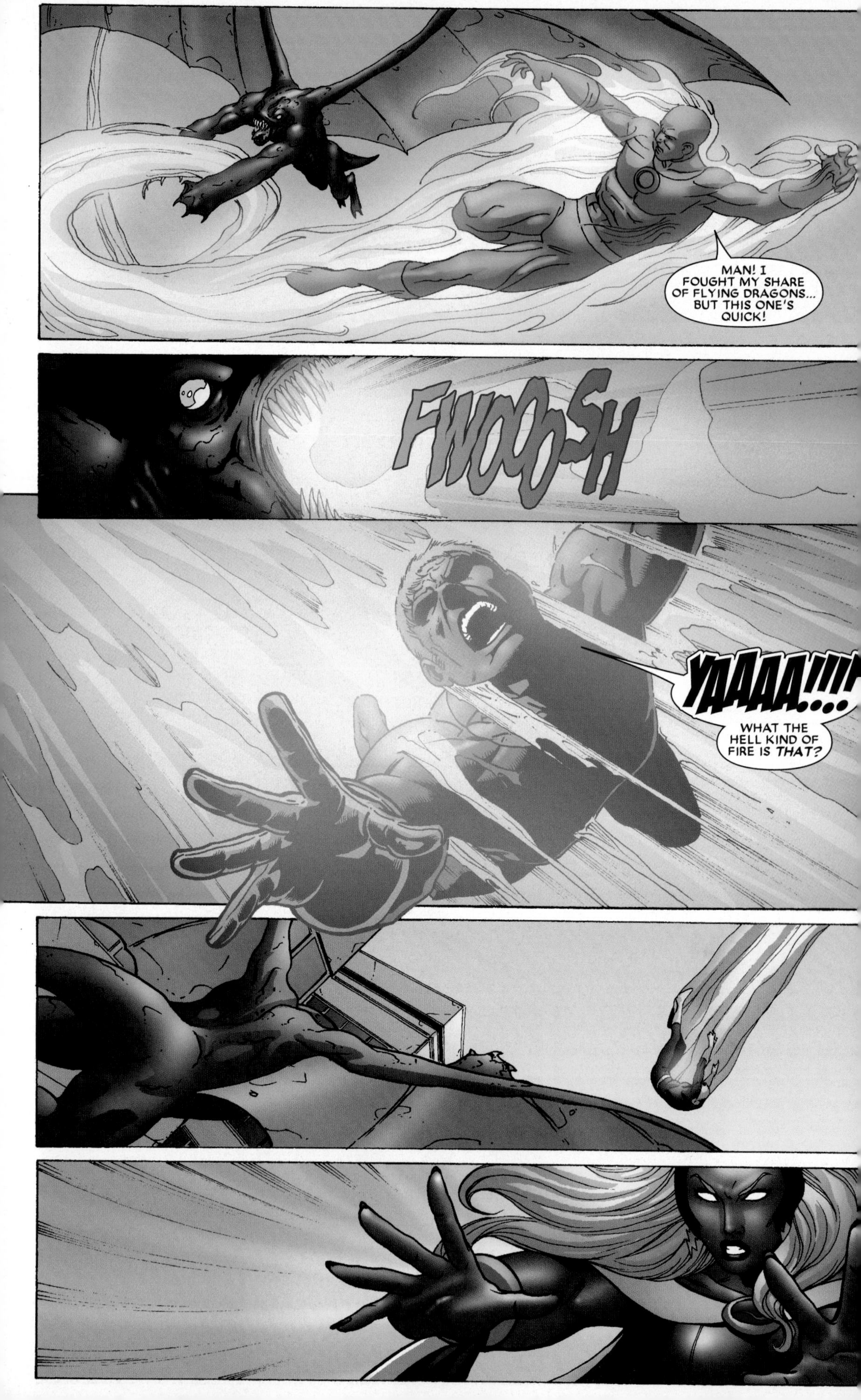
MAN! I FOUGHT MY SHARE OF FLYING DRAGONS... BUT THIS ONE'S QUICK!
FWOOO-SH
YAAAA!!!!...
WHAT THE HELL KIND OF FIRE IS *THAT?*

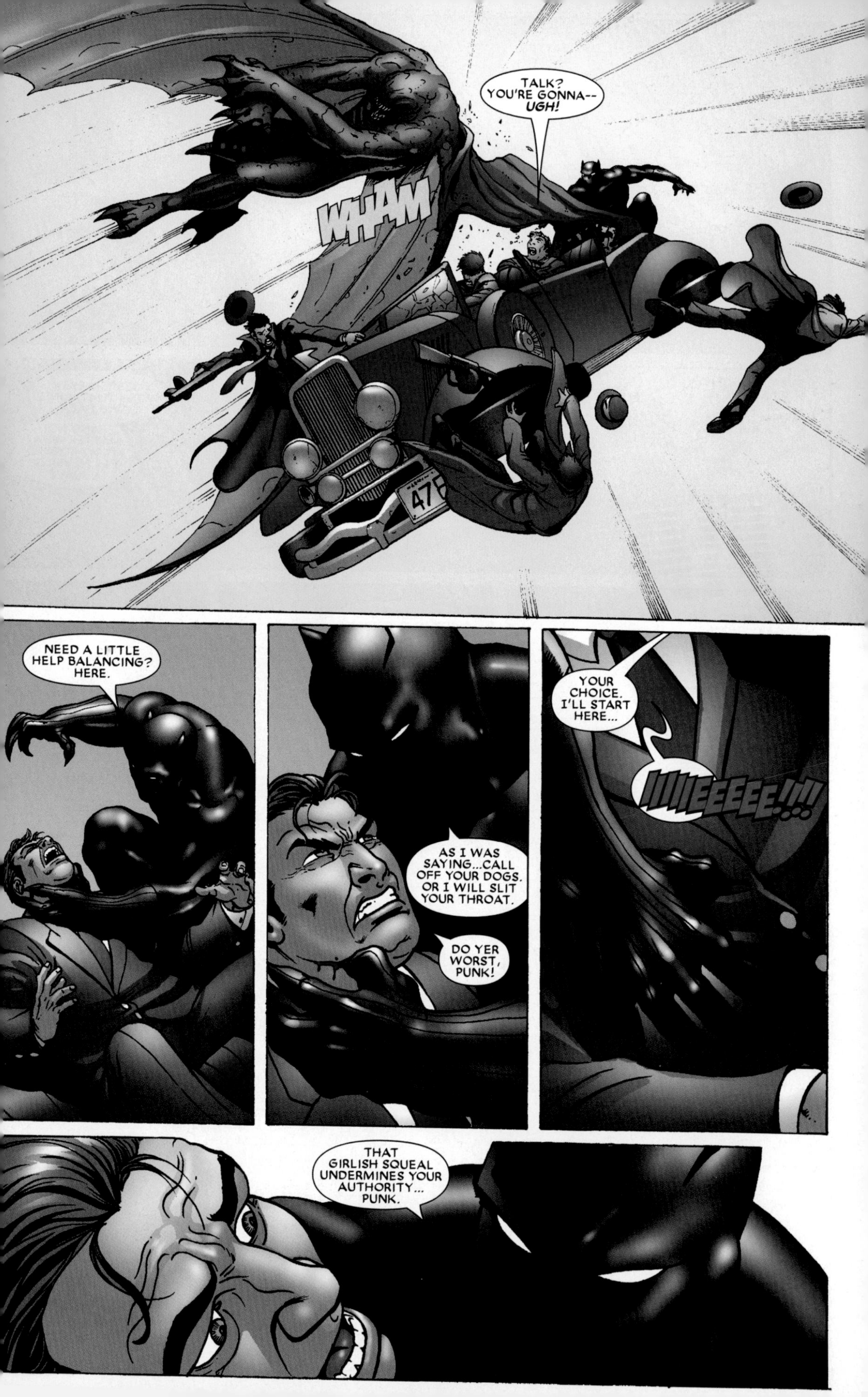
TALK? YOU'RE GONNA-- UGH!
WHAM
NEED A LITTLE HELP BALANCING? HERE.
AS I WAS SAYING...CALL OFF YOUR DOGS. OR I WILL SLIT YOUR THROAT.
DO YER WORST, PUNK!
YOUR CHOICE. I'LL START HERE...
IIIIIEEEEEE!!!
THAT GIRLISH SQUEAL UNDERMINES YOUR AUTHORITY... PUNK.

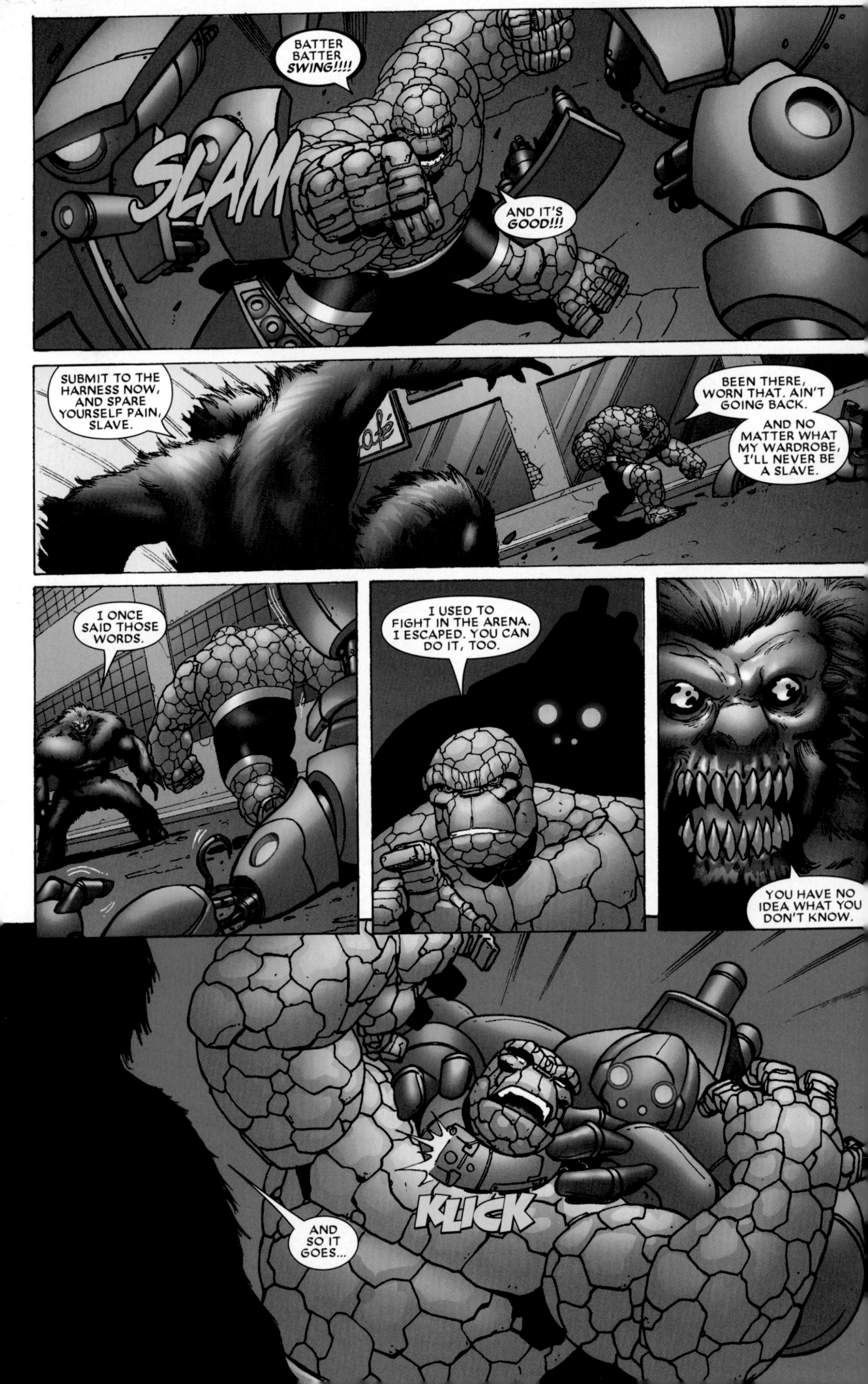
BATTER BATTER SWING!!!!
SLAM
AND IT'S GOOD!!!
SUBMIT TO THE HARNESS NOW, AND SPARE YOURSELF PAIN, SLAVE.
BEEN THERE, WORN THAT. AIN'T GOING BACK.
AND NO MATTER WHAT MY WARDROBE, I'LL NEVER BE A SLAVE.
I ONCE SAID THOSE WORDS.
I USED TO FIGHT IN THE ARENA. I ESCAPED. YOU CAN DO IT, TOO.
YOU HAVE NO IDEA WHAT YOU DON'T KNOW.
KLICK
AND SO IT GOES...

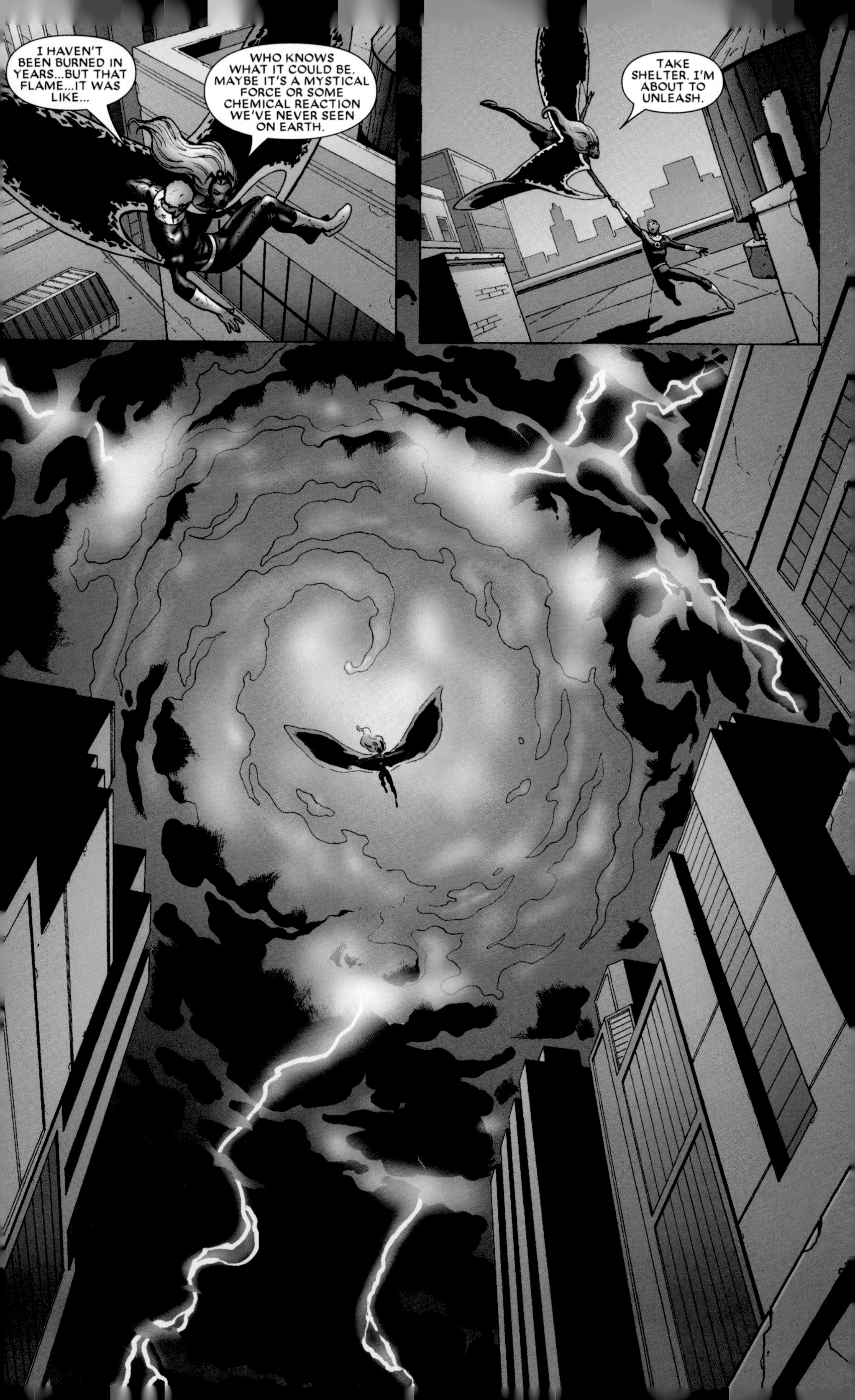
I HAVEN'T BEEN BURNED IN YEARS...BUT THAT FLAME...IT WAS LIKE...
WHO KNOWS WHAT IT COULD BE. MAYBE IT'S A MYSTICAL FORCE OR SOME CHEMICAL REACTION WE'VE NEVER SEEN ON EARTH.
TAKE SHELTER. I'M ABOUT TO UNLEASH.

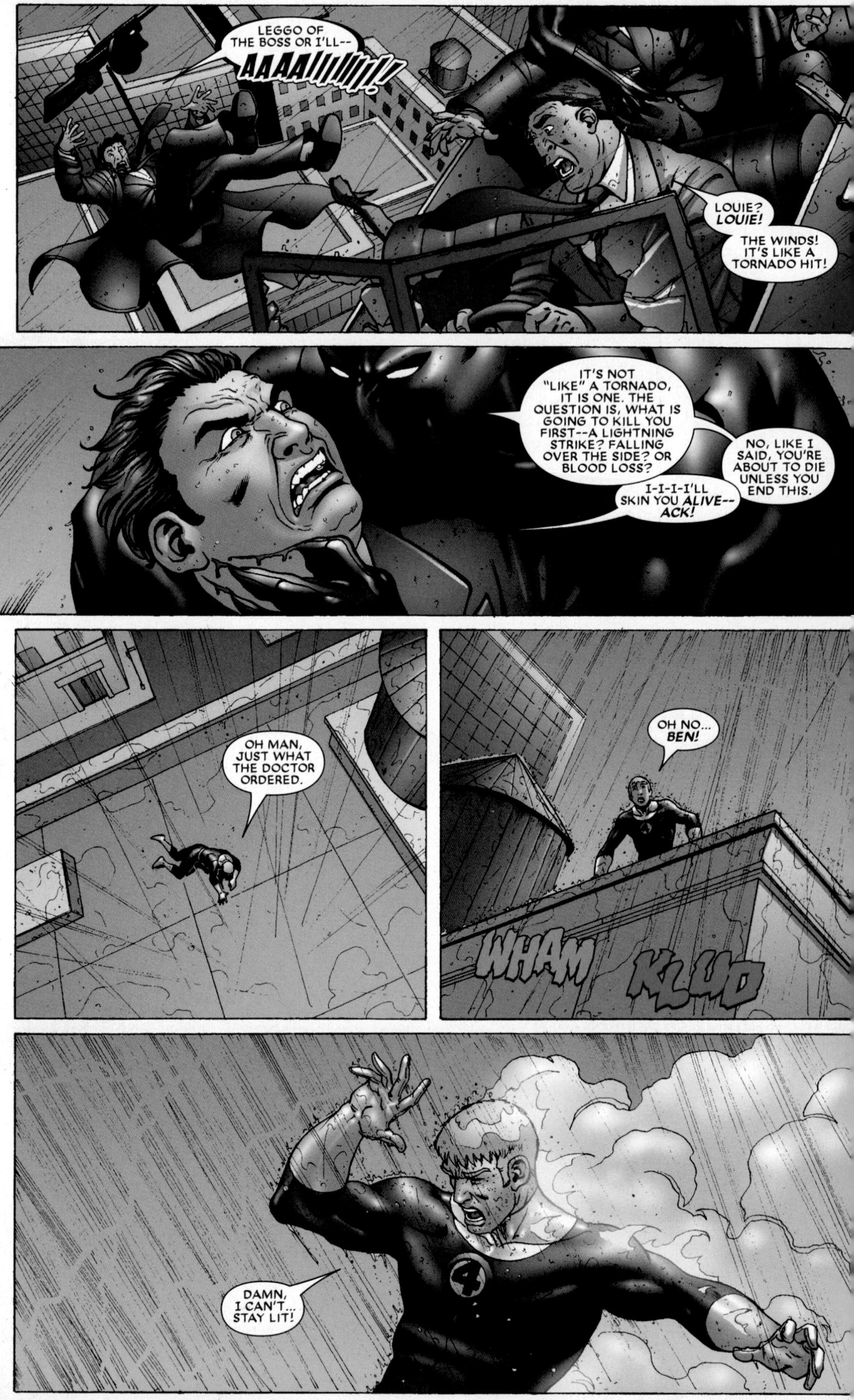
LEGGO OF THE BOSS OR I'LL--
AAAA!!!!!!!!
LOUIE? LOUIE!
THE WINDS! IT'S LIKE A TORNADO HIT!
IT'S NOT "LIKE" A TORNADO, IT IS ONE. THE QUESTION IS, WHAT IS GOING TO KILL YOU FIRST--A LIGHTNING STRIKE? FALLING OVER THE SIDE? OR BLOOD LOSS?
I-I-I-I'LL SKIN YOU ALIVE-- ACK!
NO, LIKE I SAID, YOU'RE ABOUT TO DIE UNLESS YOU END THIS.
OH MAN, JUST WHAT THE DOCTOR ORDERED.
OH NO... BEN!
WHAM
KLUD
DAMN, I CAN'T... STAY LIT!

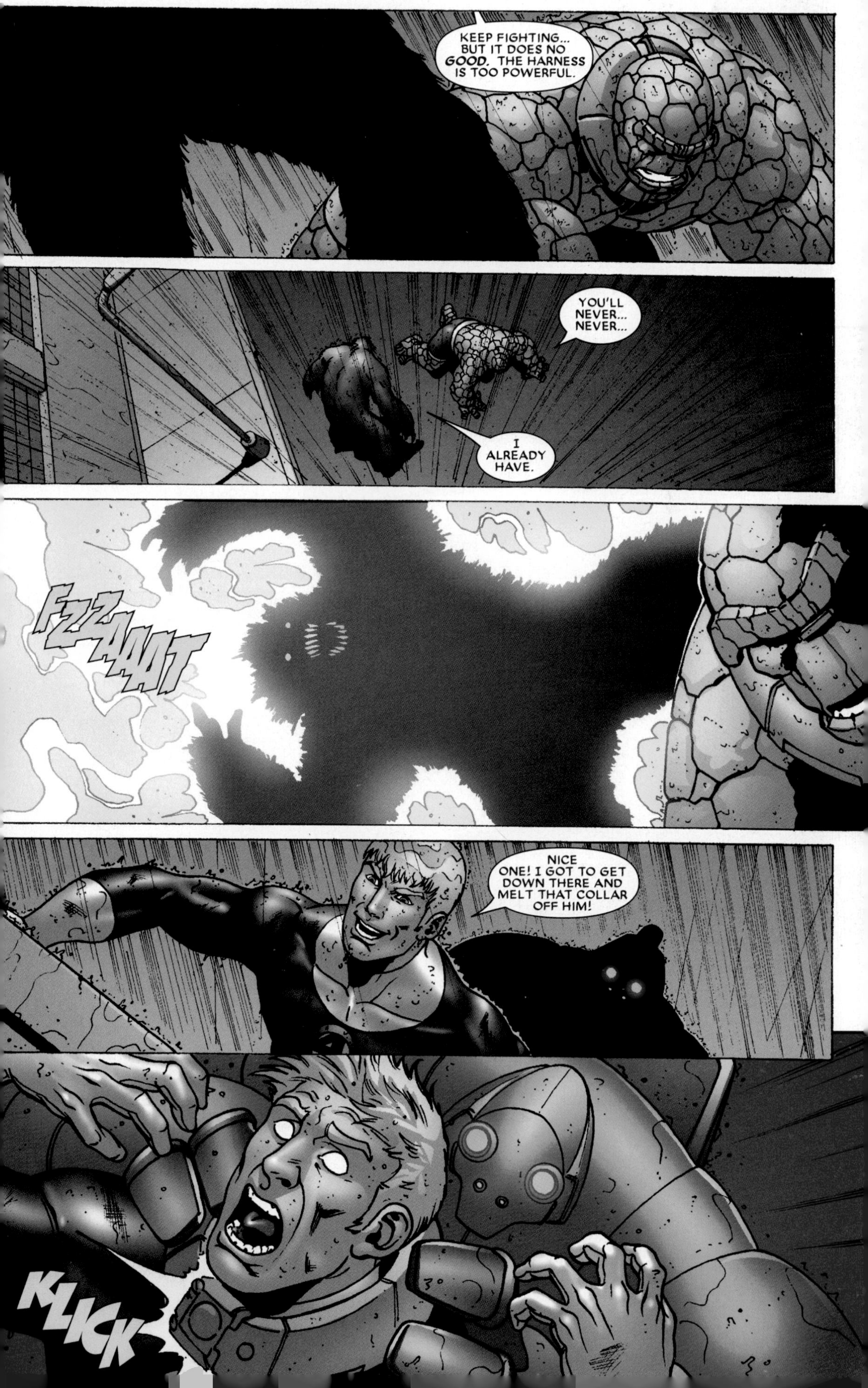
KEEP FIGHTING... BUT IT DOES NO GOOD. THE HARNESS IS TOO POWERFUL.
YOU'LL NEVER... NEVER...
I ALREADY HAVE.
FZZAAAT
NICE ONE! I GOT TO GET DOWN THERE AND MELT THAT COLLAR OFF HIM!
KLICK

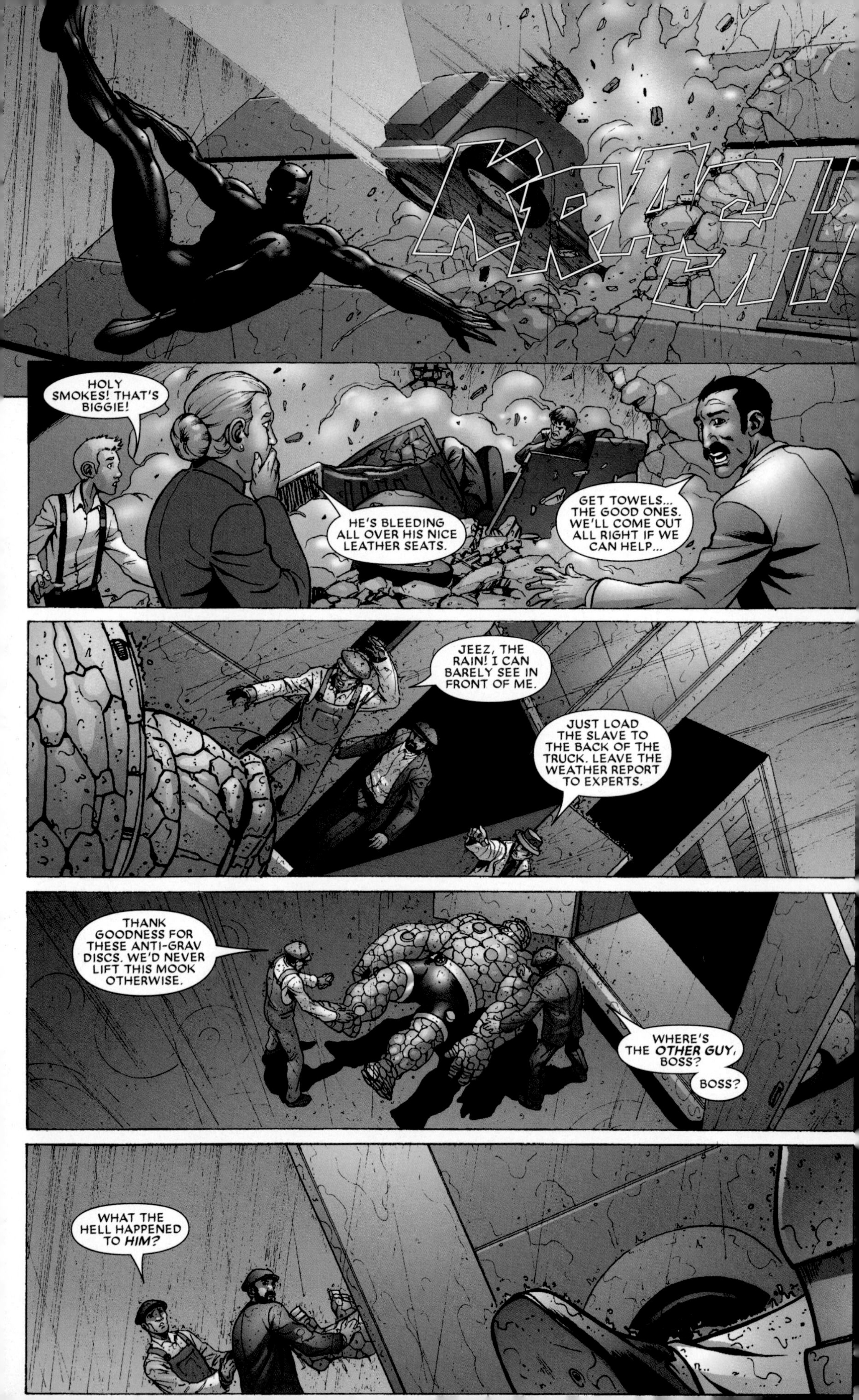
HOLY SMOKES! THAT'S BIGGIE!
HE'S BLEEDING ALL OVER HIS NICE LEATHER SEATS.
GET TOWELS... THE GOOD ONES. WE'LL COME OUT ALL RIGHT IF WE CAN HELP...
JEEZ, THE RAIN! I CAN BARELY SEE IN FRONT OF ME.
JUST LOAD THE SLAVE TO THE BACK OF THE TRUCK. LEAVE THE WEATHER REPORT TO EXPERTS.
THANK GOODNESS FOR THESE ANTI-GRAV DISCS. WE'D NEVER LIFT THIS MOOK OTHERWISE.
WHERE'S THE **OTHER GUY**, BOSS?
BOSS?
WHAT THE HELL HAPPENED TO **HIM?**

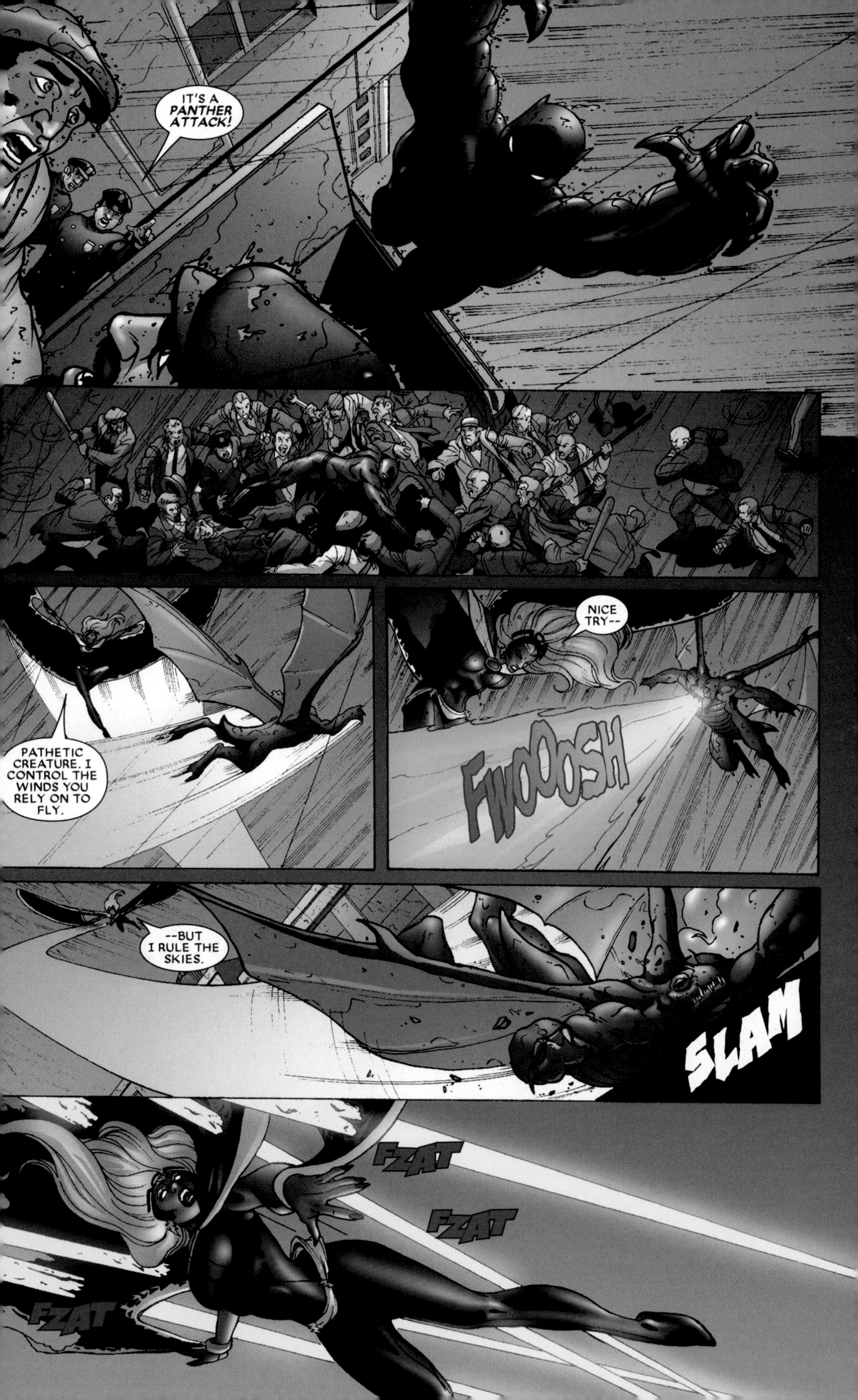

IT'S A PANTHER ATTACK!
PATHETIC CREATURE. I CONTROL THE WINDS YOU RELY ON TO FLY.
NICE TRY--
FWOOOSH
--BUT I RULE THE SKIES.
SLAM
FZAT
FZAT
FZAT

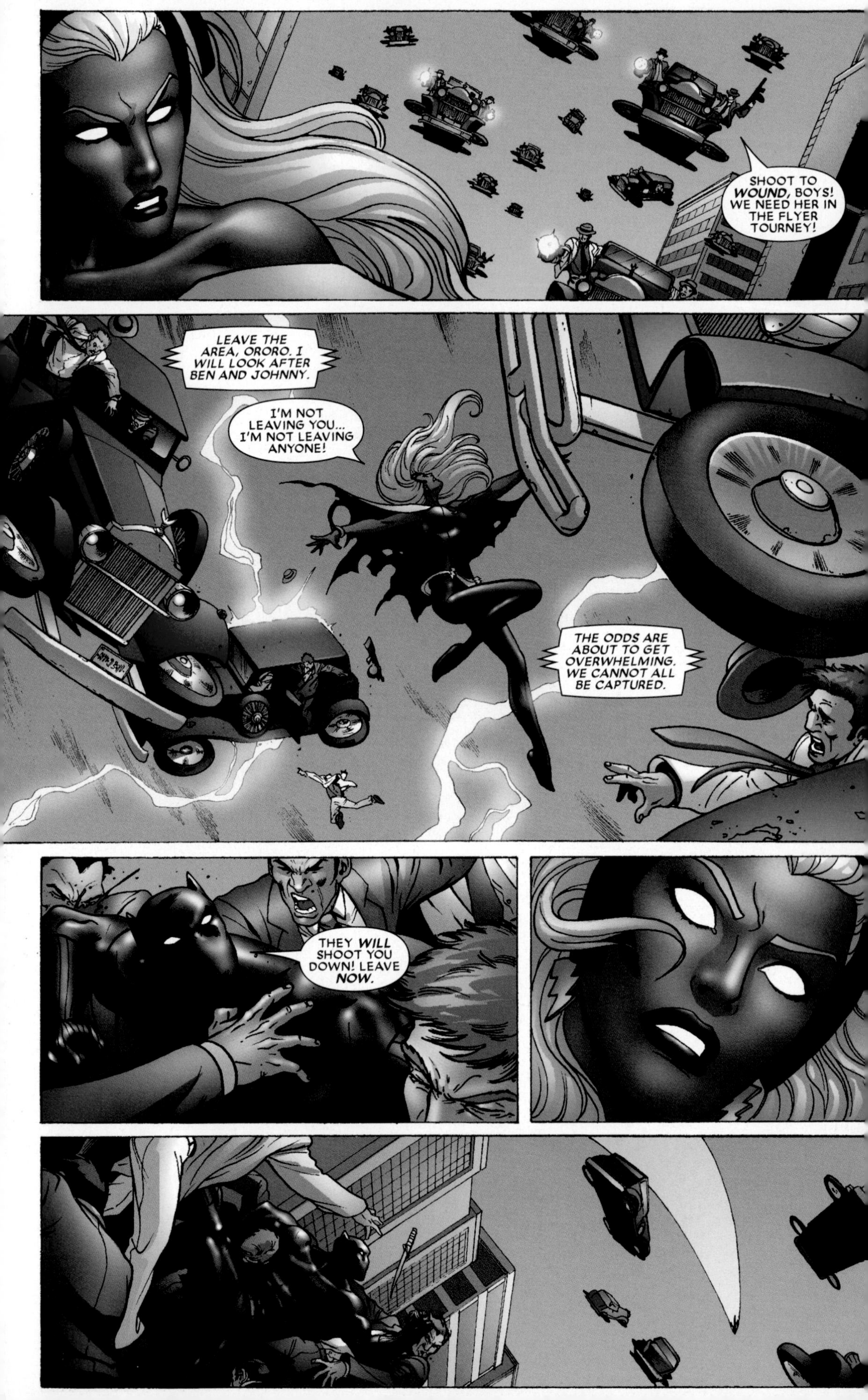
SHOOT TO WOUND, BOYS! WE NEED HER IN THE FLYER TOURNEY!
LEAVE THE AREA, ORORO. I WILL LOOK AFTER BEN AND JOHNNY.
I'M NOT LEAVING YOU... I'M NOT LEAVING ANYONE!
THE ODDS ARE ABOUT TO GET OVERWHELMING. WE CANNOT ALL BE CAPTURED.
THEY WILL SHOOT YOU DOWN! LEAVE NOW.

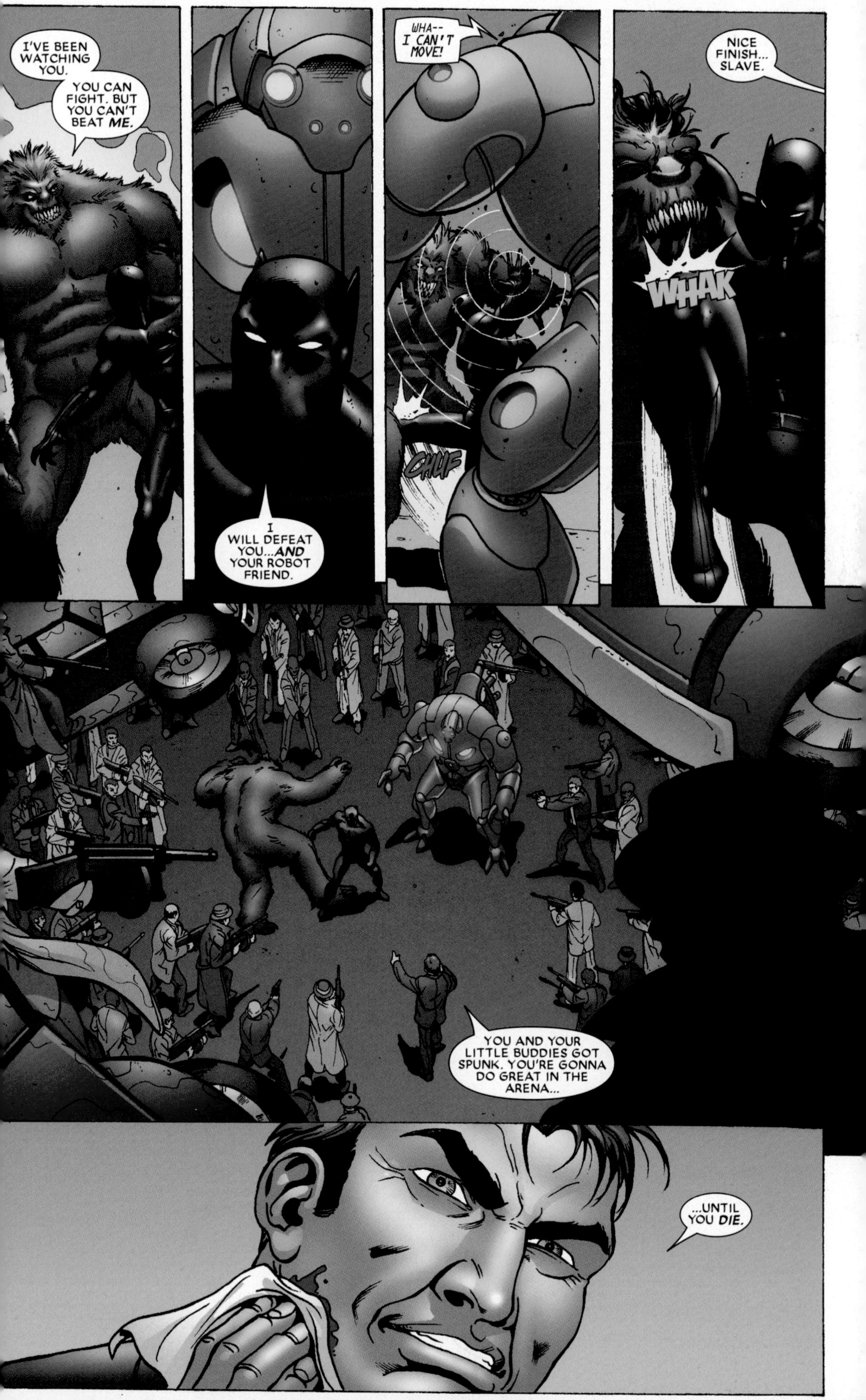
I'VE BEEN WATCHING YOU.
YOU CAN FIGHT. BUT YOU CAN'T BEAT *ME.*
I WILL DEFEAT YOU...*AND* YOUR ROBOT FRIEND.
WHA-- I CAN'T MOVE!
CHUF
NICE FINISH... SLAVE.
WHAK
YOU AND YOUR LITTLE BUDDIES GOT SPUNK. YOU'RE GONNA DO GREAT IN THE ARENA...
...UNTIL YOU *DIE.*

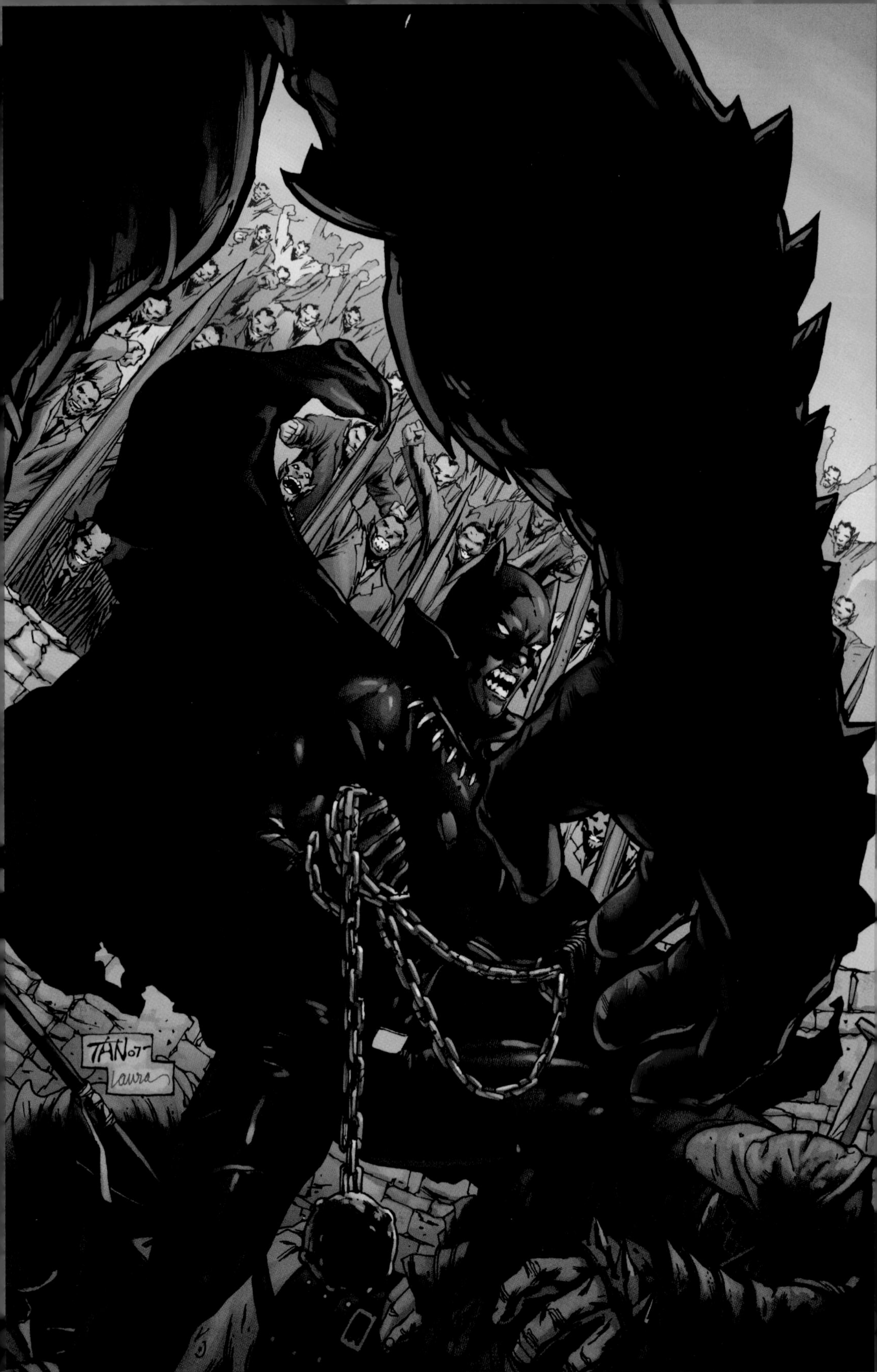
TAN07
Laura

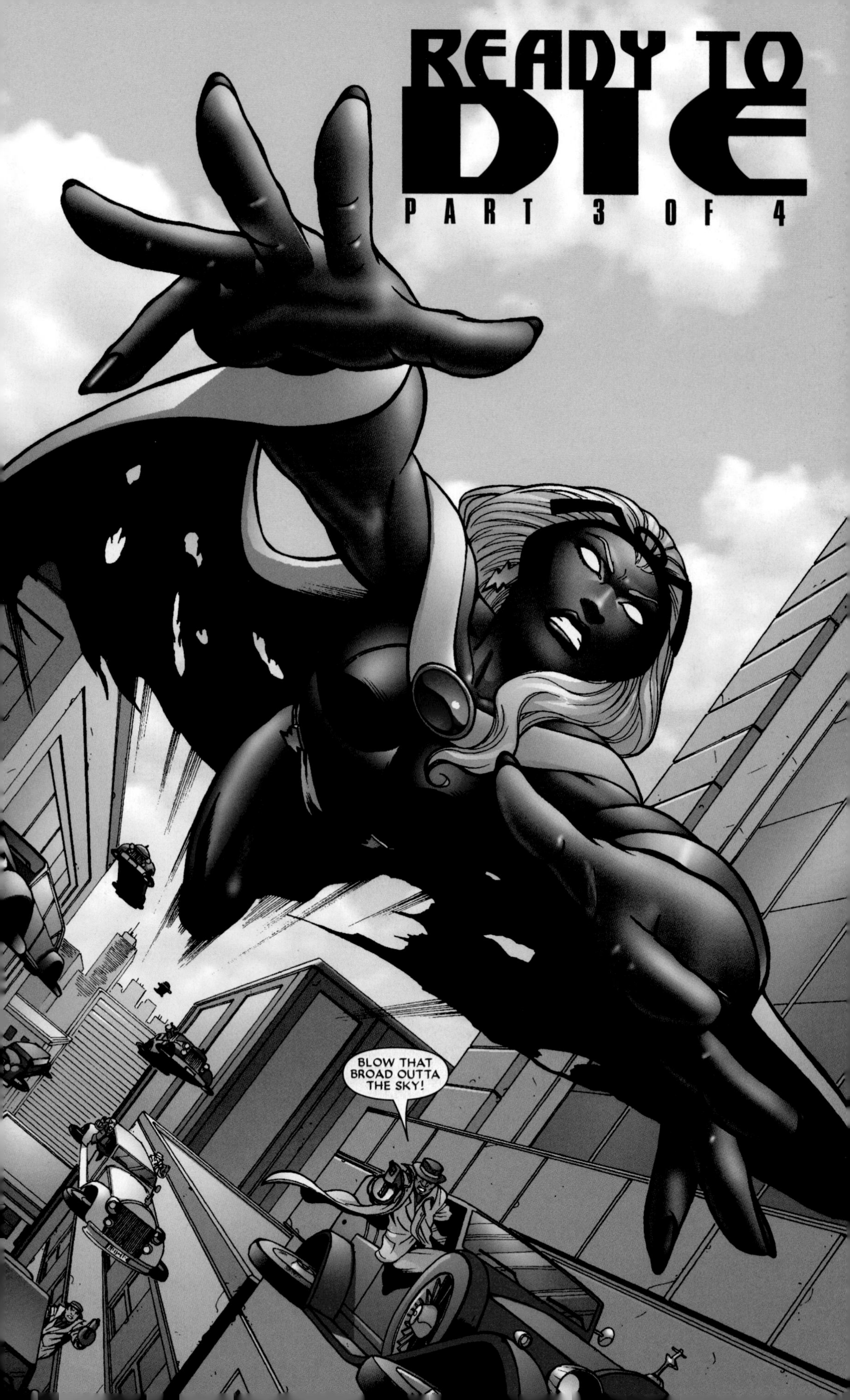
READY TO DIE
PART 3 OF 4
BLOW THAT BROAD OUTTA THE SKY!

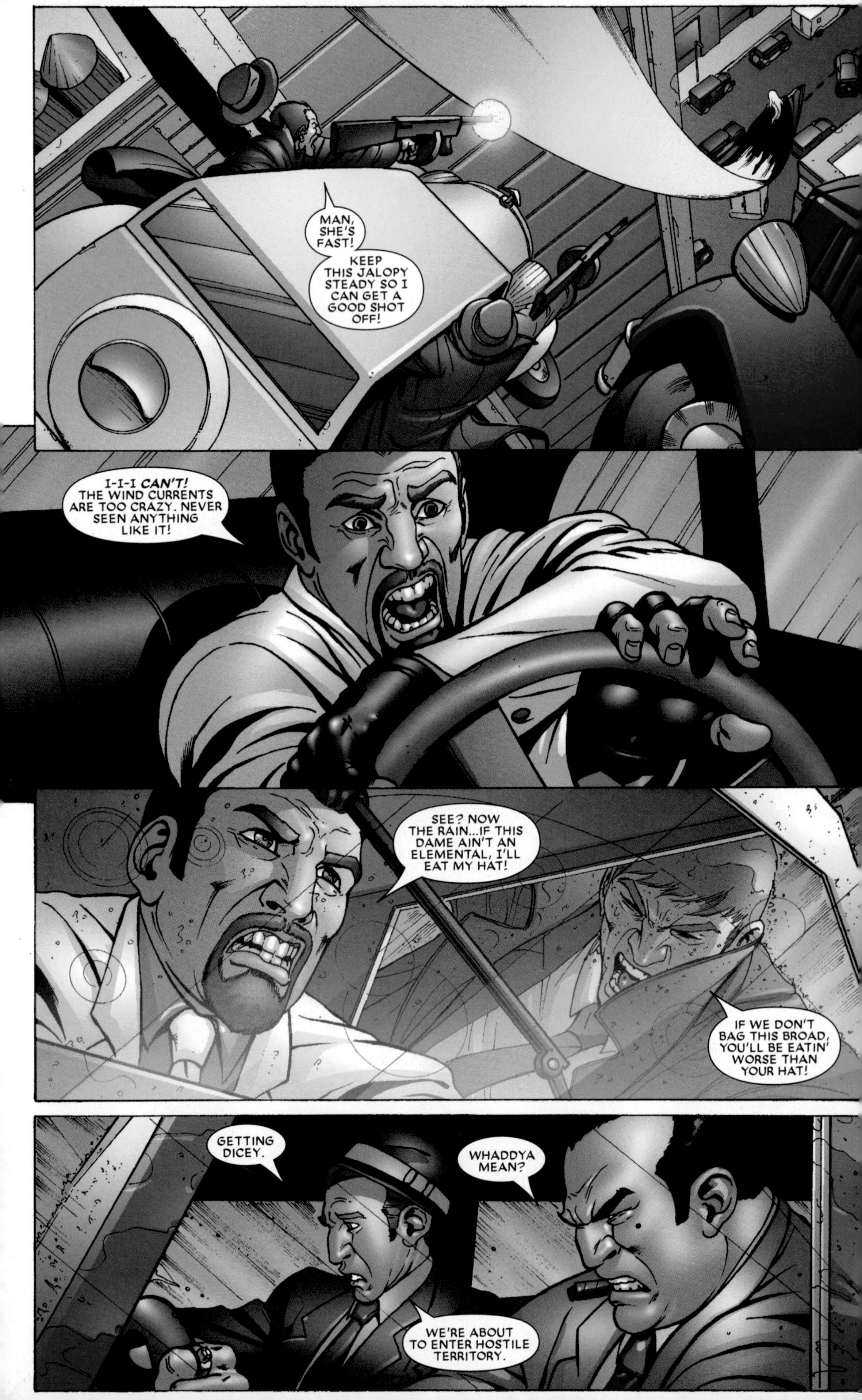
MAN, SHE'S FAST!
KEEP THIS JALOPY STEADY SO I CAN GET A GOOD SHOT OFF!
I-I-I CAN'T! THE WIND CURRENTS ARE TOO CRAZY. NEVER SEEN ANYTHING LIKE IT!
SEE? NOW THE RAIN...IF THIS DAME AIN'T AN ELEMENTAL, I'LL EAT MY HAT!
IF WE DON'T BAG THIS BROAD, YOU'LL BE EATIN' WORSE THAN YOUR HAT!
GETTING DICEY.
WHADDYA MEAN?
WE'RE ABOUT TO ENTER HOSTILE TERRITORY.

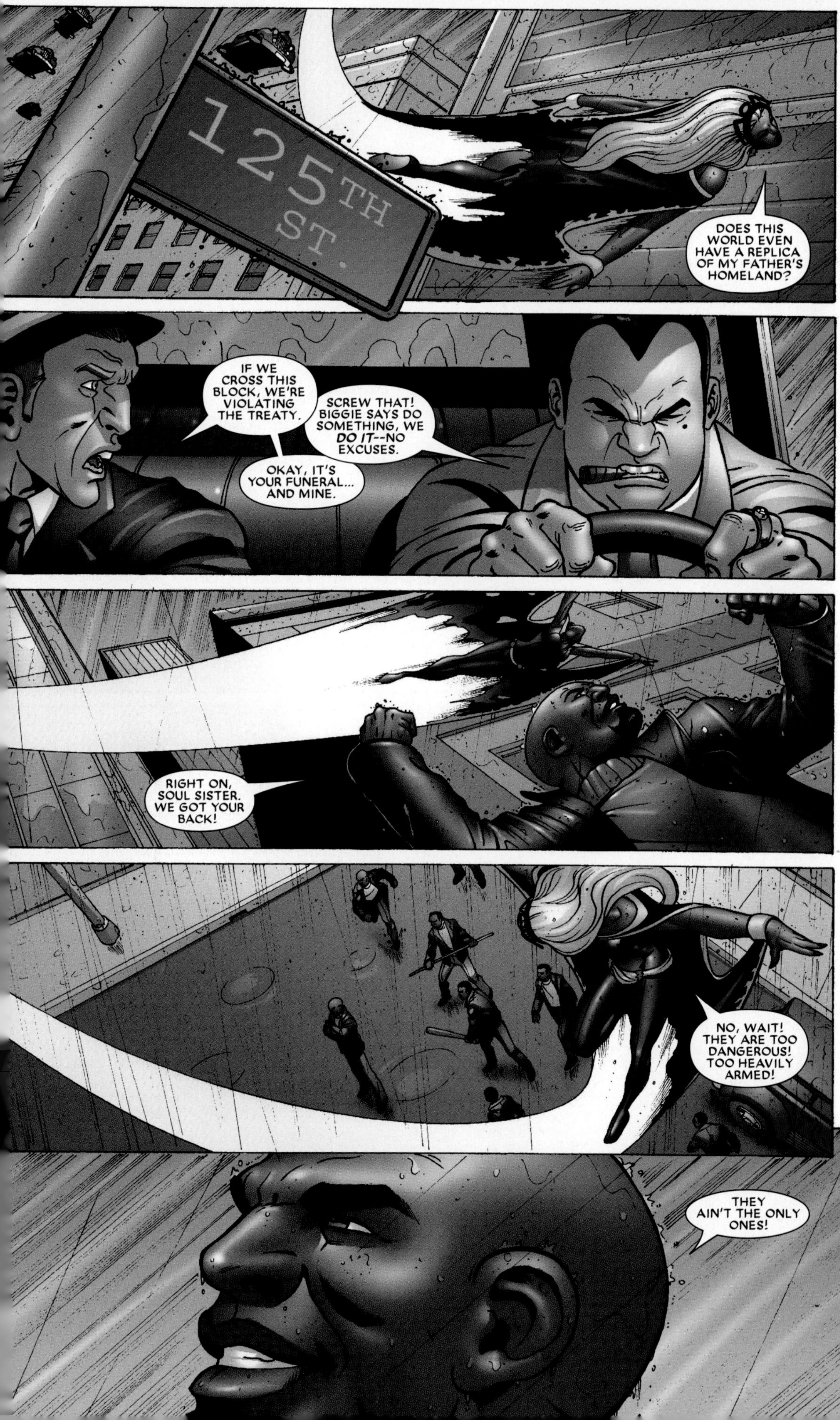
125TH ST.
DOES THIS WORLD EVEN HAVE A REPLICA OF MY FATHER'S HOMELAND?
IF WE CROSS THIS BLOCK, WE'RE VIOLATING THE TREATY.
SCREW THAT! BIGGIE SAYS DO SOMETHING, WE DO IT--NO EXCUSES.
OKAY, IT'S YOUR FUNERAL... AND MINE.
RIGHT ON, SOUL SISTER. WE GOT YOUR BACK!
NO, WAIT! THEY ARE TOO DANGEROUS! TOO HEAVILY ARMED!
THEY AIN'T THE ONLY ONES!

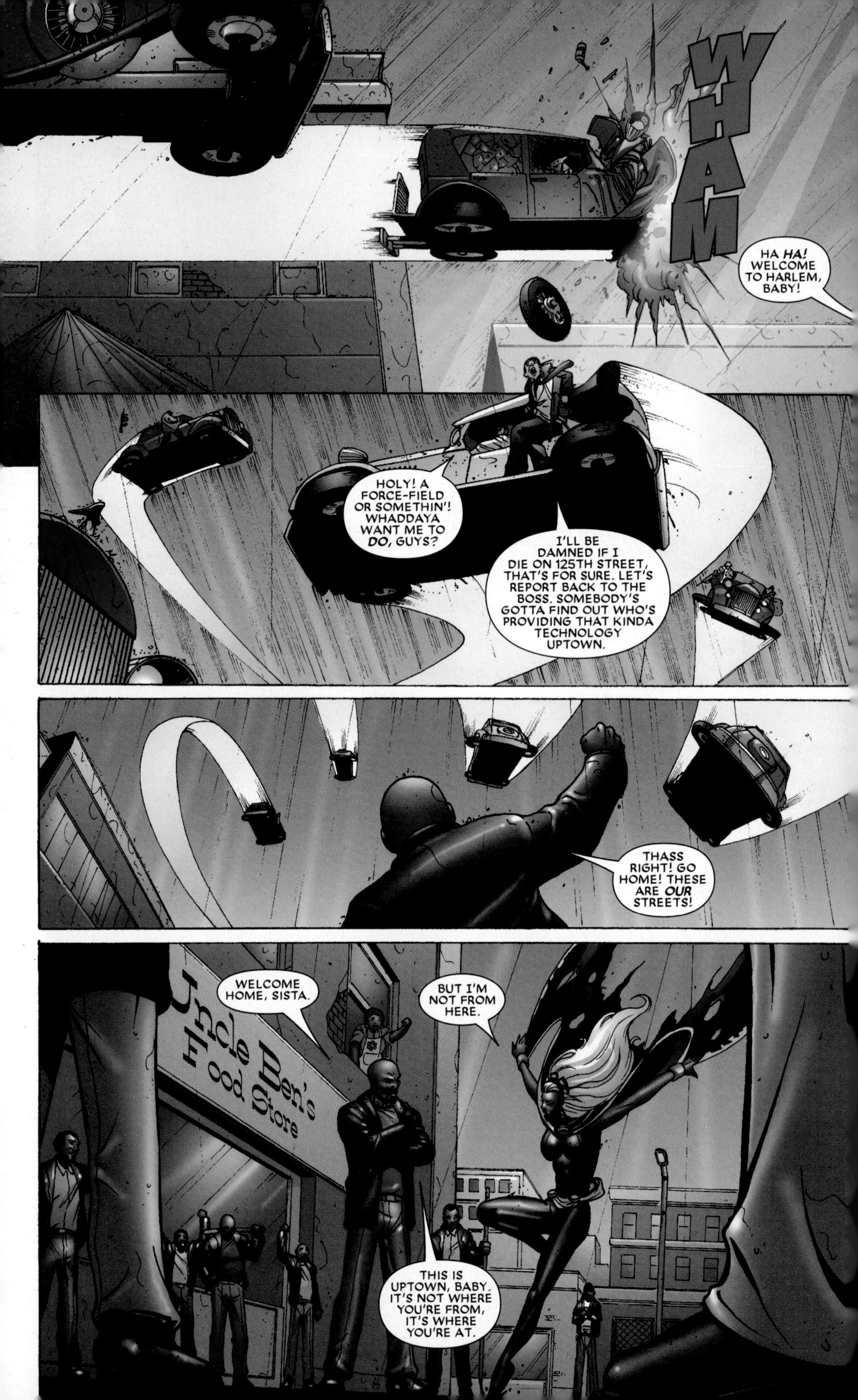
WHAM
HA HA! WELCOME TO HARLEM, BABY!
HOLY! A FORCE-FIELD OR SOMETHIN'! WHADDAYA WANT ME TO DO, GUYS?
I'LL BE DAMNED IF I DIE ON 125TH STREET, THAT'S FOR SURE. LET'S REPORT BACK TO THE BOSS. SOMEBODY'S GOTTA FIND OUT WHO'S PROVIDING THAT KINDA TECHNOLOGY UPTOWN.
THASS RIGHT! GO HOME! THESE ARE OUR STREETS!
Uncle Ben's Food Store
WELCOME HOME, SISTA.
BUT I'M NOT FROM HERE.
THIS IS UPTOWN, BABY. IT'S NOT WHERE YOU'RE FROM, IT'S WHERE YOU'RE AT.

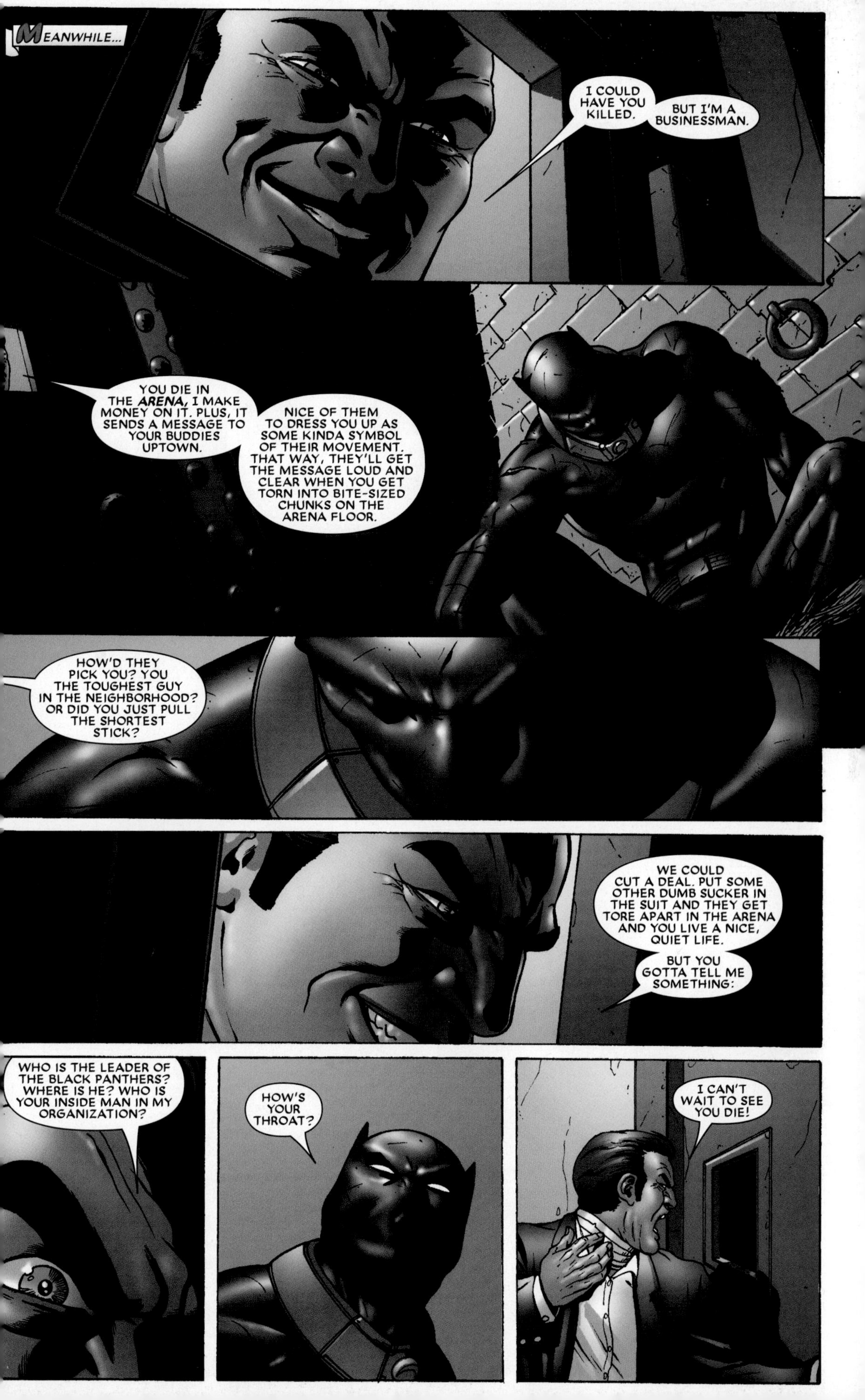
MEANWHILE...
I COULD HAVE YOU KILLED.
BUT I'M A BUSINESSMAN.
YOU DIE IN THE ARENA, I MAKE MONEY ON IT. PLUS, IT SENDS A MESSAGE TO YOUR BUDDIES UPTOWN.
NICE OF THEM TO DRESS YOU UP AS SOME KINDA SYMBOL OF THEIR MOVEMENT. THAT WAY, THEY'LL GET THE MESSAGE LOUD AND CLEAR WHEN YOU GET TORN INTO BITE-SIZED CHUNKS ON THE ARENA FLOOR.
HOW'D THEY PICK YOU? YOU THE TOUGHEST GUY IN THE NEIGHBORHOOD? OR DID YOU JUST PULL THE SHORTEST STICK?
WE COULD CUT A DEAL. PUT SOME OTHER DUMB SUCKER IN THE SUIT AND THEY GET TORE APART IN THE ARENA AND YOU LIVE A NICE, QUIET LIFE.
BUT YOU GOTTA TELL ME SOMETHING:
WHO IS THE LEADER OF THE BLACK PANTHERS? WHERE IS HE? WHO IS YOUR INSIDE MAN IN MY ORGANIZATION?
HOW'S YOUR THROAT?
I CAN'T WAIT TO SEE YOU DIE!

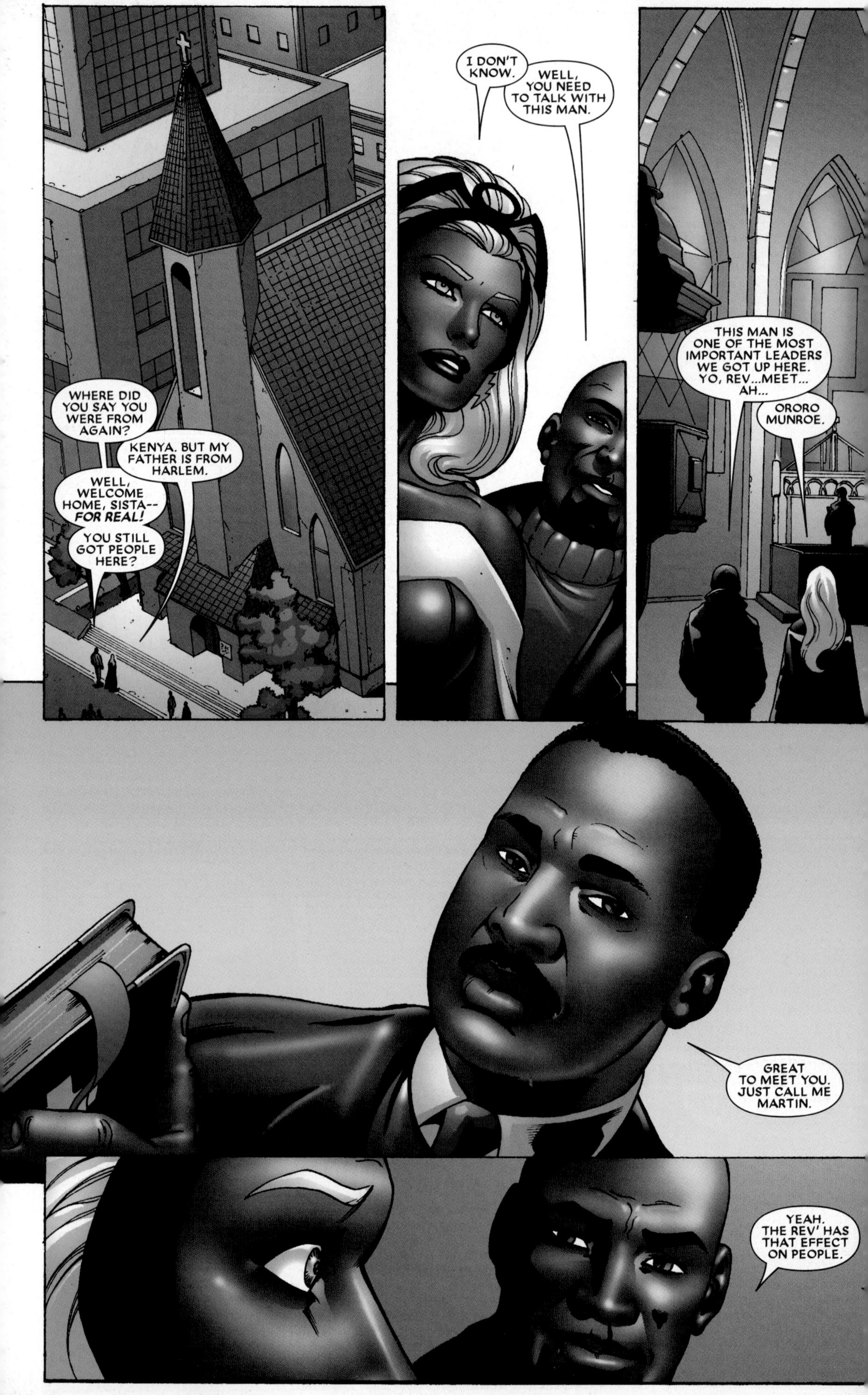
WHERE DID YOU SAY YOU WERE FROM AGAIN?
KENYA. BUT MY FATHER IS FROM HARLEM.
WELL, WELCOME HOME, SISTA-- *FOR REAL!*
YOU STILL GOT PEOPLE HERE?
I DON'T KNOW.
WELL, YOU NEED TO TALK WITH THIS MAN.
THIS MAN IS ONE OF THE MOST IMPORTANT LEADERS WE GOT UP HERE. YO, REV...MEET... AH...
ORORO MUNROE.
GREAT TO MEET YOU. JUST CALL ME MARTIN.
YEAH. THE REV' HAS THAT EFFECT ON PEOPLE.

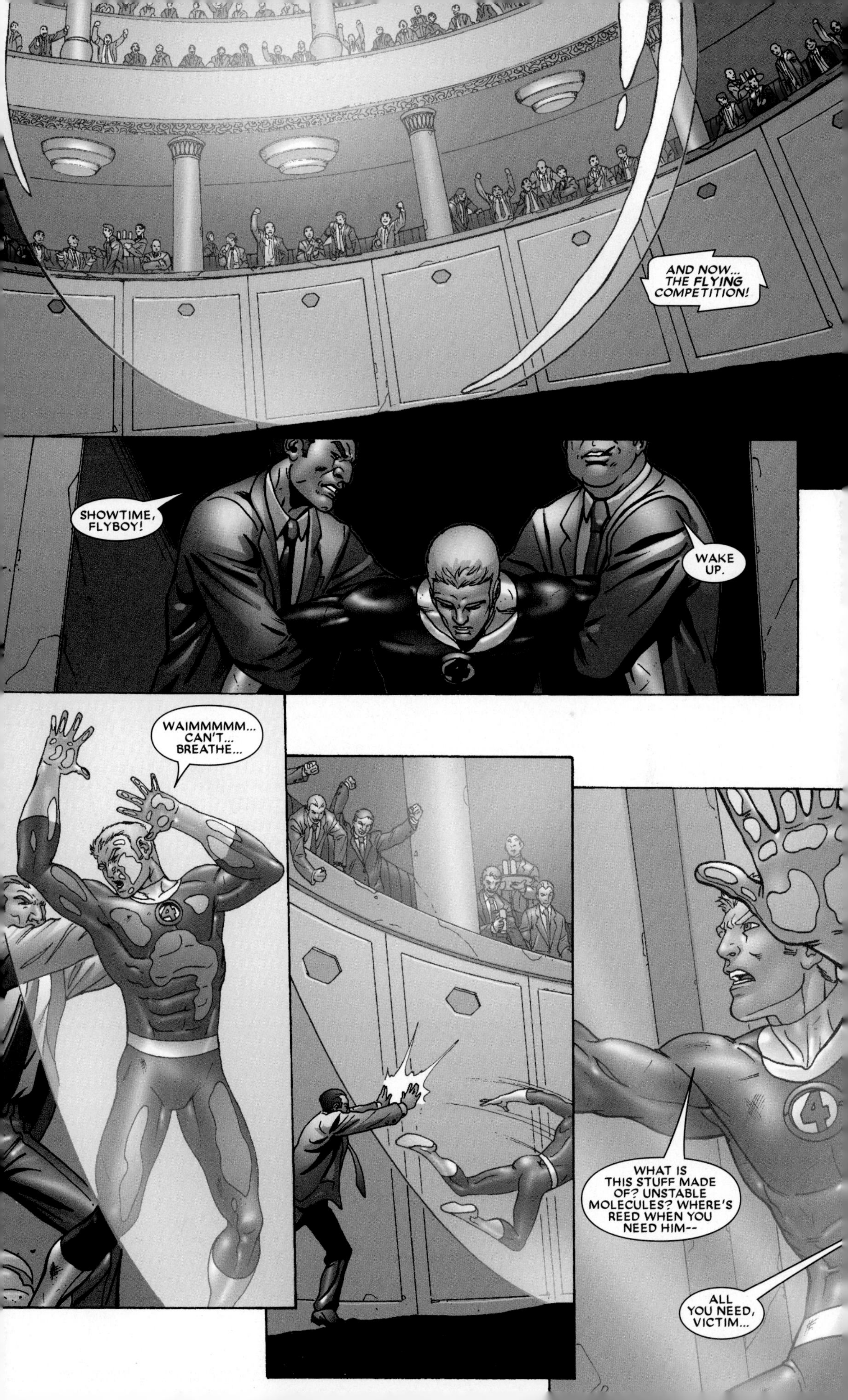
AND NOW... THE FLYING COMPETITION!
SHOWTIME, FLYBOY!
WAKE UP.
WAIMMMMM... CAN'T... BREATHE...
WHAT IS THIS STUFF MADE OF? UNSTABLE MOLECULES? WHERE'S REED WHEN YOU NEED HIM--
ALL YOU NEED, VICTIM...

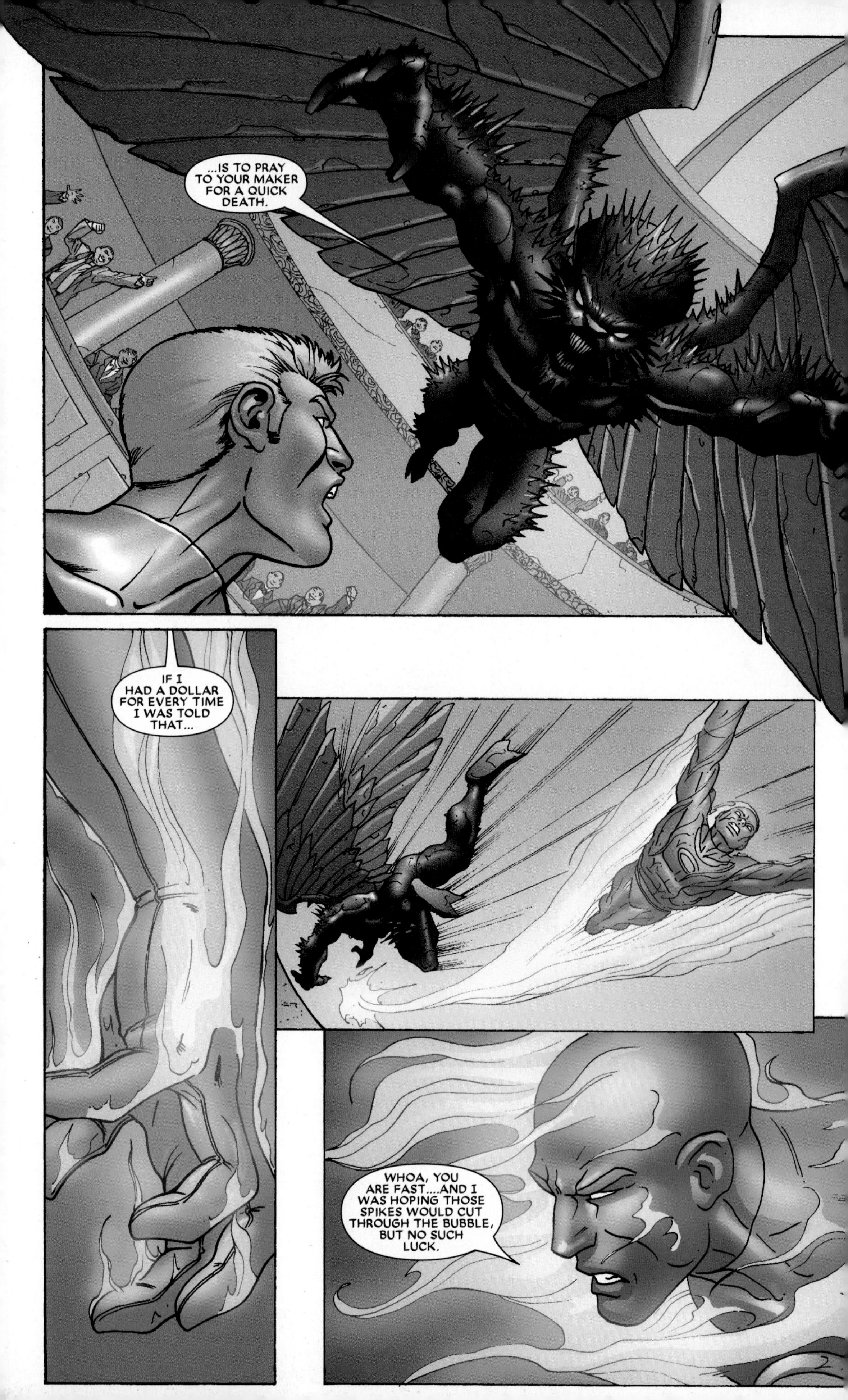
...IS TO PRAY TO YOUR MAKER FOR A QUICK DEATH.
IF I HAD A DOLLAR FOR EVERY TIME I WAS TOLD THAT...
WHOA, YOU ARE FAST....AND I WAS HOPING THOSE SPIKES WOULD CUT THROUGH THE BUBBLE, BUT NO SUCH LUCK.

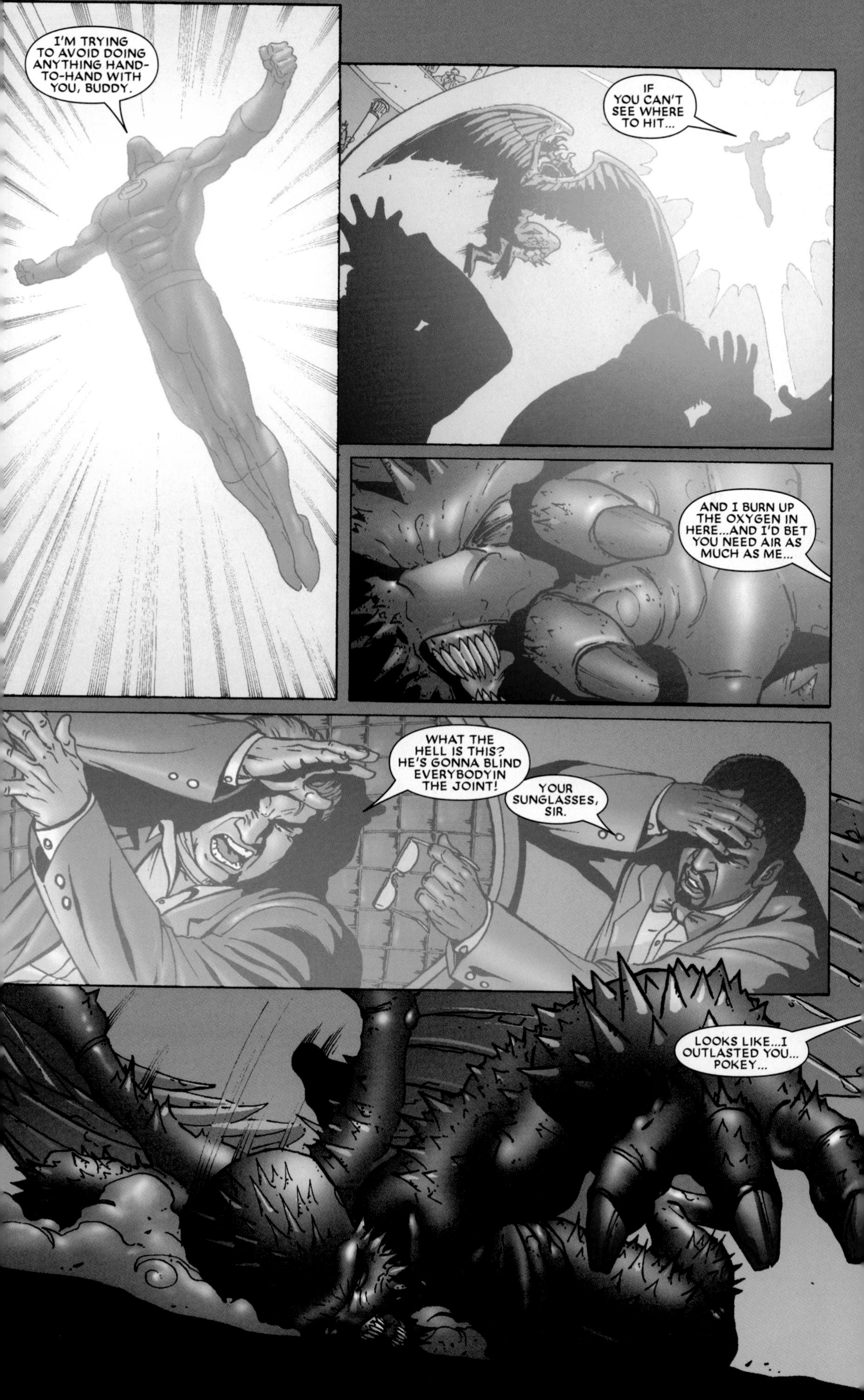
I'M TRYING TO AVOID DOING ANYTHING HAND-TO-HAND WITH YOU, BUDDY.
IF YOU CAN'T SEE WHERE TO HIT...
AND I BURN UP THE OXYGEN IN HERE...AND I'D BET YOU NEED AIR AS MUCH AS ME...
WHAT THE HELL IS THIS? HE'S GONNA BLIND EVERYBODYIN THE JOINT!
YOUR SUNGLASSES, SIR.
LOOKS LIKE...I OUTLASTED YOU... POKEY...

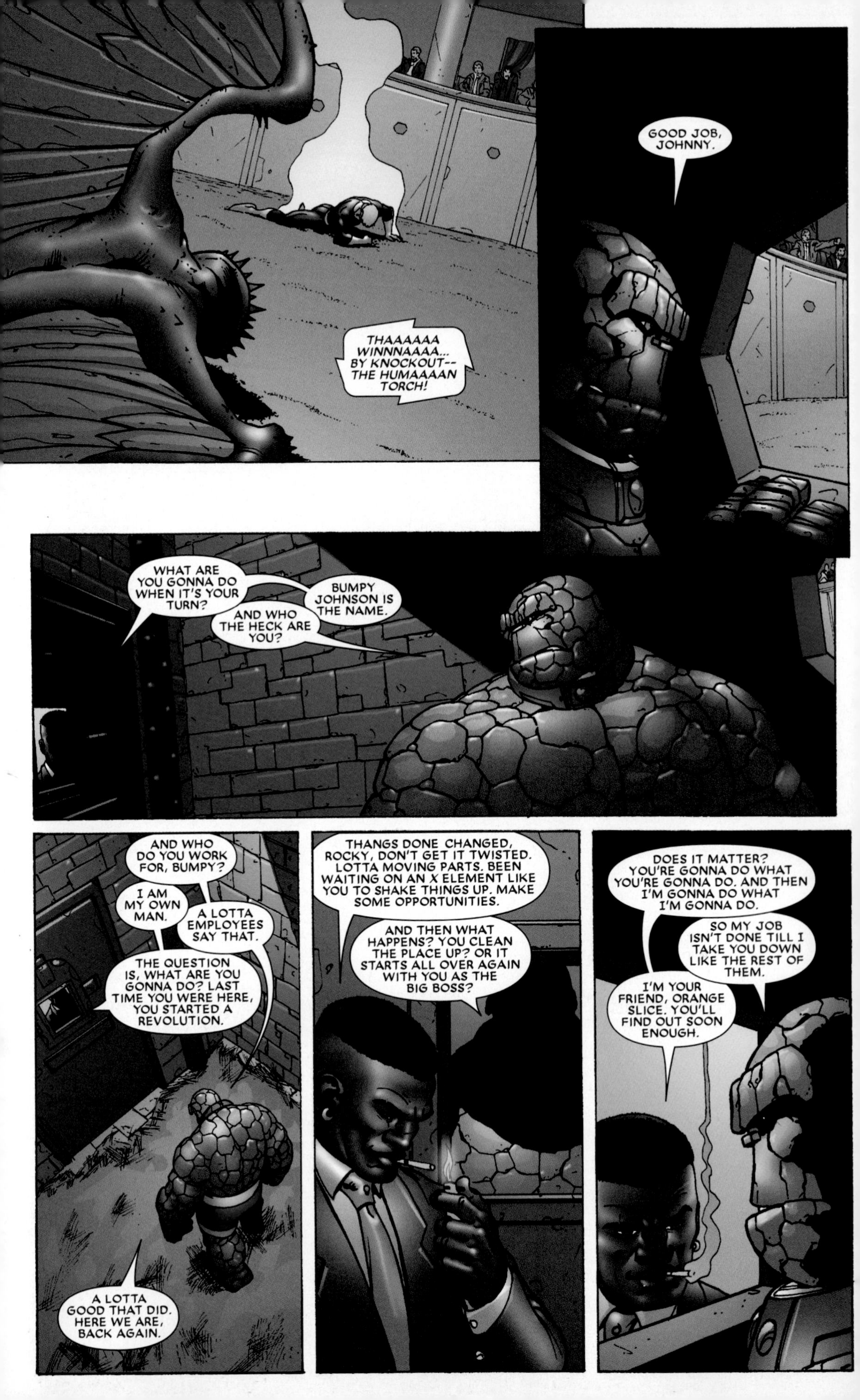
THAAAAAA WINNNAAAA... BY KNOCKOUT-- THE HUMAAAAN TORCH!
GOOD JOB, JOHNNY.
WHAT ARE YOU GONNA DO WHEN IT'S YOUR TURN?
BUMPY JOHNSON IS THE NAME.
AND WHO THE HECK ARE YOU?
AND WHO DO YOU WORK FOR, BUMPY?
I AM MY OWN MAN.
A LOTTA EMPLOYEES SAY THAT.
THE QUESTION IS, WHAT ARE YOU GONNA DO? LAST TIME YOU WERE HERE, YOU STARTED A REVOLUTION.
A LOTTA GOOD THAT DID. HERE WE ARE, BACK AGAIN.
THANGS DONE CHANGED, ROCKY, DON'T GET IT TWISTED. LOTTA MOVING PARTS. BEEN WAITING ON AN X ELEMENT LIKE YOU TO SHAKE THINGS UP. MAKE SOME OPPORTUNITIES.
AND THEN WHAT HAPPENS? YOU CLEAN THE PLACE UP? OR IT STARTS ALL OVER AGAIN WITH YOU AS THE BIG BOSS?
DOES IT MATTER? YOU'RE GONNA DO WHAT YOU'RE GONNA DO. AND THEN I'M GONNA DO WHAT I'M GONNA DO.
SO MY JOB ISN'T DONE TILL I TAKE YOU DOWN LIKE THE REST OF THEM.
I'M YOUR FRIEND, ORANGE SLICE. YOU'LL FIND OUT SOON ENOUGH.

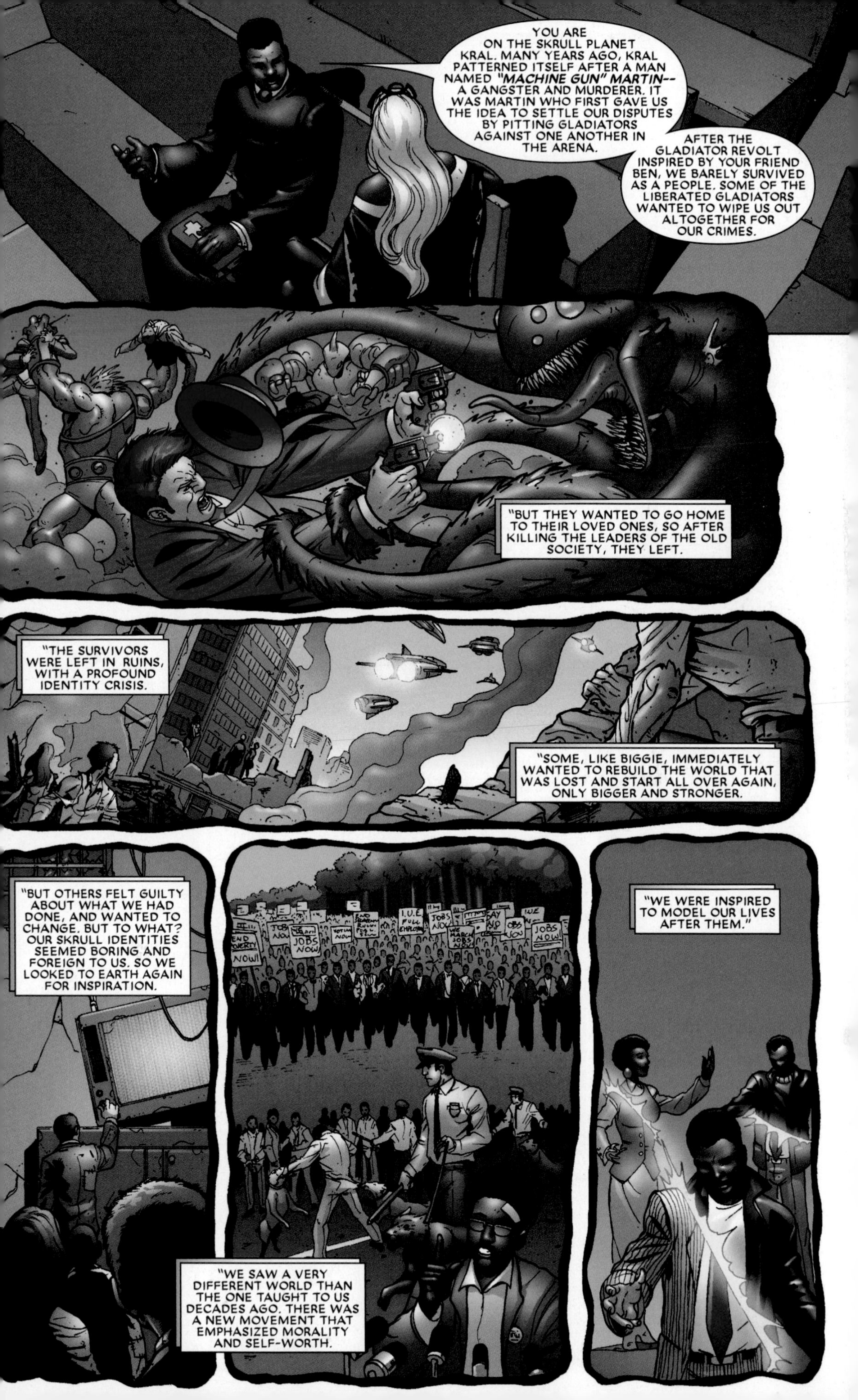
YOU ARE ON THE SKRULL PLANET KRAL. MANY YEARS AGO, KRAL PATTERNED ITSELF AFTER A MAN NAMED "MACHINE GUN" MARTIN-- A GANGSTER AND MURDERER. IT WAS MARTIN WHO FIRST GAVE US THE IDEA TO SETTLE OUR DISPUTES BY PITTING GLADIATORS AGAINST ONE ANOTHER IN THE ARENA.
AFTER THE GLADIATOR REVOLT INSPIRED BY YOUR FRIEND BEN, WE BARELY SURVIVED AS A PEOPLE. SOME OF THE LIBERATED GLADIATORS WANTED TO WIPE US OUT ALTOGETHER FOR OUR CRIMES.
"BUT THEY WANTED TO GO HOME TO THEIR LOVED ONES, SO AFTER KILLING THE LEADERS OF THE OLD SOCIETY, THEY LEFT.
"THE SURVIVORS WERE LEFT IN RUINS, WITH A PROFOUND IDENTITY CRISIS.
"SOME, LIKE BIGGIE, IMMEDIATELY WANTED TO REBUILD THE WORLD THAT WAS LOST AND START ALL OVER AGAIN, ONLY BIGGER AND STRONGER.
"BUT OTHERS FELT GUILTY ABOUT WHAT WE HAD DONE, AND WANTED TO CHANGE. BUT TO WHAT? OUR SKRULL IDENTITIES SEEMED BORING AND FOREIGN TO US. SO WE LOOKED TO EARTH AGAIN FOR INSPIRATION.
"WE SAW A VERY DIFFERENT WORLD THAN THE ONE TAUGHT TO US DECADES AGO. THERE WAS A NEW MOVEMENT THAT EMPHASIZED MORALITY AND SELF-WORTH.
"WE WERE INSPIRED TO MODEL OUR LIVES AFTER THEM."

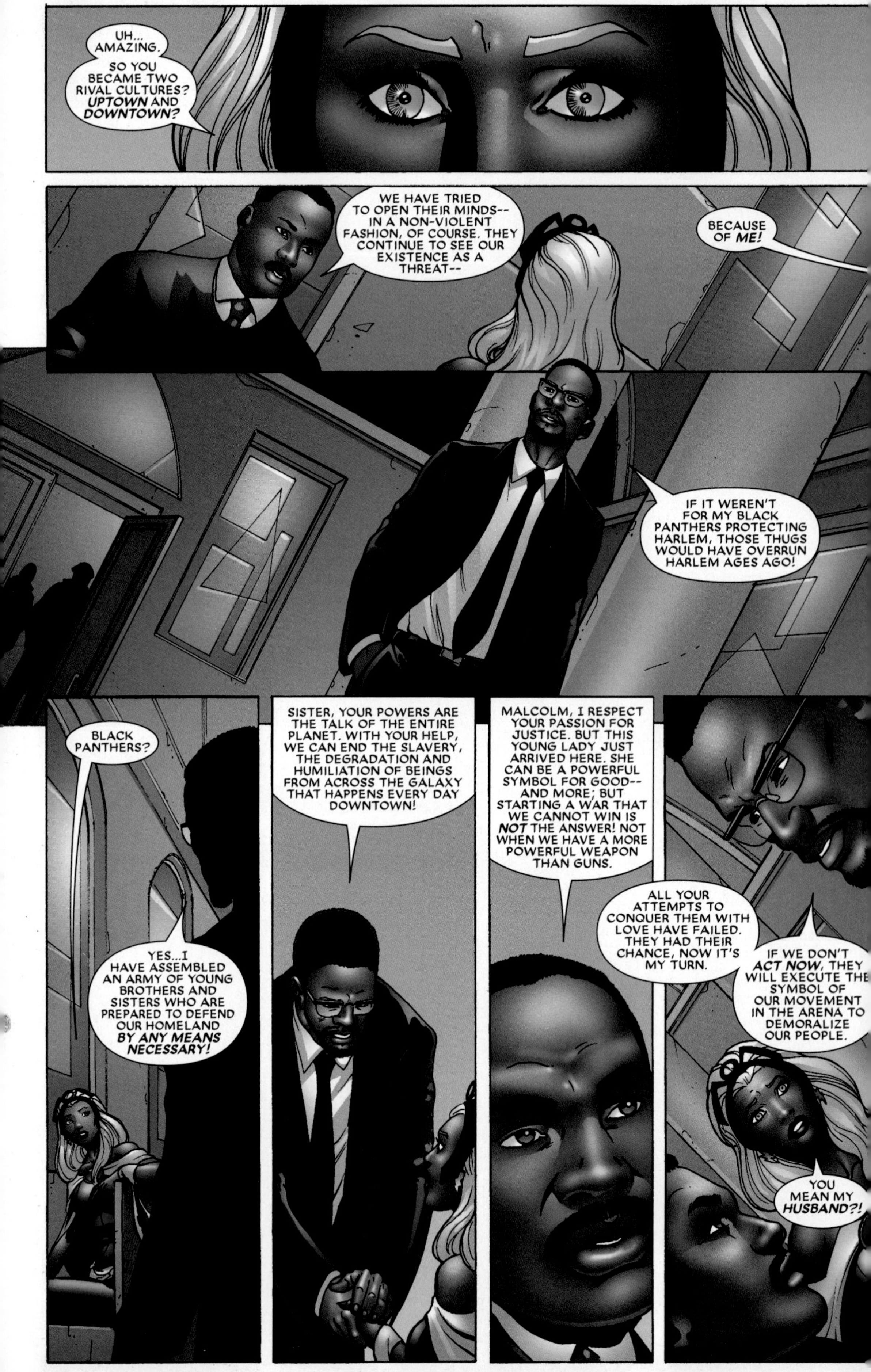
UH... AMAZING.
SO YOU BECAME TWO RIVAL CULTURES? UPTOWN AND DOWNTOWN?
WE HAVE TRIED TO OPEN THEIR MINDS-- IN A NON-VIOLENT FASHION, OF COURSE. THEY CONTINUE TO SEE OUR EXISTENCE AS A THREAT--
BECAUSE OF ME!
IF IT WEREN'T FOR MY BLACK PANTHERS PROTECTING HARLEM, THOSE THUGS WOULD HAVE OVERRUN HARLEM AGES AGO!
BLACK PANTHERS?
YES...I HAVE ASSEMBLED AN ARMY OF YOUNG BROTHERS AND SISTERS WHO ARE PREPARED TO DEFEND OUR HOMELAND BY ANY MEANS NECESSARY!
SISTER, YOUR POWERS ARE THE TALK OF THE ENTIRE PLANET. WITH YOUR HELP, WE CAN END THE SLAVERY, THE DEGRADATION AND HUMILIATION OF BEINGS FROM ACROSS THE GALAXY THAT HAPPENS EVERY DAY DOWNTOWN!
MALCOLM, I RESPECT YOUR PASSION FOR JUSTICE. BUT THIS YOUNG LADY JUST ARRIVED HERE. SHE CAN BE A POWERFUL SYMBOL FOR GOOD-- AND MORE; BUT STARTING A WAR THAT WE CANNOT WIN IS NOT THE ANSWER! NOT WHEN WE HAVE A MORE POWERFUL WEAPON THAN GUNS.
ALL YOUR ATTEMPTS TO CONQUER THEM WITH LOVE HAVE FAILED. THEY HAD THEIR CHANCE, NOW IT'S MY TURN.
IF WE DON'T ACT NOW, THEY WILL EXECUTE THE SYMBOL OF OUR MOVEMENT IN THE ARENA TO DEMORALIZE OUR PEOPLE.
YOU MEAN MY HUSBAND?!

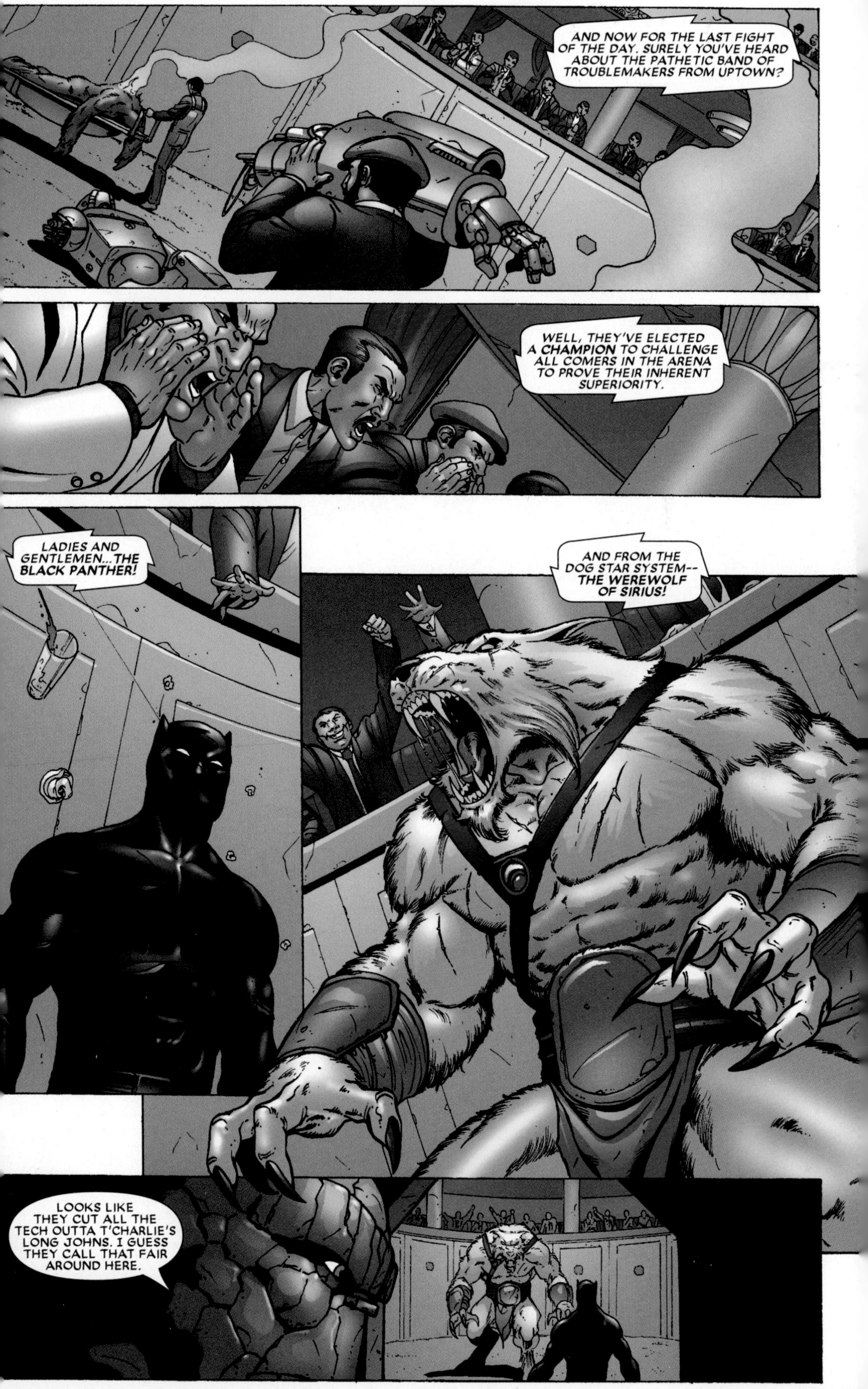
AND NOW FOR THE LAST FIGHT OF THE DAY. SURELY YOU'VE HEARD ABOUT THE PATHETIC BAND OF TROUBLEMAKERS FROM UPTOWN?
WELL, THEY'VE ELECTED A CHAMPION TO CHALLENGE ALL COMERS IN THE ARENA TO PROVE THEIR INHERENT SUPERIORITY.
LADIES AND GENTLEMEN... THE BLACK PANTHER!
AND FROM THE DOG STAR SYSTEM-- THE WEREWOLF OF SIRIUS!
LOOKS LIKE THEY CUT ALL THE TECH OUTTA T'CHARLIE'S LONG JOHNS. I GUESS THEY CALL THAT FAIR AROUND HERE.

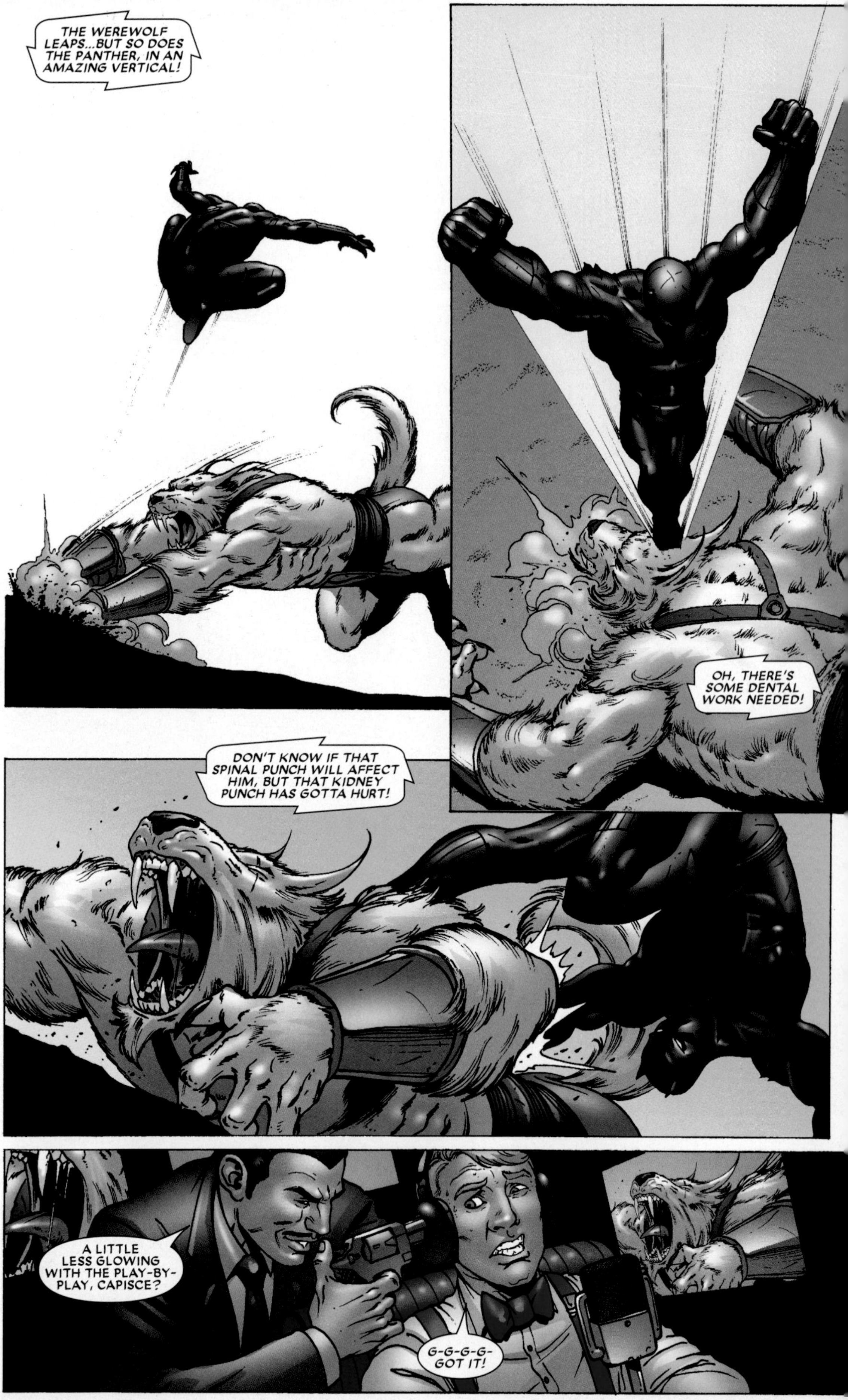
THE WEREWOLF LEAPS...BUT SO DOES THE PANTHER, IN AN AMAZING VERTICAL!
OH, THERE'S SOME DENTAL WORK NEEDED!
DON'T KNOW IF THAT SPINAL PUNCH WILL AFFECT HIM, BUT THAT KIDNEY PUNCH HAS GOTTA HURT!
A LITTLE LESS GLOWING WITH THE PLAY-BY-PLAY, CAPISCE?
G-G-G-G-GOT IT!

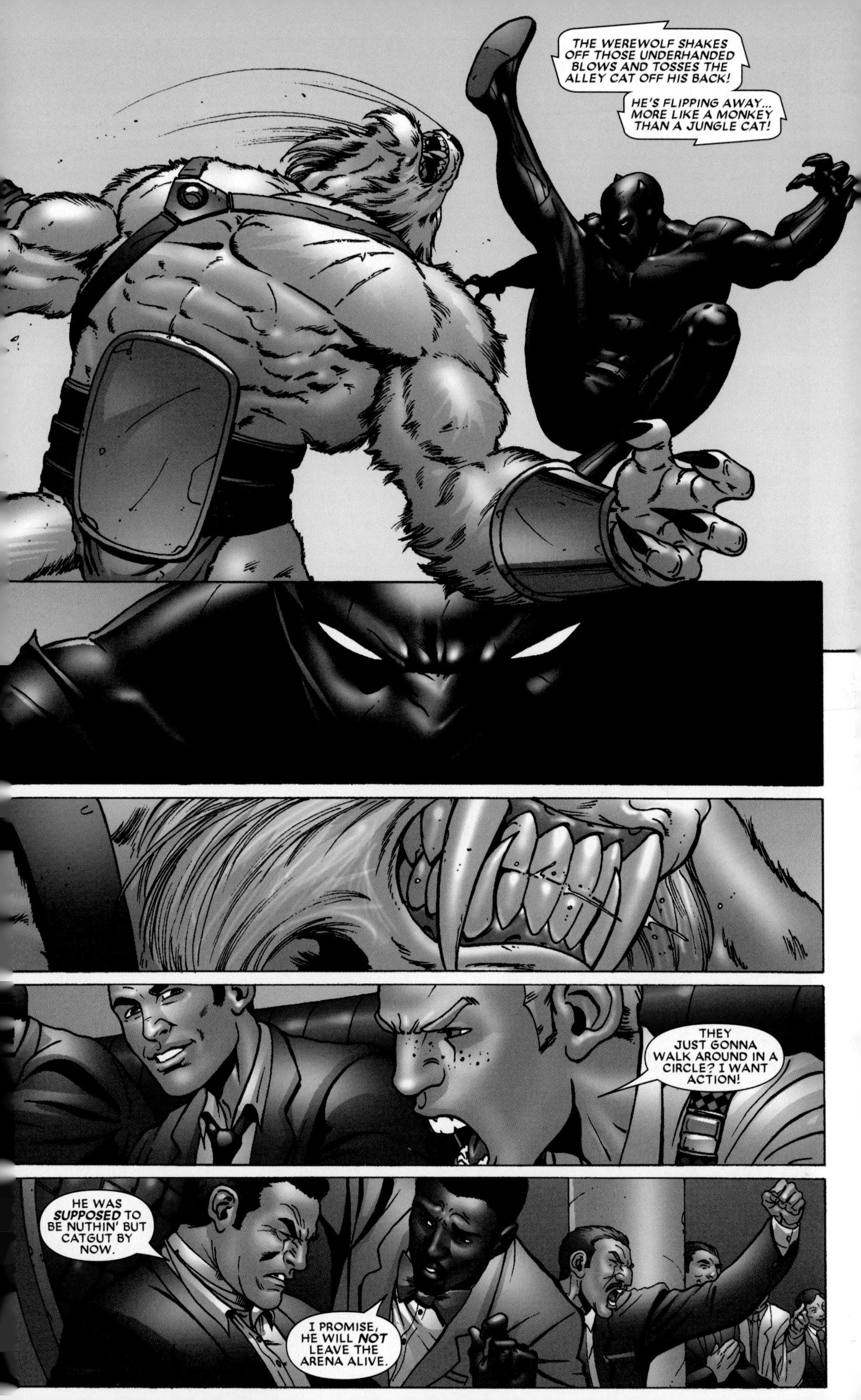
THE WEREWOLF SHAKES OFF THOSE UNDERHANDED BLOWS AND TOSSES THE ALLEY CAT OFF HIS BACK!
HE'S FLIPPING AWAY... MORE LIKE A MONKEY THAN A JUNGLE CAT!
THEY JUST GONNA WALK AROUND IN A CIRCLE? I WANT ACTION!
HE WAS *SUPPOSED* TO BE NUTHIN' BUT CATGUT BY NOW.
I PROMISE, HE WILL *NOT* LEAVE THE ARENA ALIVE.

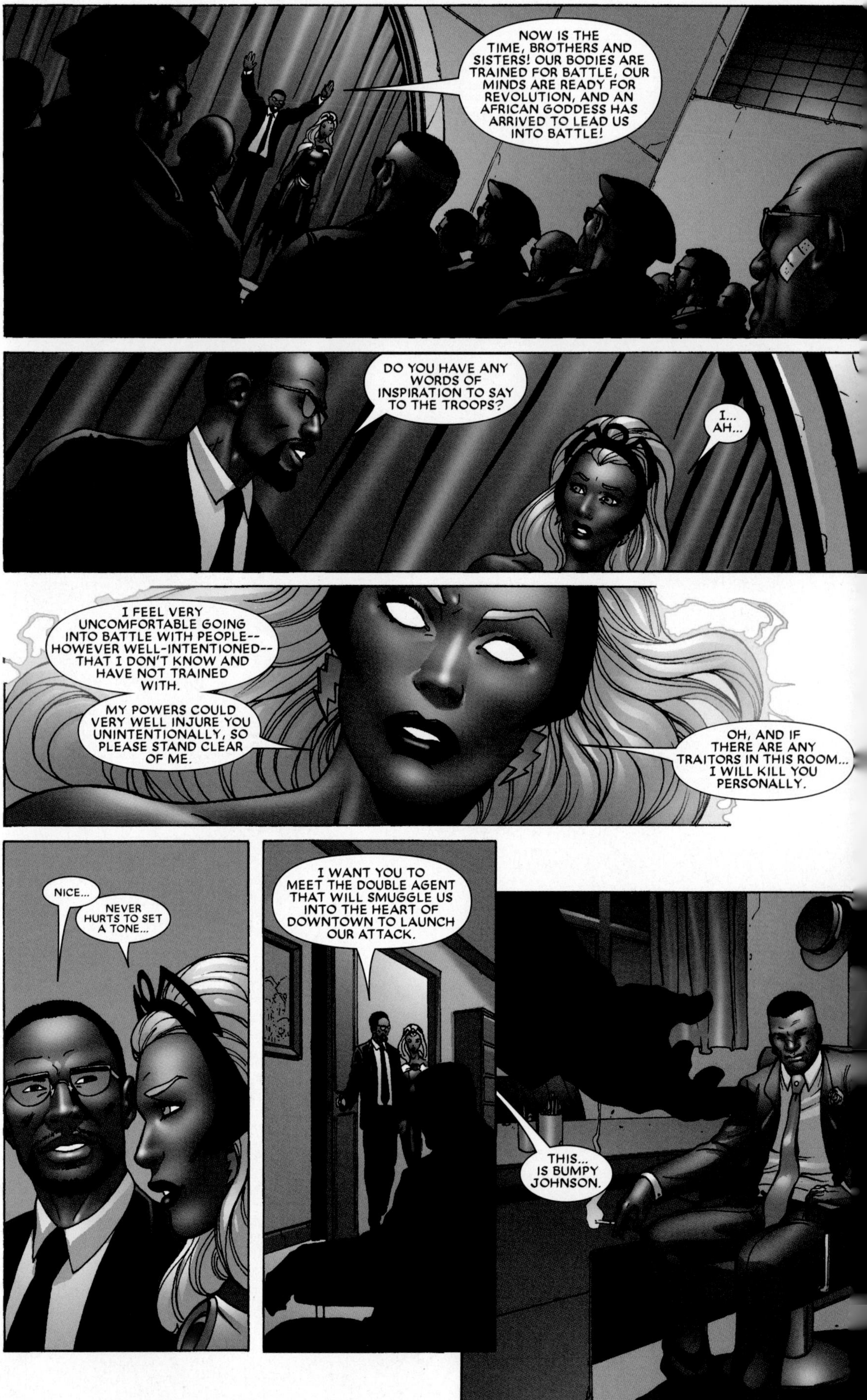
NOW IS THE TIME, BROTHERS AND SISTERS! OUR BODIES ARE TRAINED FOR BATTLE, OUR MINDS ARE READY FOR REVOLUTION, AND AN AFRICAN GODDESS HAS ARRIVED TO LEAD US INTO BATTLE!
DO YOU HAVE ANY WORDS OF INSPIRATION TO SAY TO THE TROOPS?
I... AH...
I FEEL VERY UNCOMFORTABLE GOING INTO BATTLE WITH PEOPLE-- HOWEVER WELL-INTENTIONED-- THAT I DON'T KNOW AND HAVE NOT TRAINED WITH.
MY POWERS COULD VERY WELL INJURE YOU UNINTENTIONALLY, SO PLEASE STAND CLEAR OF ME.
OH, AND IF THERE ARE ANY TRAITORS IN THIS ROOM... I WILL KILL YOU PERSONALLY.
NICE...
NEVER HURTS TO SET A TONE...
I WANT YOU TO MEET THE DOUBLE AGENT THAT WILL SMUGGLE US INTO THE HEART OF DOWNTOWN TO LAUNCH OUR ATTACK.
THIS... IS BUMPY JOHNSON.

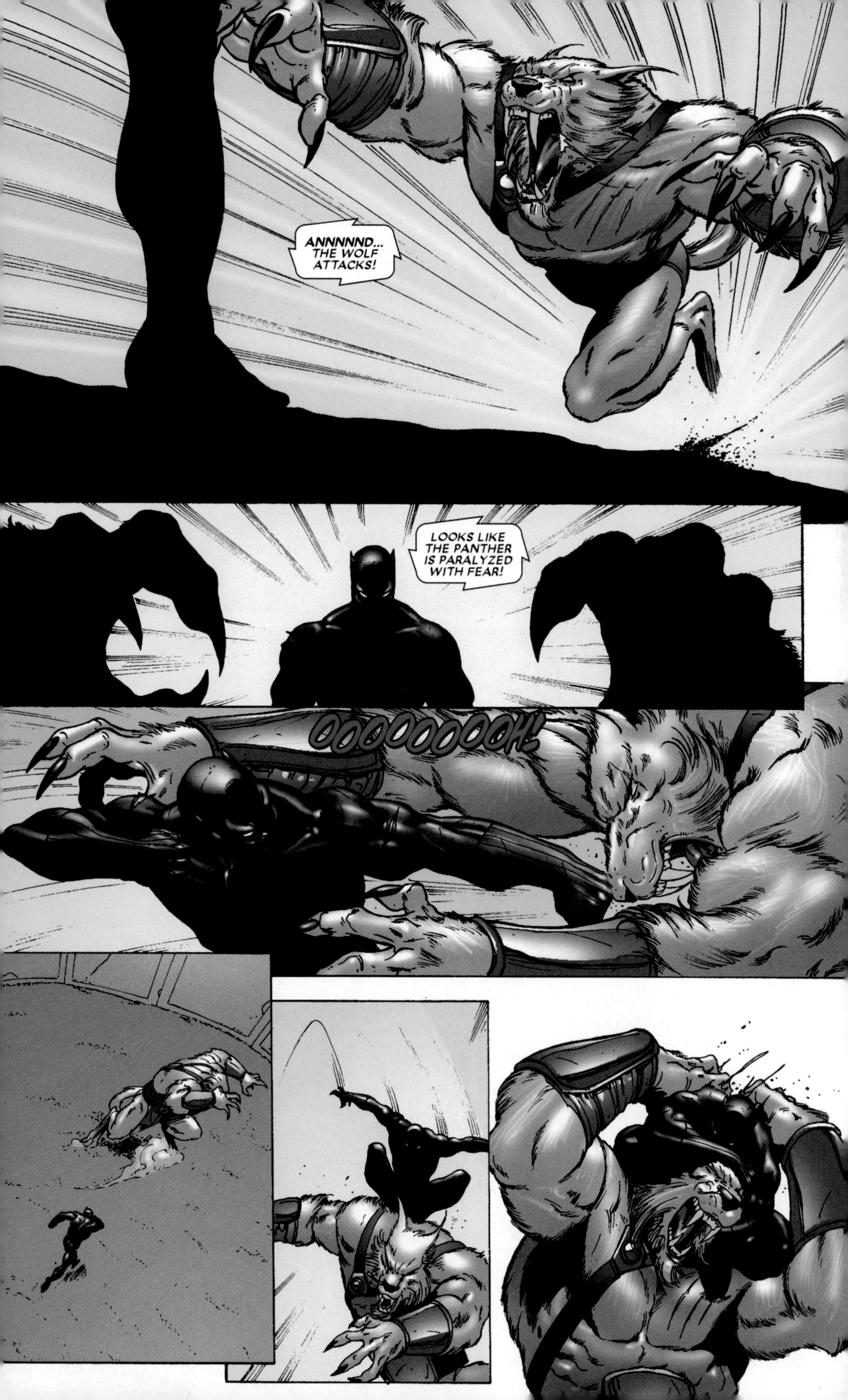
ANNNNND... THE WOLF ATTACKS!
LOOKS LIKE THE PANTHER IS PARALYZED WITH FEAR!
OOOOOOOOOH!

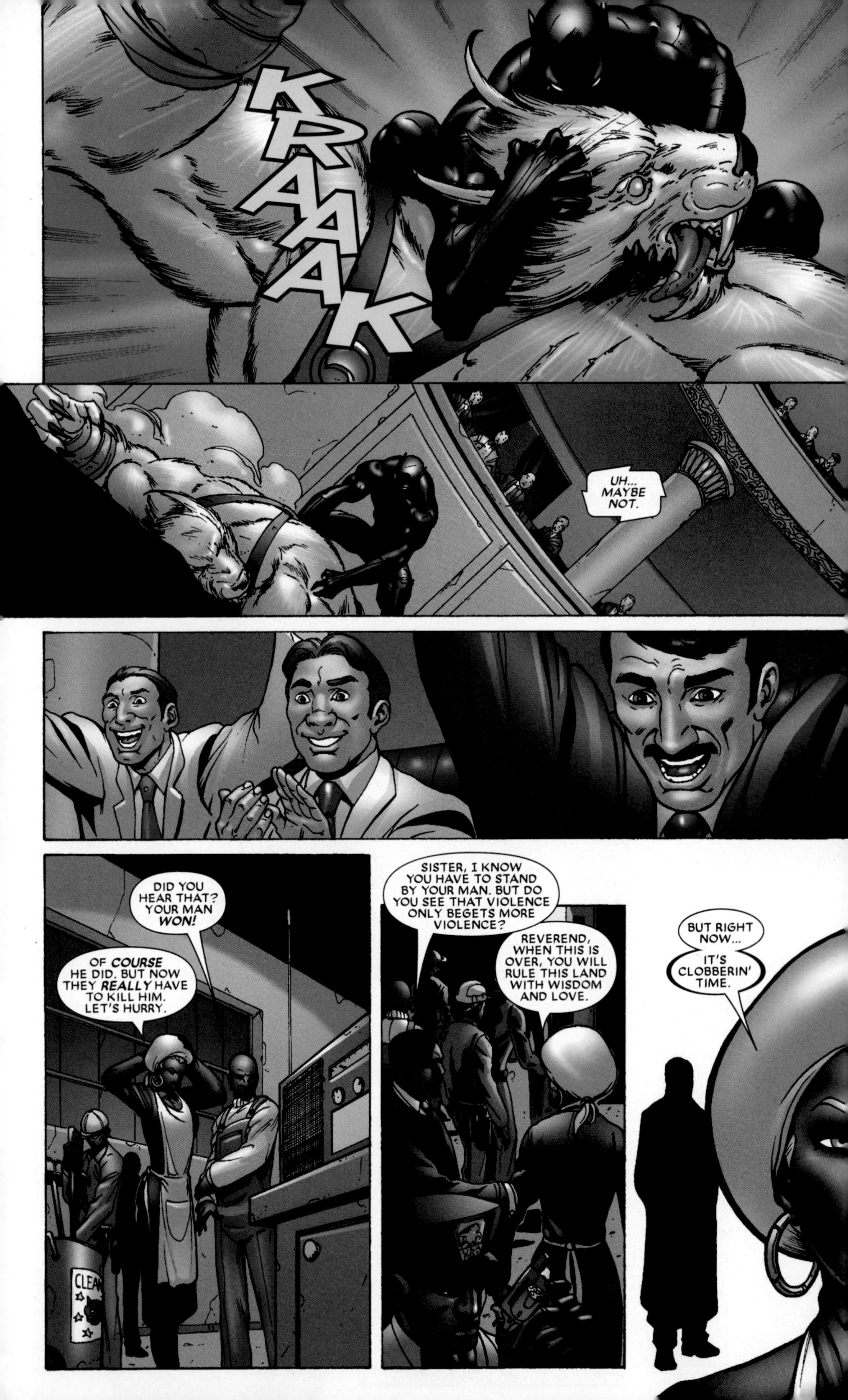
KRAAAK
UH... MAYBE NOT.
DID YOU HEAR THAT? YOUR MAN WON!
OF COURSE HE DID. BUT NOW THEY REALLY HAVE TO KILL HIM. LET'S HURRY.
SISTER, I KNOW YOU HAVE TO STAND BY YOUR MAN. BUT DO YOU SEE THAT VIOLENCE ONLY BEGETS MORE VIOLENCE?
REVEREND, WHEN THIS IS OVER, YOU WILL RULE THIS LAND WITH WISDOM AND LOVE.
BUT RIGHT NOW... IT'S CLOBBERIN' TIME.
CLEAN

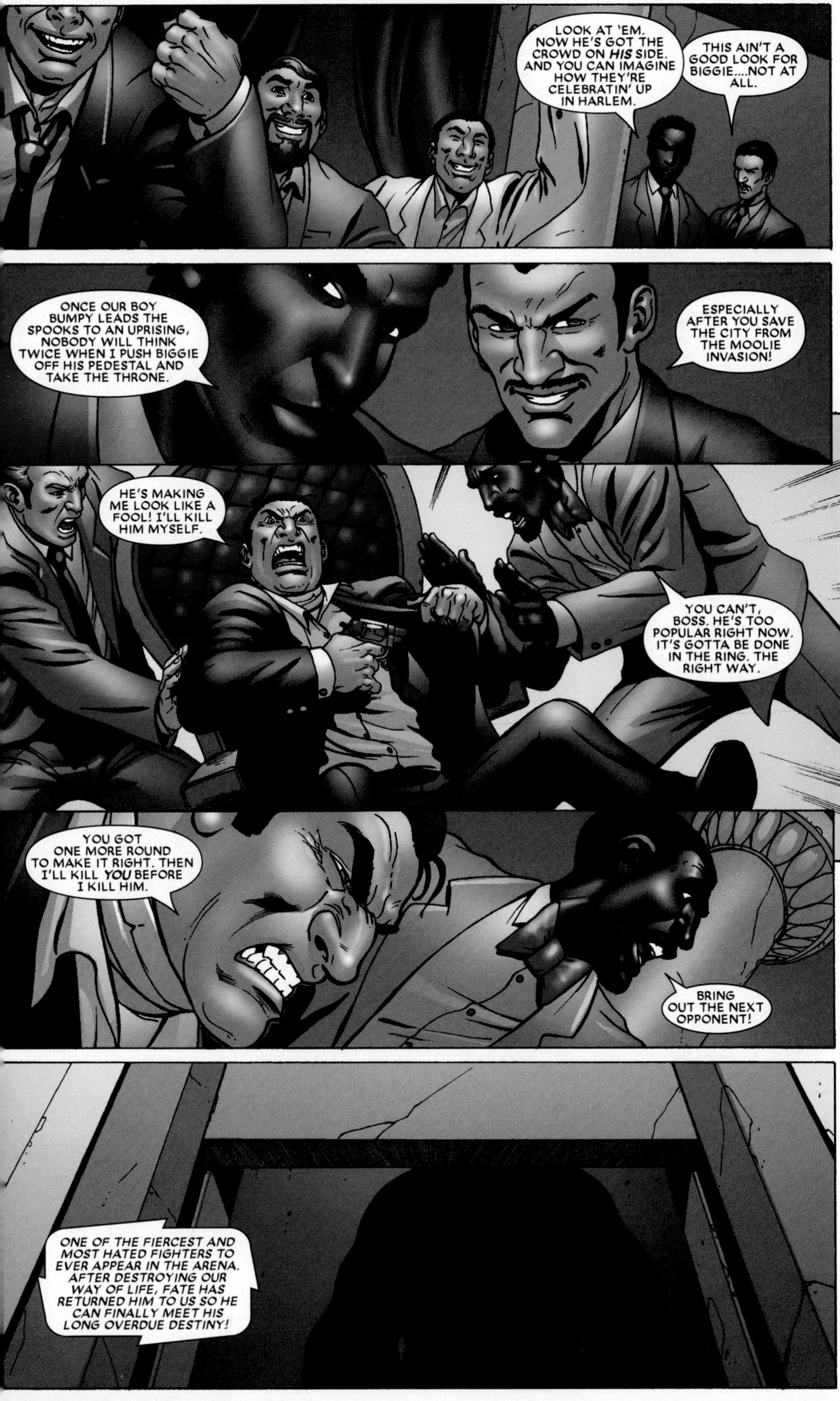
LOOK AT 'EM. NOW HE'S GOT THE CROWD ON *HIS* SIDE. AND YOU CAN IMAGINE HOW THEY'RE CELEBRATIN' UP IN HARLEM.
THIS AIN'T A GOOD LOOK FOR BIGGIE....NOT AT ALL.
ONCE OUR BOY BUMPY LEADS THE SPOOKS TO AN UPRISING, NOBODY WILL THINK TWICE WHEN I PUSH BIGGIE OFF HIS PEDESTAL AND TAKE THE THRONE.
ESPECIALLY AFTER YOU SAVE THE CITY FROM THE MOOLIE INVASION!
HE'S MAKING ME LOOK LIKE A FOOL! I'LL KILL HIM MYSELF.
YOU CAN'T, BOSS. HE'S TOO POPULAR RIGHT NOW. IT'S GOTTA BE DONE IN THE RING. THE RIGHT WAY.
YOU GOT ONE MORE ROUND TO MAKE IT RIGHT. THEN I'LL KILL *YOU* BEFORE I KILL HIM.
BRING OUT THE NEXT OPPONENT!
ONE OF THE FIERCEST AND MOST HATED FIGHTERS TO EVER APPEAR IN THE ARENA. AFTER DESTROYING OUR WAY OF LIFE, FATE HAS RETURNED HIM TO US SO HE CAN FINALLY MEET HIS LONG OVERDUE DESTINY!

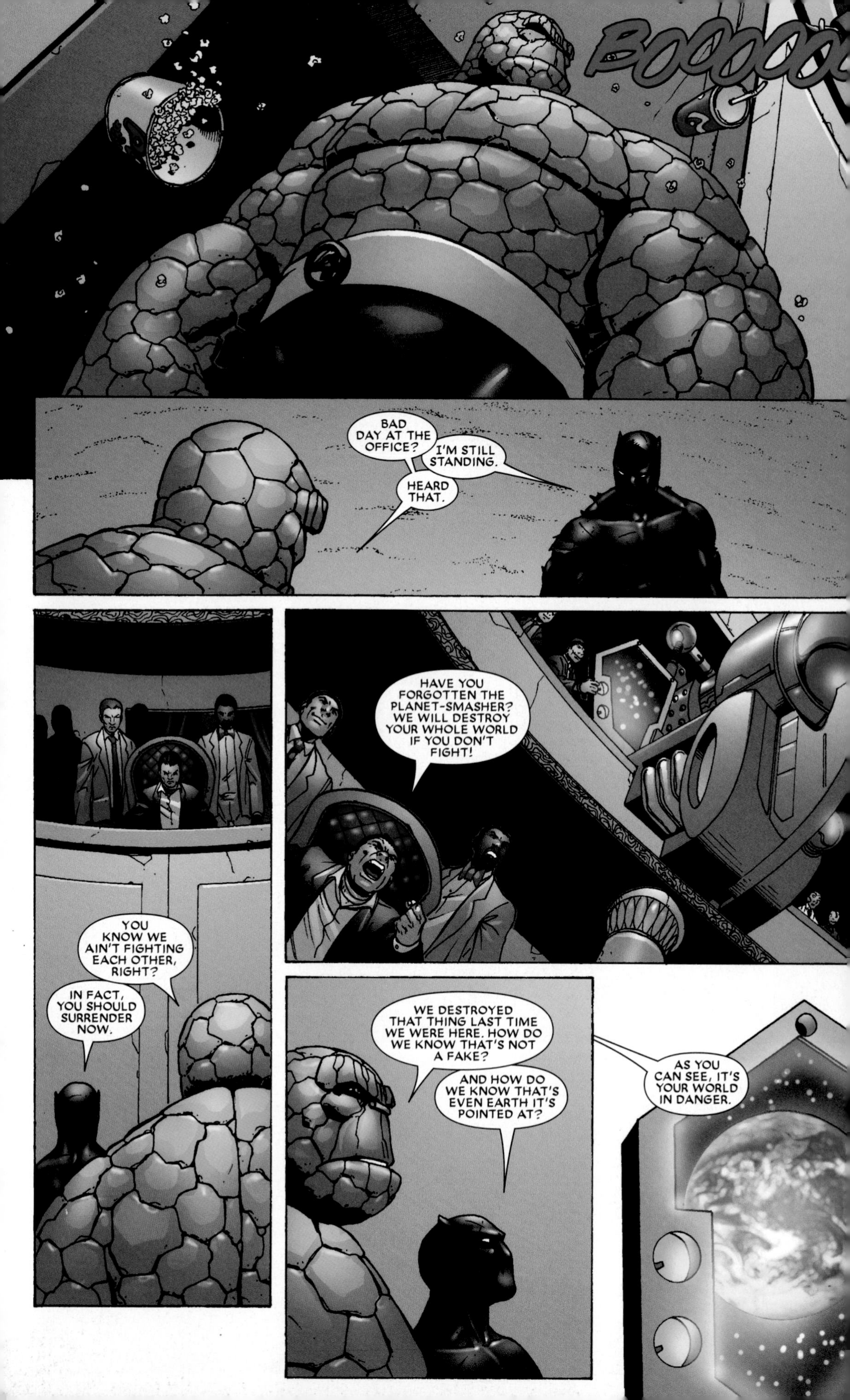
BOOOOOO
BAD DAY AT THE OFFICE?
I'M STILL STANDING.
HEARD THAT.
HAVE YOU FORGOTTEN THE PLANET-SMASHER? WE WILL DESTROY YOUR WHOLE WORLD IF YOU DON'T FIGHT!
YOU KNOW WE AIN'T FIGHTING EACH OTHER, RIGHT?
IN FACT, YOU SHOULD SURRENDER NOW.
WE DESTROYED THAT THING LAST TIME WE WERE HERE. HOW DO WE KNOW THAT'S NOT A FAKE?
AND HOW DO WE KNOW THAT'S EVEN EARTH IT'S POINTED AT?
AS YOU CAN SEE, IT'S YOUR WORLD IN DANGER.

SMOOTH MOVE, T'CHARLIE. NOW AT LEAST WE KNOW WE'RE IN THE RIGHT REALITY.

AND AS FOR THE EFFECTIVENESS OF THE WEAPON...WE CAN CHOOSE ANY OF THE LAND MASSES TO PROVE OUR POINT.

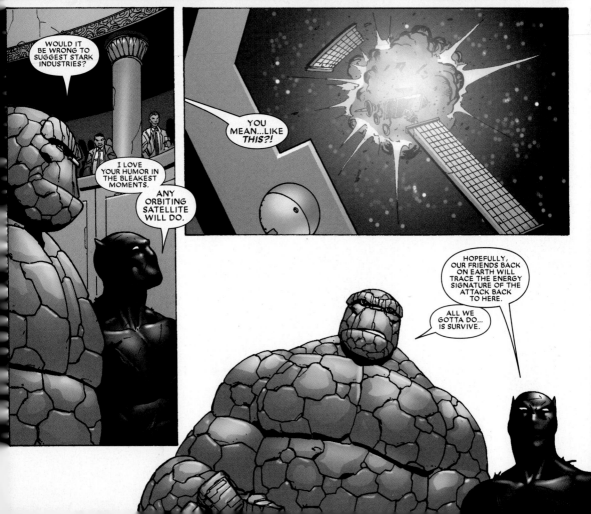

WOULD IT BE WRONG TO SUGGEST STARK INDUSTRIES?

I LOVE YOUR HUMOR IN THE BLEAKEST MOMENTS.

ANY ORBITING SATELLITE WILL DO.

YOU MEAN...LIKE *THIS?!*

HOPEFULLY, OUR FRIENDS BACK ON EARTH WILL TRACE THE ENERGY SIGNATURE OF THE ATTACK BACK TO HERE.

ALL WE GOTTA DO... IS SURVIVE.

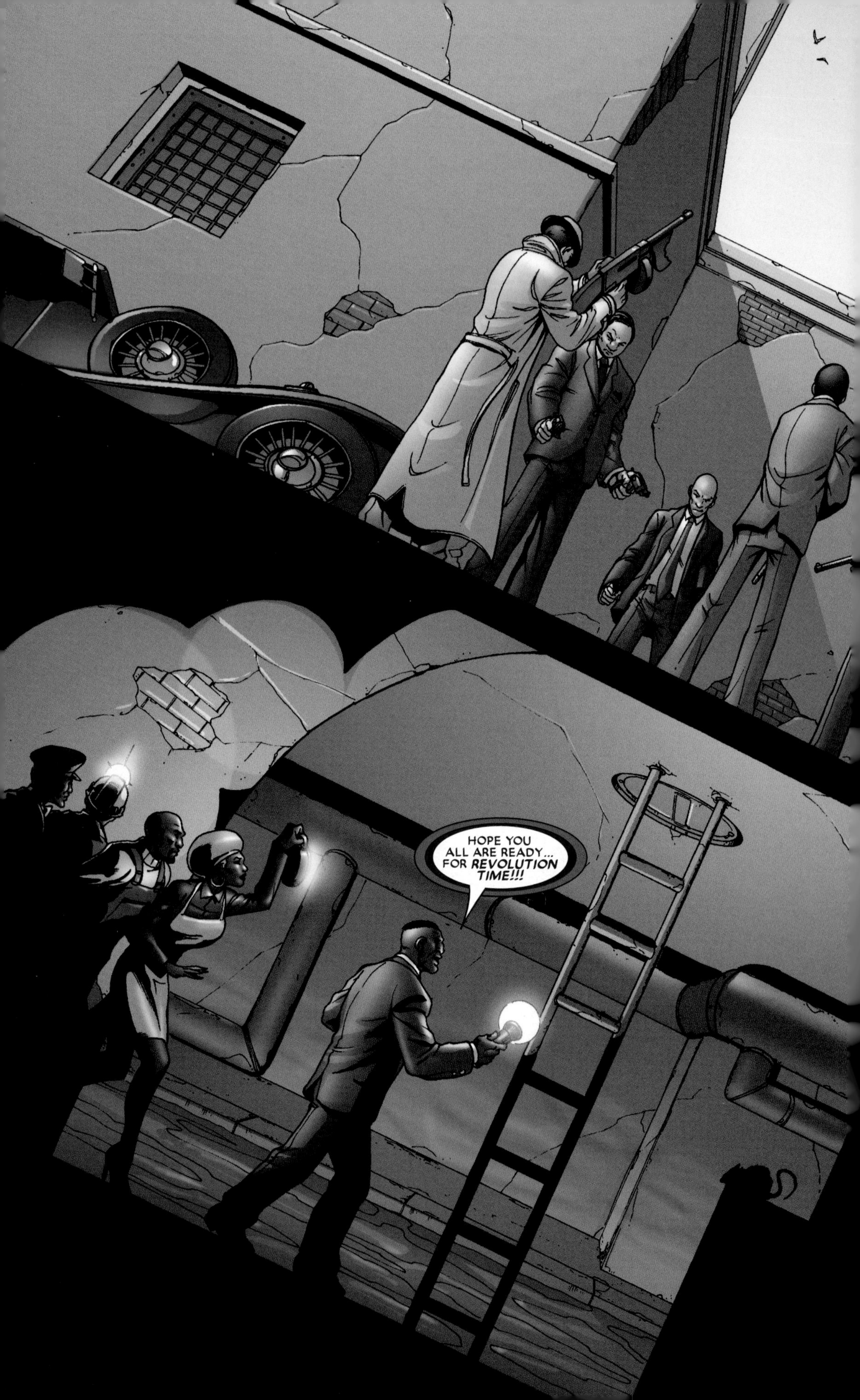
HOPE YOU ALL ARE READY... FOR REVOLUTION TIME!!!

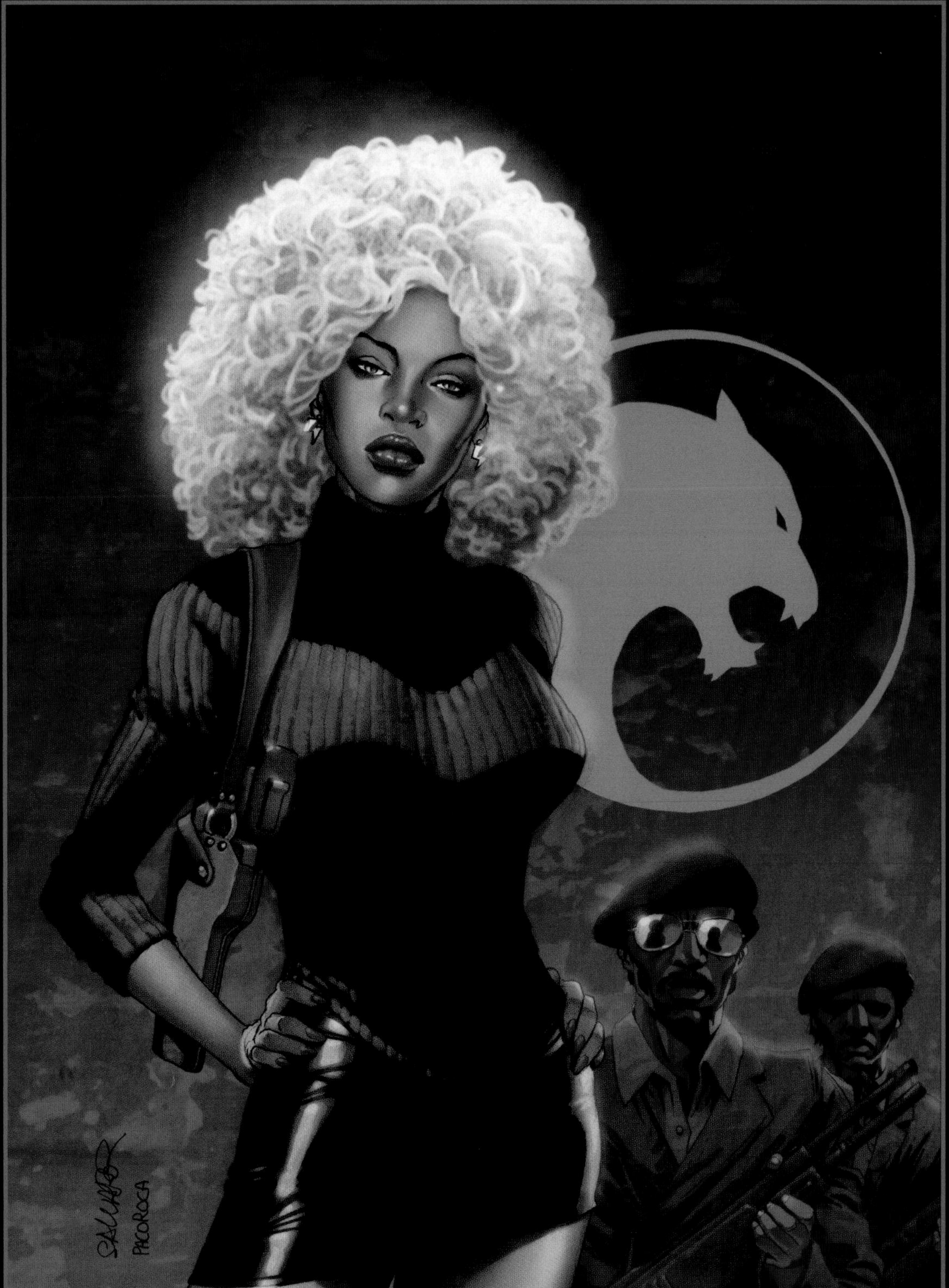
PACOROCA

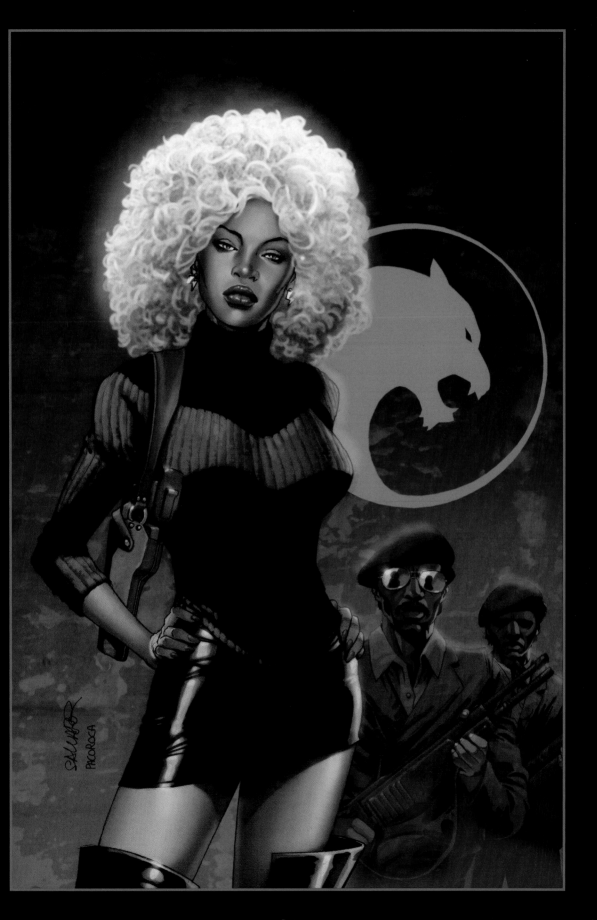

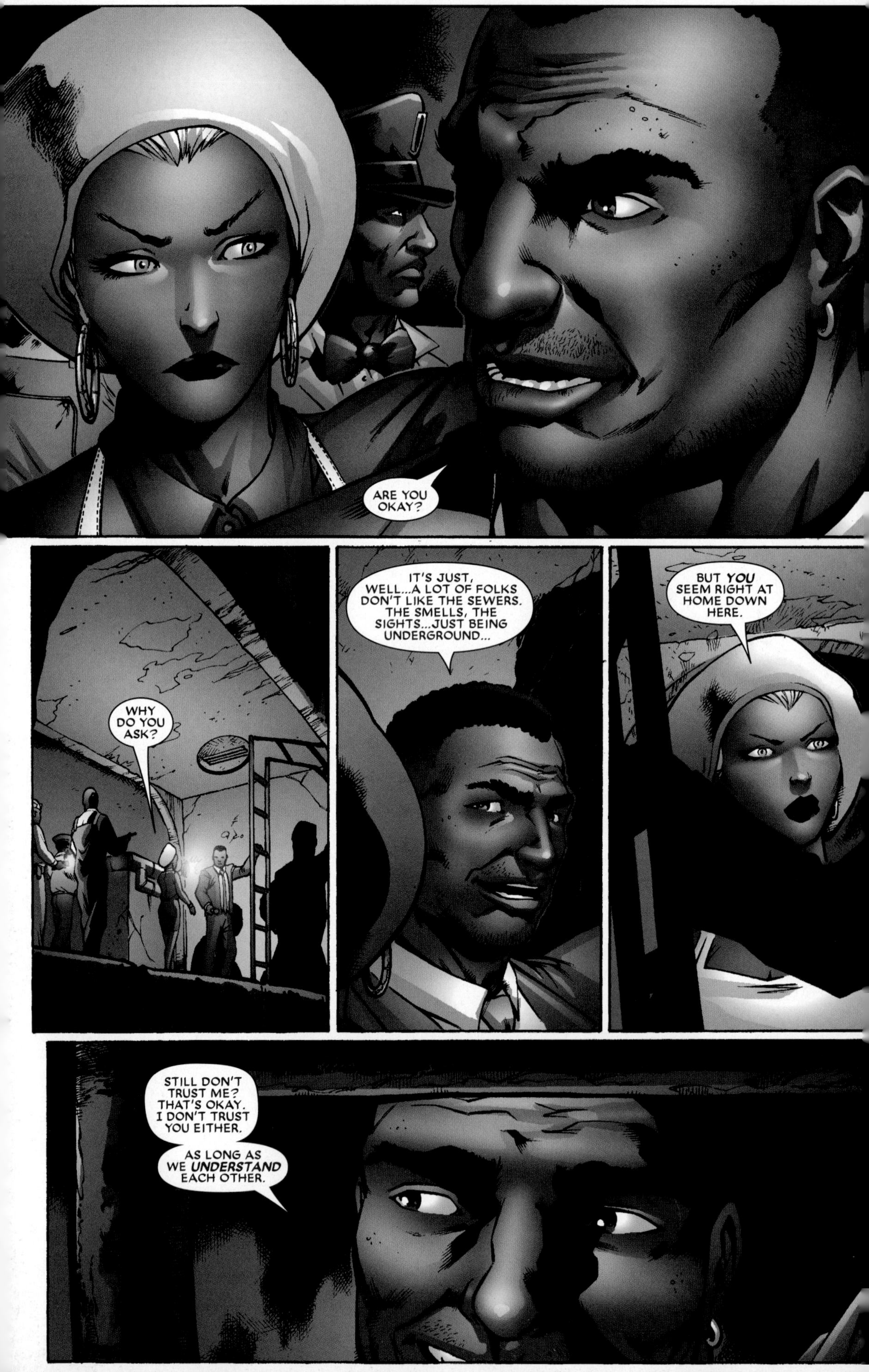

ARE YOU OKAY?
WHY DO YOU ASK?
IT'S JUST, WELL...A LOT OF FOLKS DON'T LIKE THE SEWERS. THE SMELLS, THE SIGHTS...JUST BEING UNDERGROUND...
BUT *YOU* SEEM RIGHT AT HOME DOWN HERE.
STILL DON'T TRUST ME? THAT'S OKAY. I DON'T TRUST YOU EITHER.
AS LONG AS WE *UNDERSTAND* EACH OTHER.

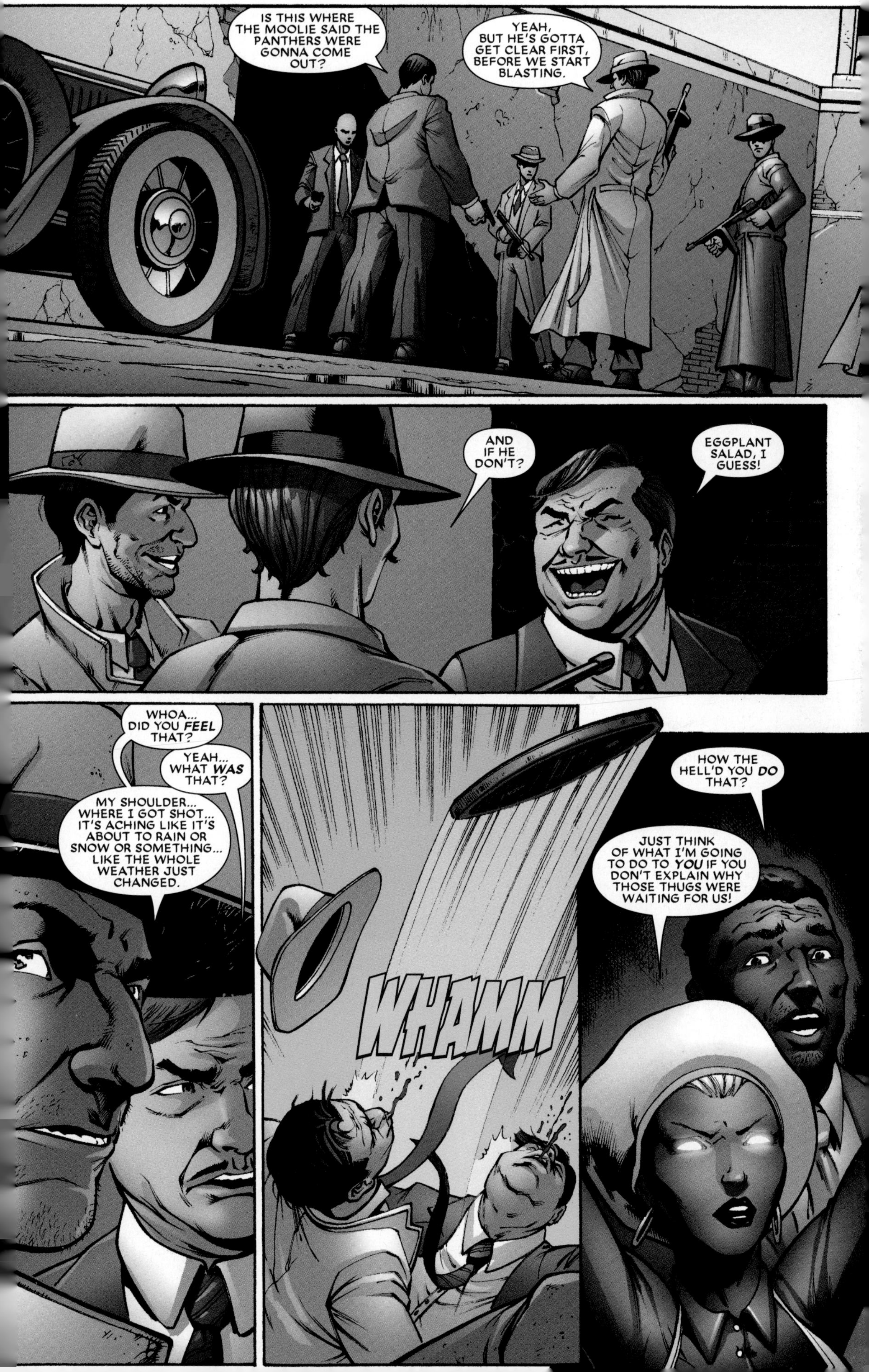
IS THIS WHERE THE MOOLIE SAID THE PANTHERS WERE GONNA COME OUT?
YEAH, BUT HE'S GOTTA GET CLEAR FIRST, BEFORE WE START BLASTING.
AND IF HE DON'T?
EGGPLANT SALAD, I GUESS!
WHOA... DID YOU FEEL THAT?
YEAH... WHAT WAS THAT?
MY SHOULDER... WHERE I GOT SHOT... IT'S ACHING LIKE IT'S ABOUT TO RAIN OR SNOW OR SOMETHING... LIKE THE WHOLE WEATHER JUST CHANGED.
WHAMM
HOW THE HELL'D YOU DO THAT?
JUST THINK OF WHAT I'M GOING TO DO TO YOU IF YOU DON'T EXPLAIN WHY THOSE THUGS WERE WAITING FOR US!

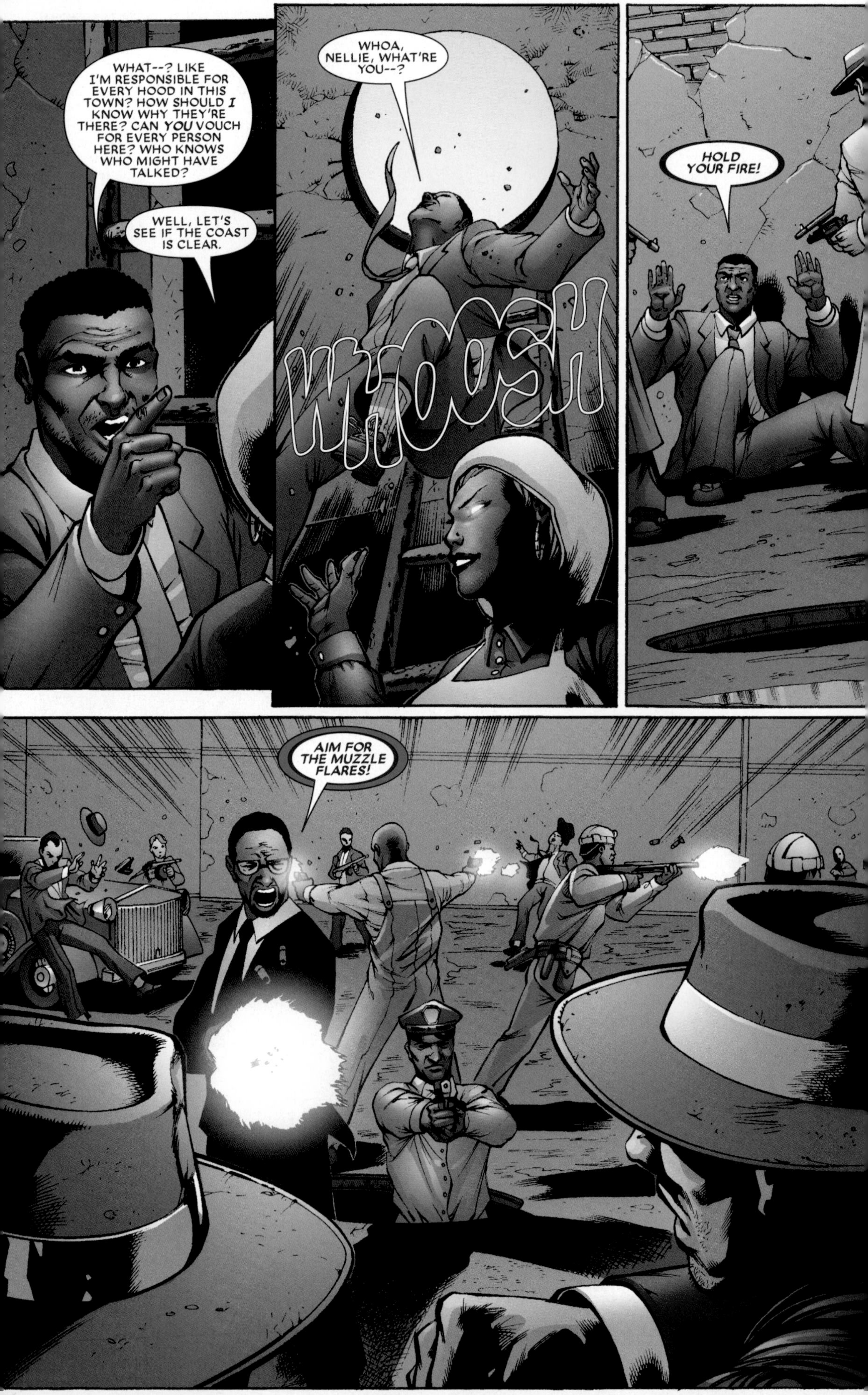
WHAT--? LIKE I'M RESPONSIBLE FOR EVERY HOOD IN THIS TOWN? HOW SHOULD *I* KNOW WHY THEY'RE THERE? CAN *YOU* VOUCH FOR EVERY PERSON HERE? WHO KNOWS WHO MIGHT HAVE TALKED?
WELL, LET'S SEE IF THE COAST IS CLEAR.
WHOA, NELLIE, WHAT'RE YOU--?
WHOOSH
HOLD YOUR FIRE!
AIM FOR THE MUZZLE FLARES!

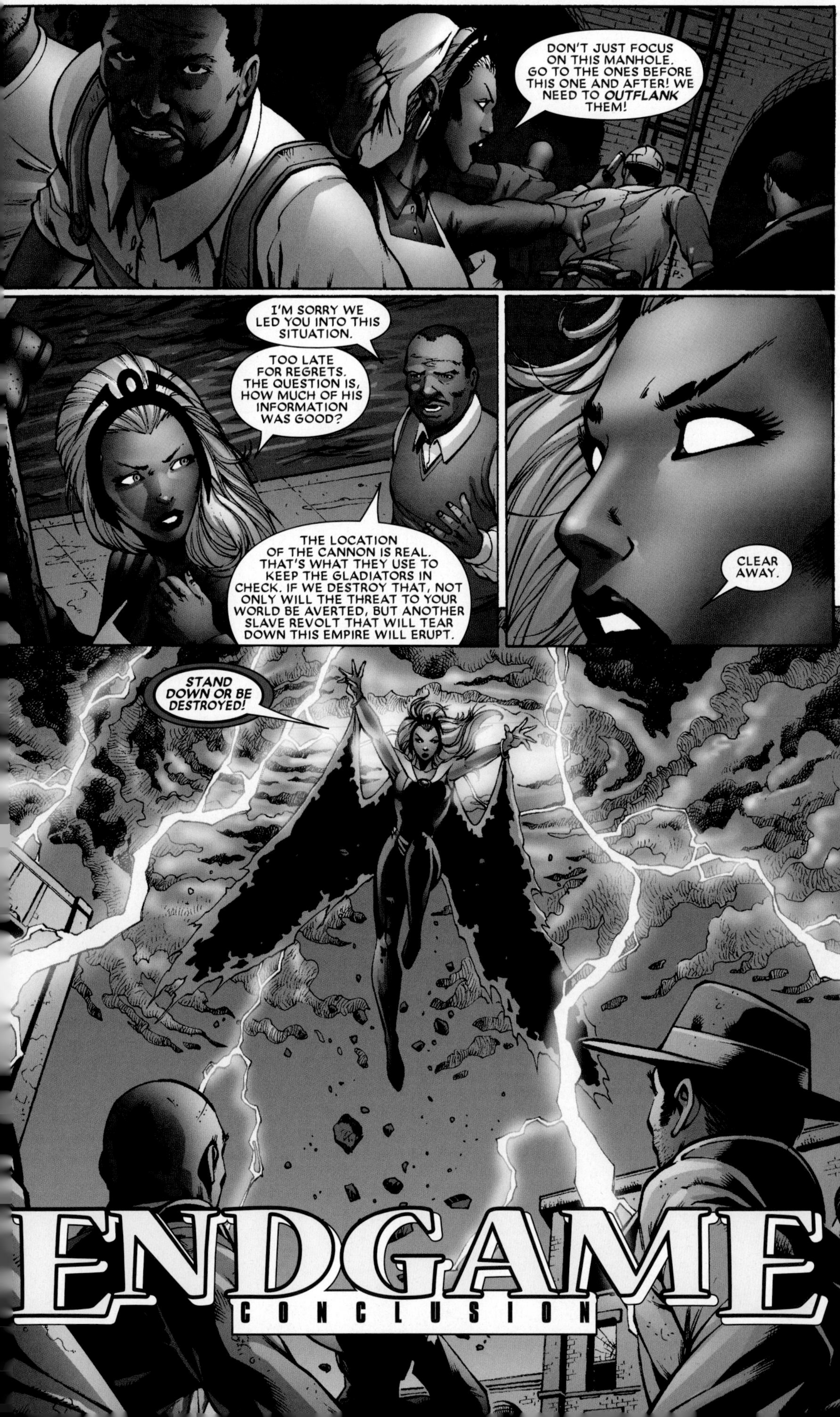
DON'T JUST FOCUS ON THIS MANHOLE. GO TO THE ONES BEFORE THIS ONE AND AFTER! WE NEED TO OUTFLANK THEM!
I'M SORRY WE LED YOU INTO THIS SITUATION.
TOO LATE FOR REGRETS. THE QUESTION IS, HOW MUCH OF HIS INFORMATION WAS GOOD?
THE LOCATION OF THE CANNON IS REAL. THAT'S WHAT THEY USE TO KEEP THE GLADIATORS IN CHECK. IF WE DESTROY THAT, NOT ONLY WILL THE THREAT TO YOUR WORLD BE AVERTED, BUT ANOTHER SLAVE REVOLT THAT WILL TEAR DOWN THIS EMPIRE WILL ERUPT.
CLEAR AWAY.
STAND DOWN OR BE DESTROYED!
ENDGAME
CONCLUSION

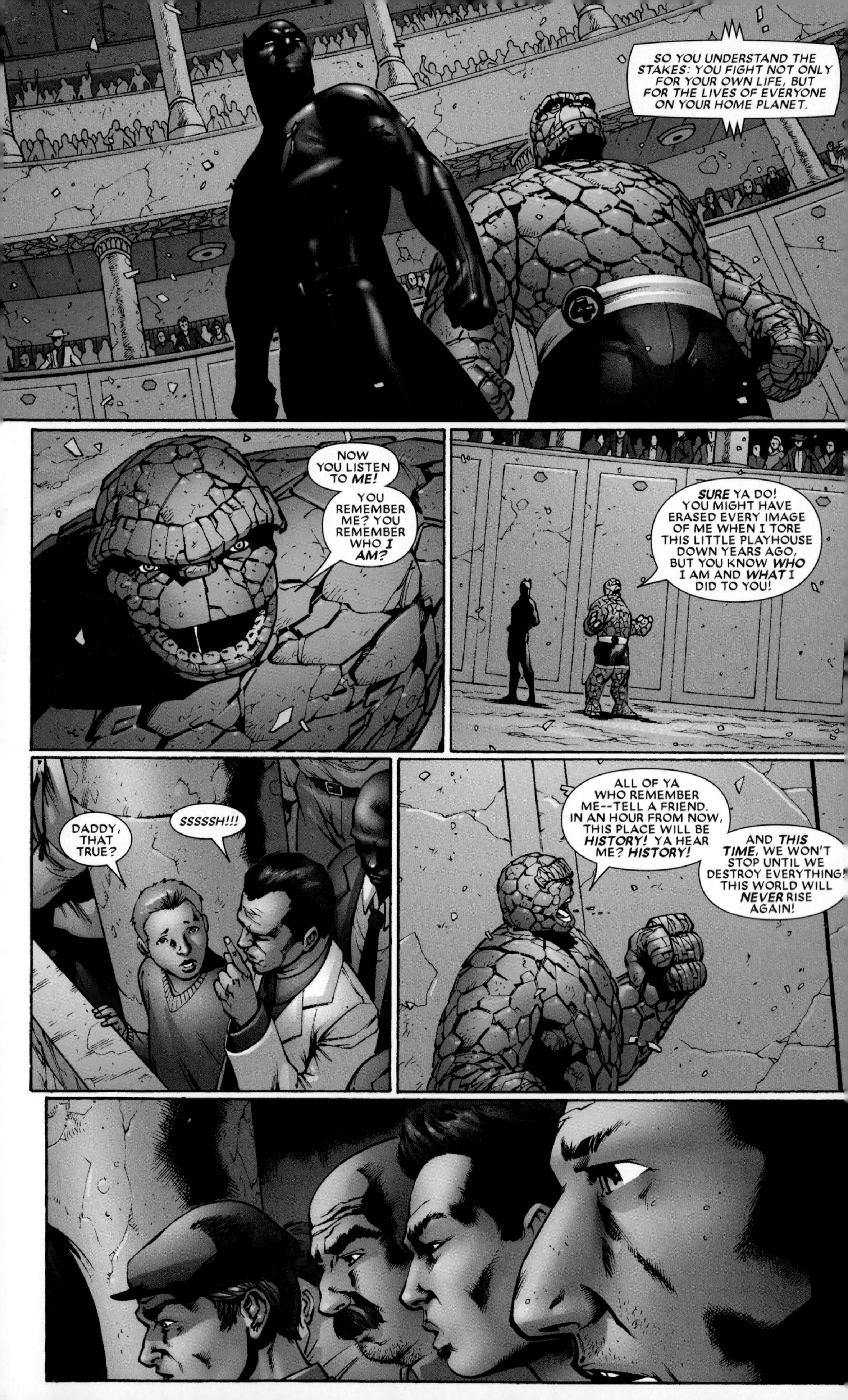
SO YOU UNDERSTAND THE STAKES: YOU FIGHT NOT ONLY FOR YOUR OWN LIFE, BUT FOR THE LIVES OF EVERYONE ON YOUR HOME PLANET.
NOW YOU LISTEN TO ME!
YOU REMEMBER ME? YOU REMEMBER WHO I AM?
SURE YA DO! YOU MIGHT HAVE ERASED EVERY IMAGE OF ME WHEN I TORE THIS LITTLE PLAYHOUSE DOWN YEARS AGO, BUT YOU KNOW WHO I AM AND WHAT I DID TO YOU!
DADDY, THAT TRUE?
SSSSSH!!!
ALL OF YA WHO REMEMBER ME--TELL A FRIEND. IN AN HOUR FROM NOW, THIS PLACE WILL BE HISTORY! YA HEAR ME? HISTORY!
AND THIS TIME, WE WON'T STOP UNTIL WE DESTROY EVERYTHING! THIS WORLD WILL NEVER RISE AGAIN!

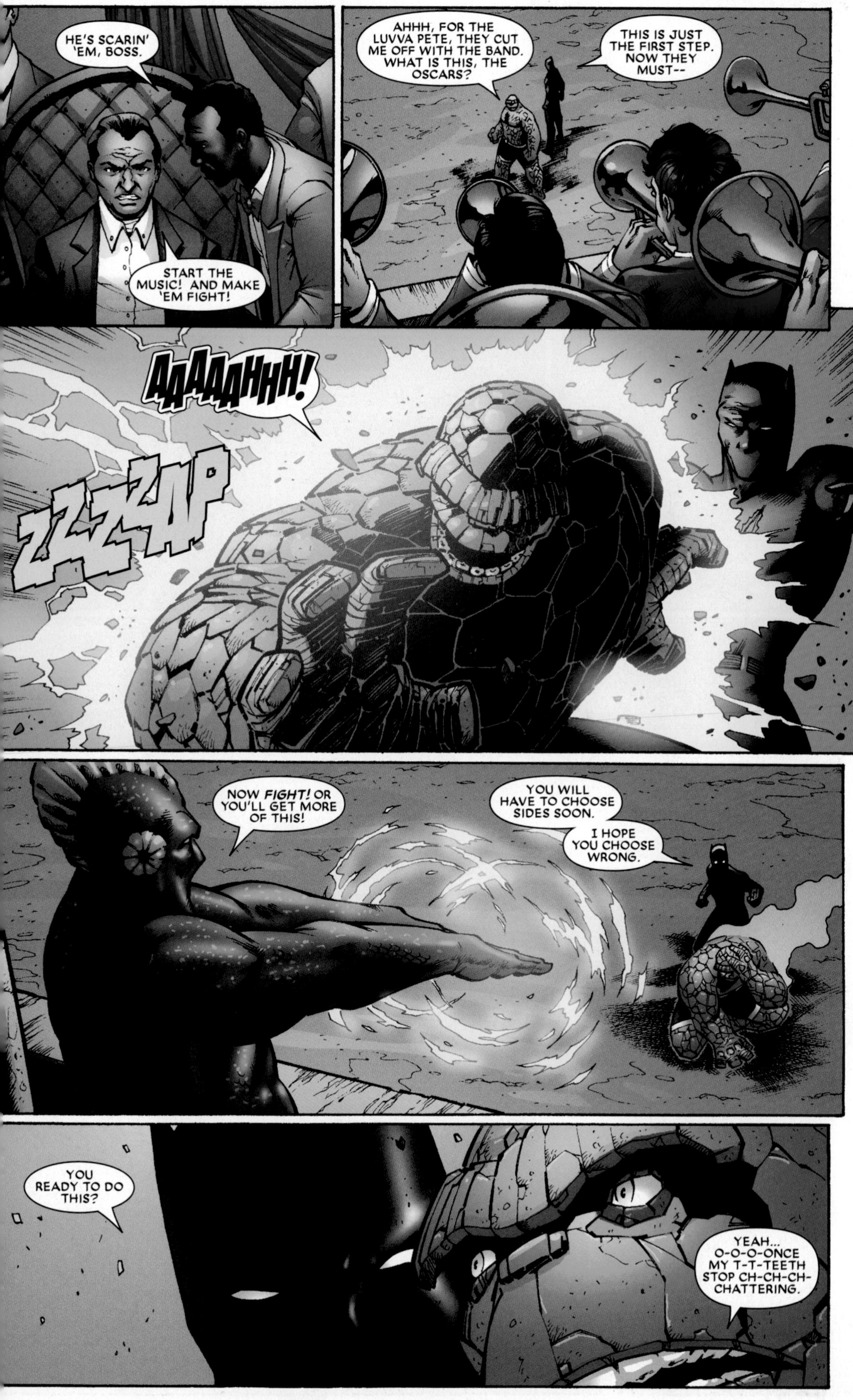
HE'S SCARIN' 'EM, BOSS.
START THE MUSIC! AND MAKE 'EM FIGHT!
AHHH, FOR THE LUVVA PETE, THEY CUT ME OFF WITH THE BAND. WHAT IS THIS, THE OSCARS?
THIS IS JUST THE FIRST STEP. NOW THEY MUST--
AAAAAHHH!
ZZZZAP
NOW FIGHT! OR YOU'LL GET MORE OF THIS!
YOU WILL HAVE TO CHOOSE SIDES SOON.
I HOPE YOU CHOOSE WRONG.
YOU READY TO DO THIS?
YEAH... O-O-O-ONCE MY T-T-TEETH STOP CH-CH-CH-CHATTERING.

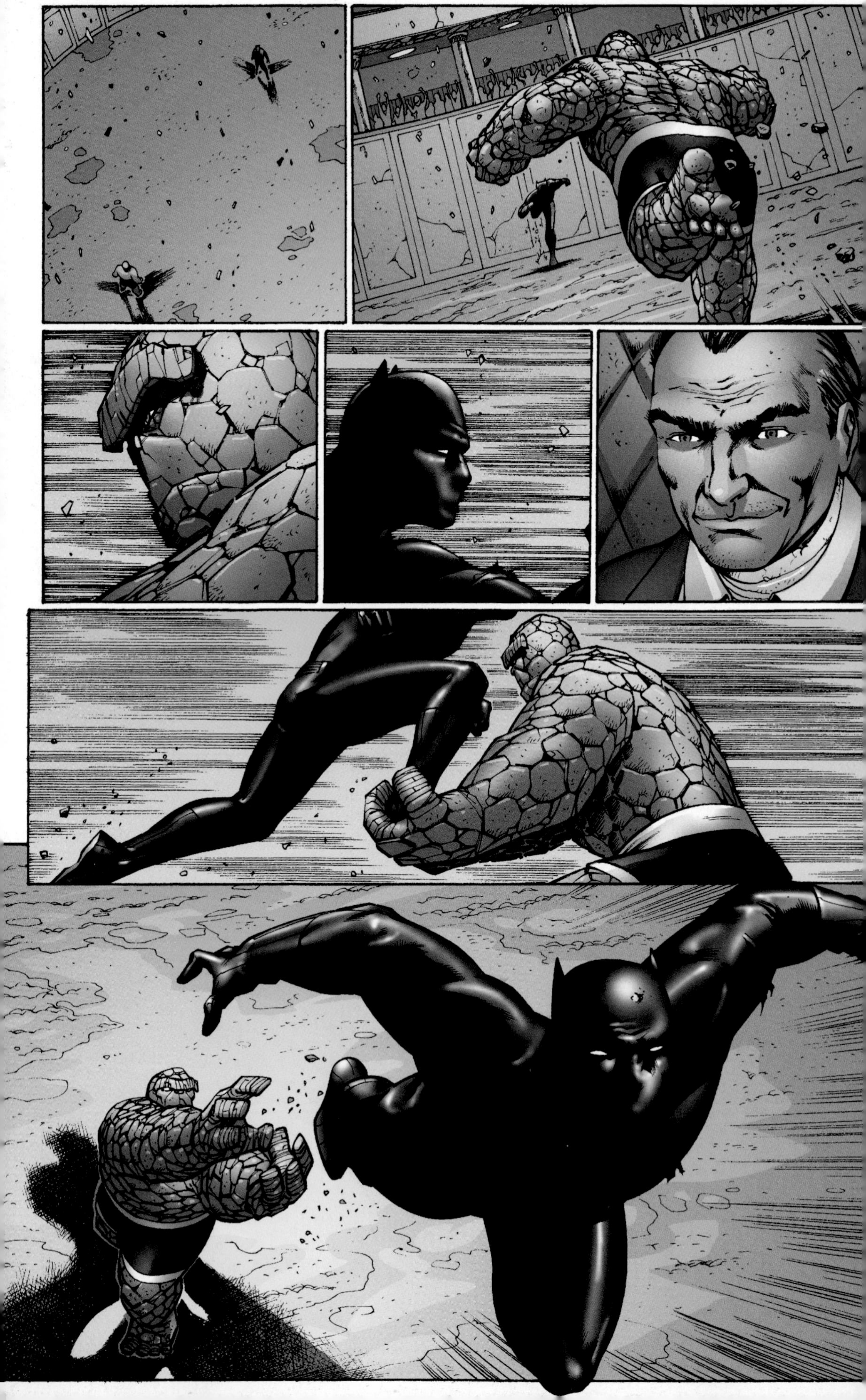

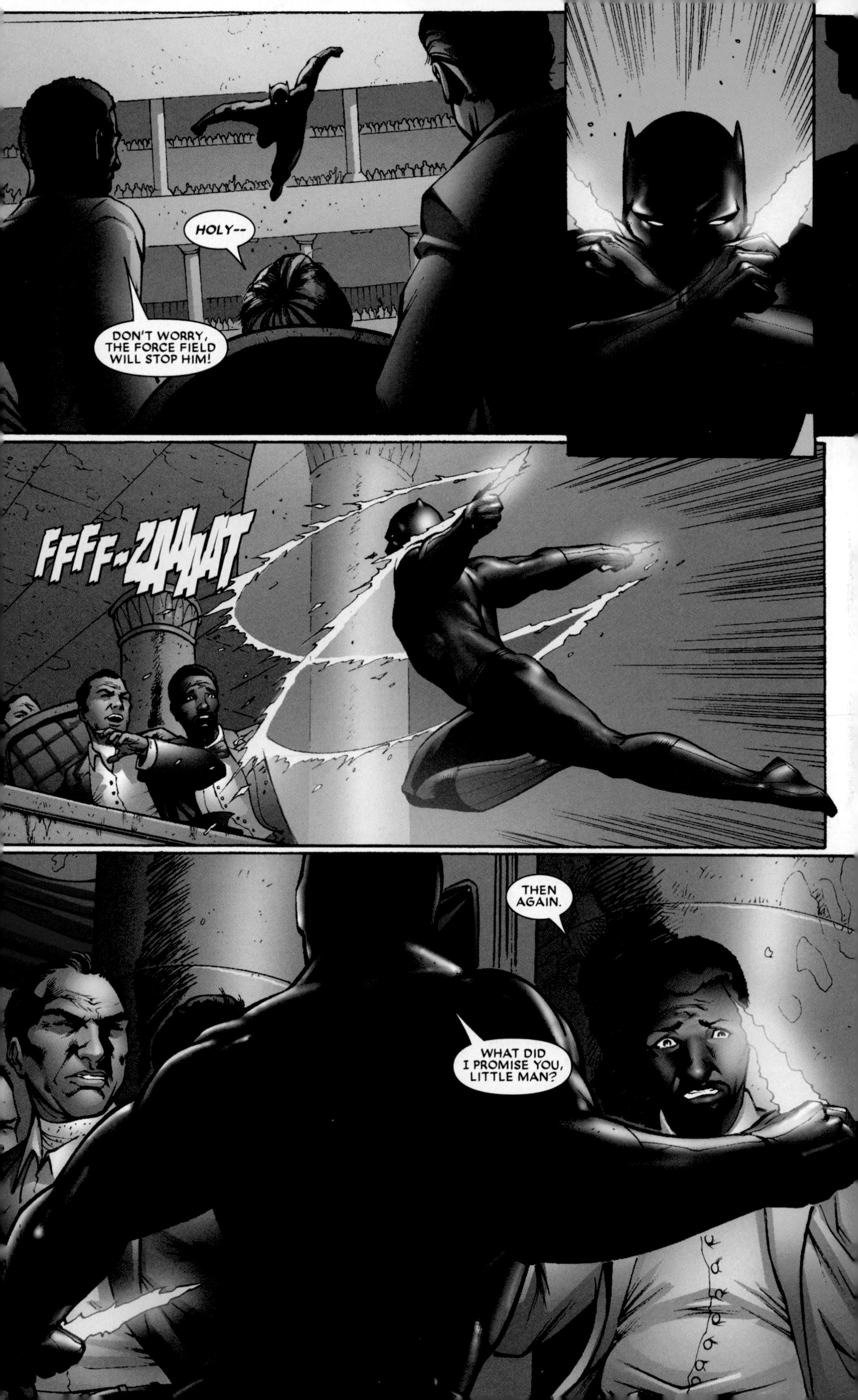
HOLY--
DON'T WORRY, THE FORCE FIELD WILL STOP HIM!
FFFF-ZAAAAT
THEN AGAIN.
WHAT DID I PROMISE YOU, LITTLE MAN?

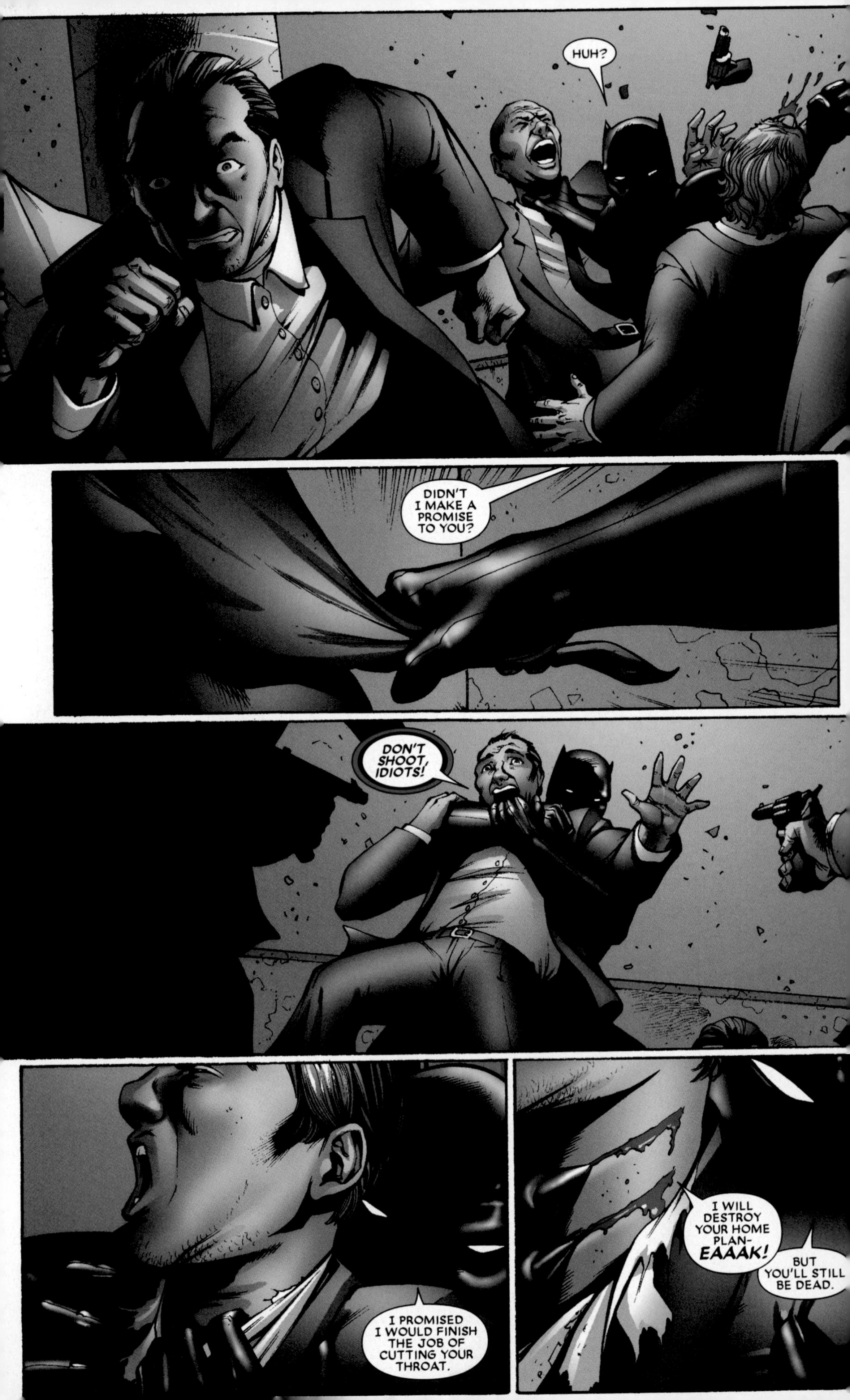
HUH?
DIDN'T I MAKE A PROMISE TO YOU?
DON'T SHOOT, IDIOTS!
I PROMISED I WOULD FINISH THE JOB OF CUTTING YOUR THROAT.
I WILL DESTROY YOUR HOME PLAN-
EAAAK!
BUT YOU'LL STILL BE DEAD.

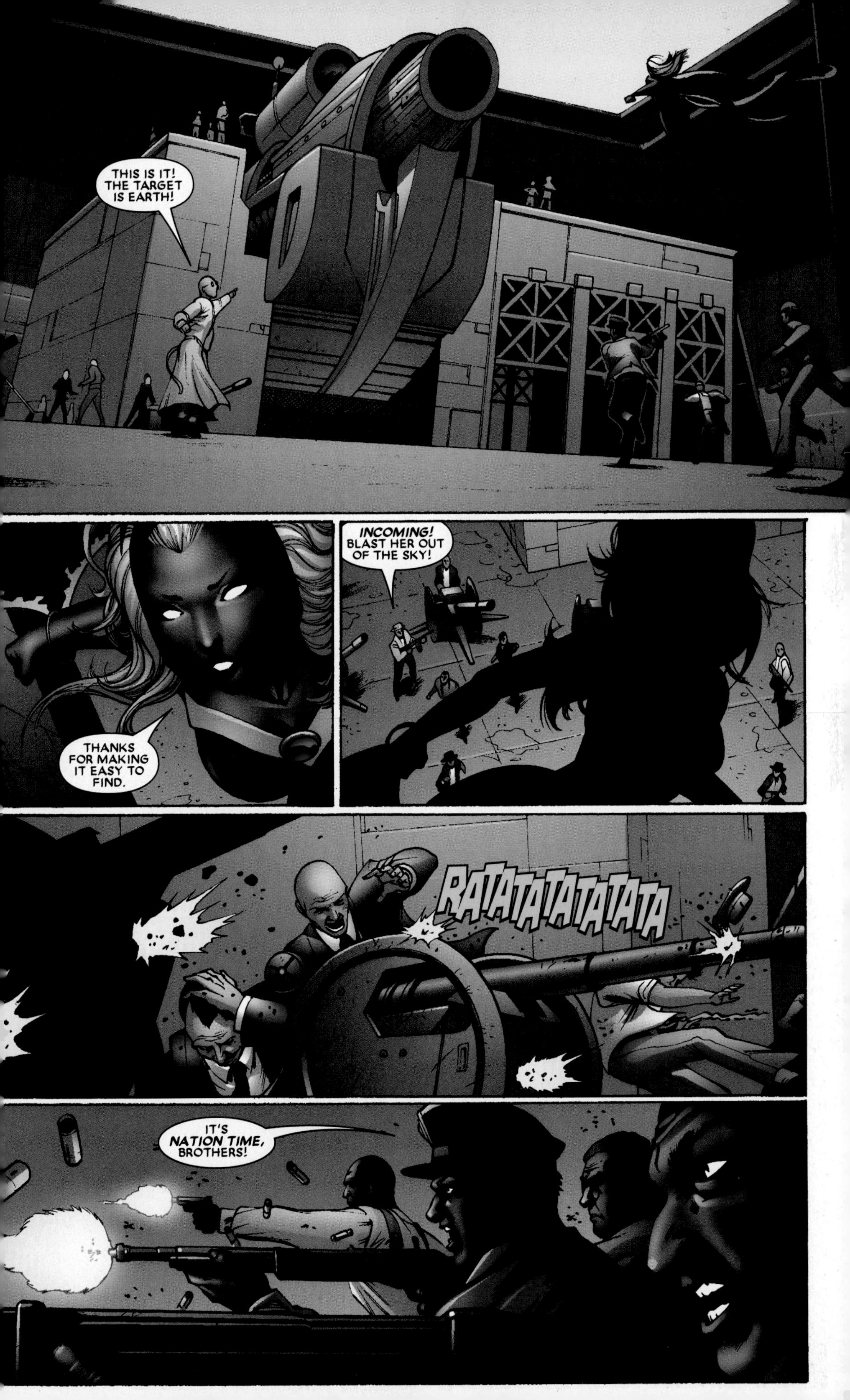
THIS IS IT! THE TARGET IS EARTH!
THANKS FOR MAKING IT EASY TO FIND.
INCOMING! BLAST HER OUT OF THE SKY!
RATATATATATATA
IT'S NATION TIME, BROTHERS!

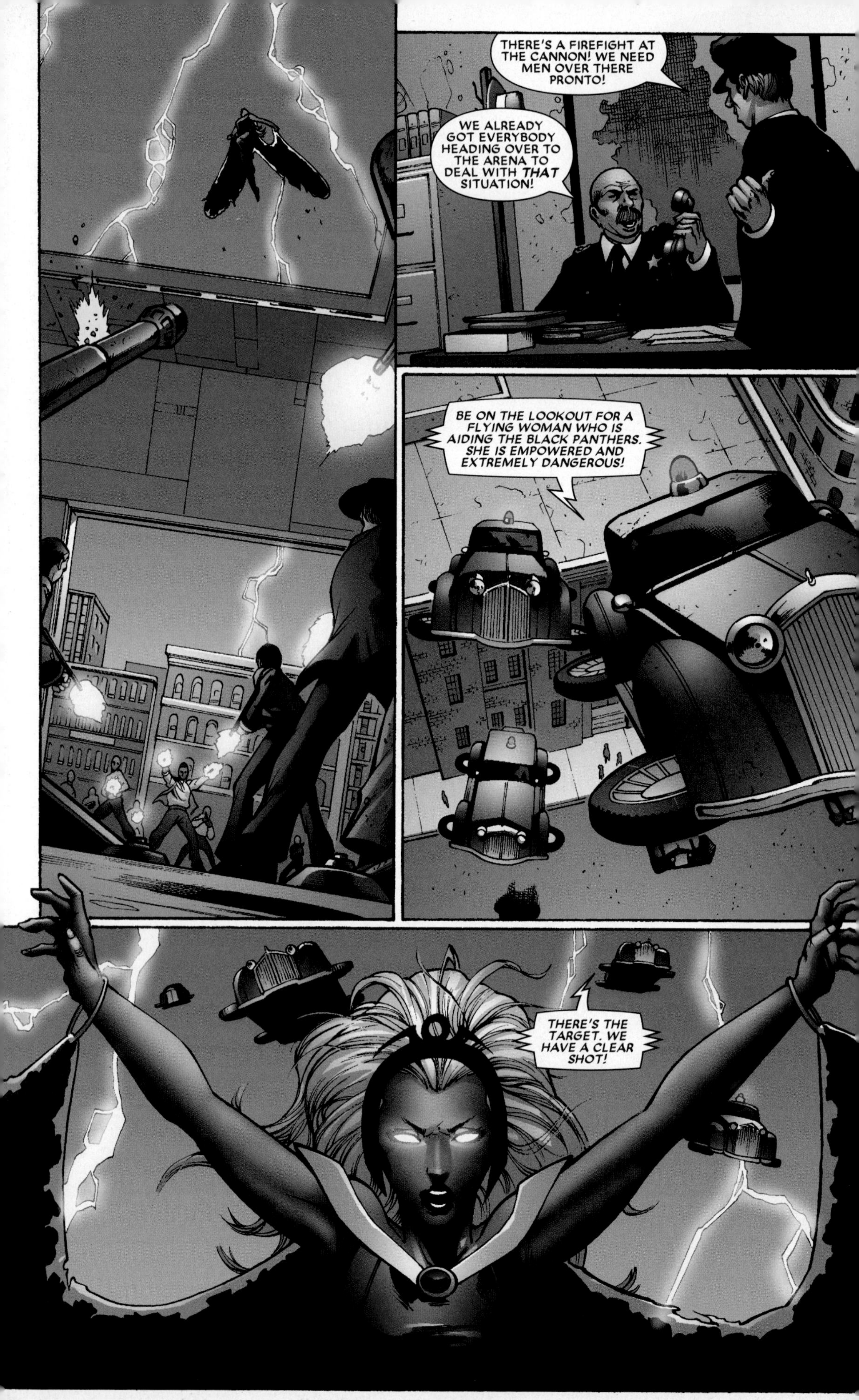
THERE'S A FIREFIGHT AT THE CANNON! WE NEED MEN OVER THERE PRONTO!
WE ALREADY GOT EVERYBODY HEADING OVER TO THE ARENA TO DEAL WITH THAT SITUATION!
BE ON THE LOOKOUT FOR A FLYING WOMAN WHO IS AIDING THE BLACK PANTHERS. SHE IS EMPOWERED AND EXTREMELY DANGEROUS!
THERE'S THE TARGET. WE HAVE A CLEAR SHOT!

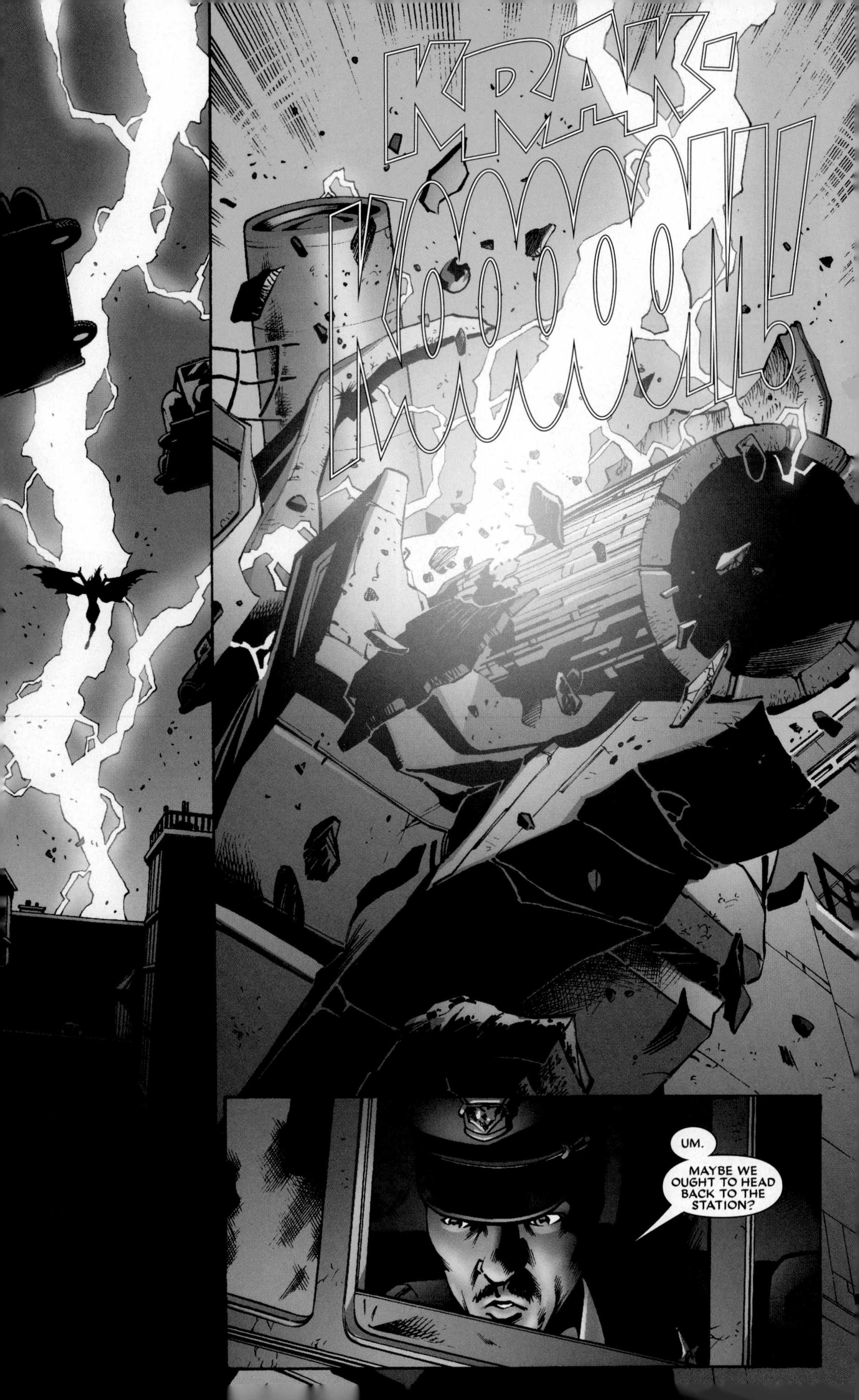
KRAK-KOOOOOOM!
UM.
MAYBE WE OUGHT TO HEAD BACK TO THE STATION?

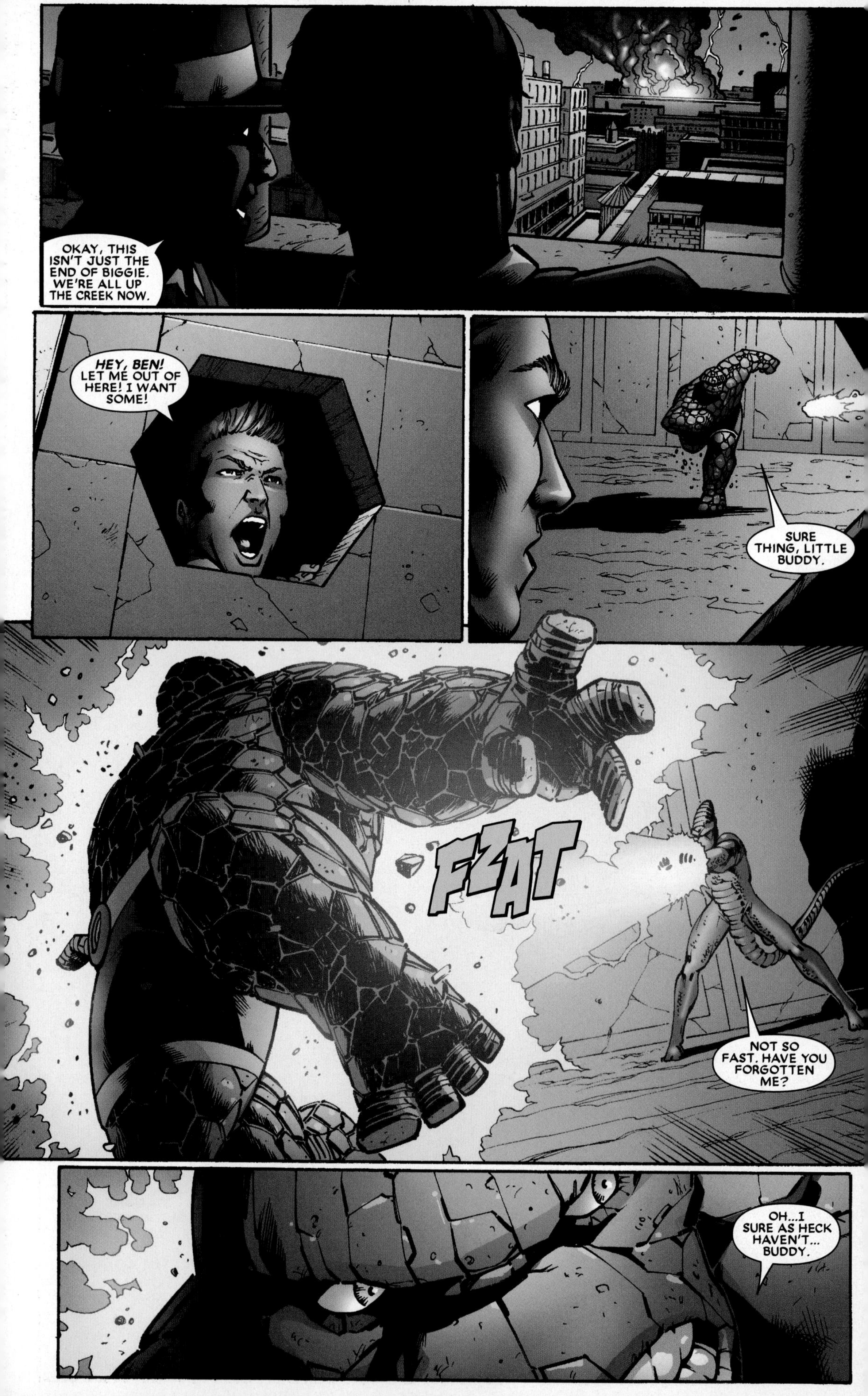
OKAY, THIS ISN'T JUST THE END OF BIGGIE. WE'RE ALL UP THE CREEK NOW.
HEY, BEN! LET ME OUT OF HERE! I WANT SOME!
SURE THING, LITTLE BUDDY.
FZAT
NOT SO FAST. HAVE YOU FORGOTTEN ME?
OH...I SURE AS HECK HAVEN'T... BUDDY.

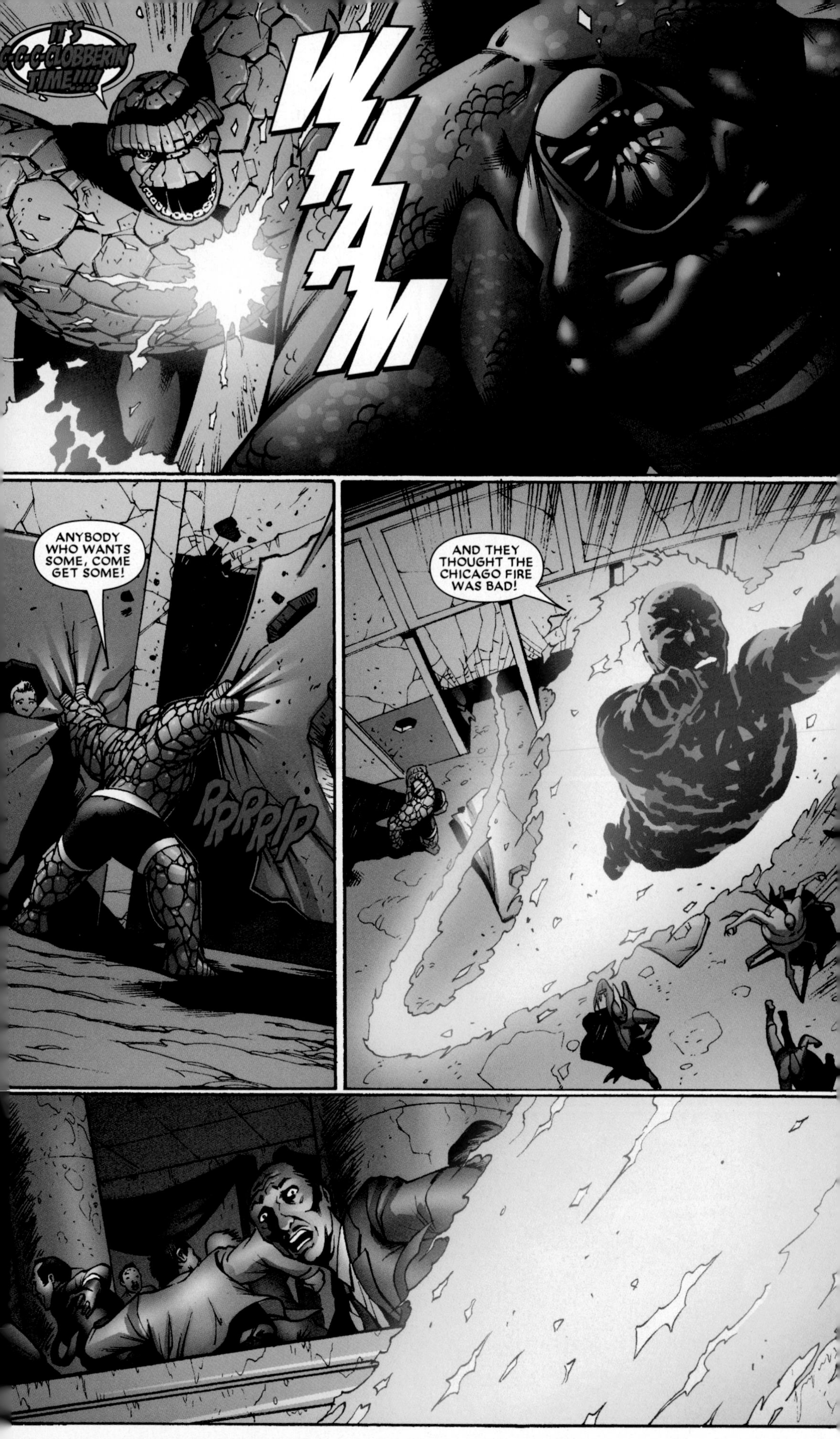
IT'S G-G-G-GLOBBERIN' TIME!!!!
WHAM
ANYBODY WHO WANTS SOME, COME GET SOME!
RRRRIP
AND THEY THOUGHT THE CHICAGO FIRE WAS BAD!

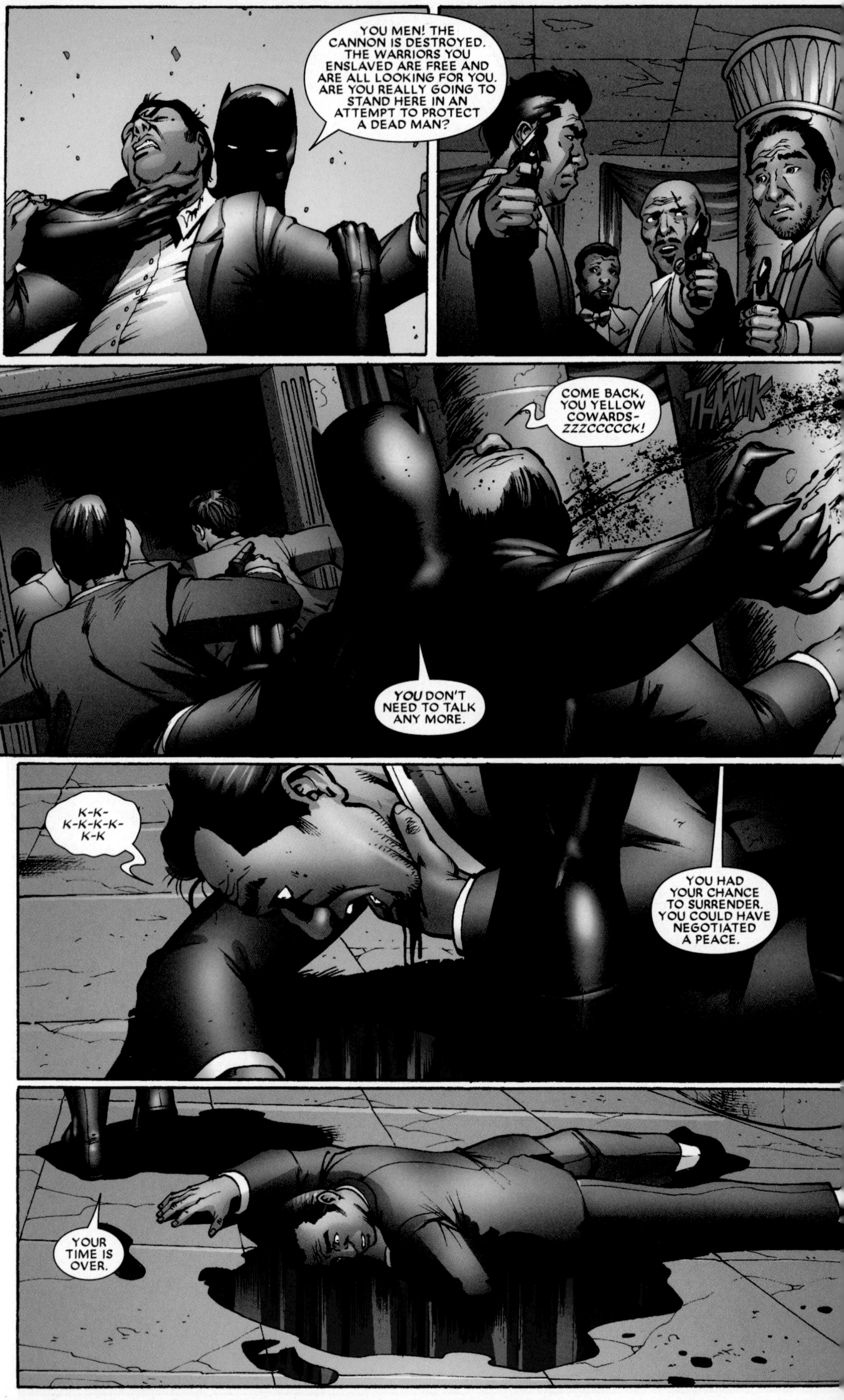
YOU MEN! THE CANNON IS DESTROYED. THE WARRIORS YOU ENSLAVED ARE FREE AND ARE ALL LOOKING FOR YOU. ARE YOU REALLY GOING TO STAND HERE IN AN ATTEMPT TO PROTECT A DEAD MAN?
COME BACK, YOU YELLOW COWARDS-ZZZCCCCCK!
THWAK
YOU DON'T NEED TO TALK ANY MORE.
K-K-K-K-K-K-K-K
YOU HAD YOUR CHANCE TO SURRENDER. YOU COULD HAVE NEGOTIATED A PEACE.
YOUR TIME IS OVER.

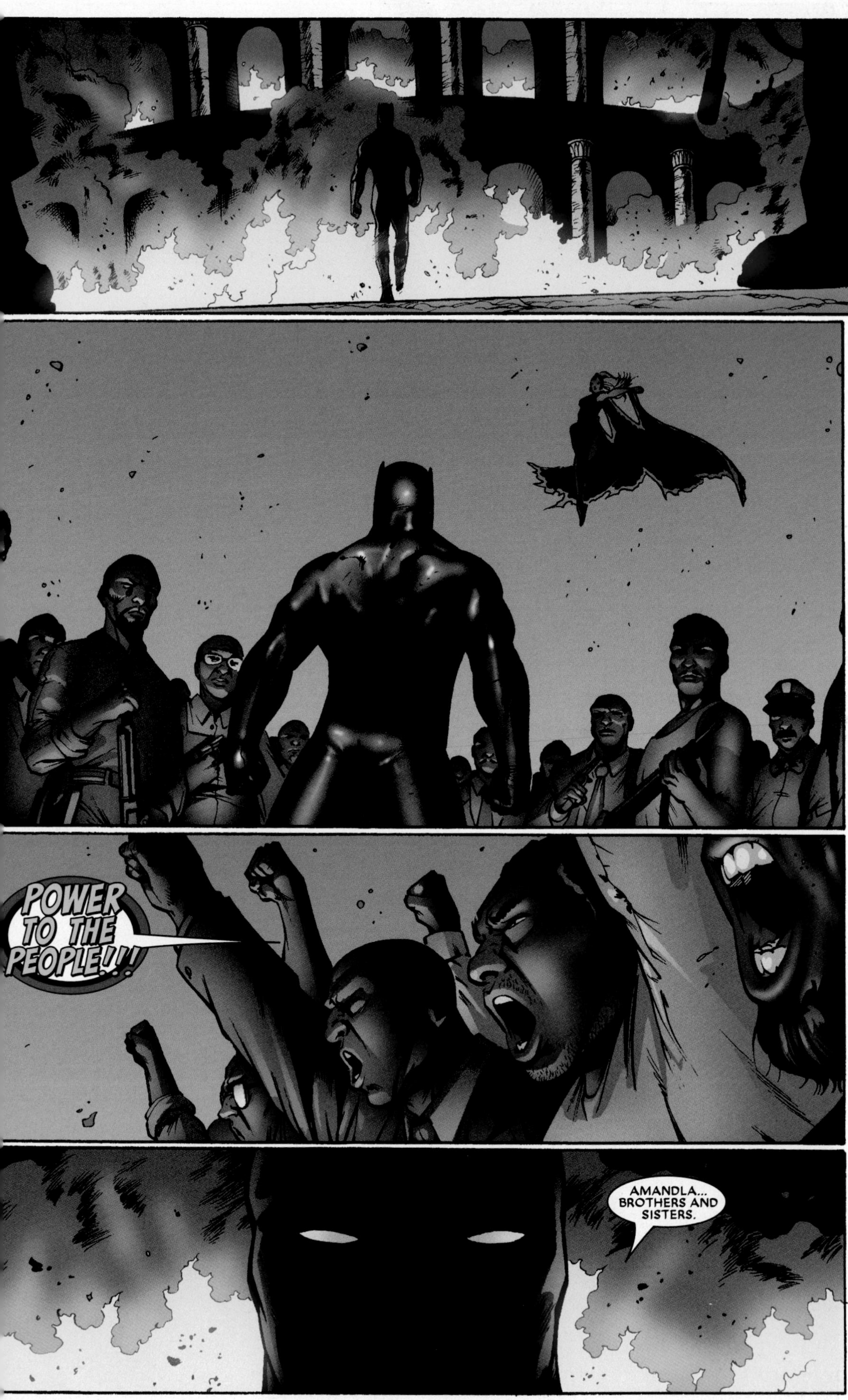
POWER TO THE PEOPLE!!!
AMANDLA... BROTHERS AND SISTERS.

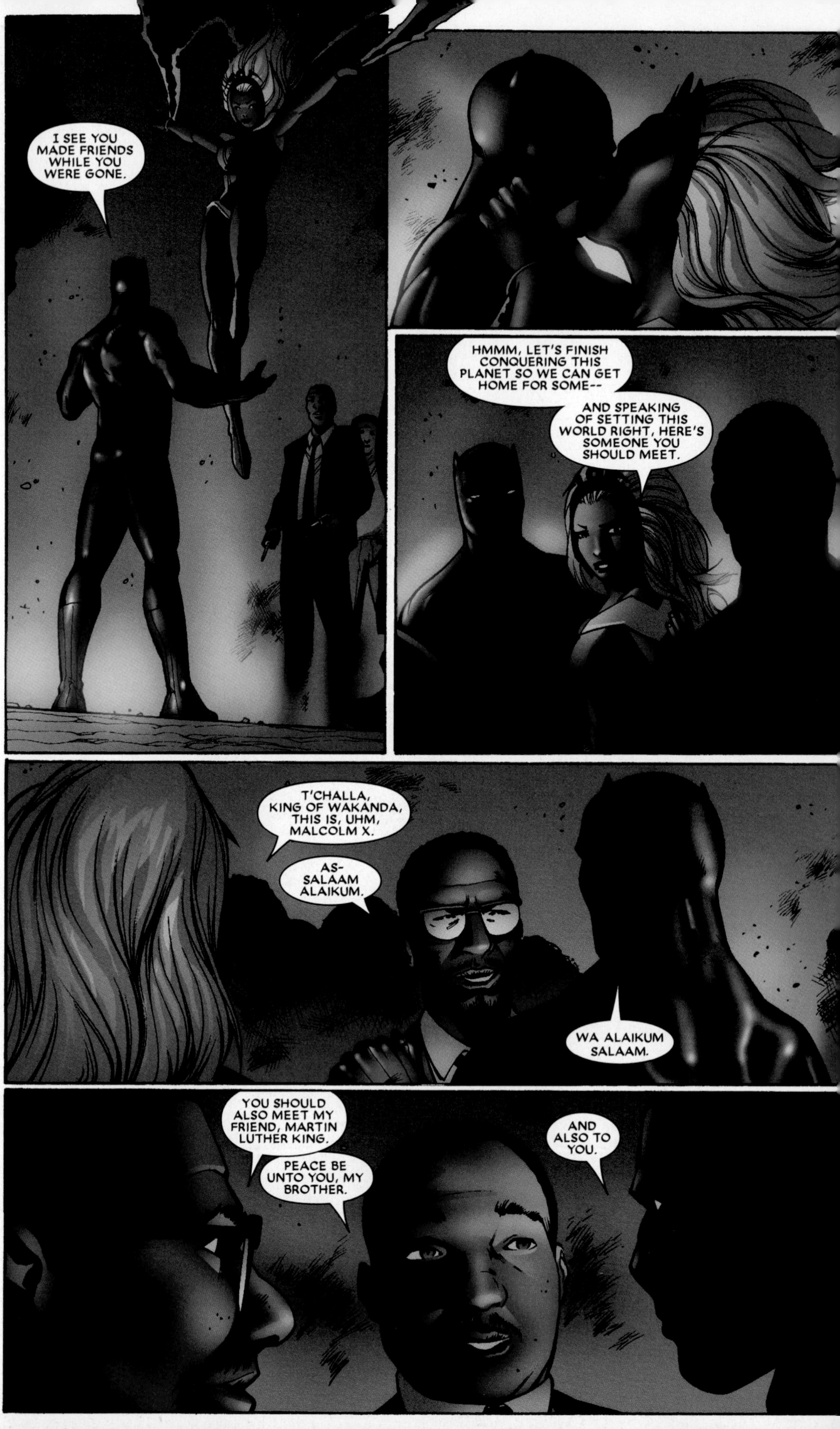
I SEE YOU MADE FRIENDS WHILE YOU WERE GONE.
HMMM, LET'S FINISH CONQUERING THIS PLANET SO WE CAN GET HOME FOR SOME--
AND SPEAKING OF SETTING THIS WORLD RIGHT, HERE'S SOMEONE YOU SHOULD MEET.
T'CHALLA, KING OF WAKANDA, THIS IS, UHM, MALCOLM X.
AS-SALAAM ALAIKUM.
WA ALAIKUM SALAAM.
YOU SHOULD ALSO MEET MY FRIEND, MARTIN LUTHER KING.
PEACE BE UNTO YOU, MY BROTHER.
AND ALSO TO YOU.

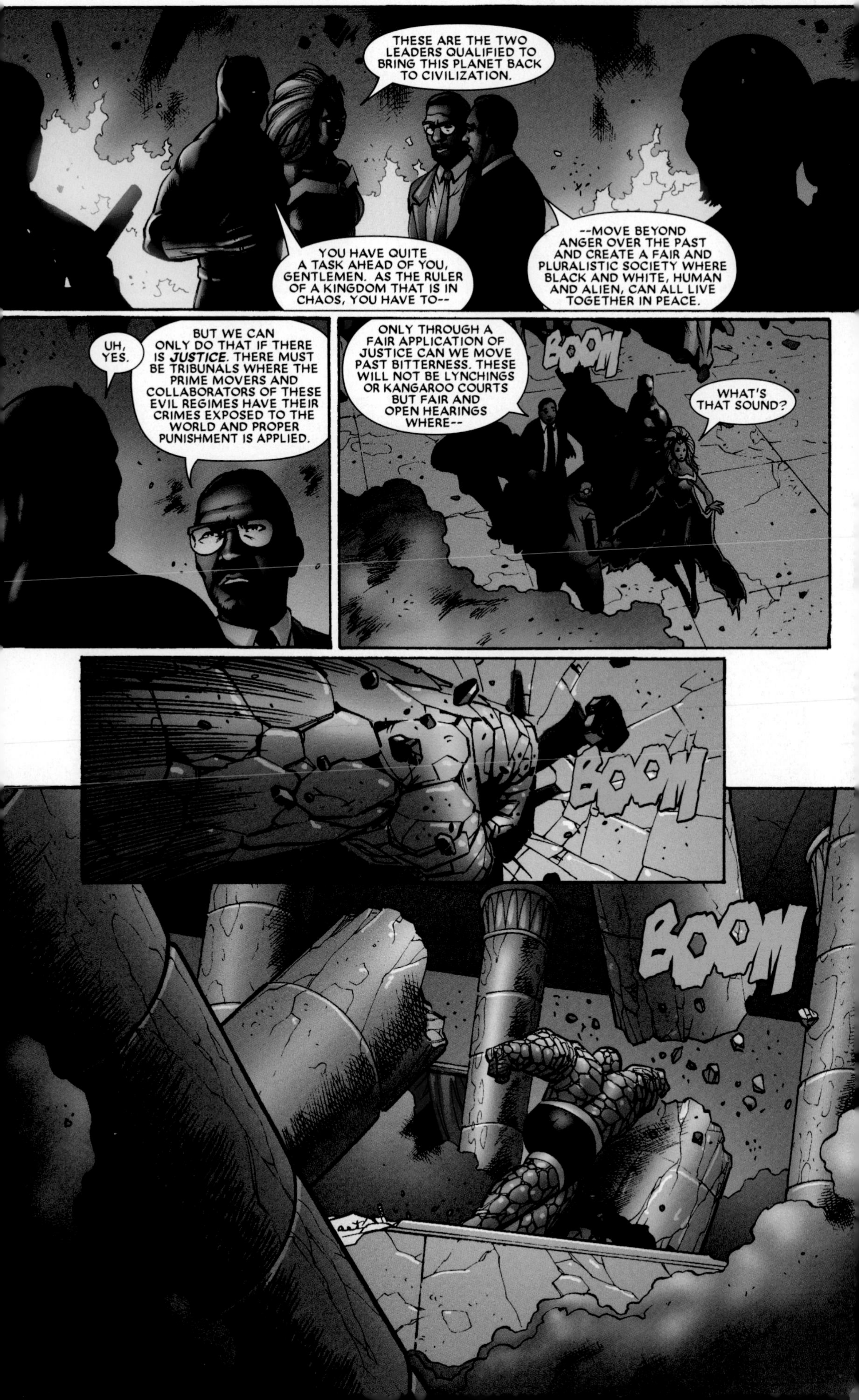
THESE ARE THE TWO LEADERS QUALIFIED TO BRING THIS PLANET BACK TO CIVILIZATION.
YOU HAVE QUITE A TASK AHEAD OF YOU, GENTLEMEN. AS THE RULER OF A KINGDOM THAT IS IN CHAOS, YOU HAVE TO--
--MOVE BEYOND ANGER OVER THE PAST AND CREATE A FAIR AND PLURALISTIC SOCIETY WHERE BLACK AND WHITE, HUMAN AND ALIEN, CAN ALL LIVE TOGETHER IN PEACE.
UH, YES.
BUT WE CAN ONLY DO THAT IF THERE IS JUSTICE. THERE MUST BE TRIBUNALS WHERE THE PRIME MOVERS AND COLLABORATORS OF THESE EVIL REGIMES HAVE THEIR CRIMES EXPOSED TO THE WORLD AND PROPER PUNISHMENT IS APPLIED.
ONLY THROUGH A FAIR APPLICATION OF JUSTICE CAN WE MOVE PAST BITTERNESS. THESE WILL NOT BE LYNCHINGS OR KANGAROO COURTS BUT FAIR AND OPEN HEARINGS WHERE--
BOOM
WHAT'S THAT SOUND?
BOOM
BOOM

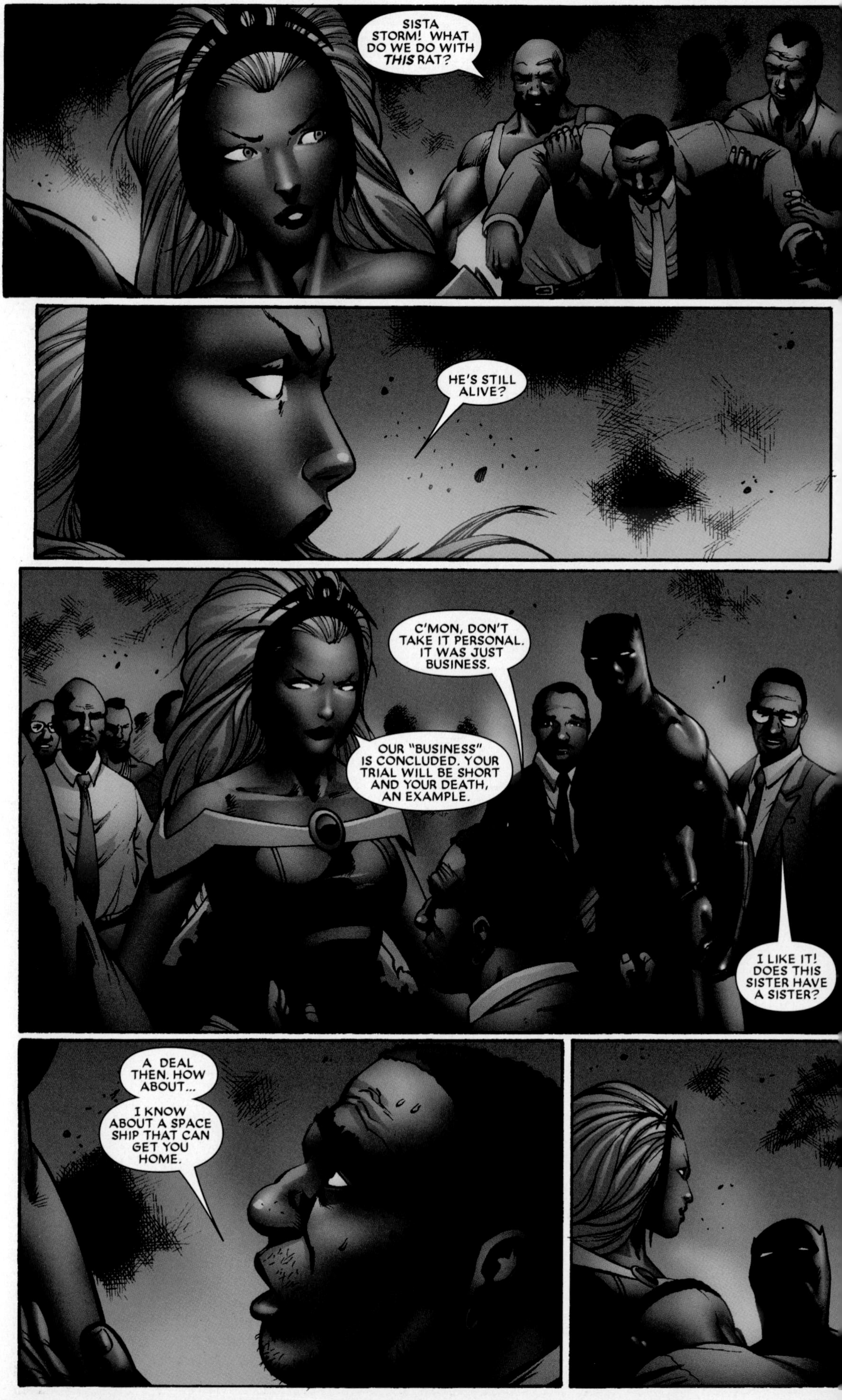
SISTA STORM! WHAT DO WE DO WITH *THIS* RAT?
HE'S STILL ALIVE?
C'MON, DON'T TAKE IT PERSONAL. IT WAS JUST BUSINESS.
OUR "BUSINESS" IS CONCLUDED. YOUR TRIAL WILL BE SHORT AND YOUR DEATH, AN EXAMPLE.
I LIKE IT! DOES THIS SISTER HAVE A SISTER?
A DEAL THEN. HOW ABOUT...
I KNOW ABOUT A SPACE SHIP THAT CAN GET YOU HOME.

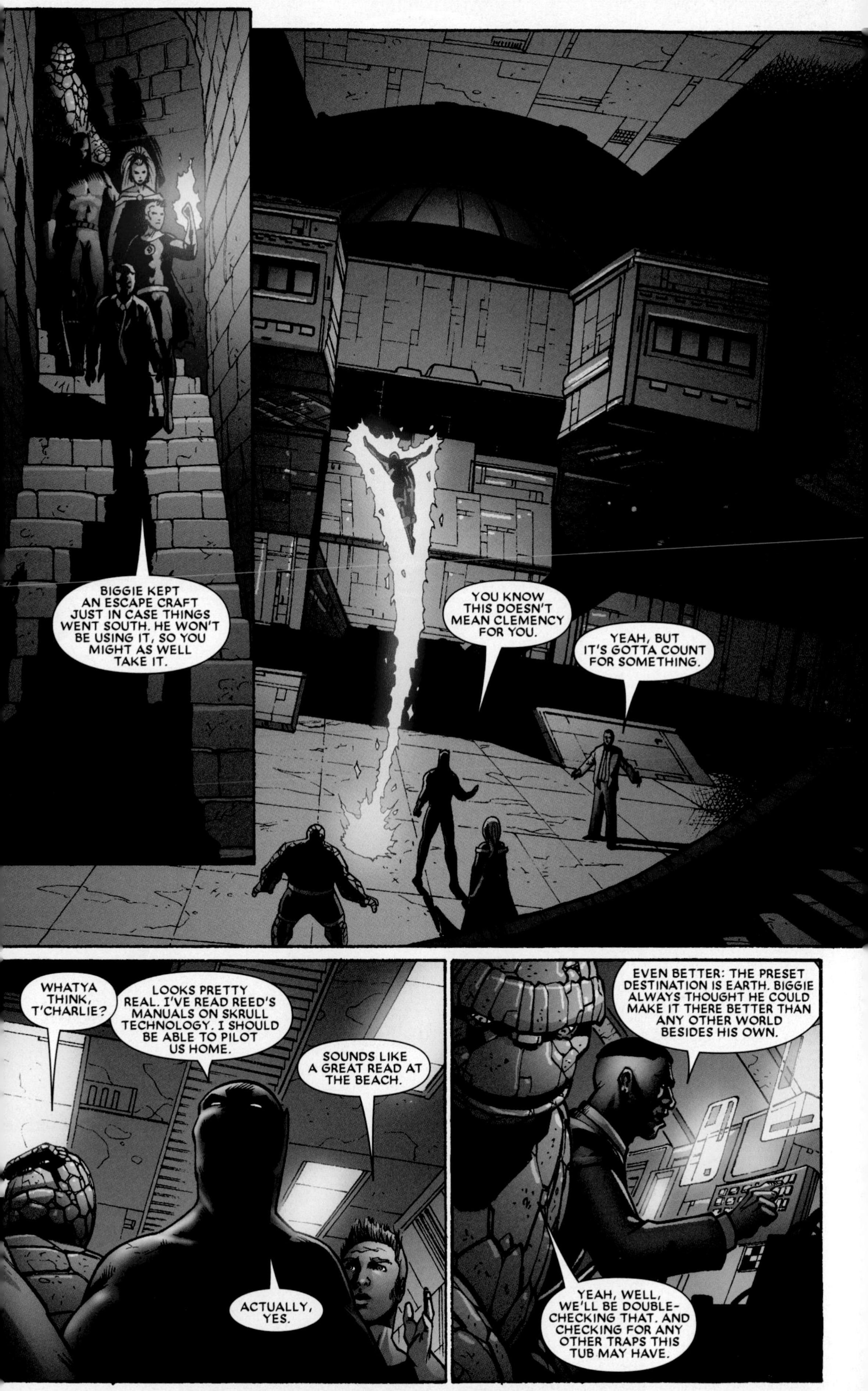
BIGGIE KEPT AN ESCAPE CRAFT JUST IN CASE THINGS WENT SOUTH. HE WON'T BE USING IT, SO YOU MIGHT AS WELL TAKE IT.
YOU KNOW THIS DOESN'T MEAN CLEMENCY FOR YOU.
YEAH, BUT IT'S GOTTA COUNT FOR SOMETHING.
WHATYA THINK, T'CHARLIE?
LOOKS PRETTY REAL. I'VE READ REED'S MANUALS ON SKRULL TECHNOLOGY. I SHOULD BE ABLE TO PILOT US HOME.
SOUNDS LIKE A GREAT READ AT THE BEACH.
ACTUALLY, YES.
EVEN BETTER: THE PRESET DESTINATION IS EARTH. BIGGIE ALWAYS THOUGHT HE COULD MAKE IT THERE BETTER THAN ANY OTHER WORLD BESIDES HIS OWN.
YEAH, WELL, WE'LL BE DOUBLE-CHECKING THAT. AND CHECKING FOR ANY OTHER TRAPS THIS TUB MAY HAVE.

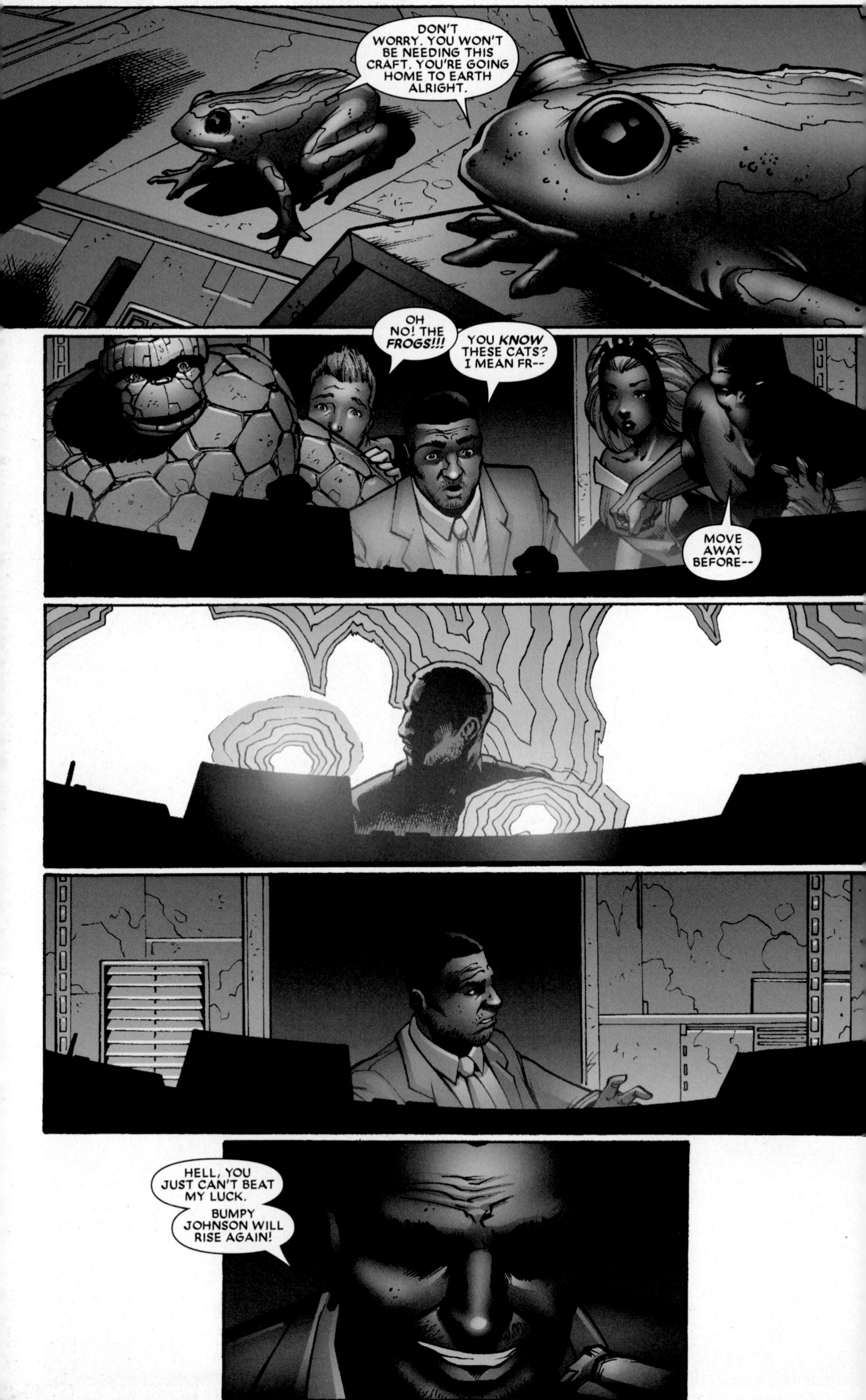
DON'T WORRY. YOU WON'T BE NEEDING THIS CRAFT. YOU'RE GOING HOME TO EARTH ALRIGHT.
OH NO! THE FROGS!!!
YOU KNOW THESE CATS? I MEAN FR--
MOVE AWAY BEFORE--
HELL, YOU JUST CAN'T BEAT MY LUCK.
BUMPY JOHNSON WILL RISE AGAIN!

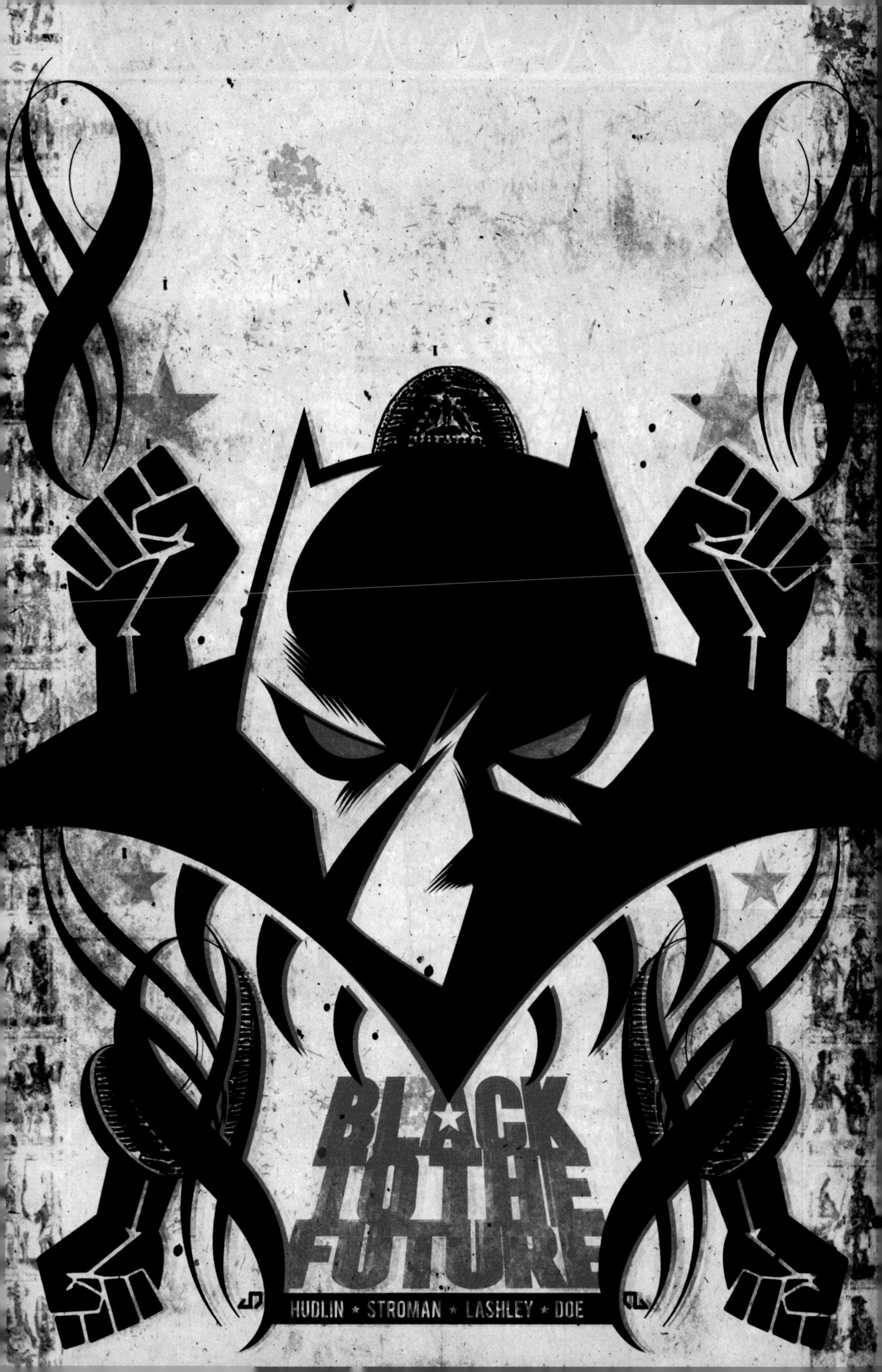
BLACK TO THE FUTURE
HUDLIN ★ STROMAN ★ LASHLEY ★ DOE

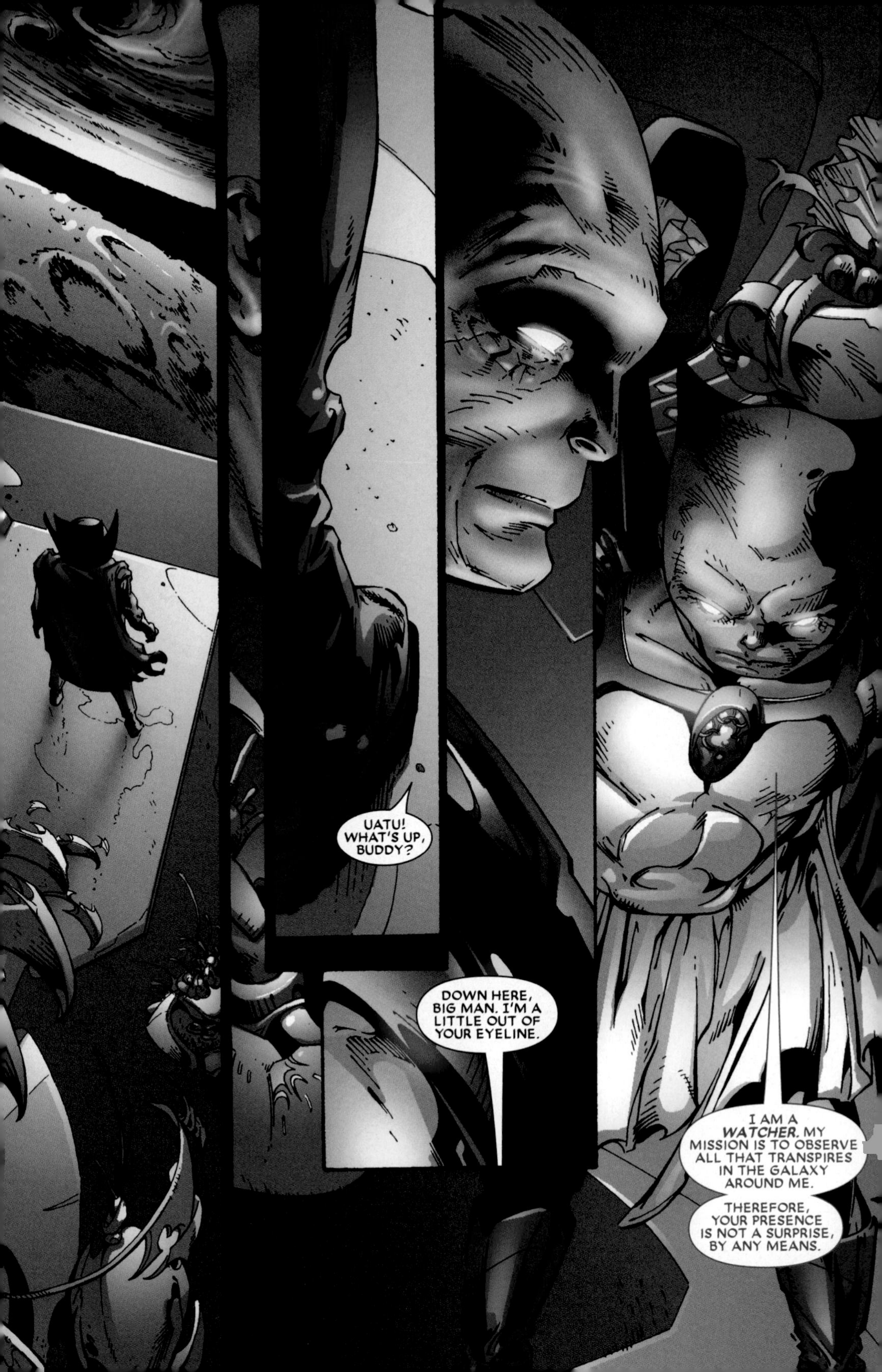
UATU! WHAT'S UP, BUDDY?
DOWN HERE, BIG MAN. I'M A LITTLE OUT OF YOUR EYELINE.
I AM A WATCHER. MY MISSION IS TO OBSERVE ALL THAT TRANSPIRES IN THE GALAXY AROUND ME.
THEREFORE, YOUR PRESENCE IS NOT A SURPRISE, BY ANY MEANS.

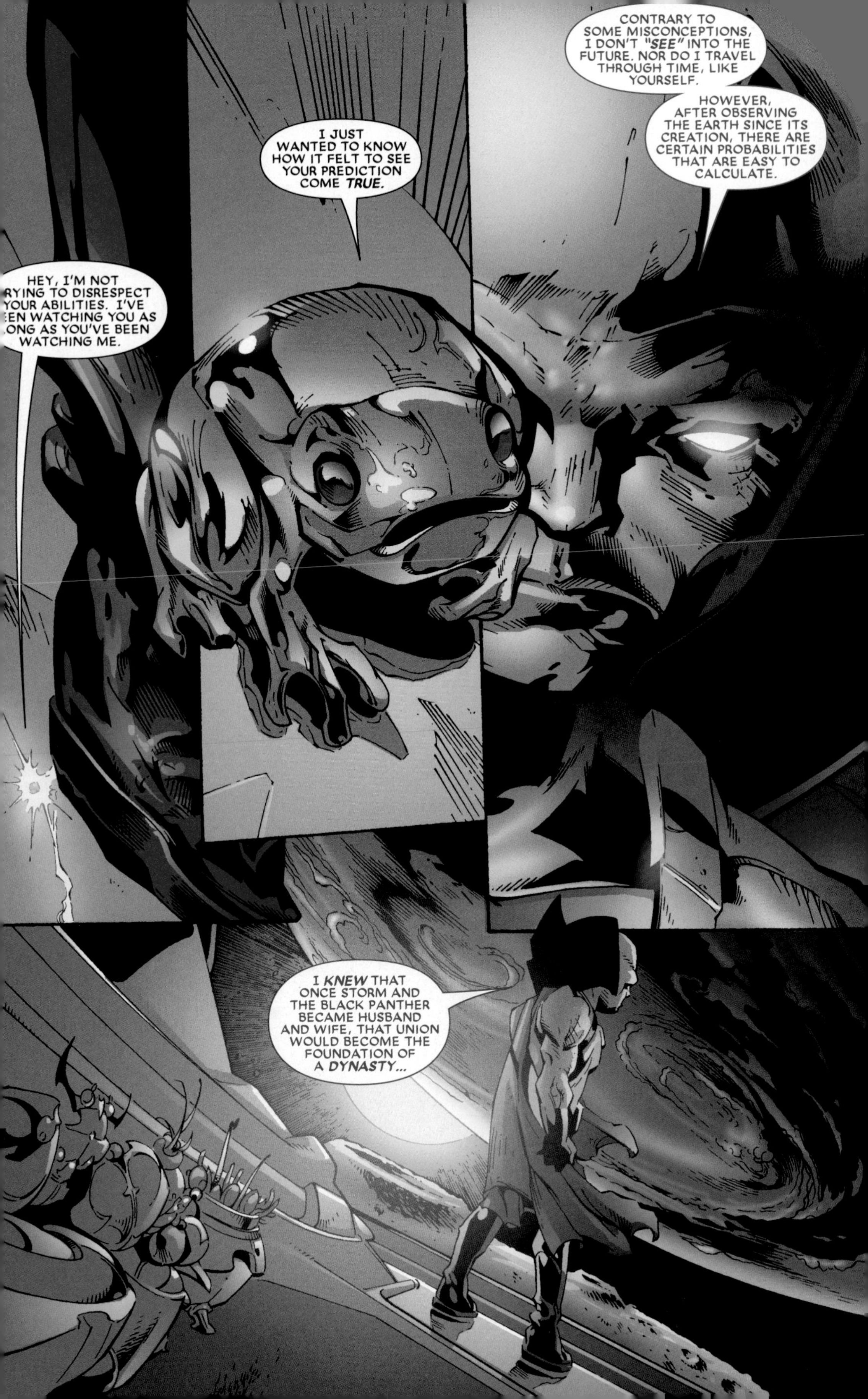
HEY, I'M NOT RYING TO DISRESPECT YOUR ABILITIES. I'VE EEN WATCHING YOU AS ONG AS YOU'VE BEEN WATCHING ME.
I JUST WANTED TO KNOW HOW IT FELT TO SEE YOUR PREDICTION COME TRUE.
CONTRARY TO SOME MISCONCEPTIONS, I DON'T "SEE" INTO THE FUTURE. NOR DO I TRAVEL THROUGH TIME, LIKE YOURSELF.
HOWEVER, AFTER OBSERVING THE EARTH SINCE ITS CREATION, THERE ARE CERTAIN PROBABILITIES THAT ARE EASY TO CALCULATE.
I KNEW THAT ONCE STORM AND THE BLACK PANTHER BECAME HUSBAND AND WIFE, THAT UNION WOULD BECOME THE FOUNDATION OF A DYNASTY...

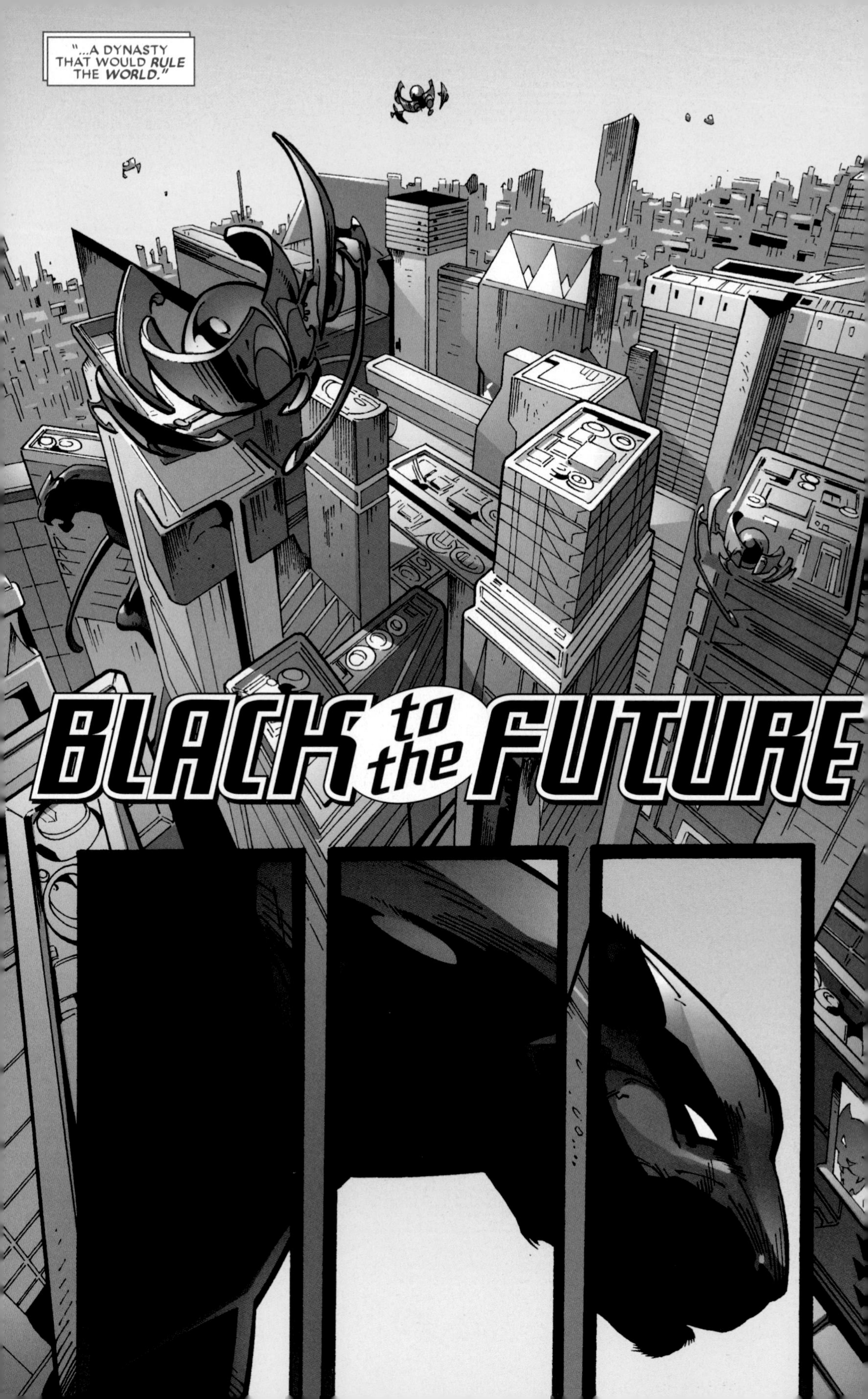
"...A DYNASTY THAT WOULD RULE THE WORLD."
BLACK to the FUTURE

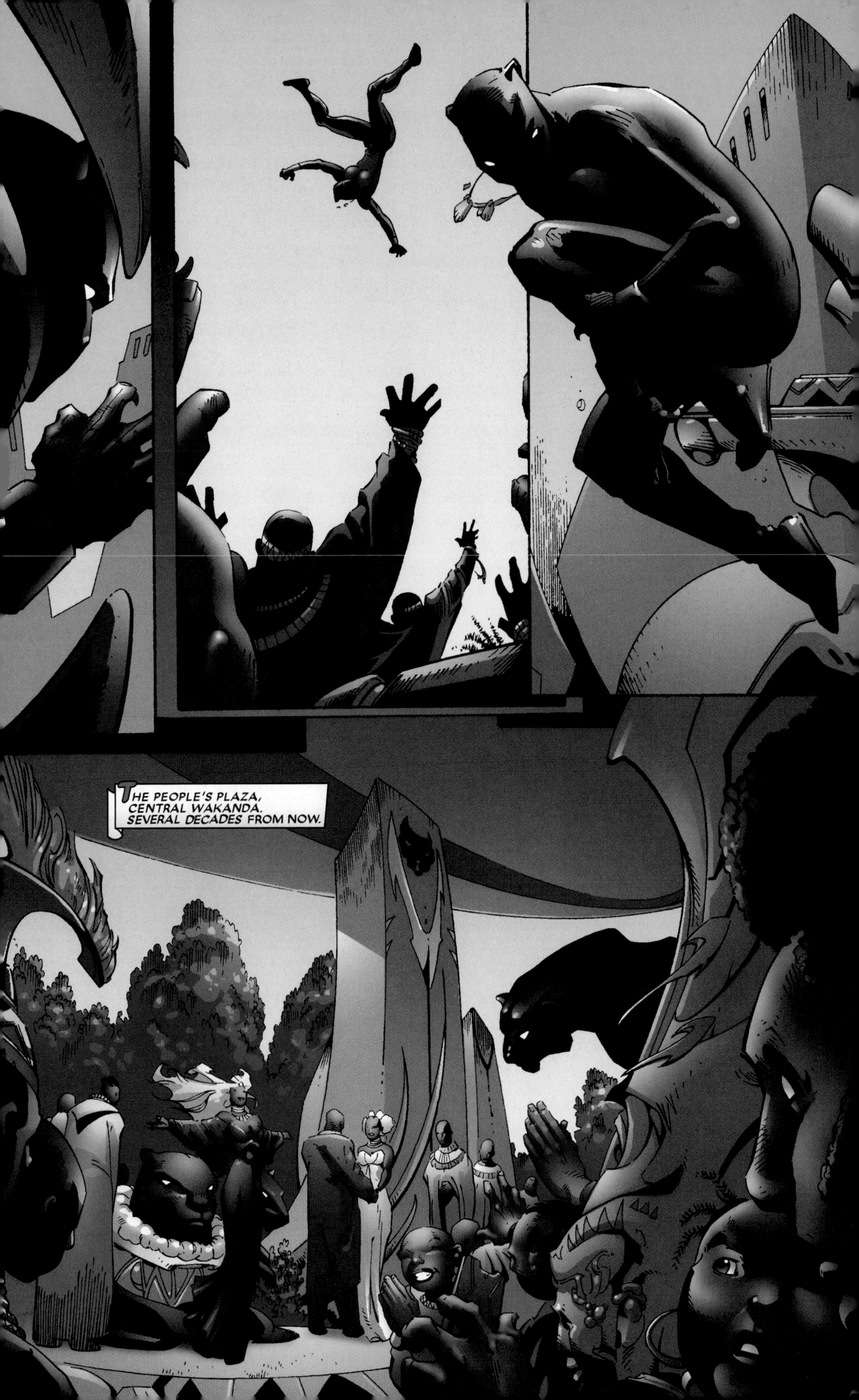
THE PEOPLE'S PLAZA,
CENTRAL WAKANDA.
SEVERAL DECADES FROM NOW.

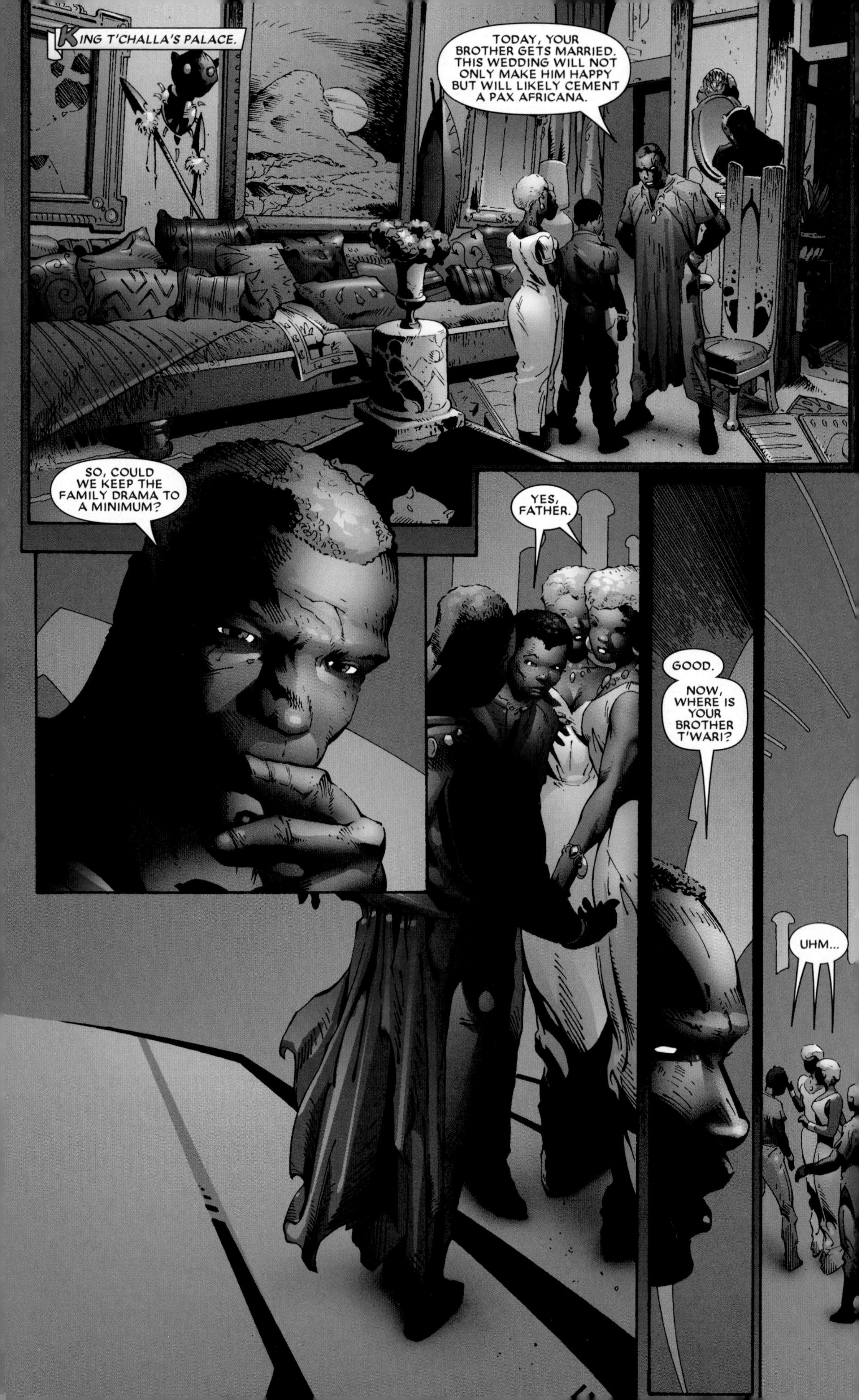
KING T'CHALLA'S PALACE.
TODAY, YOUR BROTHER GETS MARRIED. THIS WEDDING WILL NOT ONLY MAKE HIM HAPPY BUT WILL LIKELY CEMENT A PAX AFRICANA.
SO, COULD WE KEEP THE FAMILY DRAMA TO A MINIMUM?
YES, FATHER.
GOOD.
NOW, WHERE IS YOUR BROTHER T'WARI?
UHM...

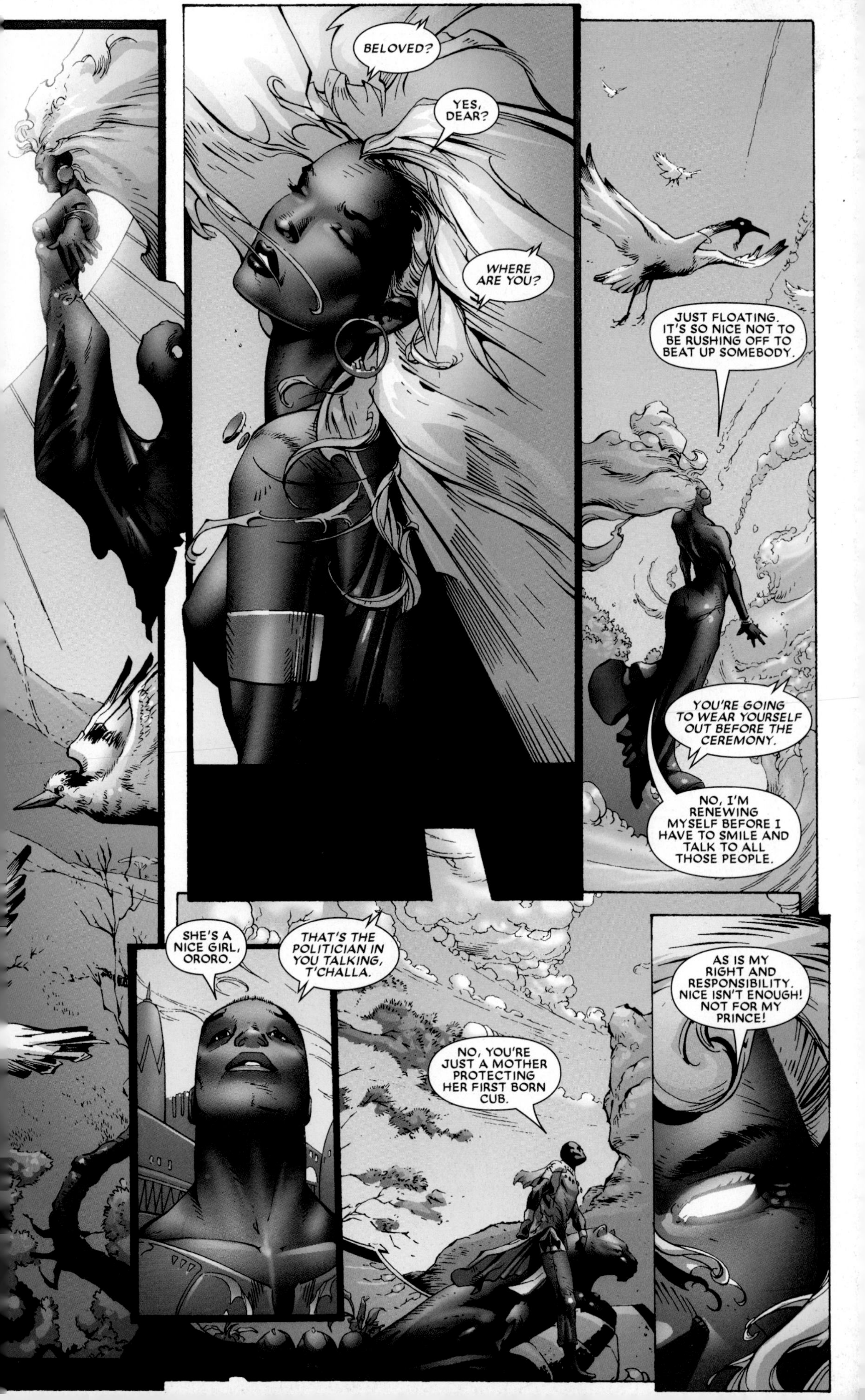
BELOVED?
YES, DEAR?
WHERE ARE YOU?
JUST FLOATING. IT'S SO NICE NOT TO BE RUSHING OFF TO BEAT UP SOMEBODY.
YOU'RE GOING TO WEAR YOURSELF OUT BEFORE THE CEREMONY.
NO, I'M RENEWING MYSELF BEFORE I HAVE TO SMILE AND TALK TO ALL THOSE PEOPLE.
SHE'S A NICE GIRL, ORORO.
THAT'S THE POLITICIAN IN YOU TALKING, T'CHALLA.
NO, YOU'RE JUST A MOTHER PROTECTING HER FIRST BORN CUB.
AS IS MY RIGHT AND RESPONSIBILITY. NICE ISN'T ENOUGH! NOT FOR MY PRINCE!

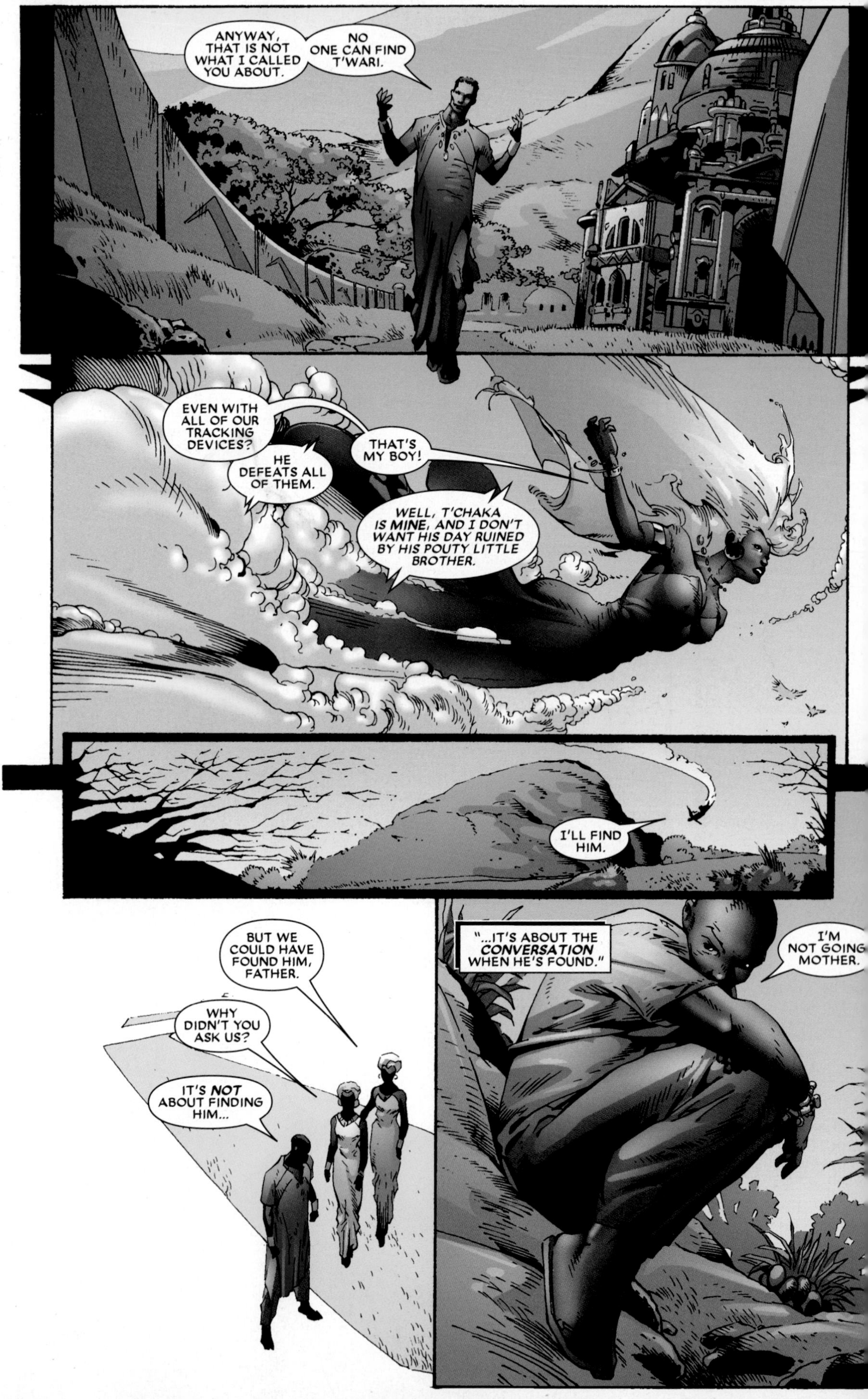
ANYWAY, THAT IS NOT WHAT I CALLED YOU ABOUT.
NO ONE CAN FIND T'WARI.
EVEN WITH ALL OF OUR TRACKING DEVICES?
HE DEFEATS ALL OF THEM.
THAT'S MY BOY!
WELL, T'CHAKA IS MINE, AND I DON'T WANT HIS DAY RUINED BY HIS POUTY LITTLE BROTHER.
I'LL FIND HIM.
BUT WE COULD HAVE FOUND HIM, FATHER.
WHY DIDN'T YOU ASK US?
IT'S NOT ABOUT FINDING HIM...
"...IT'S ABOUT THE CONVERSATION WHEN HE'S FOUND."
I'M NOT GOING MOTHER.

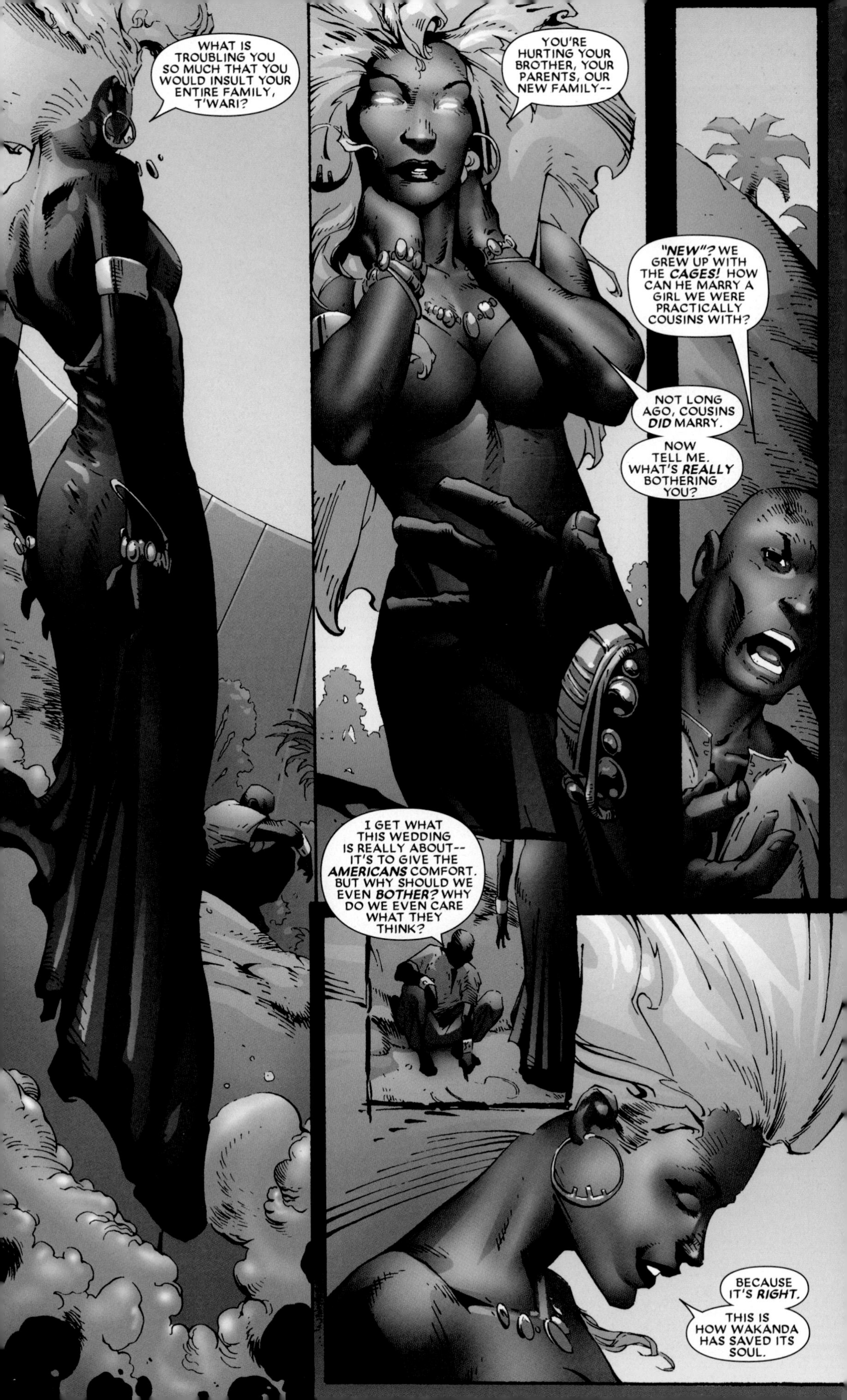
WHAT IS TROUBLING YOU SO MUCH THAT YOU WOULD INSULT YOUR ENTIRE FAMILY, T'WARI?
YOU'RE HURTING YOUR BROTHER, YOUR PARENTS, OUR NEW FAMILY--
"NEW"? WE GREW UP WITH THE CAGES! HOW CAN HE MARRY A GIRL WE WERE PRACTICALLY COUSINS WITH?
NOT LONG AGO, COUSINS DID MARRY.
NOW TELL ME. WHAT'S REALLY BOTHERING YOU?
I GET WHAT THIS WEDDING IS REALLY ABOUT-- IT'S TO GIVE THE AMERICANS COMFORT. BUT WHY SHOULD WE EVEN BOTHER? WHY DO WE EVEN CARE WHAT THEY THINK?
BECAUSE IT'S RIGHT.
THIS IS HOW WAKANDA HAS SAVED ITS SOUL.

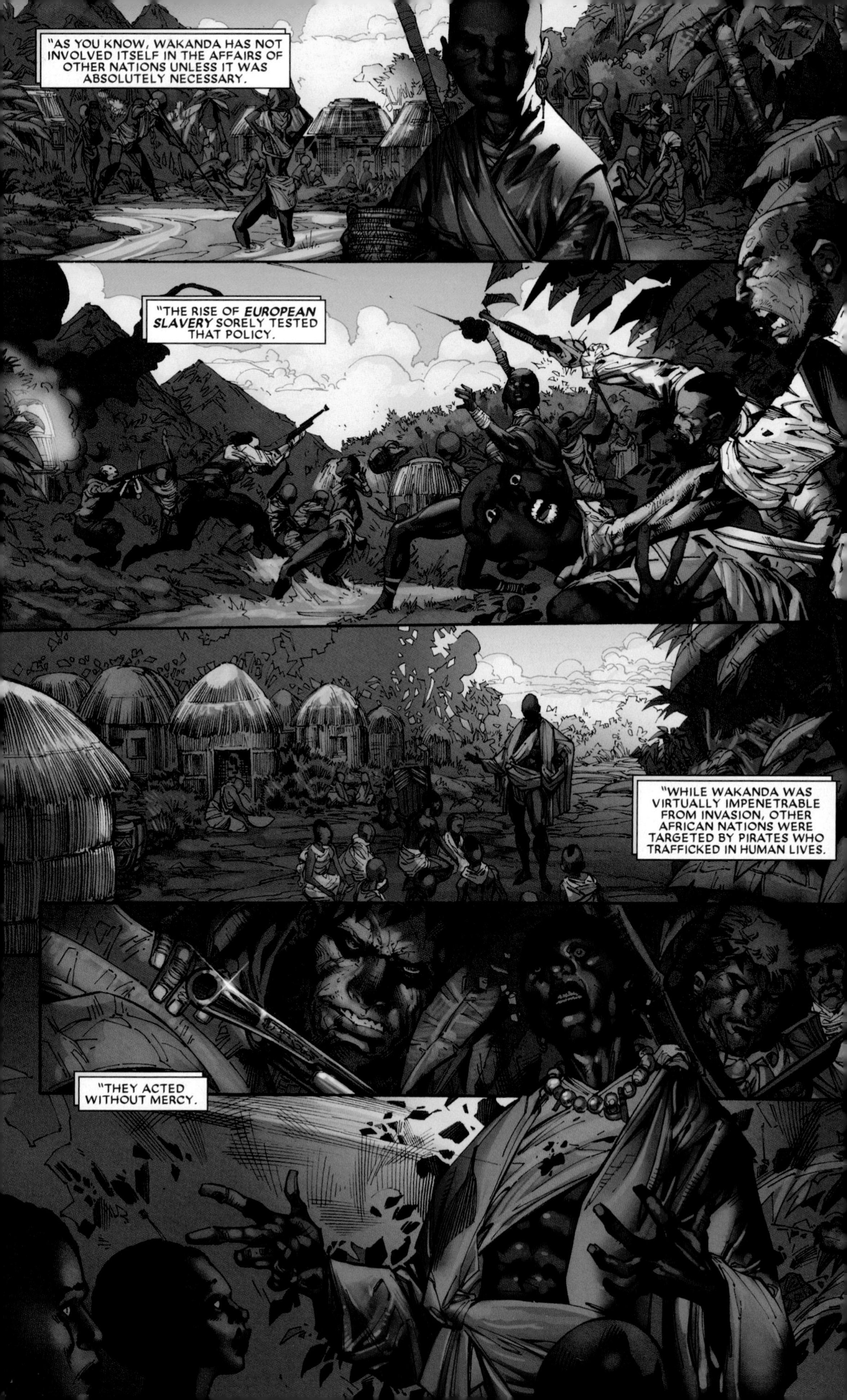
"AS YOU KNOW, WAKANDA HAS NOT INVOLVED ITSELF IN THE AFFAIRS OF OTHER NATIONS UNLESS IT WAS ABSOLUTELY NECESSARY.
"THE RISE OF EUROPEAN SLAVERY SORELY TESTED THAT POLICY.
"WHILE WAKANDA WAS VIRTUALLY IMPENETRABLE FROM INVASION, OTHER AFRICAN NATIONS WERE TARGETED BY PIRATES WHO TRAFFICKED IN HUMAN LIVES.
"THEY ACTED WITHOUT MERCY.

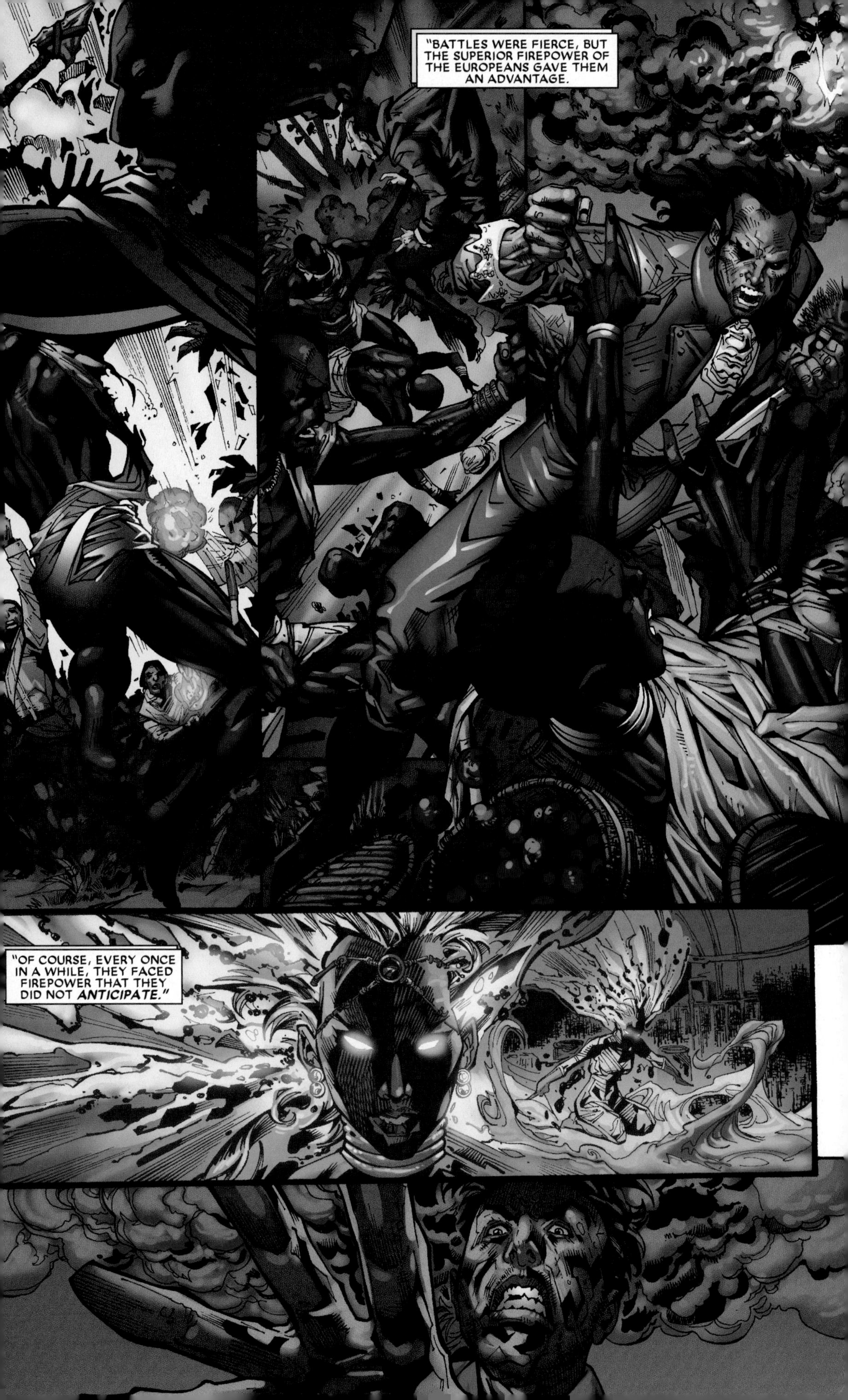
"BATTLES WERE FIERCE, BUT THE SUPERIOR FIREPOWER OF THE EUROPEANS GAVE THEM AN ADVANTAGE.
"OF COURSE, EVERY ONCE IN A WHILE, THEY FACED FIREPOWER THAT THEY DID NOT *ANTICIPATE*."

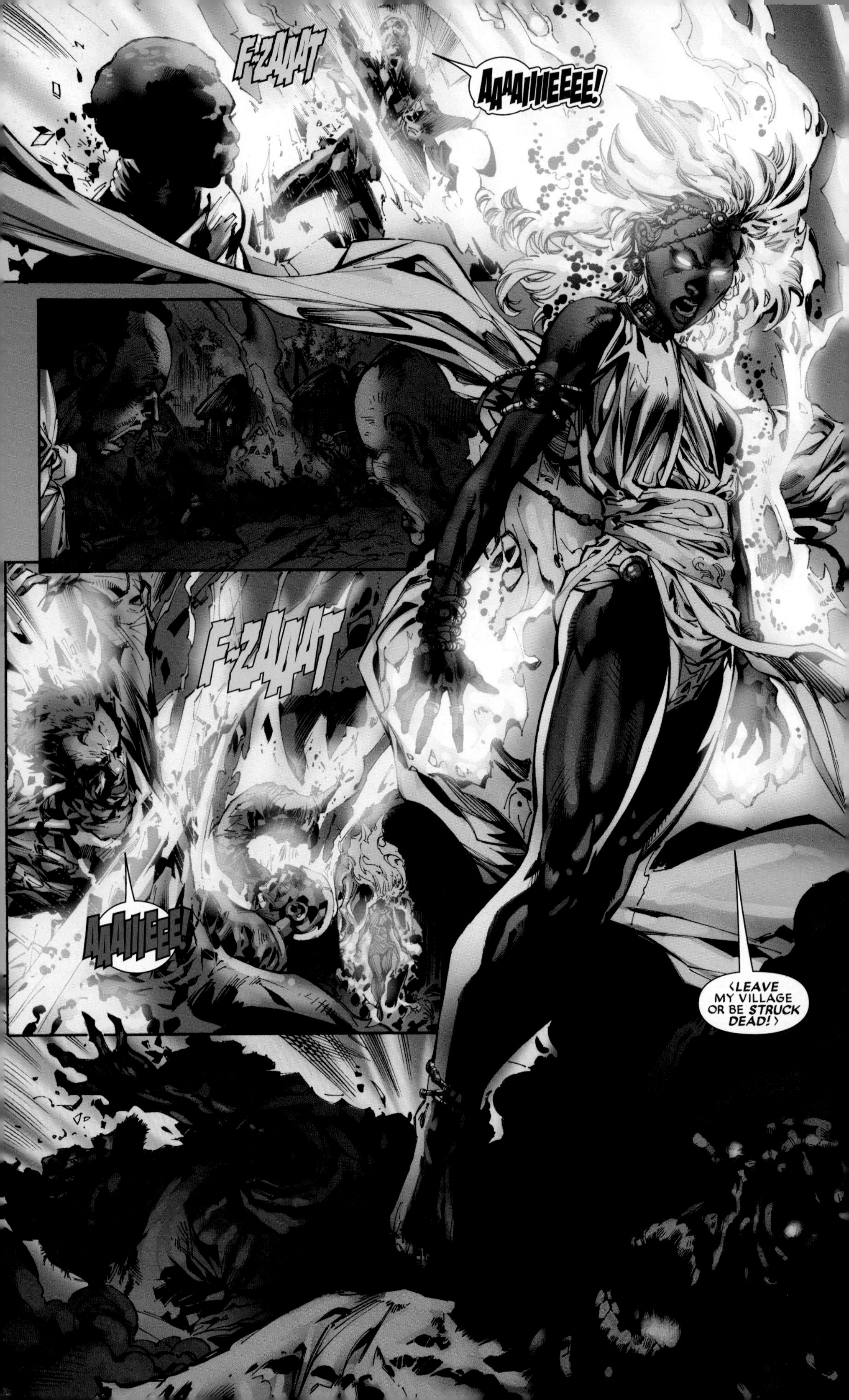
F-ZAAAT
AAAAIIIIEEEE!
F-ZAAAT
AAAIIIEEE!
‹LEAVE MY VILLAGE OR BE *STRUCK DEAD!*›

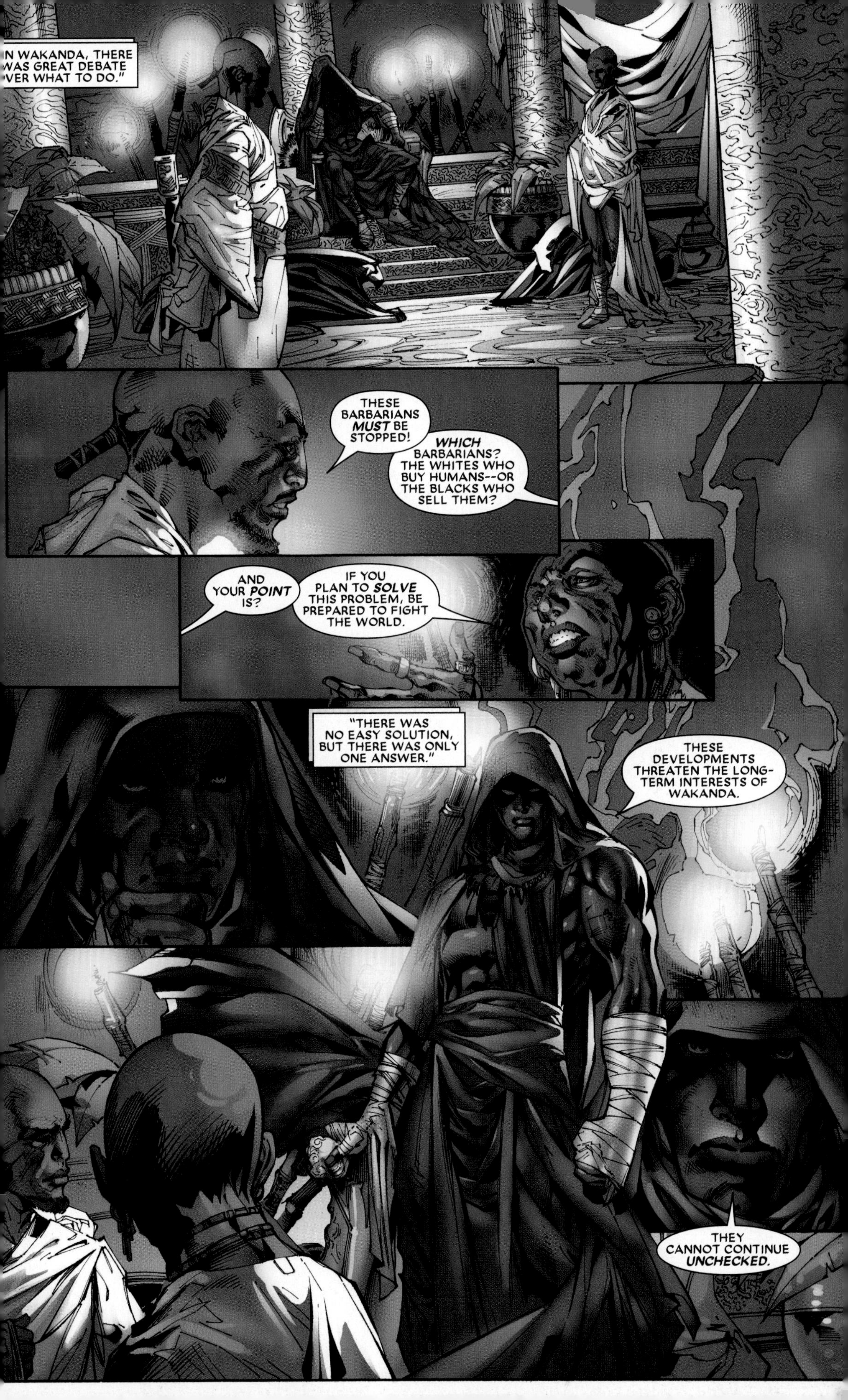

"IN WAKANDA, THERE WAS GREAT DEBATE OVER WHAT TO DO."
THESE BARBARIANS *MUST* BE STOPPED!
WHICH BARBARIANS? THE WHITES WHO BUY HUMANS--OR THE BLACKS WHO SELL THEM?
AND YOUR *POINT* IS?
IF YOU PLAN TO *SOLVE* THIS PROBLEM, BE PREPARED TO FIGHT THE WORLD.
"THERE WAS NO EASY SOLUTION, BUT THERE WAS ONLY ONE ANSWER."
THESE DEVELOPMENTS THREATEN THE LONG-TERM INTERESTS OF WAKANDA.
THEY CANNOT CONTINUE *UNCHECKED.*

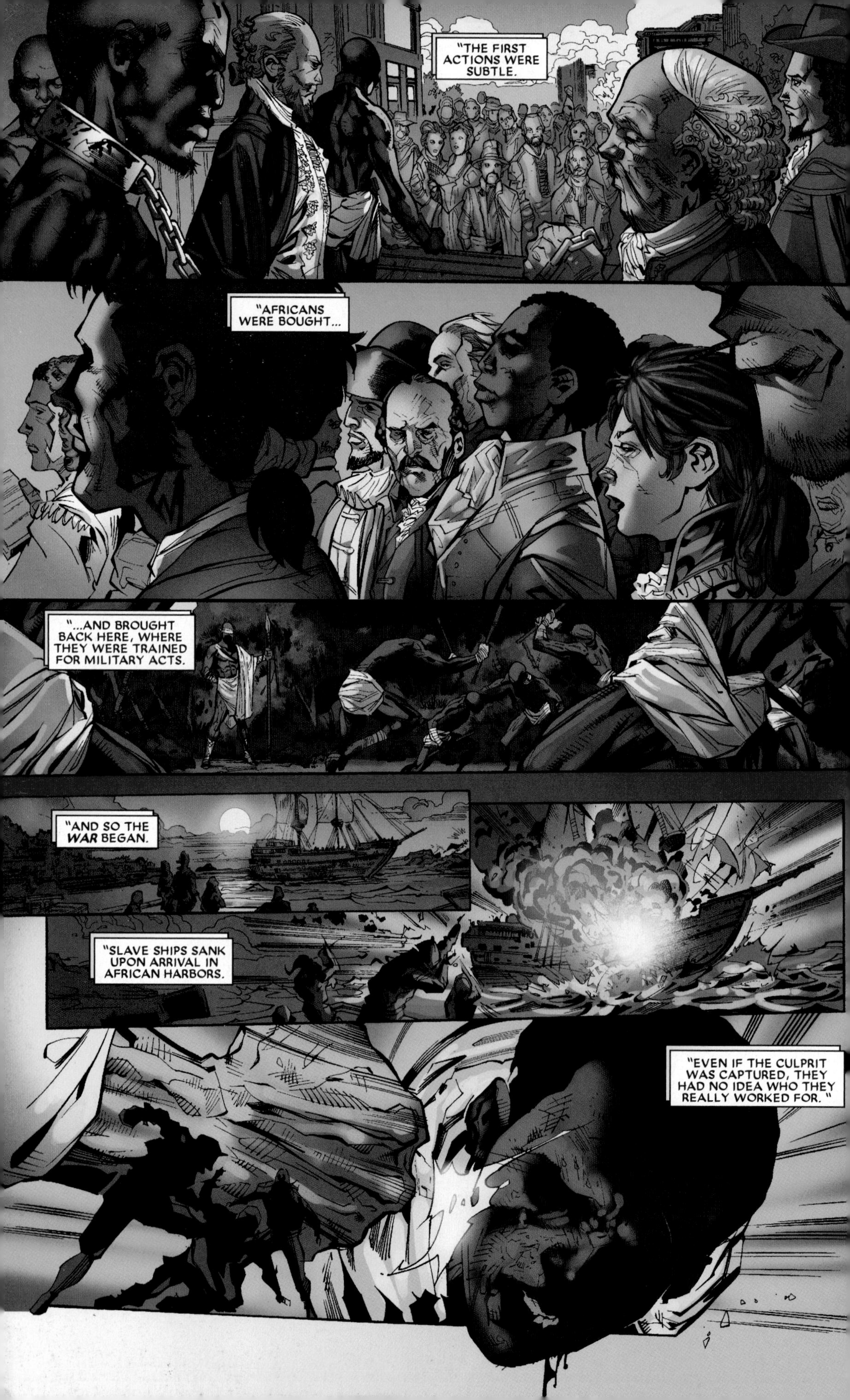
"THE FIRST ACTIONS WERE SUBTLE.
"AFRICANS WERE BOUGHT...
"...AND BROUGHT BACK HERE, WHERE THEY WERE TRAINED FOR MILITARY ACTS.
"AND SO THE *WAR* BEGAN.
"SLAVE SHIPS SANK UPON ARRIVAL IN AFRICAN HARBORS.
"EVEN IF THE CULPRIT WAS CAPTURED, THEY HAD NO IDEA WHO THEY REALLY WORKED FOR."

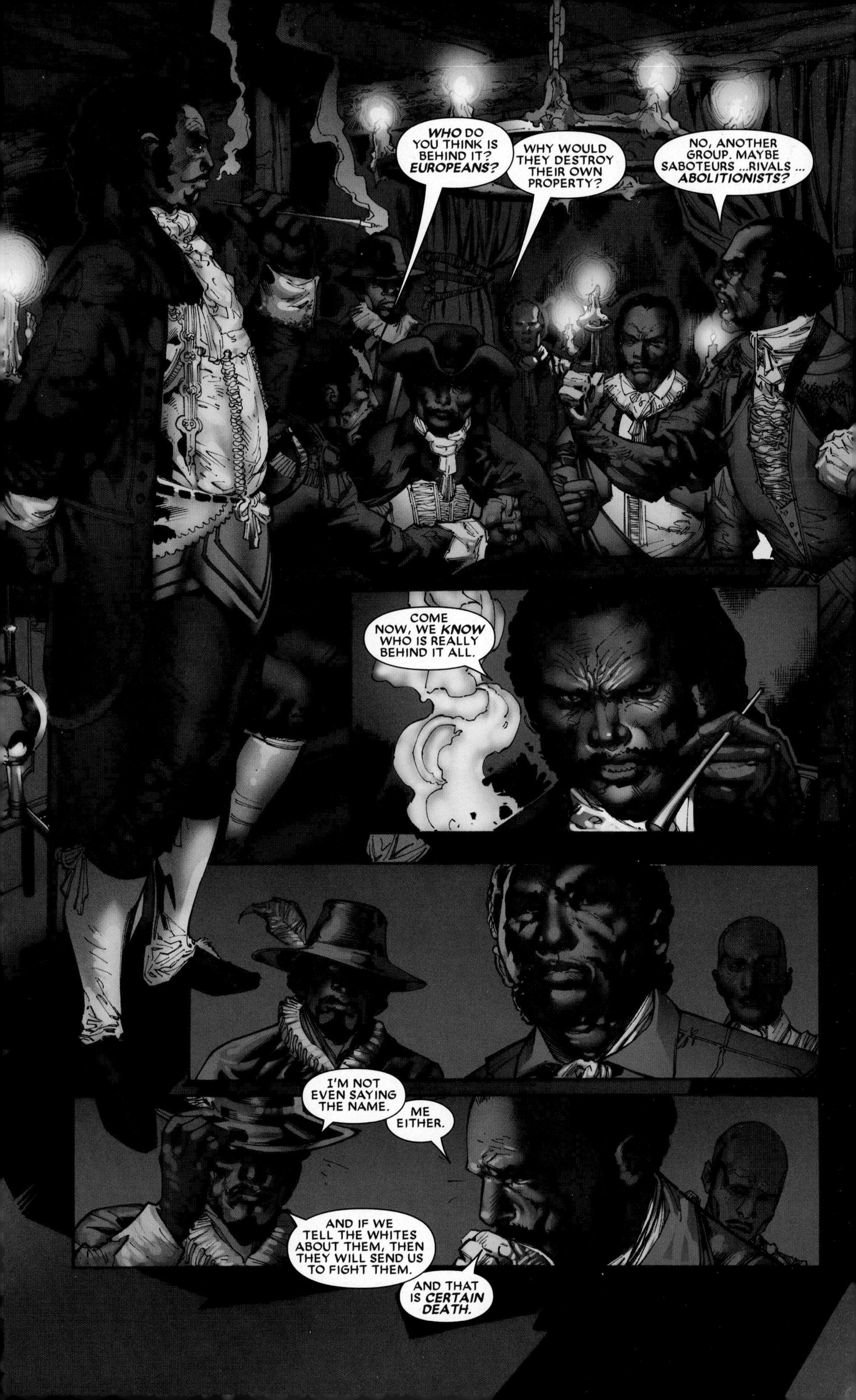

WHO DO YOU THINK IS BEHIND IT? EUROPEANS?
WHY WOULD THEY DESTROY THEIR OWN PROPERTY?
NO, ANOTHER GROUP. MAYBE SABOTEURS ...RIVALS ... ABOLITIONISTS?
COME NOW, WE KNOW WHO IS REALLY BEHIND IT ALL.
I'M NOT EVEN SAYING THE NAME.
ME EITHER.
AND IF WE TELL THE WHITES ABOUT THEM, THEN THEY WILL SEND US TO FIGHT THEM.
AND THAT IS CERTAIN DEATH.

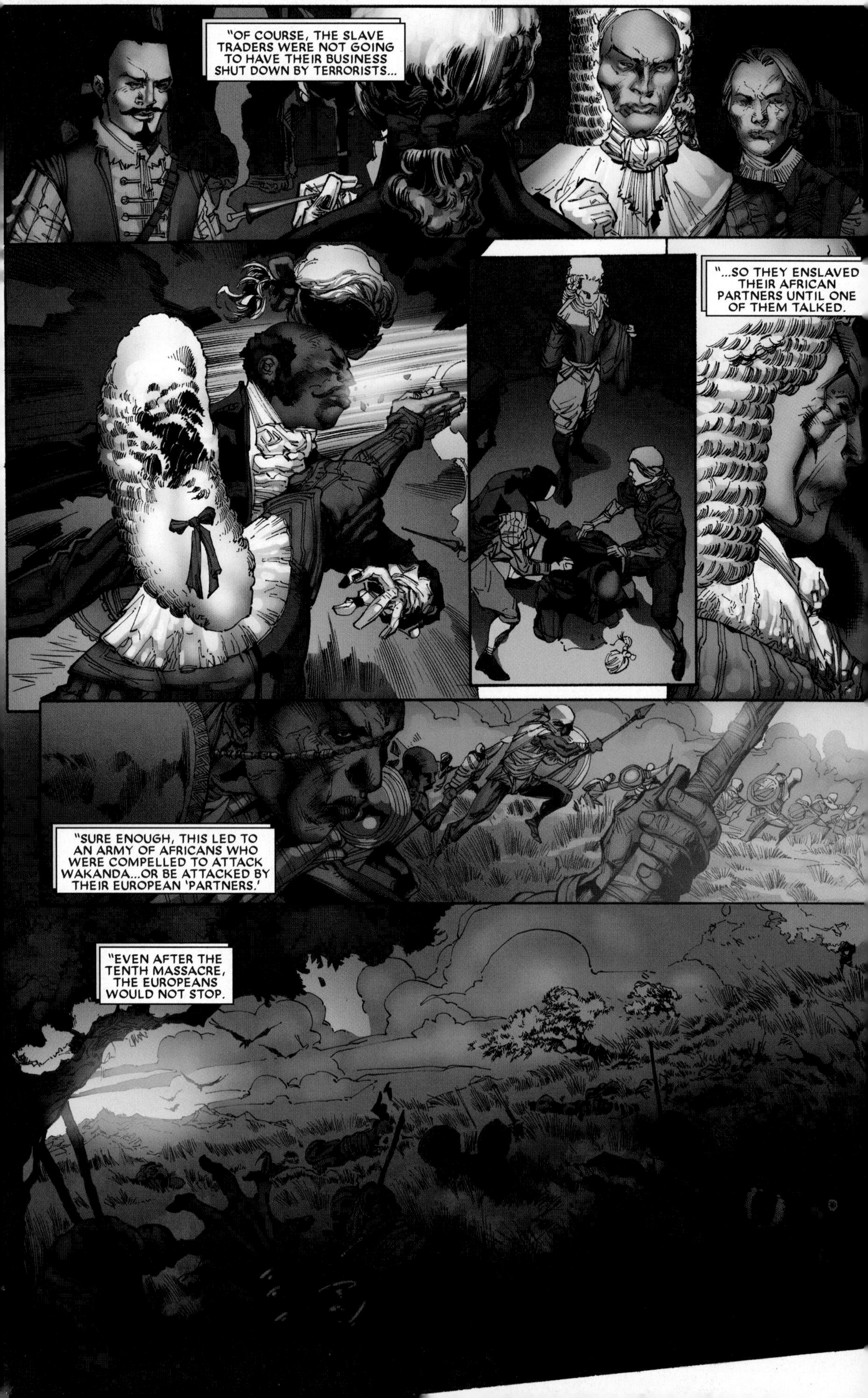
"OF COURSE, THE SLAVE TRADERS WERE NOT GOING TO HAVE THEIR BUSINESS SHUT DOWN BY TERRORISTS...
"...SO THEY ENSLAVED THEIR AFRICAN PARTNERS UNTIL ONE OF THEM TALKED.
"SURE ENOUGH, THIS LED TO AN ARMY OF AFRICANS WHO WERE COMPELLED TO ATTACK WAKANDA...OR BE ATTACKED BY THEIR EUROPEAN 'PARTNERS.'
"EVEN AFTER THE TENTH MASSACRE, THE EUROPEANS WOULD NOT STOP.

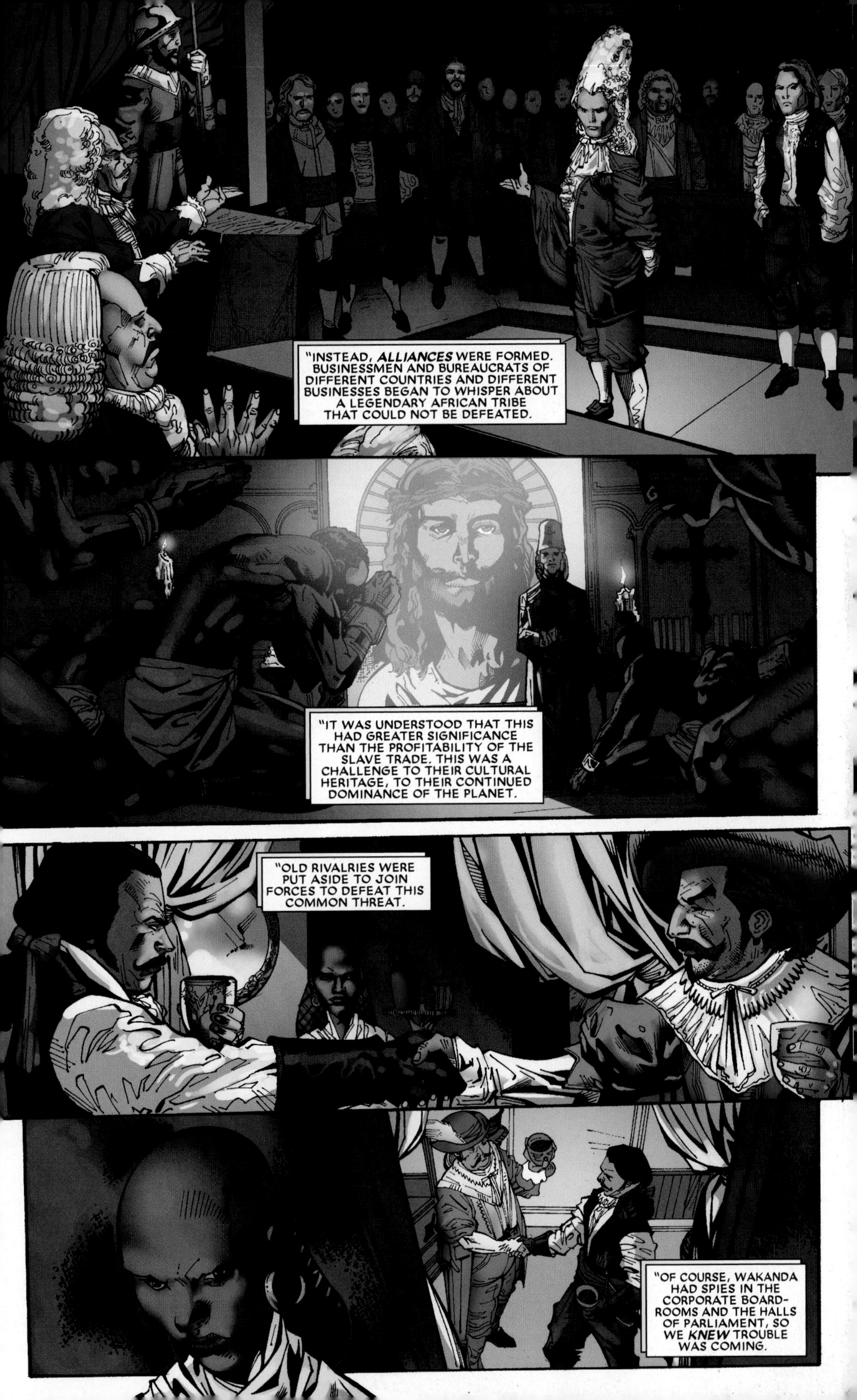

"INSTEAD, ALLIANCES WERE FORMED. BUSINESSMEN AND BUREAUCRATS OF DIFFERENT COUNTRIES AND DIFFERENT BUSINESSES BEGAN TO WHISPER ABOUT A LEGENDARY AFRICAN TRIBE THAT COULD NOT BE DEFEATED.
"IT WAS UNDERSTOOD THAT THIS HAD GREATER SIGNIFICANCE THAN THE PROFITABILITY OF THE SLAVE TRADE. THIS WAS A CHALLENGE TO THEIR CULTURAL HERITAGE, TO THEIR CONTINUED DOMINANCE OF THE PLANET.
"OLD RIVALRIES WERE PUT ASIDE TO JOIN FORCES TO DEFEAT THIS COMMON THREAT.
"OF COURSE, WAKANDA HAD SPIES IN THE CORPORATE BOARD-ROOMS AND THE HALLS OF PARLIAMENT, SO WE KNEW TROUBLE WAS COMING.

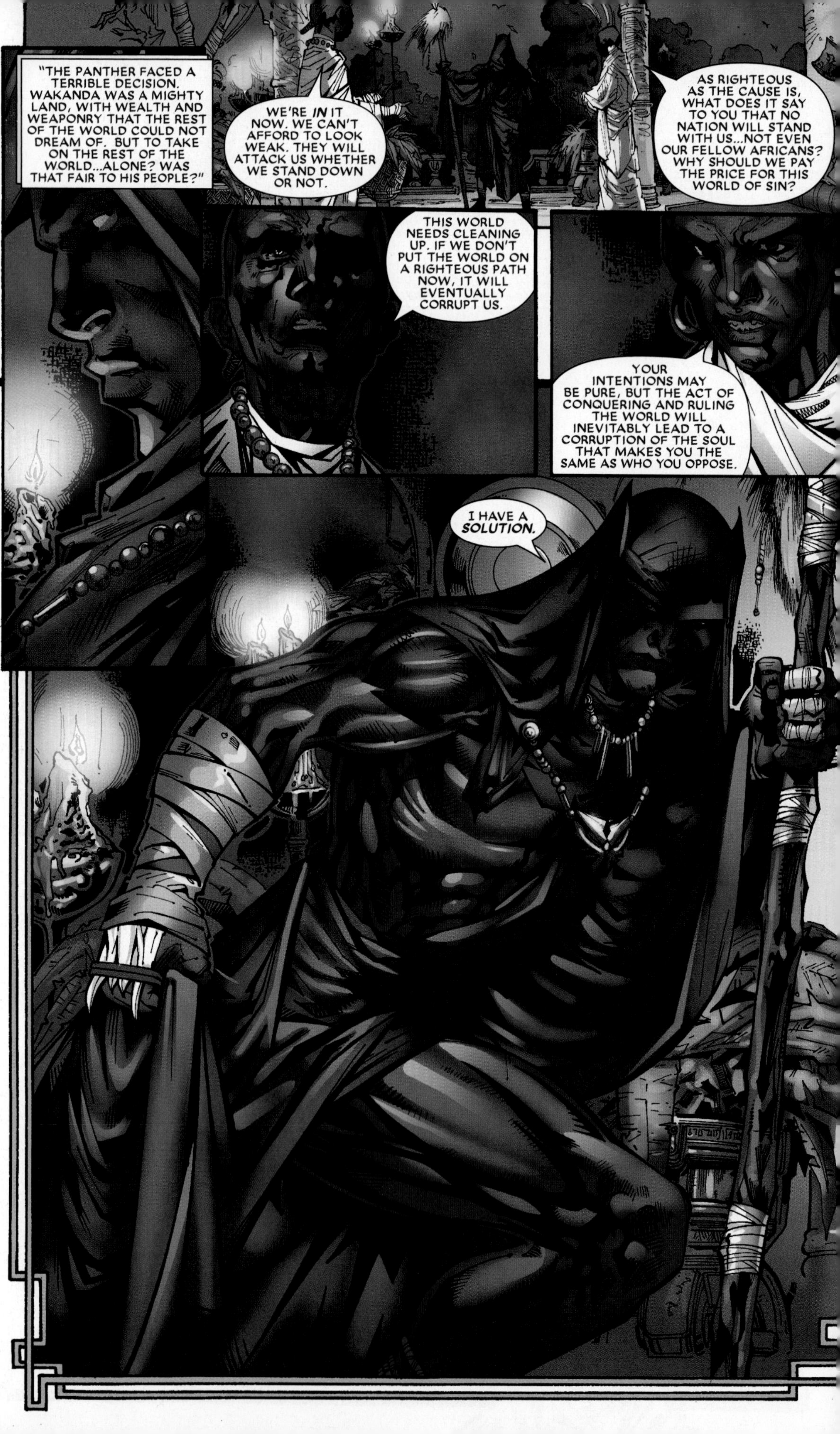
"THE PANTHER FACED A TERRIBLE DECISION. WAKANDA WAS A MIGHTY LAND, WITH WEALTH AND WEAPONRY THAT THE REST OF THE WORLD COULD NOT DREAM OF. BUT TO TAKE ON THE REST OF THE WORLD...ALONE? WAS THAT FAIR TO HIS PEOPLE?"
WE'RE *IN* IT NOW. WE CAN'T AFFORD TO LOOK WEAK. THEY WILL ATTACK US WHETHER WE STAND DOWN OR NOT.
AS RIGHTEOUS AS THE CAUSE IS, WHAT DOES IT SAY TO YOU THAT NO NATION WILL STAND WITH US...NOT EVEN OUR FELLOW AFRICANS? WHY SHOULD WE PAY THE PRICE FOR THIS WORLD OF SIN?
THIS WORLD NEEDS CLEANING UP. IF WE DON'T PUT THE WORLD ON A RIGHTEOUS PATH NOW, IT WILL EVENTUALLY CORRUPT US.
YOUR INTENTIONS MAY BE PURE, BUT THE ACT OF CONQUERING AND RULING THE WORLD WILL INEVITABLY LEAD TO A CORRUPTION OF THE SOUL THAT MAKES YOU THE SAME AS WHO YOU OPPOSE.
I HAVE A ***SOLUTION.***

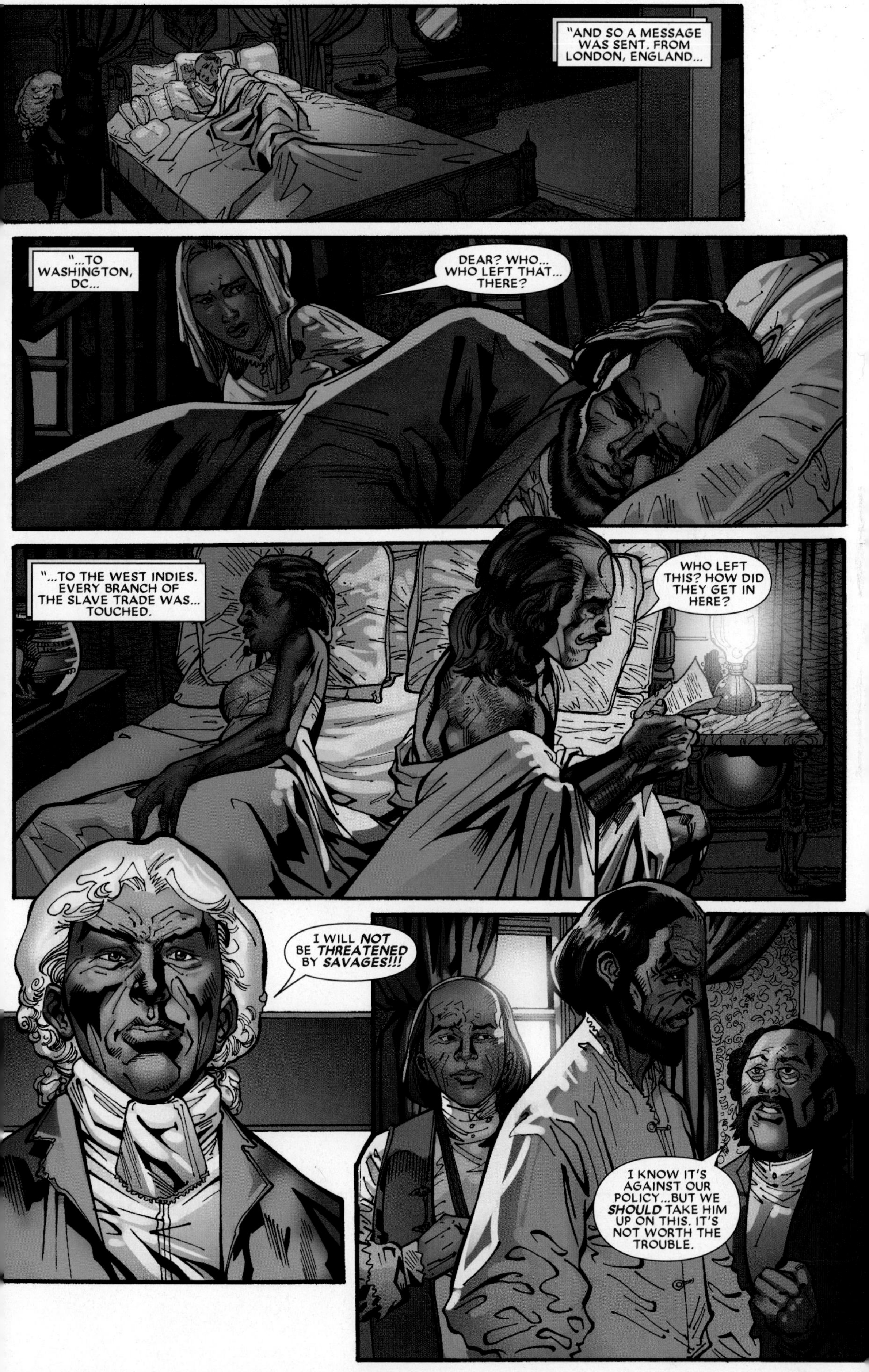
"AND SO A MESSAGE WAS SENT. FROM LONDON, ENGLAND...
"...TO WASHINGTON, DC...
DEAR? WHO... WHO LEFT THAT... THERE?
"...TO THE WEST INDIES. EVERY BRANCH OF THE SLAVE TRADE WAS... TOUCHED.
WHO LEFT THIS? HOW DID THEY GET IN HERE?
I WILL NOT BE THREATENED BY SAVAGES!!!
I KNOW IT'S AGAINST OUR POLICY...BUT WE SHOULD TAKE HIM UP ON THIS. IT'S NOT WORTH THE TROUBLE.

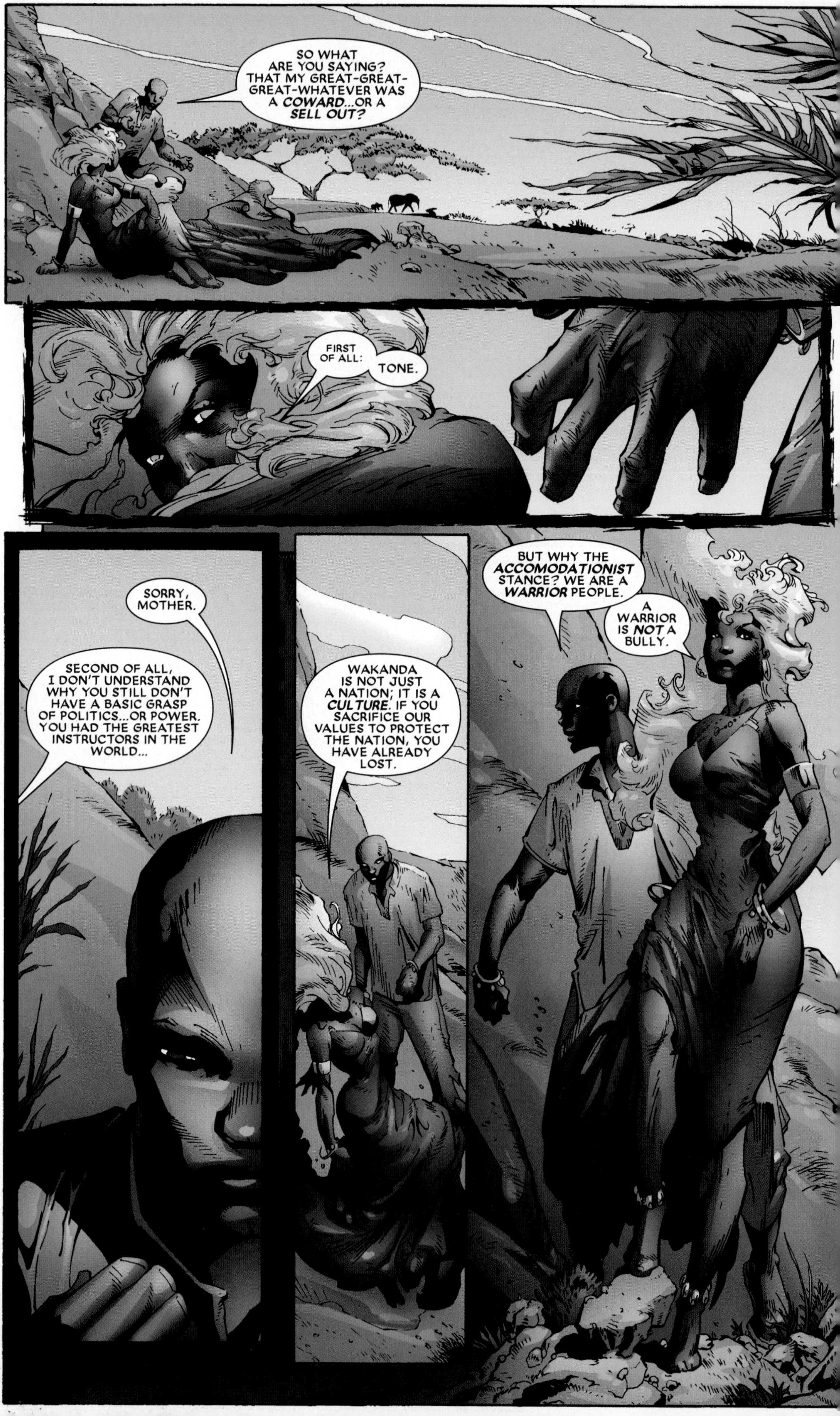
SO WHAT ARE YOU SAYING? THAT MY GREAT-GREAT-GREAT-WHATEVER WAS A *COWARD*...OR A *SELL OUT?*
FIRST OF ALL:
TONE.
SORRY, MOTHER.
SECOND OF ALL, I DON'T UNDERSTAND WHY YOU STILL DON'T HAVE A BASIC GRASP OF POLITICS...OR POWER. YOU HAD THE GREATEST INSTRUCTORS IN THE WORLD...
WAKANDA IS NOT JUST A NATION; IT IS A *CULTURE*. IF YOU SACRIFICE OUR VALUES TO PROTECT THE NATION, YOU HAVE ALREADY LOST.
BUT WHY THE *ACCOMODATIONIST* STANCE? WE ARE A *WARRIOR* PEOPLE.
A WARRIOR IS *NOT* A BULLY.

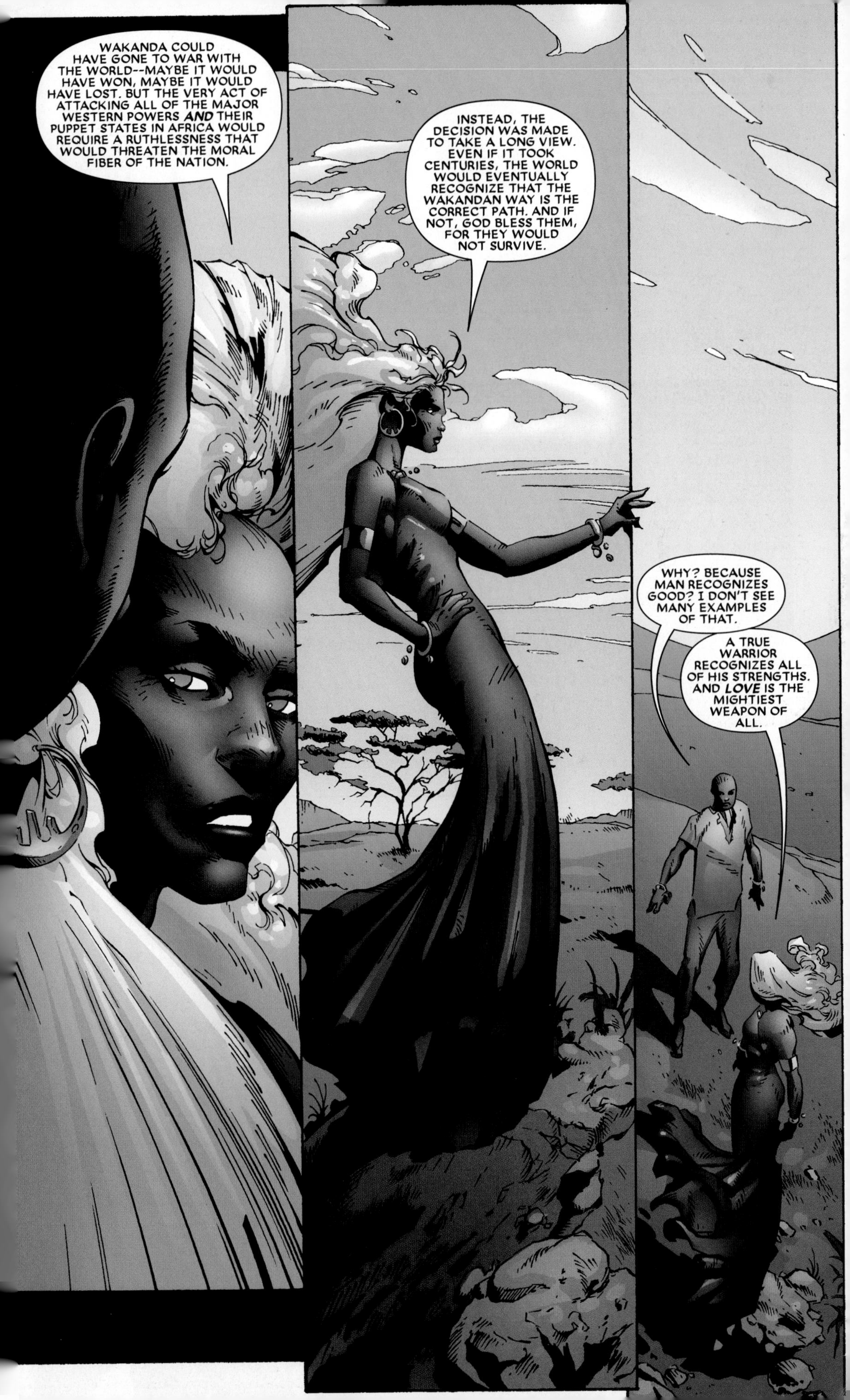
WAKANDA COULD HAVE GONE TO WAR WITH THE WORLD--MAYBE IT WOULD HAVE WON, MAYBE IT WOULD HAVE LOST. BUT THE VERY ACT OF ATTACKING ALL OF THE MAJOR WESTERN POWERS ***AND*** THEIR PUPPET STATES IN AFRICA WOULD REQUIRE A RUTHLESSNESS THAT WOULD THREATEN THE MORAL FIBER OF THE NATION.
INSTEAD, THE DECISION WAS MADE TO TAKE A LONG VIEW. EVEN IF IT TOOK CENTURIES, THE WORLD WOULD EVENTUALLY RECOGNIZE THAT THE WAKANDAN WAY IS THE CORRECT PATH. AND IF NOT, GOD BLESS THEM, FOR THEY WOULD NOT SURVIVE.
WHY? BECAUSE MAN RECOGNIZES GOOD? I DON'T SEE MANY EXAMPLES OF THAT.
A TRUE WARRIOR RECOGNIZES ALL OF HIS STRENGTHS. AND ***LOVE*** IS THE MIGHTIEST WEAPON OF ALL.

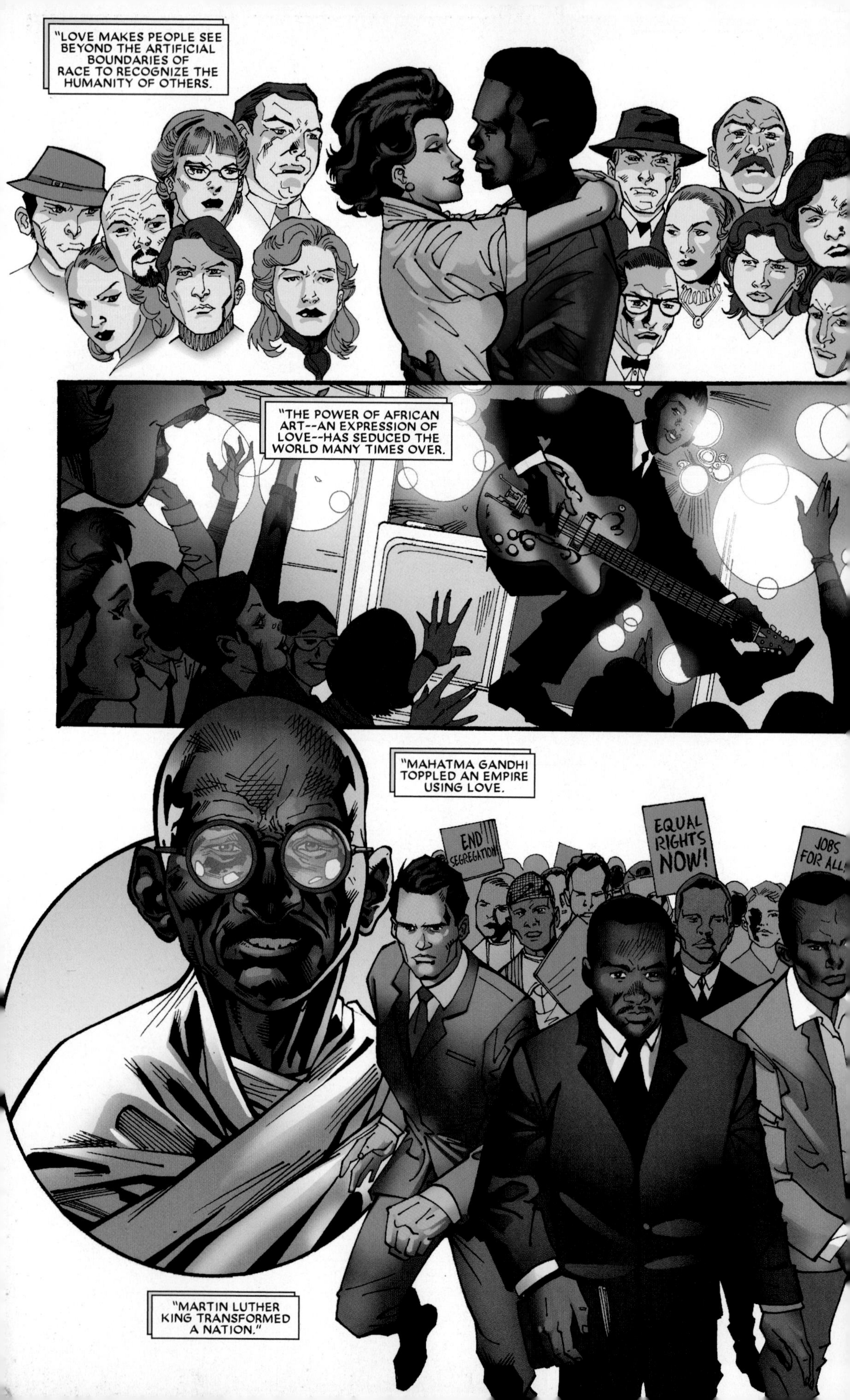
"LOVE MAKES PEOPLE SEE BEYOND THE ARTIFICIAL BOUNDARIES OF RACE TO RECOGNIZE THE HUMANITY OF OTHERS.
"THE POWER OF AFRICAN ART--AN EXPRESSION OF LOVE--HAS SEDUCED THE WORLD MANY TIMES OVER.
"MAHATMA GANDHI TOPPLED AN EMPIRE USING LOVE.
END SEGREGATION
EQUAL RIGHTS NOW!
JOBS FOR ALL
"MARTIN LUTHER KING TRANSFORMED A NATION."

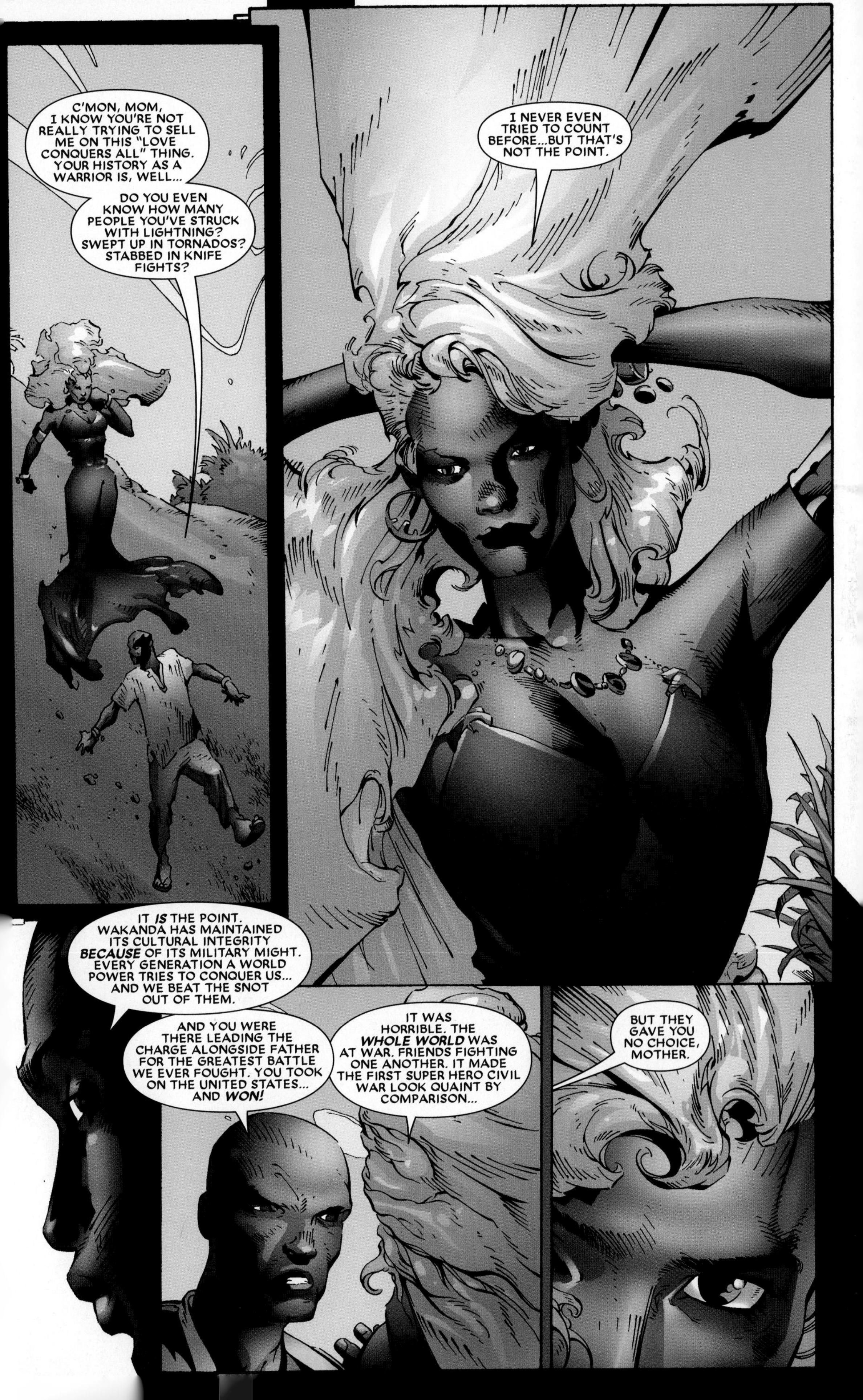
C'MON, MOM, I KNOW YOU'RE NOT REALLY TRYING TO SELL ME ON THIS "LOVE CONQUERS ALL" THING. YOUR HISTORY AS A WARRIOR IS, WELL...
DO YOU EVEN KNOW HOW MANY PEOPLE YOU'VE STRUCK WITH LIGHTNING? SWEPT UP IN TORNADOS? STABBED IN KNIFE FIGHTS?
I NEVER EVEN TRIED TO COUNT BEFORE...BUT THAT'S NOT THE POINT.
IT *IS* THE POINT. WAKANDA HAS MAINTAINED ITS CULTURAL INTEGRITY *BECAUSE* OF ITS MILITARY MIGHT. EVERY GENERATION A WORLD POWER TRIES TO CONQUER US... AND WE BEAT THE SNOT OUT OF THEM.
AND YOU WERE THERE LEADING THE CHARGE ALONGSIDE FATHER FOR THE GREATEST BATTLE WE EVER FOUGHT. YOU TOOK ON THE UNITED STATES... AND *WON!*
IT WAS HORRIBLE. THE *WHOLE WORLD* WAS AT WAR. FRIENDS FIGHTING ONE ANOTHER. IT MADE THE FIRST SUPER HERO CIVIL WAR LOOK QUAINT BY COMPARISON...
BUT THEY GAVE YOU NO CHOICE, MOTHER.

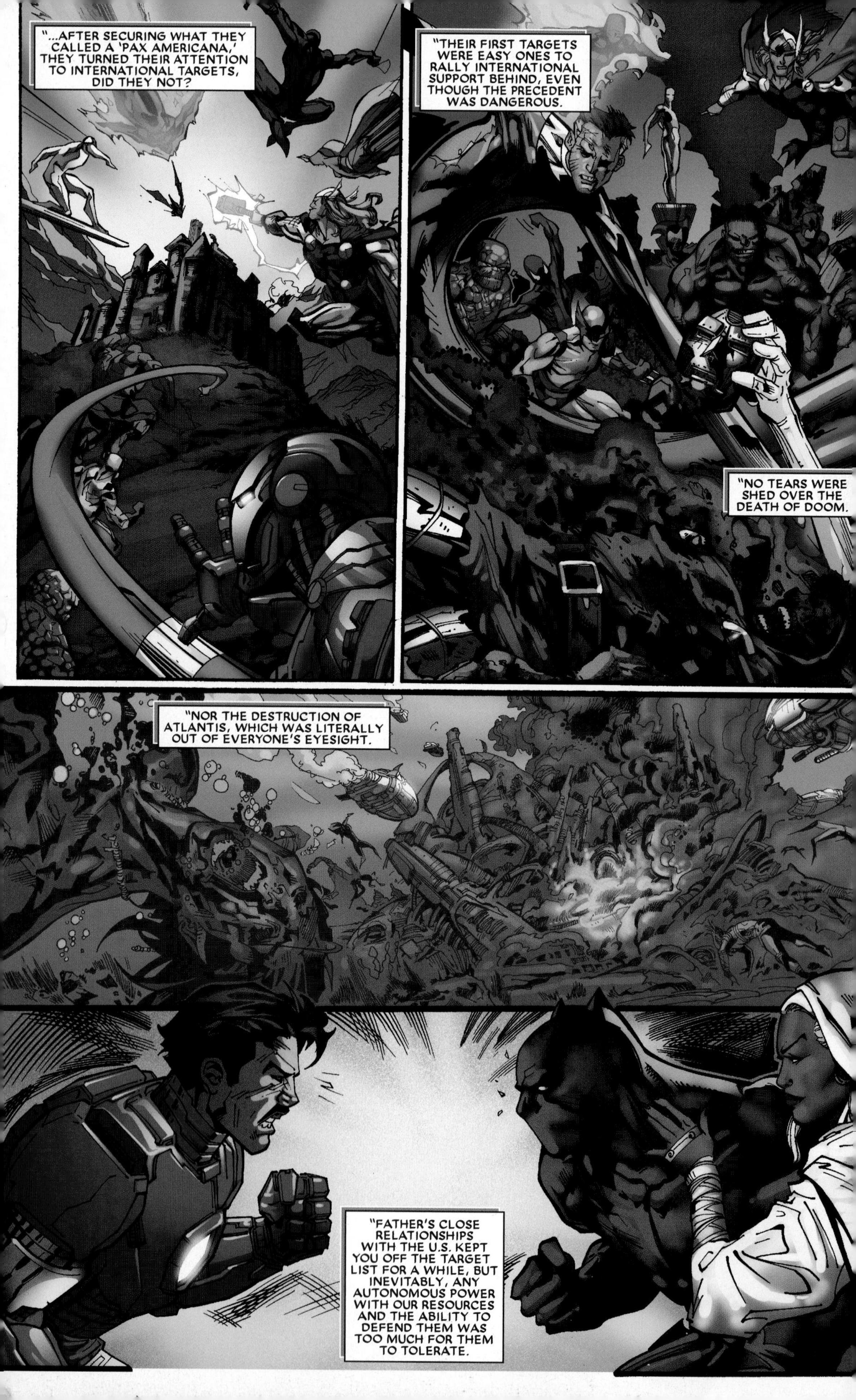
"...AFTER SECURING WHAT THEY CALLED A 'PAX AMERICANA,' THEY TURNED THEIR ATTENTION TO INTERNATIONAL TARGETS, DID THEY NOT?
"THEIR FIRST TARGETS WERE EASY ONES TO RALLY INTERNATIONAL SUPPORT BEHIND, EVEN THOUGH THE PRECEDENT WAS DANGEROUS.
"NO TEARS WERE SHED OVER THE DEATH OF DOOM.
"NOR THE DESTRUCTION OF ATLANTIS, WHICH WAS LITERALLY OUT OF EVERYONE'S EYESIGHT.
"FATHER'S CLOSE RELATIONSHIPS WITH THE U.S. KEPT YOU OFF THE TARGET LIST FOR A WHILE, BUT INEVITABLY, ANY AUTONOMOUS POWER WITH OUR RESOURCES AND THE ABILITY TO DEFEND THEM WAS TOO MUCH FOR THEM TO TOLERATE.

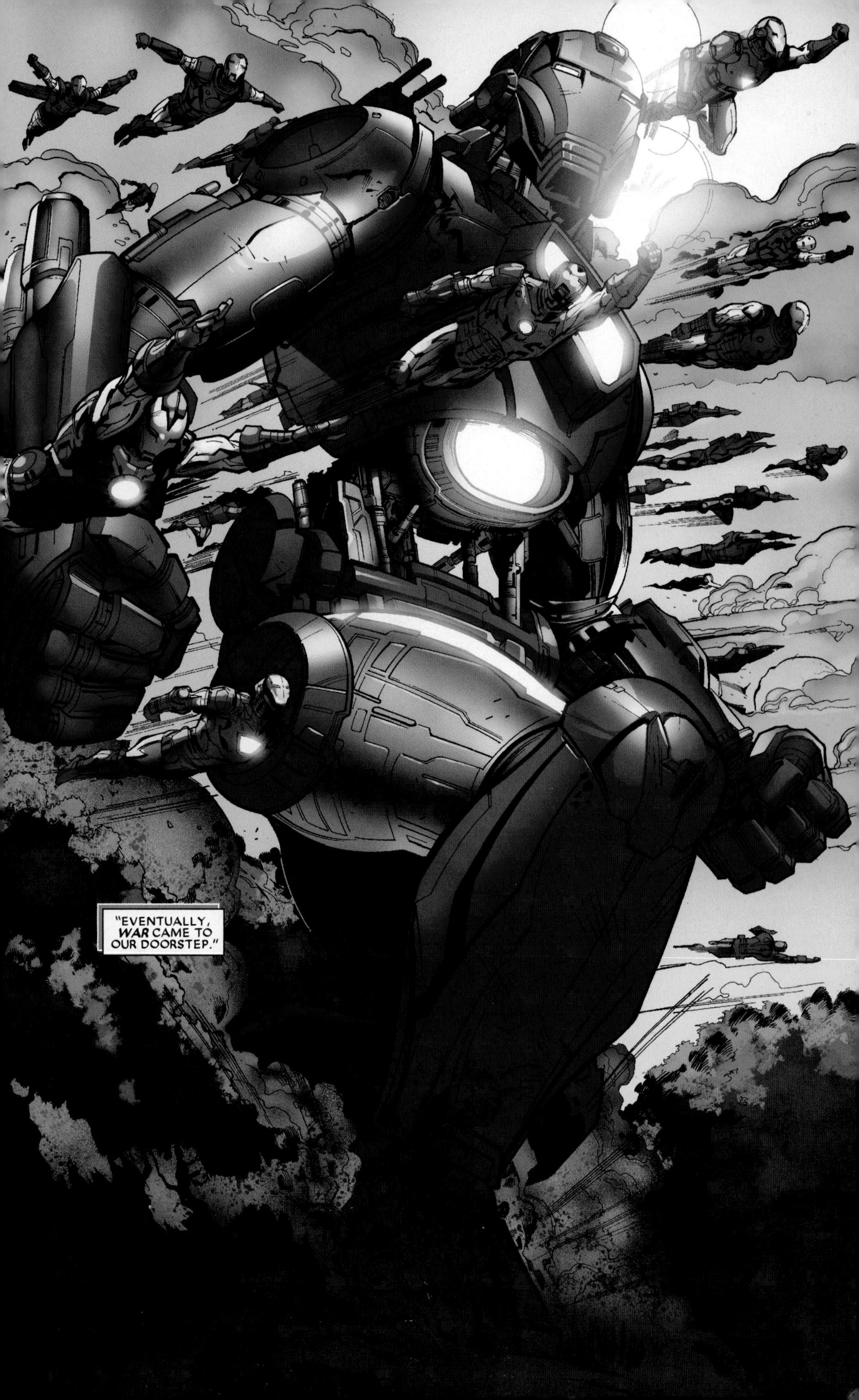
"EVENTUALLY, WAR CAME TO OUR DOORSTEP."

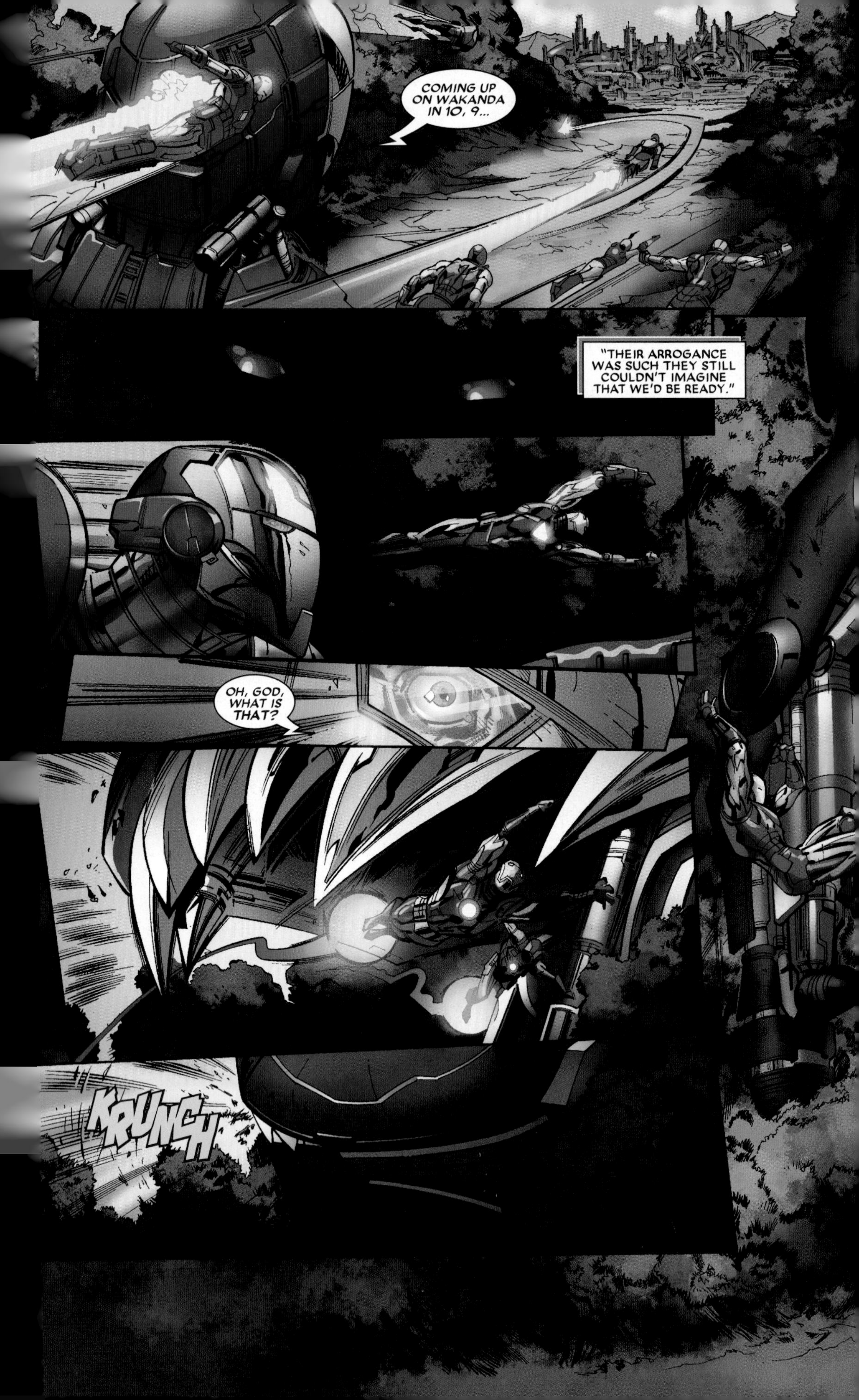
COMING UP ON WAKANDA IN 10, 9...
"THEIR ARROGANCE WAS SUCH THEY STILL COULDN'T IMAGINE THAT WE'D BE READY."
OH, GOD, WHAT IS THAT?
KRUNCH

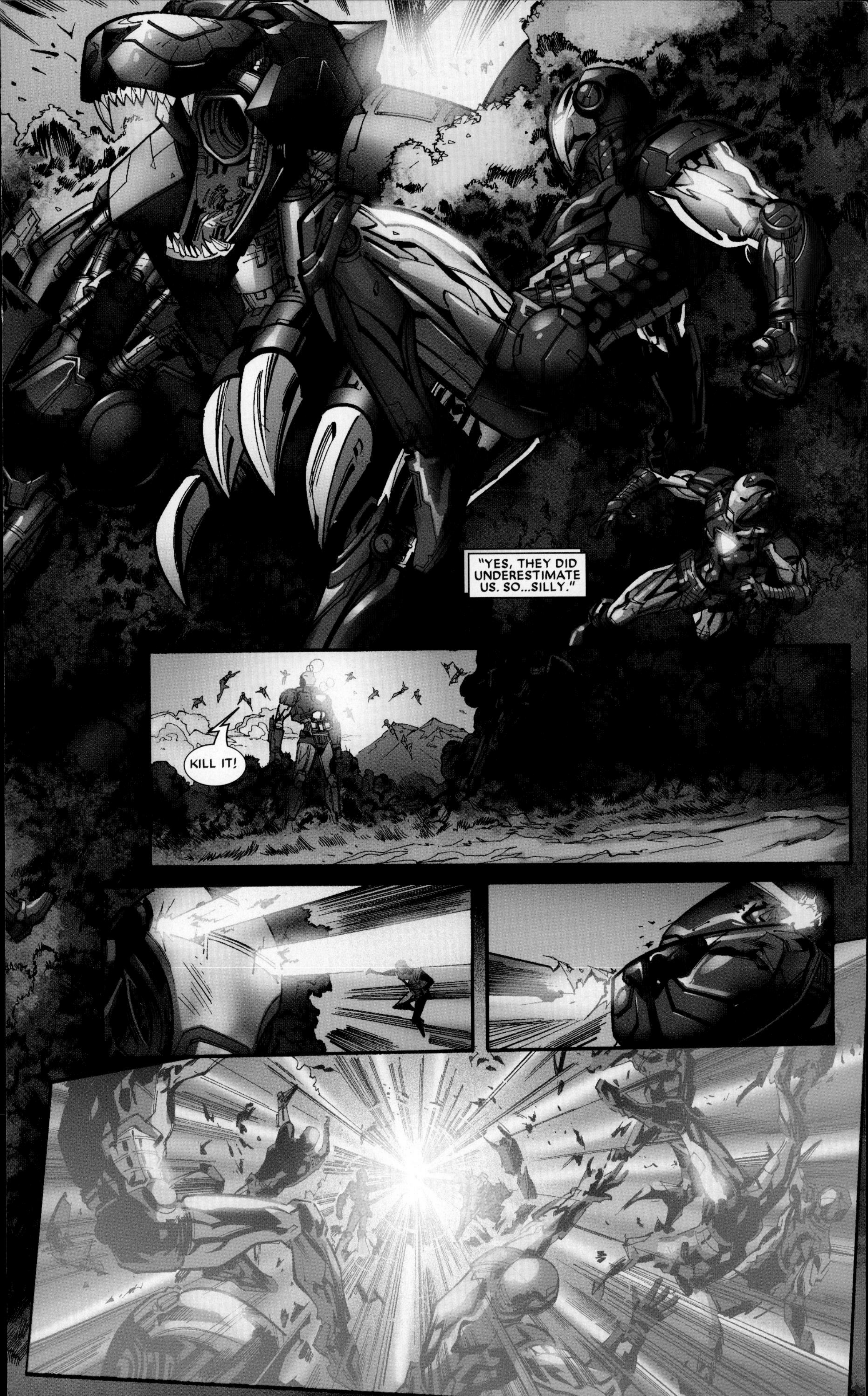

"YES, THEY DID UNDERESTIMATE US. SO...SILLY."
KILL IT!

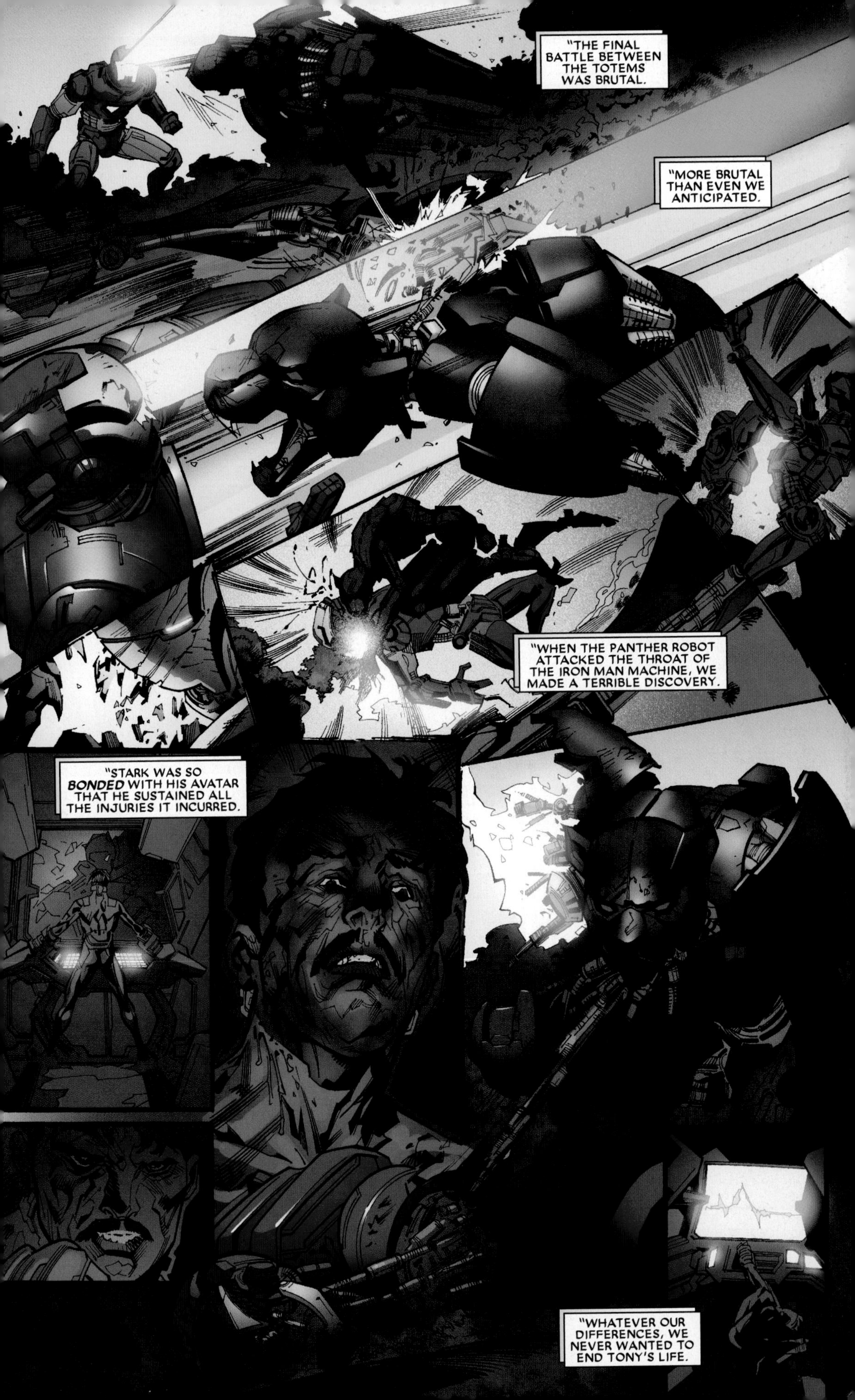
"THE FINAL BATTLE BETWEEN THE TOTEMS WAS BRUTAL.
"MORE BRUTAL THAN EVEN WE ANTICIPATED.
"WHEN THE PANTHER ROBOT ATTACKED THE THROAT OF THE IRON MAN MACHINE, WE MADE A TERRIBLE DISCOVERY.
"STARK WAS SO *BONDED* WITH HIS AVATAR THAT HE SUSTAINED ALL THE INJURIES IT INCURRED.
"WHATEVER OUR DIFFERENCES, WE NEVER WANTED TO END TONY'S LIFE.

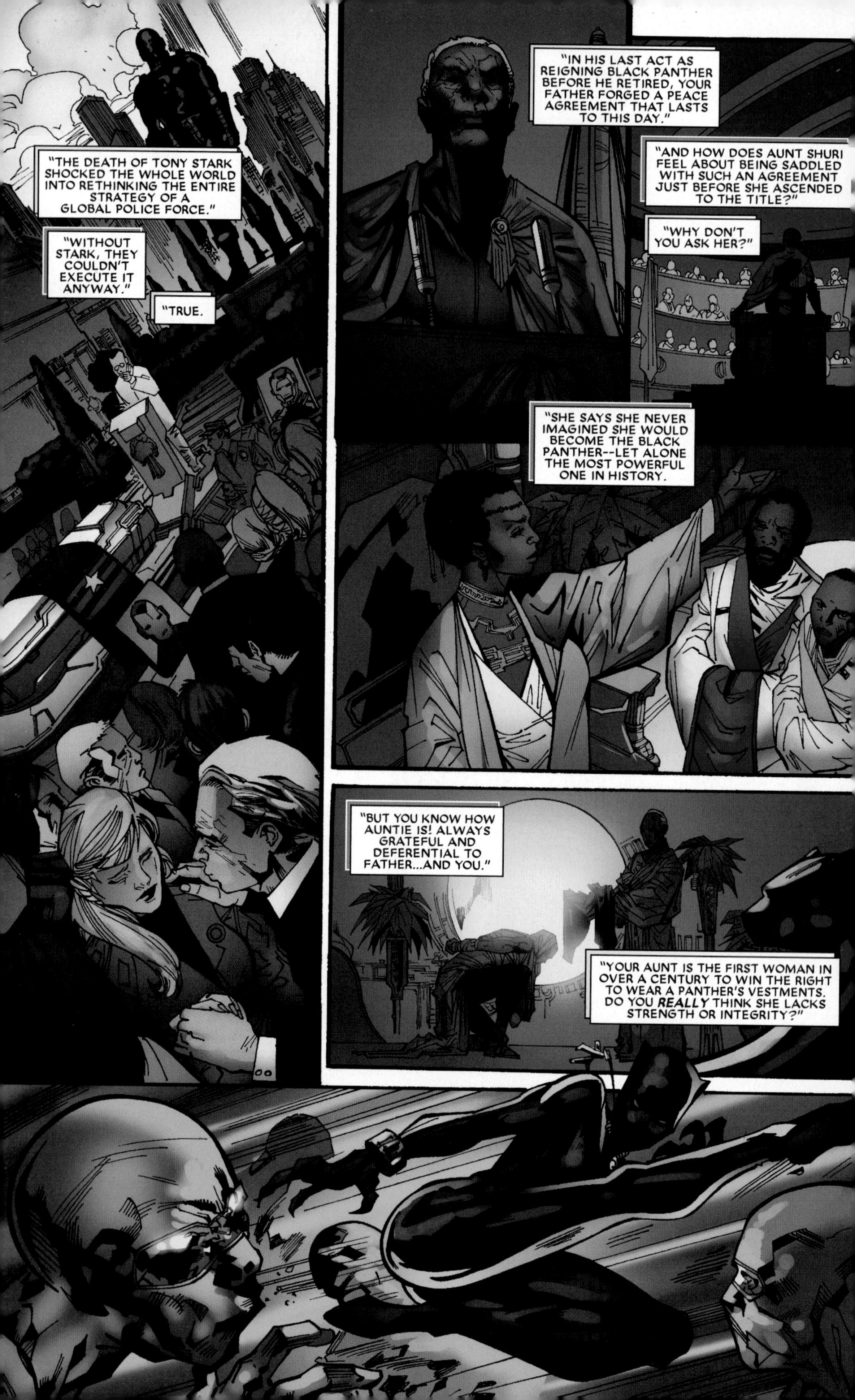
"THE DEATH OF TONY STARK SHOCKED THE WHOLE WORLD INTO RETHINKING THE ENTIRE STRATEGY OF A GLOBAL POLICE FORCE."
"WITHOUT STARK, THEY COULDN'T EXECUTE IT ANYWAY."
"TRUE.
"IN HIS LAST ACT AS REIGNING BLACK PANTHER BEFORE HE RETIRED, YOUR FATHER FORGED A PEACE AGREEMENT THAT LASTS TO THIS DAY."
"AND HOW DOES AUNT SHURI FEEL ABOUT BEING SADDLED WITH SUCH AN AGREEMENT JUST BEFORE SHE ASCENDED TO THE TITLE?"
"WHY DON'T YOU ASK HER?"
"SHE SAYS SHE NEVER IMAGINED SHE WOULD BECOME THE BLACK PANTHER--LET ALONE THE MOST POWERFUL ONE IN HISTORY.
"BUT YOU KNOW HOW AUNTIE IS! ALWAYS GRATEFUL AND DEFERENTIAL TO FATHER...AND YOU."
"YOUR AUNT IS THE FIRST WOMAN IN OVER A CENTURY TO WIN THE RIGHT TO WEAR A PANTHER'S VESTMENTS. DO YOU *REALLY* THINK SHE LACKS STRENGTH OR INTEGRITY?"

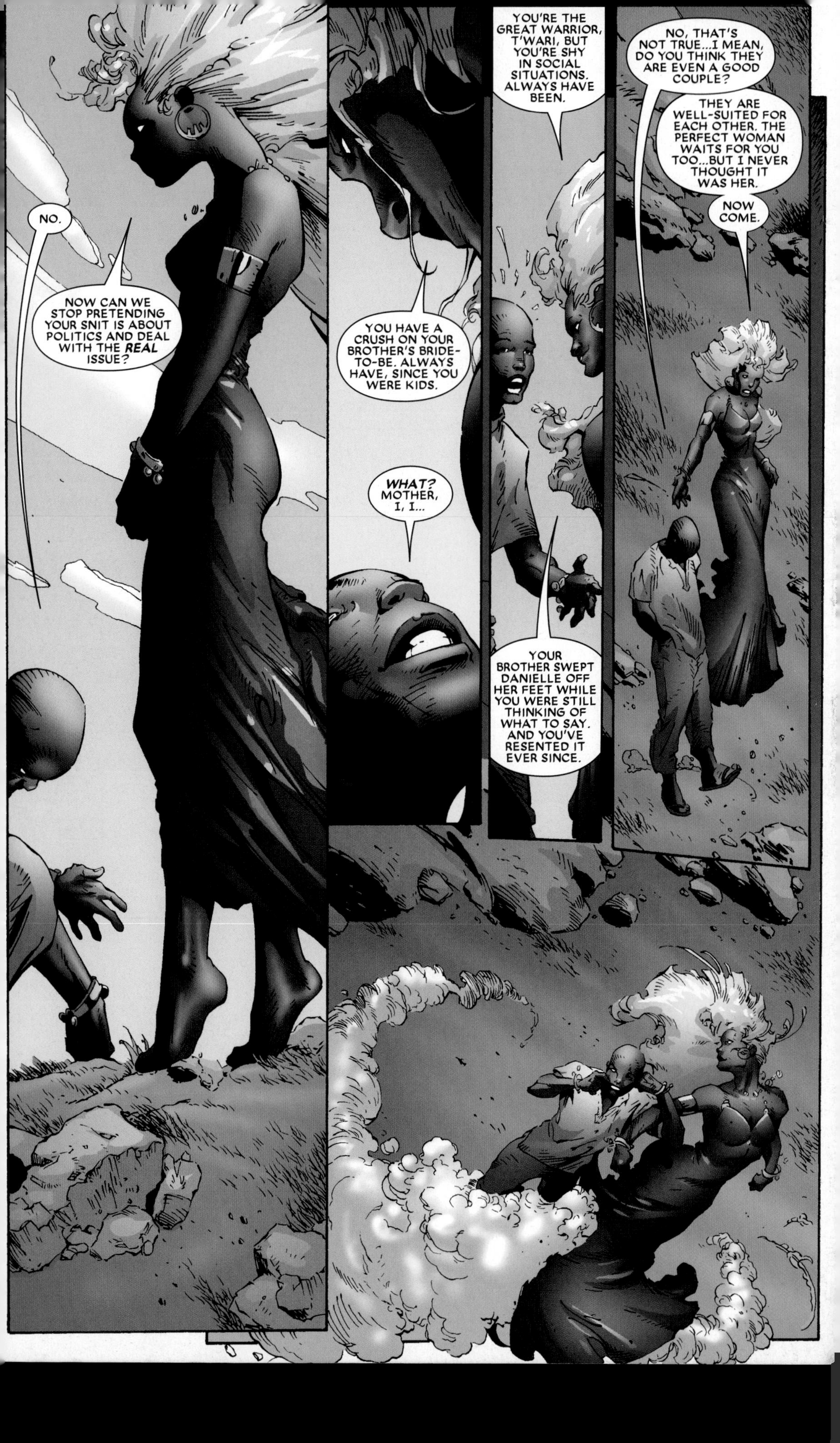
NO.
NOW CAN WE STOP PRETENDING YOUR SNIT IS ABOUT POLITICS AND DEAL WITH THE *REAL* ISSUE?
YOU HAVE A CRUSH ON YOUR BROTHER'S BRIDE-TO-BE. ALWAYS HAVE, SINCE YOU WERE KIDS.
WHAT? MOTHER, I, I...
YOU'RE THE GREAT WARRIOR, T'WARI, BUT YOU'RE SHY IN SOCIAL SITUATIONS. ALWAYS HAVE BEEN.
YOUR BROTHER SWEPT DANIELLE OFF HER FEET WHILE YOU WERE STILL THINKING OF WHAT TO SAY. AND YOU'VE RESENTED IT EVER SINCE.
NO, THAT'S NOT TRUE...I MEAN, DO YOU THINK THEY ARE EVEN A GOOD COUPLE?
THEY ARE WELL-SUITED FOR EACH OTHER. THE PERFECT WOMAN WAITS FOR YOU TOO...BUT I NEVER THOUGHT IT WAS HER.
NOW COME.

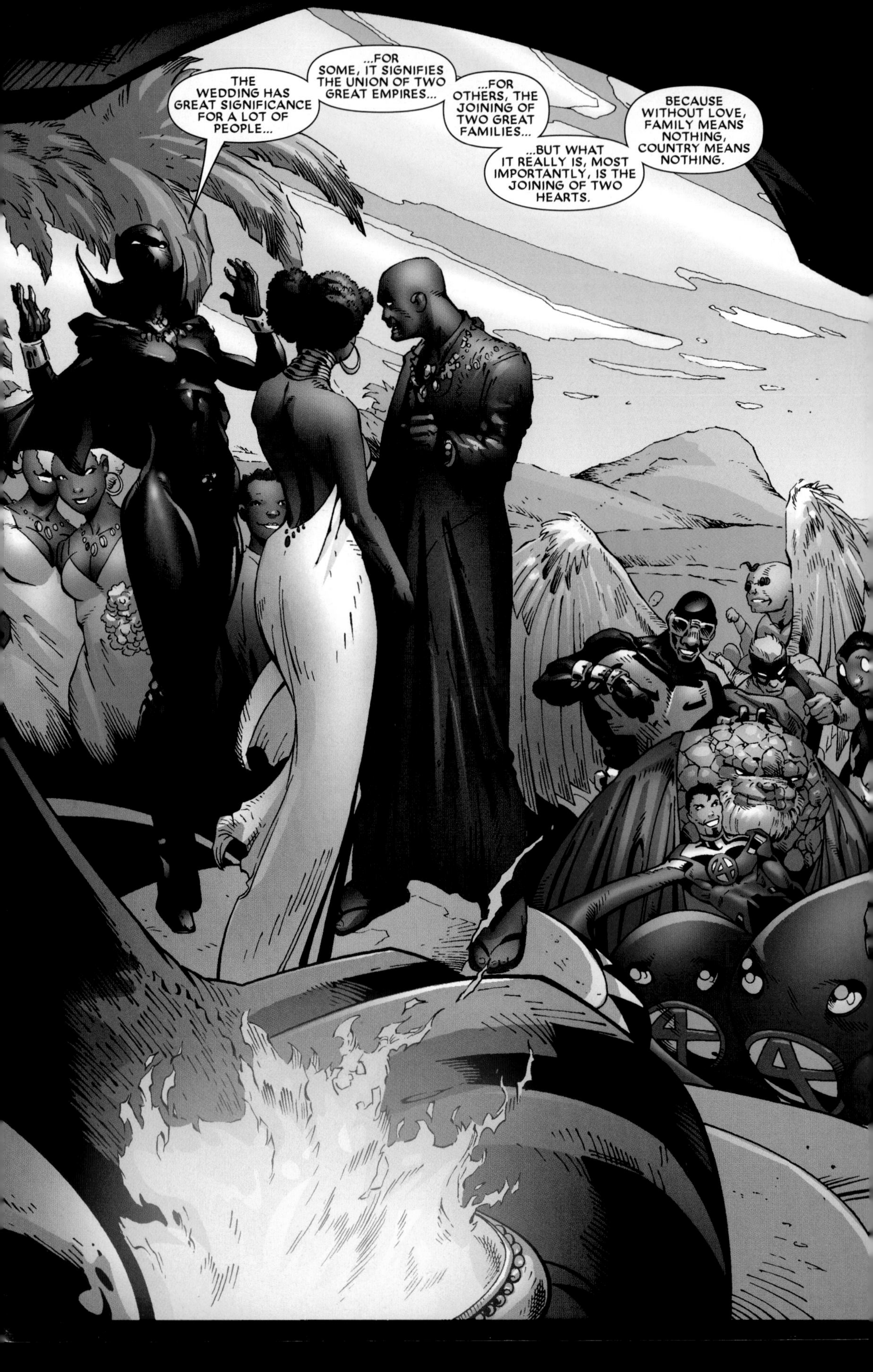
THE WEDDING HAS GREAT SIGNIFICANCE FOR A LOT OF PEOPLE...
...FOR SOME, IT SIGNIFIES THE UNION OF TWO GREAT EMPIRES...
...FOR OTHERS, THE JOINING OF TWO GREAT FAMILIES...
...BUT WHAT IT REALLY IS, MOST IMPORTANTLY, IS THE JOINING OF TWO HEARTS.
BECAUSE WITHOUT LOVE, FAMILY MEANS NOTHING, COUNTRY MEANS NOTHING.

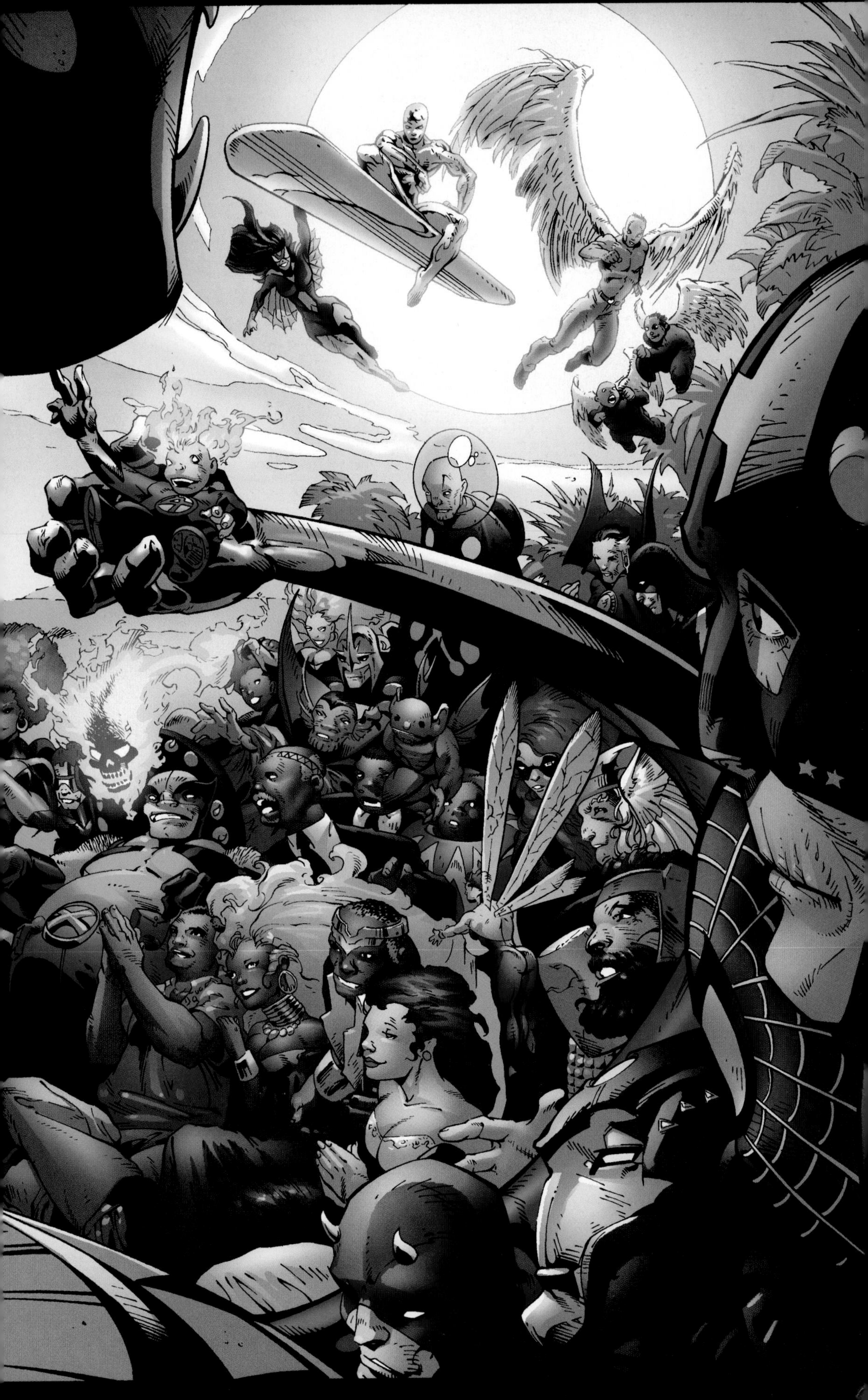

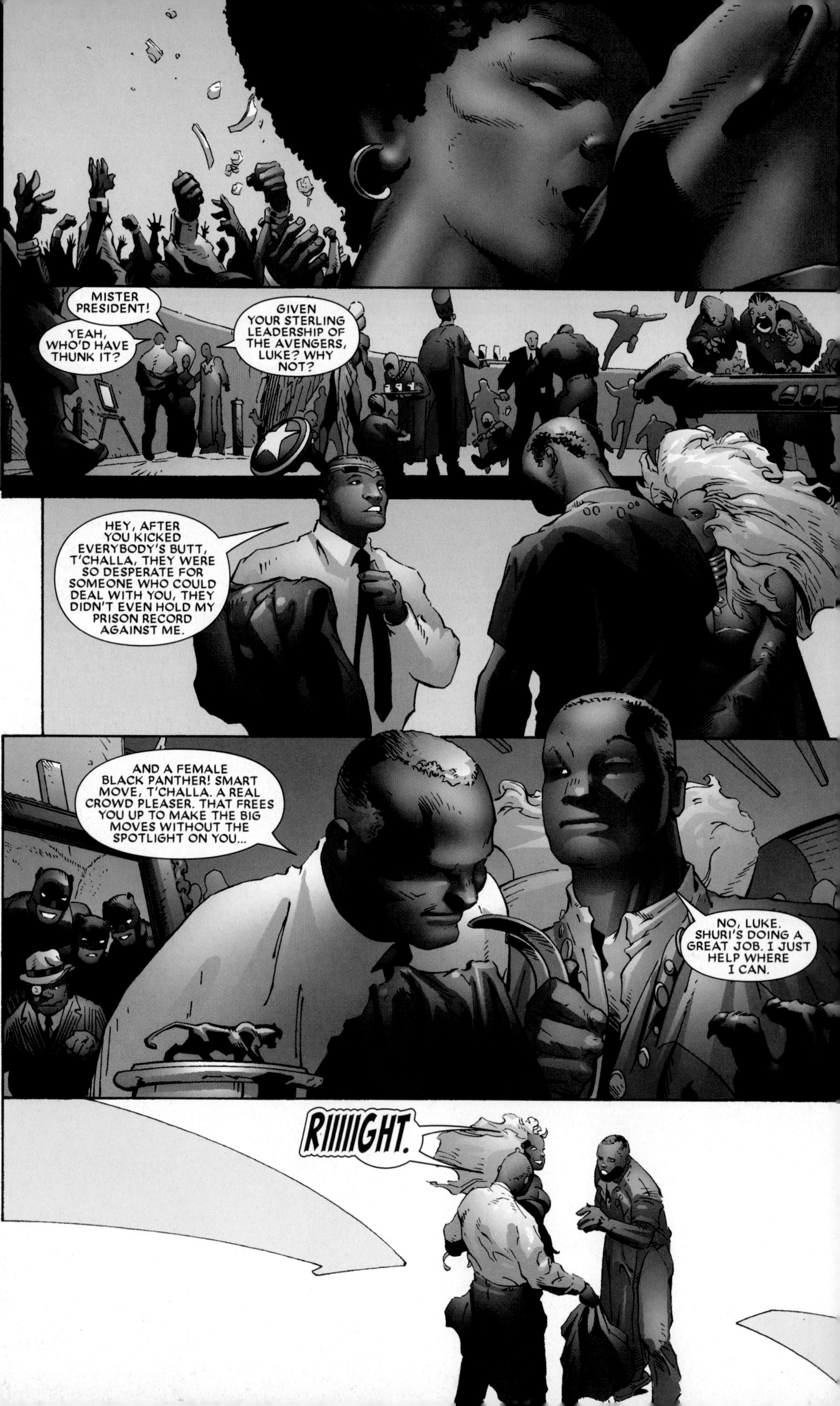
MISTER PRESIDENT!
YEAH, WHO'D HAVE THUNK IT?
GIVEN YOUR STERLING LEADERSHIP OF THE AVENGERS, LUKE? WHY NOT?
HEY, AFTER YOU KICKED EVERYBODY'S BUTT, T'CHALLA, THEY WERE SO DESPERATE FOR SOMEONE WHO COULD DEAL WITH YOU, THEY DIDN'T EVEN HOLD MY PRISON RECORD AGAINST ME.
AND A FEMALE BLACK PANTHER! SMART MOVE, T'CHALLA. A REAL CROWD PLEASER. THAT FREES YOU UP TO MAKE THE BIG MOVES WITHOUT THE SPOTLIGHT ON YOU...
NO, LUKE. SHURI'S DOING A GREAT JOB. I JUST HELP WHERE I CAN.
RIIIIIGHT.

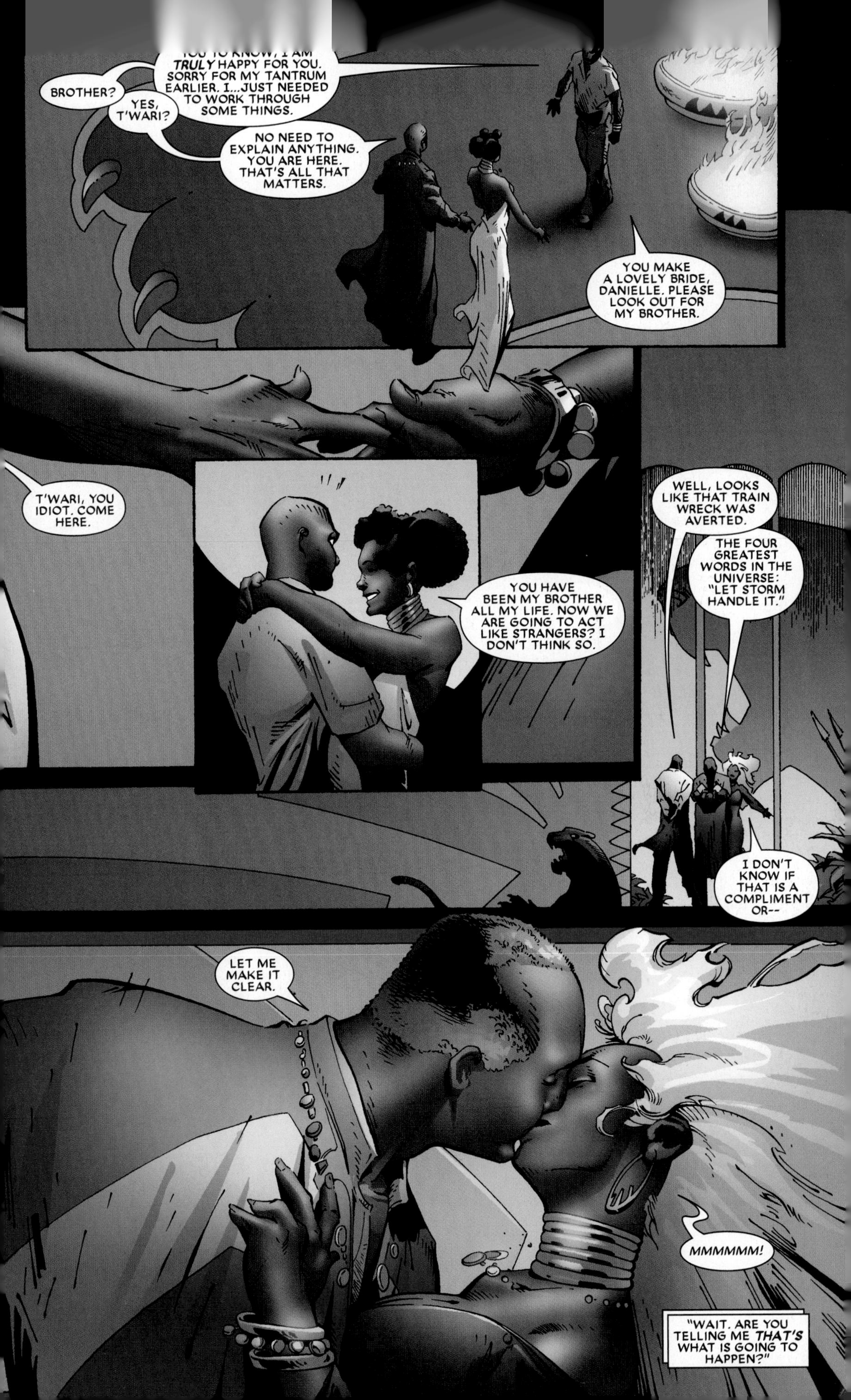

BROTHER?
YES, T'WARI?
TRULY HAPPY FOR YOU. SORRY FOR MY TANTRUM EARLIER. I...JUST NEEDED TO WORK THROUGH SOME THINGS.
NO NEED TO EXPLAIN ANYTHING. YOU ARE HERE. THAT'S ALL THAT MATTERS.
YOU MAKE A LOVELY BRIDE, DANIELLE. PLEASE LOOK OUT FOR MY BROTHER.
T'WARI, YOU IDIOT. COME HERE.
YOU HAVE BEEN MY BROTHER ALL MY LIFE. NOW WE ARE GOING TO ACT LIKE STRANGERS? I DON'T THINK SO.
WELL, LOOKS LIKE THAT TRAIN WRECK WAS AVERTED.
THE FOUR GREATEST WORDS IN THE UNIVERSE: "LET STORM HANDLE IT."
I DON'T KNOW IF THAT IS A COMPLIMENT OR--
LET ME MAKE IT CLEAR.
MMMMMM!
"WAIT. ARE YOU TELLING ME *THAT'S* WHAT IS GOING TO HAPPEN?"

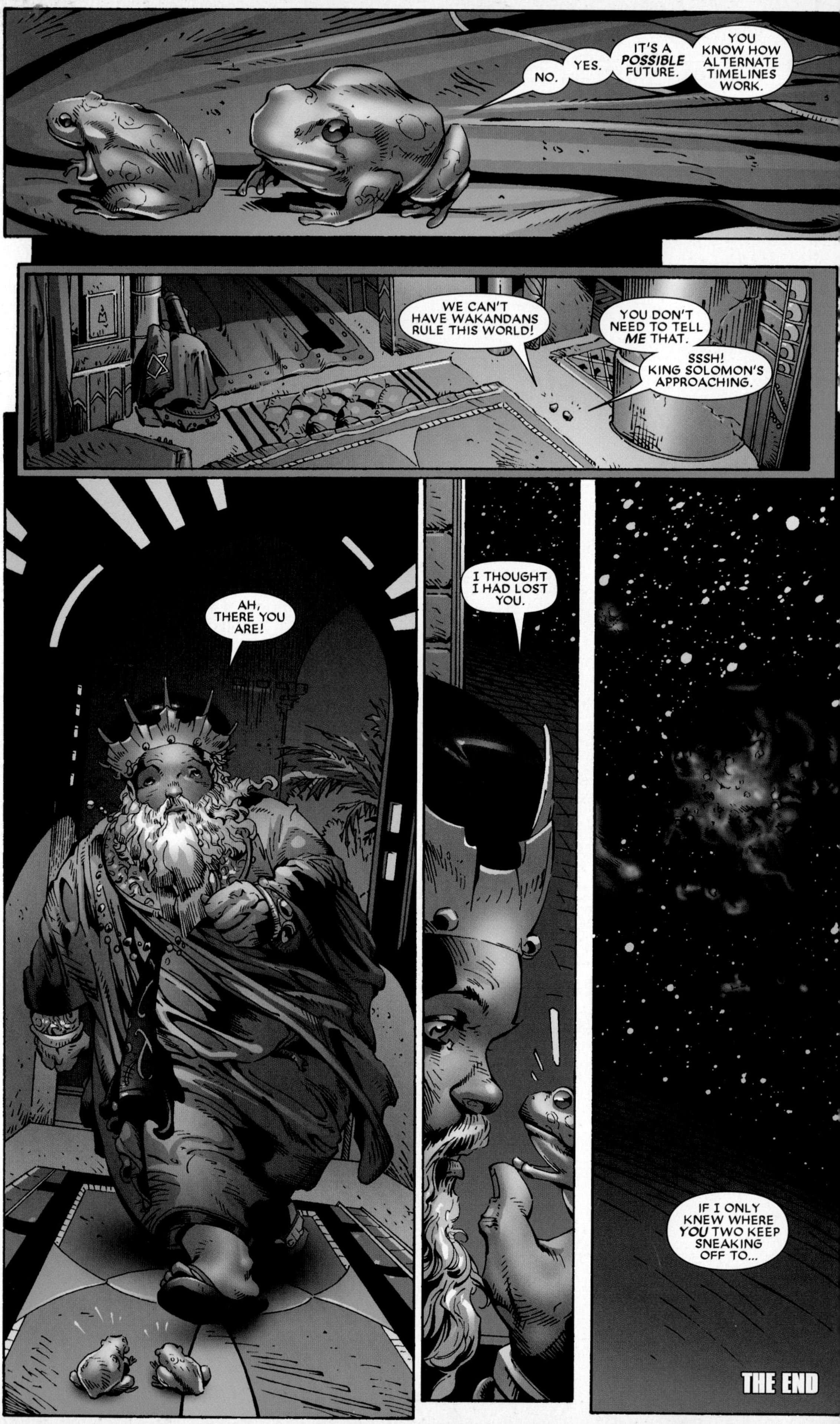

NO.
YES.
IT'S A POSSIBLE FUTURE.
YOU KNOW HOW ALTERNATE TIMELINES WORK.
WE CAN'T HAVE WAKANDANS RULE THIS WORLD!
YOU DON'T NEED TO TELL ME THAT.
SSSH! KING SOLOMON'S APPROACHING.
AH, THERE YOU ARE!
I THOUGHT I HAD LOST YOU.
IF I ONLY KNEW WHERE YOU TWO KEEP SNEAKING OFF TO...
THE END

A MARVEL COMICS EVENT®

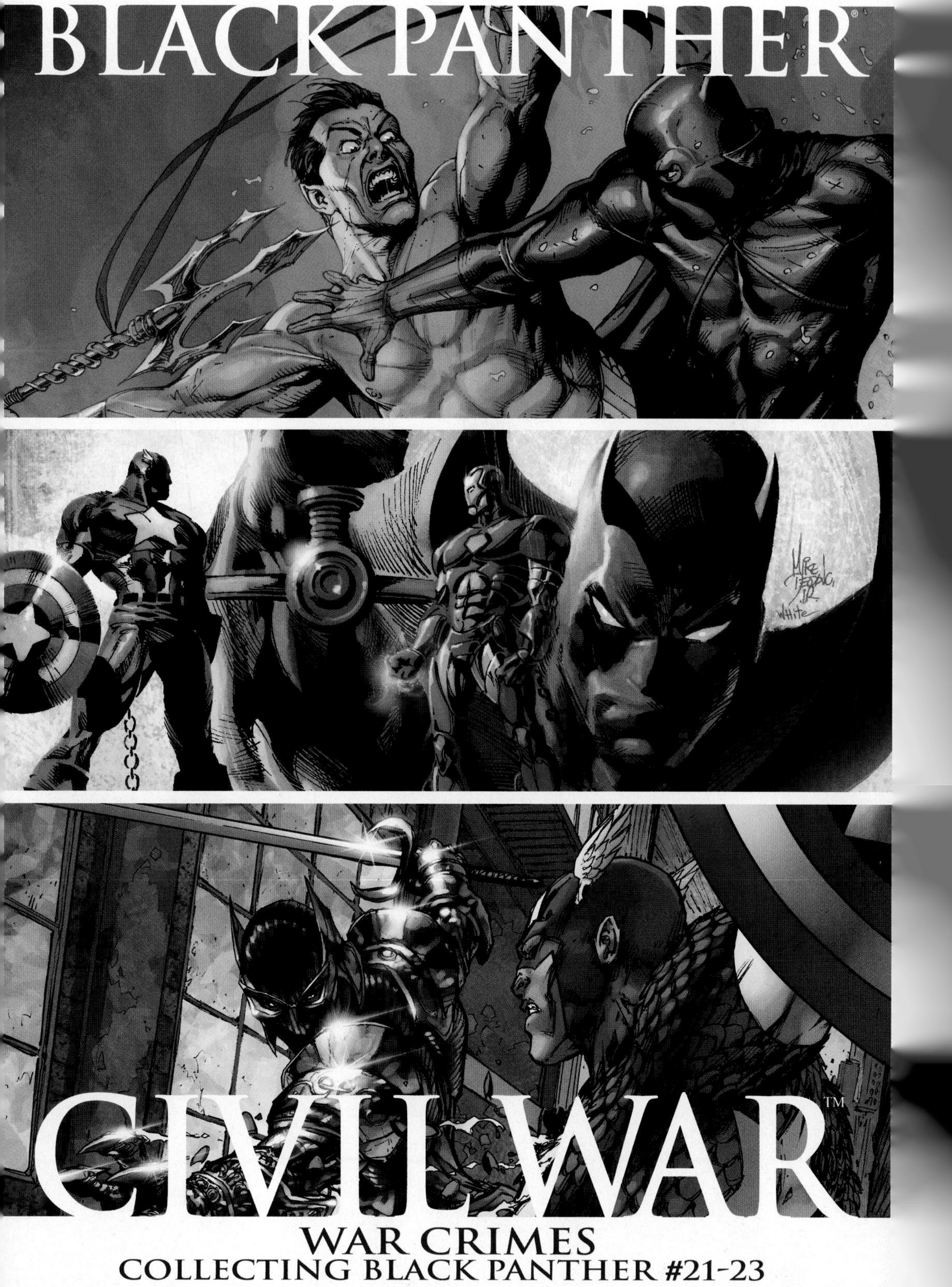
BLACK PANTHER®
CIVIL WAR™

WAR CRIMES
COLLECTING BLACK PANTHER #21-23

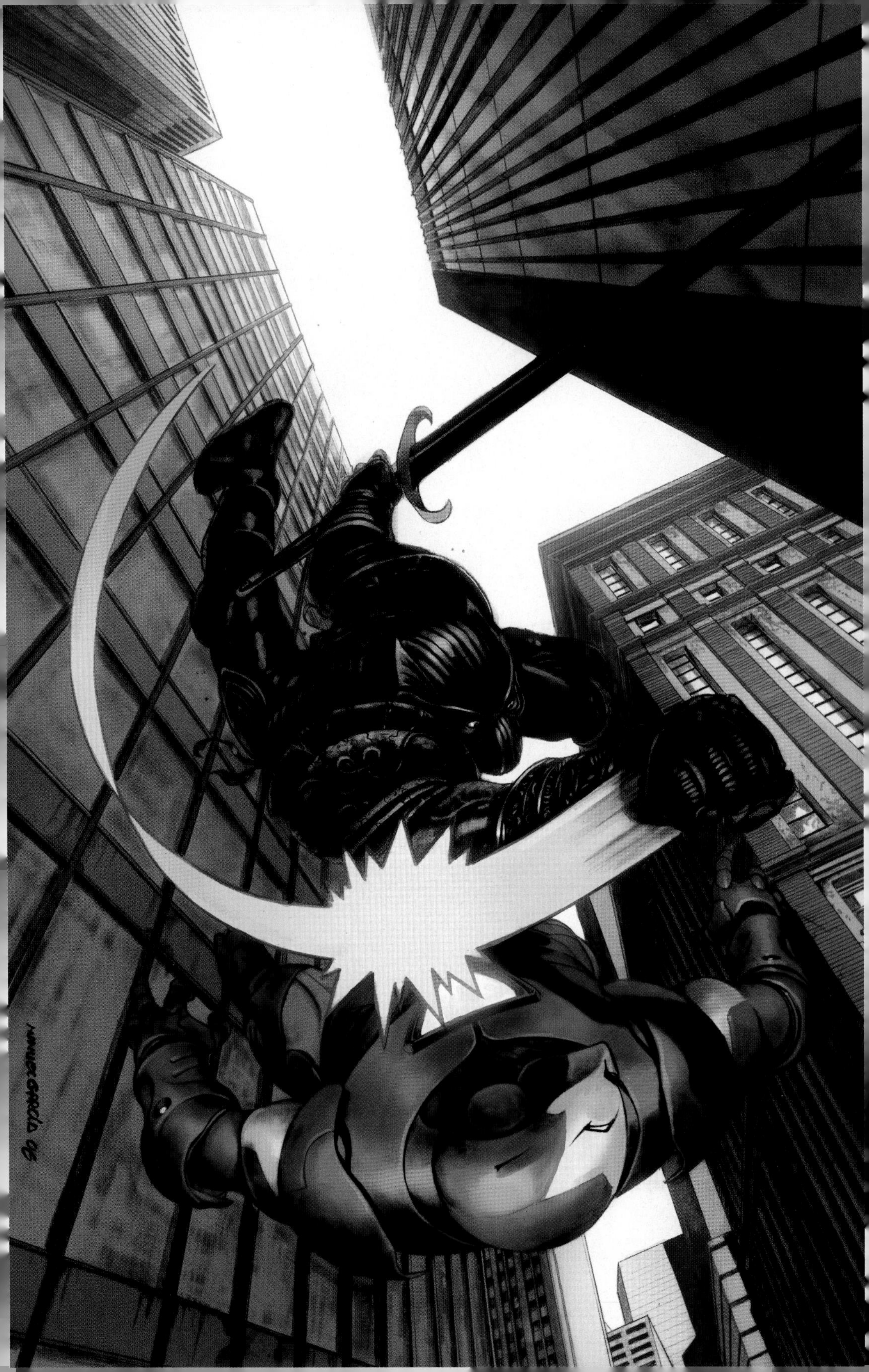

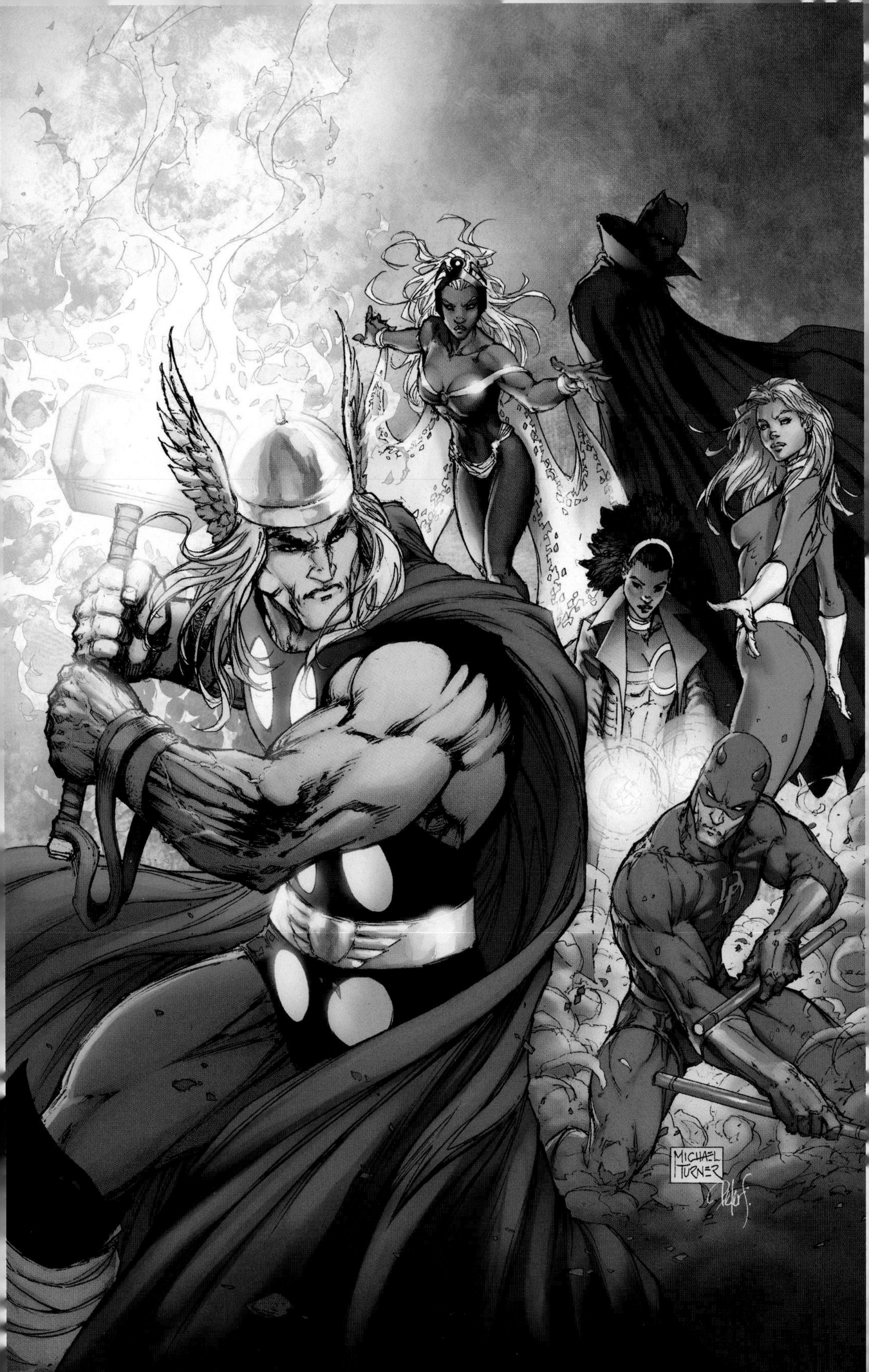
MICHAEL TURNER

CIVIL WAR
AFTERMATH

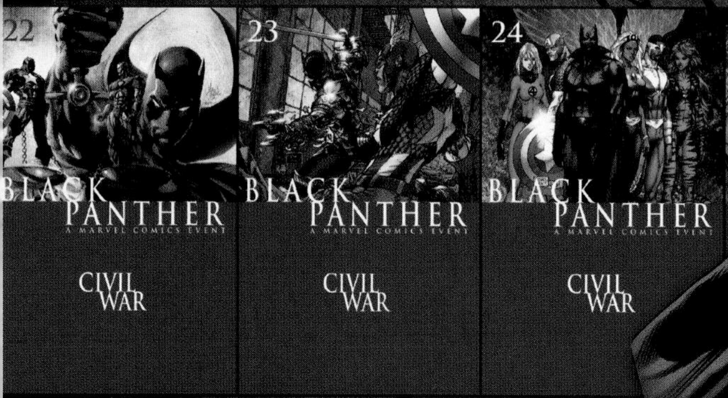

22
BLACK PANTHER
A MARVEL COMICS EVENT
CIVIL WAR
23
BLACK PANTHER
A MARVEL COMICS EVENT
CIVIL WAR
24
BLACK PANTHER
A MARVEL COMICS EVENT
CIVIL WAR
25
BL

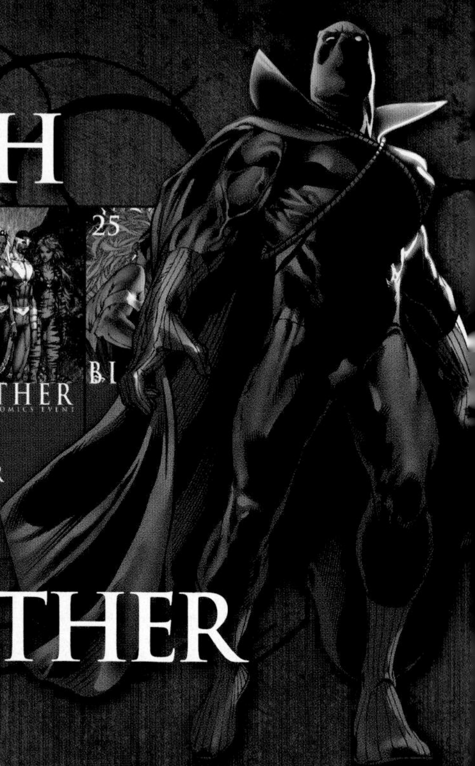

BLACK PANTHER

WRITER: REGINALD HUDLIN
ARTIST: FRANCIS PORTELLA

"Just when I thought I was out, they pull me back in!" said Michael Corleone in *The Godfather, Part III*, words that seem to haunt the Black Panther as he slips into his uneasy new role in the aftermath of the *Civil War*. After all, the marriage with his new bride Ororo was supposed to be their coming out party to the world as Wakanda's new power couple, and the resultant "world tour" with world leaders in Europe, America, Latveria and Atlantis was to seal the deal. Little did either Storm or Black Panther know that any plans they had to fulfill their royal duties as Wakandans would be merged with their obligations to help repair a super-hero world torn asunder in America – and one of those obligations would be manifested in a leadership role in the Fantastic Four!

Spotlight talked about the dynamic world of the Black Panther and his queen with writer Reginald Hudlin, who enters his third year of work on the title!

SPOTLIGHT: How much did your writing strategy for Black Panther change once you knew Civil War was coming down the pike? Is your plan for Black Panther in the post-CW Marvel Universe substantively different than what it was when you signed on, and if so, how?

REGINALD: Actually, CIVIL WAR fit perfectly into my plans for Panther. It accelerated and amplified certain ideas, which was a good thing. My plan was always to have Panther become a major player in the MU and his drafting by Namor to lead the international resistance to the SHRA and Reed turning over the FF to his leadership did that naturally.

SPOTLIGHT: The wedding of Black Panther and Storm was a huge, huge event in Marvel history, and in fact, it appears that their wedding is the last time some of the combatants of the Civil War will be in the same room (at least for some time!) Before we dip into the events of *Civil War*, let's look back at the wedding: from a creative standpoint, are you satisfied with how it played out, in terms of both the elements you brought to the story and the way the book wound up looking visually? (And how about that wedding gown?)

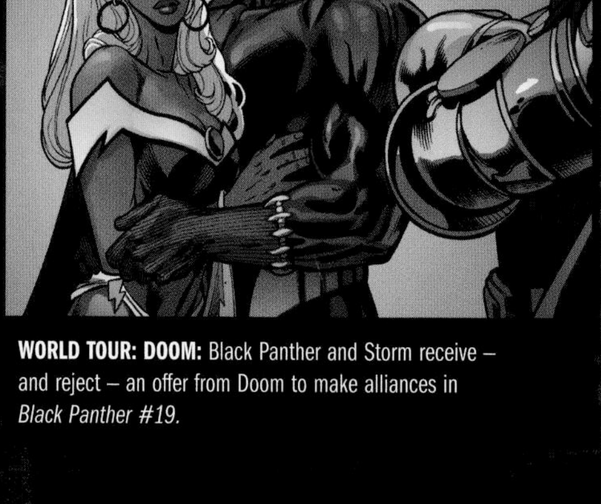

A PROVOCATIVE ANALYSIS OF WORLD EVENTS, DOOM, BUT I *CANNOT* ACCEPT YOUR OFFER. I CANNOT FORM AN ALLIANCE WITH SOMEONE I DON'T TRUST.

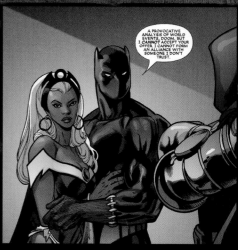

WORLD TOUR: DOOM: Black Panther and Storm receive – and reject – an offer from Doom to make alliances in *Black Panther #19.*

REGINALD: My only regret about the wedding was that I needed another ten pages! There were so many great characters all there at such an important time in history, I wanted to play out a lot more side conversations between different characters who you may have never seen in a room together. I could have had at least of page of Storm floating in that hot dress as she danced with T'Challa.

That said, Storm's grandparents from both sides reconnecting was a big moment; Panther's failed attempt to broker a peace between Iron Man and Cap was big; and Xavier telling Storm she is the now the highest profile mutant in the world – all of those are moments that will pay out over the next year or so. (More information on one of the biggest moments – the appearance of the Watcher at the Wedding – will be explained in an upcoming issue of the *Fantastic Four*.)

SPOTLIGHT: Here's one thing I've been wondering: was Reginald Hudlin on T'Challa and Storm's guest list? If you were honored with an invite, can you give us any dish on behind-the-scenes stuff we normal folk missed out on?

REGINALD: As the President of Entertainment of the world's biggest black media company of course I would insure that BET would offer complete coverage of the nuptials.

What did you miss? Well there was that cool time when The Falcon took an early flight across Wakandan skies and crossed flight paths with the Angel, who was doing the same thing in the other direction; and that whole bonding moment between Luke Cage and Isaiah Bradley, the first Captain America. Wolverine picked up a super hero hottie at the reception, but I can't say who.

SPOTLIGHT: My favorite moment, besides the actual nuptials, was the brouhaha between Spider-Man and Man Ape. That was one heck of a payoff off from a scene you wrote in *Friendly Neighborhood Spider-Man #2*. Was that a scene you were holding in your back pocket that whole time?

REGINALD: Kind of. I've just never been able to take the character seriously – he's a guy in a gorilla suit. Once I started mocking him I knew I had to pay it off and I knew I wanted Man Ape at the wedding. Since the wedding of Reed and Sue established this tradition of huge brawls, I wanted to both pay off and send up that expectation. And who better to make fun of him than the hero with the lowest self-esteem and the best wit?

SPOTLIGHT: One of the big discussions currently raging in Spider-Man circles is how the reality of marriage between Peter Parker and Mary Jane is, in some reader's minds, diluting the "everyman" status that made Peter Parker unique in the first place. Certainly, neither Black Panther or Storm are as popular as Spider-Man, but their fans still have expectations concerning their characterizations. What are your thoughts on how the marriage between Storm and BP will enhance their characters, and do you have any concerns that the marriage could potentially derail their characters?

REGINALD: As much as Peter Parker/Spider Man represents the everyman, T'Challa the Black Panther and Storm represent ideals. They make a great couple, one that many fans have been waiting to see come together for decades.

Both of them are natural leaders with strong moral centers. There's an adjustment period in any new marriage during which a couple figures out how they are going to operate as a team. It's not just a matter of who's the boss – the King or the Goddess. It's two human beings bringing out the best in each other though affection, understanding, devotion and the occasional kickboxing challenge.

SPOTLIGHT: A scene in *Black Panther #19* shows T'Challa making a witty aside to Ororo about how, if the pair's burgeoning power is perceived as too much of a threat by foreign leaders while on their "world tour," they'd have to "take over the world." Is that notion that T'Challa was cracking wise about going to be a subtle underpinning of how they do business in the future, i.e. using this kind of "power capital" they're fully aware that they possess?

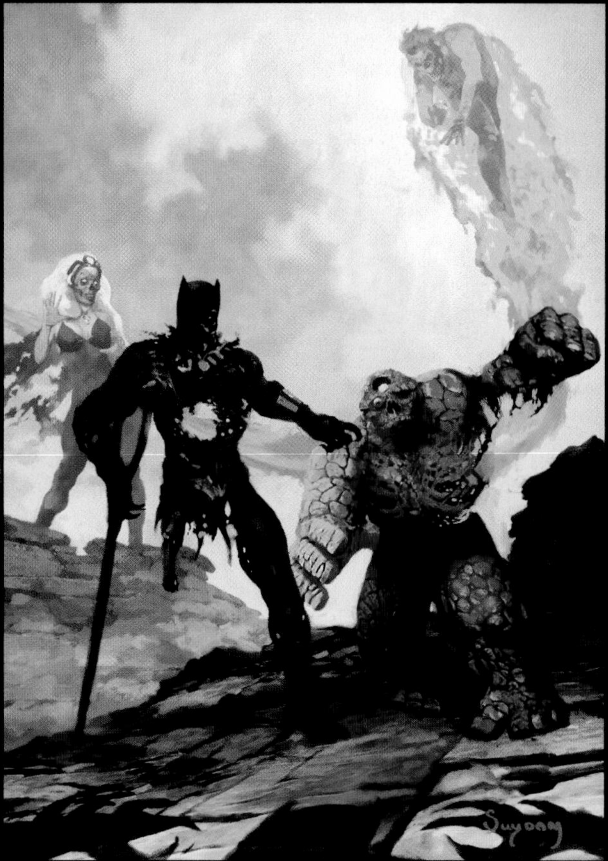
Suydam

MARVEL ZOMBIES ARE BACK? The gloriously zombiefied Arthur Suydam cover to *Black Panther #28*.

NO OFFENSE INTENDED. YOUR WIFE IS A TRUE WARRIOR.

LET *ALL THREE OF US* DISCUSS THE HARD CHOICES AHEAD.

"The pivotal moment for Panther and Storm happened at the bottom of the ocean when Namor convinces them to spearhead the international alliance against registration (in BP #21). At that moment T'Challa breaks with centuries of Wakandan policy to take a stand. He can justify it politically and morally but the aftereffects will be profound for both of them." – writer Reginald Hudlin

REGINALD: I think the first test of their newfound power capital was their taking a stand on Civil War. That act has repercussions which will cause them to invest even more heavily in bolstering their "power" leverage, which requires them to examine the roots of their abilities, both biological and spiritual.

Ultimately, they have to figure out how to balance "the greatest good" with "absolute power corrupts absolutely."

SPOTLIGHT: The first official *Civil War* crossover issue, *BP #23*, showed Black Panther and Storm leveraging their influence in a big way: they've chosen a side and are taking some proactive measures to help that side win. What events helped you connect the dots between T'Challa's initial stance of neutrality (in both *Illuminati Special* & *Civil War #3*) and this new stance?

REGINALD: I think the murder of Bill Foster, aka Goliath, was proof that whatever the intentions of the SHRA were, the execution of the idea was going terribly wrong. The SHRA creates a very real super-hero arms race and if they would kill one of their close friends (even inadvertently) then what would they do to the rest of the world?

SPOTLIGHT: Is writing politics into a mainstream super-hero comic, even in subtext, a nerve-wracking experience for you? Are you ever concerned that readers will think that you are writing the characters to reflect your own personal opinions, and thus alienating them if they are faced with ideas or themes they may disagree with? If so, how do you reckon with all that and still produce a comic that deals with international intrigue and swashbuckling, adversarial action?

REGINALD: I think that is one of the beautiful things about the Marvel Universe. It has always been grounded in the real world, not made up Metropolises. Stan Lee revolutionized superheroes by introducing real life problems into the lives of characters, whether they were psychological, economic or political. I think that's why Civil War has been such a great success. It takes real world anxieties and plays them out on a gigantic scale.

As for writing those themes and issues into stories, it's actually great fun. I really enjoyed writing the debates between characters about the SHRA. When I wrote the dialogue for pro-registration characters like Captain Britain or Jim Rhodes, I only used arguments that I could agree with. I really wanted to make a strong case for both sides.

New Black Panther artist Francis Portella's character sketches for T'Challa and Storm's Fantastic new teammates!

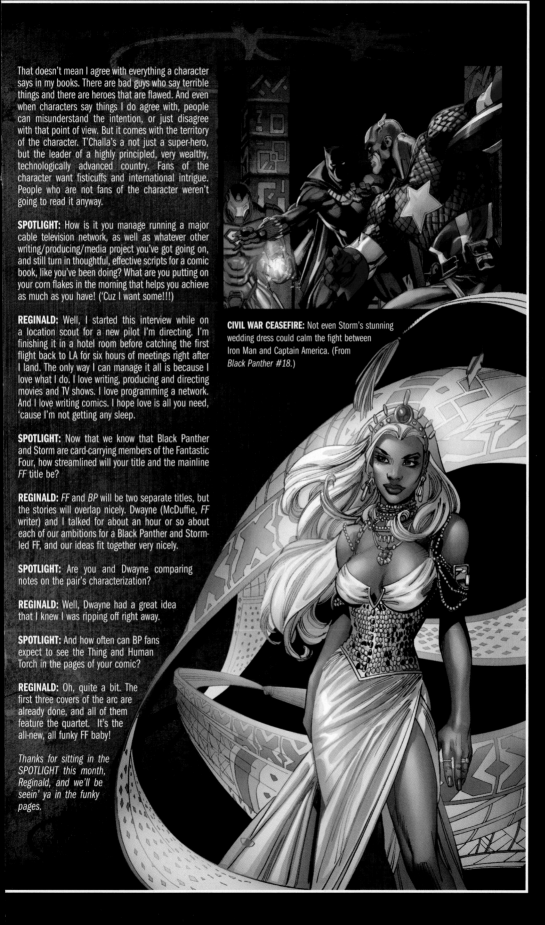

That doesn't mean I agree with everything a character says in my books. There are bad guys who say terrible things and there are heroes that are flawed. And even when characters say things I do agree with, people can misunderstand the intention, or just disagree with that point of view. But it comes with the territory of the character. T'Challa's a not just a super-hero, but the leader of a highly principled, very wealthy, technologically advanced country. Fans of the character want fisticuffs and international intrigue. People who are not fans of the character weren't going to read it anyway.

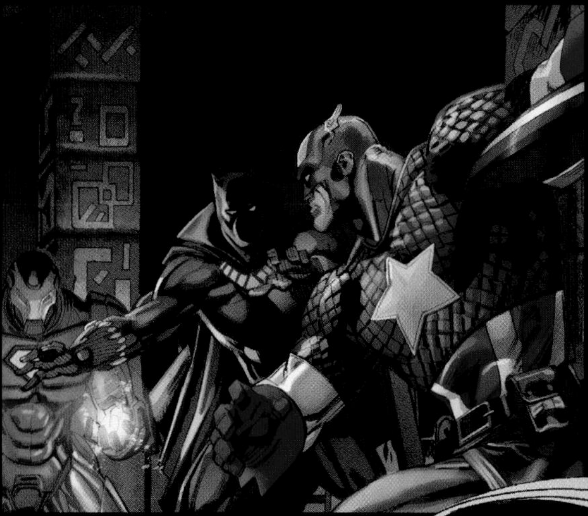

SPOTLIGHT: How is it you manage running a major cable television network, as well as whatever other writing/producing/media project you've got going on, and still turn in thoughtful, effective scripts for a comic book, like you've been doing? What are you putting on your corn flakes in the morning that helps you achieve as much as you have! ('Cuz I want some!!!)

REGINALD: Well, I started this interview while on a location scout for a new pilot I'm directing. I'm finishing it in a hotel room before catching the first flight back to LA for six hours of meetings right after I land. The only way I can manage it all is because I love what I do. I love writing, producing and directing movies and TV shows. I love programming a network. And I love writing comics. I hope love is all you need, 'cause I'm not getting any sleep.

CIVIL WAR CEASEFIRE: Not even Storm's stunning wedding dress could calm the fight between Iron Man and Captain America. (From *Black Panther #18.*)

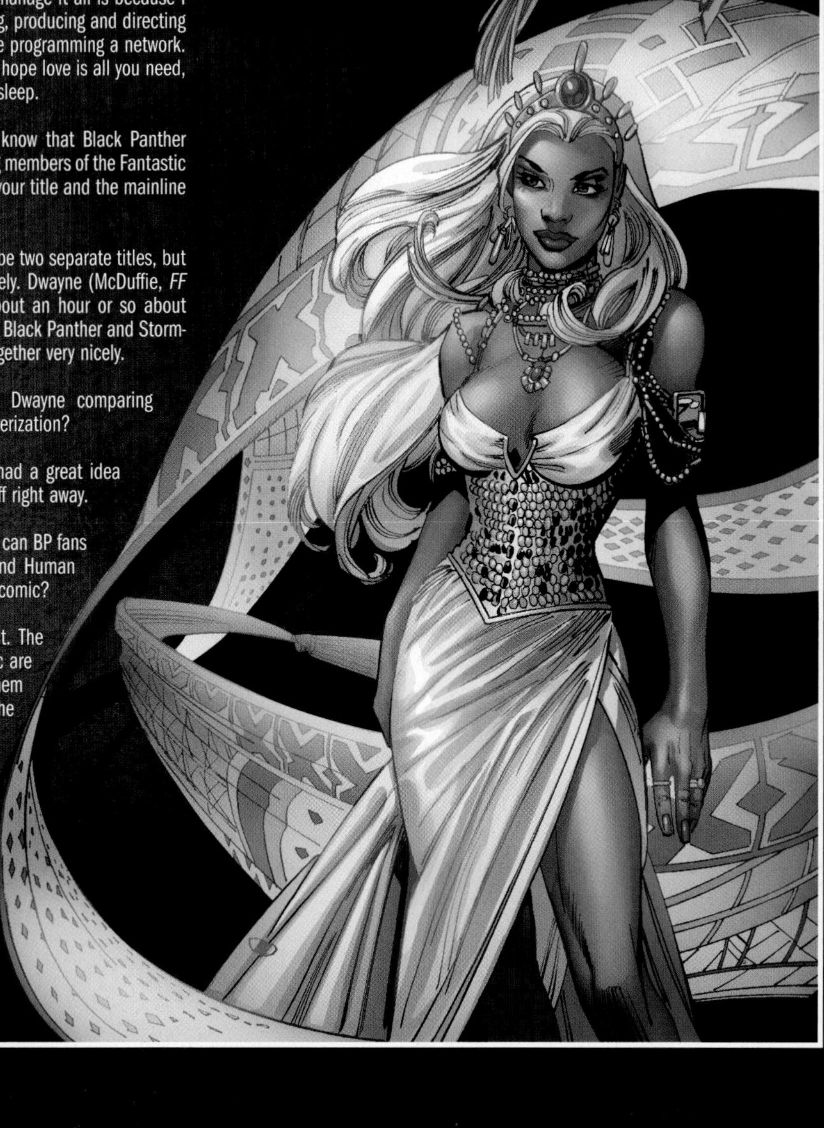

SPOTLIGHT: Now that we know that Black Panther and Storm are card-carrying members of the Fantastic Four, how streamlined will your title and the mainline *FF* title be?

REGINALD: *FF* and *BP* will be two separate titles, but the stories will overlap nicely. Dwayne (McDuffie, *FF* writer) and I talked for about an hour or so about each of our ambitions for a Black Panther and Storm-led FF, and our ideas fit together very nicely.

SPOTLIGHT: Are you and Dwayne comparing notes on the pair's characterization?

REGINALD: Well, Dwayne had a great idea that I knew I was ripping off right away.

SPOTLIGHT: And how often can BP fans expect to see the Thing and Human Torch in the pages of your comic?

REGINALD: Oh, quite a bit. The first three covers of the arc are already done, and all of them feature the quartet. It's the all-new, all funky FF baby!

Thanks for sitting in the SPOTLIGHT this month, Reginald, and we'll be seein' ya in the funky pages.

BLACK PANTHER #28-30 HOMAGE COVER COMMENTARY BY **ARTHUR SUYDAM**

FANTASTIC FOUR
MARVEL COMICS GROUP
25¢ 116 NOV
THE WORLD'S GREATEST COMIC MAGAZINE!
Fantastic Four
ALL-NEW THRILLS --AS REED RICHARDS IS REPLACED BY-- DOCTOR DOOM!
THE ALIEN... THE ALLY... AND ARMAGEDDON!

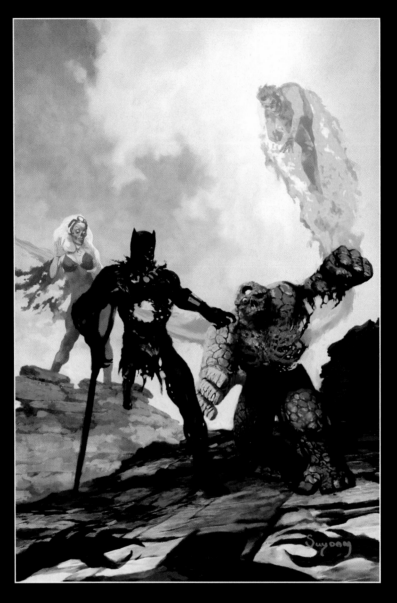

FANTASTIC FOUR #116 (November 1971)

Cover by **John Buscema** & **Joe Sinnott**

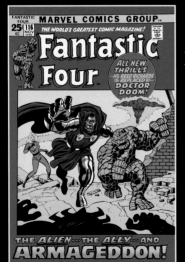

Jack Kirby was a tough act to follow, but John Buscema rose to the occasion with some sterling work on FF in the shadow of the King. This classic, double-sized issue featured a twist on the fantastic foursome that surely caused a double-sized double-take among the comic readers of the day. Dr. Doom leading the FF? Surely that can't be...

"When Jack Kirby stopped drawing FF, that's when I stopped reading it. Back then, I was following Jack and Steve Ditko — anywhere those guys went, I was following. *FF #116* was recommended by Marvel, and it was a new cover for me, one that I had never seen before.

"I tried to hold on to the substories for the characters. In a previous painting, I had painted Black Panther with big hole in him. I liked the idea of putting a big hole in him where you can see through him and see the landscape and background behind him. I thought that was a very comical thing, like a cannonball went through him but he's still walking around. The shadow figure in the foreground was also supposed to be the Black Panther. What I was told was that the shadow on the cover was going to be the Black Panther coming through.

"The element I loved most out of the whole *Marvel Zombies* series was Henry Pym keeping his secret stash away from his fellow zombies. He has the Panther hooked up to this table and keeping him alive just so he could have his midnight snacks and nibble on him. That killed me."

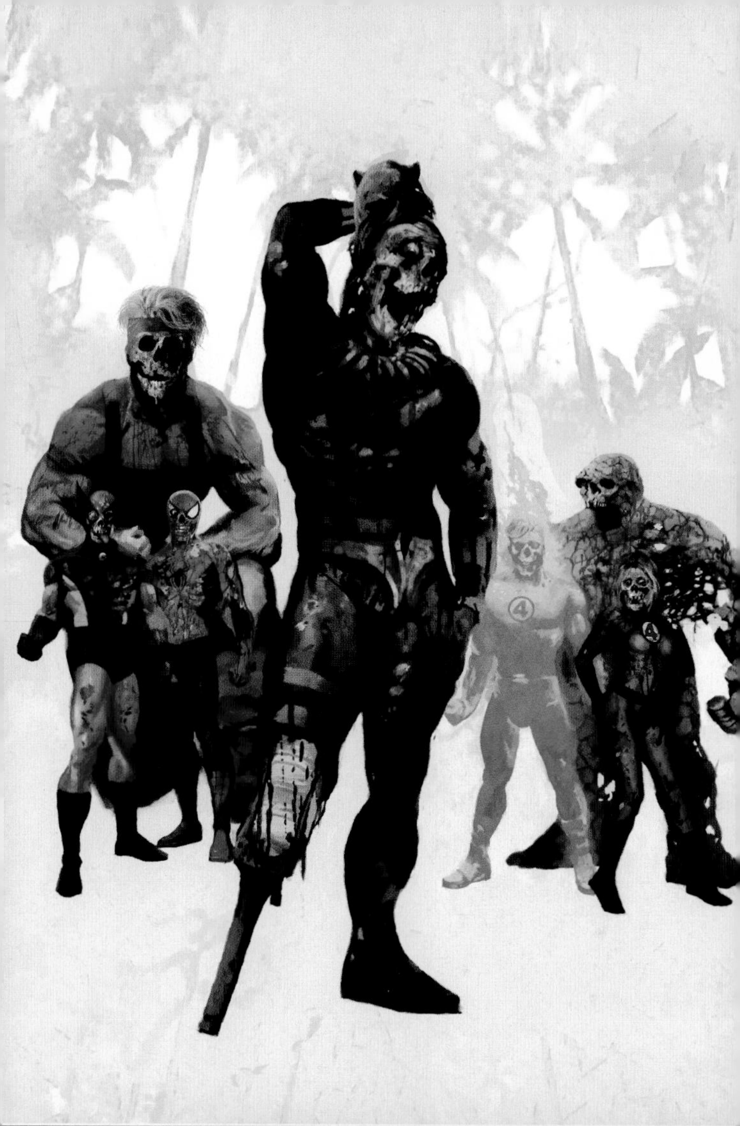

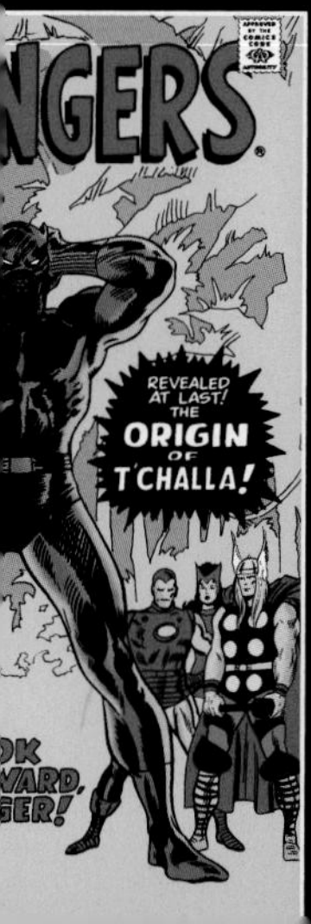
NGERS
REVEALED AT LAST! THE ORIGIN OF T'CHALLA!

AVENGERS #87 (April 1971)

Cover by **John Buscema**

The first African Avenger, the Black Panther was the first black member of Earth's Mightiest Heroes. In this origin issue, which was published right on the cusp of the classic Kree–Skrull War multi-issue event, the life story of the Wakandan king is revealed!

"Since this cover shows the unveiling of the origin of the character, I wanted to set the body language of the character to reflect that. I wanted it very much to say, 'Here's the Black Panther,' with the big surprise being that he is also a zombie. Surprise! I wanted to give him a poetic and romantic Renaissance body language, with pelvic tilts and an S-shape to his character.

"I had the hole in hi
in because what made
picture was the six-pack
the romantic gesture I w

"This is the first time
Storm appears as a z
I did that because she
zombies. I was struggli
I didn't want to zombify
her with the pretty, chee
the Black Panther was
in this picture, and she
with the zombies, I fe
wouldn't make sense t
with them but not be thr

Suydam

IND.
THE WORLD'S GREATEST COMIC MAGAZINE!
12¢
The Fantastic Four
MC
4 MAY
STOP HIM! IF THE SUB-MARINER REACHES THE WATER, HE'LL BECOME INVINCIBLE!
"THE COMING OF THE SUB-MARINER!"

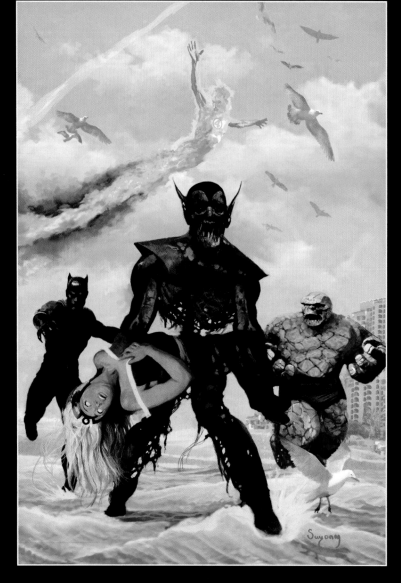

FANTASTIC FOUR #4 (May 1962)

Cover by **Jack Kirby** & **Sol Brodsky**

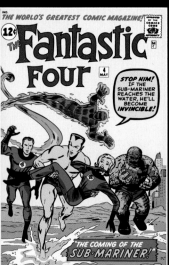

The love triangle between Reed, Sue and the arrogant, prickly Namor was a total blast in the early days of Lee and Kirby's FF. The one-upmanship between the two men, the games of jealousy played by the woman of their affections — and of course every reader of FF was right there with ol' Reed and Subby! The cover to Fantastic Four #4 *was not only the first Silver Age appearance of the underwater prince of Atlantis, but foretold the romantic troubles that loomed for all involved.*

"This was on my Top Ten list of favorite comics of all time, where Namor decides to come out of the ocean and steal Reed Richard's love interest. The ambiguity of this story was something that really stuck with me, really shocked me, because a part of Sue Storm wanted to go with him. Reed is her lifelong love interest and then she meets this fish-man and is tempted to go live under the ocean with him. That's one of my favorite Marvel stories of all time, so I couldn't wait to do this cover."

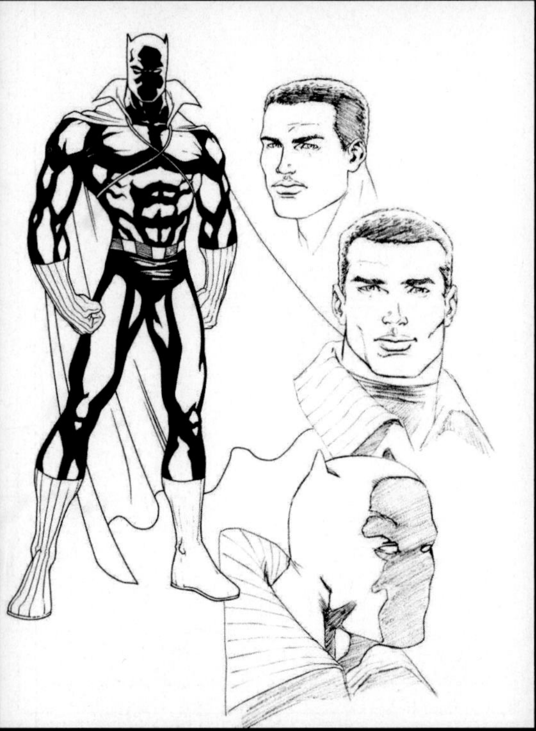
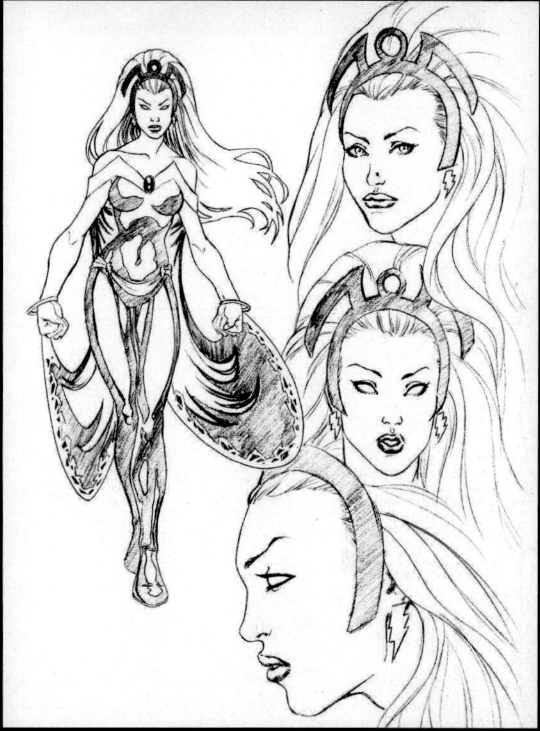
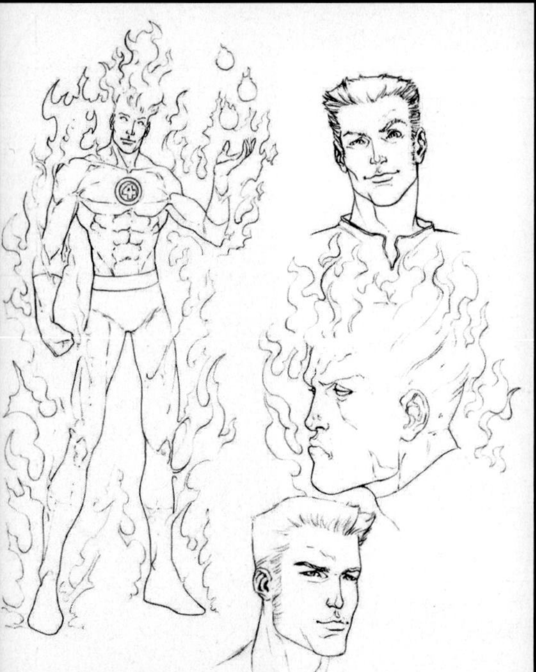
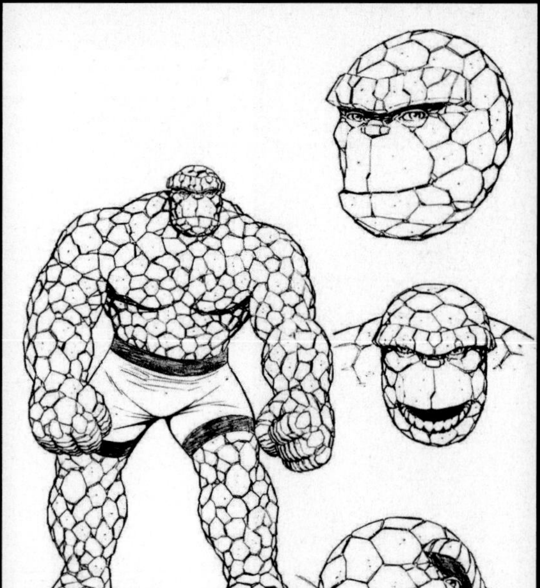

BLACK PANTHER #28, PAGES 1, 2 & 4 LAYOUTS BY **FRANCIS PORTELA**

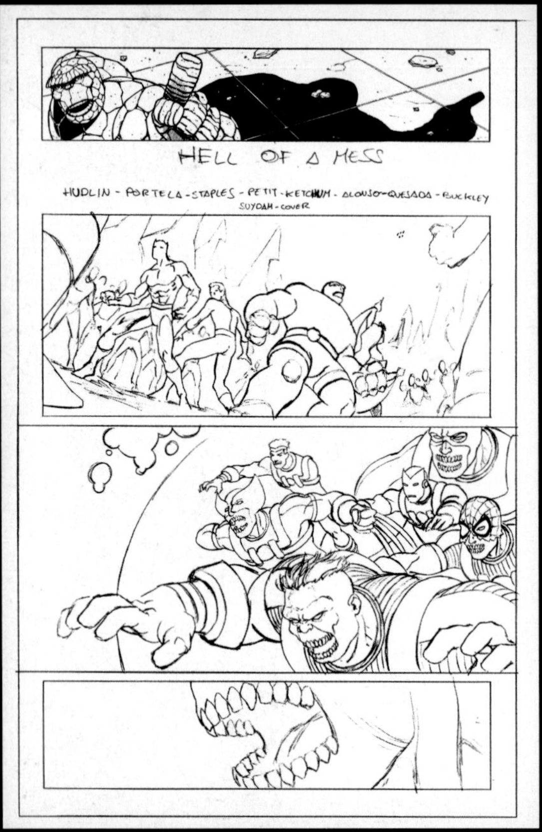

HELL OF A MESS
HUDLIN - PORTELA - STAPLES - PETIT - KETCHUM - ALONSO - QUESADA - BUCKLEY
SUYDAM - COVER

PAGE 1

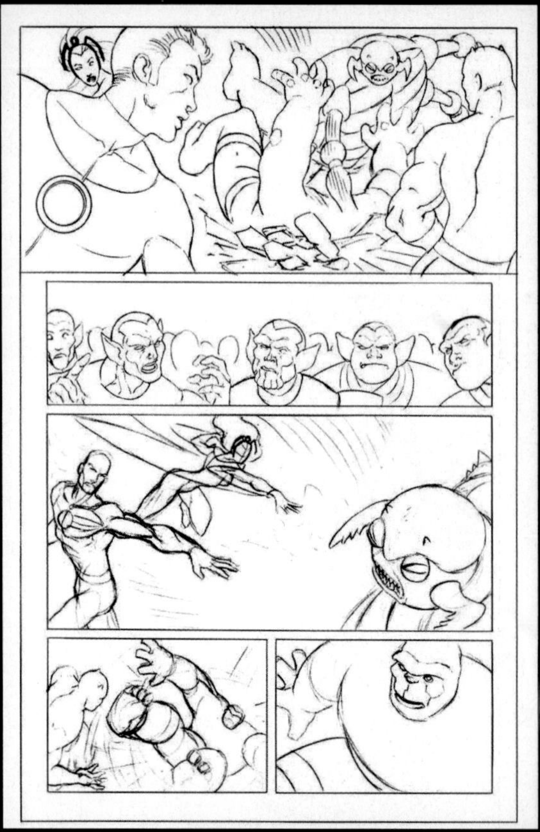

PAGE 2

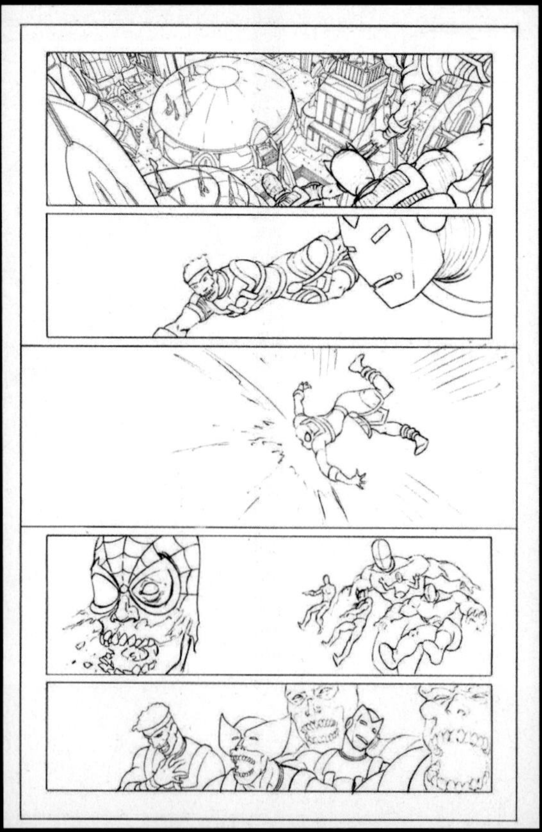

PAGE 4

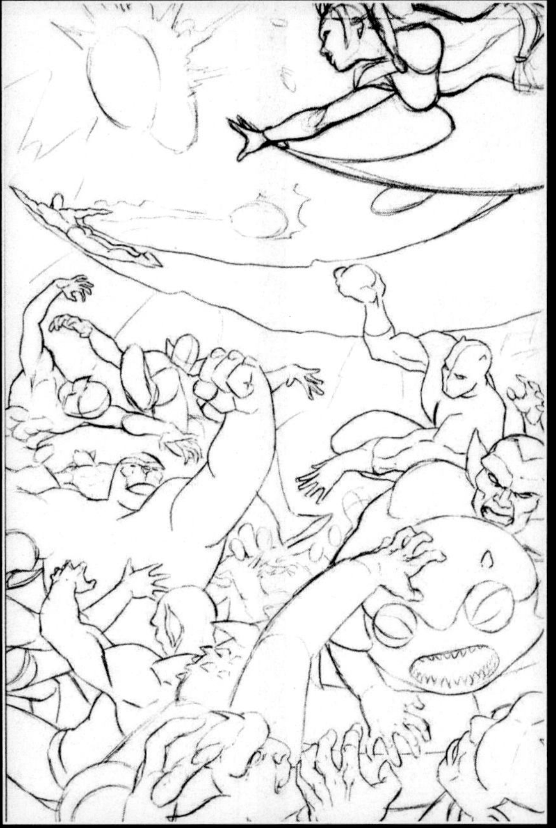

BLACK PANTHER #31-32 COVER PENCILS BY **BILLY TAN**

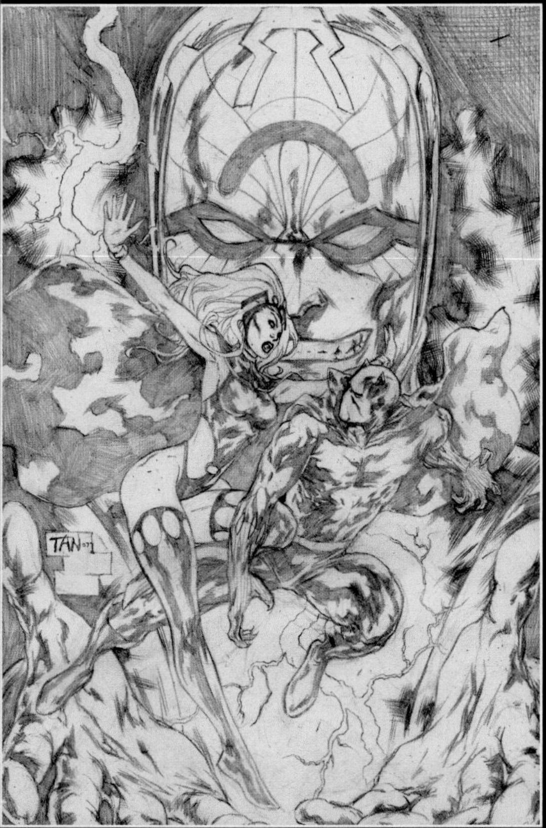
TAN

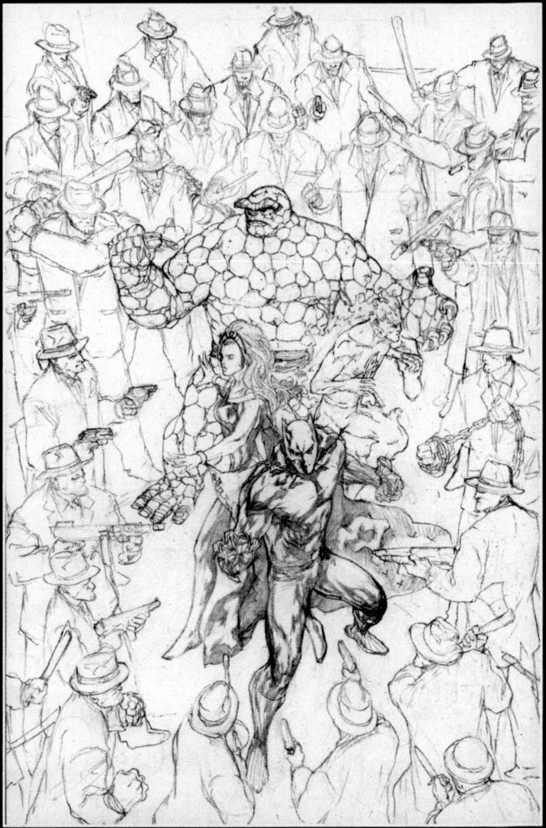

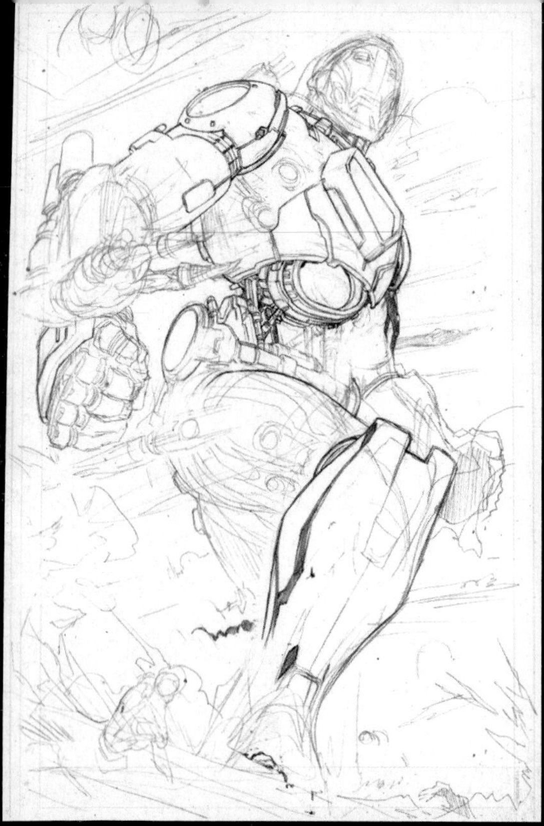
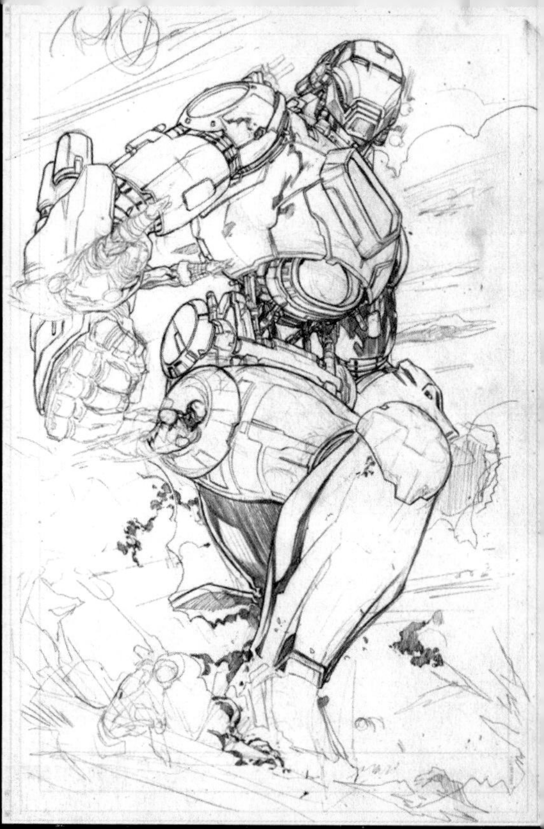
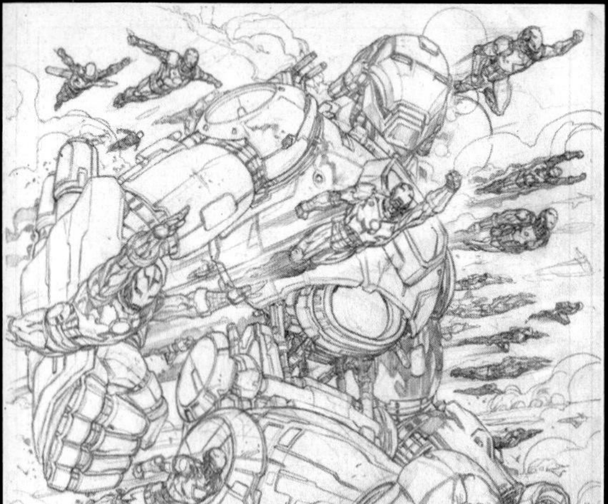
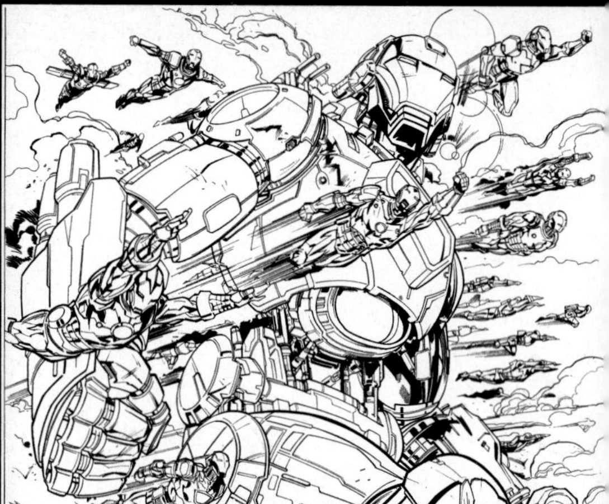

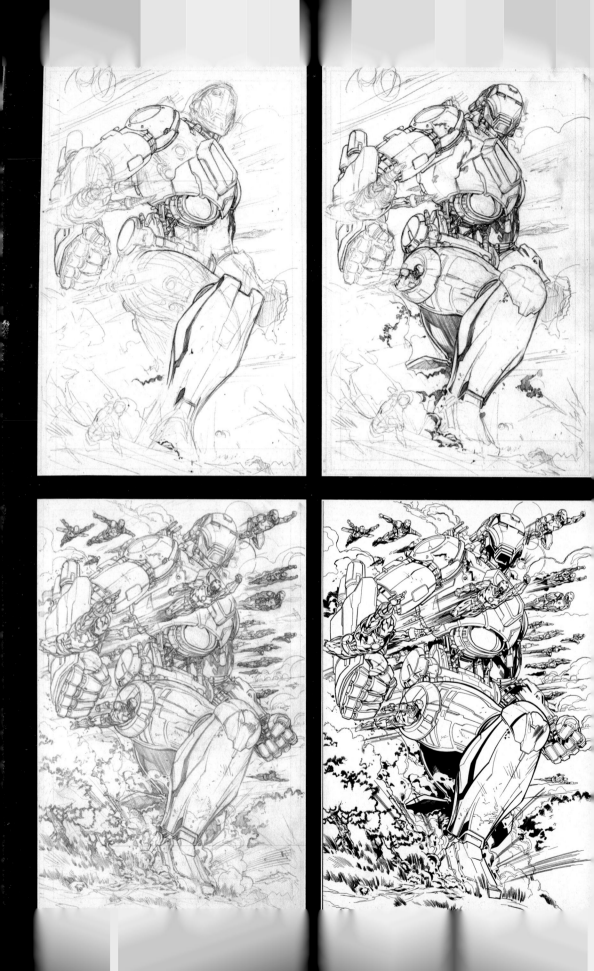